SELF-EFFICACY

SELF-EFFICACY

The Exercise of Control

Albert Bandura
Stanford University

W.H. Freeman and Company
New York

To: Ginny, Mary, Carol, and my indefatigable pals,
Andy and Timmy

Acquisitions Editor: Susan Finnemore Brennan

Project Editor: Christine Hastings

Cover Designer: Blake Logan/Michael Minchillo

Text Designer: Blake Logan

Cover Illustrator: Mark Geo

Illustration Coordinator: Susan Wein

Production Coordinator: Maura Studley

Composition: Digitype

Manufacturing: R R Donnelley & Sons Company

Library of Congress Cataloging-in-Publication Data

Bandura, Albert, 1925–
    Self-efficacy : the exercise of control / Albert Bandura.
        p.   cm.
    Includes index.
    ISBN 0-7167-2626-2 (hardcover). — ISBN 0-7167-2850-8 (softcover)
    1. Self-efficacy.   2. Control (Psychology).   I. Title.
    BF637.S38B36   1997
    155.2 — dc21   96-52118
                                                    CIP

© 1997 by W. H. Freeman and Company

Printed in the United States of America

Second printing, 1998

Contents

Preface

THE SOCIETIES OF TODAY are undergoing extraordinary informational, social, and technological transformations. Wrenching social changes are not new over the course of history, but what is new is their magnitude and accelerated pace. Rapid cycles of drastic changes require continuous personal and social renewals. These challenging realities place a premium on people's sense of efficacy to shape their future. Much contemporary theorizing depicts people as onlooking hosts of internal mechanisms orchestrated by environmental events. They are stripped of any sense of agency. People are proactive, aspiring organisms who have a hand in shaping their own lives and the social systems that organize, guide, and regulate the affairs of their society.

This book explores the exercise of human agency through people's beliefs in their capabilities to produce desired effects by their actions. It reviews in considerable detail the origins of efficacy beliefs, their structure, the processes through which they affect human well-being and accomplishments, and how these processes can be developed and enlisted for human betterment. Perceived self-efficacy plays a pivotal role in a multifaceted social cognitive theory, but it is not the sole determinant of action. This book documents the many ways in which efficacy beliefs operate in concert with other sociocognitive determinants in governing human adaptation and change.

The drastic changes taking place in societies are creating new paradoxes. On the one hand, people have greater knowledge, means, and social entitlements to exercise increased control, both individually and collectively, over their own development and the conditions that affect their lives. On the other hand, with growing transnational interdependencies, the social and economic life in the societies of today is now largely shaped by events in distant places. The globalization of human interconnectedness presents new challenges for people to exercise some control over their personal destinies and national life. These transnational realities are creating a new world culture that places increasing demands on collective efficacy to shape the quality of lives and the social future.

In the conception of human agency presented in this book, perceived self-efficacy operates within a broad network of sociostructural influences. However, this analysis goes beyond the contextualist perspective in which people adapt their actions to suit the social contexts in which they happen to find themselves. People are producers as well as products of social environments. In short, they have a hand in selecting and shaping their environmental contexts. This reciprocal causation of the characteristics of persons and their environments is better captured by a transactionalist perspective than by a contextualist perspective. In this view, sociostructural influences work largely through self-systems rather than represent rival conceptions of human behavior. Because influence flows bidirectionally, social cognitive theory rejects a dualistic view of the relationship between self and society, and between social structure and personal agency.

Human lives are highly interdependent. What they do individually affects the well-being of others, and in turn what others do affects their personal well-being. People must increasingly work together to make a better life for themselves. Social cognitive theory, therefore, extends the analysis of human agency to the exercise of collective agency. It operates through the shared efficacy beliefs and aspirations of families, communities, organizations, social institutions, and even nations so that people can solve the problems they face and improve their lives through unified effort. This volume examines the contemporary conditions of life that undermine the development of collective efficacy and the new social arrangements through which people are striving to regain some measure of control over their lives.

Theories are judged by their explanatory and predictive power. In the final analysis, the value of a psychological theory must also be judged by the power to change people's lives for the better. Self-efficacy theory provides a rich body of knowledge for social applications to varied spheres of life. The broad scope and variety of applications attests to the explanatory and operative generality of this approach. It is my hope that a better understanding of personal and collective enablement can help chart optimistic courses of human development and change.

Growth of knowledge and the technologies it spawned have vastly enhanced the human power to transform environments. People are increasingly adapting the environment to themselves rather than just adapting themselves to the environment. By their transforming actions they are exerting a stronger hand in this bidirectional evolutionary process. The impact of enhanced efficacy on the nature and quality of life depends on the purposes to which it is put. There is growing public concern over where our incentive systems and some of the technologies we create are leading us. If we continue to destroy the interdependent ecosystems that sustain life through incentive systems founded on a foreshortened perspective, it is a theory of "unnatural cultural selection" that should command our attention. The growing human domination of the environment creates interesting paradoxical effects. The very technologies that people create to alter and control their environment can, paradoxically, become a constraining force that in turn controls how they think and behave. The final chapter of this book addresses these more global issues and efficacy-based approaches to them.

Some of the material in this book was published in an earlier form in various chapters and periodical articles I wrote under the following titles: Self-efficacy mechanism in human agency, *American Psychologist*, 1982; Perceived self-efficacy in the exercise of personal agency, *The Psychologist: Bulletin of the British Psychological Society*, 1989; Self-regulation of motivation and action through goal systems, Kluwer Academic Publishers, 1988; Self-efficacy mechanism in physiological activation and health-promoting behavior, *Raven*, 1991; and Perceived self-efficacy in cognitive development and functioning, *Educational Psychologist*, 1993. This material has been substantially revised, expanded, and updated.

It is with pleasure that I take this opportunity to acknowledge my considerable debt of gratitude to the many people who have helped me in one way or another with this undertaking. I remain ever thankful to the Spencer Foundation and the Johann Jacobs Foundation for their generous support of my programs of research and the preparation of this manuscript. This book bears the name of a single author, but it is the product of the collaborative efforts of many former students and colleagues. Their creative contributions are recognized in the numerous citations throughout this book. I thank them for enriching my scholarship and for their warm friendship over the years. I also wish to express my appreciation to the numerous scholars who offered new evidence and fresh insights into the workings of the efficacy belief system. The breadth and depth of coverage in this book could not have been achieved without their informative contributions.

Self-efficacy theory is applied to strikingly diverse spheres of human functioning. Surveying this diversity has been a protracted, tortuous journey through many disciplinary terrains. I am deeply grateful to David Atkins for the countless hours he spent in the murky catacombs of those untold libraries in resilient pursuit of all too often missing and obscure periodicals. I owe an especially heavy debt of gratitude to Lisa Hellrich, who not only made my work life manageable but bettered it through her invaluable assistance. We lived through it all with our sense of humor intact.

Writing a book takes possession not only of the author but of the household as well. To my family goes the credit and my deep gratitude for their forbearance, especially when the end of this lengthy journey seemed nowhere in sight. It is to them that I dedicate this book.

1

Theoretical Perspectives

PEOPLE HAVE ALWAYS STRIVEN TO control the events that affect their lives. By exerting influence in spheres over which they can command some control, they are better able to realize desired futures and to forestall undesired ones. In primitive times, when people had a limited understanding of the world around them and few ways to alter its workings, they appealed to supernatural agents who were believed to wield control over their lives. People practiced elaborate rituals and codes of conduct in an attempt to gain favor from, or protection against, supernatural powers. Even in contemporary life, when faced with weighty matters of much uncertainty, many people employ superstitious rituals to sway outcomes in their favor. A few instances in which an irrelevant ritual happened to be accompanied by a successful outcome can easily make people believe that the ritual affected the outcome.

The growth of knowledge over the course of human history greatly enhanced people's ability to predict events and to exercise control over them. Belief in supernatural systems of control gave way to conceptions that acknowledged people's power to shape their own destiny. This change in human self-conception and the view of life from supernatural control to personal control ushered in a major shift in causal thinking, and the new enlightenment rapidly expanded the exercise of human power over more and more domains. Human ingenuity and endeavor supplanted conciliating rituals to deities as the way to change the conditions of life. By drawing on their knowledge, people built physical technologies that drastically altered how they lived their daily lives. They developed biological technologies to alter the genetic makeup of animals and plants. They created medical and psychosocial technologies to improve the quality of their physical and emotional lives. They devised social systems that placed constraints on the types of beliefs and conduct that could be subjected to coercive or punitive institutional control. These entitlements and institutional protections expanded freedom of belief and action.

The striving for control over life circumstances permeates almost everything people do throughout the life course because it provides innumerable personal and social benefits. Uncertainty in important matters is highly unsettling. To the extent that people help to bring about significant outcomes, they are better able to predict them. Predictability fosters adaptive preparedness. The inability to exert influence over things that adversely affect one's life breeds apprehension, apathy, or despair. The ability to secure desired outcomes and to prevent undesired ones, therefore, provides a powerful incentive for the development and exercise of personal control. The more people bring their influence to bear on events in their lives, the more they can shape them to their liking. By selecting and creating environmental supports for what they want to become, they contribute to the direction their lives take. Human functioning is, of course, embedded in social conditions. The environmental supports for valued life paths, therefore, are created both individually and in concert with others. Through collective action, people can improve their lives by modifying the character and practices of their social systems.

The human capacity to exercise control is a mixed blessing. The impact of personal efficacy on the quality of life depends on the purposes to which it is put. For example, the lives of innovators and social reformers driven by unshakable efficacy are not easy ones. They are often the objects of derision, condemnation, and persecution, even though societies eventually benefit from their persevering efforts. Many people who gain recognition and fame shape their lives by overcoming seemingly insurmountable obstacles, only to be catapulted into new social realities over which they have less control and manage badly. Indeed, the annals of the famous and infamous are strewn with individuals who were both architects and victims of their life courses.

The vastly enhanced human power to transform the environment can have pervasive effects not only on current life but also on future generations. Many technologies that provide current benefits also entail hazards that can take a heavy toll on the environment. Our technical capability to destroy or render uninhabitable much of the planet attests to the growing magnitude of human power. There is much public concern over where some of the technologies we create are leading us. Voracious pursuit of self-interest produces effects that collectively can be harmful to society in the long run. The exercise of social power that places individual interest above the common good creates special interest gridlock that immobilizes efforts to solve the broader problems of society. Without commitment to common purposes that transcend narrow self-interests, the exercise of control can degenerate into personal and factional power conflicts. People must work together if they are to realize the shared destiny they desire and preserve a habitable environment for generations to come. In short, the capacity for human control can be exercised for good or ill.

Because control is central in human lives, many theories about it have been proposed over the years. People's level of motivation, affective states, and actions are based more on what they believe than on what is objectively true. Hence, it is people's belief in their causative capabilities that is the major focus of inquiry. Most theories are couched in terms of an inborn drive for control. Any capability that is widely beneficial — and, thus, highly prevalent — is quickly interpreted as an inborn drive for self-determination or mastery. Theories that contend that striving for personal control is an expression of an innate drive discourage interest in how human efficacy is developed, because people allegedly come fully equipped with it. Instead, such theories dwell heavily on how the drive is socially thwarted and weakened. The fact that virtually all people try to bring at least some influence to bear on some of the things that affect them does not necessarily indicate the presence of an innate motivator. Nor is control sought as an end in itself. Exercise of control that secures desired outcomes and wards off undesired ones has immense functional value and provides a strong source of incentive motivation. The issue of whether the exercise of control is pushed by an inborn drive or pulled by anticipated benefits will be given considerable attention later.

People make causal contributions to their own psychosocial functioning through mechanisms of personal agency. Among the mechanisms of agency, none is more central or pervasive than beliefs of personal efficacy. Unless people believe they can produce desired effects by their actions, they have little incentive to act. Efficacy belief, therefore, is a major basis of action. People guide their lives by their beliefs of personal efficacy. *Perceived self-efficacy refers to beliefs in one's capabilities to organize and execute the courses of action required to produce given attainments.* The events over which personal influence is exercised vary widely, however. Influence may entail regulating one's own motivation, thought processes, affective states, and actions, or it may involve changing environmental conditions, depending on what one seeks to manage.

People's beliefs in their efficacy have diverse effects. Such beliefs influence the courses of action people choose to pursue, how much effort they put forth in given endeavors, how long they will persevere in the face of obstacles and failures, their resilience to adversity, whether their thought patterns are self-hindering or self-aiding, how much stress and depression they experience in coping with taxing environmental demands, and the level of accomplishments they realize. This chapter examines the nature of human agency and alternative conceptions of personal causation.

· ·

THE NATURE OF HUMAN AGENCY

People can exercise influence over what they do. Most human behavior, of course, is determined by many interacting factors, and so people are contributors to, rather than the sole determiners of, what happens to them. The power to make things happen should be distinguished from the mechanics of how things are made to happen. For example, in pursuing a particular strategy in an athletic contest, the players do not tell their nervous system to get the motor neurons to move their skeletal musculature in designated patterns. Based on their understanding of what is within the power of humans to do and beliefs about their own capabilities, people try to generate courses of action to suit given purposes without having the foggiest notion of how

their choices orchestrate the neurophysiological events subserving the endeavor.

In evaluating the role of intentionality in human agency, one must distinguish between the personal production of action for an intended outcome and the effects that carrying out that course of action actually produce. Agency refers to acts done intentionally. Thus, a person who smashed a set of precariously displayed dishes in a china shop upon being tripped by another shopper would not be considered the agent of the event. Davidson (1971) reminds us, however, that actions intended to serve a certain purpose can cause quite different things to happen. He cites the example of the melancholic Hamlet, who intentionally stabbed the man behind a tapestry who he believed to be the king, only to discover, much to his horror, that he had killed Polonius, the wrong person. The killing of the hidden person was intentional, but the wrong victim was done in. Effects are not the characteristics of agentive acts; they are the consequences of them. Many actions are performed in the belief that they will bring about a desired outcome, but they actually produce outcomes that were neither intended nor wanted. For example, it is not uncommon for people to contribute to their own misery through intentional transgressive acts spawned by gross miscalculation of consequences. Some of the social practices and policies that cause harm were originally designed and implemented with well-meaning intent; their harmful effects were unforeseen. In short, the power to originate actions for given purposes is the key feature of personal agency. Whether the exercise of that agency has beneficial or detrimental effects or produces unintended consequences is another matter.

Beliefs of personal efficacy constitute the key factor of human agency. If people believe they have no power to produce results, they will not attempt to make things happen. In social cognitive theory, a sense of personal efficacy is represented as propositional beliefs. We will see later that these beliefs are embedded in a network of functional relationships with other factors that operate together in the management of different realities. The fact that beliefs are described in the language of mind raises the philosophical issues of ontological reductionism and the plurality of regulatory systems. Mental events are brain activities, not immaterial entities existing apart from neural systems. Were one to perform Bunge's (1980) hypothetical brain transplant, the donor's unique psychic life would undoubtedly accompany the brain to the new host, rather than remain behind with the donor as a mental entity in a separate realm. Physicality does not imply reductionism, however. Thought processes are emergent brain activities that are not ontologically reducible. In his treatise on the paradigmatic shift to cognitivism, Sperry (1993) spells out some of the characteristics of a nondualistic mentalism. Mental states are emergent properties of generating brain processes. Emergent properties differ in novel ways from the elements of which they are created, rather than simply representing increased complexity of the same properties. To use Bunge's (1977) analogy, the emergent properties of water, such as fluidity, viscosity, and transparency, are not simply the aggregate properties of its microcomponents, oxygen and hydrogen.

Thought processes are not only emergent brain activities; they also exert determinative influence. There are many neural systems that subserve human functioning. They operate interactively at different sites and levels to produce coherent experiences out of the multitude of information processing. With regard to this ontological plurality, certain brain structures are specialized for mentation. The thought processes generated by the higher cerebral system are involved in the regulation of visceral, motoric, and other lower level subsystems. For example, a host of microsensory, perceptual, and information processing activities gives rise to a judgment of personal efficacy. Once formed, however, efficacy beliefs regulate aspirations, choice of behavioral courses, mobilization and maintenance of effort, and affective reactions. The influence between microevents and emergent macroevents operates both upwardly and downwardly. Thus, an emergent interactive agency assumes ontological nonreductionism of complex events to simpler ones and plurality of regulatory physical subsystems that function interconnectedly in a hierarchically structured system in which higher neural centers control lower ones.

The fact that cognition is a cerebral occurrence does not mean that the laws expressing functional relations in psychological theory are reducible to those in neurophysiological theory. One must distinguish between how cerebral systems function and the personal and social means by which they can be orchestrated to produce courses of action that serve different purposes. Much of psychology is concerned with discovering principles about how to structure environmental influences and enlist cognitive activities to promote human adaptation and change. Most of the subject matter of psychological theory with regard to psychosocial factors does not have a counterpart in neurobiological theory and, therefore, is not derivable from it. These factors do not appear in neurophysiological theory because many of them involve the construction and organization of events external to the organism. For example, knowledge of the brain circuitry involved in learning does not tell one much about how best to devise conditions of learning in terms of levels of abstractness, novelty, and challenge; how to provide incentives to get people to attend to, process, and organize relevant information; in what modes to present information; and whether learning is better achieved independently, cooperatively, or competitively. The optimal conditions must be specified by psychological principles. Nor does understanding how the brain works furnish rules on how to create efficacious parents, teachers, or politicians. Although psychological principles cannot violate the neurophysiological capabilities of the systems that subserve them, the psychological principles need to be pursued in their own right. Were one to embark on the road to reductionism, the journey would traverse biology and chemistry and would eventually end in atomic particles, with neither the intermediate locales nor the final stop supplying the psychological laws of human behavior.

A major challenge for a physicalistic account of the mind is to specify the mechanisms through which the brain creates mental events and explain how these events exert determinative influence. The human mind is generative, creative, and proactive, not just reactive. Hence, an even more formidable challenge is to explain how people come to be producers of thoughts that may be novel, inventive, or visionary or that take complete leave of reality, as in flights of fancy. One can intentionally originate novel coherent thoughts; for example, visualizing hippopotami attired in chartreuse tuxedos gracefully navigating hang gliders over lunar craters. Similarly, one can conceive of several novel acts and choose to execute one of them. People bring cognitive productions into being by the intentional exercise of personal agency. Intentionality and agency raise the fundamental question of how people actuate the cerebral processes that characterize the exercise of agency and lead to the realization of particular intentions. This question goes beyond the cerebral correlates of sensory input and motor output to the intentional production of cerebral events in thinking of future courses of action, evaluating their likely functional value under differing circumstances, and organizing and guiding the execution of the chosen options. Cognitive production, with its purposive, creative, and evaluative properties, defies explanation of novel thoughts in terms of external cueing of preformed cognitions. In addition to the question of how people bring about thoughts and actions is the intriguing question of how people generate self-perceiving, self-reflecting, and self-correcting activities.

Rottschaefer (1985) presents a thoughtful analysis of human agency operating through intentional and generative cognition as it bears on the nonintentionalistic views of human behavior favored by eliminative materialists. People are agentic operators in their life course not just onlooking hosts of brain mechanisms orchestrated by environmental events. The sensory, motor and cerebral systems are tools people use to accomplish the tasks and goals that give meaning and direction to their lives (Harré & Gillet, 1994). Through their intentional acts, people shape the functional structure of their neurobiological systems. By regulating their own motivation and the activities they pursue, they produce the experiences that form the neurobiological substrate of symbolic, psychomotor, and other skills. Should people

experience any loss or decline in any of their bodily systems, they devise alternative ways of engaging and managing the world around them.

The duality of self as agent and self as object pervades much of the theorizing in the field of personality. The double nature of the self merges in the case of self-influence. In their daily transactions, people analyze the situations that confront them, consider alternative courses of action, judge their abilities to carry them out successfully, and estimate the results the actions are likely to produce. They act on their judgments, later reflect on how well their thoughts have served them in managing the events at hand, and change their thinking and strategies accordingly. People are said to be agents when they act on the environment but objects when they reflect and act on themselves.

Social cognitive theory rejects the dualistic view of the self. Reflecting on one's own functioning entails shifting the perspective of the same agent rather than converting the self from agent to object or reifying different internal agents or selves that regulate one another. It is one and the same person who does the strategic thinking about how to manage the environment and later evaluates the adequacy of his or her knowledge, thinking skills, capabilities, and action strategies. The shift in perspective does not transform the person from an agent to an object, as the dualist view of the self would lead one to believe. One is just as much an agent when one is reflecting on one's experiences and exerting self-influence as when one is executing courses of action. In social cognitive theory, the self is not split into object and agent; rather, in self-reflection and self-influence, individuals are simultaneously agent and object.

HUMAN AGENCY IN TRIADIC RECIPROCAL CAUSATION

The term *causation* is used in the present context to mean functional dependence between events. In social cognitive theory, human agency operates

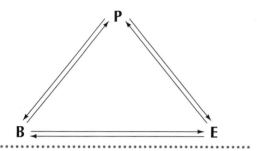

FIGURE 1.1. The relationships between the three major classes of determinants in triadic reciprocal causation. B represents behavior; P the internal personal factors in the form of cognitive, affective, and biological events; and E the external environment. (Bandura, 1986a)

within an interdependent causal structure involving triadic reciprocal causation (Bandura, 1986a). In this transactional view of self and society, internal personal factors in the form of cognitive, affective, and biological events; behavior; and environmental events all operate as interacting determinants that influence one another bidirectionally (Fig. 1.1). Reciprocity does not mean that the three sets of interacting determinants are of equal strength. Their relative influence will vary for different activities and under different circumstances. Nor do the mutual influences and their reciprocal effects all spring forth simultaneously as a holistic entity. It takes time for a causal factor to exert its influence. Because of the time lag in the operation of the three sets of factors, it is possible to gain an understanding of how different segments of reciprocal causation operate without having to mount a Herculean effort to assess every possible interactant at the same time.

Human adaptation and change are rooted in social systems. Therefore, personal agency operates within a broad network of sociostructural influences. In agentic transactions, people are both producers and products of social systems. Social structures — which are devised to organize, guide, and regulate human affairs in given domains by authorized rules and sanctions — do not arise by immaculate conception; they are created by human activity. Social structures, in turn, impose constraints

and provide resources for personal development and everyday functioning. But neither structural constraints nor enabling resources foreordain what individuals become and do in given situations. For the most part, social structures represent authorized social practices carried out by human beings occupying designated roles (Giddens, 1984). As such, they do not compel uniform action. Within the rule structures, there is a lot of personal variation in their interpretation, enforcement, adoption, circumvention, or active opposition (Burns & Dietz, in press). Efficacious people are quick to take advantage of opportunity structures and figure out ways to circumvent institutional constraints or change them by collective action. Conversely, inefficacious people are less apt to exploit the enabling opportunities provided by the social system and are easily discouraged by institutional impediments. It is not a dichotomy between a disembodied social structure and a decontextualized personal agency, but a dynamic interplay between individuals and those who preside over the institutionalized operations of social systems. This interplay involves agentic transactions between institutional functionaries and those who seek to accommodate to or change their practices. Agency is just as integral to institutional functionaries as it is to freelancing individuals. Social cognitive theory thus avoids a dualism between individuals and society and between social structure and personal agency.

Sociostructural theories and psychological theories are often regarded as rival conceptions of human behavior or as representing different levels of causation. This perspective, too, is dualistic. Human behavior cannot be fully understood solely in terms of either social structural factors or psychological factors. A full understanding requires an integrated causal perspective in which social influences operate through self-processes that produce the actions. The self system is not merely a conduit for external influences, as structural reductionists might claim. The self is socially constituted, but, by exercising self-influence, individuals are partial contributors to what they become and do. Moreover, human agency operates generatively and proactively rather than just reactively. Thus, in the theory of triadic reciprocal causation, sociostructural and personal determinants are treated as interacting cofactors within a unified causal structure.

Conceptions of agent causality have been wedded to individual agency. Social cognitive theory adopts a much broader view of agency. People do not live their lives in isolation; they work together to produce results they desire. The growing interdependence of social and economic life further underscores the need to broaden the focus of inquiry beyond the exercise of individual influence to collective action designed to shape the course of events. Social cognitive theory, therefore, extends the analysis of mechanisms of human agency to the exercise of collective agency. People's shared belief in their capabilities to produce effects collectively is a crucial ingredient of collective agency. Collective efficacy is not simply the sum of the efficacy beliefs of individuals. Rather, it is an emergent group-level attribute that is the product of coordinative and interactive dynamics. Later chapters analyze how both individual and collective efficacy beliefs contribute to human adaptation and change. Personal and social change are complementary rather than rival approaches to improving the quality of life.

··

DETERMINISM AND THE EXERCISE OF SELF-INFLUENCE

The discussion of agent causality raises the fundamental issues of determinism and the freedom to exert some control over one's life. The term *determinism* is used here to signify the production of effects by events rather than in the doctrinal sense meaning that actions are completely determined by a prior sequence of causes independent of the individual. Because most behavior is codetermined by many factors operating interactively, given events produce effects probabilistically rather than inevitably within the reciprocally deterministic system.

Freedom is often considered antithetical to determinism. When viewed from a sociocognitive perspective, there is no incompatibility between freedom and determinism. Freedom is not conceived negatively as exemption from social influences or situational constraints. Rather, it is defined positively as the exercise of self-influence to bring about desired results. This agentic causation relies heavily on cognitive self-regulation. It is achieved through reflective thought, generative use of the knowledge and skills at one's command, and other tools of self-influence, which choice and execution of action require. Self-influences operate deterministically on behavior in the same way external influences do. Given the same environmental conditions, people who have the ability to exercise many options and are adept at regulating their own motivation and behavior will have greater freedom to make things happen than will those who have limited means of personal agency. It is because self-influence operates deterministically on action that some measure of freedom is possible.

The choice of actions from among alternatives is not completely and involuntarily determined by environmental events. Rather, the making of choices is aided by reflective thought, through which self-influence is largely exercised. People exert some influence over what they do by the alternatives they consider; how they foresee and weigh the visualized outcomes, including their own self-evaluative reactions; and how they appraise their abilities to execute the options they consider. To say that thought guides action is an abbreviated statement of convenience rather than a conferral of agency on thought. It is not that individuals generate thoughts that then become the agents of action. The cognitive activities constitute the processes of self-influence that are brought to bear on the courses of action to take. Thus, for example, an individual will behave differently in an efficacious frame of mind than in an inefficacious one. But the individual remains the agent of the thoughts, the effort, and the actions. An elliptical expression should not be misconstrued as a transfer of agency from person to thought.

Agent causation involves the ability to behave differently from what environmental forces dictate rather than inevitably yield to them. In enticing and coercive situations, personal agency is expressed in the power to refrain. People construct personal standards that they then use to guide, motivate, and regulate their own behavior (Bandura, 1986a; 1991b). The anticipatory self-respect for actions that correspond to personal standards and self-censure for actions that violate them serve as the regulatory influences. People do things that give them self-satisfaction and a sense of self-worth. They refrain from behaving in ways that violate their personal standards because it will bring self-censure. After self-reactive capabilities are developed, behavior usually produces two sets of consequences — external outcomes and self-evaluative reactions — that can operate as complimentary or opposing influences on behavior. It is not uncommon for individuals to invest their self-worth so strongly in certain convictions that they will submit to prolonged mistreatment rather than accede to what they regard as unjust or immoral. Thomas More, who was beheaded for refusing to compromise his resolute convictions, is a notable example from history. In their everyday lives, people repeatedly confront predicaments in which they forgo expediency and material benefit for self-respect.

Self-influence affects not only choices but the success with which chosen courses of action are executed. Psychological analyses of the mechanisms of personal agency show that people contribute to the attainment of desired futures by enlisting cognitive guides and self-incentives and by selecting and constructing environments to suit their purposes (Bandura, 1986a). The greater their foresight, proficiency, and means of self-influence, all of which are acquirable skills, the more successful they are in achieving what they seek. Because of the capacity for self-influence, people are at least partial architects of their own destinies. It is not the principle of determinism that is in dispute, but whether determinism should be treated as a one-sided or a two-way process. Given the reciprocal interplay between people and their environment, determinism does not imply the fatalistic view that people are only pawns of external forces. Reciprocal causation provides people with opportunities to exercise some control over their destinies as well as setting limits on self-direction.

Arguments against the causal efficacy of thought and other means of self-influence usually invoke a selective regression of causes. In the operant view (Skinner, 1974), people are merely repositories for past stimulus inputs and conduits for external stimulation — they can add nothing to their performance. Through a conceptual sleight of hand, the determinants of human action are regressed to an "initiating cause" located in the environment, thus rendering human thought entirely externally implanted, acausal, and completely redundant. A detailed critique of this conceptual scheme is presented elsewhere (Bandura, 1996). Obviously, thought is partly influenced by experience, but thought is not completely shaped by past stimulus inputs. Operant analyses emphasize how people's judgments and actions are determined by the environment but disregard the fact that the environment itself is partly determined by people's actions. Environments have causes, as do actions. People create, alter, and destroy environments by their actions. The sociocognitive analysis of reciprocal causation does not invite an infinite regression of causes, because individuals originate actions from their experiences and reflective thought rather than merely undergo actions as implants of the past. The emergent creations are not reducible to the environmental inputs. For example, Bach's magnificent masterpieces, which fill sixty volumes of prolific originality, are not reducible to his prior instruction in the mechanics of musical composition, his predecessors' musical works, and the ongoing events in his everyday environment. Since Bach was not endowed with fully orchestrated Brandenburg concertos and hundreds of church cantatas, from which repository did the environmental reinforcers select these artistic creations? Reinforcement cannot select what does not exist in a repertoire. One can, of course, create simple new responses by waiting around for random variations to produce some approximate elements to reward. But given Bach's prolific output, one would have to wait around for countless lifetimes to shape such artistic creations by selective reinforcement of random variations, if it could ever be achieved at all by this slow, laborious process. Although human ingenuity incorporates some aspects of past experience, it transforms it, adds novel features to it, and thereby creates something that is not just a conglomerate or replica of the past. In short, human behavior is determined, but it is determined partly by the individual rather than solely by the environment. One does not explain a unique musical composition by attributing it to causes in the environment further back in time. The composition is an emergent creation.

The long-standing debate over the issue of freedom was enlivened by Skinner's (1971) contention that, apart from genetic contributions, human behavior is shaped and controlled by environmental contingencies. A major problem with this type of analysis is that it depicts two-way causality between people and environments as one-way control by an autonomous environment. In Skinner's view, freedom is an illusion. It is not that the interdependence of personal and environmental influences is never acknowledged by advocates of this point of view. Indeed, Skinner (1971) has often commented on people's capacity for countercontrol. The notion of countercontrol, however, portrays the environment as the instigator to which individuals can react. In fact, people are foreactive, not simply counteractive. Equivocation by the unidirectionalists created further conceptual ambiguities. Having acknowledged the reality of bidirectional influence, Skinner (1971) negated it by reasserting the preeminent control of behavior by the environment: "A person does not act upon the world, the world acts upon him." The environment thus reappears as an autonomous force that automatically selects, shapes, and controls behavior. Whatever allusions are made to two-way influences, environmental rule clearly emerges as the reigning metaphor in this view of reality.

It is the height of irony when people who exercise the liberties guaranteed by institutions of freedom denigrate freedom as an illusion. Over the course of history, countless people have sacrificed their lives to create and preserve institutions of freedom that prohibit rulers from forcing obedience to unauthorized dictates. Struggles for freedom are aimed at creating institutional safeguards that exempt certain forms of behavior from coercive and punitive control. The less social jurisdiction there is over given spheres of activities, the greater is the causal contribution of self-influence to choice of action in those domains. After protective laws are built into social systems, there are certain things that a society may not do to individuals who choose to challenge conventional values or vested interests, however much it might like to. Legal prohibitions against unauthorized societal control create personal freedoms that are realities, not illusory abstractions. Societies differ in their institutions of freedom and in the number and types of activities that are officially exempted from punitive control. For example, social systems that protect journalists from criminal sanctions for criticizing government officials and their practices are freer than those that allow authoritative power to be used to silence critics or their vehicles of expression. Societies that possess a judiciary independent of other government institutions ensure greater social freedom than those that do not.

When it comes to social change, thoroughgoing environmental determinists become fervent advocates of people's power to change their lives for the better by applying the advocate's psychotechnology. For example, Skinner spent much of the later part of his career promoting, with missionary earnestness, operant technology as the remedy for the world's ills. Even the modest applications of operant conditioning fell short of his claims, let alone providing the panacea for growing worldwide problems. A fervent environmental determinist urging people to change their environment is amusingly self-negating because it contradicts the basic premise of the doctrine of environmentalism. If humans were, in fact, incapable of acting as causal agents, they could describe the changes they were undergoing in response to the dictates of their environment, but they could not select actions based on reasoned plans and foresight of consequences, nor could they intentionally make desired things happen. They can be conduits for environmental forces, but they themselves cannot be creators of programs for environmental change. Boring (1957) provided a thoughtful analysis of the "egocentric predicament" in which advocatory environmental determinists get themselves entangled by regarding themselves as self-directing agents but other folks as being externally determined. The advocates thus exempt themselves from the overriding environmental control that presumably shepherds the rest of the populace. Otherwise, the advocates' own views simply become utterances shaped by their insular environment and, thus, have no special truth value. However, should members of the populace adopt the technology of the advocate, they are suddenly converted into intentional agents who can improve their lives and shape their future.

RELATED VIEWS OF PERSONAL EFFICACY

Self-referent thought plays a paramount role in most contemporary theories of human behavior. Self-conceptions, of course, have many different facets. Although they are all self-referential, not all of the facets are concerned with personal efficacy, and this has been the source of some confusion in the literature. Even theories that explicitly speak to the issue of personal efficacy typically differ in how they view the nature of efficacy beliefs, their origins, the effects they have, their changeability, and the intervening processes through which they affect psychosocial functioning. Theories of the self differ not only in conceptual orientation but also in comprehensiveness. The various theoretical perspectives rarely encompass all the important aspects of efficacy beliefs. Much of the research generated by the various theories is tied to an omnibus measure of perceived control and devoted to a search for its correlates. A full understanding of personal causation requires a comprehensive theory that explains, within a unified conceptual framework, the origins of efficacy beliefs, their structure and function, the processes through which they produce diverse effects, and their modifiability. Self-efficacy theory addresses all these subprocesses at both the individual level and the collective level.

The social cognitive theory of the origin and function of perceived self-efficacy offers certain other analytic and operative advantages. It specifies other aspects of the conglomerate self system. These include, among other things, personal aspirations, outcome expectations, perceived opportunity structures and constraints, and conceptions of personal efficacy. Analysis of how these constituent factors work together and their relative contribution to adaptation and change provides an integrated view of the self (Bandura, 1986a). These sociocognitive determinants are grounded in a large body of empirical evidence about the mechanisms by which they motivate and regulate behavior. The conceptual and empirical linkages of other determinants to perceived self-efficacy deepen understanding of how people guide and shape their own destinies. By embedding the self-efficacy belief system in a unified sociocognitive framework, the theory can integrate diverse bodies of findings in varied spheres of functioning.

The value of a theory is ultimately judged by the power of the methods it yields to effect changes. Self-efficacy theory provides explicit guidelines on how to enable people to exercise some influence over how they live their lives. A theory that can be readily used to enhance human efficacy has much greater social utility than theories that provide correlates of perceived control but have little to say about how to foster desired changes. The following sections review alternative conceptions of personal efficacy, as well as constructs that are sometimes mistakenly grouped with perceived efficacy as if they resembled one another when, in fact, they are concerned with different phenomena.

Self-Concept

Self-appraisal has often been analyzed in terms of the self-concept (Rogers, 1959; Wylie, 1974). The self-concept is a composite view of oneself that is presumed to be formed through direct experience and evaluations adopted from significant others. Self-concepts are measured by having people rate how well descriptive statements of different attributes apply to themselves. Their role in personal functioning is tested by correlating the composite self-concepts, or disparities between actual and ideal selves, with various indices of adjustment, attitudes, and behavior.

Examining self-referent processes in terms of the self-concept contributes to an understanding of people's attitudes toward themselves and how these attitudes may affect their general outlook on life. There are several features of theories of this type, however, that detract from their power to explain and predict human behavior. For the most part, the theories are concerned with global self-images. Combining diverse attributes into a single index creates confusion about what is actually being measured and how much weight is given to particular attributes in the forced summary judgment. Even if the global self-conception is tied to certain areas of functioning, it does not do justice to the complexity of efficacy beliefs, which vary across different domains of activities, within the same activity domain at different levels of difficulty, and under different circumstances. A composite self-image may yield some weak correlations, but it is not equal to the task of predicting, with any degree of accuracy, the wide variations in behavior that typically occur in a given domain of activity under different conditions. Such theories fail to explain how the same self-concept can spawn different types of behavior. In comparative tests of predictive power, efficacy beliefs are highly predictive of behavior, whereas the effect of self-concept is weaker and equivocal (Pajares & Kranzler, 1995; Pajares & Miller, 1994a, 1995). Self-concept loses most, if not all, of its predictiveness when the influence of perceived efficacy is factored out. Such findings suggest that self-concept largely reflects people's beliefs in their personal efficacy.

Differentiating Self-Efficacy from Self-Esteem

The concepts of self-esteem and perceived self-efficacy are often used interchangeably as though they represented the same phenomenon. In fact, they refer to entirely different things. Perceived self-efficacy is concerned with judgments of personal capability, whereas self-esteem is concerned with judgments of self-worth. There is no fixed relationship between beliefs about one's capabilities and whether one likes or dislikes oneself. Individuals may judge themselves hopelessly inefficacious in a given activity without suffering any loss of self-esteem whatsoever, because they do not invest their self-worth in that activity. The fact that I acknowledge complete inefficacy in ballroom dancing does not drive me to recurrent bouts of self-devaluation. Conversely, individuals may regard themselves as highly efficacious in an activity but take no pride in performing it well. A skilled forecloser of mortgages of families that have fallen on hard times is unlikely to feel pride for driving them out of their homes proficiently. It is true, however, that people tend to cultivate their capabilities in activities that give them a sense of self-worth. If empirical analyses are confined to activities in which people invest their sense of self-worth, they will inflate correlations between self-efficacy and self-esteem, because the analyses ignore both domains of functioning in which people judge themselves inefficacious but could not care less and those in which they feel highly efficacious but take no pride in performing the activity well because of its socially injurious consequences.

People need much more than high self-esteem to do well in given pursuits. Many achievers are hard on themselves because they adopt standards that are not easily fulfilled, whereas others may enjoy high self-esteem because they do not demand much of themselves or they derive their esteem from sources other than personal accomplishments. Consequently, self-liking does not necessarily beget performance attainments. They are the product of toilsome self-disciplined effort. People need firm confidence in their efficacy to mount and sustain the effort required to succeed. Thus, in ongoing pursuits, perceived personal efficacy predicts the goals people set for themselves and their performance attainments, whereas self-esteem affects neither personal goals nor performance (Mone, Baker & Jeffries, 1995).

The inappropriate equation of self-esteem with perceived self-efficacy has both methodological and conceptual sources. Some of the instruments devised to measure self-esteem include self-appraisals of both personal efficacy and self-worth, thus confounding factors that should be separated (Coopersmith, 1967). Some authors mistakenly regard self-esteem as the generalized form of perceived self-efficacy. For example, Harter (1990) treats judgments of self-worth and personal competence as representing levels of generality within the same phenomenon. Self-worth is said to be global and perceived competence to be domain-specific. Global self-worth is considered to be an emergent superordinate property that is more than the sum of the domain-specific competencies. The assessment of global self-worth is disembodied from particular domains of functioning that contribute in varying degrees to one's sense of self-pride or self-dislike. That is, people are asked how much they like or dislike themselves without any regard to what it is they like or dislike. Measurement of self-worth noncontextually and perceived competence specifically presumably integrates unidimensional and multidimensional perspectives into a hierarchical model of self-evaluation.

As already noted, judgments of self-worth and personal efficacy represent different phenomena, not part-whole relationships within the same phenomenon. Moreover, self-esteem is no less multidimensional than perceived efficacy. People vary in the extent to which they derive a sense of self-worth from their work, their family life, their community and social life, and their recreational pursuits. For example, some students may take pride in their academic accomplishments but devalue themselves in their social facility. Hard-driving executives may value themselves highly in their occupational pursuits but devalue themselves as parents. Domain-linked measures of self-worth reveal the patterning of human self-esteem and the areas of vulnerability to self-disparagement. There is neither conceptual nor empirical justification for construing self-worth globally. Nor is self-esteem the generalized embodiment of specific efficacy beliefs.

There are several sources of self-esteem or self-worthiness (Bandura, 1986a). Self-esteem can stem from self-evaluations based on personal competence or on possession of attributes that are culturally invested with positive or negative value. In self-esteem arising from personal competence, people derive pride from fulfilling their standards of merit. They experience self-satisfaction for a job well done but are displeased with themselves when they fail to measure up to their standards of merit. Personal competencies that provide the means for achieving valued accomplishments afford a genuine basis of self-esteem. This source of self-evaluation enables people to exert some influence over their own self-esteem by developing potentialities that bring self-satisfactions from personal accomplishments.

People often voice evaluations that reflect their likes and dislikes of the attributes possessed by others rather than judging them by their accomplishments. In these instances, the social evaluations are linked to personal attributes and social status rather than to personal competencies. For example, people who are socially relegated to subordinate positions may be disparaged. In conflict-ridden families, parents may deprecate offspring who possess attributes resembling those of a disliked spouse. Social evaluations tend to influence how the recipients come to evaluate their own self-worthiness. Moreover, people are often criticized or deprecated when they fail to live up to the ideals or aspirational standards imposed upon them by others. To the extent that they adopt those onerous standards, most of their accomplishments will bring them nothing but self-devaluation because they fail to measure up. The roles played by personal competence and social evaluation in the development of self-esteem receive support from the studies of Coopersmith (1967). He found that children who exhibited high self-esteem had parents who were accepting, who set explicit attainable standards, and who provided their children with considerable support and latitude to acquire competencies that could serve them well in their pursuits.

Cultural stereotyping is another way in which evaluative social judgments affect a sense of self-worth. People are often cast into valued or devalued groups on the basis of their ethnicity, race, sex, or physical characteristics. They then get treated in terms of the social stereotype rather than on the basis of their actual individuality. In situations that give salience to the stereotype, those stereotyped suffer losses in self-esteem (Steele, 1996). Devaluative societal practices are usually clothed in social justifications that fault the disfavored groups for their maltreatment. Justified devaluation can have more devastating effects on judgments of self-worth than acknowledged antipathy. When blame is convincingly ascribed to a devalued group, many of its members may eventually come to believe the degrading characterizations of themselves (Hallie, 1971). Discriminatory social practices help to create some of the very failings that serve as justifications for the devaluation. Thus, vindicated inhumanity is more likely to instill self-devaluation in disparaged groups than inhumanity that does not attempt to justify itself. People who possess attributes that are socially disparaged, and who accept the stereotyped negative evaluations of others, will hold themselves in low regard irrespective of their talents.

Because self-esteem has many sources, there is no single remedy for low self-esteem. People who combine limited competencies, exacting standards of self-evaluation, and socially disparaged attributes are the ones most likely to harbor a pervasive sense of worthlessness. These different sources of self-devaluation call for different corrective measures. Self-devaluation rooted in incompetence requires the cultivation of talents for personal accomplishments that bring self-satisfaction. Those who suffer from self-disparagement because they judge themselves harshly against excessively high standards become more self-accepting and self-rewarding after they are helped to adopt more realistic standards of achievement (Jackson, 1972; Rehm, 1982). Self-devaluation resulting from belittling social evaluations requires humane treatment by others that affirms one's self-worth. Self-devaluation stemming from discriminatory disparagement of attributes requires modeling and rewarding a sense of pride in those attributes. Efforts by minorities to instill pride in racial characteristics (for example, "Black is beautiful") illustrate this approach. When self-devaluation arises

from multiple sources, multiple corrective measures are needed; for example, fostering pride in one's characteristics but also cultivating competencies that instill a high and resilient sense of personal efficacy for personal accomplishments.

Effectance Motivation

In seeking motivations for exploratory behavior, White (1959, 1960) postulated an effectance motive. This motive is conceptualized as an intrinsic need to deal effectively with the environment. The production of effects through exploratory activities builds competencies and is said to be satisfying in its own right. The effectance motive presumably develops through cumulative acquisition of knowledge and skills in managing the environment. In these conceptual papers, White argues eloquently for a competence model of human development that is rooted in nonbiologic drives. Behavior is pursued for the feelings of efficacy derived from it. White provides only a general conceptual framework, however, rather than a particularized theory from which testable deductions can be made. How an effectance motive is created by effective transactions with the environment is never spelled out. The impact of failed efforts, which are all too common, receives no mention. Nor is the nature of the intrinsic reward of effective action specified in a way that would be subject to test. Harter (1981) has elaborated White's formulation into a developmental model of intrinsic mastery motivation.

It is difficult to verify the existence of an effectance or mastery motive because the motive is inferred from the very exploratory behavior it supposedly causes. This creates problems of circularity. Without an independent measure of motive strength, one cannot tell whether people explore and manipulate things because they are propelled by a competence motive to do so, or for the satisfactions they derive or anticipate from the activity. There is a marked difference between being driven by an intrinsic effectance motive and being motivated by anticipated outcomes. We will return to this issue in Chapter 6, which presents a conceptualization of intrinsic motivation within the framework of social cognitive theory.

Over the years, theorists have argued about whether it is the push of boredom and apprehension or the pull of novelty that rouses organisms to exploratory action (Berlyne, 1960; Brown, 1953; Harlow, 1953; Mowrer, 1960b). Critics of exploratory drives have been able to explain and to alter some forms of exploratory behavior by the outcomes it produces without recourse to an underlying drive (Fowler, 1971). However, theories concerned solely with external prompts and immediate rewards for action are hard-pressed to explain the directedness and persistence of behavior over extended periods when immediate situational inducements are weak, absent, or even negative. This type of sustained involvement in activities requires self-regulatory capabilities that operate anticipatorily. Efficacy beliefs play a crucial role in the ongoing self-regulation of motivation, as will be shown later.

The theory of effectance motivation has not been formulated in sufficient detail to permit extensive theoretical comparisons. Nevertheless, effectance theory and social cognitive theory clearly differ over several issues. In the sociocognitive view, choice behavior, effort, and persistence are extensively regulated by beliefs of personal efficacy rather than by an effectance drive. Because efficacy beliefs are defined and measured independently of performance, they provide a basis for predicting the occurrence, generality, and persistence of behavior. In contrast, it is difficult to explain the variability of human behavior in terms of an overall intrinsic motive drive (Bandura, 1991b). People will approach, explore, and try to manage situations within their perceived capabilities, but unless they are externally coerced, they avoid transactions with those aspects of their environment that they perceive exceed their coping abilities.

These alternative views also differ in how they explain the origins of personal efficacy. In effectance theory, the effectance motive develops gradually through prolonged transactions with the environment. The theory thus focuses almost exclusively on exploratory behavior as the source of effectance. In social cognitive theory, efficacy beliefs are developed and altered not only by direct mastery experiences but also by vicarious experience, social evaluations by significant others, and changes in physiological states or how they are construed. These differences in theoretical approach have significant implications for how one goes about creating a strong sense of efficacy.

Beliefs of personal efficacy do not operate as dispositional determinants independently of contextual factors. Some situations require greater self-regulatory skill and more arduous performance than others. Efficacy beliefs will vary accordingly. Thus, for example, the level and strength of personal efficacy in public speaking will differ depending on the subject matter, whether the speech is extemporaneous or from notes, and the evaluative standards of the audiences to be addressed, to mention just a few conditional factors. Therefore, analyses of how efficacy beliefs affect actions rely on microanalytic measures rather than global indices of personality traits or motives of effectance. It is no more informative to speak of self-efficacy in general terms than to speak of nonspecific social behavior.

In effectance theory, affecting the environment arouses feelings of efficacy and pleasure. Although such feelings may arise from performance attainments, attainments do not necessarily enhance perceived self-efficacy. Attainments may raise, lower, or leave unchanged beliefs of personal efficacy, depending on what is made of those attainments. Nor does the successful exercise of personal efficacy necessarily bring pleasure or raise self-esteem. It depends on how attainments measure up against internal standards. If the level of efficacy that is realized falls short of personal standards of merit, the accomplishment may, in fact, leave one with self-discontent. Students with stringent academic standards will not swell with pride upon achieving only modest improvements in academic activities important to them. The pace at which activities are mastered can drastically alter self-evaluative reactions (Simon, 1979a). Accomplishments that surpass earlier ones bring a continued sense of self-satisfaction. But people derive little satisfaction from smaller accomplishments, or even devalue them, after having made larger strides. Early spectacular accomplishments reflecting exemplary proficiency can thus be conducive to later self-dissatisfaction even in the face of continuing personal attainments. Nor will high self-efficaciousness in an activity boost self-satisfaction if the activity happens to be devalued. When competencies are used for inhumane purposes, performers may feel self-efficacious in their triumphs but remain displeased with themselves for the sorrow they have wrought.

The relationship between personal attainments and self-satisfaction is clearly more complex than effectance theory would lead one to believe. A theory of effectance must consider the important role played by personal standards and the cognitive appraisal of attainments in people's affective reactions to their own performances. These are some of the mechanisms that determine whether performance attainments bring pleasure or displeasure. The manner in which internal standards and efficacy beliefs operate as interrelated mechanisms of personal agency and affective self-reactions is addressed in a later chapter.

Effectance motivation is said to come into play only under certain limited conditions (White, 1959), a point that is often overlooked in overextensions of the theory to wide spheres of behavior. The effectance motive is believed to be aroused when the organism is otherwise unoccupied or is only weakly stimulated by organic drives. In the words of White (1960), effectance promotes *spare-time behavior*. In social cognitive theory, efficacy beliefs enter into the regulation of all types of performances, until they become routinized into habitual patterns. Although the theory of effectance motivation lacks verifiable particulars, considerable research disputes its two basic premises: that people are inherently driven to exercise control over their environment and that the achievement of control is inherently self-satisfying (Bandura, 1986a; Rodin, Rennert, & Solomon, 1980). We will return to a more detailed discussion of the issue of inherent motivators shortly.

Yarrow and his associates have recast effectance motivation in a more testable form (Yarrow et al., 1983). They call it mastery motivation and construe

it as a striving for competence — which, in turn, is defined as effective action in dealing with the environment. Mastery motivation is manifested in attentiveness, exploratory behavior, and persistence in goal-directed activities. Developmental tests of the nature and correlates of this postulated motive system yield equivocal findings. Behavioral indices of mastery motivation are weakly related to one another and become even more heterogeneous with increasing age of the people tested. A mastery motive that does not hang together presents conceptual problems. The same mastery behavior shows little consistency over even a short time, reflecting surprising instability. Moreover, indices of mastery motivation are not consistently linked to actual competence. The authors, however, place a positive interpretation on this extensive disconnectedness. The mastery motive simply takes on the shape of the empirical findings. The proponents argue that weak relationships between different indices of the same motive serve as evidence that mastery motivation is multifaceted. Increasing heterogeneity indicates that the motive becomes more differentiated with age. Lack of behavioral continuity indicates that the motive undergoes developmental transformation. And the inconsistent linkage between mastery motivation and actual competence is taken as evidence that they create each other interactively, although one would expect reciprocal causation to produce a strong relationship.

A more plausible conclusion to be drawn from the extensive disconnectedness is that striving for competence is not driven by an omnibus mastery motive but rather is motivated by the varied benefits of competent action. What competent functioning is differs across time, milieus, social standards, and domains of activity. Competence requires appropriate learning experiences; it does not emerge spontaneously. Hence, people develop different patterns of competencies and deploy them selectively depending on the match of efficacy beliefs to environmental demands and on anticipated outcomes. A functional analysis of striving for competence can better explain variations in the patterning of human competencies than does one cast in terms of an omnibus mastery motive.

The Exercise of Personal Control: Inborn Drive or Prevalent Incentive?

As previously noted, personal control enables one to predict events and shape them to one's liking. A major issue of contention is whether the exercise of personal efficacy is impelled by an inborn drive for control or is motivated by anticipated benefits. There is a fundamental difference between the two. Drives push action, anticipated incentives draw it (Bolles, 1975a). For example, most people are drawn to television and spend countless hours watching it for the enjoyment it provides, but one would hardly regard television viewing as impelled by an inborn drive. Being deprived of television will not cause the buildup of a drive pressing for release by exposure to televised fare. Theories in which a drive for control is inferred from the very behavior it supposedly causes are fraught with difficulties. Drive theories become testable if drives are measured independently of the behavior they supposedly activate. If variations in controlling action are taken as evidence of variations in strength of a drive for control, the circularity strips the theory of any explanatory or predictive value. Unless the strength of a drive is measured separately from its postulated effects, the functional properties ascribed to it are empirically unverifiable.

Some theorists regard the striving for control as an expression of an inborn drive (Deci & Ryan, 1985; White, 1959). For others, the striving for control is couched in the language of an inborn drive without explicitly designating it as such. Thus, it becomes an "intrinsic necessity of life" (Adler, 1956), "a primary motivational propensity" (DeCharms, 1978), "a motive system" that impels the organism (Harter, 1981), a universal "inborn desire" for competence (Skinner, 1995), and the like. Such characterizations leave considerable ambiguity about whether the motivation for control is an acquired propensity or an inherited endowment. In social cognitive theory, people exercise control for the benefits they gain by it. Some of these benefits may involve biological gratifications, but the striving for control is not a drive in its own right. Treatises on perceived and actual control typically emphasize the importance of the intrinsic value of control. But control is not exercised universally with blissful outcomes. There are many conditions under which people shun control; this fact is a serious problem for inborn drive theories but is compatible with incentive motivation theories.

When personal control is easy to exercise and enables one to deal effectively with the demands of everyday life, it is highly desired. Indeed, in laboratory studies in which aversive events can be controlled by simple acts requiring little in the way of skills, expenditure of effort, and risks, personal control is decidedly preferred (Miller, 1979). Personal control is neither universally desired nor routinely exercised, however. There is an onerous side to personal control that quickly dampens interest in it. Self-development of personal efficacy requires mastery of knowledge and skills attainable only through long hours of arduous work. This calls for the sacrifice of many gratifications. Moreover, maintaining proficiency in one's pursuits, many of which require upgrading of skills with rapid social and technological advances, demands continued investment of time, effort, and resources. A noted composer put it succinctly when he remarked, "The toughest thing about success is that you've got to keep on being a success."

In addition to the hard work of continual self-development, in many situations the exercise of personal control carries heavy responsibilities and risks. For example, managers of organizations are granted considerable controlling power, but they must bear personal responsibility for the effects of their decisions and actions, some of which have widespread repercussions. It is usually the most self-efficacious individuals who assume leadership positions of high potential stress and strain. They are held accountable but must depend on others to get things done. Their lives can be made miserable if they have to preside over conflicting social expectations, pressures, and demands (Kahn, Wolfe, Quinn, & Snoek, 1964). These burdensome aspects of personal control can dull the appetite for it. Attractive incentives, privileges, and heady social rewards are therefore needed to get people to seek control in pursuits involving complex skills, onerous responsibilities, and weighty risks.

Proxy Control

People are often willing to relinquish control over events that affect their lives to free themselves of the performance demands and hazards that the exercise of control entails. Rather than strive for direct control, they seek their well-being and security in proxy control. In this socially mediated mode of control, people try to get those who wield influence and power to act on their behalf to effect the changes they desire. Children pressure parents to get what they want; employees work through intermediaries to alter organizational practices; and the citizenry tries to shape its social future by influencing the actions of its governmental representatives and other public officials. Effective proxy control requires a high sense of personal efficacy to influence intermediaries who, in turn, operate as the agents of desired improvements.

In many areas of life, individuals do not have direct control over the institutional mechanisms of change and therefore must turn to proxy control to alter their lives for the better. All too often, however, people surrender control to intermediaries in areas over which they do have some direct influence. They choose not to exercise direct control because they have not developed the means to do so, they believe others can do it better, or they do not want to saddle themselves with the onerous responsibilities that personal control entails. Part of the price of proxy control is a vulnerable security that rests on the competence, power, and favors of others.

A low sense of efficacy fosters dependence on proxy control, which further reduces opportunities to build the skills needed for efficacious action. The influential role of comparative efficacy evaluation in proxy control is revealed in studies by Miller and her associates (Miller, 1980). People who are led to believe that they possess superior coping ability handle aversive problems by themselves, whereas those who believe themselves to be less skilled yield control to others to cope with the aversive environment. The dependent ones enjoy the protective benefits without the performance demands and attendant stress, while the controllers do the work and suffer the distress over managing arduous task demands and the risks of failure.

People who are in the habit of exercising personal control do not like to place their fate in the hands of others, even when it is advantageous for them to do so. Competitive, hard-driving, type A individuals are constantly struggling to master task demands impatiently and with a sense of time urgency (Glass & Carver, 1980). Miller, Lack, and Asroff (1985) found that people who exhibit the type A coping pattern would rather suffer aversive experiences than relinquish control to others who can manage the situation better. Type B's, who are more relaxed and easygoing, readily give up control under similar circumstances. Female type A's are willing to yield control provisionally to someone who is more skilled if they can reclaim it at will. But many male type A's will not surrender control even provisionally.

Inadvertent Relinquishment of Personal Control

Many factors operate in everyday life to undermine efficacious use of the knowledge and skills that people possess. As a result, they do not exercise the personal control that is fully within their capabilities. In a program of research on illusory incompetence, Langer (1979) has given us a better understanding of how people give up personal control, either by making erroneous inferences from their experiences or by inadvertent action. At the time the actions are taken, people do not perceive themselves as relinquishing control, nor do they realize that their actions may hinder their future competence. Since the self-debilitation goes largely unnoticed, there is little reason to resist it.

People often relinquish personal control by their actions because it is the easier thing to do at the time. Langer (1979) documents the various conditions under which this is likely to happen. In some instances, the effort involved in mastering an activity seems to outweigh its perceived potential benefits. In others, people foster self-induced dependencies when they can obtain valued outcomes more easily by having somebody else do things for them. Settings in which individuals happen to perform poorly can, in themselves, come to activate a sense of incompetence that impairs future performance in those particular contexts. The contextual activation of inefficacy is well illustrated by athletic performances in which winners regularly lose to weaker opponents in settings in which they have come to expect difficulties because of past upsets. The mere presence of an opponent exuding high confidence can undermine one's use of routine skills. Attending to what is strange in new tasks, rather than to what is familiar about them and clearly within one's capability, may similarly hinder the effective use of skills. Rigid mind-sets impede generative use of one's knowledge and skills in new situations in which they would be useful. When people are cast in subordinate roles or are assigned inferior labels, implying limited competence, they perform activities at which they are highly skilled less well than when they are not labeled negatively or placed in a subordinate role. Racial and gender stereotyping similarly undermines the effective use of cognitive skills (Steele, 1996). Thus, African-American students asked to state their race perform more poorly on standardized college entrance exams than those not asked to give their racial status. Women perform worse than men on math tests characterized as sensitive to gender differences, but they perform as well on the same tests when they are depicted as insensitive to gender. Offering unnecessary help can also detract from a sense of competence and thereby impair the execution of skills.

Mindlessness is hypothesized by Langer and Park (1990) to underlie illusory incompetence. Environmental cues suggestive of personal deficiencies are said to trigger poor performance when routine situations are no longer given thoughtful consideration. Undoubtedly, some instances of deficient skill use do reflect routinized situational control of action. But situational influences also activate other processes that can detract from the effective use of skills. Verification of an explanatory mechanism is greatly aided if the mediating process is measured rather than simply presumed

to be operating. The presumptive mediation of mindlessness could be tested by assessing whether the extent to which people think about the situations they are in accounts for variations in how much their performance is undermined by situational influences suggesting personal deficiency. The degree of mindful involvement in the activities at hand could also be varied systematically and its impact on effective use of preexisting skills measured.

We know from other lines of research that the types of situations that produce illusory incompetence diminish perceived self-efficacy, with concomitant effects on choice behavior, motivation, stress, and self-debilitating thought. For example, a formidable-looking opponent instills lower efficacy beliefs than does one who looks less impressive (Weinberg, Yukelson, & Jackson, 1980). Illusorily strengthened beliefs of personal efficacy in relation to an opponent heighten competitive performance and resilience, whereas illusorily weakened efficacy beliefs debilitate competitive performance and increase vulnerability to the adverse effects of failure (Weinberg, Gould, & Jackson, 1979). The more the efficacy beliefs are diminished, the greater is the performance debilitation.

Trivial situational factors, devoid of information that could affect competence, can nevertheless influence efficacy beliefs (Cervone & Peake, 1986; Peake & Cervone, 1989). Illusory efficacy beliefs exert a strong effect on the level of performance motivation. Dwelling on formidable aspects of a task weakens people's belief in their efficacy, but focusing on doable aspects of the same task raises self-efficacy beliefs (Cervone, 1989). The stronger the altered efficacy beliefs, the longer people persevere in the face of repeated failure. In these diverse experiments, variations in perceived self-efficacy predict variation in motivation under the same conditions as well as between different conditions. Biasing external influences impair performance through their influence on efficacy beliefs rather than directly. Once people develop a mind-set about their efficacy in given situations, they act on their established self-beliefs without further reappraising their capabilities.

Outcome Expectancy Theories

With the ascendancy of cognitive theories of behavior, the concept of expectancy assumed an increasingly prominent place in explanations of human functioning. Psychological theories postulating that expectations influence actions focused almost exclusively on outcome expectations. Irwin's (1971) theory of motivation and intentional behavior was formulated in terms of act-outcome expectancies. In Bolles's (1975b) view, learning essentially involves the acquisition of expectancies that particular situational events or behaviors will give rise to certain outcomes. Rotter's (1966) conceptual scheme centers on causal beliefs about the relationship between actions and outcomes. In a similar vein, Seligman (1975) set forth the view that people behave resignedly when they acquire expectancies that they cannot affect outcomes through their actions. According to expectancy-valence theories, performance is jointly influenced by the expectancy that behaving in a particular way will lead to a given outcome and the desirability of that outcome (Atkinson, 1964; Feather, 1982; Vroom, 1964).

The heavy emphasis on outcome expectations can be traced, in large part, to the Tolmanian roots of this line of theorizing. Tolman formulated his conceptual system at a time when competing psychological theories sought to resolve controversies about learning by examining how animals learn to solve mazes. The prevailing theories at the time viewed learning mainly as the acquisition of habits (Hull, 1943; Spence, 1956). Tolman (1932, 1951) interpreted learning as the development of expectations that behavior will produce certain outcomes. The question of whether the animals had the ability to get to the goal box was, of course, never at issue. They came fully endowed with the trivial behavioral skill needed to navigate the prefixed path. Therefore, what the animals expected to find in the goal box was considered to be the major determinant of their choice behavior. The influential role of self-referent thought in the regulation of motivation and action was understandably disregarded, because animals are not given to self-reflection and do not structure the meager options in their lives on the basis of self-beliefs of what they can and cannot do. In contrast, the self-referent belief system is fundamental to adaptive human functioning. People's beliefs in their efficacy affect almost everything they do: how they think, motivate themselves, feel, and behave.

Some of the theorizing about the controllability of outcomes is sometimes likened to the notion of perceived efficacy. According to the theory of personality proposed by Rotter (1966), behavior is influenced by generalized expectancies that outcomes are determined either by one's actions or by external forces beyond one's control. Such expectations about the instrumental value of behavior are considered to be largely the product of one's reinforcement history. Most of the research within this tradition is concerned with the extent to which behavior can be predicted by individual differences in the tendency to perceive outcomes as being either personally or externally determined (Lefcourt, 1976, 1979; Phares, 1976; Rotter, Chance, & Phares, 1972). In general, people who believe that their outcomes are determined by their behavior tend to be more active than those who perceive outcomes fatalistically.

External causality is often viewed in terms of beliefs that outcomes depend on chance factors. Gurin and her associates have argued that lack of personal control is often due not to chance or whimsy but to the unresponsiveness of social systems and the barriers they erect to protect vested interests and the status quo (Gurin & Brim, 1984; Gurin, Gurin, & Morrison, 1978). Social systems may be unresponsive because adequate solutions to problems are not yet available. More often, however, it is because they are negatively biased against certain classes of people but promote and reward the competencies of the members they favor. Institutional biases either bar access to opportunity structures or impose higher competence requirements on members of disfavored groups who are trying to attain valued outcomes. The imposition of higher competence requirements is illustrated by the changing social practices with respect to administrative roles in organizations. At one time, executive positions were closed to minorities and women, no matter how talented they were. Later, the extraordinarily talented could gain entry into lower echelons. Still later, differential competence requirements were largely removed for entry into subordinate ranks, but they still operate strongly at top executive levels.

Perceived self-efficacy and locus of control are sometimes mistakenly viewed as essentially the same phenomenon measured at different levels of generality. In point of fact, they represent entirely different phenomena. Beliefs about whether one can produce certain actions (*perceived self-efficacy*) cannot, by any stretch of the imagination, be considered the same as beliefs about whether actions affect outcomes (*locus of control*). The conceptual distinction is corroborated empirically (Bandura, 1991b). Evidence reviewed in the next chapter shows that perceived self-efficacy and locus of control bear little or no relationship to each other. With regard to their relationship to behavior, perceived self-efficacy is a uniformly good predictor of diverse forms of behavior, whereas locus of control is generally a weak or inconsistent predictor of the same behaviors. This is not to say that outcome expectations have no impact on behavior. They do, if particularized and assessed in relation to the actions that can produce them. Social cognitive theory identifies different classes of expected outcomes and measures them in discriminative ways linked to performances situated in contexts rather than in general decontextualized ways.

It is widely assumed that beliefs that personal actions determine outcomes give rise to a sense of efficacy and power, whereas beliefs that outcomes occur regardless of what one does create apathy. It should be noted, however, that Rotter's (1966) conceptual scheme is primarily concerned with causal beliefs about the relationship between actions and outcomes, not with personal efficacy. Beliefs about the locus of outcome causality must be distinguished from beliefs about personal efficacy. Beliefs that outcomes are determined by one's own behavior can be either demoralizing or empowering, depending on whether or not one believes one can produce the required behavior. People who regard outcomes as personally determined, but who lack requisite skills, would experience a low sense of efficacy and view the activities with a sense of futility. Thus, for example, children who lack understanding of arithmetic concepts and expect their course grades to depend entirely on the quality of their mathematical performance have every reason to be demoralized. It is when people have the efficacy to perform well that belief that outcomes are dependent on their actions will create a sense of causative power.

Human behavior and affective states would be best predicted by the combined influence of efficacy beliefs and the types of performance outcomes expected within given social systems. The structural features of social systems that are especially germane concern the opportunities they provide and the constraints they impose. As shown in Figure 1.2, different patterns of efficacy beliefs and outcome expectations have different psychosocial and emotional effects. A high sense of personal efficacy

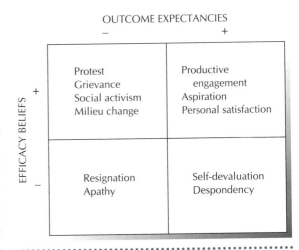

FIGURE 1.2. The effects of different patterns of efficacy beliefs and performance outcome expectancies on behavior and affective states. The pluses and minuses represent positive and negative qualities of efficacy beliefs and outcome expectancies.

in a responsive environment that rewards valued accomplishments fosters aspirations, productive engagement in activities, and a sense of fulfillment. These are the conditions that enable people to exercise substantial control over their lives through self-development.

Consider the pattern combining high personal efficacy with low environmental responsiveness. Efficacious individuals who cannot gain valued outcomes through personal accomplishments will not necessarily cease trying. Those with low perceived efficacy quickly give up when their efforts fail to produce results. But self-efficacious individuals will intensify their efforts and, if necessary, try to change inequitable social practices. This pattern in which competency goes unrewarded or is punished underscores the need to differentiate two levels of control: control over the outcomes that accomplishments bring and control over the social systems that prescribe what the outcomes will be for given endeavors. Piece-rate workers may control their incomes by how hard they work but exercise no control over the unit pay rate the system sets. Gurin and Brim (1984) and Lacey (1979a) address this issue of control over social systems, which typically receives scant attention in psychological analyses of controllability. Conditions combining high personal efficacy and environmental unresponsiveness generate resentment, protest, and collective efforts to change existing institutional practices (Bandura, 1973; Short & Wolfgang, 1972). Should reforms be hard to achieve, given better options, people will desert environments that are unresponsive to their efforts and pursue their activities elsewhere.

The joint influence of efficacy beliefs and outcome expectations provides a basis for differentiating conditions conducive to apathy from those likely to drive people to bouts of despondency. When people have a low sense of personal efficacy and no amount of effort by themselves or others like them produces valued outcomes, they become apathetic and resigned to a dreary life. If no one can succeed, people become convinced of their powerlessness to improve the human condition. As a result, they do not put much effort into effecting changes.

The pattern in which people perceive themselves as ineffectual but see others like them enjoying the benefits of successful effort is apt to give rise to self-disparagement and depression. The evident success of similar others makes it hard to avoid self-criticism. In studies instilling different beliefs about personal efficacy and the success of others, belief in one's own inability to secure valued outcomes readily attainable by others of similar standing is most conducive to depressive mood and cognitive debilitation of performance (Bloom, Yates, & Brosvic, 1984; Davis & Yates, 1982).

Self-Efficacy, Outcome Expectancies, and Control

Outcomes arise from actions. How one behaves largely determines the outcomes one experiences. Performance is thus causally prior to outcomes. Similarly, the outcomes people anticipate depend largely on their judgments of how well they will be able to perform in given situations. To claim, as some writers have (Eastman & Marzillier, 1984), that people visualize outcomes and then infer their own capabilities from the imagined outcomes is to invoke a peculiar system of backward causation in which the outcomes that flow from actions are made to precede the actions. People do not judge that they will drown if they jump in deep water and then infer that they must be poor swimmers. Rather, people who judge themselves to be poor swimmers will visualize themselves drowning if they jump in deep water. The causal relationship between beliefs of personal efficacy and outcome expectations is depicted in Figure 1.3. Perceived self-efficacy is a judgment of one's ability to organize and execute given types of performances, whereas an outcome expectation is a judgment of the likely consequence such performances will produce.

Outcome expectations can take three major forms (Bandura, 1986a). Within each form, the positive expectations serve as incentives, the negative ones as disincentives. One distinct class of outcomes is the positive and negative physical effects

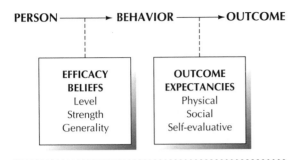

PERSON ───────▶ BEHAVIOR ───────▶ OUTCOME

EFFICACY BELIEFS
Level
Strength
Generality

OUTCOME EXPECTANCIES
Physical
Social
Self-evaluative

FIGURE 1.3. The conditional relationships between efficacy beliefs and outcome expectancies. In given domains of functioning, efficacy beliefs vary in level, strength, and generality. The outcomes that flow from a given course of action can take the form of positive or negative physical, social, and self-evaluation effects.

that accompany the behavior. These include pleasant sensory experiences and physical pleasures in the positive forms and aversive sensory experiences, pain, and physical discomfort in the negative forms. Human behavior is partly regulated by the social reactions it evokes. Positive and negative social effects form the second major class of outcomes. On the positive side, they include such social reactions of others as expressions of interest, approval, social recognition, monetary compensation, and conferral of status and power; on the negative side, they include disinterest, disapproval, social rejection, censure, deprivation of privileges, and imposed penalties.

Social cognitive theory rejects the crude functionalist view that behavior is regulated solely by external rewards and punishments. If actions were performed only in anticipation of external rewards and punishments, people would behave like weather vanes, constantly shifting direction to conform to whatever influence happened to impinge upon them at the moment. In actuality, people display considerable self-direction in the face of competing influences. Anyone who attempted to change a devoted pacifist into a cruel aggressor or a religious devotee into an atheist would quickly come to appreciate the force of self-reactive influence in the regulation of human behavior. After

people adopt personal standards, they regulate their behavior by their self-sanctions. They do things that give them self-satisfaction and a sense of pride and self-worth and refrain from behaving in ways that give rise to self-dissatisfaction, self-devaluation, and self-censure. This third major class of outcomes includes the positive and negative self-evaluative reactions to one's own behavior. To use an athletic example, the belief that one can high-jump seven feet in an athletic contest is a self-efficacy judgment, not an expected outcome. The anticipated social recognition, applause, trophies, monetary prizes, and self-satisfaction if such a jump represents a superior attainment, and the anticipated social disappointment, forfeiture of material rewards, and self-criticism if it represents a deficient level of attainment, constitute the outcome expectations. A comprehensive functionalist view encompasses all these different forms of outcomes.

As conventionally defined, a *performance* is an accomplishment; an *outcome* is something that follows from it. In short, an outcome is the consequence of a performance, not the performance itself. Serious conceptual problems are created when a performance is misconstrued as the outcome of itself, as when jumping seven feet is viewed as the outcome that flows from it. A performance must be specified by descriptive markers; for example, high jumps of five, six, or seven feet. Remove the specifying markers, and one is left with a nondescript activity. Needless confusion has been introduced into the literature by misinterpreting *markers* of different levels of performance as the outcomes of the performance (Eastman & Marzillier, 1984). Consider an example in the achievement domain. The letter grades of A, B, C, D, and F are markers of different levels of performance, not outcomes. Performance grade levels do not come with a fixed set of outcomes. Performances at the A level may bring self-satisfaction and social approval in circles that value academic achievement but social censure in subgroups of peers who devalue academic achievement and are quick to ridicule, harass, and ostracize academic achievers (Ogbu, 1990; Solomon, 1992).

The markers of different performance levels vary depending on the domain of functioning. In academic achievement, the marker may be letter grades or percentile ranks; in health-related behavior, the amount of change achieved in weight, exercise, smoking, or nutritional habits; in phobic behavior, the level of threat that is managed; in athletic activities, the speed or accuracy of performance; and in organizational functioning, the level of group productivity. But in no case is the marker of different performance levels an outcome expectation. The motivating potential of anticipated outcomes is, of course, determined largely by the subjective value placed on them. Two people may believe that a given behavioral attainment will produce a particular outcome but evaluate the attractiveness of that outcome quite differently.

Those who misconstrue a performance marker as the outcome of itself launch themselves on an endless performance regress. In the high-jump example, a six-foot leap becomes the "outcome" of a prior pattern of muscular activity, which in turn becomes an "outcome" brought about by a prior activity regulating the muscular exertion, which in turn becomes an "outcome" that is brought about by something else the agent did antecedently, and so it goes on and on endlessly with each attainment being an "outcome" of its precursor, which then becomes an "outcome" of its precursor! Similarly, an A level of academic performance becomes an "outcome" of a certain level of study behavior, but then the study behavior itself becomes an "outcome" of something else the student did to bring it about.

The conceptual confusion caused by converting part of a performance sequence into an outcome can be illustrated in another way. Behavior and the effects it produces are different classes of events. The latter can be used to influence the former. That is, behavior can be altered by the outcomes it gives rise to, be they physical, social, or self-evaluative effects. Rechristening an attainment marker as an outcome creates a logically and procedurally impossible predicament when one is asked to raise academic performance to the A level through contingent use of outcomes. Such a task would require using an A level performance (the

alleged outcome) to produce an A level performance! The misconstrual of a performance attainment as an outcome of itself and the resulting infinite regress problem can be easily avoided simply by centering the inquiry on the physical, social, and self-evaluative outcomes that flow from a given performance attainment.

Weight loss is another example of the conceptual and operational distinction between attainments and outcomes. People do not struggle to shed pounds just to shed pounds. They do so for the resulting outcomes, which include physical health benefits, social benefits, and self-evaluative benefits. If weight loss had no physical effects whatsoever, if others couldn't care less whether individuals are svelte or plump, and if their weight had no bearing on their self-satisfaction, people would not go around starving themselves endlessly solely to lose weight (the alleged outcome). The weight-reduction and diet industries would promptly go out of business. This is the conceptual muddle created by misinterpreting an attainment marker as an outcome of its prior self. If researchers choose to construe a performance marker as an outcome, this construal is their conceptual and methodological problem to defend. A view of outcomes that self-efficacy theory categorically rejects should not be foisted on it and then portrayed as its problem in separating performances from outcomes.

Self-efficacy theory distinguishes degrees of controllability by personal means. Controllability affects the extent to which efficacy beliefs shape outcome expectancies and how much outcome expectations add incrementally to prediction of performance. There is no single relationship between efficacy beliefs and outcome expectations. It depends on how tightly contingencies between actions and outcomes are structured, either inherently or socially, in a given domain of functioning. In activities where outcomes are highly contingent on quality of performance, the types of outcomes people anticipate depend largely on how well they believe they will be able to perform in given situations. For example, students do not expect to be showered with academic honors for a low level of scholarship. Athletes who concede that they cannot triumph over formidable opponents do not expect to capture top prizes in contests with them. In most social, intellectual, and physical pursuits, those who judge themselves highly efficacious will expect favorable outcomes, whereas those who expect poor performances of themselves will conjure up negative outcomes.

Where performance determines outcome, efficacy beliefs account for most of the variance in expected outcomes. When differences in efficacy beliefs are controlled, the outcomes expected for given performances make little or no independent contribution to prediction of behavior. This is true for diverse spheres of functioning, including academic attainments (Barling & Abel, 1983; Lent, Lopez, & Bieschke, 1991; Shell, Murphy, & Bruning, 1989), social behavior (Gresham, Evans, & Elliott, 1988), weight management (Shannon et al., 1990), health habits (Carey, Kabra, Carey, Halperin, & Richards, 1993; Godding & Glasgow, 1985), pain management (Jensen, Turner, & Romano, 1991; Lackner, Carosella, & Feuerstein, 1996; Williams & Kinney, 1991), phobic behavior (Lee, 1984a,b; Williams & Watson, 1985), premature attrition from counseling (Longo, Lent, & Brown, 1992), occupational performance (Barling & Beattie, 1983), and choice of cultural milieu in which to pursue one's occupation (Singer, 1993).

Lack of independent predictiveness does not mean that outcome expectations are unimportant to human behavior. Rather, where efficacy beliefs foretell the expected outcomes, the outcomes become a redundant predictor. Redundancy of predictors, however, should not be misinterpreted as indifference to expected outcomes. The fact that students' perceived scholastic efficacy determines whether or not they expect to gain academic awards does not mean that they place no value on academic awards or are not motivated by them. It is because people see outcomes as contingent on the adequacy of their performance, and care about those outcomes, that they rely on efficacy beliefs in deciding which course of action to pursue and how long to pursue it. They avoid pursuits that they believe they cannot perform successfully and that they

anticipate will invite trouble for them, but they actively pursue activities that they judge they can manage successfully and that hold promise of valued rewards. In short, people take action when they hold efficacy beliefs and outcome expectations that make the effort seem worthwhile. They expect given actions to produce desired outcomes and believe that they can perform those actions.

Efficacy beliefs account for only part of the variation in expected outcomes when outcomes are not completely controlled by quality of performance. This partial separation occurs when factors extraneous to quality of performance also affect outcomes or when outcomes are socially tied to a minimum level of performance, so that further variations in quality of performance above the standard do not produce differential outcomes. For example, the prizes granted by equestrian judges may be influenced by the attractiveness of the horse as well as by the skill of the rider. In work situations, compensation is often fixed to some normative performance standard, but a higher level of productivity does not bring larger weekly paychecks. Belief that one can do the job at the required level will produce better expected outcomes than will disbelief in one's efficacy to meet that level. Belief that one can perform above the minimal standard, however, would not give rise to different expected outcomes. And belief that one cannot meet the minimal standard would produce expectations of unemployment in that activity.

Expected outcomes are independent of efficacy beliefs when contingencies are restrictively structured so that no level of competence by certain groups can produce desired outcomes. This independence occurs in pursuits that are rigidly segregated by sex, race, age, or some other factor. Under such circumstances, people in the excluded group expect uniformly negative outcomes however efficacious they judge themselves to be. During the era when professional sports were rigidly segregated by race, minority baseball players could not gain entry to the major leagues and receive lucrative financial payments no matter how well they pitched or batted. After the social barrier was removed, perceived efficacy pretty much prescribed the expected outcomes.

Self-Guidance by Envisioned Possible Selves

Markus and her associates provide an agentic theory of self-conception that assigns an influential regulative function to envisioned possible selves (Markus & Nurius, 1986). In this view, people conjure up specific self-images of future successes and failures. These possible selves are constructed from personal experiences, the vast array of actual and symbolic models, and sociocultural influences that shape life pursuits. Possible selves that are well-articulated serve several functions. They provide a conceptual framework for interpreting our experiences. They influence the way we think about our potential and options. And they guide our courses of action and motivate our pursuit of selected goals. Self-images serve this function well when they are elaborated to include the relevant plans and procedural strategies for realizing desired futures. Ill-defined possible selves remain but idle fantasies. The nonprescriptiveness of indefinite selves is captured well in a theatrical portrayal of a character who never quite manages to get her act together (Wagner, 1987). Reflecting on her unrealized ambitions leads her to the incontrovertible insight: "All my life I've always wanted to be somebody. But I see now I should have been more specific."

In this conceptual scheme, people's personal repertoires contain a variety of possible selves that reflect their hopes and fears. Positive selves motivate and guide people to realize desired futures. By themselves, unwanted and feared selves can block action or prompt avoidance of what one is afraid of becoming. If combined with positive images, however, they can serve as additional motivators to do what is needed to avoid envisioned unwanted futures or to prepare to cope with them. Because of the additive motivational effect, the balance of positive and negative possible selves may be more influential in shaping the desired self than either the positive or negative visualized selves alone. Social circumstances activate certain subsets of possible selves that, in turn, promote the patterns of behavior appropriate to creating the desired self.

Markus and her colleagues regard anticipatory cognitive simulation as the key mechanism by which self-images get translated into behavioral competencies (Markus, Cross, & Wurf, 1990). On the assumption that perception, imagery, and action have parallel structural properties, they presume that cognitive simulation coordinates perceptual and action schemata. Viewed from the sociocognitive perspective, however, it is the individual, rather than similarities of neurophysiological structure, that forges the linkage between thought and action, often through laborious effort. If structural similarities led to automatic translation of cognitive schemata into action schemata, the development of competencies would be an easy matter. One would need only to visualize a skill to have it arise behaviorally. In actuality, proficiency is usually achieved through a long, arduous process, especially where complex skills are involved. An interpretation in terms of cross-modal coordination of perceptual and action schemata leaves unexplained the transformational mechanism by which cognition is converted into proficient action.

One solution that is widely accepted for the transformation problem relies on a dual knowledge system: declarative knowledge and procedural knowledge (Anderson, 1980). Declarative knowledge supplies the appropriate factual information; procedural knowledge supplies production systems embodying decision rules for solving tasks. Construing the acquisition of competence in terms of factual and procedural knowledge is well suited for cognitive problem solving where solutions are cognitively generated and no actions are involved or are trivially simple. One must distinguish between knowledge and performance skills, however. A novice given complete factual information about how to ski and a full set of procedural rules, then launched from a mountaintop, would most likely end up in an orthopedic ward or intensive care unit of the local infirmary. Procedural knowledge alone will not convert novices into proficient violinists, captivating orators, or graceful ballerinas. Activities requiring the construction and adept execution of complex skills call for additional mechanisms to get from knowledge structures to proficient action. Procedural knowledge and cognitive skills are necessary but not sufficient for competent performance.

In social cognitive theory (Bandura, 1986a), the mechanism for transforming thought into action operates through a conception-matching process. Conceptions of skills serve as guides for developing competencies and as internal standards for improving them. Conceptions are rarely transformed into appropriate performances without error on initial attempts. Skilled performances are usually achieved by repeated corrective adjustments of enactments to the guiding conception as the skills are being behaviorally constructed and improved (Carroll & Bandura, 1987, 1990). Observing one's enactments provides the information needed to detect and correct mismatches between conception and action. If people do not monitor what they are doing, efforts to implement a good conception will not produce proficient action.

A theory cast in terms of multiple selves plunges one into deep philosophical waters. It requires a regress of selves to a presiding superordinate self that selects and manages the collection of possible selves to suit given purposes. Actually, there is only one self that can visualize different desired and undesired futures and select courses of action designed to attain cherished futures and escape feared ones. Actions are regulated by a person, not by a cluster of selves doing the choosing and guiding. The desired future self bears close likeness to distal life goals, and the more proximal working self-concept resembles the short-run subgoals through which distal aspirations are realized. Aspirations combine with self-appraisal of capabilities in shaping life courses. People's beliefs in their personal efficacy determine the life pursuits they foreclose from consideration, as well as those they choose to follow and their level of interest, staying power, and success in them (Lent & Hackett, 1987).

The fractionation of selves poses additional conceptual problems because once one starts fractionating the self, where does one stop? For example, an athletic self can be split into an envisioned tennis self and a golfing self. These separable selves, in turn, have their subselves. Thus, a golfing self can be subdivided into different facets of the athletic ability to include a driving self, a fairway self, a sand-trapped self, and a putting self. How does one decide where to stop fractionating selves? Here, too, there is only one self that can aspire to perfect different sets of subskills encompassed by an envisioned multifaceted pursuit. Diversity arises not from a collection of agentive selves but from the different options considered by the one and the same agentive self.

People striving to realize an envisioned desired self guide and motivate their efforts through a set of self-regulatory mechanisms. These are governed by appraisal of personal capabilities for different pursuits, long-range aspiration merged with proximal subgoals that lead to its fulfillment, positive and negative outcome expectations for different life courses, the value placed on those envisioned outcomes, and the perceived environmental constraints and opportunity structures. These represent some of the influential sociocognitive determinants of the courses that lives take. One and the same person exercises these self-influences differentially in different activity domains and in different social contexts.

The research on self-images has centered mainly on the blend of positive and negative possible selves in people who differ in modes of adaptation and on how envisioned selves affect the processing of information and recruitment of imagery. Those who are coping well have a balanced mixture of possible self-images, whereas people who are exhibiting problems of adaptation envision predominantly negative selves. To date, the causal link of envisioned selves to motivation and behavior has received much less attention. The central question is whether assessment of possible selves contributes to prediction of future behavior beyond the prediction provided by the set of sociocognitive determinants mentioned above. The sociocognitive approach specifies how to influence life courses as well as predict them.

Control Beliefs

A control event consists of an agent using certain means to produce performance attainments that give rise to various outcomes. Skinner and her colleagues provide a conceptualization of perceived control that divides this fourfold sequence into three segments (Skinner, 1991; Skinner, Chapman, & Baltes, 1988). This segmentation produces three sets of beliefs about the exercise of control. Agency beliefs refer to whether one possesses or has access to the appropriate means. The means include effort, ability, luck, and the influence of powerful others or unknown factors. Means-ends beliefs refer to whether these means are effective in producing desired events or preventing undesired ones. Control beliefs refer to whether one can produce desired events or avoid undesired ones independent of any means. This view of perceived control essentially adds an actor to the standard causal factors proposed by attribution theory. As noted earlier, lack of control may arise from personal incapabilities or the social structure of outcome contingencies. These two different loci of control are distinguished in social cognitive theory because they have different motivational, affective, and behavioral effects and indicate whether personal or social remedies are required.

The tripartite scheme creates a number of conceptual puzzlements about the different aspects and sources of control. To begin with, the scheme includes only three of the four essential elements in the exercise of control. The nature of the missing element depends on how "ends" are conceptualized. If positive and negative events represent the rewarding and punishing outcomes that flow from performance attainments, then performance is missing from the tripartite scheme. Means do not operate on outcomes directly. Rather, means give rise to certain performances that then produce outcomes. It is not that effort as a means brings book royalties, but that effort produces novels that bring book royalties. I could hardly write to my publisher demanding royalties because I expended tremendous effort without producing a book. If positive and negative ends represent variations in performance attainments, then the tripartite scheme is missing outcomes. Behavior is not created and executed purposelessly. People strive to exercise behavioral control to secure valued outcomes and to prevent or escape undesired ones. In the tripartite

scheme, positive and negative ends are measured in terms of variations in level of academic performance. As noted earlier, high and low grades are markers of performance attainment, not outcomes. The same academic performance may bring rewarding or punishing outcomes depending on the value system to which performers and their reference groups subscribe.

In addition to the omission of outcomes from the control sequence, there is the problem of means. Some of the means proposed by Skinner are things people can do (effort), others are things they presumably have (ability), and still others are external forces wielding unspecified influence, such as powerful others and luck. Or they are simply unknown determinants of outcomes. To regard chance happenings as a means at one's disposal to produce performance attainments or outcomes creates conceptual problems. Luck may be regarded as a force that shapes events, but good or bad fortune is not a means one controls. Thus, luck leaves agents with no personal control over their experiences. Outcomes happen to them through inexplicable good or bad fortune rather than being the result of purposeful actions. Agency must be defined in terms of *doing*, not *undergoing* (Thalberg, 1972).

Social cognitive theory subscribes to a more dynamic conception of means and a view of operative agency. Operative agency involves more than just possessing different categories of means, as conceived in the tripartite scheme. Means are not fixed entities that one possesses. Effective exercise of control requires the orchestration of knowledge, subskills, and resources to manage changing situations. Means encompass not only cognitive and behavioral skills but also emotional and motivational self-regulative skills for enlisting motivation and managing disruptive emotional arousal. Moreover, the results people produce depend on how well they use available means as well as the potential utility of those means. The implementive aspect is an integral part of agency. Hence, people with the same means may perform adeptly or poorly under taxing circumstances because their efficacy beliefs affect how well they use the means at their disposal (Bandura, 1990a). In these instances, the problem is not the lack of means but the inadequate way in which they are applied. The operative aspect of control accords with the traditional definition of agency as the power to produce outcomes rather than as the mere possession of a set of means.

There are also major conceptual problems with control beliefs. How can an agent stripped of all means exercise control over outcomes? This would be analogous to immaculate conception. When people are asked, without suggesting any means, whether they can attain desired outcomes, they undoubtedly consider on their own the means they have at their disposal in making their judgments. In short, they add means to their exercise of agency. There are two principal ways in which people can exercise control: through direct personal control and through socially mediated proxy control. In direct personal control, people mobilize the skills and resources at their command to produce the performances that secure desired outcomes. In proxy control, they exercise influence over others who get them the desired outcomes. Gaining outcomes through intermediaries involves the exercise of agency just as it does in direct control, but proxy control banks heavily on persuasion or social coercion. Although the alternative forms of control require different types of means, both are agentive.

People may believe that good or bad things will happen to them either fortuitously or through the actions of power holders, divine agencies, or other types of supreme beings. But whether such happenings involve control beliefs depends on whether people regard the outcomes as occurring independently of anything they do or as somehow influenced by their effect on the ruling agents. Some people try to exert influence on the supernatural agents of their faith by praying to their deities, performing rituals or making material offerings to them, and behaving in ways they believe will avoid deistic punishments and bring worldly rewards or a blessed afterlife.

In their everyday lives, people repeatedly produce effects by their actions. Because they make all kinds of things happen in their immediate environment, there is every reason for them to believe that their actions will continue to have at least some effect in whatever new situations they may

encounter. Langer (1983) has shown that people are easily misled into believing they exercise some control even over outcomes determined entirely by chance events, if the activities include elements that ordinarily increase the likelihood of success on tasks of skill. For example, being given a choice or being allowed active participation and practice on chance tasks, even though this has no effect on what will happen, creates a cognitive set that carrying out these rituals of skill will provide some measure of control over chance outcomes. Apparently, people feel confident that, by their actions, they have gained some influence over chance happenings. If they believe they exert no influence on what is happening to them, however, they do not view the situation as involving personal agency.

In sum, when people are asked, in the tripartite assessments, to judge their control over life events without reference to means, they undoubtedly supply their own means in situations where they can exercise direct personal control, invoke proxy control when they have to depend on intermediaries to get what they want, or operate under an illusion of agency. They must unite agency with means; otherwise, control beliefs reduce to wishful thinking that, somehow, good things will happen without the exertion of any causal influence.

In tests of predictive power, agency beliefs predict children's academic performance, whereas control beliefs and means-end beliefs bear little or no relation to performance (Chapman, Skinner, & Baltes, 1990; Little, Lopez, Oettingen, & Baltes, 1995). The strength of the relationship between agency beliefs and performance increases with age. These findings are consistent with other lines of evidence supporting the predictive superiority of efficacy beliefs over outcome expectations. Beliefs about the effectiveness of particular types of means will not drive individuals to success if they are beset with doubts that they can develop the required means or use them skillfully in situations strewn with difficulties. Nor will individuals drive themselves to success solely by visions of good happenings without any effort or ingenuity on their part.

Weisz and Cameron (1985) segment the control process into the usual two components:

perceived capability and action-outcome expectancies. They have examined how conceptions of control change developmentally as a joint function of these two belief systems. Young children have difficulty distinguishing between outcomes caused by chance events and those that are personally controllable. As they gain knowledge about causality, they increasingly recognize that actions affect outcomes probabilistically rather than invariantly because outcomes are often the product of interacting factors that are changeable across time, places, and circumstances. With growing self-knowledge and inferential capabilities, children get better at assessing the extent to which motivation and skill, as opposed to chance events, affect the controllability of outcomes. In judging their capabilities, children change from an exaggerated sense of competence to a more modest view of their capabilities as they mature.

Interpreting developmental trends in the accuracy with which children judge their capabilities requires caution. Research often confounds the influence of two factors: the self-appraisal of capabilities and the knowledge of task demands. Perceived capability may exceed performance for three reasons. Children may exhibit inflated performance expectations because they overestimate their capabilities, they judge their capabilities accurately but underestimate the task demands, or they harbor both types of misjudgments. As children mature, they gain increasing familiarity with the level of task demands and the types of skills the tasks require, as well as knowledge about their own capabilities. Over time, they may become more realistic because they understand the complexities of their environment better, rather than because they are losing a sense of omnipotence. This is an issue to which we will return later.

Primary versus Secondary Control

People may use their efficacy to adapt to their environment or to change it. Some theorists characterize efforts to change existing realities as primary control and accommodation to them as secondary control (Rothbaum, Weisz, & Snyder, 1982). Secondary control includes two aspects: adapting to existing realities and ameliorating distress over them. The distinction between personal adaptation and social change is a useful one, but they are not mutually exclusive. Nor should they be invested with differential inherent status, as the terms primary and secondary would seem to imply. In the dual view, people first try to change the environment; when their efforts fail, they resign themselves to fitting in with it. Weisz and his colleagues liken this distinction to Piaget's (1970) theory of cognitive development wherein cognitive incongruities are resolved by assimilation or accommodation. In assimilation, people interpret reality in ways that fit their existing beliefs; in accommodation, they change their existing beliefs to fit with reality. In the dual conceptual scheme, the alternative forms of control are invested with different values and emotional consequences. In primary control, people presumably enjoy satisfying triumphs; in secondary control, they try to make the best of an unchangeable reality and to lessen the negative emotional impact of crushing defeats.

The traditional distinction between primary and secondary control is not without its problems. The portrayal of adaptational control is stereotypically narrow, the affective consequences of adaptation and social change are incompletely represented, and the Piagetian analogy is ill-fitting. In both forms of Piagetian cognitive adjustment, people try to fit themselves to an incongruent perceived reality either by reconstruing it or by altering their views to match it. In neither case are they altering the physical or social environment itself. By contrast, in the exercise of so-called primary control, people actually change the character of the environment rather than merely view it differently. There is a world of difference between intrapsychic change and social change.

Adaptation is not necessarily subordinately acquiescent and environmental change preeminently exalting. The conception of secondary control portrays accommodation to existing realities as acquiescent adaptation born of vanquishing defeat. But acquiescence is only one form of adaptation to existing realities. Many efforts to fulfill the role and task demands of life pursuits, which represent adaptations to social systems, are motivated by aspiration and rewarded by improvements in competencies and the satisfactions of a job well done. Adaptation in the service of self-development is not a consolatory fallback strategy. Both adaptation and environmental change require skills and the self-regulatory efficacy to achieve success. If one already possesses the competencies to fulfill the demands of an existing environmental system, adaptation is mainly a process of exercising one's capabilities. If, however, one lacks the necessary knowledge and competencies, as when fulfilling new occupational role requirements, adaptation is a lengthy, complex process of self-development. Effective adaptation to existing realities requires the exercise of control over the demands of those realities rather than the abdication of control. For example, in accommodating to their fixed roles, routes, and time schedules, airline pilots must be vigilantly controlling. Thus, adaptations requiring mastery of new competencies promote self-development, and successful fulfillment of roles provides a sense of personal accomplishment. Indeed, the more closely a person's interest and skills match those of the most successful members of a given occupation, the greater is his or her satisfaction with the chosen pursuit (Holland, 1985). Just as adaptation is not confined to joyless acquiescence, environmental changes are not always satisfying successes. Changes made with faulty forethought of consequences can create more problems and distress than the changes were intended to remedy. Even beneficial social changes are not free of problems.

One can distinguish between the exercise of control over the demands of existing realities and the exercise of control over the emotional impact of those realities. But that is a difference in what is being controlled, not between personal adaptation and social change. Social change efforts call for high efficacy to manage perturbing emotions because the pathways to changing the character of the environment are usually strewn with institutional barriers, stiff social resistance from vested interests, and even coercive threats and punishments.

Typically, those who attempt to shape future realities have to manage more severe personal distress — caused by the opposing social reactions to their change efforts — than those who seek to adapt to existing realities. Social changers must struggle to overcome their frustrations, apprehensions, uncertainties, self-doubts, and despair to keep going in the face of aversive obstacles and social resistance. It is not that changers are serene alterers of environments with occasional disappointments and adapters are busily tranquilizing personal distress over fitting in with the world around them. To further complicate matters, people must act together to accomplish most forms of social change, rather than try to do it by themselves. The eventual outcomes of attempts at social change remain highly uncertain, so it does not take much adversity to convince people of the futility of further effort. Although personal adaptation and social change involve many common processes, changing established environments requires some additional forms of personal efficacy.

Much of what gets included under secondary control is concerned with exercising influence over one's thinking to reduce the aversiveness of life situations that are perceived to be exceedingly difficult to modify. The cognitive strategies for ameliorating stress take a variety of forms (Pearlin & Schooler, 1978). They may involve retrenching aspirations, lowering expectations, making the best of existing realities by finding something positive in them, comparing one's own difficulties favorably with the plight of others, viewing one's current life circumstances as an improvement over the past or as a forerunner of a better future, reorganizing one's priorities, or maintaining an optimistic faith in one's future. The self-regulation of vexing emotions is not confined to positive reappraisals of bleak realities or refuge in escapist activities. Life is multifaceted. Even under the most difficult conditions, there are some aspects of life that are personally controllable. The exercise of behavioral control over events that affect one's life is a powerful way to regulate emotional states. The achievement of valued changes brings satisfactions, and the lessening of problems that one can control brings relief from stress and despair. Focus on the controllable aspects of one's life makes the uncontrollable ones more bearable.

The relationship between individuals and their social environment is reciprocally deterministic, not independent (Bandura, 1986a). They create each other. Human transactions produce changing levels of reciprocity and balances of power. If people acquiesce to environmental dictates, they relinquish power to authorities and thereby make the institutional environment more powerful. Silence gives consent. To paraphrase Edmund Burke, the only thing necessary for tyrants to triumph is for good people to do nothing. Because adaptation involves two-way influence rather than merely a one-way personal accommodation to an autonomous environment, even in acquiescing people are changing the environment, though clearly without intending to do so. Moreover, no two individuals adapting to the same objective environment do so in exactly the same way. They may adapt grudgingly, apathetically, agreeably, or eagerly. Different styles of adaptation produce different environments.

In short, human functioning is not neatly compartmentalized into changing the environment or changing oneself, nor is personal change necessarily a fallback from failure in social change. People cannot be dichotomized solely into adapters or changers, because the environment is multifaceted rather than a uniform mass. In seeking to alter their environment, people adapt to the aspects they like while at the same time trying to change the aspects they find undesirable. In effecting social change, people have to change themselves by developing the beliefs and skills needed to do so and to manage the aversive emotional effects generated by antagonistic counterreactions to their efforts. Thus, human adaptation and change are better explained by the dynamic interplay of different coping strategies than by the categorization of strategies into types and the binding of types to particular adaptational outcomes. The categorical approach spawns varied assortments of typologies and disputes over which version is the superior one. We will revisit this issue in analyzing the distinction between problem-focused coping and emotion-focused coping.

Self-Efficacy in Individualistic and Collectivistic Social Systems

People live their lives in sociocultural environments that differ in their shared values, social practices, and opportunity structures. Cultures that are individualistically oriented tend to favor self-initiative and pursuit of self-interest, whereas those that are collectively oriented place group interest and shared responsibility above self-interest (Triandis, 1995). However, these global classifications mask much diversity and variability. Bicultural contrasts, in which a single collectivistic culture is compared to a single individualistic one, can spawn a lot of misleading generalizations. To begin with, the dichotomization of cultures rests on a questionable uniformity assumption. Although collectivistic systems, such as East Asian ones founded on Confucianism or Buddhism, favor a communal ethic, they differ significantly from each other in particular values, meanings, and customs they promote (Kim, Triandis, Kâğitçibaşi, Choi, Yoon, 1994). Nor are so-called individualistic cultures a uniform lot. Americans, Italians, Germans, and the British differ in their particular brands of individualism. Even within an individualistically oriented culture, such as the United States, the New England brand of individualism is quite different from the Californian version or that of the Southern region of the nation. In addition to the diversity within and between cultures placed in the same category, even members of the same national culture adopt different orientations depending on social circumstances. Thus, for example, members of collectivistically oriented societies are highly communal with ingroup members but not so with outgroup members. But in the presence of negative sanctions against free riders they become as communal with outsiders as do people in individualistic cultures (Yamagishi, 1988). Thus, people express their cultural orientation conditionally rather than invariantly. Both intracultural and situational variation in styles of behavior underscore the need to specify mechanisms through which cultural influences exert their effects. Cultural orientations must be treated as multifaceted dynamic influences in explorations of how efficacy beliefs regulate human functioning within independent and interdependent social systems. People live their lives neither entirely autonomously nor entirely interdependently in any society. They do many things independently but must also work together to achieve desired results. Interdependence does not obliterate a personal self. Self-conceptions embody both personal and collective facets, although their relative emphasis will vary depending on the type of culture in which people are raised. Efficacy beliefs have a similar multifaceted character.

Some writers regard any reference to "self" as reflecting a pernicious individualistic bias in psychological theorizing and pit the self against collectivism. In this jaundiced view, the exercise of personal control is portrayed as an act of self-indulgence. For example, Seligman (1990) christened this allegedly self-centered character as the "California self." In point of fact, personal efficacy can serve varied purposes, many of which subordinate self-interest to the benefits of others. Gandhi provides a striking example of self-sacrifice in the exercise of commanding personal efficacy. He spearheaded the triumph over oppressive rule through unceasing nonviolent resistance and repeatedly forced concessions from ruling authorities by going on life-threatening fasts. He lived ascetically, not self-indulgently. Without a resilient sense of self, people are easily overwhelmed by adversities in their attempts to improve their group life through collective effort.

Because efficacy beliefs involve self-referent processes, self-efficacy is sometimes inappropriately equated with individualism (Schooler, 1990). But a high sense of personal efficacy is just as important to group-directedness as to self-directedness. In collectively oriented systems, people work together to produce the benefits they seek. Group pursuits are no less demanding of personal efficacy than individual pursuits. Nor do people who work interdependently in collectivistic societies have less desire to be efficacious in the particular roles they perform than do those in individualistic societies. Personal efficacy is valued not because of reverence for individualism but because a strong sense

of personal efficacy is vital for successful adaptation and change regardless of whether they are achieved individually or by group members putting their personal capabilities to the best collective use. A firm group loyalty creates strong personal obligations to do one's part in group pursuits as efficaciously as one can. Members are respected for their personal contributions to group accomplishments. Efficacy beliefs operate in complex, multifaceted ways, however the cultural pursuits are socially structured. All too often the complexities and subtleties get lost in oversimplified cross-cultural comparisons.

Group achievements and social change are rooted in self-efficacy. The research of Earley (1993; 1994) attests to the cultural universality of the functional value of efficacy beliefs. Universality does not mean a culture-free perspective. Belief in one's ability to produce desired effects fosters accomplishments in all cultures. But cultural values and practices affect how efficacy beliefs are developed, the purposes to which they are put and the way in which they are best exercised in particular cultural milieus. Thus, in cross-cultural analyses, efficacy beliefs contribute to the productivity of members of both collectivistic and individualistic cultures. Individualists are most efficacious and productive when they can manage things themselves, whereas collectivists are most efficacious and productive when they manage things together. Collectivists, however, tend to be wary of outsiders and are therefore not invariably group oriented. Indeed, collectivists have a low sense of efficacy and perform poorly in an ethnically mixed group.

The influence of individualistic and collectivistic orientations on performance operates largely through beliefs of personal and group efficacy and their motivational impact. The debates on this topic often ignore the significant variations within cultures, which are often at least as interesting as the modal variations between cultures. Efficacy beliefs function as regulative influences for collectivists in individualistic societies and individualists in collectivistic societies, regardless of whether orientations are analyzed at the cultural level or at the individual level. Earley's informative studies debunk the simplistic view that efficacy beliefs are wedded solely to Western individualism. The way in which a society is structured does not say much about how well its members perform activities when the influence of their perceived personal and group efficacy is factored out.

The cross-cultural generality of the adaptive functions of efficacy beliefs is evident in emotional well-being as well as in motivation and action. A low sense of coping efficacy is just as occupationally debilitating and stressful in collectivist cultures as in individualistic ones (Matsui & Onglatco, 1992). People who are wracked with self-doubt do not become social reformers or inspiring mentors, leaders, and social innovators. Because social reformers encounter considerable resistance and retaliatory threats, they must have a tenacious belief in their ability to produce social change through collective effort. If they do not believe in themselves, they are unlikely to empower others with the belief that they can successfully confront and change conditions that affect their lives adversely. The same is true for other members of a group or social system. Inveterate self-doubters are not easily organized into a collectively efficacious force. Indeed, a collectivistic society, populated with members who are consumed by self-doubts about their capabilities and who anticipate the futility of any effort to shape their future, would be condemned to a dismal existence.

Enablement versus Moralization

Some writers express ambivalence over the notion that people make causal contributions to their lives for fear that they will get blamed for their problems (Myers, 1990). Victimization is, of course, a common social practice that gives much cause for concern. The belief that acknowledgment of human efficacy may invite victimization, however, rests on a simplistic view of causal processes laced with moralistic overtones. Self-efficacy is concerned with human enablement, not with moral judgments. If people harbor beliefs that are self-hampering, it does not mean that the problem is exclusively an individual one and that the solution lies solely in personal change.

Human behavior is multidetermined by the reciprocal interplay of personal and environmental influences. People make causal contributions to their lives, but they are not the *sole* causes of their destinies. Numerous other influences — some social, some geographical, and some institutional — also contribute to the courses our lives take. Human life paths are thus determined by multiauthored influences. Within this multicausality, people can improve their lives by exercising influence in areas over which they have some control. The more they bring their influence to bear on changeable conditions that affect their lives, the more they contribute to their own futures. Ideological prohibition against recognizing that behavior is codetermined by the dynamic interplay of personal and social influences is self-defeating.

People change their lives for the better not only through self-development but by acting together to alter adverse institutional practices. If the practices of social systems impede or undermine the personal development of some sectors of society, then a large part of the solution lies in changing the adverse practices of social systems through the exercise of collective efficacy. To shape their social future, people must believe themselves capable of accomplishing significant social change, which rarely comes easily. In the words of John Gardner, "Getting things done socially is no sport for the short-winded." Regardless of whether efforts are directed at personal or social betterment, the overriding message of self-efficacy theory is enablement, not personal blame. Personal and social change are complementary rather than rival approaches to improving the quality of life. Because social change is a slow, tortuous process, people can ill afford to suspend personal control over things they can alter in their lives until societal changes are eventually achieved. Denial that people make any causal contributions to the paths their lives take carries the dispiriting implication that people are powerless to effect any personal changes in their lives. It is a patronizing prescription for apathy and despair.

The Self-Efficacy Component of Social Cognitive Theory

It is important to distinguish between *social cognitive theory* and the *self-efficacy component* of the theory, which operates in concert with other determinants in the theory to govern human thought, motivation, and action. Social cognitive theory posits a multifaceted causal structure that addresses both the development of competencies and the regulation of action (Bandura, 1986a). The different classes of determinants and mediating mechanisms are summarized only briefly here because they are extensively reviewed in subsequent chapters. Knowledge structures representing the rules and strategies of effective action serve as cognitive guides for the construction of complex modes of behavior. These knowledge structures are formed from the results of observational learning, exploratory activities, verbal instruction, and innovative cognitive syntheses of acquired knowledge. Knowledge structures are translated into proficient action through transformational and generative operations. Cognitive models serve as guides for the production of skilled action and as internal standards for making corrective adjustments in the development of behavioral proficiency. The situations people have to deal with are rarely, if ever, completely alike. Execution of a skill must be varied to suit changing circumstances and serve varied purposes. Adaptive functioning, therefore, requires generative conceptions that enable individuals to enact skills in a variety of ways rather than in a rigidly fixed fashion.

Cognitive guidance is especially influential in the early and intermediate phases of skill development. Knowledge structures specify how appropriate subskills must be selected, integrated, and sequenced to suit particular purposes. With continued practice, skills become fully integrated and are executed with ease. Human action is regulated by multilevel systems of control. Once proficient modes of behavior become routinized, they no longer require higher cognitive control. Their execution can be regulated largely by lower level sensory-motor systems in managing recurrent task demands, unless something goes awry. In fact, attending to the mechanics of what one is doing after proficiency is achieved is likely to disrupt skilled performance.

Partial disengagement of thought from proficient action has considerable functional value. Having to think about the details of every skilled activity before carrying it out in recurrent situations would consume most of one's precious attentional and cognitive resources and create a monotonously dull inner life. After people develop adequate ways of managing situations that recur regularly, they act on their perceived efficacy without requiring continuing directive or reflective thought. To cite a familiar example, people rely on their perceived efficacy in choosing what types of traffic situations to get into while they are developing their driving skills. But after they routinize their driving skills, it would be a considerable waste of cognitive resources if they had to continue to reappraise their driving efficacy each time they set forth on a familiar route with their automobile. This does not mean that efficacy belief is an important contributor to skill development but operates as less of a factor after the skill is routinized. Quite the contrary. As long as people continue to believe in their ability to perform a given activity, they act habitually on that belief without having to keep reminding themselves of it. Should they cease to believe in their ability, they would behave differently. If significant changes occur in task demands or situational circumstances, personal efficacy is promptly reappraised as the guide for action under the altered conditions.

Routinization is advantageous when the skills that have been acquired are the optimal ones and remain so under a variety of circumstances. Routinization can detract from the best use of personal capabilities, however, when people react in fixed ways to situations requiring discriminative adaptability. Routinization is also self-limiting when people settle for low-level pursuits on the basis of self-doubts of efficacy and no longer reappraise their capabilities or raise their vision of themselves.

When routinized behavior repeatedly fails to produce expected results, the cognitive control system again comes into play. Both the behavior and the changing environmental circumstances are monitored to identify the source of the problem. New modes are considered and tested. Control reverts to the lower control system after an adequate mode is found and becomes the habitual way of doing things.

Social cognitive theory encompasses a large set of factors that operate as regulators and motivators of established cognitive, social, and behavioral skills. These factors operate through the anticipative mechanism of forethought. Instrumental thoughts about desired futures tend to promote the type of behavior likely to bring about their realization. Forethought manifests itself in many different ways. Predictive knowledge of what is likely to happen if particular events occur fosters planfulness and foresightful adaptations. The ability to envision the likely outcomes of prospective courses of action is another way in which anticipative mechanisms contribute to human motivation and adaptation. These outcome expectancies may take the form of external outcomes produced by the behavior, vicarious outcomes as observed in the costs and benefits occurring to others, or self-evaluative reactions to one's own behavior. These different types of outcomes operate in concert to influence the course of human action. Cognized goals and internal standards rooted in value systems create further self-incentives and guides for action through self-regulatory mechanisms.

Perceived self-efficacy occupies a pivotal role in social cognitive theory because it acts upon the other classes of determinants. By influencing the choice of activities and the motivational level, beliefs of personal efficacy make an important contribution to the acquisition of the knowledge structures on which skills are founded. An assured sense of efficacy supports the type of efficient analytic thinking needed to ferret out predictive knowledge from causally ambiguous environments in which many factors combine to produce effects. Beliefs of personal efficacy also regulate motivation by shaping aspirations and the outcomes expected for one's efforts. A capability is only as good as its execution. The self-assurance with which people approach and manage difficult tasks determines whether they make good or poor use of their capabilities. Insidious self-doubts can easily overrule the best of skills. Although this book focuses on beliefs of personal efficacy, these beliefs operate within a broad system of multicausality. The next chapter addresses the basic characteristics of efficacy beliefs and the influential role they play in causal structures.

The Nature and Structure of Self-Efficacy

HUMAN COMPETENCIES ARE DEVELOPED AND manifested in many different forms. These diverse areas of functioning demand different knowledge and skills. One cannot be all things; it would require a gigantic amount of time, resources, and effort to master every realm of human activity. Hence, people differ both in the areas in which they cultivate their efficacy and in the levels to which they develop it even within their chosen pursuits. The particular patterns of competencies they acquire are products of natural endowment, sociocultural experiences, and fortuitous circumstances that alter the course of developmental trajectories (Bandura, 1986a). The particular organization of self-knowledge is shaped by these various formative influences.

Self-efficacy theory acknowledges the diversity of human capabilities. Thus, it treats the efficacy belief system not as an omnibus trait but as a differentiated set of self-beliefs linked to distinct realms of functioning. Moreover, efficacy beliefs are differentiated across major systems of expression within activity domains. Opera stars, for example, may differ in their perceived efficacy to fulfill the vocal, emotive, and theatrical aspects of their artistic craft and to fuse them into dramatic performances. Efficacy beliefs are concerned not only with the exercise of control over action but also with the self-regulation of thought processes, motivation, and affective and physiological states. This chapter analyzes the nature and structure of efficacy beliefs and their causal contribution to human well-being and accomplishments.

PERCEIVED SELF-EFFICACY AS A GENERATIVE CAPABILITY

Effective personal functioning is not simply a matter of knowing what to do and being motivated to do it. Nor is efficacy a fixed ability that one does or does not have in one's behavioral repertoire, any more than one would regard linguistic efficacy as a collection of words or a colony of preformed sentences in a verbal repertoire. Rather, efficacy is a generative capability in which cognitive, social, emotional, and behavioral subskills must be organized and effectively orchestrated to serve innumerable purposes. There is a marked difference between possessing subskills and being able to integrate them into appropriate courses of action and to execute them well under difficult circumstances. People often fail to perform optimally even though they know full well what to do and possess the requisite skills to do it (Schwartz & Gottman, 1976). Self-referent thought activates cognitive, motivational, and affective processes that govern the translation of knowledge and abilities into proficient action. In short, perceived self-efficacy is concerned not with the number of skills you have, but with what you believe you can do with what you have under a variety of circumstances.

Efficacy beliefs operate as a key factor in a generative system of human competence. Hence, different people with similar skills, or the same person under different circumstances, may perform poorly, adequately, or extraordinarily, depending on fluctuations in their beliefs of personal efficacy. Collins (1982) studied the level of problem solving by children who perceived themselves to be of high or low mathematical self-efficacy at each of three levels of mathematical ability. Mathematical ability contributed to performance. But at each ability level, children who regarded themselves as efficacious were more successful in solving mathematical problems than were children who doubted their abilities. Skills can be easily overruled by self-doubts, so that even highly talented individuals make poor use of their capabilities under circumstances that undermine their beliefs in themselves (Bandura & Jourden, 1991; Wood & Bandura, 1989a). By the same token, a resilient sense of efficacy enables individuals to do extraordinary things by productive use of their skills in the face of overwhelming obstacles (White, 1982). As these and other studies reveal (Bandura, 1992a), perceived self-efficacy is an important contributor to performance accomplishments, whatever the underlying skills might be.

Effective functioning requires both skills and the efficacy beliefs to use them well. This calls for continuous improvisation of multiple subskills to manage ever-changing situations, most of which contain ambiguous, unpredictable, and often stressful elements. Preexisting skills often must be orchestrated in new ways to meet varying situational demands. Even routinized activities are rarely performed in exactly the same way each time. Initiation and regulation of transactions with the environment are, therefore, partly governed by judgments of operative capabilities — what people believe they can do under given circumstances and task demands. Perceived self-efficacy is not a measure of the skills one has but a belief about what one can do under different sets of conditions with whatever skills one possesses.

Some writers have misconstrued beliefs of personal efficacy as judgments of motor acts in a "behavioral repertoire" or as a decontextualized quantity of perceived ability (Eastman & Marzillier, 1984; Kirsch, 1995). They detach elementary motor acts from complex adaptations and then reason that, because everyone possesses the motor acts in their behavioral repertoire, personal efficacy is not at issue. For example, perceived efficacy to protect oneself against sexually transmitted diseases is reduced to the isolated act of donning a condom, whereas in fact it involves perceived self-regulatory efficacy to surmount the numerous interpersonal impediments to condom use. It includes the perceived capability to negotiate regular condom use and to resist pressure for unsafe sex from partners, when intoxicated or high on drugs, when strongly attracted to the partner, or when caught up in an arousing intimacy without a condom. If all else fails, it means exercising control by refusing to engage in unprotected sexual activity with a partner who continues to reject condom use. In the trifling conception of personal efficacy, the fervent organ is essentially severed from the interpersonal dynamics that determine if it gets sheathed or not. This is the very depleted conception of perceived capability that self-efficacy theory rejects (Bandura, 1995a).

To take another example, in measuring people's beliefs in their driving efficacy, they are not asked to judge whether they can turn the ignition key, shift the automatic transmission, turn a steering wheel, accelerate and stop an automobile, blow the horn, interpret road signs, and change traffic lanes. Rather, they judge the strength of their perceived efficacy that they can navigate an automobile adequately under traffic conditions that present different levels of challenge. The subskills of driving are trivial, but the generative capability of maneuvering an automobile under very narrow margins of error through congested city traffic, around vehicles on crowded expressways propelled by drivers differing in proficiency, and on narrow twisting mountain roads is not. Driving under taxing and rapidly changing traffic conditions calls for high coordinative proficiency, acute vigilance, anticipatory reading of traffic patterns, and split-second decision making. A summation of decontextualized perceived efficacy for subskills would provide a misleading measure of perceived operative capability. A critique of conceptions of perceived efficacy as a repertoire of component skills or as a fixed quantity of ability has been presented elsewhere and will not be reviewed here (Bandura, 1984, 1995a,b).

The subskills necessary for performance contribute to the judgment of operative efficacy but do not substitute for it. Mone (1994) reports findings bearing on this issue. He compared the relative predictiveness of students' beliefs in their efficacy to attain different levels of performance in an academic course with beliefs in their efficacy to perform cognitive subfunctions such as concentrating in class, memorizing and comprehending material, note taking and the like. Belief in subfunction efficacy contributes independently of past performance to belief in efficacy for academic attainment. Attainment efficacy is a better predictor of level and changes in academic aspirations and performance than subfunction efficacy, however. This is because perceived efficacy to produce different levels of performance may subsume efficacy for the customary subfunctions as well as others. Judgment of attainment efficacy not only may be more inclusive but also may encompass some ways of exercising control that are idiosyncratic to individuals but are unrecognized by assessors. Belief in one's self-regulatory efficacy — which determines how well subskills are enlisted, orchestrated, and

sustained — is also an important contributor to the belief in attainment efficacy that governs behavioral accomplishments (Zimmerman & Bandura, 1994; Zimmerman, Bandura, & Martinez-Pons, 1992).

Other writers have misinterpreted markers of performance as the outcomes that flow from them (Devins & Edwards, 1988; Rooney & Osipow, 1992). Rather than measure perceived self-efficacy for different levels of performance, they fractionate the given activity into its constituent subskills and measure people's sense of efficacy to perform the detached subskills. As illustrated in the previous examples, efficacy beliefs may be high for the subskills but low for their integrated use in taxing situations. Beliefs about how well subskills can be put into practice can vary depending on the pursuits they subserve. Thus, beliefs of personal efficacy may be lower for the same quantitative skills when used in technical pursuits than when used in nontechnical ones (Matsui & Tsukamoto, 1991). Investigators would do well to follow the dictum that the whole is greater than the sum of its parts. These comments should not be misinterpreted as a prescription for vague global measures. Rather, the issue is the fragmentation and decontextualization of capabilities. Sensitive measures of efficacy beliefs link operative capabilities to levels of challenge in particular domains of functioning.

ACTIVE PRODUCERS VERSUS PASSIVE FORETELLERS OF PERFORMANCES

Self-efficacy beliefs are not simply inert predictors of future performance, as some writers have suggested. For example, strong adherents of behavioristic doctrines regard thoughts as merely residues of conditioned responses that cannot influence human motivation or action. In such an agentless view, self-beliefs reside in the host organism as mere foretellers of future behavior that gets realized in some unspecified way. An organism that forecasts its future performances but can do nothing to bring them about would be left at the mercy of environmental forces. There is nothing like a superficial explanation that rules out any personal causation to put a damper on psychological inquiry. Performances do not just happen to us; we do a lot to bring them about. People contribute to, rather than merely predict, their actions. There is a world of difference between doing and undergoing.

Later in this chapter, I will review a large body of evidence demonstrating that efficacy beliefs affect thought processes, the level and persistency of motivation, and affective states, all of which are important contributors to the types of performances that are realized. People who doubt their capabilities in particular domains of activity shy away from difficult tasks in those domains. They find it hard to motivate themselves, and they slacken their efforts or give up quickly in the face of obstacles. They have low aspirations and weak commitment to the goals they choose to pursue. In taxing situations, they dwell on their personal deficiencies, the formidableness of the task, and the adverse consequences of failure. Such perturbing thinking further undermines their efforts and their analytic thinking by diverting attention from how best to execute activities to concerns over personal deficiencies and possible calamities. They are slow to recover their sense of efficacy following failure or setbacks. Because they are prone to diagnose insufficient performance as deficient aptitude, it does not require all that much failure for them to lose faith in their capabilities. They fall easy victim to stress and depression.

In contrast, a resilient sense of efficacy enhances sociocognitive functioning in the relevant domains in many ways. People who have strong beliefs in their capabilities approach difficult tasks as challenges to be mastered rather than as threats to be avoided. Such an affirmative orientation fosters interest and engrossing involvement in activities. They set themselves challenging goals and maintain strong commitment to them. They invest a high level of effort in what they do and heighten their effort in the face of failures or setbacks. They remain task-focused and think strategically in the face of difficulties. They attribute failure to insufficient effort, which supports a success orientation. They quickly recover their sense of efficacy after failures or setbacks. They approach potential stressors or threats with the confidence that they can exercise some control over them. Such an efficacious outlook enhances performance accomplishments, reduces stress, and lowers vulnerability to depression. These findings offer substantial support for the view that beliefs of personal efficacy are active contributors to, rather than mere inert predictors of, human attainments. People make things happen rather than simply passively observing themselves undergoing behavioral happenings.

THE SELF-EFFICACY APPROACH TO PERSONAL CAUSATION

Efforts to discover how personal determinants contribute to psychosocial functioning have generally relied on omnibus tests of personal attributes designed to serve diverse purposes. The items in the scales are decontextualized by deleting information about the situations with which one is dealing. For example, people are simply asked to judge their aggressiveness in a situational void without reference to the form of aggression, who the protagonists are, the type and level of provocation, the social setting, and other circumstances that can strongly affect one's proneness to act aggressively. Such omnibus measures contain a fixed set of items, many of which may have little relevance to the particular sphere of functioning that is of interest. Moreover, in an effort to produce an all-purpose measure, the items are usually cast in a general form, requiring respondents to try to guess what the unspecified situational particulars might be. The more general the items, the greater is the burden on respondents to figure out what is being asked of them. For example, consider an item from the widely used personality measure (Rotter, 1966), the locus of control scale: "The average citizen can have an influence in government decisions." What is an average citizen? For respondents who dissociate themselves from the average citizenry because of political alienation, cynicism, or a privileged status, the item measures their perceptions of what the ordinary citizenry might believe, not their belief about how much control they can wield personally. The item also leaves unspecified which level of government is the object of influence — city, state, federal? Governmental systems can vary considerably in amenability to influence. What constitutes an influence — rectifying grievances, securing projects and services for one's community, gaining enactment of laws, ensuring enforcement of existing statutes? Decisions about what? Some governmental decisions are easy to influence, others are responsive only to concerted social pressure, and still others remain highly resistant to change even under strong public clamor. The indefiniteness of every key term in the item produces considerable ambiguity and variation among individuals in what they assume is being measured. People would undoubtedly have different beliefs about their capability to influence governmental decisions depending on the nature of the decisions and the type and level of governmental system with which they must deal. Omnibus measures create problems of predictive relevance as well as obscurity about what is being assessed. Most of the items in a measure designed to be universally applicable may be irrelevant to the particular domain of interest. Why should beliefs about the influenceability of governmental decisions, however interpreted, have much to say about how people will perform on athletic fields, in academic courses, in child rearing, or on concert stages?

It is unrealistic to expect personality measures cast in generalities to shed much light on the contribution of personal factors to psychosocial functioning in different task domains and contexts and under diverse circumstances. Efficacy beliefs in the scholastic domain are a good case in point. An all-purpose test of perceived self-efficacy would be phrased in terms of people's general belief that they can make things happen, without specifying what those things are. Such a measure would most likely be a weak predictor of attainments in a particular scholastic domain, such as mathematics. A

self-efficacy measure cast in terms of the general academic domain would be more explanatory and predictive, but still deficient because scientific, mathematical, linguistic, literary, and artistic academic subdomains differ markedly in the types of competencies they require. A self-efficacy measure tailored to the mathematical domain would be even more predictive of choice of mathematical activities, how vigorously they are pursued, and level of mathematical achievement. Particularized efficacy beliefs are most predictive because those are the types of beliefs that guide which activities are undertaken and how well they are performed. Thus, in navigating the mathematical realm, people act on their beliefs of mathematical efficacy, not on their efficacy beliefs for writing sonnets or baking soufflés.

A common misconception is that global scales requiring people to judge their *general* capabilities measure an efficacy disposition or trait. Such a presumption is highly disputable. Vague items obscure what, in fact, is being measured. In coming up with a global judgment, respondents must not only weigh and average self-referent information but also delimit the scope of activities and conjure up levels of challenges. The generality of their judgments can vary markedly, depending on the range of activities and situational demands they happen to take into consideration. Consider, for purposes of illustration, global judgment of athletic efficacy. If track runners are asked to judge their athletic efficacy in general, they probably think mainly about their capabilities across closely related pursuits rather than across divergent domains of athletic activities such as shot putting or weight lifting. Similarly, if gymnasts are asked to judge their overall athletic efficacy, they most certainly are not conjuring up images of tobogganing or wrestling in their averaging judgment. The settings in which global measures are administered may inadvertently graft a context onto decontextualized items. Thus, people asked in an academic context to judge their general beliefs about their capabilities will most likely consider their academic skills rather than their athletic or parenting skills. The predictiveness of indefinite global measures will depend on the extent to which the visualized activities on which the mental averaging is performed happen to overlap with the domain of functioning being studied.

A genuine "trait" measure of athletic efficacy should assess perceived capabilities across a full range of athletic activities that are clearly specified, such as sprinting, golfing, wrestling, and skiing. The intercorrelations among the different athletic activities identify the level of generality of perceived athletic efficacy. Domain scores provide the patterning of perceived efficacy; the mean of the different domains provides an integrative summary index if one is desired. In addition to broad assessment, trait theorists must provide consensual criteria and a persuasive rationale for how much generality across different activity domains is required to invoke a trait. Complete generality? Moderate generality? Does variability across domains mean that one is traitless or dispositionless? By masquerading traits in vague items that require reducing variability across diverse activity domains by mental averaging, the conceptual issues of what constitutes a trait are rarely raised, let alone answered. For the most part, so-called traits or global personality dispositions are creations of notoriously vague assessment.

Omnibus trait measures may have practical value in that some predictive gain, however small, is better than sheer guesswork. But major progress in understanding how personal factors operate in causal structures requires explicit measurement of the particular personal determinants that are germane to given spheres of functioning. It is regrettable that omnibus personality tests did not achieve greater success in explaining and predicting human functioning. The task of gauging personal determinants would have been greatly simplified if one could predict all kinds of behavior in different settings and under diverse circumstances with a simple general-purpose device. But life is too variegated for such an approach to have much success. Human competence is structured and manifested diversely rather than uniformly across domains of activity. The convenience of general-purpose tests of personal determinants is gained at the cost of explanatory and predictive power.

The multiple nature of efficacy beliefs raises the broader issue of how personal causation is

conceptualized and measured. The influence of personal factors on human functioning is often insufficiently recognized because the issue tends to be thought of in terms of individual differences rather than personal determinants. The difference between these conceptions is illustrated by instances in which a personal factor is necessary for certain types of performances but is developed to the same high level in different individuals. In such cases, the difference between individuals is negligible and would therefore be unrelated to performance, but the personal competence is, in fact, vital for successful performance. For example, all librarians know how to read well and do not differ in this respect, but possessing the ability to read is essential for performing the librarianship role. Personal determinants operate as multifaceted dynamic factors in causal structures rather than as static entities that people possess in differing amounts. The alternative perspective on personal causation reflects more than differences in semantic labeling. The individual differences approach is rooted in trait theory, whereas the personal determinants approach is founded on a model of functional relations between dynamic personal factors and the quality of human adaptation and change. The implications of these alternative conceptions for measurement and analysis of how personal determinants operate in causal structures are addressed in the rest of this chapter.

It is sometimes assumed, incorrectly, that a personality disposition of perceived control spawns efficacy beliefs. Any association between these factors most likely reflects some overlap in the wording of items rather than dispositional causation of efficacy beliefs. Indeed, multivariate analyses indicate that so-called dispositional measures, such as perceived control and optimism, derive their predictiveness largely from their redundancy with efficacy beliefs (Cozzarelli, 1993; Dzewaltowski, Noble, & Shaw, 1990). When the influence of efficacy belief is controlled, the relation of perceived control and optimism to psychological functioning essentially disappears.

A related common misconception is that general efficacy beliefs spawn specific efficacy beliefs. The empirical evidence has not been any kinder to this view than to presumed linkages with other global personality dispositions. General indices of personal efficacy bear little or no relation either to efficacy beliefs related to particular activity domains or to behavior (Earley & Lituchy, 1991; Eden & Zuk, 1995; McAuley & Gill, 1983; Pond & Hay, 1989). If general indices of efficacy happen to include some overlap of content with particularized efficacy beliefs, then a weak relationship may be obtained. But this is more by chance than by dispositional causation. When global efficacy beliefs are related to performance, evidence suggests that particularized efficacy beliefs account for the relation (Martin & Gill, 1991; Pajares & Johnson, 1994). Global beliefs lose their predictiveness when the influence of particular efficacy beliefs is removed.

Social cognitive theory does not cede the construct of "disposition" to trait theory. Obviously, individuals who have a resilient sense of efficacy in a given domain are disposed to behave differently in that realm of activity from those who are beset by self-doubt. Efficacy beliefs are patterned differently in different individuals. To say that personality disposition fosters efficacy belief is to say that efficacious disposition causes itself. The issue in contention is not whether people have personal dispositions but how they are conceptualized and operationalized. In social cognitive theory, an efficacious personality disposition is a dynamic, multifaceted belief system that operates selectively across different activity domains and under different situational demands, rather than being a decontextualized conglomerate. The patterned individuality of efficacy beliefs represents the unique dispositional makeup of efficaciousness for any given person.

MULTIDIMENSIONALITY OF SELF-EFFICACY BELIEF SYSTEMS

Self-efficacy theory prescribes an appropriate model of measurement along the lines already suggested. Efficacy beliefs should be measured in terms of particularized judgments of capability that may vary across realms of activity, under different levels of task demands within a given activity domain, and under different situational circumstances. Personal efficacy is not a contextless global disposition assayed by an omnibus test. Rather, it is a multifaceted phenomenon. A high sense of efficacy in one activity domain is not necessarily accompanied by high self-efficacy in other realms (DiClemente, 1986; Hofstetter, Sallis, & Hovell, 1990). Therefore, to achieve explanatory and predictive power, measures of personal efficacy must be tailored to domains of functioning and must represent gradations of task demands within those domains. This requires clear definition of the activity domain of interest and a good conceptual analysis of its different facets, the types of capabilities it calls upon, and the range of situations in which these capabilities might be applied.

Structure of Self-Efficacy Scales

Efficacy beliefs vary on several dimensions that have important performance implications. First, they differ in *level*. The perceived personal efficacy of different individuals may be limited to simple task demands, extend to moderately difficult demands, or include the most taxing performance demands within a particular domain of functioning. The range of perceived capability for a given person is measured against levels of task demands that represent varying degrees of challenge or impediment to successful performance. If there are no obstacles to surmount, the activity is easy to perform, and everyone has uniformly high perceived self-efficacy for it. For example, in measuring high-jump efficacy, athletes judge the strength of their belief that they can leap over crossbars set at different heights. One can add refinements to the assessment of efficacy beliefs that enhance predictiveness by including contextual conditions that pose additional challenges or impediments to performance. An efficacy belief is not a decontextualized trait upon which situational conditions act. Nor do situational circumstances "determine" efficacy beliefs. To continue with the high-jump example, the task demands in the successively rising height of the cross bar are not "determinants" of efficacy beliefs. Rather, situational conditions are the performance requirements against which perceived efficacy is judged.

In developing efficacy scales, researchers must draw on conceptual analysis and expert knowledge of what it takes to succeed in a given pursuit (Bandura, 1995c). This information is supplemented with interviews, open-ended surveys, and structured questionnaires to identify the levels of challenge and impediment to successful performance of the required activities. The nature of the challenges against which personal efficacy is judged will vary depending on the sphere of activity. Challenges may be graded in terms of level of ingenuity, exertion, accuracy, productivity, threat, or self-regulation required, just to mention a few dimensions of performance demands. Many areas of functioning are primarily concerned with self-regulatory efficacy to guide and motivate oneself to get things done that one knows how to do. The issue is not whether one can do them occasionally but whether one has the efficacy to get oneself to do them regularly in the face of varied dissuading conditions. For example, consider the measurement of perceived self-efficacy to stick to a health-promoting exercise routine. Individuals judge how well they can get themselves to exercise regularly under various impediments, such as when they are under pressure from work, are tired, or are depressed; in foul weather; or when they have other commitments or more interesting things to do. In the preliminary inquiry for constructing scales to assess self-regulatory efficacy, people are asked to describe the things that make it hard for them to perform the required activities regularly. In the formal scale, participants judge their ability to surmount the various impediments. Sufficient impediments and challenges should be built into efficacy items to avoid ceiling effects. When essential skills are lacking, perceived efficacy to regulate one's motivation and learning activities provides the motivational supports for mastering the needed skills.

Efficacy beliefs also differ in *generality*. People may judge themselves efficacious across a wide range of activities or only in certain domains of functioning. Generality can vary on a number of different dimensions, including the degree of similarity of activities, the modalities in which capabilities are expressed (behavioral, cognitive, affective), qualitative features of situations, and the characteristics of the persons toward whom the behavior is directed. Assessments linked to activity domains and situational contexts reveal the patterning and degree of generality of people's beliefs in their efficacy. Within the network of efficacy beliefs, some are of greater import than others. The most fundamental self-beliefs are those around which people structure their lives.

In addition, efficacy beliefs vary in *strength*. Weak efficacy beliefs are easily negated by disconfirming experiences, whereas people who have a tenacious belief in their capabilities will persevere in their efforts despite innumerable difficulties and obstacles. They are not easily overwhelmed by adversity. Strength of perceived self-efficacy is not necessarily linearly related to choice behavior (Bandura, 1977). A certain threshold of self-assurance is needed to attempt a course of action, but higher strengths of self-efficacy will result in the same attempt. The stronger the sense of personal efficacy, however, the greater the perseverance and the higher the likelihood that the chosen activity will be performed successfully.

In the standard methodology for measuring efficacy beliefs, individuals are presented with items portraying different levels of task demands, and they rate the strength of their belief in their ability to execute the requisite activities. The items are phrased in terms of *can do* rather than *will do*. *Can* is a judgment of capability; *will* is a statement of intention. Perceived self-efficacy is a major determinant of intention, but the two constructs are conceptually and empirically separable (Ajzen & Madden, 1986; Arch, 1992b; deVries & Backbier, 1994; Dzewaltowski et al., 1990; Kok et al., 1991; Wulfert & Wan, 1995). Efficacy beliefs affect performance both directly and by influencing intentions. The view that efficacy beliefs are intentions is conceptually incoherent and empirically disputed.

In the standard methodology, individuals record the strength of their belief on a 100-point scale, ranging in 10-unit intervals from 0 ("Cannot do"); through intermediate degrees of assurance, 50 ("Moderately certain can do"); to complete assurance, 100 ("Certain can do"). Efficacy scales are unipolar, ranging from 0 to a maximum strength. They do not include negative numbers because a judgment of complete incapability (0) has no lower gradations. Some researchers retain the same scale structure and descriptors but use single unit intervals ranging from 0 to 10. Scales that use only a few steps should be avoided because they are less sensitive and less reliable (Streiner & Norman, 1989). Including too few steps loses differentiating information because people who use the same response category would differ if intermediate steps were included.

Preliminary instructions should establish the appropriate judgmental set. People are asked to judge their operative capabilities as of now, not their potential capabilities or their expected future capabilities. In the case of self-regulatory efficacy, people judge their assurance that they can perform the activity regularly over designated periods of time. For example, recovered alcoholics would judge their perceived ability to refrain from drinking over specified time intervals. A practice item, such as the capability to lift objects of increasing weight, helps to familiarize respondents with the scale gauging strength of efficacy belief and reveals any misunderstanding about how to use it.

Two formats can be used to measure self-efficacy strength. In the dual-judgment format, individuals first judge whether or not they can execute given performances. For the tasks they judged they can do, they then rate the strength of their perceived efficacy using the efficacy strength scale. In the single-judgment format, they simply rate the strength of their perceived efficacy from 0 to 100 or 0 to 10 for every item in the activity domain. The single-judgment format provides essentially the same information and is easier and more convenient to use. The efficacy strength scores are summed and divided by the total number of items to indicate the strength of perceived self-efficacy for the activity domain. A measure of efficacy level can be extracted by selecting a cutoff value below which people would judge themselves incapable of executing the activities in question.

Efficacy scales vary in their structure depending on the form the competencies take in a given domain of functioning and the gradations of capabilities that are of interest. Some scales are ordered throughout their range, as when teachers rate their perceived efficacy to get their students to master particular subjects, with efficacy items representing increasing percentage of mastery. Other scales are ordered at the lower range but not at the upper region of the scale. For example, in measuring perceived coping efficacy in snake phobics, approaching, touching, and holding a snake are hierarchically ordered, but after one can handle a reptile, the higher level activities performed with it do not follow any inherent order. Still other scales include a heterogeneous set of activities that admit to no particular order. In measuring the perceived efficacy of alcoholics to resist urges to drink, the efficacy items present a variety of situational and emotional instigators to drink. The degree of strain these situations place on self-regulatory capabilities may vary idiosyncratically among individuals. What may be manageable for one person may be uncontrollable for another.

As already noted, self-efficacy scales should measure people's beliefs in their abilities to fulfill different levels of task demands within the psychological domain selected for study. Including a wide range of task demands identifies the upper limits of people's beliefs in their capabilities as well as gradations of strength of perceived self-efficacy below that point. Some researchers have relied on a single-item measure that assesses perceived efficacy for only a single level of task demand. Such measures not only yield a restricted range of scores but often fail to differentiate between individuals who, in fact, differ in their beliefs of personal efficacy. For example, a single-item measure would not distinguish between two individuals who judge themselves equally inefficacious to fulfill a selected difficult task demand but differ in their perceived efficacy for lower level demands. Similarly, a single item, representing a relatively easy task demand, would not distinguish between two individuals who judge themselves completely efficacious for that task but differ in their perceived self-efficacy to accomplish higher level tasks. Curtailed distributions lower the magnitude of correlations. In a comparison of efficacy measures, Lee and Bobko (1994) found that a single-item measure of efficacy not only was weakly related to composite measures of efficacy to fulfill graded task demands but also had lower predictive value.

Differences in precision and comprehensiveness of self-efficacy assessment are well illustrated in research on the impact of beliefs of memory efficacy on memory performance (Bandura, 1989a). In the single-item measures, people are simply asked to judge their efficacy for a memory task of moderate or high difficulty, or they judge how much material they believe they will be able to recall. In contrast to such restricted measures, Berry, West, and Dennehey (1989) have devised multidimensional self-efficacy scales that accord well with guidelines from self-efficacy theory and methodology. Separate self-efficacy scales are devised for different types of memory. The intercorrelations corroborate that the set of scales represents a common domain but taps different aspects of memory. The scales measure self-efficacy strength for gradations of memory demands rather than just a categorical judgment of whether or not one can execute a given level of memory performance. The scales are highly reliable, and they account for a good part of the variance in memory performance. The scale format can be easily extended to other types of memory.

Efficacy beliefs do not share the major properties ascribed to personality traits. This raises questions about the appropriateness of some of the trait-based psychometric procedures for evaluating self-efficacy measures. Consider the issue of reliability as estimated by invariance over time. Efficacy beliefs do not necessarily remain immutable over time. Depending on factors to be reviewed later, such beliefs vary in their changeability. Although efficacy beliefs are usually quite durable, an accurate measure of perceived self-efficacy does not necessarily demand high temporal stability. Self-efficacy scales include gradations of capability demands, so that items requiring few capabilities are not interchangeable with items making arduous capability demands.

Efficacy beliefs involve different types of capabilities, such as management of thought, affect, action, and motivation. Certain activities may draw more heavily on some aspects of perceived efficacy than on others. Moreover, the aspects of perceived efficacy that come into play during the development of mastery may differ from those required for the ongoing self-regulation of behavior. Treating multifaceted efficacy beliefs as a unitary trait that reigns supreme over all functioning sacrifices validity for internal consistency. Restricting items to those that correlate highly with one another results in a self-efficacy scale that measures redundantly only a segment of perceived efficacy and perhaps a narrow segment at that. Guided by a sound conceptual scheme in the construction of efficacy items, factor analysis can help to verify the multifaceted structure of efficacy beliefs.

The item content of self-efficacy scales must represent beliefs about personal abilities to produce specified levels of performance and must not include other characteristics. There is no absolute index of a belief against which to gauge the accuracy of a particular measure used to assess it. The adequacy of self-efficacy measures can be evaluated independently, however, by evidence that they are measuring what they are purporting to measure and by their level of specificity and the range of task demands they include. Indefinite items and those that encompass only a few levels of task difficulty provide relatively insensitive measures of perceived efficacy. The accuracy of self-efficacy measures can also be enhanced by using test procedures that minimize evaluative concerns over possible social reactions to one's self-appraisals. Evidence of validity relies heavily on construct validation. Perceived self-efficacy is based on a theory of the different ways in which self-efficacy beliefs affect human functioning. Self-efficacy measures gain validity from their demonstrated success in predicting the effects specified by the social cognitive theory in which the efficacy factor is embedded. The theory predicts a variety of effects on thought, affect, action, and motivation. Hence, there is no single validity coefficient. The vast body of research reviewed in this volume speaks to the validity of the construct.

Effects of Self-Assessment

In simple actions that can be produced at will, stating an efficacy judgment might, in itself, affect performance. Most activities, however, include various impediments demanding effort, ingenuity, and endurance if the desired performance is to be attained. Simply verbalizing an efficacy judgment that may not fully reflect what one really believes will not instantly produce the performance attainment. If merely recording a level of efficacy made it so, personal change would be trivially easy. People would rate themselves into grand accomplishments. Nevertheless, the question arises as to whether making efficacy judgments may contribute some motivational inducement to improve the match between self-judgment and performance.

Cognitive consistency theories assume that disparities between beliefs and perceived behavior are discomforting and therefore motivate people to reduce the discrepancies they experience (Abelson et al., 1968; Festinger, 1957). Although the consistency drive is often invoked, it has proved elusive in extensive empirical searches. Moreover, there is evidence that, when people err in their self-judgments, their efficacy beliefs typically exceed their behavior. This evidence indicates that they are more oriented toward self-challenge than toward simply maintaining belief-behavior consistency. Self-assessment could have other reactive effects, however, that must be ruled out.

The standard procedure for measuring beliefs of personal efficacy includes a number of safeguards to minimize any potential motivational effects of self-assessment. Self-efficacy judgments are recorded privately without personal identification to reduce social evaluative concerns. People make multiple judgments of their efficacy across the full range of task demands within the activity domain rather than making

each judgment immediately before each performance. The assessments of perceived efficacy and behavior are conducted in different settings and by different assessors to remove any carryover of social influence from assessment of one factor to the other. And finally, the instructions for self-assessment emphasize the importance of frank judgments.

Numerous tests for reactive effects of self-assessment show that people's affective reactions and performance attainments are the same regardless of whether they do or do not make prior efficacy judgments. The nonreactivity of self-efficacy assessment is corroborated for diverse activities, including coping behavior and anxiety arousal (Bandura, Adams, Hardy, & Howells, 1980), regulation of motivation (Bandura & Cervone, 1983, 1986; Cervone, 1989), pain tolerance (Reese, 1983), cognitive attainments (Brown & Inouye, 1978), recovery of functioning after coronary surgery (Thomas, 1993); and exercise adherence (Lyons, Harrell, & Blair, 1990). Also, performances are unaffected by whether people make their efficacy judgments privately or publicly (Gauthier & Ladouceur, 1981; Weinberg et al., 1980). Nor are efficacy judgments influenced by a responding bias to appear socially desirable, regardless of whether the domain of activity involves sexual behavior, alcohol consumption, smoking, dietary practices, or self-management of diabetes (Grossman, Brink, & Hauser, 1987; Seltenreich, 1989/1990; Velicer et al., 1990; Stotland & Zuroff, 1991; Wulfert & Wan, 1992).

Private recording of efficacy judgments may reduce evaluative concerns and consistency demands, but it could be argued that it does not eliminate them entirely. To the extent that people assume their private recordings will be evaluated at a later time, they may retain some evaluative concerns. Telch and his colleagues provide the most decisive evidence that making efficacy judgments does not increase congruence between perceived efficacy and behavior (Telch, Bandura, Vinciguerra, Agras, & Stout, 1982). Phobics made efficacy judgments either under high social demand for consistency or under the belief that their efficacy judgments would not be seen by anyone because they kept them for themselves, thus removing any social pressure for consistency. Unbeknownst to the latter participants, however, they left a record of their efficacy judgments on a white carbon back copy. Contrary to consistency theory, high social demands reduced rather than increased the congruence between efficacy judgment and behavior. Under high social surveillance and evaluative threat, people became more conservative in their efficacy appraisals and behaviorally exceeded their self-judgments. If actions were governed by a drive for consistency, they could have easily achieved high congruence simply by quitting after their performance matched their efficacy judgment. Instead, they continued to take on additional performance tasks. Social evaluative concerns encourage conservatism in self-appraisal mainly when ambiguity exists about the precise nature of the threat and the tasks to be performed. After people gain some information on these matters, they rely on their self-knowledge and do not let extraneous evaluative factors intrude on their self-appraisals. As a result, their actions correspond closely to their stated efficacy beliefs.

Assessment of self-efficacy should not be confounded with instruction in efficacious modes of behavior. A study by Arisohn, Bruch, and Heimberg (1988) of perceived efficacy for refusal of unreasonable requests illustrates such confounding. Each test item provided a set of effective refusal responses appropriate to each of several unreasonable request situations, and individuals were asked to judge their efficacy to execute them. Thus, in the context of assessing assertive self-efficacy, individuals were taught a variety of effective refusal strategies they may not have known. Verbal strategies are especially easy to teach by word. Not surprisingly, the confounded efficacy assessment raised perceived efficacy to turn down unwarranted demands. The more examples of effective strategies people were given, the more they raised their sense of efficacy. This is an instance of instruction effects, not reactive effects of self-assessment. An unconfounded assessment would have individuals judge their efficacy to refuse unreasonable requests without instructing them in effective ways of doing it.

Self-efficacy scales are often structured hierarchically in terms of ascending task demands. The initial reference point in a series of items can have an anchoring influence on efficacy judgments (Peake & Cervone, 1989). Given that every set of items must begin somewhere, the preferred format is the one that minimizes any anchoring influence. Berry and her associates found that a descending format ordering the items from most to least difficult task demands tended to produce slightly higher self-efficacy appraisals than did an ascending or random order, which did not differ from each other (Berry, et al., 1989). Since the ascending order of presentation does not bias self-efficacy judgment, either ascending or random orders would seem to be the preferred formats.

Omnibus versus Domain-Linked Measures

Numerous studies have compared the relative predictive power of domain-linked measures of perceived efficacy and omnibus locus of control scales. The evidence is relatively consistent in showing that perceived self-efficacy is a good predictor, whereas locus of control is either a weak predictor or is nonpredictive. This pattern of findings is replicated across diverse activities. Consider some representative examples. Efficacy beliefs predict academic performance, proneness to anxiety, pain tolerance, metabolic control in diabetes, and political participation, whereas locus of control does not (Grossman, Brink, & Hauser, 1987; Manning & Wright, 1983; McCarthy, Meier, & Rinderer, 1985; Smith, 1989; Taylor & Popma, 1990; Wollman & Stouder, 1991). More circumscribed but still general locus of control measures do not fare much better. The more specific measure of perceived locus of health control (Wallston, Wallston, & DeVellis, 1978) has been used in some of the comparative studies. It measures whether people believe that health is largely controlled by themselves, by chance factors, or by health professionals. Efficacy beliefs predict adoption of preventive dental practices, improvement in pulmonary functioning, effective breast self-examination to detect lesions, adoption of healthful nutritional and exercise habits, pursuit of smoking treatment, and long-term maintenance of smoking cessation, whereas people's general beliefs that they can control their own health does not predict any of these health behaviors (Alagna & Reddy, 1984; Beck & Lund, 1981; Brod & Hall, 1984; Kaplan, Atkins, & Reinsch, 1984; Sallis et al., 1988; Walker & Franzini, 1983). Given that people can stick to preventive dental routines but have a tough time resisting smoking urges, there is little reason to expect that the same general items regarding the personal controllability of health should have much success in predicting either or both behaviors.

Other omnibus measures of perceived personal control suffer similar low predictiveness. For example, general measures of perceived control fail to reveal any changes with increasing age, whereas more sensitive domain-linked measures do (Lachman & Leff, 1989). Similarly, measures of perceived efficacy tailored to distinct domains are much better predictors than omnibus measures of internal attributions for successes and failures (Collins, 1982), perceived self-control capabilities (Barrios, 1985), and self-concept of ability (Pajares & Miller, 1994a). These diverse comparative tests of predictiveness testify that ambiguous traitlike measures of perceived control do not provide adequate tests of self-efficacy theory. Global measures of self-efficacy suffer from more than indefiniteness and questionable relevance to the domain of functioning being explored. They typically include a confounded mixture of items that assess not only people's beliefs about their capabilities but also the emotional and motivational effects of efficacy beliefs and reports of past behavior. For this reason, this book excludes research using confounded global measures.

Harter (1981) adopted a multidimensional approach to the assessment of perceived competence. Three general areas of perceived competence—cognitive, social, and physical—are measured. Distinguishing among major classes of activities incorporates some features of the multidomain methodology. The domains are too broad and the items are too general, however, to do justice to the diverse forms human competencies take. As people develop their competencies through selective pursuits, their beliefs about their capabilities become more differentiated. This diversity requires differentiations within major activity domains. Consider perceived scholastic competence as an example. High school students often vary in the degree to which they consider themselves competent in mathematics, physical sciences, literature, social sciences, and the humanities. In one of the items in Harter's test of perceived cognitive competence, students are asked to judge their scholastic competence by rating whether they are "good at schoolwork." Because the subject matter is unspecified, they have to come up with a single judgment of their capabilities from the scholastic activity that happens to spring to mind at the moment or guesses about the scholastic activity the assessor had in mind. Otherwise, they must engage in subjective weighting and aggregation across diverse subject matters. Because the patterning of perceived scholastic efficacy across different types of "schoolwork" is likely to vary from student to student, similar scores of perceived capability may mean different things.

General items linked to major activity domains are an improvement over omnibus measures that are dissociated from clearly defined activities and contextual factors. But indefinite items still sacrifice explanatory and predictive power even though they may be tied to a designated domain. Microanalytic approaches that are sensitive to the diversity of human capabilities are better suited to clarify how self-beliefs affect human thought, motivation, affect, and action. Comparative tests would reveal whether self-efficacy measures have greater predictive utility than Harter's semiomnibus ones.

Some investigators have constructed an all-purpose measure of perceived self-efficacy and general measures of social and physical self-efficacy (Ryckman et al., 1982; Sherer et al., 1982). Such tools violate the basic assumption of the multidimensionality of self-efficacy beliefs. They are not the appropriate measures to use in tests of self-efficacy theory, nor do they have much predictive utility. Whereas domain self-efficacy measures are good predictors, these general ones account for little variance in human motivation or performance

(Earley & Lituchy, 1991; Eden & Zuk, 1995; LaGuardia & Labbé, 1993; McAuley & Gill, 1983). Sometimes evidence is presented that global measures are poor predictors of particular performances but fare better as summary ratings of behavior. The implication is that global and multidomain measures may be complementary. Such findings most likely reflect an affinity of the vagueness of efficacy measures for the vagueness of performance measures, rather than complementarity. It is more accurate to characterize omnibus measures as superficial samples of many areas of functioning using indefinite items than as comprehensive gauges of the generality of self-belief. Combining scores from multidomain measures, weighted by their relative importance, provides a more sensitive, integrated predictor of overall level of functioning. This type of integrative approach to the generality of self-belief includes both depth and breadth of assessment. The relevant issue in predicting composite performances is not specificity versus globality of measures; rather, the issue is indistinct omnibus measures versus integrated multidomain measures.

Self-efficacy is commonly misconstrued as being concerned solely with "specific behaviors in specific situations." This is an erroneous characterization. Domain particularity does not necessarily mean behavioral specificity. One can distinguish among three levels of generality of assessment. The most specific level measures perceived self-efficacy for a particular performance under a specific set of conditions. The intermediate level measures perceived self-efficacy for a class of performances within the same activity domain under a class of conditions sharing common properties. And finally, the most general and global level measures belief in personal efficacy without specifying the activities or the conditions under which they must be performed.

We have already seen that, as a rule, undifferentiated, contextless measures of personal efficacy have weak predictive value. The optimal level of generality at which self-efficacy is assessed varies depending on what one seeks to predict and the degree of foreknowledge of the situational demands. If the purpose is to explain and predict a particular

level of performance in a given situation, an efficacy measure of high specificity is most relevant. For example, to evaluate the impact of a team's sense of efficacy on its performance in a championship playoff game, one should measure the players' perceived efficacy to execute different aspects of the game against the particular opponent they have to face rather than against the whole array of teams in the league or some unspecified opponent. Similarly, in testing theoretical propositions about the processes through which efficacy beliefs affect particular courses of action, one must examine microrelations at the level of particular activities.

In many situations, self-efficacy theory seeks to explain certain classes of performances within generic or prototypic classes of settings. For this purpose, people judge their efficacy across the full range of task demands within a given domain of functioning with items cast at an intermediate level of generality. Consider a clinical example of impaired driving capability in agoraphobics. In assessing their perceived efficacy in this domain of functioning, they judge their efficacy to navigate automobiles in a wide range of generic contexts ranging from driving in residential areas to suburban business districts, crowded freeways, urban traffic, and winding mountain roads (Bandura et al., 1980). The urban context is specified as driving in city traffic rather than being tied to highly specific situations such as driving in San Francisco during Friday rush hour traffic in a downpour up Nob Hill behind a cable car.

The variations within a generic context differ in degree of representativeness. For the generic context of urban driving, flat streets are more typical of cities than precipitously hilly ones. Self-efficacy for a specified domain of functioning is usually assessed at the intermediate level of generality because the self-regulatory demands in some particular settings may be unrepresentative of the demands under the conditions that exist when people usually perform the activity. To continue with our timorous motorist, scaling the precipitous hills of San Francisco requires considerably greater self-regulatory efficacy than navigating through level urban streets. Hence, perceived efficacy for the atypical specific context of steep streets would be less predictive across the range of urban driving situations than efficacy for the generic common context of level streets.

When the situations people are likely to encounter are not fully known, one would predict better from perceived efficacy for common situations than for unusual ones. It should be noted, however, that efficacy predictiveness for common conditions is gained at the loss of some predictiveness for conditions within the same generic context that have fewer common features. If the task is to predict motoring venturesomeness in San Francisco, then the self-efficacy probes should be concerned with personal efficacy to navigate the precipitous streets of enchanting San Francisco rather than with the more common flat urban terrains. Some of the situational variants cannot be specified in advance and, even if they were known, assessing perceived efficacy for all variants of a generic context can be time-consuming. Therefore, in practice, casting efficacy items at an intermediate level of generality expands the scope of predictiveness. In short, efficacy beliefs are multifaceted and contextual, but the level of generality of the efficacy items within a given domain of functioning varies depending on the degree of situational resemblance and the foreseeability of task demands. But regardless of the level of generality, in no case are the efficacy items dissociated from context and level of task demands.

Research strategies often dictate, for better or for worse, the depth and breadth of self-efficacy assessment. Research designed to clarify a particular mechanism governing human motivation and action differs from studies that seek to maximize the percentage of variance in behavior explained by combining a host of factors that contribute to the behavior. In research aimed primarily at verifying the causal contribution of perceived efficacy to motivation and action, efficacy beliefs are systematically altered, and the other determinants are controlled by randomization or by assessment and statistical control. Because the inquiry is highly focused on clarifying how efficacy beliefs contribute to human functioning, perceived efficacy is measured in considerable detail.

Large-scale efforts to maximize the percentage of variance accounted for in behavior usually include a sizable set of possible determinants. Because people's time and patience are limited, investigators are often forced to use brief global measures for each of many different factors. In some instances, perceived efficacy is assessed by a single item, yielding scores that are severely restricted in range and of questionable reliability. Also, precision may be sacrificed for brevity by the use of general brief measures that skimp on the range of task demands for which self-efficacy is judged and that remove the contexts in which the activities are performed. Given the poor track record of undifferentiated, contextless measures, such a research strategy is likely to sacrifice predictive power for operational feasibility. Networks of relationships obtained with suboptimal measures may underestimate or actually misrepresent the causal contribution of given factors. The superiority of particular, multiple-item measures is most evident when the measures of human functioning adequately reflect the diversity of the behavior being predicted. The explanatory and predictive benefits of sensitive predictors are lost, however, when conglomerate indefinite measures of human functioning are used.

Discriminative Generalization of Self-Appraisal

A multidimensional approach does not mean that there is no structure or generality to efficacy beliefs. The development and exercise of capabilities would be severely constricted if there was absolutely no transfer of efficacy beliefs across activities or settings. People would have to establish their sense of efficacy anew for every activity that had an element of dissimilarity with familiar activities. Such extreme specificity would not be adaptive. Indiscriminate transfer of efficacy beliefs is not adaptive, either. If it were, those who harbored a low sense of efficacy would avoid all new pursuits or quickly undermine their efforts if they did try them. Conversely, those who approached every new activity with unbridled efficacy, blissfully free of any sense of personal limitations, would be in for many rude awakenings. One is not served well by either extreme specificity or indiscriminate generality. Adaptive functioning requires discriminative generalization of perceived efficacy.

Efficacy beliefs are structured by experience and reflective thought rather than being simply a disjoined collection of highly specific self-beliefs. There are at least five processes through which mastery experiences can produce some generality in personal efficacy. One such process occurs when different classes of activities are governed by *similar subskills*. Thus, executives may have comparable confidence in their ability to run a company and a community fund-raising campaign because these activities rely heavily on similar organizational and problem-solving skills. Perception of similarity of task demands is, of course, largely a personal construction, and it is not simply dictated by the number of objective common features. Few activities are entirely new. Most contain varying mixtures of familiar and novel aspects. Individuals who focus on the familiar aspects of new activities will display greater transfer of perceived self-efficacy than those who center their attention on the more novel features (Cervone, 1989).

Generalization of perceived efficacy has been studied as a function of the degree of similarity of qualitative features of activities and the skills they require. The enhancement of perceived personal efficacy through the development of coping skills generalizes across different stressors within the same activity domain (Bandura, Adams, & Beyer, 1977). The less similar the activities, however, the less perceived efficacy generalizes. Thus, for example, mastery of high-risk physical activity heightens perceived efficacy that generalizes to other types of physical stressors but not to highly dissimilar social and cognitive stressors (Brody, Hatfield, & Spalding, 1988).

Codevelopment is another process that builds generality. Even if different activity domains are not subserved by common subskills, some generality of perceived efficacy can occur if development of competencies is socially structured so that skills in dissimilar domains are acquired together. For example, if students are tutored in language and mathematics with comparable adequacy, the levels of perceived efficacy in both subjects will be positively related even though they depend on different cognitive skills. Thus, students are likely to develop relatively high perceived efficacy in these dissimilar academic domains in superior schools but relatively low perceived efficacy in ineffective schools, which do not promote much academic learning in any subject matter. Ewart and his colleagues provide evidence that both commonality of subskills and covariation of development foster generality of perceived efficacy (Ewart et al., 1986). This research also corroborates the predictive superiority of domain-related efficacy measures.

Efficacy beliefs differ widely in importance. Some forms of efficacy are more vital to one's life pursuits than others. Life pursuits are structured around roles typically requiring multiple sets of skills that must be developed together rather than resting on a single disjoined skill. Most people labor hard to master the different facets of their vocation. Therefore, the constellation of role demands partly determines how efficacy beliefs will be organized in a given life pursuit. Because the structural characteristics of different roles vary widely, the patterns of relationships among domain-specific efficacy beliefs will vary across different life pursuits.

Proficient action is not simply a mechanical expression of preformed skills. Rather, it requires selecting and orchestrating subskills guided by higher *self-regulatory skills*. These include generic skills for diagnosing task demands, constructing and evaluating alternative courses of action, setting proximal goals to guide one's efforts, and creating self-incentives to sustain engagement in taxing activities and to manage stress and debilitating intrusive thoughts. Such generalizable self-regulatory skills enable people to improve their performance in a variety of activities (Meichenbaum & Asarnow, 1979; Zimmerman, 1989). Widely applicable metastrategies learned in one realm of activity tend to be used in other activity domains (Bandura, Jeffery, & Gajdos, 1975). In addition, people's beliefs in their learning capabilities affect how they approach new challenges. Having mastered some skills, they can develop a more general sense of their efficacy to learn in other life situations. To the extent that people consider their self-regulatory capabilities in their self-appraisals, they will exhibit at least some generality in their sense of personal efficacy across different activities. But some regulative commonality does not necessarily mean high uniformity in perceived efficacy for tasks that differ substantially in the competencies they require.

Multidomain measures reveal the patterning and degree of generality of people's sense of personal efficacy. Some judge themselves highly efficacious across a wide range of domains of functioning. They believe they can succeed at most things they attempt. Others are beset by overwhelming self-doubts and anticipate that things will go wrong in whatever they try. But most people judge themselves to be relatively efficacious in domains in which they have cultivated their competencies, moderately efficacious in domains in which they are somewhat less conversant, and inefficacious in activity domains that severely strain their capabilities. Thus, the sociocognitive approach to the structure of personal agency provides profiles of efficacy beliefs across diverse domains of functioning rather than evading the distinctive patterning of human belief systems by using general measures. One can derive the degree of generality in perceived efficacy from multidomain scales, but one cannot extract the patterning of perceived efficacy from indefinite conglomerate tests.

Mastery-oriented treatments strive to expand the positive impact of success experiences on efficacy beliefs by cultivating *generalizable coping skills* that enable people to exercise control over diverse threats. Consider some examples. When women are taught powerful physical skills for disabling physical and sexual assailants, they display widespread increase in personal efficacy to control a variety of potentially threatening situations before they get out of hand. As a result, they lead safer and more active, enriched lives (Ozer & Bandura, 1990). The effect on personal efficacy is widespread because the self-protective skills are highly generalizable to different individuals, different settings, and

different activities. The self-efficacy benefits of enhancement of general physical strength in women also has positive ramifications on personal efficacy in areas of life in which physical capability enables them to exercise better control over social situations (Holloway, Beuter, & Duda, 1988). When phobics are taught generalizable coping skills, their enhanced self-efficacy and coping behavior extend beyond the particular threat for which those skills were developed (Bandura, et al., 1975; Williams, Kinney, & Falbo, 1989). Similarly, mastering stress-management skills that are serviceable across different activity domains produces general enhancement of perceived efficacy (Smith, 1989).

The impact of success experiences on efficacy beliefs can also be generalized by construing activities in ways that highlight commonalities. In this process, generality is achieved by *structuring commonalities cognitively* across diverse activities. The framing creates the self-efficacy linkages between activities (Cervone, 1989). Consider an example of widespread generality in efficacy belief. Individuals who have minor heart attacks often lead needlessly impoverished lives because they believe they have a permanently impaired heart. Some of these patients were helped to resume active and productive lives by raising their belief in their cardiac capabilities through mastery of heavy workloads on a treadmill (Taylor, Bandura, Ewart, Miller, & DeBusk, 1985). Their treadmill attainments were interpreted as generic indications of their cardiovascular capacity; they believed that the strain their heart was able to withstand on the treadmill exceeded any strains they were likely to encounter in their everyday activities. By emphasizing the commonality of cardiac robustness across diverse activities, the treadmill mastery experience raised patients' beliefs not only in their cardiac capability, but also in their efficacy to resume a wide range of activities that involve physical and emotional strain. The higher their perceived cardiac efficacy, the greater was their recovery of cardiovascular function. Had the treadmill been presented simply as an isolated motor task, it is unlikely that perceived efficacy beyond this particular activity would have been much affected by the experience.

Powerful mastery experiences that provide striking testimony to one's capacity to effect personal changes can also produce a *transformational restructuring of efficacy beliefs* that is manifested across diverse realms of functioning. Such personal triumphs serve as transforming experiences. What generalizes is the belief that one can mobilize whatever effort it takes to succeed in different undertakings. Indeed, my initial investigations into the causal contribution of efficacy beliefs to human adaptation and change was an unintended outgrowth of a different line of research. We launched a series of studies to expand the psychological impact of a powerful mastery-based treatment and to reduce vulnerability to negative experiences with phobic threats should they occur in the future. These additional benefits, we reasoned, could be achieved by having phobics pursue self-directed mastery experiences with different versions of the phobic threat after their coping capabilities were fully developed (Bandura et al., 1975). Multiple experiences in the exercise of personal control over varied threats would further strengthen and generalize their coping capabilities. Numerous positive experiences would neutralize the impact of any subsequent negative ones. Severe snake phobics who had led constricted and tormented lives for most of their lifetime were all cured within a few hours — they were permanently freed of phobic behavior, ruminative dread, anxious distress, and recurrent nightmares. Swift mastery of chronic incapacity had a transformational impact that produced profound change in participants' beliefs in their personal efficacy to exercise better control over their lives. They were putting themselves to the test in surmounting other problems and were enjoying successes, much to their surprise.

In follow-up assessments, we found that participants had improved their level of functioning in other realms completely unrelated to the treated dysfunction. Dramatic mastery of a snake phobia reduced social timidity, boosted self-expressiveness, and otherwise increased venturesome self-testing of personal capabilities: "The feeling of accomplishment I was experiencing at having overcome the fear of snakes gave me the confidence to

overcome my fear of public speaking." "I'm generally somewhat less timid than I was before." "The biggest benefit to me of the successfulness of the treatment was the feeling that if I could lick snakes, I could lick anything. It gave me the confidence to tackle, also successfully, some personal stuff." This generalized boost of personal efficacy did not follow any gradient of physical or semantic commonalities. To take but one of the generalized improvements, reptiles are poor conversationalists and provide little opportunity to practice oratorical skills. There is no gradient of stimulus generalization that could explain why overcoming a snake phobia should make one a venturesome public speaker. In the instances cited, the generality of efficacy stemmed primarily from metacognitive changes in people's beliefs concerning their agentive power for self-change rather than from skill commonalities, cognitive structuring of similarities, temporal co-development, or strategy transfer.

The point at issue is not whether efficacy beliefs can be generalized to some extent, but the processes through which generality occurs and how it should be measured. This requires a theory about the structure and processes of generality and particularized measures of personal efficacy. The previous discussion identified five processes by which efficacy beliefs generalize across domains of functioning. The assessment implications of a process-oriented approach can be illustrated with achievement of generality in self-efficacy through use of serviceable self-regulatory skills. This contributor to personal efficacy would be assessed by multifactor scales of perceived self-regulatory efficacy to plan and structure activities; to enlist needed resources; to regulate one's motivation through proximal challenges and self-incentives; and to manage the emotionally and cognitively disruptive effects of obstacles, setbacks and stressors. Empirical evidence that efficacy beliefs vary across activity domains should temper the pursuit of a psychological Grail of generality, however. To continue with the self-regulatory example, a high sense of self-regulatory efficacy can aid performance in different domains, but pursuits differ in the specialized competencies they require, and some aspects of life are considerably more difficult to modify then others. People's appraisal of their efficacy in a given domain is undoubtedly based, in part, on judgment of their general self-regulatory capabilities. Thus, generic and domain self-efficacies are not entirely independent. A process approach to generality has the added benefit of providing useful guidelines on how to structure programs of personal change to enhance their impact on general beliefs of personal efficacy.

SELF-EFFICACY CAUSALITY

A central question in any theory of the cognitive regulation of motivation and action is the issue of causality. Do efficacy beliefs operate as causal factors in human functioning? Psychological theories postulate mediating mechanisms through which external factors affect behavior. Empirical tests of causation may vary in the number of links they verify in the postulated causal chain. The weakest test provides evidence that behavior covaries with changes in external conditions that are believed to affect the postulated mediator, but they do not measure the mediator independently. Much research rests on such presumptive evidence of mediation. Covariation between instating conditions and actions increases confidence in the theory, but it does not firmly establish the theory's validity because the covariation can be mediated by other mechanisms that can produce similar effects.

The need to assess, rather than simply to presume, the mediating link can be illustrated by empirical tests of the attributional and self-perception theory of intrinsic motivation. According to this theory, children judge their motivation from the conditions under which they perform. If they are rewarded for engaging in an activity, they ascribe their heightened performance to the external inducements and lose intrinsic interest; if they perform without external inducement, they judge themselves to be intrinsically motivated and actively pursue the activity. Causal attributions are regarded as the intervening determinant of

subsequent performance. In empirical tests of the theory, however, the attributions actually evoked by external rewards are rarely measured. Because rewards can alter performance through a variety of mechanisms (Bandura, 1986a), evidence that rewards capable of affecting causal attributions influence performance provides a weak empirical test. Evidence of a linkage between incentive practices and causal attributions and between attributions and interest in the activity would constitute the strong test of the theory. Developmental analysis of how extrinsic rewards affect causal attributions reveals that, contrary to presumption, young children actually attribute more intrinsic interest to an activity when it is rewarded than when it is not (Karniol & Ross, 1976; Kun, 1978). Moreover, Morgan (1981) found that rewards given irrespective of quality of performance reduce interest, regardless of whether children subscribed to the additive principle that rewards raise interest, or to the discounting principle that rewards detract from interest. Such findings challenge the notion that, in young children, rewards reduce interest through a discounting attributional process. The mediating mechanism that governs the reductive effects of noncontingent rewards has yet to be identified. As this example shows, merely linking external influences to actions leaves considerable ambiguity about the mechanism through which the effect is produced.

Dual Causal Linkage

Verification tests of causation are much more persuasive when they rely on assessed mediation rather than on presumptive mediation. A postulated cognitive mediator is not directly observable, but it has observable indicants other than the actions it presumably governs. In the case of the efficacy mediator, people can report their beliefs. This observable indicant enables us to understand the origin and function of efficacy beliefs. The most stringent test of a theory provides evidence of dual linkage in the causal process — external influences are linked to changes in an independently measured indicant of the internal mediator, and it, in turn, is linked to behavior. Further tests can be conducted to determine whether the effect of external influence on action is mediated completely or partially through efficacy belief (Judd & Kenny, 1981). If no relation between external influence and action remains after controlling for variation in efficacy belief, then the external influence works entirely through efficacy belief. If the relation is weakened but not eliminated by controlling for efficacy belief, then the external influence operates partly through efficacy belief.

The efficacy-action link can be corroborated in two ways. The first is by verifying *microlevel* relations between particular efficacy beliefs and corresponding actions. This measure of congruence is obtained by recording whether or not individuals judge themselves capable of executing each of various levels of performance and computing the percentage of accurate correspondence between self-efficacy judgment and actual performance. Mismatches between efficacy judgment and action — judged efficacy for subsequently failed action and judged inefficacy for successful action — represent instances of incongruence. Cervone (1985) provides a randomization test for evaluating the level of significance of obtained microlevel congruences. This microanalytic procedure is well suited for examining theoretical issues about the relation of self-referent thought to action and processes that affect accurateness of self-appraisal.

We saw earlier that efficacy beliefs vary in strength. In applying the microanalytic procedure, judgments of personal efficacy must be divided into positive and negative instances based on a selected cutoff value of strength of belief. Dividing continuous measures of strength of belief on the basis of a minimal strength value inevitably loses some predictive information. For example, if a low efficacy strength value is selected as the criterion of self-judged efficacy (say, 20), a weak sense of efficacy (30) is treated the same as complete certitude (100). Such a low criterion could produce artifactual mismatches. Conversely, if the cutoff criterion is set at a high efficacy strength (say, 70) a moderately strong sense of efficacy (60) would be defined as an instance of low efficacy. This too

could produce artifactual discrepancies. The optimal cutoff criterion must be determined empirically for different domains of functioning. A more refined microanalysis of congruence is provided by computing the probability of successful performance as a function of the strength of perceived self-efficacy (Bandura, 1977). This microlevel analysis retains the predictive value of variations in strength of efficacy beliefs. Because efficacy strength incorporates efficacy level as well as gradations of certainty above any threshold value, efficacy strength is generally a more sensitive and informative measure than efficacy level.

There are a number of conditions under which the microlevel congruence procedure is unsuitable for verifying the effects of efficacy beliefs. In some instances, the modality through which self-efficacy is exercised differs from the modality in which the effects are manifested. For example, the efficacy judgments may center on behavioral coping capabilities, but their impact is assessed in terms of affective reactions of anxiety and depression or physiological activation of autonomic, catecholamine, opioid, or immunologic systems. Variations in efficacy judgments and in the affective and physiological reactions are measured on different ordinal scales. In other cases, the efficacy judgment is made about an intermediary activity that in due time produces a result of a different sort. An example is linkages between perceived self-regulatory efficacy to cut down on consumption of saturated fat and reduction in level of plasma cholesterol. In still other cases, the self-efficacy is judged for different performance attainments, and the effect is level of motivation as indexed by intensity and persistence of effort. Often, the interest is in predicting a wide range of activities from efficacy beliefs assessed across different levels or facets of functioning within a given domain. An example would be the effect on academic grade point average of perceived self-efficacy to regulate one's motivation and learning activities. In the last instance, the link between perceived self-efficacy and subsequent performance attainments is verified by macrolevel relations that correlate aggregated efficacy beliefs with aggregated academic performances.

Diverse Tests of Causality

Studies of the causal contribution of efficacy beliefs to the level and quality of human functioning test each of the postulated links in the causal process. A variety of experimental strategies have been used for this purpose. In one approach, perceived self-efficacy is raised to different preselected levels, and its effects on behavior are measured. In one such experiment (Bandura, Reese, & Adams, 1982), perceived self-efficacy was raised from virtually nonexistent to either low or moderately high levels solely by modeling. In this vicarious mode of efficacy induction, phobics observed coping strategies being modeled, but they themselves did not perform any actions. Therefore, they had to rely entirely on what they saw in forming generalized beliefs of their own efficacy. In the second phase of the study, after the behavior of groups at different levels of perceived self-efficacy was measured, each individual's perceived efficacy was successively raised to higher levels, and their behavior was again measured at each new level. This dual-phase experimental design provided an intergroup comparison with an intraindividual replication of how phobics behaved after

their beliefs about their coping efficacy were raised to different levels.

As shown in Figure 2.1, higher levels of perceived self-efficacy were accompanied by higher performance attainments. The efficacy-action relationship was replicated in comparisons of variations in both intergroup and intraindividual levels of perceived efficacy. Microanalysis of efficacy-action congruences revealed a close fit between efficacy beliefs and coping performance on individual tasks. People successfully executed tasks that fell within their enhanced range of perceived self-efficacy, but they shunned or failed those that exceeded their perceived coping capabilities.

Findings from the vicarious mode demonstrate the causal contribution of efficacy beliefs to performance especially well. Individuals simply observed models' performances, made inferences from the modeled information about their own coping efficacy, and later behaved in accordance with their efficacy beliefs. This was true even for individuals who were so phobic that they could not perform a single response in the pretest assessment and, hence, had no pretreatment performance information from which to foretell what they could

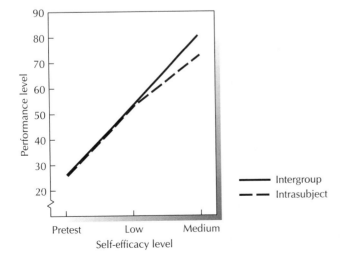

FIGURE 2.1.   Mean performance attainments as a function of created differential levels of perceived self-efficacy solely by vicarious experiences. The intergroup line shows the performance attainments of a group of phobics whose efficacy beliefs were raised to different levels; the intrasubject line shows the performance attainments for the same phobics after their efficacy beliefs were successively raised to different levels. (Bandura, Reese, & Adams, 1982)

do after observing the instructive modeling. The only thing their pretest behavior could tell them was that they could do nothing.

Another approach to the test of causality is to introduce a trivial factor that provides no information to affect competency but that can alter perceived self-efficacy. The impact of the altered efficacy beliefs on level of motivation is then measured. Studies of anchoring influences show that arbitrary reference points from which judgments are adjusted either upward or downward can bias the judgments (Tversky & Kahneman, 1974). Thus, for example, a randomly selected low number as a starting point will lead people to estimate a smaller crowd in a stadium than will a large starting number. An arbitrary starting point biases judgments because the adjustments from it are usually insufficient.

Cervone and Peake (1986) used arbitrary reference numbers to influence self-appraisals of efficacy. Judgments of personal efficacy made from an arbitrary high starting point raised students' perceived efficacy, whereas an arbitrary low starting point lowered students' appraisals of their efficacy

(Fig. 2.2). The starting level in a graded sequence of items measuring personal efficacy to fulfill different levels of performance can similarly influence self-efficacy appraisal. Peake & Cervone (1989) also biased efficacy judgment simply by having people judge their efficacy in relation to ascending or descending levels of possible performance attainments. People judged their efficacy as lower for the ascending format than for the descending one. Here the environmental input was simply a physical arrangement of scale items that neither provided any differential information about capabilities nor involved any social influences. In a further study, Cervone (1989) biased efficacy appraisal by differential cognitive focus on things about the task that might make it troublesome or tractable. Dwelling on formidable aspects weakened people's belief in their efficacy; focusing on doable aspects raised their perceived efficacy. In each of these experiments, the higher the instilled efficacy beliefs, the longer individuals persevered on difficult and unsolvable problems before they quit. Mediational analyses reveal that neither anchoring influences nor cognitive focus had any effect on motivation

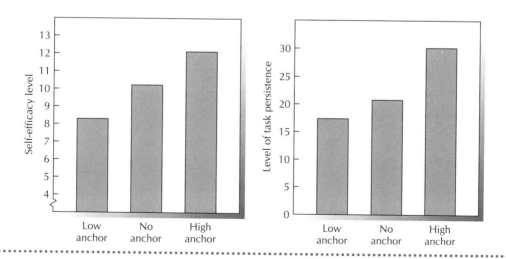

FIGURE 2.2. Mean changes induced in perceived self-efficacy by arbitrary starting points or anchoring influences and the corresponding effects of efficacy beliefs on level of perseverant effort. (Cervone & Peake, 1986)

when perceived self-efficacy was controlled. Thus, the effect of the external influences on performance motivation was completely mediated by the degree to which they changed efficacy beliefs.

A number of experiments have been conducted in which efficacy beliefs are altered by bogus feedback unrelated to one's actual performance. As we will see later, people judge their capabilities partly through social comparison. Using this type of induction procedure, Weinberg, Gould, and Jackson (1979) showed that physical stamina in competitive situations is mediated by perceived self-efficacy. They raised the efficacy beliefs of one group of individuals by telling them that they had triumphed in a competition of muscular strength. They lowered the efficacy beliefs of another group of individuals by telling them that they were outperformed by their competitor. The participants were then tested in competitive trials on a different motor task measuring physical stamina rather than strength. The higher the illusory beliefs of physical strength, the more physical stamina subjects displayed during competition (Fig. 2.3). Failure in a subsequent competition spurred those with a high sense of efficacy to even greater physical effort, whereas failure further impaired the performance of those whose efficacy beliefs had been undermined. Beliefs of physical efficacy illusorily heightened in females and illusorily weakened in males obliterated large preexisting sex differences in physical stamina.

Another variant of self-appraisal through social comparison that has been used to raise or weaken efficacy beliefs relies on bogus normative comparison. In these studies, individuals are led to believe that they performed at the highest or lowest percentile ranks of a relevant reference group, regardless of their actual performance. The regulatory role of efficacy beliefs instated by fictitious normative comparison is revealed in a study of pain tolerance by Litt (1988). After being tested for pain tolerance on a cold-pressor test, individuals were led to believe that they were either at a high (90th) or low (37th) percentile rank in pain tolerance compared to an ostensibly normative group, without regard to their actual performance. The bogus

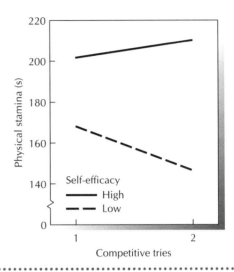

FIGURE 2.3. Mean level of physical stamina mobilized in competitive situations as a function of illusorily instated high or low beliefs of physical efficacy. The second competitive presents the level of stamina by competitors of high and low efficacy beliefs following a defeat. (Weinberg, Gould, & Jackson, 1979)

normative information produced differential levels of perceived self-efficacy that, in turn, were accompanied by corresponding changes in pain tolerance (Fig. 2.4). The greater the changes in perceived self-efficacy, the larger the changes in pain tolerance. In the next phase of the study, the bogus normative feedback was the opposite of that provided originally, presumably reflecting enduring capability to bear pain. Those who were led to believe that they had lost their comparative superiority lowered their perceived self-efficacy, whereas those led to believe that they had gained comparative superiority raised their belief in their capability to tolerate pain. Their subsequent level of pain tolerance changed in the direction of their altered efficacy beliefs. The condition involving alleged change from high to low normative standing is especially interesting because efficacy belief surpassed past performance as a predictor of subsequent performance.

As further verification of the causal contribution of efficacy beliefs in a markedly different domain of functioning, Bouffard-Bouchard (1990)

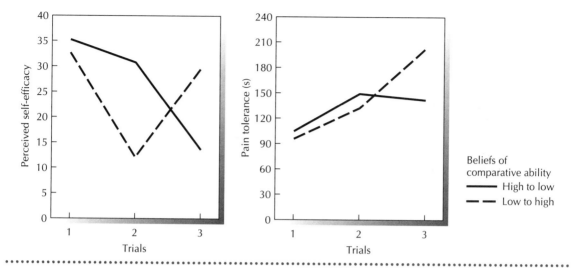

FIGURE 2.4. Changes in pain tolerance by individuals whose beliefs in their efficacy to manage pain were either raised or lowered by comparison to a bogus normative group. Trial 1 is the pretest level; in trials 2 and 3, efficacy beliefs were arbitrarily raised or lowered. (Litt, 1988)

induced high or low perceived self-efficacy in students by arbitrary comparison with peer norms irrespective of actual performance. Students whose sense of efficacy was illusorily raised set higher goals for themselves, used more efficient problem-solving strategies, and achieved higher intellectual performances than students of equal cognitive ability who were led to believe they lacked such capabilities. Jacobs and his colleagues similarly demonstrated that efficacy beliefs raised by fictitious normative comparison foster perseverant motivation in difficult problem solving (Jacobs, Prentice-Dunn, & Rogers, 1984). Instilled illusory beliefs of efficacy operate causally at the collective as well as the individual level. Arbitrary feedback to groups that they performed better or worse than a comparative normative standard altered belief in their collective capabilities (Prussia & Kinicki, 1996). The effect of this fictitious feedback on groups' aspirations and performance attainments was mediated entirely through the changes it produced in perceived collective efficacy.

Still another approach to the verification of causality employs a contravening experimental design in which a procedure that can impair

functioning is applied, but in ways that raise perceived self-efficacy. The changes accompanying psychological ministrations may result as much, if not more, from instilling beliefs of personal efficacy as from the particular skills imparted. If people's beliefs in their coping efficacy are strengthened, they approach situations more assuredly and make better use of the skills they have. Holroyd and his colleagues (Holroyd et al., 1984) demonstrated with sufferers of tension headaches that the benefits of biofeedback training may stem more from enhancement of perceived coping efficacy than from the muscular exercises themselves. In biofeedback sessions, they trained one group to become good relaxers. Another group received bogus feedback signals that they were relaxing whenever they tensed their muscles. They became good tensers of facial muscles, which, if anything, would aggravate tension headaches. Regardless of whether people were tensing or relaxing their muscles, bogus feedback that they were exercising good control over muscular tension instilled a strong sense of efficacy that they could prevent the occurrence of headaches in various stressful situations. The higher their perceived efficacy, the fewer headaches they experienced. The actual amount of change in muscular activity achieved in treatment was unrelated to the incidence of subsequent headaches.

The findings of these experiments, which rely heavily on persuasory modes of influence, should not be taken to mean that arbitrary persuasory information is a good way of instilling strong efficacy beliefs in the pursuits of everyday life. Rather, these studies have special bearing on the issue of causality because efficacy beliefs are altered independently of performance and, therefore, cannot be discounted as by-products of performance. They demonstrate that changes in efficacy beliefs regulate motivation and action. In actual social practice, however, personal enablement through mastery experiences is the most powerful way to create a strong, resilient sense of efficacy (Bandura, 1986a, 1988a). Personal enablement is achieved by equipping people with knowledge, subskills, and self-affirming experiences in the exercise of personal control. This is not to say, as is sometimes erroneously assumed, that the causal function of efficacy beliefs cannot be analyzed if the beliefs are altered by providing knowledge or cultivating skills. Efficacy beliefs are not fabricated from thin air. They are formed partly on the basis of judgment of one's knowledge and skills, but efficacy beliefs contribute to performance independently of actual skills or past performance, as will be shown shortly. Because efficacy beliefs are based on cognitive processing of multiple sources of information, actual skills often account for a relatively small amount of the variance in beliefs of personal efficacy.

The final way of verifying the causal contribution of efficacy beliefs to human functioning is to test the multivariate relations between relevant determinants and performance attainments in a theoretical causal model by hierarchical regression analysis or causal modeling techniques. These analytic tools indicate how much of the variation in performance is explained by perceived self-efficacy when the influence of other determinants is controlled. Moreover, these methods indicate the extent to which efficacy beliefs influence human functioning both directly and indirectly through their effects on other determinants.

The multivariate investigations involve panel designs in which efficacy beliefs, other possible determinants, and performance attainments are measured on two or more occasions to determine what effect these factors may have on one another. In some of these studies, efficacy beliefs are altered by naturally occurring influences during the intervening period. More often, efficacy beliefs are altered experimentally by appropriate influences. The temporal ordering and systematic variation of efficacy beliefs before the predicted behavior help to remove ambiguities about the source and direction of causality. In addition to controlled induction and temporal priority of efficacy change, controls are applied for other potentially influential factors. The results of such studies reveal that efficacy beliefs usually make substantial independent contribution to variations in motivation and performance attainments (Bandura & Jourden, 1991; Dzewaltowski, 1989; Locke, Frederick, Lee, & Bobko, 1984; Ozer & Bandura, 1990; Wood & Bandura, 1989a). The causal contribution of efficacy beliefs to human functioning is further documented in comparative tests of the predictive power of social cognitive theory and alternative conceptual models (Dzewaltowski, et al., 1990; Lent, Brown, & Larkin, 1987; McCaul, O'Neill, & Glasgow, 1988; Siegel, Galassi, & Ware, 1985; Wheeler, 1983).

Radical behaviorists typically single out studies in which efficacy beliefs are altered by enactive modes of influence because there is a behavior to latch onto. They then argue that perceived self-efficacy is a reflection of prior performance. This claim has long lost its credibility by evidence from countless studies demonstrating that perceived self-efficacy contributes independently to subsequent performance when variations in prior performance are controlled. Another argument against cognitive determinants widely used by behavior analysts is that cognitions are inferred from the behavior they seek to explain. This trite argument is inappropriate to causal tests of self-efficacy theory because beliefs of personal efficacy are conceptually and operationally distinct from the behaviors to be explained. Indeed, in tests of causal contribution where efficacy beliefs are changed without any behavior being performed, there is no relevant or informative behavior from which to infer personal efficacy.

The diverse causal tests reviewed in this section were conducted with different modes of efficacy induction, diverse populations that included both children and adults, all sorts of domains of functioning and response systems, and experimental designs comparing groups raised to differential levels of perceived efficacy or the same individuals progressively raised to higher perceived efficacy; and the results were analyzed for microlevel and macrolevel relations. Moreover, efficacy beliefs were measured by different formats and domain-linked scales, so that the results are not peculiar to a particular instrument. The evidence is relatively consistent in showing that efficacy beliefs contribute significantly to level of motivation and performance. They predict not only the behavioral changes accompanying different environmental influences but also differences in behavior between individuals receiving the same environmental influence, and even variation within the same individual in the tasks performed and those shunned or attempted but failed. Evidence that divergent procedures produce convergent results across heterogeneous areas of functioning adds to the explanatory and predictive generality of the efficacy determinant.

SOURCES OF DISCORDANCE BETWEEN EFFICACY JUDGMENT AND ACTION

People make judgments of their efficacy because these judgments serve functional purposes. Acting on sound appraisals of personal capabilities increases the prospect of success, whereas acting on gross misjudgments of what one can do may be costly to one's psyche, cash flow, and fragile body. Indeed, in situations in which missteps can be physically injurious or fatal, people have to behave proactively on the basis of sound appraisal of their capabilities, otherwise they will suffer maiming or a tragically shortened life span.

Although efficacy beliefs are functionally related to action, a number of factors can affect the strength of that relation. Efficacy beliefs alone can raise and sustain motivation, but they will not produce newfangled performances if the subskills necessary for the exercise of personal agency are completely lacking. Of course, people do not hold vacuous efficacy beliefs devoid of any underlying capabilities. Nor does perceived self-efficacy involve only a one-way dependence on subskills. People usually possess many of the basic subskills for fashioning adaptive performances. If some of the subskills are lacking, it does not mean that efficacy beliefs can do nothing. Through the proactive exercise of efficacy belief in self-development, capacity is converted to capability. Belief in one's learning efficacy activates and sustains the effort and thought needed for skill development. Conversely, self-inefficacious thinking retards development of the very subskills upon which more complex performances depend. Perceived efficacy thus contributes to the acquisition of knowledge and development of subskills, as well as drawing upon them in the construction of new behavior patterns.

The previous section analyzed the independent contribution of efficacy beliefs to thought processes, motivation, affect, and action. A number of conditions, however, can create disparity between efficacy belief and action. Some of these disparities stem from deficiencies of assessment, others arise from ambiguities of task demands or performance attainments, others violate propositions about the condition under which thought is related to action, and still others reflect genuine discordances between self-referent thought and action.

Limited Scope of Self-Efficacy Assessment

Most behavior has multiple determinants. An assessment of the full contribution of personal efficacy to level of functioning, therefore, requires a sound theory of the factors governing the activity of interest. Theory tells us what form of efficacy to target. Self-efficacy theory is often tested on a factor that exerts only partial influence over the behavior of interest. If the factor targeted is a relatively small contributor to the given performance, perceived efficacy cannot emerge as a strong predictor because the factor to which it is tied carries limited weight in the causal structure. The success with which perceived efficacy to control eating habits predicts weight reduction is a common case in point. Weight is determined by what people eat, by their level of exercise (which burns calories and can raise the body's metabolism), and by genetic factors that regulate metabolic processes. Thus, the modifiable behavioral factors (that is, food intake and exercise) exert only partial control over reducing weight and keeping it off. If efficacy beliefs are targeted solely to eating habits, even the weight reduction that is predictable by behavioral factors is restricted. One weight management program combined changes in eating habits with exercise, but only efficacy to stick to dietary changes was measured (Stotland & Zuroff, 1991). Given that exercise contributes to maintenance of weight reduction, self-efficacy theory would gain in predictiveness by also measuring beliefs in one's ability to adopt and stick to an exercise routine. As this example illustrates, performances having multifaceted determinants require multifaceted self-efficacy predictors.

A similar issue of scope of assessment arises when self-efficacy is measured for only a component function of a multifaceted capability rather than for the integrated execution of the capability. This point was illustrated in the earlier example of driving efficacy. Perceived self-efficacy is an integrated emergent judgment rather than simply the sum of microcomponent functions. In complex activities requiring a variety of capabilities, including more facets of personal efficacy in the assessment increases predictive power. The multifaceted contribution of perceived efficacy to academic attainments is a good case in point. Engagement in activities that promote intellectual development is governed by a variety of psychosocial influences. The predictiveness of perceived efficacy increases as more of its relevant facets are measured. Thus,

perceived academic efficacy to regulate one's learning activities, social efficacy to cultivate supportive social relationships, and self-regulatory efficacy to resist peer pressures for activities that undermine academic pursuits together account for substantially more of the variance in academic achievement than does perceived academic efficacy alone (Bandura, Barbaranelli, Caprara, & Pastorelli, 1996a). The improved predictiveness of multifaceted measures of efficacy is verified in other areas of functioning as well (Arch, 1992a; Lent et al., 1986).

To complicate matters further, different forms of perceived self-efficacy may come into play in different phases of a given pursuit (Poag-DuCharme & Brawley, 1993). Therefore, behavior is better explained by people's beliefs in their capabilities to do whatever is needed to succeed in given situations than by their beliefs in only one aspect of self-efficacy. Because human functioning is multifaceted and self-efficacy assessment is rarely inclusive of all facets, the contribution of efficacy beliefs to adaptation and change is probably underestimated in formal tests. Thus, we should be cautious about interpreting the explained variance in performance by perceived self-efficacy in any given study as its maximum contribution.

Mismatch between Self-Efficacy and the Performance Domains

The structure of the relationship between efficacy belief and action requires that both tap similar capabilities. To the extent that the capabilities measured in perceived efficacy differ in significant ways from those that govern performance, one would not expect efficacy beliefs and performance to be highly related. They would be measuring different types of competencies. Pajares and Miller (1994b) systematically compared the predictive power of efficacy beliefs depending on the degree of correspondence between the capabilities assessed in belief and in performance. Efficacy beliefs were stronger predictors under good matches than under partial matches. The problem of mismatch is illustrated in a longitudinal study of perceived control and intellectual functioning in the elderly conducted by Lachman and Leff (1989). Self-efficacy was measured in terms of perceived ability to perform everyday cognitive tasks and to learn new things, whereas intellectual performance was measured in terms of vocabulary and inductive reasoning. Although these different activities may involve some overlap of cognitive functions, people can be efficacious in learning common cognitive tasks but lack an expansive vocabulary.

Efforts to enhance human functioning and well-being are usually guided by theories about the ways in which desired attainments can be achieved. For example, various theories claim that mastery of general problem-solving strategies will improve decision making in different spheres of activities. For example, training in metacognitive skills independent of particular subject matter will raise academic achievement. Dietary changes will reduce plasma cholesterol. Muscular relaxation will alleviate pain. And exercise of control over perturbing thought patterns that can keep one awake will reduce insomnia. When personal efficacy to perform the prescribed means is used as a predictor in the hypothesized causal model, one is testing not only the predictive power of efficacy beliefs but also the validity of the posited influence of the prescribed means on attainments in the causal model. Suppose, for instance, that muscular relaxation does *not* affect pain. A high sense of efficacy to induce relaxation would be irrelevant to the prediction of pain. If the targeted means have little effect on the desired attainment, the prediction coefficient will be low even though perceived efficacy is highly predictive of how well the prescribed means are executed. In such an instance, the predictiveness of self-efficacy theory would be erroneously faulted when, in fact, the causal model of the means for effecting change is of questionable validity.

When the means that produce certain behavioral attainments are only partially understood or have not been adequately verified, efficacy beliefs should be measured at two levels of specificity: efficacy to execute the prescribed means successfully and efficacy to achieve different levels of

performance attainments by whatever means people choose to do so. Efficacy beliefs measured in terms of gradations of attainments have good predictive validity (Bandura & Cervone, 1986; Wood & Bandura, 1989a). Attainment efficacy is also more predictive than means efficacy, if the means selected for assessment are only a partial set of those contributing to the behavioral attainments (Mone, 1994; Stotland & Zuroff, 1991). In judging their attainment efficacy, individuals can consider all of the means they have at their disposal to exercise control. Because attainment efficacy, being more inclusive, has higher validity than means efficacy, attainment efficacy is the preferred measure. This is especially so when the causal model of optimal means has not been adequately verified and there are limits on the number of factors that can be measured.

Faulty Assessments of Self-Efficacy or Performance

Causal processes are best clarified by microanalytic measures of efficacy beliefs that are tailored to the domain of functioning being explored. Such particularized measures capture the variations in people's beliefs in their efficacy for different types of activities and under different circumstances. We have already seen that particularized domain-related measures of perceived self-efficacy surpass global measures in explanatory and predictive power. Some tests of self-efficacy theory violate the multidimensionality of the efficacy belief system. In some studies, perceived efficacy is measured by a single general item; in others, it is assessed as a global trait; and in still others, global measures designed for other constructs that appear to bear some resemblance to efficacy are simply substituted for particularized indices of personal efficacy (Rebok & Balcerak, 1989; Rosenbaum & Hadari, 1985). Data from such global or proxy measures raise questions about the relevance of these measures to the issue of self-efficacy control of motivation and action.

The activities of everyday life are strewn with frustrating, boring, stressful, and other aversive elements. This is part and parcel of daily living. In many spheres of functioning, people know full well how to perform the needed behavior. Here, the relevant efficacy beliefs concern self-regulatory capabilities — can people get themselves to stick with the behavior given the many dissuading conditions they will encounter? Those who have a high sense of efficacy accept bothersome and aversive elements as part of the price of gaining mastery over problems. In contrast, those who distrust their capabilities to surmount unpleasant factors have little reason to put themselves through misery. In familiar activities that must be performed regularly to achieve desired results, it is perceived self-regulatory efficacy, rather than perceived efficacy for the activity per se, that is most relevant. For example, in predicting the self-management of periodontal disease, the appropriate efficacy measure is not whether individuals believe they can perform the trivial act of flossing their teeth (McCaul, Sandgren, O'Neill, & Hinsz, 1993), but whether they believe they have the self-regulatory capabilities to get themselves to do so daily in the face of specified conditions that interfere with their efforts. Trivial measures will yield misinformative results.

The performance part of the causal relation must also be adequately assessed under appropriate circumstances. Performance is rarely, if ever, measured with complete accuracy, as is evident in coefficients of reliability. Extraneous situational fluctuations, transient physiological states, and imperfect scoring contribute to inaccuracy in the index of performance. Errors of measurement place an upper limit on how highly efficacy beliefs can correlate with performance. The magnitude of correlations, therefore, should not be interpreted as though the measure of performance is errorless.

The relation of efficacy beliefs to performance can be reduced by the choice of performances as well as by how reliably they are measured. Complex patterns of behavior do not lend themselves easily to assessment. To measure them well requires time, effort, resources, and ingenuity. As a consequence, some studies rely on such questionable proxy measures of behavior as people's reports of what they do or the ratings of others. Even these types of ratings often rely on global judgments that mask the diversity of the behavior to be predicted. People do not behave globally. The problem of behavioral diversity and complexity is not solved by simplifying global judgments. Sometimes, when behavior is measured directly, only a very limited sample of questionable representativeness is included because other tests would take too much time, cost too much, and be too cumbersome. Global measures of perceived self-efficacy or deficient assessment of performance will yield discordances between the two.

Ambiguity of Task Demands

Judgment of self-efficacy requires knowledge of task demands. If one does not know what demands must be fulfilled in a given endeavor, one cannot accurately judge whether one has the requisite abilities to perform the task. Activities vary widely in difficulty and in the subskills they require. They may differ in the demands they make on cognitive and memory skills, on manual facility, strength, endurance, and the ability to manage stress. Even the same activity may tap different capabilities under different circumstances. Delivering a prepared speech requires fewer generative and memory skills than producing one spontaneously. The more knowledgeable and critical the audience, the greater are the demands on emotional skills for managing disruptive ideation and stress reactions. Discrepancies between efficacy belief and performance will arise when either the tasks or the circumstances under which they are performed are ambiguous. When performance requirements are ill-defined, underestimating task demands produces errors in the direction of apparent overassurance; overestimating task demands produces errors in the conservative direction. Both types of discrepancies often stem from task ambiguities rather than from genuine misappraisals of personal efficacy. Even with adequate knowledge of task demands, if there is a fair amount of situational unpredictability, one cannot always anticipate the impediments that may have to be surmounted. Insufficient allowance for likely impediments may yield overconfident judgment.

Judgment of self-efficacy for cognitive activities presents special problems because the cognitive operations required to solve given problems are not always readily apparent from what is most easily observable. When complex cognitive operations are imbedded in seemingly easy tasks, as is often the case, appearances may be quite misleading (Bandura & Schunk, 1981). Moreover, solving problems typically requires applying multiple cognitive operations. Even if the operations are readily recognizable, judgment of cognitive capabilities for a given activity is complicated if some of the operations are thoroughly mastered while others are only partially understood. Selective attention to elements already mastered will highlight competencies, whereas focusing on what is less well understood will highlight shortcomings (Cervone, 1989). Even equal attentiveness to all aspects of the task will produce some variation in judgments of personal efficacy depending on how much weight is given to the differentially mastered cognitive skills.

In many endeavors, the adequacy of performances is judged socially rather than solely by objective qualities of the performance. Evaluators differ in the stylistic and strategic features they like and dislike. Gymnasts may bring their acrobatic routines under good self-efficacy control only to find their performances downgraded by a judge using idiosyncratic criteria. Similar artifactual discordances between efficacy belief and action are encountered in social styles of behavior and artistic endeavors if performers' criteria of adequacy are at variance with those used by others to evaluate the level of attainments. Even extraneous factors such as ethnic, racial, and gender status can sway performance judgments. Therefore, the accuracy of efficacy beliefs will depend partly on knowledge of the subjective criteria on which one's performances will be judged. When consensus about what constitutes a good performance is lacking, performers have to know the criteria of adequacy against which their performances will be evaluated. They can then judge their efficacy to fulfill the criteria. In socially appraised performances, disparities between efficacy beliefs and performance attainments can arise, not because people misjudge their capabilities, but because they do not know the evaluators' biases.

The most common form of judgmental disparity is one in which beliefs of personal efficacy exceed performance. Optimistic judgments of self-efficacy do not necessarily mean that individuals have inflated views of their capabilities, as is commonly assumed. Such disparities may stem from exaggeration of one's capabilities or from inadequate knowledge of task demands or of how the social system works. A case in point is the common finding of inflated academic expectations among disadvantaged students with deficient academic preparation and achievement. Such expectations reflect inadequate knowledge of the academic performance required to gain entry to, and succeed in, college, rather than solely overestimation of personal capabilities (Agnew & Jones, 1988). Students from low-income families are much less likely than more advantaged ones to receive informative guidance on what they need to master to gain admission to college and to realize occupational aspirations. Deficient information leads to poor academic preparation, which can foreclose entire classes of pursuits requiring advanced competencies.

Dornbusch (1994) presents disconcerting evidence that most students are grossly uninformed about the academic realities they will face. Many do not know the preparatory requirements for college. Some are even misinformed about the curriculum in which they are experiencing their successes. Many able and hard-working students who intend to enroll in college and believe they are preparing themselves for it are, unbeknownst to them, assigned to lower academic tracks that make them ineligible for four-year colleges. When students of differing ethnicity are assessed for high ability, disadvantaged minorities are more likely to be misassigned to low academic tracks, especially if the students exhibit negative social behavior and if supportive parental guidance for academic pursuits is lacking. A self-appraisal based on attainments in an elementary curriculum may be accurate but appear inflated to others when judged against higher level academic demands. In short, the academic demands for which students judge their capabilities are, in many instances, shrouded in ambiguity. Attributing misjudgment entirely to faulty appraisal of capabilities, as is commonly done, reflects faulty judgments by researchers.

The same exaggerated judgment of success can thus arise from different sources. In some instances, judgment of personal capabilities is quite accurate but task demands are underestimated. In other instances, judgment of capabilities is exaggerated but task demands are well understood. In still other instances, personal capabilities are overestimated and task demands are underestimated. Therefore, to determine whether people harbor exaggerated appraisals of their capabilities, one must also measure what they believe the task demands to be and the accuracy of those beliefs. Challenges to successful attainments usually involve more than specific task demands. Most pursuits, being embedded in institutional practices, must be coordinated socially rather than done in isolation. Therefore, to judge what one is capable of attaining requires adequate knowledge of how the social system works and an appraisal of one's ability to manage the institutional requirements.

Indefinite Aims and Deficient Performance Information

Like any other cognitive determinant, efficacy beliefs cannot operate as a regulative influence in an informational vacuum. Cognitive regulation of motivation and action requires performers to have some idea of what they are trying to attain and informative feedback about what they are doing. If they are not aiming for anything in particular or they cannot monitor their performance, they are at a loss to know what skills to enlist, how much effort to mobilize, how long to sustain it, and when to make corrective adjustments in their strategies (Bandura & Cervone, 1983; Cervone, Jiwani, & Wood, 1991). Given definite aims and feedback about one's performance, efficacy beliefs

function as influential regulators of motivation and performance attainments.

The problem of performance ambiguity arises when important aspects of one's performance are not personally observable. This is especially true in the self-regulation of manual and athletic skills when the results of one's actions are observable but the actions themselves are executed outside the field of vision (Carroll & Bandura, 1982, 1987; Feltz, 1982). In coordinated skills, such as tennis or swimming, performers cannot see much of what they are doing and must rely greatly on kinesthetic feedback and onlookers' verbal reports to inform them. As a result, they may perform deficiently, while assuming all along that they are performing the activity correctly. The same is true of social behavior. People are often surprised when they view video replays of their social behavior because, at the time, they were watching the behavior of others rather than their own. It is difficult to guide actions that are only partially observable or to make corrective adjustments in behavior that is poorly monitored. Mismatches between efficacy beliefs and action will also arise, as previously noted, when adequacy of performance is socially judged by vague criteria.

Information about one's performances can vary on many dimensions that affect ongoing cognitive regulation of motivation and action. For activities that provide objective indications of adequacy, performers can see for themselves what they are doing. But for activities judged by social standards, performers must rely on others to tell them how they are doing. Performance feedback can vary on a number of dimensions. It can be intrinsically generated by the actions themselves, or it can be provided externally, as when tennis players see where their shots land or when people rely on video replays or the reports of observers. It can focus on how well different aspects of the performance were executed or only on the final product as a success or failure. It can be qualitative or quantitative, implicit or explicit. The feedback can be given in rudimentary categorical form, as above or below a minimal standard, or in refined gradations of adequacy such as percentile ranks. It can be provided intermittently or regularly, and close in time to ongoing performance or delayed until the end of a long endeavor. Efficacy belief is more easily translated into corresponding performance when there is some destination in mind and the feedback about one's performance is timely and accurate. There is little basis for adjusting effort and action to perceived efficacy if one does not know where one should be going or have any idea what one is doing.

Temporal Disparities

The elapsed time between assessments of efficacy beliefs and performance of an action is another important factor that affects the degree of relation. In the course of their daily lives, people's competencies are repeatedly tested, if not expanded, which prompts periodic reappraisals of personal efficacy. Behavior is regulated by efficacy beliefs that are operating at the time of the behavior, rather than by those held earlier, unless they have remained unchanged in the interim.

The relation between efficacy beliefs and action is revealed most accurately when they are measured in close temporal proximity. The closer in time, the better the test of causation. To relate dated efficacy beliefs to actions creates artifactual discordances if people are acting on altered self-beliefs. For example, perceived efficacy for memory functioning predicts subsequent memory performance even when prior level of memory performance is controlled (Bandura, 1989c; Berry, 1989; Rebok & Balcerak, 1989). Long temporal disparity between assessment of efficacy beliefs and performance may misrepresent the relationship between these factors. Lachman and Leff (1989) concluded that efficacy beliefs did not affect memory performance because the performance was unrelated to efficacy beliefs measured five years earlier. Because the efficacy beliefs changed somewhat over this long period, the earlier ones would have little bearing on the issue of whether beliefs of memory capabilities affect memory performance. Correlational findings, using a more proximal assessment of efficacy beliefs, reveal a

bidirectionality of influence between efficacy beliefs and memory performance (Bandura, 1989c). Such findings are in accord with a substantial body of evidence of similar reciprocal causation in other domains of competency (Bandura, 1986a).

Problems in the interpretability of relationships involving long temporal lags arise in longitudinal panel studies in which the relative predictiveness of past efficacy beliefs is compared with that of current efficacy beliefs. When earlier beliefs are less predictive than current ones, some authors have concluded that the current ones overestimate the strength of the relationship (Krampen, 1988). This is not necessarily so. Evidence that efficacy beliefs have changed over the intervening period support the opposite interpretation, namely, that the causal contribution of past beliefs is underestimated because they no longer represent the efficacy beliefs that currently regulate level of functioning.

This is not to say that efficacy beliefs cannot predict behavior over long time periods. Although proximal measures of perceived efficacy are more predictive than prior ones, efficacy beliefs predict action under longer intervals as well (Holden, 1991; Holden, Moncher, Schinke, & Barker, 1990). The most relevant factor is not the amount of time elapsed per se, but whether efficacy beliefs have been altered by intervening experience. The stability of efficacy beliefs over time is determined, in large part, by the way in which they were acquired, by their strength, and by the potency of intervening experiences.

Efficacy beliefs exhibit a gradient of strength as a function of temporal and physical proximity to the relevant activity, especially if the activity involves elements of threat. Efficacy strength is likely to waver as the time of performance draws near. The task begins to look more formidable, and possible personal limitations may become more prominent in one's thoughts (Gilovich, Kerr, & Medvec, 1993). Of interest is the height and slope of the self-efficacy gradient and the threshold strength of efficacy for acting on one's belief. These characteristics of self-beliefs are affected by the authenticity of the efficacy information on which they were based and their resilience. Efficacy beliefs that are firmly established remain strong regardless of whether the taxing or threatening activities are far off or one is about to perform them. Such beliefs are resilient to adversity and are changeable only through compelling disconfirming experiences. Thus, a strong sense of efficacy has been shown to predict coping behavior five years later, health functioning four years later, and maintenance of habit changes over long time intervals (Coletti, Supnick, & Payne, 1985; Devins & Edwards, 1988; Holman & Lorig, 1992). In contrast, weakly held efficacy beliefs are highly vulnerable to change. Self-doubts rise as performance of taxing activities draws near (Kent, 1987; Kent & Gibbons, 1987). Negative experiences readily reinstate disbelief in one's capabilities.

Consequences of Misjudgment

The seriousness of missteps can also influence the accuracy of self-efficacy judgments. Situations in which misjudgments of capabilities carry no consequences provide little incentive for serious appraisal of personal efficacy. If such judgments are made publicly, modesty or self-flattery can take precedence over accuracy. Concern over what others might think becomes more important than how well one performs an inconsequential activity on some future occasion. People take their self-appraisal seriously when they must choose between courses of action that have significant personal consequences or when they must decide how long to continue activities that consume their time, effort, and resources without yielding appreciable benefits. When things matter, accurate self-appraisals serve as valuable guides for action. Misjudgments that are consequential do not go unnoticed or unchanged for long, unless they are insulated by tenacious construal biases.

Disincentives and Performance Constraints

People may possess the skills needed to accomplish a task and a strong sense of efficacy that they can execute them well but still choose not to perform the activities because they have no incentive to do so. In such instances, discrepancies arise from disincentives to act upon one's beliefs of efficacy. In addition, efficacy beliefs will not be expressed in corresponding action if people lack the necessary apparatus or resources to perform the activities adequately. Self-efficacious artisans and athletes cannot perform well with faulty equipment, and self-efficacious executives cannot put their talents to best use if they lack adequate financial and material resources to do so. Physical or social constraints also impose limits on what people can do in particular situations. When performance is impeded by disincentives, inadequate resources, or external constraints, efficacy beliefs will exceed actual performance. In disparities arising from constraints on action, it is not that people do not know their capabilities, but that they are prevented by external impediments from performing to the level of their efficacy beliefs.

Causal Ordering of Determinants

Analyses of human functioning often involve a multiplicity of determinants. Some of these determinants are not easily amenable to experimental variation and therefore must be studied as they operate concurrently and interactively under real-life conditions. The analytic task is to extract a causal structure from the pattern of relations among the various determinants. Such analysis requires theoretical justification of the order in which the relative contribution of the potential determinants is evaluated. For example, social cognitive theory posits that people who have a strong sense of efficacy set high goals for themselves and remain strongly committed to them in the face of difficulties. Self-efficacy will be shown to have a larger effect if, as postulated, its contribution is assessed causally prior to goals in multiple regression analyses than if the analytic order is inverted. Studies in which the analyses reverse causal priorities or let computers make the decisions are likely to underestimate the contribution of efficacy belief to performance attainments.

Statistical Overcontrol

In studies that take past behavior into consideration, it is easy to apply statistical controls ritualistically, but it requires careful analytical thought to use them appropriately. Behavior is not a cause of behavior. Correlations between prior and subsequent behavior reflect the degree of commonality of their determinants. If the determinants are similar across time, the performances will be highly correlated. If the determinants change over time, the resulting performances will differ. In causal analyses, marshalling evidence that past behavior is a predictor of future behavior reduces to the mundane the notion that unspecified causes operating similarly on different occasions will produce similar performances. Statistical controls are not removing the "effects" of past performance, but rather the effects of the determinants governing past performance.

Many motivational and self-regulatory influences contribute to level of performance. This fact calls into question the common practice of using past performance as a proxy for ability. Doing so confounds ability and nonability factors. Past performance is itself affected by beliefs of personal efficacy. It is not as though efficacy beliefs operate on later performance but are totally absent as a determinant from prior performance. Because efficacy beliefs usually affect both prior and later performance, using unadjusted past performance scores as a proxy for ability will also remove some of the effects of efficacy beliefs on future performance. Just as past performance is not an unconfounded index of ability, it is not an unconfounded index of unknown causes operating separately from the efficacy determinant. Efficacy beliefs are likely to be an important part of that constellation of unspecified causes. Controlling for the level of past performance without any regard to the determinants governing it obscures rather than clarifies the factors regulating human performance. Theoretical considerations should prescribe which determinants get controlled in causal analyses, as opposed to having a machine control indiscriminately all the determinants of prior performance. To avoid overcorrection, the contribution of self-efficacy to prior performance should be removed before prior performance is introduced into the analyses of the contribution of self-efficacy to future performance (Wood & Bandura, 1989b). Otherwise, one is controlling not only for ability but also for the prior impact of efficacy beliefs and other motivational determinants on the performances from which ability is inferred. Similarly, the contribution of efficacy beliefs must be extracted from past performance before past performance is used as a control for unknown causes.

People reappraise their efficacy and guide their actions accordingly when there is some variation in the conditions under which they have to perform. The more dissimilar the present conditions are to past ones and the more uncertain elements they contain, the greater is the need to judge personal capabilities to manage the activities or whether even to get into them. Past performance becomes a highly inflated predictor of subsequent performance when people have to perform the same actions over and over again under similar conditions in the same session. As would be expected, in judging what they can do on the next try, people simply extrapolate from their prior level of performance. Under such invariant conditions, perceived self-efficacy guides performance in initial phases of mastery where performers must make choices of what to undertake, organize appropriate courses of action, make corrective adjustments based on how well the actions work, and sustain their motivation in the face of setbacks and slowed improvement. Under invariant conditions, both perceived efficacy and performance quickly stabilize, and so there is little, if any, change to explain. Adjacent performances are highly correlated because their determinants are alike. Simply demonstrating that people do pretty much the same thing over and over again under identical circumstances does not give us information about causal contributors. In everyday life, people have to manage situations that not only vary in the demands they make but also contain many uncertain, unpredictable, and stressful elements that require judgment. Under such conditions, perceived self-efficacy influences the activities people undertake and how well they manage them.

Faulty Self-Knowledge

Under many of the conditions discussed so far, self-appraisals of efficacy are reasonably accurate, but they diverge from action because people do not know fully what they will have to do, they lack feedback information for regulating their strategies and level of efforts, they are operating under different criteria (from those of the people who are evaluating them) of what constitutes good performances, or they are hindered by external impediments from doing what they can. In addition, discrepancies often arise from misjudgments of personal efficacy rather than from performance ambiguities or constraints. Faulty self-judgments can arise from a variety of sources.

In new undertakings, people have a limited basis on which to assess the adequacy of their self-appraisals. Given limited familiarity with the new activity, they tend to make self-efficacy judgments partly from knowledge of what they could do in similar situations. Appearances of similarity or dissimilarity can be misleading, however. In the absence of an experiential base, self-efficacy judgment is easily swayed by whatever past examples of efficacious or inefficacious behavior spring to mind most readily. Self-efficacy can also be misjudged when personal factors distort self-appraisal processes. The distortions may occur at the point of perception of one's experiences, during cognitive processing of them, or during recall of efficacy-relevant experiences. At the initial perceptual stage in the process, people may misperceive the quality of their performances and thus make inferential errors in judging their efficacy. Or they may perceive their ongoing experiences accurately but introduce distortions by how they cognitively select, combine, and weight the multiform efficacy information available to them. And finally, distortions in memory of efficacy-relevant experiences and the circumstances under which they occurred will produce faulty self-appraisals. Judgment of personal efficacy can be inflated by selective recall of personal successes and deflated by selective remembrance of personal failures. The cognitive processing of efficacy information is addressed in some detail in the next chapter.

Whatever the sources of distortion might be, when people act on faulty judgment of their efficacy, they can suffer adverse consequences.

We saw earlier that human behavior is regulated by multilevel systems of control. Once skills have been developed and routinized in recurring situations, people behave in accordance with what they have come to believe they can or cannot do, without giving the matter much further thought. There are personal costs, however, when underestimated personal efficacy leads to routine thoughtless avoidance of activities well within personal capabilities that can expand one's competencies or otherwise enrich one's life. Langer (1979) verifies the self-debilitating effects that result when people judge themselves incompetent and behave ineffectually in situations that remind them of personal deficiencies.

The published research in any field of study varies in merit. It typically includes some studies that are imaginatively conceived and masterfully executed; many of high quality conceptually and procedurally that contribute to advances in the field; others that have some weaknesses but enough merit to survive the critical eye of reviewers; some that are methodologically sound but rest on faulty assumptions; and still others that are seriously flawed but are salvaged by adroit use of the pen or are published as a result of editorial lapses. The conceptual and procedural criteria that have been presented in the previous sections enable readers to judge for themselves the adequacy of specific published work. They are thus mercifully spared detailed methodological postmortems of studies plagued by defective measures or faulty experimental designs.

Veridicality of Self-Appraisal: Self-Aiding or Self-Limiting?

Assessments of the accuracy of self-appraisals typically use behavior as the standard against which judgments of personal efficacy are evaluated. Self-appraisals that exceed performance presumably reflect overconfidence, and those that fall short signify undue conservativeness. The use of performance as the unalloyed index of actual ability should be tempered by considerable caution, however, because performance is usually confounded with interacting motivational, self-regulatory, and affective nonability determinants. Hence, an individual with the same set of abilities may perform at a mediocre, adequate, or notable level depending on fluctuations in the nature and strength of the nonability contributors. Such differential attainments are due not merely to fortuitous happenings but to systematic changes in contributory self-regulatory influences. The sensitivity of performance to nonability influences will depend on the level of skill development, the complexity of the activity, and the environmental uncertainties surrounding the activity. Nonability influences operate most heavily in performance when they involve some complexities; when they are improvable by the exercise of self-guidance and self-motivation; and when the environment contains uncertainties, impediments, or stressors.

Given fluctuating performance, it is no easy matter to determine whether discrepancies between efficacy judgment and action reflect misjudgments of capability or unrepresentativeness of the particular performance sample used as the reality marker. The problem of gauging the accuracy of efficacy appraisal is compounded when quality of performance is measured by the consensual opinions of others rather than by objective criteria of adequacy. Such activities constitute the major share of human endeavors. The history of innovative attainments amply documents that the social consensus was often wrong, whereas the innovators had the better grasp of what they could accomplish.

It is widely believed that misjudgment produces dysfunction. Certainly, gross miscalculation of one's efficacy can get one into trouble. To act persistently on a belief that one can exercise control over events that are, in fact, uncontrollable is to tilt at windmills. The functional value of veridical self-appraisal, however, depends on the nature of the venture. In activities where the margins of error are narrow and missteps can produce costly or injurious consequences, personal well-being is best served by highly accurate efficacy appraisal. For example, people who seriously misjudge their swimming capabilities in tackling heavy surf may not survive for more prudent encores. Managers who get in over their heads through inflated judgments of their decision-making capabilities can create an organizational mess. Much of the research aimed at devising strategies for deflating overconfidence stems from concerns over physical risks or financial losses from faulty judgment.

Underconfidence similarly carries costly consequences. Overly conservative self-appraisal receives little attention, however, because the adverse effects of lost opportunities and underdevelopment of potentialities are usually delayed and are far less noticeable than the effects of venturesome missteps. The costs of mistaken actions taken are studied extensively, but the costs of promising courses of actions not taken are essentially ignored. Yet forsaken opportunities figure more prominently in people's regrets than do the regrets of action (Hattiangadi, Medvec, & Gilovich, 1995). Personal development requires taking risks. People's regrets commonly center on educational opportunities forsaken, valued careers not pursued, interpersonal relationships not cultivated, risks not taken, and failures to exercise a stronger hand in shaping one's life course. Concentration on the risks of optimistic self-appraisal promotes a conservative orientation toward human development.

It is a different matter when difficult accomplishments can produce substantial personal or social benefits and the personal costs involve time, effort, and expendable resources. Individuals have to decide for themselves which creative abilities to cultivate, whether to invest their efforts and resources in ventures that are difficult to fulfill, and how much hardship they are willing to endure in pursuits strewn with obstacles and uncertainties. Turning visions into realities is an arduous process with uncertain outcomes. Societies enjoy the considerable benefits of the eventual accomplishments in the arts, sciences and technologies of its persisters and risk takers. Realists trade on the merchandizable products that flow from the creations of innovative persisters. To paraphrase the astute observation of George Bernard Shaw, since reasonable people adapt to the world and unreasonable ones try to alter it, human progress depends on the unreasonable ones.

When people err in their self-appraisals, they generally overestimate their capabilities. In nonhazardous activities, optimistic efficacy appraisals are a benefit, whereas veridical judgments can be self-limiting. If efficacy beliefs always reflected only what people can do routinely, they would remain steadfastly wedded to overly conservative judgments of their capabilities that would beget only habitual performances. Under cautious efficacy appraisal, people rarely set aspirations beyond their immediate reach nor mount the extra effort needed to surpass their ordinary performances. One can easily produce veridicality of judgment, though at the cost of personal accomplishments through self-challenge, simply by deflating people's self-assurance. Indeed, in social systems where children are punished for optimistic beliefs in their capabilities, their attainments closely match their conservative view of what they come to expect of themselves (Little, Oettingen, Stetsenko, & Baltes, 1995; Oettingen, 1995).

The difficult nature of human realities makes optimistic self-efficacy an adaptive judgmental bias rather than a cognitive failing to be eradicated. A growing body of evidence reveals that human accomplishments and positive well-being require an optimistic sense of personal efficacy (Bandura, 1986a). This is the case because ordinary social realities are usually strewn with difficulties. Life is full of disappointments, impediments, adversities, failures, setbacks, frustrations, and inequities. Self-doubts can set in fast after failures or reverses. The important thing is not that difficulties arouse self-doubt, which is a natural immediate reaction, but the speed of recovery of perceived efficacy after a person encounters difficulties. Some people recover their self-assurance quickly; others lose faith in their capabilities. The acquisition of knowledge and competencies typically requires perseverant effort in the face of difficulties and setbacks. Therefore, it takes a resilient sense of personal efficacy to override the numerous dissuading impediments to

significant accomplishments. In pursuits strewn with obstacles, realists forsake the venture, abort their efforts prematurely when difficulties arise, or become cynical about the prospects of effecting significant changes. An optimistic belief in one's efficacy is thus a necessity, not a character flaw. Optimistic self-appraisals of capability raise aspirations and sustain motivation in ways that enable people to get the most out of their talents.

Affective and Motivational Benefits of Optimistic Self-Efficacy Belief

The path to innovative achievements is even more heavily strewn with impediments and inherent disincentives than are the paths to more common pursuits. Innovations demand heavy investments of time, effort, and resources. The benefits are often realized gradually through a lengthy process of developmental refinement with numerous setbacks. Indeed, many innovators never see the fruits of their labor during their lifetime. Not only are the disincentives for innovative pursuits discouraging, but the social reactions to unconventional thinking can quickly scare off the fainthearted. Innovations clash with existing preferences and practices and threaten those who have a vested interest in preserving traditional ways. Therefore, innovative efforts are more likely to bring social rejection than fame and fortune. Innovators also face a unique problem of self-validation. They cannot easily evaluate their ideas and talents against the judgments of others who subscribe to more conventional thinking and practices. Innovators often dismiss criticisms of their work as being based on the wrong standards. Critics, in turn, tend to dismiss innovators as attention-seekers or as self-deluded eccentrics doggedly pursuing ill-conceived ideas. There is no shortage of examples of misdirected ventures to reinforce social skepticism about innovators.

Clearly, innovators must be well-equipped to endure hardships and persevere against tough odds. In his review of social reactions to human ingenuity, titled *Rejection*, John White (1982) provided vivid testimony that the striking characteristic of people who have achieved eminence in their fields is an unshakable sense of efficacy and a firm belief in the worth of what they are doing. This resilient self-belief system enables them to override repeated early rejections of their work.

Many of our literary classics brought their authors innumerable rejections. The novelist Saroyan accumulated more than a thousand rejections before he had his first literary piece published. James Joyce's *The Dubliners* was rejected by 22 publishers. Gertrude Stein submitted poems to editors for about 20 years before one was finally accepted. (Now that's invincible self-efficacy!) Try to explain such resiliency by reinforcement theory or cost-benefit analysis. Fifteen publishers rejected a manuscript by e. e. cummings. When he finally got it published by his devoted mother, the dedication, printed in uppercase letters, read: WITH NO THANKS TO . . . followed by the list of publishers who had rejected his prized offering.

Early rejection is the rule, rather than the exception, in other creative endeavors. The Impressionists had to arrange their own art exhibitions because their works were routinely rejected by the Paris Salon. A Paris art dealer refused Picasso shelter when he asked if he could bring in his paintings from out of the rain. Van Gogh sold only one painting during his life. Rodin was rejected three times by the Ecole des Beaux-Arts. The musical works of most renowned composers were initially greeted with derision. Stravinsky was run out of town by an enraged audience and critics after the first performance of the *Rite of Spring*. Many other composers suffered the same fate, especially in the early phases of their careers. The brilliant architect Frank Lloyd Wright was one of the more widely rejected architects during much of his career.

Entertainers in the more contemporary culture have not fared any better. Hollywood initially rejected the incomparable Fred Astaire as "a balding, skinny actor who can dance a little." Decca Records turned down a recording contract with the Beatles with the unprophetic evaluation, "We don't like their sound. Groups of guitars are on their way out." Whoever issued that rejective pronouncement must cringe at each sight of a guitar. After Decca

Records rejected the Beatles, Columbia records followed suit. Walt Disney's proposed theme park was rejected by the city of Anaheim on the grounds that it would only attract riffraff. He persisted and eventually triumphed over his rejectors.

It is not uncommon for authors of scientific classics to experience repeated initial rejection of their work, often with hostile embellishments if it is too discordant with what is in vogue. The intellectual contributions later become the mainstays of the field of study. For example, John Garcia, who eventually was honored for his fundamental psychological discoveries, was once told by a reviewer of his often-rejected manuscripts that one is no more likely to find the phenomenon he discovered than bird droppings in a cuckoo clock. Verbal droppings of this type demand tenacious self-belief to continue the tortuous search for new Muses. Scientists often reject theories and technologies that are ahead of their time. The more innovative the work, the greater the risk of rejection. Goddard, the rocket pioneer, found his ideas bitterly rejected by his scientific peers on the grounds that rocket propulsion would not work in the rarefied atmosphere of outer space. Even Nobel Prize winners have faced rejection of the scholarship that later won them the coveted honor (Gans & Shepherd, 1994; Shepherd, 1995). The gatekeepers of scientific periodicals and their advisory panels are generally wary of new ideas until they gain acceptance. Innovative technologies do not fare any better. When Bell Telephone was struggling to get started, its owners offered all their rights to Western Union for $100,000. The offer was disdainfully rejected with the pronouncement, "What use could this company make of an electrical toy." Because of the cold reception given to most innovations, the time between conception and technical realization typically spans several decades.

The moral of *Rejection* is that rejections should not be accepted too readily as indications of personal failings. To do so is self-limiting. The next time you have one of your ideas, prized projects, or manuscripts rejected, do not despair too much. Take comfort in the fact that those who have gone on to fame and fortune have had a much rougher time. Those whose innovations were widely discordant with conventional thinking received neither fame nor fortune during their lifetimes.

Laboratory findings have supported the centrality of the motivational role of self-efficacy beliefs in human attainments. It takes a resilient sense of efficacy to override the numerous dissuading impediments to significant accomplishments. One does not find many pragmatic realists in the ranks of innovators and greater achievers.

Evidence suggests that it is often the so-called normals who distort their self-appraisals, but they distort in the positive direction (Taylor, 1989; Taylor & Brown, 1988). An optimistic sense of efficacy contributes to psychological well-being as well as to performance accomplishments. The skills and self-beliefs of anxious and depressed people have been compared with those of people who are unburdened by such problems. The groups differ little in their actual skills. But they differ substantially in their beliefs about their efficacy. People who are socially anxious are often just as socially skilled as the more sociable ones. But socially active people judge themselves much more adept than they really are (Glasgow & Arkowitz, 1975). Schwartz and Gottman (1976) have similarly shown that unassertive people know what to do but lack the efficacy to translate their knowledge into assertive action.

Depressed people usually display realistic self-appraisals of their social competencies. But people who are not depressed view themselves as much more adroit than they really are. As depressed people improve in treatment, they show the self-enhancing biases that characterize the nondepressed (Lewinsohn, Mischel, Chaplin, & Barton, 1980). A similar pattern of advantageous self-appraisal is revealed in laboratory tasks in which people perform actions and outcomes occur, but the actions exert no control over the outcomes. Those who are depressed are quite realistic in judging that they lack control. In contrast, nondepressed people believe that they are exercising a good deal of control in such situations (Alloy, Clements, & Koenig, 1993). After nondepressed people are made temporarily depressed, they become realistic in judging their personal control. When depressed people are made to feel happy, they overestimate the extent to which they exercise control (Alloy, Abramson, & Viscusi, 1981). Thus, the depressed appear as realists, the nondepressed as confident distortionists. It is another matter, of course, in the case of severe depression. Realism may be less true of the clinically depressed (Dobson & Pusch, 1995). The psychotically depressed, who blame themselves for the world's ills and regard themselves as totally worthless, are hardly realists.

Social reformers strongly believe that they can mobilize the collective effort needed to bring social change (Bandura, 1973; Muller, 1979). Although their beliefs and the collective sense of efficacy they instill in others are rarely fully realized, they sustain reform efforts that achieve lesser, but important, gains. Consummate survivors have a Phoenixlike ability to bounce back from setbacks. Were social reformers to be entirely realistic about the prospects of transforming social systems, they would either forgo the endeavor or fall victim to discouragement. Realists may adapt well to existing realities, but those with a tenacious optimistic efficacy are likely to change those realities.

The emerging evidence indicates that the achievers, the innovators, the sociable, the nonanxious, the nondespondent, and the social reformers take an optimistic view of their personal efficacy to exercise influence over events that affect their lives. If not unrealistically exaggerated, such self-beliefs sustain the motivation needed for personal and social accomplishments.

Specifying when an optimistic sense of efficacy is advantageous calls attention to important distinctions and qualifiers. Resolute strivers should be differentiated from wistful dreamers. Wistful optimists lack the efficacy strength and commitment to go through the uncertainties, disappointments, and drudgery that are part and parcel of high accomplishments. Resolute strivers believe so passionately in themselves that they are willing to expend extraordinary effort and suffer countless reversals in pursuit of their vision. They abide by objective realism when considering the normative reality but by subjective optimism when considering their personal chances of success. That is, they do not delude themselves about the tough odds of lofty attainments, but they believe they have what it takes to beat those odds. As long as subjective optimists believe that a desired attainment is probable, their belief will stand up against negative instances because such instances do not really show that the attainment is unachievable. Thus, aspiring actors who acknowledge that very few make it into the big time but firmly believe they can do it will exhibit greater staying power and achieve greater progress than those who acknowledge the long odds and view themselves as having little chance of making it. Those who operate under a dual belief that entry into the big time is easy and they can do it easily are in for a rude awakening. They would be ill-prepared to endure the many adversities of pursuits with low rates of success. In short, illusion with denial of realistic odds must be distinguished from resolute efficacy in which tough odds are acknowledged but are considered surmountable. A distinction should also be drawn between personal variation in perceived efficacy for different types of activities and categorizing people into optimistic and pessimistic types. The same individual may be unwaveringly optimistic in some activities but self-doubting in others. Typological approaches encourage selection practices that can be easily misused to cast people into self-limiting roles.

The positive effects of overoptimistic self-appraisal on achievement are sometimes interpreted as reflecting defensiveness motivated by fear (Clance, 1985; Phillips & Zimmerman, 1990). People presumably drive themselves to high achievement to avoid confirming their worst fears that they are untalented imposters. Should optimism about one's capabilities clouded by periodic self-doubts really be cast as deceit? Even the most talented people are beset by self-doubts from time to time, because no one ever experiences unceasing ever-rising accomplishments. The pursuit of standards that are difficult to fulfill provides challenges that sustain engrossment in activities but also brings periodic discouragements. Accomplishments that look good to others may prove self-disappointing when they fail to measure up to exacting personal standards. To add further strains on positive

self-appraisals, the presence of many superachievers can breed self-belittling comparisons.

It is more fruitful to analyze the motivational benefits of optimistic personal efficacy in terms of positive, affirmative processes than in terms of negative, defensive ones rooted in pretending to be what one is not. This is the difference between motivation arising from an unshakable belief in oneself and that arising from fear of being exposed as an intellectual phony. In the latter case, human strivings become largely a matter of defensive impression management. The substantial body of evidence reviewed in this chapter supports the view that an optimistic sense of efficacy fosters psychological well-being and personal accomplishments through self-challenge, commitment, motivational involvement, and nonintrusive task orientation rather than through fearful self-protectiveness.

Psychological analyses have centered heavily on human triumphs over adversities. This work vividly documents how a resilient sense of efficacy enables people to endure hardships and persevere against great odds. It also requires a strong sense of self-regulatory efficacy to overcome the many allures of luxuriant material advantage in the pursuit of self-development. When the things one desires come easily, tough challenges are lacking, and all kinds of competing attractions are constantly available, there is less incentive to endure the prolonged periods of arduous work required to develop personal potentialities. It is not uncommon for people who have struggled hard to achieve success to find that their children pay little heed to development of their talents despite the abundant resources available to them. Successful self-development under these conditions requires self-regulatory triumph over the demotivating effects of abundance available without much effort.

Differential Function of Preparatory and Performance Efficacy

Self-efficacy theory distinguishes between the effects of strength of efficacy beliefs during the development of skills and during the use of established skills to manage situational demands. (Bandura, 1986a). In the skill development phase, people who perceive themselves to be highly efficacious in the undertaking have little incentive to invest much preparatory effort in it. For example, students who greatly underestimate the difficulty of academic course demands and remain blissfully free of self-doubt are more likely to party than to hit the books to master the academic subject matter. As Confucian wisdom warns regarding preparatory self-appraisal, "Too much confidence has deceived many a one." Salomon (1984) provides some evidence bearing on this issue. He found that children who believed strongly in their learning efficacy invested high cognitive effort and learned much from instructional media they considered difficult, but invested less effort and learned less from the same information conveyed by media they believed to be easy. Thus, some self-doubt about one's efficacy provides incentives to acquire the knowledge and skills needed to function successfully. In applying skills already developed, however, a strong belief in one's efficacy is essential to mobilize and sustain the effort needed to succeed in difficult tasks. One cannot execute well what one knows while wrestling with self-doubt. In short, self-doubt creates the impetus for acquiring knowledge and skills, but it hinders proficient use of developed skills. The social management of preparatory and performance efficacy is a standard practice in athletic activities. Coaches inflate the capabilities of their opponents and underscore deficiencies of their own team to motivate their players to practice earnestly for upcoming contests. But at the time of the contest, coaches do not send their teams out on the playing field racked with self-doubt. Rather, they dispatch them in an efficacious frame of mind to get them to play to the best of their abilities.

Norem and Cantor (1990) presented the seemingly paradoxical notion that pessimistic thinking fosters good performances. They found that some people use pessimistic performance expectations as a strategy to motivate themselves and to reduce the threat of failure to their self-esteem. The anticipatory pessimism is conceptualized as a domain-linked strategy rather than a global personality trait.

These findings appear to fly in the face of a vast body of evidence that negative thinking typically impairs performance attainments. One would not recommend that people approach tasks with strong disbelief in their capabilities and anticipate the futility of their efforts as the way to promote success. The different functional value of self-doubt during preparatory and performance phases of an activity provides one answer to this apparent paradox.

Anticipatory pessimism also partly reflects superstitious thinking rather than genuine disbelief in personal capabilities. Instances in which optimistic anticipations were rudely dashed remain indelibly etched in people's minds. It is not uncommon for them to invoke anticipatory pessimism as a superstitious means of trying to sway future outcomes. They do not allow themselves to expect the best because, in some mysterious way, such optimistic thinking will bring disappointments. We know from Langer's (1975) research that rituals that are completely irrelevant to what will happen are viewed as providing some measure of control over outcomes determined entirely by chance. Anticipatory pessimistic thinking is a cognitive ritual that does heavy duty in illusory control.

The research on defensive pessimism is largely confined to successful and academically gifted students, which means that their pessimism is self-protective rather than realistic. A focus on high achievers, of course, excludes negative thinking that is distressing and impairs performance. Students who are genuinely pessimistic about their capabilities would debilitate their efforts to the point where they are unlikely to make it into selective colleges. The anticipatory pessimism of successful individuals most likely reflects superstitious thinking rather than genuine disbelief that they lack the ability to succeed. They concoct worst-case scenarios and exaggerate the formidableness of task demands, then spend many hours preparing themselves to exercise control over the challenges they face. There is some evidence to suggest that efficacious pessimists lacked structured guidance in their early family life, which required them to develop self-management skills. If carried too far, however, preparatory negative thinking can turn into a stressor and debilitator rather than a motivator. Indeed, Norem and Cantor report that academic pessimistic thinking eventually takes a heavy toll on psychosocial functioning. Those who incessantly strive to forestall anticipated misfortunes demand much of themselves, drive themselves to exhaustion through intense preparation, distress themselves, constrict their social life, gain little satisfaction from their activities, and begin to undermine their accomplishments. In the long run, optimists fare much better in psychosocial well-being and academic accomplishments.

Self-Affirmation versus Self-Deception

Illusory judgments, which involve false notions, should be distinguished from strong commitment to accomplishments that have a low probability of realization. As we have already seen, great innovators and achievers attain the supposedly unattainable, not by fervent hope but by unshakable self-belief and dogged effort in the face of innumerable obstacles. Pursuits that have only a small chance of success consume large amounts of time, effort, and resources that offer better prospects of benefit when applied to more realistic endeavors. People who expect much of themselves face a dilemma when their tenacious efficacy beliefs generate nonproductive effort. Should they continue to persevere in the hope of eventual success, or invest their efforts elsewhere? Some persist with unshakable belief in their capabilities. But most judge that superior accomplishments are personally unattainable and seek their satisfactions in what they can do reasonably well without enormous effort. The costs of exaggerated self-appraisal are usually emphasized, but the personal and social benefits from important innovations and social changes produced by persisters in the face of considerable obstacles receive little attention. Human betterment has been advanced more by persisters than by pessimists. Self-belief does not necessarily ensure success, but self-disbelief assuredly spawns failure. This point is illustrated in research on inflated academic expectations mentioned earlier (Agnew & Jones, 1988).

Among children who have little chance of academic success according to objective base rates, those with inflated self-appraisals are much more likely to make it to college than those with realistically low expectations. As T. S. Eliot put it succinctly, "Only those who will risk going too far can possibly find out how far one can go."

The ability to generalize self-knowledge gained from past experiences to new undertakings on the basis of observed similarities plays a fundamental role in successful adaptation. Because situations are rarely, if ever, identical, if people had to suspend their self-knowledge and appraise their efficacy anew in every slightly different situation, they would waste effort on needless reappraisals and accomplish little. The situations of everyday life are not unambiguously similar or dissimilar to one another. Rather, they usually contain some similarities and some dissimilarities. The relevance of different aspects of similarity and dissimilarity to one's sense of efficacy is not always instantly apparent. It may require some initial experience with the new situation to discern the competencies it requires and the opportunities it provides for the exercise of one's capabilities.

The adaptive proactive function of positive efficacy beliefs can give rise, in the short run, to what looks like illusory self-belief. Fortunately, people do not behave like weather vanes, constantly shifting their self-appraisals to conform to whatever momentary feedback they happen to receive from others. Their self-beliefs are more firmly grounded in their past mastery experiences. By acting in new situations on self-beliefs affirmed by repeated experience, people motivate themselves and construct efficacious courses of action in an anticipatory, proactive way. Evidence that people believe they exercise some control in ambiguous situations where there is no actual control does not mean that they are habitual self-deceivers. To make judgments of personal capabilities entirely dependent on the vagaries of transient experiences would raise havoc with adaptive functioning. It would mean that validated efficacy beliefs do not carry over to new situations or, if they do, they are so frail that they can be overruled easily by momentary effects. Successful functioning requires efficacy beliefs that support foresightful behavior when immediate outcomes are not especially conducive to it. Hence, validated efficacy beliefs remain in force in new endeavors until sufficient evidence suggests a need for self-reappraisal. Because most situations permit some measure of control, transfer of positive efficacy beliefs is more adaptive than carryover of self-limiting beliefs to new endeavors. People may be said to act on illusions only when their self-beliefs remain adamantly unresponsive to massive disconfirming evidence.

The issue arises as to whether unwarranted beliefs of personal control involve self-deception. Because of the incompatibility of being simultaneously a deceiver and the one deceived, literal self-deception cannot exist (Bok, 1980; Champlin, 1977; Haight, 1980). It is logically impossible to deceive oneself into believing something, while simultaneously knowing it to be false. Efforts to resolve the paradox of how one can be the agent and the object of deception at the same time have met with little success (Bandura, 1986a). These attempts usually involve creating split selves and rendering one of them unconscious. The split-self solutions fail to specify how a conscious self can lie to an unconscious self without some awareness of what the other self believes. The deceiving self has to be aware of what the deceived self believes in order to know how to concoct the deceptions. Different levels of awareness are sometimes proposed as another possible solution to the paradox. It is said

that "deep down" people really know what they believe. This attempt to reacquaint the split selves only reinstates the paradox of how one can be the deceiver and the one deceived at the same time. Of course, people may misconstrue their performances, lead themselves astray by filtering efficacy information through biases and misbeliefs, or judge their efficacy with deficient knowledge of the types of capabilities certain activities demand. To be misdirected by one's biases or ignorance does not mean that one is lying to oneself, however.

Self-deception is often invoked when people choose to ignore possibly disconfirming evidence. It could be argued that they must believe its validity in order to avoid it; otherwise they would not know what to shun. But this is not necessarily so. Staunch self-believers often choose not to waste their time scrutinizing critical social appraisals of them because they are fully convinced that their evaluators are misinformed or hopelessly biased. For example, the Impressionist artists were not self-protectively avoidant or consumed by self-doubt, nor did they abandon their creative bent when their paintings were routinely rejected by the ruling traditionalists who controlled the exhibition galleries. They created their own standards for judging their artistic talents. In endeavors in which people are heavily invested, when confronted with evidence that disputes firm self-beliefs, people question its credibility, dismiss its relevance, or twist it to fit their views. If the evidence is compellingly persuasive, however, most eventually alter their self-beliefs.

Sources of
Self-Efficacy

PEOPLE'S BELIEFS ABOUT THEIR PERSONAL efficacy constitute a major aspect of their self-knowledge. Self-efficacy beliefs are constructed from four principal sources of information: enactive mastery experiences that serve as indicators of capability; vicarious experiences that alter efficacy beliefs through transmission of competencies and comparison with the attainments of others; verbal persuasion and allied types of social influences that one possesses certain capabilities; and physiological and affective states from which people partly judge their capableness, strength, and vulnerability to dysfunction. Any given influence, depending on its form, may operate through one or more of these sources of efficacy information.

Information that is relevant for judging personal capabilities — whether conveyed enactively, vicariously, persuasively, or physiologically — is not inherently enlightening. It becomes instructive only through cognitive processing of efficacy information and through reflective thought. Therefore, a distinction must be drawn between information conveyed by experienced events and information as selected, weighted, and integrated into self-efficacy judgments. A host of personal, social, and situational factors affect how direct and socially mediated experiences are cognitively interpreted.

The cognitive processing of efficacy information involves two separable functions. The first pertains to the types of information people attend to and use as indicators of personal efficacy. Each of the four modes of conveying information about personal capabilities has its distinctive set of efficacy indicators. The array of factors selected provides the information base upon which the self-appraisal process operates. The second function relates to the combination rules or heuristics that people use to weight and integrate efficacy information from different sources in constructing beliefs about their personal efficacy. This chapter examines the principal sources of efficacy beliefs and the processes governing the selection, interpretation, and integration of efficacy information into appraisals of personal efficacy.

ENACTIVE MASTERY EXPERIENCE

Enactive mastery experiences are the most influential source of efficacy information because they provide the most authentic evidence of whether one can muster whatever it takes to succeed. Successes build a robust belief in one's personal efficacy. Failures undermine it, especially if failures occur before a sense of efficacy is firmly established. If people experience only easy successes, they come to expect quick results and are easily discouraged by failure. A resilient sense of efficacy requires experience in overcoming obstacles through perseverant effort. Some difficulties and setbacks in human pursuits serve a beneficial purpose in teaching that success usually requires sustained effort. Difficulties provide opportunities to learn how to turn failure into success by honing one's capabilities to exercise better control over events. After people become convinced that they have what it takes to succeed, they persevere in the face of adversity and quickly rebound from setbacks. By sticking it out through tough times, they emerge from adversity stronger and more able. Elder and Liker (1982) provided a good example of this effect in their analysis of the enduring impact of hard times during the Great Depression on women's lives. Among women who had some adaptive resources, early economic hardships left them more self-assured and resourceful in later years than if they did not have to struggle through hard times. But for women who were less well equipped to cope with adversity, severe economic hardship left them less intellectually astute and with a sense of ineffectualness and resignation in their later years.

The relative power of guided enactive mastery to create and strengthen efficacy beliefs has been compared with other modes of influence such as modeling of strategies, cognitive simulations of successful performances, and tutorial instruction (Bandura et al., 1977; Biran & Wilson, 1981; Feltz, Landers, & Raeder, 1979; Gist, 1989; Gist, Schwoerer & Rosen, 1989). Enactive mastery produces stronger and more generalized efficacy beliefs than do modes of influence relying solely on vicarious experiences, cognitive simulations, or verbal instruction.

Complex performances are neither the products of an act of will nor simply the emissions of implants of external rewarding and punishing experiences. Rather, they are constructions that are organized and controlled, in large part, by cognitive and other self-regulatory subskills. Building a sense of personal efficacy through mastery experiences is not a matter of programming ready-made behavior. It involves acquiring the cognitive, behavioral, and self-regulatory tools for creating and executing effective courses of action to manage ever-changing life circumstances. The development of efficacy beliefs through enactive experience creates the cognitive and self-regulative facility for effective performance. We will see in subsequent chapters that this development is best achieved by organizing mastery experiences in ways that are especially conducive to the acquisition of generative skills (Bandura, 1986a). Knowledge of the rules and strategies for constructing effective courses of behavior provides people with the tools to manage the demands of their everyday life. Development of the cognitive basis of human competencies is facilitated by breaking down complex skills into easily mastered subskills and organizing them hierarchically.

People need not only to be provided with effective rules and strategies but to be persuaded that they can exercise better control by applying them consistently and persistently. We saw earlier that having knowledge and skills does not produce high attainments if people lack the self-assurance to use them well. Indeed, impaired functioning arises more often from disuse than from deficiency of cognitive skills (Flavell, 1970). A good case in point is research on the benefits of strategy training. Schunk and his colleagues taught children with severe academic problems how to diagnose cognitive task demands, construct solutions, monitor their adequacy, and make corrective changes when they erred (Schunk & Rice, 1987). Instruction in cognitive strategies and practice in applying them improved neither children's sense of personal efficacy nor their academic attainments. Even repeated feedback of success did not help in this regard. But reminding them that they were exercising better control over academic tasks by using the strategies and conveying the success feedback as evidence that they were applying the strategies well substantially enhanced the children's efficacy beliefs and their subsequent intellectual attainments. The more their beliefs of personal efficacy were raised, the better they performed. Thus, skill transmission and success feedback alone achieved little with individuals beset with strong doubts about their capabilities. But skill transmission with social validation of personal efficacy produced large benefits. Improvements in functioning are also more likely to endure if skill development emphasizes the personal power to produce results through the exercise of the skills.

People act on their efficacy beliefs and assess the adequacy of their self-appraisal from the performances they manage to achieve. Performance successes generally raise beliefs of personal efficacy; repeated performance failures lower them, particularly if the failures occur early in the course of events and do not reflect lack of effort or adverse external circumstances. Although performance successes are forceful persuaders, they do not necessarily raise efficacy beliefs, nor do performance failures necessarily lower them. Changes in perceived efficacy result from cognitive processing of the diagnostic information that performances convey about capability rather than from the performances per se. Therefore, the impact of performance attainments on efficacy beliefs depends on what is made of those performances. The same level of performance success may raise, leave unaffected, or lower perceived self-efficacy depending on how various personal and situational contributors are interpreted and weighted (Bandura, 1982a). A small performance success that persuades individuals they have what it takes to succeed often enables them to go well beyond their immediate performance attainment to higher accomplishments and even to succeed at new activities or in new settings (Bandura, 1978b; Bandura et al., 1980; Williams et al., 1989).

Performance alone does not provide sufficient information to judge one's level of capability, because many factors that have little to do with ability can affect performance. Therefore, there is no simple equivalence of performance to perceived self-efficacy. Appraisal of personal efficacy is an inferential process in which the relative contribution of ability and nonability factors to performance successes and failures must be weighted. The extent to which people will alter their perceived efficacy through performance experiences depends upon, among other factors, their preconceptions of their capabilities, the perceived difficulty of the tasks, the amount of effort they expend, the amount of external aid they receive, the circumstances under which they perform, the temporal pattern of their successes and failures, and the way these enactive experiences are cognitively organized and reconstructed in memory. Performance alone thus leaves uncertainty about the amount of information it conveys about personal capabilities. Perceived self-efficacy is often a better predictor under variable conditions than past performance, because efficacy judgment encompasses more information than just the executed action. The simplistic view that efficacy beliefs are solely reflections of past performance does not survive empirical scrutiny. Knowing how various factors affect the cognitive processing of performance information clarifies the conditions under which people get the most out of their mastery experiences.

Preexisting Self-Knowledge Structures

The development of self-knowledge is a cognitive construction rather than simply a mechanical audit of one's performances. People do not approach tasks devoid of any notion about themselves or the world around them. Through transactional experiences, they evolve a structured self-system with a rich semantic network. These self-schemata of personal efficacy influence what people look for, how they interpret and organize the efficacy information generated in dealings with their environment, and what they retrieve from their memory in making their efficacy judgments. Some transactions provide redundant information that reveals nothing new about one's efficacy. Redundant indicators do not alter self-appraisal. Many transactions yield mixed patterns of evidence over time and place that allow room for interpretive biases to operate. The weight people give to new experiences and how they reconstruct them in memory also depends, in part, on the nature and strength of the self-beliefs into which those experiences must be integrated (Bandura, 1992c). Efficacy beliefs are thus both products and constructors of experiences.

The biases exerted by preexisting self-schemata on the cognitive processing of efficacy information contribute to their stability. The efficacy beliefs that one already holds are strengthened by treating redundant indicators as further evidence of personal efficacy and by construing mixed indicators of efficacy in self-confirming ways. Experiences that are inconsistent with one's self-beliefs tend to be minimized, discounted, or forgotten in reconstructed memory. In contrast, those that are congruent with self-beliefs are readily noticed, given significance, and remembered. Thus, people who doubt their efficacy are more likely to view repeated successes as products of laborious effort than as evidence of their own capability, whereas self-assured people believe even more highly in their capabilities following similar successes (Alden, 1987).

The power of preset efficacy beliefs to reduce the impact of discordant efficacy information is strikingly illustrated in studies in which people's efficacy beliefs are raised or lowered by arbitrarily telling them that they performed well or poorly in a novel activity (Ross, Lepper, & Hubbard, 1975). They continue to adhere to the fictitiously instilled efficacy beliefs even after the persuasory basis for those beliefs has been thoroughly discredited. Efficacy beliefs created arbitrarily survive behavioral experiences that contradict them for some time (Cervone & Palmer, 1990). Lawrence (1988) provides suggestive evidence that efficacy beliefs created by fictitious success may gain strength through a cognitive self-persuasion process. Upon being told of their alleged attainments, people enlist supporting evidence from their past success experiences and thereby persuade themselves of their capabilities in that activity. Later, persuasory evidence to the contrary does not eradicate their entrenched self-belief. When there is much subjectivity in judging the adequacy of one's performances, as in social competency, an illusorily created low sense

of efficacy endures despite repeated performance attainments that indicate personal capabilities (Newman & Goldfried, 1987). Dislodging a low sense of personal efficacy requires explicit, compelling feedback that forcefully disputes the preexisting disbelief in one's capabilities.

Although attentional and interpretive biases can lead one astray, they also provide essential continuity to one's self-conception. Without their stabilizing effect, people's views of themselves would shift continuously at every momentary success or failure. Stabilizing self-schemata serve one well when they are advantageous. After a strong sense of efficacy is developed through repeated successes, occasional failures or setbacks are unlikely to undermine belief in one's capabilities. People with a high sense of efficacy are inclined to look to impeding situational factors, insufficient effort, or poor strategies as likely causes for deficient performances. When people ascribe poor performances to faulty strategies rather than to inability, failure can, paradoxically, raise efficacy through belief that better strategies will bring future successes (Anderson & Jennings, 1980). A self-enhancing confirmatory bias is likely to pay off in performance accomplishments. It is a different matter when people hold firmly to a low belief in their capabilities. A confirmatory bias for one's inefficacy tends to breed poor performances that further undermine a sense of personal efficacy.

Task Difficulty and Contextual Factors in the Diagnosticity of Performance Information

The self-diagnostic value of successes and failures for judging personal efficacy will depend on the perceived difficulty of a task. To succeed at an easy task is redundant with what one already knows and, therefore, does not call for any efficacy reappraisals. Mastery of difficult tasks, however, conveys new efficacy information for raising belief in one's capabilities. In performing activities, people may discover new things about the task as well as about themselves. These discoveries can sometimes produce the seemingly paradoxical effect of success lowering perceived self-efficacy. For example, if in the course of completing a challenging task, performers discover potentially formidable aspects of the undertaking or possible limitations to their mode of coping, they lower their perceived efficacy despite their successful performance (Bandura, 1982a). In such instances, a singular success leaves them shaken rather than emboldened.

The difficulty of most new, complex tasks is usually not fully known. In addition, complex pursuits call upon diverse subskills that vary in importance and in the level to which they have been developed. Task difficulty must be inferred not only from the features of the tasks but also from the perceived similarity to other activities for which the difficulty and requisite skills are better known (Trope, 1983). Ambiguity about task demands adds an element of uncertainty in the appraisal of personal efficacy from enactive experiences. In gauging the difficulty of tasks, people often fall back on normative information about the success rates of others who have performed the activities. Variations in the assessment of task difficulty will yield different appraisals of personal efficacy from performance attainments.

Performances always occur in contexts containing a constellation of factors that can hinder or facilitate accomplishments. These contextual factors include situational impediments, assistance provided by others, the adequacy of the resources or equipment available, and the circumstances under which an activity is performed. Thus, successes achieved with external assistance carry little efficacy value because they are likely to be credited to external aids rather than to personal capabilities. Similarly, faulty performances under adverse conditions will have much weaker efficacy implications than those executed under optimal circumstances. The more nonability factors operate on performance, the less diagnostic performance is of personal capability. But judgments about how much a performance might reveal about one's efficacy will be affected by how many nonability factors are noticed and how much weight they are given. This appraisal process is guided by one's intuitive causal model about the factors that determine performance attainments in given domains of activity (Trope, 1983).

Self-beliefs that have served a protective function for years are not quickly discarded. People who doubt their coping efficacy are more likely to distrust their success experiences than to risk more involving encounters with threats they doubt they can adequately control. When experience contradicts firmly held beliefs of weak efficacy, people resist changing their views of themselves if they can find grounds to discount the diagnostic value of the success experience. In such instances, producing enduring, generalized changes in personal efficacy requires powerful confirmatory experiences in which people successfully manage, under diverse conditions, task demands that far exceed those commonly encountered in their daily lives (Bandura, 1988b). They hold their efficacy beliefs in a provisional status, testing their newly acquired knowledge and skills before raising their judgments of what they are able to do. As they gain increasing ability to predict and manage potential threats, they develop a robust sense of efficacy that serves them well in mastering new challenges.

Effort Expenditure

Performance attainments are partly determined by how hard one works at a given pursuit. Therefore, the amount of effort expended affects inferences of capability from task performances. Nicholls and Miller (1984) report that effort has different ability implications for children and adults. For young children, high effort means the acquisition of more ability, whereas for adults the need to exert high effort to achieve things implies low ability. Because ability and effort are seen as interdependent determinants of performance, the amount of effort expended influences how much perceived efficacy is derived from performance accomplishments. Other researchers have found, however, that many adults also believe that effort enhances ability, while others believe that effort compensates for limited ability (Surber, 1985). Whether resolute effort signifies high or low ability thus varies among individuals rather than across age groups.

The inference rules for judging underlying ability from task performances are likely to include the perceived normative difficulty of tasks and circumstances as well as the level of effort. Success with minimal effort on tasks others find difficult signifies high ability, but similar attainments gained through laborious struggle imply lower ability and are thus less likely to raise perceived self-efficacy. Even in the absence of information about how others performed, success achieved through laborious effort can lower people's beliefs in their efficacy to muster the same level of effort again (Bandura & Cervone, 1986).

Effort is also an important factor in self-appraisal of efficacy from failures (Trope, 1983). Low effort renders failures nondiagnostic of personal capabilities. That is, to perform poorly without really trying tells little about what one can do. Failures on tasks of high or moderate difficulty speak more strongly to underlying abilities when much effort has been exerted under conditions conducive to high performance. To try hard and fail under optimal conditions signifies limited capability. To fail under such conditions on tasks known to be relatively easy would, of course, have a crushing effect on perceived personal efficacy.

Studies conducted within the attributional framework (Frieze, 1980; Weiner, 1986) have examined how causal judgments of effort and task difficulty affect performance. The attributional scheme singles out two dimensions of causality: the locus of the causes and their stability over time. The analytical procedure is usually confined to four categories of information representing ability, effort, task difficulty, and luck. Ability is regarded as a stable internal cause and task difficulty as a stable external cause; effort is treated as an unstable internal cause and luck as an unstable external factor. Attribution theory has stimulated considerable research into the judgment of causality. Most of this research is based on judgments of hypothetical scenarios, however, and not much of it addresses the relationship between causal attribution and action.

This approach also raises a number of conceptual and methodological issues. On the conceptual side, it tends to treat judgmental factors as discrete entities when, in fact, they derive their significance relationally. For example, task difficulty is not a stable external cause but a relational property involving the fit between perceived capabilities and task demands. The same arithmetic task that is trivially simple for an accomplished mathematician is inordinately difficult for someone lacking elementary arithmetic skills. Nor is ability necessarily a stable internal attribute, inasmuch as ability is changeable. Even effort is not as easily controllable as attribution theorists would lead one to believe. People often doubt their efficacy to mount and sustain the high level of effort needed to succeed in difficult endeavors. Many failures reflect an inability to regulate one's motivation rather than a deficiency of knowledge or basic skills. The weaker people's sense of efficacy that they can control their level of effort, the lower is their performance motivation (Bandura & Cervone, 1986). Controllability of effort and growth of capableness are rooted in a firm sense of self-regulatory efficacy (Bandura, 1991b, 1993).

Attribution theory usually includes only a few categories of information relevant to the judgment of personal efficacy. In a sociocognitive analysis, these types of factors serve as conveyors of efficacy information rather than as categories of causes of behavior. Moreover, causal factors other than perceived effort, task difficulty, and luck are also important in people's judgment of their capabilities. Such factors include situational conditions, physical and emotional states, contextual influences, and the temporal patterning of performance attainments, just to mention a few. Moreover, people draw on information gained from modeling, social comparisons, and social evaluations as well as from their performance experiences in forming beliefs about their personal efficacy. Therefore, the inferential processes that govern the self-appraisal of efficacy are better elucidated by analyzing how people select and integrate multidimensional efficacy information than by having them rate the relative weight they give to a few preselected factors. Efficacy beliefs bias the attention and relative weight given to the subset of factors singled out by attribution theorists. Thus, people who have a high sense of efficacy tend to ascribe their failures to insufficient effort or unfavorable circumstances, whereas those who regard themselves as inefficacious view the cause of their failures as stemming from low ability (Alden, 1986; Grove, 1993; McAuley, Duncan, & McElroy, 1989; Silver, Mitchell, & Gist, 1995). Weighting such factors as effort, task difficulty, and circumstances is not a matter of attributions shaping efficacy beliefs but of using efficacy-relevant information to appraise one's personal efficacy.

The process of forming efficacy beliefs is a matter of integrating diverse sources of information considered diagnostic of personal capabilities rather than a matter of integrating sociocognitive theory with attribution theory. Sociocognitive theory favors a dynamic integrative approach to the judgment process rather than a limited categorical one. The attribution and information integration approaches, therefore, differ not only in the number of judgmental factors encompassed but also in their analytical methods for determining which factors people use and how heavily they weight them in their efficacy judgments. The attribution approach relies on self-reported weighting in which individuals are simply asked to rate the relative contribution of ability, effort, task difficulty, and luck to their performances. There is a marked difference between asking people to reconstruct their judgment processes and identifying their judgment processes as revealed in their actual judgments. This is not only a matter of whether people have insight into their judgment processes. Retrospective reports leave some uncertainty as to whether they reflect judgments of the causes of one's performances or socially desirable excuses for one's performances (Covington & Omelich, 1979). Information integration approaches favor an inferential weighting procedure using analysis of variance, multiple regression techniques, or algebraic models that can reveal the cognitive integration processes underlying summary judgments (Anderson, 1981; Surber, 1984). Performance situations contain constellations of factors that convey efficacy information. Which factors people select and how they

weight and combine them are revealed by the amount of variance in efficacy judgments accounted for by the different diagnostic factors and their interactions. This procedure makes explicit the judgment rules people are actually using in forming their efficacy judgments. Analytical methods for determining how people integrate multiform efficacy information in arriving at beliefs of personal efficacy are discussed more fully in the concluding section of this chapter.

We will see later that the particular factors picked by attribution theorists influence performance largely through their intervening effects on beliefs of personal efficacy. For example, attributing deficient performance to insufficient effort will heighten motivation only to the extent that individuals believe they have the capabilities to succeed. Those who don't believe in their efficacy anticipate the uselessness of additional effort. Because people usually consider more factors than the attributional subset in forming the efficacy beliefs on which they act, perceived self-efficacy has the greater predictive power.

Selective Self-Monitoring and Reconstruction of Enactive Experiences

Perceived self-efficacy is affected not only by how performance successes and failures are interpreted but also by biases in the self-monitoring of the performances themselves. Every endeavor involves some variation in the quality of performance. Many factors contribute to this variability, including fluctuations in attentional, physical, and emotional states and changes in thought processes, contextual influences, and situational demands. Performances at early and intermediate phases of development, when skills have not yet been fully organized and refined, are especially vulnerable to such influences. Variability allows some leeway in whether one's good performances or poor ones are most closely observed and best remembered. People who selectively attend to and recall their poorer performances are likely to underestimate their efficacy even though they may process what they remember correctly. In such instances, the problems reside in biased attentional and memory processes rather than in the inferential judgments made about the causes of one's successes and failures.

Selective self-monitoring can enhance beliefs of personal efficacy if one's successes are especially noticed and remembered. Research on self-modeling provides evidence suggesting that efficacy is enhanced by selective focus on personal attainments. In these studies, people observe themselves in video replays performing successfully, with missteps and external aids edited out. These self-portrayals of efficaciousness convey no new factual information for improving actual skills (Dowrick, 1983; Schunk & Hanson, 1989a). After observing their edited successes on videotape, people display substantial gains in perceived efficacy and performance.

Attainment Trajectories

Most competencies must be developed over a long period. For complex ones, different subskills must be acquired, integrated, and hierarchically organized under continually changing conditions that can enhance or mar particular performances. Because attainments are governed by many interacting processes, the road to proficiency is marked by spurts, setbacks, and periods of little or no progress. Rate of improvement varies with stage of skill acquisition. Improvements come easily at the outset, but rapid gains are harder to come by in late phases of skill development. By then, gross mistakes have been eliminated and more intricate skills are demanded than in early or intermediate phases. Much time is spent on plateaus with small gains in between.

Temporal changes in attainments carry efficacy implications. People read their rate and pattern of attainments as indicants of personal efficacy. Those who experience periodic failures but continue to improve over time are more apt to raise their sense of efficacy than those who succeed but see their performances leveling off compared to their prior rate of improvement. If they interpret a temporary plateau as evidence that they are approaching the limits of their capacity, they may not expect much more of themselves in that particular activity. Consequently,

they do not invest the additional time and effort needed to attain a higher level of proficiency.

The way in which cumulative experiences affect the self-appraisal of efficacy depends on how they are cognitively represented. The cognitive representation involves memory for the relative frequency of successes and failures, their temporal patterning, and the circumstances under which they occurred. As Bunge (1980) puts it succinctly, memory is a reconstruction of the past, not simply a reproduction of it. The ability to integrate experiences dispersed widely over time and place will vary developmentally. Young children, whose cognitive integrational capabilities are less well developed than those of adults, have special difficulty appraising their efficacy in terms of aggregate experiences spread out over a long time. The more recent experiences are likely to be easier to recall and thus carry the greater weight. If these experiences are not fully representative of personal capabilities, they provide a biased information base for self-appraisal. Development of memory skills through experience enables better reconstruction of patterns of past successes and failures widely distributed over time and the variable conditions under which they had occurred.

VICARIOUS EXPERIENCE

People do not rely on enactive experience as the sole source of information about their capabilities. Efficacy appraisals are partly influenced by vicarious experiences mediated through modeled attainments. So modeling serves as another effective tool for promoting a sense of personal efficacy. Personal capabilities are easier to judge for activities that produce independent objective indicants of adequacy. There is little ambiguity about whether one can swim, fly an aircraft, or balance a checkbook. High jumpers can assess their proficiency and rate of improvement from the heights they clear. For most activities, however, there are no absolute measures of adequacy. Therefore, people must appraise their capabilities in relation to the attainments of others. A student who achieves a score of 115 points on an examination would have no basis for judging whether it is a good or poor performance without knowing how others have performed. When adequacy must be gauged largely in relation to the performance of others, social comparison operates as a primary factor in the self-appraisal of capabilities (Festinger, 1954; Goethals & Darley, 1977; Suls & Miller, 1977).

The referential comparisons with others may take different forms for different activities. For some regular activities, standard norms of how well representative groups perform given activities are used to determine one's relative standing. The impact of normative comparison on self-appraisal of efficacy is well documented in studies in which individuals are given bogus feedback that their attainments place them in either a high or a low rank according to the norms of a reference group of similar status (Jacobs et al., 1984; Litt, 1988). Efficacy beliefs are heightened by alleged performance superiority in relation to group norms but diminished by alleged low normative standing. More often in everyday life, people compare themselves to particular associates in similar situations, such as classmates, work associates, competitors, or people in other settings engaged in similar endeavors. Surpassing associates or competitors raises efficacy beliefs, whereas being outperformed lowers them (Weinberg et al., 1979). Self-efficacy appraisal will vary substantially depending upon the talents of those chosen for social comparison (Bandura & Jourden, 1991; Wood, 1989).

Processes Governing the Impact of Modeling on Self-Efficacy

There are several processes by which modeling exerts its effects on efficacy beliefs. As already mentioned, through social comparative inference, the attainments of others who are similar to oneself are judged to be diagnostic of one's own capabilities. Thus, seeing or visualizing people similar to oneself perform successfully typically raises efficacy beliefs in observers that they themselves possess the capabilities to master comparable activities. They persuade themselves that if others can do it, they too have the capabilities to raise their performance (Bandura, 1982a; Schunk, Hanson, & Cox, 1987). By the same token, observing others perceived to be similarly competent fail despite high effort lowers observers' judgments of their own capabilities and undermines their efforts (Brown & Inouye, 1978). The greater the assumed similarity, the more persuasive are the models' successes and failures. If people see the models as very different from themselves, their beliefs of personal efficacy are not much influenced by the models' behavior and the results it produces. Self-modeling, in which people observe their own successful attainments achieved under specially arranged conditions that bring out their best, is directly diagnostic of what they are capable of doing. This form of modeling also strengthens beliefs in personal efficacy (Schunk & Hanson, 1989a).

There are several conditions under which self-efficacy appraisals are especially sensitive to vicarious information. The amount of uncertainty about one's capabilities is one such factor. Perceived efficacy can be readily changed by relevant modeling influences when people have had little prior experience on which to base evaluations of their capabilities. Lacking direct knowledge of their own capabilities, they rely more heavily on modeled indicators (Takata & Takata, 1976). This is not to say that a great deal of prior experience necessarily nullifies the potential influence of social modeling. Quite the contrary. Life is too changeable to create such fixedness. Mixed experiences of success and failure can instill self-doubts requiring periodic personal reappraisals. Moreover, activities and associates change from time to time, so that social comparative information continues to carry self-diagnostic value. Modeling that conveys effective coping strategies can boost the self-efficacy of individuals who have undergone countless experiences confirming their personal inefficacy (Bandura, 1977). Even those who are highly self-assured will raise their efficacy beliefs if models teach them even better ways of doing things.

The different forms of efficacy influences rarely operate separately and independently. People not only experience the results of their efforts but also see how others are faring in similar pursuits and, from time to time, receive social evaluations of the adequacy of their performances. Because these influences affect one another, the power of a given mode of efficacy influence can change markedly depending on the strength of the other modes of influence. Therefore, generalizations about the relative power of different modes of efficacy influence must be qualified by the sway of interacting influences.

The power of vicarious experience to enhance or neutralize the impact of direct experience is a good case in point. Although vicarious experiences are generally weaker than direct ones, under some conditions vicarious influences can override the impact of direct experience. The comparative information conveyed by modeling may alter the diagnosticity of failure experiences and foster behavior that confirms the vicariously based self-conception. Thus, people convinced of their inefficacy by seeing similar others fail are quick to accept their own subsequent failures as indicants of personal deficiencies. They then behave in ineffectual ways that generate confirmatory behavioral evidence of inability. Conversely, modeling influences that convince people of their efficacy weaken the impact of direct failure experiences and sustain effort that supports performance in the face of repeated failure (Brown & Inouye, 1978; Weinberg et al., 1979). A given mode of influence can thus set in motion processes that strengthen its effects or weaken the effects of otherwise powerful influences.

Modeling influences do much more than simply provide a social standard against which to appraise personal capabilities. People actively seek proficient models who possess the competencies to which they aspire. By their behavior and expressed ways of thinking, competent models transmit knowledge and teach observers effective skills and strategies for managing environmental demands (Bandura, 1986a). Acquisition of effective means raises beliefs of personal efficacy. The instructive contribution of modeling is especially important when perceived inefficacy reflects skill deficits rather than misappraisals of the skills already possessed. Aspirational modeling guides and motivates self-development.

Models do not behave like mute automatons. They model efficacy by word as well as by action. While struggling with problems, they may voice hopeful determination and the conviction that problems are surmountable and valued goals are achievable, or discouragement and the futility of continued effort. Models who express confidence in the face of difficulties instill a higher sense of efficacy and perseverance in others than do models who begin to doubt themselves as they encounter problems (Zimmerman & Ringle, 1981). Undaunted attitudes exhibited by perseverant models as they cope with obstacles repeatedly thrown in their path can be more enabling to others than the particular skills being modeled. Evidence of progress toward aspirational standards provides a source of self-efficacy and self-satisfaction. In addition to their instructive and motivational function, modeled events convey information about the nature of environmental tasks and the difficulties they present. Modeled transactions may reveal the tasks to be more or less difficult, and potential threats more or less manageable, than observers originally believed. Adoption of serviceable strategies and altered perceptions of task difficulty will change beliefs in one's capabilities.

Modeled performances designed to alter coping behavior emphasize two factors — predictability and controllability — that are conducive to the enhancement of efficacy beliefs (Bandura et al., 1982). In demonstrating predictability, models repeatedly engage in threatening activities in ways that exemplify how feared persons or objects are most likely to behave in each of many different situations. Predictability reduces stress and increases preparedness for coping with threats (Averill, 1973; Miller, 1981). In modeling controllability, the model demonstrates highly effective strategies for handling threats in whatever situation might arise. What phobic thinking renders frightening, instructive modeling makes predictable and personally controllable.

There are some conditions under which modeled strategy information can alter the usual efficacy effects of social comparative information. Seeing a skilled person fail by use of deficient strategies can boost the perceived efficacy of observers who believe they have more suitable strategies at their command. Observed failure is most likely to raise perceived efficacy when seeing what has not worked for others raises the observer's confidence in better alternatives. Conversely, observing a skilled person barely succeed despite the most adroit tactics may lead observers to reevaluate the task as much more difficult than they had previously assumed. To clarify how factors in modeled portrayals affect self-efficacy appraisals, research should focus on strategy exemplification and task evaluation as well as on social comparative indicants of ability.

Social comparison theory was originally designed to explain self-appraisal of ability in the absence of objective criteria and self-regulation of distress and self-esteem through comparison with others who are worse or better off (Festinger, 1954). This theory has since been expanded to encompass additional psychological functions that are socially mediated (Wood, 1989). As its scope has broadened, the theory has lost its distinctiveness and explanatory and predictive power. For example, one of the incorporated functions is self-improvement of capabilities. People turn to proficient models for knowledge, skills, and effective strategies. Social comparison theory has little to say about how people acquire sociocognitive skills from observing proficient models. By contrast, social cognitive theory provides a large body of verified knowledge about the determinants and psychological mechanisms governing observational learning of behavioral and social competencies, cognitive skills, and emotional propensities (Bandura, 1986a; Rosenthal & Zimmerman, 1978).

Observational learning is governed by four subfunctions, which are summarized in Figure 3.1. Attentional processes determine what is selectively observed in the profusion of modeling influences and what information is extracted from ongoing modeled events. A number of factors influence the exploration and construal of what is modeled in the social and symbolic environment. Some of these factors involve the cognitive skills, preconceptions, and value preferences of the observers. Others are related to the salience, attractiveness, and functional value of the modeled activities themselves.

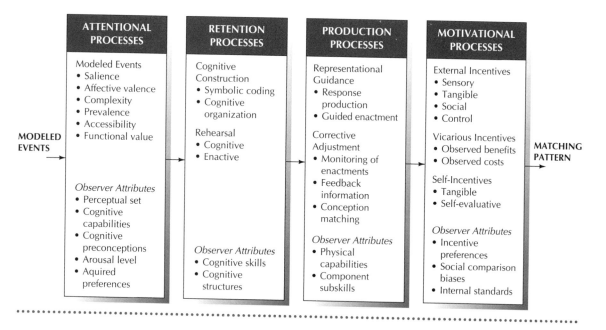

FIGURE 3.1. Four subprocesses governing observational learning. (Bandura, 1986a)

Still others pertain to the structural arrangements of human interactions. Associational networks largely determine the types of models to whom people have ready access and the styles of behavior they repeatedly observe and learn.

People cannot be much influenced by modeled events if they do not remember them. A second major subfunction governing observational learning relates to cognitive representational processes. Retention involves an active process of transforming and restructuring information about events for memory representation in the form of rules and conceptions. Behavioral conceptions should be distinguished from scripts, which are sometimes used to characterize the cognitive representations of modeled styles of behavior. Behavioral conceptions embodying production rules serve as generative guides for constructing actions to fit changeable circumstances, whereas scripts are akin to robotic enactment of fixed action sequences. Retention is greatly aided by symbolic transformations of modeled information into memory codes and by cognitive rehearsal of the coded information. Generative codes that extract the underlying structure from specific behavioral instances enable observers to create new variants of actions that fit the structure but go beyond what was seen or heard. Preconceptions and affective states exert biasing influences on these representational activities. Similarly, recall involves a process of reconstruction rather than simply retrieval of registered events.

In the third subfunction of modeling — the behavioral production process — conceptions are translated into appropriate courses of action. Earlier, we saw that this translation is achieved through a conception-matching process. Conceptions guide the construction and execution of behavior patterns, and the adequacy of the action is compared against the conceptual model. The behavior is then modified on the basis of the comparative information to achieve close correspondence between conception and action. The more extensive the subskills that people possess, the easier it is to integrate them based on modeled information to produce new behavior patterns. When deficits exist, the subskills required for complex performances must first be developed by modeling and guided enactment.

The fourth subfunction of modeling involves motivational processes. Social cognitive theory distinguishes between acquisition and performance, because people do not perform everything they learn. Performance of observationally learned behavior is influenced by three major types of incentive motivators: direct, vicarious, and self-produced. People are more likely to exhibit modeled behavior if it results in valued outcomes than if it has unrewarding or punishing effects. The observed detriments and benefits experienced by others influence the performance of modeled patterns in much the same way as do directly experienced consequences. People are motivated by the successes of others who are similar to themselves but are discouraged from pursuing courses of behavior that they have seen often result in adverse consequences. Personal standards of conduct provide a further source of incentive motivation. The evaluative reactions people have to their own behavior regulate which observationally learned activities they are most likely to pursue. They pursue activities that they find self-satisfying and that give them a sense of worth and reject those of which they personally disapprove.

As this discussion has shown, altering efficacy beliefs through vicarious influence is not simply a matter of exposing people to models. Modeling operates through a complex set of interrelated subfunctions. Social cognitive theory provides a conceptual framework for how to mobilize attentional, representational, production, and motivational subfunctions to enhance the development of personal efficacy by vicarious means. Also, a multifunction analysis of observational learning helps to explain variations in the impact of modeling influences on efficacy beliefs and sociocognitive functioning.

Another way in which vicarious influences can affect the self-appraisal of efficacy is through the affective states aroused by comparative self-evaluation. The characteristics of the people one chooses to observe or that are forced upon one have affective consequences (Bandura & Jourden, 1991; Goethals & Darley, 1987). Seeing the accomplishments of similar others can gladden or depress observers, depending on how they fare in the social comparison. Competitive comparisons with superior performers give rise to self-deprecation and despondency, whereas advantageous comparisons with equally talented individuals can produce positive self-evaluations. People who are insecure about themselves generally avoid social comparisons that are potentially threatening to their self-esteem. When threatened, they tend to compare themselves either with subordinates who make them look good or with eminent figures who are much too far removed to pose any serious evaluative threats. Testa and Major (1990) offer evidence that, following failure, social comparison with people who do better than oneself is emotionally and motivationally debilitating mainly when accompanied by a low sense of personal control. Seeing others do well when one believes that one cannot get better is depressing, angering, and demotivating. In contrast, upward comparison after failure is neither dispiriting nor motivationally hindering as long as people believe they can improve.

Observing oneself model positive affective states videotaped at an earlier time can similarly reduce depressive mood in adolescents and adults (Dowrick & Jesdale, 1990; Kahn, Kehle, Jenson, & Clark, 1990). Evidence will be reviewed later that efficacy beliefs are raised under a positive mood but diminished under a despondent mood. Self-modeling can activate additional processes that affect one's sense of personal efficacy. Creer and Miklich (1970) found that observing oneself performing successfully not only improves the targeted performance but also leads people to exercise better control over other aspects of their daily functioning. Such findings suggest that successful self-modeling may produce a general increase in self-efficacy that has a positive impact on a variety of activities.

The acquisition of knowledge about skills and strategies by observing proficient models is evident even in infants and toddlers (Bandura, 1986a; Kaye, 1982; Meltzoff & Moore, 1983). The subfunctions governing observational learning, of course, improve with maturation and experience. Although developmental growth increases how much one can profit from vicarious influences, a sense of efficacy can be enhanced by the instructive function of modeling at all ages. There

are developmental constraints, however, on the use of social comparison information for the self-appraisal of capabilities. Developmental studies of comparative appraisal of capabilities indicate that young children make little use of social comparison information. Thus, young children's judgment of their ability is affected by how well they perform but unaffected by information that children their age perform poorly or well (Ruble, 1983). This is true even when strong incentives are provided for accuracy in judging their relative ability. As children get older, their evaluation of their ability is affected by how well other children do.

The age at which children begin to use social comparison information for self-appraisal may depend partly on the nature of the activity and the people available for comparison. Young children are apt to ignore comparative information when it is in the form of general social norms of how most children their age perform or when the activity does not hold much significance for them. In activities that are part of daily life and can secure recognition from peers, children recognize the relevance of comparative information for assessing personal capabilities at an earlier age (Morris & Nemcek, 1982). Nevertheless, their facility to use such comparative information self-diagnostically lags behind their facility to distinguish differences in ability among their peers.

In a review of the relevant literature, Ruble (1983) shows that young children have the cognitive abilities to make social comparisons, periodically check how their peers are doing, and know which comparative information would tell them the most about their own level of ability. The evidence Ruble cites suggests that the developmental delay in comparative self-appraisal stems more from other cognitive limitations. Forming a belief about one's capabilities calls for skills in inferential reasoning and information integration. Young children have difficulty inferring internal attributes from concrete performances. This is especially true when such judgment requires integrating information from multiple performances that is not always unambiguous or consistent across time and place. Young children do not regard personal determinants of performance as having much stability over time. Nor are very young children given to self-reflection about the relevance of diverse comparative experiences to their personal capabilities. These various cognitive factors would reduce the perceived self-diagnostic value of social comparison information. A motivational factor may also be involved. Children may simply avoid determining their relative standing because all too often they do not like what they find. Evaluative school practices, however, quickly impose comparative appraisals whether children like it or not. Because relative standing among one's peers has social consequences, social comparison cannot be ignored for long.

Development of skill in comparative self-appraisal is a mixed blessing. Social comparison can take a variety of forms, and it can have negative as well as positive effects. Well-founded appraisal of personal capability has considerable adaptive value. People who undertake activities without appraising their efficacy can get themselves into difficulties. Missteps can result in wasted effort or produce costly or irreparable harm. On the other hand, heavy focus on comparison with high achievers can make the less talented miserable and wreck their sense of efficacy. There is no shortage of superstars to occasion humbling social comparisons. Nicholls (1990) calls attention to the paradox that developmental maturity, which enables people to assess their capabilities against the success rates of others, is often self-debilitating.

In analyzing comparative self-appraisal, Ruble and Frey (1991) provide evidence that interest in, and use of, social comparison information may vary during different phases of skill and knowledge acquisition. Temporal or self-comparison is of special interest when skills are being developed. Evidence of progressive improvement sustains a sense of personal efficacy and provides a continuing source of self-satisfaction. As skills are formed or progress slows, however, people turn to social standards to appraise and validate their capabilities. At the more advanced phase of skill development, they measure their capabilities by how well they perform compared to others.

According to the sociocognitive theory of self-appraisal (Bandura, 1986a), different sources of comparative information — normative comparative, specific social comparative, and personal comparative — are weighted and integrated in judging personal efficacy. Shifts in self-diagnostic strategies are reflected in the relative weight given to different forms of comparative information rather than in changes from exclusive reliance on a self-comparative standard to a social-comparative one. Evaluative social practices force people to compare their rate of progress against that achieved by others throughout the course of skill acquisition. Slow comparative progress signifies low efficacy; rapid progress compared to others indicates high efficacy. The relative weighting of different forms of comparative information may vary across domains of functioning and social evaluative practices as well as across stages of competency development.

Modeling influences can be structured in ways that instill and strengthen a sense of personal efficacy while avoiding the personal costs of adverse social comparison. This is achieved by maximizing modeling's instructive function and minimizing its comparative evaluative function. The modeling situation is construed as an opportunity to develop one's knowledge and skills through the aid of proficient models. Under this cognitive set, observers regard their own skill at any given time as a transitory level in a process of growth rather than as an indicant of basic capability (Frey & Ruble, 1990). Self-comparison of skill improvement combined with anticipatory upward comparison with esteemed proficient models helps to support an optimistic personal appraisal despite current deficiencies in skill.

Modes of Modeling Influence

Modeling influences take different forms and serve different functions depending on the types of information they convey (Bandura, 1986a). A great deal of psychological modeling occurs in everyday association networks. The people with whom one regularly associates, either through preference or imposition, determine the types of competencies, attitudes, and motivational orientations that will be repeatedly observed. (The way in which a society is structured and socially differentiated along age, gender, ethnic, and socioeconomic lines largely determines the types of models to which its members have ready access.

Another prevalent source of vicarious influence is the abundant and varied symbolic modeling provided by television and other visual media. The accelerated growth of video technologies has vastly expanded the range of models to which people are exposed day in and day out. Whereas modeling influences used to be largely confined to the behavior exhibited in one's community, nowadays symbolic modeling enables people to transcend the bounds of their immediate social life. They can observe the attitudes, styles of competencies, and attainments of members of different segments of their society, as well as those of other cultures. Exposure to actual or symbolic models who exhibit useful skills and strategies raises observers' beliefs in their own capabilities (Bandura, 1982a; Schunk, 1987). The same is true at the collective level. Seeing effective problem-solving strategies modeled raises the performance attainments of groups partly by enhancing their members' collective sense of efficacy (Prussia & Kinicki, 1996). The impact of symbolic modeling on efficacy beliefs can be further enhanced by cognitive rehearsal. Visualizing oneself applying the modeled strategies successfully strengthens self-belief that one can do it in actuality. Thus, modeling with cognitive rehearsal builds stronger perceived efficacy than modeling alone; modeling alone, in turn, surpasses verbal instruction in the same strategies (Maibach & Flora, 1993).

Modeling is not confined to behavioral competencies, nor is it merely a process of behavioral mimicry. Highly functional patterns of behavior, which constitute the proven skills and established customs of a culture, may be adopted in essentially the same form as they are exemplified. There is little leeway for improvisation on how to drive automobiles or solve arithmetic problems. In many activities, however, subskills must be improvised to suit different situations. Modeling influences can

convey rules for generative and innovative behavior as well. In abstract modeling, people learn thinking skills and how to apply them by inferring the rules and strategies that models use as they arrive at solutions. Once observers learn the rules, they can use them to generate new instances of behavior that go beyond what they have seen or heard (Bandura, 1986a; Rosenthal & Zimmerman, 1978). Providing many modeled examples demonstrates how the rules can be widely applied and adjusted to fit changing circumstances.

Much human learning involves the development of cognitive skills to gain and use knowledge for various purposes. It is difficult to acquire cognitive skills through modeling when covert thought processes are not adequately reflected in modeled actions. The problem of observability is overcome simply by having models verbalize their thought processes and strategies aloud as they engage in problem-solving activities. The covert thoughts guiding the actions are thus made observable through overt representation. In conveying cognitive skills by verbal modeling of thought processes, models verbalize their thoughts about how to use cognitive plans and strategies to diagnose and solve problems, generate alternative solutions, monitor the effects of their actions, correct errors, use coping self-instructions to overrule self-doubts, use self-praise to provide motivational support for their efforts, and manage stress (Meichenbaum, 1977, 1984; Schunk, 1989). In complex activities, the verbalized thinking skills that guide actions are generally more informative than the modeled actions themselves. People who lack problem-solving skills benefit more from observing others model self-guiding thoughts in conjunction with actions than from seeing their actions alone (Sarason, 1975b). Verbal modeling of cognitive skills builds self-efficacy and promotes cognitive skill development (Schunk, 1981; Schunk & Gunn, 1985; Schunk & Hanson, 1985). It can do so more effectively than direct instruction in the same cognitive operations (Gorrell & Capron, 1990). Cognitive modeling with skill enactment heightens efficacy beliefs and attainments more than does cognitive modeling alone (Fecteau & Stoppard, 1983).

Self-modeling of capabilities also enhances personal efficacy and performance. In this approach, which has been developed and applied widely by Dowrick (1983, 1991), people who exhibit deficient skills or coping capabilities are helped by a variety of aids to perform at a level that exceeds their usual attainments. The hesitancies, mistakes, and external aids are then edited from videotape recordings to show the individuals performing much more skillfully than they normally do. Sometimes the edited versions include recoupling of successful performances to more demanding situations than those in which they originally occurred. After observing themselves perform effectively, people display substantial improvement in performance compared to their baseline level or to other activities that are filmed but not observed. Self-modeling is more effective than didactic instruction in raising perceived efficacy (Scraba, 1990). The performance improvements accompanying successful self-modeling are mediated by increases in beliefs of personal efficacy (Bradley, 1993). Self-modeling has remarkably wide applicability and often succeeds with inveterate self-doubters where other instructional, modeling, and incentive approaches fail (Dowrick, 1991; Meharg & Woltersdorf, 1990). Apparently, it is hard to beat observed personal attainment as a self-persuader of capability.

Self-modeling can be effectively applied without requiring extensive editing. This is achieved by structuring performance tasks in ways that ensure progressive mastery or by arranging conditions that bring out the best of one's capabilities. The successes are authentic rather than partially contrived. These favorable performances are captured on videotape for subsequent replay to raise and strengthen a sense of personal efficacy. Schunk and Hanson (1989) used this self-modeling strategy to develop cognitive skills in children. Those who had the benefit of observing themselves perform successfully in the initial phase of learning developed a stronger belief in their learning efficacy. As a result, they subsequently mastered the full range of cognitive skills faster, had a higher eventual sense of cognitive efficacy, and outperformed their counterparts who received the same instructive guidance but did not observe a replay of their early successes. Successful self-modeling was as effective as observing successful peer modeling.

Positively structured self-modeling should be distinguished from unedited replays of one's performances. Observing one's prior successful attainments enhances level of functioning, whereas simply observing unedited replays of one's deficiencies as well as strengths has mixed results (Dowrick, 1986; Hung & Rosenthal, 1981). Observing one's faulty performances tends to undermine belief in one's efficacy and impair performance, unless one figures out better strategies from observing what does not work. People who have already gained some competence may possess sufficient self-assurance and knowledge to profit from observing their errors in unedited replays. But the failures of those who suffer from self-doubts are unlikely to serve as a fertile source of promising strategies. Self-modeling of deficiencies, however, loses its negative impact when the deficiencies occur early in the process of gaining mastery. Self-modeling of progress in skill acquisition is as effective as self-modeling of successes only in enhancing self-efficacy and competencies (Schunk & Hanson, 1989a).

Seeing oneself perform successfully can enhance proficiency in at least two ways: It provides clear information on how best to perform skills, and it strengthens beliefs in one's capability. In a study designed to separate these two effects, Gonzales and Dowrick (1982) had subjects observe their own skilled performances with good results or their mediocre performances to which good results were spliced in the videotapes to create the illusion of skillfulness. Self-observation of illusory skillfulness improved performance just as effectively as self-observation of actual skillfulness. These findings suggest that self-modeling of skillfulness operates largely by enhancing belief in one's capability rather than by improving one's skills. These findings are further corroborated by Schunk and Hanson (1989a). In the studies just cited, the videotapes portray skills that observers have already thoroughly learned, so that they cannot improve upon them.

By raising beliefs in their learning capabilities through self-observed successes, people acquire new skills more rapidly and profit more from their subsequent experiences.

Dowrick (1991) distinguishes between reconstructive and constructive self-modeling. In the reconstructive form, individuals perform activities with facilitative aids, and their performances are then edited to remove deficiencies. In the constructive form, people perform activities, and relevant subskills are extracted from the videotaped performances. Competencies not yet achieved are then created by splicing together existing subskills into new forms of capability. Individuals then observe themselves on the edited videotape realizing their potential by doing things they had never done before in their entirety. Self-review of constructed capabilities raises efficacy beliefs and level of performance (Dowrick, Holman, & Kleinke, 1993). Degree of efficacy change predicts amount of performance improvement.

Cognitive self-modeling serves as another means of enhancing efficacy beliefs. In this particular mode of self-influence, people visualize themselves repeatedly confronting and mastering progressively more challenging or threatening situations. Cognitive simulations of skilled performances improve subsequent performance (Bandura, 1986a; Corbin, 1972; Feltz & Landers, 1983). The benefits of cognitive self-modeling are partly mediated by boosts in perceived self-efficacy, although the gains tend to be modest (Bandura et al., 1980; Kazdin, 1979).

Even the most resilient individuals often find themselves struggling with self-doubts in the face of setbacks and adversities. We will see later that the speed of recovery of self-efficacy from setbacks and defeats is one of the factors that separates higher achievers from those who settle for lesser accomplishments. Dowrick reports that a review of self-modeling of earlier successes can help sustain efficacy beliefs through tough times. Bringing one's successful past to bear on present difficulties weakens their negative impact. Whether self-modeling does this through its efficacy-mediated increases in motivation or through reduction in negative affective states remains to be determined. Review of videotapes of oneself at an earlier time in a positive mood or behaving in a socially skilled way has been shown to reduce anxiety and depression in depressed individuals (Dowrick & Jesdale, 1990). Further work is needed, however, on how to structure self-modeling reviews to ensure that self-comparison of favorable past with troublesome present is uplifting rather than discouraging.

All of the vicarious modes of influence — whether conveyed through effective actual modeling, symbolic modeling, videotaped self-modeling, or cognitive self-modeling — enhance efficacy beliefs and improve performance. The level to which perceived efficacy is raised is a uniformly good predictor of subsequent performance attainments. The higher the perceived self-efficacy, the greater are the performance accomplishments.

New technologies alter the mode of modeling to boost its instructive power. For example, modeling via computer graphics is being used increasingly to cultivate physical skills. Some skills are difficult to grasp and perfect because the constituent actions may occur in a split second. Learners have difficulty not only in seeing what is being modeled but also in monitoring their own enactments, because much of the activity occurs outside their visual field. Ultra-high-speed cameras are used to capture what the eye cannot easily see in modeled performances (Gustkey, 1979). The picture frames are then translated into moving figures of the performance on a computer screen, enabling observers to discover what best to do at any given point in the action. The instructiveness of performance feedback can be augmented by this means as well. Electronic analysis of filmed enactments graphically pinpoints mistakes in the execution of skills.

As in the case of direct mastery experiences, the impact of modeled information on self-appraisal of efficacy, whether conveyed normatively or individually, depends on how that information is cognitively processed. The factors that are especially relevant to the cognitive processing of modeled information are examined in the sections that follow.

Performance Similarity

Cognitive processing of vicariously derived information will depend on the indicants of personal efficacy conveyed by the modeled events. We noted earlier that people judge their capabilities partly by comparing their performances with those of others. Similarity to a model is one factor that increases the personal relevance of modeled performance information to observers' beliefs of their own efficacy. Persons who are similar or slightly higher in ability provide the most informative comparative information for gauging one's own capabilities (Festinger, 1954; Suls & Miller, 1977; Wood, 1989). Neither outperforming those of lesser ability nor being surpassed by the vastly superior conveys much information about one's own level of capability. In general, modeled successes by similar others raise observers' beliefs in their efficacy, and modeled failures lower them.

In judging personal efficacy through social comparisons, observers may rely on similarity either to the model's past performances or to the model's attributes that are presumably predictive of the ability

in question. The influential role of prior performance similarity on vicarious efficacy appraisal is revealed in a study by Brown and Inouye (1978). Observers performed a cognitive task along with the model and received preset feedback that they were either equal in ability to the model or more able than the model. When they later saw the model fail repeatedly, those who believed themselves to be superior to the failing model maintained a high sense of personal efficacy on similar tasks that were exceedingly difficult and did not slacken their effort at all, despite repeated failure. In contrast, modeled failure had a devastating effect on observers' efficacy beliefs when they perceived themselves of comparable ability to the failing model. They expressed a very low sense of personal efficacy and gave up quickly when they encountered difficulties. The lower their perceived self-efficacy, the quicker they gave up. The longer they engaged in the activity, the more their sense of personal efficacy and motivation deteriorated. The powerful way in which vicariously instilled self-beliefs accented or neutralized the negative impact of failure on performance motivation is revealed in Figure 3.2.

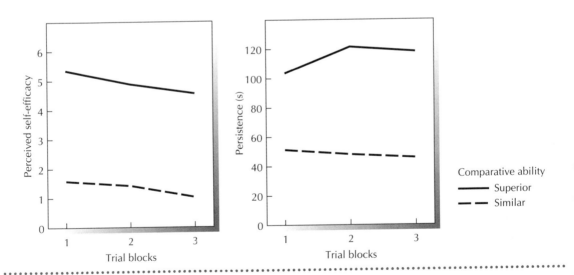

FIGURE 3.2. Level of perceived self-efficacy and persistence in cognitive problem solving for students after they had observed a model alleged to be of equal or lesser ability to them fail repeatedly in trying to solve similar types of problems. Each trial block contains five problems. (After Brown and Inouye, 1978)

Even minimal indicants of past experiences suggesting similarity or dissimilarity to the model can substantially alter the impact of instructive modeling on perceived efficacy and corresponding behavior. Exposure to a filmed model successfully performing mathematical operations increased students' beliefs in their own mathematical capabilities when the model was depicted as having had little prior experience with mathematics and was thus presumably similar to them (Prince, 1984). But the students' perceived efficacy was unaffected by exposure to the same successful modeling when they assumed the model was very different from them by being portrayed as well versed in mathematics. That perceived dissimilarity can override the benefits of modeled strategies is further shown in the modification of phobic behavior through vicarious influence. Brief information given to spider phobics that the model had fed tarantulas in a pet shop created perceived dissimilarity that greatly reduced the impact of filmed modeling of effective coping strategies on phobics' perceived coping efficacy and avoidant behavior. Seeing the same coping strategies performed by the same model but with the model depicted as apprehensive of insects reduced the observers' fear and phobic behavior.

Some writers have commented on the apparent paradox that one uses prior knowledge of similarity to ascertain similarity in capabilities (Goethals & Darley, 1977). The paradox exists only if old and new activities are identical and situational demands remain invariant. This is rarely the case. Both the activities and the situations in which they are performed vary to some degree. Therefore, in arriving at a self-efficacy appraisal, observers must extrapolate from past performance similarities and knowledge of the model's attainments in the new situations. For example, students judge how well they might do in a chemistry course from knowing how peers, who performed comparably to them in physics, fared in chemistry.

The research on self-appraisal of capability via social standards has centered mainly on why people engage in social comparison, whom they choose to compare themselves with, the role of perform-

ance and attribute similarity in the selection of social referents, and the self-evaluative consequences of such choices (Suls & Miller, 1977; Suls & Mullen, 1982; Wood, 1989). Results of these studies have helped to clarify some important aspects of comparative self-appraisal. The laboratory situations, however, generally differ in several respects from how socially comparative influences operate under natural conditions. In laboratory situations, people can choose from a set of social referents whose accomplishments they want to hear about to determine whether they prefer upward or downward comparisons. The comparative self-appraisal is usually made only once. By contrast, under natural conditions, people are continually confronted with comparative information with social consequences whether they seek it or not. They see the accomplishments and rates of progress their associates are attaining, and from time to time they see how others of similar status are doing. Moreover, comparative evaluation is an ongoing process that often involves changes in the level, rate, and direction of performance discrepancies. Comparative self-appraisal, therefore, entails interpreting the ability implications of changing patterns of comparative information over time. Moreover, a full understanding of how social comparative influences affect human functioning requires broadening this line of inquiry to include the impact of these influences on ongoing performance and the mediating mechanisms through which such influences produce their performance effects.

The impact of different patterns of social comparison on efficacy beliefs and level of functioning is strikingly revealed in a study that investigated management of a simulated organization (Bandura & Jourden, 1991). Managers served as organizational decision makers and received accurate feedback of how well their organization was performing under their direction along with one of four prearranged patterns of comparative feedback. They were lead to believe they performed as well as a comparison group of decision makers; consistently surpassed them; achieved progressive mastery in which they started out poorer than their managerial counterparts but gradually closed the gap and eventually surpassed them; or exhibited progressive decline, starting out better than their managerial counterparts but then falling further and further behind them.

The comparative decliners displayed a precipitous drop in their perceived efficacy, their analytic thinking became erratic, and their organization's performance progressively deteriorated. By contrast, the comparative masterers heightened their perceived efficacy, improved their use of efficient analytic strategies, and raised their organization's performance. The comparative masterers were more likely to adopt the type of task-diagnostic focus that ensures success. Those who experienced progressive decline in their comparative status were more prone to a self-referent focus on their inability to do their job and experienced despair over their repeated failure to reverse the downward slide. Performing as well as others of similar status sustained a sense of efficacy.

Comparison of managers who allegedly achieved superiority easily with those who had to struggle to gain mastery suggests that easy comparative triumphs may support a sense of efficacy and good analytic thinking but have demotivating effects. The easy triumphers set lower goal challenges for themselves than did the masterers and were highly satisfied with declining performance attainments because they happened to surpass the performances of their comparators. Complacent self-assurance creates little incentive to expend the increased effort needed to attain high levels of performance.

Attribute Similarity

Self-efficacy appraisals are often based not on comparative performance experiences but on similarity to models in terms of personal characteristics that are assumed to be predictive of performance capabilities (Suls & Miller, 1977). People develop preconceptions of performance capabilities linked to age, sex, educational and socioeconomic level, race, and ethnic designation, even though the individuals within these groups differ widely in their capabilities. Such preconceptions usually arise from a combination of cultural stereotyping and overgeneralization from salient experiences. Attributes that get invested with predictive significance operate as influential factors in comparative self-appraisals.

Among the attributes that affect the perceived diagnosticity of modeled performances for personal capabilities, age and gender often carry heavy weight. Thus, the same physical stamina modeled by a nonathletic female raises women's perceived physical efficacy and muscular endurance, whereas that of an athletic male model does not (Gould & Weiss, 1981). Nonathletic individuals exhibit higher efficacy beliefs and physical stamina after observing persevering nonathletic models than after observing athletic models displaying the same level of sturdiness (George, Feltz, & Chase, 1992). When exposed to skilled peer or adult models exemplifying the same cognitive skills, children derive a stronger sense of personal efficacy from peer modeling (Schunk & Hanson, 1985). They become more assured in their efficacy to learn things, they infer a higher level of efficacy from their developmental progress, and they perform the cognitive activities more competently. If the activity is not stereotypically linked to gender, however, the functional value of the modeled skills can override the influence of the model's gender on observers' judgments of their efficacy. Although the impact of dissimilar modeling in terms of age on perceived efficacy is weaker, it still operates as an efficacy builder if dissimilar models provide valuable skills. The enhanced persuasiveness of model similarity is further revealed in adoption of self-diagnostic health practices promoted by health communications (Anderson & McMillion, 1995). Models of similar race and gender are viewed as more credible and instill stronger efficacy beliefs and behavioral intentions than do models of different race and gender.

Attribute similarity generally increases the power of modeling influences even when the personal characteristics may be spurious indicants of performance capabilities (Rosenthal & Bandura, 1978). For example, similarity in age and sex to coping models emboldens phobic observers, although these characteristics do not really affect how well one can perform the feared activities. Such misjudgments reflect overgeneralization from other activities in which these attributes may predict performance, at least to some extent. Indeed, when model attributes irrelevant to the new task are salient and overweighted in their predictive value, these irrelevant model characteristics sway observers more than do relevant indicators of ability (Kazdin, 1974c). When the successes of models who possess similar attributes lead others to try things they would otherwise shun, spurious indicants can have beneficial social effects. But comparative efficacy appraisals through faulty preconceptions often lead those who are uncertain about their abilities to judge valuable pursuits to be beyond their reach. In such instances, judging personal efficacy by social comparison based on irrelevant attributes is self-limiting, especially if the models express self-doubts about their own capabilities (Gould & Weiss, 1981).

Multiplicity and Diversity of Modeling

In everyday life, appraisal of personal efficacy is rarely based on the performances of a single model. Rather, people have ample opportunities to observe the attainments of many individuals of similar status. The successes and failures of a particular individual are easily discountable as an atypical case. But similar attainments by many individuals carry persuasive force. Through the persuasive power of numbers, multiplicity of modeling augments the strength of vicarious influence (Perry & Bussey, 1979). Indeed, exposure to multiple skilled models produces stronger belief in one's efficacy to learn, higher perceived efficacy for notable attainments, and higher development of competence than does observing a single skilled model (Schunk, Hanson, & Cox, 1987).

Diversified modeling, in which different people master difficult tasks, is superior to exposure to the same performances by a single model (Bandura & Menlove, 1968; Kazdin, 1974a, 1975, 1976). If people of widely differing characteristics can succeed, then observers have a reasonable basis for increasing their own sense of efficacy. The augmenting factor is not diversity per se. Observing the performances of different people who all happen to be of superior capability will not necessarily heighten observers' beliefs in their own efficacy. It is modeled successes by individuals of similar or lesser ability within the diversity that is the major carrier of the effect. Thus, observers who are deficient in cognitive skills acquire more perceived efficacy and cognitive competencies from observing a single similar model eventually gain mastery by tenacious effort than they do from observing multiple skilled models (Schunk et al., 1987).

Coping versus Masterly Modeling

Modeling formats may rely on masterly models, who perform calmly and faultlessly, or on coping models, who begin timorously but gradually overcome their difficulties by determined coping efforts. Observers may benefit more from seeing models overcome their difficulties by tenacious effort than from observing only facile performances by adept models (Kazdin, 1973; Meichenbaum, 1971). Coping modeling can boost efficacy beliefs in several ways. Observers who are unsure of themselves are likely to regard coping models as more similar to themselves than masterly ones. Showing the gains achieved through perseverant effort can reduce the negative import of failure or setbacks by demonstrating that perseverance eventually brings success. Such displays help to create the cognitive set that failures reflect insufficient effort or limited experience rather than lack of basic ability. Such an orientation would help to sustain motivation in times of difficulty. If coping models voice faith in their capabilities for self-improvement as they struggle with problems, they can promote efficacious thinking in observers directly by the efficacy beliefs they model.

Some of the benefits commonly attributed to coping modeling may be overstated because variations on the coping-masterly dimension have, in fact, produced mixed behavioral results. In some studies, coping surpasses masterly modeling

(Kazdin, 1974d; Meichenbaum, 1971); in others, coping modeling aids the process of change when it is combined with model similarity in personal attributes, but not by itself (Kazdin, 1974c); and in still others, coping and masterly modeling are equally effective (Kato & Fukushima, 1977; Klorman, Hilpert, Michael, LaGana, & Sveen, 1980). A social influence containing multiple factors of differing strength will yield mixed results if the separate factors vary unsystematically in the relative weight they are given in different studies.

Coping modeling usually contains several separable factors: Models display decreasing distress as they struggle with difficulties or threats; they demonstrate strategies for managing difficult situations; and they voice self-efficacious beliefs. Instruction in coping strategies is more helpful than emotive modeling. Therefore, whether coping modeling is weaker, equipotent, or stronger than masterly modeling may depend, in large part, on the number of serviceable strategies these two forms of modeling deliver. Masterly modeling that conveys a lot of functional information on how to exercise control over environmental demands is uniformly effective in raising and strengthening efficacy beliefs (Bandura, 1986a; Rosenthal & Steffek, 1991). In the cultivation of cognitive competencies, when observers' attention is explicitly focused on the cognitive skills being modeled, coping and masterly modeling are either equally effective in enhancing efficacy beliefs and competencies or multiple coping modeling is more influential if embellished with modeled expressions of self-efficaciousness (Schunk & Hanson, 1985; Schunk et al., 1987). Masterly self-modeling is just as effective in raising perceived efficacy and performance as is self-modeling of improvement (Schunk & Hanson, 1989a,b).

Individuals who are racked with self-doubt need to be convinced of their learning capabilities if they are to gain much from the information conveyed by models. Coping modeling, in which people like themselves of limited competence achieve progressive mastery by stick-to-itiveness, can help to build a stronger sense of learning efficacy than masterly modeling. It should be noted, however, that the differences are small and equivocal because even dissimilar proficient models who demonstrate valuable skills in explicit, easily mastered steps raise perceived learning efficacy in inveterate self-doubters (Schunk & Hanson, 1985; Schunk et al., 1987). These findings suggest that greater attention should be placed on how to structure modeling influences to enhance their instructive value than on contrived coping displays. Individuals who already have some belief in their capabilities convert initial model dissimilarity in competence to eventual perceived similarity by observational learning of the models' skills and strategies (Schunk & Hanson, 1989b). Their sense of learning efficacy and their eventual level of perceived efficacy and performance are raised just as much by masterly modeling as by coping modeling.

If modeling progressive mastery aids personal change by increasing model similarity, it is possible to capitalize on the motivational benefits of likeness by historical modeling without temporarily exacerbating problems by initial modeled displays of distress and ineptness. For instance, while demonstrating effective ways of coping, models can describe, and even show, how they had previously suffered from similar problems but overcame them by determined effort. In this approach, which is a common rehabilitative practice especially in self-help groups, progressive mastery of problems is described historically rather than enacted presently. Recovered alcoholics need not get soused and then model regained sobriety to convey self-regulatory skills to recovering alcoholics, nor must surgery instructors begin by modeling shaking ineptness to motivate and instruct surgical skills in their aspiring students. Modeling influences can be enhanced by recounted historical similarity combined with proficient modeling.

Coping modeling is more likely to contribute to resilience in personal efficacy under difficult circumstances where the road to success is long and full of impediments, hardships, and setbacks and where evidence of progress may be a long time in coming. These are the usual conditions faced by innovators and those seeking to effect fundamental social change. Inspiring resilient persisters can help to sustain a collective sense of efficacy to keep going in the face of adversities.

Model Competence

The skills and strategies that models exhibit vary in their functional value for managing environmental demands. Among the various characteristics of models, their level of competence carries especially heavy weight. Competent models command more attention and exert greater instructional influence than do incompetent ones (Bandura, 1986a). In virtually all of the studies examining the impact of model attributes on efficacy beliefs, the models are highly competent but vary in age, sex, or other personal attributes. Embedding such attributes in competent models may invest those attributes with greater influence than they ordinarily carry on their own. Thus, for example, when both model competence and age are varied, model competence overrides age dissimilarity in promoting efficacy beliefs and skill development (Lirgg & Feltz, 1991). Model competence is an especially influential factor when observers have a lot to learn and models have much they can teach them by instructive demonstration of skills and strategies. People are not about to discard information that makes them more efficacious just because it comes from a dissimilar source.

Most of the studies of model attributes are patterned after real-life conditions in which individuals of limited competence seek to develop their knowledge and competencies by drawing on the skills and strategies discovered by successful models. In aspirational modeling, people actively select proficient models from whom they can learn what they aspire to become. If they believe in their learning capabilities, they do not need to observe coping models moving from distressing incompetence to undaunted competence in order to raise their own sense of personal efficacy after being shown by models how to manage problems effectively. Progressive mastery of modeled skills and strategies through observational learning increases perceived similarity to initially dissimilar proficient models.

VERBAL PERSUASION

Social persuasion serves as a further means of strengthening people's beliefs that they possess the capabilities to achieve what they seek. It is easier to sustain a sense of efficacy, especially when struggling with difficulties, if significant others express faith in one's capabilities than if they convey doubts. Verbal persuasion alone may be limited in its power to create enduring increases in perceived efficacy, but it can bolster self-change if the positive appraisal is within realistic bounds. People who are persuaded verbally that they possess the capabilities to master given tasks are likely to mobilize greater effort and sustain it than if they harbor self-doubts and dwell on personal deficiencies when difficulties arise. To the extent that persuasive boosts in perceived efficacy lead people to try hard enough to succeed, self-affirming beliefs promote development of skills and a sense of personal efficacy. Persuasory efficacy attributions, therefore, have their greatest impact on people who have some reason to believe that they can produce effects through their actions (Chambliss & Murray, 1979a, 1979b). To raise unrealistic beliefs of personal capabilities, however, only invites failures that will discredit the persuaders and further undermine the recipients' beliefs in their capabilities.

Framing of Performance Feedback

Persuasory efficacy information is often conveyed in the evaluative feedback given to performers. It can be conveyed in ways that undermine a sense of efficacy or boost it. The effects of evaluative feedback on efficacy beliefs have been examined extensively by Schunk and his colleagues. In these studies, children with mathematical or reading deficits pursue a program of self-directed instruction during which they receive prearranged attributional feedback, regardless of their actual performance, that carries efficacy implications. They are told from time to time that their work shows that they are capable, that they have been working hard, or that they need to work harder (Schunk, 1982; Schunk & Cox, 1986). Evaluative feedback highlighting personal capabilities raises efficacy beliefs. Feedback that the children improved their capabilities through effort also enhances perceived efficacy, although not as much as being told that their progress shows they have ability for the activity. Ability feedback in the early stages of skill development has an especially notable impact on the development of a sense of personal efficacy (Schunk, 1984b).

Effort attributions for progress are often touted as a preferred remedial strategy: Hard work produced the improvement. This may sustain motivation in the short run. But to be told repeatedly that one's progress is a product of high effort eventually conveys the message that one's talents must be quite limited to require such unending arduous work (Schunk & Rice, 1986). Indeed, telling people that they have ability and that they gained it by hard work produces a lower sense of efficacy than does telling them that their progress shows they have ability without reference to the effort they had to exert (Schunk, 1983b).

In these studies, the more the persuasory feedback raised children's beliefs in their efficacy, the more persistent they were in their efforts and the higher the level of competence they eventually achieved. Because judgment of efficacy is influenced by many factors, skill development only partially affects children's beliefs in their personal efficacy. Perceived self-efficacy contributes to performance accomplishments over and above the effects of skill development.

Social evaluations of capability are often conveyed indirectly and subtly toward people believed to be of limited aptitude. When social customs frown on voicing devaluation of others, the low social evaluations are usually masked in disingenuous comments or in social practices that convey the message that one does not expect much of the recipients. They are assigned unchallenging tasks, praised excessively for mediocre performances and treated indifferently for faulty performance, repeatedly offered unsolicited help, or given less recognition than others when they perform as well. The individuals at the receiving end of such indirect appraisals are generally well practiced in seeing through thinly veiled devaluations. Such practices tend to lower recipients' judgments of their capability (Lord, Umezaki, & Darley, 1990; Meyer, 1992). However, young children, who are less skilled in deciphering the meaning of indirect appraisal actions, read high praise for ordinary performances as an indicant of high capability (Lord et al., 1990; Meyer, 1992).

The way in which persuasory influences and performance feedback are framed or structured can affect the appraisal of personal efficacy. People are generally more motivated to avoid potential losses in the present than to secure potential future gains (Tversky & Kahneman, 1981). Temporally remote benefits are likely to exert less influence when they are perceived as less certain, appear less salient, and are less affectively compelling than current aversive losses. To the extent that people believe they can exercise greater control over negative predicaments in the short run than over positive payoffs in the future, they may judge themselves more efficacious for the same courses of action construed as serving safety functions than for actions serving gainful functions.

Some of the empirical support for the effects of framing influences on perceived efficacy comes from efforts to get people to adopt health-promoting behavior. Meyerowitz and Chaiken (1987) report that health communications emphasizing the potential health losses from nonadherence to self-protective practices were more successful in raising efficacy beliefs and adoptive behavior than communications emphasizing the long-term health benefits of adhering to such practices. Whether the threat of losses for nonadherence to healthy practices is more behaviorally persuasive than the prospect of gains for adherence depends on the strength of preexisting efficacy beliefs (Wilson, Wallston, & King, 1990). Persuasive health influences framed in terms of threat of losses lead people with a high sense of efficacy to intensify efforts at self-directed change but undermine the efforts of those who believe they cannot exercise much control over their risky health behavior.

The persuasory framing influences that bear directly on self-efficacy appraisal are most evident in social evaluations of performance attainments. In their various pursuits, people strive for certain goals or levels of performance. These desired accomplishments are reached gradually rather than fulfilled instantly. The point of reference from which successive attainments are socially evaluated can affect appraisal of personal capabilities. Social evaluations that focus on achieved progress underscore personal capabilities, whereas evaluations that focus on shortfalls from the distant goal highlight existing deficiencies in capabilities.

In systematic tests of framing effects, the performance feedback is factually equivalent but simply varies whether the evaluative reference point is the performance level at which one began or the level to be fulfilled. Thus, for example, if an individual performs at a 75 percent level of a selected standard, the gain framing highlights the 75 percent progress already achieved, and the deficit framing highlights the 25 percent shortfall. Feedback framed as gains is likely to support self-efficacy

development, whereas informative feedback that is objectively equivalent but framed in terms of shortfalls is apt to diminish a sense of personal efficacy by highlighting one's deficiencies. These efficacy effects are corroborated by Jourden (1991) in a study in which people managed a simulated organization and received feedback of organizational attainments as percent progress toward a desired standard or as percent shortfall from it. Casting evaluative feedback for the same accomplishment in terms of performance gains enhanced efficacy beliefs and subsequent rate of accomplishment, whereas centering the evaluative feedback on how far one still has to go detracted from a sense of personal efficacy and accomplishment (Fig. 3.3). The latter pattern, in which good work is taken for granted but shortfalls bring ready criticism, is all too common in everyday life.

Deficient performances often draw harsh criticism that berates the performer rather than offers helpful guides on how to improve performance. Devaluative feedback not only creates social estrangement but undermines people's belief in

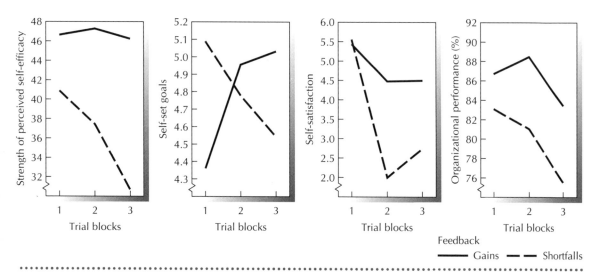

FIGURE 3.3. Changes in self-regulatory factors and performance attainments depending on whether performance feedback is given as level of progress toward a selected standard (mastery) or as shortfalls from the same standard (deficit). Each trial block includes six different production tasks. (Jourden, 1991)

themselves. Given the same level of performance, disparaging criticism lowers perceived efficacy and aspirations, whereas constructive criticism sustains aspirations and upholds or even bolsters a sense of personal efficacy (Baron, 1988). These findings take on added significance because of the debilitating and enabling effects of evaluative feedback generalized across different types of activities.

It is more difficult to instill enduringly high beliefs of personal efficacy by persuasory means alone than it is to undermine such beliefs. Unrealistic boosts in efficacy are readily disconfirmed by disappointing results of one's actions. By acting on highly inflated self-beliefs, one quickly finds out what one cannot do. But people who have been persuaded that they lack capabilities tend to avoid challenging activities that cultivate competencies and give up quickly in the face of difficulties. By constricting choice of activities, undermining motivation, and discouraging explorations that cultivate interests and competencies, disbeliefs in personal efficacy can create their own behavioral validation.

Knowledgeableness and Credibility

For many activities, people cannot rely solely on themselves in evaluating their level of ability because such judgments require inferences from indicants of talent about which they may have only limited knowledge. To complicate this inferential appraisal, not only are the relevant indicators imperfect predictors but they must be combined and weighted in insightful ways. Success in a given pursuit involves more than just natural endowment. There are many people with a world of talent who do little with it. A crucial predictor of self-development is the self-regulatory capability to mobilize and sustain the perseverant effort needed to convert potential to behavioral fulfillment. Even if people do develop their talents, they may be chronic underachievers if they do not handle pressure and failure well. Self-motivational and self-management capabilities are, therefore, important factors in the diagnostic analysis.

Self-appraisals are partly based on the opinions of others who presumably possess diagnostic competence gained through years of experience with aspirants in a given field. Of course, people do not always believe what they are told about their abilities. Skepticism develops from personal experiences that often run counter to what one has been told. Were this always the case, performers would eventually turn a deaf ear to their persuaders. But there are many occasions when individuals are persuaded to try things they routinely avoid or to persist at tasks they were ready to discontinue, only to discover, much to their surprise, that they were capable of mastering them. This is because performance attainments on many tasks are determined more by how hard one works at them than by inherent capacity.

Mixed experiences with persuasory efficacy appraisals are common because they are used for diverse purposes. Persuaders may laud the talents of others for flattery, perfunctory encouragement, self-ingratiation, or manipulative "hype," as well as for realistic assessments of people's capabilities to manage task demands. Consequently, persuasory efficacy appraisals have to be weighted in terms of who the persuaders are, their credibility, and how knowledgeable they are about the nature of the activities. Deferral to supposedly objective indicants of capability can boost persuaders' influence on people's beliefs in their efficacy. This is revealed most strikingly in studies in which people are taught to alleviate stress and pain by self-relaxation (Holroyd et al., 1984; Litt, 1988; Litt, Nye, & Shafer, 1993, 1995). Some are arbitrarily told that their recorded physiological reactions show them to be good relaxers; others receive no social feedback. The persuasory affirmation of capability, though unrelated to the actual physiological indicants, boosts people's beliefs in their efficacy to manage pain. The more their efficacy beliefs are raised, the better they tolerate acute pain, the less physical and emotional distress they experience during oral surgery, and the more successful they are in alleviating tension headaches.

Differences between personal and social appraisal of efficacy raise questions about whose judgments are more accurate. Most people believe they know themselves and their predicaments better than others do, and this belief creates some resistance to social persuasion. The impact of persuasory opinions on efficacy beliefs is apt to be only as strong as the recipient's confidence in the person who issues them. This confidence is mediated through the perceived credibility and expertness of the persuaders. The more believable the source of information about one's capabilities, the more likely are judgments of personal efficacy to change and to be held strongly. People are inclined to trust evaluations of their capabilities by those who are themselves skilled in the activity, have access to some objective predictors of performance capability, or possess a rich fund of knowledge gained from observing and comparing many different aspirants and their later accomplishments (Crundall & Foddy, 1981; Webster & Sobieszek, 1974).

Skill in a given pursuit, of course, does not necessarily confer competence in gauging talent for it. For example, not all superstar athletes are insightful judges of athletic talent. Sound diagnostic and prescriptive skills require intricate knowledge about the development of proficiency in given pursuits. For performers who realize this, evidence of success in judging talent is apt to be the more persuasive indicant of evaluative competence. Others often voice opinions of what performers can do without being thoroughly acquainted with the difficulty of the tasks or with the circumstances under which they will have to be performed. Knowledge of the realities that performers will have to manage is, therefore, another consideration in evaluating the credibility of social persuaders. Even the judgments of otherwise credible advisors may be discounted on the grounds that they do not fully understand the task demands. When individuals are more confident in their self-appraisals than in the judgments of others, they are not swayed by what they are told about their capabilities.

Degree of Appraisal Disparity

Social appraisals vary in how discrepant they are from people's own beliefs about their capabilities. What they are told may differ minimally, moderately, or markedly from how they view themselves. The optimal level of disparity will depend on the temporal proximity of pursuits and the nature of the activity. Social appraisals that differ markedly from people's judgments of their current capabilities may be considered believable for the distant future but not in the short run. The optimal level of disparity, therefore, will be much lower for proximate level of functioning than for future functioning.

Persuasory efficacy appraisals are likely to be most believable when they are only moderately beyond what individuals can do at the time. At this level of discrepancy, better performances are achievable through better strategy selection and extra effort. Those who are persuaded they can succeed are more likely to test different strategies and expend the necessary effort than those who are troubled by uncertainties. Performance successes, in turn, raise the perceived diagnostic competence of the persuaders. Inflated persuasory appraisals that mislead performers to repeated failures undermine the diagnostic credibility of the persuaders and further reinforce performers' belief in their inherent limitations.

The optimal level of disparity will also vary depending on whether deficient performances reflect basic skills deficits or ineffectual use of preexisting skills. In the misuse case, performance gains are achievable by convincing people they have what it takes to succeed. Self-efficacious thinking fosters effective use of skills. Where requisite skills are lacking, however, social persuasion alone cannot substitute for skill development. Simply telling people they are much more capable than they believe themselves to be will not necessarily make it so. Efficacy beliefs are best instilled by presenting the pursuit as relying on acquirable skills, raising performers' beliefs in their abilities to acquire the skills, modeling the requisite skills, structuring activities in masterable steps that ensure a high level of initial success, and providing explicit feedback of continued progress. Social persuasion serves best as part of a multifaceted strategy of self-development. People who are struggling with self-doubts rooted largely in skill deficits are likely to view optimistic social appraisals as more believable if the judgments focus on efficacy for self-development rather than on high current accomplishments.

Persuasory modes of instilling a sense of efficacy should not be misconstrued as limited to brief verbal influence attempts. Social persuasion involves much more than fleeting pep talks. During formative years, the significant models in people's lives play a key role in instilling beliefs of their potential and power to influence the direction their lives take. These self-beliefs shape basic orientations to life. People who triumph over severe adversities provide some of the most striking testimony of enduring persuasory influences. To cite but one example (Mandel, 1993), a single minority mother raising nine daughters on a $2.00 an hour wage as a cook refused to have her life dictated by adverse circumstances. During these trying times, she would sing her daughters to sleep with the blues song, "We may not have a cent to pay the rent, but we're gonna make it." She acted on this inspiring affirmation of efficacy in the face of severe adversity. Through extraordinary resourcefulness and self-sacrifice, she not only made it but presides over five barbecue restaurants attracting customers from far and wide. She traces the roots of her resilience to her mother, who instilled in her a firm sense of personal agency, "Work hard and you can get anything. Don't wait for someone to give it to you."

Social persuasion serves as a useful adjunct to more powerful efficacy-promoting influences. Skilled efficacy builders, therefore, do more than simply convey positive appraisals or inspirational homilies. In addition to cultivating people's beliefs in their capabilities, they structure activities for them in ways that bring success and avoid placing them prematurely in situations where they are likely to experience repeated failure. To do this effectively, persuasory mentors must be good diagnosticians of strengths and weaknesses and knowledgeable about how to tailor activities to turn potentiality into actuality. Moreover, to ensure progress in personal development, skilled efficacy builders encourage people to measure their successes in terms of self-improvement rather than in terms of triumphs over others. Mere pronouncements of capacity to shape the course of one's life without providing efficacy-affirming experiences along the way become empty homilies.

PHYSIOLOGICAL AND AFFECTIVE STATES

In judging their capabilities, people rely partly on somatic information conveyed by physiological and emotional states. Somatic indicators of personal efficacy are especially relevant in domains that involve physical accomplishments, health functioning, and coping with stressors. People often read their physiological activation in stressful or taxing situations as signs of vulnerability to dysfunction. Because high arousal can debilitate performance, people are more inclined to expect success when they are not beset by aversive arousal than if they are tense and viscerally agitated. Stress reactions to inefficacious control generate further stress through anticipatory self-arousal. By conjuring up aversive thoughts about their ineptitude and stress reactions, people can rouse themselves to elevated levels of distress that produce the very dysfunctions they fear. Treatments that eliminate emotional reactions to subjective threats through mastery experiences heighten beliefs in coping efficacy with corresponding improvements in performance (Bandura, 1988c). Physiological indicators of efficacy are not limited to autonomic arousal. In activities involving strength and stamina, people read their fatigue, windedness, aches, and pains as indicants of physical inefficacy. Mood states also affect people's judgments of their personal efficacy. Physiological indicators of efficacy play an especially influential role in health functioning and in activities requiring physical strength and stamina. Affective states can have widely generalized effects on beliefs of personal efficacy in diverse spheres of functioning. Thus, the fourth major way of altering efficacy beliefs is to enhance physical status, reduce stress levels and negative emotional proclivities, and correct misinterpretations of bodily states (Bandura, 1991a; Cioffi, 1991a).

People differ in their proneness to dwell on their somatic states and reactions. Some are quick to focus inwardly on their sensory experiences, others are more externally oriented (Carver & Scheier, 1981; Duval & Wicklund, 1972). Apart from attentional biases, a number of conditions increase the salience of somatic indicators of efficacy. The level of attentional involvement in activities is one such condition. Attention has a very limited capacity, so there are only a few things to which one can attend at any given time (Kahneman, 1973). When situational matters command attention, one cannot be focused both inwardly and outwardly simultaneously. Hence, the less absorbed people are in activities and events around them, the more they focus attention on themselves and notice their aversive bodily states and reactions in taxing situations (Pennebaker & Lightner, 1980).

Perceived vulnerability to psychological stressors heightens the level and salience of physiological reactions. It is difficult to ignore internal visceral agitation when one is hyperventilating; sweating; tensing; trembling; and experiencing a pounding heart, stomach upsets, and bouts of insomnia. The self-directed attention further highlights the internal agitation (Scheier, Carver, & Matthews, 1983). A high level of physical activity also produces a lot of somatic information that carries efficacy implications (Bandura, 1992b). During physical pursuits, evident indicators of strength and stamina — and fatigue, aches, and pains — do not escape notice. In efforts at self-assessment, some people push themselves to their limits to gain knowledge of their physical capabilities. The more sedentary ones would just as soon not know the degree to which their capabilities have declined and scale down their physical activities to minimize reminders of inefficacy. And finally, physical maladies and dysfunctions can draw dispiriting attention to physical limitations (Cioffi, 1991a). People who suffer such disorders often become vigilant self-monitors of their physical condition and are prone to ascribe impediments arising from other sources, such as sedentariness or natural fluctuations in physical states, solely to physical impairment.

As in the other modes of influence, the information conveyed by physiological states and reactions is not, by itself, diagnostic of personal efficacy. Such information affects perceived self-efficacy through cognitive processing. A number of factors — including cognitive appraisal of the sources of physiological activation, its intensity, the circumstances under which the activation occurs, and construal biases — affect what is made of physiological conditions. The presumed diagnosticity of emotional arousal for performance enhancement or impairment is also an important factor in the cognitive processing of somatic efficacy information.

Perceived Source of Activation

Activities are often performed in situations that contain varied evocative events. This creates ambiguity about what caused the physiological reactions. Environmental factors exert strong influence on how an internal state is interpreted. The efficacy impact of physiological arousal on self-efficacy, therefore, will vary depending on the situational factors singled out and the meaning given to them. Speakers who ascribe their sweating to the physical discomforts of the room read their physiology quite differently from those who view it as distress reflecting personal failings.

Self-appraisal of efficacy from arousal cues raises a number of intriguing developmental questions. How do young children come to view bodily states as emotional conditions? How do they learn to tell what emotion they are experiencing? How do they learn that arousal cues signifying particular emotions are predictive of level of functioning? In the sociocognitive view (Bandura, 1986a), knowledge about bodily states is acquired, in large part, through social labeling coordinated with experienced events. Arousing experiences contain three significant events, one of which remains private and two of which are publicly observable. These include environmental elicitors, expressive reactions, and social labeling. Visible situational affective elicitors activate internal arousal and visible expressive reactions signifying positive or negative experiences. Both the observable situational events and the expressive reactions carry affective meaning for observers. This enables them to read the emotion children are likely to be experiencing at the moment.

The internal arousal itself cannot play a differentiating role in the social labeling of emotion because the arousal is unobservable to others. Moreover, phenomenologically different emotions appear to have too many similar physiological reactions to be differentiable by the person experiencing them. Therefore, adults must infer the presence of the internal affective state in young children from their expressive reactions and from environmental elicitors known to produce particular types of emotions. Drawing on these observable events, adults describe and differentiate the emotions children are experiencing (for example, happiness, sadness, anger, fear) and explain their causes. Thus, parents label children's bodily tension and other expressions of somatic agitation as fear in threatening situations and as anger in irritating or thwarting situations.

Through repeated social linkage of situational elicitors, expressive reactions, and internal arousal, children learn to interpret and to differentiate their affective experiences. Within the first few years of life, children come to understand which situations produce which emotions (Harris, 1989). The final step in investing emotional states with self-efficacy implications involves recognizing relations between inferred emotions and performance attainments. By observing how well they perform under different emotional conditions, children eventually form a belief about how emotional arousal might affect their personal efficacy. Different interpretations of internal arousal (for example, "frightened," "fired up," "angered") will have different impact on perceived self-efficacy.

By commanding attention, salient situational factors strongly determine how physiological arousal is judged. Indeed, because most somatic activity is diffuse, people rely more heavily on situational information than on visceral information to judge what they are feeling. Thus, visceral arousal occurring in situations that contain threatening cues is interpreted as fear, arousal in thwarting situations is experienced as anger, and arousal resulting from

irretrievable loss of valued objects is experienced as sorrow (Hunt, Cole, & Reis, 1958). In many situations, people experience mixed emotions rather than only a single one. They vacillate, often rapidly, between anxiety and depression, fear and anger, apprehension and excitement. The mixed emotional arousal or residual arousal from a prior experience may be misassigned to a prominent element in a new situation, as when residual sexual arousal is misjudged as anger in the presence of anger-provoking cues (Zillmann, 1983). Even the same source of physiological arousal may be interpreted differently in ambiguous situations depending on the emotional reactions of others in the same setting (Mandler, 1975; Schachter & Singer, 1962). Because of their selective attention to threatening cues, those who perceive themselves to be inefficacious are especially prone to misjudge arousal arising from other sources as a sign of coping deficiencies.

Level of Activation

It is not the sheer intensity of emotional and physical reactions that is important but rather how they are perceived and interpreted. The diagnostic implications of physiological arousal for self-efficacy judgment derive from past experiences with how labeled arousal affects performance. For people who generally find arousal facilitory, arousal will have different efficacy meaning than for those for whom arousal has been debilitating. Indeed, high achievers view arousal as an energizing facilitator, whereas low achievers regard it as a debilitator (Hollandsworth, Glazeski, Kirkland, Jones, & van Norman, 1979). The judgmental process is complicated by the fact that it is not arousal per se but rather its level that carries the greater weight in judging personal capabilities. As a general rule, moderate levels of arousal heighten attentiveness and facilitate deployment of skills, whereas high arousal disrupts the quality of functioning. The optimum level of activation will depend on the complexity of the activity. Simple activities and those that are overlearned are not easily disruptable. But performance of complex activities requiring intricate organization and precise execution are more vulnerable to impairment by interfering processes that accompany high emotional activation.

Construal Biases

Preexisting efficacy beliefs create attentional, interpretive, and memory biases in the processing of somatic information, as they do in the other sources of efficacy information. A low sense of efficacy is likely to heighten sensitivity to bodily states of arousal in the domains of functioning in which people distrust their coping capabilities. Cognitive biases in the interpretation of bodily sensations are graphically revealed when people are given false feedback of changes in their physiological arousal. In one such study, individuals who are prone to misinterpret bodily sensations as foreboders of panic attacks received fictitious feedback of a sudden unexplained rise in their heart rate (Ehlers, Margraf, Roth, Taylor, & Birbaumer, 1988). Because individuals with panic disorders feel powerless to exercise control over panic attacks, they conjure up catastrophic outcomes, heighten their anxiety, accelerate their heart rate, and drive up their blood pressure. In contrast, secure individuals view the same abrupt rise in heart rate as a benign event and remain physiologically unperturbed. Bodily sensations are likewise experienced differently when the interpretive biases are experimentally induced rather than developed naturally (Salkovskis & Clark, 1990). The same heightened bodily sensations are experienced as pleasant states under an instilled positive construal bias but as aversive states under a negative construal bias. The more intense the physiological sensations, the stronger are the emotional reactions in line with the interpretive predilections. Thus, the problem is not arousal per se but the view one takes of it. In fact, to read arousal as challenge can boost perceived efficacy. For panicky individuals, who are prone to misread somatic states, treatments that alter catastrophic thinking or teach ways of controlling emotional arousal reduce negative biases in interpreting bodily sensations (Westling & Öst, 1995).

Physiological activity typically involves a variety of somatic events. How people read their bodily states will depend partly on which aspects of their multifaceted somatic experiences they observe. Moreover, many somatic events do not convey distinct meaning. For example, all emotions are characterized by elevation in autonomic arousal. The extensive similarities in the autonomic accomplishments of different emotions overshadow any small differences (Frankenhaeuser, 1975; Levi, 1972; Patkai, 1971; Schwartz, Weinberger, & Singer, 1981). The heart races alike in fear, euphoria, and vigorous physical exertion. Any small differences in an otherwise common elevated pattern of autonomic activation is not sufficiently distinguishable to tell one which emotion is being experienced. Thus, preexisting cognitive biases can convert the same pattern of autonomic activation into different experienced emotions, the same tactile sensations into painful or pleasant experiences, and the same bodily states into innocuous physical expressions or illness symptoms (Cioffi, 1991a; Schachter, 1964; Skelton & Pennebaker, 1982). The presence of identifiable situational determinants of somatic states, of course, places limits on interpretive biasing. Persons who are viscerally agitated at the sight of a snarling dog will not believe they are experiencing euphoria.

What constitutes an optimal level of activation depends not only on the nature of the activity but on how the arousal is construed. People vary in the beliefs they hold about the source of their emotional arousal and how it will affect their performances. Those who are prone to construe their arousal as stemming from personal inadequacies are more likely to lower their perceived efficacy than those who regard their arousal as a common transitory reaction that even the most competent people experience from time to time. Accomplished theatrical performers, who often become highly anxious before a performance but lose their apprehensiveness once they appear on stage, are likely to ascribe their anticipatory arousal to normative situational reactions rather than to personal deficiencies. Sir Laurence Olivier, the renowned actor, used self-efficacy orations to combat stage fright by appearing on stage before a show began and proclaiming behind the curtain that he was a superb actor whose performance would captivate the audience that evening. Given a predilection to attribute arousal to personal deficiencies, heightened attention to visceral cues can result in reciprocally escalating arousal (Sarason, 1975a).

In a discerning analysis of construal of somatic information, Cioffi (1991a) argues convincingly that it is not the sheer intensity of physical sensations or the amount of attention paid to them that is of import, but rather how they are perceived and interpreted. Somatic information is processed into percepts. It is the percepts that serve as the information base for judgment. The relationship between perceived and actual autonomic reactions is surprisingly low and highly variable across different types of bodily sensations (Pennebaker, Gonder-Frederick, Cox, & Hoover, 1985; Steptoe & Vögele, 1992). Given this disparity, it is to be expected that judgments of personal efficacy are affected by perceived, rather than by actual, autonomic activation in situations involving risks (Feltz & Albrecht, 1986).

Somatic information comes in different forms and varies in sensory qualities even within the same modality. In reading their physiological states and reactions, people may experience the same somatic activation differently depending on the sensory qualities to which they selectively attend. Thus, people find pain and the discomfort of physical exertion less distressing and more tolerable if they focus on the concrete characteristics of the sensations they are experiencing rather than on their aversiveness, or if they try to divert their attention from the sensations (Ahles, Blanchard, & Leventhal, 1983; Cioffi, 1993; Leventhal & Mosbach, 1983). In extended physical exertion, masterly marathon runners monitor their bodily sensations as information for adjusting their pace to avoid risk of physical exhaustion or injury, whereas the less proficient ones experience the sensations of exertion as an aversive state from which they continuously try to divert their attention by cognitive distraction strategies (Morgan & Pollock, 1977). That heightened attention to the same somatic sensations can carry markedly different meaning is further revealed in research in which a strenuous physical activity is performed in the presence or absence of an uncontrollable threat (Cioffi, 1991b). Close sensory monitoring produced a negative interpretation of one's somatic sensations under uncontrollable

threat but a more positive interpretation under no threat, even though the sensations were just as pronounced and noticeable under both conditions. Somatic construal and personal efficacy involve two-way causation. Compared to individuals who judge themselves physically inefficacious, those who have a high sense of physical efficacy perceive less physiological strain and experience their somatic activation more positively during the same level of taxing exertion after controlling for aerobic capacity (McAuley & Courneya, 1992; Rudolf & McAuley, 1996). Perceived high physiological strain and the experience of somatic activation as aversive, in turn, weaken belief in one's physical efficacy.

In taxing activities, people have to process constellations of physiological indicators of physical efficacy. The relative weight they give to positive and negative indicators will affect how they judge their capabilities. The cognitive processing of efficacy information generated by treadmill tests of cardiovascular capacity is illustrative of this point (Juneau, Rogers, Bandura, Taylor, & DeBusk, 1986). Treadmill performances produce many negative signs, such as fatigue, pain, and shortness of breath, which mount as the task continues. Feedback that highlights physical attainments on the treadmill raises women's judgments of their cardiac capabilities. In the absence of such feedback, women read the mounting negative sensations accompanying increasing exertion on the treadmill as indicants of cardiac limitations and lower their judgments of their cardiac efficacy.

Somatic information occurs in the context of other diagnostic indicators of self-efficacy. These include prior mastery experiences, validation of capability in comparison with others, and appraisals by knowledgeable others. Sometimes these indicators conflict, as when people who are assured of their capabilities experience anticipatory arousal as they are about to perform before critically evaluative audiences. The other indicators of self-efficacy are usually given greater weight because they are more reliably diagnostic of personal capabilities than are diffuse, transitory states of the viscera. This was corroborated by Katz and his colleagues (Katz, Stout, Taylor, Horne, & Agras, 1983) in a study with phobics comparing the contribution of mastery experiences and autonomic arousal to judgments of coping self-efficacy. In the context of mastery experiences, which greatly heightened efficacy beliefs, reduction of peripheral autonomic arousal by beta blocking medication had no effect on judgment of coping efficacy. Perceived autonomic arousal may contribute to judgment of personal efficacy when a risky activity is first tried. But with further task engagement, mastery experience increases, and perceived autonomic arousal fades in importance as determinants of efficacy beliefs (Felz & Albrecht, 1986).

At other times, the somatic source provides supporting or redundant efficacy information. A common example is when individuals beset with self-doubts derived from other efficacy indicators experience intense emotional arousal. In areas of functioning that draw heavily on physical resources, physiological states and reactions contribute unique efficacy information for judging the functional capabilities of one's biological systems and physical capabilities (Bandura, 1992c). The way in which such information is cognitively processed can affect how active a life people lead. Those who read their fatigue, aches, and lowered stamina as signs of declining physical capacity are likely to curtail their activities more than those who regard such signs as the effects of sedentariness.

The cognitive processing of physiological information figures prominently in psychological recovery from physical disorders (Ewart et al., 1983; Taylor et al., 1985). For example, patients who have had a heart attack are likely to base their level of activity on their perceived cardiac capability, which they infer from observable signs such as fatigue, shortness of breath, pain, and reduced stamina. Different physical conditions, including a sedentary life-style, can produce these same effects. Such signs, therefore, are easily misread as evidence of cardiac impairment. When patients perform treadmill tests, those who selectively focus on the fatigue and discomfort accompanying intense exertion during the test will perceive a debilitated cardiac capability, whereas those who focus on the strenuous workloads they had accomplished will perceive a more robust cardiac capability. Differential cognitive processing of physiological information can lead to quite different perceptions of one's physical capabilities.

Impact of Mood on Self-Efficacy Judgment

Most of the discussion so far has centered on how physiological activation may be read as an indicator of personal efficacy. Moods provide an additional source of affective information for judging personal efficacy because they often accompany changes in quality of functioning. Mood states can bias attention and affect how events are interpreted, cognitively organized, and retrieved from memory (Bower, 1981, 1983; Eich, 1995; Isen, 1987). People can learn faster if the things that they are learning are congruent with the mood they are in, and they recall things better if they are in the same mood as when they learned them. Intense moods exert stronger effects than weak ones, except for despondency, which retards almost everything. It is assumed that emotional arousal primes affective themes, thus making congruent information more salient, learnable, and memorable. Memory involves an associative network of concepts and propositionally encoded events. In Bower's network theory of how emotional arousal affects thought processes, emotions become associated in memory with different events, thus creating multiple linkages within the associative network. Activating a particular emotion unit in the memory network will facilitate recollection of events linked with it.

Mood-biased recollection can similarly affect people's judgments of their personal efficacy. Two biasing processes have been postulated. These include affective priming and cognitive priming. According to the affective priming theory proposed by Bower, past successes and failures are stored as memories along with their affect (Bower, 1983). The set of memories provides the database on which judgments are made. Mood activates the subset of memories congruent with it through an associative mood network. Thus, a negative mood activates thoughts of past failings, whereas a positive mood activates thoughts of past accomplishments. The spread of activation from the emotion node makes mood-congruent memories salient. Appraisal of personal efficacy is enhanced by selective recall of past successes and diminished by recall of failures. According to Teasdale (1988), negative episodes and depressed mood activate a global view of oneself as inadequate and worthless rather than just activating unhappy memories. Perceived inadequacy, which is akin to perceived inefficacy, exacerbates and prolongs depression through a sense of futility of effort to exercise any control over aversive aspects of one's life situation. In the cognitive priming view, specific successes or failures that induce the affect also produce cognitions that directly cue thoughts of other past successes and failures. This view places greater emphasis on the thought content of the inducing event than on the aroused affect as the primer of other positive or negative thoughts. Cognitive availability biases self-efficacy judgment.

Affective state can influence evaluative judgment directly through its perceived informative value as well as indirectly by activating selective recall of mood-congruent memories (Schwartz & Clore, 1988). In this process, people use their perceived affective reactions rather than recalled information to form their evaluations. They make positive evaluations when they are in good moods and negative evaluations when they are in bad moods. Therefore, the impact of mood on evaluative judgment can be altered by varying the information provided by the affective state itself. Thus, if the meaning of an affective state is altered by attributing it to a nonemotional or transient irrelevant source, the state does not affect evaluative judgment because it is considered uninformative for the judgment at hand. For example, interviewers who attribute their accelerated heart rate to having rushed up a set of stairs are less likely to wonder about their capabilities to manage the interview situation than interviewers who read their pounding heart as a sign of distress. It is not the arousal state per se but the meaning given to it that affects judgment. Current mood can override the influence of the content by which it was induced to produce similar generalized effects on evaluative judgment irrespective of the content domain. And finally, the mood experienced at the time the judgment is made can bias that judgment regardless of the mood in which memories of past experiences with the same events are preserved.

Schwartz and Clore (1988) specify a number of conditions — mainly in the form of strains, pressures, complexities, and ambiguities — that lead people to rely on their affective states as a basis for their judgments. They are especially prone to rely on their "gut reactions" when faced with judgmental tasks requiring integration of a large amount of information, when they make global rather than specific judgments, when the affect involves diffuse mood states rather than clearly identifiable emotions, when relevant information is not readily recallable, when feelings are so strong as to shut out competing thoughts on the matter, and when judgments must be made quickly. Simply using how one feels simplifies the judgmental task. However, the numerous qualifiers that have been proposed greatly limit the conditions under which mood itself can affect judgment. Many limiting conditions that are not that easily identifiable or measurable provide a fertile ground for the growth of conflicting findings.

Induced positive mood enhances perceived efficacy, whereas induced despondent mood diminishes it (Forgas, Bower, & Moylan, 1990; Salovey & Birnbaum, 1989). The more intense the induced mood, the greater is its impact on efficacy beliefs. Moreover, Kavanagh and Bower (1985) have shown that the impact of induced mood on efficacy beliefs is widely generalized rather than confined to the particular content domain of functioning in which happiness or sadness were experienced. Moods aroused by recall of happy and sad romantic experiences affect not only perceived heterosexual efficacy but also social efficacy and athletic and others types of coping efficacy (Fig. 3.4). These authors note, however, that the range of past failings and attainments represented in memory sets limits on how much change in self-appraisal mood can produce. Thus, elated mood will not elevate mediocre achievers to a superstar level of perceived efficacy, nor will sad mood lower superstars to a mediocre level of perceived efficacy. Or, to put it in the authors' more graphic metaphor, mood will not transform a mouse into a mighty lion or a lion into a cringing mouse.

Wright and Mischel (1982) further document that mood can bias how much perceived self-efficacy is derived from ongoing success and failure experiences. Successes under positive mood spawn a

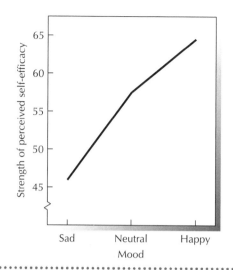

FIGURE 3.4. Mean strength of perceived self-efficacy for heterosexual, social, and athletic domains of functioning when self-efficacy was judged in a positive, neutral, or negative mood state. (Kavanagh & Bower, 1985)

high level of perceived efficacy, whereas failures under negative mood breed a low sense of personal efficacy. The efficacy-biasing impact of mood is especially evident when mood mismatches performance attainments. People who fail under a happy mood overestimate their capabilities. Those who succeed under a sad mood underestimate their capabilities. They recall many more successes from events that occurred in the happy mood than in the sad mood. These findings suggest that the impact of mood on efficacy beliefs is at least partially mediated by selective recall of past successes and failures.

Kavanagh (1983) tested whether inducing events influence efficacy beliefs through affective or cognitive priming. Happy and sad moods were induced by vivid recall of either a personal triumph or a failure, or by a positive or negative fortuitous experience devoid of successful or failed efforts, as when thoughts of winning a lottery creates euphoria and loss of a pet arouses sorrow. If thought content is the main influencer, then judgmental bias should be more pronounced in conditions emphasizing personal success or failure than in those in which people are made elated or sad by events over

which they exercise no control. The results, though qualified by gender differences, indicate that affect, rather than achievement cognition, is the main carrier of the effect. Efficacy beliefs were raised in a positive affect state and lowered in a negative affect state, regardless of whether the mood was induced by fortuitous events or by success or failure. People then act in accordance with their mood-altered efficacy beliefs, choosing more challenging tasks in a self-efficacious frame of mind than they do when they doubt their efficacy. The relationship between perceived efficacy and challenge seeking is strongest under fortuitously induced affect.

Despondency can lower efficacy beliefs; the lowered beliefs, in turn, weaken motivation and spawn poor performance, breeding even deeper despondency in a downward cycle. In contrast, by raising efficacy beliefs that heighten motivation and performance accomplishments, good mood can set in motion an affirmative reciprocal process. Consider an example in the area of health recovery. Following coronary angioplasty, the more positive the patients' mood, the higher is their sense of personal efficacy and the greater is their engagement in activities that restore cardiovascular function and help to prevent future coronary disease (Jensen, Banwart, Venhaus, Popkess-Vawter, & Perkins, 1993). Mood and efficacy beliefs are related both concurrently and predictively.

The preceding analyses examine only the effects of mood states on efficacy beliefs. Other lines of research that are reviewed in the next chapter reveal a bidirectionality of influence between efficacy beliefs and depression. A low sense of efficacy to gain the things in life that bring self-satisfaction and self-worth breeds depression, and depression, in turn, diminishes belief in one's personal efficacy.

INTEGRATION OF EFFICACY INFORMATION

Our discussions to this point have explored the efficacy implications of diagnostic factors unique to each of the four major modalities of influence. In forming their efficacy judgments, not only do people have to deal with different configurations of efficacy-relevant information conveyed by a given modality but they also have to weight and integrate efficacy information from these diverse sources. To complicate matters, the weights assigned to different types of efficacy information may vary across different domains of functioning. For example, the set of indicants most diagnostic of cognitive capabilities will differ in important respects from those most relevant to physical capabilities. There has been little research on how people process multidimensional efficacy information. There is every reason to believe, however, that efficacy judgments are governed by some common judgmental processes.

The factors that carry efficacy value vary in their informativeness and degree of interrelatedness. Some may be highly reliable indicants of personal capability; others may be much less so and therefore should be given lesser weight. Some factors contribute unique information; others may be highly redundant and therefore do not add any new self-diagnostic information. Relevant factors also vary in the complexity of their relations to judgment of personal capabilities. Some are linearly related, so that the higher the level of a given factor, the stronger the perceived efficacy. Others are related curvilinearly, as, for example, when moderate arousal is regarded as optimal activation for effective performance, but low levels of activation are viewed as demotivating and high levels as disrupting. Linear relationships are much easier to learn than curvilinear ones. Many of these generic judgmental processes have been widely studied within the framework of social judgment theory (Brehmer, 1980; Brehmer & Joyce, 1988; Brunswick, 1952; Hammond, McClelland, & Mumpower, 1980).

The integration rules that people use in forming their efficacy judgments also vary. Some may combine efficacy-relevant factors additively — the more indicants there are, the stronger is the belief of personal capability. Others may use a relative weighting rule in which some factors are weighted more heavily than others. Still others may use a multiplicative combination rule. Here the conjoint impact of factors on efficacy beliefs is greater than simply their additive effect. Efficacy-relevant factors can also be combined configurally. In this type of integration rule, a particular factor is given different weight depending on other available sources of efficacy information. For example, perceived efficacy is unaffected by repeated failure in the context of seeing a person of lesser ability fail on similar problems but is greatly diminished by failure in the context of seeing a person of assumed similarity fail (Brown & Inouye, 1978). Much of the research of Anderson and his colleagues is aimed at identifying the rules people use in integrating multidimensional information into a unitary judgment (Anderson, 1981; Surber, 1984).

In analyzing cognitive integration rules, different judgmental elements are varied factorially and people are asked to make a summary judgment for each particular combination of factors. How they weight the different factors and the rules they use to integrate them are inferred from their judgments across different configurations of information. This type of integration analysis is easy to perform when situations involve only a few judgmental factors. But a large set of judgmental factors, each presented in several levels, produces a large number of different configurations of information. Numerous judgmental situations create a formidable assessment task. For convenience, most of the research on human judgment examines covariations of only a few factors and relies heavily on hypothetical scenarios. Questions arise about the generalizability of findings from placid hypothetical situations to real situations that are emotionally involving, psychologically taxing, and socially consequential. Ebbesen and Konecni (1975) provide some evidence that people's judgments are more complex for hypothetical scenarios than for the commotion of everyday life. They draw on a wide range of factors in judging hypothetical situations but fall back on only a few salient factors in actual situations.

Although common cognitive processes undoubtedly operate in both self-efficacy and nonpersonal judgments, forming conceptions of oneself undoubtedly involves some distinct processes as well. It is a rare person who is entirely dispassionate about himself or herself. Self-referent experiences are more likely to pose threats to self-esteem and social valuation than are experiences involving other persons or objects. Such threats can produce self-exaggeration or self-belittlement in judgments of personal capabilities. Affect can have markedly different effects on personal and social judgment. Thus, depressive mood lowers judgments of efficacy to control events but inflates judgments of the controlling efficacy of others under identical outcome feedback (Martin, Abramson, & Alloy, 1984). Activation of self-referent processes may distort self-monitoring of multiform experiences and how they are remembered, organized, and retrieved. The research reviewed earlier documents about the way in which emotional states bias these different cognitive processes.

In addition to the judgmental biasing effect of emotional states, people are poor at weighting and integrating multidimensional information (Nisbett & Ross, 1980; Slovic, Fischhoff, & Lichtenstein, 1977; Tversky & Kahneman, 1974). When faced with multiform information, they typically handle the cognitive strain by relying on only a few factors and simplified judgmental rules rather than engaging in detailed analyses of all potentially relevant factors. They pay little attention to redundancy in the diagnostic information conveyed by different factors and thus raise their self-assurance on the basis of noninformative factors. They are easily swayed by salient instances that spring readily to mind. Their judgments can be unduly biased by the standards of attainment exemplified by others to whom they happen to be exposed or whom they select without much consideration of their appropriateness. Such tendencies can lead people to ignore or to misweight relevant information. Although simplifying heuristics often aid judgment, they produce cognitive biases that can easily lead one astray. People's descriptions of the factors they used in making their judgments have been compared with computed weights of how heavily different factors contributed to their actual judgments. The findings show that when people describe what they believe influenced their judgment, they tend to underestimate their reliance on important factors and overweight those of lesser value.

The ability to discern, weight, and integrate relevant sources of efficacy information improves with the development of cognitive skills for processing information. These include attentional, memory, inferential, and integrative cognitive capabilities for forming self-conceptions of efficacy. The development of self-appraisal skills also relies on growth of self-reflective metacognitive skills to evaluate the adequacy of one's self-assessments. Evaluation of one's self-diagnostic skills requires not only self-knowledge of capabilities but also understanding of the types of skills needed for different activities. The adequacy of one's self-assessments is tested by comparing the goodness of the match between self-appraisals and actual attainments. Good matches corroborate one's self-appraisal skills; repeated mismatches question one's ability to judge what one can do. Continuing misjudgments call for self-corrective changes in how efficacy information is selected and cognitively processed. The development of self-appraisal skills is analyzed in a later chapter on developmental changes in personal efficacy across the life span. Later chapters also address issues of how to alter dysfunctional self-efficacy appraisals.

The multiple benefits of a strong sense of personal efficacy do not arise simply from the incantation of capability. Saying something should not be confused with believing it to be so. Simply saying that one is capable is not necessarily self-convincing, especially when it contradicts preexisting beliefs. For example, no amount of self-declaration that one can fly will be personally persuading that one has the efficacy to get oneself airborne and remain aloft. A sense of personal efficacy is constructed through a complex process of self-persuasion. Efficacy beliefs are the product of cognitive processing of diverse sources of efficacy information conveyed enactively, vicariously, socially, and physiologically. Once formed, efficacy beliefs contribute to the quality of human functioning in diverse ways. They do so by enlisting cognitive, motivational, affective, and decisional processes through which accomplishments are realized. These efficacy-regulated processes are examined next.

4

Mediating Processes

THE DISCUSSION SO FAR HAS addressed issues related to the nature and structure of efficacy belief systems, the influential role they play in causal structures, and the experiential sources of personal efficacy. This chapter is concerned with the processes through which efficacy beliefs produce their effects. Such beliefs influence how people feel, think, motivate themselves, and act. A substantial body of literature shows that efficacy beliefs regulate human functioning through four major processes. They include cognitive, motivational, affective and selective processes. Some of these efficacy-activated events, such as emotional states, are of interest in their own right rather than merely as intervening influencers of action. These different processes usually operate in concert, rather than in isolation, in the ongoing regulation of human functioning.

COGNITIVE PROCESSES

Efficacy beliefs affect thought patterns that can enhance or undermine performance. These cognitive effects take various forms. People who have a high sense of efficacy take a future time perspective in structuring their lives. Much human behavior, being purposive, is regulated by forethought that embodies cognized goals. Personal goal setting is influenced by self-appraisal of capabilities. The stronger the perceived self-efficacy, the higher the goals people set for themselves and the firmer their commitment to them (Bandura & Wood, 1989; Locke & Latham, 1990). Perceived collective efficacy similarly raises the goals that groups set for themselves in collective endeavors (Prussia & Kinicki, 1996). Challenging goals raise the level of motivation and performance attainments.

Cognitive Constructions

Most courses of action are initially shaped in thought. The cognitive constructions then serve as guides for action in the development of proficiencies (Bandura, 1986a; Carroll & Bandura, 1990). People's beliefs about their efficacy influence how they construe situations and the types of anticipatory scenarios and visualized futures they construct. Those who have a high sense of efficacy view situations as presenting realizable opportunities. They visualize success scenarios that provide positive guides for performance. Those who judge themselves as inefficacious construe uncertain situations as risky and are inclined to visualize failure scenarios (Krueger & Dickson, 1994). Cognitive negativity that dwells on personal deficiencies and how things are likely to go wrong is a good way to undermine self-motivation and performance. It is difficult to achieve much while fighting self-doubt. Numerous studies have shown that cognitive simulations, in which individuals visualize themselves executing activities skillfully, enhance subsequent performance (Bandura, 1986a; Corbin, 1972; Feltz & Landers, 1983; Kazdin, 1978). Visualizing successful actions improves performances; imaging faulty ones impairs them (Powell, 1973). Perceived self-efficacy and cognitive simulation affect each other bidirectionally. A high sense of efficacy fosters cognitive constructions of effective courses of action, and cognitive enactments of efficacious actions, in turn, strengthen efficacy beliefs (Bandura & Adams, 1977; Kazdin, 1979).

Inferential Thinking

A major function of thought is to enable people to predict the likely outcomes of different courses of action and to create the means for exercising control over those that affect their lives. Many activities involve inferential judgments about how actions affect outcomes. Such problem-solving skills require effective cognitive processing of multifaceted information that contains many complexities, ambiguities, and uncertainties. The fact that predictive factors are usually related probabilistically, rather than invariably, to future events creates some degree of uncertainty. The fact that the same predictor may contribute to different effects and the same effect may have multiple predictors creates additional uncertainty as to what is likely to lead to what in probabilistic environments. In ferreting out predictive rules, people must draw on their preexisting knowledge to construct options, to weight and integrate predictive factors into composite rules, to test and revise their judgments against the immediate and distal results of their actions, and to remember which factors they have tested and how well they

have worked. It requires a strong sense of efficacy to remain fully task oriented in the face of causal ambiguities, pressing situational demands, and judgment failures that can have important personal and social repercussions.

The powerful influence of efficacy beliefs on self-regulatory cognitive processes is revealed in a program of research on complex organizational decision making (Wood & Bandura, 1989a). Much of the research on human decision making involves discrete judgments in static environments under nontaxing conditions (Beach, Barnes, & Christensen-Szalanski, 1986; Hogarth, 1981). Judgments under such circumstances may not provide a sufficient basis for developing either descriptive or normative models of decision making in dynamic naturalistic environments. In such environments, decisions must be made from a wide array of information within a continuing flow of activity under time constraints and social and self-evaluative consequences. Moreover, prior decisions shape or impose constraints on later ones. To complicate matters further, organizational decision making requires working through others and coordinating, monitoring, and managing collective efforts. Many of the decisional rules for effective management of dynamic environments must be learned through exploratory experiences while coping with ongoing organizational activities. Under these more complex transactional conditions, self-regulative, affective, and motivational factors can exert substantial impact on the quality of decision making.

In research that encompasses these dynamic aspects of decision making, business school graduates manage a computer-simulated organization devised by Wood and Bailey (1985). They must match employees to subfunctions based on information about the employees' unique skills, experiences, and job preferences. They also have to make decisions about three motivational factors they could use to optimize the group's performance. For each employee, they must decide what goals to set, the type and amount of supervisory feedback to provide, and how to use social incentives to enhance motivation. They manage varying production activities and receive feedback on the level of organizational performance achieved based on the quality of their managerial decisions. In short, the managers must discover how personnel assignments and motivational factors affect group performance. Some of these factors involve nonlinear rules. For example, goals that provide an optimal level of challenge are motivating, whereas those that are too easy or unattainably difficult are demotivating. Other decisions involve compound rules in which several factors have to be considered together. Thus, level of commendation must consider not only quality of work but equity in the group as a whole. These types of relations between decisional actions and group performance are more difficult to learn than are linear ones in which the higher the factor, the better the outcome (Brehmer, Hagafors, & Johansson, 1980). Moreover, managers must figure out the best way to integrate the set of rules and to apply them discerningly to each member of the group in a coherent managerial effort. At periodic intervals, the managers are assessed on their perceived managerial efficacy, the goals they seek to achieve, the adequacy of their analytic thinking in discovering managerial rules, and the level of organizational performance they realize.

Organizational characteristics and belief systems that can enhance or undermine cognitive functioning are varied experimentally to evaluate the contribution of self-regulatory factors to complex decision making. One important belief system concerns the conception of ability (M. Bandura & Dweck, 1988; Dweck, 1991; Nicholls, 1984). Some people regard ability as an *acquirable skill* that can be increased by gaining knowledge and perfecting competencies. They adopt a functional learning goal. They seek challenges that provide opportunities to expand their knowledge and competencies. They regard errors as a natural part of the learning process. One learns from mistakes. Missteps and setbacks are viewed not as personal failures but as learning experiences indicating that greater effort or better strategies are needed to succeed. Such people judge their capabilities and measure their successes more by personal improvement than by comparison against the achievement of others. When skill is viewed as something that is changeable, rate

of self-improvement is of greater interest than how one's transitory level of attainment happens to compare with that of others. Failure leads these individuals to seek more information about their capabilities that can help to guide further self-development (Dunning, 1995). By contrast, people who view ability as a more or less *inherent aptitude* regard performance level as diagnostic of endowed capacity. Errors and deficient performances carry high evaluative threat because they signify intellectual limitations. Therefore, such individuals prefer tasks that minimize errors and permit ready display of their intellectual proficiency at the expense of expanding their knowledge and competencies. In self-protection, they shun opportunities to learn more about their proficiencies when they do poorly. High effort is also threatening because it presumably reveals low ability. These people are prone to measure their ability by social comparison and to belittle their own accomplishments when others surpass them.

Conceptions of ability as either an acquirable skill or an inherent aptitude, instilled experimentally, exert strong effects on the self-regulatory mechanisms governing cognitive functioning and performance accomplishments (Wood & Bandura, 1989b). These conceptions of ability bias how substandard performances are cognitively processed. Construal of low attainments as indicants of inherent personal deficiencies erodes a sense of efficacy, whereas construal of the same low attainments as instructive guides for enhancing personal competencies sustains it. Such evolving self-beliefs further bias cognitive processing of attainments and promote actions that create confirmatory behavioral evidence for them. This produces an exacerbation cycle of motivational and performance impairment under the inherent capacity view and proficient functioning under the acquirable skill view. Thus, managers who view decision-making ability as reflecting inherent cognitive aptitude are beset by increasing self-doubts about their efficacy as they encounter problems (Fig. 4.1). They become more and more erratic in their analytic thinking. They lower their organizational aspirations. They achieve progressively less with the organization they are

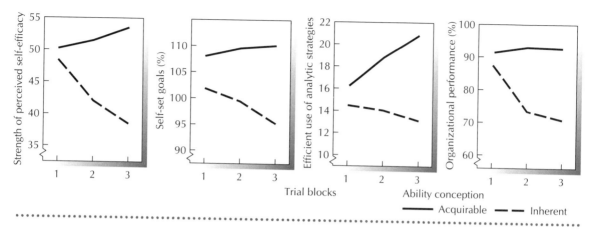

FIGURE 4.1. Changes in perceived managerial self-efficacy, the performance goals set for the organization relative to the present standard, effective use of analytical strategies, and achieved level of organizational performance across blocks of production tasks under instilled conceptions of ability as an acquirable skill or as an inherent intellectual aptitude. Each trial block includes six different production tasks. (Wood & Bandura, 1989b).

managing. In contrast, construal of ability as an acquirable skill fosters a highly resilient sense of personal efficacy. Under this belief system, the managers remain steadfast in their beliefs in their managerial efficacy even when performance standards are difficult to fulfill. They continue to set themselves challenging organizational goals, and they use analytic strategies in efficient ways that aid discovery of optimal managerial decision rules. Such a self-efficacious orientation pays off in high organizational attainments.

People often forsake realizable challenges because they believe they require extraordinary aptitude. Inborn capacities, of course, place constraints on what is achievable. Potentialities are converted to functioning realities through extensive guided effort. People see the extraordinary feats of others but not the unwavering commitment and countless hours of perseverant effort that produced them. Such partial information generally leads people to overestimate inherited endowments and underestimate self-regulatory factors in human accomplishments. Viewing ability as an inherent capacity lowers perceived self-efficacy, retards skill development, and diminishes interest in the activity

(Jourden, Bandura, & Banfield, 1991). Although belief in the acquirability of talent is conducive to high personal development, it does not necessarily ensure it. Many people are reluctant to go through the drudgery of perfecting skills that enable them to perform at extraordinary levels.

Conceptions of ability should not be viewed as monolithic traits that govern the whole of life. The same person may view ability differently in different domains of functioning. For example, a novelist might regard writing as a perfectible craft but mathematical competencies as heavily dependent on inborn aptitude, whereas a mathematician might make the opposite differentiation in the ease of acquirability of competencies in these two domains. Preexisting conceptions of ability are changeable through social influence. Thus, children who were easily debilitated by failures because they regarded them as indicative of inherent deficiencies take failures in their stride and perform more competently after being persuaded that ability is an acquirable skill (Elliott & Dweck, 1988). The studies discussed above identify self-regulatory mechanisms through which conceptions of ability affect learning and performance.

We saw in Chapter 3 that social comparison operates as a pervasive influence in the self-appraisal of capabilities. The research on organizational decision making provides confirmatory results that the impact of comparative influences on performance attainments is mediated through self-regulatory mechanisms (Bandura & Jourden, 1991). Business graduates managed the simulated organization and received accurate feedback about their own performance attainments but preset feedback on how well others allegedly performed the role. In the *similar* condition, the comparative information showed the managers performing as well as the comparison group of decision makers; in the *superior* condition, they consistently surpassed the comparison group; in the *progressive mastery* condition, the managers were shown performing more poorly than the comparison group at the outset but gradually closing the gap and eventually surpassing their counterparts; and in the *progressive decline* condition, they were shown doing slightly better than their counterparts at the outset but then beginning to fall behind and ending well below the comparison group of decision makers.

The contrasting conditions of comparative mastery and decline are of special psychological interest (Fig. 4.2). The comparative decliners displayed a precipitous drop in their perceived managerial efficacy, their analytic thinking remained erratic, and they were unremittingly self-critical of their performance attainments. By contrast, the comparative masterers heightened their perceived self-efficacy, they improved their use of efficient analytic strategies for ferreting out predictive rules, and their affective self-reactions provided a dual source of motivation — namely, self-discontent with comparative substandard performances but a self-rewarding sense of satisfaction with their rising accomplishments. These divergent patterns of self-regulatory influence were accompanied by corresponding divergent changes in performance attainments. Whereas the decliners produced a progressive deterioration of group performance, the masterers boosted the level of their group's attainments as their comparative status ostensibly improved. Path analyses corroborate previous findings that, with cumulative experience, efficacy beliefs exert increased impact on performance attainments.

Another important belief system that affects how efficacy information is cognitively processed is people's beliefs about the extent to which their environment is influenceable or controllable. People who are

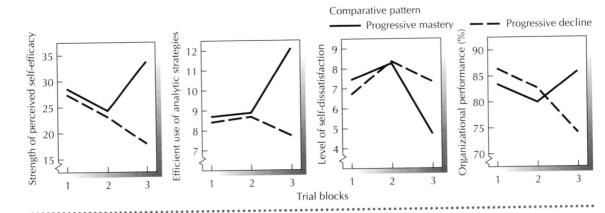

FIGURE 4.2. Changes in perceived managerial self-efficacy, quality of analytical thinking, level of self-satisfaction, and achieved level of organizational performance across blocks of production tasks under comparative appraisals suggesting progressive mastery or progressive decline relative to a similar comparison group of managers. Each trial block includes six different production tasks. (Bandura & Jourden, 1991)

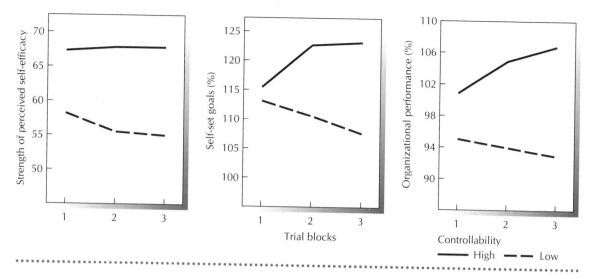

FIGURE 4.3. Changes in strength of perceived managerial self-efficacy, the performance goals set for the organization, and level of organizational performance for managers who operated under an instilled cognitive set that the organizations are controllable or difficult to control. Each trial block includes six different production tasks. (Bandura & Wood, 1989)

harried by self-doubts anticipate the futility of efforts to modify their life situation. They are much less likely to undertake and sustain actions designed to improve their circumstances than are those who have a firm belief in their efficacy to bring about meaningful social change. The organizational simulation research underscores the strong impact of perceived controllability on the self-regulatory factors governing decision making that can enhance or impede performance (Bandura & Wood, 1989). People who managed the simulated organization under an instilled cognitive set that organizations are not easily changeable quickly lost faith in their decision-making capabilities even when performance standards were within easy reach (Fig. 4.3). They lowered their aspirations. Their group's performance deteriorated. Those who operated under an instilled cognitive set that organizations are controllable exhibited high resiliency of self-efficacy even in the face of numerous difficulties. They set themselves increasingly challenging goals and used good analytic thinking to discover effective managerial rules. Their group performed at a high level and continued to get even better over time.

Path analyses of the pattern of influences confirm the postulated causal ordering of self-regulatory determinants. When initially faced with managing a complex unfamiliar environment, people relied heavily on their past performance in judging their efficacy and setting their personal goals. But as they began to form a self-schema about their efficacy through further experience, the performance system was regulated more strongly and intricately by efficacy beliefs (Fig. 4.4). As self-conceptions get affirmed through growing experience, performance becomes more heavily laden with nonability self-regulatory determinants. Efficacy beliefs influence performance both directly and through their strong effects on personal goal setting and proficient analytic thinking. Personal goals, in turn, enhance performance attainments through the mediation of analytic strategies.

The combined findings from this series of experiments document that diverse psychosocial influences alter efficacy beliefs, which, in turn, influence performance attainments both directly and through their effects on cognized goals and efficiency of analytic thinking. Regardless of whether it

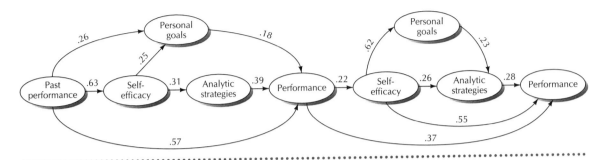

FIGURE 4.4. Path analysis of causal structures of organizational management. The numbers on the paths of influence are the significant standardized path coefficients. The network of relationships on the left side of the figure are for the initial managerial efforts, and those on the right side are for later managerial efforts. (Wood & Bandura, 1989a)

is conceptions of ability, social comparison, or beliefs about the influenceability of the environment, these influences work in part through efficacy beliefs and the aspirational and strategic thinking they promote. Other studies provide further evidence that efficacy beliefs affect the generation and use of problem-solving strategies. Among students equated for ability but differing in perceived self-efficacy, those with a strong sense of efficacy are quicker to discard faulty cognitive strategies in the search for better ones and are less inclined to reject good solutions prematurely (Bouffard-Bouchard, Parent, & Larivée, 1991; Collins, 1982). Our discussion in this chapter focuses on the impact of efficacy beliefs on the use of cognitive guides and skills. We will see in Chapter 6 that efficacy beliefs affect the rate with which cognitive skills are acquired as well as how effectively preexisting cognitive capabilities are used.

MOTIVATIONAL PROCESSES

The capability for self-motivation and purposive action is rooted in cognitive activity. Future states cannot be causes of current motivation or action. The projected future can be brought into the present through forethought, however. By being cognitively represented in the present, conceived future states are converted into current motivators and regulators of behavior. In this functional explanation of purposive behavior, having adopted a certain goal, people then act for the sake of realizing it. Yet a goal is not the agent of its own realization. Forethought is translated into incentives and courses of action through the aid of self-regulatory mechanisms. Most human motivation is cognitively generated. In cognitive motivation, people motivate themselves and guide their actions anticipatorily through the exercise of forethought. They form beliefs about what they can do, they anticipate likely positive and negative outcomes of different pursuits, and they set goals for themselves and plan courses of action designed to realize valued futures and avoid aversive ones. Efficacy beliefs play a central role in the cognitive regulation of motivation.

One can distinguish three different forms of cognitive motivators around which different theories have been built. These include *causal attributions*, *outcome expectancies*, and *cognized goals*. The corresponding theories are attribution theory, expectancy-value theory, and goal theory. Figure 4.5 summarizes these alternative conceptions of cognitive motivation schematically. Outcome and goal motivators clearly operate through

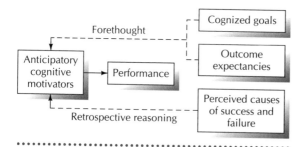

FIGURE 4.5. Schematic representation of conceptions of cognitive motivation based on cognized goals, outcome expectancies, and causal attributions.

the anticipation mechanism. Causal reasons conceived retrospectively for prior attainments can also affect future actions anticipatorily by altering judgment of personal capabilities and perception of task demands. The self-efficacy mechanism of personal agency operates in all of these variant forms of cognitive motivation.

Attribution Theory

According to the attribution theory of motivation (Weiner, 1985), retrospective judgments of the causes of one's performances have motivational effects. People who credit their successes to personal capabilities and their failures to insufficient effort will undertake difficult tasks and persist in the face of failure. They do this because they see their outcomes as influenceable by how much effort they expend. In contrast, those who ascribe their failures to deficiencies in ability and their successes to situational factors will display low strivings and give up readily when they encounter difficulties.

Some writers have argued that reasons offered retrospectively should not be regarded as causes. This is obviously true for past actions, which precede ascribed causes and would, therefore, involve backward causation. But reasons for past performances that affect beliefs of personal capability can serve as causes of future actions. Thus, people who believe they failed because they did not work hard enough are likely to strive harder, whereas those

who believe they failed because they lack the ability are apt to slacken their efforts and become easily discouraged. Causal attributions can serve different purposes, however. For example, Covington and Omelich (1979) provide evidence that causal attributions may sometimes function as self-serving excuses that do not affect future performances. The question of when causal attributions function as excuses and when as motivators warrants investigation.

The role of attributional judgments in human motivation is clarified by research in which causal attributions for ongoing performances are systematically varied by providing arbitrary explanations for successes and failures. Changes in efficacy beliefs and performance attainments are then measured. The results indicate that causal attributions can influence achievement strivings, but the effect is mediated almost entirely through changes in perceived self-efficacy (Relich, Debus, & Walker, 1986; Schunk & Gunn, 1986; Schunk & Rice, 1986). The more the arbitrary reasons raise efficacy beliefs, the higher are the subsequent performance attainments.

Attributions of success to ability are accompanied by heightened beliefs of personal efficacy, which, in turn, predict subsequent performance attainments. Effort attributions, on the other hand, have variable effects on efficacy beliefs. These diverse findings raise questions about the conception of ability espoused by attribution theory and how effort is related to it. Attribution theorists usually treat ability as a stable or enduring internal characteristic of the person. High effort needed to achieve success is taken as an indicant of low ability (Kun, 1977). In actuality, people vary in their conceptions of ability and alter their views about the relation between effort and ability with increasing experience (M. Bandura & Dweck, 1988; Dweck & Leggett, 1988; Nicholls & Miller, 1984). The presumptions of attributional theory fit the subgroups of people who regard ability as a stable inherent attribute. Many individuals, however, construe ability as an acquirable skill that is developed through effort: The harder you work at it, the more capable you become. For them, errors reflect inexperience in the activity, which effort rectifies, rather than inherent inability. High effort that begets rising accomplishments can thus enhance efficacy beliefs (Schunk & Cox, 1986). We have already seen that conception of ability as a stable internal attribute often serves as an impediment to the development of complex competencies and increases vulnerability to distress and dysfunction in the face of difficulties.

Just as ability is not necessarily fixed and personally uncontrollable, effort is not necessarily easily controllable. People who labor hard without success do not believe that they can mount and sustain higher effort (Bandura & Cervone, 1986). Many of those who succeed through extraordinary effort seriously doubt they can repeat the feat. The impact of effort attributions on efficacy beliefs will vary under different conceptions of ability and differing views of the controllability of effort. For example, high effort will be positively correlated with beliefs of personal efficacy for individuals who consider ability acquirable by hard work, but negatively correlated for those who regard ability as an inherent attribute so that struggle signifies deficient capability. Because people view the conditional relations among factors differently, it is not entirely surprising that effort attributions do not bear a uniform relationship to efficacy beliefs. Regardless of whether effort attributions correlate positively or negatively with perceived efficacy, however, the stronger the efficacy beliefs, the higher the subsequent performance attainments (Schunk & Cox, 1986; Schunk & Gunn, 1986; Schunk & Rice, 1986).

In judging their efficacy from performance attainments, people use much more varied sources of enactive efficacy information than the four causal factors (effort, ability, task difficulty, chance) routinely assessed in attributional research. As will be recalled from the earlier discussion, in addition to perceptions of task difficulty and amount of effort expended, people consider whether they performed under favorable or unfavorable circumstances, the amount of external aid they received, their physical and emotional state at the time, and the pattern of their successes and failures with continued engagement in the activity. Positive or negative biases in the self-monitoring, cognitive representation, and retrieval of past successes and failures also affect judgments of personal efficacy. Whereas attribution theory is concerned solely with perceived causes of performance successes and failures, self-efficacy theory encompasses modeling and persuasory and affective sources of efficacy information as well as enactive ones. The competencies and strategies that models exhibit and the comparative ability information that they convey figure prominently in people's judgment of their efficacy. Indeed, when personal capability is gauged relationally, as is often the case, modeled efficacy information can override the influence of performance experiences in appraisal of personal efficacy (Brown & Inouye, 1978). Moreover, the appraisals of significant others and perceptions of somatic and affective states enter into the process of judging personal efficacy.

The relative weight given to information about perceived adeptness, effort, task complexity, and situational circumstances will affect appraisal of personal efficacy. Efficacy beliefs, in turn, bias causal attributions. Self-efficacious individuals view attainments as personally controllable. Therefore, those who regard themselves as highly efficacious tend to ascribe their failures to insufficient effort or situational impediments, whereas those with a low sense of efficacy view the cause of their failures as stemming from lack of ability. The influence of efficacy beliefs on causal attributions is highly reproducible across cognitive attainments (Matsui, Konishi, Onglatco, Matsuda, & Ohnishi, 1988; Silver et al., 1995), interpersonal transactions (Alden, 1986), physical performances (Courneya & McAuley, 1993; McAuley et al., 1989), and management of health habits (Grove, 1993). Performance feedback that is inconsistent with perceived self-efficacy is dismissed as less accurate and is more apt to be attributed to extraneous factors than is feedback that is consistent with one's sense of efficacy.

The overall evidence reveals that causal attributions, whether in the form of ability, effort, or task difficulty, generally have weak or no independent effect on performance motivation. Perceived self-efficacy mediates the effect of causal attributions on performance across such diverse activities as academic performances (Relich et al., 1986; Schunk & Gunn, 1986) and occupational burnout (Chwalisz, Altmaier, & Russell, 1992). The types of factors singled out by attribution theory serve as conveyors of efficacy-relevant information that influence performance attainments mainly by altering people's beliefs in their efficacy. Sometimes, ability attribution emerges as an independent contributor to performance motivation, but such direct effects tend to be small and equivocal.

It is no easy matter to devise interventions to raise human motivation and accomplishments solely by changing causal attributions. Prediction studies abound, but intervention studies designed to produce enduring personal change by attribution retraining are hard to come by. To begin with, there is some disagreement about the types of causal attributions that should be promoted (Grove, 1993). If people are led to believe that their difficulties stem from internal but changeable factors, the net result may be self-blame rather than heightened motivation if the personal impediments do not lend themselves readily to modification without additional resources and mastery performance aids. Conversely, if difficulties are attributed to external changeable factors, people have less incentive to build their competencies and easily fall back on situational excuses if their situations do not change for the better. Causal attributions can temporarily raise motivation, but the boost will not survive for long in the absence of affirming accomplishments. To keep telling individuals who lack essential skills that their failures are due to insufficient effort can be demoralizing. To keep telling them they have high capabilities while their repeated failures tell them otherwise only discredits the attributers. Not surprisingly, efforts to alter refractory behavior by attribution retraining alone have met with limited success, whereas sociocognitive programs fostering personal enablement produce uniformly beneficial changes (Bandura, 1986a). Persuasory attributions can serve as supplementary motivators but not as a primary mode of generating human motivation and accomplishments.

Expectancy-Value Theory

People also motivate themselves and guide their actions anticipatorily by the outcomes they expect to flow from given courses of behavior. Expectancy-value theory was designed to account for this form of incentive motivation (Ajzen & Fishbein, 1980; Atkinson, 1964; Rotter, 1982; Vroom, 1964). These various formulations all assume that strength of motivation is governed jointly by the expectation that particular actions will produce specified outcomes, and the attractiveness of those outcomes. They differ mainly in what additional determinants are combined with expectancy and outcome value. Atkinson adds an achievement motive; Rotter adds a generalized expectancy that actions control outcomes; Ajzen and Fishbein add perceived social pressures to perform the behavior and proneness to compliance; Vroom adds belief that the behavior is achievable through effort.

In its basic version, the expectancy-value theory predicts that the higher the expectancy that certain behavior can secure specific outcomes and the more highly those outcomes are valued, the greater is the motivation to perform the activity. The findings generally show that outcome expectations obtained by adding or multiplying these cognitive factors predict performance motivation (Feather, 1982; Mitchell, 1974; Schwab, Olian-Gottlieb, & Heneman, 1979). The amount of variance in performance motivation explained by this model is generally smaller than might be expected, however. This has stimulated spirited debates about the scope of the expectancy-value theory, its major assumptions, and the methodologies used for assessing and combining the cognitive factors.

According to maximizing expectancy models, people seek to optimize their outcomes. But people are not as systematic in considering alternative courses of action and in weighing their likely consequences as expectancy-value models assume. The issue in question is not the rationality of the judgmental process. People often have incomplete or erroneous information about alternatives and their probable consequences, they process information through cognitive biases, and what they value may be rather odd. Decisions that are subjectively rational to the performer, given the basis on which they were made, may appear irrational to others. Subjective rationality often sponsors faulty choices. The judgmental process encompasses too many aspects where one can go astray to achieve objective rationality (Brandt, 1979). The main issue in dispute is the disparity between the postulated judgmental process and how people actually go about appraising and weighing the probable consequences of alternative courses of action. Chapter 10 addresses this issue in some detail.

The types of anticipated incentives singled out for attention is another dimension on which expectancy-value theory often departs from actuality. Some of the most valued rewards of activities are in the self-satisfactions derived from fulfilling personal standards. The self-satisfaction for personal accomplishments may be valued more highly than tangible payoffs. When these two sources of incentives conflict, self-evaluative outcomes often override the influence of tangible rewards (Bandura, 1986a). Because incentive theories of motivation tend to neglect affective self-evaluative outcomes, self-incentives rarely receive the consideration they deserve in the option-outcome analysis. Predictiveness is sacrificed if influential self-incentives are overlooked. With regard to the scope of the expectancy-value model, even the elaborated versions include only a few cognitive motivators. In actuality, forethought of outcomes influences effort and performance through additional intervening mechanisms.

People act on their beliefs about what they can do as well as their beliefs about the likely effects of various actions. The motivating potential of outcome expectancies is partly governed by beliefs of personal capabilities. There are many activities that, if done well, guarantee valued outcomes, but they are not pursued by people who doubt they can do what it takes to succeed (Beck & Lund, 1981; Betz & Hackett, 1986; Dzewaltowski et al., 1990; Wheeler, 1983). An example would be students who expect that a medical degree will bring highly valued social status and material rewards but shy away from medical studies because they believe they lack the ability to master the heavy scientific premedical course work. A low sense of efficacy can thus nullify the motivating potential of alluring outcome expectations. Conversely, firm belief in one's efficacy can sustain efforts over prolonged periods in the face of uncertain or repeated negative outcomes. Indeed, high accomplishments require a resilient sense of personal efficacy because the road to success is usually strewn with countless impediments.

In activities that call upon competencies, efficacy beliefs affect the extent to which people act on their outcome expectations. Thus, in activities in which outcomes depend on quality of performance, efficacy beliefs determine the types of outcomes that are foreseen. When variations in efficacy beliefs are controlled statistically, the outcomes expected for given performances contribute little to the prediction of behavior, as previously documented. Some expectancy-value theories include an expectancy that effort will beget the needed performances (Vroom, 1964). In these theories, the effort factor is usually construed as a generalized expectancy that effort can beget certain performances. In contrast, efficacy beliefs are concerned with personal capabilities to produce certain performances. Expectancies about the general value of effort bear little relationship to beliefs of personal efficacy (Danehower, 1988). People regulate their performances by beliefs of what they can do rather than by expectations of what effort can do for others. Danehower shows this to be the case. Efficacy beliefs contribute to performance, whereas generalized effort expectancy does not.

It should also be noted that perceived self-efficacy is a broader construct than effort expectancy because it encompasses much more than effort determinants of performance. Effort is but one of many factors that govern the level and quality of performance. People judge their capabilities for challenging activities in terms of the knowledge, skills, and strategies they have at their command rather than solely on how much they can exert themselves. Performances that call for ingenuity, resourcefulness, and adaptability depend more on adroit use of skills, specialized knowledge, and analytic strategies than on simple dint of effort (Wood

& Bandura, 1989a). Moreover, people who cope poorly with stressors expect that marred performances in intimidating situations will be determined by their self-debilitating thought patterns rather than by how much effort they mount. Indeed, the harder they try, the more likely they are to impair their execution of the activity. Expectancy theorists probably singled out effort as the sole cause of performance because the theory has usually been concerned with how hard people work at routine activities unimpeded by obstacles or threats. Hence, the aspect of self-efficacy that is most germane to how much is accomplished is people's perceived perseverant capabilities — that is, their belief that they can exert themselves sufficiently to attain required levels of productivity.

Recent efforts to increase the predictiveness of expectancy-value models have added an efficacy-like factor to the usual set of predictors. For example, in the Ajzen and Fishbein (1980) model of reasoned action, the intention to engage in a course of action is governed by two components: a personal determinant in the form of perceived outcomes and their valuation; and a subjective normative determinant combining perceived social pressures by significant others to perform or refrain from a given behavior and one's motivation to comply with their expectations. Ajzen (1985) expanded this model by including perceived behavioral control, which presumably comes into play when there are difficulties in performing a behavior. This version is called a theory of planned behavior. Ajzen and his colleagues have shown that perceived behavioral control affects performance both directly and indirectly through its effects on intention (Ajzen & Madden, 1986; Schifter & Ajzen, 1985). Perceived self-efficacy exerts similar direct and indirect influence on performance in conjunction with perceived outcomes and social pressures (deVries & Backbier, 1994; deVries, Dijkstra, & Kuhlman, 1988; Dzewaltowski et al., 1990; Kok, deVries, Mudde, & Strecher, 1991; Schwarzer, 1992). Therefore, when perceived self-efficacy is added to the original set of expectancy predictors, perceived control makes no independent contribution to performance motivation (Dzewaltowski, 1989). In activities that are not subject to much social pressure, efficacy beliefs carry most of the explanatory power, and perceived outcomes and normative influences do not account for variations in motivation (Dzewaltowski et al., 1990). The predictiveness of other versions of expectancy-value theory is enhanced by including the self-efficacy determinant (McCaul et al., 1988; Wheeler, 1983).

In the theory of reasoned action, perceived behavioral control is defined and measured in terms of perceived ease or difficulty in performing a required behavior. Perceived difficulty is, of course, a relational concept involving perceived capability to fulfill perceived task demands. The less efficacious people judge themselves to be, the more difficult the tasks will appear to them. Indeed, the research of Dzewaltowski and his colleagues indicates that perceived behavioral control corresponds to the self-efficacy determinant, as suggested by Ajzen. In some studies, the constructs appear to differ, but the measure of perceived behavioral control is a confounded one that bears little resemblance to perceived difficulty. For example, some researchers combine intentions with perceived efficacy of the behavioral strategy rather than measuring perceived difficulty (McCaul et al., 1993). Others include a mixture of knowledge of what to do, ability to influence outcomes, and understanding of social expectations, which also have little to do with perceived difficulty (Stevens, Bavetta, & Gist, 1993). Still others treat perceived efficacy as perceptions of task difficulty, which is actually Ajzen's operationalization of perceived control (Terry & O'Leary, 1995). Barring insurmountable environmental constraints, highly self-efficacious individuals may view certain undertakings as inherently difficult but believe firmly that they can succeed through ingenuity and perseverant effort. This is precisely what characterizes notable achievers, innovators, and social reformers. Comparative tests of the two constructs should use measures that are equivalent in scope but differ in whether they center on perceived capability or perceived difficulty. Moreover, efficacy beliefs should be measured against levels of challenge rather than by a few indefinite items.

The contribution of efficacy beliefs to incentive-based motivation has also been evaluated when people are given actual monetary incentives for performance attainments rather than just assessed for the types of benefits they would expect for given performances. Lee, Locke, and Phan (in press) examined performance under hourly, piece rate, or bonus compensation tied to fulfillment of different performance standards. They also measured a variety of possible mediators of the incentive effects. After controlling for ability, perceived efficacy and personal goals were the key mediators through which pay incentives affected level of performance. Regardless of the incentive system, persons of high efficacy and goals outperformed those who doubted their efficacy to meet difficult standards and scaled down their aspirations accordingly.

Goal Theory

The capacity to exercise self-influence by personal challenge and evaluative reaction to one's own performances provides a major cognitive mechanism of motivation and self-directedness. In this form of anticipatory self-regulation, behavior is motivated and directed by cognized goals rather than being pulled by an unrealized future state. The causal agency resides in forethought and in the self-regulatory mechanisms by which forethought is translated into incentives and guides for purposive action. Motivation through pursuit of challenging standards has been the subject of extensive research on goal setting. Evidence from numerous laboratory and field studies shows that explicit, challenging goals enhance motivation. This is a remarkably robust effect that is replicated across diverse activity domains, settings, populations, social levels, and time spans (Locke & Latham, 1990; Mento, Steel, & Karren, 1987). Goals operate largely through self-reactive influences rather than regulating motivation and action directly. Perceived self-efficacy is one of the important self-influences through which personal standards create powerful motivational effects.

Motivation based on personal standards involves a process of cognitive comparison of perceived performance to an adopted personal standard. By making self-satisfaction conditional on matching the standard, people give direction to their actions and create self-incentives to persist in their efforts until their performances match their goals. They seek self-satisfactions from fulfilling valued goals and are prompted to intensify their efforts by discontent with substandard performances. Activation of self-evaluation processes through cognitive comparison requires both comparative factors: a personal standard and knowledge of one's performance level. Simply adopting a goal without knowing how one is doing, or knowing how one is doing in the absence of a goal, has no lasting motivational impact (Bandura & Cervone, 1983; Becker, 1978; Strang, Lawrence, & Fowler, 1978). But the combined influence of goals with knowledge of performance heightens motivation substantially.

Self-Reactive Influences as Mediators of Goal Motivation

Cognitive motivation based on goals or standards is mediated by three types of self-influences. They include affective self-evaluative reactions to one's performance, perceived self-efficacy for goal attainment, and adjustment of personal standards in light of one's attainments. As already noted, goals motivate by enlisting self-evaluative involvement in the activity. The anticipated self-satisfaction gained from fulfilling valued standards provides one source of incentive motivation for personal accomplishments. Self-dissatisfaction with substandard performances serves as another incentive motivator for enhanced effort. Both the positive and negative affective self-motivators operate in human pursuits, although discontent is more salient when performances fall substantially or moderately short of what one seeks. But without the prospect of self-satisfaction from personal accomplishments, unremitting discontent would eventually take a toll on self-motivation (Bandura & Jourden, 1991).

Efficacy beliefs contribute to motivation in several ways. It is partly on the basis of beliefs of personal efficacy that people choose what challenges to undertake, how much effort to expend in the endeavor, and how long to persevere in the face of difficulties (Bandura, 1986a; 1991b). Whether negative discrepancies between personal standards and attainments are motivating or discouraging is partly determined by people's beliefs that they can attain the goals they set for themselves. When faced with obstacles and failures, people who distrust their capabilities slacken their efforts or abort their attempts prematurely and settle for mediocre solutions. Those who have strong belief in their capabilities intensify their efforts when they fail to achieve what they seek and persist until they succeed (Bandura & Cervone, 1983; Cervone & Peake, 1986; Jacobs et al., 1984; Peake & Cervone, 1989; Weinberg et al., 1979). Strong perseverance usually pays off in performance accomplishments.

The goals people set for themselves at the outset of an endeavor are likely to change, depending on how they construe the pattern and level of progress they are making. They then readjust their aspirations accordingly (Campion & Lord, 1982). They may maintain their original goal, lower their sights if they are not making much headway, or adopt an even more challenging goal. As people approach or surpass their adopted standard, they often set new goals for themselves that serve as additional motivators. The higher the self-set challenges, the more effort invested in the endeavor. Thus, notable attainments bring temporary satisfaction, but people who are assured of their capabilities enlist new challenges as personal motivators for further accomplishment. Thus, the third constituent self-influence in the ongoing regulation of motivation is the readjustment of personal goals in light of the progress being made. Csikszentmihalyi (1979) examined what it is about activities that fosters continuing deep engrossment in life pursuits. The common factors found to be conducive to enduring motivation include adopting personal challenges in accordance with one's perceived capabilities and having informative feedback of progress.

The contribution of these self-reactive influences to motivation is strikingly revealed when the direction and magnitude of discrepancy between performance and a difficult assigned standard are

systematically varied (Bandura & Cervone, 1986). After performing a strenuous activity, individuals received prearranged feedback either that their effort fell markedly, moderately, or minimally short of the adopted standard or that it exceeded the standard. They then recorded their perceived efficacy for goal attainment, their self-evaluation, and self-set goals, whereupon their motivational level was measured. Inspection of Figure 4.6 shows that the more sources of self-influence individuals brought to bear on themselves, the greater the effort they exerted and sustained to attain what they sought. Taken together, this set of self-reactive influences accounts for the major share of variation in motivation.

The way in which the three self-influences operate together in regulating motivation varies somewhat depending on the degree to which performance falls short of the valued standard. Perceived efficacy contributes to motivation at all discrepancy levels. The more strongly people believe that they can meet challenging standards, the more they intensify their efforts. Discontent operates as an influential affective motivator when attainments fall substantially or moderately short of a comparative

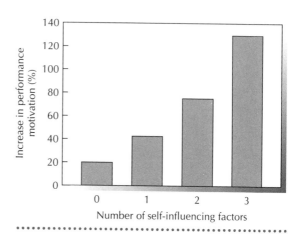

FIGURE 4.6. Mean change in motivational level as a function of the number of self-reactive influences operating in given individuals. The three self-reactive factors include strong perceived self-efficacy for goal attainment, self-dissatisfaction with substantial performance, and adoption of challenging standards. (After Bandura & Cervone, 1986)

standard. The more self-dissatisfied people are with substandard attainments, the more they heighten their efforts. If they are satisfied with approximating or matching the standard again, however, they do not invest increased effort in the pursuit. As people approach or surpass the initial standard, they set new goals for themselves that serve as further motivators. The higher the self-set goals, the more effort invested in the endeavor.

It is commonly assumed that accomplishments raise performance standards. Evidence from research on level of aspiration shows that, indeed, people generally set their goals above their immediately preceding level of attainment (Festinger, 1942; Ryan, 1970). The use of simple tasks that call for little effort limits the generality of these findings, however. This is because, in everyday life, difficult accomplishments usually require arduous effort over an extended period. People do not necessarily expect to surpass each past attainment in an ever-rising series of triumphs. Lofty accomplishments achieved through sustained extraordinary effort are not easily repeated or excelled.

Accomplishments are related to perceived efficacy and personal goal setting in a more complex way than might appear to be the case intuitively. Knowledge of having surpassed a demanding standard through laborious effort does not automatically strengthen efficacy beliefs and raise aspirations. Many people respond to their success by affirming a strong sense of efficacy and setting themselves even more challenging goals to accomplish. But some are left with self-doubts that they can muster the same level of laborious effort again, and they set their sights on simply trying to match the standard they had previously surpassed. Having driven themselves to success, others judge themselves inefficacious to repeat the demanding feat and lower their aspirations.

Self-reactive influences predict the impact of success, as well as of failure, on motivation (Bandura, 1991b). After a difficult accomplishment, those who hold a strong belief in their efficacy motivate themselves by setting even higher goals that create new challenges to be mastered. Thus, notable attainments bring temporary satisfaction, but people enlist new challenges as personal motivators for further attainments. Those who doubt they can muster the same level of effort again lower their goals. Their motivation declines.

The experience of struggling hard but falling just short of a difficult standard produces several interesting patterns of self-reactions. Some individuals become demoralized. Their perceived efficacy plummets, and they abandon pursuit of the goal. Others remain self-efficacious and aspiring but are insufficiently discontent to motivate themselves to do better. Still others remain aspiring, although somewhat less certain of their capabilities, and pleased with having performed as well as they did. A good number become overcomplacent. They view themselves as highly efficacious in meeting the challenge, but they are too content with a near miss to mobilize the effort needed to do better. Folk wisdom cautions that too much confidence has deceived many a person. Indeed, Salomon (1984) has found that a high level of perceived self-efficacy as a learner fosters a heavy investment of cognitive effort and superior learning when the task is considered difficult, but less investment of effort and poor learning when the task is believed to be easy. Motivation is perhaps best maintained by a strong sense of efficacy to withstand failure, coupled with some uncertainty that is ascribed to the challenge of the task rather than to fundamental doubts about one's abilities to put forth the effort needed to fulfill personal challenges. That efficacy beliefs enhance motivation is further corroborated in field studies of productivity in diverse human pursuits (Barling & Beattie, 1983; Earley, 1986; Taylor, Locke, Lee, & Gist, 1984).

Self-Regulation and the Negative Feedback Model

Many theories of self-regulation are founded on a negative feedback control system. Negative feedback is the basic regulator in control theory (Carver & Scheier, 1981; Lord & Hanges, 1987; Powers, 1973); in psychobiologic homeostatic theories (Appley, 1991); and in the cybernetic model presented by Miller, Galanter, and Pribram (1960). Equilibration is also the sole motivational mechanism in Piaget's theory (1960). The basic structure of this type of regulatory system includes a behavior sensing operation, an inner comparator, and an error correction routine. The system functions as a motivator and regulator through a discrepancy reduction mechanism. Perceived discrepancy between performance feedback and an inner reference standard automatically triggers adjustments to reduce the incongruity.

Control theories that portray humans as nonconscious organisms locked in negative feedback loops and driven to reduce disparity between sensed feedback and inner referents have come under some fire. Locke (1991a, 1994) has argued that much of control theory involves translation of the principles and knowledge of goal theory into a stilted machine language without providing a new perspective or predictive advantages. He further shows that adherents of control theory have now grafted so many ideas from other theories on the negative feedback loop to remedy its prediction problems that control theory has lost any distinctiveness. Various adherents espouse different versions of control theory. For example, in a recent enlargement of control theory in the name of theoretical integration, the standards or referents in the feedback loop have been redefined to include virtually everything and anything (Lord & Levy, 1994). This expanded cybernetic analogue is now endowed with a consciousness and even an enigmatic "will" that other versions either do not have or disallow. In the absence of a determinate set of propositions, is "control theory" ever capable of verification?

Discrepancy reduction clearly plays a central role in any system of self-regulation. In the negative feedback control system, however, if perceived performance matches the standard, the person does nothing. A regulatory process in which matching a standard begets inertness does not characterize human self-motivation. Such a feedback control system would produce circular action that leads nowhere. Nor could people be stirred to action until they receive feedback of a shortcoming.

Although comparative feedback is essential in the ongoing regulation of motivation, people initially raise their level of motivation by adopting goals before they receive any feedback about their beginning effort (Bandura & Cervone, 1983). Self-regulation via negative discrepancy tells only half the story and not necessarily the more interesting half. People are proactive, aspiring organisms. Their capacity to exercise forethought enables them to wield adaptive control anticipatorily rather than being simply reactive to the effects of their efforts.

Different self-regulatory systems govern the mobilization of motivation and its continued regulation. Human self-motivation relies on both *discrepancy production* and *discrepancy reduction*. It requires *proactive control* as well as *reactive control*. People initially motivate themselves through proactive control by setting themselves valued performance standards that create a state of disequilibrium. They then mobilize their effort on the basis of their anticipatory estimation of what it would take to reach those standards. Reactive feedback control comes into play in subsequent adjustments of effort expenditure to achieve desired results. After people attain the standard they have been pursuing, those who have a strong sense of efficacy generally set a higher standard for themselves. The adoption of further challenges creates new motivating discrepancies to be mastered. Similarly, surpassing a standard is more likely to raise aspiration than to lower subsequent performance to conform to the surpassed standard so as to reduce disequilibrium. Self-regulation of motivation and action thus involves a dual hierarchical control process of disequilibrating discrepancy production followed by equilibrating discrepancy reduction.

Of course, an evaluative executive control system with a proactive component can be superimposed on a negative feedback operation that keeps changing aspirational standards either upward or downward depending on how performance attainments are construed. To capture the complexity of human self-regulation, such an executive control system must be invested with the evaluative and agentive properties previously shown to play an important role in self-directedness. These include (1) proactive adoption of aspirant standards rooted in a value system and subserving advantageous purposes; (2) self-appraisal of personal efficacy to fulfill particular goal challenges; (3) anticipatory regulation of the strategies and effort needed to turn cognized standards into reality; (4) material and social outcome expectations for fulfillment or unfulfillment of standards; (5) affective self-evaluative reactions to one's performances; and (6) self-reflective metacognitive activity focused on the accuracy of one's efficacy appraisals, the suitability of one's standard setting, and the adequacy of one's strategies. Evaluation of personal efficacy relative to task demands indicates whether the standards being pursued are within attainable bounds or beyond one's reach.

In human endeavors, goal adjustments do not follow a neat pattern of ever-rising standards after personal accomplishments, nor do failures necessarily lower aspirations. Rather, because of interacting cognitive and affective factors, feedback of discrepancy has diverse effects on the self-reactive influences that mediate motivation and aspiration (Bandura & Cervone, 1986). When people fail to fulfill a challenging standard, some become less sure of their efficacy and others lose faith in their capabilities, but many remain unshaken in their belief that they can attain the standard. Surpassing a taxing standard through sustained strenuous effort does not necessarily strengthen efficacy beliefs. Although, for most people, high accomplishment strengthens beliefs of personal efficacy, a sizable number who drive themselves to hard-won success are left with self-doubts that they can duplicate the feat. These findings raise the important issue of resiliency of efficacy beliefs in the face of difficulties.

Negative Discrepancy as Automotivator

Self-motivation has been explained by some theorists in terms of an inborn automotivator operating through cognitive incongruity reduction. According to Piaget (1960), discrepancies between the cognitive schemata people already possess and perceived events create internal conflict that motivates exploration of the source of discrepancy until the internal schemata are altered to accommodate the contradictory information. In this view, moderately discrepant experiences, rather than markedly or minimally discrepant, are the ones that presumably arouse the cognitive perturbations regarded as necessary for cognitive change.

The conceptual and empirical problems associated with this equilibration model have been addressed elsewhere in some detail and will not be reviewed here (Bandura, 1986a; Kupfersmid & Wonderly, 1982). The findings show that arousal of interest is not confined to events that differ only slightly from what one already knows. Also, a moderate discrepancy of experience alone does not guarantee cognitive learning, nor does acquisition of knowledge necessarily depend on internal cognitive conflict. Simply demonstrating that people are bored by what they already know and easily discouraged by information that exceeds their cognitive processing capabilities is a mundane finding that can be explained by any theory without requiring an automotivating mismatch mechanism. There are many other motivators for bettering one's knowledge and thinking skills. The substantial benefits of being able to predict events and to exercise control over those that affect one's own well-being or that of significant others provide positive incentives for acquiring knowledge and adaptational competencies (Bandura, 1986a). The self-satisfaction gained from progressive mastery and fulfillment of personal challenges serves as another enduring motivator of pursuits. People often drive themselves for material gain, for social recognition, or in the pursuit of excellence.

There are other reasons that an automotivational system of the type proposed by Piaget might be viewed with considerable skepticism. An automatic self-motivator explains more than has ever been observed. If disparities between perceived events and mental structure were, in fact, automatically motivating, learning would be unremitting and much more unselective than it really is. As a rule, people do not persist in exploring most activities that differ moderately from what they know or can do. Indeed, if they were driven by every moderately discrepant event encountered in their daily lives, they would be rapidly overwhelmed by innumerable imperatives for cognitive change. Effective functioning requires selective deployment of attention and inquisitive effort. When faced with contradictions between evidence and their conceptions, people are much more likely to discount or reinterpret the "evidence" than to change their way of thinking. If they were motivated by an innate drive to know powered by negative discrepancy reduction, they should all be highly knowledgeable about the world around them and continually advancing to ever higher levels of reasoning. The evidence does not bear this out.

In the social cognitive view, people function as active agents in their own motivation rather than being simply reactive to discordant events that produce cognitive perturbations. Self-motivation through cognitive comparison requires distinguishing between standards of what one knows and standards of what one desires to know. It is the aspirational standards, together with perceived self-efficacy, that exert selective influence over which of many activities will be actively pursued. Aspirational standards determine which discrepancies are motivating and which activities people will strive to master.

Goal Properties and Self-Motivation

Goal intentions do not automatically activate the self-reactive influences that govern level of motivation. Certain properties of goal structures determine how strongly the self-system will become enlisted in any given endeavor. The relevant goal properties are addressed next.

Goal Specificity. The extent to which goals create personal incentives and guides for action is partly determined by their specificity. Explicit standards regulate performance by designating the type and amount of effort required to attain them, and they generate self-satisfaction and build personal efficacy by furnishing unambiguous signs of personal accomplishments. General intentions, which are indefinite about the level of attainment to be reached, provide little basis for regulating one's efforts or for evaluating one's capabilities. In studies of the regulative function of goals differing in specificity, clear, attainable goals produce higher levels of performance than general intentions to do one's best, which usually have little or no effect (Locke & Latham, 1990; Bandura & Cervone, 1983). Specific performance goals serve to motivate the unmotivated and to foster positive attitudes toward the activities (Bryan & Locke, 1967).

Goal Challenge. The amount of effort and satisfaction that accompany different goals depends on the level at which they are set. Strong interest and involvement in activities is sparked by challenges. For example, to mountain climbers, it is not crawling on slippery rocks in foul weather that is intrinsically satisfying. It is the satisfactions derived from personal triumphs over lofty peaks that sustain deep engrossment in the activity. When self-satisfaction is contingent on attainment of challenging goals, more effort is expended than if one adopts only easy goals. Locke postulates a positive linear relationship between goal level and performance motivation. A large body of evidence does show that the higher the goals, the harder people work to attain them and the better their performance (Locke & Latham, 1990). The linear relationship is assumed to hold, however, only if performers accept the goals and remain strongly committed to them. Most people, of course, eventually reject performance goals they consider unrealistically demanding or well beyond their reach. Yet people often remain surprisingly steadfast in pursuing goals they have little chance of fulfilling, even when given normative information that others reject the goals as unrealistic (Erez & Zidon, 1984). When assigned goals are beyond their reach and when failure to attain them carries no cost, people try to approximate high standards as closely as they can rather than abandon them altogether (Garland, 1983; Locke, Zubritzky, Cousins, & Bobko, 1984). As a result, they achieve notable progress even though the accomplishment of distal goal aspirations eludes them.

The generality of the evidence for unshaken pursuit of unreachable goals must be qualified, however, by the fact that laboratory simulations may differ from everyday conditions in several important respects. The simulation usually involves only a brief effort, failure carries no costs, and no opportunities exist for alternative pursuits. Unattainable goals are more likely to be abandoned when the activities require extensive investment of effort and resources, failure to meet the goals produces negative consequences, and other activities are available in which one's efforts might be more fruitfully invested. When goals are set unrealistically high, strong effort produces repeated failure that eventually takes its toll on personal efficacy. In the sociocognitive view, strength of self-motivation varies curvilinearly with the level of discrepancy between goals and attainments. Relatively easy goals are insufficiently challenging to arouse much interest or effort; moderately difficult ones maintain high effort and produce satisfactions and a growing sense of efficacy through subgoal attainments; goals set well beyond one's reach can be demotivating by undermining beliefs in one's efficacy and creating discouragement.

Much of the experimentation on level of goal challenges involves a single effort to achieve an individual goal. Social cognitive theory distinguishes between complementary regulative functions of distal goals and a graduated system of proximal subgoals in ongoing endeavors (Bandura, 1986a). Superordinate distal goals give purpose to a domain of activity and serve a general directive function, but subgoals are better suited to serve as the proximal determinants of the specific choice of activities and how much effort is devoted to them. Self-motivation is best sustained through a series of proximal subgoals that are hierarchically organized to ensure successive advances to superordinate goals. The relation between probability of goal attainment and expenditure of effort will differ for subgoals and end goals. Pursuit of a formidable distal goal can sustain a high level of motivation if it is subdivided into subgoals that are challenging but clearly attainable through extra effort (Bandura & Schunk, 1981). To strive for unreachable subgoals is to drive oneself

to unrelenting failure. By making complex tasks easier through subdivision into more manageable units, one can retain the power of goals that tend to have less impact on complex activities than on simpler ones (Wood, Mento, & Locke, 1987). It is not that challenging goals are necessarily ineffective or debilitating for complex pursuits but that complex activities must be structured in ways that goals enhance and helpfully channel efforts rather than misdirect them. When complex tasks are aidfully structured, challenging goals are transformed from debilitators to enhancers of performance (Earley, Connolly, & Ekegren, 1989; Earley, Connolly, & Lee, 1989).

The complementary regulation of motivation by hierarchical goals of differential achievability characterizes most of the strivings of everyday life. Long-range aspirations may remain unfulfilled, but personal and social advancements are realized in the process of successful striving. In an ongoing pursuit, of course, the perceived difficulty of a superordinate goal does not remain constant. Progress toward a superordinate goal in the distant future alters subjective estimates of eventual success. As one comes closer to realizing distal goals, their attainment appears less formidable than when originally viewed from far down the line.

Goal Proximity.   As suggested in the preceding discussion, the effectiveness of goal intentions in regulating motivation and action depends greatly on how far into the future the goals are projected. Proximal subgoals mobilize self-influences and direct what one does in the here and now. Distal goals alone are too far removed in time to provide effective incentives and guides for present action. In the face of many competing attractions, focus on the distant future makes it easy to put off matters in the present in the belief that there is always ample time to mount the effort later. In the absence of proximal goals to concentrate their efforts, people postpone taking needed steps; find convenient detours in other activities; and, when they do get on track, dawdle along the way.

Subgoals not only enlist self-reactive motivators, they also figure prominently in the development of self-efficacy (Bandura & Schunk, 1981). Without standards against which to measure their performances, people have little basis for gauging their capabilities. Subgoal attainments provide rising indicants of mastery that enhance efficacy beliefs. By contrast, distal goals are too far removed in time to serve as favorable markers of progress along the way to ensure a growing sense of personal efficacy. The enhancement of motivation by achievable proximal subgoals is governed by increases in perceived self-efficacy (Stock & Cervone, 1990). In highly complex activities, lofty distal goals alone can impair performance by diverting attention from devising effective strategies to self-defeating concern over failure. The same distal goals combined with challenging interim goals builds a sense of efficacy, which, in turn, is accompanied by enhanced performance attainments (Latham & Seijts, 1995).

The diverse effects of proximal self-motivation are revealed in a study in which children who were grossly deficient and uninterested in mathematics pursued a program of self-directed learning under conditions involving proximal subgoals leading to a distal goal, involving only the distal goal, or without any reference to goals (Bandura & Schunk, 1981). Within each of the goal conditions, children could observe how many units of work they had completed in each session and their cumulative attainment. Under proximal subgoals, children progressed rapidly in self-directed learning, achieved substantial mastery of mathematical operations, and developed an increased sense of efficacy (Fig. 4.7). Distal goals had no demonstrable effects. Subgoal attainments also created intrinsic interest in arithmetic, which initially held little attraction for the children. The value of proximal subgoals in cultivating intrinsic interest and promoting academic attainment was further corroborated by Morgan (1985) in an extended field experiment designed to improve the academic competence of college students. Not only do people perform better under goal proximity, but they much prefer a proximal to a distal focus (Jobe, 1984).

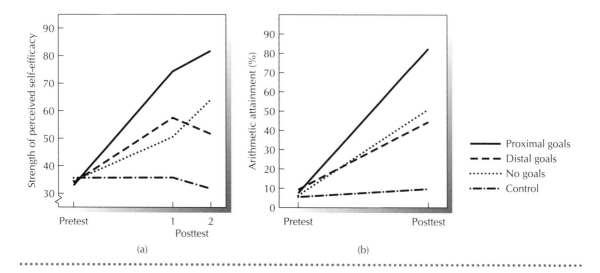

FIGURE 4.7. (a) Strength of children's perceived arithmetic efficacy at the beginning of the study (pretest), after they completed the self-directed learning (posttest 1), and after they took the arithmetic posttest (posttest 2). Children in the control group were assessed without the intervening self-directed learning. (b) Children's level of arithmetic achievements before and after the self-directed learning. (Bandura & Schunk, 1981)

Hierarchical Structure of Goal Systems

So far, the discussion has centered on goal systems as directive and motivational devices and on the self-referent mechanisms through which these systems exert their effects. Goal systems, of course, usually involve a hierarchical structure in which the goals that operate as the proximal regulators of motivation and action subserve broader goals that reflect matters of personal import and value. Proximal goals are not simply subordinate servitors of valued loftier ones, however, as is commonly depicted in machinelike hierarchical control systems. Through engagement of the self-system, subgoals invest activities with personal significance. Proximal goals generate self-satisfaction from personal accomplishments that operates as its own reward during the pursuit of higher level goals. When the reward of personal accomplishment is linked to indicants of progress, individuals contribute continuing self-motivation quite apart from the incentive of the loftier goal. Indeed, subgoal challenges often outweigh the lure of superordinate goals as ongoing motivators (Bandura & Schunk, 1981). In this motivational process, people gain their satisfaction from progressive mastery of an activity rather than suspending any sense of success in their endeavors until the superordinate goal is attained. In short, the reward is in the ongoing process of mastery rather than solely in the attainment of the end goal. The model of self-motivation as a process of recurrent proximal self-challenge and evaluative reward differs from one in which a linear series of subordinate goals is powered entirely by a superordinate one.

Self-motivation through proximal self-influence does not imply any restriction in the future time perspective of aspirations. Nor does the focus on the process of mastery imply disinterest in the products of one's efforts. Progress toward valued futures is best achieved by combining distal aspirations with proximal self-guidance. Progress on the path of mastery is likely to produce better results and greater self-satisfaction along the way than is preoccupation with the destination. One must distinguish between goals as self-motivating devices and goals as onerous external dictates. Goals are resisted when they are externally imposed to heighten productivity but increased performance brings no personal benefits. People willingly adopt and stick to goals when their self-interests are linked to goal attainments. They recognize that they are better off by adopting goals than by performing aimlessly.

Causal Ordering of Efficacy and Goal Influences

There is a good deal of evidence, much of which has already been reviewed, that efficacy beliefs have several effects on the operation of personal goals. Efficacy beliefs influence the level at which goals are set, the strength of commitment to them, the strategies used to reach them, the amount of effort mobilized in the endeavor, and the intensification of effort when accomplishments fall short of aspirations. Some authors posit that goal setting affects efficacy beliefs (Garland, 1985) or that they influence each other bidirectionally (Eden, 1988). Efficacy beliefs, in turn, influence performance.

In evaluating the direction of influence between efficacy beliefs and goal setting, it is important to distinguish between their causal ordering during acquisition of competencies and during ongoing regulation of motivation and action. In the regulation of action, basing personal goals on perceived capabilities has considerable functional value. Otherwise, people would burden themselves with onerous dictates they could not fulfill. To judge personal efficacy from the goals one happens to select would not only be a peculiar causal ordering but could carry heavy costs. People do not choose the goal of swimming a treacherous body of water and then wonder whether they have the swimming capabilities to reach the opposite shore. Rather, they tend to select proximal goals they judge to be within their reach. Goals may have some effect on efficacy beliefs, however, when they are socially assigned. Setting challenging goals for others conveys belief in their abilities to attain them. This raises belief not only in one's own efficacy but in the efficacy of one's reference group (Gellatly & Meyer, 1992). It is not the goals per se but the persuasory message that one has what it takes to succeed that is the carrier of the effect.

In the acquisition of competencies, goals help to build a sense of efficacy by structuring activities and providing incentives and markers for gauging personal capabilities. Accomplishments with subgoal markers increase perceived efficacy and self-satisfaction; the same accomplishments without subgoals by which to evaluate the progress being made have little effect (Bandura & Schunk, 1981; Schunk, 1991; Stock & Cervone, 1990). As efficacy beliefs develop, they affect the operation of goals so that motivation and accomplishments are a product of reciprocal causation. Earley and Lituchy (1991) tested the alternative causal relations between personal goals and efficacy beliefs in a series of experiments on regulation of performance. The comparisons yielded the strongest support for the causal sequence in which efficacy beliefs affect personal goals rather than the other way around.

Research on the motivational effects of perceived personal efficacy has usually focused on achievement and occupational activities. Efficacy beliefs operate motivationally in the social domain as well. Research on persuasory attempts in organizational decision making corroborates the generality of the effect (Savard & Rogers, 1992). Effective managers continue to try to persuade others of the value of their proposed solutions when they meet with resistance, whereas those of low efficacy are quick to conclude that additional efforts would be futile. Perceived efficacy supports perseverance regardless of whether the social transaction involves superiors, coworkers, or subordinates. Given that innovations typically meet stiff resistance at their inception, organizations need foresightful persisters if they are to continue to prosper.

AFFECTIVE PROCESSES

The self-efficacy mechanism also plays a pivotal role in the self-regulation of affective states. One can distinguish three principal ways in which efficacy beliefs affect the nature and intensity of emotional experiences: through the exercise of personal control over *thought*, *action*, and *affect*. The thought-oriented mode in the regulation of affective states takes two forms. Efficacy beliefs create attentional biases and influence whether life events are construed, cognitively represented, and retrieved in ways that are benign or emotionally perturbing. The second form of influence centers on perceived cognitive abilities to control perturbing trains of thoughts when they intrude on the flow of consciousness. In the action-oriented mode of influence, efficacy beliefs regulate emotional states by supporting effective courses of action to transform the environment in ways that alter its emotive potential. The affect-oriented mode of influence involves perceived efficacy to ameliorate aversive emotional states once they are aroused. These alternative paths of affect regulation are amply documented in the exercise of control over anxiety arousal, depressive mood, and biological stress reactions. Before analyzing these three modes of affect regulation, let us consider briefly a number of alternative perspectives on anxiety arousal.

Anxiety is defined as a state of anticipatory apprehension over possible deleterious happenings. Some theorists, however, endow the construct of anxiety with its presumed causes and effects as if they constituted defining properties of the construct itself. Thus, for example, in the tripartite conception (Lang, 1977), anxiety is characterized as a set of loosely coupled components embodying apprehensive cognitions, physiological arousal, and avoidant behavior. Because these three modes of expression are believed to be only loosely coupled, they may appear in varied patterns of interconnectedness. Indeed, reports of fear, visceral reactions, and avoidance acts may cohere, diverge, or remain independent of one another (Eriksen, 1958, 1960). Even the so-called components themselves are diverse and interact in complex ways. Physiological indices are often poorly interrelated (Lacey, 1967). There is much specificity to actions, and when they do cluster, the ways in which behaviors covary differ in different social settings (Wahler, Berland, & Coe, 1979). The tripartite view presupposes concordance of indices within modalities. But this is clearly not the case. Because responsiveness within each of the three systems is so multifaceted and discordant, any tripartite pattern obtained with a particular set of modality indices can change markedly if other indices of the same expressive modalities are selected. Other conceptual and empirical problems associated with tripartite conceptions of anxiety have been addressed in some detail elsewhere (Bandura, 1986a; Williams, 1987).

The tripartite notion is primarily a conception of the construct of anxiety, not a theory about its causes, mechanisms, or effects. It is conceptually problematic even as a specification of anxiety. To make cognition, affect, and action all aspects of anxiety precludes meaningful theoretical analysis of its origins and functions. If avoidant behavior is anxiety, then the theoretical issue of whether anxiety causes avoidant behavior is reduced to the empty question of whether anxiety causes itself. The assumption that anxiety arousal controls avoidant behavior will be analyzed in a later chapter. Similar conceptual problems arise when cognitions are regarded as anxiety. Apprehensive cognitions may cause anxiety arousal, but they are not in themselves anxiety. If anxiety is characterized as apprehensive cognitions, this renders meaningless the proposition that cognitions generate anxiety because both are defined as part of the same thing.

Although, in definition, anxiety has often been invested with multifaceted properties, in theorizing about it and testing for its origins and effects, the confounding cognitive and behavioral properties are appropriately jettisoned. Anxiety is then meaningfully conceptualized as an emotion of fright indexed by physiological arousal or subjective feelings of agitation. Theories about whether or not anxiety controls self-protective behavior and whether apprehensive thoughts generate anxiety then become testable.

Lang (1985) has incorporated the multisystem notion in a bioinformational theory of anxiety. In this view, anxiety is an action disposition that is centrally represented by an associative network of propositionally coded information about evocative stimuli, multisystem responses, and their meaning. This information is organized into an emotion prototype. The more closely input information matches the emotion prototype, the more likely it is to enervate the entire network, including visceral and motor systems. This theory is not easy to test. It provides no measure of the emotion prototype and its propositional content. It does not explain how an emotion prototype is acquired. And it does not specify a process model of how input factors are selected, weighted, and integrated, either additively or configurally, to produce something to match against the prototype. Given the substantial disconnectedness of elements within each of the tripartite response systems, it is unclear how the same emotion prototype triggers such mixed emotional expressions that usually do not covary.

Empirical tests of the bioinformation theory have centered largely on predictions that are neither distinctive to the theory nor especially germane to its basic assumptions about prototype matching and activation. The tests include demonstrations that imaging different thematic contents produces different physiological responses: Fear-provoking depictions elicit stronger physiological responses than neutral ones; snake phobics are more emotionally aroused by snakes than by public speaking, whereas speech phobics are more perturbed by public speaking than by snakes; visualizing vigorous physical exercise produces higher muscle potential levels than does visualizing a fearful situation; telling people to focus on physiological reactions gets them to generate stronger physiological activation while imaging fearful situations, and good imagers are better at it than poor imagers; and exposure to enactments of feared activities is more physiologically arousing than exposure to descriptions of them. Such findings can be easily explained by any number of more parsimonious and testable theories. Bioinformation theory would prescribe modification of the emotion prototype as the way to eliminate anxiety. But the theory provides little guidance on how to do it or any evidence for the efficacy of such an approach (Williams, 1996).

Anxiety involves anticipatory affective arousal that is cognitively labeled as a state of fright.

The process of labeling one's state of affective arousal as anxiety or some other emotion is heavily influenced by the cognitive and situational context in which the arousal occurs. Situational instigators give emotional specificity to physiological commonality. Thus, affective arousal in the presence of perceived threats is experienced as anxiety or fear, arousal occurring in thwarting and insulting situations as anger, and arousal produced by irretrievable loss of what is highly valued as sorrow (Hunt et al., 1958).

According to the two-factor theory of emotion proposed by Schachter (1964), different emotions have a similar physiological state. How people experience the undifferentiated visceral reactions depends on how they interpret their causes. When people experience arousal for which they have no plausible explanation, their cognitive appraisal of situational factors will determine what emotion they feel. Physiological arousal will be labeled and felt as anger in hostile contexts and as euphoria in joyful contexts. Schachter's cognitive labeling view of emotion was recast in attributional terms. How people interpret their emotional state depends on what they perceived the causes to be. Thus, athletes will believe they are frightened if they attribute their racing heart to the threat of the situation but as a state of competitive readiness if they attribute it to being "psyched up."

There are limits to the cognitive reconstruals of the same arousal state. The source of the arousal must be ambiguous. If external instigators are apparent, arousal states are less susceptible to arbitrary interpretation by social influences that suggest otherwise about what one is feeling. Individuals who are viscerally agitated at the sight of a menacing reptile cannot be easily talked into believing they are experiencing a state of euphoria. Moreover, the social factors that influence cognitive appraisal must occur before the rise in arousal, otherwise the arousal will be attributed to whatever has just happened. Given people's strong propensity to interpret events, it is unlikely that they will experience arousal for long without producing an explanation for it. Attributions are typically presumed from situational factors to be operating rather than actually measured at the time of arousal. When attributions are assessed, it is usually after the happening. Presumptive causation and post hoc assessment create problems of verifiability of the theory.

Most theories of anxiety assign an important role to cognitive appraisal in determining how visceral reactions are experienced phenomenologically. There is some dispute, however, over the aspect of the theory that involves misattribution or mislabeling of arousal. The issue is whether people who are physiologically aroused but misinformed about what caused the arousal can be made to feel their arousal as different emotions in different emotional contexts, such as hostile, comic, or frightening ones (Marshall & Zimbardo, 1979; Maslach, 1979; Schachter & Singer, 1979). Unexplained arousal tends to be experienced as negative affect. As Maslach (1979) suggests, it signifies a lack of personal control that can be highly disconcerting. Unexplained arousal, therefore, does not lend itself readily to mislabeling as a positive affect. Efforts to reduce anxiety and phobic behavior by misattributing arousal by threats to benign sources have also met with little success (Bootzin, Herman, & Nicassio, 1976; Gaupp, Stern, & Galbraith, 1972; Kellogg & Baron, 1975; Kent, Wilson, & Nelson, 1972; Nisbett & Wilson, 1977; Rosen, Rosen, & Reid, 1972; Singerman, Borkovec, & Baron, 1976; Sushinsky & Bootzin, 1970).

Cognition plays a broader role in human emotion than simply providing labels for physiological states. Cognitive conceptions of emotion have focused almost exclusively on appraisal of externally generated arousal. Social cognition theory underscores the self-arousal power of cognition. Indeed, physiological arousal itself is often generated cognitively by arousing trains of thought (Beck, 1976; Schwartz, 1971). People frighten themselves by scary thoughts, they work themselves into a state of anger by ruminating about social slights and mistreatments, they become sexually aroused by conjuring up erotic fantasies, and they become depressed by dwelling on gloomy scenarios. The trains of thoughts that occupy one's consciousness thus create physiological arousal as well as help to define what one is feeling. Thoughts about one's coping efficacy figure prominently in the self-arousal of anxiety.

Psychodynamic theories generally attribute anxiety to intrapsychic conflicts over the expression of forbidden impulses. The threat posed by the impulse is presumably displaced and projected outward on some object. The selected object or situation is then irrationally feared and phobically avoided. For example, in the psychoanalytic theory of a snake phobia, the censoring ego projects the sexual id impulse onto a snake so that "the conscious idea of snake replaces the unconscious one of penis" (Fenichel, 1945). The external object of anxiety is considered to be of no special significance because the threat can be projected onto any number of external things. In this approach, anxiety is seen to be rooted in the unconscious conflict over the prohibited impulse. The external threats vary depending on what object happens to be selected as the danger, but the internal threat is much the same across different types of phobias.

The patterning of phobic reactions is better explained by direct and vicarious aversive experiences that undermine a sense of personal control than by appeal to repressed internal dangers (Bandura, 1969a; Bandura, Blanchard, & Ritter, 1969). The application of psychodynamic theory has not been rewarded by either predictive or therapeutic success (Erwin, 1996; Rachman & Wilson, 1980; Zubin, Eron, & Schumer, 1965). Although the psychodynamic view was once the principal line of theorizing about the determinants of anxiety, it has now largely fallen out of vogue.

Conditioning theory assumes that formerly neutral events acquire anxiety-provoking properties by association with painful experiences. If a neutral event is paired with one that is painful, the formerly neutral one is said to become aversive (Hineline, 1977). This theory essentially externalizes the cause in the stimulus — it is the stimulus that presumably acquires aversive properties. Painful experiences change judgments of one's controlling capabilities and appraisal of external stimuli, not the stimuli themselves. Thus, for example, if individuals develop a phobia of mountain driving as a result of a

mishap on a hairpin turn, it is not the mountain road that has acquired aversive characteristics. Rather, it is the individuals' beliefs about their capability to manage risky driving situations and the anticipatory thought patterns they spawn that undergo change. Getting phobics back on the mountain roadway requires restoring confidence in their driving capabilities rather than changing the valence of the roadway by pairing it with benign stimuli.

Efficacy Regulation of Anxiety through Attentional and Construal Processes

In social cognitive theory (Bandura, 1986a), perceived efficacy to exercise control over potentially threatening events plays a central role in anxiety arousal. Threat is not a fixed property of situational events. Nor does appraisal of the likelihood of aversive happenings rely solely on reading external signs of danger or safety. Rather, threat is a relational matter concerning the match between perceived coping capabilities and potentially hurtful aspects of the environment. Therefore, to understand people's appraisals of external threats and their affective reactions to them, it is necessary to analyze their judgments of their coping capabilities. Efficacy beliefs determine, in large part, the subjective perilousness of environmental events.

Efficacy beliefs affect vigilance toward potential threats and how they are perceived and cognitively processed. People who believe they can exercise control over threats do not conjure up calamities and frighten themselves. But those who believe that potential threats are unmanageable view many aspects of their environment as fraught with danger. They dwell on their coping deficiencies, magnify the severity of possible threats, and worry about perils that rarely (if ever) happen. Through such inefficacious trains of thought, they distress themselves and constrain and impair their level of functioning (Lazarus & Folkman, 1984; Meichenbaum, 1977; Sarason, 1975b).

Several converging lines of evidence corroborate the influential role of perceived control in anxiety and stress reactions (Averill, 1973; Levine &

Ursin, 1980; Miller, 1980). In cognitive control, individuals operate under the belief that they are capable of managing threatening situations should they arise. People who are led to believe they can exercise some control over painful stimuli display lower autonomic arousal and less performance impairment than do those who believe they lack personal control, even though they are equally subjected to the painful stimuli (Geer, Davison, & Gatchel, 1970; Glass, Singer, Leonard, Krantz, & Cummings, 1973). Repeated failures arouse anxiety when ascribed to personal incapability, but the same painful experiences leave people unperturbed if ascribed to situational factors (Wortman, Panciera, Shusterman, & Hibscher, 1976).

Beliefs of coping efficacy, instilled illusorily, can boost the ameliorative value of common procedures for diminishing distress. Patients about to undergo oral surgery received either sedative medication, relaxation training, or self-efficacy enhancement combining relaxation with false physiological feedback that they were highly effective relaxers (Litt, Nye, & Shafer, 1993, 1995). The illusory feedback raised patients' beliefs in their efficacy to cope with the different aspects of oral surgery. Efficacy enhancement surpassed relaxation and sedative drugs in reducing self-rated anxiety as well as anxiety and behavioral agitation during surgery as rated by the oral surgeon and dental assistant. Regardless of treatment condition, the higher the preexisting efficacy beliefs and the more the beliefs were raised, the lower the anxious agitation. The ameliorative benefits of beliefs of coping efficacy remain after controlling for dental anxiety. Illusorily created efficacy beliefs similarly reduce cardiovascular reactivity to cognitive stressors when it is possible to exercise some control over them (Gerin, Litt, Diech, & Pickering, 1995).

That perceived control can cognitively transform threatening situations into safe ones and thereby obviate anxiety is graphically illustrated in a laboratory study of agoraphobics by Sanderson, Rapee, and Barlow (1989). Inhaling air enriched with carbon dioxide typically provokes panic attacks in agoraphobics. Comparable groups of agoraphobics received the same amount of carbon dioxide but under different beliefs of control. One group could do nothing to control the amount of carbon dioxide they received. A second group was led to believe they could regulate the amount of carbon dioxide they received by closing a valve. In fact, the valve had no effect on the flow of carbon dioxide, so the control was illusory. Agoraphobics who believed they were exercising control remained calm and rarely experienced panic attacks or catastrophic thoughts (Fig. 4.8). But those who knew they could not exercise any control experienced mounting anxiety and had a high rate of panic attacks and catastrophic thoughts about dying, losing control, and going crazy.

The power of efficacy belief to influence construal processes is further corroborated with radically different stressors: migrants seeking to build a new life in a dissimilar societal milieu (Jerusalem & Mittag, 1995). Those with a high sense of efficacy viewed their new social reality as a challenge, whereas those with low perceived efficacy viewed it as a threat. In contrast to the more benign construal, which made adaptation less stressful, construal of the new circumstances as a threat was accompanied by high anxiety and health problems. Belief in coping efficacy exerted its protective function regardless of social support or employment status.

Efficacy Regulation of Anxiety through Transformational Actions

People who have a high sense of coping efficacy adopt strategies and courses of action designed to change hazardous environments into more benign ones. In this mode of affective control, efficacy beliefs regulate stress and anxiety through their impact on coping behavior. The stronger the sense of efficacy, the bolder people are in taking on the problematic situations that breed stress and the greater their success in shaping them more to their liking. Major changes in aversive social practices are usually achieved through the exercise of efficacy collectively rather than just individually. We will return to this mode of lowering human anxiety in the analysis of perceived collective efficacy.

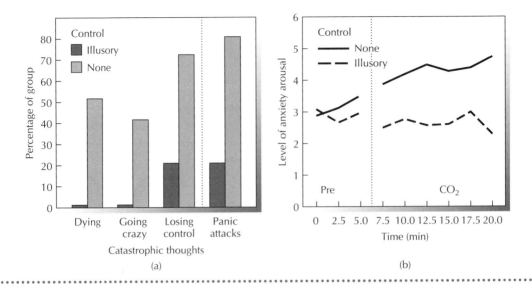

FIGURE 4.8. Rate of (a) panic attacks and catastrophic thoughts and (b) level of anxiety exhibited by agoraphobics under illusory control or no control over threatening physical events. (After Sanderson, Rapee, & Barlow, 1989)

Efficacious exercise of control diminishes anxiety by reducing or preventing painful experiences (Notterman, Schoenfeld, & Bersh, 1952). Anxiety reduction by behavioral control involves much more than simply curtailing painful events, however. In some studies of behavioral control, threatening events occur undiminished, but they are promptly transformed subjectively to nonaversive events when their occurrence is personally controlled (Gunnar-vonGnechten, 1978). Infants are frightened by a noisy mobile toy that is out of their control, but it becomes a pleasant toy when they can activate it. In such instances, it is simply the exercise of initiatory control, not the curtailment of the events themselves, that reduces anxiety. If one can control events, one can predict when they will occur. The effects of predictability must be disentangled from those of controllability. Evidence indicates that anxiety reduction stems from the sense of personal control rather than from increased predictability of aversive events (Gunnar, 1980b).

That a sense of control can diminish anxiety, even across markedly different domains of functioning, is tellingly demonstrated by Mineka, Gunnar, and Champoux (1986) in a developmental study. Monkeys who had been reared from birth under conditions in which they exercised control over access to food showed little fear or avoidance of novel threats months later. The same threats were highly frightening to monkeys who could not develop a sense of control because food had been given to them independently of their actions. This is a remarkable transfer of the anxiety-reducing benefits of control from appetitive activities to threatening ones. In situations in which the opportunity to wield behavioral control exists but is unexercised, it is the self-knowledge that one can exercise control should one choose to do so, rather than the actual application of control, that reduces anxiety reactions (Glass, Reim, & Singer, 1971). These converging lines of evidence indicate that much of the anxiety-reducing effects of behavioral control stem anticipatorily from belief that one can wield control over aversive events rather than simply from attenuating them when they occur.

The experiences that accompany the exercise of behavioral control produce substantial cognitive changes in efficacy beliefs that continue to affect autonomic arousal after the behavioral episodes have ceased (Bandura, Cioffi, Taylor, & Brouillard, 1988). In this study, perceived efficacy was strengthened by exercise of full control over problem-solving demands and substantially weakened by inability to wield adequate control. People who perceived themselves as efficacious exhibited little autonomic arousal during the problem solving, whereas those who had a weak sense of efficacy experienced a high level of subjective stress and autonomic arousal (Fig. 4.9). Perceived coping inefficacy not only was accompanied by higher autonomic arousal during the problem solving but left individuals with a sense of inefficacy that affected autonomic arousal beyond that experience. Thereafter, simply judging one's capabilities after the problem-solving activity was over activated divergent autonomic reactions — a rise in autonomic arousal in those of low perceived efficacy and a sharp drop in arousal in those with high perceived efficacy. The greater the increase in perceived coping efficacy, the larger the drop in autonomic arousal.

Microrelationships between Efficacy Beliefs and Anxiety Arousal

Studies of controllability create the conditions for illusory or actual control but do not measure the extent to which those conditions, in fact, alter people's beliefs in their efficacy to manage environmental threats and stressors. The more stringent verification of cognitive regulation of affective arousal requires that thoughts about coping capabilities be measured. That perceived self-efficacy operates as a cognitive regulator of anxiety arousal has been tested directly by creating different levels of perceived efficacy in phobics and relating them at a microlevel to different manifestations of anxiety as they cope with phobic threats varying in degree of intimidation. This research links perceived coping efficacy not only to subjective emotional reactions but also to the neurobiological aspects of emotional states. People display little anxiety arousal while coping with potential threats they regard with high efficacy. But as they confront threats for which they distrust their coping efficacy, their anticipatory and performance subjective anxiety mounts, their heart rate accelerates, and their blood pressure rises (Bandura et al., 1982). This pattern of activation is replicated across different phobic dysfunctions with subjective stress and different physiological indices of anxiety arousal. The consistency of findings adds to the generality of the influence of perceived inefficacy and anxiety.

Understanding of the physiological mechanisms through which efficacy beliefs affect anxiety arousal was carried one step further by linking strength of perceived efficacy to release of catecholamines (Bandura, Taylor, Williams, Mefford, & Barchas, 1985). Phobics exhibit low epinephrine and norepinephrine levels while performing coping activities within their high perceived efficacy range. They display substantial increases in these catecholamines during threatening activities that approach the upper bounds of their perceived coping efficacy. Catecholamines drop

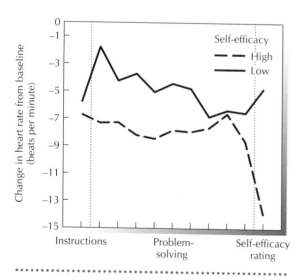

FIGURE 4.9. Changes in heart rate displayed by students of perceived high and low efficacy while they received instructions for a cognitive problem-solving task, coped with the task demands, and later appraised their perceived self-efficacy. (Bandura, Cioffi, Taylor, & Brouillard, 1988)

sharply when they withdraw from threats that exceed their perceived coping capabilities.

In these experiments, after level of anxiety is measured as a function of different strengths of perceived efficacy, a guided mastery procedure is used to strengthen perceived coping efficacy to the maximum level for all previous coping activities. After a strong sense of coping efficacy is instilled, the previously intimidating threats no longer elicit differential autonomic or catecholamine reactivity. The combined results are consistent in showing that anxiety reactions to coping activities differ when perceived self-efficacy differs, but anxiety reactions to the identical activities are uniformly low when perceived self-efficacy is raised to the same maximum level. Thus, perceived mismatch between beliefs of coping efficacy and task demands, rather than properties inherent in the tasks themselves, is the source of variation in anxiety reactions. Efficacy beliefs determine the subjective perilousness of situations. People view contact with potential threats as hazardous when they believe they cannot manage them safely, but they regard such encounters as benign when they believe they can wield control over them.

The effects of a weak sense of coping efficacy on anxiety arousal have been amply documented in diverse spheres of functioning. Leland (1983) examined the level of precompetition anxiety as a function of perceived self-efficacy, proneness to competitive anxiety, and a host of experiential factors and situational stressors that could be anxiety-provoking. In a multiple regression analysis in which each factor was treated on an equal footing, perceived self-efficacy emerged as the major predictor of how anxious players felt before athletic contests. Anxiety proneness was a weak predictor. The greater their self-doubts, the more agitated the athletes became. In a longitudinal study, Krampen (1988) similarly found that perceived capability predicted academic test anxiety, but general anxiety proneness did not. Declines in perceived efficacy to control perturbing thoughts are accompanied by increased academic anxiety over time, whereas expectations of negative outcomes are unrelated to changes in anxiety (Kent & Jambunathan, 1989). In social situations, perceived self-efficacy predicts the level of anxiety experienced and manifested in interpersonal transactions (Alden, 1986).

Environmental Controllability and Anxiety Arousal

Many deleterious events are not completely under personal control. Although perceived coping efficacy is a major contributor to anticipatory anxiety and stress reactions, it is not the sole determinant. For example, the more efficacious people judge themselves as drivers, the less anxious they will be on busy thoroughfares. Even highly efficacious drivers, however, will experience some apprehension because they cannot always spot and forestall reckless drivers from ramming them or sideswiping them through disregard of traffic signals. In situations where the margins for error are narrow, mistakes produce serious consequences, and some limits exist on how much personal control can be wielded over potential threats, the exercise of high perceived efficacy will be accompanied by some apprehension. The more predictable and personally controllable potentially deleterious events are, the smaller will be the contribution of extraneous factors to anxiety arousal. People who judge themselves to be highly efficacious are prone to take on risky activities, however. To continue with the driving example, individuals of high efficacy venture into congested freeway and urban traffic and thereby create for themselves more risky and frightening environments than do individuals of low perceived efficacy who confine their driving to relatively safe situations. This applies equally to other stressors. When people can impose high performance demands on themselves, those whose efficacy beliefs are illusorily raised drive themselves harder and have more concomitant autonomic arousal than those who forego tough demands after their sense of personal efficacy is illusorily lowered (Gerin et al., 1996). In evaluating the role of perceived coping efficacy in anxiety arousal, therefore, one must consider how risky and demanding are the activities people choose to pursue.

Although perceived self-efficacy emboldens venturesomeness, it does not incite recklessness. With a low sense of efficacy, both safe and risky aspects of the environment are seen as fraught with danger, whereas assurance in one's coping capabilities increases ability to judge the potential riskiness of situations (Ozer & Bandura, 1990). After inefficacious individuals develop a strong sense of coping efficacy, they replace rigid self-protectiveness with flexibly adaptive behavior that is cognitively controlled by judgments of the probable effects of prospective actions. They engage in activities of interest to them when it is relatively safe to do so, but they refrain from those that carry high risk.

Alleviation of human distress by actions that alter environmental threats is by no means confined to struggles at the individual level. Much stress and despondency arise from institutional practices that are deleterious to human welfare. Therefore, self-efficacy theory is equally concerned with enabling people to act together to change their lives for the better. Those who feel powerless to alter detrimental life conditions accept things as they are. Those who have a resilient sense of collective efficacy find ways to improve their living conditions in the face of seemingly insurmountable obstacles. The development and exercise of collective efficacy for social change are addressed in Chapter 11.

Regulation of Affective States by Thought Control Efficacy

People possess the capacity to manage their own thought processes. Because one has to live continuously with a psychic environment that is largely of one's own making, the exercise of control over one's own consciousness is of considerable import to personal well-being. To the extent that people can regulate what they think, they can influence how they feel and behave. Some people can control what they think. Others feel powerless to rid themselves of perturbing or dejecting intrusive thoughts. Many human distresses are exacerbated, if not created, by failures of thought control. The self-regulation of thought processes, therefore,

plays a significant role in the maintenance of emotional well-being.

Human activities are rarely devoid of risk. It is natural to give some thought to potential risks in any undertaking and to have some apprehension about them. But where the risks are extremely low, it is dysfunctional to conjure up magnified subjective dangers or to ruminate apprehensively about highly improbable risks to the point where such thoughts create self-inflicted misery and impair psychosocial functioning. The exercise of control over anxiety arousal in activities involving some risks may require development not only of coping efficacy but also of efficacy in controlling dysfunctional apprehensive cognitions. The process of efficacious cognitive control is summed up well in the Chinese proverb: "You cannot prevent the birds of worry and care from flying over your head. But you can stop them from building nests in your hair." Self-generated distress is likely to be kept at a relatively low level when control over both thoughts and coping actions is fully exercised.

The influential role played by thought control efficacy in anxiety arousal is corroborated in an interesting line of research examining the different properties of perturbing cognitions and their affective correlates. The characteristics of intrusive cognitions include their frequency, intensity, acceptability, and controllability. The results show that it is not the frequency of aversive cognitions per se that accounts for anxiety arousal but rather the strength of perceived efficacy to control or dismiss them (Kent, 1987; Kent & Gibbons, 1987). Hence, the frequency of aversive cognitions is unrelated to anxiety level when the influence of perceived thought control efficacy is removed, whereas perceived thought control efficacy is strongly related to anxiety level when extent of aversive cognitions is removed.

Churchill (1991) devised a multifaceted measure of the capability to manage unwanted thoughts. It assesses perceived capability to divert attention from unwanted thoughts, to tolerate them, and to reconstrue them in benign ways. Perceived efficacy to exercise diversionary attentional control carries the heaviest weight in this set of cognitive management skills. People who have a low sense of efficacy to control what they think experience more unwanted intrusive thoughts, find them more distressing, are more recurrently plagued by them, and engage in more obsessive-compulsive rituals. Thought control efficacy predicts the distressfulness of intrusive thoughts, whereas when perceived efficacy to manage intrusive thoughts is controlled, frequency of intrusive thoughts or their degree of unpleasantness has little effect on distress (Churchill & McMurray, 1989). It appears that people who have a high sense of efficacy that they can control their thought processes are relatively unperturbed by apprehensive cognitions because they believe they can abort their escalation or perseveration. Repetitious intrusions of unwanted thoughts is a major feature of obsessive-compulsive disorders. Analysis of the aversiveness of obsessional ruminations provides further support for efficacious thought control as a key factor in the regulation of cognitively generated arousal (Salkovskis & Harrison, 1984). It is not the sheer frequency of intrusive thoughts but rather the perceived inefficacy to turn them off that is the major source of distress arising from obsessional thinking.

In a series of studies, Wegner (1989) has examined different strategies of thought control and the effects they have. Efforts to banish unwanted thoughts by simply trying to suppress them not only may be ineffective but may exacerbate the problem. This is because the very negation of a thought contains the thought. Thus, the suppressive self-instruction "Quit thinking of a giraffe" invariably activates the unwanted thought of a towering giraffe. Thoughts that were the object of direct suppression come to preoccupy later thinking. The reason is that, through repeated association, situations in which the thought suppression occurred become reminders of unwanted thoughts that keep activating them. Use of multiple distractors can create many reminders of unwanted thoughts, which only adds to the problem of cognitive control.

An elaboration of the theory places limits on when intentional efforts to suppress unwanted thoughts paradoxically tend to activate them (Wegner, 1994). Mental control is said to involve dual regulatory systems: an effortful operating process that seeks to produce the desired state of mind and an automatic monitoring process that notes failed instances and thereby undermines control efforts by reinstating the very unwanted thoughts. Other demands on mental resources, stress, and time pressure sidetrack the operating control process or undermine its effectiveness. Under weakened control, unwanted thoughts become more salient. Therefore, efforts at thought control are likely to backfire under cognitive or emotional strain but not under nonpressured conditions. There are several possible explanations for failure in cognitive control of thought processes under strain that require verification. Is the failure due to a vigilant monitoring system scanning for unwanted mental contents, the direct disruptive effects of cognitive and emotional strain, or perceived inefficacy to exercise thought control under taxing conditions that undermines effort and generates stress and dysfunctional trains of thought?

Self-distraction by becoming absorbed in other trains of thought can be more effective than suppression in banishing unwanted thoughts. Distraction escapes paradoxical activation because drawing one's mind away to replacement thoughts instates the very thoughts one seeks. Wegner (1989), however, has shown that, through association, cognitive distractors can become reminders of the unwanted thoughts. He portrays the process of thought control in predominantly avoidant negative terms. Unwanted thoughts intrude forcefully into one's consciousness. In trying to rid oneself of them, both situational cues and cognitive distractors become reminders that bring back the unwanted thoughts repeatedly to haunt one. It should be noted, however, that suppression of unwanted thoughts does not always increase their intrusiveness (Mathews & Milroy, 1994; Roenor & Borkovic, 1994). Nor are suppressed emotional thoughts more likely to rebound than neutral ones. So the conditions under which thought suppression backfires are still not well understood. Intrusive thinking often takes the form of worrying in which people torment themselves with nagging thoughts about impending imagined or authentic threats. Thought that is meant to serve an anticipatory protective function by creating possible solutions to problems becomes a debilitator in chronic worriers. The cause of worrying stems more from perceived inefficacy to implement solutions than to generate them. Indeed, Davey, Jubb, and Cameron (1996) demonstrate experimentally that belief in one's capability to solve life problems has causal influence on catastrophic worrying. People whose sense of efficacy was undermined by fictitious comparison with superior capabilities of others experienced higher anxiety and engaged in more catastrophic worrying while examining vexing problems in their life than did those whose beliefs about their capabilities were raised by favorable social comparison. A low sense of problem-solving efficacy predicted catastrophic worrying, whereas level of anxiety did not. These findings are fully in accord with those of other studies showing that perceived efficacy surpasses anxiety as a predictor of diverse forms of functioning.

Borkovec and his colleagues tested the effectiveness of postponement as a means of shutting off worrisome ruminations (Borkovec, Wilkinson, Follensbee, & Lerman, 1983). Rather than worrying throughout the day, chronic worriers are instructed to postpone their worrying to a particular time and place each day. By applying this mode of thought control, they spend less time worrying and are less distressed than those who do not receive this mode of thought management.

Human thought can be positively proactive as well as avoidantly reactive. Thought control through production of wanted trains of thoughts involves self-attraction to desired thoughts rather than solely self-distraction from unwanted thoughts. The same is true for diversionary activities. There is a marked difference between keeping busy to avoid thinking about unpleasant matters and engrossment in activities for the enjoyment they provide. In forming associations between different types of thoughts, the principles of associative learning would suggest that forward cueing of positive diversions by unwanted thoughts should be more reliable than backward cueing of unwanted thoughts by positive diversions. Wegner emphasizes the backward cueing effect but does not explain why, through cognitive association, unwanted thoughts do not become reminders of positive diversions. Nor is there any reason that situational cues should not become reminders of triumphant diversionary thought rather than only prompters of supplanted thoughts.

People often enlist external aids for thought control rather than trying to control their thinking solely by cognitive diversions (Wegner, 1989). Situational cues that command attention wield influence over thoughts. A change in environmental setting can instantly alter what preoccupies one's thinking. Similarly, absorption in novels, movies, or television quickly turns off negative cognitive carryovers of the workday. Such attentional diversions illustrate the power that situational events exert over thinking. People can influence what they think about by enlisting events that occupy their attention or by surrounding themselves in their immediate environment with cues that foster beneficial engrossments.

An even more effective enactive mode of thought control is achieved through immersion in engrossing activities. People can occupy themselves for hours on end with occupational, social, or recreational pursuits. Aversive rumination is supplanted by positive engrossment. Life-threatening illnesses, such as cancer, evoke repeated intrusions of perturbing thoughts about the illness and the possibility of death. Perceived self-efficacy to cope with thoughts of dying and to engage oneself in activities that give meaning and satisfaction to one's everyday life help to reduce vexing intrusive thoughts and despondency (Joss, Spira, & Speigel, 1994). Nolen-Hoeksema (1990) explains the self-perpetuation of depression and gender differences in depression in terms of ability to use engrossing action to turn off depressive rumination. The nondepressed are prone to work their way out of depressive episodes by immersing themselves in activities that distract them from their problems or alter them for the better. The depressed are more inclined to engage in ruminative thinking about their dysphoric condition that sustains or exacerbates despondent mood. In controlled studies, depressed ruminators remain depressed; depressed distractors lift themselves out of their despondent state and pessimistic thinking. Introspective preoccupation with one's sorrowful state is clearly not the remedy for despondency.

When depressed individuals try to rid themselves of depressive rumination by cognitive self-distraction, they usually resort to a self-defeating strategy. Whereas the nondepressed distract themselves with positive thoughts, the depressed use negative self-distractors that are only likely to reinstate depressing trains of thought (Wenzlaff, Wegner, & Roper, 1988). Depressed people acknowledge that dejecting thoughts are more readily turned off by positive than by negative self-distractors, but they cannot get themselves to exercise the necessary thought control. Even when positive distractors are provided for them, they have difficulty sticking to them. Actions known to alleviate depression and bring some enjoyment to everyday life are constrained by perceived inefficacy to do them (Lyubomirsky & Nolen-Hoeksema, 1994; Ross & Brown, 1988).

The strategies of thought control discussed so far rely primarily on attentional regulation of thought processes. Unwanted thoughts are combated by competing thoughts. Even when action is used to change thought, the focus is on attentional diversion. These are reactive strategies rather than ones that remove the source of the perturbing rumination. The most powerful way of eliminating intrusive ideation is by gaining mastery over threats and stressors that repeatedly trigger the perturbing trains of thought. As we will see later, this is best achieved by guided mastery experiences that equip people with the knowledge, skills, and beliefs of personal efficacy to manage the things that disturb them. Through personal enablement, people gain some measure of mastery over themselves. Those who are assured of their capability to cope with threats have little reason to ruminate about them.

The dual control of anxiety and behavior by perceived coping efficacy and thought control efficacy is revealed in a study of the mechanisms governing personal control over pervasive social threats (Ozer & Bandura, 1990). Sexual violence toward women is a prevalent problem. Because any woman is a potential victim, the lives of many women are distressed and constricted by a sense of inefficacy to cope with the threat of sexual assault. To address this problem at a self-protective level,

women participated in a mastery modeling program in which they perfected trustworthy physical skills that enabled them to disable unarmed assailants instantly by powerful strikes to vital areas of the body. Mastery modeling enhanced perceived coping efficacy and cognitive control efficacy, decreased perceived vulnerability to assault, and reduced intrusive aversive thoughts and anxiety arousal. These changes had a liberating effect. The women expanded the activities they engaged in and reduced the number of everyday activities they avoided out of perceived vulnerability. The efficacy to defend themselves physically was liberating emotionally and psychologically as well as behaviorally. The self-assurance also helped them to set firm limits verbally, which helps to prevent coercive or assaultive treatment. Path analysis of the causal structure revealed a dual path of regulation of avoidant behavior and active engagement in activities by enhanced self-efficacy (Fig. 4.10).

One path of influence is mediated through the effects of perceived self-protective efficacy on perceived vulnerability and risk discernment. Much of the research on risk perception has been concerned with estimating the likelihood of future environmental events that are not personally controlled. Studies aimed at elucidating the determinants of risk perception have focused mainly on mood states and accessibility of salient examples of events (Bower, 1983; Kahneman, Slovic, & Tversky, 1982). In transactions involving the exercise of personal competencies, estimations of risk require a relational judgment of the match between perceived coping capabilities and environmental challenges. Perceived efficacy operates as a key factor in judgments of the riskiness of environmental situations and personal vulnerability to social threats. In the absence of self-protective efficacy, most situations appear scary and risky. But after a strong sense of efficacy is acquired, people are better able to distinguish between risky and safe situations and regulate their behavior with realistically based precaution.

The second path of influence operates through the impact of perceived cognitive control efficacy on intrusive aversive thoughts (see Fig. 4.10).

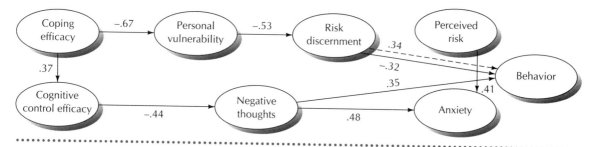

FIGURE 4.10. Path analysis of the causal structure of coping behavior involving interpersonal threats. The numbers on the paths of influence are the significant standardized path coefficients. The solid lines to Behavior represent avoidant behavior; the dotted line represents participant behavior. (Ozer & Bandura, 1990)

When people have a strong sense of efficacy to control their own thinking, they are less burdened by negative thoughts and experience a low level of anxiety. A strong sense of coping efficacy rooted in performance capabilities enhances perceived efficacy to control the escalation or perseveration of perturbing cognitions. Belief that one can exercise control over potential threats thus makes it easier to dismiss intrusive aversive thoughts. The affective benefits of thought control efficacy result not only from better regulation of one's consciousness but also from its effects on construal processes. The same unwanted thoughts are likely to be viewed as benign if one can easily dismiss them but as pernicious if they repeatedly disrupt productive thinking and one cannot get rid of them.

In information-processing models of anxiety and phobic dysfunctions, environmental threats activate a self-schema of personal vulnerability. The self-schema in turn guides how information is processed and acted upon. How the self-schema begets action and emotional states remains unclear, however. In social cognitive theory, as shown in Figure 4.10, beliefs of personal inefficacy underlie perceptions of vulnerability. The theory specifies in some detail the causal structure governing anxiety arousal and avoidant styles of coping. Knowledge on how to build a resilient sense of coping efficacy provides explicit guidelines for eradicating debilitating phobic dysfunctions. Drawing on the conception of coping by Lazarus and Folkman (1984), writers often dichotomize the coping process into problem management and emotion management. In the former case, they try to get rid of the problem; in the latter case, they try to get rid of the distress caused by the problem. People presumably resort to problem-solving coping when difficult situations are changeable, but they turn to stress-reducing coping by cognitive reappraisal and diversion when they cannot change difficult situations. This is a misleading dichotomy when these alternative strategies are tied to changeability of situations. In actuality, successful coping usually requires both problem solving and stress management. This is because most difficult situations that are changeable involve some degree of stress. Thus, in academic examinations, students have to keep in check anticipatory anxiety and control distressing intrusions while solving problems. While executing problem-solving strategies, tournament tennis players have to rid themselves of perturbing thoughts and stress reactions, especially when things go wrong. Conversely, there are few problem situations in which there is absolutely nothing people can change. Life is not one-dimensional. Even those in terminal illness try to do things that ease their daily problems and add purpose to their remaining life. The aversive emotional impact of what is uncontrollable is diminished by exercising influence over the aspects of one's life that are controllable. Thus, among patients with life-threatening renal disease about which they can do little, those who act on their sense of efficacy in social, occupational, and community activities suffer less depression than patients who show resignation in all aspects of their life (Devins et al., 1982).

The dichotomization of coping into problem management and emotion management also confounds means and ends. The strategies for reducing stress require cognitive and behavioral skills that have to be learned and applied strategically and persistently. Both task management and emotion management involve problem solving but at a different locus. In task management, people are solving mainly an external problem; in emotion management, they are solving an internal problem. As indicated by the causal structure shown in Figure 4.10, human adaptation requires concurrent regulation of thought, affect and action.

The powerful impact of mastery experiences on perturbing ideation is vividly revealed in the treatment of severe phobic disorders (Bandura et al., 1985; Bandura et al., 1977; Bandura et al., 1975; Bandura et al., 1982; Wiedenfeld et al., 1990). Virtually all of the participants were tormented by intrusive thoughts and recurrent nightmares that they felt helpless to control: "I have had nightmares about spiders at least once a week for 10 to 15 years. They are always on my mind in the evening when I have to turn on a light in a dark room." "Every time I went outside I was on my guard. During my waking hours a lot of 'what ifs' about snakes entered my mind." Constant apprehensive vigilance detracted from enjoyment of everyday activities and produced chronic distress: "I could not watch TV, read, enjoy any of the things I normally did at home since I was always uncomfortable and watchful of a possible spider in the room." Even a picture or mere mention of the phobic object triggered perturbing ruminative thoughts.

During the process of gaining coping mastery, habitual modes of phobic thinking were transformed into benign reappraisals of former threats, as these snake phobics reveal: "My whole way of thinking was changed. I used to loathe them, now I appreciate them and admire their refined engineering!" "I've gone from fear to fascination. Before I saw them as threatening monsters." The sight or mention of the phobic object no longer triggered perturbing ruminations as it did in the past: "I no longer have afterthoughts after an encounter with a snake." The phobics reported fascinating metamorphic alterations of dream activity. At the beginning of treatment, the snakes in their dreams were terrorizing: "At the beginning of the program I dreamt about scary snakes growing larger and larger. Now I don't have those dreams at all." The former threats then began to be invested with positive attributes: "I had a dream in which a boa constrictor became my friend and even washed the dishes. This is a marked improvement over my recurrent dream of being terrorized by snakes." With further growth of perceived self-efficacy, scenarios of personal mastery supplanted concern over the characteristics of snakes: "I had a dream but it was only what I had accomplished that day." Eventually, dreams inhabited by phobic objects simply ceased: "I haven't had a dream about snakes." The chronically perturbing ruminations were eliminated in all phobics within several sessions of guided mastery.

After acquiring a maximal sense of coping efficacy, participants experienced complete relief from perturbing ruminations and nightmares. Their peace of mind was gained through confidence in their power to exercise control over threats and stressors should they encounter them: "I just don't worry about the possibility of encountering a snake now. If it happens I can deal with it." Coping efficacy built through mastery experiences had profound impact not only on intrusive thought but also on emotional distress and action. As these findings indicate, intractable ruminations are more effectively eradicated by personal enablement than by trying to combat unwanted thought with competing thought. The cognitive thought control strategies that receive the greatest attention are the ones that usually meet with limited success.

Theories about intrusive thought typically center on the negative valence of the thoughts' content. Their frequent recurrence and persistence are presumed to be motivated by pressing problems, conflicts, or taboo impulses seeking expression. People struggle to rid themselves of such thoughts because of their aversiveness or because they fear that their thoughts will trigger foolish, detrimental, or dangerous action. Evidence suggests that the heavy emphasis on thought content and frequency may be misplaced. Rather, people become perturbed about perceived inefficacy itself. We saw earlier that it is not the frequency of negative thoughts but the sense of inability to control them that is the major source of distress. There are several ways in which perceived inefficacy in thought control can be distressing and depressing. First, a sense of helplessness to control one's thinking can be highly upsetting in itself because it is a constant reminder of self-regulatory weaknesses. Second, uncontrollable thinking can create stress by persistently intruding on, and impairing concentration and performance of, tasks at hand. Third, intrusions that occur uncontrollably may involve upsetting contents. And finally, perceived inefficacy to control intrusive thoughts involving taboo activities can create doubts about personal efficacy to restrain oneself from acting out those thoughts in real life.

Comparisons of the stressfulness of inefficacy to control positive and negative intrusions suggests that the first two processes may be the main contributors to distress. Difficulty of thought control does not seem to be a function of the unpleasantness of its content. Pleasant intrusive thoughts are just as difficult to dismiss as unpleasant ones, and both forms are more persistent than neutral thoughts (England & Dickerson, 1988). Moreover, perceived inability to exercise control over pleasant intrusions is just as depressing as inability to control unpleasant intrusions (Edwards & Dickerson, 1987). Both signify a sense of powerlessness. Both can disrupt performance. These different lines of evidence underscore the importance of perceived efficacy in anxious arousal by ruminative thought.

Affective Control Efficacy

The analyses so far have centered on the regulation of affective states by exercising behavioral control over potential threats and stressors and cognitive control over perturbing intrusive thoughts. In addition, people can exercise control over their affective states by palliative means without altering the environmental or cognitive sources of emotional arousal. Self-relaxation, calming self-talk, engrossment in diversionary recreational activities, and seeking solace in social supports are examples of palliative means for allaying anxiety and mollifying anger arousal (Meichenbaum & Turk, 1976; Novaco, 1979). Belief that one can relieve unpleasant emotional states, whatever their source, makes them less aversive.

Arch (1992a) has given special attention to affective control efficacy. Some of her research has examined the independent contribution of beliefs in personal efficacy to control the behavioral, cognitive, and affective aspects of functioning in taxing achievement situations. These aspects include perceived behavioral efficacy to fulfill stressful task demands, to control apprehensive thoughts, and to manage the emotional distress accompanying performance. Each facet of efficacy predicts level of anticipatory anxiety. The stronger the sense of efficacy, the weaker the anxious expectations. Each of the three facets of personal efficacy also predicts willingness to undertake the activity. Men and women seem to differ in how heavily they weight the different facets of personal efficacy in deciding whether to pursue stressful activities (Arch, 1992b). Men consider mainly their efficacy to do the job adequately, whereas women place greater weight on their perceived efficacy to control their affective arousal in performance situations.

Positive diversions and beneficial lifestyle perspectives provide further means of managing the stressors of everyday life (Rosenthal, 1993). Physical exercise, recreational activities, and enjoyable avocational pursuits help to relieve pressures and restore restful balance to lives. Humor tempers the sting of adversities. Ervin summed it up well when he said, "Humor makes our heavy burdens light and smooths the rough spots in our pathways." Much human distress is self-inflicted by personal demands for accomplishments that are exceedingly difficult to fulfill. Relaxing stringent self-imposed standards relieves stress. Taking one day at a time curtails unbridled apprehensions about the future. Setting priorities among multiple activities so that full attention is given to the task at hand without worrying about tasks still to be done reduces the stressfulness of workloads and time pressures. Putting petty concerns within the larger scheme of things makes them less stressful.

Lifestyle orientations are easy to prescribe but difficult to follow, especially for stress-prone individuals. They are reluctant to take time from their pressing schedules to restructure stressful aspects of their lives. People differ widely in their perceived efficacy to adopt lifestyle practices that bring some balance and periods of tranquillity to their harried lives (Rosenthal, Edwards, & Ackerman, 1987). Although perceived efficacy to alter lifestyle practices can have a general impact on stress and anxiety, its role in the regulation of affective arousal has been largely ignored. Admittedly, some of the lifestyle orientations are not easily measurable, but most do involve concrete practices. The relative neglect probably reflects the pathologic bias of research on anxiety that pays little heed to salutary ideational and behavioral orientations in human adaptation and change.

Interactive but Asymmetric Relationship

Social cognitive theory posits an interactive, though asymmetric, relation between beliefs of coping efficacy and anxiety arousal, with efficacy beliefs exercising the much greater sway. That is, perceived inefficacy to cope with potential threats leads people to approach such situations anxiously, and experience of disruptive arousal may further lower their sense of efficacy that they will perform skillfully. However, people are much more likely to act on their efficacy beliefs inferred from other dependable sources of information indicative of personal capabilities than to rely primarily on visceral cues. This is not surprising, because self-knowledge based on information about one's coping skills, past accomplishments, and comparative appraisals is considerably more reliable than are the indefinite

stirrings of the viscera. Seasoned performers on theatrical stages, athletic fields, and lecture circuits interpret their anticipatory apprehension as a normative situational reaction rather than as an indicant of personal incapability. They know what they can do once they get started, however much their viscera may be agitating anticipatorily.

The impact of perceived coping inefficacy on anxiety arousal is well established. But the influence of anxiety arousal on efficacy beliefs is equivocal. Actual level of physiological arousal has little or no effect on judgments of personal efficacy, but perceived autonomic arousal can affect such judgments (Feltz & Mugno, 1983). In prospective studies, perceived self-efficacy predicts subsequent level of anxiety, but anxiety level has only a weak relation to subsequent beliefs of personal efficacy (Krampen, 1988). The indistinct diagnosticity of visceral information about personal capabilities probably explains why the effect of physiological arousal on efficacy beliefs is ambiguous and inconsistent.

The initial investigations into the contribution of efficacy beliefs to stress and anxiety centered solely on efficacy to exercise behavioral control over the stressors themselves. Subsequent research verified that affective arousal is regulated by thought control efficacy, which can take three different forms: suppression of perturbing thoughts; cognitive diversion to positive trains of thought; and cognitive reconstrual of intimidating situations, as when problems are looked upon as challenges rather than as threats. The extension of self-efficacy theory to the management of affective arousal accounted for additional variation in anxiety. Therefore, a full test of self-efficacy theory in the affective sphere should incorporate all three facets of perceived efficacy — personal control of coping action, thought, and affect — that regulate level of anxiety arousal.

Catastrophic outcome expectations are often invoked as explanations for severe clinical dysfunctions. For example, agoraphobics are said to constrict their lives because they fear they will be overcome by a panic attack. Catastrophic misinterpretation of bodily sensations as foreboders of physical and mental breakdown is considered to be the crucial determinant of panic reactions (Barlow,

1986; Clark, 1988). Anticipated catastrophic outcomes further heighten anxiety and physiological arousal in an upward cycle, culminating in a panic attack. In the fear of fear explanation, which is simply a milder version of the fear of panic notion, agoraphobics presumably shun activities because they anticipate they will become anxious. Another variant of expected outcomes commonly invoked is in terms of perceived danger. Agoraphobics presumably forsake activities because they believe all kinds of harmful consequences will befall them.

Explanations in terms of aversive or catastrophic outcome expectations beg the question of what fuels the catastrophic thinking. In short, the outcome expectations themselves need explanation. People who believe they can exercise control over potential threats or over their emotional states do not conjure up catastrophic outcomes (Ozer & Bandura, 1990; Sanderson et al., 1989). The stronger the perceived efficacy to exercise behavioral, cognitive, and affective control, the weaker the anxious expectations. Anticipated panic, anticipated anxiety, or perceived danger do not predict degree of change in agoraphobic reactions following treatment when the influence of efficacy beliefs is controlled. In contrast, efficacy beliefs are highly predictive of changes in agoraphobic reactions regardless of whether variations in anticipated panic, anticipated anxiety, perceived danger, maximal performance during treatment, and level of anxiety arousal accompanying performance are controlled (Williams et al., 1989; Williams & Watson, 1985).

Perceived Self-Inefficacy and Depression

The inability to influence events and social conditions that significantly affect one's life can give rise to feelings of futility and despondency as well as anxiety. A theory must specify when perceived inefficacy will generate anxiety and when depression. The nature of the outcomes over which personal control is sought is an important differentiating factor. People experience anxiety when they perceive themselves as ill equipped to manage potentially injurious events. Attenuation or control of aversive outcomes is central to anxiety. People are saddened and depressed by their perceived inefficacy to gain highly valued outcomes. Irreparable loss or failure to gain desired rewarding outcomes figures prominently in despondency. In extreme cases, individuals become so chronically preoccupied with self-depreciation and their sense of worthlessness that the pursuit of personal satisfactions becomes futile (Beck, 1973).

There is a dichotomous view in the clinical lore that anxious people have an attentional bias toward threats, but depressed people have a memory bias for past failures and other negative events. This dichotomization of biases in information processing is probably an artifact of the types of events presented and whether one examines forethought or afterthought. If presented with choice situations involving both potential losses and opportunities, there is every indication that depressed individuals would show a pessimistic attentional bias toward likely losses of future ventures. Nor are the depressed mired solely in negative remembrances of the past. Indeed, hopelessness about the future is one of the major features of depression.

Human distress does not come packaged in neatly separable forms. Perceived inefficacy in gaining highly valued outcomes is often anxiety-provoking as well. When losses of what one values highly produce aversive outcomes, as when failure to secure a job jeopardizes one's livelihood, a sense of powerlessness to control vital aspects of one's life is both distressing and depressing. The fact that attainment failures and losses that portend aversive consequences are both distressing and depressing may be upsetting to nosologists and proponents of discrete emotions but is hardly perplexing to sociocognitivists. Because of the common co-occurrence of privations and threats, both apprehension and despair often accompany perceived inefficacy to alter miserable life circumstances.

There is more than one process through which people can become depressed. In the model of triadic reciprocal causation, each of the three classes of causal factors — cognitive and other personal factors, behavior, and environmental events — contribute to depression interactively. Adverse life events — in the form of failures, hardships, and lack or loss of emotional relationships — can instill a sense of worthlessness and despondency over one's life situation (Krantz, 1985; Lloyd, 1980; Oatley & Bolton, 1985). This is the environmental contributor. Yet most people who struggle with negative realities do not lapse into chronic depression. The emotional effects of adverse life events depend, in large part, on how they are construed. People who have developed a negatively biased self-system tend to interpret adverse life events in pessimistic ways that produce, exacerbate, and prolong bouts of depression (Beck, 1984; Kuiper & Olinger, 1986; Peterson & Seligman, 1984; Rehm, 1988). This is the cognitive contributor. Depressed people create depressing environments by their behavior. Those who are markedly lacking in social competencies experience impoverished, rejective relationships that contribute to feelings of dejection, inadequacy, and worthlessness (Lewinsohn, Hoberman, Teri, & Hautzinger, 1985). When they interact with others, their dejective alienating behavior makes those around them morose, hostile, rejecting, and guilty (Coyne, 1985; Joiner, 1994). The negative social evaluations and reactions they elicit from others provide social validation for their morose outlook on life. This is the behavioral contributor to despondency. Thus, depressed people not only have a gloomy view of their environment, they also create gloomy social environments for themselves to view.

Different theories of depression — cognitive, behavioral, and environmental — have been built around each of the three major contributors to depression. Viewed from an interactional perspective, depression is better understood by examining how these major classes of determinants act together to produce despondency than by treating them as rival determinants that operate independently to create depressive reactions. We turn now to analyses of the ways in which efficacy beliefs operate as shapers and mediators of the cognitive, behavioral, and environmental contributors to depression.

Inefficacy and Biased Cognitive Processing of Experiences

A weak sense of personal efficacy operates on the cognitive source of depression in several ways. One cognitive path of influence involves the impact of efficacy beliefs on cognitive processing of positive and negative experiences. A low sense of efficacy creates negative biases in how personally relevant experiences are cognized, organized, and recalled. Research on dysfunctions in self-regulatory thought conducive to depression has clarified different aspects of this process. Depression is often generated by negative cognitive biases in the constituent subfunctions of self-regulation of performances invested with self-evaluative significance (Kanfer & Hagerman, 1981; Rehm, 1982). The three major subfunctions include self-monitoring and cognitive processing of one's successes and failures; judging of one's ongoing performances against the standard one seeks to fulfill; and affective self-reactions to one's accomplishments.

Beliefs of personal inefficacy operate in these various subfunctions in ways that increase vulnerability to depression. In the self-monitoring domain, people who are prone to depression misperceive their performance attainments or distort their recollections of them in self-slighting directions. They dwell on their failures rather than savoring their successes. In contrast, the nondepressed display a self-enhancing bias in which they remember their successes well but recall fewer failures than they have actually experienced (DeMonbreun & Craighead, 1977; Nelson & Craighead, 1977; Wener & Rehm, 1975). Minimizing one's successes while accenting one's failures can give rise to despondency. The nondepressed also have an exaggerated belief in their social efficacy and the degree of control they exercise over positive outcomes (Alloy & Abramson, 1988; Lewinsohn et al., 1980). Belief in personal control serves as a protective factor against depressive reactions to aversive life events (Alloy & Clements, 1992).

Efficacy beliefs influence causal explanations of performance attainments (Alden, 1986). People with a high sense of efficacy accept successes as indicants of their capabilities but dismiss the diagnostic import of failures and attribute them to external impediments. Those who harbor a low sense of efficacy readily accept failures as evidence of their personal deficiencies but view their successes as dependent on situational aids. These differential explanatory patterns are very much in evidence in depressive dysfunctions. The nondepressed credit successes to themselves and failures to situational factors. Such favorable causal appraisals serve to heighten positive affect. Depressed persons are not especially charitable to themselves in how they judge their performance determinants. While not always discounting their contributions to successes, they are quick to blame themselves for their failures (Kuiper & Higgins, 1985; Peterson & Seligman, 1984; Rizley, 1978).

Being outperformed by others in matters of personal importance arouses self-disparaging emotional reactions (Bandura & Jourden, 1991). Dysphoric individuals are especially prone to use unfavorable social comparative information in self-depreciating ways. When exposed to the high attainments of others, depressed people judge their own accomplishments as less praiseworthy than do nondepressed people (Ciminero & Steingarten, 1978). Self-devaluation for performances that fall short of those achieved by others is more pronounced in depressed women than in depressed men (Garber, Hollon, & Silverman, 1979). Davis and Yates (1982) created conditions in which they raised or lowered people's beliefs in their cognitive efficacy and told them that others performed either well or poorly on the same intellectual activity. The experience of seeing themselves as unable to realize valued accomplishments while others readily attained them induced a depressed mood and debilitated intellectual performance. Similar mood-related biases operate when despondent and nondespondent people can choose with whom to compare themselves after they perform poorly (Swallow & Kuiper, 1993). Picking those who perform well provides opportunities to improve one's competencies. But simply comparing oneself against superior attainments

without examining how those successes were achieved is likely to perpetuate a sense of inadequacy and despondency.

To mitigate the deleterious effects of social comparison, it is often recommended that human endeavors be structured so that people judge themselves in reference to their own capabilities and standards, rather than by comparing themselves against others. In this process, people set themselves the goal of progressive improvement and judge their accomplishments against their personal standards. Self-comparative standards provide the benefits of personal challenge and success experiences for self-development without the cost of invidious social comparison. In competitive, individualistic societies, however, where one person's success is another person's failure, social comparison inevitably enters into self-appraisal.

Continued progress in a valued activity does not necessarily ensure perpetual self-fulfillment. The pace at which activities are mastered can drastically alter self-evaluative reactions (Simon, 1979a). Accomplishments that surpass earlier ones bring a continued sense of self-satisfaction. But people derive little satisfaction from smaller accomplishments, or even devalue them, after having made larger strides. Early spectacular accomplishments reflecting notable proficiency can thus be conducive to later self-dissatisfaction even in the face of continuing personal attainments. For example, it is not uncommon for great achievers to suffer depression upon receiving a prized award if they judge their current accomplishments as falling short of the earlier triumphs that brought them the social acclaim. This is the price of early success. When Linus Pauling was asked what one does after winning the Nobel Prize, he replied, "Change fields, of course!" After a phenomenal long jump that shattered the existing record by two feet, Beamon avoided self-disfavor by never jumping again. In short, self-discontent can be created by self-comparative standards just as it can by social-comparative standards.

Depression through Inefficacy for Unfulfilled Aspirations

Another cognitively mediated path to depression is through a low sense of efficacy to realize unfulfilled aspirations. The satisfactions people derive from what they do are largely determined by their self-evaluative standards. A sure way of inducing self-discouragement and a sense of personal inefficacy is to impose on oneself lofty or globally vague standards for gaining a sense of self-worth. Evidence indicates that faulty goal setting is indeed conducive to despondency and performance debilitation. Compared to nondepressed persons, the depressed generally set higher standards for themselves relative to their attainments (Golin & Terrill, 1977; Loeb, Beck, Diggory, & Tuthill, 1967; Schwartz, 1974; Simon, 1979a). Goal difficulty is a relational characteristic reflecting the match between personal capabilities and goals, not a matter of absolute level. Thus, a medium-level goal beyond one's reach is a difficult one, whereas a high goal readily within one's reach is an easy one. Depression is most likely to arise when personal standards of merit are set well above one's perceived efficacy to attain them (Kanfer & Zeiss, 1983). A sense of inefficacy to fulfill valued standards gives rise to self-devaluation.

Self-regulatory theories of motivation and of depression make seemingly contradictory predictions about the effects of negative discrepancies between attainments and standards. Standards that exceed attainments are said to enhance motivation through goal challenges, but negative discrepancies are also invoked as activators of despondent mood. Moreover, when negative discrepancies do have adverse effects, they may give rise to apathy rather than to despondency. A conceptual scheme is needed that differentiates the conditions under which negative discrepancies will motivate, depress, or induce apathy.

In accord with social cognitive theory, the directional effects of negative goal discrepancies are predictable from the relationship between perceived efficacy for goal attainment and level of self-set goals (Bandura & Abrams, 1986). Failure produces high motivation and low despondent mood when people believe they have the efficacy to fulfill

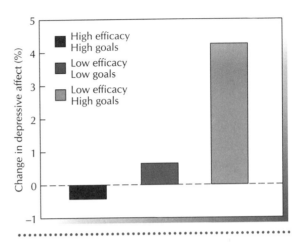

FIGURE 4.11. Change in depressive mood of people combining strong perceived self-efficacy with goal adherence, weak perceived self-efficacy with goal adherence, and weak perceived self-efficacy with goal abandonment. (Bandura & Abrams, 1986)

difficult goals and continue to strive for them (Fig. 4.11). Failure diminishes motivation and generates despondent mood when people judge they lack the efficacy to attain difficult goals but continue to demand those difficult attainments of themselves for any sense of satisfaction or success. People who judge they lack the efficacy to attain difficult goals and abandon them as unrealistic for themselves become apathetic rather than depressed.

People who judge themselves unfavorably are not inclined to treat themselves positively. Not surprisingly, the negative bias extends to the affective self-reaction component of self-regulation. Compared to nondepressed persons, those who are prone to depression react less self-rewardingly for similar successes but more self-critically for similar failures (Gotlib, 1981; Lobitz & Post, 1979; Nelson & Craighead, 1977; Rehm, 1982). Self-devaluation and despondent mood feed on each other in a self-demoralizing cycle. Repeated self-devaluation creates a depressive mood, which, in turn, further diminishes self-rewarding reactions and enhances self-critical ones. It is difficult to maintain interest and involvement in activities in which one's performances produce mainly self-denigration.

Depression through Inefficacious Thought Control

The previous analyses of cognitive causality focused mainly on how personal inefficacy breeds depression by fostering demoralizing and self-disparaging thought. Another way in which efficacy beliefs affect the cognitive source of depression is through the exercise of control over depressing thoughts themselves. We saw earlier that perceived inability to turn off ruminative thought gives rise to depression. People who are highly prone to depression display a notable inability to rid themselves of negative thoughts. When they try to distract themselves, they often use faulty cognitive strategies that, if anything, trigger further negative trains of thought (Wenzlaff et al., 1988). Even though they know that positive distractors are more effective than negative ones, they usually try to combat the negative thoughts that preoccupy their thinking with other negative thoughts. Through cognitive and affective associations, negative cognitive distractors are likely to activate trains of thought that rekindle the unwanted ones. While depressed people are inefficacious in banishing negative thoughts, they are good at eliminating positive ones. The breakdown in thought control is attributed to the salience and ready accessibility of negative cognitions under depressive mood states.

All people experience depressive episodes from time to time in response to rejections, losses, failures, and setbacks. But they vary in how quickly they get over them. Most rebound rapidly, whereas some sink into a deepening despondency that lasts for a long time. Nolen-Hoeksema (1990, 1991) has demonstrated, in a series of laboratory and field studies, that ruminative reactions to adversity partly determine the severity and duration of depressive episodes. Recurrent rumination about dejecting life events and one's despondent state amplifies and prolongs depressive reactions, whereas engrossment in activities that command attention or improve one's life terminates depressive episodes. Dwelling on negatives only dredges up more negatives, activates faulty modes of thinking, and debilitates motivation and performance, all of which give further cause for despondency.

In laboratory tests, reducing intrusive negative thinking alleviates depression (Teasdale, 1983). Research into the mechanisms by which cognitive behavior therapy abates depression reveals that perceived inefficacy to exercise control over ruminative thought figures prominently in the occurrence, duration, and recurrence of depressive episodes. Kavanagh and Wilson (1989) found that the weaker the perceived efficacy to regulate ruminative thoughts, the higher the depression. The stronger the perceived thought control efficacy instilled by treatment, the greater the decline in depression and the lower the vulnerability to recurrence of depressive episodes. Perceived self-efficacy retains its predictiveness of improvement and reduced vulnerability to relapse when level of prior depression is controlled.

Depression through Social Inefficacy

An additional route to depression is through a low sense of social efficacy to develop interpersonal relationships that provide models of coping competency, cushion the adverse effects of chronic stressors, and bring satisfaction to people's lives. It is now well established that socially supportive relationships reduce vulnerability to stress, depression, and physical illness. Analyses of paths of influence indicate that social competencies and environmental stressors exert their effects on depression primarily through the mediation of perceived self-efficacy. Supporting evidence for causal mediation comes from depressive reactions to markedly different social stressors. Cutrona and Troutman (1986) examined postpartum depression as a function of the temperamental difficulty of the infant and the quality of social support in the mother's networks of relationships. The paths of influence are shown in Figure 4.12. Temperamental difficulty of the infant undermined mothers' beliefs in their parenting capabilities. Social support exerted its protective function indirectly by enhancing parenting efficacy beliefs. Mothers who had others to turn to for support and guidance were more assured in their parenting capabilities. A high sense of efficacy, in turn,

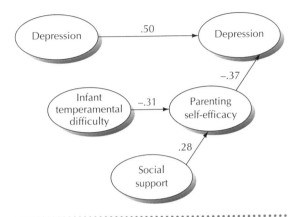

FIGURE 4.12. Path analysis showing that the influence of social support and temperamental difficulty of infants on postpartum depression is mediated through the effects on mothers' beliefs in their parenting efficacy. (Cutrona & Troutman, 1986)

protected them from becoming depressed over the daily hassles of caring for their infants. That a sense of inefficacy to fulfill parental role demands is a predisposer and maintainer of depression is further corroborated by Olioff and Aboud (1991). Strength of perceived parenting efficacy, measured prepartum, predicted postpartum depression when preexisting level of depression and self-esteem were held constant. Postpartum depression also showed a concurrent dependence on perceived parenting efficacy.

In a program of research on adaptation to abortion, Major and her colleagues have shown that a high sense of coping efficacy is accompanied by fewer adverse physical reactions and lower depression both immediately after an abortion and in subsequent adjustment (Major, Mueller, & Hildebrandt, 1985). Successful coping is better predicted by efficacy beliefs than by causal attributions for unwanted pregnancies. Moreover, the coping benefits of a high sense of efficacy remain even when the immediate reactions to abortion are controlled. A low sense of coping efficacy predicts persistence of postabortion depression when preabortion depression is controlled, whereas preabortion depres-

sion is related to immediate postabortion depression directly and via perceived coping efficacy but is unrelated to subsequent depression (Cozzarelli, 1993). That a sense of personal efficacy operates as a protective personal factor against depression is further corroborated when women's beliefs in their coping efficacy are enhanced (Mueller & Major, 1989). Women received preabortion counseling aimed either at enhancing their perceived coping efficacy or at shifting causal attributions for unwanted pregnancies from characterological weaknesses to heterosexual behavior that is personally controllable. Both interventions facilitated adjustment, but the one designed to enhance efficacy beliefs had the greater impact on depression. Women high in perceived efficacy dwelled less on potential negative difficulties and were less depressed than those who had a low sense of coping efficacy.

Because of the personal and social conflicts surrounding abortion, social support is likely to be an especially important factor in adjustment following termination of an unwanted pregnancy. Indeed it is, but it operates through perceived coping efficacy rather than directly (Major et al., 1990). Efficacy beliefs were measured in terms of perceived capability to resume normal activities, maintain good sexual relations, and cope with situational reminders of abortions. The greater the social support women received while making their decision and the more support they anticipated from their partner, family, and friends, the stronger was their belief in their coping efficacy. A high sense of efficacy was accompanied by low depressive reactions. Social support attenuated depression entirely through its effects on perceived coping efficacy. Evidence that social support increases activity patterns only indirectly by strengthening beliefs of personal efficacy adds to the generality of their mediational role in supportive influences (Duncan & McAuley, 1993).

The model of proactive, reciprocal causation that characterizes social cognitive theory applies to the role of social support in depression. A sense of personal efficacy not only mediates the impact of social support on depression but also functions as a determinant of social support. Social support is not a self-forming entity waiting around to buffer harried people against stressors. Rather, people have to go out and find or create supportive relationships for themselves. Given the prevalence of social reservedness, this is not an easy matter (Zimbardo, 1977). The lower the social efficacy, the more reticent people are, even though they know how to behave socially (Hill, 1989). Their efficacy beliefs override their knowledge. It requires a strong sense of social efficacy to cultivate and maintain beneficial relationships (Glasgow & Arkowitz, 1975; Leary & Atherton, 1986).

The studies by Cantor and Harlow (1994) underscore the heavy demands placed on social efficacy as people struggle to enlist the help of others in overcoming setbacks in the pursuit of their life goals. If help is sought in the wrong way, from the wrong people, at the wrong time, in the wrong settings, and without sensitivity to the needs of others, it strains relationships and eventually exhausts the network of supporters. Socially efficacious individuals create more supportive environments for themselves than do those who have a low opinion of their social capabilities. Supportive relationships, in turn, can enhance personal efficacy. Supporters can raise efficacy in others in several ways. They can model effective coping attitudes and strategies for managing problem situations, demonstrate the value of perseverance, and provide positive incentives and resources for efficacious coping.

The social cultivative function of perceived efficacy becomes especially important during transitional periods in life when established emotional ties are left behind and new ones must be formed. The Holahans have conducted longitudinal studies on the path of influence from perceived social inefficacy to social isolation to depression (Holahan & Holahan, 1987a,b). The elderly often experience disruption or loss of close relationships due to retirement, geographic relocation, and loss of friends and spouses through death. The loss of social supports with aging places new demands on social capabilities to develop a dependable social network. In accord with the proposed causal model, perceived social efficacy predicts the level of social support achieved a year later (Holahan & Holahan,

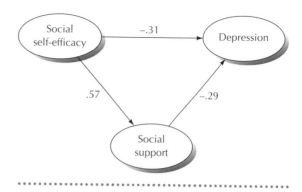

FIGURE 4.13. Path analysis of the contribution of perceived social inefficacy to depression both directly and through its influence on development of socially supportive relationships. (Holahan & Holahan, 1987a)

1987a). Perceived personal efficacy influences depression both directly and indirectly by fostering social support that reduces depressive reactions to chronic stressors (Fig. 4.13).

The analysis so far corroborates the path of influence from the perceived inefficacy to gain what one longs for to depression. The causal contribution is established both experimentally by altering the level of depression through differentially instilled efficacy beliefs and by demonstrations under natural conditions that dysphoric conditions give rise to depression through their effect on efficacy beliefs. Tests of alternative mediators reveal that an optimistic disposition alone does not affect depression, but perceived inability to exercise control over life events breeds despondency (Marshall & Lang, 1990). People are spared depression not by an optimistic disposition but because belief in their abilities to master events that befall them fosters an optimistic outlook on future outcomes. When variations in perceived efficacy are controlled, optimism has no independent effect on depression. Optimism devoid of a sense of personal efficacy to bring about the longed-for outcomes would be little more than wishful thinking, which cannot sustain coping efforts for long under recurrent adversity. In other multivariate prospective studies, a sense of inefficacy to master activities of personal importance predicts depression when multiple controls are applied for variations in preexisting depression, social support, stressful life events, and faulty automatic thinking (Olioff, Bryson, & Wadden, 1989).

Research linking perceived inefficacy to a vulnerability to feelings of futility and despondency has focused almost exclusively on adults. Adolescence is a critical period of development that places heavy demands on simultaneously managing stressful biological, educational, and social changes. Children who are beset by self-doubt and who lack supportive guidance have a lot they can get depressed about during this vulnerable time. Indeed, perceived intellectual and social inefficacy is as depressing for children as it is for adults. Those who believe they cannot manage scholastic demands and form and maintain satisfying peer relationships suffer frequent bouts of depression (Bandura et al., 1996a). Gender differences emerge in adolescence, with girls being more prone to depression than boys. Examination of different facets of perceived personal efficacy provides some insight into the differential risk of depression. Whereas boys get depressed mainly over perceived inefficacy to fulfill academic demands, girls get depressed over perceived inefficacy in academic, social, and self-management aspects of their lives (Pastorelli, Barbanelli, Bandura, & Caprara, 1996). Evidence that efficacy beliefs contribute similarly to adult and childhood depression lends support to the generality of the self-efficacy mechanism in depression.

In the previous chapter, we saw that mood states bias the way in which events are interpreted, cognitively organized, and retrieved from memory. Thus, mood and perceived efficacy can influence each other bidirectionally. Perceived inefficacy breeds depression. Despondent mood diminishes perceived efficacy; positive mood enhances it (Kavanagh & Bower, 1985). People then act in accordance with their mood-altered efficacy beliefs, choosing more challenging activities in a self-efficacious frame of mind than if they doubt their efficacy (Kavanagh, 1983). Despondency can thus lower efficacy beliefs, which undermines

motivation and spawns deficient performances, causing even deeper despondency. In contrast, by raising beliefs of personal efficacy that facilitate motivation, aidful cognitive self-guidance, and accomplishments, positive mood can set in motion an affirmative reciprocal process.

SELECTION PROCESSES

So far, we have discussed efficacy-activated processes that enable people to create beneficial environments and exercise control over them. People are partly the products of their environment. By selecting their environment, people can have a hand in what they become. Choices are influenced by beliefs of personal capabilities. Hence, beliefs of personal efficacy can play a key role in shaping the courses lives take by influencing the types of activities and environments people choose to get into as well as the types of environments they produce. In self-development through choice processes, destinies are shaped by selection of environments known to cultivate certain potentialities and lifestyles. People avoid activities and environments they believe exceed their capabilities, but they readily undertake activities and pick social environments they judge themselves capable of handling. The higher their perceived self-efficacy, the more challenging the activities they select (Kavanagh, 1983; Meyer, 1987).

People of high efficacy not only prefer normatively difficult activities but also display high staying power in those pursuits. Any factor that influences choice behavior can profoundly affect the direction of personal development. This is true because the social influences operating in selected environments continue to promote certain competencies, values, beliefs, and interests long after the decisional determinant has rendered its inaugurating effect and faded from the picture (Bandura, 1986a; Snyder, 1987). Thus, seemingly inconsequential efficacy determinants of choices can initiate selective interpersonal associations that produce major and enduring personal changes. The more encompassing the social milieus to which one gravitates, the more the course of one's life is affected (Bandura, 1982b).

People foreclose realization of certain aspects of their potentialities by the options they disregard because of a low sense of efficacy. Therefore, in elucidating efficacy effects mediated through selection processes, one is just as concerned with options of merit that are given short shrift as with those that are actively pursued. Selection processes are differentiated from cognitive, motivational, and affective processes because, in prompt dismissal of certain courses of action on grounds of personal inefficacy, the latter regulative processes never come into play. It is only after people choose to engage in an activity that they mobilize their efforts; generate possible solutions and strategies of action; and become elated, anxious, or depressed over how they are doing.

In their daily lives, people repeatedly confront situations in which they must choose among different possible activities. Many of these choices have short-run effects that are of no lasting consequence. Of greater import are efficacy-based choices that leave more enduring marks or even alter the course lives take. Choices made during formative periods of life carry special weight because they initiate concatenating experiences that create the prerequisites for desired futures or foreclose them. The choices made at crucial turning points usually do not appear all that important at the time. This is because their significance derives from the channeling flow of influences they inaugurate. It is in hindsight that turning points stand out.

The power of efficacy beliefs to affect the course of life paths through selection processes is most clearly revealed in studies of career choice and development (Betz & Hackett, 1986; Lent & Hackett, 1987). The stronger people's belief in their efficacy, the more career options they consider possible, the greater the interest they show in them, the better they prepare themselves educationally for different occupational careers, and the greater their staying power in the chosen pursuits. Multivariate studies include a variety of possible determinants of vocational choice and preparatory accomplishments in addition to beliefs of personal efficacy, such as ability level, past achievements, and vocational interests (Lent, Brown, & Larkin, 1986). Even when perceived efficacy is entered last in hierarchical regression analyses, it predicts the range of career options seriously considered and persistence and academic success in chosen options above and beyond the other predictors.

Hackett and Betz (1981) provide a conceptual analysis of career development in which perceived self-efficacy functions as a key mediator. Most occupational pursuits depend on cognitive and social competencies that may require years to master. Hackett and Betz document the diverse ways in which institutional practices and socialization influences contribute to developmental paths by the types of competencies and self-beliefs they promote in childhood. Experiences during this formative period leave their mark on personal efficacy, which, in turn, sets the future direction of a life course by affecting the career choices made and the successes attained.

Efficacy beliefs contribute to the course of social development as well as to occupational pursuits. For example, children who judge themselves highly efficacious in getting things they want by aggressive means adopt aggressive styles of behavior (Perry, Perry, & Rasmussen, 1986). Those who develop aggressive styles are inclined to select activities and associates who share similar aggressive orientations, thereby mutually reinforcing preexisting bents (Bandura & Walters, 1959; Bullock & Merrill, 1980). Developmental processes thus involve bidirectional causation. Beliefs of personal efficacy determine choice of associates and activities. Affiliation patterns, in turn, shape the direction of efficacy development. The next chapter analyzes the development of personal efficacy throughout the life span.

5

Developmental Analysis of Self-Efficacy

DIFFERENT PERIODS OF LIFE present certain proto-typic competency demands for successful functioning. Changing aspirations, time perspectives, and social arrangements over the course of the life span alter how people structure, regulate, and evaluate their lives in the lifelong journey. Changes with age in requisite normative competencies do not represent lock-step stages through which everyone must inevitably pass. Adolescence is not necessarily a period of adaptational turbulence, for example, nor are the middle years necessarily a period of "midlife crisis" as part of a preordained developmental sequence. There are many pathways through life, and at any given period, people vary substantially in how successfully they manage their lives in the milieus in which they are immersed. The beliefs they hold about their capabilities to produce results by their actions are an influential personal resource as they negotiate their lives through the life cycle.

Social cognitive theory analyzes developmental changes in perceived self-efficacy in terms of evolvement of human agency across the life span. When viewed from a life course perspective, the paths that lives take are shaped by the interplay of diverse influences in ever-changing societies. The environment in which people live their lives is not a situational entity that ordains their life course. Rather, it is a varied succession of transactional life events in which individuals play a role in shaping the course of their personal development (Baltes, 1983; Brim & Ryff, 1980; Hultsch & Plemons, 1979). Some of the influential events involve biological changes. Others are normative social events linked to people's age status and their roles in educational, familial, occupational, and other institutional systems. Virtually everyone engages in these latter activities at certain phases in their development. Still other life events involve unpredictable occurrences in the physical environment or irregular life events such as career changes, divorce, migration, accidents, and illnesses. Lives are historically situated and are socially developed in milieus that present unique opportunities, constraints, and threats. Elder (1994) has argued eloquently for the analysis of people's lives over time as they are shaped by the distinctive life experiences provided by the eras in which they live. Major sociocultural changes that make life markedly different — such as technological innovations, economic depressions, military conflicts, cultural upheavals, and political changes — modify the character of the society in ways that have strong impact on life courses. Life trajectories differ depending on where people are in their lives at the time of such changes (Elder, 1981).

Whatever the social conditions might be, personal lives take varied directions at any given time and place. It is the way in which people take advantage of opportunity structures and manage constraints under the prevailing sociocultural conditions that make the difference. There is also an element of fortuity to life courses. People are often brought together through a fortuitous constellation of events that can shape the course of their lives. Indeed, some of the most important determinants of life paths often arise through the most trivial of circumstances. In these instances, seemingly minor events have important and enduring impact on the courses lives take. There are many fortuitous elements in the events people encounter in their daily lives. Many chance encounters touch people only lightly, others leave more lasting effects, and still others thrust people into new life trajectories. Although many social encounters occur more by chance than by design, people exert some control over what they derive from those experiences. The power of fortuitous influences to initiate enduring personal changes is determined by the reciprocal interplay of personal attributes and the characteristics of the social milieus into which one is inaugurated (Bandura, 1982b). The particular patterning of biopsychosocial changes interwoven with fortuitous occurrences during the life course contribute to the uniqueness of individual life and its continuities and discontinuities.

The exercise of personal agency over the direction one's life takes varies depending on the nature and modifiability of the environment. Operative environments take three different forms: those that are *imposed*, *selected*, and *created*. There is the physical and sociostructural environment that impinges on people whether they like it or not. They do not have much control over its presence, but they do have leeway in how they construe it and react to it. They can view it favorably, neutrally, or negatively, depending on how well it serves them.

There is a major difference between the potential environment and the actual environment. For the most part, the environment is only a potentiality with different rewarding and punishing aspects. The environment does not come into being until it is selected and activated by appropriate action. Which part of the potential environment becomes the actual environment that is experienced thus depends on how people behave. This constitutes the selected environment. Under the same potential environment, some people take advantage of the opportunities it provides and its rewarding aspects; others get themselves enmeshed mainly in its punishing and debilitating aspects.

And finally, there is the environment that is created. It did not exist as a potentiality waiting to be selected and activated. Rather, people create social systems that enable them to exercise greater control over their lives. Gradations of environmental changeability require increasing levels of personal agency, ranging from cognitive construal agency to selection and activation agency to creative agency. People's beliefs in their personal efficacy play a paramount role in how they organize, create, and manage the environment that affects their developmental pathways.

As previously noted, appraisal of one's own capabilities is highly advantageous and is often essential for effective functioning. Those who seriously misjudge what they can do may put themselves at high risk should they engage in activities in which faulty performances produce detrimental consequences. Very young children lack knowledge of their own capabilities and the demands and potential hazards of different courses of action. They would get themselves into dangerous predicaments repeatedly were it not for the guidance of others. They can wander into dangerous thoroughfares, jump into deep pools, and wield sharp knives before they develop the necessary skills to manage such situations safely (Sears, Maccoby, & Levin, 1957). Adult watchfulness and guidance see young children through this early formative period until they gain sufficient knowledge of what they can do and what different situations require in the way of skills. With development of cognitive self-reflective capabilities, self-efficacy judgment increasingly supplants external guidance.

ORIGINS OF A SENSE OF PERSONAL AGENCY

The newborn arrives without any sense of self. The self must be socially constructed through transactional experiences with the environment. The developmental progression of a sense of personal agency moves from perceiving causal relations between events, through understanding causation through action, and finally to recognizing oneself as the agent of the action. Infants exhibit sensitivity to causal relationships even in the first months of life. For example, they express surprise at seeing a hand appear to move an object without touching it (Leslie, 1982; Mandler, 1992). Infants most likely begin to learn about action causation through repeated observation of contingent occurrences in which the actions of others make things happen. They see inanimate objects remain motionless unless manipulated by others (Mandler, 1992). Moreover, infants personally experience the effects of actions directed toward them, which adds salience to the causative functions of actions. Sociocognitive theory encompasses a wider set of developmental influences than do theories that assume that a sense of personal agency develops solely out of one's actions (Flammer, 1995; Gecas, 1989; Piaget, 1952). The observational learning that actions produce effects plays a leading role in the initial development of a sense of action causation. As infants begin to gain some behavioral capabilities, their understanding of agent causation is fostered by both observing and directly experiencing the results of actions.

In developing a conception of personal agency, infants must gain self-recognition and learn that they can make things happen. Infants' exploratory experiences in which they see themselves produce effects by their actions provide the initial basis for moving beyond understanding action causation to

developing a sense of personal agency. Newborns' immobility and limited means of action upon the physical and social environment greatly restrict their domain of influence, however. The initial enactive experiences that contribute to development of a sense of personal agency are tied to infants' ability to control the sensory stimulation from manipulable objects and the attentive behavior of those around them. Infants behave in certain ways, and certain things happen. Shaking a rattle produces predictable sounds, energetic kicks shake cribs, tossing objects makes them fall with a loud impact, and screams bring adults.

Recognition That Actions Produce Outcomes

Realization of personal agency requires both self-observation that outcomes flow from actions and recognition that the actions are part of oneself. By repeatedly observing that environmental events occur with action, but not without it, infants learn that actions produce effects. Initially, infants produce outcomes through flailing action. But as they come to recognize that their actions affect the environment, they begin to test their sense of agency through more planful, intentional action. They do things and look for expected affects. They alter their actions and watch for the different effects they produce. Through such exploratory tests, they verify their agentive capabilities. They now know they can make things happen.

Environments that are responsive to infants' actions promote the development of causal agency. Infants who experience success in controlling environmental events by their actions become more attentive to their own behavior and more competent learners than infants for whom the same environmental events occur regardless of how they behave. Experiences in which effects appear independently of action not only retard learning of personal agency in infants but also impair future learning in situations where outcomes are controllable through actions (Finkelstein & Ramey, 1977; Ramey & Finkelstein, 1978). Early experiences in lack of control have the power to undermine the exercise of agency in situations where infants can make things happen. These effects can be long-lasting and widely generalized. Thus, infants in homes where they make mobiles or hanging toys move by striking them are quick to learn how to make things happen in laboratory situations, whereas infants exposed to automatic wind-up mobiles at home become deficient learners (Watson, 1977). Noncontingent happenings teach infants that they lack controlling capabilities. So they make little effort to master activities that would enable them to exercise influence over their immediate environment. After repeated experiences of inefficacy in influencing events, even adults can lose their sense of personal agency and become apathetic in situations where the opportunity to exercise control exists (Garber & Seligman, 1980).

Watson (1977) identifies a number of factors that can impede infants' perceptions of control. Some of these factors involve the hazy functional relations between events in everyday life, such as delays between actions and outcomes, imperfect linkage between actions and outcomes, multidetermination of outcomes, and ambiguous environmental signaling of the events that are controllable and those that are not. There are a number of personal impediments to discernment of control. Infants have poorly developed attentional and memory functions; have limited capacity to construct actions; and have difficulty repeating the same actions in rapid succession, which increases opportunities to observe that they can make things happen. During the initial months of life, the exercise of influence over the physical environment may contribute more to the development of a child's sense of personal agency than does influence over the social environment (Gunnar, 1980a). This is because there is considerably less ambiguity about personal causation of outcomes in the realm of manipulative physical activities. Manipulating physical objects produces quick, predictable, recurrent, and easily observable effects. After shaking a rattle repeatedly and hearing the resultant sound, infants cannot help but notice that their actions produce environmental effects. Highly noticeable correlation between actions and effects facilitates perception of

personal agency in infants whose attentional and representational capabilities are initially limited.

The production of sounds, sights, and shapes with inanimate objects requires that they be manipulated in appropriate ways. In describing the order in which manipulative skills develop, Karniol (1989) notes that adults can facilitate the development of infants' sense of personal control by providing them with objects within their manipulatory capabilities to activate what the objects can do. This calls for simple objects when manipulatory capabilities are minimal. As infants become more capable of acting on their environment through development of manipulatory skills, they are given progressively more complex objects to explore and master. Increasing challenges expand their sense of controllability. The enabling benefits of challenging play materials are enhanced if parents use them interactively in ways that build their infants' competencies (Parks & Bradley, 1991).

Younger infants have difficulty with contingency learning, even from salient physical effects of their actions, if the effects are widely separated in time or place. When the outcomes of actions are delayed, the activities that occur during the intervening period create some confusion as to what produces what. To learn from outcomes appearing long after the actions have occurred one must attend to disparate events, code them symbolically for memory, recall them, and relate them cognitively. Thus, when actions and their full effects are widely separated in time, distal outcomes are often difficult to link to their behavioral causes or are easily misjudged as resulting from irrelevant actions that happened to occur more closely in time.

Infants and young children have difficulty not only in recognizing that what they do has effects later but in representing such agentive knowledge symbolically. During the first few months of life, infants do not possess the attentional and memory capabilities to profit much from contingent experiences, even when the effects of their actions are delayed only briefly (Millar, 1972; Watson, 1979). The problems of contingency learning are compounded when delayed outcomes of actions are also separated in where they occur. This is shown in studies by Millar and his associates on how attentional strategies reflecting cognitive competencies affect contingency learning from perceptual feedback. Younger infants are as adept as older ones at contingency learning when their actions and the sounds and sights they produce are spatially contiguous. This makes it easy for infants to attend to both sets of events (Millar & Schaffer, 1972). But younger infants fail to learn that actions produce outcomes when the outcomes are spatially displaced. They watch what they are doing but, because they have difficulty remembering where the delayed effects occur, they do not notice and relate them to their actions. Older infants, by contrast, adopt an effective attentional strategy for integrating actions and outcomes: They manipulate objects while at the same time looking where they expect the effects to appear. If younger infants are provided with an external cue that tells them where to look for the effects of their actions, they become more observant of the happenings around them and learn from them (Millar, 1974). Such findings suggest that deficits in infant contingency learning may often reflect failures in the deployment of attention, rather than cognitive incapacity to integrate contingent events. The informative value of contingent experience for personal agency can be greatly enhanced by creating conditions that encourage infants to try controlling actions, by linking outcomes closely to actions, by using aids to channel infants' attention to the outcomes they are producing, and by heightening the salience and functional value of the outcomes.

Causal agency is more difficult to discern in noisier social contingencies. The social effects of infants' behavior, depending as they do on the availability and vagaries of others, are not only more delayed and variable but often occur independently of the infants' behavior. That is, others frequently attend to infants and initiate activities with them regardless of what the infants may be doing at the time. A cry may bring others instantly, some time later, or not at all. Yet others often appear in the absence of crying. It is difficult to learn from such mixed social experiences, in which actions do not always produce social reactions and social reactions

often occur on their own through the initiative of others (Watson, 1979).

Microanalyses of familial interactions show that parents often structure contingent experiences in ways that help infants discover that their actions have social effects (Papousek & Papousek, 1979). This is achieved in several ways. Parents establish close eye contact with the infant to ensure adequate attentiveness. They react to their infant's actions quickly and animatedly to create highly noticeable proximal effects. Further, to aid the infant's perception that actions produce outcomes, the transactions are often repeated in rapid succession. Should the contingencies escape the infant's notice during the initial transactions, it has many additional opportunities to discover them without having to draw on an infirm memory capability.

A high level of adult contingent responsiveness helps newborns and infants to learn that they can make things happen by their actions. As infants' mobility develops, the instant effects of their acts on the physical environment provide clear evidence of causal agency. A toy that is dropped or is used as a percussion instrument produces interesting sounds and sights. Infants soon discover to their delight that they can create outcomes promptly by their actions, especially if a parent is present to retrieve flung objects. Proximal contingent experiences, whether they occur directly or are revealed by the actions of others, create a causal cognitive set to look for relations between events when the actions are less clearly related to their effects. As infants begin to sense that they can produce effects, they engage in exploratory activities in which they vary their actions and observe what outcomes flow from them. The adoption of a causal cognitive set with exploratory verification accelerates the development of a sense of personal agency. With the development of representational capabilities, infants can begin to learn from probabilistic and more distal outcomes of personal actions. Before long, the exercise of control over the social environment begins to play an important role in the early development of self-efficacy. The experience of making social events happen generalizes to the exercise of control over nonsocial events (Dunham, Dunham, Hurshman,

& Alexander, 1989). Thus, infants who have been exposed to contingent social responsiveness act on their physical environment to produce sights and sounds, whereas infants who received the same amount of attention but independently of how they behaved make little effort to change aspects of their environment that are under their control.

The previous discussion documents how spontaneous enactive experience reveals the power of action to produce certain results. The development of a sense of personal agency is not entirely the result of solitary exploratory endeavor, however. After infants discover that they can exercise some control over aspects of their immediate environment, they draw on vicarious experiences to expand and verify their sense of personal efficacy. They observe the models around them achieve certain effects by appropriate courses of action. When the modeled strategies are within the infants' capabilities, they adopt the same strategies to achieve similar results (Kaye, 1982). Moreover, on later occasions, they use novel manipulative skills they had seen modeled when the model is no longer around (Meltzoff, 1988a,b). Thus, modeled performances not only instill views of agent causation but also convey skills to infants that increase their success in the exercise of control.

There is also a great deal of intentional guidance in fostering infant mastery (Heckhausen, 1987). Mothers segment activities into manageable subskills. They set challenges for their infants just beyond their existing competencies. They adjust their level of assistance across phases of mastery, offering explicit guidance in earlier phases of skill acquisition but gradually withdrawing aid as infants become more competent in mastering tasks on their own. These types of instructional strategies are highly conducive to the development of a sense of personal agency during the initial years of life.

Recognition and Differentiation of the Self

Development of a sense of personal efficacy requires more than simply producing effects by actions. Those actions must be perceived as part of oneself and one must recognize that one is the agent of those actions. This additional understanding shifts the perception of agency from action causality to personal causality. The differentiation of oneself from others is the product of a more general process of the construction of the self. Intentional production of effects creates a rudimentary sense of agentive self. Personal effects resulting from self-directed actions help to underscore the presence of a recipient experiencing those effects. Thus, if striking oneself causes pain, feeding oneself brings comfort, and entertaining oneself with manipulable objects generates enjoyment, one begins to recognize an experiential self. The self becomes differentiated from others through rudimentary dissimilar experiences. If hitting oneself brings pain, whereas seeing others hit themselves brings no pain, one's own activity becomes distinct from that of all other persons. The earliest differentiations between self and others probably involve activities that have salient somatic effects that make the self distinct from others.

Infants acquire a sense of personal agency when they recognize that they can make things happen and they regard themselves as the doers. The construction of self is not entirely a matter of private reflection on one's experiences. As children begin to mature and acquire language, those around them refer to them by personal names and treat them as distinct persons. Understanding language accelerates self-recognition and development of self-awareness of personal agency. Indeed, by about 18 months, infants have self-referent verbal labels and apply them only to pictures of themselves (Lewis & Brooks-Gunn, 1979). They clearly differentiate themselves from others in their verbal labeling. As they become increasingly aware that they can produce effects by their actions, by about 20 months, they spontaneously describe themselves as agents of their actions and their intentions as they engage in activities (Kagan, 1981). Before long, they begin to describe the psychological states accompanying their actions. Based on their growing personal and social experiences, they eventually form a symbolic representation of themselves as a distinct self capable of making things happen.

The emergence of awareness of one's own efficacy has received little attention. Admittedly, this is a very difficult methodological challenge. Children who do not yet understand language cannot be asked to judge their abilities to produce given results. The affective and behavioral indicators that have been explored usually confound affective self-reaction with perceived capability. Knowing that one can make things happen is different from experiencing sadness, happiness, pride, or distress over what one has done. The former is a judgment of personal agency to produce certain results; the latter is an affective self-reaction to the results one has produced. Affective self-reaction presupposes self-recognition of personal agency and adoption of a standard for evaluating one's conduct. But feeling good or bad about one's performance is not a measure of perceived capability. During the preverbal period of development, a sense of personal agency is perhaps better reflected in evidence that courses of actions are intentionally selected, self-monitored, and self-corrected in the face of impediments to achieve particular outcomes.

FAMILIAL SOURCES OF SELF-EFFICACY

Children must gain self-knowledge of their capabilities in broadening areas of functioning as they expand their transactions with the environment. They have to develop, appraise, and test their physical capabilities, their social competencies, their linguistic skills, and their cognitive skills for comprehending and managing the many situations they encounter daily. Development of sensorimotor capabilities greatly enlarges the infant's available environment and the means for acting upon it. These early exploratory and play activities, which occupy much of an infant's waking hours, provide opportunities to expand and refine their basic skills.

While developing their capabilities during this initial period of immaturity, most of the infant's gratifications and well-being must be mediated by adults. Neonates have to depend on others to feed them, clothe them, comfort them, entertain them, and furnish the play materials for their manipulative exploration. Because of this physical dependency, infants quickly learn how to influence the actions of those around them by their social and verbal behavior. Many of these transactions involve the exercise of proxy control; young children get adults to produce desired outcomes that the children themselves cannot bring about. Efficacy experiences in the exercise of personal control are central to the early development of social and cognitive competence. Parents who are responsive to their infant's communicative behavior and who create opportunities for efficacious actions by providing an enriched physical environment, freedom for exploration, and varied mastery experiences have infants who are relatively accelerated in their social, linguistic and cognitive development (Ainsworth & Bell, 1974; Ruddy & Bornstein, 1982; Yarrow, Rubenstein, & Pedersen, 1975).

Impact of Early Mastery Experiences on Social and Cognitive Development

Longitudinal studies in which parents are explicitly taught how to provide their infants with experiences of mastery furnish even stronger evidence that enabling influences during infancy build a sense of agency conducive to cognitive development. Infants who are taught how to be causative are more cognitively competent in childhood than those who have not had the benefit of early mastery experiences (Ramey , McGinness, Cross, Collier, & Barrie- Blackley, 1982). Premature infants of disadvantaged, unmarried mothers make big gains in cognitive development when the mothers are taught how to give them challenging tasks that encourage them to initiate activities and produce effects with manipulable objects (Scarr-Salapatek & Williams, 1973). The more enabling mastery activities the mothers provide their infants, the better is their cognitive development.

Other lines of research further document the substantial developmental benefits of early interventions that build the competencies of children at high risk for future intellectual disabilities (Ramey & Ramey, 1992). Intensive preschool programs that provide rich mastery experiences permanently raise the intellectual level and academic attainments of children from economically impoverished and undereducated families. The most disadvantaged benefit the most. The earlier and more intensive the enablement program, the greater the lasting intellectual benefits. High-risk children without such enablement programs end up functioning at borderline or retarded levels of intelligence and tend to repeat grades. These long-term results suggest that efficacy-enhancing programs can alter adverse intergenerational patterns of intellectual functioning.

The level of efficacy-promoting influences in the home environment carries the major explanatory weight in the commonly observed relationship between socioeconomic background and children's cognitive functioning (Bradley et al., 1989). Simply possessing socioeconomic advantages does not necessarily lead parents to create cognitively stimulating home environments for their children. It is what parents do with their advantages that makes the difference. Hence, parental influences that enable their children to interact effectively with their environment predict the course of their cognitive development when socioeconomic level is controlled, but socioeconomic level makes little unique contribution to cognitive development when variations in enabling parental influences are controlled.

Efficacy-promoting influence does not flow solely in one direction. Even in the initial period of development, infant and environment operate as reciprocal interactants. Parental enabling activities increase infants' exploratory and cognitive competence, and infant capabilities elicit greater parental responsiveness in a process of reciprocal causation (Bradley, Caldwell, & Elardo, 1979). The influence from parent to infant, however, is stronger than from infant to parent (Bradley et al., 1989). Mastery experiences in infancy initiate the developmental course. But the types of enabling experiences parents provide during the early childhood years contribute to the future direction the

developmental course takes irrespective of the quality and stability of the early home environment (Bradley, Caldwell, & Rock, 1988). The course of children's cognitive development is evidently shaped by both the carryover effects of early enablement and the more contemporary experiences of mastery in the broader social environment.

Acquisition of language provides children with the symbolic means to reflect on their experiences and on what others tell them about their capabilities. Through reflective thought, they begin to build self-knowledge of what they can and cannot do. Once children can understand speech, parents and others express judgments of children's capabilities to guide them in foreseen situations where the parents may not be present. To the extent that children's appraisals of their capabilities are partly shaped by the efficacy appraisals of others, they can affect their children's rate of personal development by influencing whether and how they approach new tasks. Thus, for example, overprotective parents, who are oversolicitous and dwell on potential dangers, constrain development of their children's capabilities, whereas more secure parents are quick to acknowledge and encourage their children's growing capabilities (Levy, 1943). In the early years, mothers' judgments influence their children's self-appraisals of capability more than do fathers' (Felson & Reed, 1986).

The initial efficacy experiences are centered in the family. But as growing children's social world rapidly expands, peers assume an increasingly important role in their development of self-knowledge of their capabilities. It is in the context of peer interactions that social comparison processes come forcefully into play. At first, the closest comparative age-mates are siblings. Families differ in number of siblings, how far apart in age they are, and their sex distribution. Different family structures — as reflected in family size, birth order, and sibling constellation patterns — create different social references for comparative appraisal of personal efficacy. Firstborns and only children have different bases for judging their capabilities than do children with older brothers and sisters. Parents have more time and opportunity to provide firstborns and only children with richer and more plentiful enabling experiences. Ordinal position, therefore, can have differential effects on the development of intellectual and social efficacy (Zajonc & Markus, 1975). Comparative evaluations of efficacy by siblings close in age will be stronger than evaluations by siblings spaced further apart in age. Similarly, siblings of the same sex force more competitive evaluations of efficacy than do those of the opposite sex. The potential for rivalrous comparisons favoring the older sibling is strongest between same-sexed siblings who are not too far apart. Younger siblings find themselves in the unfavorable position of judging their capabilities in relation to older siblings who are several years advanced in their development. Therefore, close age spacing may create pressures on younger children to differentiate themselves from older siblings by developing dissimilar personality patterns, interests, and vocational pursuits (Leventhal, 1970). The self-evaluative habits developed in sibling interactions undoubtedly affect evaluations of personal capabilities in later life. Self-efficacy rooted in sibling rivalry is especially likely to create hypersensitivity to judging personal efficacy against the accomplishments of others.

Development of Self-Appraisal Skills

With cognitive development through exploratory experiences, modeling, and instruction, children gradually improve their self-appraisal skills. The self-knowledge gained by applying those appraisal skills enables them to judge their efficacy on their own as guides for their actions in whatever situations may arise. How children learn to use diverse sources of efficacy information in developing a stable and accurate sense of personal efficacy is a matter of considerable interest. Functional self-appraisal is no easy matter.

Accurate appraisal of one's capabilities depends on a number of constituent skills that develop through direct and socially mediated experiences. While engaging in activities, children must attend simultaneously to multiple sources of efficacy information conveyed by the nature of the task, situational factors that aid or impede

performance, the characteristics of their actions, and the results they produce. Because activities are performed on repeated occasions, children must be able to transcend particular instances and integrate efficacy information from rises and falls in performance over time. The presence of many interacting determinants places heavy demands on children's ability to monitor ongoing events, to evaluate the causes of fluctuations in performances and outcomes, and to represent and retain efficacy information derived from numerous prior experiences under varying circumstances.

Research on development of metacognitive skills has explored how children gain knowledge about cognition, task goals, and strategies for achieving them, as well as how they learn to reflect on the adequacy of their own thinking (Brown, 1984; Flavell, 1979). Gaining self-knowledge of capabilities as a doer requires appraisal of considerably more skills than judging one's capabilities merely as a thinker. Exercise of personal efficacy requires improvisation of multiple cognitive, social, manual, and motivational skills. Activities vary substantially in the demands they make on cognitive and memory skills, motor facility, strength, endurance, and stress tolerance. In addition to appraising the versatility of their skills, children have much to learn about the difficulty of environmental tasks, the abilities the tasks require, and the types of problems likely to arise in executing different courses of action. Moreover, they must judge their capability to withstand stressors. Disparities between efficacy beliefs and action may stem from misjudgment of task demands as well as from faulty self-knowledge. With wider experience, children gain better understanding of themselves and their everyday environment. This knowledge enables them to judge their efficacy in particular areas of functioning more realistically.

Because of their limited cognitive skills and experience, young children have sketchy knowledge of their cognitive and behavioral capabilities. They have difficulty in attending simultaneously to multiple sources of efficacy information, in distinguishing between important and minor indicants of capability, and in processing efficacy information distributed over long stretches of time. As a result, their self-appraisals are apt to be quite dependent on immediate, salient outcomes and, hence, to be relatively unstable.

As children become more proficient with age in their self-appraisal skills, reliance on immediate performance attainments declines in importance in judging what they can do. These changes are accompanied by developmental increases in children's use of more diverse, less salient, and sequential efficacy information (Parsons, Moses, & Yulish-Muszynski, 1977; Parsons & Ruble, 1977). With experience, they begin to understand how expenditure of effort can compensate for lack of ability (Kun, 1977). Through more extensive use of efficacy information provided across tasks, time, and situations, older children judge their capabilities and limitations more accurately. As they get older, they begin to use inference rules or heuristics in processing efficacy information; for example, inferring that the more effort expended, the lower the capability.

We saw earlier that people judge their capabilities partly through social comparison with the performances of others. Evaluating personal efficacy by social comparison involves greater complexities than do self-appraisals based on direct experience. In comparative appraisals of personal efficacy, children not only have to evaluate their own performances but also must monitor how well others do, recognize nonability determinants of their performances, and understand that it is others slightly better than themselves who provide the most informative social criterion for gauging capabilities. With development, children become increasingly discriminative in their use of comparative efficacy information. Developmental analyses conducted by Morris and Nemcek (1982) show that effective use of social comparative information lags behind perception of ability rankings. Except for the very young (for example, three-year-olds), who do not discern differences in ability, with increasing age children are progressively more accurate in appraising their own abilities and those of their peers. Not until about age six, however, do they realize that it is the performances of others who are like themselves, but slightly better, that are most informative for comparative purposes.

A problem for future research is to clarify how young children learn what type of social comparative information is most useful for efficacy evaluation. Such knowledge is probably gained in several ways. One process undoubtedly operates through success and failure experiences of acting on comparative self-appraisals based on people of different levels of ability and different attributes. Children repeatedly observe their own behavior and the attainments of others. We know from the work of Morris and Nemcek that, at least in some areas of functioning, children begin to discern differences in ability at a very early age. Given that they can rank ability, they would soon learn that neither the successes of the most talented nor the failures of inept peers tell them much about how well they are likely to perform new activities. Rather, it is the attainments of others similar to themselves that are most predictive of their own operative capabilities. Acting on appropriate comparative self-appraisal thus maximizes the likelihood of success. Attribute similarity would also gain informative value for comparative appraisal of capabilities through differential experiences. To the extent that children with similar attributes achieve comparable performance levels, comparing oneself with peers of similar attributes is likely to yield more accurate self-appraisal than would basing self-appraisal on the accomplishments of dissimilar peers.

Children do not rely solely on the behavioral consequences of comparative efficacy judgments in learning to select similar others for evaluating their capabilities. They receive direct instruction from time to time about the appropriateness of various social comparisons. Because of their limited experience, young children are quick to try what they see others doing even though it is well beyond their reach. Acting on faulty self-evaluation can undermine their developing sense of efficacy or, if the activities are potentially dangerous, result in injury. To minimize such consequences, parents explain to their children who is appropriate and who is not for comparison in gauging their capabilities.

Measuring the accuracy with which children at different ages judge their efficacy can shed some light on developmental trends in how children use different sources of efficacy information in their self-appraisals. Such research does not say much about how proficiency in self-appraisal is acquired, however. Knowledge of how determinants and self-appraisal skills are developed can be advanced by experiments designed to increase efficacy-appraisal skills where they are lacking. Cognitive modeling provides one effective means of increasing children's understanding of the value of relevant sources of efficacy information.

In cognitive modeling (Meichenbaum & Asarnow, 1979), models verbalize aloud their thoughts as they form judgments and solve problems. Their covert thought processes are thus made fully observable. In applying cognitive modeling to the development of self-appraisal skills, models identify cues indicative of efficacy and verbalize rules for interpreting and integrating the efficacy information while performing different tasks. Functional rules for evaluating social comparative information can be modeled in a similar fashion so that the performances of others serve as instructive guides and motivators rather than as demoralizers.

Research aimed at building efficacy-appraisal skills offers therapeutic benefits as well as knowledge about developmental processes. Many children are severely handicapped by disbelief in their efficacy stemming from faulty self-appraisal. They misconstrue performance difficulties arising, in large part, from nonability factors as due entirely to personal deficiencies and undermine their efforts by adverse social comparisons (Bandura, 1990a; Sternberg & Kolligian, 1990). They have much to gain from changing a negatively biased system of self-appraisal that leads them to belittle their capabilities and increases their vulnerability to stress and despondency.

Surmounting Childhood Adversities

Studies of the life trajectories of children burdened with unrelenting childhood adversity provide additional insights into the origins and growth of human efficacy (Masten, Best, & Garmezy, 1990; Rutter, 1990; Werner, 1992). These are children who grow up in families plagued with chronic poverty, discord, physical abuse, divorce, parental alcoholism, or serious mental disorders. Remarkably, a goodly

number of children surmount such enormous hardships and develop into efficacious, caring, and productive adults. Their personal triumphs have given us a better sense of some of the determinants of extraordinary resilience. Resilience is reflected in positive developmental outcomes in the face of severe adversity. These outcomes include social competence, academic achievement, a favorable sense of self, absence of psychosocial pathology, and successful fulfillment of essential roles in adult years.

The development of a stable social bond to a competent, caring adult is a crucial factor in the management of risk and adversity (Egeland, Carlson, & Sroufe, 1993). Such caregivers offer emotional support and guidance, promote meaningful values and standards, model constructive styles of coping, and create numerous opportunities for mastery experiences. Enabling caretaking builds trust, competencies, and a sense of personal efficacy. Physical attractiveness and sociable temperamental qualities help to draw nurturing caretaking. As children develop positive attributes, they become more engaging to others and attract support from them. Supportive teachers are often important enabling influences in the lives of children who surmount severe adversities. Social connectedness to a variety of other caring persons outside the family provides continuing guidance and opportunities for self-development. Intellectual competencies, which are essential tools for managing the demands of everyday life, are also uniformly strong predictors of successful adaptation.

Given impoverished or disordered home lives, resilient children play a proactive role in shaping their life courses. They become highly resourceful in finding and creating environments conducive to their personal development. They take upon themselves the responsibilities of managing the household and care of younger siblings when their parents are unable to do so, which is often the case. They cultivate interests that bring satisfactions and save them from becoming engulfed by the turbulent home life. Resiliency is reflected in the ability not only to withstand adverse circumstances but to recover from a disordered life course. Disordered life courses are notoriously difficult to change, but they can be changed through extensive supportive enablement. Those who have failed to escape from childhood adversities are better able to turn their lives around as they enter young adulthood if they have developed their intellectual skills; pursue opportunities to acquire vocational skills; form a stable, supportive partnership; and affiliate with religious or other community groups that provide support and meaning to their lives (Werner & Smith, 1992). Personal attributes operate interactively with environmental aids in achieving such major redirection of life paths. The personal and social resources enable them eventually to free themselves from their troublesome impoverished lives.

Longitudinal studies of the sources of childhood resilience have focused, for the most part, on broad classes of social influences. Much has been learned from these efforts. The appropriate next stage for research is to identify which aspects of these multifaceted influences contribute to different types of developmental change and the mechanisms through which they promote human resilience. Werner (1992) reports that a sense of personal control over one's life circumstances is a key factor in resilience. Childhood control beliefs predict less distress and high enlistment of social supports for successful adaptation in adulthood. One would not prescribe adversity alone as the way to build human resilience. But adversities combined with enabling social supports that instill a sense of personal efficacy and self-worth and provide paths to success can promote masterful resilience.

PEERS AND THE BROADENING AND VALIDATION OF SELF-EFFICACY

Children's efficacy experiences change substantially as they move increasingly into the larger community. It is in peer relationships that they broaden and particularize knowledge of their capabilities. Peers serve several important efficacy functions. Activities are extensively age-graded so that much of children's interactions are with age-mates. Those who are most experienced and competent provide models of efficacious styles of thinking and behavior (Bandura, 1986a; Perry & Bussey, 1984). A vast amount of social learning occurs among peers. In addition, because of similarities in age and experiences, age-mates provide the most informative points of reference for comparative efficacy appraisal and verification. Children are, therefore, especially sensitive to their relative standing among the peers with whom they affiliate in activities that determine prestige and popularity.

Peers are neither homogeneous nor selected indiscriminately. Children tend to choose close associates who share similar interests and values. Selective peer association will promote self-efficacy in directions of mutual interest, leaving other potentialities underdeveloped (Bandura & Walters, 1959; Bullock & Merrill, 1980; Ellis & Lane, 1963; Krauss, 1964). The social influences are undoubtedly bidirectional: Affiliation references affect the direction of efficacy development, and personal efficacy, in turn, partly determines choice of peer associates and activities. Because peers serve as a major agency for the development and validation of self-efficacy, disrupted or impoverished peer relationships can adversely affect the growth of personal efficacy. A low sense of social efficacy, in turn, can create attitudinal and behavioral obstacles to favorable peer relationships (Connolly, 1989; Wheeler & Ladd, 1982). Thus, children who regard themselves as socially inefficacious exhibit social withdrawal, perceive low acceptance by their peers, and have a low sense of self-worth. A high sense of efficacy for some forms of behavior, such as coercive styles, can be socially alienating rather than socially affiliating.

Developmental psychology has been moving away from studying individual differences in global decontextualized traits to studying individual differences in cognitive processes regulating behavioral proclivities in different types of social situations (Crick & Dodge, 1994). For example, children differ in how they respond to ambiguous provocations. Some react aggressively, others withdraw to avoid further harassment, and still others choose constructive ways of managing such situations. Children's beliefs in their efficacy to carry out different types of solutions predict their social goals and how they are likely to behave (Erdley & Asher, 1996). Children with a high sense of efficacy for aggressive means favor hostile goals expressed in retaliative actions, whereas those of high perceived efficacy for prosocial means pursue friendly goals aimed at resolving interpersonal problems amicably. Attributing hostile intent to others does not provoke retaliative acts in children who distrust their efficacy to wield control by aggressive means. This is another example where efficacy beliefs mediate the effects of attributions on behavior. Children with a high sense of efficacy for aggressive means are quick to use them without needing provocation. Perry and his associates report that two sociocognitive determinants — efficacy beliefs and outcome expectations — operate in concert in supporting aggressive or prosocial behavioral styles (Perry et al., 1986). Thus, children who judge themselves to be efficacious for aggression and believe that they can get what they want by this means readily resort to aggression in peer interactions. Although the development of personal efficacy in coercive styles of behavior permits easy control over others, it is estranging in ways that can lead down a transgressive life path.

The work of Patterson and his colleagues amply documents that coercive conduct is an important precursor of deviant and delinquent development (Patterson, DeBaryshe, & Ramsey, 1989; Patterson, Di_____ on, & Bank, 1984). Aggressive disorders ofte_____ _____ n families with low positive interactions _____ _____ n degree of punitive reciprocity. Un____ _____ _____ itions, children become opposi-_____ _____ _____ stile. Parents try to get them to behave by _____ _____ rcive, punitive means. This results in escalating power struggles in which about half the time the parents reinforce the child's coercive behavior by giving in and the other half the parents' coercive behavior pays off because the child eventually gives up. The family members thus learn to control each other by coercion and aggression. The antagonistic coercive style of conduct evolves into a physically aggressive coping style, which the child generalizes to peers and teachers. Such conduct provokes rejection from prosocial peers, which only activates

further alienating behavior toward them. In the pre-delinquent phase, peer rejection, academic failure, and poor parental monitoring of the child's activities outside the home foster selective association with a delinquent peer group. Antisocial peers model, teach, and reward delinquent behavior.

SCHOOL AS AN AGENCY FOR CULTIVATING SELF-EFFICACY

During the crucial formative period of children's lives, the school functions as the primary setting for the cultivation and social validation of cognitive capabilities. School is the place where children develop the cognitive competencies and acquire the knowledge and problem-solving skills essential for participating effectively in society. Here their knowledge and thinking skills are continually tested, evaluated, and socially compared. The role of educational systems in the development of children's cognitive efficacy is addressed in a later chapter and will be reviewed only briefly here.

As children master cognitive skills, they develop a growing sense of their intellectual efficacy. Many social factors apart from the formal instruction — such as peer modeling of cognitive skills, social comparison with the performances of other students, and instructors' interpretations of children's successes and failures in ways that reflect favorably or unfavorably on their ability — also affect children's judgments of their intellectual efficacy (Schunk, 1984a; 1987; 1989a). A strong sense of efficacy fosters a high level of motivation, academic accomplishments, and development of intrinsic interest in academic subject matter (Bandura & Schunk, 1981; Relich et al., 1986; Schunk, 1984a).

A fundamental goal of education is to equip students with self-regulatory capabilities that enable them to educate themselves. Self-directedness not only contributes to success in formal instruction but also promotes lifelong learning. Self-regulation encompasses skills for planning, organizing, and managing instructional activities; enlisting resources; regulating one's own motivation; and applying metacognitive skills to evaluate the adequacy of one's knowledge and strategies. A high sense of self-regulatory efficacy contributes to mastery of academic subject matter by building a sense of cognitive efficacy and raising academic aspirations in those domains (Zimmerman, Bandura, & Martinez-Pous, 1992). Much learning occurs outside the confines of formal instruction. The stronger the students' self-instructional efficacy, the more learning they engage in on their own outside the school (Bergin, 1987). We will return later to a detailed analysis of how belief in one's self-regulatory efficacy promotes cognitive growth.

Students who come well-prepared cognitively and motivationally learn quickly and are adequately served by the prevailing educational practices. There are numerous social critics, however, who believe that, for many children, the school falls short of accomplishing its purposes. Not only does it fail to prepare the youth adequately for the future, but all too often it undermines the very sense of personal efficacy needed for continued self-development. Recurring difficulties encountered with low-achieving students erode teachers' sense of instructional efficacy (Bandura, 1993). Inefficacy feeds on itself.

There are a number of school practices that, for the less talented or ill-prepared, tend to convert instructional experiences into education in inefficacy. These include lock-step sequences of instruction, which lose along the way many children who fail to learn at the required pace. Sorting students into ability groupings further diminishes the perceived self-efficacy of those cast into lower academic tracks where little is expected of them, and so they continue to fall further behind academically. Socially competitive grading practices convert educational experiences into ones where many are doomed to failure for the high success of a few.

Classroom structures affect perceptions of cognitive capabilities, in large part, by the relative emphasis they place on social-comparative versus self-comparative appraisal. Self-appraisals of less able students suffer most when the whole group studies the same material and teachers make frequent comparative evaluations (Rosenholtz &

Rosenholtz, 1981). Under such a uniform structure, which highlights social comparative standards, students rank themselves according to capability with remarkably high consensus. Once established, reputations are not easily changed. In a diversified classroom structure, individualized instruction tailored to students' knowledge and skills enables all of them to expand their competencies and provides less basis for demoralizing social comparison. As a result, students are more likely to compare their rate of progress to their personal standards than to the performance of others. They have greater leeway in selecting others with whom to compare themselves, should they choose to do so. Personalized classroom structures produce higher perceived capability and less dependence on the opinions of teachers and classmates than does the monolithic structure.

Whether activities are structured cooperatively or competitively also affects children's judgments of their capabilities and the esteem with which they hold themselves and their associates. Results of comparative studies show that cooperative structures, in which members encourage and teach one another, generally promote higher performance attainments than do competitive or individualistic ones (Johnson, Maruyama, Johnson, Nelson, & Skon, 1981). Less talented members fare much better in successful cooperative systems than in competitive ones. They judge themselves more capable, they feel more deserving of recognition, and they are more self-satisfied. These personal benefits do not come at costs to highly capable members when the group effort works well. Skilled performers evaluate themselves just as positively as they do in competitive systems. When cooperative efforts fail, however, the more skilled feel less satisfied than if they can gain benefits independently, and they view those who perform poorly as less deserving of reward. The less able performers also think less well of themselves under these circumstances. In competitive systems, the successes of skilled members spell failures for the less able. Victors enhance their self-appraisal. Losers suffer self-devaluation. The negative impact may be lessened if different people find different things at which they can excel. In any event, the combined findings suggest that both performance attainments and favorable self-appraisals are best achieved through co-operative effort that is organized to work well.

Children have to learn to face displeasing realities about gaps in their knowledge and competencies. Classroom practices that undermine students' sense of efficacy and thereby lower their future academic performances, however, partly contribute to these displeasing realities. Educational practices should be gauged not only by the skills and knowledge they impart for present use but also by what they do to children's beliefs about their capabilities, which affects how they approach the future. Students who develop strong belief in their efficacy are well-equipped to educate themselves when they have to rely on their own initiative.

Children's beliefs in their cognitive efficacy have repercussions in the course of their social development as well as their intellectual growth. Those who are confident of their abilities to master academic skills and to regulate their own learning are more prosocially inclined and enjoy greater popularity and less rejection by their peers than do children who are too burdened with intellectual self-doubts to put much effort into academic activities (Bandura, 1993). A low sense of cognitive efficacy not only curtails positive peer relationships but fosters socially alienating aggressive and transgressive behavior. The negative impact of perceived cognitive inefficacy on the course of social development becomes stronger as children grow older and gravitate to peer groups that can get them into all kinds of trouble.

Lifelong health habits are formed during childhood and adolescence. Children need to learn nutritious eating patterns; recreational skills for lifelong fitness; and self-management skills to avoid substance abuse, delinquency and violence, and sexually transmitted diseases (Hamburg, 1992; Millstein, Petersen, & Nightingale, 1993). Health habits are rooted in familial practices, but schools also have a vital role to play in promoting the health of a nation. This is the only place where all children can be easily reached regardless of their age, socioeconomic status, cultural background, or ethnicity. But harried educators do not want the additional responsibilities of health promotion and disease prevention, nor are they adequately equipped for the role even if they were willing to undertake it. Moreover, schools are reluctant to get embroiled in social controversies over drug use, sexuality, and the various social morbidities that place youth at risk. Many educators argue that it is not their responsibility to remedy society's social ills. They have enough problems fulfilling their basic academic mission.

The traditional style of health education provides students with factual information about health without attempting to change the social influences that shape and regulate health habits. These influences from family members, peers, mass media, and the broader society are often in conflict. As a general rule, school health education is long on didactics but short on personal enablement. School-based informational approaches alone do little to change health behavior (Bruvold, 1993). Effective programs to promote healthy lifestyles must address the social nature of health behavior and equip youth with the means to exercise control over habits that can jeopardize their health. This requires a multifaceted approach to the common determinants of interconnected health habits rather than piecemeal targeting of a specific behavior for change. A comprehensive approach is called for because problem behaviors usually go together as part of a distinctive lifestyle rather than appearing in isolation. It is not indefinite holism that is being recommended but rather focus on the broad network of psychosocial influences that shape and support interrelated clusters of health habits. Categorical funding of school health programs for specific health-risking behaviors encourages the fragmentation, often with bureaucratic impediments. When the more comprehensive approaches are grudgingly allowed into the schools, they are typically applied in a superficial way under time constraints that strip them of their effectiveness.

Schools are an advantageous place for health promotion and early intervention, but that does not mean that educators must be the standard-bearers for the health mission. Health promotion must be structured as part of an overall children's health policy that makes health a crucial issue and provides the multidisciplinary personnel and resources needed to foster the health of youth. This requires creating new school-based models of health promotion that operate together with the home, the community, and the society at large. Issuing health mandates without supporting resources, explicit plans of action, and a system for monitoring progress will not beget a healthy society. Successful models of personal change rely on guided mastery experiences in managing problem situations as the principal vehicle of change. Success in discouraging the adoption of injurious health habits is best achieved by guided mastery approaches that combine school-based health programs with family and community efforts (Perry, Kelder, Murray, & Klepp, 1992; Telch, Killen, McAlister, Perry, & Maccoby, 1982). The effectiveness of such programs depends partly on their success in instilling and strengthening a sense of personal efficacy to manage one's health habits.

GROWTH OF SELF-EFFICACY THROUGH TRANSITIONAL EXPERIENCES OF ADOLESCENCE

Each period of development brings with it new competency requirements and challenges for coping efficacy. Adolescence is an important transitional phase in the life course that presents a host of new challenges. It is a crucial formative period because this is when the roles of adulthood must begin to be addressed in almost every dimension of life. Adolescents must begin to consider seriously what they want to do with their lives. During this time, they have to master many new skills and the ways of adult society. They must do all this in a society that does not provide many meaningful roles for them. As adolescents expand the nature and scope of their activities into the larger social community, they have to assume increasing responsibility for conduct that plays a more decisive role than do childhood involvements in fostering or foreclosing various life courses. The way in which adolescents develop and exercise their personal efficacy during this period can play a key role in setting the course their life paths take.

Adolescence has often been characterized as a period of psychosocial turmoil. While no period of life is ever free of problems, contrary to the stereotype of "storm and stress," most adolescents negotiate the important transitions of this period without undue disturbance or discord (Bandura, 1964; Petersen, 1988; Rutter, Graham, Chadwick, & Yule, 1976). By the time youngsters reach adolescence, most have adopted values and standards of conduct compatible with those in the home so that externally imposed controls are largely unnecessary (Bandura & Walters, 1959; Elkin & Westley, 1955). Adolescents tend to choose friends who share similar value systems and behavioral norms. Consequently, the peers with whom they associate are more likely to uphold their behavioral standards than to breed family conflicts.

The passage through adolescence to adulthood has become riskier than it was in the past, especially for youth growing up in conflicted and fractured families in impoverished neighborhoods. Substance abuse, unprotected sexuality, and delinquent and violent activities can seriously jeopardize realization of successful development. Most of our theories of human behavior greatly overpredict the incidence of psychosocial pathology under adversity. Although some youths in high-risk environments are defeated by their pernicious circumstances, remarkably, most manage to navigate the hazardous terrain without developing serious personal problems. Such findings dispute the gloomy overpredictions by theories that are more preoccupied with how people are defeated by inimical life circumstances than with how they transcend them. Focus solely on life risks fails to explain resilience to adversity. One must look to sources of personal enablement for the answer.

Sociocognitive theory construes the positive contributors to adaptation within an agentic perspective as enablement factors rather than as protective or sheltering factors, as typically characterized in epidemiological theories of psychopathology. Protectiveness shields individuals from harsh realities or may weaken their impact. Enablement equips them with the personal resources to select and structure their environments in ways that set a successful course for their lives. This is the difference between proactive recruitment of sources of positive guidance and support and reactive adaptation to life circumstances. An agentic view of resilience also differs from the dualistic diathesis-stress model of psychopathology in which external stressors act upon personal vulnerabilities. Individuals play a proactive role in their adaptation rather than simply undergoing happenings in which environments act upon their personal endowments. The success with which the risks and challenges of adolescence are managed depends, in no small measure, on the strength of personal efficacy built up through prior mastery experiences. Youngsters who enter adolescence beset by a disabling sense of inefficacy transport their vulnerability to stress and dysfunction to the new environmental demands and to the pervasive biopsychosocial changes they find themselves undergoing.

Adolescents have to manage major biological, educational, and social role transitions concurrently. Learning how to deal with pubertal changes, emotionally invested partnerships, and sexuality becomes a matter of considerable importance. To begin with, adolescents must cope with the extensive biological changes of pubescence (Hamburg, 1974). The accelerated rate of physical development during this period heightens concerns over bodily states and physique that have social ramifications, especially in peer relationships. Pubertal changes contribute to the development of self-efficacy in interaction with psychosocial factors rather than directly. Biological maturation can affect physical prowess and social status among one's peers in ways that have significant impact on self-schemata of efficacy in physical and psychosocial domains of functioning.

The timing of pubertal changes and the self-evaluative and social reactions to them serve as important determinants of how the passage through pubescence is weathered. Pubertal precocity can affect boys and girls differently (Brooks-Gunn, 1991; Petersen, 1987). Early maturation builds the musculature and strength of boys, which can benefit their self-evaluation and enhance their social status. Developmental lag for boys is a personal handicap. In contrast, pubertal precocity is more likely to present some adaptational difficulties for girls. They have to cope with weight gains that violate cultural ideals of attractiveness and lead them to devalue their body image. They also have to deal with the physical effects accompanying menstrual function. Moreover, early maturers get initiated sooner by older peers into dating situations, sexual and drinking activities, and transgressive behavior that heighten the risk of social and academic problems (Magnusson, Stattin, & Allen, 1985). These precocious involvements in problem behaviors exact a toll on educational aspirations and achievements.

Adolescents must manage not only pervasive pubertal changes but difficult educational transitions as well. The transition to middle-level schools involves a major environmental change that taxes personal efficacy. Adolescents move from a personalized school environment of familiar peers to an impersonal, departmentalized one with curricular tracking into college preparatory, general, or vocational paths. Under these new social structural arrangements, they have to reestablish their sense of efficacy, social connectedness, and status within an enlarged heterogeneous network of new peers and with multiple teachers in rotating class sessions. During this adaptational period, young adolescents sense some loss of personal control, become less confident in themselves, are more sensitive to social evaluation, and suffer some decline in self-motivation (Eccles & Midgley, 1989). But these initiatory adverse effects are neither universal nor enduring for every adolescent. Like other new demands and challenges, school transitions can be detrimental or beneficial to the growth of personal efficacy. For example, adolescents who have a high sense of efficacy weather inefficacious teachers in the move to junior high school, whereas inefficacious students become even more self-doubting of their capabilities (Midgley, Feldlaufer, & Eccles, 1989). Many adolescents manage the transitional stressors in ways that sustain or increase their sense of personal competence (Nottelmann, 1987). If they are instructed through mastery modeling about how to exercise control over peer pressures, they are much less vulnerable to enlistment in drug use during difficult transition periods to junior and senior high school (Pentz, 1985).

Adolescents' beliefs in their efficacy in social and academic realms affect their emotional well-being as well as their development. Close personal ties bring satisfactions and render the stressors of everyday life more bearable. Adolescents who are assured in their social efficacy are better at cultivating supportive friendships than those who are beset with self-doubt (Connolly, 1989; Wheeler & Ladd, 1982). Navigating one's way in isolation through adolescence — with its unsettling pubertal, social, and academic changes — carries high risk of despondency. Girls are generally more prone to depression than boys (Nolen-Hoeksema, 1990). Longitudinal research into the role of efficacy belief in adolescent depression sheds some light on gender differences in the paths of influence through which perceived inefficacy breeds despondency (Pastorelli et al., 1996). Boys become despondent over perceived social inefficacy and indirectly over a low sense of academic efficacy that gives rise to problem behaviors, low prosocialness, and deficient academic performance, each of which contributes to depression. In contrast, girls get depressed by a low sense of academic efficacy regardless of how well they are doing in school. Moreover, perceived inefficacy in academic activities, interpersonal relations, and self-regulatory capability to resist peer pressure to engage in potentially risky activities reduces prosocialness, which, in turn, increases proneness to depression. The direct impact of perceived social inefficacy on depression is stronger for girls than for boys. Thus, girls get depressed over a low sense of efficacy in more aspects of their lives that impinge more heavily on interpersonal relations than do boys.

The mediational role of perceived social efficacy in adolescent depression is further corroborated in a study by McFarlane, Bellissimo, and Norman (1995). Supportive family and peer relationships operate as safeguards against depression. Family support lowers depression both directly and by strengthening adolescents' belief in their social efficacy, whereas supportive peers do so only to the extent that they promote a sense of social efficacy. Including more facets of personal efficacy, as in the previous study, would probably reveal an even greater mediational role for perceived efficacy in adolescent depression.

Management of Sexuality

With achievement of reproductive maturity, which is occurring earlier than it did in the past, adolescents must learn how to manage their sexuality long before they are ready to take on the functions of parenthood. While the mass media serve up a heavy dose of sprightly sexual activity, mainly by unmarried partners in uncommitted relationships, societal practices largely foster sexual ignorance and unpreparedness (Brown, Childers, & Waszak, 1990). Unlike with most other activities, sexual unpreparedness does not dissuade sexual ventures. Teenagers engage in a high rate of sexual activity and are initiating it at a younger age (Brooks-Gunn & Furstenberg, 1989). Early sexual activity is more prevalent among adolescents from disadvantaged backgrounds and those who have low educational aspirations. Much of this sexual activity is unprotected by regular contraceptive use. All too often, this results in sexually transmitted diseases, unwanted pregnancies, abortions, or unmarried teenage parenthood.

Our society has always had difficulty providing comprehensive sex education and contraceptive services for its youth. Nor is much sex education provided in the home (Koch, 1991). Because many parents do a poor job of it, most youngsters pick up their sex information and a good deal of misinformation late in their development primarily from peers and, to a lesser extent, from the media and from the adverse consequences of uninformed sexual experimentation. Socially oriented efforts at sex education are often thwarted by sectors of the society that lobby actively for maintaining a veil of silence regarding protective sexual practices in the belief that such information will promote indiscriminate sexuality. They vigorously oppose sex education programs in the schools that talk about contraceptive methods. Even adults who view sexual development more open-mindedly are uneasy talking frankly about sexual matters with their children and evade the subject as much as possible. They have learned to talk a good line, but they convey anxious attitudes about sexual relations. Many impart sexual information to their children only after they suspect their children have already learned "too much" from other sources (Bandura & Walters, 1959). Because of anxious evasion and moral opposition, efforts at sex education are usually couched in desexualized generalities about reproduction processes that leave much ignorance in their wake. The net result is that teenagers in our society are more sexually ignorant and are getting pregnant at higher rates than in other societies that address the informational, attitudinal, and interpersonal aspects of sexual development openly and provide ready access to contraceptive services.

Most efforts to prevent the adverse consequences of early sexual activity center on educating teenagers about sexual matters and contraceptive use, encouraging them to postpone sexual intercourse, and providing the sexually active ones with contraceptive services. It is widely assumed that if teenagers are adequately informed about sexuality they will take appropriate self-protective action. Heightened awareness and knowledge of risks are important preconditions for self-directed change. Unfortunately, information alone does not necessarily exert much influence on sexual behavior. Translating sexual knowledge into effective self-management of sexuality requires social and self-regulative skills and a sense of personal efficacy to exercise control over sexual situations. As Gagnon and Simon (1973) have correctly observed, managing sexuality involves managing interpersonal relationships. Thus, sexual risk reduction calls for enhancing interpersonal efficacy rather than simply targeting a specific behavior for change (Bandura, 1994). The major problem is not teaching teenagers sex guidelines, which is easily achievable, but equipping them with skills that enable them to put the guidelines into practice consistently in the face of counteracting social influences. Difficulties arise because knowledge and intentions often conflict with interpersonal pressures and sentiments. In these interpersonal predicaments, the sway of allurements, heightened sexual arousal, desire for social acceptance, coercive pressures, situational constraints, and fear of rejection and personal embarrassment can override the influence of the best informed judgment. The weaker the perceived

self-efficacy to exercise personal control, the more such social and affective factors can increase the likelihood of early or risky sexual behavior.

In managing sexuality, people have to exercise influence over themselves as well as over others. This requires self-regulative skills in guiding and motivating one's behavior. Self-regulation operates through internal standards, evaluative reactions to one's conduct, use of motivating self-incentives, and other forms of cognitive self-guidance. Self regulative skills thus form an integral part of sexual self-management. They partly determine the social situations into which people get themselves, how well they navigate through them, and how effectively they can resist social inducements to risky sexual behavior. It is easier to wield control over preliminary choice behavior that may lead to difficult social predicaments than to try to extricate oneself from such situations while enmeshed in them. This is because the antecedent phase involves mainly anticipatory motivators that are amenable to cognitive control; the entanglement phase includes stronger social inducements to engage in unprotected sexual behavior, which are less easily manageable.

The influential role played by efficacy beliefs in the management of sexual activities is documented in studies of contraceptive use by teenage women at high risk for unwanted pregnancy because they often engage in unprotected intercourse (Kasen, Vaughan, & Walter, 1992; Levinson, 1986). Such research shows that perceived efficacy to manage sexual relationships is associated with more effective use of contraceptives. The predictive relationship remains when controls are applied for demographic factors, knowledge, and sexual experience. Favorable attitudes toward contraceptives increases intentions to use them, but efficacy beliefs determine whether those intentions are put into practice (Basen-Engquist & Parcel, 1992). Even women who are sexually experienced, knowledgeable about contraception, and highly motivated to prevent pregnancy because it would jeopardize career plans fail to use contraceptives consistently and effectively if they lack a sense of personal efficacy (Heinrich, 1993). Alcohol and drug use in the context of sexual activities fosters unprotected sex. Drugs and alcohol lower perceived efficacy to adhere to safer sex practices (Kasen et al., 1992). Experiences of forced unwanted intercourse, which are not uncommon, also lower women's sense of efficacy to exercise control over contraceptive practices (Heinrich, 1993).

A low sense of self-regulatory efficacy in the presence of social influences promoting risky sexual practices spells trouble. Indeed, the psychosocial profile of teenagers who engage in unprotected intercourse includes a low sense of efficacy to exercise self-protective control in sexual involvements, association with peers who sanction intercourse and are risky in their own sexual behavior, and misconceptions about the prevalence of unprotected intercourse among students their age (Walter et al., 1992). This combination of psychosocial influences overrides beliefs about personal susceptibility to sexually transmitted diseases and about their severity. Perceived efficacy and peer influence similarly predict whether or not teenagers intend to become sexually active in the next year, have multiple partners, and use condoms (Walter et al., 1993). Values about sexual involvement at their age also affect behavioral intentions. Whether sexual values and standards determine peer affiliations or affiliations shape sexual standards remains to be determined. There is every indication that these types of influences operate bidirectionally (Bandura & Walters, 1959).

Gilchrist and Schinke (1983) applied the main features of a self-regulative model of personal change to teach teenagers how to exercise self-protective control over sexual situations. They received essential factual information about high-risk sexual behavior and self-protective measures. Through modeling, they were taught how to communicate frankly about sexual matters and contraceptives, how to deal with conflicts regarding sexual activities, and how to resist unwanted sexual advances. They practiced applying these social skills by role-playing in simulated situations and received instructive feedback. The self-regulative program significantly enhanced perceived efficacy and skill in managing sexuality. Botvin and his associates provide a comprehensive school-based program that teaches generic self-regulative skills for managing sexual activities and social pressures for

alcohol and drug use (Botvin & Dusenbury, 1992). These personal and social life skills include, in addition to strategies for resisting coercions for detrimental conduct, skills in problem solving, decision making, self-guidance, and stress management. Educational aspirations delay initiation into sexual activity. Therefore, efforts to reduce early childbearing should also be directed at promoting educational self-development and aspiration.

Many adolescents engage in unprotected sex with multiple partners, which puts them at risk of sexually transmitted diseases, including HIV infection. Change programs incorporating elements of the self-regulative model produce significant reductions in risky sexual behavior in male and female adolescents alike (Jemmott, Jemmott, & Fong, 1992; Jemmott, Jemmott, Spears, Hewitt, & Cruz-Collins, 1992). Those who had the benefit of the program were more knowledgeable about infective risks and more likely to use contraceptives to protect themselves against sexually transmitted diseases and unwanted pregnancies than did those who received no instructive guidance or were only given detailed information on the causes, transmission, and prevention of sexually transmitted diseases. The findings of these studies indicate that simply imparting sexual information without developing the self-regulative skills and sense of efficacy needed to exercise personal control over sexual relationships has little impact on patterns of sexual behavior.

Teenage parenthood imposes socioeconomic hardships and jeopardizes certain life courses for young mothers and their offspring. Young childbearers are more likely to drop out of school and find it harder to secure gainful employment or achieve stable marriages than do late childbearers (Hayes, 1987; Hofferth & Hayes, 1987). Although it is difficult to disentangle the determinants of life courses, the evidence suggests that many of these detrimental effects stem from preexisting socioeconomic disadvantages (Furstenberg, 1976). These adversities are further exacerbated by the multiple strains of young parenthood and the constraints it places on self-development.

As in other life adaptations, there is variability in the long-term consequences of teenage parenthood (Furstenberg, Brooks-Gunn, & Morgan, 1987). Adolescent childbearers who develop their intellectual competencies and efficacy in managing their later life fare much better than their counterparts who do not. These personal resources enable them to exert greater influence over the future direction their lives take. Those who make the more successful readjustment complete their schooling, which provides them with tools for securing stable employment, and they postpone additional childbearing. Providing opportunities for continued education is an important vehicle for minimizing the cumulative adverse effects of early childbearing. Although the detrimental effects commonly attributed to teenage parenthood may be overgeneralized, early childbearing restricts the types of life options that are considered and pursued. Moreover, many of the women continue to be plagued by marital instability, and their offspring exhibit relatively high rates of behavior problems, academic failures, and early pregnancies.

The consequences of adolescent parenthood differ across race and ethnicity. Adverse effects are more likely to persist if they create educational disadvantage. Premature entry into parenting roles seems to be more detrimental to the educational development of Latinas than to that of African-American and white teenagers (Forste & Tienda, 1992). The rate of teenage childbearing is higher for African-Americans than for whites or Latinas; but whereas almost all the African-Americans and white teenagers complete their secondary schooling, Latinas tend to drop out of school. Mothers' education increases the likelihood of their daughters completing high school for African-Americans and whites. Forste and Tienda explain the ethnic and racial differences in educational pursuits in terms of structural support systems and cultural factors. High rates of joblessness among African-American males create incentives for their female counterparts to pursue schooling as a means to economic self-sufficiency. African-Americans approve of women working. For Latinos, the emphasis on traditional family values and disapproval of mothers working discourages school completion following childbearing.

Management of High-Risk Activities

With growing independence during adolescence, some experimentation with risky activities is not all that uncommon in the passage out of childhood status (Jessor, 1986). These activities include alcohol and marijuana use, smoking, tooling around in automobiles, and early sexual activity. Adolescents expand and strengthen their sense of efficacy by learning how to deal successfully with potentially troublesome situations in which they are unpracticed, as well as with advantageous life events. This strengthening of self-efficacy is best achieved through guided mastery experiences that provide the knowledge and skills needed to exercise adequate control over situations that place one at some risk (Bandura, 1986a). Development of resilient self-efficacy requires some experience in mastering difficulties through perseverant effort. Success in managing problem situations instills a strong belief in one's capabilities that provides staying power in the face of difficulties. Adolescents who have been sheltered and left ill-prepared in terms of coping skills are highly vulnerable to distress and behavioral problems when they encounter difficult interpersonal predicaments that are not completely avoidable.

Most adolescents who experiment with hazardous behaviors quit them after a while, but some become deeply and chronically involved in them. Activities rarely occur in isolation. Rather, they are clustered by structural and normative influences of the environment. Sets of behaviors are blended by social custom, such as the idea that drinking goes with partying, and create separate clusters of activities through incompatible demands, such as the fact that heavy partying detracts from serious studying. Distinctive patterns of activities are also structured by socioeconomic status, sex, and age-graded practices. Whatever the sources of the activity patterning may be, frequent engagement in some problem behaviors leads to involvements in other ones and to forming a high-risk lifestyle. Such behavior usually includes a constellation of activities such as heavy drinking, drug use, delinquent conduct, early sexuality, and disengagement from academic pursuits (Donovan & Jessor, 1985; Elliott,

1993). Such a lifestyle often has reverberating consequences that jeopardize physical health and self-development. Some of the detrimental effects produce irretrievable losses of life options.

A number of factors can influence whether some experimentation with problem behavior protects against adoption of detrimental lifestyles or inaugurates one into them. The intensity of early involvement and the reversibility of effects are relevant considerations. Intense early involvement with habit-forming substances can create dependencies and lifelong personal vulnerabilities that make it hard to give them up. Experimentations that have benign effects are a different matter from those that place one at danger of injurious consequences or produce irreversible outcomes that shape life courses. For example, drunken driving that leaves one a paraplegic is a tragic event that has lifelong consequences. Another important factor is the amount of social guidance provided in the development of self-regulatory skills to manage potentially risky activities and to extricate oneself from detrimental ones. Good guidance can turn beginning involvement in potentially troublesome activities into opportunities to develop self-regulatory skills to avoid future problems.

The impact of engagement in risky activities on association networks is another predictor. Experimentations within prosocial peer networks carry much less risk than those that inaugurate one into peer networks deeply enmeshed in a deviant lifestyle. Adolescents vary widely in their perceptions of the extent of peer involvement in problem behavior. Perceived normativeness comes into play. Adolescents who have an exaggerated view of peer involvement are more likely to continue risky activities than those who believe that such involvement is less widespread. The final consideration is the degree of intrusion of risky activities into prosocial development. The more the problem behavior competes with and impairs prosocial development, the more it jeopardizes successful trajectories. Competitive intrusion on intellectual development is of special importance because intellectual development provides a major means for successful pursuit of prosocial lifestyles.

Thus, whether adolescents forsake risky activities or become chronically enmeshed in them is determined, in large part, by the interplay of personal competencies, self-regulatory capabilities, and the nature of the prevailing social influences in their lives. Those who adopt the hazardous pathway generally place low value on academic self-development and are heavily influenced by peers who model and approve engagement in problem behaviors (Jessor, 1986). Both academic self-development and management of peer pressures for risky activities rest partly on a firm sense of self-regulatory efficacy. Thus, adolescents who are insecure in their efficacy are less able to avoid or curtail involvement in drugs, unprotected sexual activity, and delinquent conduct that jeopardize beneficial life courses than are those who have a strong sense of self-regulatory efficacy (Allen, Leadbeater, & Aber, 1990).

Substance abuse further weakens perceived efficacy to resist interpersonal pressures that lead to drug use, thus creating a self-debilitating cycle (Pentz, 1985). Impoverished, hazardous environments present harsh realities with minimal resources, models, and social supports for culturally valued pursuits but extensive modeling, incentives, social supports, and opportunity structures for antisocial pursuits. Such environments severely tax the coping efficacy of youth embedded in them to make it through adolescence in ways that do not irreversibly foreclose many beneficial life paths. That most adolescents in hazardous environments manage to overcome their adverse circumstances without serious involvement in self-ruinous pursuits is testimony to their resilience and that of their caretakers. But it places a heavy burden on personal efficacy to socially structure beneficial life paths under such conditions.

The prototypical self-regulatory program developed by Gilchrist and Schinke (1985) has been successfully extended to the prevention and reduction of drug abuse by adolescents. This type of program informs adolescents about drug effects, provides them with interpersonal skills for managing personal and social pressures to use drugs, lowers drug use, and fosters self-conception as a nonuser (Gilchrist, Schinke, Trimble & Cvetkovich, 1987). These findings are all the more interesting because they were achieved with ethnic and minority youth who have to contend with repeated inducements to use alcohol and drugs. Regarding oneself as a nonuser can produce important lifestyle changes by restructuring peer relations and the kinds of activities in which one gets involved (Stall & Biernacki, 1986).

The task of choosing what lifework to pursue also looms large during adolescence. The preparatory choices made in this realm play a key role in shaping the pathways adolescents follow into adulthood. Efficacy beliefs influence the range of career options seriously considered, the degree of preparation for them, and the vocational paths that are likely to be pursued (Betz & Hackett, 1986; Lent & Hackett, 1987). A low sense of efficacy to master academic subjects forecloses a variety of vocational options. The self-impeding consequences of perceived inefficacy are fully experienced in young adulthood when individuals confront their job options in seeking employment.

SELF-EFFICACY CONCERNS OF ADULTHOOD

The change from adolescence to adulthood involves a number of major role transitions. Young adulthood is a period when people have to learn to manage many new social demands arising from lasting partnerships, marital relationships, parenthood, entry into vocational careers, and management of financial resources. This is the phase in life when personal factors come strongly into play with sociostructural and economic conditions of the larger society. Young adults have to contend with societal norms associated with the diverse roles of adult status and the concomitant socioeconomic constraints and opportunity structures. The passage to adulthood is less well marked than it was in the past. Family patterns have become more varied, occupational pursuits are less stable and predictable, and normative consensus is harder to come by. Given the increased ambiguity and diversity of the society, individuals have more leeway to determine

the course their lives take by cultivating their competencies and selecting, shaping, and modifying their environments. The interactional effects of personal and sociostructural determinants during this major transitional phase in life are important contributors to the organization of personal life courses. As in earlier mastery challenges, a firm sense of efficacy is an important contributor to the type of social reality individuals construct for themselves. Those who enter adulthood poorly equipped with skills and plagued by nagging doubts about their capabilities find many aspects of their adult life aversive, full of hardships, and depressing.

Fulfillment of Occupational Roles

Beginning a productive vocational career poses a major transitional challenge in early adulthood. The youth who pursue careers via higher education follow a structured pathway. They are extensively counseled, fully informed about college entry requirements, adequately prepared in the requisite academic subjects, and financially supported in one way or another during their schooling. They have the benefit of advanced academic preparation, which not only expands career options but provides access to them through informal social networks and established institutional linkages. The development and successful pursuit of occupational roles requiring advanced preparation are addressed in Chapter 10. The transition from school to vocational career is a much more difficult problem for the non-college-bound youth, especially in the U.S. educational system. Schools offer them little occupational counseling or help in vocational placement. Many are inadequately prepared in the basic skills required for the technologies of the modern workplace. Some prefer a period of freedom to explore things before settling on a particular vocational pursuit. The vast majority, however, find themselves in a marginal work status by exclusion from the primary labor market rather than by choice. The problem does not reside solely in the deficiencies of youth. Social hiring practices and the lack of functional linkages between schools and the workplace create institutional impediments to employability.

Societies differ in how they structure the transition from school to vocation. These variations are rooted in broader cultural orientations and conceptions of youth development. In American society, the transition routes for noncollege youth are unstructured, marked by early detours and directional changes, and left largely to individual initiative. The youth who develop their capabilities and get sound guidance end up in skilled occupations. Those who, for one reason or another, become only marginally involved in systems of education and occupational training generally find themselves embedded in a disadvantaged life with recurrent spells of unemployment. Youth adrift with no stake in the system breed social problems. Some who see no legitimate pathway to an adequate subsistence level turn to illegal pursuits for their livelihood.

Rosenbaum and his colleagues analyze at some length the different sources of the vocational-entry problem (Rosenbaum, Kariya, Settersten, & Maier, 1990). Academic achievement is a good predictor of vocational productivity at the outset and in the long term, but employers do not use this information in their hiring decisions (Bishop, 1989). Successful school performance reflects a constellation of personal competencies, including motivational and self-management capabilities as well as cognitive skills. The development of sound measures of self-regulative capabilities could further increase the prediction of occupational potential. A high school diploma is all that is usually asked for, even though it is often gained with serious deficiencies in basic skills. Quality of school performance does not affect the entry-level jobs students get or their wages, so there is little incentive to master basic academic skills. A system in which educational effort and accomplishment do not bring better jobs and pay strips teachers of their instructional influence and breeds student apathy by providing little incentive for learning. Peers may deprecate academic efforts and achievements. If students collectively do poorly in their schoolwork, they cannot all be failed, so they are all promoted. By making level of academic performance inconsequential, business hiring practices partly contribute to the poor quality of high school graduates about whom employers

complain. They bear some of the responsibility for the educational disincentives. Lack of incentive and guidance for academic preparation also handicaps students bound for colleges that have low admission requirements. Most end up in junior colleges without pursuing higher education. Our educational system provides strong incentive for intellectual development mainly for the students who wish to attend elite universities.

When noncollege students first leave school, they have no job, find part-time work, or end up performing simple functions in dead-end jobs in retail and service sectors that offer little training or opportunity to advance in a stable career path. Not surprisingly, turnover rates are high during this period. For the most poorly educated and unskilled, this is not a passing phase. They remain permanently trapped in a marginal employment status. This problem is most pervasive among minority youth (Hotz & Tienda, in press). Employers come to regard recent school graduates as too immature and unreliable to invest the time and effort to develop their vocational competencies. They rarely hire new high school graduates. Employers prefer older applicants who have already passed through the presumed probationary period of instability and are ready to settle down to a stable vocational career. So after they leave school, many young workers find themselves in a moratorium status, drifting between short-term jobs that require few skills and offer little future (Osterman, 1980). The long delay between leaving school and being seriously considered for permanent employment may partly explain employers' disinterest in academic predictors of vocational success.

Given adequate cognitive skills, the specialized knowledge and technical skills required for many vocational activities do not take all that long to develop. They are typically learned on the job. Although much emphasis is being placed on the need to develop higher cognitive skills, the capability to manage one's motivational and interpersonal functioning is another set of foundation skills that largely determines success on the job. Hence, in preparing youth for the world of work, the development of self-management skills is crucial. It comes as no surprise that hiring decisions are based more on employers' judgments of dependability of work habits than on potentiality for vocational learning. The combined effect of poorly educated students and disfavoring hiring practices make the transition from school to work a protracted and often demoralizing process. The vocational-entry problem is exacerbated for disadvantaged youth. Superficial business involvements in schools such as donations of equipment, sponsorship of particular schools, provisions of short-term apprenticeships, and offers of incentives for getting a high school diploma that says little about actual abilities do not do much to improve the situation.

Other societies create more formal social mechanisms for getting young adults started early on valued vocational careers and provide them with incentives to develop their intellectual competencies. Training in vocational skills is founded on a solid base of academic skills. In the Japanese system, schools and employers form close partnerships, with a mutual commitment of schools to educate their students well and businesses to provide vocational career paths for them upon graduation (Rosenbaum & Kariya, 1989). The close partnership not only provides transition routes but also restores the functional value of educational development for noncollege youth. Just as selective colleges foster development of cognitive skills through their admission standards, hiring standards do so by rewarding educational attainments. Employers hire graduates on the basis of their academic skills and provide them with the necessary vocational skills after they join the workforce. The more students cultivate their academic competencies, the better the jobs they can get. If schools turn out deficient graduates, they jeopardize their various partnership arrangements, and if businesses fail to provide satisfactory vocational pathways, schools will not place their students with them. These contingencies of mutual benefit provide students with positive incentives to develop their competencies, schools with instructional influence and incentive to produce well-educated graduates, and employers with applicants proficient in higher order skills. In short, all the constituencies have strong incentives to perform well because they all benefit from doing so.

Many educational systems are modeled on some form of dual-track structure in which students pursue either an academic route or a vocational route through an apprenticeship system. In the German system, where industry and schools share responsibility for occupational development, educational programs for the non-college-bound youth are linked to occupational career lines by combining academic instruction with intensive apprenticeships at worksites that lead to skilled employment (Hamilton, 1987). Academic achievement is rewarded with preferred apprenticeships. Because many technical skills become outmoded by technological changes, apprenticeship programs must have a substantial educational component that builds versatile higher order skills. These intensive apprenticeships are held in high status and serve as good means for career advancement. Evans and Heinz (1991, 1993) found that there are really four different paths that students take within an institutionalized dual-track system. In addition to the academic pathway leading to professional occupations and the apprenticeship vocational pathway leading to skilled employment, some youth find themselves on two other trajectories. These are the dropouts from apprenticeships who are on an uncertain life course. They quit apprenticeships because the quality of training leaves much to be desired, because they lose out in the competition for the apprenticeships of their choice, or for personal reasons. Then there are the educationally detached youth who are not even considered for apprenticeships because of deficient academic records and remain only marginal players in the system. The dropouts and the educationally detached youth find themselves in unstable or low-level employment with bleak prospects of ever improving their vocational livelihood. Within trajectories, especially those rooted in higher level competencies, personal career patterns vary depending on whether occupational interests are pursued planfully, challengingly, or reactively to fluctuating market conditions. The apprenticeship system is not easily transplantable to societies favoring a single educational path for their students and where employers do not want to encumber their work routines and incur costs training apprentices for the society at large (Kempner, Castro, & Bas, 1993). Most countries opt for vocational training poorly coordinated with workplaces or on-the-job training for those who get hired.

Increasing automation of the more technical aspects of work is placing heavier weight on versatile cognitive and self-management skills that can be used flexibly to fulfill rapidly changing occupational roles and demands. These higher order skills enable individuals to master changing technologies throughout their vocational careers. Therefore, in preparing students for the occupational roles of the future, instructional systems must cultivate generic cognitive skills as well as specialized technical skills. The apprenticeship system encourages earlier vocational specialization than does the partnership system. Highly structured transitional systems provide a more secure passage to occupational careers but may allow less flexibility and room for changing directions along the way (Hurrelmann & Roberts, 1991).

It is an open question as to which type of system produces the more talented and versatile workforce. The answer may lie in the quality of the training in generic intellectual and self-management skills rather than in the timing of the occupational specialization. High specialization reduces mobility across occupational activities, which presents problems when the world of work is rapidly changing. Whatever system is adopted should provide opportunities to pursue higher levels of learning to create the means for continual self-renewal. Because of the rapidly changing nature of work, such a system should not foreclose chances to shift occupational pursuits to take advantage of future opportunities. The career benefits may also stem partly from the motivational incentives these systems provide for personal development rather than solely from the form of collaborative arrangement. Some of the key features of transitional systems — provision of incentives for school achievement by linkage to employment opportunities, quality instruction in higher order skills, and structured pathways for entry into the workforce — can be implemented by an active public-private partnership in ways that improve the occupational development of youths without requiring wholesale adoption of a particular system.

Transition systems with positive incentives for learning enable students to exercise some control over their vocational future by developing their talents and self-directive capabilities. It is difficult to get people to invest a great deal of time and effort in uncertain occupational futures. A major determinant of unemployment is poor economic conditions of the society (White & Smith, 1994). Societies must do more than institute transitional programs that integrate academic activities with vocational pursuits. They must also create conditions conducive to the expansion of opportunity structures and support social policies for equitable sharing of costs during displacements by technological change and economic turndowns. Being trapped in unemployment despite high levels of education and technical training can be profoundly demoralizing.

The benefits of efforts to raise the educational and occupational competencies of individuals are sometimes trivialized on the grounds that, unless the pool of jobs is expanded, such efforts merely rearrange the unemployment line (Hamilton, 1994). This type of argument rests on the simplistic assumption that development of competencies enables people merely to fill existing jobs but creates no new ones. This zero-sum view, where one person's gain is another's loss, ignores the fact that the quality of a workforce has significant impact on the economic vitality of a nation. Businesses do not spring up by happenstance; they are human creations. The volume and types of jobs available within a society are, in large part, the product of entrepreneurial minds rather than institutional edicts. Hewlett, who with Packard started an electronic venture during the Depression, summed it up well when he said, "There were no jobs then, so we created our own!" The Hewletts, Packards, Jobs, and Wozniaks did not simply rearrange people in the unemployment line. They created the vast electronics industry of Silicon Valley through their own ingenuity and initiative (Rogers & Larsen, 1984). They launched their entrepreneurial ventures on a shoestring in their garages. Entrepreneurs are often forced to strike out on their own because their ideas are summarily rejected by established corporations.

The frosty reception given to innovations is further testimony to the influential role of tenacious innovators in creating and expanding the pool of jobs in a society. Not only do efficacious innovators create productive jobs, but the quality of workforces determines how effectively innovations are commercialized. The higher the perceived efficacy of workforces and their overseers, the greater is their productivity (Sadri & Robertson, 1993). Competitive advantage in the global marketplace rests largely on the quality of the workforce. Industries with efficacious workforces thrive and expand the pool of jobs by their success in the competitive marketplaces of the world economy. Industries with poorly trained workforces lose jobs through economic noncompetitiveness. The rapid rate of technological change is placing an increasing premium on education for the types of abilities that contribute to both innovation and productivity. It is not as though people are simply plugged into jobs like automatons. They are highly influential in creating and expanding jobs.

There are a number of ways in which efficacy beliefs contribute to career development and success in vocational pursuits. In preparatory phases, students' beliefs in their efficacy partly determine how well they develop the basic sociocognitive skills on which vocational careers are founded (Multon, Brown, & Lent, 1991). Creation of opportunity structures and positive incentives for self-development play an important role in the structuring of vocational paths. Opportunities alone, however, do not ensure that people will take advantage of them. Requisite competencies are not mastered without sacrifice and hard work. It requires a high level of self-regulatory efficacy to mount and sustain the effort needed to prepare oneself adequately for given vocational pursuits. Conversely, even under depressed labor market conditions, individuals who have a resilient sense of efficacy perceive greater employment opportunities and are more successful in finding employment than those who anticipate the futility of their efforts. Thus, a full understanding of occupational development and

pursuits must recognize the interplay of sociocultural determinants and personal determinants. It is not as though the courses that vocational lives take are dictated by structural factors and personal factors are significant contributors mainly in youth who cannot find or hold jobs because of psychological hang-ups (Osterman, 1980).

Beliefs about one's capabilities are influential determinants of vocational life paths (Betz & Hackett, 1986; Lent & Hackett, 1987). Young adults forgo vocations they see as providing valued benefits and rewards if they believe they lack the efficacy to fulfill the entry requirements and occupational demands (Wheeler, 1983). A low sense of efficacy thus forecloses consideration of vocational options despite opportunities and attractive incentives. Beliefs of occupational efficacy are largely the product of socioeducational experiences and prevailing cultural attitudes and practices. The adverse experiences associated with low socioeconomic status breed a low sense of occupational efficacy regardless of the prestige level of the vocation. Efficacy beliefs are diminished by experiences arising from gender barriers as well as social class barriers (Hannah & Kahn, 1989). Cultural changes have expanded the array of career options for women compared to the opportunity structures for them in the past. But ingrained stereotyping practices change slowly. Women's lowered sense of efficacy for traditionally male-dominated occupations constrains their occupational development and pursuits (Betz & Hackett, 1981).

It is one thing to get started in an occupational pursuit and another thing to do well or advance in it. Most occupational disruptions arise more often from interpersonal and motivational problems than from lack of technical skills. The climate of a workplace reflects, in large part, the bidirectional effects that employees and their overseers have on each other. Supervisors who are inefficacious in working through others create a dispirited or aversive environment for the employees. Improving supervisory skills through guided mastery programs enhances organizational morale and productivity (Latham & Saari, 1979; Porras et al., 1982). The interpersonal problems that people experience in their everyday lives often intrude on their work. Guided mastery programs that teach employees the skills needed to manage social problems at home and at work, control substance abuse, and raise self-motivation produce lasting increases in perceived self-regulatory efficacy (Frayne & Latham, 1987; Latham & Frayne, 1989). The stronger the sense of self-regulatory efficacy, the greater the improvement in work involvement. It should also be noted that most people work in service jobs rather than production jobs. In such activities, personal efficacy to manage services and interpersonal relationships are the heavy contributors to occupational success.

Economic recessions and displacement by automation and geographic relocation of manufacturing functions put people out of work. Although technological innovations eliminate some traditional types of jobs, they also create new ones requiring retraining and new adaptations. Such rapid changes in the modern workplace put a premium on higher generic skills, versatility, and resilient personal efficacy to manage effectively the changing demands accompanying job displacements and restructuring of vocational activities. Several longitudinal studies corroborate that perceived efficacy is a significant determinant of reemployment following job loss (Kanfer & Hulin, 1985; Clifford, 1988). The unemployed who have some sense of efficacy that they can find job leads and prepare adequately and follow them up are more active in their job search and achieve higher and quicker reemployment success than those who doubt they can mount a successful job search. They quickly give up trying. Age, employment history, education, depression, and cause of termination do not differentiate the reemployed from those who remained unemployed. The jobless face harsh realities that can easily overwhelm them, but those who persevere in their efforts through belief that they can exercise some control over their employability increase their prospect of eventual success.

Drawing on knowledge of coping and self-efficacy, researchers at the Michigan Institute for Social Research devised a multifaceted program to immunize laid-off workers against the debilitating effects of job loss and to restore their efficacy to secure reemployment in quality jobs (Vinokur, van Ryn, Gramlich, & Price, 1991). They were taught and rehearsed in role enactments how to carry out effective job searches. They identified potential obstacles and developed problem-solving strategies for generating alternative solutions. They received resilience training by anticipating potential barriers and setbacks and developing coping strategies that enabled them to persist despite disappointments during their search. They also received social support from the staff and other participants to sustain their efforts. In follow-up assessments conducted shortly after the program and several years later, the project participants had a higher sense of job-seeking efficacy, found jobs more quickly, got better quality jobs, and earned higher wages than did those who did not receive the program. In a mediational analysis, van Ryn and Vinokur (1992) found that the effect of the reemployment program on job search behavior was entirely mediated by perceived self-efficacy. The stronger the participants' beliefs in their efficacy to do the things that gain employment, the more positively they viewed job search efforts both personally and normatively. Perceived self-efficacy determined job search behavior both directly and indirectly through its effects on attitudes and intention to mount a vigorous job search. The mediational role of efficacy beliefs was verified after controlling for the effects of age, sex, family income, and education. In assessments conducted four months later, efficacy beliefs continued to mediate the influence of the intervention on job searches, but they were also linked directly to the intervention. The authors speculate that this later emerging link may be due to the intervention creating a social network among the participants, which could effect job searches.

Eden and Aviram (1993) further corroborate that a high sense of efficacy, whether preexisting or raised by guided mastery of job search skills, intensifies job search activities, which, in turn, greatly increases the likelihood of reemployment. Efficacy beliefs affect emotional as well as behavioral reactions to the hardship of losing one's job (Mittag & Schwarzer, 1993). The stress of unemployment drives men of low perceived efficacy to heavy drinking but does not increase the use of alcohol in those who believe that they can surmount their life problems. A sense of inefficacy both influences and is influenced by substance abuse in a cycle of functional impairment.

An unstable pattern of employment creates severe hardships and stressors for young families. Males who cannot earn a sufficient income to support a family do not marry, resulting in a rise in single-parent households headed by a single mother (Wilson, 1987). Most of these families are relegated to a life of persistent poverty from which it is difficult to break out. They find themselves trapped in impoverished neighborhoods lacking resources, opportunities, quality schools, helpful social networks, and successful models for personal advancement. The youth brought up in poverty face the difficult task of mastering with meager resources the competencies that enable them to escape from it.

Fulfillment of Family Roles

The transition to parenthood suddenly thrusts young adults into the expanded roles of both parent and spouse. Parents not only have to deal with ever-changing challenges as their children grow older but also have to manage interdependent relationships within a family system and social transactions with a host of extrafamilial social systems including educational, recreational, medical, and care-giving facilities. Thus, the transformation from a marital dyad to a family triad greatly increases the scope and diversity of coping demands (Michaels & Goldberg, 1988). Many parents manage to acquire sufficient knowledge and skills in one way or another to shepherd their children adequately through the various phases of development without serious problems or severe strain on the marital relationship. But it can be a trying period for those who are ill-prepared to take on the parenting role because of a lack of effective parental modeling during their own childhood and an insecure sense of personal efficacy to manage the expanded familial demands.

Evidence that perceived parenting efficacy plays a key role in adaptation to parenthood comes from longitudinal research conducted by Williams and her colleagues (Williams et al., 1987). Mothers who had strong belief in their care-giving capabilities, as measured before the birth of their first child, experienced more positive emotional well-being, closer attachment to their baby, and better adjustment to the parenting role during the postpartum phase. They also experienced less conflict over the parenting role and a better marital relationship during the toddler period than did mothers who held weaker beliefs about their parenting capabilities. These family outcomes do not merely reflect a general positive affectivity. Mothers' emotional well-being prior to the birth of the child was related neither to the development of the attachment relationship to the infant nor to the quality of the marital relationship. Moreover, perceived parenting efficacy predicts child and marital relationships over and above the prior quality of those relationships.

Family systems vary in the amount and quality of social support they provide for coping with familial stressors. Temperamentally difficult infants can quickly overtax shaky parenting efficacy. Cutrona and Troutman (1986) found that both lack of social support and difficult temperamental qualities of the infant undermine perceived parenting efficacy, which, in turn, predicts postpartum depression. A longitudinal study by Olioff and Aboud (1991) further confirms that a strong sense of parenting efficacy serves as a protective factor against postpartum depression. Low perceived parenting efficacy fosters depression in mothers of toddlers as well (Gross, Conrad, Fogg, & Wothke, 1994). Difficult toddler temperament has a weak, but significant, negative impact on mothers' beliefs in their parenting efficacy. A low sense of efficacy for child rearing contributes longitudinally to chronicity of maternal depression.

Recurrent bouts of depression can weaken maternal attachment and impede the quality of child-care. Maternal despondency is often associated with indecisiveness, unresponsiveness, disciplinary ineptness, and negative reactivity (Gelfand & Teti, 1990). Observational studies of interactions of clinically depressed mothers with their infants, however, reveal that the adverse effects of depression on caretaking activities are mediated through mothers' beliefs in their parenting efficacy (Teti & Gelfand, 1991). Depression impedes various domains of infant care only to the extent that it affects perceived parenting efficacy. Thus, severity of depression and level of social and marital support are unrelated to how competently mothers perform caretaking activities when maternal perceived efficacy is controlled, but mothers' beliefs in their parenting efficacy predict their caretaking competence when social and marital support and depression are controlled. Similarly, difficult, irritable infants impair caretaking to the extent that they affect mothers' beliefs in their parenting efficacy. Those who have a firm belief in their parenting abilities are quite resourceful in managing temperamentally difficult infants despite struggling with despondency.

Parental efficacy is also taxed when children suffer ongoing health problems, especially if they impair the child's ability to perform the tasks of daily life. Some parents manage these problems well; others are severely distressed by them. The severity of the medical condition itself does not account for the variation in parental functioning. A low sense of maternal efficacy, however, has been shown to heighten the risk of emotional distress (Silver, Bauman, & Ireys, 1995). The relationship remains after controlling for the severity of the children's functional impairment and a variety of sociodemographic factors, including education, ethnicity, maternal employment, and economic hardship.

Building parenting efficacy can help eliminate child behavioral problems while they are still minor and thus prevent more serious ones from becoming entrenched styles of conduct. Gross, Fogg, and Tucker (1995) tested such a prevention program founded on mastery modeling. Parents with difficult preschool children watched and discussed videotaped vignettes on how to help children learn, play with them, encourage them, set limits, and manage misbehavior. Mothers who had the benefit of the program increased their sense of parenting efficacy and experienced lower familial stress and child behavior problems. They differed in this regard from mothers in a nontreated group. In home observations, mothers whose efficacy was raised interacted more positively with their preschoolers, while nontreated mothers became more critical and negative in their interactions with their children over time.

The research just reviewed shows that a strong sense of parental efficacy yields dividends in the emotional well-being of mothers raising children who present special difficulties. Parents who believe that they have a key role to play in their children's development act on that belief in ways that cultivate their potential. They build their children's sense of intellectual efficacy and aspirations, which, in turn, contributes to their social relations, emotional well-being, and academic development (Bandura et al., 1996a). Moreover, self-efficacious parents are strong advocates for their children in interactions with social institutions that can have an important impact on their children during the formative period of their lives. We will return to these issues later.

The family has been undergoing major structural changes (South & Tolnay, 1992). Marriage is in decline and cohabitation and single-parent families are on the rise. These changes are often attributed to women's growing economic independence, but they also reflect men's efforts to escape the constraints of marriage. Women's roles are changing, which poses the new challenge of how to strike a balance between fulfillment of family needs and personal needs. Women are educating themselves more intensively in growing numbers, which opens up a much wider array of options than was available for women in the past. Women work as a matter of personal satisfaction and identity, not just economics. They seek fulfillment in career pursuits as well as in their family life.

Astin (1984) has identified a number of factors that contribute to the occupational aspirations of women. Increased longevity creates the need for purposeful pursuits that provide satisfaction and meaning to one's life over the full term of the expanded life span long after the offspring have left home. A sharp drop in the birthrate, in which having one or two children has become the norm, reduces the time spent rearing children and makes it easier for women to care for the family and pursue careers. Women increasingly postpone childbearing until they have completed higher education and established themselves in an occupational path. Nontraditional lifestyles are becoming more common; many women elect to remain single, marry but remain childless, or live with a partner without marrying. In these arrangements, most women pursue independent careers. The rising divorce rate adds further incentive for women to develop a career that would enable them to exercise control over their livelihood should their marriage be dissolved. Occupational attainments and earning power weaken the economic pressure on women to remain in an unsatisfying marriage. Reform legislation removing sex discrimination practices in education and employment has also expanded occupational opportunities for women.

Major demographic changes in the composition of the population and the occupational structure of the modern workplace require greater participation of women in the labor force. College enrollments reveal proportional declines of white males and increases in females and ethnic minorities. With automation and computerization of manufacturing enterprises and services in the modern workplace, most occupational pursuits require brains rather than brawn. The economic vitality and competitiveness of our society will depend increasingly on the talents and educational advancement of women and ethnic minorities. And finally, women work for the supplementary income needed for the family's subsistence or higher education of their children. For these various reasons, the traditional nuclear family of a working father, homemaker mother, and several children is on the decline.

Increasing numbers of married women are joining the work force by either economic necessity or personal preference. The burden of change is falling on the shoulders of women who find themselves managing the major share of the family demands as well as the demands of their occupational roles. Social practices lag far behind the changes in family life in which most married women are now working outside the home. The social changes call for equitable division of

household labor and equality of occupational opportunities in the workplace. Some of these changes require adjusting work arrangements to promote sharing of family responsibilities. The families of today need more social supports to safeguard their children's futures.

There is considerable variability among working women in the types of role demands they face; in the degree to which work and family demands conflict and disruptively intrude into one another; in the level of shared responsibility for the care of children and household; in the availability of adequate childcare; and in the types of stressors, satisfactions, and feelings of accomplishment women experience at home and at work. Given the wide diversity of conditions, it is not surprising that evidence on the effects of managing multiple role demands is ambiguous and inconsistent. Even under similar conditions, effects differ among individuals depending on the coping resources they bring to bear in efforts to fulfill the various role demands.

It is not workloads per se but the degree to which one can exercise control over them that largely determines their effects. These processes, of course, operate at the level of perceived capability to manage perceived workloads. Thus, there are women who thrive on the challenge of managing multiple roles and others who feel overwhelmed by them. In addition to socially imposed demands, women must contend with the self-imposed demands and standards by which they judge the adequacy of their homemaking and occupational accomplishments.

Ozer (1995) presents evidence that perceived efficacy to manage different aspects of multiple role demands is an influential factor in how women's lives are affected by these demands. Married women who pursued professional, managerial, and technical occupations were tested before the birth of their first child for their perceived efficacy to manage the demands of their family and occupational life. Their physical and psychological well-being and the strain they experienced over their dual roles were measured after they had returned to work. Although, the women contributed approximately half the family income, they bore most of the childcare responsibility. This is the prototypical social pattern. The division of household labor continues to lag behind the changing family pattern in which both spouses are employed. The minimal involvement of husbands in the housework and childcare explains the glaring absence of research on how working fathers juggle dual roles. Rather, the research focuses on how the social support of the home buffers working fathers against the stressors of the workplace.

Family income, heaviness of occupational workload, and division of childcare responsibility had no direct effect on women's well-being or emotional strain over the dual roles. These factors operated through their effects on perceived self-efficacy. Women who had a strong sense of efficacy that they could manage the multiple demands of family and work, exert some influence over their work schedules, and enlist their husbands' aid with various aspects of childcare experienced a low level of physical and emotional strain and a more positive sense of well-being. The effects of combining dual roles are generally framed negatively in the literature in terms of conditions under which interrole conflicts breed family discord and distress and the buffering role of protective factors. There are countless studies on the negative spillover of job pressures on family life but few on how job satisfaction enhances the quality of family life. Ozer's research shows that a sense of efficacy in managing dual roles contributes to personal well-being and better health rather than merely protecting against distress. Family income and perceived self-efficacy to enlist spousal aid with childcare is also associated with lowered vulnerability to physical symptoms. Women who are beset by nagging self-doubts in their ability to combine the dual roles, however, suffer physical health problems and emotional strain.

Women's beliefs in their efficacy to combine occupational and familial responsibilities may shape their career choices and development. Unmarried college women express a higher sense of efficacy that they can combine family responsibilities with traditionally female occupations than with male-dominated occupations (Stickel & Bonett, 1991). A low sense of efficacy to manage the latter dual role may discourage women who seek a married life from pursuing nontraditional careers. Men doubt

their efficacy to handle competently the combined demands of job and parenthood. Most elude the difficulties of juggling multiple roles by minimal involvement in housework and childcare.

Low-income families experience considerable economic hardships. The needs of family members exceed scarce resources and often require severe reductions or trade-offs of basic necessities. Not only do the families have to cope with problems of subsistence, but the impoverished communities in which they live provide meager positive resources for their children's development and heavy exposure to dangerous activities that can set a negative developmental course during the early years of life. Yet most poor parents manage to raise their children successfully despite the adversities. A major question of interest concerns the mechanisms governing parental triumph over economic hardships and community perils.

Elder and his associates shed light on psychosocial processes through which economic hardships alter parents' perceived efficacy, which, in turn, affects how they raise their children (Elder, Eccles, Ardelt, & Lord, 1995). Poor parents living in high-crime neighborhoods need to exercise three major types of child management (Furstenberg, Eccles, Elder, Cook, & Sameroff, in press). The first is the exercise of parental efficacy to promote their children's competencies. Successful parents place a high value on academic development, become involved in the school systems to ensure that their children are well taught, enroll them in community programs, cultivate peer relationships that are likely to be beneficial for their children, and encourage development of leisure time skills. The second aspect of child management relies on parental efficacy to exercise control over their children's involvement in high-risk behavior. This includes limiting where the children can go; keeping track of what they are doing outside the home; and discouraging them from engaging in drug use, alcohol, and premature sexual activity. The third aspect of efficacy in child management includes active parental involvement in beneficial community organizations. Efficacious parents carve out functional subcommunities through these affiliations that link their children to positive models, constructive activities, supportive social networks, and the values and social norms parents hold dear. These social ties compensate for meager neighborhood resources and protect against a neighborhood's dangerous aspects.

The findings show that objective economic hardship, by itself, has no direct influence on parents' perceived efficacy. Rather, objective financial hardship creates subjective financial strain (Fig. 5.1). Families who feel overwhelmed by the hardships experience high strain, whereas those who feel they can make it through tough times experience less emotional strain. In intact households, subjective strain impairs parental efficacy by fueling marital discord. A supportive marital relationship enables parents to withstand poverty without having it undermine their belief in their ability to guide their children's development. Indeed, in families with strong positive ties, hard economic times bring the members closer together and increase parents' sense of efficacy to guide their children's development.

The detrimental effects of financial strain on parents' sense of efficacy are greater in families living in impoverished neighborhoods than in those living in better-off ones. In poor, crime-infested neighborhoods, parents must work hard to protect their children and to promote their development. Parents' beliefs that they can affect the course of their children's lives have stronger impact on beneficial child guidance under disadvantaged conditions than under advantaged conditions. With more

plentiful material resources, social supports, and neighborhood controls, parents can get by with a lower sense of parenting efficacy. They have fewer stressors to cope with and more supplemental social aids to guide their children's development. Given the fragmentation of social life and the paucity of resources in impoverished communities, parents have to turn inward for their support in times of stress. If support is lacking in the home, the mounting stressors begin to overwhelm their coping efforts. Thus, for single parents, financial strain weakens parents' sense of efficacy both directly and indirectly by creating feelings of despondency. Regardless of family structure, parents who have a high sense of efficacy are active in encouraging their children's competencies both at home through promotive and protective strategies and outside the home through close ties to religious and social organizations in the broader community. In short, they refuse to let adversity get them down. In the face of scarce resources and demoralizing constraints, however, poor parents have to sustain extraordinary effort and make huge personal sacrifices to achieve a decent life path for their children.

In tracing the path of influence from economic conditions through familial processes to perceived parental efficacy and child management practices, Elder and his associates advance our understanding of how personal agency operates within a broad network of sociostructural influences. This pattern of

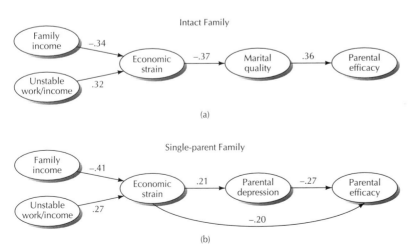

(a)

(b)

FIGURE 5.1. Path analysis showing that the effect of objective economic hardship on parents' sense of efficacy to guide their children's development operates through psychosocial processes rather than directly. Marital discord is the mediator in intact households (a), and depression is the mediator in single-parent households (b). (Elder & Ardelt, 1992)

causation is supported by research in other spheres of functioning to be reviewed later.

In many societies and familial structures grandparents are an important part of their grandchildren's lives. Through the ongoing relationships they have with their grandchildren, they contribute in many ways to their development. This source of emotional support and guidance, which can be especially influential in early formative years, has been seriously neglected in investigation of factors that shape the course of child development. King and Elder (1996) remedy this neglect in their research on perceived efficacy of grandparenthood. Grandparents vary in the beliefs they hold about their efficacy to influence their grandchildren's academic and social lives and peer associations. Their sense of efficacy is unaffected by sociodemographic characteristics, but it is enhanced by positive images of their own grandparents, religious connectedness and quality of the bond with the parent. Self-efficacious grandparents take a more active role in their grandchildren's lives than less self-efficacious counterparts. They spend time with their grandchildren, do things together in recreational and community activities, serve as a companion and mentor for them and discuss their personal problems and how they plan to make their way through life. Grandparental perceived efficacy is even more predictive of high quality relationships with grandchildren in divorced families, where their resourcefulness can be of considerable help.

Families that have an efficacious outlook are likely to experience greater community satisfaction and attachment because they believe they can change things for the better. Economic adversities exact a lower toll if they are viewed as surmountable. In contrast, families that believe there is little they can do to improve the quality of life in their communities feel dissatisfied with and estranged from their communities. Rudkin and his colleagues provide evidence that how families feel about their communities is partly mediated through their sense of efficacy rather than being simply a reflection of the objective economic conditions in their communities (Rudkin, Hagell, Elder, & Conger, 1992). Parents who believe they can exercise some control over their everyday lives feel more positive about their communities

and have less desire to move elsewhere. Economic conditions per se have only a weak direct effect on community satisfaction and only indirectly influence desire to move to the extent that hard times create dissatisfaction with the community.

The influence of perceived familial efficacy on community attachment will vary, of course, depending on the level of economic adversity and the responsiveness of institutional systems to change. When both adversity and prospects for change are dismal, families with a high sense of efficacy are apt to move elsewhere in search of a better life. Selective migration of the more efficacious residents contributes to the further deterioration of the socioeconomic life of a community (Wilson, 1987). Even under the most blighted community conditions, however, some individuals with a tenacious sense of efficacy and social purpose remain and labor tirelessly to get people to work together to improve their conditions of life.

Developed countries are experiencing mass migration of people seeking a better life. Some are fleeing the devastation of armed violence and political persecution. Others are deserting disintegrating countries that were held together by authoritarian rule. Many people living under impoverished and desperate circumstances are moved by televised visions of prosperity in other societies. Migratory pressures will persist or intensify as long as large economic disparities exist between nations. Rich nations pick off the most skilled and talented members of poorer nations, which only exacerbates the disparities. In addition to the international migrations, there are the extensive domestic migrations from rural to urban areas with progressive elimination of family farms as no longer economically viable. Rural towns wither as farming families depart.

Efforts to build a new life elsewhere run up against untold stressors, especially when migrations involve radical changes in sociocultural patterns and an influx of migrants creates backlashes toward them as foreign intruders. A prospective longitudinal study by Jerusalem and Mittag (1995) reveals that an efficacious outlook contributes in many ways to successful migratory adaptation. Migrants who were assured in their coping efficacy felt more challenged than threatened by the impediments to a new life. They also experienced less stress and better health than those who distrusted their abilities to cope with the vast changes in their lives. During the difficult transitional period, a high sense of efficacy enabled them to weather severance from supportive relationships and the misery of unemployment without undue stress and health impairment.

Midlife Changes

By the middle years, people settle into established lifestyles that stabilize their sense of efficacy in major areas of functioning. The popular literature portrays midlife as a period when personal growth has plateaued, youthful aspirations are retrenched, and efforts to come to terms with a static life heading toward inevitable decline creates an emotional crisis. These gloomy accounts misconstrue stabilization of career and family life as curtailment of further growth and challenge. In fact, gaining some measure of control over major spheres of life frees one to explore new activities of interest with greater resources to do so. Conditions of life never remain static. Human development is a lifelong process rather than one that is arrested at a midlife stage with an arbitrary beginning and end.

Rapid technological and social changes constantly require adaptations calling for reappraisals of personal efficacy. In the occupational sphere, the middle-aged find themselves pressured by younger challengers. Managers find younger rising aspirants vying for their positions. Younger athletes supplant their older teammates when their physical skills begin to wane. Situations in which people must compete for promotions, status, and even work itself force constant self-appraisals of capabilities by means of social comparison with younger cohorts unless one forsakes one's regular pursuits (Suls & Mullen, 1982).

Occupational advancement within an organization requires perceived efficacy to master the new roles and skills of different job assignments over the span of a career. Moreover, reduced organizational stability has made occupational pursuits much less secure. People lose jobs as a result of corporate restructuring through acquisitions, mergers, divestitures, and subcontracting of functions. Such changes usually include reductions in workforces and replacement of management teams. Formerly stable jobs also vanish through geographical relocations of production facilities and technological innovations. These new organizational realities have made work life more uncertain and occupational changes more common. To navigate their work lives successfully, people must develop skills and efficacy beliefs that enable them to manage periodic changes in jobs, companies, and even occupations to fulfill new job demands and roles. This places increased responsibility on individuals to take charge of their work lives. A high sense of efficacy to master multiple jobs and careers will be essential for a secure and satisfying occupational life in the transnational economy of the future. This is not solely a matter of personal adaptability, however. Societies must provide structural supports to facilitate the restructuring of work lives and ease the personal strains and costs of doing so.

During the middle years, people typically confront declining opportunities for career growth. Most will have gotten as far as they will in their vocations. They see time and opportunities to realize the ambitions that sustained them over the years slipping away. Visions of a future lacking variety and prospects for new challenges and accomplishments may give rise to strains, especially for people who harbor doubts that what they are doing is worthwhile. Upward mobility in organizational hierarchies, which is a prevailing career path, decreases with age. A consequence of hierarchical systems is the structural plateauing of employees in occupational roles lacking diversity, challenges, and opportunities to expand and exercise their competencies fully (Dewhirst, 1991). In the absence of preventive measures against occupational stagnation, plateaued employees are likely to experience a growing sense of obsolescence of their efficacy. This takes a toll on their health as well as the quality of their work life (McAteer-Early, 1992). Work enrichment through job rotation and teamwork approaches with flexible structures provide diversity and new challenges. These types of occupational arrangements help to maintain a satisfying and productive work environment. Employees who are assured of their learning efficacy are more receptive to opportunities to expand their knowledge and expertise, and benefit more from training programs, than do the less efficacious ones (Gist et al., 1989; Hill & Elias, 1990). Successes in managing job transitions further strengthen efficacy beliefs for occupational learning.

The way work is organized is undergoing major changes calling for greater personal efficacy and self-directedness than ever before. Much of the world of work is no longer being packaged into fixed activities presided over by multilayered administrators. Hierarchical structures are giving way to flexible, flattened organizational structures in which work is being configured around projects for which workers assume functional authority within self-managed teams. Teams are reshaped into whatever clusters of competencies are needed to achieve optimal results. Increasing reliance on temporary and part-time employees, job sharing, subcontracting, teleworking at home, and freelancing places an increasing premium on self-efficaciousness, self-directedness, and continuing self-development. Successful functioning under changing patterns of teamwork requires a high level of interpersonal as well as technical efficacy. While the new world of work gives people more leeway to manage their own vocational careers, it also creates uncertainty and job insecurity. For the less self-efficacious, this can be a source of perpetual stress.

Some life pursuits demand heavy investment of time and effort in the service of short-term careers. For those whose livelihood and self-esteem rest mainly on physical strength, such as professional athletes, reduced physical adeptness or injuries bring early forced retirement. This requires redirection of life pursuits posing new challenges to personal efficacy. A life devoted almost exclusively to professional sport, to the neglect of competencies required for other occupational pursuits, is not easy to redirect (McPherson, 1980). To find oneself unemployed with abrupt loss of income and status and poorly equipped with skills necessary for another occupation creates severe personal strains. The transition from sports careers to new life paths

is most difficult for athletes who have invested their sense of efficacy and identity almost entirely in the competitive activity. This is true even for competitive amateur athletes (Werthner & Orlick, 1986). Perceived self-efficacy and satisfaction with one's life drop during the period of transition. Those who cultivate other interests and competencies during their competitive years fare much better in moving on to new life pursuits. They regain a sense of efficacy in their new lives.

The need to restructure overambitious goals and self-doubts about the meaning and directions of one's life are by no means unique to the middle years. But when such reactions occur at this developmental phase, they are quickly seized upon as symptoms of midlife crisis. The alleged crisis resides more in the rhetoric of the popular media than in the actual experiences of people in their midlife, however this period is demarcated. Midlifers do not hold a monopoly on stocktaking. Younger and older folks do a lot of it too because disappointments, which arouse reappraisals of one's future, abound throughout life. Reactions to taking stock of one's life in the middle years take varied forms. Some people continue to expand their competencies in the domains around which their lives are structured. Many scale down their ambitions or reorder their goals but continue to update and upgrade their knowledge and skills to pursue their activities as competently as they can. In the occupational arena, except for nonskilled manual workers, people who remain in the same job increase their level of skill and responsibility over time, often due to advancements in technology (Gallie, 1991). Opportunities for further self-development always exist. Many people who find themselves in routine jobs, however, cease developing their capabilities, do their work perfunctorily, and seek satisfaction elsewhere. Most people try to keep their lives interesting by selecting pursuits that provide them with continuing challenges (Brim, 1992).

The paucity of research on psychosocial functioning in the midlife period has encouraged sensationalistic portrayals of the middle years as a time of midlife crisis. In the absence of countervailing knowledge, atypical examples of marked lifestyle changes come to be regarded as the normative pattern. Research on psychosocial functioning in the advanced years is dispelling the myth of uniform decline. But the myth of midlife plateau with internal upheavals is still very much part of the folklore. Most people navigate through the middle years efficaciously. Some do not. Like other developmental phases, midlife is a point in a personal life trajectory, not a unique stage that spawns distinct forms of behavior. Adaptation in midlife is best predicted by the interplay of personal attributes and life circumstances rather than by one's age.

In late adulthood, most people begin to consider leaving their main occupational role. Since work takes up much of everyday life, this change constitutes another major transition in the life course. People's beliefs in their efficacy to manage life in retirement as it nears determine whether they approach this transition apprehensively and despondently, as a welcome diversion freeing time for other interests, or as an opportunity for personal renewal (Fretz, Kluge, Ossana, Jones & Merkangas, 1989). Perceived efficacy remains a significant factor in the emotional adaptation during this transitional period after controlling for sociodemographic factors, quality of health, and level of retirement income. The traditional notion of "retirement" as withdrawal from working life is becoming a vestige of an era when work was packaged in fixed roles that changed little over time, society imposed arbitrary terminal limits, and life was short beyond that period. Major structural and personal changes have created a substantial lag between the thinking from this earlier era and current realities (Riley, Kahn, & Foner, 1994). People are now living a good deal longer, most are aging well physically and cognitively, they are changing their work activities and roles rapidly under flexible organizational arrangements, arbitrary age barriers to employment have been removed, and new educational technologies enable people to acquire advanced knowledge and competencies through self-directed learning. In the current realities of late adulthood, life is characterized more by a shift in pursuits and personal renewal than by withdrawal from an active life. The problems created by sociostructural lag reappear even more pervasively in the advanced years of life.

REAPPRAISALS OF SELF-EFFICACY WITH ADVANCING AGE

The prolongation of life underscores the need to alter social attitudes and institutional practices in ways that are conducive to healthy, productive aging. The self-efficacy issues for older adults center on reappraisals and misappraisals of their capabilities. Biological conceptions of aging focus extensively on declining capacities. Advancing age is said to produce losses in physical stamina, sensory functions, intellectual facility, memory, and the speed with which cognitive operations are executed. Many physical capacities do decrease as people grow older, thus requiring reappraisals of personal efficacy for activities in which the mediating biological functions have been significantly affected. People are equipped with excess biological reserve, however, so that some loss of reserve capacity with aging does not necessarily impair the level of psychosocial functioning because the remaining reserve function is ample for what is needed (Fries & Crapo, 1981). Moreover, gains in knowledge, skills, and expertise compensate for some loss in reserve capacity. The biopsychosocial conception of aging highlights the adaptive capacities of older adults and their potential to enhance their level of functioning.

In cultures that revere youth and negatively stereotype the elderly, age becomes a salient dimension for self-evaluation. Once chronological age assumes great significance, changes in performances over time stemming from sociocultural factors are easily misattributed to biological aging. The widespread belief in intellectual decline with age is a good case in point. Baltes and his colleagues have argued cogently for a more enlightened perspective on cognitive functioning in adulthood and advanced age (Baltes, Lindenberger, & Staudinger, in press). They marshal numerous lines of evidence that refute the stereotype of a single monolithic trajectory of intellectual growth followed by a uniform decline in all intellectual abilities. Rather, they show that intellectual development and functioning across the life span include diverse changes characterized by several distinctive features.

Heterogeneity of Cognitive Changes

Intellectual development is multifaceted and encompasses different types of abilities that vary in how heavily they draw on such component cognitive processes as attention, memory, time-sharing, information integration, and level of knowledge and expertise. Cognitive functioning is multidirectional, following different trajectories of change for different abilities. Some improve, others remain stable, and still others decline with age. Tests for the upper limits of functioning reveal some decline with aging in speed and flexibility of cognitive processing of information and psychomotor facility. Some reduction in maximum capacity does not necessarily detract from performance of daily cognitive activities, however, because most of them do not call for a sustained level of intense cognitive effort near the upper limits of functioning. Intellectual growth and decline exist together. Reasoning, problem-solving, and wisdom, which rely heavily on accumulated expert knowledge, remain stable or may actually increase into advanced age (Baltes & Smith, 1990). Because experienced judgment and wisdom do not lend themselves as easily to study as do the mechanics of cognitive processing, these facets of cognitive functioning that improve with age get neglected. The contributions that the elderly can make to the quality of life in a society receive little attention.

Wisdom is traditionally characterized by advanced understanding, keen discernment, and sound judgment. In psychological treatises, however, wisdom is all too often restricted to profundities about the meaning and existential problems of life. When wisdom is invested with metaphysical exclusionary criteria, only a select group of philosophizers and secular gurus end up possessing it. Counselors who impart insights about life would also come out looking wise even though their particular brands of insights often reflect their own theoretical allegiances and are easily predictable from their theoretical affiliations (Bandura, 1969a). The "wisdom" about the human condition dispensed by psychoanalysts differs predictably from that of Jungians or Skinnerians. Each claims superiority for their preferred brand of insight about life. Self-styled gurus dispensing inner bliss would also qualify as bearers of wisdom. The more metaphysical definitions of wisdom thus raise questions not only about whom they exclude but also about whom they include. A theory of wisdom must be concerned not only with the forms that wisdom takes but also with how to evaluate its usefulness. Unless the wiseness of judgment is verifiable, inspirational homilies about life enjoy the same status as deep understanding of the nature of things and human affairs.

An example of wisdom born of rich reflected experience that extends beyond abstract profundities is well illustrated by the 90-year-old oenologist, André Tchelistcheff, who was the unrivaled guru of California winemaking. Aspiring oenologists sought his wise counsel on how to conduct every phase of the winemaking process to bring out the best in the noble grape (Whiting, 1991). He bequeathed to them his vast knowledge of viticulture and winemaking, critiqued their wine samples with his refined palate, and counseled them in progressive thinking about winemaking. He did this daily with infectious enthusiasm for the life of a winemaker. A generation of winemakers regarded him as a font of wisdom. According to the criteria of wisdom emphasizing abstract profundities about life, a bartender who periodically counsels drinkers about their life problems would be exhibiting wisdom, but a master mentor like Tchelistcheff would not, even though he conveyed rich understanding that went well beyond technical viticultural skills.

Every human pursuit presents dilemmas and problems of how to conduct one's life to gain a sense of purpose and fulfillment. Wise judgment applies to pursuits around which people structure much of their lives as well as to ponderous issues about the meaning of human existence. Wisdom exists in degrees in all walks of life. Although wisdom is founded on expert knowledge, it encompasses much more. Experts who take a narrow technical view of their field of endeavor or use their advanced knowledge for selfish or destructive purposes would not be regarded as paragons of wisdom. Wisdom requires, in addition to superior judgment, a broad social and temporal perspective on matters and concern for human well-being. Baltes (in press), who has a lot of wise things to say about wisdom, defines it as expert knowledge about life and sound judgment in managing life's complexities and uncertainties. Wisdom need not be confined to social dilemmas. Many of the complexities and uncertainties of life involve nonsocial aspects of human pursuits, such as occupational activities requiring wise judgments.

Analyses of wisdom focus heavily on advice on how to deal with life matters. Wisdom not only is imparted verbally but also is conveyed by modeled self-management of important aspects of life. Those who are venerated for their wisdom not only talk wisely but exemplify their wisdom in the way in which they conduct their own lives. Since wisdom is often conveyed through modeling, rather than through lengthy discourse, we need criteria for measuring the wisdom of living as well as the wisdom of words. If wisdom is defined out of existence for the common endeavors of life by metaphysical criteria, a human capability that benefits from growing experience with age will continue to be slighted in the characterization of cognitive changes accompanying aging.

Component cognitive functions are easier to measure and quantify than expertise, wisdom, and creativity. The psychometric assessment of subfunctions is usually disconnected from belief systems and contextual influences known to affect intellectual functioning. So decontextualized component functions get emphasized over adaptive use of complex competencies, even though the latter accomplishments are the important measure of human cognitive functioning. It is of no great consequence that the Verdis, Toscaninis, Picassos, Rubinsteins, George Bernard Shaws, Martha Grahams, Georgia O'Keefes, Bertrand Russells, Winston Churchills, and Frank Lloyd Wrights may have been a bit slower in processing bits of information or less facile in trying to do several things simultaneously in their 80th and 90th years of life but continued to excel in

their vocations. Societies are the beneficiaries of their extraordinary later life accomplishments.

The discussion so far has distinguished intellectual functioning as comprising diverse types of abilities that follow different trajectories of change. A third distinguishing feature is the substantial differences among individuals in level and pattern of cognitive growth and functioning. Pursuit of dissimilar life careers cultivates different types of cognitive competencies. Differential experiences accompanying diverse roles, lifestyles, positions in socioeconomic strata, and historical periods of development further contribute to differences among individuals in the cognitive competencies they develop and how well they maintain them over time. Gender is another source of variation in which certain types of cognitive competencies are cultivated while others remain underdeveloped. Given huge variability within age levels, averages mask more than they reveal.

The modifiability of cognitive functioning even in advanced old age is an additional feature of intellectual change highlighted by Baltes and his associates. When the elderly are taught cognitive strategies to make better use of their cognitive capabilities, they substantially improve their level of cognitive functioning (Baltes & Lindenberger, 1988; Willis, 1990). Indeed, elderly persons experiencing cognitive decline with aging can achieve gains in cognitive functioning that offset the cognitive decrements over two decades spanning the advanced years of life. The elderly who experience no cognitive decline over the long time span improve their cognitive functioning beyond their earlier level following instruction. The improvements in cognitive functioning are maintained well into advanced age. Under an unhurried pace, the trained elderly are just about as adept cognitively as young adults, but under severe time pressure, the cognitive gains achieved by the elderly are much smaller than those of young adults. Declines in cognitive functioning with age thus partly reflect disuse of latent capacity and a drop-off in cognitive efficiency at upper limits of cognitive strain. Theorists who view cognitive development as a lifelong process are not unmindful of some regularities in the changes that occur with age, but the diversity and plasticity of cognitive functioning are the more impressive features.

Longitudinal studies reveal no universal or general decline in intellectual abilities until the very advanced years, but in cross-sectional comparisons of different age groups, the young do surpass the old (Baltes & Labouvie, 1973; Schaie, 1995). The extended longitudinal study by Schaie suggests that a major share of age differences in intelligence, until the very advanced years, is due to differences in the intellectual experiences across generations rather than solely to biological aging. To paraphrase Schaie, cultures age as do people. The changes that individuals undergo over their life course are extensively examined, but commensurate in-depth assessments of the changes that societies undergo over time are lacking. Age trends in functioning are especially likely to be overattributed to inherent biological aging when life course changes are disembodied from societal changes. Many age differences are partly the product of sociocultural changes in formal education and accelerated dissemination of information by new communication technologies. It is not so much that the old have declined in intelligence as that the young have had the benefit of richer intellectual experiences, enabling them to function at a higher cognitive level. To take one example, computers were nonexistent in the formative periods of today's elderly, whereas today's youngsters are taught computer literacy to expand their cognitive competencies in areas that interest them. Not surprising, the level of cognitive functioning of same-age adults has been rising across generations. Hence, cross-sectional age differences in cognitive functioning overestimate decline with aging.

Changes in intellectual functioning with age vary across individuals as well as across cognitive abilities and cultural periods. Individual diversity in patterns of aging reveals psychosocial determinants of successful aging. Elders who maintain high levels of intellectual functioning into very advanced age have educated themselves, pursued intellectually stimulating activities, exhibited flexibility and satisfaction with their life accomplishments in midlife, and maintained lifestyles that preserve their physical health (Schaie, 1995). Maintenance of

cognitive functioning in the advanced years reflects successful aging. Efficacy beliefs that support an active lifestyle sustain cognitive capabilities (Seeman, McAvay, Merrill, Albert, & Rodin, 1996). In a comprehensive longitudinal analysis of successful cognitive aging, Albert and her colleagues examined a host of potential predictors, including a variety of sociodemographic statuses and numerous lifestyle, psychosocial, and physiological factors (Albert et al., 1995). Four factors emerged from the large set as independent contributors to maintenance of cognitive functioning in the elderly: a sense of efficacy to influence the events of everyday life, educational level, a physically active lifestyle, and pulmonary capacity. Among elders exhibiting intellectual decline, brief training in cognitive strategies produces enduring gains in cognitive functioning (Willis & Schaie, 1986). Intellectual offerings on the Internet provide seniors with vast learning opportunities that can be pursued in the home at a time of their own choosing. These educational technologies enable them to exercise greater control over their intellectual functioning. This form of self-regulated learning provides an ongoing natural vehicle for promoting cognitive competencies.

Memory Functioning

Older people tend to judge changes in their intellectual capabilities largely in terms of their memory performance. This is because memory lapses in everyday life are highly noticeable and disruptive. Memory functioning, therefore, gets invested with a lot of diagnostic significance. Lapses and difficulties in memory that young adults dismiss are inclined to be read by older adults as indicators of shrinking intellectual capacities. Older adults use memory strategies less than do younger adults and favor external reminders over cognitive memory aids. Reduced cognitive effort contributes to forgetfulness, whatever the physical capacity might be. The elderly vary in how they construe memory and its changes with age (Lachman, M. Bandura, Weaver, & Elliott, 1995). Some view memory as a biological capacity that inevitably shrinks with age and is not personally controllable. Others view it as a set of cognitive skills that can be developed and maintained with effort. These divergent conceptions of memory can have varied effects on the quality of functioning. Belief in memory as a controllable skill is associated with confidence in one's ability to improve it, to generate solutions to everyday problems, and to live independently. This efficacious outlook is accompanied by low depression. In marked contrast, people who believe memory to be a shrinking biological capacity feel inefficacious to do anything about it, harbor doubts about their continued ability to solve problems and to live independently, fear that memory lapses may signify development of Alzheimer's disease, and suffer depression. These different conceptions of memory are also related to memory performance, with belief in memory as a cognitive skill facilitating memory performance and belief in memory as a shrinking capacity impairing it.

Because people rely heavily on memory performance as an indication of their cognitive capabilities, research on the effects of perceived efficacy for memory carries special significance (Bandura, 1989c; Berry, 1989). Human memory is an active constructive process in which information is semantically elaborated, transformed, and reorganized into meaningful memory codes that aid recall. People who view memory as a cognitive skill that they can improve are likely to exert the cognitive effort needed to convert their experiences into recallable symbolic forms. Those who regard memory as an inherent physical capacity that shrinks with biological aging have little reason to try to exercise control over their memory functioning. They are quick to read instances of normal forgetting as indicants of declining cognitive capacity. Older adults with a low sense of memory efficacy believe that they have a limited memory capacity, that they can do little to affect their memory, and that it is easily disrupted by stress and inevitably declines with age (McDougall, 1994). These belief correlates of perceived inefficacy remain after controlling for demographic factors, health status, and depression. The more the elderly disbelieve their memory capabilities, the poorer use they make of their cognitive capabilities.

People who have a strong belief in their memory capabilities do a good job of remembering things (Berry et al., 1989; Lachman, Steinberg, & Trotter, 1987). Moreover, level of perceived memory efficacy predicts degree of improvement in memory performance in young and old adults alike following training in mnemonic aids (Rebok & Balcerak, 1989). Self-efficacy retains its predictiveness when prior level of memory performance is controlled (Bandura, 1989c). After brief training in memory aids, however, young adults are more likely than older adults to raise their beliefs in their memory efficacy and to use the memory aids they have been taught in other types of memory tasks. Memory training in the elderly clearly requires more persuasive demonstrations that they can exercise some control over their memory in their everyday life by using cognitive strategies. This can be achieved by efficacy demonstration trials in which the elderly perform memory tasks with and without cognitive aids and observe that their memory improves when they use them. Modeling influences can be used to demonstrate how others have been able to improve their memory by habitual use of mnemonic aids. Persuasory influences that instill beliefs conducive to the use of memory skills can also help to raise elderly people's beliefs in their memory capabilities.

There are different types of memory, and they are differentially affected by the aging process. Forms of memory requiring active processing and restructuring of material generally decline with age, but those that make fewer processing demands are well-maintained. Such variations in developmental trajectories provide further evidence of cognitive diversity even for different facets within the same sphere of functioning. Moderate intercorrelations of memory efficacy scales measuring this diversity indicate that they represent a common domain but also tap unique aspects of memory (Berry et al., 1989). Efforts to enhance memory functioning, therefore, must provide people not only with general strategies but also with cognitive aids tailored to a particular type of memory.

We saw earlier that efficacy beliefs exert their effects on performance through cognitive, affective, and motivational processes. Efficacy beliefs can enhance memory performance by motivating deeper levels of cognitive processing of experiences. These cognitive memory aids may involve organizational strategies, mental rehearsal, and elaborative and associative coding that makes new information memorable by relating it to what is already familiar and meaningful. The more strongly older adults believe in their memory capabilities, the more time they devote to cognitively processing memory tasks (Berry, 1996). Higher processing effort, in turn, produces better memory performance. In the analysis of the causal structure, efficacy beliefs affect actual memory performance both directly and indirectly by increasing cognitive effort (Fig. 5.2). The findings of West, Berry, and Powlishta (1983) suggest that efficacy beliefs can operate on memory functioning through the affective modality as well. Many of the psychosocial and physical changes associated with aging give rise to bouts of despondency. Depression is accompanied by a weak sense of memory efficacy, which, in turn, is associated with deficient memory performances. The decline in perceived efficacy and intellectual performance associated with impaired health (Lachman & Leff, 1989) may arise more from depression over physical impairments than from the physical condition itself.

Because of the many ways in which efficacy beliefs affect performance, programs designed to enhance the cognitive functioning of elderly people must be aimed at raising their sense of cognitive efficacy as well as imparting memory skills. Debilitating beliefs of memory capacity have been modified by correcting faulty memory beliefs and modeling adaptive memories, along with providing practice in generating strategies for remembering (Lachman, Weaver, M. Bandura, Elliott, & Lewkowicz, 1992). The combined influence fosters a conception of memory as an influenceable skill and instills a sense of efficacy that one can improve it. Training memory skills on isolated laboratory tasks raises perceived efficacy for those tasks, but the elderly do not generalize the enhanced self-efficacy to their everyday cognitive functioning nor do they see much utility to the strategies being taught (Dittmann-Kohli, Lachman, Kliegl, & Baltes, 1991).

The generalization problem is in no way unique to memory functioning or to the elderly. Cognitive training without providing varied experiences in the applicability of the skills being taught usually produces weak generalization and maintenance of new cognitive skills. To promote generalized use, the elderly need efficacy verification experiences that they can produce good results with the new cognitive skills in their everyday memory functioning. Once self-persuaded that they have the capability to exercise control over their memory functioning, they will neither ignore nor abandon the means by which they do so. This persuasion is best achieved by instilling, for personally meaningful activities, a sufficiently generalized sense of cognitive efficacy to short-circuit the need for tedious transfer training in every setting in which the cognitive skills should be used.

As in earlier periods of development, the elderly use the major sources of efficacy information in reappraising their personal efficacy. In judging their capabilities from enactive experiences, they evaluate their performance attainments and compare them to their level of functioning at earlier periods of their life (Suls & Mullen, 1982). The accomplishments of others provide modeled information for gauging personal efficacy through social comparison. The different age trends in intellectual functioning, which have been revealed by longitudinal and cross-sectional comparisons, can have quite different impact on how much change is

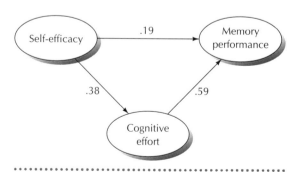

FIGURE 5.2. Path analysis showing that belief in one's memory enhances memory performance both directly and by increasing cognitive processing of information. (Berry, 1987)

perceived in cognitive capability. The elderly who weight self-comparison in functioning over time more heavily than social comparison with younger cohorts are less likely to view themselves as declining in capabilities than those who use younger cohorts extensively in comparative self-appraisals.

Physical and Health Functioning

Misappraisals of capabilities with aging occur in physical and health functioning as well as in cognitive functioning. Declines in stamina and functional health status are attributed, all too often, solely to biological aging. Some of the decline in physical stamina reflects decrements in beliefs of physical efficacy. In laboratory studies of this mediating mechanism, reductions in perceived physical efficacy, induced vicariously through exposure to supposedly superior performances of others, lower observers' physical endurance (Weinberg et al., 1979; Weinberg et al., 1980). The more perceived physical efficacy is diminished by arbitrary social comparison, the greater is the decline in physical stamina. The reduction of strength and stamina by a sedentary lifestyle is more likely to be attributed to biological aging by older than by younger people. The incomparable Satchel Paige alluded to the self-limiting effects of age-graded beliefs when he queried: "How old would you be if you didn't know how old you was?" Although most people enjoy good health, illnesses in the later years of life take their toll on both psyche and body. The damage to a sense of personal efficacy is no small matter.

Physical inactivity has more profound effects than simply sapping neuromuscular strength and stamina. It weakens the functioning of biological systems, resulting in negative changes in cellular and metabolic processes, loss in lean body mass, cardiovascular decline, and diminished immunocompetence. Bortz (1982) has marshaled a large body of evidence showing that declines in many physical functions commonly attributed to biological aging are similar to those produced by physical inactivity. Cardiovascular diseases cause over half the deaths in the elderly and continue to take an increasing toll in the advanced years. The major share of the decline in cardiovascular function with age can be offset by regular exercise (Bortz, in press; Hagberg, 1994).

Functional decline in other bodily functions, due to a sedentary lifestyle, can also be reversed or greatly attenuated by a physically active life. Regular exercise provides a reliable means for improving health and extending life (Winett, 1996). Despite the substantial health benefits of aerobic activity and strength development, adults who have a low sense of self-regulatory efficacy cannot get themselves to adopt a regular exercise regimen and stick to it (McAuley, Lox, & Duncan, 1993). Most older adults settle into a sedentary life believing in the inevitable and unchangeable withering of their physical capabilities. Chapter 9 reviews strategies for promoting active lives by enhancing a sense of efficacy to regulate one's motivation and health habits. Regular exercise is an important part of aging successfully.

The contribution of perceived personal efficacy to health promotion and disease prevention is addressed fully in Chapter 7. Although older adults benefit as much from health promotion programs as do younger counterparts, the elderly receive fewer preventive services. Grembowski and his associates examined the health benefits of reimbursed preventive services for the elderly designed to change a variety of habit patterns that create health risks (Grembowski et al., 1993). When preventive services are made available, older adults with strong belief in their efficacy to manage health-related behavior take advantage of the services. They lower their health risks and achieve better health.

There is substantial evidence that socioeconomic level is related to longevity and good health throughout gradations of the socioeconomic hierarchy (Adler et al., 1994). Because the association is present at upper as well as lower socioeconomic levels and occurs even under nationalized health care, access to medical services does not adequately account for the differences in health status. The mechanisms underlying the graded association between socioeconomic level and health are far from clear. In Grembowski's research with the elderly, higher socioeconomic level was associated with better functional health status, but the strength of that association was reduced when the effect of efficacy beliefs was removed. These findings indicate that perceived self-efficacy accounts for part of the association between socioeconomic level and functional health status.

Instilling personal efficacy to exercise some control over health habits clearly can benefit people at all ages and socioeconomic levels. Fostering health in the elderly is of special importance because health problems that create functional impairments threaten loss of autonomy. Efficacy beliefs function as a protective factor against the adverse effects of debilities. With development of functional limitations over time, elders who have a low sense of personal efficacy give up trying to manage on their own and suffer a lowered quality of life (Zautra, Reich, & Newsom, 1995). Elders with similar levels of physical impairment but with belief in their efficacy to produce desired results and cope with stressors enjoy greater autonomy and psychological well-being. Their level of depression is determined more by beliefs in their physical inefficacy than by declines in their physical status (Davis-Berman, 1989).

The mass media play an influential role in shaping images of reality (Bandura, 1986a; Signorielli & Morgan, 1989). The elderly are rarely seen in televised representations of society, as though people after midlife cease to be significant contributors to the life of a society. On the infrequent occasions they appear in the symbolic world of television, they are often cast in comical or eccentric roles rather than shown leading productive, self-fulfilling lives (Signorielli, 1985). In more recent televised representations, the elderly are portrayed a bit better than they used to be. In exploiting the physical changes and common ailments associated with aging, the world of television advertising is heavily populated with negative stereotypes of the elderly either as idle simpletons or as leading impoverished, debilitated lives requiring countless medical remedies. The pejorative stereotypes of enfeebled old persons shape, through persuasory means, cultural expectations and evaluative reactions of inefficacy toward the elderly. Researchers

reinforce the stereotype by studying mainly low-functioning adults in care facilities for the elderly rather than the successful elderly who are pursuing active, productive lives. As aches and pains increase with advancing age, physical states gain importance as indicators of capability. The elderly tend to pay increasing attention to somatic states and are more inclined to read unpleasant bodily states as indicators of loss of capability due to the biological aging process. Level of functioning cannot be adequately gauged from assessment of biological factors alone. Therefore, people of similar biological status but with differing efficacy beliefs will vary in how well they use the capabilities they possess.

Aging and the Exercise of Control

The study of aging has been largely confined to cognitive functioning. The scope of inquiry must be broadened to provide a deeper understanding of how people adapt and change in their later years. Even in the cognitive domain, the issue of interest is not only what cognitive capacities the elderly have, but how they use them to construct and manage their social realities. A key issue in this expanded perspective is how the elderly maintain a sense of personal agency and exercise it in ways that give meaning and purpose to their lives. This is no easy matter given the major life transitions, biopsychological changes, and social barriers with which they have to cope.

The maintenance of social connectedness is an important aspect of successful aging. Major life changes in social ties in later years are brought about by retirement, relocation, and loss of friends or spouses. Such changes place demands on interpersonal skills to cultivate new social relationships that can contribute to positive functioning and personal well-being. A low sense of social efficacy increases older people's vulnerability to stress and depression both directly and indirectly by impeding development of social supports (Holahan & Holahan, 1987a,b). The benefits of social support are usually explained in terms of its function as a buffer against life stressors. But social support is more than just a protective cushion against environmental on-slaughts. As noted earlier, acquaintances model coping attitudes and skills, provide incentives for engagement in beneficial activities, and motivate others by showing that difficulties are surmountable by perseverant effort. The enabling function of social support enhances perceived coping efficacy (Major et al., 1990). Indeed, the combined findings suggest a bidirectional relationship between efficacy belief and social support: A strong sense of social efficacy facilitates development of socially supportive relationships, and social support, in turn, enhances perceived efficacy.

Social dependency is commonly regarded as a concomitant of the aging process, presumably due to physical impairments. The inevitability of dependency is another aspect of the stereotypical view of aging. The majority of the elderly are quite independent in managing their daily activities. Others, who may suffer some disability, live independently with a few supportive services. Even in the more frail elderly, the biological determination of dependent behavior is overstated. In microanalytic studies of interactional patterns in nursing homes, Baltes (1988) found that social factors are influential contributors to dependent behavior in the elderly. The social environment fosters dependency in the residents but offers little support for expressions of independence. Being able to do things by oneself can secure numerous benefits, so that social discouragement of such behavior does not eliminate it. Even dependency does not necessarily indicate helplessness (Baltes, 1996). In an institutional milieu, dependency is a highly effective way of gaining social contact. Moreover, as daily routines take longer and become harder to do in advanced years, the elderly get others to help do some of them. It is important to distinguish between dependence on others and seeking help in areas of functional limitations to preserve one's autonomy. Selective dependence frees elders' time to pursue other activities of special interest to them independently.

All too often, the lives of residents of institutions are routinized and extensively controlled to maintain institutional efficiency and economy. Institutional constraints on the exercise of personal control can take a toll on psychobiological well-being. Residents of nursing homes who are given opportunities to exercise some control over events in their daily lives are more active socially, more engaged in activities, happier, remain in better health, and live longer than those who are kept dependent on the staff (Langer & Rodin, 1976; Rodin & Langer, 1977). Programs that increase residents' sense of control by developing coping skills lower their stress and neuroendocrine activation and make them better problem solvers (Rodin, 1986). Neuroendocrine changes can affect immunological competence. Indeed, Rodin presents some evidence that enhanced perceived control improves health status in the elderly by mitigating the adverse effects of psychosocial stressors on immunocompetence.

A sense of personal efficacy not only promotes health but also aids physical and social recovery from injuries common to older people, such as hip fractures and coronary artery surgery (Carroll, 1995; Ruiz, 1992; Ruiz, Dibble, Gilliss, & Gortner, 1992). Surgical procedures expand physical capacity, but paradoxically, the expanded physical capacity is often unaccompanied by functional improvements in the social, physical, and leisure activities of daily living (Allen, Becker, & Swank, 1990). The people who are confident of their efficacy to manage situational demands are the ones who resume a more active life postoperatively. The relationship remains after controlling for variations in physical capacity, sociodemographic status, and preoperative physical functioning. Efficacy belief heavily outweighs physical capacity in how active a life people lead postoperatively.

The elderly vary in how they respond to opportunities to exercise greater control over their daily lives. Compared to young adults, older adults generally express less desire for personal control (Woodward & Wallston, 1987). These variations in desire for personal control, however, are heavily determined by efficacy beliefs. The elderly desire control in areas in which they believe they can achieve results but not in domains they doubt they can do much to influence. Some domains of functioning are, of course, more subject to personal control than others. The mediation by self-efficacy of desire for personal control is especially evident in the area of health functioning, where some people view health as biologically ordained and others regard it as modifiable by psychosocial means. Age differences in desire for personal control over health services and health information disappear when variations in perceived efficacy are controlled. Regardless of age, those with a high sense of efficacy seek an active role in their health care; the less efficacious ones relinquish control to health professionals. Age effects on the desire for personal control over daily activities are partially mediated by variations in efficacy beliefs as well.

Age trends in cross-sectional studies of desire for control should be interpreted with caution because, as Woodward and Wallston acknowledge, it is difficult to disentangle the effects due to aging from those due to cultural changes over a long time. The elderly of today grew up in an era when the active exercise of personal control was not especially encouraged. The young adults of today are continuously swamped with prescriptive tracts on how to take charge of their lives. Similarly, today's young adults are repeatedly urged to reduce health habits that risk disease and adopt those that enhance vitality, whereas most of today's elderly were not brought up with the belief that they can command goodly control over their physical well-being by psychobehavioral means.

Many adults manage to preserve a favorable sense of personal efficacy well into the later years (Baltes & Baltes, 1986; Lachman, 1986). This is a reassuring finding provided it does not reflect insensitivity of global measures of personal efficacy. General measures often fail to reveal age differences where more sensitive domain-linked ones do. As we have already seen, people vary in their capabilities and developmental trajectories across domains of functioning. Some capabilities are on the rise over the life span, others are on the decline, and still others remain relatively stable. Given the diversity of functioning, analysis of changes in efficacy beliefs as a function of aging clearly requires domain-linked assessments.

People hold beliefs not only about how well they can manage the demands of their daily lives but also about how much control they can exert over their future personal development and the course their lives take. Brandtstädter (1989, 1992) reports a gradual decrease with advancing age in perceived control over personal development. Belief that one can exert influence over the developmental changes in one's life is associated with better health; more effective intellectual and occupational functioning; and reduced vulnerability to stress, despondency, and resignation. The findings also reveal that people seek to regain some control over the direction of their lives in behavioral domains that are personally improvable. They do so not only by acting on their sense of personal efficacy but also by drawing more heavily on support from their marital partners. This can be an optimizing strategy if proxy efficacy is used in some areas of functioning to free time and effort to enhance personal efficacy in other areas. The exercise of such dual efficacy is not unique to the elderly. No one has the time, energy, and limitless skills to manage adequately all the adaptational demands of everyday life. Those who optimize their talents concentrate their efforts on pursuits of focal interest and get others to help them manage the many other functions that must be attended to in their daily life. If it becomes harder to maintain or improve one's skills with age, the need for proxy efficacy increases.

Sociostructural Constraints

Aging does not happen in isolation but occurs in a societal context. The course of aging, therefore, is affected by the structure of society within which it occurs. The roles into which older adults are cast impose sociocultural constraints on maintenance and cultivation of cognitive competencies. It is easier to age successfully for those who experience little discontinuity in their major life pursuits as they grow older. Writers continue to write, artists to paint, conductors to conduct, professors to teach, farmers to cultivate the land; other nonprofessional pursuits for which one possess the necessary resources can be long-lived. Among the people who have had to give up their lifework because of mandatory age limits, those who developed transferable skills and expertise can construct new pursuits for themselves that give them a sense of purpose and satisfaction. As people move to older age phases, however, most suffer losses of resources, productive roles, and access to opportunities and challenging activities. Monotonous environments that require little thought or independent judgment diminish cognitive functioning; intellectually challenging ones enhance it (Schooler, 1987). The more the environment in which the elderly live limits them, the more they will decline in their sociocognitive functioning.

Discussions of aging in different social contexts often treat persons and contexts as though they were independent entities that jointly shape the course of personal change. In fact, they determine each other. People are producers as well as products of contexts. Individuals who differ in personal efficacy will create different social realities for themselves within the same structure of society. Therefore, the courses that lives take in the advanced years are the product of transactions between personal attributes and the opportunity structures and constraints that societies provide their elderly (Featherman, Smith, & Peterson, 1990).

Some of the declines in cognitive functioning with age result from sociocultural dispossession of the environmental substructures for it, rather than being inherent in the aging process. It requires a strong sense of personal efficacy to reshape and maintain a productive life in cultures that cast their elderly into powerless roles devoid of purpose and do not expect much of them. Because people rarely exploit their full potential, elderly persons who invest the necessary time and effort can function at the higher levels of younger adults. By affecting level of involvement in activities, a sense of personal efficacy contributes to the maintenance of cognitive functioning over the adult life span. Structural changes that expand the roles and opportunities available for older people would make it easier for them to pursue fulfilling, productive activities over their entire lifetime.

The people of today are aging more effectually than those of yesteryear. They are exercising greater control over their self-development and health in ways that foster efficacious longevity. As a result, today's elderly are healthier, more knowledgeable and intellectually agile, and more proactively oriented toward life than previous generations. These changes over time are creating a mismatch or "structural lag" in which the vast majority of people are growing older more effectually but societal institutions and practices are slow in accommodating their expanded potentials (Riley et al., 1994). The structural impediments to the continuance of productive lives include institutional arrangements, role expectations, and social norms that curtail opportunities and withdraw incentives to exercise the competencies the elderly possess. These social expectations and practices touch most aspects of life. They affect work opportunities, retirement practices, educational pursuits, and how people fill their unstructured leisure time. Because social practices have not kept pace with improved aging, the problems of the elderly are partly due to the failure of social systems to support the personal efficacy they possess. Handicapping environments produce functional declines that readily get misattributed to biological aging. Some of the social impediments to the exercise of personal efficacy are easing, with less rigid structuring of work and education by age. But institutional practices still lag behind the capabilities of the elderly. Their skills and wealth of knowledge go untapped despite a critical social need for their contributions. As the ranks of the elderly grow in the age structure of societies, social pressure increases to remove cultural exclusions and barriers to the continuation of purposeful lives.

Maintenance of Self-Efficacy with Decline in Capacity

Because of the many processes by which efficacy beliefs enhance human functioning, there is considerable adaptive value to maintaining a sense of personal efficacy despite some diminishment in capacity. Otherwise, if people exhibited a collapse in perceived efficacy mirroring the actual decline in reserve capacity, they would be condemned to a mounting sense of resignation and futility. In short, a self-efficacious outlook is no less functional in old age than in earlier periods of life when individuals struggled to make it in pursuits strewn with obstacles.

There are several processes by which older adults can sustain a high sense of efficacy in spite of declines in reserve capacity. One such process operates through strategies of social comparison. The capabilities of those used for comparative self-appraisal have strong impact on people's beliefs of their personal efficacy, which, in turn, affect the quality of their functioning (Bandura & Jourden, 1991). Whom the elderly compare themselves against, therefore, can contribute much to their differences in perceived efficacy. If older adults do not experience a significant decline in a given area of functioning and avoid social comparison with younger cohorts, they can achieve an enduring sense of personal efficacy through favorable self-comparison over time. They can do things about as well as they did before. Even if they experience a decline in capability, they can sustain their sense of efficacy by ignoring younger cohorts and appraising their capabilities through selective social comparison with their age-mates. By maintaining or improving their relative standing among age-mates, they can preserve an efficacious outlook in the face of declining capabilities. The trend may be downward, but as long as one excels relative to one's age-mates, the favorable comparison sustains a sense of personal efficacy (Bandura & Jourden, 1991).

Frey and Ruble (1990) indicate that the elderly can maintain a sense of efficacy and self-satisfaction in the face of changing capabilities by shifting standards of self-appraisal depending on phase of skill development and on age-related changes in capabilities. Self-comparison of changes over time is most conducive to positive self-appraisal when skills are being improved. Evidence of progressive improvement sustains a high sense of efficacy and provides a continuing source of self-satisfaction. When skill levels have stabilized or capabilities begin to wane with increasing age, however, self-satisfaction and perceived efficacy are better served by use of social comparative standards. Surpassing comparative age-mates can contribute to positive self-appraisal even though personal capabilities are no longer improving or may even be declining. In a study of older runners, Frey and Ruble provided evidence that self-appraisal strategies are indeed adapted to the direction of performance change. The runners shifted their evaluative standard from self-comparison to social comparison as the course of their performance changed from improvement to decline in the maximum level they could achieve.

A word of caution is in order about overgeneralizing these findings to pursuits that are socially structured in a different manner. Runners are free to choose where and when they will compete. In addition to the exercise of control over the selection of performance situations, the contests are carefully age-graded, which constrains performance comparison mainly to age-mates. This is not the way things work in the real world. In the important pursuits of everyday life, older persons have to compete with younger cohorts whether they like it or not. Competitively structured systems in which one person's success is another person's failure force social comparison unless one forgoes the activity. In most pursuits, comparative self-appraisal does not shift dichotomously between social and self-comparison across age and phase of skill development. People may give more or less weight to social and self-standards but they usually consider both how they are changing and how they compare with others in appraising their capabilities.

Frey and Ruble (1990) further note that older adults who keep up their skills can maintain a high sense of efficacy and self-satisfaction by exploiting age norms. In such normative comparisons, they come out looking superior to their age-mates. This self-enhancement strategy is beneficial for those who exceed the normative age standard. But those who have let their skills go to pot would do better to avert their gaze from normative standards unless they want to arouse self-discontent as a motivator for a program of self-reinvigoration. There is, however, some latitude for self-enhancement through normative comparison even though, objectively, one does not surpass one's age level. This is because people usually make their comparative appraisals in terms of their impressions of the norms rather than in terms of the actual norms, which most may not even know. In examining the use of subjective norms in appraisal of personal capabilities, Heckhausen (1992) found that people believe they are better able to exercise control over their attributes and to counteract their decline than most others at their age level can do. Advantageous social comparisons, whatever form they take, help to preserve a sense of personal efficacy.

Another process in the maintenance of perceived self-efficacy amidst some decline in reserve capacity operates through selective integration of multifaceted efficacy information. Multiple experiences in using different skills in diverse activities provide a heterogeneous base of information for judging personal efficacy. Therefore, people have some leeway in self-appraisal by how heavily they weight different domains or facets of functioning. For example, if they remain good problem solvers and bring a broad perspective to bear on judgments of important matters, they will not necessarily downgrade their sense of personal efficacy because they process information a bit slower or have experienced some decline in physical stamina. By weighting heavily the domains of functioning at which they excel and minimizing those they consider of lesser import, people can preserve their sense of efficacy amidst a decline of functioning in their advanced years.

Another major process of efficacy maintenance late in life operates through selective optimization and compensation (Baltes & Baltes, 1990). With some cognitive slowdown and reduction in stamina with age, it takes more time and effort to improve performance. The elderly can optimize their level of functioning by concentrating their efforts on things that are important to them and forgoing activities that are of lesser consequence to their lives. Selectivity enables them to maintain or even improve their skills in the selected pursuits. Performance improvement with some decline in reserve function can also be achieved by compensatory changes in how activities are managed. Better knowledge and strategies can compensate for loss in speed or stamina (Salthouse, 1987). External memory aids can substitute for cognitive aids in remembering and regulating activities in daily life (Kotler-Cope & Camp, 1990). With declining physical functioning in advanced age, control over daily life is maintained by simplifying activities, pacing them so that they are not too taxing, and restructuring the physical environment to make it more manageable.

The Baltes provide a telling example of selective optimization and compensation in Rubinstein's account of how he had remained an inimitable pianist beyond his 90th year of life: "First, he reduces his repertoire and plays a smaller number of pieces (selection); second, he practices these more often (optimization); and third, he slows down his speed of playing prior to fast movements, thereby producing a contrast that enhances the impression of speed in the fast movements (compensation)." In organizational functioning, adoption of compensatory self-regulatory strategies that enable one to exercise good control over heavy workloads can raise perceived efficacy despite some decline in particular information-processing skills (Birren, 1969; Rebok, Offerman, Wirtz, & Montaglione, 1986).

A related strategy for maintaining a sense of efficacy and positive well-being is to scale down one's pursuits or adopt new roles. To make one's self-esteem dependent on performance attainments for which one lacks efficacy breeds despondency (Bandura, 1991b). In activities in which skills wane, individuals struggle with decisions about whether to continue pursuits that may be getting beyond their reach or to set their sights on more attainable ones (Brandtstädter & Baltes-Götz, 1990). Successful adaptation to loss of reserve function can be achieved by transferring one's area of expertise to new pursuits that are fulfillable and thus efficacy enhancing. Former athletes become coaches, media commentators, and administrators of athletic franchises; former opera singers become voice teachers; former ballerinas become dance instructors; and former truck drivers become dispatchers and shipping overseers. The changes in roles provide new sources of personal efficacy.

Although optimization strategies play an especially important role in successful aging, the Baltes emphasize that such strategies are important to successful functioning throughout life (Baltes & Baltes, 1990). Those who make the most of their talents structure their activities around a selective set of meaningful life pursuits and strive for excellence in those they undertake. They stick to their priorities and do not fritter away their time and effort on whatever demands on their time happen to come their way. People also become more selective late in life in the social relationships they cultivate and maintain (Carstensen, 1991). They prefer established relationships that provide positive emotional experiences, but they are reluctant to devote the time and effort it takes to explore new ones that often entail some strains and other negative aspects during the acquaintance process. Reduction in the number of social contacts with age may reflect social selectivity rather than disengagement from emotional involvements.

A declining sense of efficacy, which may stem more from disuse and undermining cultural practices than from biological aging, can set in motion a negative spiral of self-debilitating appraisals that result in diminishing cognitive and behavioral functioning. People who are insecure about their personal efficacy not only curtail the range of their activities but diminish their efforts in those they undertake. The spiraling weakening of perceived self-efficacy results in a progressive loss of motivation, interest, and skill. In societies that emphasize the potential for self-development throughout the life span, rather than psychophysical decline with aging, the elderly lead productive and purposeful lives.

6

Cognitive Functioning

EDUCATIONAL SYSTEMS HAVE UNDERGONE fundamental change during historical periods of cultural and technological transitions. Educational systems were originally designed to teach low-level skills in agricultural societies. When industrialization supplanted agriculture as the major economic enterprise, the educational system was adapted for the needs of heavy industry and manufacturing. Most of the occupational pursuits required rote performance without many cognitive skills. Increasing complexities in technologies, social systems, and the international economy present different realities demanding new types of competencies. In the modern workplace, sweeping changes in technologies are mechanizing many of the everyday transactions and activities that were formerly done manually. In contemporary production systems, people manage computer-controlled machines that perform most of the routine work. We retool our production machines by changing the computer software. We design and test things using computer graphics and thus do not have to construct prototypes. The offices of today are run, in large part, by computerized information-management systems. New technologies are displacing traditional jobs even in the delivery of services. We

bank with automatic tellers, talk to operatorless recording machines that shepherd us through tortuous paths, and pump gas from computerized equipment monitored by a single person sitting in a booth. Bar code scanners tied to automated inventory management systems reorder merchandise without requiring inventory clerks and purchasing agents. Many workers have been displaced by automation.

The advent of the information era does not mean that the workplace is now solely concerned with managing data and transacting messages. Rather, the information technology is operating automated production and service systems. These electronic technologies are run by structuring and manipulating information. The historical transition from the industrial to the information era has profound implications for educational systems. In the past, youth with limited schooling had recourse to well-paying industrial and manufacturing jobs demanding minimal cognitive skills. Such options are rapidly shrinking. The emerging opportunities require communication and thinking skills to fulfill the more complex occupational roles and to manage the intricate demands of contemporary life. Education has now become vital for a productive life. Moreover, the rapid pace of social and technological change requires people to learn new competencies or to adapt preexisting ones to changing conditions to keep their skills from becoming outmoded. Moreover, computerized systems provide a handy vehicle for transactive construction of knowledge. Educational systems, therefore, must teach students how to educate themselves throughout their lifetime. They have to be adaptable, proficient learners. The hope and future of individuals and their societies reside in their capacities for self-renewal.

Societies pay dearly for the educational neglect of their youth. School failure often foreshadows delinquency, substance abuse, teenage pregnancies, and heavy involvement in other high-risk behaviors that jeopardize the chances of having a productive and satisfying life. Intellectually deficient youth become occupationally disadvantaged adults with unstable means of livelihood that have severe repercussions on patterns of family life (Wilson, 1987). In the new global economy, even the better educated now have to compete with well-educated labor abroad where companies are quite willing to relocate their development and production systems to places where they can hire workers at lower wages. There is little support for family life if wage earners cannot provide for the family's economic welfare. A society with a poorly educated work force cannot compete successfully in the international marketplace. The net result is a decline in the quality and standard of living.

The impact of the information era on educational systems extends well beyond matters of occupational preparation. The information technologies are transforming the educational enterprise itself. Easy electronic access to well-organized instruction in virtually any subject creates extensive learning opportunities that transcend time and place. The process of learning is individualized and enables students to exercise considerable control over their own education. They can construct their own learning environment and structure their knowledge by drawing on the vast educational resources available. This enables people in all walks of life to take a stronger hand in

shaping their own development. If people form interactive networks, they can learn from one another through collaborative instruction. Multilinked collaborative and mentoring relationships can accelerate the mastery of difficult subjects and the construction of new understandings. Multimedia educational resources available on the network similarly enable teachers to create and tailor learning environments in their classrooms to suit particular purposes.

Much learning will be occurring outside the confines of schools. Students will be educating themselves with multimedia instruction presented electronically by master teachers via the global Internet. This educational technology can greatly expand the learning opportunities of children in school systems with limited resources. The students can pursue courses taught by gifted faculty in distant locales. They can have the best libraries, instructional sites, and museums at their fingertips. Electronically mediated instruction also provides a convenient vehicle for gaining specialized knowledge long after one's formal schooling has ended. People can expand their knowledge and skills at a time, place, and pace of their own choosing through the offerings in the network. The Internet will serve as the main instructional medium for lifelong learning. Virtual institutions increasingly will provide multimedia higher education both nationally and internationally.

Telelearning must be placed in proper perspective. Educational technologies can do only so much. Children can learn a lot from computer terminals, but they need human teachers to help build their sense of efficacy, to cultivate their aspirations, and to find meaning and direction in their pursuits. The content of early schooling is perishable and long forgotten, but the interpersonal and self-development effects endure. If students are to make the most of these opportunities, they must develop the ability to regulate their own motivation and learning activities. Those who are most at risk of educational failures are likely to be the ones who are least prepared to use such instructional systems or who have limited access to them. Because of limited resources, the disadvantaged are likely to be left out of these educative systems. Unless the poor are provided with home computers and access to on-line services, the knowledge gap between rich and poor nations and between advantaged and disadvantaged sectors within nations will widen. Information technologies provide educational opportunities, but self-motivation and aspirations will determine, in large part, what is made of those opportunities. Under self-managed instruction, the knowledge gap between wavering self-regulators and proficient self-regulators will widen, whatever their socioeconomic status might be.

Software producers who offer telelearning and resource indexing will be increasingly influential players in the educational process. As in other technologies, the benefits of electronic education come with social costs. Market forces and production gimmickry may come to dictate educational content. The divisive social effects of inequitable access have already been noted. Open access to the Internet enables students to explore not only educational resources but also materials that parents and schools consider highly objectionable. Moreover, students can use the Internet for offensive purposes (Futoran, Schofield, & Eurich-Fulcer, 1995). Therefore, parents and educators will have to grapple with the troublesome side of electronic instructional systems.

Much of the fervor over the development of national talent is fueled by an ethic of competitive triumphs in the global marketplace. Not all of this productivity uses resources wisely or improves the human condition. The pursuit of continuous economic growth through high consumption exacts a heavy toll on finite resources and widespread environmental degradation. All too often, the heavy demands of work life leave little time or energy for family, recreation, and civic life. Schools carry a broader social responsibility in educating a society's youth. Good schooling fosters psychosocial growth that contributes to the quality of life beyond the vocational domain. The major goal of formal education should be to equip students with the intellectual tools, efficacy beliefs, and intrinsic interests needed to educate themselves in a variety of

pursuits throughout their lifetime. These personal resources enable individuals to gain new knowledge and to cultivate skills either for their own sake or to better their lives.

The various psychosocial processes over which efficacy beliefs exercise some control are intimately involved in the cultivation of cognitive competencies. The principal mediators, which were extensively reviewed earlier, include cognitive, motivational, affective, and selective processes. These efficacy-regulated processes not only play a key role in setting the course of intellectual development but also exert considerable influence on how well-established cognitive skills are used in managing the demands of everyday life. There are three main ways in which efficacy beliefs operate as important contributors to the development of cognitive competencies that govern academic achievement: students' beliefs in their efficacy to master different academic subjects; teachers' beliefs in their personal efficacy to motivate and promote learning in their students; and faculties' collective sense of efficacy that their schools can accomplish significant academic progress.

STUDENTS' COGNITIVE SELF-EFFICACY

Considerable progress has been achieved in clarifying the role of efficacy beliefs in the growth of cognitive competencies and their use in adapting to and changing the environment. The initial research verified that perceived efficacy beliefs contribute independently to intellectual performance rather than simply reflecting cognitive skills. Collins (1982) selected children who judged themselves to be of high or low efficacy at each of three levels of mathematical ability. They were then given difficult mathematical problems to solve. Within each level of ability, children who had the stronger belief in their efficacy were quicker to discard faulty strategies, solved more problems (Fig. 6.1), chose to rework more of those they failed, and

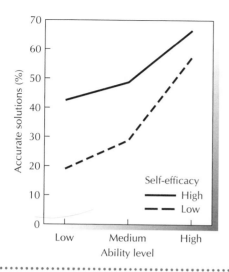

FIGURE 6.1. Mean levels of mathematical performance achieved by students as a function of mathematical ability and perceived mathematical self-efficacy. (After Collins, 1982)

did so more accurately than children of equal ability who doubted their efficacy. Children's causal attributions for their academic successes and failures were unrelated to their mathematical performances. Efficacy beliefs predicted interest in, and positive attitudes toward, mathematics, whereas actual mathematical ability did not. As this study shows, students may perform poorly either because they lack the skills or because they have the skills but lack the perceived personal efficacy to make optimal use of them.

Bouffard-Bouchard, Parent, and Larivée (1991) not only corroborated the independent contribution of efficacy beliefs to cognitive performance but also identified some of the self-regulative processes through which they do so. Regardless of whether children were of superior or average cognitive ability, those with a high sense of efficacy were more successful in solving conceptual problems than were children of equal ability but lower perceived efficacy. The more self-efficacious students at each ability level managed their work time better, were more persistent, and were less likely to reject correct solutions prematurely.

The causal contribution of efficacy beliefs to cognitive functioning is verified even more directly by Bouffard-Bouchard (1990), in a study cited earlier. High or low efficacy beliefs were instilled in students by comparison with fictitious peer norms irrespective of their actual performance. Students whose sense of efficacy was raised set higher aspirations for themselves, showed greater strategic flexibility in the search for solutions, achieved higher intellectual performances, and were more accurate in evaluating the quality of their performances than were students of equal cognitive ability who were led to believe they lacked such capabilities. Efficacy beliefs contributed to accomplishments both motivationally and through support of strategic thinking.

In an extensive series of studies, Schunk and his coworkers have employed an informative experimental paradigm that has added greatly to our understanding of the many factors that affect children's perceived cognitive efficacy and its impact on scholastic performance (Schunk, 1989). The participants are children who present severe deficits in mathematical and language skills. They pursue a program of self-directed learning in which the material is structured for them in easily mastered subskills. The children learn the basic principles and practice applying them to mathematical problems. The self-directed learning is supplemented with instructional social influences that can affect children's beliefs of their cognitive efficacy. These influences include modeling of cognitive operations, instruction in higher order strategies, use of different forms of performance feedback that can influence self-appraisal of capabilities, and addition of positive incentives and aspirational goals as further motivators for the development of cognitive skills.

This paradigm includes several positive features for causal analyses. The children have little in the way of preexisting skills to serve as a source of perceived efficacy. Their sense of efficacy is instilled to differential levels through systematic variation of instructional influences applied over an extended period. Experimental variation removes ambiguity about the source and direction of causation. The acquisition of cognitive subskills is continuously monitored, thus permitting evaluation of the unique contribution of efficacy beliefs to academic performance over and above that of acquired skills. And finally, the treatments create complex sets of academic skills in natural educational settings. This makes the results highly generalizable to the very scholastic tasks children have to master in their classroom assignments.

The research using this standardized paradigm is reviewed in the sections that follow. In these numerous studies (Schunk, 1989), analyses of the contribution of efficacy beliefs to level of cognitive performance are uniform in their findings: Efficacy beliefs are influenced by acquisition of cognitive skills, but they are not merely a reflection of them. Children with the same level of cognitive skill development differ in their intellectual performances depending on the strength of their perceived efficacy. Several factors may account for the predictive superiority of efficacy belief over acquired skills. Children vary in how they interpret, store, and recall their successes and failures. As a result, they differ in how much self-efficacy they derive from similar attainments. Moreover, in judging their capabilities, children evaluate social influences that contribute to efficacy beliefs independently of skills. Academic performances are the products of cognitive capabilities implemented through motivational and other self-regulatory skills. The efficacy beliefs that children form affect how consistently and effectively they apply what they know. Perceived self-efficacy, therefore, is a better predictor of intellectual performance than skills alone.

Studies in this series that include path analyses shed further light on the different paths through which efficacy beliefs influence intellectual performance (Schunk, 1984a). Figure 6.2 provides one illustration of the causal structure. Skill development has small direct effects on academic performance and on children's beliefs of their academic efficacy. Perceived efficacy exerts a more substantial impact on academic performance, both directly by affecting quality of thinking and good use of acquired cognitive skills and indirectly by heightening persistence in the search for solutions.

If self-efficacious individuals find solutions readily, they have no need to persist. Therefore, the

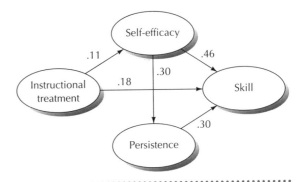

FIGURE 6.2. Path analysis showing the mediating role of perceived mathematical self-efficacy in the mastery of mathematical competencies through self-directed instruction. (Schunk, 1984a)

motivational link in causal structures is best tested with intractable problems. When successes are hard to come by, individuals of high efficacy are persisters and those of low efficacy are rapid quitters (Bandura & Schunk, 1981). The motivational link is even more convincingly demonstrated when efficacy beliefs are altered by arbitrary means without changing skills, and then people are observed to see how long they persist in trying to solve intractable or insoluble intellectual problems (Brown & Inouye, 1978; Jacobs et al., 1984; Lyman, Prentice-Dunn, Wilson, & Bonfilio, 1984). Raising belief in their efficacy makes them more perseverant.

Efficacy beliefs play an influential mediational role in academic attainment. The extent to which such factors as level of cognitive ability, prior educational preparation and attainment, gender, and attitudes toward academic activities influence academic performance is partly dependent on how much they affect efficacy beliefs. The more they alter efficacy beliefs, the greater the impact they have on academic attainments. The unique contribution of beliefs of cognitive efficacy to academic performance is highly replicable in analyses of the direct and mediated effects between these diverse types of determinants (Hackett, 1985; Pajares & Kranzler, 1995; Pajares & Miller, 1994a; Pajares, Urdan, & Dixon, 1995; Randhawa, Beamer, & Lundberg, 1993).

Development of Cognitive Self-Efficacy through Aspiration

The development of cognitive competencies requires sustained involvement in activities. If appropriately structured, such pursuits provide the mastery experiences needed to build intrinsic interest and a sense of cognitive efficacy when they are lacking. This type of enduring self-motivation is best achieved through personal challenges that create a sense of efficacy and self-satisfaction in performance accomplishments (Bandura, 1991b). The motivating power of personal goals is partly determined by how far into the future they are projected. Short-term, or proximal, goals provide immediate incentives and guides for current pursuits. Distant goals are too far removed in time to be effective self-motivators. Usually, there are too many competing influences in everyday life for distant aims to exert much control over current behavior. By focusing on the distant future, it is all too easy to keep putting off difficult activities to some future time. Self-motivation is best sustained by combining a long-range goal that sets the course of one's endeavors with a series of attainable subgoals to guide and sustain one's efforts along the route.

In addition to serving as cognitive motivators, proximal goals serve as an effective vehicle for developing a sense of personal efficacy. Without standards against which to measure their performances, people have little basis for judging how they are doing or for gauging their capabilities. Subgoal attainments provide rising indicants of mastery that help to instill and verify a growing sense of personal efficacy. Making complex activities easier by breaking them down into a series of attainable subgoals also helps to reduce the risk of self-demoralization through high aspiration. The same accomplishment that indicates significant progress when evaluated against a short-term subgoal may appear trifling and disappointing when compared against lofty long-range aspirations. People can be acquiring skills but deriving little sense of efficacy because of the wide disparity between current attainment and distal standard. The less individuals believe in themselves, the more they need explicit, proximal, and frequent feedback of progress that provides repeated affirmations of their growing capabilities.

The efficacy-promoting effects of subgoal challenges are revealed in a study in which children pursued self-directed learning with either proximal subgoals for mastering different mathematical skills, a distal goal of mastering all the skills by a future time, or without any goals (Bandura & Schunk, 1981). Those who motivated themselves with proximal subgoals made rapid progress, achieved substantial mastery of mathematical operations, and developed a strong sense of mathematical efficacy (see Fig. 4.7). Distal goals had no demonstrable effects. Children who pursued the self-directed learning with distal goals or no goals retained self-doubts about their capabilities and achieved much less through their efforts. Regardless of variations in goal systems, the more children raised their sense of efficacy, the greater were their mathematical accomplishments. Acquired skill alone was a weak predictor of how well children applied their mathematical knowledge in solving problems.

The benefits of goals in promoting cognitive development are replicated across different scholastic domains and types of goals. Children from remedial classes who receive instruction in reading comprehension achieve higher perceived efficacy and reading performances under goals either to raise their comprehension attainments or to increase their proficiency in using comprehension strategies than do children with only a general goal in mind (Schunk & Rice, 1989). By highlighting the progress one is making, learning goals for gains in knowledge and skill are more effective in developing a sense of personal efficacy and proficiency than goals that focus solely on level of performance accomplishment (Schunk, 1996). These alternative goal orientations, of course, can serve complimentary purposes. Proximal learning goals help to create the means for hoped-for accomplishments.

Effective goal systems embody a hierarchical structure in which proximal subgoals regulate motivation and action designated to fulfill loftier aspirations. As previously shown, however, proximal goals are not simply subordinate conveyances to valued loftier goals. By enlisting self-evaluative involvement, subgoals invest activities with personal significance. The satisfaction derived from advancing accomplishments operates as its own reward during the pursuit of higher distal goals (Bandura & Schunk, 1981).

Efficacious self-regulators invest activities with proximal challenges on their own by adopting goals of progressive improvement when they can get feedback of how they are doing (Bandura, 1991b; Bandura & Cervone, 1983). Those who set no goals of improvement achieve no change and are outperformed by those who set themselves the challenging goal of bettering their past accomplishments. The need to focus on progress rather than on distal products is particularly important for individuals who are convinced of their personal inefficacy and who need repeated self-persuasive evidence that they have what it takes for high attainments. It is easier to instill beliefs of personal efficacy if the instruction and informative feedback center on mastery of strategies that enable one to achieve progress rather than only on level of performance attainments. Knowing the means for becoming adept in given endeavors instills a sense of personal control over one's own development.

Schunk and Rice (1991) corroborate the value of strategic agency goals. Remedial readers who focused their efforts on mastering comprehension strategies and were given feedback of successful use of the strategies gained a higher sense of efficacy and outperformed students who pursued strategy acquisition goals without feedback or who affixed their goals to level of performance attainment. For children who have serious deficits, instruction in strategies alone does not increase their efficacy or cognitive skill (Schunk & Rice, 1992). They require repeated verification that they can produce results with those strategies. The more their perceived efficacy is raised, the more they use the strategies in guiding their behavior. The benefits of combining training in strategies with feedback of progress in mastering them are even greater where learned skills must be transferred to new situations and adhered to over time (Schunk & Swartz, 1993).

Goals are unlikely to have much effect if there is little personal commitment to them. Goal commitment can be affected by the degree to which they are personally determined. When people select their own goals, they are likely to have greater self-involvement in achieving them. If goals are prescribed by others, however, individuals do not necessarily accept them or feel obligated to meet them. When it is a matter of simply using existing skills productively, people perform better with goals. Self-set goals increase satisfaction but do not produce improvements in performance over and above assigned goals (Locke & Latham, 1990; Locke & Schweiger, 1979). Self-determination of goals may be more influential in the development of skills, especially for those who harbor doubts about their capabilities. Thus, under self-set goals, children with serious mathematical deficits have higher initial expectations of goal attainment, develop a stronger sense of mathematical efficacy, and achieve higher mathematical performances than if comparable goals are prescribed for them or they pursue the self-directed learning without any goal challenges (Schunk, 1985).

Another way of increasing personal commitment to self-development of cognitive skills in activities that hold little interest is to link positive incentives to goal attainment. Adopting proximal goals for self-directed learning and gaining rewards for meeting them raise perceived efficacy, expectations for goal attainment, and academic performances to a higher level than do goals alone or positive incentives alone (Schunk, 1984c). Increased perceived efficacy is accompanied by higher academic attainments.

Cultivating Intrinsic Interest through Development of Self-Efficacy

Most of the things people enjoy doing for their own sake originally held little or no interest for them. Children are not born innately interested in singing operatic arias, playing contrabassoons, solving mathematical equations, writing sonnets, or propelling shot-put balls through the air. But with appropriate learning experiences, almost any activity, however trifling it may appear to others, can become imbued with consuming personal significance. Good instruction should promote interest as well as technical skill in subject matter. Teaching that instills a liking for what is taught fosters self-initiated learning long after the instruction has ceased.

The process by which people develop interest in activities in which they initially lack skill, interest, and self-efficacy is an issue of some importance. The major conceptual and empirical issues involved in the development of intrinsic interest have been addressed elsewhere (Bandura, 1986a). The present review analyzes mainly the contributory role of efficacy beliefs to the development of intrinsic interest. According to social cognitive theory, growth of intrinsic interest is fostered through affective self-reactive and self-efficacy mechanisms. People display enduring interest in activities at which they feel efficacious and from which they derive self-satisfaction. Both of these self-functions rely on personal standards. In most activities from which people gain lasting enjoyment, neither the behavior itself nor its natural feedback is inherently rewarding. Although behavior is not its own reward, it can provide its own rewards once it gets invested with personal significance. Once self-involvement in activities gets tied to personal standards, variations in performance attainments activate self-satisfying or self-dissatisfying reactions. To mountaineers, the toilsome activity of crawling over slippery rocks in foul weather is not inherently joyful. It is the self-satisfaction derived from personal triumphs over lofty peaks that provides the exhilaration. Remove the personal challenges, and crawling over rocks becomes quite boring. It is people's affective self-reactions to their own performances that constitute the principal source of reward. To cite an uncommon example, there is nothing inherently gratifying about playing a tuba solo. To an aspiring tuba instrumentalist, however, a performance that fulfills a hoped-for standard is a source of considerable self-satisfaction that can sustain much tuba blowing. Improvements in intellectual, athletic, and artistic pursuits similarly activate self-reactions that provide a sense of fulfillment and create personal incentives for accomplishments.

People differ widely in the pursuits in which they invest their self-evaluation. Hence, what is a source of self-satisfaction for one person may be devalued or of no consequence for another.

Personal standards can contribute to enhancement of interest in activities in at least three ways. Challenging standards enlist the sustained involvement in activities needed to build competencies. Csikszentmihalyi (1975; 1979) examined what it is about activities that fosters deep engrossment and enjoyment in different types of life pursuits. He found that almost any activity can be made intrinsically interesting by selecting challenges that match one's perceived capabilities and getting feedback of progress. One of the most important structural features of activities that captivate attention for hours on end is whether or not the activity has a personally challenging goal (Malone, 1981). When people aim for and master valued levels of performance, they experience a sense of satisfaction (Locke & Latham, 1990). The satisfactions derived from goal attainments build intrinsic interest. Standards also foster development of personal efficacy by providing markers for verifying the level and growth of capabilities. Without standards, self-appraisal of capabilities is left in foggy ambiguity. A sense of personal efficacy in mastering tasks is more apt to spark interest in them than is perceived inefficacy in performing competently.

That subgoal accomplishments can build intrinsic interest in disvalued activities receives support from the study just cited in which children pursued self-directed learning of mathematics with proximal subgoals, with distal goals, or without any reference to goals (Bandura & Schunk, 1981). It was mainly the children given subgoal challenges, all of whom developed a strong sense of efficacy, who became intrinsically interested in mathematical activities. Difficult and remote challenges, which diminish the significance of modest progressive gains, neither promote perceived efficacy nor cultivate intrinsic interest. The value of proximal subgoals in fostering interest is further corroborated by Morgan (1985) in a study in which college students improved their academic attainments over the course of an academic year. Compared to students who aimed for a distal goal, those who set interim goals for themselves not only achieved more but developed a greater interest in the subject matter. A sense of personal efficacy promotes interest and enjoyment in physical activities as well as in intellectual ones (McAuley, Wraith, & Duncan, 1991).

The nature of the relation between the growth of perceived efficacy and the increase of interest warrants systematic investigation. There may be a temporal lag between newly acquired efficacy beliefs and growth of interest in activities that are disvalued or even disliked. In the temporal lag pattern, a high sense of efficacy promotes mastery experiences that, over time, provide self-satisfactions conducive to growth of interest. If, in fact, growth of interest follows such a temporal course, then increased interest would emerge as a later, rather than as an instant, consequence of enhanced self-efficacy. The threshold notion suggests an alternative relation. At least moderate perceived efficacy may be required to generate and sustain interest in an activity, but increases in perceived efficacy above the threshold level do not produce further gains in interest. Indeed, supreme self-assurance may render activities unchallenging and, thus, uninteresting. Evidence lends some support for the threshold view (Bandura & Schunk, 1981). Regardless of the goals children were pursuing, efficacy beliefs of moderate to high strength predicted high intrinsic interest. Harackiewicz, Sansone, and Manderlink (1985) have similarly found that perceived self-efficacy mediates task enjoyment, but these factors are not linearly related. Temporal lag and threshold effects are by no means incompatible. In fact, both probably operate in the development of intrinsic interest.

Most academic activities present ever-rising challenges. Whatever knowledge and cognitive skills are acquired, there is always more to learn. Past accomplishments are quickly outdistanced, and self-satisfactions are sought in higher accomplishments. Thus, in the pursuit of excellence, the higher the students' efficacy beliefs, the higher the academic challenges they set for themselves and the greater their intrinsic interest in scholastic matters (Pintrich & DeGroot, 1990). Beliefs of personal efficacy predict level of interest in different occupational pursuits as well as in specific academic subjects even when the influence of ability is removed (Lent, Larkin, & Brown, 1989; Lent, Lopez, Bieschke, & Socall, 1991).

Like any other form of influence, goals can be applied in ways that breed dislikes rather than nurture interests. Personal standards promote interest when they create challenges and serve as guides for aspirations. But if goals assigned by others impose constraints and performance burdens, the pursuit can become aversive. Propositions about goal setting, therefore, must be qualified by the form they take and how they are used. Mossholder (1980) reports that goals enhance interest in dull tasks by infusing them with challenge but reduce interest in interesting tasks. Self-development would be poorly served if aspirations and challenges became dysfunctional for activities that normally hold some interest. Fortunately, this is not the case. An interesting activity with a rising standard of excellence, which continues to present new challenges, enhances intrinsic interest, whereas the same activity with a low level of challenge does not (McMullin & Steffan, 1982). If subgoals for an interesting activity pose little challenge because they are easily attainable, then distal goals that are viewed as less readily achievable may hold greater interest (Manderlink & Harackiewicz, 1984). Routine successes with no corresponding growth of competence are not especially good sources of enjoyment. In the studies in which it is found that proximal goals cultivate perceived efficacy and intrinsic interest, each proximal subgoal presents new challenges in mastery of subskills (Bandura & Schunk, 1981).

Positive incentives are widely used to raise interest in academic activities. Some writers (Deci & Ryan, 1985; Lepper & Greene, 1978) have questioned the wisdom of this practice on the grounds that rewarding people for engaging in an activity is more likely to reduce than to increase subsequent interest in it. Extrinsic incentives presumably decrease interest by weakening competency drives or by shifting causal attributions for performance from internal motivators to external rewards.

Innumerable studies have found that the effects of incentives on interest are much more complex than commonly claimed: Rewards can increase interest in activities, reduce interest, or have no effect (Bandura, 1986a; Bates, 1979; Kruglanski, 1975; Morgan, 1984; Ross, 1976). In evaluating the impact of incentives on interest, it is important to distinguish whether incentives are used to manage performances or to cultivate personal efficacy. Extrinsic incentives are most likely to reduce interest when they are given for merely performing over and over again an activity that is already of high interest (Lepper, 1981). With this type of loose contingency, rewards are gained regardless of the level or quality of performance. Even when rewards are given indiscriminately, however, they sometimes enhance interest (Arnold, 1976; Davidson & Bucher, 1978), boost low interest but diminish or do not affect high interest (Calder & Staw, 1975; Loveland & Olley, 1979; McLoyd, 1979), or reduce low interest but do not significantly affect high interest (Greene, Sternberg, & Lepper, 1976). Conflicting findings occur when a given factor exerts a weak influence so that co-occurring influences can easily alter or override its effects. Many possible contributing factors have been studied, often with inconclusive results. They include how closely rewards are linked to performance; the level of preexisting interest and ability; the size, salience, and value of rewards; the type of activity performed; and how, when, and where intrinsic motivation is measured. Indiscriminate indictment of positive incentives as underminers of interest reflects, for the most part, the triumph of doctrine over evidence.

Incentives for mastering activities contribute to the growth of interest and perceived efficacy. Positive incentives foster performance accomplishments. The resultant acquisition of knowledge and skills that enable one to fulfill personal standards of merit tend to heighten beliefs of personal efficacy. Thus, for children hampered by mathematical deficits, incentives for mastering subskills accelerate acquisition of mathematical competency and raise perceived mathematical efficacy, whereas noncontingent rewards or the pursuit of self-instruction without incentives produces a much lower level of competency and a weaker sense of efficacy (Schunk, 1983a).

Diverse lines of research indicate that positive incentives promote interest when they either enhance or authenticate personal efficacy. Both children and adults maintain or increase their interest in activities when they are rewarded for performance attainments, whereas their interest declines when rewarded for undertaking activities irrespective of how well they perform (Boggiano & Ruble, 1979; Ross, 1976). The larger the extrinsic reward for performance signifying competence, the greater is the increase in interest in the activity (Enzle & Ross, 1978). When rewards are tied to levels of competence, greater interest in the activity is produced if competence is generously rewarded than if it is meagerly compensated (Rosenfield, Folger & Adelman, 1980). When material reward for performance attainments is accompanied by either self-verbalization of competence or social feedback of competence, both children and adults sustain high interest in the activity (Pretty & Seligman, 1984; Sagotsky & Lewis, 1978). Even incentives for undertaking a task, rather than for performing it well, can raise interest if engaging in the activity provides information about personal competence (Arnold, 1976).

In some of the studies cited, the mediating cognitive mechanism is measured globally as perceived competence. Rewarding quality of performance enhances perceived competence, which, in turn, predicts intrinsic interest. People who subscribe to high standards strive for a job well done even though they may be rewarded simply for performing the activity without regard to quality (Simon, 1979b). Therefore, sometimes interest is predicted by perceived competence regardless of whether people are rewarded for only engaging in activities or for doing them well (Arnold, 1985). A global self-conception is not the most sensitive measure of perceived capability. Research using microanalytic measures provides the most direct evidence that incentives linked to standards of excellence work in part through their effects on efficacy beliefs in promoting intrinsic interest (Schunk, 1983a).

According to Deci and Ryan (1985), rewards diminish interest when they appear to be controlling but increase it when they convey information about competency. Distinctions are easy to draw, but actual incentive systems are difficult to classify because they usually embody a number of different properties. Moreover, incentive transactions usually involve bidirectional rather than unidirectional influence. People who possess valued skills regard their competent performances as the reason for the rewards they receive, rather than viewing the rewards as the cause of their competent performances (Karniol & Ross, 1976). They do not view themselves as objects of coercion but as controllers of deserving recompense for their talents.

Research on how incentives affect interest has rested on intuitive and post hoc classifications of incentive systems. Originally, rewards requiring performance achievements were regarded as more controlling, and hence more detrimental to interest, than rewards that make no performance demands. This supposition did not fare well empirically because rewarding people regardless of how they perform, although clearly less controlling than requiring them to meet certain performance standards, is more likely to dampen their interest. Rewards for performance accomplishments, which generally increase interest, were then redefined as being informative. There are inconsistencies across studies in the classification of similar types of incentives as predominantly controlling or as informative. This illustrates the arbitrariness of the controlling-informative distinction and its limitations as an organizing principle. Until objective criteria are provided for classifying rewards as controlling, as informative, or as expressing some other aspect of a rewarding transaction, the theory is not easily testable.

The controlling-informative dichotomy by no means exhausts the properties of incentives that may affect self-efficacy, interest, and motivation. Incentives can also serve as challenges. When people are provided with incentives for fulfilling certain standards, they tend to set goals for themselves. The extent to which positive incentives enhance accomplishments is partly mediated through the level of self-set challenges they prompt (Locke & Latham, 1990; Wright, 1989). Challenges motivate people to develop and exercise their efficacy, and they serve as a major determinant of interest. In evaluating incentive systems, therefore, one must distinguish between the recompense of an incentive and its challenge. To someone working on an assembly line, the incentive system pays but does not challenge. To aspiring Olympic athletes, the prospect of a medal presents a challenge that motivates arduous, endless perfection of athletic competencies. The more that extrinsic incentives provide challenges, the more likely they are to foster development of self-efficacy, interest, and deep involvement in an activity. Just as incentive systems are not necessarily the foes of self-determination, nor is competency feedback alone necessarily the interest builder it is made out to be. It depends on whether that competency feedback conveys good or bad news. Feedback of poor progress or deficient performances can create internal barriers to self-determination by undermining a sense of personal efficacy.

The previous discussion should not be misinterpreted as advocating wholesale use of extraneous incentives. One can point to numerous instances in which such incentives are applied thoughtlessly and more for purposes of social regulation than for personal development. Incentives should be used, if necessary, mainly to cultivate competencies, a sense of personal efficacy, and enduring interests. As involvement and skills in activities increase, social, symbolic, and self-evaluative rewards assume the incentive functions. Activities can be creatively structured in ways that capture and heighten interest (Hackman & Lawler, 1971; Malone, 1981; Malone & Lepper, 1985). This is achieved by building positive features into tasks that make them enjoyable, creating personal challenges through goal setting, adding variety to counteract boredom, encouraging personal responsibility for accomplishments, and providing feedback of progress. Moreover, the enthusiasm exhibited by models imparts interest to activities that might otherwise be regarded indifferently. Mentors who seek challenges, enjoy what they are doing, and do not let problems get them down often lead others by their example to seek their identity and fulfillment in similar pursuits. The less interestingly activities are structured and modeled, the more people are likely to resort to extrinsic incentives as motivators.

Self-Efficacy in the Use of Cognitive and Metacognitive Skills

Psychology has focused heavily on issues of how the mind works in processing, representing, organizing, and retrieving information. Research has clarified many aspects of cognitive functioning. This insulated cognitivism does scant justice, however, to the diverse self-regulatory processes governing human development and adaptation. Effective intellectual functioning requires much more than simply understanding the factual knowledge and reasoning operations for given realms of activities. It also requires metacognitive skills for how to organize, monitor, evaluate, and regulate one's thinking processes (Brown, 1984; Flavell, 1978a; Meichenbaum & Asarnow, 1979). Thus, an integral part of effective instruction is teaching students how to regulate their own learning. Metacognition involves thoughts about one's cognitive activities rather than simply higher order cognitive skills. In constructing solutions, people must channel their attention, decipher environmental task demands, draw on relevant factual and operational knowledge, appraise the adequacy and versatility of their skills, conduct tests of their understanding, and evaluate and revise their plans and strategies depending on the results their efforts produce. Operative competence entails improvisation of multiple cognitive, social, affective, and motivational skills.

Adding metacognitive skills broadens the scope of a theory of cognition but still neglects self-referent, affective, and motivational processes that play a vital role in cognitive development and functioning. There is an important difference between metacognitive skills and their effective use. Knowing what to do is only part of the story. Failures in intellectual performance often arise from disuse or deficient use of cognitive and metacognitive skills rather than from lack of knowledge (Flavell, 1970; Bandura,

1986a). People need a sense of efficacy to apply what they know consistently, persistently, and skillfully, especially when things are not going well and deficient performances carry negative consequences. Given appropriate subskills, successful performance is often as much a matter of perceived efficacy as of capability. This is strikingly revealed by the marked differences in how well talented individuals use their knowledge and cognitive skills under altered efficacy beliefs (Wood & Bandura, 1989a). Theories can be evaluated for the determinants and processes they ignore as well as for those they explain. We will return shortly to a detailed analysis of the scope of theories of educational self-directedness.

Evidence for the contribution of efficacy beliefs to the self-regulation of cognitive development and functioning comes from two lines of inquiry. The first approach is primarily concerned with how task-related strategies are acquired, applied, and monitored for effectiveness. The second approach adopts a broader scope that encompasses not only execution of task strategies but also how people structure for themselves environments conducive to learning and regulate their own motivational, affective, and sociocognitive skills to realize their aspirations. The strategy regulative functions will be considered first, and the broader self-regulatory functions will be reviewed later in this chapter.

That the influence of strategy instruction on intellectual performance is partly mediated through efficacy beliefs is amply documented in a series of studies by Schunk (1989). Children presenting deficiencies in mathematics and reading comprehension are provided with strategy knowledge and taught how to monitor their level of comprehension and take corrective action when necessary. Task strategies enhance level of performance both directly and by raising beliefs of personal efficacy (Schunk & Gunn, 1986). Locke and his colleagues found a similar dual path of influence of strategy instruction on creativeness with level of ability controlled (Locke et al., 1984).

Some theories of human development focus heavily on the self-regulative function of speech. Luria (1961) proposed a three-stage developmental process in which children's behavior is initially regulated by verbal instructions from others. Later, children guide their actions by overt self-instruction and eventually by covert self-instruction. In Vygotsky's (1962) theory, inner speech similarly serves as the principal vehicle of thought and self-direction. A major part of Meichenbaum's (1977; 1984) approach to enhancing human competence is aimed at developing beneficial self-guiding speech. In applications of this type of approach, the cognitive skills are described and then modeled by having models think aloud the thought processes and strategies they are following while solving problems. Individuals then practice verbalizing the modeled plans and strategies as they guide their own problem solving. In addition, they use coping self-instructions to counteract self-debilitating thought patterns when problems arise. Deficient and faulty habits of thought are corrected during this period of overt self-regulation. Individuals then practice the verbal self-guidance covertly. After new skills become routinized, they no longer require conscious guidance unless they fail to produce results.

There are several ways in which verbal self-guidance can enhance competence. Self-guiding speech heightens attentional and rehearsal involvement in the cognitive skills being taught, which can facilitate their learning and retention. But guided self-instruction does more than impart strategy information. To the extent that using the strategies produces good results, it confirms their value. Anticipated benefits produce incentive motivation to apply cognitive aids that work well. In addition, successful self-guidance provides repeated affirmations of personal agency — that one has gained the ability to exercise control over one's own thinking processes and performances.

Self-guidance training has been shown to be a self-efficacy builder in promoting self-expressiveness through proficient interpersonal communication (Fecteau & Stoppard, 1983). The more the training in self-guidance raises people's beliefs in their efficacy, the greater are their performance attainments. Support for the mediating role of efficacy beliefs in the development of scholastic competencies by instruction in self-guidance is provided by Schunk and his colleagues. Low-achieving children who verbalize cognitive strategies as they solve problems exhibit greater increases in perceived self-efficacy and achieve higher proficiency in mathematics and reading comprehension than do children who are equally trained in the strategies but do not engage in verbal self-guidance (Schunk, 1982b; Schunk & Rice, 1984; 1985). The more extensive the self-guidance, the greater its impact on efficacy beliefs and performance (Schunk & Cox, 1986).

Children who have major language deficiencies require a lot of persuasive evidence to overcome their doubts about their learning capabilities and the instructional value of cognitive strategies. Such students were taught strategies for increasing reading comprehension, practiced verbalizing the strategic steps aloud and fading them to covert self-instruction, and received repeated feedback on the usefulness of the strategies (Schunk & Rice, 1993). Adding practice in internalizing verbal self-guidance and utility feedback increased perceived reading efficacy, use of the strategies, and skill in reading comprehension. Combining verbal fading with utility feedback produced more enduring use of reading strategies. The more the children's efficacy was raised, the more they used the cognitive strategies and the more skilled they became in reading comprehension.

Opportunities to improvise self-guidance convey a more generalized sense of personal causation than self-instruction in strategies provided by others. One can repeat what one has been told without much understanding or proficiency in adapting cognitive subskills that were taught in variable circumstances. By contrast, improvisation involves the exertion of personal agency. Of course, no amount of improvisational self-talk alone will create cognitive skills where they are grossly lacking. Given information on cognitive operations and strategies, however, improvisational self-guidance produces a higher sense of personal efficacy and intellectual performance than does externally prescribed self-guidance (Schunk, 1982b).

In the previous studies, people are explicitly taught strategies for solving intellectual problems. Many problem-solving activities are more open-ended with regard to means. They usually involve multiple tasks, some of which may be ill-defined. There are different possible solutions, some of which work better than others. Sufficing solutions tend to discourage a search for optimal ones (Schwartz, 1982). To complicate matters further, what works well under some circumstances may be ineffective under others. Given such variable conditions, people often have to discover effective strategies on their own. Even established strategies must be adapted to particular circumstances rather than simply applied ritualistically. In managing such situations, people must draw on a reliable knowledge base, use their cognitive skills efficiently to ferret out relevant information, construct options, and test and revise their strategic knowledge based on the results of their decisions.

We saw earlier that perceived efficacy promotes self-generated analytical strategies that benefit performance of complex activities (Wood & Bandura, 1989a). When good results are hard to come by, people with a high sense of efficacy maintain strategic thinking in the search for optimal solutions, whereas those with a weak sense of efficacy have difficulty finding good exploratory strategies and end up deploying their efforts erratically and ineffectively. Janis and Mann (1977) similarly provide evidence that self-doubt following failure prompts a shift to suboptimal strategies. These include inadequate identification and evaluation of options, deficient use of outcome information, and faulty recall of the results of previous efforts. The findings taken as a whole thus indicate that perceived efficacy both facilitates the development of strategies and affects how well they are used once they are acquired.

Impact of Performance Feedback on Perceived Self-Efficacy

During instructional transactions, teachers repeatedly convey evaluations of their students both directly and indirectly. In the explicit evaluations, they rate their students' academic performances, comment on the causes of their success and failures, and compare their standing among their classmates. The more subtle evaluative reactions take diverse forms. They include the differential attention paid to students, what teachers expect of them academically, the standards they set for them, how they group them instructionally, and the difficulty level of the academic tasks they assign to them. Teachers' evaluative reactions can influence students' judgments of their capabilities and scholastic performances (Jones, 1977; Meyer, 1992; Rosenthal, 1978). Not surprisingly, students' appraisal of their academic capabilities are closely related to teachers' judgments of them (Rosenholtz & Simpson, 1984). The way in which school practices function as conveyors of efficacy information will be addressed later. The present analysis is concerned with the efficacy effects of teachers' direct evaluative reactions.

The power of causal evaluations to shape students' efficacy beliefs is demonstrated by Schunk and his co-workers. Crediting children's progress in academic tasks to ability promotes a greater sense of efficacy and achievement than attributing their progress to hard work (Schunk, 1983b; 1984b). Being told that one achieved improvements through one's own efforts raises perceived efficacy and performance achievements more than pursuing the same self-directed learning without any social feedback (Schunk & Cox, 1986). Crediting early progress to ability and later progress to hard work, however, can detract from perceived efficacy and performance if the feedback conveys the impression that improvement by arduous effort signifies that one must be approaching the limits of one's capabilities (Schunk, 1984b; Schunk & Rice, 1986).

Whether effort attributions carry positive or negative efficacy connotations may depend partly on the conceptions of ability within which they are embedded. For people who believe that ability is built through sustained effort, attributions of accomplishments to effort will enhance efficacy. But those who believe that ability is an inherent aptitude, and thus not subject to much personal control, are likely to question their efficacy upon being told that their improvements were due to hard work. People differ in their conceptions of ability and whether they view effort as creating ability or as compensating for low ability (M. Bandura & Dweck, 1988; Dweck,

1991; Surber, 1984). Therefore, feedback that credits attainments to effort will have more variable effects on efficacy beliefs and performance than crediting attainments to personal capabilities. As in other sources of influence, efficacy beliefs altered by different types of attributional feedback are good predictors of academic achievement.

Causal evaluations given to entire classes of students affect their sense of efficacy and mathematical achievements in much the same way as when the feedback is given on an individual basis (O'Sullivan & Harvey, 1993). Classes who are told that their progress reflects ability for the subject matter markedly increase their sense of efficacy and outperform classes whose achievements are ascribed to high effort. Effort attributions do not do much for perceived efficacy, accuracy of self-appraisal, or mathematical achievement. Indeed, students in a low ability class who are led to construe their improvements as signs of growing ability eventually match the level of perceived efficacy and mathematical achievement of more able students whose performances are credited to hard work.

The inconsistent effects of effort attributions on efficacy beliefs and performance raise questions about attribution retraining in which low-achieving students are told that their performances are due to how hard they work to get them to perform better. Since effort is personally controllable, such feedback presumably motivates them to greater achievements. This approach may be fine in theory, but it is inconsistent in results. For individuals seriously lacking requisite subskills, to keep telling them in a roundabout way that they should work harder without providing them with the means to translate effort to success eventually can be demoralizing. They've heard that sermonette many times before. Nor can one keep telling students who are encountering considerable difficulties that they are highly talented. Under such conditions, perceived efficacy is best promoted by ascribing failures to lack of knowledge and cognitive skills that are acquirable and by using guided mastery with proximal subgoals to highlight the growth of personal capabilities. Focusing on the acquirable means to mastery provides instructive guidance and more persuasive

evidence of aptitude than simply ascribing performance to effort or to inherent ability. The evidence also raises concerns over the way in which ability and effort are usually construed in attribution theory — ability as a stable disposition and effort as a changeable factor. In point of fact, people vary in their conceptions of ability (M. Bandura & Dweck, 1988). Construing ability as an inherent aptitude tends to undermine self-development of capabilities (Jourden et al., 1991; Wood & Bandura, 1989b). In contrast, viewing ability as an acquirable skill fosters a resilient sense of efficacy, adoption of challenging personal aspirations, proficient analytical thinking, and performance attainments.

Another form of teacher feedback that carries efficacy implications highlights the quality of academic work. This is illustrated in studies of self-regulated productivity in which students can earn grade bonuses by voluntarily constructing items of inquiry for the subject matter they are studying (Tuckman & Sexton, 1991). Feedback that one's work is of good quality progressively raises perceived efficacy, which, in turn, predicts subsequent performance. In contrast, factual feedback of how much work one produced without reference to its quality improves neither perceived efficacy nor level of productivity.

Social cognitive theory advocates a multifaceted approach to promoting student achievement as an alternative to the approach prescribed by attribution theory. Ability is construed as a changeable attribute over which one can exercise some control. Guided mastery serves as the principal vehicle for the cultivation of competencies (Bandura, 1986a). In this enablement approach, cognitive modeling and instructional aids are used to convey the relevant knowledge and strategies in graduated steps. A variety of opportunities are provided for guided practice in when and how to use cognitive strategies in the solution of diverse problems. The level of social guidance is progressively reduced as competencies are being acquired. Activities, incentives, and personal challenges are structured in ways that ensure self-involving motivation and continual improvement. Growing proficiencies are credited to expanding personal capabilities. Self-directed mastery experiences are then arranged to strengthen and generalize a sense of personal efficacy. Each of these modes of influence is structured in ways that build self-regulative capabilities for exploratory learning and strengthen students' beliefs that they can exercise some control over their intellectual self-development.

Guided mastery by mutual structuring of environments conducive to growth of knowledge, competencies, and affirmative self-beliefs bears some likeness to Vygotskian tutoring by social guidance. Social cognitive theory, however, specifies motivational and self-regulatory mechanisms that provide numerous guidelines for promoting cognitive development. Moreover, social cognitive theory focuses more on evolvement of agency as central to personal development than on internalization of social functions as private self-regulators. The agentic view addresses itself to how people construe, select, and construct learning environments. As documented in this chapter, the social genesis of cognitive competencies encompasses much more than collaborative instruction. Although much learning is socially situated, after people develop self-regulatory capabilities, they learn a lot on their own.

Cognitive development, of course, is situated in sociocultural practices. These influences operate interactively through familial, peer, educational, neighborhood, media, and other cultural subsystems. For all too long, cognitive development was regarded as an intrapsychic activity largely severed from its social roots. Proclamations that human development and functioning are socially situated are no longer newsworthy, however. Significant advances require moving beyond this truism to verification of the paths of influence through which these various sociocultural practices exert their effects. These causal structures are addressed in succeeding sections of this chapter.

Self-Efficacy in Self-Regulated Cognitive Development

Development of capabilities for self-directedness enables individuals not only to continue their intellectual growth beyond their formal education but to advance the nature and quality of their life pursuits. Changing realities are placing a premium on the capability for self-directed learning throughout the life span. The rapid pace of technological change and the accelerated growth of knowledge require continual upgrading of competencies if people are to survive and prosper under increasingly competitive conditions. Moreover, people are now living much longer than previous generations did. Self-development with age partly determines whether the expanded life span is lived self-fulfillingly or apathetically. These changing realities call for lifelong learners.

As students progress in their education, they are expected to become more self-directing in their learning. Not all do so. Teachers face the challenge of adapting their instruction to students' differing levels of educational self-directedness in ways that build underdeveloped self-regulatory skills (Grow, 1991). Analyses of the role of self-regulation in the acquisition of knowledge and cognitive skills have been largely confined to enhancement of academic learning by use of task-related metacognitive strategies. In this approach to self-regulation, metacognitive thought is usually categorized into declarative or factual knowledge and procedural knowledge about the steps involved in solving problems. There is a major difference, however, between possessing knowledge and being capable of proficient action. Knowledge and cognitive skills are likewise necessary but not sufficient for academic attainments. Students often know what to do but cannot translate that knowledge into proficient performance. Even if they can make skilled translations of knowledge, they often fare poorly when left on their own because they cannot get themselves to put in the necessary effort to fulfill difficult task demands.

One of the major advances in the study of lifelong cognitive development concerns the mechanisms of self-regulated learning. Metacognitive theorists have addressed the pragmatics of self-regulation in terms of selecting appropriate strategies, testing one's comprehension and state of knowledge, correcting one's deficiencies, and recognizing the utility of cognitive strategies (Brown, 1984; Paris & Newman, 1990). Metacognitive training aids academic learning. Such training contains a number of different ingredients. The independent contribution of expected utility and self-correction skills to academic achievement and their transferability to situations where students have to assume major responsibility for their own learning has yet to be systematically tested. There is every reason to believe that adding these forms of self-management to strategy instruction improves scholastic learning. But self-corrective use of cognitive strategies is only a small part of the way in which people regulate their own cognitive development and functioning.

Social cognitive theory integrates the cognitive, metacognitive, and motivational mechanisms of self-regulation (Bandura, 1986a). This theory expands the conception of self-regulation in two directions. First, it incorporates a larger set of self-regulatory mechanisms governing cognitive functioning. Second, it encompasses social and motivational skills as well as cognitive ones. As mentioned briefly before, knowledge structures are translated into proficient performances through a conception-matching process that includes both transformational and generative operations (Bandura, 1989b). In academic learning, this process involves comparing what one knows against the level of understanding one seeks and then acquiring the requisite knowledge.

It is commonly acknowledged that self-directed learning requires motivation as well as cognitive and metacognitive strategies. Motivation is a general construct that encompasses a system of self-regulatory mechanisms. Attempts to explain the motivational sources of behavior must specify the determinants and intervening mechanisms that govern the three main features of motivation: selection, activation, and sustained direction of behavior toward certain goals (Bandura, 1991b). All too often, interlinked facets of a motivational mechanism are fractionated into separate constructs drawn from divergent theories. The medley of constructs then gets called integrative theorizing.

The motivational facet of self-directed learning encompasses a variety of interlinked self-referent processes including self-monitoring, self-efficacy appraisal, personal goal setting, outcome expectations, and affective self-reactions. These component activities promote engrossment in academic activities through investment of the self-system in them. Moreover, cognitive development and functioning are embedded in social relations. Skill in using social resources and managing the social consequences of one's school experiences, therefore, is another important facet of self-directed learning. The various forms the social aspects take will be considered later.

Zimmerman (1989, 1990) has been the leading exponent of an expanded model of academic self-regulation. Viewed within the conceptual framework of social cognitive theory, people must develop skills to regulate the motivational, affective, and social determinants of their intellectual functioning as well as the cognitive aspects. This requires bringing self-influence to bear on every aspect of their learning experiences. To begin with, students must learn how to select and structure environmental settings in ways that are conducive to learning. Choosing a regular time and place to work on academic activities increases the chances that they will get done. Other strategic aids to learning involve study strategies of how to condense, paraphrase, and synthesize relevant information for future use. Daily life presents a wide array of social and recreational activities that can be considerably more attractive than struggling with academic assignments, many of which include their share of vexations. The imbalance of attraction disfavoring scholastic matters is particularly great at the earlier levels of education and among older students who do not view academic pursuits as their calling. If study is to triumph over inviting competitors, students have to mobilize and sustain their motivation for academic pursuits. In the exercise of self-directedness (Bandura, 1986a, 1991c), people monitor their learning activities, set goals and performance standards for themselves, and enlist self-incentives by making engagement in leisure activities contingent on completing academic assignments.

Because self-regulation involves temporary self-denial of inviting activities, it might appear at first sight to be self-inflicted drudgery. In analyzing the regulation of behavior by personally marshaled motivators, however, one must distinguish between two sources of incentives. First, there are the conditional self-incentives that provide guides and proximal motivators for pursuing particular activities. Second, there are the more distal personal benefits of attainments that create incentives to exercise self-regulative influence. Self-incentives enable people to develop potentialities and competencies that serve them well in their everyday life. With growing efficacy comes increased attraction to academic activities and a rewarding sense of fulfillment through personal accomplishments. Indeed, perceived efficacy and interest may develop to the point where academic pursuits eventually surpass other activities in attractiveness.

In managing task demands, people who have developed their self-regulatory capacity not only do what needs to be done more efficiently but spare themselves a lot of needless strain. Failure to complete academic assignments makes educational pursuits aversive. Failure to perform the tasks of one's trade well and on time makes occupational pursuits stressful and insecure. When self-regulatory skills are lacking, people defer tasks to the last moment and do them minimally or not at all. Competencies that can be cultivated only through sustained effort remain underdeveloped. Moreover, when people procrastinate in doing required tasks, thoughts about what they are putting off continuously intrude on, and detract from, their enjoyment of other activities they are pursuing. Those who can mobilize themselves to get things done are spared such intrusive self-reminders. Self-directedness thus provides an important and continuing source of personal satisfaction, interest, and well-being. Without aspirations and evaluative involvement in activities, people remain unmotivated, bored, and underdeveloped in their capabilities.

The critical role of self-regulation in human accomplishments is nowhere better illustrated than in the writing habits of successful novelists. They must depend on their own self-discipline if they are going to get much writing done because they have no resident supervisors issuing directives and overseeing daily writing activities. As Wallace and Pear (1977) clearly document, novelists influence how much they write by making the pursuit of other activities contingent on either completing a certain amount of writing each day or writing for a

designated length of time. Most acclaimed novelists write regularly for a fixed number of hours per day. For example, once he launched a novel, Jack London wrote a thousand words per day, six days a week, whether inspired or not. Hemingway, who closely monitored his daily writing output, demanded more of himself on days preceding his fishing trips (Plimpton, 1965). As these examples illustrate, in self-directed pursuits, people must exercise personal discipline if they are to accomplish what they seek. Considerable research shows that both children and adults accomplish much more with the exercise of self-regulative influence than without it (Bandura, 1986a).

Another aspect of self-directed learning centers on the cognitive skills needed to make academic subjects more understandable, recallable, and usable. The strategic skills needed to exercise control over one's own learning and memory processes take three different forms. The first involves information-processing skills for identifying important information, transforming it to improve its meaningfulness, organizing it into easily recallable and generalizable forms, and rehearsing what has been learned (Bauer, 1987; Palincsar & Brown, 1989; Paris, Cross, & Lipson, 1984; Weinstein & Mayer, 1986). In addition to skills for acquiring knowledge, students need cognitive operational skills for structuring problems in ways that specify goals and possible routes to them, selecting appropriate strategies, and applying them effectively to solve the problems. The operational thinking about how to frame the problems, construct appropriate solutions, and translate them to action constitutes the second form of cognitive guidance. Evidence that efficacy beliefs mediate the influence of task-related strategies on learning and cognitive functioning has already been reviewed (Wood & Bandura, 1989a). The third cognitive means by which academic learning is self-regulated is through the use of metacognitive skills (Brown, 1984; Flavell, 1979).

Much confusion has been created by the failure to distinguish between cognition and metacognition. Metacognition has traditionally been defined as general knowledge about cognitive processes and their conscious control, but the term is now widely applied to almost any rules or strategies. In this overextended usage, metacognition is essentially indistinguishable from cognition, and the meta prefix becomes superfluous. In the sociocognitive framework, metacognition refers to cognitive appraisal and control of one's cognitive activity; that is, thinking about the adequacy of one's own thinking. In metacognitive functioning, individuals monitor their regulative thought; evaluate its adequacy in the solution of problems; and, if necessary, make corrective adjustments in the way in which they structure problems, construct solutions, and select strategies to implement them. In short, using regulative thought to guide action and self-reflective thought to guide the regulative thought represents separable levels of cognitive control.

The cognitive aspects of self-regulated learning cannot be divorced from the motivational and self-reactive aspects. One can have serviceable cognitive and metacognitive skills, but they will contribute little to performance if one cannot get oneself to use them. It is commonly assumed that metacognitive training produces widespread improvement in performance, because the generic skills taught can be readily applied to differing tasks in diverse settings. Evidence reaffirms that there are no easy solutions to the transferability of skills. Although metacognitive training aids learning, it usually delivers less than it promises when assessed in terms of transferability and habitual use of skills (Deshler, Warner, Schumaker, & Alley, 1983; Tharp & Gallimore, 1985). Learned cognitive skills and strategies tend to be applied to tasks and contexts in which they were developed but are not necessarily transferred spontaneously to dissimilar pursuits. Nor does metacognitive training necessarily ensure their continued use. People learn cognitive skills but do not always use them regularly.

It is a common finding that people who learn rules in the abstract do a poor job of applying them to particular situations (Nisbett, 1993; Rosenthal & Zimmerman, 1978). Teaching abstract rules with applications to everyday examples produces greater use of rules than does abstract rule instruction or concrete applications alone. Although some cognitive skills are highly generalizable, many are specific to particular domains of functioning. Metacognitive training that teaches students much about cognitive processes but little about how to apply cognitive operations to particular problems may not achieve much. Some researchers are retreating to an even higher abstraction by seeking regulators of cognitive functioning in meta-metacognition (Kitchener, 1983) — the extended lineage of metas takes the form of epistemic thinking about the adequacy of one's self-reflective thinking about one's regulative thinking! The issue in question is not the existence of high-level thinking but the proliferation of metas. Grafting another level of cognitive oversight will not solve the difficulties of deficient cognitive control of problem solving.

To promote transferability of cognitive skills, people need repeated experiences in applying their knowledge and skills to diverse tasks in diverse settings. To ensure continued use of cognitive skills and strategies, people need repeated demonstrations of their effectiveness. Simply instructing people in self-regulative processes and strategies will not automatically instill them. People need to learn how to monitor their functioning and the effects it produces and how to structure motivating challenges and self-incentives. These different affirmative experiences must be structured in ways that instill a strong sense of personal efficacy to master intellectual task demands when successes do not come easily.

People do not develop their knowledge and their cognitive competencies entirely by themselves. In gaining mastery over difficult subject matter, they must seek academic assistance from time to time from knowledgeable adults and classmates to gain important information they lack. Social cognitive theory acknowledges the social nature of self-regulated development. Newman (1991) distinguishes seeking academic assistance in the service of self-development from simply soliciting help to complete assignments. Effective self-regulators seek needed information from others to achieve higher levels of mastery self-directedly. This form of social assistance requires effective exercise of self-directedness. Students must monitor their level of understanding and problem-solving activities to know when further independent effort will prove unproductive and they must turn to knowledgeable others for help. To enhance their competency, they have to figure out what information they lack, how best to frame their inquiry, from whom to seek assistance, and how to overrule any social hesitancy they feel to do so. As students progress to the high school level, the sources of assistance on which they rely shift from parents to teachers, especially for students who have a high sense of academic efficacy (Zimmerman & Martinez-Pons, 1990). Thus, the final set of strategies for self-regulated learning includes the social skills needed to secure information from others about problematic matters.

Zimmerman and Martinez-Pons (1986, 1988) measured the extent to which high school students used the multifaceted strategies for self-regulated learning in different contexts — in the classroom, when preparing scholastic assignments at home, in studying for examinations, and when poorly motivated. High academic achievers make much greater use of all the self-regulative strategies than do low achievers. By managing their own learning, good self-regulators do much better academically than poor self-regulators. Self-regulative strategies account for variation in achievement in both language and mathematics even when the effects of gender and socioeconomic status are removed. Low achievers rely mainly on rote memorization, which does not produce much learning that is transferable to different situations (Pintrich & DeGroot, 1990). The instructional benefits of self-management are corroborated in experimental research (Young, 1996). Students skilled in self-regulation learn much more than their less skilled counterparts from computer-based instruction when they can control the type and amount of information needed to master a given subject area. Children who are good at managing their own learning activities have parents who cultivate such capabilities by modeling, guiding, and rewarding self-directedness (Martinez-Pons, 1996). These parental efforts affect academic attainments through their children's acquired self-regulatory capabilities rather than directly.

It is one thing to possess self-regulative skills but another to be able to adhere to them in taxing situations when activities hold little interest or allurements are beckoning. An unwavering sense of efficacy is needed to overrule such subverters of self-regulative efforts. Zimmerman, Bandura, and Martinez-Pons (1992) provide evidence of this fact. High school students, predominantly minorities, were tested for belief in their personal efficacy to execute the different facets of self-regulation. These included their ability to structure environments conducive to learning, to plan and organize their academic activities, to use cognitive strategies to gain better understanding and memory of the material being taught, to obtain information and get teachers and peers to help them when needed, to motivate themselves to do their school work, to get themselves to complete scholastic assignments within deadlines, and to pursue academic activities when there are competing interesting things to do. Interestingly, students registered the highest perceived efficacy to manage the content aspects of instruction but a low sense of efficacy to manage themselves to get their academic activities done. Indeed, they expressed their lowest sense of efficacy to stick to academic tasks when there were other interesting things to do. Thus, the aspect of self-directed learning that plays a pivotal role in academic achievement — the ability to mobilize, direct, and sustain one's instructional efforts — has been sorely neglected. Neither cognitive processing skills nor metacognitive skills will accomplish much if students cannot get themselves to do academic assignments. A strong sense of efficacy to regulate one's motivation and instructional activities undergirds belief in one's academic efficacy and aspirations.

In this study, the contributory role of perceived self-regulatory efficacy in academic achievement was examined within a broader causal structure that included prior academic achievement, parental goals for their children's academic pursuits, and children's beliefs in their ability to master academic subject matter and the academic goals they set for themselves. These factors were assessed at the beginning of the semester and related to academic achievement at the end of the semester. Figure 6.3 shows the paths of influence. The higher the students' self-regulatory efficacy, the more confident they were in their efficacy to master academic subjects. In accord with the pattern of influence

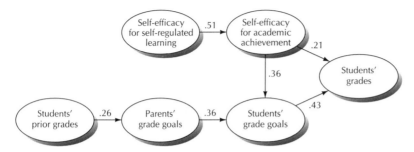

FIGURE 6.3. Path analysis of the influence of perceived self-efficacy and parents' and children's academic aspirations on children's academic achievement. (Zimmerman, Bandura, & Martinez-Pons, 1984a)

in other domains of functioning, efficacy beliefs promoted academic achievement both directly and by raising personal goals. When the effects of children's self-influence were controlled, their prior academic achievement was significantly linked only to parental goal setting. The parents' aspirations, in turn, influenced academic achievement only indirectly through their effects on their children's personal goals. The findings of this research add to our understanding of how beliefs in one's self-regulatory efficacy operate in concert with personal aspirations to contribute to academic accomplishments. Evidence that children base their academic aspirations on their efficacy beliefs as well as on the standards their parents set for them has significant implications for parental guidance of educational development. It is not enough for parents simply to set academic standards for their children. Unless parents also help to build their children's sense of efficacy, the children are likely to view high standards as beyond their reach and disregard them.

Skill in formulating ideas and expressing them well in written form is an important contributor to success in all types of academic and occupational pursuits. All too often, promising ideas are mangled, if not massacred, by a deadening impenetrable prose. Writing presents special challenges to self-regulation (Bandura, 1986a; Bereiter & Scardamelia, 1987; Wason, 1980). This is because writing activities are usually self-scheduled, are performed alone, and require creative effort sustained over long periods with all-too-frequent stretches of barren results. What is eventually produced must be revised repeatedly to fulfill personal standards of quality. Not surprisingly, even professional writers must resort to varied techniques of self-discipline to

promote their writing activities (Barzon, 1964; Gould, 1980; Plimpton, 1965; Wallace & Pear, 1977).

Mediational analyses attest to the influential role of efficacy beliefs in writing activities. The effects of gender and writing aptitude on quality of writing are largely mediated by efficacy beliefs. The higher the students' beliefs in their writing capabilities, the less apprehensive they are about writing, the more useful they regard such skills for personal accomplishments, and the better are their writing performances (Pajares & Valiante, in press). Instruction in writing strategies and verbal self-guidance has been shown to enhance perceived writing efficacy and improve the schematic structure and quality of compositions (Graham & Harris, 1989a, 1989b; Schunk & Swartz, 1993).

Research on the development of writing proficiency further clarifies how efficacy beliefs operate in conjunction with other self-regulatory influences in the mastery of this vital skill (Zimmerman & Bandura, 1994). Instruction in creative writing builds students' sense of efficacy to produce written work and to get themselves to do it. Self-efficacy is weakest for taking the first steps in writing a piece. A sense of efficacy to regulate writing activities affects writing attainments through several paths of influence (Fig. 6.4). It strengthens efficacy beliefs for academic activities and personal standards for the quality of writing considered self-satisfying. Verbal aptitude affects writing attainments only indirectly by raising personal standards of writing, which, in turn, raises goals for mastering the craft of writing. The increased sense of academic efficacy promotes writing attainments both directly and by heightening writing aspirations.

As with other types of skills, self-regulatory skills will not contribute much if students cannot get themselves to apply them persistently in the face of difficulties, stressors, and competing attractions. Within the sociocognitive framework of bidirectional causality, acquisition of cognitive subskills strengthens beliefs in one's academic efficacy (Bandura & Schunk, 1981). Both academic and self-regulatory efficacy, in turn, have reciprocal effects on cognitive and metacognitive learning strategies. Compared to students low in perceived self-efficacy, those who have a high sense of academic efficacy make greater use of cognitive strategies, manage their time and learning environments better, and monitor and regulate their learning more closely (Pintrich & Schrauben, 1992). A high sense of academic efficacy similarly is accompanied by extensive use of self-directed learning strategies (Zimmerman & Martinez-Pons, 1990).

There are gradations of prescriptiveness for self-regulation of cognitive development. The preceding analyses were primarily concerned with managing one's own learning of subject matter being taught at school. Here, the failures in self-directedness rooted in perceived inefficacy occur despite repeated external pressure to fulfill academic assignments. Greater self-initiative is called for under conditions in which teachers provide students with opportunities to raise their academic attainments by performing cognitive tasks on their own

without being required to do so. Those who believe strongly in their own efficacy exploit the opportunities through highly productive engagement in the supplementary cognitive activities (Tuckman & Sexton, 1990). By contrast, those who do not believe in their own efficacy cannot get themselves to put in the effort, and so they accomplish little supplementary work. Even additional inducements in the form of personal commitments and shared group benefits do little to override the disbelievers' self-doubts (Tuckman, 1990).

The highest level of self-initiative in the exercise of self-regulatory efficacy involves learning on one's own subjects that are neither taught at school nor socially imposed. A major aim of education is to prepare students to continue self-directed learning throughout their lifetimes. Indeed, many people actively pursue self-instruction to gain new knowledge and cultivate skills either to enrich their lives or to advance their careers. Despite its importance, self-instruction outside the school setting has not received the attention it deserves (Tough, 1981). It requires greater personal resourcefulness to be self-taught than to master activities that are structured and guided by others. Not surprisingly, students have a much lower sense of efficacy for self-instruction beyond the confines of the school than for formal instruction in school (Bergin, 1987). But the more strongly they believe in their efficacy to teach themselves, the more they get involved in extracurricular self-instructional

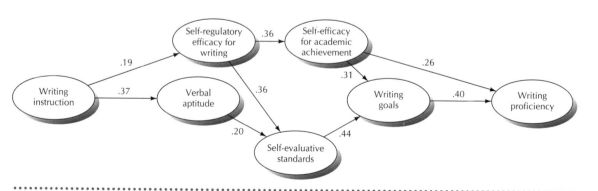

FIGURE 6.4. Path analysis of the pattern of influence through which cognitive self-regulatory factors mediate the impact of writing instruction on the development of writing proficiency. (Zimmerman & Bandura, 1994)

pursuits. With ready access to prime instruction on the Internet, self-regulated learning outside the confines of the school will play an increasingly influential role in the educational development of students. The interplay of self-instruction and school-based instruction clearly warrants increased study.

Peer Influences in the Social Construction and Validation of Self-Efficacy

Peers can operate as a potent force in the development and social validation of intellectual self-efficacy. This source of influence tends to increase in importance as children grow older. There are several ways in which peers contribute to the social construction of intellectual self-efficacy. In their academic work, students receive a great deal of comparative information about their capabilities from grading practices and teachers' evaluations of their scholastic performances (Marshall & Wienstein, 1984; Rosenholtz & Simpson, 1984). These unremitting ability evaluations shape students' collective appraisals of one another. Even in the absence of teachers' appraisals, students can readily judge how well they perform compared to others and their rate of progress on similar academic tasks. As a result, there is high consensus among peers in their perceptions of one another's relative abilities. The peer comparisons go beyond private perceptions. Students publicly label, rank, and discuss with one another how smart their classmates are. Shared social appraisals serve as persuasory modes of influence on beliefs of personal efficacy. Thus, students' self-appraisals of their intellectual capabilities are closely related to the appraisals by their peers. Classroom structures that prescribe similar academic tasks for all students, group them by achievement level, and permit them little choice of activities to show their particular talents lend themselves to stable ability ranking. The more educational practices are structured along these monolithic lines, the greater the consensus about students' ability levels and the more closely students'

self-appraisals of their abilities match their teachers' and classmates' evaluations of them (Rosenholtz & Wilson, 1980).

Peers also shape efficacy beliefs by their instructive function. Students learn much from one another through direct tutelage and modeling of academic proficiencies. In formal tests of this facet of peer influence, students with academic deficits observe videotaped peer models verbalize appropriate cognitive skills and strategies as they perform academic tasks (Schunk & Hanson, 1989b). Peer modeling of academic skills raises students' beliefs in their efficacy for learning, their efficacy for the subject matter, and their actual achievement. Students generally gain more from coping peer models shown developing their cognitive skills and self-assurance than from masterly peer models exhibiting high proficiency from the outset. Evidence for the superiority of coping modeling, however, is weak and equivocal (Schunk & Hanson, 1985, 1989b; Schunk et al., 1987). In seeking to acquire functional skills, children seem to weight heavily the competence of peer models regardless of their initial level of skills. The more similar they perceive themselves to be in competence to the peer models, the more firmly they believe in their learning efficacy and the higher the intellectual performances they achieve.

Modeling influences do not transmit competencies unless observers attend to the relevant information and process it cognitively into recallable and widely usable forms (Bandura, 1986a). Given large perceived disparities in expertise, children are likely to view skills exemplified by an experienced model as beyond their reach and are thus disinclined to invest the effort needed to master them fully. Perceived dissimilarity is, of course, considerably greater in relation to teacher models than even to masterly peer models. Exposure to peers modeling cognitive skills, therefore, boosts children's sense of efficacy and achievement more than observing teachers modeling the same cognitive skills (Schunk & Hanson, 1985).

Peer modeling can alter efficacy beliefs through the influence of social comparison independently of any skill transmission. Knowledge of modeled successes by social equals boosts individuals' appraisals of their own capabilities, whereas modeled failures tend to leave them shaken about their own prospects. Efficacy beliefs instilled by social comparison alone can influence performance through their major mediating processes — by affecting level of effort, perseverance, cognitive efficiency, choice predilections, and stress and demoralization. In studies verifying these mediating mechanisms in cognitive functioning, observers are informed of how well others are performing without knowing the means by which they do so (Bandura & Jourden, 1991; Brown & Inouye, 1978). Thus, social comparative information is the sole source of influence. Comparative efficacy appraisals affect how well children use cognitive strategies they have been taught. Among children equally instructed in cognitive strategies, those who are led to believe that their peers achieve high success using them exhibit a higher sense of efficacy and intellectually outperform their counterparts who are told nothing about peer attainments (Schunk & Gunn, 1985).

The final way in which peers shape personal efficacy for academic pursuits is by influencing interpersonal affiliations. The peers with whom one associates partly determine which potentialities will be cultivated and which will be left undeveloped. The way in which peer affiliations can affect the entire course of intellectual development is shown in studies of children from impoverished backgrounds who went on to college and professional careers at a time when it required overcoming daunting barriers to do so (Ellis & Lane, 1963; Krauss, 1964). In these families, the parents themselves could not provide the necessary resources and preparatory academic skills because of their limited schooling. However, a parent or a family acquaintance who valued education highly usually played a key role in setting the course of these children's intellectual development during their formative years. The valuation of education they instilled was further developed by teachers who took special interest in the children's talents. These evolving value preferences led to selective association with college-oriented peers who, by their interest and example, promoted attitudes, achievement standards,

and sociocognitive skills conducive to intellectual pursuits. Efficacy beliefs are both products and determiners of peer affiliations. The processes by which a sense of intellectual efficacy can influence scholastic development through its effects on interpersonal ties are analyzed in a later section of this chapter.

Perceived Self-Efficacy and Academic Anxiety

Academic activities are often infused with perturbing elements. Many parents impose on their children stringent academic demands that are difficult to fulfill. Accomplishments that fall short of those standards are devalued and lead to unpleasantness at home. A similar drama is played out in schools, where academic deficiencies displease teachers and lower status and evaluation by one's peers. To add further to the stress, students who adopt stringent standards for themselves, as indeed many do, must contend with self-censuring reactions to their own substandard performances as well as with the reactions of others.

The stakes become considerably higher at upper levels of schooling where performance grades determine entry to future pursuits that affect life courses. To excel academically opens up a wide range of options for career development. Academic deficiencies foreclose many life paths and erect barriers to others that are difficult to surmount. To add to the strain, scholastic and occupational life paths have become more fiercely competitive and more demanding of higher levels of cognitive skills. There is less leeway for missteps along the way. Many of the opportunities lost through school failure become essentially irretrievable. As a result, for most children, the social pressures for academic achievement are exerted much earlier and more passionately than ever before. In short, there is a lot to be anxious about in scholastic life.

Students who have a low sense of efficacy to manage academic demands are especially vulnerable to achievement anxiety. Rather than concentrate on how to master the knowledge and cognitive skills being taught, they magnify the formidableness of the tasks and their personal inadequacies, ruminate about their past failures, worry about the calamitous consequences of failing, imagine perturbing scenarios of things to come, and otherwise think themselves into emotional distress and faulty performances (Sarason, 1975a; Wine, 1982).

The influence of efficacy beliefs on anxiety over scholastic activities has been examined most extensively in relation to mathematics, which is a common source of apprehension among students. A low sense of mathematical efficacy is accompanied by high math anxiety both concurrently and longitudinally (Betz & Hackett, 1983; Krampen, 1988). Past performance experiences with mathematics do not affect anxiety directly. Rather, the impact of past successes and failures on anxiety is mediated entirely through their effects on beliefs of personal efficacy (Meece, Wigfield, & Eccles, 1990). If failures weaken students' sense of efficacy, they become anxious about scholastic demands, but if their efficacy beliefs are unshaken by failures, they remain unperturbed. The self-efficacy mediation of the emotional effects of failure in intellectual activities is further corroborated by Wortman and her co-workers (Wortman et al., 1976). Students are left anxious by repeated failures when they view them as due to personal incapabilities, but they are unruffled by failures when they construe them as due to situational factors. Although female students are more mistrustful of their mathematical capabilities and experience higher anxiety than do males, efficacy beliefs mediate the effect of past scholastic experiences on anxiety in the same way for both gender groups (Meece et al., 1990). At the college level, a low sense of efficacy to manage the academic demands and interpersonal aspects of college life is accompanied by high levels of anxiety and stress-related physical symptomatology (Solberg, O'Brien, Villareal, Kennel, & Davis, 1993). Parental and peer support bolsters personal efficacy to cope with college stressors.

In the preceding analyses, scholastic anxiety is examined solely as a function of perceived self-efficacy to fulfill academic demands. Much of the distress over scholastic matters is cognitively generated by perturbing anticipatory thought. This self-perturbing focus is exacerbated in test situations where disruptive thought continuously intrudes on, and impairs, academic performances. Thought control efficacy is an integral part of the sociocognitive theory of anxiety arousal. The full impact of perceived self-efficacy on academic anxiety is best revealed by multifaceted assessment of belief in one's efficacy to fulfill academic demands, to exercise control over intrusive thinking, to ameliorate experienced distress, and to regulate one's study activities. Smith, Arnkoff, and Wright (1990) report that, in addition to faulty study habits and perturbing thinking, a low sense of efficacy to manage one's study activities and examination stressors contributes to scholastic anxiety. Different studies use different bits of personal efficacy, but the full scope of this determinant is rarely measured.

Chapter 8 will present a large body of evidence demonstrating that, in activities posing threats, anxiety and impaired performances are coeffects of a low sense of coping efficacy, rather than anxiety causing impaired performances. This finding is replicated in academic activities as well. Students' beliefs in their efficacy to master academic subjects predicts their subsequent academic attainments, whereas their level of scholastic anxiety bears little or no relationship to their academic performances (Pintrich & DeGroot, 1990; Siegel et al., 1985). When anxiety correlates with academic performance, the relation usually disappears or is markedly diminished when the influence of perceived self-efficacy is removed (Pajares, in press; Pajares & Johnson, 1994; Pajares & Valiente, in press).

These findings carry important implications for how to alleviate scholastic anxiety. Such anxiety is best allayed not by anxiety palliatives but by building a strong sense of efficacy through development of cognitive capabilities and generalizable self-regulatory skills for managing academic task demands, self-debilitating thought patterns, and aversive affective states. The research already reviewed provides many treatment strategies for enhancing perceived scholastic efficacy through cognitive skill development. The competency development aspect of treatment is essential for students who are handicapped by extensive cognitive deficits. Development of self-regulatory efficacy provides the means for improving one's cognitive skills and for controlling self-impairing thought processes and emotional states (Rosenthal, 1980; Smith, 1980).

The multifaceted treatment of scholastic anxiety devised by Smith (1980) addresses the situational, cognitive, affective, and skill aspects of the problem. Students are taught effective self-instruction techniques, how to manage their time and available academic resources better, how to structure their environment in ways conducive to study, and how to motivate themselves through goal setting and contingent use of self-incentives. Students are also taught cognitive coping strategies that encourage more benign appraisals of academic stressors and enlist cognitive self-guidance through supportive self-instruction and cognitive rehearsal of strategies for dealing with problem situations. Finally, to ameliorate aversive physical arousal by stressful anticipation or threatening situations, students master stress-reduction techniques by visualizing taxing situations and alleviating their anxiety reactions by relaxing and supplanting stressful thought patterns. Training in these generalizable self-regulatory skills raises the perceived efficacy of students whose academic performances are impaired by self-debilitating reactions to academic stressors (Smith, 1989). The more their sense of efficacy is raised, the greater is the reduction in their anxiety and the more they improve their grades.

Impact of Cognitive Self-Efficacy on Developmental Trajectories

So far, the analyses have been confined to the effects of perceived cognitive efficacy on academic aspirations, motivation, intrinsic interest, and level of academic attainment. Children's intellectual development cannot be isolated from the social relations within which it is embedded or from its interpersonal effects. It must be analyzed from a social perspective. A secure sense of intellectual and self-regulatory efficacy not only promotes academic successes but also is influential in fostering satisfying and supportive social relationships and positive emotional development. Children who are considerate of their peers and are accepted by them are more likely to experience a favorable school environment as conducive to learning than are children who behave in socially alienating ways and are repeatedly rejected by their peers. A negative emotional and social life can erode a sense of intellectual efficacy and self-worth. Despondency undermines academic performance (Nolen-Hoeksema, Girgus, & Seligman, 1986). Moreover, students who doubt their intellectual efficacy tend to gravitate to peers who devalue academic pursuits. Disengagement from academic activities often means engagement in a constellation of problem behaviors that jeopardize the prospects of a successful future (Jessor, Donovan, & Costa, 1991; Patterson et al., 1984).

Not all children who experience academic difficulties display troublesome patterns of behavior. In the course of socialization, children adopt social and moral standards that serve as guides and deterrents for conduct. The sanctions children apply to themselves keep conduct in line with internal standards. Self-sanctions do not operate unless they are activated, however, and there are many psychological processes by which self-restraints can be disengaged from detrimental conduct. Personal control is selectively disengaged by reconstruing negative conduct as serving worthy purposes, obscuring personal agency by diffusion or displacement of responsibility, disregarding or minimizing the injurious consequences of one's actions, and blaming and dehumanizing those who are mistreated (Bandura, 1991d; Bandura, Barbaranelli, Caprara, & Pastorelli, 1996b). Propensity to disengage restraining self-sanctions from detrimental conduct increases the likelihood that academic inefficacy will give rise to aggressive and other forms of socially alienating conduct.

Social cognitive theory adopts an ecological perspective on the contribution of efficacy beliefs to cognitive and social development. Chapters 1 through 6 have provided a wealth of information about the separate impact of family, educational, and peer influences on the development of personal efficacy and its various regulative functions. Further research elucidates how they operate together as multiple interacting influences in shaping the course of children's development (Bandura, Barbaranelli, Caprara, & Pastorelli, 1996a). Figure 6.5 summarizes the pattern of influences. The intricate network of influences stands in stark contrast to the insulated cognitivism that has dominated the field of cognitive development.

Family socioeconomic status affects children's academic achievement only indirectly by promoting parental aspirations and children's prosocialness. Parents with a high sense of efficacy that they can influence their children's intellectual development hold high aspirations for their children and raise their children's beliefs in their capabilities to regulate their own learning and academic attainments. Different aspects of children's efficacy beliefs contribute to their academic attainments but, interestingly, through partially different paths of influence. Perceived academic efficacy raises academic attainments both directly and by fostering

academic aspirations and prosocial relationships and counteracting despondency. Children's beliefs in their efficacy to resist peer pressures for risky activities contribute to academic attainment directly and by supporting adherence to self-sanctions against detrimental conduct that can subvert academic pursuits. Perceived social efficacy contributes to academic attainments principally by promoting academic aspirations and reducing vulnerability to feelings of futility and depression. The other paths of influence reveal the ways in which emotional well-being and interpersonal relationships affect the course of cognitive development. Strong prosocial connectedness and peer popularity promote academic achievement directly and by curbing socially alienating conduct. Evidence that different facets of perceived self-efficacy contribute to academic achievement through different mediational paths which global measure cannot reveal attests to the explanatory value of microanalytic measures.

The findings of the research just discussed document the interplay of the diverse types of

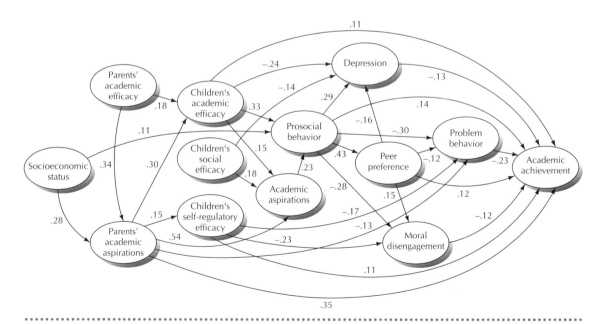

FIGURE 6.5. Path analysis of the pattern of influence through which parents' and children's efficacy beliefs and academic aspirations promote children's academic development. All of the path coefficients are significant beyond the *p* < .05 level. (Bandura et al., 1996a)

influences that shape developmental trajectories. Perceived inefficacies that impair cognitive functioning, sap aspirations, generate despondency, and breed socially alienating adaptations produce increasing academic deficiencies. Over time, growing doubts about intellectual capabilities and deficiencies in cognitive competencies foreclose many occupational life courses, if not prosocial life paths themselves. Indeed, among the different types of competencies, academic deficiencies are the ones most likely to foreshadow adoption of antisocial styles of behavior (Hinshaw, 1992; Rutter, 1979). In these different ways, beliefs of cognitive efficacy have reverberating effects on developmental trajectories well beyond the academic domain.

Self-Efficacy in Advanced Cognitive Functioning

The previous sections have been primarily concerned with the way in which efficacy beliefs foster development of cognitive competencies and academic achievement in formal instruction under the guidance of teachers. If anything, efficacy beliefs are even more crucial at advanced levels of cognitive functioning where pursuits are complex and demand a high level of self-directedness. Many of the problems of everyday life do not have a single fixed solution but rather permit different solutions of varying adequacy. Uncertainty about the range of possible solutions and their relative effectiveness increases the complexity of monitoring and evaluating one's understanding of problems and personal efficacy to come up with good courses of action. To complicate matters further, changing social practices and technological innovations continually demand new adaptations. Moreover, many of the pursuits call for prolonged laborious effort without the benefit of quick triumphs. Success under such conditions requires people to deploy their knowledge and cognitive skills flexibly, creatively, and persistently.

At the college level, students must choose which educational directions to pursue and assume major responsibility for their own learning. Those who have a high sense of efficacy are more successful in regulating their own learning and do better academically than those who are beset with uncertainties about their intellectual capabilities (Pintrich & Schrauben, 1992; Wood & Locke, 1987). Multon and her colleagues summarize by meta-analysis the findings of a large number of studies of academic achievement conducted with both children and adults (Multon et al., 1991). The results are consistent in showing that efficacy beliefs contribute significantly to scholastic performance. Beliefs in personal efficacy have substantially greater impact on academic performance than the personal, social, and occupational outcomes expected for proficient performance (Shell, Murphy, & Bruning, 1989).

Considerable research reveals that perceived academic efficacy plays an influential role in career choice and development. It predicts academic grades, the range of career options considered, and persistence and success in chosen fields (Betz & Hackett, 1986; Lent & Hackett, 1987). Perceived self-efficacy accounts for variations in these different intellectual aspects of occupational pursuits when past academic achievement, scholastic ability, and occupational interests are controlled (Lent et al., 1986, 1987). When differences in efficacy beliefs are controlled, however, ability no longer accounts for course planning, course selections, and academic grades, suggesting that students' beliefs in their academic efficacy mediates the relationship between ability and educational pursuits and attainments (Lent et al., 1993). By influencing preparatory development and occupational choices, efficacy beliefs partly shape the courses that lives take.

Creativity constitutes one of the highest forms of human expression. Innovativeness largely involves restructuring and synthesizing knowledge into new ways of thinking and of doing things. It requires a good deal of cognitive facility to override established ways of thinking that impede exploration of novel ideas and search for new knowledge. But above all, innovativeness requires an unshakable sense of efficacy to persist in creative endeavors when they demand prolonged investment of time and effort, progress is discouragingly slow, the outcome is highly uncertain, and creations are socially devalued when they are too incongruent with preexisting ways.

Locke, Frederick, Lee, and Bobko (1984) examined the role of perceived cognitive efficacy in creative thinking when individuals were taught cognitive strategies for thinking creatively. Both level of cognitive skills and strategy instruction raised belief in cognitive innovativeness. The increased perceived efficacy promoted creative thinking both directly and by adoption of motivating personal challenges. Creative scholarship in academic settings benefits from the exercise of some of the self-regulative influences reviewed earlier. Research projects often require a long lead time because of false starts and inevitable delays caused by difficulties in coordinating time schedules with availability of personnel, facilities, and resources. If a project does not pan out, time has been lost with nothing to show for it. Efforts are more productively deployed by working concurrently on several projects at varying stages of completion and shifting among them as circumstances dictate. It requires considerable self-regulatory efficacy to pursue multiple projects concurrently. Moreover, without personal goals to strengthen commitment to creative endeavors, people succumb to impediments and ever-present distractions. It also requires a high sense of efficacy to submit the products of one's labors to the critical scrutiny of others and to gain their acceptance. The research of Taylor and her colleagues (Taylor et al., 1984) sheds light on the impact of efficacy beliefs on these processes in scholarly productivity. The results of path analysis indicate that professors' high confidence in their efficacy to produce publishable research affects their scholarly productivity both directly by fostering goal setting and indirectly by concurrent involvement in multiple projects.

Perceived self-efficacy figures prominently in scholarly productivity even during development of academic careers. Research training exerts its impact on the productivity of graduate students to the extent that it influences their efficacy beliefs (Brown, Lent, Ryan, & McPartland, 1996). The mediational role of perceived efficacy is stronger for males than for females. These findings suggest that in cultivating scholarly careers, mastery

experiences, modeling of research strategies, and supportive feedback should be structured in ways that build a robust sense of efficacy as well as technical competencies. Research, by its very nature, requires resilience and a firm sense of purpose.

Human accomplishments in virtually all the domains of functioning reviewed in the various chapters of this book depend, in part, on effective use of specialized knowledge and cognitive skills. Recall the earlier causal analysis of how efficacy beliefs govern complex decision making in the social management of organizational performance (Wood & Bandura, 1989a). The contribution of efficacy beliefs to complex decision making, entrepreneurship, and receptivity to innovations are reviewed in greater detail in a later chapter.

TEACHERS' PERCEIVED EFFICACY

The task of creating learning environments conducive to development of cognitive competencies rests heavily on the talents and self-efficacy of teachers. Evidence indicates that teachers' beliefs in their instructional efficacy partly determine how they structure academic activities in their classrooms and shape students' evaluations of their intellectual capabilities. Gibson and Dembo (1984) measured teachers' beliefs in their efficacy to motivate and educate difficult students and to counteract adverse home and community influences on students' academic development. Teachers with a high sense of instructional efficacy operate on the belief that difficult students are teachable through extra effort and appropriate techniques and that they can enlist family supports and overcome negating community influences through effective teaching. In contrast, teachers who have a low sense of instructional efficacy believe there is little they can do if students are unmotivated and that the influence teachers can exert on students' intellectual development is severely limited by unsupportive or oppositional influences from the home and neighborhood environment.

Gibson and Dembo conducted a microanalytic observational study of how teachers of high and low perceived efficacy manage their classroom activities. Teachers who have a high sense of instructional efficacy devote more classroom time to academic activities, provide students who encounter difficulties with the guidance they need to succeed, and praise their academic accomplishments. In contrast, teachers of low perceived efficacy spend more time on nonacademic pastimes, readily give up on students if they do not get quick results, and criticize them for their failures. Thus, teachers who believe strongly in their ability to promote learning create mastery experiences for their students, but those beset by self-doubts about their instructional efficacy construct classroom environments that are likely to undermine students' judgments of their abilities and their cognitive development. The less time spent on academic instruction, the lower the students' academic progress (Cohn & Rossmiller, 1987). In studies of student teachers, those with a higher sense of efficacy do a better job in presenting lesson plans, drawing students out in discussions, and managing their classrooms during the subsequent course of their training (Saklofske, Michayluk, & Randhawa, 1988).

Educational systems will be relying increasingly on electronically mediated instruction. These new realities call for special types of teacher efficacy. Technologies change rapidly, requiring continual upgrading of knowledge and skills. Teachers' beliefs in their efficacy affect their receptivity to, and adoption of, educational technologies. Teachers of low perceived mathematical efficacy distrust their capacity to make good instructional use of computers (Olivier, 1985). Similarly, school administrators who have a low sense of computer efficacy resist adopting computers for instructional purposes (Jorde-Bloom & Ford, 1988). The availability of electronic media to deliver the more traditional instruction shifts the emphasis in teachers' pedagogical efficacy from rote instruction to training in how to think creatively, evaluate the deluge of information with which people are being overdosed, and use available knowledge productively. The efficacy issue of interest concerns teachers' beliefs in their abilities to integrate these pedagogical practices

successfully within a broad perspective of education.

Teachers' beliefs in their efficacy affect their general orientation toward the educational process as well as their specific instructional activities. Those who have a low sense of instructional efficacy favor a custodial orientation that takes a pessimistic view of students' motivation, emphasizes control of classroom behavior through strict regulations, and relies on extrinsic inducements and negative sanctions to get students to study (Woolfolk & Hoy, 1990; Woolfolk, Rosoff, & Hoy, 1990). Melby (1995) finds that teachers with a low sense of efficacy are mired in classroom problems. They distrust their ability to manage their classrooms; are stressed and angered by students' misbehavior; are pessimistic about students' improvability; take a custodial view of their job; resort to restrictive and punitive modes of discipline; focus more on the subject matter than on students' development; and, if they had to do it all over again, would not choose the teaching profession. In path analyses, the influence of perceived inefficacy on punitive classroom management is mediated through stress and anger. Heavy reliance on coercive practices to get things done fosters devaluation of others and their level of ability (Kipnis, 1974), which can further undermine students' academic interest and motivation. Teachers who believe strongly in their instructional efficacy tend to rely on persuasory means rather than authoritarian control and to support development of their students' intrinsic interest and academic self-directedness.

The preceding research delineates some of the classroom social processes through which teachers' efficacy beliefs can affect students' self-conceptions, aspirations, and academic learning. Ashton and Webb (1986) document the cumulative impact of divergent levels of teachers' perceived efficacy. They studied seasoned teachers who taught students placed in classes for basic skills because of severe academic deficiencies. Teachers' beliefs about their instructional efficacy predicted their students' levels of mathematical and language achievement over the course of the academic year with variations in the students' entering ability controlled. Students learned much more from teachers imbued with a sense of efficacy than from those beset with self-doubts. Teachers with a high sense of efficacy tend to view difficult students as reachable and teachable and regard their learning problems as surmountable by ingenuity and extra effort. Teachers of low perceived efficacy are inclined to invoke low student ability as an explanation for why their students cannot be taught.

The early school years are an important formative period in children's development of conceptions of their intellectual capabilities. Their beliefs about their intellectual efficacy are, in large part, a social construction based on appraisals of their performances in different academic subjects, repeated social comparisons with the attainments of their peers, and construals of the academic expectations and ability evaluations conveyed by their teachers either directly or in subtle indirect ways. A teacher's sense of efficacy is likely to be especially influential on young children because their beliefs about their capabilities are still relatively unstable, peer structures are relatively informal, and young children make little use of social comparison information in evaluating their capabilities. In accord with this expectation, Anderson, Greene, and Loewen (1988) report that teachers' beliefs in their instructional efficacy is a much stronger predictor of the academic attainments of younger students than of older students.

Socioeducational transitions involving new teachers, regroupings of classmates, and different school structures confront students with adaptational pressures that inevitably shake their sense of efficacy. These adaptational problems are likely to be exacerbated if the teachers to whom the students are entrusted doubt they can achieve much success with them. Students whose sense of efficacy is well-grounded in academic self-regulatory capabilities are less vulnerable to the possible adverse effects of teachers with a low sense of efficacy than are students who are struggling with self-doubts about their academic abilities. This differential effect is corroborated by Midgley, Feldlaufer, and Eccles (1989) in a longitudinal study of the transition from elementary to junior high school. High-achieving students were not much affected by their teachers'

sense of instructional efficacy during transition periods. In contrast, low-achieving students who had teachers low in perceived efficacy in both school environments or who moved from teachers' of high perceived efficacy to ones of low perceived efficacy suffered declines in academic expectations and evaluations of their academic performances. Transitions from teachers of low to high perceived efficacy led low-achieving students to expect more of themselves academically.

Some teachers find themselves beleaguered day in and day out by disruptive and nonachieving students. Eventually, their sense of inefficacy to fulfill academic demands takes a stressful toll. Burnout in academia is not all that uncommon. It encompasses a syndrome of reactions to prolonged occupational stressors that includes physical and emotional exhaustion, depersonalization of the people one is serving, and lack of any sense of personal accomplishment (Jackson, Schwab, & Shuler, 1986; Kyriacou, 1987; Maslach, 1982). Chwalisz, Altmaier, and Russell (1992) clarify the causal path through which a sense of coping inefficacy is linked to burnout in teachers. When faced with academic stressors, teachers of high perceived efficacy direct their efforts at resolving problems. In contrast, teachers who distrust their efficacy try to avoid dealing with academic problems and, instead, turn their efforts inward to relieve their emotional distress. The pattern of coping by withdrawal heightens emotional exhaustion, depersonalization, and a growing sense of futility.

Some of the avoidant means of coping involve disengagement from the instructional activities themselves. Thus, teachers who lack a secure sense of instructional efficacy show weak commitment to teaching (Evans & Tribble, 1986), spend less time on subject matter in their areas of perceived inefficacy (Enochs & Riggs, 1990), and devote less total time to academic matters (Gibson & Dembo, 1984). Teacher efficacy in science education is of particular concern, given the increasing importance of scientific literacy and competency in the technological transformations occurring in society. In a study including a variety of factors, Coladarci (1992) found that teachers' sense of instructional efficacy was the best predictor of commitment to the teaching profession. Strong educational leadership by the principal also contributed to teachers' commitment, but a school climate of collegiality and support, salary, and teaching experience did not. Attrition rates are high for teachers. Those of low perceived efficacy are the ones most likely to drop out of the teaching profession (Glickman & Tamashiro, 1982). Strategies for preventing and alleviating occupational burnout, which require both personal and organizational changes, are reviewed in Chapter 10.

As in other areas of research on the regulative function of efficacy beliefs, the assessment of teachers' perceived self-efficacy should be broadened to gauge its multifaceted nature. Teachers' sense of efficacy was initially conceptualized as a global construct measured by one item involving teachers' efficacy to educate difficult and unmotivated students and by a second item involving the efficacy of teachers in general to overcome the negative impact of adverse home environments on students' academic motivation (Berman, McLaughlin, Bass, Pauly, & Zellman, 1977). Gibson and Dembo (1984) improved the assessment procedure by measuring these two facets of teachers' perceived efficacy with multiple items. Multiform measures reduce the problems of low reliability, deficient sampling of variant manifestations of a particular facet, and restricted variability of scores that plague single-item measures and diminish relationships between variables. Efficacy to surmount taxing conditions, however, should be measured in terms of teachers' beliefs about their own efficacy to do so rather than about the efficacy of teachers in general. Teachers' instructional efforts are governed more by what they believe they can accomplish than by their view of other teachers' abilities to prevail over environmental obstacles by effective teaching.

Multi-item measures are an improvement over single-item ones, but teacher efficacy scales are, for the most part, still cast in a general form rather than being tailored to domains of instructional functioning. Teachers' sense of instructional efficacy is not necessarily uniform across different subjects. Thus, teachers who judge themselves highly efficacious in mathematical or science instruction may be much less assured of their efficacy in language instruction

and vice versa. Therefore, teacher efficacy scales should be linked to the various knowledge domains. Because omnibus measures sacrifice predictive power, they probably underestimate the degree to which teachers' sense of efficacy contributes to students' academic attainments.

Teachers' perceived efficacy rests on much more than the ability to transmit subject matter. Their effectiveness is also partly determined by their efficacy in maintaining an orderly classroom conducive to learning, enlisting resources and parental involvement in children's academic activities, and counteracting social influences that subvert students' commitments to academic pursuits. Multifaceted teacher efficacy scales (Bandura, 1990b) enable researchers to select those that are most germane to the domain of functioning the research is designed to elucidate.

COLLECTIVE SCHOOL EFFICACY

Teachers operate collectively within an interactive social system rather than as isolates. Therefore, educational development through efficacy enhancement must address the social and organizational structure of educational systems. Educational organizations present a number of distinct challenges and stressors. Many of the adverse conditions with which schools have to cope reflect the broader social and economic ills of the society. These adverse realities affect student educability and impair the school environment. In the 1940s teachers identified as the top disciplinary problems: students making noise, talking, running in the halls, and chewing gum. In the 1980s, the leading problems included drug and alcohol abuse, assault and vandalism, extortion, pregnancy, gang warfare, and rape. To make matters worse, there are a host of problems endemic to the teaching profession, some of which are not easily amenable to personal control. These are well documented by Ashton and Webb (1986). They include heavy workloads requiring constant intensive interactions, little say in how the educational enterprise is run but responsibility to meet high public demands, disconcerting bureaucratic practices, variable quality of administrative leadership, insufficient resources, lack of advancement opportunities, a sizable share of problematic students, insufficient pay, low occupational status, and inadequate public recognition of accomplishments. There are even contentious battles over what should be taught in schools, what subjects should be forbidden, and what criteria should be used to evaluate the effectiveness of educational systems. The public demands objective measures of academic achievement, whereas teachers generally prefer more subjective indicants of educational development. In short, educational systems are strewn with conditions that can easily erode teachers' sense of efficacy and occupational satisfaction. Given these numerous impediments, it is remarkable that so many schools attain the academic successes that they do.

Much has been written about the attributes of efficacious schools. Given some variability in achievement across grades and subjects within schools and fluctuations over time, identifying effective schools is not as easy as it might appear at first sight. The analyses that are most informative control for background factors associated with level of academic achievement, such as the ethnic and socioeconomic composition of the schools' student bodies. Without such controls, school differences may simply reflect what students bring to those schools. The characteristics of high-achieving schools that enroll a high proportion of economically disadvantaged students are of special interest. Effectiveness is generally measured in terms of rate of absenteeism, behavior problems, and academic achievement on standardized tests. There is much commonality in educational practices among high-achieving schools (Edmonds, 1979; Good & Brophy, 1986; Levin & Lockheed, 1993; Mortimore, 1995). Rather than simply provide a bare catalogue of correlates of efficacious schools, the present review will focus on how the identified features operate psychosocially to produce their effects and on how they can be instituted. The things that make schools effective typically include strong academic leadership by the principal, high academic standards with firm belief in student's capabilities to fulfill them, mastery-oriented instruction that enables students to exercise control over their academic performances, good management of classroom behavior conducive to learning, and parental support and involvement in their children's schooling.

Attributes of Efficacious Schools

In highly efficacious schools, in addition to serving as administrators, principals are educational leaders who seek ways to improve instruction. They figure out ways to work around stifling policies and regulations that impede academic innovativeness. In low-achieving schools, principals function more as administrators and disciplinarians. Masterful academic leadership by the principal builds teachers' sense of instructional efficacy (Coladarci, 1992).

High expectations and standards for achievement pervade the environment of efficacious schools. Teachers regard their students as capable of high scholastic attainments, set challenging academic standards for them, and reward behaviors conducive to intellectual development. High standards will not accomplish much, and can actually be demoralizing, unless learning activities are structured and conducted in ways that ensure they will be mastered. Deeper analysis would probably reveal that efficacious schools not only endorse high standards but back them up with mastery aids for success. In such schools, teachers maintain a resilient sense of instructional efficacy and accept a fair share of responsibility for their students' academic progress. Poor academic performances are not excused on the grounds of low inherent ability or adverse family backgrounds that supposedly render students uneducable. By contrast, in low-achieving schools, teachers do not expect much academically of their students, spend less time actively teaching and monitoring their academic progress, and essentially write off a large part of the student body as uneducable (Brookover, Beady, Flood, Schweitzer, &

Wisenbaker, 1979). Not surprisingly, students in such schools have a high sense of academic futility.

Students are often stratified into academic tracks oriented toward vocational, general, academic, or honors instruction. Tracking practices determine the level of intellectual challenge and career guidance students receive. In efficacious schools, when subgroup instruction is used for students who fall behind in a given academic skill, it is designed to accelerate learning so that they can make up their deficits and become part of the regular instructional life of the school. In low-achieving schools, teachers spend less time on academic instruction and more time as disciplinarians trying to maintain order in the classroom. Students who have difficulty with their schoolwork, as many from disadvantaged backgrounds do, are set apart by placement in slow-learner tracks where little is expected of them academically. They remain permanently segregated in a socially stigmatized status as they continue to fall further behind. Whatever praise they receive is unlikely to do them much good academically because they are often rewarded for substandard performances or merely for effort, without much reinstruction on poorly done assignments.

A disproportionately high percentage of disadvantaged minorities of high ability are also misplaced in low academic tracks with watered-down curricula that leave them ineligible for higher education (Dornbusch, 1994). Such instructional practices foreclose occupational opportunities to escape impoverished lives of socioeconomic disadvantage. Peterson (1989) documents the debilitating effects of remedial academic grouping. Low-achieving students assigned to a program for accelerated students achieved substantial academic gains, whereas those assigned to a remedial program created disciplinary problems and made little academic progress over the course of the year. Similarly, able students are academically handicapped by placement in lower educational tracks (Dornbusch, 1994). Remedial tracking further undermines academic strivings by fostering affiliation with low-achieving peers who are apathetic or antipathetic toward schooling. Assignment to low academic tracks eventually takes a toll on teachers' sense of instructional efficacy as

well as breeding perceived inefficacy in students (Raudenbush, Rowan, & Cheong, 1992).

The family plays a key role in children's success in school. It is often said that parents are the first teachers and the home is the first school. Parents continue to exert influence on their children's academic progress, especially in their earlier years of schooling. Hence, another distinguishing feature of efficacious schools is their heavy involvement of parents as partners in their children's education. Parents contribute to their children's intellectual growth in a variety of ways. They prepare their children for school, place a value on education, convey belief in their children's scholastic ability, set standards for them, establish regular homework habits, help them with their schoolwork at home, encourage language development and comprehension through reading, keep track of their academic progress, reward their efforts, support school-related functions, assist with school activities, and participate in school governance or community advocacy groups for school improvement (Epstein, 1990). Among students equated for ability, parental guidance and encouragement of academic activities increases the likelihood that children will be placed in high academic tracks (Dornbusch, 1994).

Educationally advantaged parents often go to great lengths to prepare their children socially, cognitively and motivationally for academic learning and are not at all timid about influencing school practices to serve their children's scholastic progress. In addition to participating actively in their children's schooling, the parents supplement their children's formal educational experiences with many after-school programs. These activities not only further their children's development but also create helpful social ties among parents in the school community, through which they learn about other opportunities for their children (Lareau, 1987). The informal social networks spawn a lot of learning outside the confines of the school. Disadvantaged families lack the means to provide their children with such developmentally enriching experiences unless the parents make considerable self-sacrifices by dedicating a great deal of their time, effort, and meager resources to such purposes.

It is usually disadvantaged parents who have low involvement with schools and provide little educational guidance for their children. Many do not know what to do or how to help their children at home with learning activities, and this lack of knowledge is easily misconstrued as lack of caring. They are often intimidated by schools and rarely initiate contact with them (Lareau, 1987). They have few economic resources at their disposal to enrich their children's schooling. As might be expected, they have a low sense of efficacy that they can influence their children's school learning (Hoover-Dempsey, Bassler, & Brissie, 1992).

Self-efficacious parents regard education as a shared responsibility. The higher their sense of efficacy to instruct their children, the more they guide their children's learning and participate actively in the life of the school (Hoover-Dempsey et al., 1992). In contrast, parents who doubt their efficacy to help their children learn turn over their children's education entirely to teachers. School staff have mixed feelings about parental involvement in schooling, especially when it subjects teachers to critical scrutiny and pressures to produce higher academic achievement. Parental participation can be easily dismissed on the grounds that many parents, especially the less educated ones, are not really interested in becoming involved in their children's academic activities.

Teachers' sense of efficacy partly determines the level of parental participation in children's scholastic activities. Teachers who are secure in their perceived capabilities are most likely to invite and support parents' educational efforts. Thus, the stronger the teachers' perceived instructional efficacy, the more parents seek contact with them, assist them in the classroom, provide home instruction on plans devised by the teacher, help their children with their homework, and otherwise support the teacher's efforts, as reported by the teachers (Hoover-Dempsey, Bassler, & Brissie, 1987, 1992). These findings most likely reflect a process of mutual efficacy enhancement. Self-efficacious teachers increase parents' ability to help their children learn, and the resultant scholastic progress and parental support of school activities, in turn, raise teachers' sense of instructional efficacy. Because of the centrality of family influence on children's scholastic success, the contribution of teacher efficacy to parental involvement in educational activities is of considerable import.

If family involvement is to become more inclusive, schools must instruct uninvolved parents whose children are most in need of educational guidance about how to promote their children's academic development. Building family connectedness to schools is becoming increasingly important with the decline in the traditional family structure and the increase in multicultural school populations unaccustomed to sharing responsibility for the intellectual life of schools (Epstein & Scott-Jones, 1988). An effective efficacy-building program would include videotaped modeling of family tutorial skills as well as guided practice in their use. Strategies for how to serve as an advocate for children's development would also be modeled.

Another element in a productive family program is a regular system of communication between school and home that forges a collaborative partnership (Brandt, 1989). Families that avoid contact with schools because they feel inefficacious and intimidated by the staff benefit from a home visitor program conducted by trained parents from the community (Davies, 1991). They provide information about the school, housing, health services, and extracurricular programs for children. They instruct parents about ways to help their children increase their interest and involvement in academic activities. These outreach activities help to build parents' beliefs that they can influence their children's educational development. When low-achieving schools are being restructured, initial efforts to enlist parental involvement will not evoke an outpouring of family response. Parental participation must be cultivated by forging links to parents, demonstrating their importance to the educational effort, and enlisting the aid of involved parents to broaden and strengthen connections of families to schools. As more and more families become involved in various aspects of school life, the rate of active parental participation rises rapidly (Levin, 1991). To maintain high participation, parents need to see that their involvement makes a difference in their children's education.

Another distinguishing feature of efficacious schools is the structuring of learning activities in ways that promote a sense of personal capability and scholastic accomplishment in all students. Such schools generally favor a mastery model of learning in which students' progress in various areas of instruction is closely monitored and they get quick corrective feedback and reinstruction when they encounter difficulties until they master the relevant knowledge and cognitive skills (Block, Efthim, & Burns, 1989). With supportive guidance, all students achieve a high level of mastery. Some simply take longer and require more help than others. Extensive interactive instruction saves slower learners from falling farther and farther behind and becoming demoralized. In addition to the usual didactic instruction, students often work together in small groups and help one another in their school work. Academic tasks are carefully structured for them, but students are encouraged to manage their own learning as much as possible to enable them to become self-directed learners. In efficacious schools, students are not sorted into homogeneous tracks of fast and slow learners.

In efficacious schools, classroom behavior is managed successfully. This is achieved more by promoting, recognizing, and praising productive activities than by punishing disruptive behavior. This approach follows the trusty dictum that adverse developmental courses are better altered by rewarding constructive patterns of behavior than by punishing detrimental ones. If troublesome behavior threatens to get out of hand, however, it is dealt with quickly and firmly. Good classroom management creates an orderly and safe learning environment. Mutual respect and safety assume special significance because young children are much more apprehensive about social maltreatment at school than about academic achievement.

Other attributes appear from time to time on listings of correlates of efficacious schools, but they are not as central or as replicable as the major ones already reviewed. Brookover and his colleagues have shown that the quality of the school environment contributes substantially to differences in academic achievement among schools (Brookover et al., 1979). When the influence of the attributes of the school social system are controlled, the proportion of variance uniquely attributable to socioeconomic, ethnic, and racial factors is considerably reduced. It should be noted, however, that much of the effect of schools on achievement is accounted for by students' sense of academic utility. This is both a product of social conditions and a characteristic of the school culture.

Collective Instructional Efficacy

As illustrated in the previous review, the quality of school environments is generally characterized in terms of a set of dimensions that mainly reflect teachers' attitudes and behavior conducive to academic learning. Perceived self-efficacy operates as a higher order determinant with broad impact on attitudinal, affective, motivational, and behavioral aspects of functioning. Therefore, perceived collective efficacy represents an overriding quality that affects different aspects of a social system. In the study by Gibson and Dembo (1984) cited earlier, teachers with a strong sense of instructional efficacy created a positive climate for academic learning by devoting the major share of time to academic activities, conveying positive expectations of student achievement, and instilling and rewarding academic success. These different expressions of teachers' sense of personal efficacy usually appear as separate dimensions of environmental qualities in studies of school climate.

Another benefit of characterizing the social environments of school systems in terms of perceived collective efficacy is that the construct is grounded in a theory and a body of knowledge about its psychosocial determinants and mechanisms of operation. It thus provides explicit guidelines for how to structure interventions to change social systems. In efforts to delineate the crucial functional properties of social systems, the goal should be to reduce lists of seemingly heterogeneous variables to a small set of supraordinate determinants and mediating mechanisms that can account for the major share of variance among schools in academic attainments. Schools in which the staff collectively judge themselves as relatively powerless to get their students to achieve academic success are likely to convey a group sense of academic futility that can pervade the entire life of the school. In contrast, schools in which staff members collectively judge themselves highly capable of promoting academic success are likely to imbue their schools with a positive atmosphere for sociocognitive development.

School systems rank at an intermediate level of interdependence. Schools include team planning of curricula and social functions and some team teaching. In addition, the functioning of the school system relies on joint responsibility for the academic and social norms of the system and hierarchical dependence on the adequacy of student socioeducational preparation in prior grades. Students who are inadequately prepared scholastically and motivationally in lower grade levels tax teachers' ability to promote academic accomplishments at higher levels. Quality of leadership by the principal also affects the milieu in which teachers work. Thus, although the level of academic progress achieved by a school largely reflects the summed contributions of the individual teachers, these various organizational interdependencies contribute to the teachers' instructional efficacy.

Effective schooling involves reciprocal causation. Teachers' sense of instructional efficacy partly determines how much their students learn. In turn, a number of factors in the school environment can alter teachers' beliefs in their efficacy to produce scholastic attainments. Some of these factors stem from the characteristics of students and their family backgrounds. Parental influences contribute to scholastic attainments through the resources, guidance, modeling, and incentives the home provides for academic learning. Teachers' sense of instructional efficacy can be gradually eroded by student bodies composed of many low-achieving students and those from disadvantaged socioeconomic backgrounds that leave them ill-prepared motivationally and cognitively for academic progress.

The belief systems of the staff also create an organizational culture that can have vitalizing or demoralizing effects on the perceived efficacy of its members. Teachers who view intelligence as an acquirable attribute and believe they can attain academic successes despite students' disadvantaged backgrounds promote a collective sense of efficacy, whereas teachers who believe that intelligence is an inherent aptitude and there is little they can do to overcome the negative influence of adverse social conditions are likely to undermine one another's sense of efficacy. The quality of leadership is often an important contributor to the production and maintenance of organizational climates. In the educational domain, strong principals excel in their ability to get their staff to work together with a strong sense of purpose and belief in their abilities to surmount obstacles to educational attainments. Such principals display strong commitments to scholastic attainment and seek ways to enhance the instructional function of their schools. Interpersonal supportiveness by principals may contribute to a positive climate in the school but does not, in itself, build teachers' sense of instructional efficacy. Rather, principals who create a school climate with a strong academic emphasis and serve as advocates on behalf of teachers' instructional efforts with the central administration enhance their teachers' beliefs in their instructional efficacy (Hoy & Woolfolk, 1993). The mutual modeling of beliefs and social practices of staff members are likely to have a significant impact on the sense of collective efficacy that pervades a school environment.

Some of the dynamics of collective school efficacy are revealed in a study that measured teachers' beliefs about the efficacy of their school to promote different levels of academic gains in a large school district (Bandura, 1993). Teachers' beliefs in their schools' efficacy to promote academic achievement was measured at the outset of the academic year, before the teachers could become familiar with the students in their classrooms. This provided an index of their preexisting beliefs about their school's instructional efficacy. Schools were used as the unit of analysis. Standardized tests assessed the level of school achievement in reading and mathematics before and at the end of the academic year. A number of factors concerned with socioinstructional influences and the sociocultural composition of student bodies that can enhance or undermine teachers' sense of collective efficacy were also assessed.

The issue of school effectiveness is often approached as though a school environment is a massive undifferentiated entity. In fact, some educational attainments are more difficult to produce than others, and students at different phases of their education present differential psychosocial competencies, motivational orientations, and instructional challenges. In schools using academic grouping, teachers instructing less able students experience different classroom environments than those instructing gifted students. Teachers are thus producers and products of microenvironments within a larger school milieu. Although some schools clearly do a much better job than others across a variety of educational activities, there are variations in views among teachers within schools as well as variations between teachers in different schools. This applies equally to perceived collective efficacy. The differences between schools are greater than among teachers within schools, but collective efficacy is by no means a unitary characteristic.

Teachers' sense of collective efficacy varies across grade level and subjects (Fig. 6.6). This is true for both aggregated teachers' beliefs of instructional efficacy in their own classrooms and aggregated teachers' beliefs in the instructional efficacy of their school as a whole. Teachers express a relatively low sense of efficacy to promote learning in students at the entry level. Since scholastic demands are minimal at entry, the low sense of instructional efficacy may partly reflect the perceived unpreparedness of students for classroom instruction. In the middle grades, when students are better acclimatized to school routines and academic demands are not too rigorous, teachers express a stronger belief that they can educate their students. In succeeding grades, however, when the complexities of academic demands increase and scholastic deficits become increasingly salient, teachers view their schools as declining in instructional efficacy. Teachers judge themselves more efficacious to promote language skills than

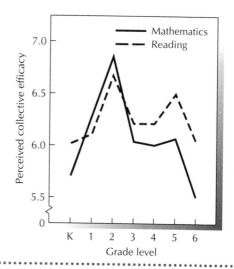

FIGURE 6.6. Changes in teachers' perceived collective efficacy to promote mathematical and reading competencies across different grade levels. (Bandura, 1993)

mathematical skills. This rise and demoralizing decline in perceived school efficacy is thus more pronounced for teaching mathematical skills than for teaching reading skills.

The decline in staff's beliefs in their instructional efficacy in later grades assumes special significance from evidence that teachers' efficacy beliefs affect how well students manage school transitions (Midgley et al., 1989). Students who end up being taught by teachers with a low sense of efficacy suffer a loss in perceived academic efficacy and lowered performance expectations in the transition from elementary school to junior high school. Students' self-doubts become even more severe if they are struggling academically and if the teachers to whom they transfer harbor doubts about their own abilities to promote academic attainments.

When no special effort is made to enhance the collective efficacy of schools composed of students predominantly from disadvantaged backgrounds, socioeconomic status and racial composition of the student bodies are likely to account for much of the variance between schools in collective efficacy and achievement level. This is because there are not many schools of low socioeconomic status with lofty collective efficacy and superior achievements or of high socioeconomic status with a sense of academic futility and meager achievement. Such findings have sometimes been interpreted to mean that factors related to student background create both the school psychological environment and the difference between schools in scholastic attainments. To assume that socioeconomic disadvantage and racial status ordain low scholastic attainment implies that poor and minority students have limited learning capability and that teachers are relatively powerless to promote academic success if their students are not socioeconomically advantaged. Superior academic attainments by efficacious schools serving almost entirely disadvantaged minority students belie this view (Bandura, 1993; Brookover et al., 1979). The collective beliefs of school faculties to motivate and educate socioeconomically disadvantaged students are, of course, modifiable.

Analyses of the relative contribution of student characteristics and school environments to school-level achievement often treat two-way causation as though it flowed unidirectionally. Because influences are bidirectional, statistical controls for students' entering scholastic attainments can seriously distort the contribution of school influences to the course of children's academic development. As previously noted, teachers' beliefs in their instructional efficacy affect their students' academic progress, which, in turn, affects teachers' beliefs in their efficacy to motivate and educate students who have difficulty academically. Negative reciprocal causation can create a demoralizing descent of staff efficacy and student efficacy and achievement, whereas positive bidirectional influences can produce mutual enhancement of efficacy and scholastic achievement. Students' entry-level skills thus reflect not only ability but also the prior impact of cognitive, affective, and motivational factors that are partly the products of instilled efficacy beliefs.

To evaluate the role of perceived collective efficacy in how well schools perform, the pattern of hypothesized influences among factorially verified indices of teacher and student body characteristics, collective efficacy, and prior level of school achievement were tested by path analysis (Bandura, 1993). Perceived collective efficacy was measured in terms of the summed beliefs of teachers in their school's capability to promote different levels of academic attainment. Figure 11.1 in the chapter on collective efficacy summarizes graphically the causal structure of the factors measured at the beginning of the academic year and school-level achievement in reading and mathematics at the end of the academic year. Adverse characteristics of student body populations that largely reflect socioeconomic disadvantage erode schools' sense of instructional efficacy. Thus, the higher the proportion of students from low socioeconomic levels and the higher the student turnover and absenteeism, the weaker are the faculties' beliefs in their collective efficacy to achieve academic progress and the poorer the schools fare academically. Student body characteristics reflecting low racial and ethnic diversity have no direct influence on subsequent school achievements. Rather, they operate indirectly by affecting earlier school achievement, which, in turn, shapes teachers' beliefs in their collective efficacy about the educability of their students. Thus, student body characteristics influence school attainments more by altering faculties' beliefs about their collective instructional efficacy than by direct impact on school achievement. Longevity in teaching has a small positive effect on school achievement but also seems to create in teachers a jaundiced view of their schools' collective instructional efficacy.

Staff's collective sense of efficacy that they can promote high levels of academic progress contributes significantly to their schools' level of academic achievement. Indeed, perceived collective efficacy contributes independently to differences in school achievement levels after controlling for the effects of the characteristics of student bodies, teachers' characteristics, and prior school level achievement. With staff who firmly believe that, by their determined efforts, students are motivatable and teachable whatever their background, schools heavily populated with poor and minority students achieve at the highest percentile ranks based on national norms of language and mathematical competencies.

Models for Enhanced Education of Disadvantaged Youth

Our nation's schools are not serving disadvantaged children well. Most children in inner city schools display major deficits in their educational development. Compensatory education programs have met with limited success. Whatever gains are achieved in academic competencies are small compared to the huge and widening gaps in achievement that persist between advantaged and disadvantaged children. The educationally disadvantaged represent about a third of the nation's student population. African-American and Latino students also drop out of school at much higher rates than do white students. Increasing ethnic diversity creates further challenges in educating students differing in norms, values, and styles of behavior. These demographic changes are likely to create a growing proportion of marginalized students. The continuing failure of educational programs for disadvantaged youth underscores the need for more radical restructuring of the school environment. Educationally disadvantaged students require accelerated rather than remedial education with instructional strategies that promote success (Levin, 1987). Education is the major path out of poverty. New technologies demanding rising levels of cognitive competencies are placing an even greater premium on educational development for success.

Faced with chronic deficiencies in the educational system, many people favor a competitive market solution to the problem. They want a voucher system that enables them to purchase educational services for their children from public or private schools of their choosing. Providing options presumably creates performance accountability and incentives for schools to increase their effectiveness — otherwise, they lose their patronage. The notion of educational choice and diversity appeals to constituencies who view it in terms of empowerment or entrepreneurial market forces. A market solution that does not provide equitable access and better education for all, however, is a socially segmenting remedy that can breed social polarization. The concern is not with competition among public schools through open enrollment, but with private schools picking off with public subsidy the more talented students from public school systems. If vouchers do not cover the full tuition costs of private schools, advantaged families can benefit from them, but most poor families may end up keeping their children in deteriorating public schools or sending them to cheaper ones with fewer educational resources. Weak schools would become worse and efficacious schools would maintain their superiority. This would create a widening educational gap between children from advantaged and disadvantaged sectors of society.

Open enrollment in the public school system does not necessarily provide much choice and competition if enrollment in quality schools is quickly closed by high demand. Mediocre schools can be put out of business faster if, in addition to open enrollment, parents can join forces with efficacious educators to create public schools that provide quality education for their children. Creating new schools and operating them successfully, however, presents formidable organizational, instructional, and financial challenges. There is no evidence as yet that charter schools run by operators under public contract are producing higher student achievement than are regular public schools. However a society chooses to educate its children, it must evaluate the results of its educational system in the aggregate. The social and economic health of a society requires effective education for all students rather than separating them into efficacious schools and mediocre schools that produce an uneducated underclass. A society that writes off its disadvantaged members pays a heavy price in social strife and the quality of its economic future. To achieve efficacious schools for all segments of society, people need to work together with a vested interest in one another's successful development and achievement. A civil society with a valued quality of life requires recognition of people's interdependence and commitment to an ethic of inclusion.

School failure reflects a broader sociocultural problem (Comer, 1988; Payne, 1991). Many children of low-income families are ill-prepared cognitively, motivationally, and socially to meet normative educational demands. They receive little help in school in developing the motivation and skills needed for academic success. Aversive experiences in school breed antagonistic reactions and behavior problems. Many teachers come to regard students who show little interest in schoolwork as unteachable and hold low academic expectations for them. Much of the communication with parents centers on disciplinary problems and learning deficiencies. These adverse experiences foster distrust, estrangement, and conflict between home and school. In the past, schools tended to be an integral part of the neighborhood and the community in which they were located. Often, there were shared values and close links between home and school. Teachers resided in the neighborhoods they served and had frequent informal contact with the students and families in their daily life. The weakening of communal bonds and the fragmentation of family and community life, especially in socioeconomically disadvantaged urban areas, has created estrangement between parents and schools. Rebuilding connectedness among school, home, and community with a common sense of purpose and shared responsibility for the intellectual life of schools is crucial in restructuring schools for academic success.

Mass migration of people seeking a better life is altering the demographic characteristics of school populations. Migrants are uprooted from their culture and thrust into a foreign one where they have to learn new languages, social norms, values, worldviews, and unfamiliar ways of life, many of which may clash with their native culture. As countries become more ethnically diverse, educational systems face the difficult challenge of fulfilling their mission with students of diverse backgrounds and adequacy of academic preparation. To further complicate matters, cultural and racial conflicts in the larger society get played out in the educational system as well. We saw earlier that many school staff have a low sense of efficacy to educate poor and minority students and do not expect much of them academically. The more culturally diverse the composition of student bodies, the poorer is the staff's implementation of programs conducive to academic learning.

The characteristics of efficacious schools have been amply documented. But there is a vast difference between knowing what makes schools academically effective and being able to create them. Occasionally, particular schools achieve spectacular results with disadvantaged ethnic minorities through the inspired leadership of a charismatic principal and the dedicated efforts of the instructional staff. In such atypical instances, success lies in the hands of the particular educators. Accelerating the education of disadvantaged youth requires well-founded models for restructuring school systems that make atypical scholastic triumphs common ones. Several such models for school development have been devised.

Ineffective schools require major restructuring of their customary practices rather than piecemeal remedies. If the changes are to have much impact and durability, they must be accomplished largely through collective initiative of the various constituencies of each school. Comer's (1980, 1988) collaborative program for creating educational environments conducive to sociocognitive development provides one model of social enablement for educational change. This program specifies social mechanisms for enlisting the often disparate social constituencies — teachers, administrators, parents, and the larger community — to adopt shared responsibilities and mutual assistance in the service of the socioeducational development of children.

Officials often mandate school reforms and improvement initiatives but give little attention to the skills, resources, and structural supports needed to successfully implement them. In schools serving students predominantly from educationally and economically disadvantaged backgrounds, the more instructional supports and help teachers receive in managing educational activities, the better they sustain their sense of instructional efficacy (Hannaway, 1992). Educational improvement depends on the establishment of partnerships of mutual trust; understanding; respect; and sensitivity to ethnic, racial, and gender differences. The improved relationships within the school and with the larger community enable the participants to build a collective sense of efficacy and responsibility that converts academic malaise into educational interest, challenge, and achievement. School restructuring models that produce educational benefits largely through collective effort rather than by revamping teaching methods or basic educational content or by requiring expensive new resources are more easily adoptable. In Comer's view, once a supportive community is established, it will create the intellectual and social conditions conducive to scholastic development. If schools create the motivational conditions for learning and provide educational guidance and challenging standards to which children can aspire, they will become good learners.

The Comer model includes three major structural components. The key component is a governance and management team composed of representatives of the different social constituencies — teachers, parents, guidance counselors, and the support staff — chaired by the principal. This collaborative governance team develops a comprehensive school plan covering academic and social programs, establishes priorities for the school, mobilizes needed resources, promotes staff development, sets clear academic standards, conveys expectations of achievement, and monitors the progress of the various programs. Minority students have the added burden of developing sets of competencies to negotiate the demands of both the mainstream society and their ethnic minority. Bicultural efficacy and identity are not easily achievable when the multiple demands clash in important spheres of functioning. In addition to developing academic skills, the program cultivates the many social skills needed for success in the mainstream society. Positive ethnic and racial identity are supported in ways that build a sense of personal efficacy and self-worth without fostering antieducational attitudes. Such attitudes impede the development of competencies and, in so doing, foreclose many life pursuits in the mainstream society. Students get shortchanged when ethnic identities are promoted at the expense of intellectual competencies.

The governance and management body of the school adopts a style of decision making that forces members to work in partnership to promote educational development instead of championing the self-interests of their constituencies (Anson et al., 1991). They follow a no-fault policy that focuses on constructive problem-solving rather than assigning blame to one another. Decisions are made by consensus rather than by vote. This avoids the cleavages, power maneuverings, coalition formations, and victors and disgruntled losers that breed conflicts and resentments. Consensus decision making fosters collaboration and mutual respect. To get beyond just talk that evades coming to grips with difficult problems, the team seeks closure with practical courses of action on whatever issues they discuss. And finally, the governance team shares power with the principal but does not undermine the principal's leadership.

A second component of the model is the parent-participation program that links parents to the sociocognitive development of their children and helps to improve the school climate. Parents assist at all levels of school activities as teachers' aides and as assistants in the libraries, resource centers, cafeterias, and playgrounds. They also develop a social program for the year that promotes the children's educational development and reestablishes close relations between the home and school. The parents thus gain a sense of control and responsibility for the academic and social life of their school. As parents are made to feel wanted and important, estrangement gives way to growing parental involvement in the life of the school.

The third component is the student services team, which includes school counselors, nurses, and other support staff. Their main role is to develop and implement individualized programs that reduce particular behavior problems and to devise changes in the socioeducational practices of the school to prevent behavior problems from arising. The management of behavior problems is similarly achieved in partnership with parents and teachers. The help of the counseling team frees teachers to pursue academic matters rather than operate as disciplinarians. Students are likely to be most responsive if they have a vested interest in the life of their school. Therefore, as they progress in their development, they should play an increased role in upholding the quality of their school life.

Informal assessments of this approach to the education of socioeconomically disadvantaged children indicate that it eliminates absenteeism, markedly reduces behavior problems, and raises academic achievement (Comer, 1985, 1988). Carefully controlled studies are needed, however, to determine how well this approach to restructuring deficient schools works and maintains its success over time and in new sites. The model provides explicit guidelines on how to create the structural components and get them to work in partnership. But it says little about how to overcome social obstacles to its adoption and ensure its successful implementation. Until formal tests verify the degree of success that this approach can achieve under good implementation, it, like other school restructuring models, must be accepted with reservation.

Levin (1996) has also devised a promising model, called the accelerated school, to enhance learning by disadvantaged youth who do not benefit much from conventional instruction. Enhanced learning is achieved through multifaceted restructuring of the social, motivational, and instructional practices of the school within existing resources. The accelerated school is founded on the principles of unity of purpose, collective enablement, shared responsibility, and building on strengths. Parents, teachers, and students commit themselves to working in close partnership toward a common set of goals of academic achievement. Explicit goals set academic standards for the school and guide and mobilize the effort required for their realization. Goals without ongoing feedback of progress achieve little (Bandura, 1991b; Locke & Latham, 1990). In the accelerated school, goals are combined with an assessment system using learning trajectories to monitor academic progress. Timely feedback provides the basis for corrective adjustments. A major goal is to close the achievement gap so that educationally disadvantaged children can benefit from regular instruction requiring a good deal of scholastic self-directedness.

The school operates using a collaborative decision-making system with a shift of control over, and responsibility for, academic practices from the central administration to the individual schools. Schools are accountable for results. Local governance without central oversight for accountability can create schools that do a poor job in fulfilling their mission. The central office provides support services and technical assistance rather than operating as the prescriber and regulator of academic activities. In this school-based management, the staff make the decisions about curriculum, modes of instruction, and how to allocate their resources and personnel. Allowing the faculty some control over school policies, instructional practices, the curriculum, and other aspects of their working conditions raises their sense of instructional efficacy (Hannaway, 1992; Raudenbush et al., 1992). Because of the primacy of language in the instruction and development of higher level competencies, heavy emphasis is placed on the mastery of communication and linguistic skills. To enhance meaningfulness, educational subjects are related to children's daily lives and experiences. The instruction underscores the usefulness of the conceptual and analytical tools being taught.

The accelerated school uses a number of instructional strategies that are effective in promoting learning and developing the capability for self-instruction. One such procedure is peer tutoring in which older students who are more knowledgeable teach younger ones. If well structured, peer tutoring includes a number of desirable features: It provides ongoing individualized instruction, social supports for learning, and the instructional advantage of close similarity to tutors who model sociocognitive skills and valuation of learning in the process of teaching the subject matter. In fulfilling the instructor role, tutors gain better mastery of academic domains, develop social and communication skills, and verify their own scholastic efficacy. Therefore, not only do tutored students improve academically, but tutors benefit as well (Cohen, 1986).

Cooperative learning strategies, in which students work together and help one another, are also used extensively in the accelerated school. Cooperative structures generally promote more positive self-evaluation and higher academic attainments than do individualistic or competitive ones (Ames, 1984; Johnson & Johnson, 1985). Cooperative learning is especially beneficial in heterogeneous classrooms with educationally disadvantaged and culturally diverse students. They differ in social status, academic skills, and access to educational resources. Group learning must be interdependently structured, however; otherwise, the preexisting status hierarchies and inequities get even more deeply entrenched. Under unstructured cooperative learning, high achievers dominate the academic activities and thrive intellectually, whereas low achievers get relegated to subordinate positions where they suffer further losses in academic interest, perceived efficacy, and achievement. These adverse effects create further barriers to participation and learning. Disadvantaged ethnic minorities are most likely to find themselves at the bottom of status hierarchies. To rectify this problem, Cohen and her colleagues (Cohen, 1990; 1993) devised intellectually challenging curricula in which academic tasks must be solved cooperatively by drawing on many different skills and role assignments. In this way, tasks, specialized skills, and roles are linked interdependently. The interdependent curricular structure enables each student to make a significant contribution to the group's success. As a result, students gain acceptance and perceived competence by their peers and achieve substantial academic progress.

Another distinguishing feature of the accelerated school is its emphasis on building on the existing strengths of the students, staff, parents, and community. Any special abilities the children possess are used to accelerate learning. In nonaccelerated schools, the talents of staff members and parents are usually underused. Teachers are urged to generate productive ideas for promoting students' progress. In school programs, families are encouraged to exercise their inherent strengths and to share their cultural and ethnic uniqueness.

In a school climate that values diversity united by common purposes, ethnicity becomes an enriching contribution to the educational process rather than a barrier to intellectual development or to a sense of common civic responsibility.

A key element in accelerated schools is the heavy parental involvement in the education of their children. Parents serve on the governance body and various task-oriented committees and assist with school programs. They are taught how to increase their children's involvement in school matters, set academic standards, and monitor and help them with their academic assignments. Students are given homework assignments to help them gain skill in self-directed learning. The school also draws on community resources. Retirees and personnel from local businesses are enlisted to assist teachers.

Although both the Comer and Levin models for school improvement include self-governance and extensive parental involvement as vital elements, they differ in some important respects. Comer relies heavily on a positive interpersonal climate to promote educational growth, whereas Levin makes greater use of curriculum changes and a variety of proven instructional strategies to help bring this about. A positive school climate will not necessarily cultivate high-level competencies if it is lacking in educational substance and informative ongoing monitoring of children's educational progress. School restructuring can maximize intellectual benefits by combining social conditions conducive to learning with instructional practices that guide it.

Accelerated schools with prior failures can achieve impressive academic gains and declines in disciplinary problems with the same disadvantaged student populations and the same teachers and without any more resources (Levin, 1996). Achievement gains are corroborated in preliminary comparative studies with matched pairs of schools. Students show increased academic achievement in accelerated schools but declines in control schools over the same period. Such results with individual schools, while most promising, require confirmation by more extensive controlled studies that include ongoing assessment of quality of implementation. This is easy to prescribe but difficult to do. It takes time to restructure schools. Educational administrators are understandably reluctant to assign some of their schools, over a long period, to control conditions that deny them programs for self-improvement. Moreover, some schools that are randomly selected for structural change may be set against the reforms imposed upon them and thus subvert their implementation. In addition to the control group design, reformative school practices can be evaluated by implementing them in different schools at staggered points in time. If the reforms are effective, schools that receive them should show greater academic gains than those still in the baseline condition. The staggered baseline design, however, requires that schools be adequately matched on relevant characteristics and that other educational changes not be introduced during the comparative period. Educational innovations have been hailed enthusiastically in the past only to be later retired by close empirical scrutiny. All too often, premature widespread diffusion, driven by the urgency of educational problems, precedes empirical verification of the model being diffused.

If self-empowering schools can transform failing systems into academically distinguished ones for disadvantaged students with little or no new resources, it does not mean that society need not invest additional resources in its educational enterprises or remedy the many demoralizing conditions endemic to the teaching profession. The academic successes are achieved through heavy investment of uncompensated time and effort added to already overloaded work schedules of teachers. School staff must be provided with the time required to gain understanding of and skill in the new practices. This can be achieved by restructuring teaching schedules and using an experienced cadre of substitute teachers to release the participating faculty for training during the workday and provide them with intensive in-service training outside the school sessions (Levine, 1991). Provision of helpful resources tied to a system of accountability rooted in performance evaluation can make school successes more prevalent and easier to achieve.

Implementation Models for School Enhancement

There are no quick fixes to educational maladies. The impediments to educational innovation have many sources and take many forms. Instituting innovations adds to teachers' already heavy workloads. Having previously seen touted educational reforms fall victim to their own inflated claims, many teachers meet proffered remedies with indifference or masked resistance. Teachers' sense of efficacy is one of the best predictors of their willingness to adopt new educational practices and to stick with them (Berman & McLaughlin, 1977). Educational staff whose sense of instructional efficacy has been eroded in schools populated with failing students tend to view new efforts to raise their schools' attainments as another exercise in futility. If the innovations lack programmatic specificity, even more receptive members do not change their practices because they do not know what to do or they misapply what was intended, with negative results. The leadership of the principal plays a vital role in adoption and continuance of new educational practices. Getting principals to share authority is no easy task. Some are reluctant to share power for fear that it will only create a gridlock of rivalries over which they will have to preside. Successful trial provides the best reassurance, but skepticism undermines serious trial efforts. Nor will parents, who feel alienated and consider themselves ill-equipped to deal with school affairs, be especially eager to take on the restructuring of their school system. The various constituencies must learn to work collaboratively. They need confirming experiences that they can influence the socioeducational life of the school. In the face of many barriers to change, new modes of governance and school practices prescribed from above are likely to be resisted by school staff or implemented half-heartedly as mere add-ons in ways that ensure their failure and quick discontinuance.

It takes time, hard work and a robust sense of efficacy to build the broad-based support needed to transform ineffectual schools into successful ones. Eventually, all constituencies benefit from school improvement. Teachers gain the advantage of a positive school climate in which the prevailing expectations and norms support educational development. Such changes enable them to devote their efforts to instruction rather than to serving as disciplinarians of students who have a high sense of futility about their academic learning. Principals find it easier and more rewarding to manage schools characterized by mutual trust, respect, and dedicated partnership. Parents gain a communal bond to their schools and the considerable satisfaction of seeing their children achieve academic success. Because it takes time and a lot of hard work by all the constituencies working in concert to turn deficient schools around, it is not uncommon for promising programs to be poorly implemented or aborted before any benefits can be realized. This is especially true when the school staff itself doubts that the required changes are achievable without heavy infusion of new resources.

The conceptual and operational models for building effective schools, just described, share many common features that characterize effective schools. Levin put it well when he noted that the field of education does not suffer from a shortage of good ideas but from a shortage of effective means of implementing them. Designing an efficacious school is one thing. Implementing it successfully is quite another. Major work remains to be done in devising and testing effective implementation models for creating a strong sense of collective school efficacy. That is the vital, but weakest, factor in the models of educational change. Implementation programs typically try to do too much with too little in too short a time. Informative evaluation research requires assessment of quality of implementation; otherwise, there is no way of knowing whether weak results reflect a deficient model or deficient application of a good one.

In the Comer model, principals; administrators; and subsets of teachers, parents, and counselors participate in an extended workshop where they receive didactic and videotaped instruction in the principles of child development, the structure of the model, and its application in multiethnic schools. Potential adopters also observe how the key components operate in a school that is applying the model successfully. A person from the school district is trained as a facilitator who conducts the staff training in the local setting and oversees the implementation of the program.

The implementation model for the Levin accelerated schools similarly relies heavily on the workshop format. School staff are instructed on how to create an accelerated school in which the principles of unity of purpose, school-based empowerment, and building on strengths govern all school activities. A receptive school within the district is first restructured to serve as a training site and to provide the power of successful example to embolden wary adopters. Regional training centers linked through an electronic network that provides ready access to new information on different aspects of accelerated schools serve to promote the dissemination of the model. Serious questions remain about whether brief didactic training can serve as an adequate vehicle of implementation, however.

Variability in quality of implementation underscores the need for more intensive training of implementers in the local sites. Educational systems operate within a sociopolitical context. It is in regard to interventions that power relations get played out in ways that all too often impede change. The various constituencies in a community have different self-interests and views on how schools should be run. Modes of implementation must go beyond didactic instruction to guidance on how to enlist the broad-based support needed to alter the governance and social practices of schools.

The development of implementational strategies must be of primary concern to any model of school development. No model, however promising, will have much social impact if its successful application is left to the vagaries of local circumstances. As previously noted, the normative reactions to innovations include a heavy blend of indifference, cynicism, and active resistance that can easily override more accepting factions. Some of the strategies needed to overcome entrenched instructional practices are discussed in the chapter on collective efficacy and will not be reviewed here. With regard to promoting adoption, a model for educational change must provide explicit guidelines for how to enlist and develop local leaders who can serve as effective emissaries for the program to the community and help to transform factional political disputes to a collective sense of responsibility for improving the schools. A system of communication must be developed to inform parents of the educational benefits achieved by other school districts that have adopted the model. Given widespread apathy, advocates must devise ways of reaching the families in the community rather than waiting for the parents to come to them. Other strategies address the issues of how to reconcile conflicting interests, develop a common sense of mission and purpose, and mobilize community support for educational improvement.

Another vital component of an effective model of implementation is staff development to ensure that the required structures and practices are implemented successfully. The creation of cooperative partnerships, new styles of school management, school climates conducive to learning, and communal bonds in fragmented communities do not come easily or without social strains. These implementational roles and skills are difficult to master. The school staff and their various constituencies need intensive on-site training during the formative period through videotaped modeling, guided practice, and corrective feedback about how to translate the conceptual model into desired school practices. With staff members who doubt that they can exercise much influence over apathetic students and who view innovations skeptically, staff training must build a sense of instructional efficacy as well as skill in new school practices. Explicit subgoals of change with feedback of progress can lessen mistrust and aid restoration of a sense of collective school efficacy. It is especially important to provide efficacy-building social supports during early phases of implementations when discouragement over inevitable problems can set in fast.

School staff members are more likely to adopt new practices and continue to use them if they have a sense of ownership of the program (Berman & McLaughlin, 1977). They work harder at implementing innovations and derive a greater sense of efficacy and satisfaction from their accomplishments. Therefore, promoters of school improvement should help school staff members to help themselves rather than imposing new practices on them. A generic model usually requires some adaptation to particular local conditions. A sense of ownership can be fostered by having school staff play an active role in devising the ways in which the general principles of a model can best be translated into effective practice in their setting. Local adaptations should be made within the guidelines of the school development model, however. Otherwise, if left to their own devices, people adopt the trappings of a model without making the fundamental changes it requires. In short, the major features of the model are prescriptive but its local adaptation is collaborative. After the elements of the program are in place, the quality of implementation must be assessed periodically to determine how well the various components are working by themselves and with one another. Such probes of how the social system is functioning identify the needed corrective adjustments to ensure that the program is being implemented productively. And finally, effective social mechanisms must be created for replacing leadership and staff members who remain recalcitrant to essential changes despite substantial offers of assistance.

7

Health Functioning

In recent years, we have witnessed a major change in the conception of human health and illness. The traditional approaches relied on a biomedical model that places heavy emphasis on infectious agents, ameliorative medications, and repair of physical impairments. The newer approaches adopt a much broader biopsychosocial model (Engel, 1977). Viewed from this broader biopsychosocial perspective, health and disease are the products of interactions among psychosocial and biological factors. Analysis of psychobiological linkages reveals that psychosocial factors affect biological systems in ways that can impair bodily functions and alter vulnerability to infectious agents (Ader & Cohen, 1993; Bandura, 1991a; Cohen & Herbert, 1996). Moreover, health habits exert a major impact on the quality of psychological and physical well-being. Many chronic health problems are partly the cumulative products of unhealthy behaviors and harmful environmental conditions. As health economists fully document, medical care cannot substitute for healthful habits and environmental conditions (Fuchs, 1974; Lindsay, 1980). Self-management of habits that promote health is good medicine.

Health is not merely the absence of physical impairment and disease. The biopsychosocial perspective not only underscores the multiple determination of health functioning but also emphasizes health enhancement and disease prevention. This orientation is a major change from a disease model to a health model. It is just as meaningful to speak of degrees of vitality as of degrees of impairment. Thus, for example, there are different levels of immunocompetence; cardiovascular robustness; physical strength, stamina, and flexibility; and quality of cognitive functioning. Health enhancement seeks to raise the level of psychobiological functioning and slow the rate of biological aging.

In a comprehensive analysis of mortality rates within and between countries, Fuchs (1974) has shown that expenditures for medical care have only a small impact on life expectancy. Improvements in the quality of preventive medicine and immunization programs have extended life expectancy. Apart from genetic endowment, however, physical health is largely determined by lifestyle habits and environmental conditions. People suffer physical impairments and die prematurely mostly because of preventable detrimental habits. Their nutritional habits place them at risk for cardiovascular diseases and certain types of cancer; being sedentary weakens cardiovascular capabilities and vitality; cigarette smoking creates a major health hazard for cancer, respiratory disorders, and heart disease; alcohol and drug abuse take a heavy toll on the body; sexually transmitted diseases can produce serious health consequences; people are maimed or their lives cut short by physical violence and other activities fraught with physical risks; and dysfunctional ways of coping with stressors can impair the immune system's ability to fight disease.

With regard to injurious environmental conditions, industrial and agricultural practices inject carcinogens and harmful pollutants into the air we breathe, the food we eat, and the water we drink, all of which take a heavy toll on the body. From the psychobiological perspective on health, changing lifestyle habits and environmental conditions yields large health benefits. The substantial decline in premature mortality and morbidity has resulted more from widespread adoption of healthier lifestyles than from medical technologies. Health benefits are accelerated by community-wide efforts to reduce habits that impair health (Puska, Nissinen, Salonen, & Toumilehto, 1983). Psychosocial methods have become the major public health tool.

Fries and Crapo (1981) have marshaled a large body of evidence that the upper limit of the human life span is fixed biologically. People are equipped with reserves in organ functions far in excess of what they need. As they grow older, they experience a gradual decline in the large biological reserve, which increases susceptibility to disease and debility. The elimination of infectious diseases has increased life expectancy, so that minor dysfunctions have more time to develop into chronic diseases. Figure 7.1 shows the mortality curves for the United States at different periods of time. People are now living longer. For example, about 30 percent of the people lived to age 70 in 1900, whereas over 75 percent reached that age in 1980. Psychosocial factors partly determine how much of the potential life span is realized and the quality of life that is lived. By exercising control over modifiable behavioral factors that slow the process of aging and forestall the

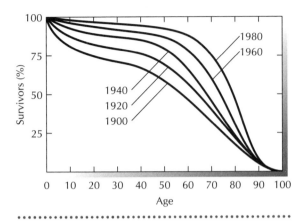

FIGURE 7.1. National survival curves in the United States for different periods of time. In the ideal survival curve for a society, people exercise control over modifiable aspects of disease and aging so that they live their expanded life span with minimum dysfunction. (Fries, 1989)

development of chronic diseases and disabilities, people live not only longer but healthier. The goal is to enable people to live their expanded life span productively with minimum dysfunction, pain, and dependence. By delaying the onset of dysfunction, the physical problems of "old age" get compressed into a short period at the very end of the life span (Butler & Brody, 1995). One makes a rapid, dignified exit when a vital system finally gives out.

The biomedical approaches that are heavily oriented toward treating bodily dysfunctions are limited in how much they can contribute to the quality of health in a society. Disease-oriented services may alleviate some of the adverse effects of debilities and provide some relief from ailments. But physicians cannot restore what detrimental habits have impaired. Chronic, degenerative diseases, which are increasing in prevalence as people live longer, further underscore the limitations of biomedical approaches developed primarily to treat acute illnesses. Biomedical research increases our understanding of the biochemical process of disease and aging. But these processes are heavily influenced by modifiable behavioral and environmental factors. Thus, a broad socially oriented approach is needed to enhance and maintain physical well-being in the society at large. People's health is partly in their own hands rather than in those of physicians. As a comedian who sipped generously of distilled spirits once remarked: "Had I known I would live this long, I would have taken better care of myself." To prevent the ravages of disease, people must be provided with the knowledge and skills needed to exercise control over their habits and the environmental conditions that impair their health.

Psychosocial approaches to health are not confined to habits that contribute directly to health status. Dangerous microbes are breaking out of their isolated locales and creating emerging diseases, such as AIDS, that are transmitted behaviorally. Knowledge of how a disease is contracted provides the basis for preventive environmental and behavioral programs to control its spread. Indeed, the McKinlays marshal an impressive body of evidence that marked declines in infectious diseases, commonly attributed to vaccines, actually occur prior to the introduction of the vaccines (McKinlay & McKinlay, 1986). This is true for the major infectious diseases except poliomyelitis. Across all disease sources, nonmedical practices account for the major share of the decline in mortality. These findings underscore the need to enlist psychosocial influences in the control of infectious diseases. Instead, a conceptual virus pervades the health field that trivializes psychosocial approaches by regarding them as merely stopgap measures until vaccines or treatments are discovered. This type of attitude reflects how disappointingly little has been learned from past experiences with behaviorally transmitted diseases.

Some viruses have thwarted our efforts to develop vaccines or antiviral treatments; for example, sexually transmitted diseases, such as gonorrhea and syphilis, have been with us for ages. The rapidly mutatable AIDS virus has effectively foiled our advanced biotechnology. Defeating AIDS would require new vaccines for changing viral strains. Even the more limited goal of slowing the progress of diseases or keeping them in check with antiviral medications presents major problems of compliance with drug regimens. To further complicate the problem, drugs that attack nonresistant viral strains spawn more virulent strains that resist the drugs. Discovery of effective treatments lowers the prevalence of a disease but does not eradicate it. Extensive worldwide travel magnifies the risk of exposing populations to deadly microbes. Medical measures can breed complacency. For example, with the development of a simple treatment for venereal disease, support for psychosocial control programs was curtailed, which resulted in a rise in infection rates (Cutler & Arnold, 1988). The history of efforts to control diseases transmitted by behavior underscores the need for a multifaceted approach combining medical measures with psychosocial preventive programs. It is not that psychosocial preventive programs are of value because they provide the only means available to stem the spread of infectious disease in the absence of vaccines or effective treatments; it is that psychosocial programs constitute an integral part of a multifaceted public health strategy not only before but also after effective treatments are found. The lessons from the past with regard to behaviorally transmitted diseases should not be lost as we attempt to deal with newly emerging viral diseases.

There are two levels of research on the psychosocial determinants of health functioning in which perceived self-efficacy plays an influential role. The more basic level examines how perceived coping efficacy affects the biological systems that mediate health and disease. The second level studies the exercise of direct control over modifiable behavioral and environmental determinants of health status and the rate of aging. This chapter examines the biochemical effects of perceived efficacy and the impact of perceived efficacy on health status and functioning through its effects on health habits. A substantial part of medical practice centers on diagnosing physical dysfunctions and prescribing remedies for them. The psychological aspects of these prognostic and remedial activities have received surprisingly little attention. A section of this chapter is devoted to an analysis of how prognostic judgments and medical interventions alter beliefs of personal efficacy in ways that can affect health outcomes. The research conducted within the conceptual framework of social cognitive theory has added greatly to our understanding of self-regulative processes. This body of knowledge provides explicit guidelines for how to structure psychosocial programs to produce widespread changes in health habits and how to restructure medical services to enhance their effectiveness and social impact. The main features of effective self-regulative programs for health promotion, disease prevention, and rehabilitation are also presented in this chapter.

of progression of disease (Peterson & Stunkard, 1989; Schneiderman, McCabe, & Baum, 1992; Steptoe & Appels, 1989).

The issues of major interest are the direction of causation and the mechanisms by which lack of perceived control over stressors produce adverse health outcomes. These questions are best addressed by converging evidence from experimental studies of the impact of perceived control on biological systems that govern health functioning and from prospective longitudinal studies of the relationship of stressful life events to health status, with statistical controls for other possible contributing factors.

BIOLOGICAL EFFECTS OF PERCEIVED SELF-EFFICACY

A sense of efficacy can activate a wide range of biological processes that mediate human health and disease. Many of these biological effects of efficacy beliefs arise while coping with acute or chronic stressors in everyday life. Stress, an emotional state generated by perceived threats and taxing demands, has been implicated as an important contributor to many physical dysfunctions (Krantz, Grunberg, & Baum, 1985). Experiments, performed mainly with animals, have identified controllability as a key organizing principle in explaining the biological effects of stress. Exposure to stressors with the ability to control them has no adverse physical effects. Exposure to the same stressors without the ability to control them activates neuroendocrine, catecholamine, and opioid systems and impairs the functioning of the immune system (Bandura, 1991a; Maier, Laudenslager, & Ryan, 1985; Shavit & Martin, 1987). The intensity and chronicity of human stress is governed largely by perceived control over the demands of one's life. Epidemiological and correlational studies indicate that lack of behavioral or perceived control over environmental demands increases susceptibility to bacterial and viral infections, contributes to the development of physical disorders and accelerates the rate

Biochemical Effects of Perceived Self-Efficacy in Coping with Stressors

Social cognitive theory views stress reactions primarily in terms of a low sense of efficacy to exercise control over aversive threats and taxing environmental demands. As previously shown, if people believe they can deal effectively with environmental stressors, they are not perturbed by them. But if they believe they cannot control aversive circumstances, they distress themselves and impair their level of functioning. Our understanding of the biological effects of exposure to uncontrollable stressors is based mainly on experimentation with animals involving uncontrollable physical stressors. Stressors take diverse forms and can produce different patterns of physiological activation. This limits extrapolation of conclusions across different species, stressors, and patterns of controllability. Uncontrollable physical stressors are not only stressful but also inflict some physical trauma that can activate confounding physiological processes. Most of the important stressors with which humans have to cope involve psychological threats (Lazarus & Folkman, 1984). Moreover, stress reactions are governed largely by beliefs of coping efficacy rather than being triggered directly by the objective properties of threats and environmental demands (Bandura, 1988c). It is the perception of life events as overwhelming one's coping capabilities that becomes the stressful reality.

Efforts to verify that a low sense of efficacy to manage stressors can impair human health have relied extensively on correlational or quasi-experimental studies. The incidence of stressful life events is related to indices of biological functioning or to infectious illnesses. The evidence shows that exposure to uncontrollable stressors is correlated with illness. Such studies, however, leave some ambiguity about the source and direction of causality. If other potential influences are overlooked, it is difficult to evaluate whether the observed biological effects are due to the stressor or to other unsuspected factors operating at the time. Studies in which potential determinants are controlled provide more persuasive evidence of psychosocial contribution. The common cold, which plagues us all from time to time, provides but one example of the power of psychological stress to increase susceptibility to viral infection (Cohen, Tyrrell, & Smith, 1991). People reporting different levels of life stress were given nasal drops containing one of five respiratory viruses or neutral saline. They were then quarantined and monitored for incidence of infection as indicated by antibody increases and development of cold symptoms. The higher the life stress, the higher was the rate of respiratory infection and cold symptoms. The relationship between stress and vulnerability to infectious illness is not altered when the influence of other possible determinants is removed. Whereas stress can impair immune function, positive mood can enhance it. Stone and his colleagues examined how fluctuations in pleasant and aversive experiences in everyday life affected protective antibody response to an orally ingested antigen (Stone et al., 1994). Antibody levels were higher on pleasant days but lower on aversive ones.

Causality is best verified, of course, through experimentation in which the relevant psychosocial determinant is systematically varied and its health-related effects are assessed. This approach cannot be applied where the determinant is not easy to create or it would be unethical to do so because it could have adverse health effects. To overcome these problems, we devised a research paradigm combining preexisting phobic stressors that plague people's lives with a mastery treatment that instills a strong sense of coping efficacy and permanently eliminates this source of stress. This paradigm enabled us to examine how changes in perceived coping efficacy affect biological systems under laboratory conditions with a high degree of control over other possible sources of influence. Participants cope with a uniform stressor that can be varied in intensity. Because a high sense of controlling efficacy can be quickly instilled in everyone through guided mastery experiences, we can create conditions of exposure to chronic stressors with, and without, perceived controlling efficacy. By the end of each study, the phobia is eradicated in all participants, so they all gain lasting relief from a chronic stressor while contributing to knowledge. The findings of these experiments reveal that perceived coping efficacy operates as a critical cognitive mediator of biological stress reactions.

Autonomic Activation

In the studies of autonomic activation, phobics' perceived coping efficacy was raised to different levels by modeling or mastery experiences. They were then tested for their level of subjective stress and of autonomic activation in response to progressively more intimidating interactions with the phobic threat (Bandura et al., 1982). Following the measurement of stress reactions, the phobics underwent guided mastery experiences until they perceived themselves to be maximally efficacious for all the previous coping activities. Then their autonomic reactions were measured again.

Figure 7.2 shows the change from the baseline level of heart rate and blood pressure under different strengths of perceived coping efficacy. Snake phobics were viscerally unperturbed by coping tasks they regarded with utmost self-efficacy. On tasks about which they had moderate doubts about their coping efficacy, however, their heart rate accelerated and their blood pressure rose during anticipation and performance of the intimidating activities. When presented with coping tasks in their perceived weak efficacy range, they promptly

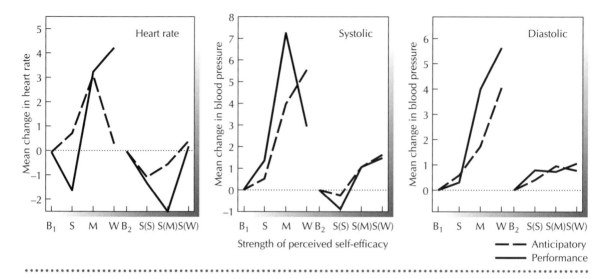

FIGURE 7.2. Mean change from the baseline level in heart rate and blood pressure during anticipatory and performance periods as a function of differential strength of perceived efficacy. B refers to baseline level, and S, M, and W signify strong, medium, and weak efficacy beliefs. For each physiological measure, the lines on the left in each panel show the autonomic reactions related to efficacy beliefs of differing strengths (performance arousal at perceived weak self-efficacy is based on only a few subjects who were able to execute only partial performances). The lines on the right of the same panel show the autonomic reactions to the same set of tasks after efficacy beliefs were strengthened to the maximal level. (Bandura, Reese, & Adams, 1982)

rejected them as too far beyond their coping capabilities. Indeed, only a few of the phobics were able to do any of them, so there was little performance-related arousal to analyze. But data from the anticipatory phase shed light on how autonomic reactions change when people withdraw from transactions with threats they judge will overwhelm their coping capabilities. Cardiac reactivity promptly declined, but blood pressure continued to climb. After beliefs of coping efficacy were strengthened to the maximal level, everyone performed these previously intimidating tasks without any rise in autonomic activation.

Heart rate is affected more quickly than blood pressure by withdrawal from intimidating task demands. This may explain the different pattern of autonomic reactivity at the low level of perceived efficacy. Catecholamines, which govern autonomic activity, are released in different temporal patterns during encounters with external stressors (Mefford et al., 1981). Heart rate is especially sensitive to momentary changes in catecholamine pattern; epinephrine, which is rapidly released, has a more pronounced effect on cardiac activity than on arterial blood pressure.

Gerin and his colleagues provide further evidence about the role of perceived coping efficacy in cardiovascular reactivity to cognitive stressors (Gerin et al., 1995). When task demands are personally controllable, people whose perceived coping efficacy was illusorily raised achieved higher levels of performance with lower blood pressure and cardiac reactivity than those whose efficacy beliefs were illusorily lowered. When situations impose constraints on personal initiative, the benefits of a sense of efficacy are better realized by supporting courses of action designed to relax the constraints than they are by struggling with them.

Catecholamine Activation

Investigation of the biochemical effects of a low sense of efficacy was further extended by linking strength of perceived coping efficacy to plasma catecholamine secretion (Bandura et al., 1985). Catecholamines are neurotransmitters that play a crucial role in brain-body mechanisms and in stress-related hormones that mobilize bodily systems to deal with perceived threats. Intense and prolonged physiological mobilization can have deleterious effects. In examining catecholamine activation, the range of perceived coping efficacy in severe phobics was broadened by having them observe models managing the phobic threats successfully. The models conveyed predictive information about the characteristic actions of the phobic objects and demonstrated effective strategies for exercising control over them. The participants were then presented with coping tasks they had previously judged to be in their low, medium, and high efficacy range, during which continuous blood samples were obtained through a catheter.

Figure 7.3 shows the microrelationship between efficacy beliefs and plasma catecholamine secretion.

Catecholamine secretions essentially mirror strength of beliefs of coping efficacy. Levels of epinephrine, norepinephrine, and dopac, a dopamine metabolite, were low when phobics coped with threats they believed they could control. Self-doubts in coping efficacy produced substantial increases in these catecholamines. When presented with tasks that exceeded their perceived coping capabilities, the phobics instantly rejected them. With removal of the threat, catecholamines dropped sharply.

The dopac response differs markedly from that of the other catecholamines. Whereas epinephrine and norepinephrine dropped upon rejection of the threatening task, dopac rose to its highest level, even though the phobics had no intention of coping with the threat. Dopac seems to be triggered by the mere perception that environmental demands would overwhelm one's coping capabilities. These data suggest that under some conditions, plasma dopac could reflect activity of brain dopamine neurons. After perceived coping efficacy was strengthened to the maximal level by guided mastery, performance of the previously intimidating tasks no longer elicited differential catecholamine

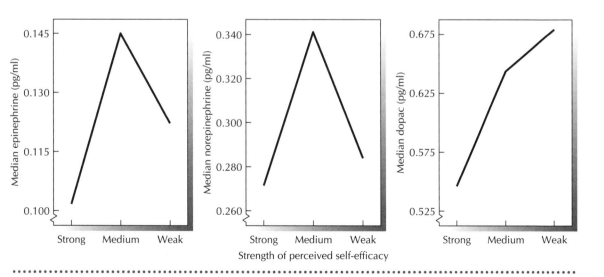

FIGURE 7.3. Microrelationships among weak, medium, and strong beliefs of coping efficacy and level of plasma catecholamine secretion. The coping task corresponding to the weak sense of efficacy was rejected by the participants, thus removing the threat. (Bandura et al., 1985)

secretions. Thus, the elevated catecholamine secretions observed in the initial test resulted from a perceived mismatch between coping capabilities and task demands, rather than from properties inherent in the coping tasks themselves.

The crucial role of controllability in biological activation is further shown in microanalysis of changes in catecholamine secretion as phobics gain mastery over phobic threats through guided mastery treatment (Bandura et al., 1985). Figure 7.4 presents the plasma catecholamine levels at five distinct phases in treatment. During the initial phases, when phobics lacked a sense of coping efficacy, even the mere sight of, or minimal contact with, the phobic threat activated catecholamine responses. After they gained controlling efficacy, their catecholamine reactivity dropped and remained relatively low, even on the most intimidating interactions. When participants were asked to relinquish all control, which left them completely vulnerable, catecholamine reactivity promptly rose. This pattern of results supports a mechanism involving controllability rather than simple extinction or adaptation over time.

We saw in an earlier chapter that autonomic arousal to stressors is reduced by belief that one

can wield control over them, even though that controlling capability is unexercised. Choosing not to exercise control at a particular time, but being able to do so whenever one wants to, should be distinguished from relinquished control in which one is deprived of all means of control while subjected to stressors. Relinquished control leaves one completely vulnerable, whereas freely usable control, even though unexercised on a particular occasion, leaves one in full command. In sum, examination of various stressors and biological expressions of stress under different levels of perceived coping efficacy yield uniform findings. Beliefs of coping efficacy affect the perceived threateningness of the environment. Perceived coping inefficacy is accompanied by elevated biological stress reactions, but the same threats are managed without stress when beliefs of coping efficacy are strengthened.

Opioid Activation

The body produces its own painkillers called endorphins. Aversive stimulation triggers release of these morphinelike chemicals, which block neural transmission of pain impulses. Endogenous opioids play a paramount role in the regulation of pain and in mediating the effects of uncontrollable stressors on immunocompetence (Kelley, 1986; Shavit & Martin, 1987). Studies with animals subjected to painful stimulation show that stress can activate endogenous opioids that block pain transmission (Fanselow, 1986). Opioid involvement is indicated by evidence that insensitivity to pain is reduced by opiate blockers. It is not the physically painful stimulation, per se, but the psychological stress over its uncontrollability that seems to be a key factor in opioid activation (Maier, 1986). Animals that can turn off shock stimulation show no opioid activation, whereas yoked animals that experience the same shock stimulation without being able to control the offset of the shock give evidence of stress-activated opioids.

In human adaptation, it is a sense of perceived inefficacy to cope with taxing environmental demands that produces endogenous opioid

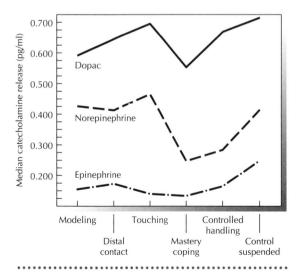

FIGURE 7.4. Changes in level of catecholamine secretion as phobics master effective coping techniques through guided mastery treatment. (Bandura et al., 1985)

activation (Bandura et al., 1988). Different levels of perceived coping efficacy were created by having people exercise control over the pace of cognitive demands or by having the same demands controlled externally at a pace that strained cognitive capabilities. A strong sense of efficacy to manage the cognitive workload was accompanied by low stress, whereas a weak sense of efficacy produced high subjective stress and autonomic arousal. Naloxone is a substance that blocks the analgesic action of opioids by attaching to the opiate receptors. To test for opioid activation, participants were administered either naloxone or an inert saline solution. They were then tested at periodic intervals for how long they could tolerate mounting pain in their hand, which was immersed in ice cold water. Efficacious individuals, whose high sense of control kept stress low, gave no evidence of opioid activation; their pain tolerance was unaffected by naloxone (Fig. 7.5). In contrast, those of low perceived efficacy, who experienced high stress, gave evidence of opioid-mediated analgesia. They displayed high pain tolerance under saline, but found pain difficult to bear under naloxone opioid blockage.

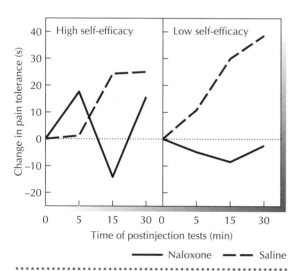

FIGURE 7.5. Change in pain tolerance as a function of (1) perceived self-efficacy to exercise control over cognitive demands and (2) whether people received saline or the opiate antagonist, naloxone. (Bandura et al., 1988)

Opioid and Cognitive Mechanisms in Pain Control

Pain is a complex psychobiologic phenomenon influenced by psychosocial factors, rather than simply a sensory experience arising directly from stimulation of pain receptors. The same intensity of pain stimulation can give rise to different levels of conscious pain depending on how attention is deployed, how the experience is appraised cognitively, the coping strategies used to modulate pain, and how others are observed to react to painful stimulation (Cioffi, 1991a; Craig, 1986; Turk, Meichenbaum, & Genest, 1983). Pain can be regulated through different mechanisms. We have already examined how pain sensations can be counteracted by opioid blockage of neural transmission of pain impulses. Pain can also be regulated by nonopioid brain processes. These include attentional and other cognitive activities that reduce consciousness of pain sensations or alter their aversiveness by how they are construed.

The Rosses (1984) provide vivid examples of cognitive pain control techniques discovered by children on their own. Many relied on attentional strategies. An 11-year old boy described how he reduces the experience of pain by competing thoughts that command attention: "When the dentist says, 'Open,' I have to say the Pledge of Allegiance to the Flag backwards three times before I even am allowed to think about the drill. Once he got all finished before I did." Whatever children discover works in coping with stress, they use it to manage pain as well. An 8-year old boy described the multipurpose value of the cognitive distraction technique: "I can get through most anything as long as there's something to count — like those little holes in the squares on the ceiling at the dentist. When I got sent to the school office for getting into trouble, I saw all the principal's freckles. The whole time he was giving it to me, I started at the top of his face and counted his freckles all the way down."

When pain sensations are hard to displace from consciousness, they are easier to bear if their meaning is transformed. An 8-year old girl coped effectively with a painful ear procedure by cognitive reconstrual: "I pretended I was in a space ship and the pressure was making my ears hurt and I was the only one who could get it back to earth." The cognitive transformation of the pain situation can take quite an elaborate form, as this next child reveals: "As soon as I get in the dentist chair, I pretend he's the enemy and I'm a secret agent and he's torturing me to get secrets and if I make one sound, I'm telling him secret information, so I never do. I'm going to be a secret agent when I grow up so this is good practice." Occasionally, he got carried away with his fantasy roleplaying. One time the dentist asked him to rinse his mouth. Much to the child's own surprise, he snarled, "I won't tell you a damn thing," which momentarily stunned the dentist.

There are several ways by which perceived coping efficacy can bring relief from pain by cognitive means. People who believe they can alleviate pain enlist whatever ameliorative skills they have learned and persevere in their efforts to reduce their discomfort. Those who judge themselves as inefficacious give up readily in the absence of quick relief. Findings of studies of chronic clinical pain accord with this view (Jensen et al., 1991). Perceived self-regulatory efficacy predicts the use of behavioral and cognitive strategies to relieve pain after controlling for pain severity and outcome expectations. Consciousness has a very limited capacity (Kahneman, 1973). It is hard to keep more than one thing in mind at the same time. If pain sensations are supplanted in consciousness, they are felt less. Dwelling on the aversiveness of pain sensations only makes them more noticeable and, thus, more difficult to bear. Perceived efficacy can lessen the extent to which painful stimulation is experienced as conscious pain by diverting attention from pain sensations to competing engrossments. For example, people can become totally oblivious to their bodily sensations while deeply engrossed in television programs or novels.

In chronic clinical pain, engrossment in meaningful activities that are attentionally demanding diverts attention from pain sensations in a more enduring fashion than trivial diversionary thought conjured up to engage one's consciousness. Trivial thought may serve as a distractor for a short time, whereas engrossing activities can fully occupy one's consciousness for hours on end without requiring deliberate effort. The absorbing continuity of the activity captures and holds attention. Control of consciousness through engrossment in activities of high interest is a positive engagement strategy rather than an avoidant or inhibitive one. Finally, people who believe they can exercise some pain control are likely to interpret unpleasant bodily sensations and states more benignly than those who believe there is nothing they can do to alleviate pain (Cioffi, 1991a). Focusing attention on the sensory, rather than the affective, aspects of pain also reduces distress and raises pain tolerance (Ahles et al., 1983).

Perceived efficacy can mediate the analgesic potency of various psychological procedures. Reese (1983) found that cognitive techniques for alleviating pain, self-relaxation, and placebos all increase perceived efficacy both to endure and to reduce pain. The more self-efficacious people judged themselves to be, the less pain they experienced in later cold pressor tests, and the higher was their pain threshold and pain tolerance. Bogus feedback that one's pain tolerance is high or low compared to that of others similarly alters people's beliefs in their efficacy to manage pain, which, in turn, affects their actual pain tolerance (Litt, 1988). Believers in their efficacy tolerate higher levels of pain; disbelievers are less able to endure pain. Arbitrarily instilled beliefs of inefficacy discourage pain coping behavior even when the opportunity to exercise personal control exists. In contrast, instilled perceived efficacy largely overrides ostensible external constraints on the exercise of personal control over pain. We saw earlier that the benefits of biofeedback training stem more from boosts in perceived coping efficacy than from the muscular exercises themselves (Holroyd et al., 1984). A high sense of efficacy, created by false feedback that one is a skilled relaxer who can control pain, predicted reduction in tension headaches, whereas actual changes in muscle activity achieved in treatment were unrelated to the incidence of subsequent headaches.

Several studies have compared the relative power of perceived efficacy to manage pain and outcome expectations of the amount of pain anticipated to predict level of pain tolerance (Williams & Kinney, 1991). Following training in different cognitive pain control techniques, efficacy beliefs predicted endurance of cold pressor pain when outcome expectations, level of experienced pain, and amount of attention devoted to pain sensations were controlled. Anticipated painful outcomes did not independently affect how much pain people could endure, however, when variations in efficacy beliefs were controlled.

Research on pain management typically centers on how efficacy to withstand or alleviate pain affects the ability to endure it. Lackner and his associates extended the analysis to beliefs in efficacy to perform physical activities essential for everyday functioning that generate pain (Lackner et al., 1996). The patients were chronic pain sufferers with low back pain. This research is of special interest because of the prevalence of low back disorders and the weak relationship between pain and functional disability. Occupationally injured patients judged their efficacy for lifting, bending, carrying, pushing, and pulling objects. To test alternative regulatory mechanisms, the patients also rated their expectations that these physical activities would cause pain and reinjury. They were then tested for how many graded levels of these physical activities they could perform. Perceived efficacy predicted physical function after controlling for pain and reinjury expectations. Neither expectations of pain intensity nor reinjury predicted level of physical function when the effects of efficacy beliefs were removed. These findings indicate that expectations of pain and catastrophic harm are largely products of perceived efficacy and, therefore, do not contribute independently to prediction of behavior that can be painful when the influence of efficacy beliefs is factored out.

That perceived efficacy makes pain easier to manage is further corroborated by other studies of acute and chronic clinical pain (Council, Ahern, Follick & Kline, 1988; Dolce, 1987; Manning and Wright, 1983; Holman & Lorig, 1992). Treatment gains in perceived efficacy to override pain not only reduce intensity of experienced pain in long-term assessments but also increase physical functioning as measured by trunk strength and range of motion and flexion-extension movements in patients suffering from degenerative disc disease (Altmaier, Russell, Kao, Lehmann, & Weinstein, 1993; Kaivanto, Estlander, Moneta, & Vanharanta, 1995). Belief that one can exercise some control over pain and one's physical functioning is also accompanied by fewer pain behaviors, less mood disturbance, better psychological well-being, and more active involvement in everyday activities (Affleck, Tennen, Pfeiffer, & Fifield, 1987; Buescher et al., 1991; Buckelew et al., 1994; Jensen & Karoly, 1991). Perceived coping efficacy predicts level of pain after controlling for disease severity, demographic factors, and depression. A strong sense of efficacy to manage pain similarly predicts use of pain medication during recovery from coronary artery surgery (Bastone & Kerns, 1995). The stronger the perceived self-efficacy assessed preoperatively, the less pain experienced and the less sleep medication taken postoperatively. Neither demographic characteristics nor medical or surgical status accounted for use of medications.

As explained earlier, efficacy beliefs affect pain by supporting palliative coping activities and the motivation to stick with them. Lin and Ward (1996) provide evidence that perceived efficacy does indeed work in part through these processes. People's beliefs in their pain-management efficacy affect the intensity of low back pain and how much it interferes with daily life both directly and by fostering the use of cognitive and behavioral strategies that help to relieve pain. In pain management, as in other activities where actions determine outcomes, the benefits people expect depend on their belief that they can perform the required activity successfully. Lin and Ward report that outcome expectations indirectly affect pain intensity and interference through coping effort. The latter finding, however, is based on an analysis of backward causation of factors in which the effect (outcome expectancies) precedes its cause (coping efficacy). Evaluation of the contribution of expected outcomes to pain management requires an analysis founded on forward causation of expectation, with coping behavior preceding the outcomes that flow from it.

At first sight, helplessness theory and self-efficacy theory appear to be at odds over how controlling efficacy relates to pain tolerance and the mechanisms mediating it. Endurance of pain is associated with deficient control over stressors in helplessness theory, but with perceived control in self-efficacy theory. There are several possible explanations for this seeming contradiction. A high sense of coping efficacy renders aversive situations less stressful, thus producing less stress-activated opioids to decrease pain. This would suggest that coping efficacy must increase pain endurance through a nonopioid cognitive mechanism. Although there may be less opioid blockage of pain, exercise of personal efficacy that occupies consciousness with engrossing matters can block awareness of pain sensations by the nonopioid cognitive mechanism.

A second plausible explanation for the paradoxical findings is the markedly different consequences of control in the types of coping situations used. Exercise of control produces entirely different conditions of pain stimulation in the situations commonly used in animal and human studies of pain. These differences would argue for some opioid involvement with high perceived efficacy. In the usual animal experimentation, control promptly terminates pain stimulation. By contrast, in the human situation, efficacious exercise of cognitive control that blocks pain sensations from consciousness enables people to tolerate high levels of pain stimulation. In so doing, perceived efficacy promotes even more active engagement in activities that can heighten the level and duration of pain stimulation. Indeed, a strong sense of coping efficacy often increases engagement in pain-producing activities to the point that it can create stressful predicaments. Thus, self-efficacious people suffering from arthritis generate pain and discomfort when they first take on more vigorous activities. Activity eventually reduces pain and swelling in the joints but increases pain and distress in the short term. Similarly, people experience mounting pain the longer they keep their hand immersed in icy water in the cold pressor task. In the latter situation, continued exercise of controlling efficacy through cognitive means eventually heightens pain to the point that it begins to overwhelm people's coping capabilities,

and they begin to experience the intense pain stimulation as unbearable. The stress of failing control with mounting pain in later stages of coping would activate opioid pain reduction systems.

In this conception of the human coping process, both opioid and nonopioid mechanisms operate in the regulation of pain, but their relative contribution varies with degree of controlling efficacy and phases of coping. A nonopioid cognitive mechanism would subserve pain tolerance, whereas cognitive control would effectively surmount pain sensations. But an opioid mechanism would come into play in later stages of coping when control becomes insufficient to attenuate mounting pain or to block it from consciousness. Thus, opioid activation would remain low during successful phases but become high during failing phases of cognitive control. Research in which exercise of personal efficacy lowers stress rather than creating mounting aversiveness that eventually overwhelms coping capabilities yields findings similar to those from studies in which control terminates physical stressors (Bandura et al., 1988).

Evidence for pain control through dual mechanisms is provided by a study in which individuals were taught cognitive methods of pain control, were administered a placebo presented as a medicinal analgesic, or received no intervention (Bandura, O'Leary, Taylor, Gauthier, & Gossard, 1987). Following the treatment phase, we measured their perceived efficacy to manage and to reduce pain and their tolerance of cold pressor pain. Participants in all conditions were then administered either naloxone, the opioid blocker, or an inert saline solution. Thereafter, their pain tolerance was measured at periodic intervals.

Training in cognitive control heightened efficacy beliefs to endure and reduce pain (Fig. 7.6). Placebo medication had a different impact on perceived efficacy to endure pain and perceived efficacy to reduce its intensity. People believed they were better able to withstand pain with the aid of a supposedly pain-relieving medication. Success in reducing experienced pain, however, depends on effective exercise of pain-reducing skills, which medication alone does not provide. Placebo medication did not persuade people that they became more capable of reducing the intensity of pain. These findings underscore the value of measuring different aspects of perceived self-efficacy in research designed to elucidate the exercise of control over pain. Efficacy beliefs predicted how well people managed pain. The stronger their beliefs in their ability to withstand pain, the longer they endured mounting pain, regardless of whether their efficacy beliefs were enhanced by cognitive means or by placebo medication. Moreover, a strong sense of efficacy to endure pain predicts tolerance of mounting pain after controlling for initial differences in pain tolerance.

The findings provide evidence for both an opioid and a nonopioid mechanism for attenuating pain by cognitive means. As can be seen in Figure 7.7, cognitive copers who were administered saline displayed a sizable increase in pain tolerance. In contrast, when pain-reducing opioids were blocked by naloxone, cognitive copers found it difficult to bear pain. Cognitive copers were able to increase their pain tolerance even under opioid blockage, however, which lends support to a nonopioid

component in the exercise of cognitive control as well. For cognitive copers administered saline, the combined effect of both opioid action and cognitive control contributed to their ability to achieve sizable increases in pain tolerance.

The correlational findings shed further light on how different forms of perceived efficacy relate to opioid activation under different modes of coping. Coping with heightened pain under opioid blockage requires the use of strategies to alleviate pain rather than mere forbearance. Efficacious pain copers would be especially distressed by their eventual inability to manage their pain effectively. Thus, the degree of opioid activation is best predicted by perceived capability to reduce pain. The stronger peoples' perceived efficacy to reduce pain, the greater the opioid activation. The strength of this relationship increased when variation in initial ability to tolerate pain was controlled.

The findings also provide some evidence that placebo medication may activate some opioid involvement. After the full time had elapsed for naloxone to exert its antagonistic effect, people given naloxone were less able to tolerate pain than

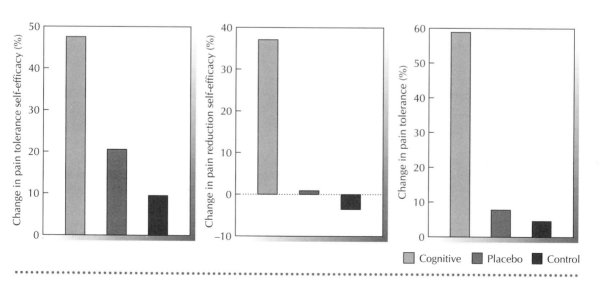

FIGURE 7.6. Change from pretest level in perceived efficacy to reduce pain and in pain tolerance achieved by people who were taught cognitive pain control techniques, administered a placebo, or received no intervention. (Bandura et al., 1987)

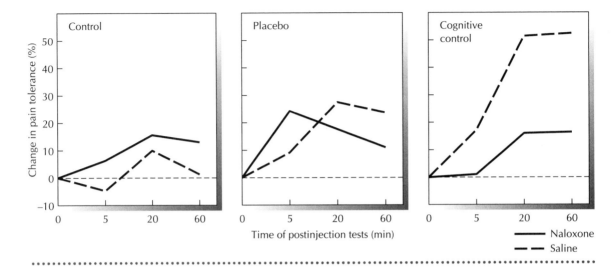

FIGURE 7.7. Change in pain tolerance from the posttreatment level at each of three postinjection periods as a function of type of treatment and whether people received saline or the opiate antagonist, naloxone. (Bandura et al., 1987)

those who had been given saline. These findings are in accord with those of Levine and his associates showing that endogenous opioids can be activated by placebo medication to reduce postoperative dental pain (Levine, Gordon, & Fields, 1978; Levine, Gordon, Jones, & Fields, 1978). A socially administered placebo produces analgesia, whereas unsignaled mechanical infusion of the placebo solution that goes undetected by patients has no analgesic effect (Levine & Gordon, 1984). Placebo-induced analgesia may involve both a nonopioid cognitive component and a stress analgetic component that is antagonizable by naloxone (Gracely, Dubner, Wolskee & Deeter, 1983). In the study discussed earlier comparing placebo and cognitive pain control, placebo medication had its major impact on perceived efficacy to withstand pain. Therefore, it was this expression of efficacy that predicted degree of opioid involvement.

So far, the discussion has focused on self-efficacious regulation of pain by cognitive override of pain sensations and stress-induced opioid activation. There is a third possible mechanism that merits consideration as well. Efficacy expectations may

directly activate the central nervous system to release pain-blocking opioids independently of stress. Animals can learn to activate their endogenous opioid systems anticipatorily in the presence of cues formerly predictive of painful experiences (Watkins & Mayer, 1982). Such findings add some credence to the possibility of direct central activation of opioid systems through learned expectations.

Pain Regulatory Efficacy in Placebo Analgesia

Placebo effects can potentiate effective medications and endow ineffective ones with therapeutic potency. Indeed, the placebo effect is so pervasive that evaluations of medications require placebo conditions to separate the contribution of psychological action and pharmacologic action. Placebos work partly through efficacy beliefs. Having been persuaded of their enhanced coping capabilities, people then behave in ways that produce beneficial effects. In the case of pain management, the strength of the placebo analgesic response is predictable from how placebos affect beliefs in the efficacy to endure pain (Bandura et al., 1987). People who judge themselves efficacious to withstand pain given the supposed medicinal aid are good pain endurers, whereas those who continue to distrust their efficacy to manage pain despite receiving the placebo medication are less able to bear pain. For people who lack assurance in their efficacy, the evident failure to achieve relief from pain, even with the help of an alleged medicinal analgesic, is only further testimony to their coping inefficacy.

The variable effects of placebos on efficacy beliefs to manage pain most likely reflect past correlated experiences with active medication. If acting on efficacy beliefs in conjunction with medication had usually brought substantial pain relief, then people would come to judge themselves more efficacious to ameliorate pain with a medicinal aid. The regulatory function of efficacy beliefs would be enlisted as well by placebo medication given on later occasions as a painkiller. The enhanced sense of coping efficacy evoked by placebo medication would activate the pain-relieving processes described earlier. In contrast, people who had often experienced little relief or heightened pain despite medication would not be at all persuaded by placebo medication that it would enable them to relieve pain. Indeed, a low sense of efficacy to exercise control over pain may even diminish the potency of genuine analgesics by discouraging the use of cognitive aids. That past correlated experiences affect how people respond to placebo medication was demonstrated by Voudouris, Peck, and Coleman (1985). They arbitrarily paired placebo medication with pain reduction for one group but with pain increases for another group. Those for whom the placebo had repeatedly brought pain relief experienced lower pain in response to painful stimulation when given a placebo, whereas those for whom the placebo previously exacerbated pain found the pain stimulation more painful when given a placebo. An appropriate next step in this line of research is to test whether the effects of positive or negative correlated experiences are mediated by changes in perceived coping efficacy to manage pain.

Combining Medications with Psychosocial Treatments

The effects of pharmaceuticals on efficacy beliefs have received scant attention but raise issues with important implications for treatments that rely solely or partly on medication. A perceived efficacy that rests entirely on medicinal aid will not survive withdrawal of medication. Chambliss and Murray (1979a, 1979b) gave smokers and obese people placebo pills but described them as medications to aid their self-control efforts. When the pills were later discontinued, the people who were left with the belief that they were aided by medication quickly reverted to their old habits, but those who were told that they succeeded through their own efforts because the medication was a placebo achieved further reductions in weight and smoking. The beliefs of children treated with drugs for hyperactivity provide vivid testimony to the readiness to ascribe psychosocial improvements to the action of medication (Whalen, 1989). In the animated words of one youngster, "It (hyperactivity) is caused by hyper cells that do bad things in your body and make you act crazy. The medicine is a little boss inside your body that sees everything that's going on in the body, even the bones. When you are acting bad, the boss sprays the bad cells with medicine, and they fall asleep, and when they wake up, they're good cells." When asked what would happen if they ceased taking their medication, some children explained that they would be socially rejected and unable to perform their schoolwork. In point of fact, medication may calm down the children socially, but the evidence is equivocal as to whether medication adds much to well-designed psychosocial programs in improving academic achievement (Gadow, 1985).

Programs that combine medication with development of self-regulatory skills can have diverse effects on efficacy beliefs depending on how the relative contributions of these two factors are cognitively appraised and weighted. If medication helps to create conditions that enable people to acquire generalizable self-regulative skills they might otherwise fail to develop, then medication can enhance perceived self-efficacy. This is most likely to occur if skill development is highlighted as they are being weaned off drugs. If medication facilitates skill development and the contribution of the skill component is emphasized whereas medication is given little weight, the medication may have no additive effect. And finally, medication can undermine the efficacy-enhancing value of skill development if coping successes are ascribed to medicinal aids rather than to improved capability. That medication can detract from the power of a psychosocial treatment was shown in a study by Craighead, Stunkard, and O'Brien (1981). An appetite suppressant, a self-management program, and a combination of these treatments produced equivalent reductions in weight. Those who lost weight with the medication alone or combined with self-management, however, rapidly regained most of the pounds they shed after the medication was withdrawn, whereas those who succeeded by self-management alone maintained most of their weight loss over a period of a year.

Treatment of depression provides another example in which medication sometimes has a negating rather than an additive effect (Simons, Murphy, Levine, & Wetzel, 1986). Sociocognitive treatment produces sustained improvement of depression, whereas adding antidepressant medication to sociocognitive treatment results in high relapse rates. Leitenberg (1995) reports a similar detracting effect of medication when added to cognitive-behavior treatment of bulimia. Some studies report peculiar findings in which adding medication to an effective sociocognitive treatment has no effect either at the time it is applied or months after the drug has been discontinued, but a small gain appears a long time later. Clearly, something other than pharmacology must be at work in this distally disjoined outcome.

Perceived Coping Self-Efficacy and Immunocompetence

Several lines of evidence suggest that psychosocial factors modulate the immune system in ways that can influence susceptibility to illness (Herbert & Cohen, 1993b; Kiecolt-Glaser & Glaser, 1988;

O'Leary, 1990). This immunoregulatory influence operates through neuroanatomical, neurochemical, and neuroendocrine linkages of the central nervous system to the immune system. Biological systems are highly interdependent. The types of biological reactions that accompany perceived coping efficacy — such as autonomic activation, catecholamines, and endogenous opioids — are involved in the regulation of the immune system. There are three major pathways through which perceived self-efficacy can affect immune function. They include mediation through stress, depression, and expectancy learning.

Stress Mediation. The inability to exercise control over potential stressors can impair immune function in ways that can be damaging to health. Exposure to intermittent stressors without the ability to control them suppresses the activity of different facets of immune function. In contrast, exposure to the same stressful events, but with efficacy to control them, has no adverse effects on immune function (Maier et al., 1985). These findings, which are based on experimentation with animals involving uncontrollable physical stressors, are quite reproducible, although they vary somewhat depending on the intensity, intermittency, and chronicity of the stressors. Because the immune cells have receptors for endogenous opioids, opioid peptides can affect immunologic processes (Plotnikoff, Faith, Murgo, & Good, 1986). There is evidence that some of the immunosuppressive affects of the inability to control stressors, such as reduced natural killer cell cytotoxicity, are mediated by the release of endogenous opioids (Shavit & Martin, 1987). When opioid mechanisms are blocked by opiate antagonists, the stress of coping inefficacy loses its immunosuppressive power.

As just mentioned, our understanding of the effects of uncontrollable stressors on immunocompetence is based mainly on experimentation with animals involving uncontrollable physical stressors. Human coping involves an important feature that is rarely examined systematically in either animal laboratory paradigms or human field studies. In animal experimentation, controllability is usually studied as an all-or-none condition. Animals either exercise complete control over physical stressors or have no control whatsoever. In contrast, human coping usually entails an ongoing process of developing and reappraising coping efficacy rather than involving an unalterable personal inefficacy in the face of unremitting bombardment by stressors. Most human stress is activated while learning how to manage environmental demands and expanding one's competencies. The challenges to competence change across the life span. Thus, coping with stressors and new mastery demands is a continuing process. Stress activated while acquiring a sense of coping efficacy is likely to be construed positively and, therefore, may have different effects than stress experienced in onerous situations with no prospect in sight of ever gaining any sense of control. There are substantial evolutionary benefits to experiencing enhanced immunocompetence during development of coping capabilities that are vital for effective adaptation. It would not be evolutionarily advantageous if acute stressors invariably impaired immune function, because they are highly prevalent in everyday life. If this were the case, people would experience high vulnerability to infective agents that would leave them chronically bedridden with infectious illnesses or quickly do them in.

Correlational and quasi-experimental studies show that exposure to stressors is usually accompanied by impairment of the immune system. This impairment is reflected in decreased lymphocyte proliferative response to mitogen stimulation, reduced number of helper T lymphocytes and natural killer cell activity, weaker immunological control over latent herpes viruses, depressed interferon production, and poorer DNA repair in lymphocytes exposed to X irradiation (Kiecolt-Glaser & Glaser, 1987). These lines of research have clarified some aspects of inefficacious control of stressors, but experimental studies are needed to remove any ambiguities about the direction of causality.

That stress aroused while gaining coping mastery over intimidating activities can enhance different components of the immune system was revealed in a study of exposure to a chronic stressor with experimentally varied perceived coping efficacy (Wiedenfeld et al., 1990). In this experiment involving extreme phobics, we measured strength of perceived coping efficacy, autonomic and neuroendocrine activation, and different aspects of the immune system at three phases: a baseline control phase involving no exposure to the phobic stressor; an efficacy acquisition phase in which phobics gained an increasing sense of coping efficacy over the stressor through guided mastery; and a perceived maximal efficacy phase during which they coped with the same stressor after they had developed a complete sense of coping efficacy.

Development of a strong sense of efficacy to control stressors enhanced different components of the immune system (Fig. 7.8). A small subgroup of individuals, however, exhibited a decrease in immune system status during the efficacy acquisition phase. The rate of efficacy acquisition is a good predictor of whether exposure to stressors enhances or attenuates the immune system. Rapid growth of perceived coping efficacy reduces stress, with concomitant immunoenhancing effects. But slow growth of perceived coping efficacy is associated with prolonged high stress and immunosuppressing effects. High autonomic and neuroendocrine activation also attenuates components of the immune system, but the impact is somewhat weaker.

Acquisition of perceived efficacy to control stressors produced more than transient changes in immunity. The increase in immunologic competence was generally sustained over time, in that the immune system status was significantly higher in the maximal perceived efficacy phase than in the baseline phase. Rapid growth of perceived efficacy also predicted maintenance of immunoenhancement during the maximal perceived efficacy phase. These findings indicate that firm mastery of chronic stressors not only instills a strong sense of efficacy but leaves lasting changes that can serve as protective factors against adverse immunologic effects of psychological stressors. Personal efficacy gained commandingly may convey a more generalized sense of coping capability than efficacy gained laboriously with prolonged stress. Hoffman (1969) has shown that uncontrollable physical stressors can create vulnerabilities that leave some sensitivity to aversive events even after acquired fears have been eliminated through repeated

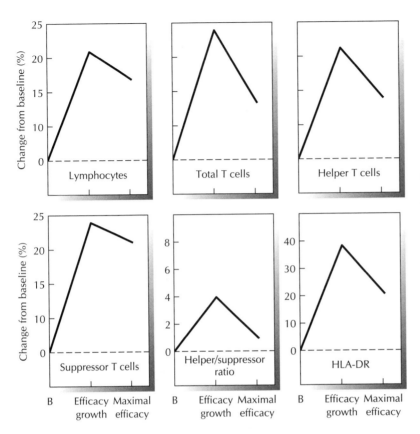

FIGURE 7.8. Changes in components of the immune system expressed as a percentage of baseline (B) values during exposure to the phobic stressor while acquiring perceived coping self-efficacy (efficacy growth) and after perceived coping self-efficacy had been developed to the maximal level (maximal efficacy). The baseline mean values for the different immune functions were as follows: total lymphocytes, 1572; T lymphocytes, 1124; helper T cells, 721; suppressor T cells, 370; helper/suppressor ratio, 2.22; HLA-DR, 216. (Wiedenfeld et al., 1990)

neutral exposure to them. Guided mastery, of course, does much more than provide neutral encounters with threats. It also equips individuals with coping strategies and a resilient sense of efficacy to exercise control over potential threats. Rapid development of perceived efficacy to exercise control over psychological stressors can thus instill a durable protection against aversive events.

These findings support other lines of evidence showing that development of skills to manage stress can enhance immunologic functioning. Stress-management skills decrease immunologic vulnerability to recurrent stressors in healthy individuals (Kiecolt-Glaser et al., 1985; Kiecolt-Glaser et al., 1986), increase immune function in metastatic cancer patients (Gruber, Hall, Hersh, & Dubois, 1988), and enhance cellular and humoral immune functioning in seropositive men in asymptomatic stages of HIV infection (Antoni et al., 1990).

Psychological analyses of health functioning have been heavily preoccupied with the physiologically debilitating effects of stressors. Self-efficacy theory, which highlights mechanisms of successful functioning, also acknowledges the physiologically strengthening effects of mastery over stressors. A growing number of studies are providing empirical support for physiological toughening by successful coping (Dienstbier, 1989). The psychosocial modulation of health functioning is concerned with the determinants and mechanisms governing the physiological toughening effects of coping with stressors as well as their debilitating effects.

Depression Mediation. Depression and bereavement have been shown to reduce immune function and to heighten susceptibility to disease. The more severe the depression, the greater the reduction in immunity (Ader & Cohen, 1993; Herbert & Cohen, 1993a). Thus, depression is often associated with increased incidence of infectious disease, development and spread of malignant neoplasms, and accelerated rate of tumor cell growth. Although the way in which depression affects immune function has not been fully explored, there is some evidence that the lower immunologic functioning is mediated mainly by affective processes rather than by concomitant behavioral changes in activity level or eating and sleeping patterns.

The latter findings indicate that another possible influence by which a weak sense of efficacy can affect immunity operates through the mediating effects of depression. We saw earlier that a low sense of personal efficacy contributes to depression in several ways. The perceived inability to fulfill stringent standards of self-worth and to secure things that bring satisfaction to one's life creates depression (Bandura, 1988b; Kanfer & Zeiss, 1983). A sense of cognitive inefficacy to turn off dejecting ruminations further contributes to the recurrence, depth, and duration of bouts of depression (Kavanagh & Wilson, 1989).

Supportive relationships help to lessen the aversive impact of adverse life events that can give rise to depression. When the perceived inefficacy involves social relationships, it can induce depression both directly and indirectly by curtailing the cultivation of the very interpersonal relationships that can provide satisfactions and buffer the effects of chronic daily stressors (Cutrona & Troutman, 1986; Holahan & Holahan, 1987a,b). O'Leary and her associates report evidence to suggest that depression arising from perceived inefficacy mediates immunity (O'Leary, Shoor, Lorig, & Holman, 1988). A low sense of efficacy to exercise control over one's health functioning was accompanied by high levels of stress and depression, each of which, in turn, was associated with lowered functioning of different facets of the immune system.

Central Mediation. The central nervous system can exert regulatory influence on immune function. Thus, a third possible path of influence of perceived self-efficacy is through central expectancy

modulation of immunologic reactivity. If physiological reactions are often activated in the presence of certain environmental cues, then those cues alone can acquire the capacity to activate the physiological reactions through expectancy learning. Ader and Cohen (1993) have shown in animal experimentation that immune function can be similarly influenced by expectancy learning. After a neutral environmental cue had been paired with a pharmacologic agent that delays the development of an autoimmune disease, the occurrence of the cue alone retarded the onset of the disease and lengthened the survival period.

In studies with humans, induced expectations have been shown to affect physical reactions to allergens and antigens (Fry, Mason, & Pearson, 1964; Smith & McDaniel, 1983). After repeated pairings of the hospital setting with the immunosuppressive effects of chemotherapy, patients exhibited anticipatory immune suppression in hospital visits but not in the preceding days at home (Bovbjerg et al., 1990). The anticipatory decrease in immune function occurred independently of anxiety. Expectancy learning can enhance immune function as well as impair it (Buske-Kirschbaum, Kirschbaum, Stierle, Lehnert, & Hellhammer, 1992). After a neutral cue has been repeatedly associated with a substance that increases natural killer cell activity, exposure to the neutral cue alone enhances killer cell function. Such cells detect and destroy virally infected cells and tumor cells.

Experiences involving successful or failed efforts to manage environmental demands produce cognitive changes in beliefs about personal coping efficacy that have significant physiological consequences when the environmental stressors are no longer present (Bandura et al., 1988). Thereafter, mere thoughts about one's coping efficacy lower autonomic activation in those whose efficacy beliefs were enhanced but heighten autonomic reactions in those whose sense of coping efficacy was diminished. Such findings raise the possibility that, depending on their nature, situationally aroused beliefs of coping efficacy may produce anticipatory immunosuppressive or immunoenhancing effects.

The immune system includes multiple interacting subprocesses with intricate interconnections to other biological systems, all of which complicates evaluation of the level of immunity. Whether the alterations in immune function accompanying changes in perceived coping efficacy are of sufficient magnitude to affect vulnerability to physical illness requires further examination. Although the picture is complex, there is evidence that the impairment of immune function by stress is substantial enough to affect the onset and progression of infectious disease (Cohen et al., 1991). Because perceived coping efficacy modulates stress, it can help explain who is most susceptible to infection. Knowledge of how efficacious control over aversive life events affects different aspects of the immune system is, therefore, important to an eventual full understanding of how psychosocial factors influence immune function, which, in turn, affects disease processes.

The preceding discussion documents the diverse ways in which inefficacy in exercising control over stressors affects the body's regulatory systems that mediate health and illness. The findings also verify the lasting beneficial changes in biological reactivity to psychosocial stressors that can be achieved by instilling a strong sense of coping efficacy. When deleterious biological effects stem from inefficacious control of adverse life events, the self-efficacy aspect of the psychobiological mechanisms of bodily dysfunctions is the optimal locus of intervention. People are taught how to manage their everyday problems of living effectively so that they are no longer chronically stressed. All too often, however, the convenience and profitability of drugs prescribe a biochemical locus of intervention. This is the difference between building people's coping capabilities and altering aversive life conditions versus medicating their distresses. Consider, for purposes of illustration, recent advances in the understanding of the psychobiological mechanisms of gastrointestinal disorders, which are a common affliction. Stress produces stomach upsets manifested in abdominal pain, heartburn, nausea, bloatedness, and diarrhea. Uncontrollable stressors trigger brain chemicals that wreak havoc on gastrointestinal functions. Discovery of the biochemical link has led to the development of a synthetic compound that partly blocks the action of the brain chemicals activated by stressors. Before long, millions of stressed people with upset stomachs will be popping prescribed pills for symptomatic relief rather than gaining permanent mastery over the stressors in their lives that continually agitate their viscera. Treatment of the psychosocial sources of gastrointestinal agitation would quickly take priority if it involved a merchandizable product that is readily prescribable, demands little effort, and requires repeated purchase and use to sustain its profitable production. The biotechnology industry is quick to capitalize on new knowledge of the neurochemical workings of the brain with marketable drugs for conditions that are sufficiently widespread to provide large sales. Because the behavioral sciences produce enabling methods that gradually make their way into public practices rather than commercial products that are aggressively marketed as breakthrough remedies, their scientific advances do not gain as much notice.

Efforts to combat the adverse effects of deficient self-regulation of health habits and the anxieties and despondencies of common problems of life increasingly seek remedies in drugs rather than in psychosocial change. Patients are routinely prescribed drugs in general practice settings for conditions that can be ameliorated by changes in health habits. For example, a diet low in fat but high in fruits and vegetables achieves blood pressure reductions similar to those from drug treatment in people suffering from hypertension. Reid and his colleagues studied how substituting lifestyle changes for patients on drug therapy affected long-term management of high blood pressure (Reid et al., 1994). General practitioners discontinued the medication and encouraged dietary and exercise changes with the aid of self-help materials. The vast majority of the patients succeeded in keeping their blood pressure down by lifestyle changes alone. The thought of lifelong drug taking with attendant risks and side effects provided strong incentives for patients to undertake lifestyle changes. Success in exercising personal control over their health without having to rely on drugs had the additional benefit of raising their positive self-evaluation. More intensive psychosocial systems for building self-regulatory efficacy, to be reviewed later, hold even greater promise of advancing the self-management of health.

PERCEIVED SELF-EFFICACY IN HEALTH-PROMOTING BEHAVIOR

We saw earlier that lifestyle habits can enhance or impair health. Thus, people can exert some behavioral control over the vitality and quality of their health. Social cognitive theory distinguishes among three basic processes of personal change: the adoption of new behavior patterns, their generalized use under different circumstances, and their maintenance over time (Bandura, 1986a). Efficacy beliefs affect each of these phases of personal change: whether people even consider changing their health habits, whether they can enlist the motivation and perseverance needed to succeed should they choose to do so, their success in restoring control after setbacks, and how well they maintain the changes they have achieved. These change processes are discussed in the sections that follow.

Initiation of Personal Change

People's beliefs that they can motivate themselves and regulate their own behavior plays a crucial role in whether they even consider changing detrimental health habits or pursuing rehabilitative activities. The perceived inefficacy barrier to preventive health is all too familiar in people's resignation about health risks, such as smoking or obesity, over which they can exercise control. They see little point in even trying if they believe they do not have what it takes to succeed. If they make an attempt, they give up easily in the absence of quick results or in the face of setbacks. Thus, smokers who judge themselves incapable of quitting smoking do not even try (Brod & Hall, 1984). If they do try, they give up easily, however concerned they may be about the health hazards of smoking. In a longitudinal study of heavy smokers who tried to stop

smoking on their own, the successful quitters had a stronger sense of efficacy at the outset than the relapsers and continuous smokers (Carey & Carey, 1993). Those who believe they can succeed mount the effort needed to override their cravings and break their smoking habit. Even people who acknowledge that their habits are harming their health achieve little success in curtailing their behavior unless they judge themselves as having some efficacy to resist situational and emotional instigators (Strecher, Becker, Kirscht, Eraker, & Graham-Tomasi, 1985).

DiClemente and his colleagues examined cross sectionally the level of perceived efficacy at different phases of habit change (DiClemente et al., 1991; DiClemente, Prochaska, & Gilbertini, 1985). They found that perceived efficacy rises as people move from disregarding habit change to contemplating it seriously, to initiating change, and to maintaining the changes they have achieved. Relapses undermine faith in one's self-regulatory efficacy. People with a low sense of efficacy forgo preventive practices. If they judge themselves incapable of managing pain, they avoid corrective treatment as well (Klepac, Dowling, & Hauge, 1982).

The media, especially television, play a major role in informing the public about health risks. Efforts to get people to adopt health practices that prevent disease, therefore, rely heavily on persuasive communications in health education campaigns (McGuire, 1984). The success of these efforts depends on knowing what makes health communications effective in promoting preventive action. In most health messages, appeals to fear by depicting the ravages of disease and personal susceptibility to it are often used as motivators, and recommended preventive practices are provided as guides for action. Excessive scare tactics can backfire. They run the risk of creating avoidance of self-diagnostic behavior that can detect disease processes and unnerving people already beset with self-doubts about their ability to control health threats (Beck & Frankel, 1981; Kegeles & Lund, 1982; Leventhal, 1970). Efforts to scare people into adopting preventive health practices have divergent effects on those of low and high perceived efficacy. Heightening the level of fear appeals about sexually transmitted diseases prompts increasing adoption of safer sex practices when perceived efficacy is raised, but decreasing adoption when perceived efficacy is lowered (Witte, 1992). Too much fear without a sense of personal control makes self-protection seem like an exercise in futility. Thus, a threat that is viewed as personally uncontrollable is best tuned out.

Beck and Lund (1981) studied the persuasiveness of health communications in which the seriousness of periodontal disease, and susceptibility to it, was varied. Patients' beliefs in their efficacy to stick to the required hygienic routine was a good predictor of whether they adopted the preventive practices. Fear arousal had little effect on whether or not they did so. Belief in the efficacy of a preventive method should be distinguished from belief in one's efficacy to use that method consistently. Public service campaigns increasingly target method efficacy but generally ignore personal efficacy. This is consequential neglect. People see little point in undertaking potentially beneficial activities if they seriously doubt their efficacy to stick with them. Seydel, Taal, and Wiegman (1990) report that increasing risk perception by emphasizing the severity and personal susceptibility to disease has little or no influence on adoption of preventive practices related to cancer. But belief in one's personal efficacy to carry out the activities and belief in the efficacy of the self-protective activities to detect incipient problems are uniformly good predictors.

People need enough knowledge of potential dangers to warrant action, but they do not have to be scared out their wits to act, any more than homeowners have to be terrified to purchase fire insurance for their households. What people need is knowledge about how to regulate their behavior and firm belief in their personal efficacy to turn concerns into effective preventive actions. Thus, a shift in emphasis is required, from trying to scare people into health to providing them with the tools needed to exercise personal control over their health habits. Interventions designed to get people to alter their health habits must be tailored to their level of perceived efficacy. Those who have come to believe in the futility of any effort to change need a guided self-enablement program that provides graduated

mastery experiences in the exercise of personal control. Those with sufficient perceived efficacy to entertain the prospect of lifestyle changes can be persuaded by less intensive measures.

People interpret information about risky activities in terms of potential gains and potential losses. They are generally more inclined to pursue options that guard against losses than options that would bring benefits. There is some evidence to suggest that health communications to get people to check for maladies are more persuasive if framed in terms of health losses, but to get them to adopt preventive behavior, such communications are more persuasive if framed in terms of health benefits (Rothman, Salovey, Antone, Keough, & Martin, 1993). Meyerowitz and Chaiken (1987) found that health communications emphasizing health benefits had less impact on efficacy beliefs and behavior designed to detect maladies than did communications emphasizing health losses. They examined four alternative mechanisms through which health communications could alter health habits: by transmission of factual information, fear arousal, change in risk perception, and enhancement of perceived personal efficacy to do what is needed. Health communications fostered adoption of preventive health practices mainly by their effects on efficacy beliefs.

Analyses of how mass media campaigns change health habits similarly reveal that both the preexisting and altered efficacy beliefs play an influential role in the adoption and social diffusion of health practices (Maibach, Flora, & Nass, 1991; Slater, 1989). The stronger the preexisting efficacy beliefs and the more the media campaigns enhance people's beliefs in their self-regulative efficacy, the more likely they are to adopt the recommended practices. The relationship remains even when multiple controls are applied for a host of other possible influences.

Positive emotions increase the availability of thoughts about personal successes, whereas negative emotions make personal failures more salient. These affective biasing processes can alter the impact of health communications. Public health messages that elicit positive emotions make people feel more efficacious and optimistic about the benefits of new healthful practices than do messages that arouse fear (Schooler, 1992). Modeling effective strategies for increasing healthful behavior, however, overrides the undermining effects of negative emotions on adoption of healthful practices. Regardless of the induced emotional states, increases in efficacy beliefs and positive outcome expectations promote adherence to healthy behavior.

Effective health communications must be tailored to the psychosocial determinants governing the behavior of any given individual. Computer-based technologies allow tailoring of health messages individually simply by combining key factors in ways that are most personally relevant. Strecher and his colleagues have shown that individualized messages on risk reduction from family practice physicians are more effective than standardized ones in getting people to quit smoking, adopt healthy eating, and follow regular screening for cancer (Campbell et al., 1994; Strecher et al., 1994). These variations in format affect how deeply the information is cognitively processed. Personalized messages are read more thoroughly, are remembered better, and are more likely to be acted upon than standardized ones that contain a lot of information that is personally irrelevant (Skinner, Strecher, & Hospers, 1994). The effectiveness of tailored guides can be further boosted by adding a brief telephone contact that provides help in overcoming problems, strengthens perceived efficacy, and supports continued effort (Rimer et al., 1994).

The benefits of personalization of interventions depend heavily on which kinds of determinants are targeted. Sophisticated tailoring to weak determinants will yield poor results. Sociocognitive theory singles out level of efficacy beliefs, health goals, outcome expectations, and perceived impediments as key factors predictive of health behavior in the computer algorithms for personalized combination. Most health communications target perceived risks and benefits and sometimes perceived barriers. They succeed mainly with people who believe they have the capacity to change their lifestyle habits (Maibach et al., 1991; Strecher et al., 1994).

To be most effective, health communications should be framed in ways that instill in people the belief that they have the capability to alter their health habits and should instruct them in how to do it. Communications that explicitly do so increase people's determination to modify habits detrimental to their health (Maddux & Rogers, 1983). Entrenched habits rarely yield to a single attempt at self-regulation. Success is usually achieved through renewed effort following failed attempts. Human attainments, therefore, necessitate a resilient sense of personal efficacy. To strengthen the staying power of self-beliefs, health communications should emphasize that success requires perseverant effort and recovery from temporary behavioral breakdowns, so that people's sense of efficacy is not undermined by a few setbacks.

People who can get themselves to start a program of self-directed change quickly confront the problem of whether they can stick to it. Studies of adherence to health-promoting regimens during the adoption phase reveal high attrition and irregular adoption of healthful practices by many of the remaining participants (Dishman, 1982; Meichenbaum & Turk, 1987). It requires self-regulatory efficacy to get oneself to continue the health habits one has started, because there is never any shortage of dissuading influences. For example, regular aerobic exercise reduces risk of coronary heart disease, lowers hypertension, sheds pounds, and enhances physical fitness and psychological well-being. Sedentary individuals who have persuaded themselves to inject some motion into their otherwise inactive lifestyle often have difficulty getting themselves to exercise when they are busy, tired, dejected, have other interesting things to do, or face inclement weather. Enduring success requires overriding recurrent impediments.

Perceived self-regulatory efficacy has been found to be a significant predictor of adherence to habit change programs. People who have a low sense of efficacy are quick to drop out, and those who remain tend to be sporadic attendees and irregular practitioners of healthful habits (McAuley, 1991; McAuley & Jacobson, 1991; McAuley & Rowney, 1990; Mitchell & Stuart, 1984). Of course, not all participants who embark on a program of self-change with a shaky self-efficacy necessarily continue to be troubled by self-doubt. Quick success can turn self-doubters into self-believers. Conversely, initial self-believers can become self-doubters if the challenge turns out to be much more formidable than originally imagined. The predictiveness of self-efficacy theory will be underestimated if the initial efficacy beliefs used as predictors are no longer the ones operating at the time that attrition and level of behavioral adherence are assessed.

Conceptual Models of Health Behavior

Research guided by various psychosocial theories of human behavior have added to our understanding of how cognitive and social factors contribute to human health and disease. However, the recent years have witnessed a proliferation of conceptual models of health behavior formed by various combinations of constructs drawn from the different theories. Table 7.1 presents the main determinants in social cognitive theory and their areas of overlap with those of some of the widely applied models of health behavior. These are the aspects of sociocognitive theory that are especially relevant to the self-management of behavior. The theory in its

totality specifies factors governing the acquisition of competencies as well as the self-regulation of action.

If people lack awareness of how their lifestyle habits affect their health, they have little reason to put themselves through the drudgery of changing bad health habits they enjoy. People are lectured more than they want to hear about their bad health habits. The various conceptual models presuppose adequate knowledge of health risks and usually find it to be high. *Knowledge* creates the precondition for change. But additional self-influences are needed to overcome the impediments to adopting new lifestyle habits. Beliefs of personal efficacy occupy a pivotal regulative role in the sociocognitive causal structure because, as previously noted, such beliefs not only operate on health behavior in their own right but also act upon other classes of determinants that contribute to motivation and self-regulativeness. Most conceptual models of health behavior now include perceived efficacy to get oneself to adopt and stick to healthful behavior as an influential contributor (Ajzen, 1985; Maddux & Rogers, 1983; Rosenstock, Strecher, & Becker, 1988; Schwarzer, 1992). Those that do not sacrifice explanatory and predictive power.

TABLE 7.1 Psychosocial Determinants of Health Behavior

| Theory | Self-efficacy | Outcome Expectations | | | Goals | | Impediments | |
		Physical	Social	Self-evaluative	Proximal	Distal	Personal & Situational	Health System
Social cognitive theory	X	X	X	X	X	X	X	X
Health belief model		X	X				X	X
Theory of reasoned action		X	X		X			
Theory of planned behavior	X	X	X		X			
Protection motivation	X	X						

In addition to the regulative function of *efficacy beliefs*, outcome expectations about the effects produced by different forms of behavior contribute to health behavior. As in other classes of behavior, these outcome expectations may take the form of detrimental or beneficial physical effects, favorable or adverse social reactions, and positive or negative self-evaluative reactions. Most of the factors in the various conceptual models of health behavior correspond to these different types of outcome expectations. The health belief model is the forerunner of the various conceptual schemes (Becker, 1974; Rosenstock, 1974). According to this model, preventive health efforts and adherence to prescribed medical regimens are influenced by four factors. They include perceived threats, benefits, barriers, and cues to action. Health threat is measured in terms of perceived seriousness of a given health condition and perceived personal susceptibility to contracting it. Perceived physical threats provide the motivation for health action. The anticipated benefits of different courses of action and perceived barriers in the form of negative effects and environmental constraints influence which course of health action will be preferred. Experienced symptoms, media communications, and social prompts serve as cues that trigger the decisional process for health-related action.

Rogers's (1983) model of protection motivation includes the physical threat component of perceived severity and susceptibility but adds two perceived efficacy determinants. The first, response efficacy, is concerned with belief in the effectiveness of the prescribed means to prevent illness or promote health. The second is the strength of perceived personal efficacy to carry out those means. Perceived response efficacy should be distinguished from outcome expectations. Response efficacy is concerned with whether a given course of action can produce a particular attainment; outcome expectations are concerned with the consequences that flow from that attainment. Thus, belief that breast self-examination is effective in detecting a cancerous growth is response efficacy; the physical, social, and self-evaluative consequences believed to flow from detecting a lump are outcome expectations. The subdivision of efficacy into agent and means requires brief comment. In acting on

their belief that they can make things happen, people must resort to certain means. They do not consider themselves efficacious if they judge they lack any means to exert influence over events. Hence, a view of personal efficacy devoid of any means does not make sense. People can, of course, have high efficacy to use certain means but low efficacy to produce desired results because the means do not, in fact, exert much control over the health behavior. For example, alcoholics may judge themselves highly efficacious to relax but remain unconvinced of their efficacy to abstain from alcohol because they believe that relaxation in no way affects their desire for liquor or their ability to resist social pressure to drink. Some of the means that are ritualistically prescribed in habit change programs have not been shown to be of value. Perceived efficacy for ineffectual means will not foretell success.

The predictiveness of personal efficacy and means efficacy diverges when particular means are socially prescribed but recipients question their usefulness. Means produce performances through the efforts of the agent wielding them. If perceived response efficacy predicts how individuals behave, it is because they believe they can carry out the means and that doing so has some effect. Otherwise, they would give little heed to the means. In short, in judging their efficacy, individuals necessarily unite personal agency with means. They act on beliefs of how well they can use prescribed means, however valuable the means may be in fact. Thus, sedentary individuals, who acknowledge that regular vigorous exercise is a good means for building cardiovascular capacity, will not be moved to action if they believe that they cannot get themselves to stick to the exercise routine. Moreover, people may consider other helpful means at their disposal in judging their efficacy rather than just the one prescribed for them by others. Separating personal efficacy from the means by which it is exercised, or restricting judgment of personal efficacy to particular means, will underestimate the contribution of personal efficacy to performance. Personal agency and means are best left united rather than arbitrarily detached.

Multivariate analyses have been conducted for health programs designed to foster various health-related activities. They include seeking medical examinations for potential health problems, performing self-diagnostic tests for early detection of illnesses, and adopting practices that reduce the risk of illness and enhance the quality of health. The relative contributions of the different determinants are usually assessed in relation to intentions to perform the health practices, less often to the actual behavior itself. The findings are highly consistent in showing that perceived personal efficacy and response efficacy are reliable determinants of health actions across diverse domains of health behavior. The effects of perceived threat, especially perceived severity, are much weaker and inconsistent (Kasen et al., 1992; Maddux & Rogers, 1983; Rippetoe & Rogers, 1987; Stanley & Maddux, 1986; Taal, Seydel, & Wiegman, 1990; Wurtele & Maddux, 1987). Indeed, high perceived personal threat to health often leads to dysfunctional thinking and avoidance of protective action. Perceived barriers fare better as predictors of preventive behavior in the original version of the health belief model (Janz & Becker, 1984). It remains to be determined whether perceived barriers account for variation in health behavior when the influence of negative outcome expectations and perceived self-efficacy are removed.

The perceived severity of, and susceptibility to, health impairment in the health belief model represents the detrimental side of expected physical outcomes in social cognitive theory. The perceived health benefits of preventive action represent the positive *outcome expectations.* In the theories of reasoned action (Ajzen & Fishbein, 1980) and planned behavior (Ajzen, 1985), intentions determine behavior. Intentions, in turn, are governed by attitudes toward the behavior and by subjective norms. The labels differ, but, as operationalized, these two sets of determinants correspond to different classes of outcome expectations. Attitude is measured in terms of expected behavioral outcomes and the value placed on those outcomes. Norms are measured by expectations of how other people are likely to react to the behavior and by one's motivation to comply with their likes and dislikes.

In social cognitive theory, normative influences regulate behavior through two systems: social sanctions and self-sanctions (Bandura, 1986a). Social norms influence behavior anticipatorily by the social consequences they provide. Behavior that violates prevailing social norms brings social censure or other punishing consequences, whereas behavior that fulfills socially valued norms is approved and rewarded. People do not act solely on the basis of anticipated social sanctions, however. Rather, they adopt certain standards of behavior and regulate their actions anticipatorily through self-evaluative consequences they create for themselves. Social norms also convey standards of conduct. Adoption of personal standards creates a self-regulative system that operates largely through internalized self-sanctions (Bandura, 1991c). People behave in ways that give them self-satisfaction, and they refrain from behaving in ways that violate their standards because such behavior will bring self-censure. Although the central constructs in the Ajzen and Fishbein models are labeled as attitudes and social norms, both are operationalized as beliefs about outcomes. The attitudinal determinant refers to anticipated costs and benefits of the behavior; the normative determinant refers to anticipated social outcomes. Social cognitive theory encompasses these two types of outcome expectations plus the influential third type rooted in personal standards and self-sanctions.

Ajzen (1985) has extended the conceptual model of reasoned action by adding perceived behavioral control. The research of Dzewaltowski (1989) indicates that perceived behavioral control essentially measures people's sense of personal efficacy. Hence, when perceived self-efficacy is included as a predictor, perceived behavioral control makes no independent contribution to performance. In comparative tests, the expanded model, which is called the theory of planned behavior, has greater predictive power than the original version without the efficacy-like determinant (Ajzen & Madden, 1986). Beliefs in personal efficacy affect behavior both directly and by influencing intention. Given that perceived self-efficacy affects thinking, motivation, and affective states, all of which act upon behavior, it is not surprising that intention is not the sole proximal determinant of behavior. The move from intention to action is far from automatic. These other factors can overrule the best of intentions.

In sociocognitive theory, *cognized goals* rooted in a value system provide further self-incentives and guides to health behavior. Goals may be distal ones that serve an orienting function or specific proximal ones that regulate effort and guide action in the here and now. Intentions are essentially equivalent to proximal goals. "I aim to" and "I intend to" both refer to what a person proposes to do. Goals are an interlinked facet of a motivational mechanism that operates through self-monitoring, aspirational standards, and affective self-reaction rather than simply a disjoined predictor to be tacked onto a conceptual model. In causal structures, efficacy beliefs affect goal setting and whether substandard performances spark greater effort or are demoralizing. But goals make an independent contribution to performance (Bandura, 1991b).

Personal change would be trivially easy if there were no *impediments* or barriers to surmount. Hence, perceived barriers are an important factor in the health belief model (Becker, 1990; Rosenstock, 1974), and elaborated versions of it (Schwarzer, 1992). Social cognitive theory distinguishes between different types of barriers: cognitive, situational, or structural. Some of the barriers are conditions that impede performance of the health behavior itself. These types of impediments form an integral part of self-efficacy assessment. Efficacy beliefs must be measured against gradations of challenges or impediments to successful performance. Thus, for example, in assessment of exercise efficacy, individuals judge the strength of their capabilities to get themselves to exercise regularly in the face of a variety of situational, social, and personal hindrances. If there are no impediments to surmount, the behavior can be performed easily and everyone is totally efficacious. The regulation of health behavior is not solely an intrapsychic matter. Some impediments to healthful living reside in health systems rather than in cognitive or situational impediments. Unavailability of health resources or lack of access to them presents a second major class of impediments to healthful behavior. These barriers are rooted in how health services are structured socially and economically. Thus, in social cognitive theory, the multifaceted construct of perceived barriers is differentiated into three major forms: perceived self-inefficacy to surmount the obstacles to the adoption and maintenance of healthful habits; negative expected outcomes associated with lifestyle changes; and unavailability of health resources.

The theory of planned behavior has been tested in a series of studies of health practices with efficacy beliefs substituted for perceived behavioral control (deVries et al., 1988; deVries, Kok, & Dijkstra, 1990; Kok et al., 1991). Efficacy beliefs predict both intentions and health behavior even after controlling for attitudinal and normative social influences. They do so longitudinally as well as concurrently. When causal priority is not imposed in the analyses, efficacy beliefs make a substantially greater contribution to health behavior than do the other two determinants. The normative determinant typically makes a negligible contribution to health behavior. This raises the issue of whether it is unimportant, which seems unlikely, or whether a better conceptualization and detailed assessment of it in terms of social outcome expectations would reveal that it has some effect on adoption and maintenance of health habits.

We are now in the era of cafeteria-style theorizing in which constructs are plucked from divergent theories and strung together in various combinations as alternative conceptual schemes in the name of theoretical integration. Hybrid models proliferate even though they rarely generate much interest. The development of a comprehensive theory of human behavior should focus on broad integrative constructs. The cafeteria style of theorizing unnecessarily multiplies predictors in several ways. Similar factors, but bearing different names, are often included in the same composite model as though they were separate classes of determinants. This creates needless redundancy among predictors. Moreover, facets of a higher order construct are sometimes treated as entirely different types of determinants, as when attitudes, normative influences, and outcome expectations are included in a conglomerate model as different constructs when, operationally, they represent different types of outcome expectations. Following the dictum 'the more the better', some researchers overload their conceptual model with a host of factors that contribute trivially to health habits. All too often, the eclectic additive approach gets passed off as integrative theorizing presumably combining the best of different approaches. Scientific progress is better achieved by encompassing more fully the determinants within an integrated theory than by creating conglomerate models with constructs picked from divergent theories with the attendant problems of redundancy, fractionation, and theoretical disconnectedness.

Some researchers have tested whether factors included in alternative conceptions of health behavior add incremental prediction over and above a subset of sociocognitive determinants. In several of these studies, the sociocognitive determinants included efficacy beliefs, expected health benefits, and satisfaction or dissatisfaction with the changes achieved in health habits (Dzewaltowski, 1989; Dzewaltowski et al., 1990). Both efficacy beliefs and affective self-reactions to personal progress contributed to adherence to healthful behavior. Attitudes and perceived social pressure similarly accounted for healthful behavior, but they did not improve prediction when added to the subset of sociocognitive determinants. Such findings suggest redundancy of determinants under different names rather than dissimilar determinants. However, the generality of construct redundancy needs to be tested further across different types of health behavior.

Most of the models of health behavior are concerned mainly with predicting health habits but offer little guidance on how to change them. In addition to providing a unified conceptual framework, social cognitive theory embeds the sociocognitive determinants in a large body of knowledge that specifies their origins, the processes through which they produce their effects, and how to modify them to enhance human health (Bandura, 1986a). A theory that offers both predictive and operative power has greater utility than one that is limited mainly to prediction.

Achievement of Personal Change

Effective self-regulation is not achieved through an act of will. It requires the development of self-regulatory skills. To build a sense of controlling efficacy, people must develop skills for regulating their own motivation and behavior. They must learn how to monitor the behavior they seek to change, set short-range attainable subgoals to motivate and direct their efforts, and enlist positive incentives and social supports to sustain the effort needed to succeed (Bandura, 1986a). Once empowered with skills and belief in their capabilities, people are better able to adopt behaviors that promote health and to eliminate those that impair it. They also benefit more from treatments for physical disabilities.

A growing body of evidence, to be reviewed shortly, reveals that the impact of various therapeutic interventions on health behavior is partly mediated by their effects on efficacy beliefs. The stronger the efficacy beliefs the interventions instill, the more likely people are to enlist the personal resources and sustain the level of effort needed to adopt and maintain health-promoting behavior. This has been shown in studies conducted in such diverse areas of health as enhancement of pulmonary function in patients suffering from chronic obstructive pulmonary disease; recovery of cardiovascular function in postcoronary patients; reduction of pain and dysfunction in rheumatoid arthritis; amelioration of tension headaches; control of labor and childbirth pain; management of chronic low back, neck, and leg pain and impairment; stress reduction; weight reduction; exercise of control over bulimic behavior; reduction of cholesterol through dietary means; adherence to prescribed remedial activities; adoption and long-term adherence to a regular program of physical exercise; maintenance of diabetic self-care; successful coping with painful invasive medical procedures; effective management of sexual coercions and contraceptive use to avoid unwanted pregnancies; postabortion adjustment; control of sexual practices that pose high risk for transmission of AIDS; and control of addictive habits that impair health such as alcohol abuse, smoking, and use of opiate drugs.

A sense of personal efficacy not only facilitates the self-management of physical disorders but also lessens their unsettling emotional effects. When equated for severity and chronicity of physical disorders, individuals of high perceived efficacy are less stressed and less depressed by their condition and use better coping strategies than those of low perceived efficacy (Martin, Holroyd, & Rokicki, 1993). Self-efficacy beliefs can vary, often substantially, across different domains of functioning. For example, perceived efficacy to control overeating is only weakly related ($r = 21$) to perceived efficacy to control smoking (DiClemente, 1986). Nor does perceived efficacy to stick to a healthy diet bear much relationship to perceived efficacy to adhere to an exercise regimen (Hofstetter et al., 1990). The role of efficacy beliefs in health-related behavior is best elucidated by efficacy measures tailored to particular domains of health functioning rather than as a global trait assessed by an omnibus test. Thus, an omnibus test of personal control over health is a poor predictor of smoking relapse, whereas a measure of perceived self-efficacy to exercise control over smoking urges under different situational instigators is a good predictor of vulnerability to smoking relapse (Walker & Franzini, 1983). In comparative studies, domain efficacy scales typically predict changes in health behavior better than do general measures of perceived personal control (Manning & Wright, 1983) or perceived personal control over one's own health (Alagna & Reddy, 1984; Beck & Lund, 1981; Brod & Hall, 1984; Kaplan et al., 1984; Walker & Franzini, 1983).

Maintenance of Personal Change

Habit changes are of little consequence unless they endure. Many of the lifestyle habits that impair health are subjected to strong instigative influences in everyday life. Habits that are imbedded in interpersonal relationships and form part of organized patterns of daily activities are not easy to break. Self-changers have to contend not only with social pressures to engage in the consummatory activities but also with the gratifications inherent in them. To add to the instigative pressures to resume detrimental styles of behavior, healthful practices are not entirely free of onerous aspects, especially in the earlier phases of change. Maintenance of habit change relies heavily on self-regulatory capabilities and the functional value of the behavior. Development of self-regulatory capabilities requires instilling a resilient sense of efficacy as well as imparting skills. Experiences in exercising control over troublesome situations serve as efficacy builders. This is a crucial aspect of self-management. If people are not fully convinced of their personal efficacy, they undermine their efforts in difficult situations and readily abandon the skills they have been taught when they suffer reverses or fail to get quick results. Multifaceted efficacy scales reveal not only areas of vulnerability in clients that must be improved to prevent relapse but also deficiencies in treatments that fail to instill perceived efficacy to manage certain types of troublesome situations (Clark, Abrams, Niaura, Eaton, & Rossi, 1991). Unless the treatment is strengthened or augmented, it leaves clients ill-equipped to handle difficult situations.

Each of the modes for enhancing personal efficacy can help people to develop the resilient sense of efficacy needed to override difficulties that inevitably arise from time to time. In the enactive mastery mode, a resilient sense of efficacy is built through structured demonstration trials in the exercise of control over progressively more challenging tasks. For example, as part of instruction in cognitive pain control strategies, arthritic patients were given efficacy demonstration trials in which they performed selected pain-producing activities with and without cognitive control and rated their pain level (O'Leary et al., 1988). Explicit evidence that they achieved substantial reduction in experienced pain with cognitive control persuaded the patients that they could exercise some control over pain by enlisting cognitive strategies. Self-efficacy validation trials not only serve as efficacy builders but also test the value of the techniques being taught. Ineffectual techniques are readily exposed.

In using modeling for this purpose, other patients demonstrate how to cope and reinstate control should setbacks occur; they also make clear that success usually requires tenacious effort. Such knowledge can strengthen the self-beliefs of others struggling with similar problems. Moreover, modeled perseverant success can alter the diagnosticity of failure experiences. People can come to see failures as caused partly by difficult situational predicaments rather than solely by inherent personal limitations. Difficulties and setbacks prompt redoubling of efforts rather than provoking self-discouraging doubts about one's coping capabilities. For example, pain threshold and tolerance is affected by modeling influences (Craig, 1983). People who have seen others persevere despite pain function much more effectively when they themselves are in pain than if they had seen others give up quickly (Turkat & Guise, 1983; Turkat, Guise, & Carter, 1983).

Persuasory influences that instill efficacy beliefs conducive to optimal use of skills can also contribute to staying power. As a result, people who are persuaded they have what it takes to succeed and are told that the gains they achieved in treatment verify their capability are more successful in sustaining their altered health habits over a long time than are those who undergo the same treatment without the efficacy-enhancing component (Blittner, Goldberg, & Merbaum, 1978; Nicki, Remington, & MacDonald, 1984; Weinberg, Hughes, Critelli, England, & Jackson, 1984). If, in conveying positive appraisals of people's capabilities, social persuaders structure tasks for them that bring success and avoid premature failure, the impact of their influence is likely to stick. By maintaining an efficacious outlook that gains are attainable when clients are beset with self-doubts, they can help clients to sustain their coping efforts in the face of reverses and discouraging obstacles. Construing a slip as an occasion for improving one's coping capabilities supplants self-debilitating thinking with constructive problem-solving thinking.

Some interventions are aimed at altering health habits; others equip people with skills for managing chronic physical conditions. Long-term success in both types of endeavors depends on steadfast self-regulation. Nonadherence to healthful practices is a prevalent problem. Perceived self-efficacy is a good predictor of how well people stick to the behaviors that enable them to manage their own health. For example, in regulating hypertension by self-relaxation,

the more firmly people believe in their self-regulative efficacy, the more they practice relaxation in their daily life and the greater the reductions they achieve in their blood pressure (Hoelscher, Lichstein, & Rosenthal, 1986). Efficacy beliefs similarly predict adherence to healthful habits that enhance cardiovascular function and help to prevent heart attacks in people suffering from coronary heart disease (Ewart, 1992; Jensen et al., 1993). In the self-management of arthritis, a low sense of self-regulatory efficacy predicts difficulty in adherence to recommended health practices even after controlling for degree of disease activity, functional incapacity, and level of pain. The problem of noncompliance with therapeutic regimens is most strikingly revealed in conditions where failure to take one's medication regularly is potentially life-threatening. Perceived efficacy increases the likelihood that organ transplant recipients will stick to immunosuppressive medication to prevent rejection episodes or graft loss (DeGeest et al., in press). Compliers suffer fewer rejection episodes than do noncompliers.

Among the conditions requiring continual self-management, none is more demanding than diabetes. Diabetics have to maintain normal blood glucose levels by coordinating a variety of self-care activities including diet, exercise, daily self-monitoring of glucose levels, and careful timing of self-administration of insulin. A strong sense of self-regulatory efficacy is associated with good self-management of diabetes regimens (Crabtree, 1986; Grossman, 1987; Hurley & Shea, 1992; Padgett, 1991). Efficacy beliefs predict adherence to glucose testing, dieting, and exercise and also predict level of glycemic control over the follow-up period after controlling for previous adherence behavior, blood glucose level, type of treatment, negative mood states, and a host of demographic characteristics (Kavanagh, Gooley, & Wilson, 1993). In a comparison of possible predictors (McCaul, Glasgow, & Schafer, 1987), neither knowledge of regimens for maintaining glycemic control nor skills in dealing with social situations that create difficulties in doing so predicted adherence to diabetes regimens. Environmental supports aided self-testing for glucose levels. Perceived efficacy was the only factor that predicted adherence to every aspect of the diabetes regimen: diet, glucose monitoring, and self-administration of insulin.

Relapse Prevention and Management

The role of perceived efficacy in the maintenance of health-promoting behavior has been examined most extensively in regard to vulnerability to relapse in addictive behavior. Marlatt and Gordon (1985) provide a conceptual model of the relapse process. They have identified a common relapse process for heroin addiction, alcoholism, and smoking in which perceived self-regulatory efficacy operates as a contributing factor. The common precipitants of breakdowns in self-regulation include inability to manage negative emotional states such as stress, depression, loneliness, boredom and restlessness; social pressures to use the substance; and interpersonal conflict, as when an argument provokes a drunken episode. Efficacy assessments confirm that such conditions weaken perceived efficacy to resist use of the substances (Barber, Cooper, & Heather, 1991; Barrios & Niehaus, 1985). The emotional and situational underminers of beliefs of personal efficacy are very similar across cultures (Sandahl, Lindberg, & Rönnberg, 1990).

Marlatt's relapse model highlights social and affective instigators for resumption of substance use. Some researchers have added situational precipitants, including the settings and other reminders of the effects of previous drug use (Heather & Stallard, 1989). There are several mechanisms through which situational reminders can prompt relapses. Exposure to situational cues can produce both biological and cognitive changes. Situations in which drugs have been repeatedly used activate, through expectancy learning, anticipatory biochemical reactions that originally served to counteract the pharmacologic effects of the drug (Siegel, 1983). These anticipatory counterreactions, known as withdrawal symptoms, are experienced as aversive physical states. For example, following detoxification in a treatment facility, drug addicts often find themselves reexperiencing the biochemical counterreactions upon return to settings in which they took drugs.

Situational reminders also activate positive outcome expectancies of the pleasurable effects of the drug experienced in past use. The anticipated pleasure and relief from aversive biochemical states create motivators for drug use that further tax self-regulatory capabilities. In addition, exposure to situations in which one formerly exercised poor control over substance use can activate thoughts of past failures that weaken beliefs in one's current self-regulatory efficacy. These cognitive changes are well documented by Cooney and his associates (Cooney, Gillespie, Baker, & Kaplan, 1987). Upon smelling their favorite alcoholic beverage, abstinent alcoholics lowered their perceived self-efficacy, raised expectations of the pleasurable effects of alcohol despite experiencing unpleasant physical reactions, and increased their desire to drink.

Repeated prolonged exposure to problem substances without consuming them can produce enduring abstinence (Jansen, Broekmate, & Heymans, 1992). Further studies are needed to clarify whether the mediating mechanisms involve extinction of aversive physical reactions, reduction of pleasurable outcome expectations (which get dubbed as "cravings"), or strengthening of perceived self-regulatory efficacy. Struggled resistance to substance use in response to a brief inducement can shake perceived efficacy despite successful self-control (Cooney et al., 1987). In the course of coping with an inducement, individuals may experience it as more powerful than they thought or notice possible limitations in some aspects of their mode of coping. This is also true in coping with threats (Bandura, 1982a). Experiencing high-risk situations with guidance, however, provides a vehicle for testing and practicing effective coping strategies. Repeated affirmation of resistive capabilities strengthens a sense of self-regulatory efficacy.

The relative importance of different facets of personal efficacy in the exercise of control over refractory unhealthful habits may change across phases of development. For example, the powerful sway of peers during adolescence particularly strains personal efficacy to resist peer influences. Thus, perceived efficacy to withstand social pressures from smoking peers is much more successful in predicting future smoking status than is perceived efficacy to withstand emotional distress (Lawrance & Rubinson, 1986). A low sense of efficacy predicts not only whether adolescents take up a smoking habit but also whether they quit it (deVries, Dijkstra, Grol, Seelen, & Kok, 1990).

The nature of the challenges to self-regulatory efficacy likewise vary across phases of personal change (Velicer et al., 1990). When people begin to consider seriously overcoming an addictive habit, negative emotional states and positive social pressures pose the major obstacles to the exercise of personal control. During early phases of abstinence, physical withdrawal symptoms and envisaged gratifications from use of the substance present additional new threats to the exercise of personal control. Situational and emotional events that activate anticipated gratifications gain strength as relapse precipitants during this transition phase. If this troublesome period is successfully weathered, cognized inducements weaken and eventually fade.

People who have the skills and assurance in their self-regulatory efficacy mobilize the cognitive and behavioral coping strategies needed to succeed in high-risk situations. Successful resistance of drug use in problematic situations further strengthens their sense of efficacy to exercise control over future risky situations (Garcia, Schmitz, & Doerfler, 1990). In contrast, when coping skills are underdeveloped and deficiently used because of disbelief in one's efficacy, a relapse is likely to occur in the presence of instigators for drug use. Selective recall of the pleasurable effects, but not the adverse effects, of substance use further strains efforts at self-regulation.

The course of behavioral change includes improvements, plateaus, setbacks, and recoveries. Faultless self-control is not easy to come by even for more pliant habits, let alone for entrenched ones. People often have to go through several cycles of mastery and relapse before they finally succeed. Slips expose vulnerabilities and provide opportunities to learn from mistakes how to manage potentially risky situations effectively. For example, lapses are not uncommon in the struggle to gain mastery over addictive behavior. When setbacks occur, it is not the relapse per se but how it is viewed and what

is learned from it that determine whether it has a positive or negative impact on the subsequent course of personal change. Personal efficacy influences how setbacks are interpreted and managed. The self-diagnostic significance given to lapses can bolster or undermine self-regulative efforts. Viewed from a self-efficacious frame of mind, a slip is a temporary setback brought about by strong situational inducements, which may be avoidable or alterable, or by particular deficits in self-regulative skills, which are improvable. Self-efficacious people redouble their efforts and improve their strategies to reinstate control. In contrast, those who distrust their coping capabilities are prone to ascribe a slip to pervasive personal incapacity and become easily overwhelmed by inducements to use the substance. Having construed themselves as powerless, further coping efforts are abandoned as futile, resulting in a total breakdown of self-control. Thus, strength of perceived self-regulatory efficacy at the time of a relapse crisis predicts who is most likely to get through it and remain abstinent by redoubled efforts at control or by successful requitting (Ossip-Klein et al., in press).

Self-regulatory efficacy is exercised by the environments people choose to get into as well as by what they do once they are in them. It is easier to wield control over initiatory choice behavior likely to lead to situations conducive to drug use than to try to extricate oneself from such situations while enmeshed in them. This is because the antecedent phase involves mainly anticipatory motivators that are amenable to cognitive control. The entanglement phase includes much stronger inducements for drug use that are less easily manageable. People must develop strategies for how to avoid problematic situations that present high risk of overwhelming their self-regulatory capabilities. In strengthening decisional self-efficacy, people have to become skilled at identifying and interrupting seemingly innocuous early choices in a chain of decisions that eventually leads to high-risk situations (Carroll, Rounsaville, & Keller, 1991). They must also safeguard against precipitating relapses by venturing prematurely and without adequate guidance into highly risky situations to test their self-regulatory capabilities. Premature tests are more likely to beget self-regulatory failures than efficacy affirmations.

Studies of behavior that is amenable to change but difficult to sustain over an extended period show that a low sense of efficacy increases vulnerability to relapse. Much of the research addressing this issue involves smoking behavior, which can be biochemically verified. People who have quit smoking through various means judge whether or not they can resist smoking in different situations known to arouse smoking urges (Carey & Carey, 1993; Coelho, 1984; Coletti et al., 1985; Condiotte & Lichtenstein, 1981; Devins & Edwards, 1988; DiClemente, 1981; Haaga, 1989; McIntyre, Lichtenstein, & Mermelstein, 1983). Although participants have stopped smoking, they differ in their perceived efficacy that they can continue to resist the desire for cigarettes. Perceived self-efficacy to resist predicts, months later, which participants will relapse and how soon they will relapse. In the most stringent tests, smoking behavior cannot predict relapse because the follow-up assessments are confined to participants who had all ceased smoking. This removes the pseudo explanation that past behavior "produces" the future behavior. In analyses that include people who are still smoking to some extent at the end of treatment, perceived self-regulatory efficacy predicts future smoking rates even when level of smoking behavior at termination is controlled (Baer, Holt, & Lichtenstein, 1986; Shadel & Mermelstein, 1993). When the influence of perceived efficacy is removed, the predictiveness of smoking rate at termination is either reduced or eliminated (Kavanagh, Pierce, Lo, & Shelley, 1990). The spontaneously expressed thoughts of personal efficacy by recent ex-smokers exposed to simulated situations conducive to smoking similarly predict success in maintaining abstinence (Haaga, Davison, McDermut, Hillis, & Twomey, 1993).

Neither demographic factors, length of smoking history, number of past attempts to break the smoking habit, length of prior abstinence, nor degree of physical dependence on nicotine differentiates relapsers from abstainers, whereas perceived efficacy does (Barrios, 1985; Haaga, 1989; Killen,

Maccoby, & Taylor, 1984; Shadel & Mermelstein, 1993; Yates & Thain, 1985). Evidence that the number of past attempts to quit smoking is unrelated to perceived efficacy indicates that efficacy beliefs do not simply reflect past coping experiences (Reynolds, Creer, Holroyd, & Tobin, 1982).

It should be noted that some of the characterizations of the process of reversion to drug and alcohol use in terms of "conditioned cravings," "urges," and other animated descriptors are vestiges of the disease model. "Urges" are heavily rooted in cognitions. Beliefs of self-regulatory efficacy and outcome expectations about the pleasurable effects of the substance are strong predictors of urges (Shadel & Mermelstein, 1993). Readoption is a common process in all types of consummatory habits. In a thoughtful critique of the surplus meaning of "relapse," Saunders and Allsop (1989) argue that readopting a behavior does not mean that one has succumbed to the grips of a pathologic condition. Just as people decide to give up a troublesome habit they may later decide to readopt it. If they do so, it does not mean that they revert to their former state. Depending on how they construe the readoption and what they learn from it, it can reflect progress in the struggle to gain mastery over substance abuse rather than an ominous backslide.

People struggle to exercise control over instigators for substance use that threaten to overwhelm their self-regulatory capabilities. It is easier to control the use of some substances than the use of others. Withdrawal of addictive substances quickly eliminates the aversive biological motivators. It is mainly psychosocial motivators that present the continuing challenges to the maintenance of abstinence or control of substance abuse. Programs for personal change must instill the resilient sense of coping and self-regulatory efficacy needed to resist drug abuse in the face of social, affective, and situational inducements. People who have structured much of their lives around substance use may find their lives in abstinence rather dreary. This in itself can drive them to drink and shoot drugs. A successful program must aid them to make broader changes that will make life in abstinence considerably more attractive than life in a drugged state.

Relapse to heavy drinking is of central concern in the management of alcoholism. It is widely claimed that alcoholics greatly underreport their level of drinking and exaggerate their ability to handle alcohol. Neither of these claims receives empirical support in formal assessments. Alcoholics' reports of their drinking behavior generally agree with those of people who know them well (Maisto, Sobell, & Sobell, 1979). In assessing self-regulatory efficacy, alcoholics judge their ability to resist the urge to drink in a variety of high-risk drinking situations (Annis, 1982; DiClemente, Carbonari, Montgomery, & Huges, 1994). Their perceived efficacy is measured before and after treatment designed to accomplish abstinence from alcohol or a reduced level of controlled drinking. Perceived self-regulatory efficacy predicts level of control of alcohol consumption over follow-up periods even when the effect of severity of alcohol dependence is controlled (Sitharthan & Kavanagh, 1990; Solomon & Annis, 1989). The outcomes that clients anticipate for ceasing or reducing their drinking do not make a significant contribution to prediction of drinking behavior over and above that of efficacy beliefs.

As in other domains of habit change, perceived inefficacy undermines the initial phase of personal change as well as control of drinking behavior after completion of treatment. In a comparison of multiple factors, Schimmel (1986) found that a low sense of self-regulatory efficacy is one of the best predictors of premature termination of treatment for alcoholism. Severe self-doubts raise questions about whether a prescribed treatment is worth the effort. If self-doubters are to achieve success, their belief in their self-regulatory efficacy must be enhanced by helping them to exercise control over manageably short intervals and providing them with a good deal of social support and guidance by close associates and self-help groups.

Some efforts have been made to assess the role of perceived self-efficacy in successful recovery from opiate addiction. In an analysis of possible determinants of abstinence from opiates conducted by Gossop and his colleagues, (1990), social supportive factors and perceived self-regulatory capability emerged as consistent predictors of abstinence over

various time periods. The more support from associates and engagement in beneficial activities that helped them remain drug free, and the stronger the belief in their ability to exercise control, the more successful were ex-addicts in sustaining abstinence. Perceived efficacy and social support also predicted reinstatement of abstinence following renewed drug use. Having many coping strategies helped in the short run, but supportive experiences and a strong sense of personal efficacy operated as the sustaining influences in staying off drugs. These findings are consistent with those cited earlier (Schunk & Rice, 1987) that it is not strategies per se, but the efficacy to use them consistently and persistently in the face of difficulty that usually determines success. Without the staying power of efficacy belief, all too often serviceable strategies are abandoned or used ineffectually.

Self-regulatory skills and belief in one's capabilities are built, in large part, through mastery experiences. Substance abuse poses special challenges in this regard. For example, as a way of reducing vulnerability to complete relapse following a slip, Marlatt and Gordon (1985) suggest use of a programmed relapse after abstinence has been achieved. The person consumes the substance and then reinstates control under the guidance of the therapist, thus gaining mastery experiences in self-recovery. Some have argued that a programmed relapse carries high risks. Triumphs over slips can strengthen perceived coping efficacy but, in so doing, they may foster periodic lapses into old habits through assurance that one can always reinstate control. A counterargument is that since most people relapse anyway, usually in pressing situations that overwhelm unpracticed recovery efforts, the risk is worth taking. Simulated lapses in visualized high-risk situations can be used to some advantage without the potential risks of programmed lapses. Individuals imagine themselves reverting to their old behavior and debilitating styles of thinking. They then rehearse how they would think and behave differently to achieve self-regulatory success.

Those who conquer substance abuse usually go through repeated cycles of abstinence and relapse. Because serious attempts to quit are typically followed by lapses and relapses, the mastery process is better viewed in terms of relapse management rather than relapse prevention (Curry & McBride, 1994). Like any other skill, gaining proficiency in self-regulation is an arduous process requiring perseverant effort in the face of setbacks. Participants need to maintain the belief that their problems are surmountable if they are to learn from mistakes rather than be demoralized by them.

Efficacy analyses of relapse processes must distinguish between perceived capabilities to exercise two distinct forms of behavioral control: perceived resistive efficacy to withstand pressure to engage in detrimental activities and perceived recovery efficacy to reinstate control after a setback. In studying the effects of controlled relapse, Cooney, Kopel, and McKeon (1982) had participants in a smoking cessation program smoke a relapse cigarette and then resume control, while others were told to avoid the cigarette because control is unachievable after relapse. Controlled relapse strengthened perceived efficacy to regain control after a slip. Abstinence admonitions lowered people's efficacy belief that they could recover from a slip. But participants who had gained a high sense of recovery efficacy resumed smoking sooner. Hill (1986) reexamined the effects of controlled relapse with a more intensive treatment in which participants resumed smoking but in a rapid puffing style that sapped any pleasure from it, whereupon they regained control. This mastery experience was designed to build recovery skill and to displace any pleasurable expectations about resumed use of the substance. The experience of reinstating control over a programmed relapse enhanced long-term abstinence.

The challenge is to strengthen both resistive and recovery efficacy so that self-belief in each of these capabilities serves the purpose of abstinence. This would require instilling strong resistive efficacy and only moderate recovery efficacy, sufficient to counteract judgment of complete inefficacy should a slip occur, but not so strong as to embolden trial of the substance. Haaga and Stewart (1992) provide some evidence to this effect. Ex-smokers who judged themselves to be moderately efficacious to regain control after a relapse were more successful at maintaining abstinence than those who either had little faith in their recovery capability or were highly confident that they could readily reestablish control.

Ecological Perspective on Efficacious Self-Regulation

Relapse prevention models focus heavily on the afflicted individuals as the locus of effort to control reversion to substance abuse. They are taught social and problem-solving skills for managing problematic situations and cognitive strategies for controlling self-debilitating thought processes that lead down a relapse path. Training in coping skills reduces relapse episodes, at least in the short run, but does not make a major dent on the relapse problem (Chaney, O'Leary, & Marlatt, 1978; Stevens & Hollis, 1989). Relapse management and prevention clearly require an expanded focus.

Viewed from the model of triadic reciprocal causation, each of the three classes of causal interactants — environmental factors, the self-system, and behavioral competencies — contribute to the long-term control of substance abuse. As we have already seen, skills and strategies are quickly abandoned if people lack the strength of self-efficacy to stick with them through tough times. Moreover, efforts at relapse prevention must be extended beyond personal changes to the social environment. Social support and guidance during difficult times bolster the maintenance of abstinence (Ossip-Klein, et al. 1991). People who have become deeply enmeshed in a subculture of substance abuse have to restructure their way of life radically if they are to conquer their addiction. Recovered substance abusers need life satisfactions in social, occupational, and recreational activities that diminish the attraction of addictive substances. In addition, they need social supports when life events threaten to overwhelm their self-regulatory capabilities. Supportive social relationships not only reduce stress and compete with substance use but also strengthen self-regulatory efficacy by enabling those struggling with self-control to weather adversities.

Quality of social aid is a predictor of abstinence (Cohen & Lichtenstein, 1990; Gossop, Green, Phillips, & Bradley, 1990). Environmental contributors involve much more than shoring up infirm self-regulation with social supports. Environmentally oriented approaches create social structures that enable people to exert satisfying proactive control over their familial, occupational, and recreational lives (Azrin, 1976). This enlarged sociocognitive model of relapse prevention is discussed at greater length in Chapter 8.

Expansion of the relapse model to include environmental change does not minimize self-efficacy contributors but rather extends them to broader domains of functioning. The environment is not simply a fixed entity that inevitably impinges upon individuals. People select, construct, and negotiate environments partly on the basis of their efficacy beliefs. The courses of behavior they pursue determine which aspects of the large potential environment will come into play and what forms they will take. People are thus interacting determiners of how their lives become structured environmentally. Indeed, within the same potential environmental structure, people can create beneficial or detrimental environments depending on their efficacy beliefs (Wood & Bandura, 1989a).

Treatments that foster the conception of oneself as a nonuser can also contribute to the maintenance of abstinence, because adoption of a self-conception as a nonuser can produce profound lifestyle changes. Such changes are most likely to occur when the emergent new self-conception leads to severance of social ties with substance abusers and sufficient social support is provided for immersion in nonuser social networks (Stall & Biernacki, 1986). Those who lead bored or aversive lives are quick to seek escape in addictive substances. They need to find involvements in activities that provide some satisfaction and meaning to their lives. These broader changes enable them to realize a satisfying life without alcohol or drugs. Engrossment in meaningful pursuits contributes to the exercise of control over substance abuse (Gossop et al., 1990). Meaningful work provides structure to one's daily life, a sense of purpose, and a set of communal relationships, and it contributes to one's sense of identity. Joblessness and vocational drudgery foster substance abuse. A multifaceted approach to relapse prevention calls for a multifaceted assessment of perceived self-regulatory efficacy that includes not only strength of efficacy to manage relapse precipitants but also perceived efficacy to cultivate and maintain helpful social relationships and to adopt and stick with activities that override the appeal of addictive substances.

Dynamics of Self-Regulation

The self-efficacy regulation of refractory behavior over extended intervals is poorly elucidated by the static investigation procedure that is routinely used. It is a method of convenience rather than of explanatory merit. The behavior of interest is simply measured at a few arbitrary follow-up points, but the factors that supposedly regulate it at those times are not studied. The behavior is thus disembodied from its current determinants and instead linked to past determinants. Maintenance processes are best clarified by microanalyses of ongoing self-regulation, rather than by changing behavior and then merely reassessing it weeks, months, or years later (Bandura & Simon, 1977). Diverse changes can and often do occur during those prolonged intervals. Some people maintain steadfast control, others lapse but recover quickly, others escalate lapses into prolonged relapses, and still others may have cycled from relapse to abstinence one or more times. The status at any point in time in this fluctuating dynamic process may or may not be representative of the self-regulatory attainments. Repeated analysis of covariation of behavior and its postulated determinants sheds light on how self-regulatory mechanisms operate and the conditions under which they malfunction, either temporarily or more enduringly.

An efficacy belief system is not an immutable trait. Understanding how perceived self-regulatory efficacy contributes to behavioral maintenance requires ongoing assessment of the fluctuations in the strength of efficacy beliefs as well as the behavior they can influence. It is the proximal efficacy beliefs that regulate behavior, not those held a year or so earlier, unless they have undergone no change in the interim. Relating posttreatment self-efficacy to behavioral status at distant occasions provides information of practical utility by identifying areas of vulnerability and potential relapse precipitants. But exclusive reliance on past efficacy beliefs underestimates their regulatory role in behavioral maintenance processes. If the magnitude of the predictive relation shrinks over time, it is probably because a dated efficacy belief is selected rather than because self-regulatory beliefs have mysteriously lost their power to influence human motivation and action at later periods. Indeed, when perceived efficacy is measured at each of several follow-up points, the closer in time the assessed efficacy belief, the better it predicts the subsequent level of smoking behavior (Becoña, Frojan, & Lista, 1988; Nicki et al., 1984).

In behavior that taxes self-regulatory efficacy, the drop-out rate increases over successive follow-up periods (McAuley, 1991). If the quitters are predominantly the less self-efficacious ones, as is usually the case, the variability in perceived efficacy in the shrinking sample is progressively restricted to those at higher levels of perceived efficacy. Range restriction lowers correlations. Correlations based on predictors that are dated and restricted in range can substantially underestimate the contribution of efficacy beliefs to the ongoing regulation of behavior.

Self-Regulatory Model of Health Promotion and Risk Reduction

Health care expenditures are soaring at a rate that is consuming an increasing proportion of the gross national product of developed nations (Fuchs, 1990). Despite the huge outlays for health services, millions of people receive no health care, and even those who can afford it are often poorly served by traditional health delivery systems and the insurance systems that pay them. Health care has thus become a major domestic problem. With people living longer, nations are confronted with the major

challenges of how to keep people healthy throughout their life span; otherwise, they will be swamped with staggering health costs that drain resources needed for national programs. Nations that provide universal health care are forced to impose increasing delays in treatment services and rationing of costly medical interventions. Clearly, the growing health care crisis requires intensifying health promotion efforts and restructuring health delivery systems to make them more productive. There is growing evidence that people are adopting beneficial health practices and living longer with fewer diseases and disabilities. Much more can be done in health promotion to produce a healthy elderly population.

It is sometimes argued that health promotion might raise health costs by increasing longevity, with a concomitant need for more health services. The evidence does not bear this out (Fries et al., 1993). People who adopt healthful habits live not only longer but healthier, with less need and demand for medical services. It is not as though those with detrimental health habits remain healthy and then die a quick death. Rather, they accumulate a lifetime of costly medical services and interventions. For example, the lifetime medical costs alone for smokers are much higher than those for nonsmokers, despite their shorter lives. The more risk factors, the higher the lifetime medical costs of morbidity. Moreover, one must look beyond longevity to the quality of life. A life impaired by physical dysfunction incurs heavy personal and social costs that must be factored into health promotion policies.

Health promotion and risk reduction programs are often structured in ways that are costly, cumbersome, and minimally effective. Services funneled through physicians often create a bottleneck in the system. Many physicians do not know how to change high-risk behavior. Even if they did, they cannot spare much time for any individual or make much money doing it. The net result is minimal prevention and costly remediation. Efforts to slow the soaring health costs of aging populations are aimed mainly at rationing or curtailing health services.

Self-management programs based on the self-efficacy model improve the quality of health and reduce the need for medical services. DeBusk and his colleagues devised an efficacy-based model combining self-regulatory principles with computerized implementation that promotes habits conducive to health and reduces those that impair it (DeBusk et al., 1994). The system is founded on knowledge of the major subfunctions of self-regulation. These include self-monitoring, proximal goal setting, strategy development, and self-motivating incentives. This computerized self-regulatory system equips participants with the skills and personal efficacy needed to exercise self-directed change. It includes exercise programs to build cardiovascular capacity; nutrition programs to reduce risk of heart disease and cancer; weight reduction programs; smoking cessation programs; and stress management programs.

For each risk factor, individuals are provided with detailed guidance about how to alter their habits. Participants monitor the behavior they seek to change, set short-range, attainable subgoals to motivate and guide their efforts, and receive detailed feedback of progress as a further motivator for self-directed change. The system is structured in this way based on the knowledge that self-motivation requires both goal challenges and performance feedback. A single program implementer, assisted by the computerized system, manages the behavioral changes of large numbers of participants. Figure 7.9 portrays the structure of the self-regulatory system. At selected intervals, the computer generates and mails to participants individually tailored guides for personal change. These guides specify subgoals and chart the participants' progress toward their subgoals and their month-to-month changes. The participants, in turn, send data cards to the implementer reporting the changes they have achieved and their level of personal efficacy in the various domains for the next cycle of self-directed change. Efficacy ratings identify areas of vulnerability and difficulty and foretell likely relapse. The tailored feedback also suggests strategies for overcoming the identified difficulties. The program implementer maintains telephone contact with the

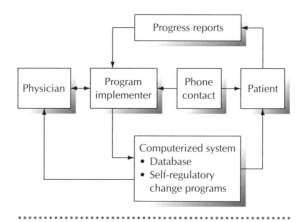

FIGURE 7.9.   Computer-assisted self-regulatory system for altering health habits.

participants and is available to provide extra guidance and support should they encounter difficulties. The implementer also serves as the liaison to medical personnel, who are called upon when their expertise is needed.

The self-regulatory operations are computerized, but participants do not have to use computers. This health delivery system can be easily linked to on-line computer services, of course. Computerized communication vastly expands the applicability and convenience of the system. Moreover, the amount of personalized service can be readily tailored to fit the needs of participants. Those with good self-management capabilities can reduce health risks with little direct social guidance (Clark et al., in press). Others need some personalized assistance as well. Those who harbor grave doubts that they can change their health habits require more intensive personalized guidance to succeed with the self-management system.

The effectiveness of this self-regulatory system was initially tested in a cholesterol reduction program conducted with employees drawn from work sites who had elevated cholesterol levels. This risk factor was selected because each 1 percent reduction in serum cholesterol produces about a 2 percent reduction in risk of heart attack. Through self-regulatory dietary change, participants reduced their intake of cholesterol and saturated fat and lowered their serum cholesterol (Fig. 7.10). The more room for change in nutritional habits, the greater the cholesterol reduction. They achieved even greater risk reduction if their spouses also took part in the program. The system works equally well in clinical settings with patients with elevated cholesterol (Clark et al., in press).

Most patients who suffer heart attacks have detrimental health habits that put them at risk for another one. They receive intensive treatment in the hospital but little help following discharge in changing health habits that contribute to further coronary artery disease. The success of the self-regulatory system in reducing risk factors in postcoronary patients was compared against the standard medical postcoronary care in five hospitals (De-Busk et al., 1994). In this effort to reduce the likelihood of future heart attacks, a number of risk factors — including elevated cholesterol, smoking, and being sedentary — were selected for change us-

ing the computer-assisted case management system. The cardiac patients who had the benefit of this system lowered their low-density lipoprotein (LDL) cholesterol and raised their beneficial high-density lipoprotein (HDL) cholesterol by a combined diet-drug therapy. They also were more successful in quitting smoking and achieved greater increases in functional cardiovascular capacity than did patients who received the standard medical care (Fig. 7.11). These preventive health benefits were achieved at minimal cost.

Further research with people suffering from coronary artery disease reveals that this personalized system for risk reduction slows the rate of arterial narrowing, which can block blood flow and cause chest pains or heart attacks (Haskell et al., 1994). At the end of four years, those receiving the usual medical care by their physicians showed no change or a worsening of their condition. In contrast, those aided in self-management of health habits lowered their intake of dietary fat, lost weight, lowered their bad cholesterol and raised their good cholesterol, and increased their exercise and cardiovascular capacity (Fig. 7.12). The program altered the physical progression of the artery disease. Those receiving the self-management program had 47 percent less buildup of plaque on artery walls, a higher rate of reversal of atherosclerosis, and fewer hospitalizations for coronary problems and deaths than did those receiving the usual care by their physician.

The self-regulatory system is well received by participants because it is individually tailored to their needs; it provides them with continuing personalized guidance and informative feedback that enables them to exercise considerable control over their own change; it is a home-based program that does not require any special facilities, equipment, or attendance at group meetings that usually have high drop-out rates; its use is not constrained by time and place; and it can serve large numbers of people simultaneously. The substantial productivity gains are achieved by process innovations combining self-regulatory and computer technologies that provide effective health-promoting services in ways that are individualized, intensive, highly convenient, and inexpensive.

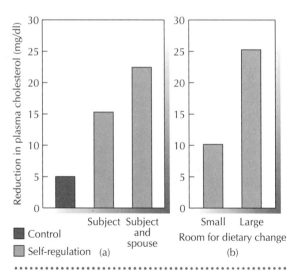

FIGURE 7.10. Levels of reduction in plasma cholesterol achieved with the computerized self-regulatory system. (a) Mean cholesterol reductions achieved in applications in the workplace by participants who used the system by themselves or along with their spouses; those who did not receive the system provided a control baseline. (b) Mean cholesterol reduction achieved with the self-regulatory system by patients whose daily cholesterol or fat intake was high or relatively low at the outset of the program.

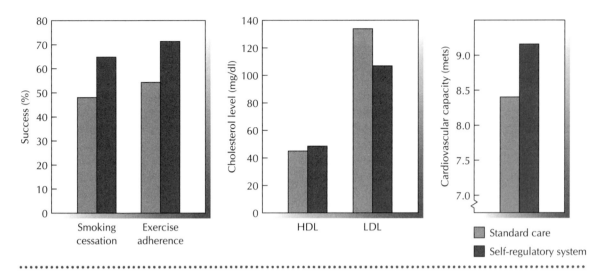

FIGURE 7.11.   Changes in coronary risk factors of patients during the first year after acute myocardial infarction depending on whether they received the usual medical care or training in self-management of health habits. (After DeBusk et al., 1994)

Because the computerized self-regulatory system can serve a vast number of participants concurrently at low cost, it lends itself readily to preventive purposes. Indeed, with this type of guidance system, adolescents achieve greater reductions in weight and consumption of saturated fat and cholesterol and eat more fiber and complex carbohydrates than those given the same strategies for weight management but without the individualized feedback (Burnett, Nagel, Harrington, & Taylor, 1989).

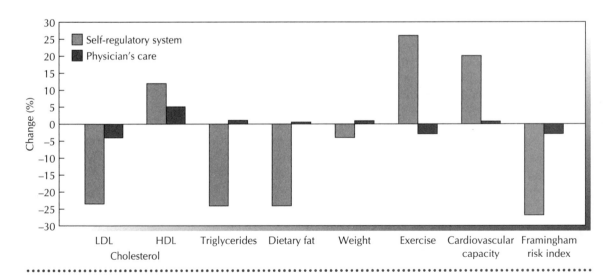

FIGURE 7.12.   Reduction in multiple risk factors of patients with coronary atherosclerosis depending on whether they received the usual care of their physician or training in self-management of health habits. (After Haskell et al., 1994)

The preceding studies attest to the efficacy and effectiveness of the self-regulatory model for reducing risk of cardiovascular disease, which is a leading cause of disability and premature mortality. This model can also serve as an effective vehicle for preventing major cancers, because it targets the behavioral risk factors for them. Approximately 60% of cancers are the products of nutritional factors and smoking (Trichopoulos and Willett, 1996). Molecular and cell biology have given us a better understanding of how food substances not only promote cell mutations but provide protection by altering the metabolism of potential mutagens. Cigarette smoking is a major carcinogen that contributes to a wide range of cancers including lung, respiratory tract, bladder, kidney, and pancreatic cancers. Physical exercise affects biochemical processes that help to protect against colon cancer. Reducing carcinogens in the workplace and living environment provides additional behavioral means of cancer prevention. In sum, over two-thirds of cancers are behaviorally preventable by psychosocial means that help people to avoid smoking, exercise more, and eat healthier. Although the psychosocial approach offers the most promise for preventing major human diseases, that is not where the major share of resources in the health field are invested.

Self-Management of Chronic Diseases

Chronic disease has become the dominant form of illness and the major cause of disability. Such diseases do not lend themselves well to biomedical approaches devised primarily to treat acute illness, so their management has not been given much attention. Rather than receiving enabling guidance, most people suffering from chronic disease are heavily medicated or simply given health guidelines that, all too often, they fail to put into practice. Their problems of adherence stem more from disbelief in their efficacy to do what they are prescribed than from physical debility, pain, or disease activity (Taal, Rasker, Seydel, & Wiegman, 1993). The treatment of chronic disease must focus on self-management of physical conditions over the lifetime rather than on cure. This requires, among

other things, pain amelioration, enhancement and maintenance of functioning with growing physical disability, and development of self-regulative compensatory skills. The goal is to retard the progression of impairment to disability and to improve the quality of life of people with chronic disease.

Holman and Lorig (1992) have devised a prototypic model for the self-management of different types of chronic diseases. The self-management skills include cognitive pain control techniques, self-relaxation, proximal goal setting combined with self-incentives as motivators to increase level of activity, problem-solving and self-diagnostic skills for monitoring and interpreting changes in one's health status, and skills in locating community resources and managing medication programs. The way health care systems deal with clients can alter their sense of efficacy in ways that support or undermine their restorative efforts (Bandura, 1992b). Clients are therefore taught how to take greater initiative for their health care and dealings with health personnel. These capabilities are developed through modeling of self-management skills, guided mastery practice, and informative feedback.

In managing chronic diseases, people not only must alleviate symptoms that are more or less personally controllable but also must exercise personal control over the medical care and treatments that are prescribed for them. Exercise of participatory influence over the design of treatment regimens contributes to positive mood and functioning (Affleck et al., 1987). Therefore, in the self-management program, people are taught how to take greater initiative for their health care and dealings with health personnel to optimize health benefits.

The effectiveness of this self-regulative approach has been tested extensively for ameliorating the debility and chronic pain of arthritis (Holman & Lorig, 1992). The degree of physical impairment does not foretell quality of functioning. Some people with extensive impairment lead active, productive lives despite the constraints, whereas others with minimal impairment restrict their activities and despair over the prospect of progressive infirmity. Formal tests indicate that functional limitations may be governed more by

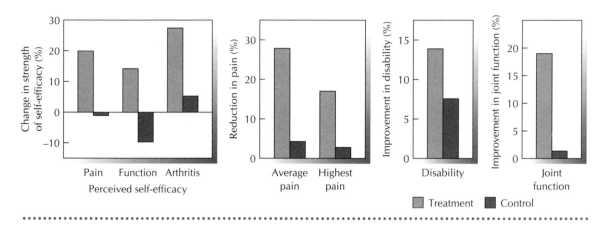

FIGURE 7.13. Changes exhibited by arthritic patients in perceived self-efficacy and reduction in pain and impairment of joints as a function of training in self-regulatory techniques. (O'Leary et al., 1988)

beliefs of capability than by degree of actual physical impairment (Baron, Dutil, Berkson, Lander, & Becker, 1987).

Fluctuations in the disease activity convey the impression that the condition is neither predictable nor personally controllable. The restoration of a sense of regulatory efficacy is therefore of major importance. In a study by O'Leary and her associates, patients suffering from rheumatoid arthritis substantially improved their psychophysical functioning following training in self-management compared to matched controls who received an arthritis help book describing self-management techniques and were encouraged to be more active (O'Leary et al., 1988). The self-management program increased patients' perceived efficacy to reduce pain and other debilitating aspects of arthritis and to pursue potentially painful activities (Figure 7.13). Activity can retard disease progression by increasing nutrients to joint cartilage and stabilizing joint tissue. The treated patients reduced pain and inflammation in their joints and were less debilitated by their arthritic condition. The higher their perceived coping efficacy, the less pain they experienced, the less they were disabled by their arthritis, and the greater the reduction they achieved in joint impairment. The more efficacious were also less depressed and less stressed, and they slept better.

The treatment did not alter immunologic function, but significant relationships were found between perceived coping efficacy and immunologic indices. There is some evidence that in the arthritic disorder, the suppressor T-cell function of the immune system is depressed. This results in proliferation of antibodies, which is aided by helper T cells. Rheumatoid arthritis is an autoimmune disorder in which the immune system produces antibodies that destroy joints and surrounding tissues. Increases in suppressor T cells, which tend to inhibit production of antibodies, suggest improvement in the immune system in this disorder. Perceived coping efficacy was associated with increases in the number of suppressor T cells and with a decrease in the ratio of helper to suppressor T cells.

This self-management approach to arthritic conditions has been applied on a large scale. In follow-up assessments conducted four years later, arthritis patients who had the benefit of self-management training displayed increased self-efficacy, reduced pain, and slower biological progression of their disease over the four-year period (Holman & Lorig, 1992). They also reduced their physician visits by 43 percent. Figure 7.14 presents the results. These enduring health benefits represent huge reductions in health costs. Enhancement of functioning despite some progression of the disease attests to the influential role of

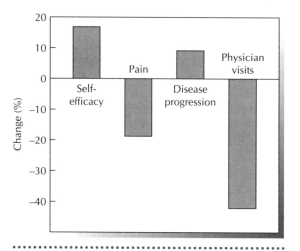

FIGURE 7.14. Enduring healthful changes achieved by training in self-management of arthritis as revealed in a follow-up assessment four years later. The 9 percent biological progression of the disease is less than half the 20 percent disease progression one would normally expect over four years for this age group. (After Lorig, 1990)

psychosocial factors in how people live with chronic disease. Tests of alternative mediating mechanisms reveal that neither increases in knowledge nor degree of change in health behaviors are appreciable predictors of health functioning (Lorig, Chastain, Ung, Shoor, & Holman, 1989; Lorig, Seleznick et al., 1989). Both baseline efficacy beliefs and changes in efficacy beliefs to exercise some control over one's arthritic condition instilled by treatment explain level of pain experienced four years later (Lorig, 1990). When patients are equated for degree of physical debility, those who believe they can exercise some influence over how much their arthritic condition affects them lead more active lives and experience less pain (Shoor & Holman, 1984).

Perceived self-efficacy similarly predicts functional disability regardless of pain level or duration of the disease (Schiaffino & Revenson, 1992; Schiaffino, Revenson, & Gibofsky, 1991). A high sense of efficacy fosters beneficial coping strategies, which, in turn, lessen functional disability. Beckham and his associates (1994) compared the quality of adaptation to rheumatoid arthritis as a function

of efficacy beliefs and faulty patterns of thinking, such as anticipating catastrophic outcomes and dwelling on negative events. Patients with higher perceived efficacy were less functionally debilitated by their condition and less bothered by pain, anxiety, and depression after controlling for age, sex, and actual severity of their disease. Faulty thinking was a much weaker and less consistent predictor of the different adaptational reactions.

Different types of chronic diseases present many similar problems of how to manage pain, overcome obstacles created by physical impairments, maintain self-sufficiency, and exercise control over medical services to achieve the best results. The self-management program, therefore, serves as a generic model that can be adapted to different chronic diseases. Indeed, it produces similar health benefits for people suffering from heart disease, lung disease, and stroke as well as arthritis (Lorig, Sobel, Bandura, & Holman, 1993). Adding to the generic model special mastery components that address problems unique to particular chronic diseases may further enhance health benefits.

Part of the challenge in maintaining the quality of life with chronic disease or the aftermath of serious illness is the exercise of control over emotional distress associated with such physical conditions. Active engrossment in meaningful activities is a good antidote to ruminative distress and feelings of despondency and futility. In addition, some of the coping strategies are directed at managing emotional states (Lazarus & Folkman, 1984). These strategies include more positive reappraisals of one's life situation, reordering one's lifestyle priorities, controlling perturbing ideation, alleviating stress by cognitive means, and seeking social support. Medical conditions that pose serious threats to life give rise to prolonged pain, emotional distress, and uncertainty about one's prospect of survival. Many forms of cancer typify this condition. Adaptation to the diagnosis and treatment of cancer varies widely. Some patients feel a profound sense of helplessness and react with despair. Others believe they can exercise some control over their psychosocial functioning and strive to improve their quality of life (Taylor, 1989). Cunningham, Lockwood, and Cunningham (1991) report that perceived coping efficacy accounts for a major share of the adaptational variation. The more patients' perceived coping efficacy was raised by training in coping skills, the better they were in warding off anxiety and despair and the more they improved their quality of life. The predictiveness of perceived coping efficacy remained unchanged by multiple controls for demographic characteristics and disease status. These findings underscore the value of combining medical treatments with psychosocial treatments that counteract collapse of personal efficacy to maintain quality of life with adverse physical conditions.

The extent to which patients applied their coping skills was unrelated to the improvements they achieved, which is similar to what Lorig and her colleagues have found. There are several possible reasons that improvements in well-being and functioning are not simply products of mechanical application of skills. It was shown earlier that perceived capability to exercise control, whether illusory or real but unexercised, decreases emotional distress over aversive events. Thus, belief in one's personal efficacy can, in itself, produce benefits. Additionally, positive cognitive reappraisals that focus on the aspects of one's life that are personally controllable can raise perceived efficacy, which activates many adaptive processes extending well beyond the particular coping skills taught in an intervention.

Social Diffusion of Health-Promoting Practices

Knowledge of mechanisms of self-directed change specifies the essential elements for broad socially oriented approaches to enhance and maintain the quality of health in a society. An effective program of widespread change in health practices includes four major components. The first is informational and is designed to increase people's awareness and knowledge of the health risks and benefits of different patterns of behavior. The second component involves development of the social and self-regulative skills needed to translate informed concerns into effective preventive action. The third

component is aimed at building a robust sense of efficacy to support the exercise of control in the face of difficulties that inevitably arise. This is achieved by providing repeated opportunities for guided practice and corrective feedback in applying the skills successfully in simulated high-risk situations people are likely to encounter in their everyday lives. The final component involves enlisting and creating social supports for desired personal changes.

Informational Component. The first set of determinants concerns the motivational preconditions for adopting patterns of behavior conducive to health. Aversive experiences usually serve as forceful inducements for personal change. Tension, discomfort, and pain motivate people to consider changes that might bring relief from distress. It may take years for detrimental habits to produce recognizable impairments to health. Hence, these aversive motivators of change are too weak to prompt people to adopt habits conducive to health or to forsake potentially detrimental ones that have not yet produced any pain or noticeable adverse effects.

Not only are the aversive motivators weak, but the process of change itself often creates temporary discomforts. Many detrimental habits are immediately rewarding, whereas the adverse effects accumulate slowly and are considerably delayed. To a gourmand, the delectable taste of appetizing food easily outweighs the imperceptible effects of the increments in weight it produces. To a chain smoker, the immediate distress accompanying cigarette withdrawal is a more powerful motivator for smoking than are the health benefits years later for nonsmoking. It takes some time before their smoking urges abate and people begin to feel better. Therefore, self-incentives must be used to provide immediate motivational inducements for self-regulatory behavior until the benefits that eventually accrue from healthful habits assume the rewarding function.

In fostering self-directed change, it is necessary to enlist potential sources of motivation and to develop new ones. Mass media can be used effectively to inform the public about how personal habits affect the risk of premature disease and how to alter risk-related behaviors of long standing (Solomon & Maccoby, 1984). Multimedia campaigns serve to arouse interest in health programs and to translate the likely future debilities of detrimental habits into current concerns. People are moved more by evidence of current adverse health effects of their behavior than by distal illnesses that affect only some people, which can be discounted as a low personal risk. Therefore, health risks must be proximated and personalized to enhance their motivational impact. For example, evidence that smoking stunts lung growth and breathing capacity and impairs other physiological functioning in everyone, along with the long-term health hazards (Evans et al., 1981), will arouse greater concern than will focus solely on the long-term risk of cancer.

The optimal way of structuring health communications was addressed earlier and will not be reviewed here. Given full information about the health risks and benefits, those with a high sense of efficacy mount the effort needed to succeed (Carey & Carey, 1993). The limitations commonly attributed to health information partly reflect the selective focus on recurrent failures. To keep matters in perspective, the relapse curves for smoking cessation, for example, should be superimposed on curves for the 40 million smokers who quit on their own. Admittedly, for most heavy smokers, quitting the habit is a difficult struggle, often with disheartening setbacks, but those who persist in their efforts eventually succeed. Factual information alone, however, usually produces little change in the more refractory cases. Despite a high level of knowledge about health risks, many people continue health-impairing practices. They need to be provided not only with reasons to change but also with the means to do it and the sense of efficacy to persevere at it until they succeed. Anticipatory concern combined with self-regulatory competencies is more likely to motivate preventive and remedial action than is concern alone.

Self-Regulatory Skills. It is one thing to convince people that they should alter detrimental health habits. It is another to get people to act on their concerns and to ensure that their efforts will bring successful results. Motivation alone is not enough. Like any other endeavor, effective self-regulation of health behavior requires certain skills. Thus, motivation facilitates self-directed change when people are taught skills for self-influence, but motivation without the requisite subskills produces little change (Bandura & Simon, 1977). Social cognitive programs that cultivate skills for exercising control over health habits instill a stronger sense of personal efficacy and firmer intentions to adopt preventive health practices than simply providing factual information on the causes of a particular disease and how to prevent it (Jemmott et al., 1992).

Self-regulation operates through three main subfunctions, each of which has been the subject of much research (Bandura, 1986a; Kanfer & Gaelick, 1986). They include self-monitoring, goal setting, and enlistment of self-incentives for personal change. As the first step in the process, people must monitor the behavior they seek to alter (Kazdin, 1974b). Keeping track of the behavior and the events that foster it serves several purposes. Observing covariations of behavior and the conditions under which it occurs serves as a self-diagnostic device for identifying determinants of one's behavior. Self-monitoring also provides the information needed for setting realistic subgoals, evaluating one's progress, and increasing one's sense of self-regulatory efficacy. Continuing feedback about how one is doing is thus essential in sustaining the process of change.

Self-directed change requires goals for motivating and guiding one's efforts. We saw earlier that self-motivation is best maintained by proximal subgoals that are instrumental in achieving larger future goals. Proximal subgoals provide incentives and guides for action, and subgoal attainments bolster self-efficacy and produce self-satisfactions that sustain one's efforts at personal change along the way.

The third component of self-regulation involves the tangible and evaluative self-incentives people create for their own behavior. People can get themselves to do things they would otherwise put off or avoid altogether by arranging incentives for themselves for subgoal attainments. They achieve greater self-directed change if they reward their successful efforts than if they provide no incentives for themselves (Bandura, 1986a). Evaluative self-incentives also serve as important self-motivators and guides for behavior. People get themselves to put forth the effort necessary to accomplish what they value for the satisfaction they derive from fulfilling the goals they have set for themselves.

Theories about the human capacity for self-regulation can be easily distorted by selectively examining only the most refractory cases while ignoring the vast population of people who achieve notable success in regulating their own behavior. Consider the theories constructed to explain the refractory nature of overeating: Food is a powerful primary reinforcer that produces instant gratification; households are filled with foodstuffs that whet the appetite; people have to eat it at periodic intervals; food is advertised, displayed, and prepared in the most appetizing forms; social custom continuously forces food on people; and it is a handy tranquilizer for deprivation and distress. These powerful conditions presumably compel overeating and swamp people's efforts at self-regulation. Were one to present this theory to the proverbial Martians, they would fully expect all Earthlings to be very obese. Yet most people manage to stay reasonably slim amidst all this appetizing abundance and recurrent social pressures to eat fattening foods. Animal studies document the serious health consequences of unlimited access to appetizing fare without self-regulatory control. Rats given access to a rich assortment of junk food quickly ballooned in weight to miniature blimps (Sclafani & Springer, 1976). Smoking is another case in point. Smoking is presumably intractable because it is compelled by two types of dependencies: nicotine dependence, in which each puff sends a reinforcing nicotine shot to the brain; and psychological dependence, which creates a craving for cigarettes. The high relapse rates of those smokers who have sought professional help supposedly attest to the intractable nature of smoking. In point of fact, the millions of people who have quit smoking on their own testify to human self-regulatory capabilities.

Full understanding of self-regulatory mechanisms requires examination of successful self-regulators as well as the intractable cases. Naturalistic studies of self-directed change show that successful self-regulators are highly skilled in enlisting the component subfunctions of self-regulation. They track their behavior; set proximal goals for themselves; draw from an array of coping strategies, rather than relying on a single technique; and create positive incentives for their efforts (Perri, 1985; Perri, Richards, & Schultheis, 1977). Moreover, they apply multifaceted self-influence more consistently and persistently than do ineffectual self-regulators. Successes achieved through sustained self-directed effort strengthen belief in one's self-regulatory capabilities. When the methods developed by skilled self-regulators are given to others to change their own problematic behavior, the naturally evolved methods produce better results than those used in standard counseling practice (Heffernan & Richards, 1981).

Self-regulatory development occupies a central position in the community-oriented model of health promotion and disease prevention devised by Maccoby and Farquhar (1975). The success of health promotion programs rests on three requisite sources of knowledge and psychosocial methods: the ability to identify risk factors that predict future health status, the ability to assess them adequately, and the ability to change them enduringly. The model devised by Maccoby and Farquhar addressed each of these issues by drawing on knowledge of epidemiology, mass communications, self-regulatory mechanisms, and community mobilization for change.

Residents are taught self-regulatory skills through self-help manuals that provide explicit guides for reducing weight; exercising; eliminating smoking; and changing dietary patterns to decrease consumption of saturated fat, salt, cholesterol, and alcohol. In follow-up assessments, residents in a control community showed little change in the risk factors for cardiovascular disease, whereas residents in two communities who received the media program in self-directed change were more knowledgeable about how health habits contribute to coronary disease and achieved a 20 percent reduction in risk of cardiovascular disease (Farquhar et al., 1977; Meyer, Nash, McAlister, Maccoby, & Farquhar, 1980). Participants at high risk, who had more to change, achieved an even greater risk reduction of 30 percent. The risk index included smoking, systolic blood pressure, plasma cholesterol, and weight. In one of the treatment communities, a subset of residents at high risk for heart disease also received personalized instructions by health personnel using modeling and guided practice of self-regulatory skills. The addition of personalized guidance increased diffusion of information in the community about ways of preventing heart disease (Meyer, Maccoby, & Farquhar, 1977), accelerated reduction in risk factors, and contributed to effective maintenance of those changes in subsequent years. The added benefits of personalized influence were especially evident in refractory habits, such as smoking. As people change, they serve as diffusers of health habits to others in the community. Perhaps for this reason, at least some personalized guidance can improve long-term maintenance of changes in the community at large.

Health Promotion in Childhood.   Preventive efforts are especially important because many of the patterns of behavior that can seriously compromise health typically begin in early adolescence and continue in adulthood. It is easier to prevent detrimental health habits than to try to change them after they have become deeply entrenched as part of a lifestyle. Because of the heavy costs of treatments and their restorative limitations, prevention should be given priority but rarely is. Economic forces, fueled by the rising health costs of chronic diseases, are more likely to raise the priority of prevention than is the medical establishment. The biopsychosocial model provides a valuable public health tool for this purpose.

Schools are a natural setting for preventive programs, especially for habits plied by peers. One must distinguish the locus of change from the implementers of change, however. As noted earlier, schools are inadequately equipped with the necessary resources, training, and incentives to seriously undertake health promotion and early intervention in habit patterns that jeopardize health.

Like other professionals, educators devote a major share of their efforts to the activities on which they are evaluated. As long as health promotion is regarded as tangential to the central mission of schools, it will continue to be slighted. However, schools can adopt some health promoting practices with

beneficial results that do not require time, new resources, or the restructuring of social relations. Schools provided with a brief health promotion curriculum and encouraged to lower the fat content of their lunch offerings and enhance their physical activity offerings produce lasting improvements in children's eating and exercise habits (Luepker et al., 1996).

A serious societal commitment to fostering the health of its youth must provide the multidisciplinary personnel and resources needed to do the job effectively. This calls for new school-based models of health promotion that operate in concert with the home, the community, and the society at large. The programs are in school but not of school. Implementers must have the operational control needed to do the job well. Without it, preventive efforts do more to discredit psychosocial approaches through deficient implementation than to advance health.

School health education provides factual information about health, but does not do much in the way of changing the social influences that shape and regulate children's health habits. These efforts are usually heavy on didactics but short on personal enablement. Enablement means more than simply teaching a stock set of refusal tactics. Rather, it involves equipping children with skills and efficacy beliefs that enable them to regulate their emotional states and manage the diverse pressures for detrimental conduct in interpersonal relationships.

Findings on the efficacy of prevention models must be viewed cautiously given the reluctance of most schools to devote much time to such activities, and outcome studies rarely assess the quality of implementation. It is exceedingly difficult to achieve high-quality implementation of programs that carry low priority, have no ongoing monitoring, lack an instructive feedback system linked to explicit implementation standards, and provide no means for improving the quality of implementation where it is weak or inconsistent. Sound models grounded in theory that achieve good results when applied well typically produce variable outcomes in large-scale interventions if the implementation quality is left to the vagaries of local circumstances. The commitment and efficacy of the social system become the major determinants of the outcomes. Many states mandate health education in schools but neither provide much in the way of training in how to do it effectively nor evaluate the results of such offerings. The lower the teachers' instructional efficacy in this subject, the less time and effort they devote to it, the greater their skepticism that their efforts will produce health benefits, and the less value they attach to health skills (Everett, Price, Tellijohann, & Durgin, 1996).

The more comprehensive approaches address values, normative beliefs, outcome expectations, and self-regulatory skills. The programs that have proved most effective in preventing substance abuse strip the substance of its glamorous image; make known that regular use of injurious substances is not normative behavior for young adolescents, as is widely misbelieved; personalize how the substance adversely affects current physiological functioning in everyone and increases long-term health risks; and model strategies for resisting social coercions to use the substances (Evans et al., 1981; McAlister, Perry, Killen, Slinkard, & Maccoby, 1980). Older peers model tactics for resistance, and children learn and practice, in role-playing, counterarguments to peer pressures. In this way, students develop a sense of efficacy to resist coercive pressures and the skill to do it. Some prevention models have been expanded to include, in addition to resistive skills, more general self-management skills in problem solving, stress management, and interpersonal communication (Botvin, 1990).

Health promotion programs that encompass the essential elements of the self-regulatory mastery model prevent or reduce injurious health habits, whereas those that rely mainly on providing health information are relatively ineffective. The more behavioral mastery experiences provided, the stronger the effect (Bruvold, 1993; Murray, Pirie, Luepker, & Pallonen, 1989). The more intensive the program and the better the implementation, the stronger the impact (Connell, Turner, & Mason, 1985). Health knowledge can be conveyed readily, but changes in attitudes and behavioral

practices require greater effort. Moreover, comprehensive approaches that integrate guided mastery health programs with family and community efforts are more successful in preventing adoption of detrimental health habits than are programs in which the schools try to do it alone (Perry et al., 1992; Telch et al., 1982). These effects are all the more interesting because they are achieved by a brief intervention at an early period carried out under operational constraints. Alcohol, drug abuse, and other health-related habits can also be changed by this means (Botvin & Dusenbury, 1992; Gilchrist et al., 1987; Killen et al., 1989).

A central premise of the self-regulatory model is that risk reduction often calls for enhancement of personal efficacy to exercise self-protective control in interpersonal relationships rather than simply targeting a specific habit for change. This is amply illustrated in the high prevalence of unprotected sexual activity among adolescents, which places them at risk for sexually transmitted diseases and unwanted pregnancies. Safer sex guidelines can be readily taught, but they do not provide much self-protection unless adolescents are equipped with the necessary social skills and sense of personal efficacy to resist peer pressures to engage in high-risk sexual practices. Even though individuals acknowledge that safer sex practices reduce the risk of AIDS infection, they do not adopt them if they believe they cannot exercise personal control in sexual relationships (Siegel, Mesagno, Chen, & Christ, 1989). The weaker the perceived efficacy to exercise control over contraception use, the more interpersonal pressures and sentiments increase the likelihood of unprotected intercourse (Levinson, 1986). Perceived efficacy to negotiate condom use predicts safer sex practices in both adolescents (Kasen et al., 1992; Rosenthal, Moore, & Flynn, 1991) and adults (Brafford & Beck, 1991; O'Leary, Goodhart, Jemmott, & Boccher-Littimore, 1992).

Gilchrist and Schinke (1983) used the self-regulatory model to teach teenagers how to exercise self-protective control over sexual situations. The program included factual information about high-risk sexual behavior and self-protective measures, modeling of how to communicate frankly about sexual matters and ensure self-protective sexuality, and role playing in simulated situations to develop interpersonal skills for managing sexual activities. The program significantly enhanced perceived efficacy and skill in managing sexuality. Research by Kelly similarly attests to the substantial value of self-regulative programs for AIDS risk reduction (Kelly, 1995). The findings of other studies indicate that self-regulatory programs for self-protective sexuality work in part through enhancement of perceived efficacy to exercise personal control over sexual practices (Jemmott et al., 1992; Jemmott, Jemmott, Spears et al., 1992).

Primary care physicians are ideally situated to foster preventive and health promotive habits. But not many seriously practice preventive medicine. This lack is not simply a matter of deficient knowledge or unfavorable reimbursement practices. Part of the problem lies in disbelief that their preventive efforts will really produce results. Physicians feel efficacious to counsel healthful habits, but they have a low sense of efficacy that they can get their clients to adopt and stick to them (Hyman, Maibach, Flora, Fortmann, 1992). It is easy to advise without any evaluative follow-through. But there are many impediments to effecting change. To achieve results, physicians must assess patients' social realities, have good strategies to offer, manage resistances, gauge progress and readjust strategies accordingly, deal with the interpersonal strains of noncompliance, and support patients through failures and setbacks. It is hardly surprising that physicians give up trying what they doubt they can achieve. It is the more self-efficacious ones who take prevention seriously in their clinical practice. They place importance on reducing detrimental health habits, view them as changeable, and assist their clients in adopting a self-change program (Stoffelmayr, 1994). Other primary care services should be enlisted more heavily in early health promotion. For example, a brief intervention in which nurses informed mothers about health risks and taught them regulatory strategies enduringly raised their efficacy to reduce exposure of their infants to tobacco smoke, which has adverse cardiorespiratory effects (Strecher et al., 1993).

Social Supports for Personal Change. People achieve self-directed change when they understand how personal habits threaten their well-being, are taught how to modify them, and believe in their capabilities to marshal the effort and resources needed to exercise control. Personal change occurs within a network of social influences, however. Depending on their nature, social influences can aid, retard, or undermine efforts at personal change. This is especially true for behavioral practices that are subjected to strong social normative influences (Bandura, 1994). For example, in the case of sexually transmitted diseases such as AIDS, strong involvement in a social network supportive of self-protective practices increases knowledge of risky behaviors, strengthens personal efficacy to manage sexual relationships, and fosters adoption of safer sex practices (Fisher, 1988; McKusick, Coates, Morin, Pollack, & Hoff, 1990; Wulfert & Wan, 1995). Kelly and his associates devised an imaginative means for altering community normative influences. They trained a cadre of respected and popular patrons of gay bars to adopt protective sexual practices and persuade acquaintances to adopt them (Kelly et al., 1992). This effort at community diffusion through peer implementers raised social norms supportive of safer practices and produced significant reductions in high-risk behavior.

Risk reduction through alteration of subcommunity norms is also an especially important vehicle for curbing the spread of AIDS among intravenous drug users. This is because drug use is often a socially shared activity involving contaminated drug injection equipment (Friedman, de Jong, & Des Jarlais, 1988). Emerging subcommunity norms against needle-sharing behavior is a good predictor of reduction in risky injection practices among intravenous drug users (Des Jarlais & Friedman, 1988a). In short, if health promotion and risk reduction programs are to achieve much success, they must address the sociocultural realities that impose constraints on the exercise of personal control.

The models of disease prevention and health promotion have undergone four generational changes. The initial approaches tried to scare people into health by informing them about the grave health risks of detrimental habits and the benefits of healthful habits. It did not take long to discover the limitations of information about health risks alone. Faced with refractory cases, the next approach tried to reward people into health by linking health habits to extrinsic rewards and penalties. The changes achieved by imposed incentive control were modest to begin with and usually dissipated after control was lifted. One-sided environmental determinism eventually gave way to models of interactive causation in which individuals operate as proactive agents with self-directing capabilities. This generational change focused on development of self-regulatory capabilities. People were equipped with motivational and self-management skills and resilient beliefs in their efficacy to exercise control over their health habits. The final evolution of the health promotion model treated personal change as occurring within a network of social influences. It added socially oriented interventions designed to provide social supports in the wider community for personal change and to alter the practices of social systems that impair health and to foster those that enhance it.

We saw earlier that social norms exert a regulative influence on human behavior via two types of sanctions, social and personal. Normative consensus strengthens both the modeling impact on personal standards and the social sanctioning function. Because of their proximity, immediacy, prevalence, and significance, the interpersonal influences operating within one's immediate social network exert a stronger regulatory function than do general normative sanctions. Overlaying norms are more distal and are applied only infrequently to the behavior of any given individual because unfamiliar others are not around to react to it. Even when they are, if the norms of one's immediate social network are at odds with those of the larger group, the reactions of outsiders carry lesser weight, if they are not disregarded altogether.

Social influences rooted in indigenous sources generally have greater impact and sustaining power than those applied by outsiders for a limited time. A major benefit of community-mediated programs is that they can mobilize the power of formal and informal networks of influence for transmitting knowledge and cultivating beneficial patterns of behavior. A community-mediated approach is a potentially powerful vehicle for promoting both personal and social change. It provides an effective means for creating the motivational preconditions of change, for modeling requisite skills, for enlisting natural social incentives to adopt and maintain beneficial habits, and for establishing health-promoting practices as the normative standard. Generic principles of effective programs are readily adaptable at the subcommunity level to sociocultural differences in the populations being served. In the social diffusion of new behavior patterns, indigenous adopters usually serve as more influential exemplars and persuaders than do outsiders. Moreover, behavioral practices that create widespread health problems require group solutions that are best achieved through community-mediated efforts. Some of the most sweeping social changes for risk reduction have been achieved largely by self-enabling community organizations (Bandura, 1994; McKusick et al., 1990).

In their pioneering health-promoting programs, Farquhar and Maccoby have drawn heavily on existing community networks for transmitting knowledge and cultivating beneficial patterns of health behavior (Farquhar, Maccoby, & Solomon, 1984). This work provides guidelines for mobilizing community resources to disseminate health information and to convey explicit guides on how to change refractory health habits. A large-scale test of community-wide efforts to modify detrimental health habits produced a 16 percent reduction in risk of coronary heart disease and a 15 percent reduction in risk of mortality from various types of diseases (Farquhar et al., 1990). Cities providing the preventive program achieved significantly greater risk reductions than those that did not.

Programs of self-directed change should be applied in ways that create self-sustaining structures within the community for promoting practices conducive to health. Community ownership is best achieved through community enablement for conducting effective health promotion programs. In this approach, a cadre of community health educators and providers is taught how to design, coordinate, implement, and evaluate specific programs for disease prevention and health promotion (Jackson et al., 1994). This type of expertise, as well as knowledge about how to enlist needed resources, enables the participants to continue to tailor health programs to particular community needs. By teaching communities how to take charge of their own change, self-directedness is fostered at the community level as well as at the personal level. Winett, King, and Altman (1989) discuss, in some detail, how the mass media and other community-based influences operating through community centers, schools, shopping centers, workplaces, and health advocacy groups can be used in concert in a social-systems approach to health promotion and disease prevention.

Some researchers call for sharper focus in future community-based efforts to enhance their impact (Luepker et al., 1994; Winkleby, 1994). In this model, large-scale public health campaigns are combined with community programs designed around public policy initiatives. It is easier to mobilize, guide, and sustain the effort needed to succeed by adopting focused smaller scale programs in the community. Because the types of behavior that contribute to diseases are established in childhood, promoting healthful practices in youth should be an integral part of community-oriented efforts. Given the heterogeneous nature of communities, the health promotion programs must be tailored to the psychosocial characteristics of the various subcommunities. Moreover, innovative approaches must be designed to reach high-risk groups that traditional health campaigns typically bypass. In a carefully tailored partnership model, health promotion programs are of the community rather than externally injected into the community.

Health promotion programs modeled on community efforts to reduce risk factors are being increasingly applied and tested. The most efficacious models combine psychosocial and policy-oriented programs. The evidence from studies where sufficient time has elapsed indicates that the preventive community efforts reduce not only risk factors but morbidity and morality as well (Puska et al., 1983; Toumilehto et al., 1986). Fewer people die of cardiovascular disease in a community where health habits are changed than in a matched community not receiving the health-promoting program, or in the society at large. There is a lot of room for improvement in how to implement knowledge of self-regulation, enlist community engagement, and promote policy remedies. Improved models of implementation should produce even greater changes in self-injurious habits.

Average community change masks wide variation in individual health benefits, which requires explanation. Maibach, Flora, and Nass (1991) examined the role played by efficacy beliefs in adoption of health habits promoted by community-wide health campaigns. They found that people's preexisting beliefs that they can exercise some control over their health habits and the degree of enhancement of their perceived self-regulative efficacy by the multifaceted campaign contribute independently to healthy eating habits and regular exercise (Fig. 7.15). Preexisting efficacy beliefs have little predictive value when they are uniformly low. When interventions produce significant changes, the altered efficacy beliefs are the relevant predictors. In the health domain, however, preexisting efficacy beliefs also serve as predictors because

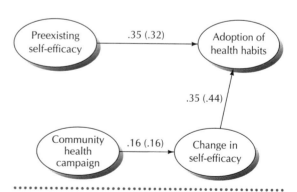

FIGURE 7.15. Path analysis of the influence of perceived self-efficacy on health habits in community-wide programs to reduce risk of cardiovascular disease. The initial numbers on the paths of influence are the significant path coefficients for adoption of healthy eating patterns; the numbers in parentheses are the path coefficients for regular exercise. (Maibach et al., 1991)

pervasive social efforts to raise health consciousness and reduce behavioral health risks create variability in perceived efficacy to manage health habits.

People are repeatedly urged by the mass media to quit smoking, lose excess weight, exercise more, lower alcohol consumption, eat foods high in fiber, and cut down on fatty foods that increase risk of cancer and coronary heart disease. Healthful practices are being modeled increasingly in the community at large. General improvements in health habits are producing declines in mortality rates. Formal community health campaigns are thus superimposed on informal social campaigns that achieve risk reductions in the easier cases that are most amenable to change. Because of the public's saturation with health information, in some studies control communities have just as much exposure to health promotion activities as do communities receiving the special health campaign (Luepker et al., 1994). In some instances, the preventive procedures that have proved effective in community-wide studies are promulgated nationwide (Toumilehto et al., 1986). Greater power is required of formal programs to produce changes in health habits over and above those already taking place in the society at large. With declining national baselines in morbidity and mortality, formal health-promotion programs have to produce faster declines in these rates.

Health Enhancement through Health Policy Initiatives and Environmental Change

A social model of health must be distinguished from an exclusively personal model of health. Health habits are not totally under personal control. They are the products of the reciprocal interplay of personal and social influences. Thus, the quality of the health of a nation is a social matter rather than just a personal one. A comprehensive approach to health promotion requires changing practices of social systems that have widespread detrimental effects on

health rather than solely changing the habits of individuals. Some of the changes require removal of hazardous conditions in the environment and workplaces. Disadvantaged groups, who generally feel politically inefficacious, experience the highest exposure to unhealthy living and work environments. Other efforts are aimed at changing health-related policies to ensure the safety of service systems and the products made for public consumption. Still other changes involve community efforts to make life more healthful and to increase the availability of health services. The social approach to health promotion is directed, in large part, at resource managers and policymakers who legislate and regulate practices that affect public health. Vigorous economic and political battles are fought over environmental health and safety. It takes a great deal of organized social pressure to dislodge entrenched detrimental practices and to remove the impediments often erected by lawmakers beholden to corporate lobbyists. People are swayed by their efficacy beliefs, aspirations, outcome expectations, and perceived impediments, regardless of whether they act individually or collectively. Thus, personal and sociostructural approaches to health promotion involve commonality of regulative influences but differences in the unit of agency, scope of intervention, and object of change.

People's beliefs in their collective efficacy to accomplish social change play a key role in the policy and public health perspective on health promotion and disease prevention. A structuralist approach to health promotion must provide people with the knowledge, skills, and sense of collective efficacy needed to undertake social and policy initiatives that affect human health (Bandura, 1986a; Wallack, Dorfman, Jernigan, & Themba, 1993). Such collaborative efforts take a variety of forms. They raise public awareness of health hazards, educate and influence policymakers and resource managers, mobilize public support for policy initiatives, and monitor and ensure enforcement of existing health regulations. In getting things done collectively, efficacy involves people's beliefs in their joint capabilities to do the various things required to accomplish change: unite different self-interests into a shared agenda, enlist supporters and resources for collective action, devise effective strategies and execute them successfully, and withstand forcible opposition and discouraging setbacks. To enhance their leverage, people must work together by forming alliances with groups of similar purpose (Butterfoss, Goodman, & Wandersman, 1993). All of this requires sustained collective effort. We do not lack sound policy prescriptions in the field of health. What is lacking is the collective efficacy to realize them. Knowledge about how to develop and wield collective efficacy provides the guidelines for moving us further in the enhancement of human health.

The tobacco industry provides a notable example in the struggle to regulate injurious products. Cigarette smoking is the single most personally preventable cause of death. It kills more than 400,000 people annually in the United States and aggravates health problems in millions of others (McGinnis & Foege, 1993). More people die annually from smoking than from alcohol, heroin, cocaine, AIDS, suicide, homicide, automobile accidents, and fires combined. About 3000 children take up smoking each day, a third of whom will die of tobacco-related diseases. Even though tobacco products are the most toxic legalized substances, they are the least regulated and most vigorously promoted. The industry spends billions of dollars each year on attractive image advertising and promotional activities that appeal to young people (Lynch & Bonnie, 1994). Unless people take up the smoking habit as youngsters, they rarely become smokers during adulthood. Policy remedies that raise tobacco taxes, limit juvenile access to tobacco products, and ban smoking in public places to remove the health hazard of secondhand smoke lower the smoking rates in a society (Lewit, 1989; Woodruff, Rosbrook, Pierce, & Glantz, 1993). Regulating the nicotine dosage in cigarettes below addictive levels would aid those struggling to quit the smoking habit.

Enactment of policies designed to reduce public health risks does not, in and of itself, guarantee widespread adoption. Regulations help to codify and legitimize social practices that society considers important to its well-being. But informal social influences are needed to foster adoption of social standards as personal ones. The members of the general public who are inclined to get others to observe health codes have a high sense of efficacy for affirmative action, place a positive value on civic action, acknowledge the public harmfulness of the regulated practices, and have associates who also take action against nonobservance of health codes (Willemsen & deVries, 1996).

Environmental degradation and pollutants and hazardous workplaces similarly take a heavy toll on health and impair the quality of life. Health protection in production worksites is achieved largely through legislative measures to minimize exposure to toxic materials, debilitating physical demands, and dangerous equipment. Protracted battles are fought over where to set the limits of acceptable risk in occupational health and safety standards. Demanding conditions of work over which employees have little control can contribute to a variety of illnesses and emotional dysfunctions. It is not the work demands per se but the lack of control over them that is the main source of distress and health impairment. Perceived efficacy moderates the adverse effects of work environments that do not afford much personal control over how jobs are structured. Thus, employees who believe they can fulfill occupational demands experience less stress and health problems than those who distrust their ability to do so (McAteer-Early, 1992).

Perceived efficacy does more than improve personal management of taxing work demands. Employees who are assured in their efficacy are inclined to take actions to improve their work situations (Parker, 1989, 1993). Such an efficacious orientation reduces depression and health problems that accompany lack of control over organizational decision making. Technological changes that now make heavy demands on cognitive competencies are shifting occupational strains from physical to mental ones. Health protection from debilitating occupational stressors requires redesign of the conditions of working life (Karasek & Theorell, 1990). The beneficial changes include decentralization of authority, participant decision making, and greater latitude for employees to exercise initiative and control over the conditions of their working life.

The advantaged sectors of society exert their collective influence to rid their immediate environment of hazardous conditions. The less advantaged have deficient health services and inadequate sanitation and often live amidst industrial pollutants and a host of other health-impairing conditions. Most feel powerless to change their living conditions. Achievement of fundamental structural changes that improve conditions of life is a slow, arduous process. While concerted efforts are made to produce such changes, people need to gain current control over aspects of their lives over which they do have some command. Impoverished communities can achieve health benefits through efficacy-oriented programs that foster collective self-help. Efforts to reduce infant mortality resulting from unsanitary conditions in poor Latino neighborhoods typify this community enablement approach (McAlister, Puska, Orlandi, Bye, & Zbylot, 1991). The community was fully informed of the impact of unsanitary conditions on children's health through the local media, churches, schools, and neighborhood meetings conducted by influential persons in the community. The residents were taught how to install plumbing systems, sanitary sewerage facilities, and refuse storage. They were taught how to secure the financing needed from various local and governmental sources. This enabling self-help program greatly improved sanitation and markedly reduced infant mortality.

As cities swell uncontrollably, centralized urban systems, especially in poor countries, fail to provide adequate human services. Through community enablement, people can work together to improve problems of sanitation, safe water, health, and public safety in their localities. Many of these pandemic problems require some material resources, however, if collective self-help is to achieve much success. Otherwise, simply telling people to fend for themselves with intractable problems is an evasion of social responsibility. Unsupported prescription of local self-help can be easily used as a political subterfuge for civic neglect. Given that health depends heavily on behavioral, environmental, and economic factors, adverse changes in living conditions in poor nations — burgeoning population, poverty, malnutrition, environmental deterioration and toxification, desertification of productive land — will present major challenges to preservation of health in the coming years (Hancock & Garrett, 1995). Some of the growing health hazards require international solutions. For example, destruction of the ozone shield against solar ultraviolet radiation by use of Freon as a refrigerant and aerosol propellant is causing an increase in skin cancers and eye disorders worldwide. International collective action is needed to phase out this destructive chemical. Chapter 11 addresses in some detail issues of how people can gain control over conditions that affect their lives through development and exercise of collective efficacy.

In community-oriented programs for health enhancement, not all adoption failures are due to deficiencies in social diffusion strategies. Some people lack the financial resources to exercise much control over their own health, even if given the knowledge and skills to do so. Poor people struggling to survive in disease-infested environments do not have the luxury of making large changes in lifestyle. Some people who have the means to exercise control over their health are poorly informed on how personal habits can impair their health. Even with smoking, one of the more publicized health risks, they may know that smoking increases the risk of lung cancer but not know that it also contributes to atherosclerosis, emphysema, and bronchitis and retards fetal development. Diffusion influences directed at lifestyles do not operate in isolation. Those who seek to improve health habits run into formidable competition. Billions of dollars are spent annually by the tobacco, dairy, liquor, pharmaceutical, and fast food industries on lobbying, advertising, and marketing campaigns to promote the very unhealthful habits the community campaigns seek to change. Adoption rates partly reflect the pervasiveness and strength of competing influencers of public consumer habits.

Health diffusion programs provide people with knowledge and the means to exercise choice rather than dictating how they should live. It is in a society's interest to do so for both humanitarian and economic reasons. Diseases caused by preventable, injurious habits and environmental conditions impair human lives and impose financial burdens on the whole society. Many people pursue unhealthful habits not through informed choice, but because they do not know the effects of such habits or how to change their own behavior. Disadvantaged and minority groups suffer most from deficits in knowledge and means. By providing a more equitable distribution of psychobiological knowledge, diffusion programs help to close the knowledge gap between advantaged and disadvantaged segments of society. Huge sums of money and medical services are spent on the ravages of diseases, but little on preventing them. Lengthened life expectancies that usher in progressive diseases resulting from unhealthy practices, and social values that people are entitled to health care whether they can afford it or not, call for radical restructuring of health services. It does not cost much to inform the public and teach people how to exercise control over their own health. Failure to do so diminishes the quality of life in later years and imposes mounting financial burdens on society.

PROGNOSTIC JUDGMENTS AND PERCEIVED SELF-EFFICACY

Much of the work in the health field is concerned with diagnosing maladies from collections of symptoms, predicting the likely health outcomes of alternative interventions, and prescribing optimal remedies. Medical prognostic judgments involve probabilistic inferences from knowledge of varying quality and inclusiveness about the multiple factors governing the course of a given disorder. Because psychosocial factors account for some of the variability in health functioning, they must be included in prognostic schemes to enhance their predictive power. Prognostic judgments activate psychosocial processes that can influence health outcomes rather than simply serving as nonreactive forecasts of things to come (Bandura, 1992c). In this section, we will examine how prognostic judgments and clinical interventions can alter efficacy beliefs in ways that affect the likelihood of different health outcomes.

Scope of Prognostic Schemes

One important issue regarding prognosis concerns the range of factors included in a prognostic scheme. Level of health functioning is determined not only by biologically rooted factors but also by patients' self-beliefs and a network of social influences that can enhance or impede the progress they make. To the extent that psychosocial influences contribute to health outcomes, giving these factors some weight in prognostic schemes will enhance their predictive utility. To take no notice of them leaves one with puzzling variations in the courses that health changes take and with unexplained differences in functional attainments by people who are equally physically impaired. For example, research on enhancement of efficacy beliefs for postcoronary recovery in patients who have had an uncomplicated heart attack reveals that belief in one's cardiac capabilities is a psychological prognostic indicator of the course that health outcomes are likely to take.

Having patients master increasing workloads on the treadmill strengthens their belief in their physical capabilities (Ewart et al., 1983). The stronger their perceived physical efficacy, the more active they become in their everyday life. Maximal treadmill attainment itself is a weak predictor of patients' level and duration of activity. Thus, treadmill experiences exert their influence indirectly, facilitating recovery by raising patients' beliefs about their physical and cardiac capabilities. Enhanced perceived efficacy, in turn, fosters more active pursuit of everyday activities. Coronary artery bypass surgery improves physical capacity, but for some patients it produces little improvement or even deterioration in physical and social functioning. Studies of this paradoxical effect reveal that preoperative belief in one's physical efficacy is a good predictor of engagement in everyday physical and social activities, whereas physiological capacity, preoperative severity of cardiac disability, number of coexisting medical problems, number of bypass grafts, age, or perceived exertion are nonpredictive (Allen,

Becker, & Swank, 1990; Oka, Gortner, Stotts, & Haskell, 1996). Restoration of self-efficacy for an active life, therefore, is an essential aspect of treatments for heart disease. The focus on physical recovery alone is not enough.

Ewart and his colleagues have further shown that patients' beliefs about their physical efficacy predicts compliance with prescribed exercise programs, whereas actual physical capability does not (Ewart et al., 1986). This corroborates the earlier findings that the effect of treadmill experiences on activity level is largely mediated by changes in perceived self-efficacy. Following coronary angioplasty, patients who have a high sense of efficacy are more successful in following prescribed exercise and dietary regimens than those who doubt they can get themselves to adhere to the new health habits (Jensen et al., 1993). Perceived self-efficacy also aids occupational readjustment following coronary angioplasty. Patients with a high sense of physical efficacy before hospital discharge were twice as likely to resume work early than those with low perceived efficacy even though they were physically capable of doing so (Fitzgerald, Becker, Celentano, Swank, & Brinker, 1989). Neither physical status nor demographic or job characteristics contributed independently to resumption of work.

Psychological recovery from a heart attack is a social rather than an individual matter. Spouses' judgments of their partners' physical capabilities can have a strong impact on the course of postcoronary recovery. A program designed to aid postcoronary recovery in uncomplicated cases used the treadmill activity to raise patients' and spouses' beliefs in the patients' ability to withstand cardiovascular strain (Taylor, Bandura, Ewart, Miller, & DeBusk, 1985). Several weeks after male patients have had a heart attack, their beliefs about how much strain their heart could withstand were measured. They then performed a symptom-limited treadmill, mastering increasing workloads with three levels of spousal involvement in the treadmill activity. The wife was either uninvolved in the treadmill activity; was present to observe her husband's stamina as he performed the treadmill under increasing workloads; or observed her husband's performance, whereupon she performed the treadmill exercises herself to gain firsthand experience of the physical stamina required. It was reasoned that having the wife experience the strenuousness of the tasks, and seeing her husband match or surpass them, would convince her that her husband had a robust heart.

After the treadmill activities, couples were fully informed by the cardiologist about the patients' level of cardiac functioning and their capacity to resume activities in their daily life. If the treadmill is interpreted as an isolated task, its impact on perceived cardiac and physical capability may be limited. To generalize the impact of enhanced efficacy on diverse domains of functioning, the stamina on the treadmill was presented as a generic indicant of cardiovascular capability. The patients were informed that their level of exertion exceeded whatever strain everyday activities might place on their cardiac system. This would encourage them to resume activities in their everyday life that placed weaker demands on their cardiac system than the heavy workloads on the treadmill. The patient's and spouse's beliefs about his physical and cardiac capabilities were measured before and after the treadmill activity and again after the medical counseling.

Figure 7.16 shows the patterns of changes in beliefs about the patients' physical and cardiac capabilities at different phases of the experiment with varying degrees of spousal involvement in the treadmill activity. Treadmill performances increased patients' beliefs in their physical and cardiac capabilities. Initially, the beliefs of wives and their husbands were highly discrepant. Husbands judged themselves moderately hearty, whereas wives judged their husbands' cardiac capabilities severely impaired and incapable of withstanding physical and emotional strain. Spouses who were either uninvolved in, or merely observers of, the treadmill activity continued to believe that their husbands' physical and cardiac capabilities were severely impaired. Even the detailed medical counseling by the cardiology staff did not alter their preexisting beliefs of their husbands' cardiac debility. Wives who had personally experienced the strenuousness of the treadmill and saw their husbands match and surpass them, however, were persuaded that their husbands had sufficiently robust hearts to withstand the normal strains of everyday activities. As a result, the wives

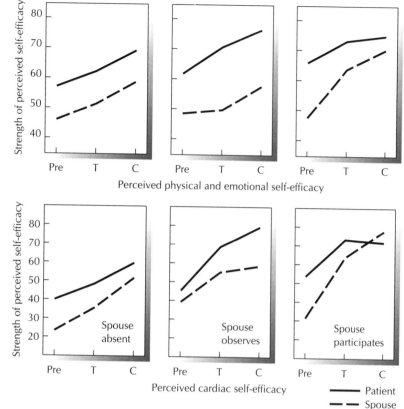

FIGURE 7.16. Changes in perceived physical and emotional efficacy and in cardiac efficacy as a function of level of spouse involvement, patients' treadmill exercises, and the combined influence of treadmill exercises and medical counseling. Perceived efficacy was measured before the treadmill (Pre), after the treadmill (T), and after the medical counseling (C). (After Taylor et al., 1985)

gave greater weight to indicants of cardiac robustness than to symptomatic signs of cardiac debility. Interestingly, efficacy beliefs also affect receptivity to prognostic information: The wives were more accepting of the cardiologists' favorable diagnoses. Following the medical counseling, couples in the participant spouse group had congruently high beliefs in the patients' cardiac capabilities.

Beliefs of cardiac capabilities affected the course of recovery from myocardial infarction. In follow-up assessments, the more the marital couples were convinced of the patients' cardiac capabilities, the greater the improvement in cardiovascular functioning, as measured by peak heart rate and maximal workload achieved on the treadmill six months later. The couple's joint belief in the patient's cardiac efficacy proved to be the best predictor of cardiac functional level. Initial treadmill performance did not predict level of

cardiovascular functioning in the follow-up assessment when the influence of efficacy beliefs was removed. But perceived cardiac efficacy predicted the level of cardiovascular functioning when initial treadmill performance was controlled. As these findings reveal, the direction that social support takes within the family system and its likely effects are partly determined by judgments of efficacy. Spouses are likely to curtail activities if they judge their partners' heart to be impaired and vulnerable to further damage but to encourage engagement in activities if they judge their partners to have a robust heart. Pursuit of an active life improves patients' physical abilities to engage in vigorous activities without overtaxing their cardiovascular system.

Prognostic judgments are not simply non–reactive forecasts of a natural history of a disease. Except in extreme pathologies that may be overwhelmingly determined by biological factors, the nature and course of clinical outcomes is partly dependent on psychological sources of influence. Strong belief in one's efficacy to exercise some control over one's physical condition serves as a psychological prognostic indicator of the probable level of health functioning. People with similar levels of physical impairment can achieve different functional outcomes depending on their efficacy beliefs (Holman & Lorig, 1992; Kaplan et al., 1984; Lorig, Chastain et al., 1989; O'Leary et al., 1988). For example, many people with severe osteoarthritis lead productive, satisfying lives, whereas others with much milder forms of the disease remain despondent and functionally incapacitated. Even in the case of severe permanent impairment, where only partial recovery is possible, psychosocial factors will affect how much of the remaining functional capacity is realized. Because prognostic information can affect patients' beliefs in their physical efficacy, diagnosticians not only foretell but may partly influence the course of recovery from disease. This proactive influence will be examined shortly in greater detail.

Perceived coping efficacy enhances recovery from surgical interventions as well as retarding progression of functional disability in chronic disease. For example, sociodemographic factors and objective physical status are poor predictors of postoperative adjustment to intestinal stoma surgery (Bekkers, van Knippenberg, van den Borne, & vanBerge-Henegouwen, 1996). On the other hand, patients' perceived efficacy to manage their physical condition and social lives, measured a few days after surgery, predicts the level of distress and quality of family, social, and vocational functioning a year later.

Mode of Conveying Prognostic Information

Another important issue in the clinical management of patients is the way in which prognostic information is conveyed to them. This is usually done by describing possible outcomes and the probabilities associated with them. Verbal prognostications alone may not have the intended impact, however, especially when they contradict strong preexisting beliefs. This is true even for positive prognostications if patients invest prescribed restorative activities with grave risks. For example, in the study of postcoronary rehabilitation, wives were not at all reassured of their husbands' hardiness by the positive prognostic judgments of the medical staff unless they had benefit of direct confirmatory experiences. To increase their persuasive influence, clinicians may have to convey positive prognostic information to their patients not only by word but also by structuring performance tasks for them that provide self-convincing experiences.

Psychological Impact of Diagnostic Procedures

The manner in which diagnostic tests are conducted can influence patients' beliefs about their efficacy. The cognitive processing of somatic information from the treadmill test is a case in point. Treadmill activity produces many negative signs, such as fatigue, pain, shortness of breath, and other exercise-induced symptoms that mount as the workload increases. Patients who focus on their physical stamina as they master increasing workloads will judge their cardiac system as more robust than will patients who selectively attend to and remember the negative somatic signs. Positive indicants of capability can be made more salient if patients receive ongoing feedback of their performance attainments as they master heavier workloads. Judgment of cardiac efficacy will vary depending on how this diverse symptom information and the indicants of cardiac robustness are weighted and integrated.

This was shown in a study of a group of healthy men and women who completed a symptom-limited treadmill task before entering an exercise program (Juneau et al., 1986). Half the participants received concurrent feedback of the workloads they mastered on the treadmill task. The other half received the feedback about their physical attainments just after they had completed the treadmill task. Their perceived cardiac efficacy was measured before and after the treadmill performance. They also recorded the physical signs they recalled having experienced during the treadmill activity. Figure 7.17 shows how treadmill performances with and without concurrent feedback affect beliefs of cardiac capabilities.

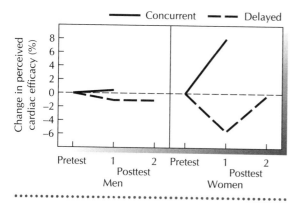

FIGURE 7.17. Impact of treadmill performances on judgment of cardiac efficacy under conditions of concurrent and delayed feedback. (After Juneau et al., 1986)

Without feedback of positive indicants of capability, exercise-induced symptoms completely dominate attention and memory representation of the treadmill experience. For healthy men, who generally have a strong view of their cardiac capabilities, a taxing treadmill test without feedback did not alter their beliefs that they had a robust cardiac system. Positive feedback that made physical attainments on the treadmill more noticeable, however, raised women's beliefs of their cardiac capabilities. In the absence of such positive feedback, women read the mounting negative physiological sensations accompanying increasing exertion on the treadmill as indicants of cardiac limitations and lowered their beliefs of their cardiac efficacy. Women did not experience any more negative physiological sensations than men. Therefore, the adverse impact of treadmill experiences without positive feedback stemmed from negative cognitive processing of symptom information rather than from greater amounts or salience of such symptoms.

Preconceptions tend to bias how information is weighted and integrated (Bandura, 1986a; Nisbett & Ross, 1980). A similar process is indicated in women's reactions to delayed positive feedback about their treadmill performances. When told of their notable physical attainments, they raised their perceived cardiac efficacy to the pretreadmill level but achieved no net gain from the treadmill experience. Positive signs of cardiac capability are difficult

to assimilate after conceptions of one's efficacy have already been formed under conditions in which negative signs clearly dominate. A coronary can markedly undermine beliefs about one's cardiac efficacy. A strong preconception of physical impairment makes negative physiological reactions to performance tests highly salient and recallable. Therefore, concurrent positive feedback of physical stamina would be especially important for countering beliefs of a frail cardiac capability in postcoronary patients who have not suffered clinical complications.

A diagnostic procedure that measures impairments and capabilities with progressively harder tasks provides early successes followed by mounting performance difficulties as the upper limits of capability are approached. Patients who selectively notice and recall their performance deficiencies will judge their capabilities as lower than those who notice their strengths as well. As shown by the treadmill example, the adverse impact on efficacy beliefs of diagnostic procedures that generate negative experiences can be reduced or counteracted by structuring performance tests in ways that give salience to one's remaining strengths. In addition to the type and timing of verbal feedback given to patients, some evidence suggests that diagnostic tasks that create mounting failure by an ascending order of difficulty produce more adverse effects than tasks of different levels of difficulty intermixed to maintain a sense of attainment (Zigler & Butterfield, 1968). Analysis of how the structure of diagnostic procedures and preconceptions of personal efficacy bias attention to, and cognitive processing of, somatic and behavioral information is clinically important and theoretically interesting (Cioffi, 1991a). The knowledge gained from these types of microanalytic studies would add greatly to our understanding of the psychological impact of diagnostic procedures.

Self-Validating Potential of Prognostic Judgments

Health outcomes are related to predictive factors in complex, multidetermined, and probabilistic ways. Prognostic judgments, therefore, involve some degree of uncertainty. The predictiveness of a given prognostic scheme depends on the number of relevant predictors it encompasses, the relative validities and redundancies among the predictors, and the adequacy with which they are measured. There is much leeway for expectancy effects to operate because prognostic schemes rarely include all the relevant biological and psychosocial predictors, and even the predictors that are singled out usually have less than perfect validity. Therefore, diagnosticians not only foretell the course of recovery but may partly influence it. Based on selected sources of information, diagnosticians form expectations about the probable course of a disease. The more confident they are in the validity of their prognostic scheme, the stronger are their prognostic expectations.

Prognostic expectations are conveyed to patients by attitude, word, and the type and level of care provided to them. As mentioned earlier, prognostic judgments have a self-confirming potential. Expectations can alter patients' efficacy beliefs and behaviors in ways that confirm the original expectations. Evidence indicates that the self-efficacy mechanism operates as one important mediator of self-confirming effects. This is clearly revealed in laboratory studies in which people's beliefs in their efficacy are altered by bogus information about their personal capabilities. Those whose efficacy beliefs were raised exhibited functional improvements in physical stamina and pain management, whereas those whose efficacy beliefs were lowered displayed functional declines (Holroyd et al., 1984; Litt, 1988; Weinberg et al., 1979).

The preceding analysis of self-confirming processes focused solely on how people's efficacy beliefs and behavior are affected by what they are told about their capabilities. Other evidence suggests that prognostic judgments may bias how people are treated as well as what they are told. In these experiments, individuals are arbitrarily led to form either high or low expectations for others. They treat others differently when they have high or low expectations in ways that confirm the original expectations (Jones, 1977; Jussim, 1986). Although there is some variation in the results, the findings generally show that caregivers pay more attention to those in their charge, provide them with more emotional support, create greater opportunities for them to build their competencies, and give them more positive feedback under high expectations than under induced low ones.

Differential care that promotes in patients different levels of personal efficacy and skill in managing health behavior can exert stronger impact on the trajectories of health functioning than care that simply conveys prognostic information. The effects of verbal prognostications alone may be short-lived if they are repeatedly disconfirmed by personal experiences due to deficient capabilities. A sense of personal efficacy rooted in enhanced competencies, however, fosters functional attainments that create their own experiential validation. Clinical transactions operate bidirectionally to shape the course of change. Improvements by patients strengthen clinicians' positive expectations and sense of efficacy to aid therapeutic progress. In contrast, negative expectations that breed functional declines can set in motion a downward course of mutual discouragement.

Medical conditions that produce severe permanent impairments can be devastatingly demoralizing to patients and their families. Patients have to reorganize their perspective to learn alternative ways of regaining as much control as possible over their life activities. They need to focus on their remaining capabilities rather than dwell on their disabilities. Goals must be restructured in ways that capitalize on remaining capacities. Ozer (1988) illustrates effective ways of structuring goals couched in functional terms to minimize disabilities created by chronic neurological impairment. Focus on achievement of functional improvements rather than on degree of organic impairments helps to counteract self-demoralization. Making difficult activities easier by breaking them down into graduated subtasks of attainable steps helps to prevent self-discouragement of rehabilitative efforts and enhances functional attainments. Recovery of some sense of efficacy and hopefulness enables those who have suffered impairments to make the most of their capabilities.

8

Clinical Functioning

THE GREATEST BENEFITS THAT psychological treatments can bestow are not specific remedies for particular problems but the sociocognitive tools needed to deal effectively with whatever situations might arise. To the extent that treatment equips people to exercise influence over events in their lives, it initiates an ongoing process of self-regulative change. Self-enablement is achieved by providing people with the knowledge, competencies, and resilient self-belief in their capabilities to exercise some measure of control over the quality and direction of their lives. Effective functioning requires developing the means for exercising control over self-debilitating patterns of thought, emotional distress, and behavior patterns that impair people's relationships with themselves and others. This chapter examines perceived self-efficacy as a common cognitive mechanism through which different modes of treatment achieve such therapeutic changes.

ANXIETY AND PHOBIC DYSFUNCTIONS

Anxiety and phobic dysfunctions are the most prevalent forms of human distress. Most people suffer from social anxieties that are viewed as shyness. They are plagued by social evaluation anxieties in which they constantly worry about what others will think of them. Most people admit to some phobic tendencies of varying intensity. Those who are burdened by acute misgivings about their coping capabilities suffer chronic distress and expend much effort in defensive forms of behavior (Bandura, 1978). They cannot get themselves to do things they find subjectively threatening even though the activities are objectively safe and offer many potential satisfactions. In the eloquent words of Shakespeare, "Our doubts are traitors, and make us lose the good we oft might win, by fearing to attempt." People even shun easily manageable activities because they see them as leading to more threatening events over which they will be unable to exercise adequate control. As a result, their lives are constricted by defensive avoidance of social, recreational, and vocational activities that might expose them to threats, however remote the possibility. But even restricting daily activities does not ensure relief from distress. People are repeatedly tormented by perturbing ruminations about possible calamities and by recurrent nightmares.

Even seemingly circumscribed phobias can profoundly impair the quality of life. For example, consider the diverse ways in which a snake phobia constrains and inflicts suffering on human lives (Bandura et al., 1969; Bandura et al., 1975). Virtually all snake phobics abandon one or more recreational activities such as camping, hiking, and swimming in rivers and lakes. They cannot walk through grassy or wooded areas, go bicycling, or do any gardening for fear of encountering snakes. They refuse to reside in rustic areas and are reluctant to visit friends living in such areas. Some are unable to conduct their vocational activities adequately, as in the case of biologists and geologists who dread field trips, plumbers who cannot work outdoors, firemen who cannot fight grass fires, and telephone repairmen who are terrified of snakes lurking near telephone poles. In some cases, phobics require their spouses to inspect every newspaper and magazine delivered to the household to delete any items referring to reptiles. Some phobics are incapacitated in more unique ways. In the true spirit of the Western frontier, a male phobic shot himself in the foot while trying to kill a harmless snake with his shaky aim. A woman was unable to use her bathroom in San Francisco upon reading that a snake had escaped into the municipal sewer system in the distant city of Santa Barbara, despite repeated appeals to reason and insistent coaxing. Even elaborate defensive constraints do not ensure serenity. The vast majority of phobics are repeatedly plagued by ruminative thoughts and nightmares over which they can exercise little control. Perturbing ruminations about snakes become especially troublesome during the summer months.

Tiny, harmless spiders similarly immobilize and torment the lives of spider phobics in every imaginable way (Bandura et al., 1985; Bandura et al., 1982). Because spiders are not especially choosy about their habitats and often appear as uninvited houseguests, they make life miserable for their phobic hosts. In some instances, if such phobics see a spider in their house, they flee the place until the spider is destroyed: "I would have to call on my neighbor to come over to kill them in my apartment." Some are immobilized by their phobia: "One day I walked into the room and saw a spider on the wall so I ran to the bathroom in which another one was on the wall. I ran into the living

room and another one showed up. I ran into the kitchen and sat in the chair in the middle of the room and cried until someone came home to kill them." Sometimes the phobia fuels marital conflicts: "Because I feel a wave of nausea and panic upon sighting a spider, I have made it a habit for years of quickly checking all four walls and ceiling of any room upon entering it, looking for spiders. The subject has been a sore one with my husband. Spiders have been the primary source of arguments between us." Spider phobics cannot enter places in the house where they have seen a spider: "If I saw one in my closet I could not go in it for days without help." Some do the laundry and get in and out of cars in garages in record speed, because they regard these places as favorite hangouts for spiders. Others are unable to enter places where they have previously seen a spider or even imagined spiders might inhabit. Chance encounters with spiders convert harmless settings into frightening places: "I got to the point where I wouldn't take a bath because I was surprised by a spider in the tub once." In some cases, the phobia endangers life and limb; for example, a woman promptly leaped out of an automobile she was driving upon noticing a spider in it. Phobics abandon enjoyable pastimes and recreational activities that might bring them into contact with spiders: "I don't garden or go hiking and camping though I love these activities"; "I have been reluctant to even just sit in the yard."

In addition to their phobic behavior, phobics are tormented by apprehensive vigilance, intrusive ruminations, and recurrent nightmares about spiders: "I could not watch TV, read, enjoy any of the things I normally did at home since I was always uncomfortable and watchful of a spider in the room." The mere sight or picture of a spider often elicits such intense physiological reactions as "convulsive shivers," "vomiting for hours," and "heart pounding and shortness of breath." Even sleep itself is fitful and provides no deliverance from apprehensive vigilance: "I'd wake up three or four times a night to see if there was a spider on the ceiling. If there was, I'd get my step stool and spray and kill it. If it fell alive in the shag rug I would lie awake for hours to see if it began its climb up the wall." They all suffer recurrent nightmares: "At night I have nightmares and wake up and turn on the light, I am scared one might be in my car while I am driving"; "I have had nightmares about spiders at least once a week for 10–15 years. They are always on my mind in the evening when I have to turn on a light in a dark room. I'm hysterical if surprised by a spider, so I always have a light on in the bedroom." In formal assessments, phobic individuals express a complete collapse of their perceived efficacy to cope with their phobic nemeses. Evidence will be presented later showing that development of a sense of coping efficacy through guided mastery experiences quickly eradicates such widespread phobic dysfunctions.

Some human debilities stem not so much from perceived inability to control environmental threats as from perceived inefficacy to control oneself or from brief lapses in one's mental functioning. Otherwise skilled actors may regard themselves as vulnerable to forgetting their lines, singers their lyrics, and concert soloists passages in their musical selections. In such well-rehearsed activities, the inefficacy concerns involve control of memory lapses rather than skillful execution of the activities. Some performing artists give up promising careers because of their inordinate apprehension over their perceived vulnerability to blacking out in the midst of a performance (Zailian, 1978). In other activities, the inefficacy concerns may center more on the ability to control potentially dangerous lapses in attentional and physical aspects of performance than on momentary cognitive failings. Thus, drivers who distrust their ability to avoid any slips in attention or motor adroitness in congested freeway traffic will shun busy roadways.

Inefficacy sometimes involves perceived vulnerability to total loss of personal control rather than momentary lapses in functioning. Some people believe they will lose consciousness, disintegrate psychologically, or be unable to restrain themselves from behaving in grossly inappropriate ways that will bring public embarrassment (Beck, Laude, & Bohnert, 1974). For example, those who doubt they can resist jumping or can retain consciousness when looking down from heights will avoid heights. Aerophobics, who perceive themselves as

being vulnerable to disintegrative loss of control while traveling in an airplane, remain on the ground. A few trips with guided modeling that convince them they are fully capable of controlling themselves in an aircraft, however, will get them to travel by airplane, even though they do not give up their beliefs that airliners occasionally crash or make hazardous landings.

Many people who undergo traumatic experiences continue to exhibit severe stress reactions long after the trauma. The posttraumatic reactions include intrusive reexperiencing of the traumatic event in flashbacks and recurrent nightmares, hypervigilant arousal, depression, self-devaluation, emotional detachment from others, and disengagement from aspects of life that can provide meaning and fulfillment. These recurrent reactions can seriously impair psychosocial functioning. The key features of traumatic stressors are their perilousness and their uncontrollability. They overwhelm coping capabilities. The experience of powerlessness exacts a heavy toll on a sense of personal efficacy, which becomes a persisting impediment to successful adaptation.

The effects of traumatic experiences on perceived self-efficacy have been examined longitudinally by Solomon and her colleagues in Israeli soldiers who suffered breakdowns in military combat (Solomon, Benbenishty, & Mikulincer, 1991; Solomon, Weisenberg, Schwarzwald, & Mikulincer, 1988). The trauma severely undermined the soldiers' perceived efficacy to cope with combat situations. The lower their perceived efficacy, the greater the perturbing intrusive thinking and avoidant tendencies in subsequent years. Interestingly, the predictors of beliefs of coping efficacy changed with the passage of time. Initially, the severity of emotional debility during the traumatic incident predicted level of perceived efficacy. But over time, its importance declined and premilitary coping capabilities and adaptability to current stressors took precedence as predictors. Soldiers who received immediate frontline treatment and returned to their units had a higher sense of efficacy and less posttraumatic stress reactions following the war than those who were evacuated to distal treatment facilities and never returned to the combat situation. Reengagement with traumatic situations in actuality or cognitively is an important part of recovery. However, it is not merely reexperiencing a traumatic event but confronting it in a way that restores a sense of control through reconstrual or improved coping that alleviates stress reactions and behavioral impairments. Indeed, renewed successful coping with an intense threat is an effective way of restoring a sense of personal efficacy. The possibility that the different treatment effects partly reflect selection of who gets shipped back and who stays cannot be ruled out, however.

This informative program of research focused solely on perceived efficacy to cope with combat situations. Analysis of the role of efficacy beliefs in the persisting aftereffects of trauma should be expanded to include perceived efficacy to control intrusive thinking, to alleviate emotional distress, and to manage the stressors in important domains of current life. The benefits of an expanded focus are revealed in the treatment of army veterans suffering from chronic posttraumatic stress (Freuh, Turner, Beidel, Mirabella, & Jones, 1996). Repeated imaginal coping with traumatic combat situations reduced stress reactions. Cultivation of social and emotional skills through modeling, behavioral rehearsal, and supportive feedback, however, not only further reduced stress reactions but improved the quality of social and emotional life. The combined enablement treatment alleviated anxiety, flashbacks, nightmares, and autonomic hyperreactivity and enhanced overall social functioning. It should be noted that the terror of combat also provides striking testimony to extraordinary human resilience. Most soldiers withstood the horrors of the battlefield without debilitating impairments either in battle or in their civilian life. But resilience to trauma recives little investigatory attention.

Research into the psychological aftermath of natural disasters further corroborates that a low sense of coping efficacy heightens vulnerability to posttraumatic disorders. One such study involved a devastating hurricane that left widespread destruction in its wake (Benight et al., 1996). The amount of damage suffered, perceived severity of the life threat during the hurricane, or level of education

or income did not account for enduring posttraumatic stress reactions. But perceived efficacy to manage the security, financial, lodging, and affective problems caused by the devastation predicted who remained traumatized by the events. The victims who were assured in their restorative capabilities escaped unscarred, however much damage they suffered. Perceived coping inefficacy also heightened neuroendocrine reactivity among the inhabitants infected with the AIDS virus.

Potential loss of life and the destruction of one's home in a natural disaster present a prolonged traumatic experience. Murphy (1987) studied the intensity of symptomatic distress after the volcanic eruption of Mount St. Helens and three years later as a function of the severity of disaster loss, perceived coping efficacy, and social support. Magnitude of disaster loss and perceived efficacy predicted severity of distress shortly after the volcanic destruction. Three years later, however, the loss suffered was no longer a predictor, but perceived coping efficacy accounted for even more of the variation in distress than it did originally. Social support did not affect distress at either period. As long as the victims believed that they could deal with the devastating aftermath they were not chronically overwhelmed with distress. Baum, Cohen, and Hall (1993) similarly found that a traumatic event is necessary but insufficient to produce chronic stress. Victims with a low sense of control that puts them at the mercy of circumstances and who cannot turn off perturbing ruminations are the ones who continue to experience elevated stress over the disaster years later. When people cannot control unwanted thoughts, they keep reliving the traumatic experience.

Many traumatic social experiences involve physical and sexual assault. The sense of inefficacy to exercise control over interpersonal threats torments and constrains women's lives. Development of self-protective capabilities through repeated mastery experience in simulated assaults goes a long way toward eradicating the perceived personal vulnerability (Ozer & Bandura, 1990). The guided mastery instills a strong sense of coping efficacy and thought control efficacy. The restored personal efficacy is accompanied by large reductions in perceived personal vulnerability, perturbing intrusive thinking, and behavioral avoidance and by expanded engagement in activities that bring satisfaction to everyday life.

Social anxiety is a less debilitating but widespread human problem. Socially anxious people tend to be excessively concerned about what others might think of them. As a result, they shy away from many social activities, are reluctant to express themselves publicly, and suffer much discomfort in social interactions they cannot avoid. The problem does not lie in the evaluative standards by which the socially anxious believe they will be judged by others. Rather, the source of the anxiety is the disparity between perceived social standards and perceived personal efficacy to fulfill them (Alden, Bieling, & Wallace, 1994; Wallace & Alden, 1991). Socially anxious people believe they lack the social efficacy to meet others' evaluative standards, whereas the nonanxious are confident that they can match them. Socially anxious individuals differ from those who are not anxious mainly in dysfunctional beliefs of inefficacy rather than in their actual social skills (Glasgow & Arkowitz, 1975).

Brief social successes do little for the perceived efficacy of the socially anxious. Positive heterosocial experiences leave them still doubting their social abilities but believing that others expect even more from them socially (Wallace & Alden, 1995). The increased disparity between perception of personal efficacy and social expectation under positive feedback creates even more cause for anxiety. By contrast, nonanxious individuals respond to social successes by raising belief in their social efficacy, but they do not alter their view of others' evaluative standards for their behavior. Consequently, they end up believing that they can surpass others' expectations for them. They maintain this self-enhancing belief even in the face of negative social experiences. Once people form beliefs about their social efficacy, they construe their social successes and failures in accordance with those beliefs (Alden, 1986). When given arbitrary feedback about their social performances, those of low efficacy discount social successes as due to situational factors but accept failures as accurate reflections of their performances. Self-efficacious individuals exhibit the opposite interpretive bias. They discount the personal significance of

social failures but readily embrace feedback of successes as faithful reflections of their social exploits. Construal biases in the cognitive processing of social experiences thus provide self-validating support for preexisting efficacy beliefs.

Self-Efficacy and Anxiety Control Theories

For years, avoidant behavior has been explained in terms of a dual-process theory (Dollard & Miller, 1950; Mowrer, 1950). This theory keeps reappearing in different guises. According to this view, avoidant behavior is motivated by an anxiety drive. Escape from threats or avoidance of them presumably reinforces the avoidant pattern of behavior through anxiety reduction. To eliminate avoidant behavior, it was considered necessary to eradicate the underlying anxiety. Therefore, many therapeutic procedures have been keyed to extinguishing anxiety arousal.

The notion that anticipatory anxiety controls avoidant behavior has been investigated extensively and found seriously wanting (Bandura, 1986a; Bolles, 1975; Herrnstein, 1969; Schwartz, 1978). In some studies, feedback of autonomic arousal, which is the principal index of the anxiety drive, is eliminated surgically or blocked pharmacologically. In other studies, the occurrence of avoidant behavior is measured after anxiety arousal to threats has been thoroughly eliminated. In still other studies, changes in anxiety arousal are related to changes in avoidant behavior during and after treatment. The evidence from these diverse procedures is highly consistent in showing that avoidant behavior is not controlled by anticipatory anxiety.

To begin with, autonomic reactions take much longer to activate than do avoidant responses, so the latter can hardly be caused by the former. Indeed, in laboratory tests, defensive reactions to threats occur instantly, even before autonomic reactions can be elicited. A cause cannot appear after the effect it supposedly produces. Psychological principles need not be reduced to physiological ones, but a postulated psychological mechanism about the relationship between autonomic arousal and avoidant behavior cannot violate what is known about the physiological systems that subserve them. Consistent with the difference in speed of the two reactive systems, routine avoidant acts prevent anxiety arousal rather than being motivated by it. Autonomic sensory feedback is not required to learn avoidant behavior, nor does it affect the speed with which such behavior is eliminated (Rescorla & Solomon, 1967; Wynne & Solomon, 1955). Avoidant behavior is often performed without autonomic arousal and can persist long after autonomic reactions to threats have been completely eradicated (Black, 1965; Rescorla & Solomon, 1967).

Assessments conducted during treatment of phobic disorders reveal no consistent relationships between changes in anxiety arousal and phobic behavior (Barlow, Leitenberg, Agras, & Wincze, 1969). Elimination of phobic behavior can be preceded by increases in autonomic arousal, by reductions in autonomic arousal, or by no change in autonomic arousal. Neither the pattern nor magnitude of change in autonomic arousal accompanying treatment correlates significantly with the degree of behavioral change (O'Brien & Borkovec, 1977; Orenstein & Carr, 1975; Schroeder & Rich, 1976).

The anxiety control theory does not fare any better when subjective indices of anxiety are used rather than autonomic ones (Williams, 1992). This is not surprising, because the anticipated anxiety reflects the aversive biological states experienced as intense anxiety; that is, sweating, pounding heart, tenseness, faintness, nausea. One would not expect anticipation of anxiety to control behavior when the physical agitations in which the expected effects are rooted do not. Anxious expectations are not sourceless. To attribute avoidant behavior to anxious expectations simply begs the question, because the source of the anxious expectations needs explaining. Chapter 4 reviewed the diverse lines of corroborating evidence that subjective anxiety and biological stress reactions are largely the products of perceived inefficacy to exert control over potentially aversive events.

In social cognitive theory (Bandura, 1986a), it is mainly perceived inefficacy in coping with potential threats that gives rise to both anticipatory anxiety and avoidant behavior. People avoid situations and activities that can be aversive not because they are beset with anxiety but because they believe they will be unable to manage the risky aspects. Those who judge themselves as efficacious in managing threats neither fear nor shun them. But those who regard themselves as inefficacious in exercising control over potential threats envisage their inept coping as producing all kinds of aversive outcomes. So they avoid potentially threatening activities without waiting for aroused viscera to tell them to do so. It is a good thing that anxiety does not control actions. If people fled from what they were doing or froze every time they felt highly tense or anxious, their lives would be immobilized much of the time. Human accomplishments and survival require efficacious thought to overrule visceral arousal in the regulation of behavior.

That people base their actions on efficacy beliefs in situations they regard as risky receives considerable empirical support. Williams (1992) and his colleagues have analyzed by partial correlation numerous data sets from studies in which efficacy beliefs, anticipated anxiety, and phobic behavior were measured (Table 8.1). Perceived efficacy accounts for a substantial amount of variation in phobic behavior when anticipated anxiety is controlled, whereas anticipated anxiety does not predict phobic behavior when perceived efficacy is controlled. Schoenberger, Kirsch, and Rosengard (1991) further confirm that phobic behavior is governed by perceived coping efficacy and that anticipated anxiety has no independent effect on phobic avoidance.

The popular explanation for why agoraphobics constrict their lives is that they fear they will become anxious or be overcome by a panic attack, or that catastrophic consequences will befall them. The findings, however, show that neither anticipated anxiety, anticipated panic, nor perceived danger predicts agoraphobic behavior after controlling for the influence of efficacy beliefs. In contrast, efficacy beliefs are highly predictive of agoraphobic behavior when variations in anticipated panic, anticipated anxiety, and perceived danger are controlled (Williams, Turner, & Peer, 1985; Williams & Watson, 1985; Williams & Zane, 1989). These findings indicate that treatment

TABLE 8.1 Comparison of the Relation between Perceived Self-Efficacy and Coping Behavior When Anticipatory Anxiety is Controlled, and the Relation between Anticipated Anxiety and Coping Behavior When Perceived Self-Efficacy Is Controlled

	Coping Behavior	
	Anticipated Anxiety with Self-Efficacy Controlled	*Perceived Self-Efficacy with Anticipated Anxiety Controlled*
Williams & Rappoport (1983)		
Pretreatment 1[a]	−.12	.40*
Pretreatment 2	−.28	.59**
Posttreatment	.13	.45*
Follow-up	.06	.45*
Williams et al. (1984)		
Pretreatment	−.36*	.22
Posttreatment	−.21	.59**
Williams et al. (1985)		
Pretreatment	−.35*	.28*
Posttreatment	.05	.72**
Follow-up	−.12	.66***
Telch et al. (1985)		
Pretreatment	−.56***	−.28
Posttreatment	.15	.48**
Follow-up	−.05	.42*
Kirsch et al. (1983)		
Pretreatment	−.34*	.54***
Posttreatment	−.48**	.48**
Arnow et al.		
Pretreatment	.17	.77***
Posttreatment	−.08	.43*
Follow-up	−.06	.88**
Williams et al. (1989)		
Midtreatment	−.15	.65***
Posttreatment	.02	.47**
Follow-up	−.03	.71***

[a]The pretreatment phases of some of these experiments include only subjects selected for severe phobic behavior. They have a uniformly low sense of coping efficacy. In such instances, the highly restricted range of self-efficacy scores tends to lower the correlation coefficients in pretreatment phases.
*$p < .05$, **$p < .01$, ***$p < .001$.

should be directed at building people's sense of coping efficacy rather than trying to correct catastrophic outcome expectations while ignoring the profound sense of inefficacy that spawns those expectations. Agoraphobics who suffer from panic attacks are prone to catastrophic misinterpretations of bodily sensations. It is not bodily sensations, however, but perceived lack of control that panics them and leads them to conjure up all kinds of catastrophic outcomes (Sanderson et al., 1989).

The predictive superiority of efficacy belief over anxiety arousal is corroborated across a variety of threats. Perceived self-efficacy accounts for variation in academic performances that entail threats, but anxiety arousal does not (Meece et al., 1990; Pajares & Johnson, 1994; Pajares & Miller, 1994a; Pajares et al., 1995; Siegel et al., 1985). Efficacy beliefs predict performances on intimidating athletic tasks; anxiety arousal does not (McAuley, 1985). Belief in one's problem-solving efficacy predicts catastrophic worrying; anxiety level does not (Davey et al., 1996). Perceived physical efficacy in elderly persons predicts engagement in a physically active lifestyle, whereas fear for one's safety in carrying out vigorous activities does not (Tinetti, Mendes de Leon, Doucette, & Baker, 1994). A low sense of efficacy to control negative ruminations generates self-debilitating thought patterns that give rise to anxiety and avoidant behavior. Here, too, self-protective social behavior in risky environments is governed by perceived behavioral and thought control efficacy but not by anxiety arousal (Ozer & Bandura, 1990).

This diverse body of evidence is highly consistent in showing that the effect of perceived efficacy on phobic behavior is not mediated by anxiety arousal. Researchers who correlate anxiety with phobic behavior without including perceived self-efficacy in the causal analysis are reporting spuriously inflated relationships between anxiety and phobic behavior that essentially disappear after the influence of perceived coping efficacy is controlled. Given the influential role that efficacy beliefs play in the causal structure, they should be included in tests of causal models of phobic dysfunctions and their treatment.

It is interesting to speculate about why the belief that anticipatory anxiety controls avoidant behavior remains firmly entrenched in psychological thinking despite massive evidence to the contrary. A possible answer may lie in the force of confirmatory biases in human judgment of causality (Nisbett & Ross, 1980). Confirming instances, in which anxiety and avoidance occur together, are likely to remain highly salient in people's minds. Nonconfirming instances, in which approach behavior occurs with anxiety or avoidance occurs without anxiety, are less noticeable and memorable. It is not that the nonconfirming instances are any less prevalent. Quite the contrary. People regularly perform activities at low strengths of perceived efficacy despite high anxiety. For example, actors appear on stage even though they may be intensely anxious while waiting to go on, athletes engage in competitive athletic activities despite a high level of precompetition anxiety, and students take intimidating examinations although they may be beset by aversive anticipatory anxiety. Similarly, people regularly take self-protective action without having to wait around for anxiety to impel them to action. They disconnect electrical appliances before repairing them without having to scare themselves with visions of electrocution. These various types of disconfirming occurrences are often ignored in judging the relationship between anxiety and avoidant behavior. There is more to the story than just biases in assessing covariations between anxiety and action, however. The research on causal paths just reviewed may also account for the imperviousness of anxiety control theories. An incomplete theoretical specification of determinants that omits perceived efficacy generates spurious correlations that continue to reinforce the belief that anxiety causes avoidant behavior.

Therapeutic Strategies: Stimulus Exposure versus Mastery Experiences

Theories shape therapeutic practices and the locus of intervention. The anxiety control theory sponsors treatments that emphasize repeated exposure to threatening situations until anxiety is extinguished. All therapists need do, according to this view, is to persuade clients to expose themselves to threatening situations without any adverse consequences and to remain there until their anxiety subsides (Marks, 1987). If such exposure is repeated often enough, phobics will eventually lose their anxiety and cease their avoidant behavior. In this approach, the prescribed therapist's role offers little in the way of enabling guidance when phobics cannot get themselves to confront what they find threatening. Since the treatment is aimed at eradicating anxiety rather than developing coping capabilities, little explicit instruction is provided about how to exercise control over threats once clients force themselves to face them. In practice, most therapists who use this approach wisely ignore the sterile exposure doctrine and adopt a more enabling role when therapeutic progress is discouragingly slow or arrested. To the extent that therapists adhere to the relatively inactive role prescribed by the exposure doctrine, they weaken and needlessly prolong treatment. Therapists can increase the power of treatment and reduce its stressfulness by being more than merely prompters for scared people to enter and remain in threatening situations.

The mechanism hypothesized to underlie the effects of exposure is habituation. Yet proponents of the habituation notion provide no independent measure of habituation to permit empirical tests of this view. The unpredictiveness of the anxiety extinction doctrine does not bode well for habituation, which is akin to it. Enactive modes of treatment using guided mastery should be distinguished from those relying mainly on exposure assignments. Guided mastery is the more powerful form for enhancing beliefs of personal efficacy, reducing anxiety, and restoring behavioral functioning (Bandura, Jeffery, & Wright, 1974; Williams, 1992). Figure 8.1 summarizes graphically the comparative power of guided mastery and exposure treatments to restore successful coping behavior in agoraphobics.

The concept of "exposure" reduces to the simple notion that modification of phobic behavior requires some contact with relevant threats. It has little explanatory or predicative value, however, and offers few prescriptive guidelines for how to accelerate the process of change. By analogy, to say that academic learning requires exposure to instructional material is to say little that is explanatory or prescriptive. Like the anxiety-extinction notion, the exposure-habituation notion does not withstand close scrutiny. Different modes of treatment with equivalent actual exposure produce markedly different changes in efficacy beliefs and accompanying coping

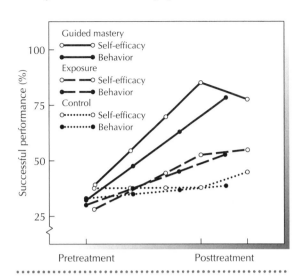

FIGURE 8.1. Mean level of perceived self-efficacy and percentage of coping tasks successfully performed by agoraphobics who received guided mastery treatment, exposure treatment, or no treatment. Perceived efficacy was measured both before and after the behavioral posttreatment test. (Williams, Dooseman, & Kleifield, 1984)

behavior. Regardless of the form these treatments take, subsequent behavioral change is highly predictable from level of self-efficacy change (Bandura et al., 1977; Bandura et al., 1974; Williams, Dooseman, & Kleifield, 1984).

In other studies, phobics receive equivalent exposure to threats but under cognitive sets that carry different efficacy implications. Phobics who have had the same amount of exposure to threatening events display higher efficacy beliefs and coping behavior under a cognitive set that treatment had imparted all the requisite coping skills than under a cognitive set that only a portion of the skills had been imparted (Laberge & Gauthier, 1986). The more their efficacy beliefs were raised by the alleged completeness of treatment, the more boldly they behaved. Phobics who perform the same types of coping tasks for the same length of exposure exhibit higher efficacy beliefs and behavioral improvement under a cognitive set that their coping activity is part of a therapeutic procedure for enhancing their coping skills than under a cognitive set that the coping activity is part of a diagnostic procedure for assessing their existing coping skills (Gauthier, Laberge, Frève, & Dufour, 1986). The amount of nonreinforced elicitation of anxiety arousal during the exposure, which presumably governs habituation and anxiety extinction, has no consistent effect on treatment outcomes (Emmelkamp & Mersch, 1982; Hafner & Marks, 1978; Mathews, Gelder, & Johnston, 1981).

According to the anxiety extinction-habituation notion, phobics should remain in threatening situations until their anxiety subsides. If they withdraw from the threatening situation as their anxiety mounts, the avoidance brings prompt relief and only reinforces their avoidant behavior. This is another deduction from anxiety control theory that has not survived empirical scrutiny. Rachman and his colleagues instructed one group of agoraphobics to cope with threats but to exercise personal control by withdrawing temporarily when they felt highly anxious and to try again (Rachman, Craske, Tallman, & Solyom, 1986). Brief avoidance under high anxiety with renewed effort was construed as exercise of personal control over one's change rather than as a sign of coping inefficacy. A second group was instructed to cope with the threats but to remain in the situation until their anxiety diminished. Contrary to anxiety control theory, withdrawal at high anxiety with renewed coping increased efficacy beliefs and reduced anxiety and phobic behavior just as much as did stoic endurance of anxiety until it subsided. In treatments relying on unassisted exposure, brief distributed encounters with threats that limit opportunities to gain a sense of coping efficacy produce little change, whereas prolonged coping that ensures confirmatory mastery experiences achieves positive results. The therapeutic changes not only are more enduring but also continue to increase after treatment by unassisted coping if, during exposure, clients are encouraged to make positive self-appraisals of their efficacy. Therapeutic changes are less enduring and do not increase after treatment if phobics undergo the behavioral changes without the positive self-affirmation (Marshall, 1985).

As these diverse lines of research demonstrate, people do things to bring about personal change,

rather than exposure to threats automatically habituating or extinguishing their anxious reactivity. This is the difference between a proactive mastery view of personal change and a reactive extinction view that harks back to the behaviorism of yesteryear. In enactive modes of treatment, it is not mere exposure to threats but mastery experience gained through exercise of personal agency that provides the basis for change. The earlier chapters provide considerable evidence that people are influenced by how they evaluate their performance attainments rather than by the attainments per se. This is well documented in microanalyses of growth of self-efficacy during the course of treatment relying on performance mastery experiences (Bandura, 1982a). Phobics register increases in their perceived coping efficacy when their mastery experiences disconfirm misbeliefs about their coping capabilities. They hold weak efficacy beliefs in a provisional status, testing their newly acquired self-knowledge and skills before consolidating their altered view of their capabilities. If, in the course of completing a task, they discover something that appears intimidating about the undertaking or that suggests certain limitations to their mode of coping, they register a decline in self-efficacy despite their successful performance. In such instances, performance successes leave them self-doubting rather than emboldened.

In vicarious modes of treatment, it is not mere exposure to models but the exemplification of effective coping strategies and socially comparative indicants of capability that constitutes the critical influence. Thus, phobics who have been exposed to a videotaped model coping successfully raise their efficacy beliefs and coping behavior and experience less fear when the model is alleged to be fearful and like them, but they do not benefit from the same exposure to the same modeling if the model is presented as nonfearful and thus different from them (Prince, 1984). The dissimilar model is dismissed as not informative of what they personally can do. In persuasory modes of influence, it is not mere exposure to talk about capability to manage threats but the social power and credibility of the persuader that convinces participants that they have the capability to perform more effectively.

Guided Mastery

Over the years, efforts to treat human dysfunctions have relied extensively on the interview as the principal means of psychological change. Although verbal analysis and social persuasion can produce some results, it is difficult to achieve consistently major changes in human behavior by talk alone. It is one thing to analyze and talk about beneficial changes but quite another to realize them in the troublesome realities of everyday life. Nor have behavioral techniques fared well when applied as if humans were unthinking organisms. Earlier reviews document that behavioral techniques depend on cognitive mediation for their effects (Bandura, 1969a; Brewer, 1974). Thus, neither verbalism insulated from action nor actionism insulated from thought harvests superior results.

Social cognitive theory prescribes mastery experience as the principal vehicle of personal change (Bandura, 1986a). When people diligently avoid what they fear, they lose touch with the reality they shun. Guided mastery provides a quick and effective way of restoring reality testing. It provides disconfirming tests of phobic beliefs. But even more important, mastery experiences that are structured to develop coping skills provide persuasive confirmatory tests that one can exercise control over potential threats. Intractable phobics, of course, are not about to do what they dread. Therefore, therapists must create enabling environmental conditions so that incapacitated phobics can perform successfully despite themselves. Enabling conditions are created proactively by enlisting a variety of performance mastery aids (Bandura et al., 1969; Bandura et al., 1974). Feared activities are first modeled to show people how to cope effectively with threats and to disconfirm their worst fears. Modeling aids that cultivate competencies are especially important when skill deficits must be overcome. In using modeling to eradicate faulty thinking, therapists create disconfirmatory tests for misbeliefs by enacting sequences of events that repeatedly demonstrate that the catastrophic outcomes phobics expect do not, in fact, occur. Modeling alone produces some heightening of perceived self-efficacy, but additional mastery aids are usually required to achieve full recovery of functioning in the more refractory cases. The transmission of coping strategies and the disconfirmation of misbeliefs through modeling increase the effectiveness of other mastery aids.

Difficult or intimidating tasks are broken down into subtasks of readily mastered steps. At any given step, people are asked to do what is within their capabilities with some extra effort and persistence. A program to eliminate a driving phobia might start with brief trips on secluded streets in minimal traffic, advance to longer drives on more active routes with scattered traffic, and culminate in lengthy excursions on crowded freeways under difficult weather conditions. If phobics fail in their initial attempts, they are quick to ascribe their difficulty to inherent incapability. The therapist ascribes the difficulty to the size of the task demands: The step was too large. More easily achieved tasks are selected and attempted. Treatment is conducted in this stepwise fashion until the most taxing or threatening activities are mastered.

Joint performance of intimidating activities with the therapist further enables phobics to attempt activities they resist doing by themselves. A participant therapist can facilitate the rate of change in several ways. The mere presence of a familiar person reduces stress reactions and increases boldness in threatening situations (Epley, 1974; Feist & Rosenthal, 1973). Self-development of coping capabilities is much easier in the absence of disruptive stress reactions. People are not always acutely attentive to coping strategies modeled in safe settings. But they become highly vigilant of helpful strategies modeled for them in contexts in which they themselves are coping with actual threats and see where they are succeeding and where they are faltering. They benefit greatly from ongoing corrective modeling specifically focused on the problematic aspects of their capabilities.

Participant involvement of the therapist serves additional important functions. People often come to believe that certain rituals, which actually carry no influence, increase the exercise of control over outcomes (Langer, 1983). This is especially true in coping with threats. For example, agoraphobics can get themselves to perform feared activities only by including ritualistic elements or executing the activities in a constricted way (Williams, 1990). For example, an agoraphobic who dreaded driving would manipulate keys ritualistically in intimidating traffic situations or cling unwaveringly to the safer right lane once she became bold enough to venture on the freeway. Encapsulated performances limit the generalizability of the efficacy benefits of successful experiences. When perceived coping efficacy is partially tied to certain rituals or to a restricted set of conditions, clients need efficacy-instilling trials that persuade them they have the capability to perform successfully without rituals or self-protective constraints. Participant therapists can quickly spot such efficacy-delimiting maneuvers and diversify the mastery experiences to generalize their impact on beliefs of personal efficacy.

Another way in which participant involvement of the therapist can accelerate the process of change is by naturalistic modification of faulty thought patterns. Most treatments try to alter dysfunctional modes of thought through interpretive interviews. Clients report the thoughts they habitually generate in problem situations or in imagined ones. They are then helped to restructure their detrimental ways of construing events and their faulty styles of thinking (Beck & Emery, 1985; Ellis & Dryden, 1987; Meichenbaum, 1977). Recollections and cognitive simulations, however, often do not fully capture the perturbing trains of thought aroused in direct encounters with threats. Moreover, clients may adopt positive thoughts in benign interview settings only to revert to faulty ones in the face of actual threats (Biran & Wilson, 1981; Emmelkamp, Kuippers, & Eggaraat, 1978). In the participant arrangement, the therapist is present to identify and correct dysfunctional patterns of thinking as they arise in taxing situations and to suggest cognitive strategies that foster successful performance (Williams & Rappoport, 1983).

Another way of overcoming resistance is to use graduated time. Phobics will refuse threatening tasks if they will have to endure stress for a long time, but they will risk them for a short period. As their coping efficacy increases, the length of time they perform the activity is gradually extended. Initially, claustrophobics might be able to endure confinement for just seconds; durations are gradually increased until minutes and later hours can be tolerated. Similarly, obsessive-compulsive clients who spend countless hours cleansing themselves against dreaded contamination or repugnant thoughts engage in the "contaminant" activity and thoughts but refrain from the cleansing rituals for increasing periods until they can do so for an extended time with equanimity (Meyer, 1966; Rachman & Hodgson, 1980).

Protective aids that reduce the likelihood of feared outcomes can be introduced as still another facilitator of change. Peering down from lofty places can be made less frightening at first for height phobics by providing secure structural guards. Contact with feared animals can be prompted if their movements are first restrained or protective gear is provided. Most of the mastery aids described so far reduce avoidant behavior while keeping the threat at a challenging level. If these strategies prove insufficient to embolden coping behavior, resistance can be surmounted by reducing the severity of the threat. Task graduation varies the complexity of the coping activity in a situation of high threat; threat graduation varies the degree of intimidation of the conditions under which the full coping activity is performed. The difference between grading coping activities and grading the threateningness of settings can be illustrated in the treatment of agoraphobics who dread grocery shopping. In activity graduation, phobics confront the most intimidating store and first get themselves to enter it, then to purchase one item in the express checkout line, and eventually to transact progressively larger purchases. In threat graduation, they make the full purchases at the outset in a small, nonthreatening store and then tackle scarier places. Severe phobics usually require both threat and activity graduation. Thus, getting an intractable agoraphobic to purchase a single item in a benign setting may be the initial coping challenge.

The severity and type of dysfunction will determine the particular mastery aids that may be required. Initially, therapists use however many mastery aids are needed to restore belief in coping capabilities and to achieve effective functioning. As treatment progresses, the provisional aids are withdrawn to verify that coping attainments stem from the exercise of enhanced personal efficacy rather than from mastery aids. Extrapolations from attribution and self-perception theories to the field of personal change often imply that people must labor unaided or under inconspicuously managed prompts if they are to convince themselves of their personal capabilities (Kopel & Arkowitz, 1975). Otherwise they misattribute their success to the external arrangements. Such prescriptions require major qualification. Any possible risk of external misattribution for performance successes is quickly eliminated in guided mastery treatment without sacrificing the enormous benefits of mastery aids. This is achieved simply by providing clients with opportunities for self-directed accomplishments after functioning has been restored. They succeed on their own without any supportive aids. Such experiences remove any lingering doubts individuals may harbor about their power to exercise control over potential threats. In the final phase of treatment, self-directed mastery experiences, designed to provide varied confirmatory tests of coping capabilities, are arranged to strengthen and generalize the sense of coping efficacy (Bandura et al., 1975).

The various components of guided mastery treatment have been analyzed for their contribution to perceived efficacy and coping behavior. Treatment drawing upon the wide array of mastery aids when needed produces huge increases in perceived personal efficacy and coping behavior, whereas minimally aided treatment achieves only modest improvements (Bandura et al., 1974; Williams et al., 1984). In Figure 8.2, the percentage of phobics achieving complete coping success is plotted as a function of the level of mastery aids provided by the treatment. With few mastery aids, treatment is discouragingly slow and needlessly distressing. With a full set of mastery aids used selectively, phobics achieve continuous, rapid progress with minimal stress. The more severe and generalized the phobic dysfunction, the greater is the need for mastery aids

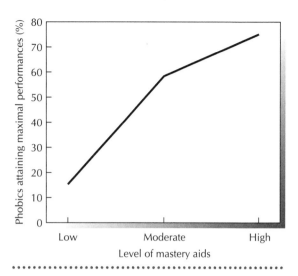

FIGURE 8.2. Percentage of phobics who successfully performed all of the threatening coping activities in the post-treatment assessment depending on the level of mastery aids in the treatment they received. (Bandura, Jeffery, & Wright, 1974)

to ensure continued progress. Some agoraphobics perform dreaded activities but do so in a rigidly self-protective manner with high anxiety. Guided mastery can get them to engage in those activities flexibly and proficiently (Williams & Zane, 1989). As they shed the defensive maneuvers imbedded in their actions and gain confidence in their capabilities, their performance anxiety essentially disappears. Guided mastery enlisting a variety of mastery aids is considerably more effective in eliminating anxiety in anxious performers than is minimally aided exposure. Mastery aids thus enable therapists to exercise substantial control over the speed and power of treatment. Enabling treatments benefit everyone. Some people simply require more aid than others.

The simulation technology of virtual reality lends itself to mastery-oriented treatment of some types of phobic dysfunctions. Rather than coping with actual threats, phobics manage progressively more threatening aspects in a computer-generated environment (Lamson & Meisner, 1994). For example, people who dread heights don a helmet containing a computer screen that displays a simulated environment containing the threatening elements. They move through this environment at their own pace by pressing a button. They inch their way across elevated walkways, look over edges at the ground below, and manage other situations that mimic scary heights. They continue their coping efforts until they gain mastery. One can accelerate mastery by introducing and fading out mastery aids either within the simulated environment or by voice-over accompaniments. The range of applications can be extended by enhancing the realness and interactivity so that actions elicit reactions from the environments in which individuals immerse themselves.

Phobics react emotionally during these simulated interactions, which suggests some sense of realness. Anecdotal reports claim widespread transfer from virtual to actual reality. Claims by enthusiastic advocates should be accepted with skepticism in the absence of controlled empirical tests, however. The amount of change that can be achieved in simulated environments clearly merits investigation. In a controlled study, height phobics reported reductions in anxiety, distress, and avoidance of heights after mastering graded virtual threats, but, surprisingly, no formal assessment of phobic behavior was conducted (Rothbaum et al., 1995). If this approach produces high success rates, it would be a significant advance in the field because of its versatility. A variety of environments could be simulated for mastery that might be difficult or inconvenient to arrange in actuality. Moreover, constructed virtual environments permit greater control over the severity of the threats phobics try to manage. If virtual mastery achieves only partial transfer, as is likely, virtual therapy can serve as a convenient adjunct but not a substitute for actual mastery experiences.

Facets of Personal Change

Social cognitive theory distinguishes among four basic processes of change: the acquisition, generality, durability, and resilience of psychological functioning (Bandura, 1986a). Acquisition involves the development of knowledge, skills, and self-beliefs that govern human thought, affect, and action. Generality has to do with how widely acquired capabilities are used. The scope of the changes can take varied forms. These include generality across different situations, toward different persons, and across modalities of thought, affect, and action. Durability is concerned with how well changes are sustained over time. Resilience refers to the ability to recover readily from adverse experiences.

Rather than framing the evaluative issue in global terms of whether a given treatment approach is effective, sociocognitive theory asks more analytic questions: What is the power of treatment to produce personal change to begin with? Do the changes generalize, or are they narrow in scope? How well are the changes maintained over time? Does the treatment build resilience to adversity? A treatment that achieves circumscribed, transitory change is of little interest. One that produces generalized but short-lived change requires a maintenance component. One that produces enduring but circumscribed change requires a transfer component. The goal is to create treatments that realize all four facets of personal change — acquisition, generality, durability, and resilience. Appropriate conditions must be arranged to achieve them. They do not necessarily occur spontaneously upon induction of personal change.

The evidence just presented verifies that mastery aids accelerate the acquisition process and reduce its stressfulness. Self-directed mastery, in which individuals manage progressively more difficult situations on their own after effective functioning has been established, contribute to the generality and durability of change. For example, recovered automobile phobics are given mastery assignments to drive on their own in heavily trafficked city streets and highways. Social phobics pursue mastery assignments in which they attend intimidating social functions. Varied coping tasks are selected that provide rising levels of challenge with growth of personal efficacy. Gradations of challenge ensure optimal rates of success in self-directed mastery. It should be noted that self-directed mastery refers to unaided performance of challenging activities, not to who suggests the coping tasks (O'Brien & Kelley, 1980). Such independent accomplishments enhance beliefs of personal efficacy and further increase the level and generality of behavioral change (Bandura et al., 1975). In follow-up assessments extending over a five-year period, the individuals remain fully self-efficacious and bold in their behavior.

Another important facet of personal change for which treatments should be evaluated is how the treatments affect vulnerability to aversive experiences. Treatments should be structured in ways that build resilience as reflected in the ability to bounce back rapidly from adverse experiences. A resilient sense of efficacy is not created by a few successes. It requires learning how to handle adversity and mastering increasingly tougher challenges through perseverant effort. Independent personal accomplishments help to build resilience to adverse experiences, thereby reducing vulnerability to relapse. The capacity of aversive events to reinstate dysfunctions depends on the nature and strength of preexisting efficacy beliefs into which new experiences are integrated, rather than on the properties of the events alone. Triumphs over diverse tough challenges build a resilient sense of efficacy that neutralizes the negative impact of an untoward experience. To take a simple example, dog phobics who develop a firm belief in their coping capabilities through many masterful encounters with diverse breeds during self-directed mastery are unlikely to experience a complete collapse of self-efficacy because of a negative encounter with a certain canine. They may be wary of that particular one, which is adaptive, but maintain belief in their capability to handle others. If they have no further mastery experiences with dogs after functioning is established, widespread self-doubt will set in fast after a negative encounter and reinstate a generalized pattern of phobic behavior. Some of the most important therapeutic benefits can be achieved after a "cure" is attained by structuring opportunities for varied mastery experiences that reduce vulnerability to the negative effects of adversity.

Removal of phobic dysfunction through restoration of a sense of coping efficacy does not mean that ex-phobics will start acting recklessly. Elimination of phobic dread of automobile traffic does not dispose unimpeded clients to rush headlong into onrushing traffic on busy thoroughfares. Rather, debilitating routinized avoidance is replaced by flexibly adaptive behavior that is cognitively controlled by judgments of personal efficacy and expected outcomes of prospective actions. The ex-phobics engage in the activities when it is advantageous to do so but not if it places them at risk.

Distinguishing between Mechanisms and Modes of Change

There is a common misconception that the modality of treatment must match the modality of dysfunction: Behavioral dysfunctions presumably require an action-oriented treatment; emotional distress requires an emotive-oriented treatment, and faulty thinking requires a cognitively oriented treatment. In fact, powerful experiences produce changes in all modalities of functioning — behavioral, cognitive, and affective. A person who had the misfortune to be mauled by a Doberman pinscher, for example, would avoid them like the plague, show visceral agitation at the mere sight of them, develop phobic thinking about them, and loathe them. Powerful enactive mastery experiences eliminate defensive behavior, physiological stress reactions, and faulty thought patterns (Bandura, 1988b). In short, the potency of the treatment rather than the modality in which it is conveyed largely determines the nature and scope of change.

It is sometimes claimed that enactive treatments reduce agoraphobic behavior but not panic attacks, whereas cognitive therapies that seek to correct catastrophic misinterpretations of bodily sensations reduce panic attacks but not agoraphobia. In fact, guided mastery treatment not only reduces panic attacks but also is more effective than cognitive therapy in raising perceived efficacy to control perturbing thoughts and panicky reactions, reducing catastrophic outcome expectations, and abating other types of fears (Williams & Falbo, 1996). Even the weaker form of enactive treatment relying solely on exposure to threats is just as effective in reducing debilitating cognitions and panic reactions as is cognitive restructuring (Bouchard et al., 1996). The same is true for social phobias (Feske & Chambless, 1995). The research by Williams and Falbo further reveals that panic attacks are much easier to treat in mildly agoraphobic people than in highly agoraphobic ones. Thus, therapy outcome studies confined to panicky people without agoraphobic disability may yield an inflated portrayal of therapeutic power through exclusion of the tougher cases. Other studies, to be reviewed later, similarly demonstrate that guided mastery is more effective than cognitive restructuring in eliminating both behavioral dysfunctions and faulty patterns of thinking.

Developments in the field of psychological change reveal two major divergent trends. On the one hand, explanations of psychological change rely increasingly on cognitive mechanisms. On the other hand, performance-based treatments operating through mastery experiences are proving most powerful in producing cognitive, affective, and behavioral changes (Bandura, 1977; Williams, 1992). The apparent divergence between cognitive theory and enactive treatment can be reconciled by distinguishing between process and means. Cognitive processes mediate psychological change, but the cognitive events can be developed and altered most readily by enactive mastery.

Common Mediating Mechanism

The aim of a comprehensive theory is to specify basic mechanisms of sufficient scope of operation to account for the effects of diverse modes of influence across different domains of functioning. A field is not much advanced by postulating different mechanisms for each mode of influence or each class of behavior. The net result is a large collection of disconnected explanatory factors. In social cognitive theory, perceived self-efficacy operates as one common mechanism of behavioral change: Different modes of treatments enhance coping behavior partly by creating and strengthening beliefs of personal efficacy. The higher order function of perceived efficacy is evident

in its impact on ideational, motivational, and affective processes. The contribution of these processes to action, therefore, can be partly reduced to the workings of efficacy belief. This chapter examines the generality of self-efficacy theory across diverse human dysfunctions and therapeutic interventions. The other chapters address the generalizability of the theory to strikingly different domains of functioning in markedly different classes of contexts.

The generality of the explanatory and predictive power of self-efficacy theory has been tested in a series of experiments in which severe phobics received treatments relying on each of the four major modes of influence — enactive, vicarious, cognitive, and emotive — conveyed through different brands of therapy (Bandura & Adams, 1977; Bandura et al., 1977; Bandura et al., 1980). In each study in this series, the level, strength, and generality of efficacy beliefs for a variety of coping activities with the phobic threat were measured before and after treatment and at follow-up periods.

The treatment employing enactive guided mastery as the principal vehicle of change has already been described in some detail. In the mode of treatment relying on vicarious influence, phobics merely observe a model exercise control over progressively more threatening interactions with the phobic object. The modeling conveys information on the predictability and the controllability of threats (Bandura et al., 1982). Predictability is modeled through enacted sequences showing how the phobic object is likely to behave under different circumstances. Knowing what is likely to happen under given circumstances reduces the stress of foreboding uncertainty and provides the basis for developing good ways of managing potential threats. In modeling controllability, models exhibit coping strategies for exercising control over phobic threats in whatever situations might arise. Thus, what inefficacious thinking renders frightful, instructive modeling makes predictable and personally controllable. To potentiate the power of modeling, factors that increase perceived similarity to the model are embedded in the coping demonstrations.

In the third treatment approach tested, which draws heavily on a cognitive modality (Kazdin, 1978), phobics generate cognitive scenarios in which they repeatedly confront threatening situations and gain mastery over them. Such cognitive simulations have been shown to increase assertiveness and reduce phobic behavior (Kazdin, 1979; Thase & Moss, 1976).

As a further test of the generality of efficacy theory, an emotive-oriented method was also examined. This emotional desensitization mode of treatment seeks to eliminate avoidant behavior by eradicating anxiety arousal (Wolpe, 1974). Threats are broken down into a graded hierarchy of menacing encounters for visualization. For example, if a person is unable to behave assertively, the visualized situations include expressions of assertiveness toward increasingly intimidating figures. Relaxation is repeatedly paired with successive visualized threats until the most intimidating one ceases to arouse any anxiety. The rationale for this treatment approach was originally cast in terms of conditioning relaxation responses to anxiety cues. This method, however, produces similar improvement regardless of whether the visualized scenarios are paired with relaxation or not (Kazdin & Wilcoxon, 1976;

Wilkins, 1971). Such evidence is inconsistent with a conditioning mechanism. In actuality, the desensitization method serves as a conveyance for several forms of efficacy information. First, repeated visualization of oneself coping successfully with varied threats can boost beliefs in one's efficacy through self-persuasion. Second, if people are less perturbed by threats, they are likely to judge themselves better able to manage them. Third, acquisition of a self-relaxation skill may lead people to approach stressful situations more self-efficaciously through belief that they have a means to alleviate stress.

Results of the series studies confirm that different modes of treatment all raise and strengthen beliefs of coping efficacy (Bandura & Adams, 1977; Bandura et al., 1977; Bandura et al., 1980). In microanalyses of the congruence between efficacy beliefs and performance on individual coping tasks, behavior corresponds closely to level of perceived self-efficacy regardless of the method by which a sense of coping efficacy is instilled. The higher the level of perceived self-efficacy, the greater are the performance accomplishments (Fig. 8.3). Strength

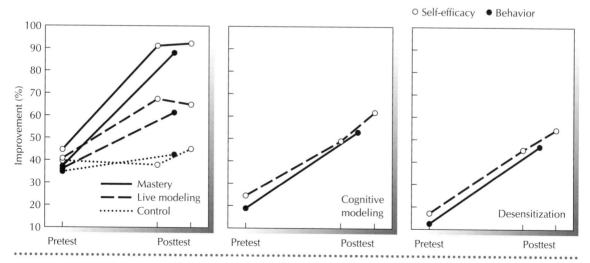

FIGURE 8.3. Mean increases in perceived self-efficacy and coping behavior accompanying treatments relying on enactive mastery experience, vicarious experiences through live modeling, cognitive modeling, or emotive desensitization. In the posttest phase, level of perceived efficacy was measured before and after the test of coping behavior. (Bandura & Adams, 1977; Bandura, Adams, & Beyer, 1977; Bandura et al., 1980)

of efficacy beliefs also predicts behavior change (Bandura, 1977). The stronger the efficacy beliefs, the more likely people are to undertake difficult activities and to persist in their efforts until they succeed.

Consistent with self-efficacy theory, enactive mastery produces the highest, strongest, and most generalized increases in personal efficacy. It eliminates phobic behavior and subjective and physiological anxiety reactions, transforms abhorrent attitudes toward phobic objects to positive ones, and eradicates phobic ruminations and nightmares in all clients within a relatively short time. Evidence that an enhanced sense of coping efficacy profoundly affects dream activity is a particularly striking generalized impact. Such marked transformations of cognitive activity in dream states indicate that nightmarish dreaming is more amenable to change by coping mastery than by interpretive dream analysis.

The superiority of treatment based on enactive guided mastery is corroborated by other comparative studies demonstrating that enactive mastery surpasses verbal persuasory, emotive, and vicarious modes of influence in enhancing efficacy beliefs and performance accomplishments (Biran & Wilson, 1981; Feltz et al., 1979; Katz et al., 1983; Williams et al., 1985). When phobics who have benefited only partially from persuasory, vicarious, or emotive treatments subsequently receive enactive guided mastery treatment, their efficacy beliefs are raised to the maximal level and their behavioral functioning is fully restored regardless of the severity of their dysfunction (Bandura & Adams, 1977; Bandura et al., 1977; Bandura et al., 1969; Biran & Wilson, 1981; Thase & Moss, 1976). These findings suggest that in treatments that yield only partial improvements, the major deficits may reside in the method of treatment rather than in the client. All too often, the poor results of weak methods get attributed to clients' resistance.

Self-efficacy theory explains rate of change during the course of treatment as well as eventual outcomes (Bandura & Adams, 1977). In microanalyses of degree of progress during treatment, coping tasks are segmented hierarchically into progressively more taxing and threatening ones. Phobics are treated with guided mastery on the lowest failed coping task in the series until they master it, whereupon they are tested for their perceived efficacy and performance attainments on all succeeding tasks that they had been unable to perform previously. Phobics differ in the amount of self-efficacy they derive from the same level of behavioral mastery. Some judge their efficacy to be only slightly beyond their prior attainments and behave accordingly; others express more substantial self-efficacy gains; and still others judge themselves supremely efficacious to fulfill all higher levels of coping demands. Efficacy beliefs formed at different points in treatment predict with considerable accuracy subsequent coping successes on tasks the phobics had never done before. Assessments of perceived self-efficacy during the process of change provide important guides for treatment. They show the progress clients are making and their remaining areas of vulnerability. Moreover, efficacy probes indicate the optimal timing and level of coping challenges that will be manageable for clients and the particular blend of mastery aids that will enable them to achieve rapid, continuous progress. Finally, ongoing efficacy assessments can reveal which aspects of a given treatment are having an impact and which are without effect (Clarke et al., 1991).

Understanding the nature and structure of multifaceted phobic dysfunctions provides guidelines for how to treat them. Agoraphobia is especially well suited for clarifying this issue because it usually takes multiple forms in the same individual. Agoraphobics cannot shop in stores and supermarkets because they find the long impersonal lines of shoppers, turnstiles, and milling crowds too intimidating. Public facilities such as theaters and restaurants, which arouse feelings of being helplessly trapped in crowds, become dangerous territories to be avoided. Fear of elevators, escalators, and heights further constricts the range of the phobics' navigable environment. The world of those who cannot use public transportation or venture forth in automobiles even as passengers is confined to what is within walking distance of their homes. The boundaries shrink even more drastically for those who feel so inefficacious in dealing with everyday realities that they become virtual prisoners in their homes. If agoraphobia is a unitary disorder, then eliminating any given phobia should produce widespread reductions in the whole assemblage of phobias. If agoraphobia is simply a collection of independent phobias, however, then each phobia would have to be treated separately.

Williams, Kinney, and Falbo (1989) addressed this issue by examining the generality of change accompanying guided mastery treatment in agoraphobics presenting different constellations of phobias. In each case, one phobia was treated and the degree of behavioral improvement in the nontreated phobias was measured. For example, a given agoraphobic might be tested for improvement in phobic avoidance of shopping and scaling heights after being treated for a driving phobia. The findings reveal that agoraphobia is neither a unitary disorder nor a collection of autonomous phobias. Treating one phobia produced improvements in untreated ones. The patterns of transfer benefits were highly variable, however, and did not necessarily conform to any gradient of physical similarity of activities. A given individual might show large improvement in one untreated phobia but little change in another. Sometimes untreated phobias that were similar to the treated one did not change much, but dissimilar ones were much improved. Thus, the phobias were complexly patterned rather than unitary or disconnected.

Williams and his colleagues examined several factors that are commonly invoked, in addition to self-efficacy, as possible mediators of transfer benefits. The pattern of efficacy beliefs proved to be an excellent predictor of the pattern of generalized changes across different domains of behavioral functioning (Williams et al., 1989). Regardless of whether the generalization domains were similar or dissimilar to the treated one, the higher the efficacy beliefs for a particular type of phobia, the greater the behavioral improvements. The structure of the self-efficacy belief system in any given case reflects the subjective construction of perceived coping efficacy rather than the objective similarity of threatening elements. Moreover, efficacy beliefs are

consistently strong predictors of both treated and untreated phobic behavior at midtreatment, posttreatment, and follow-up. Efficacy beliefs retain their predictiveness when anticipated panic, anticipated anxiety, perceived danger, maximal performance in treatment, and level of anxiety accompanying the behavior are controlled. These factors lose their predictiveness, however, when beliefs of personal efficacy are controlled. Now that perceived efficacy has been identified as an important transfer mechanism, the next step for research is to clarify the idiosyncratic ways in which agoraphobics cognitively process their successes and difficulties in restructuring their efficacy beliefs.

The preceding analyses have centered mainly on the relative power of treatments relying on mastery experiences and empirical tests of alternative mechanisms of change. Cognitive-behavior therapy is another approach that is widely used. The basic tenet of cognitive-behavior therapy is that human problems and distresses arise from faulty thinking. Treatments founded on this conceptual scheme, therefore, seek to eradicate phobic dysfunctions by altering faulty modes of thinking. Although thought is the principal locus of intervention, proponents of this approach have different views on what form the troublesome thoughts take. Some emphasize dysfunctional global beliefs (Ellis & Dryden, 1987); others single out self-debilitating internal dialogues (Meichenbaum, 1985); and still others focus on faulty ways of thinking that create and sustain negative self-schemata (Beck & Emery, 1985).

Modes of treatment that rely heavily on verbal analyses of faulty thinking and on verbal persuasion are generally labeled cognitive-behavior therapy. Such approaches have come under fire from behaviorists (Ledwidge, 1978). They raise the specter of disembodied mentalism. They relabel thought as verbal behavior and argue that behavior cannot cause behavior; only influences outside the organism can do so. They point to evidence that verbal modes of treatment are no more effective, and often are less so, than are behavioral techniques. Close scrutiny of such critiques underscore the need to recast the issues in less evangelical form. Thoughts are brain activities, not disembodied mental entities. To christen thought as verbal behavior is to stretch the definition of behavior to the point where it ceases to have any meaning. One can have thoughts without words. Preverbal children, deaf-mutes, and aphasics are not thoughtless. People often engage in extended trains of thought without uttering a single word. To equate thoughts with verbalism is to confuse the form of the thought probe with the cognitive phenomenon being assessed.

The field of psychological change is not well served by false dichotomies that there exist pure cognitive and behavioral treatments. Because behavior therapists structure and implement contingent rules, incentive systems, and social sanctions by verbal means that must be processed cognitively, one would be hard pressed to find a "behavioral" method of treatment that does not rely, at least in part, on cognitive conveyance. Nor is one likely to find a "cognitive" method of treatment that is devoid of any performance elements in the likeness of a behaviorectomy. To label verbal modes of influence as cognitive and action modes as behavioral is to confuse means and mechanisms of change. Human thought is changed by informative experiences flowing from actions as well as by conversations. Indeed, even Piaget's theory, which is the hallmark of cognitivism, depends almost entirely on exploratory actions as the prime source of knowledge and thinking skills. Because thought is changeable by the influence of word, action, and example, treatments relying on these different modalities are all cognitive. The relevant issue is their relative power. Conversational treatments have no special claim on cognitive change.

Within the model of triadic reciprocal causation, action, cognition, and environmental factors operate interactively to produce changes. Distressed people create perturbing realities by how they behave as well as by misreading what they encounter in their everyday life. The causal contribution of cognition, therefore, is best understood and enlisted in concert with behavioral and environmental interactants. The treatment of phobic disorders illustrates this point. Phobias are rarely eradicated by thought analysis alone. Although performance attainments are forceful persuaders, they do not necessarily ensure generalized enduring changes. The impact that performance attainments exert depends on what is made of them. Among driving phobics, all of whom have been helped to navigate the same difficult routes, some judge themselves thoroughly efficacious and drive around unimpededly; others retain some misgivings about their capabilities and drive circumscribedly; while still others judge their capabilities as largely confined to the particular route mastered but remain otherwise immobilized by their perceived inefficacy, despite their performance successes (Bandura et al., 1980). The degree and generality of change is mediated by perceived efficacy gleaned from performances rather than being directly forged by the performed responses.

When self-referent thought weakens the impact of performance accomplishments, this does not mean that enactive mastery should be abandoned for talk. Rather, analysis of how people are evaluating their performances provides guides for how to structure mastery experiences to make them more self-persuasive. Once individuals specify what would convince them of their coping capabilities, their sense of efficacy can be enhanced by helping them to manage successfully the activities that carry high diagnostic import for them. In short, the choice and structuring of mastery tasks is largely determined by their potential impact on beliefs of personal efficacy. Those who are convinced of their efficacy by performance successes on a few challenging tasks do not require repetitive proof of coping capabilities. Highly self-inefficacious drivers need more substantial successes on tasks they regard as especially diagnostic of coping efficacy before they alter their self-beliefs. The most recalcitrant ones need multiple self-affirming experiences on diverse routes, under diverse circumstances, with different field workers to persuade them of their capabilities. Because of the interactive relationship among thought, affect, and action, psychological influences are not exclusively cognitive or behavioral. Nor does the power of treatment depend simply on adding or deleting cognitive and behavioral elements as though they were independent modules of influence. Rather, they act bidirectionally to shape the course of change.

Cognitive behavioral therapies produce improvements in varied dysfunctions (Hollon & Beck, 1994; Meichenbaum & Jaremko, 1983). The question of theoretical interest is not whether such methods work, especially if supplemented with behavioral assignments, but rather the power of cognitive restructuring through verbal means alone to alter behavior. Therapeutic power is best gauged by comparing cognitive restructuring with methods of proven strength, rather than with untreated controls or with weak treatments. Evidence of comparative power is also affected by the types of outcome measures that are selected. Words come easier than deeds or physiological tranquillity. Self-reports usually exaggerate degree of change compared to actual improvement in behavioral functioning (Williams & Rappoport, 1983). Therefore, measures of coping behavior and physiological reactivity are better at detecting differences between treatments than are verbal reports of change (Paul, 1986). Therefore, results of comparative studies relying solely on self-report measures of outcomes should be accepted with reservation.

Biran and Wilson (1981) treated phobics either with guided enactive mastery or with cognitive restructuring that included the three major variants of this procedure. Irrational beliefs were corrected as phobics verbalized their thoughts while visualizing threatening situations; they were taught how to supplant self-debilitating ideation with coping self-instruction and how to reconstrue situations to make them less intimidating. Enactive mastery instilled a strong sense of coping efficacy, diminished physiological stress reactions, and eradicated phobias in virtually everyone (81 percent). Cognitive restructuring alone created a weaker and less realistic sense of coping efficacy, did not affect physiological stress reactions, and produced few cures (9 percent). When the phobics who had achieved only partial improvement through cognitive restructuring were given enactive mastery, almost all were cured (86 percent).

Others have found enactive mastery to be considerably more powerful than multifaceted cognitive restructuring not only in eradicating phobic behavior but also in eliminating agoraphobic thinking (Emmelkamp et al., 1978). While imagining threatening situations, phobics can supplant scary thoughts with bold internal dialogues, only to revert to phobic thinking when actual threats are confronted. In contrast, people who gain a strong sense of coping efficacy through enactive triumphs over actual threats have little reason to engage in phobic thinking. Altering thought through enactive experience accords with social psychological approaches that use behavior change to alter attitudes (Abelson et al., 1968; Festinger, 1957).

The efficacy information conveyed by enactive mastery experiences can easily preempt the weaker redundant information provided by verbal restructuring (Rosenthal & Bandura, 1978). Perhaps for this reason, adding cognitive restructuring to enactive mastery does not promote greater self-efficacy and behavioral change than does enactive mastery alone (Emmelkamp & Mersch, 1982; Emmelkamp, van der Helm, van Zangen, & Plochg, 1980; Fecteau & Stoppard, 1983; Ladouceur, 1983; van den Hout, Arntz, & Hoekstra, 1994; Williams & Rappoport, 1983). Cognitive restructuring by verbal means is more likely to potentiate enactive modes of treatment in interpersonal dysfunctions where events contain many ambiguities that can be easily misconstrued to fit distorted views of reality.

Cognitive-behavior therapy, of course, does not rely solely on verbal analysis of thought processes. Erroneous beliefs and faulty habits of thinking are analyzed by examining the evidence for and against the misbeliefs. But to correct faulty ways of thinking, new ways of behaving are also prescribed as an integral part of this approach. In the more action-oriented forms of cognitive-behavior therapy, new ways of behaving not only are discussed but also are often modeled and practiced in role playing to develop effective styles of thinking and behaving. Much of the time in the treatment session is devoted to analyzing what impact the behavioral assignments have had, altering problematic aspects, and devising new ways of behaving to explore. The substantial contribution of enactive mastery to successful outcomes is revealed in a self-efficacy analysis of cognitive behavior treatment of speech anxiety with and without mastery trials in which clients put their speaking skills into practice in role playing (Fecteau & Stoppard, 1983). Instruction in cognitive coping skills and stress management raises perceived self-efficacy. But adding performance mastery heightens efficacy beliefs, reduces anticipatory and performance anxiety, and improves behavioral functioning. Including more cognitive components does not strengthen the treatment, but providing opportunities to validate one's efficacy through enactive mastery increases the power of treatment. In all variants of treatment, whether predominantly verbal or supplemented with coping action, the stronger the instilled efficacy beliefs, the better the public speaking and the lower the anxiety in intimidating situations.

In treatments using multiple cognitive procedures, a few of them usually work as well as the full set (Jaremko, 1979). Several factors may account for why more is not better. It may be that some of the seemingly different cognitive procedures convey redundant information about cognitive strategies for effective action. Outcomes will not be much affected by deletions or additions of redundant cognitive aids. A second possibility is that people may already possess many of the requisite cognitive skills but make little use of them. Indeed, deficient functioning often arises more from disuse than from deficits of cognitive competencies (Flavell, 1970). Intensive instruction in cognitive strategies may serve mainly to increase motivation to put into practice known strategies. When part of a method works as well as the complete one, the similarity in results may also be due to reduced adherence to the enlarged method. If people are prescribed many things to do, they may abandon most of them because it is too much bother. An expanded method will fail to produce superior results if it is not fully adopted and consistently applied. A final explanation, which might subsume most of the others, lies in the self-efficacy mediator of change. Instruction in cognitive self-guidance serves as a self-efficacy builder. A few component influences may be as persuasive of improved personal capabilities as the full complement of cognitive procedures.

Cognitive-behavior therapists prescribe certain behaviors for clients to carry out in their everyday interactions. Such behavioral assignments are designed to create both disconfirming evidence for faulty beliefs and misconstruals and confirming evidence of personal capabilities. Neimeyer and Feixas (1990) tested the effectiveness of cognitive therapy alone or with behavioral assignments to monitor dysfunctional thoughts, test the validity of beliefs by corrective actions, and promote better ways of behaving. Behavioral assignments enhanced therapeutic changes. The more skilled clients were in cognitive self-guidance, the better they maintained their therapeutic changes. Evidence for the benefits of behavioral assignments, however, is far from conclusive (Edelman & Chambless, 1995).

It is one thing to prescribe corrective actions and another to get people to carry them out successfully on their own, especially when they involve onerous or threatening aspects. Simply telling clients beset with self-doubts to embark on courses of action designed to change faulty thought does not mean they all rush out and do so consistently and self-persuasively. People vary in self-application of prescribed regimens (Primakoff, Epstein, & Covi, 1986). The contribution of behavioral assignments, therefore, is best revealed by assessing the degree to which prescribed activities are implemented. Belief in the efficacy of a prescribed regimen and in one's capabilities to perform it regularly predicts level of subsequent adherence as measured objectively (Hoelscher et al., 1986). The higher the sense of efficacy, the better the adherence and the greater the therapeutic benefits that are realized. Adherence to prescribed activities that yield evident benefits provides further verification of personal efficacy. A sense of self-regulative efficacy thus promotes adoption of corrective activities, which, in turn, is likely to strengthen efficacy beliefs.

Despite the importance attached to ameliorative behavioral assignments in cognitive-behavior therapy, guidelines for structuring this aspect of treatment are undeveloped. Selecting the enactive experiences best suited to disconfirm faulty thought patterns rests largely on intuition. When individuals are instructed to pursue beneficial courses of action but are left to their own devices to carry them out, the successes achieved will depend on a number of factors: Are individuals provided with the sociocognitive skills and the efficacy beliefs needed to perform effectively? Do they know how to improvise behavioral prescriptions under changing circumstances to disconfirm misbeliefs and to expand competencies? Have they anticipated possible difficulties in carrying out the prescribed activities and rehearsed strategies for surmounting them? Is their sense of efficacy strong enough to withstand setbacks and failures? Do they have sufficient positive incentives and social supports to invest the effort needed for personal change? If these facilitative factors are lacking, therapists will find themselves wrestling with covert or open resistance to their behavioral assignments. People who distrust their efficacy to produce good outcomes are not about to thrust themselves into difficult predicaments.

Therapeutic outcomes remain uncertain when intimidated persons have to create by themselves the conditions necessary for their own change. Guided mastery treatment circumvents the resistance problem by providing enabling mastery aids that bring success. Conditions conducive to personal change can also be reliably achieved by enlisting the assistance of significant others in the treatment (Bandura, 1988b; Williams, 1990). Indeed, when mastery modes of treatment are well developed, nonprofessionals given appropriate training and guidance can serve as well as or better than professionals in creating corrective and growth-promoting mastery experiences for those seeking personal change (Mathews, Teasdale, Munby, Johnson, & Shaw, 1977; Moss & Arend, 1977). Nonprofessionals are well situated to offer intensive help at opportune times in the very settings in which the problems arise. A cognitively oriented treatment combining verbal restructuring, simulated practice, and socially aided mastery will produce better results than if corrective action is verbally prescribed but its realization is left unguided.

The preceding evidence indicates that efforts to enhance the power of cognitive-behavioral treatments might be most fruitfully directed at advancing knowledge about how to structure corrective

and growth-enhancing forms of behavior in the transactions of everyday life. Procedures of enablement must be an integral part of effective ameliorative efforts. If clients cannot get themselves to translate new ways of managing their realities into action, they will not achieve much change. Instead of addressing challenging enablement and sociostructural issues, many proponents of the cognitive-behavioral approach are moving in the opposite direction in search of unconscious motivators and integration with psychodynamic theories that have spawned cumbersome, protracted talking treatments of limited effectiveness and social utility. These hybridized theories are becoming more interiorized in the mechanics of information processing but give short shrift to the societal conditions that influence the course and quality of lives. Human problems are treated as though they arise solely from personal dysfunctions. An interactive ecological model that considers the life circumstances with which people have to cope is better suited to explain human adaptation and change.

Let us first consider the unconscious odyssey. When people are acquiring cognitive skills, behavioral competencies, and adaptational patterns, they are very much aware of what they are thinking and doing. They do not rely on an unconscious mind to teach them how to fly airplanes, perform brain surgery, or solve problems. Rather, they use thought to construct, motivate, and regulate their actions. Eventually, people routinize their habits of thought and action through repeated use to the point where they execute them with little accompanying awareness. This routinization is achieved through several different processes, all of which involve transfer of control to nonconscious regulatory systems (Bandura, 1986a). As a result, people often react with fixed ways of thinking unreflectively and with habitual ways of behaving unthinkingly. Nonconscious information processing and routinization of thought and action should be distinguished from an unconscious mind acting as a concealed agent orchestrating behavior in an unwitting host organism. To reify, from evidence of automatic and routinized responses, a subterranean agent steering perceptions and actions is to commit a serious metaphysical transgression. Therapists who are making forays into the thicket of unconsciousness have not been rewarded with gains in predictive and therapeutic power.

Much psychological theorizing is characterized by rampant pluralism. Constructs are picked from divergent theories, some of which disagree in their fundamental assumptions. The batch of constructs is then packaged in conceptual boxes and strung together by presumptive causal chains. A weary reviewer once characterized this cafeteria style of theorizing as boxology run amok. One author, in presenting his conglomerate scheme as an integrated causal model, unwittingly labeled it a casual model, which was a remarkably insightful portrayal. There have been recent appeals for integration of social cognitive and psychodynamic theories. The belief that combining elements from diverse theories is the way to advance a field has more intuitive appeal than empirical support (Wachtel, 1977). What exactly does the unification mean? If it is unification at the conceptual level, how does one combine theories that rest on incompatible assumptions about human behavior and retain any conceptual coherence? If integration means drawing methods from divergent sources regardless of their conceptual bases, than one is left with unenlightened technical eclecticism. If the integration specifies generic mechanisms that operate across diverse spheres of functioning, then the mechanisms should be grounded in a unified theoretical framework.

Psychological theories provide abstractions about human phenomena, but the particular set of phenomena that happens to be singled out for attention by different theorists is not the patented possession of the theories. Nor do the phenomena have to be permanently saddled with the explanations imposed upon them by particular conceptual schemes. Important advances in the understanding of human behavior are often impeded when deficient theories claim jurisdiction over significant phenomena. Progress is achieved when the phenomena are reconceptualized within a more fruitful theoretical framework. Witness the limited and impoverished yield of research spawned by the psychoanalytic theory of identification and the voluminous cumulative research stimulated by the social cognitive theory of the determinants, mechanisms, diverse effects, and operative power of psychological modeling (Bandura, 1969b, 1986a; Bronfenbrenner, 1958; Rosenthal & Zimmerman, 1978).

Of course, a comprehensive theory of human functioning must encompass the factors that govern human thought, affect, and action, whatever Aristotle, Comte, Freud, Jung, Mead, Montesquieu, or one's grandmother may have had to say about some of them at one time or another. But the multiform factors must be integrated within a unified conceptual framework, or one ends up with discordantly fragmented eclecticism. There is a marked difference between seeking theoretical inclusiveness by expanding the range of phenomena explained within a unified theory and seeking that inclusiveness by ad hoc combinations of constructs from divergent theories. Significant advances require theoretically integrated efforts that extend the explanatory and operative power of theories of demonstrated value.

The basic human phenomena have been charted by the ancient psychic mariners and are not new to any particular theory. The challenge is to provide conceptions of them that have explanatory, predictive, and operative power. Ecumenical appeals for unification of social cognitive and psychodynamic theories are unsupported by any empirical evidence for the superiority of the theoretical hybridization. Close empirical scrutiny has repeatedly shown that psychodynamic assessments are relatively poor predictors of human behavior (Dawes, Faust, & Meehl, 1989; Mischel, 1968; Wiggins, 1973). Indeed, actuarial systems combining a few psychosocial factors are typically superior to psychodynamic assessments in predicting how people will behave. Similarly, under most conditions, self-appraisals, based as they are on extensive self-knowledge, are better predictors than psychodynamic assessments, which supposedly measure critical determinants of people's behavior of which they are unaware (Kaplan & Simon, 1990; Osberg & Shrauger, 1990; Shrauger & Osberg, 1982).

Efforts at laboratory tests of some of the less loosely specified tenets of such theories have floundered in conceptual and methodological quagmires (Erwin, 1996; Eysenck & Wilson, 1973; Gruünbaum, 1984). Psychodynamic approaches have been shown to be wanting not only in predictive power but also in their efficacy to alter human behavior. The burden of proof rests with the unificationists to demonstrate empirically that psychodynamic grafts produce a theory that has superior predictive and operative power. Such evidence has yet to be provided. Doctrine cannot continue to substitute for empirical evidence.

DEPRESSION

Depression has come to be regarded as the "common cold" of psychosocial functioning. Everyday life presents adversities that are not always easily controllable. Hence, no one is immune to periodic experiences of ineffectualness, discouragement, and purposelessness. Depressive reactions seriously impair functioning when they become severe and prolonged. The different ways in which a sense of personal inefficacy contributes to depression were analyzed in some detail in an earlier chapter. The present discussion is concerned with the amelioration of depression and the extent to which various treatments developed for this purpose alleviate depression through the mediating link of perceived self-efficacy. Before reviewing evidence bearing on the self-efficacy mechanism, a few general comments about the nature and treatment of depression are in order.

There is more than one way in which people drive themselves to despondency. Therefore, there is no one treatment that is effective for all sources of depression. Separate etiological theories and therapeutic approaches have been built around these different sets of causal processes. Most of the theories, however, share a common emphasis on the causative role of faulty thinking in depression. Some people suffer depression because they lack the competencies and interpersonal skills to gain satisfactions and minimize aversive experiences in their lives. Lewinsohn and his colleagues have centered their theory of depression on such *skill deficits*. In this conceptualization, depression arises from an inability to produce pleasurable experiences and to forestall aversive ones (Lewinsohn et al., 1985). Under these disheartening conditions, people become dejected and lethargic and find little pleasure in what they do. The treatment cultivates social and self-change skills that increase engagement in enjoyable activities and reduce aversive experiences or encourage people to construe them in ways that weaken their painfulness (Lewinsohn, Hoberman, & Clarke, 1989; Lewinsohn, Antonuccio, Steinmetz, & Teri, 1984). This is achieved by a psychoeducational approach that provides explicit guidelines, role-playing exercises, and performance assignments of enjoyable activities. The self-change exercises are structured so that this approach can be used preventively with people at high risk of developing depression as well as with those already suffering from depression (Muñoz & Ying, 1993).

People's satisfaction with their lives, their sense of worthiness, and their ability to withstand stressors are strongly affected by the quality of their interpersonal relationships. Those whose lives are devoid of affection and companionship or beset by interpersonal discord and severed affectional relationships are prone to suffer bouts of depression (Coyne, 1990). Despondency, in turn, distresses others or drives them away. Although initially supportive, after a while intimates become perturbed and impatient with repeated expressions of pessimism, hopelessness, listlessness, and despair (Coyne, 1976b; Marcus & Nardone, 1992). Growing social strains and rejection by intimates escalate depressive behavior that only make matters worse. For proponents of the *interpersonal model*, depression is rooted in relationship problems. They regard dysfunctional marital relationships as a major source of depression. Marital problems are less distressing if couples believe they can resolve them. They are more likely to suffer hopelessness and despair if they find themselves trapped in unfulfilling or aversive marital relationships that they feel inefficacious to change. Such conditions are especially depressing for women whose lives are more constrained by economic dependencies and social role dictates (Pretzer, Epstein, & Fleming, 1991). Treatments that address interpersonal sources of depression seek to improve skills in communication, interpersonal problem solving, social functioning, and negotiating mutually satisfying relationships and social roles (Coyne, 1988; Gotlib & Colby, 1987; Jacobson & Holtzworth-Munroe, 1986; Klerman & Weissman, 1982).

Some people get themselves into despondent states by faulty habits of thinking. Beck (1984) developed a *self-schema theory* around the notion that depression is basically a thinking disorder. People who are prone to depression negatively distort and misinterpret events. They make erroneous inferences from flimsy evidence; take things out of context and give them the wrong meaning; overgeneralize personal deficiencies from isolated failures; turn ordinary mistakes and setbacks into catastrophes by magnifying their seriousness; personalize negative happenings that have little or nothing to do with them; think dichotomously so that one is either astute or stupid, courageous or cowardly with nothing in between; and become skilled at discounting their successes and positive experiences. These routinized faulty habits of thinking create a negative self-schema that biases people's attentional, interpretive, and memory processes toward the miserable aspects of their lives (Kuiper, Olinger, & MacDonald, 1988; Teasdale, 1983). Through this distorted cognitive processing of experiences, they disparage their capabilities, find no satisfaction or meaning in the world around them, and become pessimistic about their future. The treatment includes two major components. The first involves analysis of erroneous assumptions, inferences, and conclusions in the routinized faulty habits of thinking. The second includes graded behavioral assignments to disconfirm misbeliefs and provide mastery experiences that affirm personal capabilities and help to restore positive self-evaluations.

Seligman and his colleagues similarly regard depression as a thinking disorder, but they focus their theory on biased causal explanations of good and bad outcomes (Peterson & Seligman, 1984). In this view, depression arises from a *pessimistic explanatory style*. The nondepressed favor a self-enhancing explanatory style in which they credit their successes to personal characteristics that are enduring and generalized and ascribe their failures to transient or external factors. In contrast, depressed people exhibit a pessimistic explanatory style, downgrading their successes as due to external factors but ascribing their failures to personal deficiencies of a generalized and enduring nature. The self-blame for failure seems to be a stronger tendency than the self-negation of success. Ascribing one's failures to personal deficiencies that pervade everything one tries and cannot be changed reflects a profound sense of personal inefficacy. A treatment explicitly grounded in this theory has not been developed for correcting causal misattributions. Instead, Beck's mode of treatment is usually prescribed for this purpose.

Many people experience depression not because they are socially inept, debilitated by faulty habits of thinking, or beset by a generalized sense of helplessness but because they adopt stringent standards of self-worth that they are unable to fulfill. All people have their ups and downs from time to time, but those who are burdened with taxing performance standards find it hard to gain satisfaction from what they do, because they rarely measure up. To make matters worse, such standards are often accompanied by self-belittling comparisons with the extraordinary achievements of others. Examples readily spring to mind of individuals who drive themselves relentlessly in pursuit of unachievable goals and whose ever-rising standards negate any sense of self-fulfillment along the way. Ironically, it is talented individuals with high aspirations, which are possible but exceedingly difficult to realize, who are especially vulnerable to despondency despite notable achievements. Nobel Prize announcements depress potential contenders who were bypassed, not those whose aspirations are more modest.

It is not uncommon for depressive reactions to be precipitated by promotion to a higher rank, although such an event might appear to be cause for joy. High positions carry heavy responsibilities for diverse activities that can be managed effectively only through the efforts of others. Those who adopt demanding standards and are unskilled in guiding the work of others, or are reluctant to delegate responsibility because they believe they are the only ones capable of doing the work well, try to do much of it themselves. The problem is compounded by ruminative self-blame for the work of others that falls short of one's exacting standards. The net effect is a burdensome workload that diminishes any pleasure the work may hold.

In its more extreme forms, harsh standards of self-evaluation give rise to chronic depression, feelings of worthlessness, and lack of purposefulness. Chronic self-disparagement is, in fact, the chief feature of depression. Ernest Hemingway, who died by suicide, suffered from this type of self-generated tyranny (Yalom & Yalom, 1971). Throughout his life he imposed upon himself demands that were unattainable, pushed himself to extraordinary feats, and constantly demeaned his accomplishments. The depth of self-inflicted misery and despair of severely depressed persons is poignantly revealed when their lives are examined over an extended period. Binswanger (1958) provides a detailed account of one such case. This woman was constantly tormented by the relentless pursuit of unattainable standards. Anything short of perfection was a crushing failure. As a child, she would weep for hours if she did not outrank all others in what she was doing. But even peerless attainments brought no satisfaction because she set her sights on magnificent achievements that would ensure her undying fame. Living by the motto, "Either Caesar or nothing," she looked upon her performances as dismal failures, although judged by any other standards they were superior. Not only was she cruel to herself, but she constantly judged others harshly by the same extraordinary standards. As her paralyzing despair began to destroy her effectiveness, she became deeply preoccupied with a sense of worthlessness and futility. Only death could provide a welcome relief from her torment, which she sought through repeated suicide attempts.

Depression arising from a *dysfunctional self-evaluation system* is addressed by Rehm's (1988) theory. In Chapter 4, we saw how dysfunctions in each of the constituent processes of self-evaluation contribute to depression. People who are prone to depression are not charitable with themselves in how they monitor their successes and failures and what they make of them. They are self-belittling when others happen to surpass them. They impose standards on themselves that are beyond their reach. And they are more self-denying and self-punitive for failures and less self-rewarding for successes than are the nondepressed. People who have such a burdensome evaluative self-system are especially vulnerable to depression in the face of adverse life events (Heiby, 1983a,b; Rehm, 1988). They lack the self-support to sustain them through difficult times.

Rehm (1981) has devised a well-structured treatment aimed at remedying each of the dysfunctional aspects of the self-system. This treatment produces consistently good results. Dysfunctions in self-monitoring are corrected by systematic self-recording of experiences in ways that bypass attentional and memory distortion and accent positive experiences. Clients' self-belittling interpretive biases are altered by analyzing recent events to reduce excessive self-blame for things that go wrong and to increase self-credit for successes. Self-debilitating goal setting is modified by having clients set explicit, attainable subgoals for activities of personal significance. They need not give up high aspirations but rather focus their efforts and self-reactions on progress toward those aspirations. Satisfactions are thus derived from the process of mastery rather than tied only to the distal products of one's efforts. And finally, austere and deprecating self-evaluations are supplanted by more positive ones by structured assignments that get clients to reward themselves with enjoyable activities and self-approval for subgoal attainments.

Some forms of depression may result from *biochemical dysfunctions*. Depletion of neurotransmitters that impairs neural communication is considered to be the major determinant. But the task of distinguishing between endogenous depression and depression arising from adaptational problems is no easy matter because they are inferred from overlapping sets of characteristics. The differences in depressive reactions are usually ones of intensity rather than of kind. Not surprisingly, efforts to sort depressive reactions into "endogenous" and "reactive" types have met with little success (Free & Oei, 1989). Nor is it an easy task to determine whether a biochemical malfunction is a cause, effect, or concomitant of depression. Human functioning is governed by interactive processes rather than dualistically by disjoined biological and psychological processes. Biological and psychological dysfunctions operate bidirectionally. For example, depletion of neurotransmitters, which serve as chemical messengers of signals between neurons, can retard thought and impair adaptive action. Research with animals shows that the inability to exercise control over recurrent stressors is an environmental condition that depletes central neurotransmitters and produces helpless reactions to subsequent controllable aversive conditions (Weiss, 1991).

Perceived inefficacy to manage threats has been shown to affect neurotransmitter functioning in humans (Bandura et al., 1985). Mastery-oriented treatment that instills a strong sense of coping efficacy normalizes neurotransmitter functioning. If depression reflects extensive involvement of biochemical dysfunctions, which is estimated to be true in about 10 percent of depressions, then antidepressant medication would aid treatment (Kessler, 1978). Even under conditions in which endogenous factors contribute to depressive reactions, however, despondency impairs cognitive and interpersonal functioning in ways that perpetuate psychosocial problems. Continuing medication with some support is no better, and sometimes is even less effective, than cognitive-behavior therapy for faulty thinking in the short term. Moreover, individuals receiving the sociocognitive mode of treatment maintain their improvement better than those treated by antidepressant drugs alone, who are much more likely to relapse once the drug is discontinued (Blackburn, Eunson, & Bishop, 1986; Evans et al., 1992; Simons et al., 1986). Psychosocial treatments are better at changing dejecting thinking than is medication. The more psychosocial treatments change faulty thinking, the lower the risk of future depression (DeRubeis et al.,

1990). Adding antidepressant drugs to cognitive-behavior therapy does not produce further therapeutic gains. The medical risks and aversive side effects of drugs drive some clients out of treatment. It is highly questionable whether the proportion of cases in which depression stems from a biochemical dysfunction justifies the widespread use of drug treatments for human despondency.

Sustained improvement can be achieved in most people suffering from bouts of despondency by enabling them through improved personal and social skills to find more satisfaction in their lives, altering their faulty styles of thinking, and getting them to relax stringent standards of self-evaluation. Despite the long-term benefits of psychosocial treatments, antidepressant medication remains the most common treatment for depression. There are several reasons for the excessive medicalization of human despondency. The pharmaceutical industry vigorously promotes drug treatments, and the payment systems in many health plans favor the cheaper drug treatment over psychosocial treatment (Antonuccio, Danton, & DeNelsky, 1995). It is easier to prescribe drugs than to enable people to improve their life circumstances or to cope better with them.

Common Mechanism of Action for Divergent Treatments

A number of comparative studies report similar success for divergent modes of treatment of depression (Elkin et al., 1989; Free & Oei, 1989; Rehm, in press; Zeiss, Lewinsohn, & Muñoz, 1979). Several factors may account for this apparent similarity in effectiveness. One possibility is that the results reflect weak outcome measures. The assessments rely almost exclusively on self-ratings of symptoms on depression inventories. Self-report measures have been shown to be less sensitive than behavioral measures to the differential power of treatments. Another possibility is that divergent processes are highlighted in theoretical conceptions, but many common methods are used in therapeutic practice. Similar practices will produce similar results.

Another plausible explanation is that the apparent comparability is an artifact of deficient experimental design. Because depression has many causes, it requires a multiplicity of treatments, each suited for a particular set of causes. If a mode of treatment is applied indiscriminately, it will benefit only the individuals for whom it happens to be appropriate. Consider, for purposes of illustration, a hypothetical study in which three types of treatments are each applied to a sample containing three subtypes of depression in equal proportion. Each treatment would benefit only the third of the clients for whom the treatment matched the source of depression. Such a design, which is blissfully oblivious to different causal subtypes of depression, would convey the erroneous impression that the varieties of treatment are equally ineffective whereas, in fact, they are highly successful in alleviating the subtype of depression for which they are designed but are ineffective for mismatched subtypes.

The importance of matching treatment to source of depression is impressively documented by Heiby (1986) using a crossover design. She selected two subtypes of depression, one rooted in deficient interpersonal skills and the other in stringent self-evaluation. Matching treatments (competency enhancement for the socially deficient; training in positive self-evaluation for the self-devaluators) produced large stable reductions in depression. Mismatching treatments (training in social skills for self-devaluators; boosting positive self-evaluation for the socially deficient) produced no benefits. When an appropriately matched treatment was then provided, depression abated. Rehm and his associates have similarly shown that self-devaluators achieve greater reduction in depression from a treatment that addresses their negative self-regulative system than from one that enhances their social skills (Rehm, Fuchs, Roth, Kornblith, & Ramono, 1979). Comparative studies that fail to match treatments to causal subtypes of depression may be not only uninformative but seriously misleading in their conclusions.

The final explanation for why diverse treatments might produce similar outcomes is in terms of the self-efficacy mediator of psychosocial change. The things about which people get depressed take varied forms, but a profound sense of personal inefficacy to bring about positive outcomes that give satisfaction to one's life is the central common factor in the different subprocesses of depression. The perceived inefficacy may involve yearned-for relationships, coveted achievements, or control of despairing trains of thought. As depressed individuals keep reaffirming the futility of their efforts through listless, ineffectual action, they sink into a deepening despair and sense of worthlessness. Although the various treatments address different facets of competencies and self-deprecating thinking, each seeks to restore a sense of personal capability to do the things that provide purpose and satisfaction to one's life. Therapeutic approaches that promote social and self-change skills enhance emotional satisfactions and social support. It will be recalled from previous analyses that perceived social efficacy alleviates depression through reciprocal causation. A sense of social efficacy supports positive interpersonal engagements and development of satisfying emotional relationships that reduce vulnerability to depression (Holahan & Holahan, 1987a, 1987b; Stanley & Maddux, 1986a). Supportive relationships, in turn, raise perceived self-efficacy to manage stressors without apprehension or despair (Cutrona & Troutman, 1986; Major et al., 1990).

In treatments aimed at counteracting depression by eradicating negative self-schemata, much of the thought analysis and performance assignments are designed to persuade depressed individuals that they are masterful rather than helpless. Attributional retraining approaches to depression similarly seek to increase people's belief in their causative capabilities by crediting their successes to themselves and their failures to transitory motivational or situational factors. Perceived self-efficacy both influences causal attributions (Alden, 1986; McAuley, 1990; Silver et al., 1995) and mediates their effects on personal accomplishments (Schunk & Cox, 1986; Schunk & Gunn, 1986).

Efforts to eradicate depression by correcting dysfunctions in the self-regulative system institute self-monitoring correctives to highlight personal capabilities. Goal-setting practices that bring aspirations within the bounds of perceived efficacy provide ongoing mastery experiences. Belief that one can fulfill challenging standards turns despondency over failures into positive engrossment in activities (Bandura & Abrams, 1986; Kanfer & Zeiss, 1983).

Clients' level of engagement and continuance in treatment are typically viewed as reflections of motivation for treatment. The term *motivation* is a general descriptor that does not say much about the problem or the remedy for it. In social cognitive theory, motivation for treatment is analyzed in terms of changeable factors encompassing efficacy beliefs, personal goals, and outcome expectations. Longo, Lent, and Brown (1992) found that clients' beliefs in their efficacy to carry out therapeutic tasks, override impediments to regular attendance, and persevere despite setbacks accounted for the major share of initial motivation for treatment. The distressfulness of the personal problems and the expected outcomes from treatment also made a small but significant contribution to motivation. Beliefs of personal efficacy determined whether clients continued in treatment, but level of distress and outcome expectations did not. These findings underscore the need to raise clients' sense of efficacy for the therapeutic activities themselves to remove impediments to progress and forestall premature termination.

Successful treatment of depression requires people to engage in enabling styles of thinking and masterful activities that counteract self-deprecation and hopelessness. The treatment of depression presents unique challenges, however, because the profound sense of inefficacy extends even to the very skills taught in treatments to alleviate depressive reactions and to reduce vulnerability to self-demoralization. These treatments commonly include skills in how to identify faulty thinking and supplant it with beneficial thinking, increase the level of self-rewarding activities, and adopt ways of behaving that disconfirm faulty beliefs and provide accomplishments for enhancing a sense of personal efficacy and positive self-evaluation. At the outset of treatment, depressed people are beset by tenacious self-doubt in their ability to do the very self-enabling things their therapists are trying to persuade them to do to alleviate depression (Ross & Brown, 1988). The deeper the despair, the lower the sense of efficacy to learn skills for alleviating depression. Perceived futility of effort undermines active pursuit of personal change. Therefore, before any progress can be achieved, therapists must alter clients' self-immobilizing beliefs about their ability to carry out the necessary therapeutic tasks. Otherwise, they will keep reaffirming their ineffectualness for the treatment activity itself (Beck, 1976; Meichenbaum & Gilmore, 1982). Mastery experiences are usually more persuasive than talk alone in eliminating inefficacious thinking. Guided mastery experiences can provide confirmatory tests that what seemed hopelessly difficult is quite achievable.

Perceived self-efficacy affects not only the effort invested in corrective therapeutic assignments but also the reductions in depression achieved through treatment and how well the improvement is maintained over time. Kavanagh and Wilson (1989) tested a variety of potential predictors of treatment outcomes for depression achieved by altering faulty modes of thinking and enhancing enjoyable pursuits. Perceived efficacy to control dejecting ruminations emerged as the major predictor. The exercise of thought control prevents the escalation of transitory dejection to enduring bouts of depression. Thus, the more treatment strengthened efficacy to control dejecting thought, the greater was the reduction in depression and the less likely were recurrences of bouts of depression during the year following treatment. Beliefs in personal efficacy to regulate thoughts that affect depressive mood remain an independent predictor of attainment and maintenance of improvements in depression when variations in depression at the end of treatment are held constant.

These findings further underscore the influential role of perceived thought control efficacy in the regulation of affective states. As in the case of anxiety arousal (Kent & Gibbons, 1987; Ozer & Bandura, 1990), despondent mood depends more on one's sense of inefficacy to turn off dejecting thoughts than on one's perceived efficacy to execute coping skills or on the mere occurrence of unwanted thoughts. The sense of helplessness to control unwanted thoughts is depressing as well as distressing. People who are vulnerable to depression, therefore, must develop skill in exercising control over dejecting ruminative thought. Some researchers are exponents of the diathesis-stress model of depression. In this nonagentic defect model, people are carriers of inherent vulnerabilities that, under taxing stressors, give rise to depression. To proponents of information-processing models, the stressors activate a self-schema of inadequacy and worthlessness that breeds depression. Social cognitive theory adopts a transactional agentic model in which depression is linked to aspirations, human connectedness, and self-regulation of cognitive and affective events that have an impact on one's emotional well-being.

EATING DISORDERS

Problems associated with the regulation of weight are pervasive. Obesity not only heightens the risk of physical diseases and premature mortality but it can exact a heavy psychological toll as well. Most people, therefore, struggle to keep their weight within normative bounds. Those who fail to do so find themselves burdened with the many social and psychological consequences of obesity. Obese individuals are often stigmatized, snubbed, discriminated against, and disparaged as being unable to exercise personal control. Social rejections foster self-disparagement. While much of the general public views obesity as a product of willful self-indulgence, many professionals espouse the opposing extreme view of obesity as a product of a relentless biological drive that is personally uncontrollable. Ever ready to provide quick fixes, publishing houses run a brisk trade in self-help books and a flourishing dieting industry promises quick success without doing much to change health habits.

Overweight hopefuls shed pounds on crash diets and various liquid diets only to regain them in a short time. The body responds to weight loss by burning calories more slowly, so it takes fewer calories to put on pounds (Leibel, Rosenbaum, & Hirsch, 1995). The body also burns calories faster under weight gain but, interestingly, researchers argue that the body conspires against weight loss but not against weight gain. As people recycle themselves through dieting routines, the body learns to adjust more quickly to calorie restriction by reducing its rate of energy expenditure. These metabolic adaptations to caloric restrictions make weight reduction more difficult but weight regain easier. Wide fluctuations in body weight, as occur under cyclic dieting, increase the risk of coronary heart disease as much as does being overweight (Lissner et al., 1991).

The most disordered eating patterns appear in anorexia and bulimia. Both conditions involve extreme efforts at weight control. Anorexics impose on themselves semistarvation diets that are carried to the point of emaciation. Bulimics alternate between restrictive dieting and episodes of overeating followed by purging. Of these two disorders, bulimia is considerably more prevalent, especially in fashionable circles where svelteness has come to be revered but highly appetizing foods are ever plentiful and have lost none of their allure.

Researchers in the health field distinguish between eating disorders and obesity. Many people, particularly women who are not really overweight, are chronically starving themselves in an effort to slim down and shape their bodies to fit the svelte cultural ideal. When carried to the extreme, the disordered eating behavior takes the form of anorexia and bulimia. Given the heterogeneity of eating problems, treatments must be tailored to the nature of the problem (Brownell & Wadden, 1992). For those starving themselves in the pursuit of an aesthetic ideal, the restrictive eating pattern and self-devaluation are the problems requiring treatment. Those at moderate levels of overweight can gain significant health benefits from modest reduction in weight by altering their eating and activity habits. Such changes are easier to achieve and to maintain than are large weight reductions. The health benefits include reductions in hypertension and lowered risk of diabetes, cardiovascular disease, and various cancers. Seriously overweight people require more intensive interventions (Wadden & VanItallie, 1992).

Obesity

A variety of factors contribute to obesity — genetic makeup, number of fat cells developed during growth spurts, metabolic rate, level of caloric intake, and activity level (Stunkard, 1988). Genetic factors, as reflected in a low basal metabolism rate and fat cell number, make it easier for some people to gain weight than others. Genetic proneness does not ordain obesity, however; genetics is only part of the story. Overeating high-calorie foods, especially in a binge eating style, and low caloric expenditure through being sedentary put on pounds (Brownell & Wadden, 1992). Thus, over the past few decades, the prevalence of obesity has just about doubled although people's genetic makeup has not changed. Obesity is more prevalent among those of low socioeconomic status who are less likely to adopt physical fitness and low-calorie nutrition. Westernized regions of a country have a substantially higher rate of obesity than the traditional regions. Ethnic minorities are also more likely to become obese in the United States, where people eat too many fatty foods and exercise too little, than are their counterparts in their native countries. Such findings attest to the influential role of behavioral factors in obesity. The integrative sociocognitive approach avoids both the moralization and excessive biologization of obesity.

Efforts to reduce obesity by psychological means center on the two factors that are behaviorally controllable. These include a change in eating habits that reduces fat caloric intake and adoption of exercise habits that burn off calories. Many people overeat without hunger because food is prepared to be luringly appetizing and not because of some compelling drive. In eating disorders stemming from social, emotional, and self-evaluative influences, however, treatments must enable clients to manage these life stressors in more healthful ways. It should be noted that some of the socioemotional problems are probably effects rather than causes of disordered eating. Lasting control of obesity requires lifestyle changes that keep weight off rather than just cutting calories intermittently. Habit changes may serve a preventive, as well as a regulative, function in obesity. Control of overeating and active exercise during developmental growth spurts in the first year of life and in adolescence retard the proliferation of fat cells (Katch & McArdle, 1977), which in turn reduces biological pressure for caloric intake.

Effective self-regulation operates through a set of psychological subfunctions that facilitate and maintain habit changes. In applications to the management of obesity the strategies include regular self-monitoring of eating and exercise habits and their situational variation, adopting attainable subgoals for gradual habit change rather than rapid weight reduction, arranging self-incentives to maintain one's efforts, altering dysfunctional styles of thinking about eating behavior that undermine self-regulative efforts, substituting other activities for eating, restructuring one's environment to reduce instigators to overeating, and developing strategies for preventing self-regulative lapses in risk situations and for regaining control when lapses occur (Agras, 1987; Brownell & Jeffery, 1987; Brownell, Marlatt, Lichtenstein, & Wilson, 1986; Perri, 1985).

Because calories as fat are more readily converted to excess pounds than calories as carbohydrates or proteins, the nutritional aspect of the program concentrates on adopting balanced low-fat eating habits. The second component of weight control is aimed at changing sedentary lifestyles to more physically active ones. Exercise not only burns calories during the activity but also may produce a carryover effect by raising the rate at which the body burns calories after the exercise has ceased (Brownell & Stunkard, 1980; Thompson, Jarvie, Lahey, & Cureton, 1982). By elevating the metabolic rate that caloric restriction lowers, exercise can contribute to the reduction of obesity. This "afterburn" effect, however, is weak and variable. Exercise also facilitates change in body composition from body fat to muscle. A change in eating habits combined with regular exercise, therefore, produces greater and longer lasting fat loss than does a change in eating habits alone.

Cognitive behavioral programs help people lose weight, but many of them have difficulty keeping it off (Brownell & Jeffery, 1987). The analysis of maintenance processes in Chapter 7 suggested directions in which maintenance strategies need to be extended to sustain hard-won changes. Long-term control of obesity requires continuing, rather than spasmodic, self-management. Programs that address the maintenance problem not only equip people with strategies for regulating eating habits and exercise activities but also provide periodic assistance in overcoming problems of adherence (Perri, Nezu, & Wiegener, 1992). Obese people who have the benefit of the multifaceted program with posttreatment assistance not only lose substantial weight but succeed in keeping it off, whereas those who receive only the multifaceted program regain much of what they have lost.

Evaluations of the modifiability of obesity usually center on average weight losses of treated clinical cases without much attention to the problems of generalizing from the more refractory cases who seek professional help to the population at large. There is some evidence to suggest that people who undertake to lose weight on their own achieve higher success rates than those who seek treatment (Brownell & Rodin, 1994). Successful self-changers employ a wider array of self-regulative influences and use them more consistently and persistently than do the unsuccessful ones (Perri, 1985). There is substantial individual variability in the weight losses people achieve in treatment programs and how well they maintain them (Brownell & Rodin, 1994; Stunkard, 1975). Some lose a substantial amount of weight and keep most of it off, others lose a fair amount but regain most of it, still others who make only a half-hearted effort lose little, and a few who vacillate between exerting dietary control and overeating may actually gain some weight. Even those who regain much of what they lost might be better off than if they would have continued to gain weight without the self-regulatory effort. Partial success can bolster a sense of efficacy that lasting changes can be achieved by redoubled

efforts. Arresting beginning rises in weight can prevent escalating overweightedness (Bandura & Simon, 1977). Because of fluctuations in weight over time, repeated assessments are needed to understand fully how interventions affect weight status.

Given the wide variability in weight loss by different individuals, averages misrepresent how most of them are affected by an intervention. One is reminded of the nonswimming statistician who drowned while crossing a river that averaged three feet in depth. Where weight losses differ widely, an exclusive focus on averages not only obscures matters but also discourages process analyses of successes and failures that provide guidelines for enhancing the power of treatment. Informative analyses of the successes people achieve on their own, as well as with professional help, might also constrain the view that people are biologically driven to certain levels of caloric consumption. The rate at which calories are burned operates as only one factor among a number of cognitive, motivational, and social factors governing weight reduction.

Self-Efficacy in the Regulation of Eating and Exercise Habits

Perceived self-efficacy to exercise control over eating habits encompasses a variety of aspects (Clark et al., 1991). These include perceived efficacy to resist overeating when experiencing negative emotions or physical discomfort, when socially pressured to eat, while engaging in enjoyable activities, and when high-calorie foods are readily available. Such a multifaceted measure enables one to monitor the effectiveness of treatment and to identify potentially troublesome situations requiring self-regulatory strategies to change eating habits and reduce vulnerability to relapse.

A growing body of research reveals that perceived efficacy predicts weight management at each phase of change in eating and exercise habits. Weight reduction programs often experience high attrition rates. Beliefs in personal efficacy to achieve weight loss goals measured at the outset predict attrition from obesity treatment programs (Bernier & Avard, 1986; Mitchell & Stuart, 1984). Eventual dropouts are initially more self-doubting of their efficacy than are those who remain, and they are quick to depart even though they are achieving weight losses similar to those of individuals who remain during the first weeks of treatment.

Efficacy beliefs similarly predict magnitude of weight losses achieved by those who remain in programs designed to change eating habits. Self-efficacy for regulating eating behavior is typically measured in terms of strength of belief that one can exercise control over eating behavior in situations involving social inducements, ready availability of appetizing foods, and emotional perturbations. The more treatment strengthens people's beliefs in their efficacy to control their eating behavior, the more successful they are in losing weight and in keeping it off over the long term (Bernier & Avard, 1986; Desmond & Price, 1988; Jeffrey et al., 1984). A high sense of efficacy in controlling overeating is also accompanied by high self-esteem (Glynn & Ruderman, 1986). Many people seek to alter their eating habits not merely to slim down or to feel better about themselves but to lower their plasma cholesterol to reduce risk of coronary heart disease. The success of dietary treatment of hyperlipedemia is partly determined by the degree to which the treatment strengthens beliefs in one's efficacy to regulate consumption of food high in saturated fats and cholesterol (McCann et al., 1995). Self-efficacy to control overeating under negative emotional states is more predictive of dietary and cholesterol change than is self-efficacy to control overeating under social dining conditions where fasting is out of place. These findings about the predictiveness of self-regulative efficacy for the initiation, adoption, and maintenance of eating habits are all the more interesting because efforts to find reliable predictors of weight loss outcomes have met with little success (Wilson & Brownell, 1980).

Laboratory studies further corroborate the contribution of personal efficacy to weight reduction. People whose sense of self-regulatory efficacy is raised by verbal persuasion are more successful in losing weight than are those whose efficacy beliefs are not altered (Chambliss & Murray, 1979b; Weinberg et al., 1984). Individuals with a preexisting belief in their causative capabilities are more easily persuaded that they can control their eating behavior and subsequently act on their self-beliefs. People often overeat when they are emotionally distressed. Glynn and Ruderman (1986) report that negative emotion fosters overeating through the mediating link of perceived self-regulative efficacy. They measured how much food individuals ate in a laboratory setting when they had not been emotionally stressed and when they had been. Emotional distress itself did not predict overeating, but perceived inefficacy to control eating behavior when emotionally distressed did. Consistent with these findings, Leon, Sternberg, and Rosenthal (1984) report that beliefs of personal efficacy at the beginning of treatment predicted long-term maintenance of weight loss, whereas intensity of life stresses did not.

Shannon and her colleagues demonstrated the value of assessing different aspects of self-regulatory efficacy that extend beyond control of overeating (Shannon et al., 1990). Caloric intake is affected by the type of food that is purchased, what is added to it in preparation, and how much of it is eaten over a given time. It is easier to manage one's weight by not buying high-calorie and fatty foods than by buying them and then trying to avoid overeating them. Perceived efficacy to choose foods appropriately for weight management accounts for daily caloric and fat intake prior to treatment, when self-regulatory skills are infirm. After self-regulatory skills are developed, however, perceived efficacy to curb overeating maintains reduced caloric and fat intake, and perceived efficacy to manage what one brings home fades in importance. Apparently, savory foods are not a problem as long as one can eat them in moderation. Excessive expectations of the benefits of caloric reduction, which are likely to go unrealized, undermine efforts to stick to low-calorie eating. Social support from family and friends affected eating behavior only indirectly by raising belief in self-regulatory efficacy.

Restrained eaters who are chronically dieting are vulnerable to overeating episodes once their control is disrupted by minor dietary infractions or dysphoric mood (Herman & Polivy, 1983; Ruderman, 1986). Having breached their diet, they give up and overeat unrestrainedly in recurring famish-binge cycles. Not all restrained eaters revert to overeating following lapses, however. Most maintain a stable self-regulatory pattern with only small weight fluctuations. Stotland, Zuroff, and Roy (1992) report that efficacy beliefs account for a major share of the variability in eating behavior among restrained eaters. Women high in dietary restraint participated in an alleged taste testing of different types of appetizing cookies after they had disrupted their diet with a generous helping of chocolate cake. The participants who had a high sense of self-regulatory efficacy ate less in the cookie paradise than those who had little faith in their self-regulatory capabilities. The experience of deficient control by those of low efficacy further undermined their sense of efficacy. Tests of other possible determinants revealed that neither anxiety, dietary thoughts, nor negative patterns of thinking predicted overeating. That binge eating following breach of stringent dieting is governed more by perceived personal control than by physiological pressure of caloric deprivation is further suggested by Polivy and Herman (1985). Dieters who overate food they thought was low in calories later ate sparingly, whereas those who thought it was high in calories and thus reflected loss of personal control later gorged themselves even more.

Green and Saenz (1995) further verify the mediational role of perceived self-regulatory efficacy in breakdowns in control among restrained eaters. Physical appearance is an overriding concern of restrained eaters. Seeing others who are overweight makes dieters anxious and depressed and shakes their sense of efficacy, whereas comparisons on intellectual qualities do not. Seeing others of svelte appearance leaves restrained dieters unperturbed. Neither appearance threats nor negative mood, however, directly trigger unrestrained eating. Perceived self-regulatory efficacy determines whether negative mood leads to overeating. These findings, based on induced dysphoric mood and weakening of efficacy beliefs, add significance to the studies cited later showing that the effect

of natural fluctuations in mood on binge eating by bulimics operates through beliefs of personal efficacy.

Regular aerobic exercise produces varied health benefits as well as promoting weight reduction. Adopting and sticking to a more active lifestyle, however, does not come easily to sedentary individuals. Perceived efficacy affects every phase of habit change in physical activity as it does in eating habits. Perceived self-regulatory efficacy for regular exercise is usually assessed in terms of beliefs that one can mobilize the effort needed to perform aerobic activities in the face of various impediments such as fatigue, dysphoric mood, time constraints, competing attractions, and unfavorable environmental conditions. Even if persuaded of the physiological benefits of increased physical activity, sedentary individuals overrule any intention of becoming exercisers if they do not believe they can get themselves to stick with it (McAuley, 1992). Of the ones who get themselves to adopt regular exercise, those who have a shaky sense of self-regulatory efficacy discontinue the practice after a while (McAuley, 1992; Sallis & Hovell, 1990). It is the individuals with strong self-regulatory efficacy who become regular exercisers and resume aerobic activities should they temporarily stop engaging in them for one reason or another. We will return to a more detailed analysis of the determinants and functions of self-regulatory efficacy for exercise in Chapter 9.

In analyzing adoption of a physically active lifestyle, one must distinguish between such routine everyday activities as brisk walking and using stairs, which are easily adoptable, and vigorous aerobic exercises performed regularly at certain times (Brownell & Stunkard, 1980; Sallis & Hovell, 1990). It is the more vigorous aerobic activities that strain self-regulatory efficacy and produce high rates of quitters (Sallis et al., 1986). Fortunately, significant health benefits can be achieved simply by being more physically active in one's daily routines without having to drive oneself to painful exhaustion. There has been little systematic research on how to raise beliefs in the self-efficacy to adopt exercise habits in individuals ensconced in a sedentary lifestyle. For the most part, the programs rely simply on enrollment in exercise classes and verbal prescription of exercise routines to produce desired changes. Some of the social enhancers that have been tried, such as social contracts, extrinsic incentives, self-monitoring, and support from class members, may keep people exercising longer while the influences are in effect but are unlikely to produce permanent conversions to active lifestyles unless physical fitness comes to be highly valued in the process.

The preceding studies examined the impact of individual interventions on weight loss and exercise as a function of changes in perceived self-regulatory efficacy. The influential role of efficacy beliefs is further corroborated in analyses of the mechanisms through which public health campaigns persuade people to alter their eating and exercise habits. In these community-wide efforts, healthful habit changes are promoted by a combination of multifaceted mass media communications and organizational and informal social networks (Farquhar, Maccoby, & Wood, 1985). Adoption of healthy eating and regular exercise are influenced both by people's preexisting sense of efficacy and by the success of multifaceted campaigns in strengthening their efficacy beliefs that they can exercise some control over their health habits (Maibach et al., 1991).

Bulimia

Bulimia has attracted considerable popular and scientific attention because of its widespread incidence, especially among college females. This eating disorder is characterized by episodes of uncontrolled overeating followed by self-induced purging to prevent weight gains. Excessive exercise is also often used as a means of control. Bulimia is most prevalent among women who adopt the cultural standard of feminine beauty that places a premium on thinness and devalues stoutness (Striegel-Moore, Silberstein, & Rodin, 1986). The preoccupation with thinness has seeped downward to preadolescence, breeding eating disorders that can plague later life. About a third of young girls,

worrying about becoming fat, resort to unhealthy dieting, laxatives, or purging, which impair normal development and generate chronic self-discontent. Despite being underweight or of normal weight, bulimics hold a distorted image of themselves as displeasingly portly. In their eating behavior, they alternate between restrictive dieting and episodes of bingeing and purging.

Dysphoric emotional states in the form of anxiety, depression, anger, or loneliness often trigger binges of eating high-calorie foods followed by purging through self-induced vomiting or the use of diuretics as a drastic mode of control (Mizes, 1985). We have seen from the research of Glynn and Ruderman (1986) that it is not emotional distress per se but perceived inefficacy to manage emotional distress that gives rise to unrestrained overeating. Schneider, O'Leary, and Agras (1987) extended this finding with bulimic binge eaters. In a prospective analysis, dysphoric mood was twice as likely to precipitate binge eating when perceived self-regulatory efficacy was low (69 percent) as when it was high (31 percent). Love and her colleagues provide microanalytic evidence bearing on the ongoing self-efficacy regulation of bulimic behavior over the course of a full week (Love, Ollendick, Johnson, & Schlezinger, 1985). They examined the extent to which various factors — including mood states, stressors, perceived efficacy, thought patterns, and pleasant events — predict successive cycles of bulimic episodes. A low sense of efficacy to manage stressful events and to resist the urge to binge emerged as the most consistent predictor of bulimic behavior. The effect of stressful events and dysphoric mood states was variable, appearing as predictors in some instances but not in others. Perceived efficacy thus seems to have primacy over dysphoric affect in the regulation of bulimic behavior.

The tranquilizing effects of gorging on appetizing foods are followed by feelings of guilt and self-disgust over the lack of personal control. Purging as a means of coping with the consequences of complete self-regulative breakdown restores some sense of control. Evidence suggests that it is the restoration of a sense of controllability rather than anxiety reduction that sustains purging behavior (Leitenberg, Gross, Peterson, & Rosen, 1984; Wilson, Rossiter, Kleifield, & Lindholm, 1986). In addition to the psychosocial problems associated with bulimic behavior, repeated vomiting and heavy use of laxatives and diuretics create a variety of serious physical disorders.

Bulimia is not simply an eating problem but rather part of a larger life management problem. The bulimic adaptational reaction is rooted in dysfunctions in interpersonal relationships, high standards of performance, stereotypic sex-role functioning, and excessive investment of self-worth in physical appearance. Social and self-regulatory deficits underlie most of these adaptational problems. Stressors are part and parcel of everyday life. As in other psychosocial dysfunctions, the goal of treatment is to reduce subjectively generated distress and build the competencies needed to manage difficult life circumstances in more efficacious ways.

The treatment approach that has proved most successful with bulimia combines cognitive restructuring of self-evaluation with development of self-regulative and interpersonal skills to manage problem situations and dysphoric moods (Agras, 1987; Fairburn, 1984; Wilson, 1986, 1989). The cognitive restructuring centers on changing distorted self-images, inefficacious styles of thinking, and beliefs that a small weight gain forebodes imminent obesity. Bulimics link their self-worth mainly to physical appearance. Treatment encourages them to accept their body shape and weight and to judge their self-worth in terms of other attributes and personal accomplishments. Efforts to restore normal eating patterns are aimed at equipping bulimics with better ways to manage the problems in their everyday life. They are taught interpersonal skills for achieving more satisfying relationships, assertion skills for dealing with unreasonable demands, and coping strategies for managing stressors. To instill and validate a strong sense of self-regulatory efficacy, they eat their binge foods and learn to resist purging by cognitive and behavioral means for reducing the resultant tension. Antidepressant medications are sometimes used as well. Treatment is concluded with instruction in how to recover from lapses in control.

Several studies have examined how cognitive-behavioral treatment affects perceived self-regulatory efficacy and its impact on bingeing and purging. Schneider, O'Leary, and Agras (1987) measured perceived efficacy to exercise control over various domains of functioning relevant to bulimia, including ability to resist the urge to binge, to refrain from binge eating while consuming high-calorie foods, to substitute pleasurable activities for binge eating, to resist bingeing while in dysphoric moods, to stick to a pattern of regular eating and resist snacking on high-calorie foods, to reduce situational instigators to bingeing, to manage interpersonal relationships, and to accept normative body shape and weight. Perceived efficacy in these multifaceted domains increased over the course of treatment. The more the participants raised their belief in their self-regulatory efficacy, the less they purged. Neither efficacy change nor reduction in vomiting was predicted by degree of objective change toward ideal body weight.

Wilson and his colleagues compared the impact on perceived self-regulative efficacy and bulimic behavior of cognitive restructuring alone or combined with mastery experiences in controlling purging, after consuming foods considered fattening, beyond the point where self-induced vomiting is usually provoked (Wilson et al., 1986). The combined treatment instilled a strong sense of self-regulative efficacy and essentially eliminated bulimic behavior, whereas cognitive restructuring alone had relatively weak effects on both perceived efficacy and behavior. Perceived efficacy distinguished responders to treatment from nonresponders and identified relapsers. Although cognitive-behavior therapy generally produces good results, the benefit of behavioral practice in curbing purging after bingeing in treatment sessions is in dispute (Leitenberg, 1995).

As in other domains of functioning, therapeutic benefits derive not from the mere execution of activities but from how the attainments are construed. Examination of how behavioral control is structured and implemented and how it affects perceived controlling efficacy would go a long way toward explaining the puzzling variability in the contribution of practice in behavioral control to the effects of the multifaceted treatment. Differences across studies in the frequency, length, and timing of practice in controlling bulimic eating behavior in treatment make it difficult to evaluate the value of this factor. There is some evidence that repeated exercise of control over enticements to consume binge foods may contribute more to lasting reduction of bulimic behavior than practice in controlling purging after eating binge foods (Jansen et al., 1992). In other consummatory habits, exercise of successful control in the face of massive enticements produces lasting behavioral change partly by raising efficacy beliefs.

Comparative evaluations of treatments for bulimia are hampered by outcome measures that may be inherently problematic given the nature of the disorder and by inattention to mediating mechanisms. To be most informative, comparative outcome studies should help to clarify the mechanisms through which treatments produce their effects. Researchers rely principally on participants' reports of bingeing and purging, behaviors they regard with shame and self-condemnation. Because bulimic behavior is usually performed secretively, it is difficult to gain social corroboration of how often it is done. Self-censuring reactions to bulimic behavior may distort what bulimics report.

Socially Oriented Initiatives

The fashion and diet industries vigorously promote the svelte body as the cultural norm of feminine attractiveness. Women who aspire to this ideal become preoccupied with their weight and bodily shape. They subject themselves to chronic hunger through severe dieting for the sake of thinness and to burdensome exercises in an effort to reshape their bodies. Reduction of eating disorders, therefore, requires both personal and social change. At the personal level, undieting treatment programs are being developed to reduce some of the health risks and miseries spawned by the diet culture

(Polivy & Herman, 1992). Chronic dieters are made aware of the health hazards created by their dieting behavior and are taught how to break the dieting habit by substituting natural eating patterns for disordered ones. Those who have had the benefit of the undieting program feel more effective, are less driven to thinness, are less depressed, like themselves better, and reduce disordered eating behavior without gaining weight. This type of program is appropriate for disordered eating behavior in the service of an obsession for thinness but not for obesity that creates serious health risks.

Part of the effort to ameliorate the epidemic problem of dieting and eating disorders should be directed at raising collective efficacy to alter sociocultural values and standards of physical attractiveness that breed health problems and self-devaluation. The socially oriented approach targets the unhealthy sociocultural values as the problem needing change. The media must be sensitized to the fact that the svelte models of beauty they propagate create severe pressures on young women to try to conform to this ideal of femininity. The pressure of social forces on the marketplace may also help to exert a corrective influence on the fashion industry, which parades spindly models as the cultural ideal. The fashion industry may well be forced to alter its standard of beauty by changing demographics in which the median age of the population with expendable income is rising and women are pursuing careers in which knowledge, intelligence, maturity, and wisdom are the valued attributes. These social changes are not lost on advertisers. In the world of fashion modeling, vacuous pubescent anorexic models are being replaced with middle-age models portraying images of mature women closer to reality. Yet the multibillion dollar diet industry has a vested interest in preserving thinness as a cultural ideal for women. These marketing forces, allied with media purveyance of svelte images and remedies, are in all likelihood important contributors to the recent advent of bulimia as well as its perpetuation. Information about the health hazards of unhealthy dieting, which are not widely known, must be promulgated so that people fully understand the risks they create for themselves in the unending pursuit of slimness.

ALCOHOL AND DRUG ABUSE

Alcohol abuse is a highly prevalent problem that exacts heavy personal and social costs. Progress in reducing alcohol abuse has been hampered by ideological disputes over the nature of alcoholism and the appropriate goals of treatment. According to advocates of the medical model, which was first proposed by Jellinek (1960), alcoholism is a disease characterized by craving, compulsion, and quick loss of control. Craving presumably drives one to the bottle, and drinking even a small amount of alcohol metabolically triggers a complete loss of control. Obeying the dictum that one drink precipitates complete relapse, proponents of the disease model regard permanent abstinence as the only legitimate goal of treatment. To get alcoholics to forsake liquor, they must be convinced that they are powerless to exercise any control over the consumption of alcohol. Given the assumed inherent inability to regulate drinking behavior, maintenance of sobriety requires lifelong dependence on social supports that help one weather periods of craving for alcohol. Proponents of the disease model vigorously oppose the view that alcohol abusers can learn to control their drinking behavior.

Studies of the life course of alcohol abuse reveal that it develops gradually over a long period of social drinking rather than abruptly as the disease model would lead one to believe. At midlife, many heavy drinkers stabilize their alcohol consumption, and only some progress to uncontrolled drinking. Of those who become alcoholic, a significant proportion give up drinking as they get older or revert to lifelong moderate drinking without the benefit of any treatment (Vaillant, 1995). Such findings pose serious problems for theories that medicalize drinking behavior as a disease that renders people powerless to exercise control over the use of alcohol. It is historically interesting that, in the social construction of diseases about consummatory behavior, alcohol abuse got socially classified as a disease but nicotine and other drug abuse, which are similarly addicting, did not.

The ruling conception of alcoholism as a unitary disease eventually came under heavy fire from theorists who adopted a biopsychosocial interactional model. In this view, alcohol abuse is not a monolithic condition with an inevitable progression requiring a single remedy for all alcohol abusers. Rather, alcoholism is a multidetermined behavior pattern that varies across individuals in severity, patterns of causal influences, and amenability to personal control (Blane & Leonard, 1987; Hester & Miller, 1995; Marlatt & Gordon, 1985; Wilson, 1988). Research conducted within the interactional framework is producing major advances in the understanding and treatment of alcoholism.

Given the heterogeneity of alcohol abuse and its multiform determinants, treatment goals and strategies must be tailored to the particular constellation of determinants operating in any given case. The benefits of treatment matching were shown earlier in depression, which also has different types of causes. Treatments that match the type of etiology reduce depression, whereas mismatching treatments are of no help. To achieve benefits by client-treatment matching in alcoholism requires theoretical verification of the different causes of abusive drinking and development of effective treatments tailored to those conditions. The long history of construing alcoholism as a unitary disease has retarded development of this type of particularized knowledge. Whatever treatment is selected, its implementation must address clients' sense of efficacy to control their drinking and their outcome expectations about how they weight the benefits of sobriety against the costs of severing activities and friendships associated with their drinking lifestyle. Eventually, matching treatments to forms of alcohol abuse will provide greater benefits to those whose lives are impaired by abusive drinking.

Biogenetic susceptibility to rapid development of physical dependence on alcohol increases risk of alcohol abuse (Goodwin, 1985). Most people who would be considered susceptible do not become alcoholics, however, nor does one have to be genetically predisposed to become an alcohol abuser. Indeed, the evidence of genetic influence in alcohol abuse by women is inconsistent, and genetic factors seem to play little role in men who begin drinking heavily in adulthood (McGue & Slutske, 1996).

When most people with the biogenetic susceptibility do not have the disorder and many who lack the susceptibility have the disorder, the association is weak, even though biogenetic susceptibility increases the likelihood of developing the disorder. Considering the complete pattern of covariation underscores the power of psychosocial influences in producing the disorder.

Even when genetic factors increase vulnerability to the development of alcoholism among adolescent males, the mode of influence might not operate entirely through pharmacological sensitivity to alcohol. Genetic factors may operate indirectly through their influence on temperamental personality characteristics that predispose some youngsters not only to heavy drinking but also to a wide range of problem behaviors given appropriate environmental inducements. A prospective study by Killen and his colleagues of the onset and maintenance of drinking in adolescence bears on this issue (Killen et al., 1996). The main predictor of onset of drinking in both boys and girls was the outcome expectation that alcohol enhances social functioning. Temperament, extent of problem behaviors, self-esteem, and depression did not contribute independently to drinking onset. Although efficacy beliefs were not measured in this project, we will see shortly that they play an influential role in drinking behavior.

Sociocultural practices exert strong influence over drinking patterns, as evidenced by the marked differences in the incidence of alcoholism and how alcohol affects conduct in different cultural, ethnic, socioeconomic, and occupational groups (Bandura, 1969a; Pittman & White, 1991). It is not that the genetic makeup and brain function of Jews, Mormons, Moslems, Italians, and members of other ethnic groups who exhibit exceedingly low rates of alcoholism is fundamentally different from that of Irish, who surpass other ethnic groups in chronic alcoholism. Social modeling of drinking behavior is a powerful shaper and regulator of alcohol consumption. Televised modeling of drinking practices increases pro-drinking attitudes and alcohol use and contributes to drunken driving (Atkin, 1993; Rychtarik, Fairbank, Allen, Roy, & Drabman, 1983). Modeling is also a strong regulator of the pattern of drinking. In simulated bar settings, people's rate of alcohol consumption is promptly raised by exposure to heavy drinking models but is decreased by seeing models who drink lightly (Collins & Marlatt, 1981; Garlington & Dericco, 1977). Societies in which alcoholic beverages are used as a food rather than as a stimulant or an escape are not plagued with drinking problems.

Self-Regulatory Efficacy in Alcohol Abuse

The combined impact of social influences and perceived efficacy on early use of alcohol, cigarettes, and marijuana is documented in longitudinal research by Ellickson and Hays (1991). Prodrug social influences in the form of exposure to models who use and offer drugs, together with a low sense of efficacy to resist social pressures to use the substances, predict the extent of subsequent adolescent involvement with drugs. A low sense of resistant efficacy operates in a generalized way across the different forms of drug use (Hays & Ellickson, 1990). Deficiencies in interpersonal skills have been linked to substance abuse in adolescence. Webb and Baer (1995), however, report that social skills affect alcohol use only if they raise adolescents' beliefs that they can resist drinking when they are upset, bored, or pressured by their peers.

Alcohol is widely used by adults as a social facilitator and drinking is usually a significant part of social activities. The camaraderie, social pressures, and various gratifications associated with these social functions promote drinking behavior. A low sense of efficacy to regulate drinking in situations of social pressure is a strong predictor of alcohol consumption in young drinkers and differentiates heavy problem drinkers from light drinkers (Young, Oei, & Crook, 1991). If heavy drinkers are to manage their alcohol consumption, they must exercise control over where and with whom they hang out. If they frequent social settings that are opportunistic for drinking, they had better develop a strong sense of self-regulative efficacy if they are to be spared frequent bouts of drunkenness.

Alcohol can reduce stress, boredom, and dysphoric mood. Thus, exposure to stressors generally increases alcohol consumption. The evidence for the stress reducing effects of alcohol itself is equivocal, however (Cappell & Greeley, 1987; Wilson, 1982). People base their actions more on what they believe than on what is objectively the case. For example, males believe that liquor increases sexual prowess whereas, in fact, it impairs physiological sexual response. It is a widely shared belief that alcohol reduces tension. Therefore, stress reduction accompanying drinking may operate more through cognitive means than through the pharmacological effects of alcohol. Belief that alcohol reduces tension or enables one to deal more efficaciously with stressful situations can be calming in the short run but can exacerbate problems if it leads to overdrinking and injurious behavior. Individuals who have learned to respond to stress and dysphoric mood by heavy drinking need to develop more effective ways of managing stressors.

The findings of Young, Oei, and Crook (1991) suggest that the relative importance of different aspects of self-regulative efficacy may change depending on the phase of problem drinking. Whereas young drinkers are driven to heavy drinking more by a low sense of efficacy to resist social pressures, chronic problem drinkers are driven to heavy drinking more by a low sense of efficacy to manage aversive emotional states. Young adults who distrust their self-regulatory efficacy, expect alcohol to produce good social and emotional effects, and favor avoidant styles of coping with stressors drink excessively and experience alcohol-related problems (Evans & Dunn, 1995).

Alcoholism usually results from prolonged heavy social drinking. After people become physically dependent on alcohol, they consume large quantities of liquor to alleviate aversive physiological withdrawal reactions and to avoid their recurrence. In advanced stages of heavy drinking, biochemical as well as psychosocial factors contribute to alcohol abuse. Because a brief period of detoxification eradicates aversive withdrawal reactions, they are not the problem in resumption of drinking. Relapses usually occur when withdrawal symptoms are no longer present to drive one to resume use of addictive substances (Cummings, Gordon, & Marlatt, 1980). The major challenge is to eliminate psychological dependence on alcohol for positive effects or as an escapist mode of coping with difficult realities. This requires changing how alcoholics live their lives.

In an exhaustive review of treatments for alcoholism, Miller and his colleagues (1995) came up with a disconcerting set of findings: The treatment approaches that have proved effective in well-controlled studies are used infrequently in common practice, whereas those that are widely used, such as insight psychotherapies, lack evidence of effectiveness. The goals and strategies of treatment differ depending on whether individuals are problem drinkers without physical dependence on alcohol or chronic alcoholics. Those who drink to excess without physical dependence constitute a major share of the problem drinkers. For years they were essentially ignored in the stormy debates over whether alcoholism is a physical disease or a biopsychosocial disorder and whether abstinence is the only solution. Some heavy drinkers can be taught self-regulatory skills to drink in moderation and reduce the harm caused in their lives by periodic bouts of intoxication. In this approach, they are taught how to prevent overdrinking by monitoring their alcohol consumption and setting explicit limits; altering the alcohol content and pace of drinking to stay within those limits; avoiding or managing effectively situations at high risk for drinking; using alternative activities to drinking; and managing stressors and depressors by constructive means (Miller & Muñoz, 1982).

The disputes over the disease model of alcoholism pale in comparison to the vehement rejection of training in moderate drinking (Peele, 1992). This forceful opposition retarded development of treatments to help excessive drinkers with low dependence, who would otherwise continue this pattern, to reduce their drinking to levels that diminish the harms caused to themselves and others by bouts of drunkenness. Well-designed comparative studies with extended follow-ups reveal that about a third of the problem drinkers either abstain from alcohol or drink in moderation after learning how to exercise control over their drinking behavior (Heather & Robertson, 1981; Miller, Leckman, Delaney, & Tinkcom, 1992). Lower severity of physical dependence and social and occupational stability predict the likelihood of success in controlled drinking (Rosenberg, 1993). Problem drinkers do as well with a goal of moderation as with a goal of abstinence. A goal of moderation does not preclude a later goal of abstinence if necessary. Failure at controlled drinking helps to persuade some problem drinkers to pursue abstention.

A widespread problem is young people who are not physically dependent on alcohol but engage in periodic social drinking bouts that lead to hazardous physical and social behavior. They view their drinking as a normative social affair rather than as a problem requiring attention. Although they summarily reject treatment, they will seek help to moderate unsafe drinking. In these brief interventions, participants are taught self-regulatory skills that enable them to moderate their drinking and maintain the changes over time (Marlatt, Larimer, Baer, & Quigley, 1994). Even very brief interventions in primary health care settings for people unwilling to give up alcohol can produce lasting reductions in unsafe drinking and improvements in health (Bien, Miller, & Tonigan, 1993). In addition, these approaches to secondary prevention of alcohol abuse provide a means for early identification of problem drinkers requiring more intensive help, who would otherwise go unattended.

Severely dependent drinkers need a broad program that helps them to develop more adaptive ways of dealing with their everyday problems. They have a better chance of success if they choose as their goal abstinence from alcohol rather than drinking in moderation. Yet vestiges of "One drink, then drunk" still pervade thinking about drinking lapses after a period of abstinence. Evidence disputes the dichotomous view of either complete abstinence or full relapse (Heather, Rollnick, & Winton, 1983). In fact, participants exhibit divergent patterns of alcohol use after treatment. Many continue to abstain, some resume drinking but in moderation, some drink heavily but still at a lower level than before

treatment, and some revert to their prior level of abusive drinking. Those who judge themselves capable of exercising some control over how much they drink are the ones who succeed in sticking to a moderate pattern of drinking regardless of their prior level of physical dependence on alcohol. Those who have a low sense of recovery efficacy are better off staying away from alcohol.

The types of treatment that have been shown to contribute to successful outcomes include training in interpersonal skills and in how to counteract social pressures to drink, stress management, and development of efficacious ways of managing marital discord (Miller et al., 1995; Wilson, 1988). Preventive peer-oriented programs teach adolescents social communication and assertion skills for developing positive peer relationships, problem-solving skills for dealing with environmental demands, behavioral and cognitive skills for managing stressors, and self-regulatory skills for withstanding peer pressure to use drugs and alcohol. This type of program changes attitudes, enhances sociocognitive competencies, reduces alcohol and drug use, decreases transgressive behavior, and fosters involvement in academic activities (Tobler, 1986). Programs that merely convey information about addictive substances increase knowledge but achieve little else. Those that focus on building self-esteem and self-awareness and clarifying feelings and values achieve little if anything. Thus, development of personal efficacy is likely to foster sobriety, self-esteem, good feelings, and positive self-awareness, whereas analyzing feelings and trying to talk people into feeling good about themselves without equipping them with needed competencies is unlikely to help them much.

Much of the effort to prevent relapse has centered individualistically on development of self-regulative skills for avoiding and coping with instigators to drink. The strains imposed on self-regulation depend on the social worlds in which people live. Viewed from the sociocognitive perspective, success in relapse prevention requires, in addition to improved coping skills and lifestyle changes, restructuring and enlisting environmental supports for a satisfying and meaningful life under sobriety. Recovering alcoholics who have the assistance of a nondrinking social network of family, friends, and coworkers are more successful in remaining abstinent than are those who do not have others to turn to in times of difficulties or who associate with drinking friends and coworkers (Gordon & Zrull, 1991). Building the interpersonal efficacy of recovering alcoholics to select, create, and maintain supportive environments for themselves, therefore, should be an important goal of treatment. The environmental contributors to enduring change are especially important in chronic alcoholism, which usually calls for lifestyle changes and major restructuring of social networks.

A multifaceted community-oriented program devised by Azrin and his coworkers addresses both the personal and social sources of lifelong change (Azrin, 1976; Hunt & Azrin, 1973). It improves familial, social, vocational, and recreational functioning in ways that support sobriety. Through role playing, participants are taught how to handle stressful problems that previously led to bouts of drinking. They are taught how to identify and handle danger signals for drinking, receive marital therapy to increase reciprocal satisfactions, get intensive training on how to find meaningful employment, learn to use drugs that counteract the biological effects of alcohol as an adjunct to support their efforts to maintain sobriety, and develop pleasurable recreational activities that compete with drinking. The program also provides a self-governing social club that offers enjoyable evening and weekend activities, replaces associates who have severe drinking problems, and creates a buddy system that provides someone to turn to in time of need. This comprehensive program produces large reductions in alcoholism, improves family life, and increases satisfying employment, whereas matched control groups achieve little change. The gains are well maintained over time. Moreover, the program is vastly superior to inpatient treatment, Alcoholics Anonymous, and drug treatments that create aversive physiological reactions to alcohol. Despite its promising results, this multifaceted treatment has not been widely adopted as the treatment of choice for chronic alcoholism.

Self-Efficacy Mechanisms in Treatment Effects

Not much attention has been devoted to the mechanisms by which treatments for alcoholism achieve their effects. Research conducted within the sociocognitive framework, however, shows perceived efficacy to be an important operative factor in the initiation, attainment, and maintenance of changes in drinking behavior. Alcoholics who have a low sense of self-regulatory efficacy become resigned to their condition and do not even consider doing anything about their drinking problem (DiClemente & Hughes, 1990). Those who enter treatment with nagging doubts in their efficacy to control their drinking behavior are quick to terminate treatment when they encounter problems (Schimmel, 1986). Among those who continue, the more treatment raises their perceived efficacy to resist the urge to drink in high-risk situations, the better they control alcohol consumption over follow-up periods, regardless of how dependent they had become on alcohol (Sitharthan, 1989; Sitharthan & Kavanagh, 1990; Solomon & Annis, 1989). Although long-term abstainers have a much stronger sense of efficacy than alcoholics who have been sober for only a short time, both groups express the lowest sense of efficacy that they can take a few drinks without getting drunk (Miller, Ross, Emmerson, & Todt, 1989). These findings suggest that deliberate tests of personal control after sobriety is achieved should be avoided because they carry high risk of relapse.

Perceived self-efficacy to resist social pressure to drink distinguishes between abstainers and relapsers following training in resistive social skills, but anticipatory stress in such situations does not (Rist & Watzl, 1983). Drinking lapses are much more likely to occur under conditions of emotional distress arising from social discord and self-created stressors than from social pressures to drink (Marlatt & Gordon, 1980). Hence, self-efficacy predictors should include perceived capability to manage social and intrapersonal stressors without recourse to alcohol as well as interpersonal pressures to drink. The more comprehensive measures of self-regulative efficacy encompass these different types of instigators to drink.

In Marlatt's relapse model, a low sense of efficacy precipitates unrestrained drinking by leading individuals to attribute their drinking lapses to extensive personal deficiencies. Research conducted by Collins and Lapp (1991) indicates that perceived self-inefficacy influences unrestrained drinking directly rather than indirectly through its effects on causal attributions. A low sense of self-regulatory efficacy was a consistent predictor of excessive drinking and alcohol-related problems, whereas causal attributions for the adverse effects of overdrinking predicted alcohol-related problems but not drinking behavior. Shiffman has further shown that decreases in perceived self-efficacy after smoking lapses are not mediated by causal attributions (Shiffman et al., 1996). These findings suggest that the mediating role of the attributional component in the relapse model needs to be reexamined. Because people who suffer from a widespread sense of inefficacy regard the causes of their problems as a personal deficiency that is internal, enduring, and generalized, the question of redundancy of predictors also arises.

Sociocognitive treatments of alcohol abuse are being supplemented with practice in resistive mastery under exposure to alcoholic beverages in an effort to reduce vulnerability to relapse. In this approach, recovered alcoholics are repeatedly exposed to the sight and smell of their favorite alcoholic beverages in imaged risky drinking situations while resisting drinking. Preliminary findings suggest that repeated practice in exercising self-control in the face of strong enticements strengthens efficacy to resist drinking (Rohsenow, Niaura, Childress, Abrams, & Monti, 1990–1991).

The mechanisms governing reduced likelihood of relapse by repeated exposure to alcohol-related stimuli are thought to be extinction of conditioned responses by conditioning theorists and enhancement of self-regulatory capabilities by sociocognitive theorists. Explanations of alcoholism in terms of physical dependence have difficulty accounting for the resumption of drinking long after the physical dependence has been overcome. Situational cues were invoked as conditioned motivators. Through repeated association with alcohol use, environmental cues are said to reactivate the pharmacologic effects of drugs that are experienced as craving for alcohol. In this nonagentic view, people are acted upon by cues that drive them to drink. Repeated exposure presumably extinguishes the craving and positive effects afforded by the drinking behavior.

In encountering addictive substances, former users do not stand by passively waiting for cue exposure to extinguish aroused cravings. Rather, they resort to cognitive and behavioral self-regulatory strategies that help them resist the substance. In a multifaceted treatment program, Monti and his colleagues added exposure to alcohol with training in coping strategies to resist drinking (Monti et al., 1993). These strategies included self-instruction in delay tactics, because the urge to drink subsides over time; using imagery to weaken the urge to drink; visualizing the negative consequences of drinking and the positive consequences of sobriety; and substituting competing activities for drinking. The training in self-regulation increased use of coping strategies and rate of long-term abstinence compared to the standard treatment. At the end of the treatment program, strength of efficacy beliefs to manage situations risky for drinking predicted enduring abstinence, whereas frequency of urges to drink was unrelated to subsequent drinking behavior. Perceived efficacy and resort to resistive coping predicted abstinence after controlling for level of drinking behavior at pretreatment. This pattern of findings and instances in which relapsers reinstated lasting control after behavioral lapses argues that the benefits of exposure to alcoholic beverages are achieved through a cognitive self-regulatory mechanism rather than a cravings extinction mechanism.

The benefits drinkers expect from alcohol have been considered to be one of the factors that maintain drinking behavior. To evaluate the regulative role of outcome expectancies, Solomon and Annis (1989) measured the benefits and costs alcoholics expected should they change their drinking behavior. Chronic drinkers view life without alcohol as having both positive and negative consequences. They see curtailment of drinking as contributing to health, self-respect, improved functioning, and a better future. But they also believe that forsaking alcohol leads to loneliness through estrangement from drinking companions, reduces expressiveness and outgoingness, increases boredom, and leaves one vexed by giving up the anticipated gratifications of alcohol. Rollnick and Heather (1982) similarly report that individuals who engage in a drinking lifestyle regard curtailment of drinking as a mixed blessing.

Azrin's community-oriented approach probably owes much of its success to the fact that it cultivates new social relationships and a wide array of rewarding social and recreational activities that tip the balance of outcome expectancies in favor of sobriety. Treatment approaches that simply seek to eradicate drinking behavior without providing competing pursuits and satisfactions to those offered by drinking companions will be hard pressed to produce lasting changes. Existing self-help groups, such as Alcoholics Anonymous, offer many such supports for a new life without alcohol for those who become deeply committed members. Unfortunately, dropout rates are very high and the few controlled studies available fail to find any effect of referral to Alcoholics Anonymous as a supplementary treatment (Miller et al., 1995). If people choose Alcoholics Anonymous on their own, however, they do better than if they do not, provided they remain deeply involved in the program (Emrick, Tonigan, Montgomery, & Little, 1993; Timko, Moos, Finney, & Moos, 1994). But high attrition of nonresponders creates a self-selective bias that makes it difficult to assess the extent to which favorable outcomes are due to good prognostic attributes of the remainers or to the characteristics of the program. The relative contribution of spiritual aspects and steadfast supportive guidance remains unknown. Some alcohol abusers who would otherwise accept the supportive social network may be turned away by the decree that they view their alcoholism as a spiritual disease requiring spiritual change. Given the diversity of value orientations, alternative supportive subcommunities are needed for rebuilding and supporting an alcohol-free life.

The model devised by Azrin builds an ongoing self-governed social group for recovered alcoholics and their families and guests in their natural environment to serve the supportive and enabling function. A self-governed social system that is embedded in a multifaceted treatment and tailored to the needs of the participants is likely to be well used. Recovering alcoholics who have the benefit of such a social system drink less, achieve greater reductions in physical and behavioral impairments, and experience fewer bouts of heavy drinking than do recovering alcoholics without a supportive group (Mallams, Godley, Hall, & Meyers, 1982). The better the attendance, the greater the reductions in drinking, the fewer the drinking lapses, and the better the improvement in life functioning.

In analyzing the psychosocial regulators of drinking behavior, the order in which their relative contribution is assessed must be guided logically by their causal priority. In tests of sociocognitive theory, efficacy beliefs should be causally prior to the expected outcomes that flow from the actions taken. When the logical relationship is disregarded by placing outcomes before regulatory action, both a low sense of regulatory efficacy and positive alcohol expectations contribute to drinking behavior and alcohol-related problems (Aas, Klepp, Laberg, Aaro, 1995; Evans & Dunn, 1995). Solomon and Annis (1990) compared the relative contribution of efficacy beliefs and outcome expectancies to the maintenance of sobriety following treatment. Efficacy beliefs predicted success in controlling alcohol consumption. As in other domains of functioning, outcome expectancies did not account for variation in drinking behavior when beliefs of personal efficacy were held constant. Efficacy beliefs remain a significant predictor of future drinking behavior when severity of drinking at intake is held constant. When outcome expectations do emerge as independent predictors, they generally contribute less to variation in drinking behavior than do efficacy beliefs (Young et al., 1991).

Self-efficacy theory not only sheds light on the self-regulation of drinking behavior but also guides strategies for treatment and for development of resistance to relapse. This is well illustrated in the work of Annis and Davis (1989). Self-efficacy assessments are used to identify the types of situations in which individuals have difficulty controlling their drinking behavior. These situations are then ranked from lowest risk to highest risk of heavy drinking. After the participants develop self-regulative skills and rehearse flexible plans of action, they carry out mastery assignments in which they deal with progressively more risky drinking situations in their natural environment until they can manage them without recourse to alcohol. Drinking slips provide opportunities to remedy remaining vulnerabilities. A program of relapse management guided by microanalytic assessment of perceived coping efficacy coupled with corrective mastery experiences aids in the maintenance of sobriety. Those whose abusive drinking is widely generalized, however, need the broader social supports for a nondrinking lifestyle, in addition to self-regulative skills. The self-efficacy contributors to this expanded domain of functioning involve the development of personal efficacy for social, occupational, and recreational pursuits that provide a satisfying life without alcohol.

In other severe disorders, a sense of personal efficacy reduces distress and supports a positive adaptational orientation on reentry to the community after hospitalization (Lent, Lopez, Mikolaitis, Jones, & Bieschke, 1992). Severe alcoholics who undergo a residential treatment program are usually scheduled for periodic follow-up sessions designed to assess their status and bolster their coping efforts. Those with a high sense of efficacy who keep up their aftercare contacts achieve a relatively high rate of sobriety over the course of a year (Rychtarik, Prue, Rapp, & King, 1992). By contrast, virtually all of those low in both perceived efficacy and participation in aftercare revert to drinking by the third month. Efficacy beliefs at intake predict maintenance of abstinence after controlling for age, marital and employment status, and degree of alcohol dependence. None of these factors except efficacy beliefs predict abstinence. Upon discharge from residential treatment and shortly thereafter, recovered alcoholics are likely to receive a great deal of support, which helps to maintain sobriety. As special attention subsides, they are left to their own coping devices. With return to habitual routines, the relapse curves for individuals of high and low perceived efficacy diverge substantially with the passage of time, with the more self-efficacious ones achieving the higher rate of sobriety.

Drug Dependence

The role of perceived self-efficacy in the exercise of control over opiate drug use has received much less attention than alcoholism. The several studies that speak to this issue, however, indicate that efficacy beliefs operate as a regulative influence in opiate use in much the same way as they do in other forms of substance abuse. Perceived self-regulatory efficacy at the end of cognitive therapy partly mediates changes in marijuana use over a period of a year after controlling for use status at that time (Stephens, Wertz, & Roffman, 1995). The conditions that have been identified as relapse precipitants, such as peer pressure and aversive emotional states, exert strains on perceived self-regulative efficacy in regard to heroin use (Sitharthan, McGrath, Cairns, & Saunders, 1993). Heroin users with a low sense of efficacy cannot resist pressures to use opiates even if they are ill or refrain from sharing needles, which involves high risk of infection. The stronger the perceived self-regulative efficacy instilled by treatment, the more successful are opiate users in staying off drugs (Gossop et al., 1990). Gossop and his colleagues examined a variety of predictors of drug status at short and long follow-up periods. The two factors that consistently emerged as significant predictors of outcome were perceived self-efficacy to refrain from drug use and protective factors in the form of supportive associates and involvement in purposeful occupational activities. Positive social and occupational involvements contributed to a satisfying life that helped former users to remain drug-free. Number of coping strategies predicted short-term drug status but was unrelated to long-term status. In these regression analyses, efficacy beliefs were entered last in the order of predictive factors. Thus, they accounted for variation in drug status after multiple statistical controls were applied for the effects of protective factors, time in treatment, previous history of abstinence, and coping strategies.

Methadone programs, in which heroin abusers are placed on a synthetic narcotic either during detoxification or on a continuing basis, are widely used. Reilly and his colleagues examined changes in perceived self-regulatory efficacy during different phases of methadone detoxification treatment (Reilly et al., 1995). Perceived efficacy to refrain from opiates increased after methadone was begun, stabilized at a moderate level during a maintenance dose, and declined as the methadone dose was gradually diminished. Efficacy beliefs predicted subsequent drug use at critical junctures in the treatment. The stronger the regulatory efficacy beliefs at the start of the stabilization phase and before the tapering phase, the less the subsequent drug use. The predictive relationship remained after controlling for level of prior drug use.

Most people who seek help for drug addiction are put through an inpatient detoxification program, whereupon they are discharged and urged to seek treatment in their community. Heller and Krauss (1991) examined predictors of entry to aftercare treatment following detoxification. The importance that polydrug users attached to behaviors that would gain entry to and aid aftercare treatment, such as finishing the detoxification program, arranging and sticking to the aftercare activities, enlisting social support, and other forms of self-management, did not predict whether they sought such aftercare. But belief in their efficacy to carry out those activities predicted who entered aftercare treatment in their communities.

The severely addicted must make fundamental lifestyle changes if they are to sustain recovery from drug addiction. To begin with, they have to disabuse themselves of the belief that they can continue to engage in the same activities with the same consorts in the same settings but simply refrain from using drugs. They must learn a new way of life rather than merely change a consumptive behavior. McAuliffe and his associates graphically document the magnitude of the behavioral, cognitive, valuational, and self-conceptual changes required in the different facets of life to achieve enduring recovery from drug addiction (McAuliffe, Albert, Cordill-London, & McGarraghy, 1991). Recovery involves

the daunting dual task of casting off a detrimental way of life and adopting a beneficial one. Recovering addicts have to sever ties with drug-using friends and dealers. They have to restructure their social and recreational activities, which have been heavily oriented around drug-related routines. They have to learn to avoid permanently highly risky situations that are avoidable and to master self-regulatory skills for managing those that are unavoidable. They have to learn to exercise control over their patterns of thinking so that they are not drawn to drugs by anticipated gratifications. Those who lack a stable means of livelihood have to develop occupational competencies that structure a large part of their life and give new meaning to it.

In making the break from drug use, recovering addicts initially face a rather bleak, restrictive life stripped of the social ties and activities of their old lifestyle. Idle weekends are especially tormenting. This difficult transitional phase in the process of personal change creates the highest vulnerability to relapse. If recovering addicts are to weather it, they need a highly supportive environment as they are adopting a new way of life that will provide competing satisfactions for those they have forsaken. Treatment programs that develop the various facets of a nonaddictive life increase the success rate (Azrin et al., 1996; McAuliffe et al., 1991). Even after comprehensive treatments, however, many of the participants revert to drug use. The high relapse rate underscores the need to include, as part of the formal treatment program, an ongoing supportive subcommunity of the type devised by Azrin to counteract relapse in alcoholism (Azrin, 1976).

The severely addicted whose lives were shaped in impoverished environments and who have been deeply enmeshed in a drug user subculture face the formidable task of major lifestyle changes with few personal and social resources to do so. If they forsake drugs, they have little or nothing to return to that might help to sustain their recovery because they have always led a marginalized life. They need to immerse themselves deeply in a wide-reaching enabling environment if they are to restructure their lives. Piecemeal solutions accomplish little. The large-scale Delancy program in San Francisco is a notable example of a self-enablement model for how to transform the lives of intractable drug addicts by providing them with the competencies and opportunity structures to pursue productive prosocial lives (Hampden-Turner, 1976; Silbert, 1984). The name Delancy symbolizes the area of New York where the immigrants of yesteryear, through self-reliance, the dignity of earning one's own way, and mutual assistance, entered the mainstream life of their new society. Delancy is a self-directed community where hard-core drug addicts and alcoholics, with long histories of imprisonment, restructure their lives through their own self-initiative without public funds. They live together in the subcommunity by a set of conduct norms that promote self-development and eliminate manipulative, destructive, and antisocial conduct. Past adversities are not accepted as excuses for detrimental conduct. To overcome cognitive deficits, everyone is tutored in basic academic skills to the level of high school equivalency. Many go on to college, professional programs, and various skilled trades.

Participants run numerous training school businesses that serve to build basic occupational skills and provide capital for the program. Economic self-reliance provides the sustaining resources for the self-governing community's development and growth. The technical self-reliance provides the knowledge and competencies needed for occupational self-development. These businesses include construction trades, printing and graphic arts, moving and trucking businesses, commercial painting, service stations and auto repair shops, furniture production and sales, restaurants, advertising, and various high-tech businesses. Each resident gains considerable experience in each of three classes of occupational activities, including production work, administrative and office work, and sales-oriented work. After they develop educational, interpersonal, and occupational competencies, they enter a transitional phase in which they pursue an occupation in the community or are provided with the resources to start up their own business while still residing in the Delancy subcommunity. Once they achieve a successful adaptation to their new life, they go out on their own.

The graduates of this program are pursuing successful prosocial lives free of drugs. They are thriving in the community as contractors, truckers, medical and dental technicians, computer operators, engineers, lawyers, advertising executives, physicians, and even deputy sheriffs. They also measure their success by the principle of restitution. The participants are given the competencies and social support to escape the "social swamp." But they should help clean up the "swamp" by helping others. Delancy graduates perform public service work and fight for social changes to improve life in the community. For example, Deborah was a heroin addict at 12, a street prostitute at 13, was imprisoned often, and tried suicide three times. She received a degree in business administration and is a sales manager for a national firm. She created a community paraprofessional program for adolescent girls in trouble and helps new women residents in the Delancy program.

The Delancy program has amassed a real estate portfolio valued in the millions. After being trained by local unions, the residents built a $25 million residential-commercial complex near the San Francisco waterfront for the 500 residents enrolled at any given time. This stunning residence, adorned with loggias, flower boxes, ornamental ironwork, decorative tiles, and stained glass windows crafted in their own shops, has won architectural acclaim. Their conglomerate businesses bring a profit in the millions each year. They have achieved all this on their own without any public funds.

This self-enabling subcommunity approach transforms antisocial lives and removes barriers to better futures. In this environment, individuals who had been deeply enmeshed in lives of crime and addiction learn to be responsible, caring people. They are provided with the social and material resources needed to restructure their lives. They are not burdened with the stigma of criminal records that block access to legitimate pursuits. They develop the capabilities and sense of personal efficacy to realize a dignified prosocial life. A self-enabling social approach that addresses multiple human problems simultaneously can succeed where fragmented individualistic approaches fail.

Scope and Use of Self-Efficacy Analysis in Addictive Habits

The overall findings provide converging evidence that perceived self-regulatory efficacy partly determines success in altering detrimental addictive and consummatory habits and in adhering to altered habits over the long term. Predictors should be used constructively not to screen people out of treatments but to tailor treatments to personal factors in ways that increase the likelihood of success. Most people who suffer from detrimental habits from which they seek relief do not enter treatment highly confident of their capabilities to alter their lifestyle. They have experienced a history of failed efforts and count on the therapist's efficacy to eradicate habits they have been unable to change on their own. They are hardly gladdened by being told that therapists can provide guidance but that they themselves will have to serve as the main agents of their own change.

Progress in understanding the role of perceived self-efficacy in addictive and other refractory habits and in their enduring modification can be increased by expanding the scope of inquiry. Self-efficacy assessments have been concerned almost exclusively with perceived self-regulatory efficacy to exercise control over addictive behaviors in precipitant situations. Two other aspects of perceived self-efficacy are relevant to understanding the modification and maintenance of habit changes. The first involves beliefs in one's efficacy to carry out the therapeutic tasks needed to effect personal change. A weak sense of self-change efficacy impedes efforts to put into practice the therapeutic activities needed to modify refractory habits. The second aspect concerns recovery self-efficacy, which taps the strength of belief that one can reinstate control after a lapse or relapse. Self-change efficacy contributes to the consideration and initiation of habit changes, and self-regulatory efficacy and recovery self-efficacy contribute to the adoption and maintenance of habit changes.

These aspects of perceived efficacy are primarily concerned with the management of instigators to addictive behavior. Whether or not people turn to drugs and alcohol is governed by positive enabling factors as well as by negative instigators to substance abuse. For example, aversive emotional states and interpersonal conflicts are common precipitants of bouts of heavy drinking. Consider, by way of example, a causal process in which perceived social inefficacy breeds despondency, which prompts heavy drinking. In this case, social inefficacy is the distal cause, and the intermediary state of despondency is the proximal instigator. Development of a strong sense of social efficacy will predict reduction in drinking behavior because it removes the proximal emotional instigator for it. The patterns of determinants of abusive drinking vary among individuals. The highest self-efficacy predictiveness will be achieved by matching the self-efficacy assessment to the set of determinants of substance abuse operating in any given case.

The level of perceived self-change efficacy has important bearing on the early structuring of therapeutic tasks. There are several sources of motivation that drive people to seek help with detrimental habits. These include the aversive effects produced by such habits, social pressures to alter them, self-dissatisfactions with one's life, and the anticipated benefits of eliminating injurious habits. These motivators may bring people to treatment but will not necessarily keep them there for long. Through gradual adaptation, people can come to tolerate a great deal of aversiveness. Hope alone will not keep them going indefinitely without some positive results. They can easily ward off social pressures to change their ways by demonstrating, through half-hearted effort, that the programs prescribed for them don't work. Therefore, individuals who enter treatment with a weak sense of self-change efficacy need self-convincing early experiences of progress; otherwise, further self-doubts set in that undermine the ability to maintain and sustain the effort needed to succeed. Some people are pressured into treatment at a time when they are unprepared to undertake the intensive work required to effect lifestyle changes. Efforts can be made to increase their motivation for treatment (Miller & Rollnick, 1991). But if their commitment to personal change remains low, they might be better served by encouragement to consider treatment on some future occasion when concerns are greater than by failure through half-hearted attempts, which only strengthens their belief in the futility of efforts at personal change.

In the various lines of evidence reviewed in this chapter, self-efficacy theory accounts for initiation of self-change, for level of behavioral changes produced by different modes of treatment, for rate of change during the course of treatment, and for variations in behavioral changes achieved by individuals receiving the same treatment, and it even predicts for any given individual whether specific coping tasks will be executed successfully or failed. The theory integrates the results of heterogeneous treatment approaches for different types of dysfunctions. It proposes a common cognitive mechanism that regulates behavior and provides an explanatory framework for the impact of psychosocial treatments in general. And finally, it provides explicit guidelines for how to structure and implement powerful treatments.

9

Athletic Functioning

SPORTS ARE AN INTEGRAL PART of many people's lives. They get so passionately involved with their favorite team that its victories and defeats affect them personally, as if they were an extension of the squad. Team triumphs elate the fans, team defeats depress and anger them. Athletic contests affect more than transient mood states. Ardent fans link their personal identities to the teams they adopt and even alter judgments of their own capabilities depending on whether their teams perform well or poorly (Cialdini et al., 1976; Hirt, Zillmann, Erickson, & Kennedy, 1992). In the most popular world sport, soccer, even national identity gets strongly linked to the performance of national teams. Entire nations experience heightened pride over triumphs and mourn defeats in World Cup championships. Because of the intense cultural preoccupation with sports, many young aspirants become deeply immersed in athletic pursuits. People are not only spectators of sports but invest a lot of time and effort in developing their own athletic skills as part of their recreational lives. Thus, for vast numbers of people, athletic activities are not just a idle pastime.

Success in athletic competition requires more than physical skills. It is now widely recognized that cognitive factors play an influential role in athletic development and functioning. This chapter examines the contribution of cognitions of personal efficacy to athletic functioning. The psychological processes that are activated by efficacy beliefs affect almost every facet of athletic functioning. Athletes must labor long and hard to master the skills of their trade and be able to stick it out through tough times against stiff odds. Beliefs in athletic efficacy determine who chooses to pursue athletic activities and how much they gain from training programs. The athletes who survive the highly competitive selection process possess natural talents for their chosen pursuit and the self-motivation to put themselves through the drudgery of perfecting their athletic skills for arduous hours on end. In contests between highly skilled athletes, a brief lapse in attention, effort, or accuracy can spell the difference between triumph and defeat. It is not surprising, therefore, that a firm sense of efficacy has long been recognized in athletic circles as a key to optimal performance. To execute the skills they have perfected effectively under intense competitive pressure, athletes must exercise control over the performance-impairing effects of acute stressors, disruptive ideation, discouraging slumps and setbacks, and vexing pain, which are part and parcel of grueling athletic activities. The success of these self-regulatory efforts rests heavily on a resilient sense of personal efficacy. Because physical activity affects quality of health, the field of exercise psychology has become a subject of major interest to investigators in the sports field as well as in the health sciences. Therefore, this chapter will also examine self-efficacy determinants of adoption and adherence to physically active lifestyles.

DEVELOPMENT OF ATHLETIC SKILLS

Cognitive Phase of Skill Development

Athletic skill development proceeds through several phases involving a number of different psychomotor functions (Bandura, 1986a). In the first phase, in which cognitive factors play the major role, a cognitive representation of the skill is formed. The conception serves several proactive functions. It specifies how relevant subskills must be selected, coordinated, and sequenced to suit particular purposes, and it provides the internal standard for the self-regulation of skill development. Without some notion of how the activity is best performed, novices would be at a complete loss as to where to begin, what to do, and what to change. Cognitive representations are formed on the basis of knowledge that can be gained in a variety of ways.

The most effective way of transmitting information about a skill is through proficient modeling. The major subfunctions governing observational learning from modeled performances are summarized in Chapter 3 and addressed elsewhere in considerable detail (Bandura, 1986a). By observing modeled performances, individuals gain knowledge about the dynamic structure of the skill being acquired. Repeated opportunities to observe the modeled activities enable observers to discover the essential features of the skill, organize and verify what they know, and give special attention to missing aspects (Carroll & Bandura, 1990). People will not learn or remember much from exposure to models unless they transform the essential features of the modeled skill into easily remembered symbolic codes in the medium of imagery or words. Observers who convert a modeled activity into codes that symbolize it form a more accurate cognitive representation than they would if they just passively observed the demonstrations. The benefits of symbolic coding are reflected in performance as well. The better the symbolic coding of physical activities into memorable words and images, the better the activities are learned and retained (Carroll & Bandura, 1990; Gerst, 1971).

Some writers single out the attentional subfunction of observational learning and treat it as a competitor to complementary representational subfunctions governing acquisition processes (Scully & Newell, 1985). Presumably, the visual system automatically extracts relative motion patterns from modeled actions; thus, in this view, thought is superfluous to learning. Oh that observational learning were that simple. Obviously, observers must extract the essential elements from information conveyed by modeled skills. Although perception involves some automatic visual processing, much of it is cognitively guided by preconceptions. Cognitive sets channel what people look for, what they extract from observations, and how they interpret what they see. Extracting information is necessary but not sufficient for observational learning. Having extracted the relevant information, observers must retain it in some symbolic form and use it to construct performance skills. Moreover, they need to be motivated to do all this. Humans have evolved not only a visual system for picking up information but also an advanced cognitive system for gaining and using knowledge to manage ever-changing situations. Forethought enables them to play a proactive role in their own learning. Thus, people learn faster, remember more, and construct physical skills better with the use of cognitive aids than without them (Bandura, 1986a). In using modeling to cultivate athletic skills, one would not prescribe that individuals sit back and watch performance demonstrations thoughtlessly on faith that the visual system will do everything automatically. Research in which cognitive representation is measured independently of physical performance corroborates the vital mediational role played by cognition in skill learning (Carroll & Bandura, 1990). The more accurate the cognitive representation derived from modeling influences, the better the performance. As will be fully documented throughout this chapter, there is considerably more to physical skills than motor mechanics. Self-regulatory processes play a pivotal role in how well the biological machine operates.

In evaluating the role of cognitive factors in instructional modeling, it is important to distinguish between fixed skills and generative skills. Some athletic activities involve solo performances that have to be executed in a rigidly prescribed way. Divers must adhere to an ordained body position during their descent and entry into the water. The skill is fixed, the situation is predictable, and cognition operates in the subfunctions of observational learning during acquisition and in the self-management of competitive pressure during contests. Most athletic activities, however, call for generative skills in managing competitive events with a lot of uncertainties and unpredictable elements. Performers have to read shifting game situations, select effective strategies, predict opponents' likely actions, and improvise performances accordingly. This requires a high level of cognitive self-regulation.

Execution of most skills must be constantly varied to suit changing conditions. Adaptive performance, therefore, requires a generative conception rather than an exact one-to-one mapping between representation and action in the likeness of a fixed script. By applying the structural rules embodied in a generative conception, the skill can be enacted in a variety of ways. For example, after individuals acquire the conception of triangularity, they can generate triangles of limitless sizes; they can sketch triangular forms by hand or foot or create them by arranging objects in the appropriate pattern. Through the process of abstract modeling, which is heavily dependent on cognitive operations, observers acquire judgmental skills and generalizable rules and strategies for orchestrating athletic performances. Performers do not gain much from being given a set of rules, but rules combined with salient performance examples improve understanding and skill (Bandura, 1986a; Rosenthal & Zimmerman, 1978).

Information needed for skill learning can be modeled by physical demonstration, pictorial portrayal, or verbal instruction that describes rather than shows how to perform given activities. Actions convey more information about an athletic skill than do words. Because description helps to focus attention on relevant aspects of an activity, however, verbal instruction is typically combined with behavioral modeling as the preferred mode of guidance. New technologies are altering the mode of modeling to boost its instructive power. Computer-aided video systems with random access to instructive demonstrations provide a convenient medium for informative modeling of athletic skills and for analyzing one's own performances.

Another promising form of modeling in the early cognitive phase of learning is the use of computer graphics to convey and improve athletic skills. Action routines can be fully portrayed by a minimum number of motion cues (Johansson, 1973). This makes it feasible to model the essence of an athletic skill without depending solely on observers to extract the vital elements from the profusion of irrelevant details. Some skills are difficult to learn and perfect because certain critical elements are not easily observable or they occur in a split second that escapes notice. Learners have difficulty not only in seeing what is modeled but also in monitoring their own enactments. This is especially true if some, if not most, of their actions occur outside their visual field. Ultra-high-speed cameras are used to capture what the eye cannot easily see in modeled performances (Gustkey, 1979). The picture frames are then translated into moving figures of the performance on a computer screen, enabling observers to discover what best to do at any given point in the action. The instructiveness of performance feedback can be augmented by this means as well. Electronic analyses of filmed enactments graphically pinpoint flaws in the execution of skills.

Computerized self-modeling of optimal performances is also used to perfect athletic skills

(Grayson, 1980). In this application, a person's performances are captured on film and electronically analyzed for correctness. The film is then edited so that only a perfectly executed performance remains. Learners watch themselves performing skillfully over and over again to master the ideal conception of the activity. Self-modeling, in which people observe themselves performing at their best in edited videotape replays, has been shown to raise beliefs of personal efficacy and improve diverse athletic skills, including swimming, power-lifting, gymnastics, volleyball, and tennis (Dowrick, 1991). Successful self-modeling enhances athletic performance, whereas self-modeling of one's deficiencies has diverse effects with no overall gain (Bradley, 1993). Self-modeling affects performance through its impact on efficacy belief.

The correct form of a skill can also be discovered through the more rudimentary form of learning based on trial and error experiences. By varying their actions and observing the results they produce, novices may eventually figure out how best to perform the activity. This is a toilsome mode of acquisition, however, especially during early phases of learning of skills with complex features. One can spend many dreary hours in trial and error labor searching for the proper form of a skill without finding it. The acquisition process can be accelerated by transmitting the rule structure of the skill through modeling and then refining and perfecting it experientially.

It should be noted that learning athletic skills through direct experience is rarely, if ever, based solely on response effects. Since complete reclusiveness is a rarity, one would be hard pressed to find any individuals who learned an athletic activity they had never seen performed by others. Before children lay hands on a football, for example, they have seen the relevant skills modeled repeatedly on playgrounds and in televised contests. Experiential learning is almost invariably superimposed on ubiquitous modeling influences that short-circuit the exploratory groping by conveying the basic structure and rules of the athletic skill. Nor is the exploratory process mindless trial and error. Detailed analyses of

the technical structure of a given athletic skill suggest ways of performing it to achieve better results.

The final way in which athletic skills are developed is through creative synthesis of knowledge into new strategies and forms. In this mode of acquisition, the new ways of performing the athletic activity are the product of an innovative process. The high jump is one notable example of a sharp break with tradition. For years, contestants leaped over bars with a forward jumping style called the straddle. Fosbury fused two bygone techniques, the curved run and the back layout, to create the flop (McNab, 1980). This creative innovation, executed by a backward rotation over the bar, won him an Olympic title. Other athletes promptly adopted this backward jumping style and went on to even loftier record leaps. Athletic innovativeness is not confined to individual sports. From time to time, creative coaches devise new styles of team playmaking that transform the game.

Innovations rarely spring entirely from individual inventiveness. A lot of modeling usually goes on in innovations. In the inception phase, innovations are built in part on some of the creations of others. By refining preexisting elements, synthesizing them in new ways, and adding some novel elements, an emergent new style is born. After it is put into practice, experiences with the new form produce further evolutionary changes. The novel style of high jumping was created in this fashion. The evolution by Shaughnessy of a new style of playmaking that transformed how football is played provides another example of developmental innovation (Fimrite, 1977). He adopted an arcane offensive system that other coaches had tried with limited success and turned it into a powerful new system that no longer bore much resemblance to the original.

Transformational Phase of Skill Development

Knowledge alone will not instantly beget proficient performance unless the activity is trivially simple. Procedural knowledge and cognitive skills are necessary but not sufficient for skilled performance. For example, procedural knowledge by itself will not convert a novice into a proficient skier or a graceful ballerina. The construction and skillful execution of complex patterns of behavior require a transformational mechanism to get from knowledge structures to proficient action. In social cognitive theory (Bandura, 1986a), the mechanism for transforming cognition into action operates through a conception-matching process. Cognitive representations serve as guides for the production of skilled action and as internal standards for making corrective adjustments in the achievement of behavioral proficiency. Skills are perfected by repeated corrective adjustments in conception-matching during behavior production (Carroll & Bandura, 1985, 1987). Monitored enactment serves as the vehicle for converting conception to skilled action. The feedback accompanying enactments provides the information needed to detect and correct mismatches between conception and action. The behavior is thus modified based on the comparative information to achieve a close match between conception and action. Through this comparative process, identified errors are gradually eliminated. The amount of overt enactment needed to eliminate mismatches depends on the complexity of the activity, the informativeness and timing of the feedback information, and the extent to which the requisite subskills have already been developed.

During the transformational phase of skill development, enactments can also contribute to the refinement of cognitive representations. Putting into practice what one has learned cognitively calls attention to aspects of the skill that may be poorly articulated or lacking in the guiding conception of the activity. By revealing what one does not know, enactments help to enhance and channel attention to aspects of the skill that still need to be conceptualized. Awareness of flaws can heighten attentiveness to further performance demonstrations and verbal instructions aimed at mastering problematic features of the cognitive representation of the skill.

Making the Unobservable Informatively Observable

Error correction through conception matching relies heavily on monitoring one's enactments. People improve and perfect their performance by seeing, hearing, and feeling what they are doing. A common problem in mastering athletic skills is that performers cannot fully observe their own behavior. For example, swimmers and golfers cannot see much of what they are doing. It is difficult to guide actions that are only partially observable or to identify the corrective adjustments needed to make behavior congruent with conception. As a result, performers may practice faulty habits while assuming all along that they are following the appropriate style. When performers know what to do and can observe their actions fully, they can improve their performance by matching actions to the standard even if they do not know the results their actions produce (Newell, 1976). They simply match what they do to what was intended. When actions are only partially observable, however, performers infer what they are doing wrong from the evident results of their actions. Golfers, for example, try to diagnose and correct the faults of their swing from seeing the golf ball slice to the left or hook to the right. Their knowledge of which faulty movements produce which results indicates what needs to be corrected. The less observable actions are to performers, the more dependent they are on response-correlated results to try to match action to conception.

Augmented visual feedback, using video systems that make the unobservable observable, is increasingly used to accelerate the development of athletic proficiency. The benefits of performance feedback will depend on its timing, specificity, and informativeness. Performers do not benefit from observing their enactments of an intricate physical skill if they have not yet formed an adequate cognitive representation of the activity. Without a conception to serve as a standard, they cannot use the visual feedback correctively. After they have conceptualized the structure of the skill, however, being able to see themselves as they are performing actions that ordinarily occur outside their field of vision markedly facilitates accurate performance (Carroll & Bandura, 1982). Delayed self-observation makes it difficult to detect and correct mismatches between conception and action, because performers tend to get absorbed in their past performance without constantly comparing it to a memory of how it should be done. Consequently, delays in observing replays of prior performances can reduce the instructive value of the self-observation (Carroll & Bandura, 1985). If people visualize the modeled activity just as they are about to observe their earlier performances, then mismatches between their conception and action can become more salient and errors can be corrected. Visualization may be one way of compensating for the limitations of delayed self-observation.

Providing delayed, unguided feedback, as is commonly done in videotaped replays, usually produces poor results (Hung & Rosenthal, 1981; Rothstein & Arnold, 1976). Simply being shown replays of one's behavior or being told that one's performances were either faulty or successful has unpredictable effects. Such uninstructed replays do not necessarily ensure that observers will notice what they are doing wrong or that they will glean from their behavior the needed corrective changes. Evaluative feedback, which focuses on how good the performance is, should be distinguished from instructive feedback, which focuses on how to do it right. Summary evaluations identify whether or not one is on the right track, but they convey little information about the corrections that need to be made to improve performance. Without instructive feedback and progressive subgoals to place current attainments in the proper perspective, self-observation of flawed performances can diminish observers' judgments of their capabilities (Brown, 1980). By contrast, corrective feedback that directs attention to relevant aspects of subskills aids the development of proficiency (Del Rey, 1971).

Computerized video systems greatly enhance the instructiveness of the feedback that can now be provided to performers. Random access to performances recorded with time-code signals permits fast and efficient review of athletic performances (Franks & Maile, 1991). The enactments can be segmented into their major components and replayed in slow motion for instructive analysis of key elements. Split-screen technology facilitates the comparison process by enabling athletes to observe concurrently how well their performances match the modeled standard. Further advances in electronic technology will accelerate mastery of some of the subroutines of motor skills. Such systems electronically monitor crucial aspects of a motor activity, compare it with a programmed standard, and provide instantaneous feedback of what needs correcting. The development of virtual reality technology, which is still in its infancy, will enable future learners to practice orchestrating their skills by interacting with computer-generated environments. Emerging systems that detect body movement within a grid of invisible infrared light allow unrestricted action in a responsive simulated environment without the learner having to wear constraining paraphernalia. Flexibility increases applicability of this technology to athletic skill development.

The feedback that is especially informative and achieves big performance gains relies on corrective modeling (Vasta, 1976). In this approach, which typifies guided skill acquisition — be it virtuosity in tennis, dramatics, playing the violin, or social skills — troublesome segments of a performance are identified and adept ways of performing them are modeled by those who are proficient at it. Learners then rehearse those subskills until they master them. Periodic feedback about how one is doing fosters goal setting and heightens attentional involvement in related activities. As a result, informative feedback not only improves the behavior singled out for attention but also facilitates the observational learning of new activities in the same setting. John Wooden, who amassed a remarkable record of 10 national basketball championships in 12 years, used a discriminative mode of modeling to provide instructive feedback. He modeled how to perform the skill correctly, then enacted the faulty way in which the players did it, and then again modeled how to do it correctly (Tharp & Gallimore, 1976). Whatever form the performance feedback takes, it should be structured in ways that build a sense of personal efficacy as well as skill. This dual goal is best promoted by highlighting successes and gains, while correcting deficiencies in subskills.

Seeing themselves as they perform activities would be of little value if performers remained dependent on visual feedback, because eventually the activities must be performed under conditions where such feedback is not provided. Ballet dancers can practice with mirrors, but they must later perform without them. Eventually, enactments must be monitored by the feel and the observable correlated results of the actions. Such a transfer does indeed occur (Carroll & Bandura, 1982, 1985). After conceptions are translated successfully into visually guided enactments, the activities continue to be performed accurately after the concurrent visual feedback is discontinued.

Skills are developed and regulated by multi-level systems of control. After proficiency is acquired with cognitive guidance, the motor skills are routinized and no longer require higher cognitive control. Execution of the motor skills is largely regulated by lower level sensory-motor systems. Cognition continues to play an influential role in athletic performance, however, especially through its strategic function. Successful performance is the product of quality of anticipatory decision making as well as motor skill (Chamberlain & Coelho, 1993). Many aspects of athletic decision making and performance must be routinized through predictive knowledge and repeated practice, because most actions have to be executed very quickly. Batters facing a baseball coming at them at 90 miles an hour must anticipate the likely pitch, predict it instantly from subtle pitching cues, and adjust the swing within a split second. They must do their thinking anticipatorily because there is no time for deliberation as the activity is being performed. Coaches amass detailed conditional probabilities of what pitchers are likely to toss in particular situations at particular times with particular batters and relay this information to their batters (Will, 1990). Pitchers are similarly provided with detailed predictive information about the strengths and limitations of the batters

they face and what type of pitch to deliver to a particular batter in a particular situation. In the elaborate communications throughout the contest itself, the contestants try to anticipate and exploit one another's strategies at each instant of play. In short, there is a lot of cognitive self-regulation of seemingly routinized skills.

Compared to novices, proficient players are better at picking early predictive cues from their opponents' behavior as to what is to come and adjust their action accordingly. The proficient ones are also more confident in their predictive judgments. The latter finding suggests that the cognitive side of athleticism is not just a matter of gaining predictive knowledge but of gaining the self-assurance to act on it unhesitatingly. Since players do not always guess right, self-doubts about their predictive capabilities can quickly creep in and negate its value. Athletes' perceived decisional efficacy is an area worthy of examination.

The automation of complex skills involves at least three major processes (Bandura, 1986a). The first process is mergerization. As familiarity with the activity is gained through understanding and repeated performance, segments of the skill are merged into progressively larger skills until eventually the skill becomes a fully integrated routine that no longer requires cognitive organization and linkage. The second process of automation is the production of contextual linkages. After dealing with the same situation repeatedly, performers eventually learn what works best in that highly predictable situation. Practiced actions are linked to recurrent contexts so that performers respond instantly to predictive situational cues without having to think about what to do. The third process in the automation of skills is a shift in the locus of attention from the execution of the action to its correlated results. Actions produce correlated observable effects that indicate what one is doing and suggest needed performance corrections. For example, tennis players monitor where their shots land and make the necessary corrective adjustments rather than attending to the details of their actions. They regulate their performances by tracking the kinesthetic feedback and correlated external results of their actions.

Cognitive Enactment

Cognitive simulation, in which individuals visualize themselves performing activities correctly, improves both the development and performance of motor skills. The gains are usually smaller than those produced by physical practice, however (Bandura, 1986a; Feltz & Landers, 1983). These positive findings undoubtedly underestimate the potential of cognitive enactment because of the skimpy way in which it is typically applied. Individuals are simply instructed to visualize themselves performing an activity with little or no guidance and training on how best to use this cognitive aid. Visualization is a cognitive skill that must be developed. Although measures of imagery skills leave much to be desired, evidence shows that individuals who happen to be good visualizers profit more from cognitive enactment than do poor visualizers. Not only are performers left to their own imagery devices, but even how often they use this aid is usually not assessed. As in other activities, executional success is a matter of self-belief as well as skill. Athletes need efficacy-affirmation evidence that they can exercise better control over their performance attainments with cognitive aids than without them. Those who have a low sense of efficacy to generate and control useful cognitive enactments will abandon the practice or use it haphazardly.

In athletic applications, adherence to visualization is generally low and is confined largely to good self-motivators who can get themselves to do it (Bull, 1991). Among elite athletes, those who rise to the top in tournaments not only make greater use of cognitive enactment but also do it more vividly and exercise better control over it than their less successful counterparts (Highlen & Bennett, 1983). The significant feature of the comparative tests is not that physical enactors outperform cognitive enactors, which would be expected, but that visualization can improve skill development and performance. There are many constraints on when one can practice physically, but skilled performances can be visualized repeatedly with no sweat at any time and place. Still, cognitive enactment is best used as an adjunct to, rather than a substitute for, actual practice.

Aggregated findings that disregard the multifaceted nature and diverse functions of visualization mask the factors that determine the effectiveness of cognitive enactments. The performance benefits of cognitive enactment depend on a number of factors. Knowledge of these determinants and their mechanisms of operation provides guidelines for boosting the impact of this cognitive aid on athletic development and functioning. The content and timing of such practices are especially important. There is little value to cognitive enactment in the early phase of learning before an adequate conception of the skilled activity has been formed. Skill learning is best promoted by first structuring the behavior cognitively and then perfecting it by physical and cognitive enactments (Carroll & Bandura, 1982; Richardson, 1967).

What people visualize during cognitive enactments affects skill development. Visualizing accurate enactments improves subsequent performances, whereas visualizing faulty ones impairs them (Murphy & Jowdy, 1992). The greater the experience and aptitude in the skill being perfected, the more people benefit from cognitive rehearsal (Corbin, 1972). Some prior experience is needed to form a conception of the skilled activity. Without a clear notion of what a good performance is like, one is at a loss to know what to rehearse cognitively or how to identify errors. In fact, with a deficient conception, there is high likelihood that many faulty habits will be cognitively rehearsed. The types of subskills called for in a given activity are another factor influencing the impact of cognitive enactment on the development of proficiency. As a rule, activities that have many cognitive aspects, as most complex performances do, benefit more and benefit more quickly from cognitive enactment than do those that involve mainly manual aspects (Feltz & Landers, 1983; Perry, 1939).

In addition to facilitating acquisition and retention of skills, preparatory cognitive enactment can enhance how well routinized skills are performed. Individuals who visualize themselves performing what they are about to do generally outperform those who do not use this cognitive aid (Richardson, 1967). Almost all elite athletes practice visualization before an event in an effort to optimize their performance (Ungerleider & Golding, 1991). There is some experimental evidence that visualizers do better than nonvisualizers. Such findings are needed to confirm that visualization is a contributing determinant rather than simply a concomitant of proficient performance.

Cognitive enactment can benefit the acquisition and execution of skills through a variety of mechanisms. One such mechanism is psychoneuromuscular. Cognitive enactments activate sensorymotor brain structures that regulate motor acts (Decety & Ingvar, 1990). Moreover, when people visualize themselves performing an activity, they exhibit electromyographic changes in the same muscle groups that would have been activated had they actually performed the activity (Ulrich, 1967). During skill development, muscular innervation by cognitive enactment may improve psychoneuromuscular organization of action patterns. The evidence is conflicting, however, on whether muscle innervation during imagery predicts performance changes. A second acquisitional mechanism is cognitive. It operates on the formation of symbolic representations of athletic skills. Like the informativeness of physical enactments, evident flaws or gaps in cognitive enactment can reveal what one does not know. Although sketchy visualizations cannot supply the unknown aspects, they can point to what one should look for in refining the cognitive representation.

Additional mechanisms come into play in enhancing skilled performance through preparatory cognitive rehearsal. Visualizing the execution of the performance primes the appropriate cognitive set and enactment strategies for the activity. Evidence that cognitive simulation increases heart and respiration rate suggests that it might prime one for action physiologically as well (Decety, Jeannerod, Durozard, & Baverel, 1993). Cognitive simulation also diverts attention from disruptive thoughts in stressful competitive situations to the routines one

is about to perform. Athletes are less likely to impair their performances if they can shut down self-debilitating thinking. Moreover, having people visualize themselves executing activities skillfully raises their perceived efficacy that they will be able to perform better. Such boosts in perceived efficacy improve performance. This is true for skills in coping with stressors (Bandura & Adams, 1977; Kazdin, 1979) as well as for physical skills (Clark, 1960; Feltz & Riessinger, 1990). Because preparatory visualizations of faulty performance impair subsequent performance, positive visualizations not only can enhance self-efficacy but can prevent efficacy-eroding effects by blocking negative imagery under game pressures that lead players to wonder whether they are as good as their opponents. When positive visualization operates through efficacy beliefs, the beliefs most likely enhance performance by reducing disruptive thinking and enlisting the effort needed to do well.

Cognitive enactment is being used increasingly both to perfect athletic skills and to apply them well by executing them cognitively just before performing athletic events. Testimonials abound that preparational cognitive enactments improve athletic performance. Although evidence from controlled studies is generally supportive of the beneficial effects, it is far from conclusive. As Suinn (1983) points out, cognitive enactment is only a tool. To achieve consistent benefits with it, one has to know what to rehearse cognitively. There are many facets of athletic skills that can be the focus of attention. The *cognitive* aspects of performance include such things as plans, strategies, and self-efficacious ideation. The *motor* aspects involve the regulation of the action patterns and the accompanying sensations. The *emotive* aspects center on stress management and the reduction of muscular tension. These various ingredients of a skill are likely to contribute differently to athletic performance, depending on the nature of the skills, their phase of development, and the level of competitive stressors. The experimental research attests to the benefits of cognitive enactment. The gains this cognitive tool provides in athletic applications, however, will depend on knowing how to develop skill in cognitive enactment and how to use it most effectively.

Comparative Tests of Modes of Motor Learning

Informative comparisons of different modes of motor learning are not as common as might be expected. Even though the rules and structure of athletic skills are almost universally conveyed at the outset through modeling, until recently comparative evaluation of different modes of learning has received relatively little attention in the field of motor learning. There are several reasons for this paradoxical neglect. In the view shared widely by investigators in this field, people learn by the results of their actions. The paradigms typically used to verify feedback regulation of actions are narrowly restricted to an isolated arm movement that must be executed at a given speed or to a given end location. By contrast, most motor skills involve complex structures in which multiple subskills must be spatially organized and temporally sequenced to achieve desired results. As previously noted, it would take an inordinate amount of time to learn the dynamic structure of complex skills by response feedback alone. Intricate skills can be symbolically constructed much faster by seeing the behavior modeled in an already integrated form than by trying to construct it gradually from observing the results of one's trial and error efforts (Bandura, 1986a).

Another possible reason for the late acknowledgment of the contribution of observational learning to the acquisition and refinement of motor skills is the provincialism of psychological inquiry. Theorizing and analyses of modeling effects and their mediating processes have focused heavily on social and cognitive skills. Yet the attentional, representational, and behavioral production subfunctions of observational learning apply equally to motor skills (Carroll & Bandura, 1990; McCullagh, 1993). Development of proficiency likewise involves a similar conception-matching process regardless of whether the referential standard involves

cognitive, social, or predominantly physical attainments. Because modeling theory did not evolve in the motor skills tradition, until recently it remained divorced from it. The legacy of behaviorism further promoted the view that one can learn only by the outcomes of trial and error.

Comparisons between feedback and modeling modes of modifying elementary arm movements additionally retarded adoption of a broadened view of how skills are best acquired. Such studies focus mainly on an isolated arm movement or a simple act that performers can already do but could do faster or better with a bit of practice. This type of research is concerned with motor control rather than with motor skill acquisition. Moving an arm a short distance hardly constitutes a skill, nor does one need modeled demonstrations of how to move an arm. In fact, there is little to be learned in such tasks. In addition to the simplicity of the acts, task instructions describe in detail what action to perform, and the apparatus further ordains it by severely constraining the options. The power of modeling to accelerate skill development is strikingly demonstrated in the mastery of novel, complexly patterned behavior that would require laborious effort to shape solely by response feedback (Carroll & Bandura, 1982).

A comprehensive conception of skill development does not pit feedback and modeling modes of learning against each other as if they were rival strategies. Rather, these modes serve complementary functions and vary in their importance at different phases of learning. Proficient modeling, either alone or with observers' innovative embellishments, is ideally suited for creating the guiding conception of the skill. Response feedback best serves as the vehicle for translating that knowledge into proficient performance. This is not to say that the benefits of modeling cease after a conception of the skill is formed in the earlier cognitive phases of learning. A comprehensive theory of skill acquisition expands the scope of feedback influences as well. In the case of intricate skills, corrective modeling of flawed elements is one of the most instructive forms of feedback. Thus, for example, in teaching aspiring violinists how to become better instrumentalists, master mentors correctively model how to play troublesome passages both technically and with greater emotional expressiveness. Students are not merely told to add some life to their spiritless play. They are shown how to do it.

Because of the allegiance to simple movements in research on motor skills, comparisons between feedback and modeling modes of skill development have not been enlightening. Research into factors that influence the effectiveness of modeling has given us a better sense of how to promote motor skill learning by this means (Bandura, 1986a). Some of these facilitating factors have already been reviewed, and others will be discussed in the sections that follow. Athletic skillfulness involves much more than mastering the mechanics of action patterns. The development of athletic skills should be conducted in ways that build the self-efficacy to withstand competitive stressors as well as build technical proficiency. As is true in other spheres of functioning, guided mastery modeling best fulfills this dual purpose. Feltz, Lander, and Raeder (1979) compared the relative effectiveness of different modeling techniques in promoting skill in springboard back diving. Guided mastery, combining modeling with guided enactment, instilled a stronger sense of efficacy and greater skillfulness than did live modeling or videotaped modeling. The latter two modeling procedures produced comparable gains in perceived self-efficacy and diving accuracy. Regardless of the mode of modeling, the stronger the efficacy belief, the better the subsequent performances.

Impact of Model Attributes on Self-Efficacy and Performance

The impact of athletic models varies depending on their characteristics. Among the influential factors, assumed similarity carries especially heavy weight. It is easier for individuals to persuade themselves of their physical abilities if they see people similar to themselves perform difficult physical feats than if they observe those of superior athletic ability. Thus, women with little athletic experience increase their

perceived physical efficacy and actual stamina after watching an allegedly nonathletic female model display high physical endurance (Gould & Weiss, 1981). But they derive no benefit, either in perceived efficacy or physical performance, from observing an allegedly athletic male model perform the same feat. Model similarity is more influential than whether the models engaged in positive or negative self-talk. Women are especially inclined to act on their beliefs of physical efficacy, however, if the models voice belief in themselves during their arduous performances. The sports videos that are commercially marketed neglect the benefits of assumed similarity and typically portray superstars exhibiting their matchless performances. Such videos are usually couched in the esoteric language of neuromuscular programming. Contrary to the extravagant claims, novices gain little if anything from such videos over and above what they have already learned about the form of the skill from numerous naturalistic observations (McCullagh, Noble, & Deakin, 1996).

The extent to which model characteristics exert influence on efficacy beliefs and performance will depend, in large part, on their relevance to the particular undertaking. Similarity of a relevant attribute is apt to be considered more indicative of one's own capabilities than similarity of an attribute that may have little bearing on the activity in question. Thus, in activities requiring physical stamina, the assumed athletic ability of the model carries greater weight than the sex of the model (George et al., 1992). Female novices exhibit a stronger sense of physical efficacy and greater physical endurance after exposure to modeled stamina by males or females described as nonathletes than they do by observing models described as varsity athletes. Of special interest is the power of a presumably superior athletic model to undermine the efficacy beliefs and performances of observers who are unsure about their capabilities. Evidence that upward comparison can have unwanted evaluative effects carries important training implications. Instructional use of talented models should highlight their value as sources of athletic knowledge and skills for improving one's capabilities. Accenting the instructional function while downplaying the comparative evaluative function can build a sense of athletic efficacy without risk of demoralization. Moreover, the devaluative potential of upward comparison is abated, if not eliminated, when understudies are confident of their efficacy to learn the skills being taught and turn to proficient models as aspirational mentors.

The characteristics of models affect observational learning mainly through their influence on associational preferences (Bandura, 1986a). Given a choice, individuals are likely to select models with similar attributes and ignore those with whom they have little in common. If dissimilar models are largely ignored, their particular skills will not be observed and learned. Tests of the influence of model characteristics may yield weak or misleading results under forced exposure where individuals have no choice but to observe the models presented to them. For example, if individuals are required to observe similar and dissimilar models for an equivalent time they may learn about as much from both. Of course, models vary in proficiency. Therefore, skilled models are more worthy of attention than less skilled ones. So a major factor governing choice of models is the assumed functional value of what they have to teach. Research by Lirgg and Feltz (1991) has bearing on some of these issues. Exposure to a model exhibiting useful motor skills boosted observers' efficacy beliefs and physical performance, whereas exposure to an unskilled model lowered perceived self-efficacy and produced deficient performances. Model skillfulness overrode attribute similarity in promoting both perceived efficacy and proficiency. A higher sense of efficacy was accompanied by more proficient performance.

The findings presented in the preceding sections indicate that perceived self-efficacy is one of the mechanisms through which modeling improves physical performance. This applies equally to self-modeling. Watching oneself on edited videotapes performing at one's best raises efficacy beliefs and improves athletic performance more than does traditional instruction (Scraba, 1990). Indeed, research by Gonzales and Dowrick (1982) reveals

that self-modeling may operate more through its motivational function than through its informative function. One group of billiard players saw themselves on videotape making proficient shots that pocketed the billiard balls; a second group saw themselves making mediocre shots that were made to appear successful by splicing bogus endings showing balls falling into pool-table pockets. The latter form of self-modeling was misinformative about the skill but persuasive about personal capabilities. Both the genuine and bogus self-modeling improved shot proficiency equally, whereas controls showed no change. Novices, who have reason to doubt their capabilities, benefited the most from the self-modeling of success, whether illusory or real.

Self-Efficacy Contribution to Acquisition of Motor Skills

The cognitive aspects of motor skill acquisition are now widely acknowledged. The primary interest in the cognitive contribution, however, has centered heavily on how skill knowledge guides development of behavioral proficiency. Motor learning and performance involve much more than mastering behavioral mechanics. Indeed, there are countless athletes who have the best of physical mechanics but quickly lose their effectiveness in tough situations because they cannot handle the pressure. Efficacy beliefs play an influential role both in the development of motor skills and in how well they are executed under different circumstances.

To begin with, belief in one's efficacy to master a complex physical skill determines whether an athletic activity is even considered, how much effort is invested in the undertaking if it is chosen, and the level of stick-to-itiveness when improvements are slow or fitful. Perceived inefficacy quickly thins athletic ranks. In other types of skills reviewed earlier, a strong sense of learning efficacy accelerates progress and thereby builds high perceived efficacy and skill in the particular domain of activity. This is equally true of complex physical skills. Ferrari and Bouffard-Bouchard (1992) examined the contribution of expertise and belief in one's efficacy to learn novel tai-chi style defensive actions involving intricate combinations of arm and leg movements. Karate students of high and low efficacy beliefs at each of three levels of expertise were given control of a videoplayer for a fixed period to learn the modeled complex actions in any way they preferred. They could reexamine all or certain parts of the modeled activities and alter the speed of the demonstrations to capture nuances and transitional moves. Karate experts learned more than did intermediates or novices. Belief in one's efficacy both to learn the action patterns and to execute them successfully, however, contributed independently to higher performance mastery after controlling for level of expertise. Karate experts benefited just as much from a high sense of learning efficacy as did the novices. When individuals are given control over their skill learning, as is usually the case in everyday life, they have greater leeway to act on their efficacy beliefs. Studies using constrained exposure, where individuals have to watch modeled portrayals but cannot pursue their own learning strategies, most likely underestimate the role of perceived learning efficacy in skill development.

Most people regard athletic skills as depending heavily on innate endowment. Aptitude is converted to mastery through perseverant effort rather than inborn programming. The self-limiting effects of viewing physical ability as an inherent aptitude are well documented experimentally. Students set out to perfect a psychomotor skill under an instilled belief that it was either acquirable through practice or that it reflected innate talent (Jourden et al., 1991). Construing psychomotor ability as an acquirable skill promoted growth of belief in one's physical efficacy and progressive improvement in the psychomotor skill (Fig. 9.1). Believing that skill development is subject to personal control additionally increased self-satisfaction with one's performances and created interest in the activity. In contrast, construing physical performance as diagnostic of inherent aptitude produced no rise in perceived self-efficacy beyond that gained from the initial practice experience. The performers acted as though they had reached the limits of their ability. Moreover, this view plateaued performers' perceived efficacy and left them discontented with their performances, disinterested in the activity, and arrested at a relatively low level of skill development.

The widespread effects of these different conceptions of physical ability were also revealed in the participants' spontaneous remarks at the conclusion of the experiment. Those who approached the activity as involving an acquirable skill commented

FIGURE 9.1. Change in (a) perceived self-efficacy and (b) improvement in psychomotor skill over repeated trials under conceptions of ability as an inherent aptitude or as an acquirable skill. Each phase consisted of two trials. The improvement in phase 1 represents the initial practice effort. Phases 2 and 3 depict the subsequent rate of improvement in psychomotor skill. (Jourden, Bandura, & Banfield, 1991)

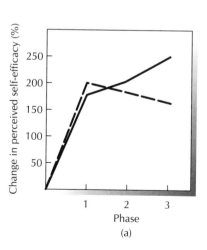

(a)

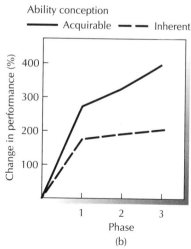

(b)

on their enjoyment of the challenge of the activity ("It was fun. I like it"), their continued interest in it ("I would like to try some more. I was getting real good at it"), their increased sense of capability ("I got pretty good"), and their ability to exercise personal control over their performance ("If you concentrate, you can get it"). In contrast, those who regarded the same activity as reflective of their inherent aptitude were more likely to express discouragement ("I tried harder and harder, and then I just gave up, especially when I got off target at the beginning of a try"), voiced their physical debility ("This really hurt my arm, and it was so tiring"), self-discontent ("I was dissatisfied"), difficulty with the task ("This was surprisingly hard"), inability to exercise control ("I thought that I'd do better, but I just couldn't"), and dispositional attributions of incapability ("I'm not very good at this sort of thing"). The benefits of focusing on self-development of capabilities are similarly revealed in research on involvement in competitive sports (Duda, 1988). Players who focus on self-improvement remain more involved in an athletic activity and practice more in their free time than do those who keep measuring their ability against the performances of others.

It should be noted that the construct of self-efficacy differs from the colloquial term *confidence*, which is widely used in sports psychology. Confidence is a nondescript term that refers to strength of belief but does not necessarily specify what the certainty is about. I can be supremely confident that I will fail at an endeavor. Perceived self-efficacy refers to belief in one's power to produce given levels of attainment. A self-efficacy assessment, therefore, includes both the affirmation of capability and the strength of that belief. Confidence is a catchword in sports rather than a construct embedded in a theoretical system. Advances in a field are best achieved by constructs that fully reflect the phenomena of interest and are rooted in a theory that specifies their determinants, mediating processes, and multiple effects. Theory-based constructs pay dividends in understanding and operational guidance. The terms used to characterize personal agency, therefore, represent more than merely lexical preferences.

Perceived athletic efficacy is a multifaceted belief system, not a unitary personality trait. Nor is it a product of a general disposition of confidence. Self-efficacy theory forces one to acknowledge athleticism as representing multiform capabilities rather than being a global entity. The incomparable Michael Jordan would regard himself as supremely efficacious to score baskets on basketball courts where he gained fame, but relatively inefficacious to hit home runs in baseball parks where he had faltered badly. The predictive deficiency of global indices of athletic efficacy is corroborated by McAuley and Gill (1983). Gymnasts' beliefs in their efficacy to execute different gymnastic feats predicted how well they performed in intercollegiate competition, whereas a general measure of perceived physical efficacy did not.

The field of sports psychology is heavily invested in personality trait measures. Such dispositional approaches not only cede predictive power but provide little guidance for how to structure training to cultivate athletic proficiency. Athletic competitiveness as a personality trait is a good case in point. In a test of comparative predictiveness, Lerner and Locke (1995) found that efficacy beliefs and personal goals contribute substantially to competitive physical performance, whereas athletic competitiveness is a much weaker predictor. When the influence of efficacy beliefs and goals is removed, athletic competitiveness loses what limited predictive weight it carried. In addition to the predictive benefits of sociocognitive determinants, one can target interventions to strengthen athletes' efficacy beliefs and goals, but one is left in foggy ambiguity about how to change personality "traits." Other trait measures, such as competitive anxiety and self-motivation, fare poorly as predictors of physical performance when the influence of efficacy beliefs is controlled. These findings will be presented later. The interventions derived from social cognitive theory are informed by knowledge of basic mechanisms of learning, self-motivation, and self-regulation.

SELF-REGULATION OF ATHLETIC PERFORMANCE

Cognitive Aspects of Athletic Ability

A common mistake is to judge ability by physical skills alone without considering efficacy to improvise them in managing ever-changing situations full of unpredictable and stressful elements. The influential role played by efficacy belief in regulating the execution of athletic skills is reflected in the astute observation of Billy Jean King, the tennis superstar, that "more matches are won internally than externally." The venerable Yogi Berra similarly underscored the cognitive aspects of athletic performance, though his mathematics leave much to be desired: "Baseball is ninety percent physical and the other half is mental." Enhancement of performance attainments requires attention to what athletes are doing cognitively as well as physically. We saw earlier that competitive success requires regulating one's actions anticipatorily on the basis of predictive cues. Self-assurance supports the strategic flexibility needed to achieve success. Insidious self-doubt can take a substantial toll on enactment of the best of skills. A hallmark of successful athletes is their ability to manage competitive stressors and setbacks with an unshakable sense of efficacy.

The annals of fleeting athletic careers are heavily populated with aspirants who possessed superior physical abilities but a fragile sense of efficacy. They quickly fell apart in times of trouble. Coaches look for resilient self-efficacy in their athletes, which is described in athletic circles as "mental toughness." For example, Mark Marquess, the distinguished baseball coach at Stanford, tests how his pitchers handle stressors as they "get knocked about a bit. Can he pitch in a pressure-game situation? Can he win when he doesn't have his good stuff?" A sturdy sense of efficacy sustains composure under pressure. Resilience is a vital attribute at the team level as well. Great teams have the efficacy to come from behind and win games when, for one reason or another, they are not playing at their best. The

emphasis on staying power in the face of high stressors has important implications for the experimental conditions under which self-efficacy determinants of athletic performances are investigated. It is easy to execute skills optimally under conditions devoid of uncertainties and stressors. Vulnerabilities to breakdown through a shaky sense of efficacy are best revealed in pressure situations.

The crucial role of perceived efficacy in athletic performance under high pressure is revealed in path analyses of determinants of wrestling performance in different phases of tournament matches (Kane, Marks, Zaccaro, & Blair, 1996). Athletes rated their efficacy for critical functions of wrestling such as performing takedowns and escaping from the bottom position. In preliminary matches, contestants with a vulnerable sense of efficacy could triumph over weaker opponents because the ability differential did not provide much of a challenge or threat. Wrestling ability, as reflected in athletic level and prior performance record, predicted competitive performance both directly and through the mediated effect of efficacy belief and personal goals (Fig. 9.2). The more prior success raises athlete's sense of efficacy, the higher the goals they set for themselves and the better they perform. It is an entirely different story in pressure-packed overtime matches where contestants are evenly matched and a mistake brings a sudden death defeat. Perceived efficacy emerges as the sole determinant of overtime performance.

These remarks are not meant to imply that perceived self-efficacy can substitute for physical talent. The relevant issue is codetermination of athletic performance. One must consider physical endowment, skill development, and resiliency of efficacy belief rather than pitting one type of contributing determinant against another. Athletic performances are the product of the reciprocal interplay of these various factors. Because human performances involve mixtures of physical endowment and experientially developed capabilities, dichotomous thinking that partitions determinants neatly into inherent and acquired forms is seriously misleading. Critics who say that confidence can take

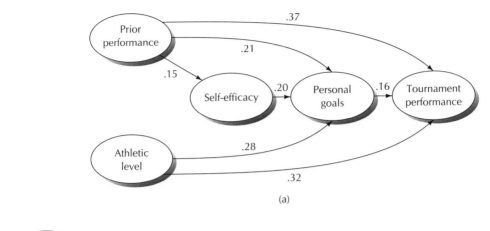

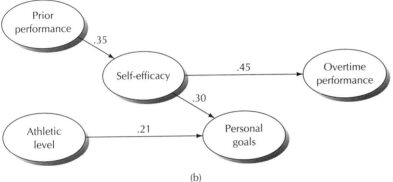

FIGURE 9.2. Role of perceived self-efficacy in the causal structure governing tournament performances (a) in preliminary matches and (b) in pressure-packed overtime matches. (After Kane et al., 1996)

you only so far are misinterpreting interactive causation as rival determinants supposedly operating in isolation. Where performers differ greatly in skill, the more able are likely to outperform the less able even if the execution is somewhat impaired cognitively. As already noted, however, the athletic survivors of severely competitive selection have the requisite talents, which they have converted into a high level of skill through laborious practice over a period of many years. One does not find the maladroit in the ranks of athletes. Any momentary mental lapse or disruptive intrusion can be one's downfall in a tight contest.

Athletic skills are not perfected at the outset. They require a prolonged period of development and refinement. During this developmental process, aspirants have to stick it out through tough times and never give up hope in the face of discouraging odds and all too often skeptical judgments as to whether

they have the talent to make it. It requires undaunted belief in one's efficacy to sustain the effort needed to convert potentiality into athletic proficiency. A baseball player who eventually became a stellar pitcher describes the sustaining motivational power of self-belief when he had to put up with repeated social discouragement: "There weren't many people out there who thought I could do it. I always thought I could. That's why I busted my butt. The day I believed I couldn't pitch in the big leagues was the day I would quit." During the years he was left behind to struggle in the minor leagues while his peers were enjoying success in the major leagues, he had little to go on but his belief in his athletic efficacy. What others thought did not deter him. To attribute the success of survivors mainly to physical talent is to take an unstudied short view of a complex process of self-selection and self-development regulated extensively by efficacy belief.

Belief in one's efficacy is no less important after athletic skills have been perfected. A capability is only as good as its execution. Where everyone is highly skilled, differences in efficacy to withstand competitive pressure can affect the adeptness of execution that spells the difference between victory and defeat. Neither talent nor cultivated subskills guarantee distinguished performance. What athletes do with what they know and what they have is partly determined by their sense of personal efficacy. It is difficult to perform well while wrestling with self-doubts about one's comparative ability. This is most evident when players have the necessary skills but lack the perceived efficacy to beat higher ranking opponents. An ascending young tennis player describes, rather graphically, the change in his comparative efficacy appraisal from conceding defeat at the outset of matches with strong opponents to affirming his competitive edge: "My biggest weakness is my head. I am starting to believe in myself to win over players I had previously only expected to get good scores against. Now I am thinking, 'Bullshit good score, I can win.'" His affirmative sense of efficacy spawned victories that formerly eluded him. Hard fought victories, in turn, do wonders for resilience of personal efficacy.

Level of perceived efficacy is the one psychological factor that most consistently differentiates successful from less successful elite athletes across a variety of sports (Highlen & Bennett, 1983; Mahoney, 1979). Weinberg and his colleagues corroborate experimentally the substantial competitive benefits of a firm sense of efficacy (Weinberg et al., 1979). In these studies, peoples' beliefs in their competitive efficacy are altered by surreptitiously predetermined victories or defeats regardless of the participants' actual capabilities. Competitors whose efficacy beliefs were illusorily raised in a contest of physical power outperformed their opponents in contests of physical stamina, whereas those whose efficacy beliefs were illusorily lowered fell easily to defeat (see Fig. 2.3). The lower the illusorily instated beliefs of physical efficacy, the weaker the competitive endurance in new physical contests. The power of efficacy belief over brawn is underscored further by evidence that beliefs of physical efficacy illusorily boosted in females and illusorily diminished in males obliterate large preexisting sex differences in physical stamina.

The findings of this experimental research also attest to the contribution of belief in personal efficacy to resilience against the adverse effects of defeat. Competitors whose efficacy beliefs were raised illusorily redoubled their efforts following defeat, whereas those whose efficacy beliefs were illusorily lowered suffered further deterioration in competitive performance following defeat. Were the contests to continue, the self-doubters would most likely exhibit progressive demoralization, whereas the self-believers would persevere in adaptive coping with setbacks. Even the mere sight of a formidable-looking opponent instills lower beliefs of competitive efficacy than does one who looks less impressive. As would be expected, preexisting efficacy beliefs have the greatest impact on initial competitive performance, whereas efficacy beliefs either raised or lowered by bogus feedback affect the subsequent course of competitive performance (Weinberg, Gould, Yukelson, & Jackson, 1981).

Shaky efficacy beliefs are most likely to set one up for failure under the pressure of face-to-face competition. Indeed, efficacy beliefs operate more powerfully under face-to-face competition than under back-to-back competition (Weinberg, Yukelson, & Jackson, 1980). It should be noted in passing that altering efficacy beliefs by bogus performance feedback is well suited for testing theoretical propositions about the regulatory power of self-belief. In such instances, the causative influence of efficacy belief on performance is clearly verified because the belief has no basis in actual capability and, therefore, cannot be dismissed as a reflection of it. In training practices, however, one would not use bogus feedback to build athletic proficiency. Rather, coaches should use modes of influence that genuinely cultivate both skills and a robust sense of efficacy. Each contributes to the quality of athletic performance.

Athletes of comparable abilities but different self-assurance do not perform at the same level. Gifted athletes plagued by self-doubts perform far below their potential, and less talented but highly self-assured athletes can outperform more talented competitors who distrust their capabilities. Many athletes with failed careers would be champions if they performed as well in contests as they did in training. Such discrepancies between capabilities and accomplishments underscore the influential contribution of efficacy beliefs to athletic adeptness. Competitive sports also reveal the fragility of perceived self-efficacy. A series of failures that can undermine belief in one's efficacy sends professional athletes into performance slumps. Because of self-misgivings, they do not execute their skills well even though they have perfected them and their very livelihood rests on their doing well.

Efficacy Beliefs in Performance Regulation by Goal Challenges

Goal challenges are ingrained in most athletic activities. In honing their skills, athletes typically set their sights at levels that surpass their prior attainments. In preparing for contests, the topmost attainments of opponents serve as the standards to beat. Personal challenges through goal setting contribute to athletic skill development and performance in several important ways (Bandura, 1986a; Locke & Latham, 1990). Challenging goals with firm self-assurance in the ability to fulfill them serve as strong motivators. In addition, subgoal attainments in the pursuit of excellence build a sense of athletic efficacy and foster interest in the activity. The motivational and efficacy effects of adopting and realizing goal challenges are well illustrated in the reports of elite athletes. As Tom Watson, a leading professional golfer, once described it, "I'm goal-oriented. I am not satisfied with what I've accomplished. I want to be better than I was last year. That (British Open victory) showed me I could win a major tournament. And it certainly magnified my confidence. Before I won the British Open, I would play poorly and it would affect me. Now I have the confidence not to let a poor round bother me."

Significant advances in sports psychology require experimental analyses of the regulatory processes reflected in anecdotal reports and correlational findings. Considerable research cited earlier provides strong and consistent support for the beneficial effects of goal setting. In extending this knowledge to athletic pursuits, Locke and Latham (1985) offer explicit guidelines for how to structure goal systems to achieve good results. Despite the evident benefits of challenging standards in other spheres of functioning, experimental tests of different aspects of goal theory in physical performance have yielded some mixed results. The sports literature conveys the impression that the benefits of goals in athletic performance have yet to be demonstrated. In fact, a meta-analysis of research by Kyllo and Landers (1995) reveals that goal setting improves athletic and exercise performances. As in other domains of functioning, combining proximal with long-term goals has sizable performance benefits, whereas long-term goals alone have no effect. Moderate goals enhance performance attainments. Neither easy goals nor very difficult ones that are likely to be rejected exert any influence.

Locke (1991b) identifies a number of factors that diminish or mask the effects of assigned goals on athletic performance. Motivation and performance are regulated by the personal goals individuals set for themselves rather than by those that others might hold for them. Some participants may have little investment in the physical activities experimenters use in their studies, especially when doing well brings fatigue and pain and mediocre performances carry no particular consequences. There is little incentive to adopt goals requiring hard work when there are no benefits to doing so and self-esteem is not at stake. In contrast, athletes invest a great deal of their personal satisfaction in their performances. Self-respect operates as a powerful self-motivator. The stellar wide receiver Gene Washington provides but one example of how athletes motivate themselves through self-evaluative aspiration: "Before each season I set certain goals for myself. They are tough ones. If I attain them then I feel I have been doing my job to the best of my ability. It gives me a great sense of satisfaction." If socially imposed goals are not accepted, they are irrelevant to the performances being studied.

When people perform activities without assigned goals but receive feedback of how they are doing, good self-motivators spontaneously set goal challenges for themselves (Bandura & Cervone, 1983; Weinberg, Bruya, Longino, & Jackson, 1988). The higher the self-set goals, the better the performance (Bandura, 1991b). Similarly, when assigned long-term goals, many performers adopt for themselves short-term ones that provide better incentives and guides for their current performances. Unbidden goal setting is especially likely when activities are structured competitively. Surpassing an opponent's level of performance becomes the personal goal for which to strive. Spontaneous goal setting converts allegedly goalless performers into goal-directed ones. Therefore, when the standards set by others do not jibe with the ones performers set for themselves, focus on socially assigned goals rather than on the personally adopted ones will yield misleading results and the erroneous conclusion that goals are not motivators in athletic pursuits.

In most studies that find no goal effects, it is not that goals fail to predict performance but that experimenters fail to prevent performers in control conditions from setting goals for themselves. Goal theory applies to the personal goals performers seek to fulfill, not to those others want them to follow. The validity of goal theory would be called into question if personal goals were unrelated to performance. In accord with goal theory, performance attainments are better predicted by personal goals than by assigned ones (Lerner & Locke, 1995). Regardless of what types of goals are assigned, the impact of competition on performance is extensively mediated through contestants' efficacy beliefs and the goals they set for themselves. The benefits of assigned goals become more evident when external inducements to set goals on one's own, such as competition or knowing how well others performed, are reduced (Hall & Byrne, 1988).

Evidence that people spontaneously set goals for themselves does not necessarily mean they all do it well. If they adopt challenging goals, they achieve higher performances than if they adopt easy ones. If they set their sights unrealistically high, they can demoralize themselves through repeated failure. If they set their goals distally without subgoals to get them there, they are unlikely to achieve much. Like other self-management skills, athletes must be taught how to set optimal goals and how to readjust them to their rate of improvement so that they motivate rather than debilitate themselves by their performance standards. Such training entails more than simply instructing them in how to set their sights for self-improvement. It requires monitoring their goal setting and providing corrective feedback when their steps are too large, too small, or too distal. Moreover, they need help on how to cope with discouragement when their efforts fall short of the gains they seek. It is at such times that athletes require the most guidance about what they demand of themselves.

The form goals take affects their motivating potential. Performers are not much stirred by goals that are vague, easy to fulfill, or remote. Lofty distal goals are fine for inspiration, but it is unwavering commitment to achievable subgoals that are hierarchically organized that gets one there. In preparing for the Olympics, John Naber estimated that he would have to shave four seconds off his best swimming time to win a gold medal. He described his strategy for realizing this enormous challenge as follows: "It's a substantial chunk. But because it's a goal, now I can decisively figure out how I can attack that" (Locke & Latham, 1985). He broke this time goal down into small, achievable steps and by this means trained himself into a gold medalist. The advantage of approaching lofty goals proximally is corroborated in formal tests of physical endurance (Tenenbaum, Pinchas, Elbaz, Bar-Eli, & Weinberg, 1991). Performers who pursued proximal goals leading to distal ones achieved a higher rate of improvement than those who focused solely on proximal goals, focused solely on distal ones, or were simply encouraged to do their best. Proximal challenge serves to optimize effort during contests as well. Cross-country skiing is the most grueling Olympic winter sport. Bjorkheim, the Norwegian superstar, describes his use of proximal focus as an ongoing self-motivating device: "I look ahead, maybe to the top of a rise and tell myself that it is near the end of the course. When I get there, I look ahead and again make believe. It usually keeps me going at my best speed."

Goals without knowing how one is doing provide little basis for regulating effort or altering strategies. For example, aspiring basketball players who could not see where their shots go would be at a loss to know what adjustments to make in the force and trajectory of their shots to realize the goals toward which they are striving. Goals alone may produce an initial spurt in performance but little or no gain thereafter (Bandura, 1991b). In contrast, goals with response feedback promote continuing gains in performance that surpass those produced by goals alone or feedback alone. This is why applications of goals under performance ambiguity yield equivocal results.

In most individual sports, the performance feedback, such as the speed of a sprint, the height of a jump, or the distance of a javelin throw, is explicitly calibrated. This makes it easy to cast the activity into quantitative goals. Team sports present a greater challenge in how to set goals and frame the feedback. This is because players serve several interdependent functions. Team attainments depend on how well players perform their individual functions and work together to produce results. Team goals, therefore, must target the level of collective performance as well as the performances of individual players. It is often said that people improve what gets measured. Goals provide the best guidance when they address separately the key skills for success. For example, Lute Olson, who builds championship basketball teams wherever he coaches, rates each player in each game on individual and coordinated performances essential for team success (Gill, 1984). The skill is broken down into the percentage of successful field goals and free throws and the number of rebounds, assists, blocked shots, personal fouls, steals, and turnovers per game. Each of these aspects lends itself to quantitative goals of improvement. Enhancement of essential performances by individualized goal setting harvests more team victories (Anderson, Crowell, Doman, & Howard, 1988).

We saw earlier that self-regulation of motivation and performance through goal aspiration relies

extensively on supporting self-influences. Therefore, to fully understand what goals can do and how they work requires analyses of the interplay of self-reactive codeterminants. In studies simulating taxing physical activities, performers achieve greater physical endurance with challenging goals than without them (Bandura & Cervone, 1983, 1986). The longer they continue building their physical stamina and athletic skills, the more goal-setters surpass their counterparts without goal assignments (Weinberg et al., 1988; Yin, Simons, & Callaghan, 1989). Virtually all of the research on athletic goal setting has focused on individual rather than team goals. Lee (1988) reports some evidence that teams that set explicit challenging goals outperform those that do not. Both team goals and strength of players' efficacy beliefs contribute to team performance.

It is easy to stick to goals when successes come readily. But it is difficult to remain wedded to arduous goals when failures, setbacks, and long stretches of no improvement make such challenges appear beyond reach. Efficacy beliefs help to fortify the sustaining power of goals under such dissuading conditions. Thus, performers who maintain firm belief in their efficacy in the face of failure redouble their efforts to realize the tough goals they have set for themselves, whereas those who harbor growing doubts about their capabilities lower their sights and slacken their efforts (Bandura & Cervone, 1986). Efficacy beliefs and personal goals also operate as codeterminants of physical performance after individuals achieve high success and must decide whether to work hard in the pursuit of an even higher performance vision. Those of high efficacy raise their aspirations and performance attainments; those of moderate efficacy are content to rest on their laurels; and those who doubt they can duplicate their hard-won success lower their aspirations and performance motivation.

Perceived Efficacy in Management of Competitive Stress and High Risks

Athletic activities include many stressful elements. Some sports, of course, carry risks of physical injury that give cause for apprehension. A slip during a backward flip on a balance beam, for example, can produce a lot of physical damage. Players vary in how much they dwell on possible injurious mishaps. Severe competitiveness linked to status and monetary consequences is an unremitting source of apprehension. Many talented players vie for a preciously small number of positions at the professional level. Comparative performances among teammates determine how fast athletes rise through the ranks, whether they make it to the top, how long they stay there, and how quickly they get demoted. These changes in status have important impacts on athletes' very livelihood. Athletic performances that fall short of personal and team standards diminish social status in the eyes of one's teammates, coaches, and others. Last, but not least, athletes have to contend with self-devaluation for deficient performances. Jimmy Connors describes how self-evaluation is both a powerful motivator and potential stressor in competitive sports: "Money is not a big enough motivation when the chips are down. Personal pride and personal satisfaction are far stronger motives. So I am preparing for Wimbledon because my pride and satisfaction will be to win Wimbledon a second time and join Laver and Newcombe and Fred Perry in that special class of player who has won Wimbledon twice." Concern over what others think and what one thinks of oneself can be a competitive stressor. Chapter 8 specifies the conditions under which stringent standards operate as stressors through evaluative self-reaction.

The relationship between anxiety and athletic performance is one of the most widely discussed issues in sport psychology but the most difficult to pin down (Gould & Krane, 1992). In conceptual analyses, what begins as anxiety quickly fades into general arousal, psychic energy, or mental alertness or gets carved up into foreboding thoughts, somatic activity, and tense behavior. Despite innumerable studies, the empirical issue remains just as unsettled as the conceptual one. Anxiety over athletic activities is often attributed to trait anxiety. Competitive situations presumably activate the personality trait, which then arouses anxiety that impairs performance. In social cognitive theory, both anxiety

and impaired performance are coeffects of a low sense of efficacy to meet competitive demands. Self-assured athletes tend to concentrate on what they need to do to push the limits of their capabilities. They accept risks as part of the price of achieving distinguished performances. In contrast, the less assured are more inclined to dwell on injurious risks, the formidableness of competitors, and the personal and social price of defeat.

Leland (1983) compared the relative power of perceived self-efficacy and competitive trait anxiety in predicting precompetition anxiety in basketball players. They were tested for dispositional anxiety about athletic contests and their perceived ability to execute different aspects of the game. These aspects covered ball-handling, outside and free throw shooting, rebounding, guarding, passing, and the ability to execute different styles of defense. In addition, the study included a host of experiential and situational predictors: players' competitive experience, their position on the team, the formidableness of the opponents and expectations about their competitive play, the importance of the game, the outcome of the prior game, and the expected crowd size. In a stepwise multiple regression analysis, perceived self-efficacy emerged from this large pool of factors as the major predictor, accounting for 40 percent of the variance in precompetition anxiety. Competitive trait anxiety accounted for 6 percent of the variation in anxiety prior to the contest. These findings further corroborate that human functioning is better predicted by multifaceted efficacy beliefs than by a global personality trait.

Recall from Chapter 4 that perceived efficacy regulates stress and anxiety through beliefs about personal control of action, thought, and affect. In the action-oriented approach, stress and anxiety are alleviated by strengthening perceived competitive capabilities through development of athletic skills. The preceding study, for example, centered on anxiety rooted in perceived performance inefficacy. The thought-oriented approach, which will be discussed more fully shortly, centers on perceived cognitive ability to control perturbing, intrusive trains of thought. Athletes become distressed over their inefficacy to control unwanted thoughts that disrupt their performances. Stress management through efficacy beliefs that center on performance capabilities and thought control serve mainly to prevent stressful activation. The affect-oriented approach seeks to raise perceived efficacy to ameliorate stress once it is aroused. Ameliorative efficacy reflects belief in one's ability to alleviate stress and anxiety by positive reappraisal of stressors, muscular relaxation, calming self-talk, shifting attention from stressors to soothers, and seeking social support. Athletes who have a low sense of efficacy to manage stress by psychosocial means are at risk of turning to drugs and alcohol for relief.

Another common assumption in sports psychology is that anxiety arousal debilitates athletic performance. Therefore, much attention is devoted to reducing anxiety. There is little evidence for such direct causation. Whatever effects physiological arousal might have are likely to depend more on how much attention is paid to it and whether it is interpreted as being psyched up or as being distressed. Research on divers by Feltz and her colleagues speaks to this issue (Feltz, Albrecht, 1986; Feltz & Mugno. 1983). Level of autonomic arousal was related neither to efficacy beliefs nor to diving performances. Although perceived autonomic arousal was related to efficacy beliefs, it did not predict performance. To the extent that perceived arousal affects performance, it does so indirectly through the influence of efficacy belief.

Tests of causality in nonathletic spheres of functioning show that efficacy beliefs influence both anxiety and quality of performance but that anxiety generally does not contribute independently to performance. McAuley (1985) has shown this to be the case in athletic performance as well. He examined alternative mechanisms through which proficient modeling improves gymnastic performance. Belief in one's gymnastic efficacy was an important determinant of performance, whereas level of experienced anxiety was unrelated to it. The competitive fleetness of distance runners is similarly predicted by efficacy belief but not by anxiety level (LaGuardia & Labbé, 1993; Martin & Gill, 1991). This pattern of results

suggests that efficacy beliefs enhance athletic performance mainly by affecting motivation and thought processes.

The preoccupation with anxiety stifles interest in the role that affect plays in athletic functioning. The literature in this field would lead one to believe that athletes experience nothing but aversive affect. Competing against tough rivals is, of course, emotionally arousing. But whether that arousal is read as energizing challenge or debilitating anxiety depends, in large part, on perceived efficacy to meet the competitive demands. In a study of efficacy and affect in athletic contests, Treasure, Monson, and Cox (1996) show that athletes also experience the exhilaration of challenge and that it makes a difference in their performance. Wrestlers who were assured in their efficacy experienced positive emotional reactions rather than anxiety just prior to competition. Perceived efficacy contributed substantially to competitive performance, but positive affect also made a small significant contribution. By contrast, anxiety bore no relation to competitive performance.

Chronic stress is often said to produce athletic burnout. Youngsters on a meteoric rise in professional tennis suddenly vanish from the scene under the intense competitive strain. Some distinguished players and coaches quit at the height of their careers because they feel emotionally drained and no longer gain any enjoyment from what they are doing (Dale & Weinberg, 1990). Other athletes hang on with cynical, spiritless play. This syndrome is usually explained in terms of the exhausting affects of chronic physiological activation by an unremitting overload of demands in competitive sports. A comprehensive theory must explain positive as well as negative adaptations to athletic stressors. After all, many players thrive under competitive pressure, continue to set new challenges for themselves, and find satisfaction in plying their trade to the best of their ability throughout their careers. We have seen that perceived efficacy is an important predictor of vulnerability to burnout in other pursuits (Chwalisz et al., 1992). Individuals of high perceived efficacy find constructive ways of handling chronic stressors; those of low efficacy resort to escapist modes of coping that only create more strain and distress. There is every indication that chronic athletic stressors work, in part, through perceived coping inefficacy in fostering burnout in sports.

Many athletic activities — such as auto racing, solo rock climbing, skiing on steep faces, low-altitude aerobatics, and skydiving — involve high physical risk. Pursuit of such activities is often attributed to sensation or thrill seeking. If it were simply a matter of thrill seeking, precious few of the extreme risk takers would survive. Slanger and Rudestam (1996) examined possible determinants of extreme and conventional risk taking in four sports: rock climbing, skiing, white water kyacking, and small plane racing and aerobatics. They found that perceived self-efficacy rather than thrill seeking separates extreme risk takers from high risk takers. The extreme risk takers felt highly secure in their efficacy to execute the activities successfully and were well prepared and willing to take the calculated risks. Neither individual differences in thrill and adventure seeking, attitudes toward death, nor sensitizing and repressive reactions to threats differentiated the two groups. It is the sense of mastery, passionately pursued, rather than mere thrill seeking, that is the motivating force. Nor did generalized measures of life efficacy or physical efficacy differentiate extreme and conventional risk takers. Evidence that athletes act on a domain-linked efficacy disposition rather than a general efficacy disposition accords with the common observation that auto racers and test pilots are quite cautious in how they drive their automobiles in daily life. The combination of superior proficiency with unwavering self-assurance built through intensive training lowers the level of risk. The romanticized stereotype of daredevil thrill seekers disregards the arduous and endless preparation required to survive activities fraught with grave physical dangers.

Thought Control Efficacy in Managing Stressors, Failures, and Slumps

Self-efficacy in the exercise of thought control is also a crucial determinant of athletic performance. Consummate athletic survivors have remarkable efficacy to block out distractions and to control disruptive negative thinking (Highlen & Bennett, 1983). Here is a relief pitcher describing his complete attentional focus on his immediate pitching task as he is brought in to quell a rally with a crucial game on the line: "I try not to worry about who's at bat, who's on base, who's up next, or what the score is." Instead, it is the next pitch that commands his full attention. As a further example, consider the concentrative efficacy of an extraordinary slugger: "I block out everything but being at the plate. It's just me and the pitcher. I'm that locked into the pitcher." It requires supreme confidence in one's capabilities to remain so task focused in high-pressure situations. Those who distrust their capabilities are likely to find themselves thinking about what is at stake and the grave consequences of fouling up.

Athletes must develop the efficacy to cope adaptively with failure because it is visited upon them unmercifully often. For example, the batting successes of even the most proficient baseball players are not much above the .300 level. This means that 70 percent of their tries end in failure. Fickle fans expect them to come through in a clutch each time they are at bat. If they fail to do so in crucial situations, the fans quickly turn on them. But much of the distress over failure is usually self-inflicted. Elite athletes drive themselves to success through stringent self-standards. To the extent that they tie their self-evaluation to standards of athletic excellence, they can be cruelest to themselves when their performance falls short in crucial situations. They dwell on their failures rather than savor their successes.

All players make mistakes from time to time. Mistakes and defeats create cognitive carryover problems with which athletes must constantly struggle. They have difficulty ridding themselves of distressing thoughts, so they carry them over to subsequent performances. They bring their psychic troubles home rather than leaving them behind. The cognitive control task is to stop rumination over a mistake or failure, which is likely to breed only further mistakes. As noted before, efforts to control unwanted thoughts by suppressing them can backfire because such attempts only draw attention to them or create reminders of them. People can better rid themselves of disruptive thinking by concentrating their attention on the task at hand and generating helpful thinking. Great players thrive on competitive challenges. For example, Joe Montana, the remarkably poised quarterback whose late-game heroics made comeback victories look ordinary, thought only about how he was going to get the job done in intense pressure situations. He never wavered in his belief that he could pull off a victory as he methodically picked apart his opponents. Because of the intense pressure of athletic competitiveness, development of efficacy in self-management of thought processes is vital to success.

Proficient athletes have the efficacy to put mistakes behind them and to continue as though they had never happened. In so doing, they do not let errors distress them or impair their future performances. Among elite athletes competing for a place on their national team, qualifiers achieve better recovery from mistakes made earlier in the events by giving them less thought than do nonqualifiers (Highlen & Bennett, 1983). Weak efficacy in the exercise of cognitive control heightens vulnerability to disintegrative response to adverse events. When they get in a jam, athletes with shaky self-efficacy get down on themselves, brood over their mistakes, and conjure up scenarios with all kinds of disastrous consequences. A low sense of efficacy feeds on itself in a downward reciprocal cycle of self-doubt and deteriorating performance. An insightful baseball catcher once described vividly this self-debilitating process when he noted that a batting slump begins at the bat, goes to the head, and ends in a chronically upset stomach.

Even otherwise hardy athletes are not immune to occasional slumps, which are characterized by a sustained collapse in performance. Whatever their origins, they instill self-doubt that then feeds on itself disruptively. By construing performance difficulties as simply unlucky aberrations, efficacy belief serves as a protective factor against slumps or their prolongation. Self-efficacious athletes do not exacerbate the performance problem by disruptive emotional reactions and interfering thought patterns. Rather, they dissociate each new attempt from how

they performed before and approach it anew with a task-oriented focus. Coaches attempt to eliminate the negative carryover effects of failure through cognitive disconnection that gets players to focus on one contest at a time and to treat every trial as a fresh start. Such cognitive restructuring shifts attention from cumulative failure to effective strategies for current performance. They try to help players regain their sense of efficacy by attributing their slump to some minor fault in the mechanics of execution, which hopefully will persuade them that all is well again. Another recovery strategy is to relax performance standards so that progress toward, rather than attainment of, restored form is viewed as success. Thus, players in batting slumps are told that they are on the road to recovery if they make good contact with the ball even though the placement and power of their hits fail to get them on base (Taylor, 1988). The favorite strategy for restoring efficacy is to prescribe a short rest with the expectation that it will help players shake their slump. Barring physical impairment, the benefits of a brief rest probably stem more from expectational changes than from inactivity or the temporary removal from the situational pressures.

Evaluation of slump interventions requires rigorous experimental analysis. Regression effects alone would predict that atypically low performances would be followed by better ones. Since everything that could go wrong to impair performance is unlikely to repeat itself in the short run, performance is apt to improve from a severe slump without any intervention. Consultants who are brought in at the lowest point in a downward slide may capitalize on regression effects and get credited as slump curers. Given the natural likelihood of an upward change in performance, almost any slump intervention is likely to raise efficacy beliefs, which, in turn, enhance the rate and level of performance recovery. Conquering a slump is not entirely an individual matter. In a later discussion, we will see that coaches' reactions can neutralize the negative impact of slumps or deepen and prolong them.

The severest test of efficacy in managing competitive stressors occurs in the Olympics. Here, a lifetime of labor comes down to a momentary performance against supreme competitors before a worldwide audience. To make matters worse, the stakes have been escalated to incredibly high levels. Competitors subordinate their lives and the lives of those around them to perfecting a particular athletic routine. With contests occurring only quadrennially, a small misstep forecloses the only lifetime opportunity for many athletes and four more years of arduous preparation for hopeful repeaters. A great deal is expected of Olympians. They have not only the overwhelming task of fulfilling personal, team, and media expectations but also that of shouldering their nation's aspirations.

Evaluative standards have been warped to the point where any medal short of gold takes on the aura of a letdown or personal failing that can haunt athletes for years to come. Where gold is the measure of success, the Olympics ironically become an exercise in failure for the most talented contestants. The loftier the expectations, the heavier the price in self-devaluation and national disappointment for bagging only a silver or bronze. Some silver medalists who treat their extraordinary attainment as a defeat are consoled by their peers for the "loss." Indeed, Olympic bronze medalists, who are content with at least winning a medal, are generally happier than silver medalists who torture themselves for having just missed the coveted gold (Medvec, Madey, & Gilovich, 1995). Efficacy belief, however, partly determines affective reaction to competitive placement. A competitor with supreme confidence of capturing the gold medal would hardly be ecstatic with bronze. One bronze medalist even refused to accept his medal. For the elitest of the elite, commercial considerations come to overshadow the manifest purpose of this quadrennial fest. Neither silver nor bronze beget the lucrative endorsements that come with gold-medal fame. Those who triumph under such unmerciful stressors have an extraordinary sense of efficacy to manage the mental aspects of competitive performance. It is not uncommon for heavily favored world champions to fade or turn in disastrous performances in pressure-packed Olympic competitions.

Self-Management of Pain and Recovery from Injury

The preceding discussion centered on the performance benefits of cognitive control of disruptive intrusive thinking. There is another important way in which exercise of control over one's own consciousness can contribute to athletic attainments. Because of the physical strains and painful contacts imposed by athletic activities, players must perform with aches, pains, and bruises; otherwise, they would spend most of their time in recuperative inaction. Athletes do not come equipped with fewer or less sensitive pain receptors than nonathletes. Nor does their physical conditioning insulate them from pain. They have to learn how to play through fatigue and pain. This does not mean playing with injury or disregarding serious pain signals, but rather playing with the soreness and aches that are part and parcel of any strenuous physical activity. Dwelling on physical discomfort detracts from effective performance. The way in which pain competes with concentration on the task demands of a game is illustrated in the comments of a pitcher who pitched an outstanding championship game while plagued with a sore hamstring: "It held up pretty well. I was able to concentrate not on my leg but on what I needed to do." He began tentatively but became oblivious to his hamstring as he devoted his sole attention to the challenges of the crucial game.

Pain can be attenuated by activation of endogenous opiates that block neural transmission of pain impulses or by cognitive activities that displace pain sensations from consciousness or alter their aversiveness. Stress, which is endemic to highly competitive athletics, activates the opiate system. Stress-activated opioids may reduce pain sensations but do not eliminate them (Bandura et al., 1988; Janal, Colt, Clark, & Glusman, 1984). If aversive sensations are supplanted in consciousness or are construed benignly (Cioffi, 1991a), they become less noticeable and less distressingly intrusive. Research reviewed earlier shows that belief that pain is controllable to some extent makes it easier to manage (Bandura, 1991a). A variety of techniques help to relieve pain. They include muscular relaxation, positive imagery, cognitive refocusing of attention from pain sensations to things of interest, and thinking differently about bodily sensations. The ameliorative effects of such pain control techniques operate partly through changes in perceived self-efficacy (Bandura et al., 1987; Dolce, 1987; Holman & Lorig, 1992). The stronger the instated perceived coping efficacy, the higher the pain tolerance and the less dysfunction pain produces.

Efficacy beliefs also enter into other aspects of recovery from physical injury. Restoration of function after an injury requires toilsome hours at graded activity programs. During this time, individuals have to struggle with tedium, pain, and discouragement over slow improvement. Management of the recovery process, therefore, requires setting interim goals to keep athletes moving ahead through satisfaction with the continual progress being made. Trying to do too much too early will only beget setbacks and despondency. A large body of evidence will be presented later showing that those who have a strong sense of self-regulatory efficacy are good adherers to rehabilitative routines. Good self-management hastens improvement. But there is more to recovery than getting physically fit. The issue of efficacy restoration also arises in recovery from temporary injuries. Skills can rapidly decline through disuse. The physical injury mends, but nagging self-doubts about existing capabilities may linger to mar performance long after physical functions have been fully regained.

The effects of pain on performance are by no means confined to the individuals experiencing it. Their reactions can also affect how those around them cope with pain. In studies of modeling influences on self-management of pain, the amount of distress models display while experiencing pain alters observers' sensory sensitivity to, and tolerance of, pain (Craig, 1978, 1983). Observers exposed to forbearing models endure high levels of aversive stimuli before experiencing them as painful, whereas observers exposed to models displaying low pain tolerance find even weak aversive stimuli painful. The altered sensitivities to painful events remain long after the modeling influence is over. On physiological

indicators of discomfort, observers of forbearing models can endure larger increases in aversive stimuli without suffering greater visceral distress than can those exposed to easily afflicted models (Craig & Neidermayer, 1974). The combined findings of Craig's research indicate that modeling affects not only the subjective experience of pain but also sensory sensitivity to painful stimulation and physiological systems that are implicated in pain.

Modeled pain tolerance also affects the ability to perform demanding tasks under pain. People who have seen models persevere under pain work much longer and are more productive when they themselves are in pain than they do if they have seen models give up quickly (Turkat & Guise, 1983; Turkat et al., 1983). Styles of pain management may have early origins. Children's ability to cope with chronic clinical pain is shaped by parents' modeling of pain coping styles (Turkat, 1982).

In the athletic sphere, where most players are plagued by aches and pains in one form or another, the modeling of pain management is ever present. Indeed, some teams look like the walking wounded. Players are often torn between safeguarding their health and contributing to the team effort by playing through pain. Because pain has few objective indicants, there is much subjectivity about the severity of pain a given player is experiencing at any given time. Teammates do not take kindly to fellow players they judge to be malingering or are quick to seek exemption from play for physical reasons. At the other extreme are the fierce competitors recovering from injuries who keep insisting on being reinstated prematurely, especially if their replacements look too good. Media commentators extol athletes' stoicism in the face of high levels of pain as though it were a virtue rather than a risk for more severe injury.

Self-Efficacy Enhancement of Athletic Performance

Some progress has been made in documenting the relation of efficacy beliefs to various types of athletic performances at the individual level. These studies cover a wide range of athletic activities including tennis, gymnastics, diving, basketball, and distance running (Barling & Abel, 1983; Feltz, 1988a; Feltz & Albrecht, 1985; Martin & Gill, 1991; McAuley & Gill, 1983; Morelli & Martin, 1982). A high sense of efficacy in the activity domain is accompanied by low precompetition stress and high athletic performance. Laboratory studies in which efficacy beliefs are raised or lowered experimentally corroborate the causal contribution of efficacy beliefs to motor performance under both competitive conditions (Weinberg, 1986; Weinberg et al., 1979; Weinberg et al., 1981; Weinberg et al., 1980) and noncompetitive ones (Gould & Weiss, 1981; McAuley, 1985). Instilled high perceived efficacy enhances motor performance and reduces vulnerability to the adverse effects of defeat.

The issue of past performance in causal analyses warrants brief comment. In studies in which individuals perform the same routine in rapid succession, efficacy beliefs contribute independently to performance, but adding prior performance increases the predictiveness of subsequent performance (Feltz, 1982, 1988b). The aim of experimental inquiry in the sports field is to verify the determinants governing athletic performance. It bears repeating that performance is not a cause of performance. Performances will correlate with one another to the extent that their determinants are the same on the different occasions. As long as the underlying determinants remain unspecified, knowing that prior performance predicts subsequent performance says nothing about causation. To advance understanding of psychosocial contributors to athletic performance requires systematic analysis of its multiple determinants. Such analysis is achieved by extracting the various sociocognitive determinants from the conglomerate set that governs performance and assessing their relative contribution. These determinants include perceived self-efficacy, goal aspirations, expected outcomes, perceived constraints, and the like. The more determinants that are removed from the conglomerate, the greater the predictive shrinkage of past performance as it

becomes the proxy residue of fewer and fewer remaining determinants. In short, analysis of causation requires a shift of attention from performance as a determinant of itself to the actual determinants of performance.

Under some conditions, prior performance is an inflated predictor of itself. One such condition occurs when a known nonability contributor to performance is not extracted in multivariate analyses from the set of contributors to performance of which it is a part. For example, efficacy beliefs influence how well people perform at the outset. The contribution of efficacy belief to subsequent performance will be artifactually reduced when variation in prior performance is statistically controlled without removing the part of that performance variation attributable to efficacy belief. In such analyses, one is controlling not only for the host of unmeasured performance determinants but also for the influence of self-efficacy itself.

The predictiveness of prior performance is also inflated when the same athletic routine is performed repeatedly in social isolation during the same session under invariant conditions. This type of paradigm usually reveals little of interest beyond the initial trial. With nothing changing situationally, little being learned, no competitive pressure to shake performers' self-assurance, and nothing to disrupt their attentional focus, performance quickly stabilizes, yielding the mundane finding that prior performance correlates virtually perfectly with subsequent performance. These types of studies can add little to our understanding of the factors that govern athletic attainments. The realities in the athleticism of everyday life are entirely different. Athletes have to perform at different times, in different places, in varying climatic conditions, under different physical and emotional states, and with varying competitors before differing audiences. Diversity in competitive conditions prompts reappraisal of personal efficacy; this reappraisal, depending on its nature, facilitates or hinders competitive performance. Thus, under competitively variable conditions, past performance fades in predictiveness, whereas efficacy belief retains its predictiveness (Lee, 1986). The differential predictiveness is especially evident under the variable conditions of team competition. In judging how well they will be able to execute their roles, players consider a host of contextual factors, not the least of which is the formidableness of their upcoming opponent. George (1994) conducted path analyses of batting performances by baseball players over a nine-game baseball season. Perceived efficacy predicted subsequent hitting performance, whereas prior performance did not.

Efficacy Belief in Transcendent Attainments

The contribution to athletic attainments of belief in one's capabilities is further indicated in the pursuit of transcendent accomplishments. Self-belief barriers can hinder even the most gifted athletes from realizing their potential. For years, each athletic activity has had a performance level that was widely regarded as a physical barrier, seemingly unattainable short of a Herculean effort. For example, year after year, even the most fleet of foot could never quite conquer the four-minute mile. Roger Bannister regarded this daunting barrier as surmountable. After he smashed it in his exhausting historic performance, high school students were beating the four-minute mark, and Kip Keino bettered it more than 50 times without much sweat. New records no longer remained durable as runners continued to lower the mark. Analysis of the effects of breaking a transcendent record reveal a common pattern. Regardless of the athletic activity, immediately after a barrier is broken, it is rapidly surpassed by others. Thus, once extraordinary performances are shown to be doable, they become commonplace. Figure 9.3 reveals that records are broken not by small uniform gradations but in step-like triumphs with plateaus between them. Just when a record appears close to the limits of human performance, a competitor with abounding efficacy cuts a large hunk off it. For example, in a more recent track meet, Marceli shattered the mile mark by the biggest margin in 28 years!

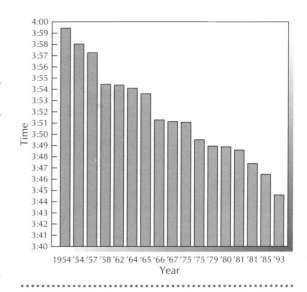

FIGURE 9.3. Successive reductions in the track record for the mile race after Bannister's historic shattering of the four-minute barrier convinced other runners that it was doable.

The interesting counterexample of the notion that demonstration of doability promptly renders the extraordinary commonplace is the long jump record, which remained as one of the most durable ones. In his stunning leap, Beamon broke the world long jump record by almost two feet at the 1968 Olympics in Mexico City. Because of the phenomenal magnitude of the feat, long jumpers attributed it largely to the lowered atmospheric resistance in the high altitude of Mexico City. They did not regard it as doable again. For example, after recording the second best long jump of all time, East German Dombrowski remarked, "I don't think that Beamon's record will ever be beaten." Barrier breakers have to be efficacious thinkers. Carl Lewis, who was never beset by uncertainties about his capabilities, began to assert both in word and in athletic deed that Beamon's unbeatable record was beatable. This altered the mind-set regarding the unattainability of the record. Although Beamon's historic record eluded Lewis, Powell (who was competing with him) smashed the 23-year mark at sea level in muggy conditions at night under threatening rain clouds. These were far from optimal physical conditions. Now that the extraordinary feat had been credited to personal capabilities rather than to atmospheric conditions, it did not take a quarter of a century to break it again. Pedroso, who was fully confident that he would set a new standard, bettered Powell's record long jump four years later in foggy, chilly weather, only to have it nullified because someone inadvertently stood in front of the wind gauge.

Elite athletes who win national or world championships face the daunting task of defending their titles. For many of them, defending their title is more taxing than winning it to begin with (Gould, Jackson, & Finch, 1993). The reported experiences of victors reveal many aversive aspects to life at the top. They become the pursued rather than the pursuers, with all the attendant pressures. There is no relief from the grueling training and competitive hurdles that got them to the top. They must continue to defer valued life pursuits outside their sport. Others come to expect bigger and better things from them. But the most aversive pressures come from the athletes' self-imposed standards. They demand of themselves flawless performances to live up to the image of a champion. Contrary to common belief, declines in motivational intensity after winning a championship are due more to burnout than to loss of competitive hunger. Victors are willing to continue to pay the price not only for the fame and fortune but to prove that they are genuine champions.

Anyone with a shaky sense of efficacy, of course, would be overwhelmed by the intense competitive pressures. The resiliency that got the competitors to the top enables them to overcome the numerous obstacles thrown in their path to repeat their triumph. But not all fare so well. Research in which people have to exert extraordinary effort to succeed has some bearing on different reactions to hard-won success (Bandura & Cervone, 1986). Most people who succeed heighten their perceived efficacy and aspiration and raise the intensity of their motivation. But others who succeed doubt their efficacy to repeat the feat, lower their aspirations, and slacken their efforts. Gould and his

colleagues report that some of the national champions had self-doubts and lapses in confidence about being able to stay on top. They are the ones who would be most vulnerable to failure in their efforts to retain their title.

Coaching Influences on Development and Maintenance of Self-Efficacy

The quality of athletic leadership contributes, in varying degrees, to team morale and performance. Much of the research in this area has centered on general leadership styles. They may be autocratic, participative, or delegative. Leadership as solely a product of personality traits was eventually supplanted by the view of leadership as a product of traits and situations acting upon one another. Social cognitive theory adopts a transactional perspective rather than focusing on global traits. In fact, effective coaches differ widely in style, but what they have in common is their remarkable efficacy as tutors and motivators. They excel at developing their players' talents, getting them to believe in themselves, and getting them to perform at their best both when things are going poorly and when they are going well. This calls for a transactional model of athletic leadership in which coaches must adapt their strategies to their players' particular talents and values and to the situational challenges they face. Functional adaptation of leadership strategies does not mean compromising standards of excellence. Because change threatens status and requires work to master new ways, it can be quite disconcerting. Many players understandably hope for a quick fix that will otherwise let things stay as they are. The type of coaching they prefer, therefore, may be harmonious but produce contented underachievers. Coaches who turn chronically losing franchises into winning ones adapt strategies to players' talents but hold them to standards that lead to success.

The task of developing resilient self-efficacy in athletes rests heavily on the managerial efficacy of coaches. This is not simply a matter of motivational pep talks or rambling encouragement. Rather, it is achieved largely through carefully graded mastery experiences. Discouragement over competitive difficulties is reduced by emphasizing self-improvement while underplaying victories and defeats. Improvement is personally controllable, whereas winning is not entirely in one's own hands. Focusing on what players can personally control provides positive guidance about what to work at to gain proficiency. Effective coaches further guide the development of athletic efficacy by modeling confidence in players' eventual proficiency and by positive corrective feedback on how to improve performance rather than by criticism of failings. Feedback about deficient performances is heavily laced with enabling reinstructions (Tharp & Gallimore, 1976). Accenting the positive does not mean lowering expectations or rewarding substandard performance. Effective coaches expect much of their players athletically and provide them with the support and guidance they need to get there through stepwise progress. Successful efficacy builders not only structure tasks for developing players in ways that bring success but avoid placing players prematurely in situations where they are likely to fail (Walsh & Dickey, 1990). Effective coaches place players in game situations and have them execute plays that have a good chance of success until the players gain self-assurance and the trust of their teammates. Inserting heralded apprentices in pressure-packed situations as a team is falling apart, which rabid fans clamor for, is a good way to destroy players' sense of efficacy and their team's confidence in them.

As players develop assurance in their capabilities, they need to be worked gradually into pressure situations that make it difficult to perform at one's best. In building resilient self-efficacy, athletes must learn how to deal with failure. Effective coaches do not give up on players when they run into difficulties. Rather, they give them support and opportunities to learn how to work their way out of troublesome situations. By maintaining confidence in their players' ability to do the job, coaches help to relieve some of the disruptive pressure in tense situations. Of course, instructive patience works well only if coaches do not place players prematurely in situations where they struggle unsuccessfully and quickly get unhinged.

If athletes are removed precipitously when they get into trouble, it undermines their sense of efficacy and strips them of opportunities to learn how to battle back from difficulties. This increases the vulnerability to self-destruction under pressure. An essential aspect of resiliency training is learning how to rebound from defeat. Athletes must learn to put mistakes behind them so that they are not encumbered with intrusive cognitive carryovers that impair their subsequent performances. Strategies for developing recovery skills should not be misread as encouraging complacency over defeat. Athletes are taught not to let mistakes get them down so that they can better manage troublesome situations when they confront them again rather than continue to get overwhelmed by them.

The ability appraisals conveyed to players by coaches through their words and actions affect the course of the players' efficacy development. Coaches who remain confident in the capabilities of players when they are struggling with difficulties or slumps weaken the negative impact of repeated failure on beliefs of personal efficacy. What counts is not the difficulty per se but the way in which it is construed and what is learned from it. It is difficulties that result in the loss of a coach's confidence in the players that have the devastating effects on athletes' personal efficacy. As one player described it, "He's not worried, so I'm not worried. He knows what I can do." This applies at the team level as well. Example exerts greater influence than preaching (Bandura, 1986a). Task-oriented composure by a coach when the team is struggling can help the players concentrate on how to regain control of their game. It is easy for coaches to model faith in their team when things are going well. It is when teams are experiencing difficulties that coaches have to work the hardest. The real test of coaching efficacy is the ability to get a team to rebound from disheartening losses. The major motivational work comes after defeats rather than in preludes to contests.

Being benched in ways that suggest loss of confidence in an athlete takes a toll on perceived self-efficacy: "When you don't play a lot of doubts begin to build in your mind. You wonder how good you are or can you still do the things you used to do." Supportive patience by a coach is especially important in sports where the development of talent takes a long time. For example, most superstar pitchers experience losing seasons early in their careers until they expand their repertoire of pitches and master the cognitive strategies of pitching. Some coaches operate well with seasoned veterans but are poor developers of young athletes because they give up on them too early. The goals of coaches are not always in harmony with those of players. Coaches whose own status is insecure seek victories because their jobs depend on amassing winning records, whereas players are more oriented toward improving their athletic proficiency. Intense pressures for short-term victories often jeopardize accomplishment of long-term successes through supportive player development.

From time to time, young athletes are thrust prematurely into the limelight only to be sent back to a lower league. The impact of such experiences on beliefs of personal efficacy is likely to be determined in part by whether the player construes the demotion as diagnostic of deficient talent or as need for further development of acquirable skills. Construal of setbacks in terms of acquirability of further proficiency fosters resilience of personal efficacy to disconcerting setbacks, as evident in the remarks of a rookie catcher returned to the minor league, "I'll be back. It's no big deal. I can't be disappointed because I'm still learning." His tenacious self-efficacy was indeed soon realized by a successful lasting return to the major leagues.

The issue of inherent talent versus acquirable skill also arises in how others judge the capabilities of professional athletes. Sports commentators have a penchant for ascribing the distinguished performances of superstars to their "natural talent," as if athletic skills spring preset from biological inheritance. For example, sportscasters commented, with monotonous regularity, on the "natural swing" of a baseball superstar vying for the national batting championship. They failed to recognize the countless dreary hours spent perfecting the so-called natural swing. This particular player was highly vulnerable to a strikeout with a particular pitch that had

become his nemesis. During the off-season, he practiced hitting about 400 pitches per day, day in and day out, to master his weaknesses. His teammates referred to him as Phi Betamax Kappa because of the endless hours he spent watching videotapes of pitchers' strategies. Tony Gwynn, a perennial baseball batting champion, wore out relief pitchers and batting machines practicing, before and after games, how to hit different types of pitches and tailor his swing to different game situations (Will, 1990). Obviously, athletic attainments depend partly on physical endowment. But intricate athletic skills are not inborn. They must be cultivated through intensive training and orchestrated by efficacious self-belief. The extraordinary self-disciplined practice required is rarely considered in studies of attributes that distinguish elite athletes from their less illustrious counterparts.

Evidence that conceptions of ability affect beliefs of physical capability in the same way as they do beliefs of cognitive capability (Wood & Bandura, 1989a) extends the generality of this form of cognitive influence. Conceptions of ability bias whether performance difficulties are viewed as indicants of inherent deficiences or as instructive guides for improving one's competency. In practical terms, those who instruct others in athletic competencies should attend not only to the specific activity and the thinking related to it but also to the more general mind-sets with which individuals approach the development of athletic skills. The experimental findings indicate that a positive approach that emphasizes the acquirability of athletic proficiency will be the most beneficial in promoting the acquisition of skills and interest in athletic activities.

Creative coaches exercise control over the process of efficacy development not only by adept structuring of mastery experiences but also by creating styles of play that capitalize on their players' unique assets. The most dramatic example of team enablement by melding talents to style of play is Shaughnessy's instant metamorphosis of the 1940 Stanford football team (Fimrite, 1977). In the previous year, the Stanford team, which had won but one game, was disparaged as the worst collection of players in the school's athletic history. The young quarterback, Frankie Albert, belittled himself as just another high school prospect who lacked what it takes to succeed in the college ranks. Upon his arrival at Stanford, Shaughnessy created a new system of play using the T formation and insightfully reassigned players to positions that capitalized on what they could do best and kept clear of their shortcomings. In his first meeting with the players, Shaughnessy announced that he had a new offensive system that, if they learned it well, would take them to the Rose Bowl. They greeted this pronouncement as a comic fantasy. The style of play substituted speed and deception for brawn in a wide-open game of elusive ball-handling, shifty running, quick openers, and players hurtling downfield as pass receivers or decoys. The speed of the offensive plays compensated for the light offensive line that could not hold off the defense for long. The talents of the formerly dispirited quarterback, who was low on strength but high on fakery, were developed to the utmost. This athletic wizardry was executed with exquisite timing through massive practice.

Before the season opened, sportswriters ignored or scoffed at Stanford's effort at athletic renewal. Several plays into the first game, the quarterback rushed back to the huddle and exclaimed, "Hey, this stuff really works!" The previously unplumbed talents thrived under this new system. The versatility produced new heroes each week. Shaughnessy had devised an alternative offense should the T formation falter, but he did not disclose or practice it for fear that it might undermine the players' confidence in the new form of playmaking. Opposing teams were totally confused by the elusive and versatile maneuvers. Stanford went undefeated that season and crowned their phenomenal metamorphosis with a victory at the Rose Bowl. The spectacular transformation was achieved without any real changes in player personnel; rather, the style of play was restructured to fit the capabilities of the existing players. This epochal venture did more than transmute a team. It revolutionized the world of football as virtually every team promptly adopted this style of play, much to the delight of the fans.

Walsh's resurrection of the formerly hapless San Francisco 49ers football team provides another striking example of building team efficacy by adapting playmaking to what the players can do best (Walsh & Dickey, 1990). The team had slow running backs but fleet receivers and a mobile quarterback. Much of the style of playmaking was adapted to the special talents of the quarterback Montana who, although not noted for his long aerial game, was unusually skilled at buying time through shiftiness in the backfield while scanning for openings to his speedy receivers. Walsh created a short-pass strategy of play to maintain ball control and put points on the scoreboard. Short passes to agile receivers would then produce long gains or coveted touchdowns.

Optimal matches that use existing talents productively and compensate for limitations facilitate the cultivation of team efficacy. The preceding examples provide graphic testimony that coaches who are creative in tailoring performance styles to players' particular talents can turn chronic losers into self-efficacious winners within a short time with little change in players. One can point to successful coaches who fit players to the coaches' preferred style of play rather than adapting their style to players particular talents. In such instances, success is achieved largely through self-selection and institutional recruitment of players for compatible matches of skills to team style of play. Successful styles, sometimes born of immediate necessity, become enduring team characteristics perpetuated by future selection of coaches and players for congruent skills. Thus, some football programs traditionally seek their success through the air while others grind it out on the ground with predictable regularity. Coaching creativity is better revealed when coaches inherit losers and turn them into winners than when they depend on selecting recruits who can do the job the coaches' set way. There is a difference between winning by developing the talents of players and winning by trading for seasoned players that creates the right mix for success.

There has been little systematic research on the strategies coaches use to promote athletic efficacy. Elite coaches of Olympic and national teams have rated their relative preference for techniques that can build athletes' sense of efficacy (Gould,

Hodge, Peterson, & Giannini, 1989). Such coaches place heavy emphasis on athletes' personal development through instructive drill; vigorous physical conditioning to build the stamina necessary to sustain high effort throughout the games; modeling confidence in their players; providing supportive feedback; and encouraging positive self-talk to aid performance and counteract self-denigration when things do not go well. They also tend to set specific performance goals and focus on skill development while downplaying wins and defeats. The coaches are less inclined to use relaxation training, positive imagery, and reattribution of tension and failure to benign or personally controllable factors. Other influential strategies for enhancing athletic efficacy, such as insightful matching of players to team subfunctions and tailoring the style of play to players' particular talents, which were not included among the rated factors, should be added in future studies of coaching practices.

The survey approach is an informative first excursion into the coaching domain. It cannot distinguish between what coaches say and what they actually do, however, or evaluate how well they use the various coaching strategies. All coaches report extensive use of efficacy-building strategies (Weinberg & Jackson, 1990). If their reports are accurate, the differences between successful coaches and less successful ones must lie in how they use the strategies or in their creativeness in structuring styles of play to capitalize on players' particular talents. The differentiating factor may be quality rather than frequency of use of particular strategies. The way in which instructional strategies are structured and implemented will have far greater impact on players' efficacy beliefs than how often they are used. For example, drill will not build efficacy if players are mismatched and ineffectual strategies are being routinized. Similarly, positive feedback may be given superficially or embedded in an instructional format that calls attention to what was done right, then models or explains how to improve problematic aspects and conveys assurance that proficiency is attainable through diligent practice (Feltz & Weiss, 1982). Given the large body of knowledge about modes of efficacy enhancement, the logical extension of research effort is to measure actual

coaching practices, how players perceive them, and how the strategies affect athletes' self-efficacy and performance. Such observational studies should examine what coaches do both during practice sessions and in games. The impact that coaches have on players needs to be further clarified by systematic experimentation on coaching practices conducive to development of athletic proficiency and competitive resilience.

Coaching efficacy extends beyond player development and motivation to guidance on personal matters and management of behavioral problems peculiar to the nature of athletic careers. Talented prospects are recruited early into athletic pursuits. Training routines command much of an athlete's time during the development phase. A life devoted almost exclusively to perfecting a particular athletic skill does not leave much time for cultivating a wide range of interests and talents. As players move into the professional ranks, team staff assume control over many aspects of athletes' lives. Their travel, accommodations, meals, and medical services are arranged for them. They have curfews and tightly prescribed time schedules for their activities. Moreover, the prized players are given vast sums of money at a young age, which creates fertile opportunities to get into trouble.

Not only are they relieved of personal control over many of the demands of everyday reality, but they are often shielded from the consequences of transgressive conduct because they are essential to their teams' success. Dependent protectiveness undermines development of personal responsibility. Highly talented players who gain wide public visibility are especially well positioned to exploit their favored status in ways that allow them to get away with exasperating work habits. Contracts with clauses permitting the players to go elsewhere after a short period provide further countercontrolling leverage. A survey of coaches revealed that disrespect from players and the inability to motivate them were their major sources of stress (Kroll, 1982). Troublesome superstars can turn coaches into ruffled guardians and social workers. For these reasons, athletics is hardly the best place to look for national role models. Coaches who are efficacious in managing such players without risking team dissension and disruptive distractions accommodate them in their teams, whereas coaches with lesser efficacy to deal with "head problems" shy away from troublesome players. Gifted players who remain highly coachable despite their triumphs continue to develop their potential and enjoy a longer and more productive athletic career.

Talented professional athletes often have greater team longevity, are paid enormously more, and receive greater public acclaim than do their coaches. It takes some doing for players to refrain from adopting a "we-be" attitude toward coaches — we-be here before you and we-be here after you. These are unique power relationships and organizational structures that are not the staples of the traditional group dynamics theorizing. Athletic teams are a special type of group. For this reason, sports psychology must create and alter, rather than simply borrow directly, principles of group dynamics. If coaches are to get players to listen to them and to achieve good team results, they must win respect from players by demonstrating efficacy and setting a good example of how to remain task-oriented through adversity rather than simply by exercising the authority of the managerial position.

Much is made of coaches' motivational and athletic tactical skills. But the importance of recruiting efficacy is rarely mentioned, let alone studied, in the analysis of successful athletic leadership. Coaches' appraisal efficacy to evaluate players and ferret out underdeveloped talent and their persuasory efficacy to recruit the right mix for success determine the caliber of players with whom they have to work. Analysis of the multicausality of coaching success should begin with player evaluation and recruitment rather than with an already assembled team. Promising candidates are vigorously courted by coaches who are vying for them. Self-efficacious coaches expect to succeed in their efforts and figure out ways to shift considerations in their favor. Those of low efficacy find many reasons that a heavily courted player is likely to go elsewhere and do not put much serious effort into their recruitment. The quality of the talent coaches manage to assemble is a major factor in the calculus of their athletic success.

Much of the discussion so far has centered on the functional role played by resilient belief in one's efficacy in the tortuous pursuit of athletic success.

Yet undaunted self-efficacy can be a liability for athletes in the twilight of their careers. Some superstars refuse to concede that the glory days are over. They continue to cling to belief in their athletic capabilities long after their skills have faded. Rather than bowing out gracefully, they hang on embarrassingly. Ironically, the unshakable efficacy belief that enabled them to rise to the top and to excel under unrelenting competition dissuades them from acknowledging that they no longer have what it takes to do the job competently. Coaches have to be skilled in managing the enlarged sense of efficacy of former superstars whose athletic careers are ending.

COLLECTIVE TEAM EFFICACY

It is one thing to build athletes' sense of personal efficacy. It is another to forge a sturdy sense of group efficacy from a collection of individuals and to sustain it in the face of setbacks and defeats. The research on the role of efficacy beliefs in athletic performance has been largely confined to the individual level. In most sports activities, athletes function as interdependent members of teams rather than as independent competitors. Hence, this line of research needs to be extended to analyses of how the perceived efficacy of a team as a whole governs its level of performance. Perceived collective efficacy is likely to influence how much effort players put forth together, their ability to remain perseverant and task oriented during periods when the team is struggling, and their capability to bounce back from wrenching defeats. Athletes' thoughts and reactions to athletic stressors often provide informative data, and some sports analysts, such as Glenn Dickey, offer especially insightful analyses of the psychosocial factors governing individual and team performance.

Informal observations indicate that successful teams have a strong group sense of efficacy and resiliency. They believe firmly that they have whatever it takes to succeed, and they never concede anything. They do not collapse or panic when they fall behind. Rather, they typically stage successful comebacks by determined effort in pressure-packed closing periods of games. In contrast, mediocre teams and those plagued by inconsistencies seem to perform much of the time in an inefficacious frame of mind. They do not expect much of themselves as a team and, as a consequence, do not do all that well. A quarterback of a professional football team that never quite makes it to the upper ranks commented after an exhibition game that, for the first time, his team has the feeling that it is going to win any given contest. This telling remark reveals that, in the past, the team essentially conceded games before the players even stepped on the field. Such teams help to beat themselves by uninspiring play and by having weak staying power in the face of mounting pressure. A resilient sense of team efficacy does not necessarily guarantee victory, but a team that disbelieves its capabilities is most likely to produce its own dispiriting validation.

From time to time, an entire team falls into a prolonged slump. There are several ways in which performance difficulties can become contagious. One likely explanation is the diffused impact of modeling influences on perceived self-efficacy. We know that mastery modeling enhances the efficacy beliefs of others, which, in turn, heighten their physical performance (Corbin, Laurie, Gruger, & Smiley, 1984; Feltz et al., 1979; Gould & Weiss, 1981; McAuley, 1985). Moreover, the enhanced sense of efficacy may generalize to other related activities (Brody et al., 1988; Holloway et al., 1988). It remains for future research to determine whether display of unsettling ineffectiveness by some players undermines teammates' sense of efficacy. In other spheres of activity, seeing others of similar ability suffer repeated failures saps observers' perceived efficacy and motivation (Brown & Inouye, 1978). Modeled ineffectiveness, especially by superstars, could also depress team performance by inflating perceptions of the overpoweringness of opponents. And finally, contagious ineffectiveness leads everyone to start pressing in ways that disrupt skills, breed mistakes, and leave players talking disparagingly to themselves. Athletic teams also experience a crisis of efficacy after the loss of a superstar, especially if they attribute much of their success to their departed teammate. They may lapse into a prolonged slump until they convince themselves of their competitive efficacy.

Collective Efficacy and System Interdependence

Athletic activities vary in the degree of mutual coordination required among team members to produce results. In the case of a gymnastics team, which represents a low degree of interdependence, the team attainment is the sum of the performances achieved independently by each of the team's members. By contrast, a basketball or soccer team requires intricate coordination, and the team attainment is highly dependent on how well its members work together. A weak link in this mutual dependence can spell disaster. By the same token, a highly gifted player in a key position on a team of an interdependent sport can raise the perceived team efficacy of mediocre teammates. The assessed perceived collective efficacy of a hockey team illustrates this point. The players collectively judged their team efficacy much higher than the sum of their own efficacies because they had a phenomenal goalie who repeatedly rescued them from their missteps. The quality of teamwork in an interdependent sport can greatly affect a team's sense of collective efficacy. A collection of superstars playing divisively in pursuit of their self-promotion will gradually erode any sense of group efficacy. It does not take many self-aggrandizing players to breed dissension in a team. Such teams look great individually but are petulant underachievers collectively. They can be beaten by less talented athletes who play well together.

Two versions of collective efficacy can be used to measure perceived team efficacy. The personal version aggregates players' judgments of their own efficacy. The group version aggregates the players' judgments of the efficacy of their team as a whole. The relative predictiveness of these two indices of collective efficacy may vary depending on the degree of interdependence in the production of team attainments. Aggregated perceived team efficacy is especially relevant when team attainments require high interdependent effort, whereas aggregated perceived personal efficacy may be adequate when team attainments largely represent the summed contributions of individual members.

The causal impact of perceived collective efficacy on team performance is verified experimentally by Hodges and Carron (1992). They raised or lowered the perceived collective efficacy of different sets of created teams by bogus feedback about their physical strength in competitive trials. Although comparable in actual strength, the teams responded in markedly different ways to subsequent preset defeats in competitive physical endurance depending on the instilled beliefs in their collective efficacy (Fig. 9.4). Teams whose collective efficacy was arbitrarily raised improved their team's performance following competitive defeat. Teams whose sense of collective efficacy was lowered suffered substantial decrements in team performance. These findings are especially interesting because collective efficacy was altered for a physical activity that differed from the competitive one. It is also interesting to note that perceived collective efficacy insulates teams against the adverse effects of competitive defeat in much the same way as it does players competing individually.

Team productivity is often attributed to group cohesiveness. In socially cohesive teams, players stick together, are united in their aspirations, and have a strong sense of collective identity. Group cohesiveness largely reflects teammates' sense of collective efficacy and shared goal imperatives. These factors are known to facilitate athletic performance by motivating and regulating effort and strategic thinking. It is difficult for team members to remain socially cohesive if they have no shared vision to strive for and they approach contests handicapped by doubts in their abilities to succeed. If they are to remain united through tough times, they have to believe in their potential to elevate their attainments through united teamwork.

Group cohesion includes both an interpersonal element, such as mutual liking and affiliation, and an aspirational element encompassing a collective sense of efficacy and shared purpose. Evidence reveals that strong commitment to shared aspirations and steadfast belief in the group's ability to realize them are the main carriers of the impact of group cohesion on team performance (Carron, 1984; Mullen & Copper, 1994). Togetherness in the pursuit of a collectively desired goal, such as a team championship, does not necessarily mean strong friendship ties among teammates. Neither interpersonal attraction nor group pride have much influence on group performance. Nor does the influence of team cohesiveness flow unidirectionally. Efficacious teamwork brings victories; victories, in turn, enhance group efficacy and aspiration that

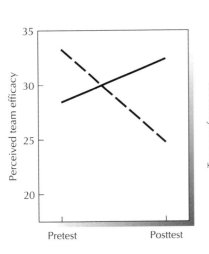

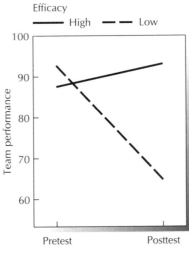

Efficacy
——— High   — — Low

FIGURE 9.4. Changes in the level of teams' competitive performance after their perceived collective efficacy was arbitrarily raised or lowered by bogus comparative feedback that they were either physically stronger or physically weaker than their opponents. The teams' level of perceived collective efficacy and competitive performance is shown before (pretest) and after (posttest) their perceived efficacy was altered. The data are based on a total of 50 teams. (After Hodges & Carron, 1992)

strengthen team unity. Perceived collective efficacy fluctuates over the course of a season. Hence, the strength of team unity will vary somewhat rather than remain fixed.

Spink (1990) documents that perceived collective efficacy is related to group processes as well as to performance attainments. Teams with a strong sense of collective efficacy have high cohesiveness, whereas those of low collective efficacy experience more factionalism. On teams with high group cohesiveness, players subordinate their self-interests for team success and coordinate their efforts in deft teamwork. Among elite volleyball teams, players' beliefs in their teams' competitive efficacy, measured before the tournament, predicted their performance success in the contests.

Preparatory versus Performance Efficacy

In social cognitive theory, the optimal strength of efficacy beliefs differs while acquiring skills and while wielding already developed skills (Bandura, 1986a). In approaching learning tasks, athletes who perceive themselves to be highly efficacious in their capabilities have little incentive to invest much effort in tedious preparatory practice. Some uncertainty clearly benefits preparation. In executing their acquired skills during competitive contests, however, a strong belief in one's efficacy is essential to mobilize the sustained effort and attentional focus needed to triumph over tough opponents or to stage successful comebacks. Thus, some self-doubt provides the driving force for perfecting athletic skills, but it impairs the execution of developed skills during contests. Players beset by self-doubts readily self-destruct under severe competitive pressure.

Coaches try to orchestrate the most advantageous mix of preparatory and performance efficacy. To motivate players to improve suspect skills and competitive strategies in preparation for upcoming contests, coaches inflate the capabilities of their opponents and highlight the vulnerabilities of their own team. Bravado self-appraisals are frowned

upon. But at the time of the contest, coaches attempt to instill a resolute sense of competitive efficacy to get the players to perform at their best. They are not sent out on the playing field infused with self-doubt.

There is another form of complacency that coaches must counteract. After a team has had a successful season, both coaches and players may fall victim to the linear projection error — that they will do as well or even better the next time around. Many extraneous factors outside a team's control affect its win record, but players may unduly credit the success to their team's capabilities. These interacting factors vary so that unusually good breaks or unusually bad ones are unlikely to repeat themselves within a short time. Performance attainments, therefore, are imperfectly correlated. Regression effects alone would predict that an atypically high win record will be followed by a lower one (Gilovich, 1984). If overinterpreted victories breed inflated self-assurance, players have less incentive to put in the laborious effort needed to maintain or improve their competitive capabilities.

History is full of teams that had a spectacular season only to be overrun the following year. The astute baseball manager Tony La Russa impresses on his players that each year presents fresh challenges and the team has to prove itself capable of repeating or bettering what it did before. Future success is not taken for granted because of past performance. By curtailing complacency, coaches create the motivational conditions needed to enhance team efficacy. The same process operates at the individual level. After a spectacular year, players who do not work seriously at their game will see their productivity decline. Therefore, players are reoriented toward challenging personal goals rather than being allowed to coast on reputation.

Coaches face especially tough challenges in strengthening their players' resilience and sustaining their motivation in contests where they are clearly outmatched and have to compete on their opponent's inhospitable turf. Under such conditions, it does not take much failure for players to start doubting themselves. As pressure mounts, they either fall apart or, having convinced themselves of the futility of their efforts, quit trying. Motivational pep talks are dismissed as unfulfillable fantasies. One strategy for neutralizing the undermining effects of being rapidly outdistanced by an opponent is to instill a firm belief that a comeback is doable. This very strategy was used to good effect by Walsh in a football match between Stanford and heavily favored Notre Dame. As part of their preparation, the players were shown film clips in which Tennessee, trailing Notre Dame by 31–7, beat them in a dramatic comeback. Filmed testimony is more informative and persuasive than verbalized hype. At the outset of the contest, fumbles and dropped passes put Stanford deep in the hole, which ordinarily would be disastrous. But the players never lost their composure or belief that they could mount a successful comeback. As the contest progressed, they took control of the game and beat the Irish in an extraordinary win.

If a successful comeback is clearly out of reach, coaches face the problem of how to keep players from conceding defeat and backsliding into spiritless or disintegrative play. The efficacy of coaches is reflected in their ability to keep their athletes playing hard when the game is lost. A meaningful strategy is to shift the focus from winning and losing to using the remainder of the contest as an opportunity to learn. The victory goal gives way to a learning goal. This strategy provides an opportunity to impress on players that it is not the athletic loss but what they learn from it that affects their subsequent performance. The renewed effort goes into trying ways of improving one's game during a losing contest. Such an exploratory approach can do more than improve aspects of the teams' playmaking. It provides opportunities to develop skill in self-management of dysfunctional thinking under stress. By getting the players to remain task-oriented persisters rather than demoralized quitters, such a strategy builds cognitive skills in refocusing goals and thinking about how to get things done rather than dwelling on failure in troublesome situations. Cognitive control efficacy can be more effectively taught by practice in focusing on performance strategies in the natural context of tough competitive situations than by rehearsing "mental toughness" exercises off the field. In other spheres of functioning, cognitive coping strategies developed and rehearsed in safe simulated contexts may be readily discarded when the actual threats are confronted (Biran & Wilson, 1981).

Perceived efficacy is a dynamic fluctuating property, not a static trait. The initial phases of contests are especially crucial in teams' reappraisals of their competitive efficacy. If a weaker opponent gets off to a superb start, the team may begin to believe it can win and play with a self-assured intensity that may produce upset victories. Substantial initial leads may also force opposing teams out of their preferred style of play and into a mode in which they are less efficacious and easier to beat. Witness the deterioration of powerful football teams fashioned for a running attack forced to play catch-up ball with an aerial attack for which their sense of efficacy and skill is shaky. A commanding performance immediately after an intermission by a team that is losing provides a strong boost in its belief in its efficacy to stage a successful comeback. Therefore, teams strive hard to overpower their opponents at the beginning of a contest to convince them that their worst doubts are warranted. Complacency over a big lead that enables an opponent to begin a comeback may also boost the opponent's sense of efficacy to the point where it is difficult to stop. Coaches try to sustain self-efficacious thinking in the face of difficulties that can shake a team's belief that the extra effort is worthwhile.

Successful streaks within games are usually characterized as shifts in momentum. Calling a streak of gains *momentum* is descriptive, not explanatory. The metaphor begs the question of what factors govern such winning sequences. The affirmation of efficacy by a positive turn of events can activate cognitive and motivational processes that elevate the intensity and level of performance. Lindsley, Brass, and Thomas (1995) provide a thoughtful efficacy analysis of the amplifying nature of reciprocal processes that can help shed light on what has been dubbed momentum. Momentum occurs when perceived efficacy and performance build on each other in an upward cycle. The larger the size and rate of the early gain, the greater the likelihood that an upward cycle will result. Small gains may be discounted as random fluctuations. Conversely, in a downward spiral, the mutual impact of self-doubt and marred performance result in mounting failure. This leads to the growing demoralization or collapse of an opponent. Some of the strategies coaches can use to arrest and reverse a downward cycle will be discussed shortly. Momentum is more apparent within games than across successive games, although even the evidence for "hot streaks" within contests is still inconclusive (Gilovich, Vallone, & Tversky, 1985; Miller & Weinberg, 1991). In championship contests requiring high team resilience to rise to the playoffs, teams are more likely to win after a defeat than after a victory, through self-corrected adjustments (Nahinsky, 1991). The changes across successive periods within a game may not, in fact, differ all that much from the cyclical changes across successive games.

The old adage that success breeds success fails to recognize the sociocognitive dynamics of performance motivation in competitive situations. Success often breeds complacency in highly efficacious players, which spawns failure. Conversely, failure can prompt efficacious contestants to alter their strategies and redouble their efforts to regain control of the game. Both phenomena — letdown after easy success and intensification after failure — are common sequences in competitive struggles. Players are likely to slacken their efforts after an impressive start in a game or after a decisive team victory in a competitive series. Resilient opponents exploit such lapses to take control of the game. This challenge, in turn, sparks comebacks by their opponents, creating an ebb and flow in athletic contests.

The diverse lines of evidence reviewed in this chapter underscore the centrality of sociocognitive factors in athletic performance. When viewed from the sociocognitive perspective, sequential fluctuations in individual or team performance called momentum are partly governed by changes in perceived competitive efficacy, the immediate strategies and microgoals adopted for regaining control, self-evaluative reactions to substandard performances, and concerns over likely outcomes.

Perceived efficacy involves control of disruptive thinking and affective states as well as physical performance. Successful streaks are the product of transactional rather than unidirectional causation. It takes two sides to have a momentum in athletic contests. What may look like a hot streak may be a temporary lapse by opponents. Reifying momentum as a cause of athletic feats diverts attention from causal analyses of interactional performance sequences.

···

PSYCHOBIOLOGICAL EFFECTS OF PHYSICAL EXERCISE

Health promotion through exercise has become a matter of considerable interest. Physical exercise yields substantial biological and psychological benefits that enhance health and extend life (Bortz, 1982; Hagberg, 1994). With regard to biological effects, physical exercise improves most bodily functions. It strengthens the cardiorespiratory system so that it takes in more oxygen and transports it more efficiently to fuel metabolism. Exercise also affects the rate of metabolic activities that provide energy for vital processes as well as altering hormonal and immunological functioning. Moreover, exercise serves as a protective factor against several major chronic diseases. It raises high-density cholesterol, which helps to prevent atherosclerosis; lowers blood pressure, which reduces the risk of stroke by artery rupture; and improves sugar absorption by the cells for carbohydrate metabolism, thereby lowering the risk of diabetes with its attendant impairment of vision and kidney and neurological function.

In addition, regular physical activity strengthens the musculoskeletal system by counteracting loss of muscle tissue and skeletal calcium and improving joint and muscle flexibility. Regular exercisers are functionally younger in these various physical capacities and aerobic power than their sedentary age-mates or even more junior individuals who are physically inactive. The rate of decline in cardiovascular function with age can be reduced by at least half through regular exercise (Bortz, in press). Lack of exercise is detrimental to one's health. Physical activity thus provides an effective means of enhancing health and retarding the aging process. Fortunately, the various detrimental biological effects of physical inactivity can be reversed by a program of regular exercise. As Bortz (1982) rightly points out, widespread improvements in vitality can be produced behaviorally that no pharmacological or medical procedures can accomplish. If medical science created a pill that could deliver these vast health benefits, it would be hailed as a spectacular breakthrough in the field of human health.

Given these diverse structural and functional benefits of physical activity, not surprisingly, physical fitness through regular exercise reduces the likelihood of physical dysfunctions including coronary heart disease, hypertension, diabetes, obesity, and osteoporosis. In the psychological realm, people generally report that they feel better after exercising. Engagement in physical activity will not solve the problems of work or family life but it helps to alleviate aversive emotional states, especially stress (Tuscon & Sinyor, 1994). Since engrossment in nonexercise activities can have similar calming effects, the stress reduction probably results mainly from shutting down distracting, perturbing ideation. While the stress-relieving effects of exercise may be primarily cognitively based, physical fitness affects how strongly people respond physiologically to stressors. The physically fit are less cardiovascularly agitated during exposure to stressors and recover more quickly than those of low aerobic fitness (Holmes, 1993).

Physical exercise has been equated all too often with monotonous, onerous exertion. Researchers who look for the psychological benefits of exercise on dreary treadmills and bicycle ergometers may be looking in the wrong place. When people lead active lives by engagement in interesting pastimes, they gain not only biological benefits but psychological well-being. They make exercising an enjoyable habit rather than a tortuous one. Considering the prevalence of physical inactivity and its contribution to diverse medical conditions, a sedentary lifestyle is clearly a major public health problem.

Impediments to Physical Exercise

Despite the multiple health benefits of physical exercise, most people lead sedentary lives, especially as they become middle-aged and older. Of those who try to get themselves to exercise regularly, most quit their routines after a short time despite the best of intentions. There are many disincentives and impediments to exercising. Therefore, if people are to reap the benefits of staying physically active, they need positive incentives and a high level of self-regulatory efficacy to override the toilsome aspects of exercise. Most people probably have a general notion that staying physically active is healthful without really knowing its full impact on biological and psychological functioning. Explicit knowledge of health benefits can provide some incentive to start exercising regularly (Sallis et al., 1986). As is true in other lifestyle changes, however, most people are not going to work up much sweat on knowledge alone. In fact, even most coronary patients discontinue prescribed exercise routines within a short time, although they know full well that physical activity strengthens their cardiovascular functioning and reduces the risk of future life-threatening coronary events.

Some of the impediments to exercise adherence stem from the nature of the physical activities and how they are structured. There are two main ways of staying physically fit. The first is by vigorous aerobic exercises performed regularly at certain times and places, such as jogging, biking, recreative sports, calisthenics, aerobic dancing, or working out on exercise equipment. The second type of exercise simply involves increasing the amount and level of physical activity in one's daily routines. It includes such things as brisk walking, climbing stairs instead of riding elevators or escalators, gardening, and exercising through enjoyable recreational activities. The latter types of activities make exercise a habitual part of one's daily life. People are more likely to remain physically active if exercises are imbedded in habitual routines and enjoyable activities than if they are isolated from daily activities at particular times and places (Epstein, Wing, Koeske, Ossip, & Beck, 1982). Unless one is highly self-disciplined, countless competing activities easily intrude on set-aside periods.

The intensity of physical activity is another factor that strains adherence. To achieve health benefits, physical activities must be performed regularly at some level of vigor. Prolonged intense exercise can be onerous and tedious. Hence, adherence to moderate activity is greater than adherence to vigorous activity (Sallis et al., 1986). Many of the health advocates of exercise approach it with missionary zeal driven unmercifully by the dictum, "No pain, no gain." The misinformation that only highly strenuous exercise provides health benefits discourages most people from adopting active habits. The minimal amount and intensity of physical activity needed for beneficial health results has yet to be determined. Evidence indicates, however, that significant health benefits are achievable even by moderate activity performed several times a week (Paffenbarger et al, 1993; Haskell, Montoye, & Orenstein, 1985). Moderate physical exercise improves health and produces bodily changes that combat disease, but more vigorous exercise is even better at extending life. Even a change in physical fitness from unfit to fit improves health and reduces risk of mortality at all age levels (Blair et al., 1995).

Regular aerobic activity retards the development of disability as well as lowering mortality rates (Fries et al., 1994). It is easier to get sedentary individuals to become moderately active than to convert them into vigorous exercisers. Moreover, different forms of physical activity may serve different protective functions (Harris, Caspersen, DeFriese, & Estes, 1989). Vigorous activity protects against coronary heart disease by improving cardiorespiratory fitness; weight-bearing activities that increase bone density protect against osteoporosis; any physical activity can reduce weight by burning calories, and engrossing physical pursuits can contribute to psychological well-being by improving health and relieving stress.

Exercises have to be performed regularly to maintain health gains. Any effortful activity requiring continuous self-regulation taxes adherence unless the activity is invested with personal value and becomes ingrained as a habitual part of one's lifestyle. It is difficult to keep people wedded to a health habit whose benefits cease once it is discontinued and that produces little in the way of accrued lasting gains from past labors. A sedentary lifestyle, of course, increases the risk of debilities that become lasting problems. We saw in Chapter 7, however, that viewing health habits as averting losses may prompt adoption of the habits, but their maintenance rests more heavily on expected gains (Rothman et al., 1993).

Self-Efficacy Determinants of Exercise Adoption and Adherence

Research has focused, for the most part, on structured aerobic types of exercise. Much of this effort is aimed at identifying the psychosocial factors that foster adoption of exercise regimens and lasting adherence to them. If people are to alter their sedentary lifestyle, they have to believe that they are capable of making exercise a regular habit. Interventions designed to get people to exercise regularly must be tailored to level of perceived efficacy. Sedentary people who have convinced themselves of the futility of any effort to increase their activity level need a guided self-enablement program to persuade them that they can lead more active lives. Those who believe that they can get themselves to exercise regularly are more persuadable by informational means alone. Given high self-efficacy readiness, even informational approaches, which ordinarily are relatively weak, can get people exercising. Nonexercisers who intend to remain so also view exercising as more troublesome than beneficial. They need some incentive if they are to become more active.

Sedentary adults who have been recruited into ongoing exercise programs are most likely to drop out if they have a weak sense of efficacy that they can motivate themselves to exercise and have inflated expectations about quick benefits they will gain from participating in such activities (Desharnais, Bouillon, & Godin, 1986). Expecting too much too soon with a weak sense of efficacy will spawn flagging effort and quickly dampen the motivation to become a devout exerciser. Inflated outcome expectations that are not easy to realize similarly undermine efforts at self-management of weight (Shannon et al., 1990).

The role played by efficacy beliefs in sustaining adherence to regular exercise has received a great deal of attention. The aspect of perceived efficacy that is most relevant is not whether one can execute the physical skills, which are readily mastered, but the self-regulatory efficacy to mobilize oneself to exercise regularly in the face of a variety of personal, social, and situational impediments (Sallis et al., 1988). People who distrust their self-regulatory efficacy are poor adherers to organized exercise programs. They attend exercise sessions irregularly; they have difficulty getting themselves to exercise at the intensity and duration required to achieve health benefits, and they are quick to drop out (McAuley, 1992, 1993). The same is true for those who choose to exercise on their own rather than in supervised programs. The higher their sense of self-regulatory efficacy, the more successful they are in getting themselves to exercise habitually at levels that are healthful.

Aging populations underscore the increasing importance of adopting active lifestyles to maintain health and well-being over the extended life span. Sedentary older adults can be helped, through graded activity programs, to adopt exercise habits that confer health benefits. By exercising regularly, they improve their level of cardiorespiratory functioning; increase their physical stamina; and lower their serum cholesterol, blood pressure, and weight (McAuley, Courneya, & Lettunich, 1991). The stronger the perceived physical efficacy prior to the exercise program, the greater the physiological benefits they derive from it. Over time, the participants experience some decline in their physical functioning. Those who have a high sense of efficacy, however, are more successful in maintaining their exercise habit and cardiorespiratory capacity (McAuley et al., 1993).

Most of the research on exercise adherence has been confined to supervised aerobic exercise programs. This research has clarified some of the determinants and psychological mechanisms that govern the self-management of exercise habits. Constraints of inconvenient time and place and imposed conformity to set routines, however, create impediments to adherence. Some of the dropouts may be exercising on their own, although probably not as intensively or as consistently as the faithful adherers. Because of greater convenience, flexibility, and naturalness, home-based activities are more likely to keep people physically active than are supervised exercise regimens outside the home (Garcia & King, 1991). The role of efficacy beliefs in long-term adherence is most clearly revealed in randomized controlled studies varying exercise intensity and whether people exercise at home or in organized programs (King et al., in press). Among sedentary men and women drawn randomly from the community, those who had a high sense of self-regulatory efficacy and exercised at home were good adherers two years later. Research on promotion of physical fitness, therefore, should devote more attention to strategies for integrating into lifestyle patterns some energetic activities that are personally suitable and enjoyable to do. If such activities are incorporated into regular activities, they do not disrupt daily routines. Sallis and his colleagues found that efficacy beliefs predict enduring changes in lifestyle activity patterns pursued on one's own as they do organized aerobic exercise, even after controlling for prior exercising level, age, gender, education, and income (Sallis et al., 1986; Sallis, Hovell, Hofstetter, & Barrington, 1992). Such confirmatory evidence attests to the generality of the efficacy determinant.

Analyses of change processes distinguish between adoption of new patterns of behavior, their generalized use under different circumstances, and their maintenance over time (Bandura, 1986a). In complex activities, the determinants of adoption differ to some extent from those governing maintenance. Adoption relies on factors that facilitate acquisition of knowledge, requisite subskills, and generative capabilities, whereas maintenance rests heavily on the ability to motivate oneself to use habitually what one has learned. There is some overlap of determinants across change processes, however, because self-regulation of motivation and affect contributes to acquisition as it does to maintenance, and maintenance may often require creative adoptions of skills to new situational constraints or demands. Like most health habits, exercise involves relatively simple performance skills that people already know how to do or can quickly learn. Success in regular exercise is heavily dependent on self-regulatory efficacy. In exercise promotion programs, the so-called adoption and maintenance phases involve pretty much the same thing: adherence to a prescribed frequency, intensity, and duration of certain exercise routines either while the program is going on or some time after it has ceased.

Although the relationship of efficacy beliefs to both adoption and maintenance of physical exercise is amply documented, the size of the relationship to exercising after long periods have elapsed may decline. This does not necessarily mean that efficacy beliefs have lessened their influence on activity habits. The self-management of health habits fluctuates, sometimes widely, over time rather than proceeding unwaveringly (Bandura & Simon, 1977). In this rocky journey, life events occur from time to time that challenge self-regulatory capabilities in ways that may strengthen, weaken, or undermine beliefs of personal efficacy. Thus, self-regulation of health habits is an ongoing struggle involving the reciprocal interplay of personal, behavioral, and situational influences. Regardless of whether it is eating habits or exercising, people go through stretches where they are good adherers, then experience lapses, and they redouble their efforts to reinstate control. Along the way, some lose confidence in their capabilities to restore and maintain adequate control to the point where they give up. The follow-up correlates, taken as a whole, indicate that individuals who embark on leading more active lives with a robust sense of efficacy are better at weathering challenges and recovering from setbacks.

If the efficacy beliefs operating in a given follow-up period differ from those that were held a year or two earlier, the distal beliefs are less relevant to the current behavior and thus are less predictive. It is the current, rather than the past, efficacy beliefs that are most relevant if causal contribution is the issue of interest. Efficacy belief retains its predictive power over increasing follow-up intervals when measured in proximity to the relapse period (Gulliver, Hughes, Solomon, & Dey, 1995).

The dynamic nature of maintenance processes is best captured by ongoing analyses of covarying fluctuations between efficacy beliefs and physical activity. To the extent that efficacy beliefs change over time, their contributory role is underestimated if level of exercising is assessed only at a single future point in time. Growing attrition over lengthening periods (McAuley, 1992) is another factor that can seriously distort the predictiveness of even distal efficacy beliefs. Among the people who try to get themselves to exercise regularly, those of weaker efficacy become poor adherers. If the inefficacious individuals selectively drop out in follow-up assessments, one ends up with the more successful ones. Restriction in the range of perceived self-efficacy and level of physical exercise shrinks the size of correlations.

Comparative Theoretical Analyses

Comparative tests have been conducted on the relative power of alternative theories to predict adherence to physical activity after involvement in exercise promotion programs. Contextualized beliefs of self-regulatory efficacy predict long-term adherence to physical exercise, whereas a trait measure of self-motivation does not foretell who will continue exercising and who will revert to a sedentary lifestyle (Garcia & King, 1991; McAuley & Jacobsen, 1991). The predictive superiority of efficacy beliefs over a trait of self-motivation is further supported in research on weight reduction in which beliefs of personal efficacy were systematically raised by persuasory means (Weinberg et al., 1984). Both preexisting and altered efficacy beliefs contribute to success. Self-motivation does not. Similar differences emerge in comparisons involving generalized beliefs either that one has some control over one's health or that it is determined by factors beyond one's influence. Efficacy beliefs predict exercise adherence; general beliefs about the locus of health control bear no consistent relationship to engagement in physical exercise (Kaplan et al., 1984; Sallis et al., 1988).

Theoretical comparisons should note that perceived self-efficacy is an important, though not the sole, determinant of health behavior in the causal structure of social cognitive theory. Some of the other contributing determinants include people's knowledge of how lifestyle habits impair and promote health, the health goals they set for themselves, the costs and benefits they anticipate for different lifestyles, the value they place on those outcomes, and the environmental facilitators and constraints on following healthful practices they encounter in their everyday lives. Dzewaltowski evaluated whether the determinants in Fishbein and Ajzen's theories add to prediction of exercise adherence over and above the predictiveness of a subset of determinants in the integrated sociocognitive theory (Dzewaltowski, 1989; Dzewaltowski et al., 1990). The sociocognitive determinants included efficacy beliefs, expected benefits of exercising, and satisfaction or dissatisfaction with the level of physical activity achieved. Both efficacy beliefs and affective self-reactions to personal progress contributed to exercise involvement. Attitudes toward exercise and perceived social pressure to become more active similarly accounted for exercise involvement, although at a lower level. The factors other than sociocognitive determinants did not improve prediction when added to the sociocognitive determinants, however. The findings of Yordy and Lent (1993) suggest that attitudes might have a residual effect after controlling for the influence of sociocognitive determinants, but the study measured the determinants of exercise intentions rather than behavior. The major challenge is to explain exercise behavior, not just the intention to exercise. Studies reviewed previously reveal that efficacy beliefs contribute to health habits both directly and by raising intentions.

The paths of influence of physical efficacy beliefs and causal attributions on progress in exercise participation have also been studied. Individuals of high perceived efficacy tend to attribute their exercise progress to personally controllable factors (McAuley, 1991). People who find exercising to be a positive experience are more likely to stick with it than those who experience it as aversive. Accomplishments in physical fitness, promoted by robust efficacy belief, can bring personal satisfaction and

improve physical well-being. Indeed, belief in one's physical efficacy contributes to positive reactions to exercising both directly and by fostering attribution of success to personal control. Efficacy beliefs reduce physiological stress reactions to vigorous exercise as well as fostering positive subjective experiences. After controlling for habitual activity level and baseline cortisol levels and aerobic capacity, confidence in one's physical efficacy predicted adrenocortical levels during treadmill running trials (Rudolph & McAuley, 1995).

Adoption of activity habits has also been examined in terms of the stage model of behavioral change proposed by Prochaska and DiClemente (1992). According to this view, in adopting new patterns of behavior, people move through a sequence of stages from precontemplators with no intention to change, to contemplators who intend to change, to actors who adopt the behavior but not yet regularly, and to maintainers who perform it regularly. Some adopters later become relapsers, reverting to their old habits. Stage theories lead one into a thicket of problems. Human functioning is simply too multifaceted and multidetermined to be categorized into a few discrete stages. For this reason, stage theories have been going out of vogue in psychological theorizing (Flavell, 1978b). People do not fit neatly into fixed stages. Predictably, substages or transitional stages must be created to encompass the human diversity. Thus, in the stages-of-change scheme, an intermediate stage of preparing for action has been inserted prior to engagement in the behavior.

A genuine stage theory has three cardinal defining properties: qualitative transformations across stages, invariant sequence of change, and nonreversibility. The classifications in the stage model under discussion are arbitrary pseudostages. In a genuine stage theory, the personal attributes at one stage are transformed into qualitatively different ones at the next stage of a fixed sequence. For example, in stage progression in biological change, a caterpillar is transformed into a butterfly. In Piaget's stage progression of psychological change, preoperational thinking is transformed into qualitatively different operational thinking. In the stage model under discussion, however, factors that vary on a continuum are arbitrarily subdivided into discrete categories called stages. The first two stages are differences in degree of intention. Precontemplators have no intention to change. Contemplators have some intention to change. Subsequent stages are simply gradations of regularity or duration of behavioral adoption rather than differences in kind, as a genuine stage theory would require. These gradations are arbitrarily dichotomized into a discrete action stage, where behavior is performed over a short time, and a maintenance stage, where behavior is performed regularly or over a long time. At the upper level of this stage view, one can continue doing the same thing but be propelled from one stage (action) to the next one (maintenance) simply by the passage of time.

In assessing stages of change, researchers try to circumvent the problem of dichotomizing a factor that varies on a continuum by requiring all-or-none judgments of intention and by arbitrarily splitting action into long or short duration or into regular or irregular categories. Where stages differ in gradation rather than in kind, the notion of stage progression is stripped of meaning or becomes a logical necessity. Thus, if exercising regularly within the last six months is the action stage and exercising regularly beyond six months is the maintenance stage (Marcus, Selby, Niaura, & Rossi, 1992), the latter is simply an extension of the former rather than a qualitative transformation of it. The subdivision of behavioral continuance at six months into different stages is arbitrary rather than grounded in a personal transformational change. One can segment the same ongoing behavior anywhere in time. Where stages differ in gradation rather than in kind, the notion of stage progression is stripped of meaning or simply acknowledges the logical necessity that a brief adoptive duration precedes a longer one.

In a genuine stage theory, the stages constitute a fixed sequence of changes that everyone must pass through. Stages cannot be skipped along the way. For example, a butterfly has to be a caterpillar first, and one cannot become an operational thinker without first being a preoperational one. For smokers who abruptly quit cigarettes and remain abstinent, there is no progression through stages. They bypass them. Most participants do not exhibit

a stable progression through the postulated sequence (Sutton, 1996). Nor does genuine stage progression permit recycling through stages. A butterfly cannot revert to a caterpillar, nor can an operational thinker go back again to a low mode of thinking. Thus, on close inspection, the stages-of-change scheme violates every major requirement of a stage theory: invariant sequence, qualitative transformation, and nonreversibility. It substitutes typecasting for analysis of the multicausation of behavior. Some researchers are now taking other continuous variables, such as degree of interest in exercising; converting them to discrete pseudostages; and then attributing effects to reified "stages" rather than to the dichotomized factor (Armstrong, Sallis, Hovell, & Hofstetter, 1993). Such arbitrary conversion and rechristening of a meaningfully labeled factor with a nondescript stage name befogs causal analyses.

The stage scheme under discussion substitutes a categorical approach for a process model of human adaptation and change. Contrary to claims, a shift from one descriptive category of intention to another or from one duration of behavior to another does not make the stage approach a dynamic process model. Even a genuine stage theory is at best a descriptive device rather than an explanatory one. For example, categorizing individuals as "precontemplators" provides no explanation for why they do not consider making changes that could benefit them. They may be disinclined to change because they are uninformed about the risks of their current habits or the benefits of alternative habits. They may know the potential risks and benefits but be convinced that they lack the efficacy to surmount recurrent impediments. Or they may have little incentive to change because they view the benefits of their current habit as greater than its potential detriments. These various determinants of inaction — risk perception, efficacy belief, and outcome expectations — call for different strategies to get "noncontemplators" to consider altering their detrimental habits. People do not recycle through stages. They fluctuate in their struggle to exercise control over their health behavior. Their attainments are a product of interactive causation involving personal factors, behavior, and environmental influences. In these behavioral fluctuations, which can occur quickly in some health domains, people are varying in their self-regulatory command, not undergoing repeated transformational changes.

Stage thinking can constrain the scope of interventions to promote change. For example, in smoking behavior, "precontemplators" have a low sense of efficacy that they can get themselves to quit, and they expect negative outcomes for quitting and little social support for the effort were they to do so (deVries & Backbier, 1994). But the prescription for change emphasizes the need to alter their outcome expectations about smoking. In point of fact, an effective intervention not only must persuade "precontemplators" of the benefits of quitting but must instill beliefs that they have the ability to succeed and enlist social supports to see them through tough times. Unlike the categorizing approach, a process model specifies the determinants and intervening mechanisms that govern different facets of change.

The basic processes of personal change have been identified and their determinants extensively researched (Bandura, 1986a; O'Leary & Wilson, 1987). They include adoption, generalization, relapse and recovery, and maintenance of new styles of behavior. The stage scheme converts these basic change processes into discrete descriptive categories stripped from their extensive knowledge base. Such knowledge provides guidelines for how to structure effective interventions to initiate, generalize, and maintain habit changes. Classifying behavior by regularity or duration says nothing about its determinants that would aid selection of appropriate interventions. What the stage scheme adds is simply the reminder that some people have no interest in changing their health habits. Others are riper for change. This common knowledge hardly requires the encumbrance of stage theorizing.

The stage model comes with a host of interventions drawn from divergent theories on the assumption that they may be incompatible in etiology but compatible for behavior change. In point of fact, the behavioristic, psychodynamic, and existential theories, from which this "transtheoretical" collection is forged, offer contradictory prescriptions for how to change human behavior. The menagerie of

interventions is not transtheoretical, which implies an overreaching integration of seeming diversity. It is atheoretical. For example, counterconditioning and altering faulty beliefs would be regarded as incompatible strategies by the proponents of these alternative approaches. In fact, conditioning theorists reject beliefs as causes of behavior and therefore consider it pointless to change them. Cognitivists, in turn, construe conditioning operations as a laborious way of creating outcome expectations that serve as motivators rather than as automatic implanters of responses. Since the stages mainly describe behavior rather than specifying determinants, the linkage of interventions to stages is rather loose and debatable rather than explicitly derivable from the stages. A self-regulation model is a process model linked to explicit interventions. Individualized interventions, tailored to personal attributes and rate of progress, are more effective than uniform ones. Effective interventions, however, must target the constellation of determinants that govern health habits, not contrived pseudostages.

The two sets of determinants — namely, perceived self-efficacy and expected costs and benefits of exercising — differentiate individuals cast into the various stages (Lechner & deVries, 1995; Marcus & Owen, 1992; Marcus et al., 1992), Individuals who have no intention of becoming physically active have a lower sense of efficacy than sedentary intenders who, in turn, express lower efficacy beliefs than those who have recently become physically active. Good adherers have the highest sense of personal efficacy. The personal and social outcome expectations for exercising similarly differentiate individuals categorized into different stages. For nonintenders, the expected disadvantages far outweigh the expected benefits; for intenders, the disadvantages and benefits are about equal; and for those who have adopted exercise and stick with it, the expected benefits outweigh the disadvantages.

Were a genuine stage theory to be devised, the issue of interest would be whether stage status retains any predictability after the influence of the full set of sociocognitive determinants is removed. The stages of change model, however, defines most of the stages in terms of the very behavior to be explained. This creates circularity of explanation and prediction. To ask whether high stage status foretells enduring change is to ask whether good maintainers (maintenance stage) are good maintainers.

Strategies for Promoting Active Lifestyles

For most people who lead sedentary lives, adoption and maintenance of lifestyle activity patterns requires development of self-regulatory capabilities. Effective self-enablement programs include a number of facets. To begin with, participants must be fully informed of the multiple health benefits of physical activity and the eroding effects of remaining sedentary. Otherwise, they have little reason to keep driving themselves to exhaustion. Linking exercise knowledge to valuation of health provides some incentive to become more physically active. If people are to convert health interests to lifestyle activity patterns, however, they must be taught how to motivate themselves to override the many impediments to exercising regularly. The inherent aversive effects of vigorous exercise — such as muscular strain, fatigue, and discomfort — are immediately felt, whereas the health benefits are slowly cumulative and are not always easy to discern. Another major impediment to exercising is that there is always a host of more interesting or pressing things to do. Without some explicit time management, exercise readily falls victim to competing activities.

A major strategy for developing the efficacy and motivational supports needed for adopting physical exercise derives from knowledge of self-regulation. This strategy involves instruction on self-monitoring of physical activity, proximal goal setting leading to more vigorous activities, and supportive feedback. Subgoal attainments build a sense of physical efficacy, and efficacy beliefs, in turn, determine the strength of commitment to exercising and perseverance in the face of contravening influences. The elements of self-regulation must be enlisted together rather than piecemeal to achieve good results. Thus, people sustain a vigorous level of physical activity when they have goals

and feedback on progress, whereas goals without feedback or feedback without any goals have little effect. When faced with slow progress or setbacks, those of low efficacy slacken their efforts or give up, but those of high efficacy redouble their efforts.

Sedentary people do not take up vigorous activity at the outset or stick with it for long. Perceived self-efficacy predicts short-term adoption of vigorous activities but long-term maintenance of moderate activities (Sallis et al., 1986). Programs designed to make exercising a habit should provide subgoal incentives for pursuits that begin at moderate levels of exertion and gradually increase the frequency, duration, and intensity of physical activity.

People need supportive feedback to sustain their efforts, especially during early phases of exercise adoption when exertion for the physically unfit is onerous and benefits are hard to find. Some of the immediate physiological benefits can be augmented and highlighted as motivators. For example, neophyte exercisers may not be moved by visions of distal risk reduction when their physical exertion fatigues and pains them, but they can be motivated to put up with the inconveniences and physical discomfort by evidence of improved cardiovascular functional capacity. By monitoring their pulse rate and respiration levels, they see that they can perform vigorous activities at lower heart rates and with quicker cardiac recovery. Miniaturized recording devices now enable people to monitor changes in the strength and efficiency of their cardiovascular system. Evidence of progress in increased activity and improvement in one's general physical condition provides another incentive that helps one to stay motivated. Progressive mastery also strengthens beliefs of physical capability. Regardless of level of physical fitness, the stronger the perceived efficacy and the higher the sense of personal accomplishment, the greater the interest and enjoyment in the physical activity (McAuley et al., 1991).

Physical activity produces affective reactions that, depending on their nature, can invest exercise with positive or negative value. Much of the interest in affect regulation has centered on the capacity of physical exercise to reduce stress and depression. Exercise can generate positive affective states as well as alleviate aversive ones. however. McAuley and Courneya (1992) show that efficacy beliefs influence affective responsiveness to physical exercise. When exercising at the same level relative to their capacity, individuals who have a high sense of efficacy feel they are exerting themselves less and find the activity more enjoyable than those who have a low perceived efficacy. Experiencing the affectivity during exercise as positive feeling states, in turn, strengthens belief of physical efficacy (McAuley, Shaffer, & Rudolph, 1995). This effect remains after controlling for age, preexisting self-efficacy, and cardiorespiratory fitness.

Adherence to lifestyle activity patterns is aided by social as well as personal determinants. The social support and modeling of active lifestyles by family members and friends contribute to perceived self-regulatory efficacy to stay physically active (Hofstetter, Hovell, & Sallis, 1990). Indeed, good adherers create environmental supports for themselves by enlisting exercise partners in aerobic and recreational activities. During early phases of exercise adoption, when discomforts far outweigh any noticeable benefits, neophyte exercisers who receive periodic support and guidance improve their functional capacity more than those who do not (King, Taylor, Haskell, & DeBusk, 1988).

Social influences produce behavioral effects largely through their impact on personal determinants. Previous analyses showed that, in the regulation of affective states, social support lessens depression to the extent that it raises perceived coping efficacy. Duncan and McAuley (1993) further corroborate the mediational role of efficacy beliefs. Social support affects exercise adherence by influencing efficacy beliefs rather than directly. Knowledge of operative mechanisms provides guidelines for how to optimize the benefits of social networks. Social support should highlight the growth of personal capabilities rather than promoting dependence on the group for one's attainments. If successes are construed as largely under social control, exercise adherence is likely to deteriorate with fluctuations or reductions in social support.

McAuley and his coworkers sought to enhance exercise adherence in sedentary adults by enlisting the four modes of efficacy development (McAuley, Courneya, Rudolph, & Lox, 1994). In the enactive mode, participants tracked the progress in their exercise activity and improvements in their aerobic capacity. In the vicarious mode, they viewed videotapes of individuals like themselves becoming stronger, fitter, and more limber by adopting an active lifestyle. In the social persuasory mode, they formed a buddy system to exercise together and encourage each other at times of difficulty. In the physiological mode, they were reassured that their somatic discomforts were natural bodily adaptations to becoming fitter. The adults who had the benefit of this program adhered better to exercise activities than their counterparts in a control group who participated with a lot of attention and health information but without the efficacy enhancement. The disparity in activity habits increased over time as the controls quickly reverted to their sedentary lifestyle. The initial perceived efficacy was assessed as the treatment was being introduced, so it could not be much influenced by it. The initial efficacy beliefs, which probably reflected preexisting levels of perceived efficacy, and the subsequent ones, supported exercise adherence, especially during periods when the best of intentions fell by the wayside. Where people get themselves to exercise together, their collective efficacy, which brings the faltering ones along, may be an even better predictor of exercise adherence than their individual levels of perceived efficacy.

Given that the route from a sedentary lifestyle to an active one is typically plagued by setbacks and aborted tries, effective interventions must include instruction in strategies for managing lapses and resuming regular exercise. Training in relapse management involves adopting the cognitive set that slips are a natural part of the process of gaining mastery rather than further verification of physical incapabilities. Such functional styles of thinking facilitate resumption of activity patterns after they have been interrupted and prevent a temporary lapse from turning into an enduring relapse. To function preventively, individuals must identify major impediments to exercising and learn how to take the preparatory action needed to surmount them.

In addition, they need to be taught skills for how to reinstate control over their exercise behavior should they lapse into inactivity. The recovery strategies include monitoring declines in physical and cardiovascular fitness with reversion to sedentary habits and enhancement of fitness with resumption of a more active lifestyle; reaffirming exercise and fitness goals and reinstating positive self-incentives to support regular exercise patterns; and managing time in ways that reduce the inconvenience of exercise activities, because time constraints are leading impediments to exercising. And finally, people need instruction about how to structure a supportive environment for their activity patterns. Simulated episodes of reversions to sedentary habits provide opportunities for participants to rehearse how they would use the different strategies to get themselves to resume exercising. Training in relapse management skills aids maintenance of activity habits, although the size and the direction of the gain leaves a lot of room for improvement (Belisle, Roskies, & Levesque, 1987; King & Frederiksen, 1984; Marcus & Stanton, 1993). To promote better exercise adherence, either the self-management procedures need to be strengthened or the programs need to be broadened to enlist social support for exercise activities, or both.

Promoting health through adoption of active lifestyles requires a broad public health approach rather than just an attempt to convert sedentary adults into devout exercisers. Schools have an essential role to play in such an effort because physical education is a regular part of the educational system. Much of this activity, however, is devoted to team sports rather than to development of recreational activities that can serve lifelong fitness. Childhood involvement in organized sports does not create a sense of physical efficacy and habits of exercise that carry over into adulthood (Hofstetter et al., 1990). It is more likely to produce avid spectators of sports than active adults. If educational systems are to prepare youth to lead active lives, they need to promote valuation of physical fitness and habits of exercise that are transferable to adulthood. Reorienting the form of physical education is especially appropriate at the secondary school level, where the transition from childhood to adult activity patterns is beginning to take shape. Families also need to be enlisted as active partners in promoting their children's physical fitness.

Exercise Efficacy in Secondary Prevention of Physical Impairment

The analysis so far has focused mainly on the contribution of efficacy beliefs to the adoption of regular exercise designed to enhance well-being and to prevent the development of major health problems. Because a sedentary lifestyle adversely affects a variety of bodily functions, physical exercise is also often prescribed to prevent further physical impairments in health problems that have already occurred. Perceived self-regulatory efficacy plays much the same role in secondary prevention of disease from getting worse as it does in primary prevention of disease from happening in the first place.

Coronary heart disease is a leading contributor to mortality. Vigorous exercise in some type of leisure activity reduces the incidence of both the first signs of heart disease and fatal heart attacks (Morris, Everitt, Pollard, Chave, & Semmence, 1980; Paffenbarger et al., 1993). The incidence of heart attacks rises slowly with age in physically active individuals but rises sharply with age in sedentary individuals. The protective function of physical activity remains very much in evidence when other factors known to influence risk of heart attack are taken into account. Given the prevalence of sedentary habits and evidence that inactive adults are about twice as likely to die of cardiovascular disease as active ones (Berlin & Colditz, 1990), physical inactivity is a serious health risk factor.

Prescription of physical exercise does not necessarily result in enduring adoption by patients even though it may lower the risk of further morbidity or mortality. As is true for asymptomatic participants from the general community, cardiac patients who have a low sense of efficacy to regulate their health habits are sporadic adopters and poor adherers to exercise regimens. Exercise prescriptions, therefore, must be merged with psychosocial programs that build patients' beliefs in their self-regulatory capabilities. Interventions designed to strengthen the cardiovascular system in postcoronary patients typify this efficacy-oriented approach.

About half the patients who experience myocardial infarctions have uncomplicated ones that leave little residual impairment (DeBusk, Kraemer, & Nash, 1983). The heart heals rapidly, and patients are physically capable of resuming an active life. The psychological and physical recovery is slow, however, for those who believe they have a chronically fragile heart. They avoid physical exertion. They fear that they cannot handle the strains in their vocational and social life. They are slow to return to work, take on only part-time work, or give up work altogether, which creates economic hardships. They give up energetic recreational activities. They fear that sexual activities will do them in, so they curtail sexual activity. The recovery problems stem more from patients' beliefs that their cardiac system has been permanently impaired than from physical debility.

The rehabilitative task is to convince patients that they have a sufficiently robust cardiovascular system to lead full, productive lives. Each of the four modes of efficacy influence can be used to enhance patients' beliefs in their cardiac capabilities. Mastery of taxing physical activities without any untoward effects provides convincing demonstrations of cardiac capabilities. Modeling influences, in which ex-patients exemplify the active lives they are leading, can strengthen belief in the restorability of cardiac function. Physicians use their expertise and prestige to persuade patients of their physical capabilities. They also correct patients' tendency to misread their physiology by incorrectly attributing fluctuations in physical functioning arising from other causes to an impaired heart.

Some of the research has examined the strength of enactive mastery and persuasive medical counseling to instill beliefs of physical and cardiac efficacy (Ewart et al., 1983). In the enactive mode, patients perform a symptom-limited treadmill routine in which they master increasingly heavier workloads to convince themselves that they have a robust cardiac system. In the social persuasive mode, the medical staff explains to patients their cardiac capabilities and encourages them to resume activities in their daily life at levels that are medically safe. Successful performance of increasing workloads strengthens patients' beliefs in their physical efficacy. Persuasive counseling has a small additive effect on perceived efficacy to withstand different types of physical strain, including sexual activity. Preexisting efficacy beliefs predict workload attainments on the treadmill that patients had not performed before. The more the intervention raises patients' efficacy beliefs, the more active they become in their everyday lives. Indeed, efficacy beliefs are more predictive of activity patterns than physical capability as measured by treadmill attainments.

Health benefits are achieved by vigorous physical activity sustained over brief periods several times per week. Postcoronary patients are usually advised to exercise at a level that ranges between 70 and 85 percent of their maximal heart rate on the treadmill. In a comparative evaluation of predictors, Ewart and his colleagues found that perceived efficacy for sustained exercise is a good predictor of adherence to the prescribed heart rate range, whereas actual physical capability is not (Ewart et al., 1986). Efficacy beliefs remain a significant predictor even after controlling for prior performance attainments on the treadmill. Patients who have a high sense of efficacy tend to overexercise. Those who doubt their physical efficacy underexercise at levels that provide little cardiovascular benefits. Type A personality orientation, depression, marital adjustment, or medication status do not predict adherence to the prescribed level of exercise.

These findings carry important clinical implications for postcoronary rehabilitation. Patients' physical activity is determined more by their perceived capabilities than by their actual physical capabilities. Exercise prescriptions made without regard to patients' beliefs in their physical capabilities may expose the overestimators to unnecessary risks through overexertion and lead the underestimators to languid exercise that provides them little health benefits. Different physical activities require different skills and levels of stamina. Domain-related beliefs of efficacy, therefore, provide better predictors of, and guides for, activity habits than do global ones (Ewart et al., 1986). Self-efficacy assessments should be tailored to the types of exercises that are being prescribed. Cardiac patients who are firmly convinced they have a debilitated heart may require a combination of exercise activities to restore a general belief in their physical capabilities. By promoting efficacy beliefs of appropriate strength for prescribed restorative activities, patients have the benefit of safe and effective exercise programs to which they are likely to adhere.

Several modes of influence have been evaluated for their power to restore a sense of physical capability in coronary patients so that they can resume active lives without constant fear of precipitating another heart attack. Fulfilling the strenuous demands of treadmill workloads is a convincing persuader, as already documented. The evident physical stamina, if underscored as a generic indicant of cardiovascular capacity, can have a generalized impact on beliefs of cardiac and physical efficacy. We saw in Chapter 7 that wives may play an influential role in whether their husbands lead active or constricted postcoronary lives (Taylor et al., 1985). Reassuring wives that their husbands can safely resume normal activities does not convince them in the least if they believe that their husbands' cardiac and physical capabilities are frail. Clearly, factual information alone is not enough. But the combined influence of experiencing firsthand the strenuousness of the treadmill and seeing their husbands withstand heavy workloads convinces them that their husbands have a robust heart. Once their efficacy beliefs have been altered, the wives are more receptive to the factual information about cardiac capabilities provided by the medical staff.

Belief in cardiac efficacy transforms construal of physical activity as dangerous to a belief that it is benign or beneficial. Anxiety over precipitating another heart attack stems from beliefs of cardiovascular frailty. Postcoronary patients who believe that they have a robust heart do not perceive physical activity as a threat or a cause for anxiety. Couples, of course, influence each other and do things together. Resumption of an active postcoronary life,

therefore, is determined mutually rather than individually. Depending on their nature, efficacy beliefs can foster overprotectiveness or an active life that strengthens the cardiovascular system in ways that protect against recurrence of coronary events.

Analysis of familial efficacy belief systems corroborates the social dynamics of postcoronary recovery (Taylor et al., 1985). Both the patients' and their wives' beliefs in the patients' cardiac and physical capabilities predicted the level of recovery of cardiovascular functioning. Couples' joint beliefs in the patients' physical capabilities, however, were more predictive of subsequent cardiovascular functioning than were their individual beliefs. Actual capability did not predict the degree of cardiovascular recovery when the effect of efficacy beliefs was removed, whereas efficacy beliefs retained their predictiveness when actual capability was removed. Interestingly, cardiovascular recovery is associated more strongly with beliefs about the strength of the heart to withstand strain than with beliefs about physical capabilities. It is the perceived fragility of the heart that weighs heavily in the regulation of physical activity. A comprehensive rehabilitation program must embrace the social and psychological aspects as well as the medical aspects of coronary heart disease.

Another way of getting patients to lead active lives that help to protect against recurrence of coronary events is by enlisting self-regulatory influence through the motivational function of goal systems. In this approach, patients monitor the health habits they seek to change, set attainable subgoals to motivate and direct their efforts, and receive supportive feedback to sustain the effort needed to succeed. The level of physical activity is geared to cardiovascular capabilities and is progressively raised as the heart is strengthened. Periodic self-efficacy assessments guide the recovery program. The usual postcoronary medical care does little to reduce detrimental health habits likely to contribute to future heart attacks. This type of self-regulatory system, which was reviewed in Chapter 7, provides an individualized case management system that is easily integrated into standard medical care to reduce multiple risk factors for coronary heart disease

(DeBusk et al., 1994). Compared to patients who receive the standard postcoronary care, those who have had the benefit of the self-regulatory system exercise more, are much better exercise adherers, and achieve greater gains in functional cardiovascular capacity.

Persuasory modes of influence have also been used to facilitate postcoronary recovery through efficacy enhancement. Gortner and Jenkins (1990) provide one such example regarding recovery from cardiac surgery involving coronary artery bypass grafting or valve replacement. Patients receive didactic instruction in the hospital on symptom interpretation, exercise, nutrition, and strategies for familial coping with the physical and emotional aspects of convalescence. Following discharge, they receive weekly telephone contacts to monitor their recovery and to provide further guidance and support with difficulties they have encountered. The intervention raises patients' beliefs in their physical efficacy and hastens their resumption of normal physical activities. Efficacy beliefs predict subsequent level of activity after multiple controls are applied for demographic characteristics, type of surgery, and baseline activity and functional status. Mood states are unrelated to physical activity during the recovery phase, but they can affect the restorative process indirectly through their impact on efficacy beliefs. Thus, for patients who have undergone coronary angioplasty, positive moods raise efficacy beliefs, which, in turn, predict adoption of lifestyle changes that can improve cardiovascular functioning (Jensen et al., 1993).

Efficacy beliefs affect personal management of chronic respiratory disease as well as coronary heart disease. These medical dysfunctions include chronic bronchitis, emphysema, and asthma. People suffering from obstructive pulmonary disease can improve their level of functioning by strengthening their cardiorespiratory system through physical activity. Many of them lead constricted lives because they distrust their efficacy to manage breathing difficulties in certain situations or while performing activities that might require physical exertion or are emotionally arousing (Wigal, Creer, & Kotses, 1991). Kaplan, Atkins, and Reinsch (1984)

tested different types of interventions designed to increase regular exercise in patients who were experiencing progressive loss of pulmonary function. One intervention combined goal setting with positive incentives for exercising. A second intervention centered on eliminating erroneous beliefs about the risks of exercise and substituting positive self-guidance; a third intervention combined the two approaches. All three interventions enhanced beliefs in physical capability, but the enactive forms proved more effective than cognitive restructuring alone. The higher the perceived physical efficacy, the better the patients adhered to prescribed exercises, improved in lung functioning, and increased their capacity for physical exertion and their sense of well-being. General beliefs about the locus of control of health were unrelated to the changes in either physical or pulmonary functioning.

Physical exercise also plays an influential role in the management of diabetes. Through its effects on metabolic function, inactivity increases intolerance of glucose, which is vital for carbohydrate metabolism. This dysfunction, which is exacerbated by sedentary habits and obesity, can be reduced by physical activity. The greater the improvement in oxygen consumption through physical exercise, the better the insulin-mediated glucose utilization (Soman, Koivisto, Deibert, Felig, & DeFronzo, 1979). Diabetes beginning in adulthood can be delayed or averted by exercise and weight control. Even early-onset diabetes can benefit from physical activity. Self-management of insulin-dependent diabetes requires strict temporal regulation of many aspects of one's daily living. To achieve optimal metabolic control, diabetics must monitor glucose levels and balance insulin doses with proper meals and exercise.

Diabetics vary in their beliefs that they can exercise adequate control over the dietary, exercise, and self-medicative aspects of their self-care regimen. Those who have a high sense of efficacy are better at managing their health behaviors, of which exercise is an important part. Efficacy beliefs predict variation in adherence after a host of other potential determinants are controlled, including demographic characteristics, type and severity of diabetes, previous level of adherence, mood states, knowledge of how health behaviors affect diabetes, and skill in managing troublesome situations (Crabtree, 1986; Hurley & Shea, 1992; Kavanagh, Gooley & Wilson, 1993; McCaul et al., 1987). These findings have significant clinical implications. Interventions designed to promote self-management of diabetes must be structured in ways that build the efficacy beliefs needed to support adherence to the arduous regimen. The preceding review amply documents that, across a variety of disabling conditions, regular exercise is an important means for restoring and maintaining functioning at the highest level possible. Beliefs of personal efficacy are influential in making exercising a habit both to enhance health and to ameliorate functional impairments.

Self-management of insulin-dependent diabetes, asthma, and other chronic illnesses presents special challenges for young children. Interactive video game systems provide a promising vehicle for raising children's perceived efficacy and enabling them to exercise control over their health by adopting beneficial self-care habits (Lieberman & Brown, 1995). For example, in a video role-playing game for diabetics, players win points depending on how well they understand the diabetic condition and regulate the diet, insulin, and blood sugar levels of the superheroes. The better they manage the superhero's diabetic condition the higher the triumphs over hostile forces. The game format for health promotion is a highly appealing approach that provides repeated opportunities to practice health-related behaviors with quick feedback of consequences for the decisions and actions taken. For children with diabetes, the health-oriented video game surpassed a control video game in boosting their perceived self-care efficacy, self-initiated discussions of their diabetic condition, and adoption of dietary and insulin practices to keep their blood sugar level under control (Brown et al., in press). Moreover, children who practiced diabetic self-care in the game format had a 75 percent reduction in urgent doctor visits for diabetes emergencies, whereas the controls increased such visits by 7 percent. The action adventure format similarly improved knowledge and enhanced perceived efficacy to avoid asthma triggers and to use emergency medications in young children suffering from asthma (Lieberman, in press). This is but the beginning in the creative use of the interactive video technology to promote child and adolescent health. Online networks, such as the Internet, present vast enabling opportunities for self-management of health.

10

Organizational Functioning

PEOPLE SPEND A MAJOR PART of their lives in occupational activities. A vocation does more than simply supply income for our livelihood. Occupations structure a large part of people's everyday reality and provide us with a major source of personal identity and sense of self-worth. The work we do determines whether a substantial part of our lives is repetitively boring, burdensome, and distressing or lastingly challenging and self-fulfilling. Work is not entirely a private matter. It is an interdependent activity that structures a good part of people's social relations. The social interconnectedness is another aspect of work that affects people's well-being. This chapter examines the role of perceived self-efficacy in what people choose as their life's work, how well they prepare themselves for their chosen pursuits, and the level of success they achieve in their everyday work. Most occupational activities are performed in concert with others rather than independently. In such instances, people's sense of collective efficacy determines their well-being and what they accomplish as a group.

CAREER DEVELOPMENT AND PURSUITS

The choices people make during the formative periods of development shape the course of their lives. Such choices determine which of their potentialities they cultivate, the types of options that are foreclosed or remain realizable over their life course, and the lifestyle they follow. Among the choices that affect life paths, those that center on career choice and development are of special import for reasons already mentioned. The process of choosing a career path is not an easy one. In making career decisions, people must come to grips with uncertainties about their capabilities, the stability of their interests, the current and long-range prospects of alternative occupations, the accessibility of potential careers, and the type of identity they seek to construct for themselves.

Career Choice and Development

A substantial body of research shows that beliefs of personal efficacy play a key role in career development and pursuits. The higher the perceived efficacy to fulfill educational requirements and job functions, the wider the range of career options people seriously consider pursuing and the greater the interest they have in them (Betz & Hackett, 1981; Lent et al., 1986; Matsui, Ikeda, & Ohnishi, 1989). Efficacy beliefs set the slate of options for serious consideration. People rapidly eliminate from consideration entire classes of vocations on the basis of perceived efficacy, whatever benefits they might hold. Efficacy beliefs predict the range of career options people consider viable for themselves when variations in actual ability, prior level of academic achievement, and vocational interests are controlled. Because mathematics is an essential entry skill for scientific and technological occupations, a low sense of mathematical efficacy operates as a barrier to a wide range of occupational pursuits requiring quantitative skills. In fact, perceived mathematical efficacy contributes more significantly to educational and career choices making use of quantitative skills than does amount of mathematical preparation in high school, level of mathematical ability and past achievement, and anxiety over mathematical activities (Hackett & Betz, 1989). Perceived mathematical efficacy affects not only occupational choices but how well students perform in mathematics course work that provides requisite skills. As these studies reveal, it is not experience or skills per se but the beliefs of personal efficacy constructed from those experiences that shape academic performance and career choices.

In much of the efficacy research on career choice, people judge their capabilities for different occupations as they perceive them. Some writers have suggested that perceived occupational efficacy should be measured in relation to the types of skills the occupations require. This prescription assumes that occupational decision making relies on sound knowledge of the actual competencies underlying various occupations. In fact, people typically consider certain occupational pursuits and stay clear of others based on their conceptions of occupations, which may be accurate or fanciful. They act on their conceptions even though those conceptions may involve misbeliefs about the actual skill requirements of the occupations. For example, many people do not pursue careers requiring computer skills in the mistaken belief that such skills call for advanced mathematical competencies. To target personal efficacy to subskills of occupations can lower the predictiveness of efficacy beliefs for the occupations people choose to pursue. We saw earlier that it is not perceived efficacy for isolated subskills but perceived efficacy to use them together under varying demands that predicts the choices people make and their performance accomplishments.

Sex differences have been examined for perceived efficacy to perform discrete work activities and to fulfill duties of various jobs involving those same activities. The findings corroborate the influential role in career choices of cultural sex-typing of occupational pursuits. Women generally judge themselves less efficacious for scientific occupations than do men. Sex differences disappear, however, when women judge their efficacy to perform the same investigative activities that scientists conduct but in everyday activities rather than in the context of scientific occupations (Matsui & Tsukamoto, 1991). Similarly, women generally express a lower sense of efficacy for occupations requiring quantitative skills, but they do not differ from men or surpass them in their efficacy to perform the same quantitative activities in stereotypically feminine tasks (Betz & Hackett, 1983; Junge & Dretzke, 1995). Such findings suggest that gender-related efficacy impediments arise less from the discrete skills themselves than from their linkage to stereotypically male occupations. Gender stereotyping of pursuits that suggests lesser ability diminishes judgments of personal efficacy for the required skills. Different types of efficacy measures serve different explanatory and predictive purposes. Assessment of efficacy to fulfill job duties is well suited for elucidating choice of occupational pursuits.

Assessment of efficacy for basic skill domains provides useful information for career guidance and training.

People act on their beliefs of vocational efficacy as well as their knowledge about potential career options. Perceived efficacy to master scientific knowledge predicts successful academic course work and perseverance in scientific fields of study (Lent, Brown, & Larkin, 1984). Students with a low sense of efficacy perform less well and are inclined to drop out of scientific fields. Perceived inefficacy is predictive of withdrawal from other occupational fields of study as well (Harvey & McMurray, 1994). Career development includes milestones of accomplishment along the way. Strong belief in personal efficacy to surmount major hurdles is a different aspect of efficacy that contributes to success and level of perseverance beyond that of belief in one's capability to master particular subjects (Lent et al., 1986). Including more facets of efficacy beliefs as they operate in a given endeavor increases their predictive power. If perceived efficacy to regulate one's study activities and to manage stress were added to other facets of personal efficacy, the expanded set of efficacy beliefs would undoubtedly account for even more of the variation in occupational development. Thus, studies measuring only a portion of the efficacy beliefs that govern motivation and performance in a given domain underestimate the magnitude of their contribution to human accomplishments. As in the determination of career consideration, perceived efficacy is not simply a reflection of actual ability. Efficacy beliefs account for students' academic attainments and steadfastness to their field of study above and beyond their actual ability and vocational interests.

The contribution of efficacy beliefs to variation in performance is also underestimated by overcontrol for ability level or past achievements. In multivariate regression analyses, perceived efficacy is routinely assessed after the effects of ability, past achievement, and high school preparation have been controlled. We saw in Chapter 6 that efficacy beliefs contribute substantially to the development of intellectual abilities and to academic achievements. It is not as though efficacy beliefs remain mysteriously inert in earlier developmental periods but abruptly arise as determinants of cognitive skill development and achievement in college. Because efficacy beliefs influence past cognitive skill development, academic achievement, and degree of interest in activities, giving these factors causal priority in multivariate analyses without removing the variance in these predictors accounted for by beliefs of personal efficacy provides a conservative estimate of the unique contribution of efficacy beliefs to career development.

Perceived efficacy can also contribute to career pursuits through its effects on the development of interests. Chapter 6 analyzed the various processes through which efficacy beliefs build enduring interest in activities. Lent and his colleagues corroborate this relationship for occupational interests (Lent et al., 1989). The higher the perceived efficacy to fulfill the educational requirements of various science and engineering fields, the stronger the interest in those occupations as measured by standardized inventories of vocational interests. Evidence that efficacy beliefs relate to interest in a selective rather than an indiscriminate way adds to the significance of the findings. Thus, a high sense of efficacy for engineering specialties is accompanied by interest in technical activities, whereas high perceived efficacy for science specialties is accompanied by interest in more theoretical abstract activities. Beliefs of personal efficacy account for interests across different occupational pursuits (Lapan, Boggs, & Morrill, 1989; Lent et al., 1991) and specialization within a career pursuit (Bieschke, Bishop, & Garcia, 1996).

Social cognitive theory posits a reciprocal but asymmetric relationship between perceived efficacy and occupational interests, with efficacy beliefs playing the stronger determinant role. As already documented, people who are beset with doubts about their efficacy either shun occupations in the corresponding domains or fail to mount the perseverant effort needed to succeed should they get into them. Neither avoidance nor failure provide much opportunity for growth of occupational interests. Perceived efficacy creates interests through engrossment in activities and the self-satisfactions derived from fulfilling personal challenges that lead to progressive mastery of occupational activities. Interest, in turn, fosters engagement in activities, which further enhances personal efficacy.

There is some evidence to suggest that perceived efficacy may influence different aspects of career pursuits through different processes. Efficacy beliefs influence career choice through their effects on vocational interests (Lent et al., 1991, 1993). It is one thing to select a career field of study but quite another to stick with it and master it when the road to success is strewn with countless difficulties. Perceived efficacy is likely to promote steadfastness to a career and high performance in it through motivational, cognitive, and affective processes. Thus, perceived efficacy contributes to persistence and performance attainments, but vocational interests do not (Lent et al., 1986).

The preceding studies have centered mainly on the career choice and development of young adults. The influential role of perceived self-efficacy in shaping occupational trajectories is indicated in research on sociostructural determinants of children's beliefs about their occupational efficacy and their consideration of different career options (Bandura, Barbaranelli, Caprara, & Pastorelli, 1997). Socioeconomic status has no direct effects on either occupational efficacy or career considerations. Rather, it has an indirect impact by influencing parents' beliefs in their efficacy to promote their children's educational development and the aspirations they hold for them. Parental efficacy and aspirations raise children's educational aspirations and their sense of academic, social, and self-regulatory efficacy.

The patterning of children's perceived efficacy influences the types of occupational activities they believe they can do, which, in turn, is linked to the kinds of jobs they would choose for their life's work. For example, children of high perceived academic efficacy have high educational aspirations and a strong sense of efficacy for scientific, educational, literary, and medical pursuits. They favor careers requiring advanced educational development. Children of high perceived social efficacy judge themselves efficacious mainly for service occupations and would choose as their life's work jobs involving public service, caregiving, and other nurturant activities. The combination of parents' low efficacy and aspirations, children's low aspirations, and weak efficacy for human service careers are the psychosocial forces that lead children to view their occupational life in jobs of manual labor. During this formative period, their actual academic achievement is not a determinant of their perceived occupational efficacy or preferred choice of work life. In short, children's anticipated occupational choices fit their pattern of perceived personal and occupational efficacy.

Perceived self-efficacy also emerges as the key mediator of socioeconomic and family influences on children's preparatory progress toward occupational goals in research conducted by Call, Mortimer, Lee, and Dennehy, (1993). Both socioeconomic status and parental support indirectly influence children's academic achievement and college preparation through their effects on children's belief in their efficacy to shape their occupational future and livelihood. The higher their perceived efficacy, the better they do academically and the more preparatory effort they invest in pursuit of higher education. Children of various backgrounds differ little in occupational aspirations, but those of high perceived efficacy are the ones who take concrete preparatory steps toward their educational goals. For those who doubt they can exercise much personal control over their occupational future, working hard is not worth the effort.

Comparative Tests of Theories of Career Choice

Another line of research that addresses itself to the impact of efficacy beliefs on career choice and development involves comparative tests of alternative theories. Lent and his colleagues compared the predictive power of perceived self-efficacy with predictors from two other theories of career development and functioning (Lent, Brown, & Larkin, 1987). According to Holland (1985), satisfying career choices and achievement depend on a good fit between a person's occupational interests and the occupational environment. Artistic types seek artistic environments, and technical types seek technical environments. In the theory of decision making advanced by Janis and Mann (1977), thinking about the potential consequences of alternative courses of action, especially the disadvantages, before making final decisions inoculates one against subsequent difficulties because they were foreseen. Consideration of negative aspects beforehand strengthens commitment to the decision that was made and thus supports persistence in occupational pursuits when things are not going well.

The explanatory power of these alternative predictors was tested with students embarking on science and engineering careers. Perceived efficacy made a unique contribution over and above ability and past academic achievement to how well students performed in science courses, their steadfastness to a science major, and the range of options they seriously considered pursuing within a variety of science and engineering fields. Neither the fit between person and environment nor anticipatory consequential thinking predicted academic achievement or occupational perseverance. Matching qualities alone will not motivate and sustain individuals in the face of difficulties if they doubt they have what it takes to succeed in pursuits that hold some interest for them. Congruence was related only to range of career considerations and vocational decisiveness. Similarly, anticipating difficulties will not necessarily stiffen persistence in the presence of nagging self-doubts in one's capability to overcome the obstacles.

Wheeler (1983) compared the relative predictiveness of self-efficacy and expectancy-value theories with regard to occupational preferences. People judged their capabilities to fulfill the requirements of different occupations. They also judged the types of outcomes each of these occupational pursuits provides and the value of those outcomes. The range of outcomes included such things as salary, security, social status, freedom to exercise initiative and use one's special abilities, variety in work assignments, chance to learn new competencies, opportunity for advancement and

leadership, congenial associates, and the social benefits of the particular line of work. These various benefits subsumed in the conception of instrumental value represent the outcome expectations in social cognitive theory. The results show that both perceived efficacy and the outcomes believed to be attainable by different pursuits are related to occupational preferences. Efficacy beliefs contribute more heavily to occupational preferences, however. This is especially true of women who base their liking of occupations much more on their perceived efficacy than on the allure of the potential benefits the vocations yield.

As mentioned before, in social cognitive theory, perceived efficacy is one of a number of determinants of human thought, motivation, and action. Lent, Lopez, and Bieschke (1993) examined the relative contribution of efficacy beliefs and outcome expectations to the development of mathematical skills, which are required for entry into a wide range of careers. Perceived mathematical efficacy contributed to prediction of mathematical interests, intent to enroll in mathematics and science courses, and actual success in such courses after the influence of mathematical ability was controlled. Beliefs of personal efficacy influenced course grades both directly and through their effects on interests. Outcome expectations predicted interests and enrollment intentions but not course grades.

The preceding analyses concern the determinants of choice of occupational pursuit from the numerous options available. The influential role of efficacy belief in shaping career paths is further corroborated in career choice of cultural milieu in which to pursue one's career. Singer (1993) examined whether Asian students pursuing education in a Western society desired to return to their homeland or to start their occupational career in the host society. Those who returned had a stronger sense of efficacy to manage their career in their native culture and expected to secure more desirable outcomes there. In contrast, those who remained believed more strongly in their efficacy to succeed occupationally in the new cultural milieu and expected equally desirable outcomes regardless of the culture in which they pursued their careers. When the contribution of efficacy beliefs and outcome expectations were analyzed together to take into account the relationship between them, however, only efficacy beliefs emerged as the predictor of where people chose to pursue their occupational life.

The combined findings of these different lines of research are consistent in showing that perceived efficacy is a robust contributor to career development. It predicts the scope of career options seriously considered, occupational interests and preferences, enrollment in courses of study that provide the knowledge and skills needed for various careers, perseverance in difficult fields, academic success in those chosen pursuits, and even the choice of cultural milieu in which to pursue one's occupational career. This independent contribution is verified in stringent empirical tests that control for the effects of actual ability, prior preparation and achievement, and level of interest.

Exploratory Decision Making and Fulfillment of Occupational Roles

The preceding discussion analyzed the contribution of perceived efficacy to career choice and development. People often avoid coming to grips with choosing a career because of the uncertain and lasting consequences it entails. Many find themselves in chronic indecision and keep postponing the matter until circumstances force them to choose some line of work. Some drift into occupations by default through failure to explore possible alternatives and to commit themselves to some occupational domain. Career decision making is not simply a matter of picking a particular occupational pursuit but rather of developing facility in solving problems when things are not easily predictable. Nor is it simply a matter of learning problem-solving skills. People who lack confidence in their judgment have difficulty making decisions and sticking with them even if they have been taught the strategies for doing so.

Under the fast pace of technological change, occupational activities shift rapidly in the modern workplace. Employees not only change jobs more often but have to develop new sets of skills to suit new growth industries. With rapid changes in the occupational structure, people must make occupational decisions recurrently rather than deciding on a pursuit that then sets the occupational path for their lifetime. Thus, efficacy in making sound choices has assumed increased importance in the realization of a satisfying occupational life.

Perceived efficacy for the various subskills of decisional thinking affects the decisiveness with which occupational choices are made and worrisome afterthoughts about the rightness of the decision. These decisional subskills include gathering information about different occupations, self-appraisal of capabilities and interests, selecting lifestyle goals that specify appropriate occupations, planning coherent courses of action to achieve the selected goals, and devising strategies for managing the host of problems that inevitably arise in any occupational pursuit (Crites, 1974). The lower the perceived efficacy to carry out these types of exploratory and planning activities needed to make career decisions, the higher the level of occupational indecisiveness (Betz, Klein, & Taylor, 1996; Taylor & Betz, 1983). People are unlikely to invest much effort in exploring career options and their implications unless they have faith in their abilities to reach good decisions. Hence, the stronger the perceived decisional efficacy, the higher the level of exploratory activity designed to aid selection and planning of a career (Blustein, 1989; Urekami, 1996).

Men and women often differ, as a group, in their perceived capabilities for various types of occupations but not in perceived capabilities for arriving at decisions about which occupation to pursue. This is not surprising because the content and process of career choice involve largely different capabilities. Men may consider themselves efficacious for a wide range of occupations but remain unsure of their efficacy to pick a suitable one. Similarly, women may exclude from serious consideration occupations traditionally dominated by men but remain unsure of their efficacy to decide which of the remaining career options to pursue. Therefore, variations in gender differences in efficacy beliefs for occupations and for making occupational decisions should not be construed as contradictory findings.

Taylor and Popma (1990) compared multiple predictors of occupational indecision, including locus of control, range of occupations seriously considered, importance attached to a career, and perceived efficacy to complete the educational and training requirements for entry into various occupations. Only perceived decision-making efficacy was a significant predictor of occupational indecision. This finding not only supports the predictive value of perceived decision-making efficacy but indicates that it reflects a distinct aspect of personal efficacy rather than simply a general sense of occupational efficacy or high occupational interest.

It is difficult for students to become engrossed in educational pursuits if they are uncertain about what to do with their lives. Those who distrust their capability to make sound decisions are not only uncertain about a vocational career but unsettled about what academic major to pursue (Bergeron & Romano, 1994). Students who enter postsecondary education both unsure of their vocational direction and only marginally prepared academically are especially prone to drop out and not return. Research by Peterson (1993) underscores the important contribution of perceived efficacy to find an occupational direction to the social and intellectual development of underprepared college students. The higher the students' beliefs in their efficacy to decide what occupational career to pursue, the more strongly they become integrated into the social and academic life of the educational environment. Academic goals also contribute, though less strongly, to academic engrossment; past academic record does so marginally, but students' sociodemographic characteristics are unrelated to level of engagement in academic activities. Thus, an important initial goal in career development is to build students' efficacy to find an occupational calling for themselves that provides structure and meaning to their educational pursuits.

Computerized career guidance programs are being used increasingly in career planning and decision making. Interactive computer systems guide self-assessment of interests, values, and abilities and provide information about a wide range of occupations and the types of training they require. These aids enable users to identify the occupations that best match their interests and perceived abilities. Computer-assisted career guidance markedly increases perceived efficacy to do what is needed to make career decisions and reduces indecisiveness about which careers to pursue (Fukuyama, Probert, Neimeyer, Nevill, & Metzler, 1988). Computerized guidance thus provides a convenient tool for building decisional self-efficacy. But one might question the wisdom of using it as the sole mode of career guidance. Individuals who downgrade their capabilities may lock themselves into low-level occupations that match their low sense of efficacy. They need help to realize that they can be more than they thought they could be. People would be best served by career exploration programs combining personal guidance that corrects faulty self-assessments of capabilities with computerized guidance of occupational matching.

Women who enter male-dominated occupations encounter considerably more obstacles and barriers to advancement than do their male counterparts. Women who are assured in their efficacy to make career decisions and have the assertiveness to manage discords that arise in the workplace are much more willing to pursue nontraditional occupations than are those who judge themselves inefficacious in making decisions and are socially unassertive (Nevill & Schlecker, 1988). Perceived decisional inefficacy breeds indecisiveness and thus influences the types of occupations eventually given serious consideration, as well as impeding the making of any occupational decision at all.

Beliefs of personal efficacy also operate in occupational decisions in the recruitment phase (Saks, Wiesner, & Summers, 1994). In recruiting newcomers, organizations often use realistic job previews as a self-selection screening device for applicants likely to drop out because their values mismatch job characteristics. Traditional job previews accent the positive features of the job. Realistic previews present not only the career opportunities but the challenges, competitive aspects, and heavy work demands required to succeed. People's beliefs in their efficacy affect how they respond to these different recruitment practices. Realistic job previews produce, through self-selection, lower job acceptance rates than do traditional ones. A foretaste of challenges and obstacles attracts applicants of high perceived efficacy but scares off those who are less self-assured. Efficacy belief influences acceptance of job offers after controlling for the degree of match in value orientation. Further research is needed to determine how self-selection in response to recruitment strategies affects career paths. Realistic previews may reduce job turnover through mismatch, but they can also foreclose promising futures in talented applicants who have some self-doubts at the outset of their career.

Perceived Efficacy in Employability and Reemployability

In most occupations, people face stiff competition in the job market. A number of factors contribute to employability. Among these is jobseekers' ability to conduct effective job searches and to convey to potential employers favorable impressions of their capabilities and promise. Ineffectual job searches harvest few employment contacts. The sway of capability is readily negated by ineffectual self-presentation in job interviews. Perceived efficacy is, therefore, an influential factor in the job-search process. Tracy and Adams (1984) taught college graduates through workshops and videotaped modeling the strategies for making contacts that lead to job interviews and for presenting themselves well in those interviews. Most job openings are discovered through friends, acquaintances, and circles of associates (Jones & Azrin, 1973). Therefore, the efficacy to enlist the aid of informal social networks is a crucial part of the process. Training in job-search skills bolsters perceived efficacy to navigate the competitive job market. The extent to which efficacy beliefs get translated into job offers, however, needs formal assessment.

Several longitudinal studies provide evidence that perceived efficacy predicts successful reemployment following job loss after job layoffs during a recessionary period. Kanfer and Hulin (1985) tested employees for their perceived efficacy to carry out different aspects of job searches. A variety of other factors that might contribute to successful reemployment were also examined. They included employee's age, marital status, length of tenure on the job, quality of job performance, depression, and perceived obstacles to reemployment. Among these multiple factors, perceived efficacy emerged as the only significant predictor of subsequent reemployment. The higher the perceived efficacy, the more extensive the job search behavior and the higher the rate of reemployment. Clifford (1988) similarly found that unemployed individuals who were assured in their job-search efficacy were more likely to be reemployed in a follow-up period, whereas neither the cause of termination nor general personality characteristics exerted any influence on reemployment status.

It is one thing to secure employment contacts, quite another to actually get hired. In keeping with the different employability demands, Kanfer and Hulin (1985) found that perceived efficacy enhanced employability beyond its effect on search behavior. Search behavior had no effect on reemployment when variation in efficacy beliefs was controlled, whereas efficacy beliefs predicted reemployment success when extent of search behavior was controlled. Given constraints on the availability of jobs, individuals who approached the employment problem with confidence in their capability to find a job were able to ferret out job opportunities and present themselves sufficiently well to gain job offers. Constraints in job markets combined with self-impediments arising from perceived inefficacy are likely to breed a sense of despondency and futility. Of particular interest are studies, reviewed earlier, that build or restore a sense of efficacy in laid-off workers through programs of guided mastery (Eden & Aviram, 1993; Vinokur et al., 1991). Enhanced efficacy increases job search activities and the likelihood of reemployment.

Career pursuits require more than the specialized knowledge and technical skills of one's trade. Success on the job rests partly on self-efficacy in dealing with the social realities of work situations, which is a crucial aspect of occupational roles. Betz and Hackett have identified a number of skills that subserve this broader function (Betz & Hackett, 1987; Hackett, Betz, & Doty, 1985). They include the ability to communicate well, to relate effectively to others, to plan and manage the demands of one's job, to exercise leadership, and to cope with stress effectively. These are the types of skills that enable people to create and take advantage of opportunities for their occupational self-development. Depending on its strength, a sense of personal efficacy in these skills aids or impedes career advancement quite apart from the technical skills one possesses. Indeed, interpersonal and self-regulatory skills contribute more heavily to career success than do occupational skills. Technical job skills can be learned readily, but psychosocial skills are more difficult to develop and often even more difficult to modify if they are dysfunctional.

Gender Differences in Occupational Self-Efficacy

Wide gender disparities exist in career aspirations and pursuits. Although women make up approximately half the total work force, not many of them are choosing careers in scientific and technical fields or, for that matter, in a variety of other occupations that traditionally have been dominated by men. Women occupy mainly clerical, service, and sales jobs. Those pursuing professional careers are largely employed in traditionally female fields. Dissuading social norms and practices continue to lag behind the changing status of women and their growing participation in the labor force. As a result, women's potential and their contribution to the creative and economic life of a society remain largely unrealized. The same is true of ethnic minorities. While women and minorities are shunning scientific and technological fields, the demographic trend is a proportional decline of white male students in college populations. This demographic change indicates that our society will have to rely increasingly on the talents of women and ethnic minorities to maintain its scientific, technological,

and economic viability. Societies must come to terms with the discordance between their occupational socialization practices and the human resources needed for their success. Societies that fail to develop the capabilities of all their youth jeopardize their social and economic progress.

Women's beliefs about their capabilities and their career aspirations are shaped by the family, the educational system, the mass media, and the culture at large (Hackett & Betz, 1981). Parents' beliefs about their children's capabilities and the achievement expectations they hold for them differ depending on the sex of the child. Phillips and Zimmerman (1990) report striking developmental gender differences in disparity between children's ability and their perceived competence. Whereas boys tend to inflate their sense of competence, girls generally disparage their capabilities. These differential patterns of self-appraisal have their origins partly in parents' gender-linked beliefs about their children's capabilities. Parents judge school to be more difficult for daughters than for sons, even though they do not differ in actual academic achievement. Girls perceive their mothers as having lower academic expectations and less stringent achievement standards for them than for boys. The more strongly girls adopt the stereotypic feminine gender-role identity, the more they underestimate their capabilities.

In longitudinal studies, Eccles (1989) found that parents generally subscribe to the cultural stereotype that girls are less talented in mathematics than boys, despite equivalent grades in mathematics. The more parents stereotype mathematics as a naturally male domain, the more they underestimate their daughters' math ability, overestimate the difficulty of the subject matter for them, attribute their successes to dint of hard work, and are disinclined to encourage them to engage in computer and mathematical activities. Not surprisingly, girls have a lower opinion of their capabilities for mathematical activities than do boys, even though they perform equally well in this subject. Although boys and girls do not differ initially in their perceived mathematical capabilities, girls begin to lose confidence in their math ability and diverge increasingly from boys in this regard as they move into high school. Females not only lose faith in their mathematical capabilities but also attach declining usefulness to quantitative skills for their future pursuits. Avoidance of mathematical activities eventually creates the very gender differences that parents originally presumed to exist.

The gender bias operates in classrooms as well as in homes. Teachers often convey, in many subtle ways, that they expect less of girls academically. This is especially evident in what they choose to criticize in boys and girls and in the feedback they provide them regarding the causes of deficient academic performances. Teachers tend to center their criticisms on boys' disruptive social behavior and to view their scholastic failures as due to insufficient effort, whereas teachers are prone to criticize the intellectual aspects of girls' academic work and to attribute their failures more to deficiencies of ability than to low motivation (Dweck, Davidson, Nelson, & Enna, 1978). Girls have higher self-appraisals and valuation of mathematics in classrooms where teachers stress the importance and usefulness of quantitative skills, encourage cooperative or individualized learning rather than competitive learning, and minimize social comparative assessment of students' ability (Eccles, 1989). Such educational practices foster higher self-appraisal of capabilities. Even for teachers who do not share the gender bias, unless they are proactive in providing equal gender opportunities to learn science and math, the more skilled male students come to dominate these instructional activities, which further entrenches differential development of quantitative competencies. It requires concerted effort to counteract the personal effects of stereotypic gender-role socialization and the social perpetuation of them.

School counselors encourage and support the interest of boys in scientific fields, but they are inclined to scale down girls' aspirations and steer them away from quantitative fields of study into vocational paths below their level of ability (Betz & Fitzgerald, 1987; Fitzgerald & Crites, 1980). Some counselors not only discourage women from pursuing nontraditional occupations but express negative attitudes toward the idea of married

women working. They view occupational careers for women as incompatible with the homemaker role and regard women's interest in occupations traditionally dominated by men as a sign of deviance. Such differential treatment lowers women's beliefs in their capabilities and constricts their career aspirations. Parents and teachers, of course, differ in their socialization practices. Although the gender bias is widespread, it does not pervade all homes or all classrooms. We will examine later factors that contribute to gender disparities in the development of perceived occupational efficacy.

The peer system is another influential agency that has an impact on children's self-conceptions. As early as the preschool years, children already stereotype occupations as to whether they befit males or females (Gettys & Cann, 1981). Moreover, preschoolers subscribe to the stereotype that boys possess higher intellectual capabilities than girls (Crandall, 1978). By behaving in ways that are more conducive to intellectual development of boys than of girls, peers create further validation for the gender stereotypes of differential capability. Even children's memory of role enactments that are incongruent with gender occupational stereotypes get distorted to fit the stereotypes. Thus, seeing a female doctor working with a male nurse produces stereotypically distorted recollections in children, in which the male becomes the doctor and the female becomes the nurse (Cordua, McGraw, & Drabman, 1979; Signorella & Liben, 1984).

Another major social influence is the pervasive cultural modeling of gender-role stereotypes. Whether it be televised representation of social roles, children's storybooks and instructional materials, or the social examples around them, children see women cast predominantly in limited nonachieving roles (Courtney & Whipple, 1974; Jacklin & Mischel, 1973; Kortenhaus & Demarest, 1993; McArthur & Eisen, 1976; Signorielli, 1990). Males are generally portrayed as directive, venturesome, enterprising, and pursuing engaging occupations and recreational activities. In contrast, women are usually cast in subordinate roles, either tending the household or performing lower status jobs and otherwise acting in dependent, unambitious, and emotional ways. Heavy viewers of television display more stereotypic gender-role conceptions than do light viewers (McGhee & Frueh, 1980). Studies in which females are portrayed as behaving counter to the traditional stereotype attest to the influence of modeling on gender-role conceptions. Nonstereo-typic modeling expands children's aspirations and the range of role options they consider appropriate for their sex (Ashby & Wittmaier, 1978; O'Bryant & Corder-Bolz, 1978). Repeated symbolic modeling of egalitarian role pursuits by males and females enduringly reduces gender-role stereotyping in young children (Flerx, Fidler, & Rogers, 1976).

Modeling continues to play an influential role throughout the process of career development and advancement. Because women are disinclined to choose careers in scientific and technical fields tra-ditionally dominated by men, such occupations lack female role models to inspire and encourage women to enter these career paths. Even as women gain more visible presence in formerly shunned oc-cupations, their scarcity in higher status positions dampens interest in the less traditional pursuits. The cumulative impact of these diverse sources of dis-suading and undermining influences exacts a heavy toll on women's self-conceptions and aspirations.

A substantial body of evidence is quite consis-tent in showing that the career interests and pur-suits of women are constricted by a sense of ineffi-cacy to master the skills necessary for traditionally male occupations (Betz & Hackett, 1981). Male college students have an equally high sense of effi-cacy for both traditionally male-dominated and fe-male-dominated occupations. In contrast, female students judge themselves more efficacious for the types of occupations traditionally held by women but have a weaker sense of efficacy that they can master the educational requirements and job func-tions of occupations dominated by males. These differential beliefs in personal efficacy are espe-cially striking because the groups do not differ in their actual verbal and quantitative ability on stan-dardized tests. The self-limitation arises more from perceived inefficacy than from actual inability. More recent evidence suggests that occupational

sex stereotyping may be weakening. Studies of stu-dents currently coming through the high school ranks reveal a smaller disparity between male and female students in their beliefs about their efficacy to pursue successfully varied careers (Post-Kammer & Smith, 1985). The social constraints against entry into managerial positions in occupations domi-nated by men are easing, but vestiges of sex segrega-tion of women to positions of lower status in organi-zational hierarchies continue to impose obstacles to their pursuit of occupations and advancement in them (Jacobs, 1989).

Special attention has been devoted to per-ceived mathematical efficacy because modern tech-nologies have made quantitative skills increasingly important to a wide range of career options and to professional advancement. Perceived mathematical efficacy operates as a significant cognitive mediator of interest and achievement in mathematical sub-ject matter (Randhawa et al., 1993). Pajares and Miller (1994a) provide further evidence for the me-diational role of beliefs of personal efficacy. Prior mathematical experience and gender affect math-ematical performance largely through their impact on efficacy beliefs. Perceived mathematical efficacy also determines the perceived usefulness of quanti-tative skills. Lack of preparation in mathematics dis-suades entry to scientific and technological careers for which it is an important prerequisite. Self-ineffi-cacy barriers in the mathematical domain, there-fore, can be particularly self-limiting and detrimen-tal by foreclosing many career futures. Because mathematics is sex-typed as a masculine activity, women harbor a lower sense of mathematical effi-cacy than do men even when they do not differ in actual math ability (Betz & Hackett, 1983; Matsui et al., 1988). The tendency for girls to underesti-mate their math efficacy and boys to overestimate theirs is even more striking among young gifted stu-dents (Pajares, in press). The more students distrust their mathematical capabilities, the more they avoid preparatory course work in mathematics and the less likely they are to select science-based fields of study.

Hackett (1985) analyzed the paths of influence through which a variety of relevant factors affect choice of academic majors that draw on mathematical skills. The results reveal that gender affects perceived mathematical efficacy through mathematical preparation in high school, mathematical achievement, and masculine gender-role orientation (Fig. 10.1). Masculine gender-role orientation and level of mathematical achievement foster math-related educational and career choices through their effects on perceived mathematical efficacy rather than directly. Perceived mathematical efficacy promotes selection of mathematically oriented educational and career pursuits both directly and by lowering vulnerability to anxiety over mathematical activities. Gender and prior mathematical preparation also have a direct effect on choice of academic major.

The research just discussed provides evidence that perceived efficacy is a central mediator through which socialization practices and past experience influence educational and career choices. The causally prior contribution of perceived efficacy to the socialization practices themselves and to children's educational preparation remains an important problem for future research to determine through longitudinal analysis. Parents' own sense of occupational efficacy is likely to influence, through modeling and expressed expectations and aspirations, the range of vocational options they consider viable for their offspring. Their children's beliefs in their capabilities and career aspirations will influence the types of courses they choose to pursue and their success in them during their secondary educational preparation.

Matsui and his colleagues shed further light on the influence of gender-role socialization and modeling on women's perceived efficacy to fulfill the educational requirements and job demands of traditionally male occupations (Matsui et al., 1989). The disparity in perceived efficacy for male-dominated and female-dominated occupations was largest for women who view themselves as highly feminine, have self-doubts about their quantitative capabilities, and believe there are few successful female models in traditionally male-dominated occupations. To the extent that stereotypic masculine attributes such as aggressiveness and competitiveness are considered essential for success in given occupations, women who have not adopted these types of attributes express a lower sense of efficacy for such fields (Matsui & Onglatco, 1991). This is true even for occupations that do not require technical and quantitative skills. Rather than emulating hard-driving competitiveness for money, power, and status, many people are redefining success to mean doing what one loves to do even if it means making less money, upholding concern for the welfare of the workforce, and seeking a balanced life between work and family.

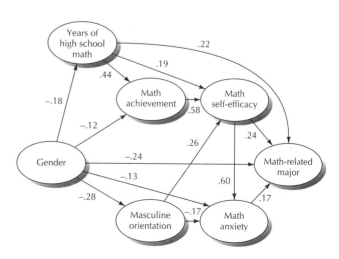

FIGURE 10.1. Path analysis showing the causal relationships among factors predicting choice of math-related college major. (Hackett, 1985)

Scheye and Gilroy (1994) report that the sex composition of the educational environment influences women's perceived efficacy for occupational pursuits traditionally dominated by males. The effect is not simple or direct, however. Women from single-sex schools who cite a male teacher as having the strongest influence on them have a higher sense of efficacy for nontraditional careers for women than those from co-educational schools. The authors offer the following interpretation for the combined benefits of male and female support. Heavy exposure to primarily female administrators and faculty provides multiple successful models for diverse occupational pursuits. Men who choose to teach in all-women's schools espouse an egalitarian orientation and actively support a wide range of aspirations and role options for women. The authors raise the alternative possibility, however, that the expanded sense of efficacy reflects self-selection rather than the impact of the educational environment. It may be that women who are already oriented toward nontraditional careers select women's schools and seek out male models in preparing for the occupational realities they will face.

The preceding research examined the role of perceived efficacy in mediating gender differences in curricular and occupational choices. A similar path analysis by Lapan, Boggs, and Morrill (1989) confirms that efficacy beliefs mediate gender differences in level of interest in scientific and technical fields as well. They found two paths through which gender affects vocational interests. First, women have weaker high school preparation in mathematics, which limits their math achievement and lowers their interest in math-related fields. Second, women have little faith in their mathematical efficacy, which lowers their sense of efficacy to perform competently in scientific and technical activities and hence lowers their interest in such occupations. The mediational role of efficacy beliefs is much stronger than that of mathematical achievement. The effects of gender on interest are entirely mediated through these two paths of influence. Thus, when differences in math achievement and efficacy beliefs are controlled, gender makes no independent contribution to vocational interests. A

low sense of mathematical efficacy arouses anxiety over mathematical activities, but anxiety has no independent effect on vocational interests. As in other areas of functioning, anxiety is largely a coeffect of perceived inefficacy rather than a causal factor.

Women's lowered sense of mathematical efficacy is, of course, changeable. Schunk and Lilly (1984) had female students pursue self-directed instruction in novel mathematical activities that they judged themselves much less capable of learning than did male students. The academic instruction was structured in ways that ensured skill development with clear feedback of success. Through mastery of mathematical operations, female students raised their perceived mathematical efficacy and mathematical skills to the level of male students. Mastery of diverse mathematical operations would eventually create a generalized sense of mathematical efficacy.

Computer systems are changing the basic structure of education by providing a ready means for self-directed learning. Disparities in computer skills can create disparities in educational development. In addition, computer literacy is increasingly important in career development and advancement. Microcomputers have now become a major information management and decision-making tool in the modern workplace. Among their myriad functions, computerized information systems are widely used for identifying trends, spotting problems, planning, forecasting, budgeting, communicating with workers both inside and outside the workplace, and guiding the activities of organizations. Computers have also become an integral part of sales and service jobs. In addition, manufacturing systems rely increasingly on computer-operated production machines to make products. The production machines are readily reprogrammable by changing the computer software to produce new products without requiring lengthy and expensive retooling. Computer skills, therefore, are essential for a wide range of occupational pursuits. Employees are working increasingly with automated and computerized systems. Men are benefiting much more than women from these technological advancements (Gallie, 1991).

The readiness with which technologies are adopted depends on their perceived complexity (Rogers & Schoemaker, 1971; Tornatzky & Klein, 1982). Complexity is not solely an inherent property of the technology. Rather, it reflects the relation between the skills it requires and individuals' capabilities. Thus, technology is complex for people who lack the capabilities to meet its task demands but simple for those who can easily fulfill the task demands. To people who have a low sense of efficacy, technologies are intimidating. This is corroborated by Hill, Smith, and Mann (1987) in regard to the development of computer skills. Belief in one's efficacy to master computers predicts enrollment in computer courses independently of beliefs about the instrumental benefits of knowing how to use them. Previous experience with computers, per se, does not affect subsequent efforts to expand computer competencies. Past experience does so only to the extent that it raises perceived self-efficacy.

Through their association with mathematics and electronics, computers have become masculinized. As a result, from an early age, boys have become more heavily involved with computers. This is a socially cultivated happening, rather than simply a spontaneous one. Boys receive greater encouragement than girls both at home and at school to develop proficiency in the use of computers. In the stereotype portrayals of the mass media, men appear as managers and experts, whereas women appear as clerical workers or merely as attractive attendants in computer work stations (Ware & Stuck, 1985). Boys are much more likely than girls to master computers, to use them extracurricularly, and to regard them as important for their futures (Hess & Miura, 1985; Lockheed, 1985). Gender differences similarly emerge in how computers are applied. They find heavier use as tools for programming, information management, and decision making by males and as word processors by females.

The adverse effects of perceived computer inefficacy extend well beyond career development and advancement. Much of the basic instruction in various subjects will be provided increasingly via computers. Computers linked to Internet services offer an unbounded new form of self-instruction and self-enablement. Computer networks enable people to gain vast amounts of information interactively in words and images on any subject that interests them. This interactive instructional system transcends the barriers of time, space, and activity constraints. A sense of inefficacy to manage computerized procedures can handicap computer-assisted instruction in the workplace, where employees work through interactive tutorials on their own.

Gender differences in perceived computer efficacy are not easily overcome. Even at an early age, girls distrust their efficacy to program and operate computers despite detailed instruction and schools' active encouragement to acquire such skills (Miura, 1987a). The lower the perceived efficacy in computer activities, the less the interest in acquiring computer competencies. School experiences with computers do not necessarily build a sense of computer efficacy or reduce gender differences. Required computer literacy courses superimposed on a pervading gender bias raise boys' self-efficacy about computer use but lower girls' self-efficacy and interest in computers (Collis, 1985). Gender differences in perceived computer efficacy extend to the college level, with males judging themselves more capable to master computer skills, especially the more advanced level skills (Murphy, Coover, & Owen, 1989). Regardless of gender, college students lacking a sense of computer efficacy are computer avoiders. They show less interest in computers, are less inclined to pursue computer course work, and see computer literacy as less relevant to their future careers (Miura, 1987b). The women who make it to the ranks of managerial personnel have more favorable attitudes toward computers.

It should be noted that the variability within the sexes is often larger than the differences between them. Therefore, modal characteristics in efficacy beliefs across sex groups should not be imputed to all members within each sex group. Moreover, sex differentiation based on biological attributes should be distinguished from gender differentiation reflecting culturally linked attributes. Although biological characteristics form a basis for some aspects of gender differentiation, most of the psychosocial attributes that get tied to masculine and feminine gender are socially conferred rather than biologically ordained. Research into what underlies sex differences in perceived efficacy for different careers and career decision making reveals sex-role orientation rather than sex per se to be the critical factor (Abdalla, 1995; Matsui et al., 1989; Matsui & Onglatco, 1991). It is women with highly stereotypic feminine orientations who harbor self-doubts about their capabilities for nontraditional pursuits. Those who take a more egalitarian view toward the roles of women display a higher sense of efficacy for traditionally male occupations and enter into them more frequently. They construct different identities and futures for themselves. Therefore, knowledge of the impact of gender-role orientation on efficacy beliefs is important to a broad understanding of sex differences in career pursuits.

In focusing on the role of efficacy beliefs in gender differences in career aspirations and pursuits, one must not lose sight of the fact that cultural constraints, inequitable incentive systems, and truncated opportunity structures are also influential in shaping women's career development. These social realities form part of the triadic model of causation. Self-efficacy theory does more than identify a contributory factor to vocational careers, however. It provides the means for enhancing the personal source of control over one's own occupational functioning. Gist, Schwoerer, and Rosen (1989) explored different ways of building self-efficacy and skill in using financial software programs applicable to varied business functions. Most of the participants were women. Those who had the benefit of helpful modeling, guided practice, and corrective feedback achieved a high sense of computer efficacy, regardless of their initial belief in their efficacy to learn such skills. The commonly used tutorial training produced some increase in perceived efficacy in participants who already believed they could learn computer skills but not in those who harbored strong doubts about their learning efficacy. Participant modeling produced higher computer proficiency as well as a stronger sense of efficacy than did the tutorial training. The higher the instilled sense of efficacy, the greater was the subsequent computer proficiency.

Cultural practices that convey lower achievement expectations for women, model stereotypic gender roles, constrain sex typing of career aspirations, and constrict opportunity structures require of women a robust sense of efficacy to pursue nontraditional vocations. Self-doubts are often difficult to override even in socially endorsed endeavors, and doubly so when nontraditional pursuits receive minimal support or are regarded with disfavor by many people. Stereotyping and discriminatory practices that channel women into tracks of lesser opportunities below their level of ability create additional impediments (Fitzgerald & Crites, 1980). Progress in a career requires considerable sustained effort to produce the results that contribute to advancements and personal fulfillment. Such effort is difficult to achieve when women have to fulfill heavy demands arising from the dual workloads of career and household without adequate help with childcare. Women's beliefs in their efficacy to manage the multiple demands of family and occupation can affect their career choices and development (Stickel & Bonett, 1991).

Ethnicity and Occupational Self-Efficacy

The previous discussion centered on the underdevelopment and underutilization of the talents of women in scientific and technological fields. Ethnic minorities are also seriously underrepresented in science and engineering, and the percentage of non-Asian minority students entering these career fields has been declining. Unlike the extensive research on gender differences in perceived occupational efficacy, however, research on minorities has been comparatively sparse. Devalued ethnicity is often accompanied by economic hardships. All too often research on the occupational pursuits of minorities confounds ethnicity with low socioeconomic status. Such confounding makes it difficult to disentangle the effects of impoverization from the effects of ethnicity. Informative research clarifies how ethnicity shapes career choice and development rather than simply compares one ethnic group against another. Such analyses must also recognize the diversity of ethnicity. For example, among Latinos, the people of Spanish, Mexican, Cuban, Puerto Rican, and Central and South American origin may differ substantially from one another economically, educationally, socially, and culturally.

Ethnicity delineates attributes that distinguish cultural groupings, but it does not explain how ethnic identity affects psychosocial functioning. There are several ways in which ethnic affiliation exerts its effects. It molds values and behavioral standards through its customs and social practices. In addition, it provides social networks that shape and regulate major aspects of life. Transactions with the social and symbolic ethnic environment help to promote a sense of collective identity. Through social stereotyping of what certain groups are like, ethnic attributes take on connotations that partly influence how people who are ethnically categorized are perceived and treated by others. Ethnicity is not simply a matter of belonging to a certain cultural grouping. Members of an ethnic group vary both in the strength of their ethnic identification and in their degree of acculturation. Some downplay or reject their ethnic origin and identify mainly with the mainstream culture. Others link their identity strongly to their ethnic culture and either pay little heed to or reject the mainstream culture. Still others develop a bicultural orientation in which they assimilate the mainstream culture while maintaining a firm ethnic identity. Another relevant factor is the degree of compatibility in values, attitudes, customs, language, and behavioral patterns between different cultural groupings. Given these complexities, simply typecasting people into different ethnic groupings is likely to yield highly variable, if not misleading, findings. Where values clash, it takes a strong sense of bicultural efficacy to function well in different subcultures. Those who pursue a bicultural identity must cope repeatedly with threats of alienation from their ethnic culture and rebuff by the mainstream culture.

The attitudinal and behavioral correlates of ethnic groups may vary due to different subcultural experiences, but the effects of sociostructural influences and the mechanisms through which they produce their effects are generalizable. The multiple benefits of a sense of personal efficacy operate similarly across gender, ethnicity, and social class. For example, the effects of efficacy beliefs on occupational choice and development exhibited by predominantly white college students are similar to those obtained for ethnic minorities who differ strikingly in educational development, age, socioeconomic status, and geographical mobility. Bores-Rangel and his associates studied Hispanic students of migrant and seasonal farm-working families who lacked a high school diploma (Bores-Rangel, Church, Szendre, & Reeves, 1990). In this economically and educationally disadvantaged minority, the stronger the children's beliefs in their academic efficacy, the higher were their educational aspirations and academic achievement on tests for certification of high school equivalency. Perceived efficacy had significant effects on academic performance even after controlling for prior achievement level. Moreover, students who had a high sense of occupational efficacy considered a wider range of occupational activities regardless of the required educational level and showed stronger interest in them than did students who had self-doubts about their capabilities. Efficacy beliefs are equally predictive of range of occupations considered by minority students regardless of ethnicity or level of acculturation (Church, Teresa, Rosebrook, & Szendre, 1992; Lauver & Jones, 1991). With regard to gender differences, minority students similarly express stronger efficacy beliefs for occupations dominated by their own gender.

Comparative studies with other ethnic minorities further attest to the generalizability of efficacy effects. Minority students generally have a low sense of efficacy for scientific and technological careers requiring quantitative skills, and many have insufficient preparatory course work in mathematics and physical sciences and are disinclined to enroll in scientific and technological fields of study or to stick with them if they are chosen. The combined influence of low academic expectations and downgrading of scientific aspirations in the students' schooling, deficient academic preparation, lack of occupational role models and support systems for pursuits in scientific and technological fields, and social barriers in opportunity structures will constrain perceived occupational efficacy in various minorities and nonminorities alike. Indeed, because the sociostructural barriers for women and ethnic minorities are similar, their patterns of perceived occupational efficacy are much the same. Access to socioeconomic resources lowers some barriers to occupational aspiration. Thus, adolescent females from families of high socioeconomic status are more likely to consider male-dominated occupations than are females of low socioeconomic status (Hannah & Kahn, 1989). One would expect socioeconomic advantages to have similar broadening effects on the occupational aspirations of ethnic minorities.

An understanding of how ethnicity contributes to career choice and development is best advanced by process analyses that link sociostructural determinants, mediating psychological mechanisms, and occupational pursuits rather than by simple comparisons of the perceived occupational efficacy of different ethnic groups. Process analyses not only verify the unique contribution of ethnicity but help to explain the wide differences in occupational pursuits among members of the same ethnic group. As with sex differences, the differences within ethnic groups are considerably larger than the differences between ethnic groups. The study of different types of ethnicity in career pursuits is of interest because some developmental experiences are unique and specific to each ethnic minority. Moreover, members of different ethnic minorities confront different social and institutional barriers that constrain occupational development and career opportunities. But the study of ethnicity should not blind us to the many commonalities among people of different ethnic backgrounds.

Enhancement of Occupational Self-Efficacy

From an interactionist perspective, solutions to restricted aspirations and occupational pursuits require both individual and social remedies. The relative contribution of personal and social factors may vary from individual to individual, but occupational paths are the product of both sources of influence. At the individual level, the different modes of building a sense of personal efficacy can be used to eliminate self-limiting barriers that have become ingrained over time through institutional practices and to create the means for exercising proactive control over one's occupational future. Mastery-oriented instruction is an enactive means for developing basic entry skills for diverse careers and persuading people that they possess the potentialities and learning capabilities to succeed in a wide range of occupational pursuits. Since skills have to be expanded and restructured with educational advances and technological changes, belief in one's learning efficacy plays an especially influential role in willingness to venture into new pursuits.

A program designed to get minorities into college illustrates how self-persuasion regarding one's efficacy through provision of relevant sample experiences of personal mastery can expand occupational aspirations and shape plans of life (Cannon, 1988). Only a handful of graduates of a large high school serving predominantly Latino students from lower socioeconomic backgrounds were entering college. Their image of themselves did not include a college education. A college course on critical thinking required at a local university was offered by a university faculty member at the high school to persuade the students that they had the capabilities to succeed. They managed the course work well. By confirming a high level of scholastic efficacy, this program substantially increased minority student enrollment in colleges. Its impact on the efficacy beliefs of minority students is summed up well by one of the students: "When I thought about college before, it seemed scary because I thought it would be too hard. Now I know I can make it." Changes in perceived efficacy produced changes in behavior patterns: "Instead of watching TV all the time, I set time aside to study for my classes."

As students' visions of themselves and their capabilities were expanded to include higher education, they worked hard at preparing themselves for college. The school, in turn, made curricular changes and provided the students with extra guidance to foster their new aspirations. Over time, increasing numbers of students enrolled in the college course, which created academic group norms and expectations that were conspicuously lacking before. Because the program was readily adoptable, other school systems instituted it. These concatenating effects illustrate how a change in perceived efficacy can set in motion behavioral changes that alter group norms and other environmental changes that are mutually enhancing.

Another way of expanding the scope of occupational self-efficacy is by exposure to models from similar backgrounds performing the occupational roles successfully. For example, in the program just described, former high school students enrolled in local colleges provide models for educational aspiration by serving as tutors. Seeing models of assumed similarity succeed in occupational pursuits considered beyond one's capabilities increases students' confidence in their own occupational potential. The growing presence of minority models in advanced pursuits raises the perceived efficacy and aspirations of students with similar backgrounds. Social support in the form of encouragement and positive feedback from instructors raises the perceived efficacy of minority students for scientific pursuits (Hackett, Betz, Casas, & Rocha-Singh, 1992). Strong perceived efficacy is accompanied by good academic performance. Training in career decision-making skills can also be used to reveal personal potentialities that broaden the scope of occupational considerations (Mitchell & Krumboltz, 1984).

The final approach to expanding occupational aspirations is aimed at eliminating self-belittling biases in the self-appraisal of capabilities and the interpretation of personal attainments. For example, when subjected to the same level of failure in mathematical activities, women judge themselves less able and treat themselves more harshly than do men (Campbell & Hackett, 1986). Women are also less likely than men to credit success in mathematics to their ability. Self-belittling habits of cognizing success and failure experiences can be altered through cognitive restructuring of belief systems

and thought processes involving standards of self-evaluation and appraisal of personal efficacy (Goldfried & Robins, 1982).

Institutional barriers to career aspirations and development require social remedies. These barriers take many forms. We have already seen how gender biases operate in major social systems to diminish the personal efficacy and aspirations of women. In the case of ethnic minorities, the adverse effects of institutional biases are often compounded by adversity. Many minority students come from households that are educationally and economically disadvantaged. Financial hardships create economic barriers that breed cycles of impoverishment and disadvantage. Negative biases in educational systems discourage high academic aspiration and erode the sense of personal efficacy needed to develop one's talents (Arbona, 1990). Disadvantaged minorities usually get tracked into general or vocational programs rather than college preparatory courses of study. Discriminatory cultural practices that stigmatize people by their race and ethnicity limit occupational opportunities and career advancement. Actual and perceived barriers to educational and vocational aspirations keep many minority groups in a disadvantaged status from which it is difficult to break out. Remedies at the social level must address the expectations, belief systems, and social practices in the home, school, mass media, and workplace. These various handicapping cultural practices need changing if people are to make the most of their talents.

MASTERY OF OCCUPATIONAL ROLES

Most of this chapter so far has focused on the influential role played by perceived efficacy in the entry and preparatory phases of career pursuits. The preparatory training provides the general knowledge and the higher cognitive skills that can serve different types of vocations. People also need to master the specialized technical skills of their chosen occupation and the generic interpersonal and self-regulatory competencies vital to the fulfillment of one's occupational role and successful management of one's career. Billions are spent annually on occupational training, but there is a paucity of reliable evidence about the effectiveness of the methods used. Most training programs do not even make a pretense at empirical verification of their effectiveness. The success of methods of training founded on social cognitive theory is evaluated by empirical tests rather than subjective claims.

Development of Competencies through Mastery Modeling

Psychological theories have traditionally emphasized learning through the effects of one's actions. If knowledge and skills could be developed only by direct experience, the acquisition of competencies would be greatly retarded, not to mention exceedingly tedious and hazardous. Errors are common during the early phases of skill development, and some of them can be highly costly. The process of acquiring skills must be abbreviated to spare people needless tedium and wasted time and effort. The tutorial approach, which is widely used in organizational training, does not serve this purpose well.

Humans have evolved an advanced capacity for observational learning that enables them to expand their knowledge and skills on the basis of information conveyed by modeling influences. Indeed, virtually all learning resulting from direct experience can occur vicariously by observing people's patterns of behavior and their consequences (Bandura, 1986a; Rosenthal & Zimmerman, 1978). Much social learning occurs either deliberately or inadvertently by observing the actual behavior of others and the consequences. A great deal of information about human values, thinking patterns, and behavior, however, is gained from models portrayed symbolically.

Chapter 3 provided analyses of the four component subfunctions governing observational learning: attending to the critical features of the skills being modeled; extracting the generative rules underlying the skilled performances; translating the

symbolic conceptions into appropriate courses of action; and enlisting motivators to engage in these acquisitional cognitive activities and to put the learned skills into practice. In the development of complex competencies, modeling involves the acquisition of knowledge and skills, not merely behavioral mimicry. One can distinguish between two broad classes of skills: *fixed* and *generative*. Fixed skills specify the optimal ways of performing an activity, with little or no allowance for variation. For example, driving an automobile requires a set pattern of activities without much leeway for deviation if one seeks to arrive at selected destinations unharmed. Fixed skills are adopted in essentially the same form as they are modeled.

In many activities, on the other hand, skills must be improvised to suit changing circumstances. In generative skills, appropriate subskills are flexibly orchestrated to fit the demands of particular situations. In cultivating generative skills, modeling influences are structured so as to convey rules for generative and innovative behavior by modeling different ways of applying the same rule under varying circumstances. For example, a model may demonstrate how to manage negotiation situations that differ widely in content and conditions using the same guiding rules and strategies. Or a model may encounter different types of moral dilemmas in business transactions but resolve them by applying the same moral standard. In this form of abstract modeling, observers extract the rules governing the specific modeled judgments or actions. Once they learn the rules, they can use them to make decisions and to generate courses of action in new situations they encounter that go beyond what they have seen or heard. Generative skills provide the tools for adaptability and innovativeness.

Mastery modeling is being widely applied with good results to develop intellectual, social, and behavioral competencies (Bandura, 1986a). It is one of the most effective modes of human enablement. The method that produces the best results includes three major elements. First, the appropriate occupational skills are modeled to convey the basic rules and strategies. Second, the learners receive guided practice under simulated conditions so they can perfect the skills. Third, they are helped to apply their newly learned skills in work situations in ways that will bring them success. These different facets of mastery modeling are reviewed next.

Instructive Modeling

Modeling is the first step in developing competencies. Complex skills are broken down into subskills. The subskills are then modeled on videotape in easily mastered steps. Subdividing complex skills into subskills produces better learning than trying to teach everything at once. It is much easier to focus attention and to learn by concentrating on component skills. After the subskills are learned by this means, they can be combined into complex strategies to serve different purposes. Effective modeling teaches general rules and strategies for dealing with different situations rather than only specific responses or scripted routines. Trainees are helped to understand the rules and strategies by voice-over narration as they are being modeled. Providing brief summaries of the rules facilitates their acquisition and retention and thereby enhances skill development and generalized application of the skills (Decker & Nathan, 1985).

People learn rules but often make little use of them because they fail to recognize their applicability to the various situations they encounter. Trainees need to learn how to apply the rules with different people performing the relevant tasks under varying circumstances. Teaching abstract rules with varied brief examples promotes generalizability of the skills being taught by showing how the rules and strategies can be widely applied and adjusted to fit changing conditions. A single lengthy example teaches how to apply the rule in that particular situation but provides no instruction on how to adapt its application to varying situations.

People also fail to apply what they have learned, or do so only half-heartedly, if they distrust their ability to do it successfully. Therefore, modeling influences must be designed to build a sense of personal efficacy as well as to convey knowledge about rules and strategies. The impact of modeling on beliefs about one's capabilities is greatly increased by perceived similarity to the models. Trainees adopt modeled ways more readily if they see individuals similar to themselves solve problems successfully with the modeled strategies than if they see the models as very different from themselves. The characteristics of models — such as their age, sex, status, the type of problems with which they cope, and the situations in which they apply their skills — should be made to appear similar to the trainees' own circumstances.

Over the years, organizational training relied almost exclusively on the traditional lecture format. Mastery modeling works much better than lectures (Burke & Day, 1986). With the advent of the computer, talking heads are being replaced by instructional diskettes that provide programmed instruction, structured drills, and feedback of accuracy. Gist, Rosen, and Schwoerer (1988) compared mastery modeling with an interactive tutorial in teaching employees how to operate a spreadsheet program and use it to solve business problems. The self-paced tutorial (on diskettes) provided step-by-step interactive instruction with appropriate performance feedback. Mastery modeling provided the same information and the same opportunities to practice the computer skills but used a videotape of a model demonstrating how to perform the computer task. The modeling approach proved superior to the computerized tutorial approach in transmitting the skills to both younger and older trainees.

The advantages of mastery modeling are even more evident when the effectiveness of alternative training methods are examined as a function of trainees' preexisting level of perceived efficacy (Gist et al., 1989). Videotaped mastery modeling instills a uniformly high sense of efficacy to acquire computer software skills regardless of whether managers begin the training self-assured or self-doubting of their computer capabilities (Fig. 10.2). A computerized tutorial exerts weaker effects on efficacy beliefs and is especially ineffective in this regard with managers who are insecure in their computer efficacy. Mastery modeling also promotes a high level of computer skill development. The higher the preexisting and instilled efficacy beliefs, the

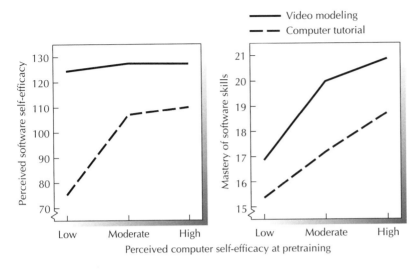

Video modeling
Computer tutorial

FIGURE 10.2. The differential impact on perceived efficacy and mastery of computer software operations of training programs based on videotaped modeling and interactive computer tutorials for managers and administrators with high and low belief in their computer efficacy. (Gist et al., 1989)

better the skill development. The influence of efficacy beliefs on computer performance remains when the effects of level of education and prior computer experience are removed. The benefits of mastery modeling extend beyond development of technical skills. Compared to tutorial training, mastery modeling produces a more effective working style, less negative affect during training, and greater satisfaction with the training program.

A great deal of professional work involves making judgments and solving problems by drawing on one's knowledge and applying decision rules. Competency in problem solving requires the development of thinking skills for how to seek and use information to solve problems. People learn thinking skills and how to apply them by observing the decision rules and reasoning strategies models use as they arrive at solutions. In teaching reasoning skills through verbal modeling, models verbalize their thought strategies aloud as they engage in problem-solving activities (Meichenbaum, 1984). The thoughts guiding their decisions and actions are thus made observable. During verbal modeling, the models verbalize their thought processes as they evaluate the problem, seek information relevant to it, generate alternative solutions, evaluate the likely outcomes associated with each alternative, and select the best way of implementing the chosen solution. They also verbalize their strategies for

handling difficulties, how to recover from errors, and how to motivate themselves.

Gist (1989) taught managers how to generate ideas to improve the quality of organizational functioning and customer service by providing them with guidelines and practice in innovative problem solving. Cognitive modeling, in which models verbalized strategies for generating ideas, proved superior to presenting the same guidelines solely in the traditional lecture format. Managers who had the benefit of cognitive modeling expressed a higher sense of efficacy and generated considerably more ideas and ideas of greater variety. Regardless of format of instruction, the higher the instilled efficacy beliefs, the more abundant and varied the generation of ideas.

Modeling thinking skills and action strategies together can aid development of reasoning skills in several ways. Watching models verbalize their thoughts as they solve problems holds attention, which is often difficult to sustain over a long period by explanation alone. Hearing the rules verbalized as the action strategies are implemented produces faster learning than only being told the rules or only seeing the actions modeled (Bandura, 1986a). Modeling also provides an informative context in which to demonstrate how to go about solving problems. The rules and strategies of reasoning can be repeated in different forms as often as needed to develop generative thinking skills, while keeping the observers' interest by using different examples. Varied application of reasoning strategies increases understanding of them. Observing models verbalize how they use their cognitive skills to solve problems highlights the capacity to exercise control over one's thought processes, which can boost observers' sense of efficacy over and above the strategic information conveyed. And finally, modeling how to manage failures and setbacks fosters resilience to difficulties. Thus, cognitive modeling can produce higher perceived efficacy and performance than verbal instruction even when the two training methods convey the same information and produce the same level of factual learning of strategies (Gist, 1989).

Guided Skill Perfection

After trainees understand the new skills, they need guidance about how to translate abstract rules into concrete courses of action and opportunities to perfect their skills. Proficiency requires extensive practice. In the venerable joke, a visitor asking how to get to Carnegie Hall is told, "Practice, practice, practice." Initially, trainees test their newly acquired skills in simulated situations where they need not fear making mistakes or appearing inadequate. This is best achieved by role rehearsal in which they practice handling the types of situations they have to manage in their work environment. Mastery of skills can be facilitated by combining cognitive and behavioral rehearsal (Bandura, 1986a; Corbin, 1972; Feltz & Landers, 1983). In cognitive rehearsal, people rehearse mentally how they will translate strategies into what they say and do to manage given situations.

In perfecting their skills, people need informative feedback about how they are doing. A common problem in using one's knowledge to achieve skilled performance is that people do not fully observe their own behavior. Informative feedback enables them to make corrective adjustments to get their behavior to fit their idea of how things should be done. Videotape replays are widely used for this

purpose. Simply being shown replays of one's own behavior, however, usually has mixed effects (Hung & Rosenthal, 1981). If performance feedback is to produce good results, it must direct attention to the corrective changes that need to be made. It should be given in such a way as to build confidence in one's capabilities. This is achieved by calling attention to successes and improvements and correcting deficiencies in a supportive and constructive way rather than by critical evaluation. Not all the benefits of performance feedback are due to skill improvement. Some of the gains accompanying informative feedback result from raising people's beliefs in their efficacy (Holman & Dowrick, 1991). By being persuaded by the feedback that they have the capabilities to succeed, they use the skills they have learned more effectively.

The feedback that is most informative and achieves the greatest improvements takes the form of corrective modeling (Vasta, 1976). In this approach, the subskills that have not been adequately learned are identified and effective ways of performing them are modeled by those who are proficient in the competencies being developed. Trainees then rehearse those subskills until they master them. The simulated practice is continued until trainees can perform the skills proficiently and spontaneously.

Effective functioning requires more than learning how to apply rules and strategies for managing given types of situations. The transactions of occupational life are littered with impediments, discordances, and stressors. Many of the problems of occupational functioning reflect failures of self-management under taxing circumstances rather than deficiencies of knowledge and skills. Therefore, an important aspect of occupational role development includes training in resiliency to difficulties. This requires skill in cognitive self-guidance, self-motivation, and strategies for counteracting self-debilitating reactions to troublesome situations that can easily unhinge one. Gist, Bavetta, and Stevens (1990) augmented a guided modeling training in negotiation with a self-management component. In the latter phase, trainees were taught how to anticipate potential stressors, devise ways of overcoming them, monitor the adequacy of their coping approach, and use self-incentives to sustain their efforts. Trainees who had the benefit of the supplemental self-management training were better at applying learned negotiation skills in new contractual situations presenting conflictful and intimidating elements and negotiated more favorable outcomes than trainees who did not. The self-managers made flexible use of the wide range of strategies they had been taught, whereas their counterparts were more likely to perseverate with only a few of the strategies when they encountered oppositional reactions.

Transfer Training by Self-Directed Success

Modeling and practice under simulated conditions are well suited for creating competencies. But new skills are unlikely to be used for long unless they prove useful when they are put into practice in work situations. People must experience sufficient success using what they have learned to believe in themselves and the value of the new ways. This is best achieved by a transfer program in which newly acquired skills are first tried on the job in situations likely to produce good results. Trainees are assigned selected problems they often encounter in their everyday situations. Then they discuss their successes and where they ran into difficulties for further instructive training. As trainees gain skill and confidence in handling easier situations, they gradually take on more difficult problems. If people have not had sufficient practice to convince themselves of their new effectiveness, they apply the skills they have been taught weakly and inconsistently. They rapidly abandon their skills when they fail to get quick results or experience difficulties.

Mastery modeling is now increasingly used to develop competencies. But its potential is not fully realized if training programs do not provide sufficient practice to achieve proficiency in the modeled skills or if they lack an adequate transfer program that helps people to experience success with their new skills in their natural environment. Such programs rarely include training in resiliency through practice on how to handle setbacks and failure. When instructive modeling is combined with guided role rehearsal and a guided transfer program, this mode of organizational training usually produces excellent results. Because trainees learn and perfect effective ways of managing task demands under lifelike conditions, problems of transferring the new skills to everyday life are markedly reduced.

Let us now consider some examples in which guided mastery modeling has been used fully to promote organizational development with stringent evaluation of its effectiveness in work organizations. Supervisors have an important impact on the morale and productivity of an organization. Yet they are often selected for their technical competencies and job-related knowledge, whereas their success in the supervisory role depends largely on their interpersonal skills to guide and motivate those they supervise. Mastery modeling programs have been devised to teach supervisors the interpersonal skills they need to work effectively through others.

Latham and Saari (1979) provide one such example in a very well designed field study. They used videotape modeling to teach supervisors how to manage the demands of their supervisory role. They were taught how to increase motivation, give recognition, correct poor work habits, discuss potential disciplinary problems, reduce absenteeism, handle employee complaints, and overcome resistance to changes in work practices (Goldstein & Sorcher, 1974). Summary guidelines defining key steps in the rules and strategies being modeled were provided to aid learning and memory. The group of supervisors discussed and then practiced the skills in role-playing scenarios using incidents they previously had to manage in their work. They received instructive feedback to help them improve and perfect their skills.

To facilitate transfer of supervisory skills from the training situation to their work environment, at the end of each session the supervisors were given written copies of the guidelines. They were instructed to use the skills they had learned with one or more employees on the job during the next week. They later reported their successes or difficulties in applying the skills. If they encountered problems, the incidents were reenacted and the supervisors received further training through instructive modeling and role rehearsal on how to manage such situations. A control group of supervisors was given the same set of supervisory guidelines but without the mastery modeling.

The supervisors' skill in managing problems was tested in role-play situations three months later and assessed by ratings of their performance on the job one year after training. Supervisors who had received the mastery modeling training performed more skillfully both in role-playing situations and on the job than did supervisors who did not receive the training. Because the skills proved highly functional, the supervisors adhered to them; whereas the effects of weak training programs, relying heavily on enthusiastic persuasion, rapidly dissipated as the initial burst of enthusiasm faded through failure to produce good results. Simply explaining to supervisors in the control group the rules and strategies for how to handle problems on the job without modeling and guided role rehearsal did not improve their supervisory skills. To enhance their skills, supervisors need instructive modeling, guided practice with corrective feedback, and help in transferring the new skill to the job situation. Indeed, when supervisors in the control condition later received the mastery modeling training, they improved their supervisory skills to the level achieved by the supervisors who had originally undergone the training. Because this approach provides supervisors with the tools for solving the problems they face, they express very favorable reactions to it.

Porras and his colleagues carried the research one step further by demonstrating that the supervisory skills instilled by mastery modeling improve the morale and productivity of organizations (Porras & Anderson, 1981; Porras et al., 1982). In one production plant, first-line supervisors participated in the mastery modeling program to improve their supervisory skills with methods similar to those used by Latham and Saari. Two other plants from the same manufacturing organization did not receive the training. Supervisors who had the benefit of the mastery modeling program improved and maintained their supervisory problem-solving skills as rated by their employees over a six-month period. The employees judged their supervisors as better able to pinpoint problems, to explain the need for change, to enlist their ideas about causes and possible solutions, to follow up on agreed-upon solutions, and to commend improved performances. The plant in which the modeling program was applied had a significantly lower absentee rate, lower turnover of employees, and a 17 percent increase in the monthly level of productivity over a six-month period, which surpassed the productivity of the control plants.

Mastery modeling produces multiple benefits in sales similar to those in production (Meyer & Raich, 1983). Salespersons in one set of chain retail stores learned and rehearsed different aspects of sales transactions with the aid of videotaped modeling, whereas salespersons in a matched set of stores did not. The modeling program produced a 7 percent increase in average commission earnings, compared to a 3 percent decline in average earnings in the control stores. In the ensuing year, 22 percent of the salespersons in the control stores quit their jobs, whereas only 7 percent of those in the stores that had offered the modeling training did so. The difference in sales performance between the two sets of stores would probably have been even greater were it not for the differential turnover, because it is the less successful performers who are most likely to leave. In any event, the modeling training not only increased sales but also produced organizational cost savings by reducing the rate of turnover in personnel.

Self-Efficacy in Occupational Socialization

New employees undergo training programs designed to prepare them for the occupational roles they will be performing. Not only do they have to develop their technical skills, they also have to learn the nature and scope of their occupational role; what is expected of them; how to manage their workload, time pressures, and other job-related stressors; and how to work effectively with their coworkers. The sense of efficacy that newcomers bring and further develop during the course of their occupational training at the beginning stage of their careers contributes to the success of this socialization process. Newcomers who come with a secure sense of efficacy learn more and perform better during the period of training than do their low self-efficacy counterparts.

Tailoring training strategies to employees' perceived efficacy facilitates acquisition of occupational competencies. It also alleviates anxiety in newcomers over the ambiguities and uncertainties of organizational life. Saks (1994, 1995) conducted an extensive analysis of newcomers' occupational development and functioning in a longitudinal field study of newly hired accountants in different accounting firms. The lower their sense of technical, educational, and interpersonal efficacy, the more anxious they were during the organizational entry. For those of low perceived efficacy, structured guidance on how to manage organizational activities calmed them, whereas self-study tutorials seemed to make them even more anxious. Those of high perceived efficacy remained unperturbed regardless of whether the instruction initiation was formally structured or self-managed. Training contributed to growth of occupational self-efficacy. Organizations that provided their new employees with mastery experiences, successful coworker models, and encouraging performance feedback enhanced their sense of occupational efficacy, which, in turn, predicted their occupational success and satisfaction many months later. Newcomers who had a high sense of efficacy at entry coped better with situational demands and performed the technical, interpersonal, and professional aspects of their job more successfully. Their efficacy beliefs following training had an even wider range of work-related effects. Compared to employees of low perceived efficacy, those who developed a high sense of efficacy not only coped better but were more satisfied with their jobs, had stronger commitment to their profession and organizations, and had less intention to quit their profession or job; fewer of them, in fact, left their firm.

In his analysis of occupational functioning, Ilgen (1994) distinguishes between fulfilling specified job duties and performing occupational roles. In role adoption, individuals can restructure their jobs to some extent by adding innovative elements or new functions to the customary job duties. Thus, one individual may perform a given role prosaically, whereas another individual may perform the same role prolifically. Jobs vary in the size of the task component and the role component and the latitude they permit for innovative role embellishment. Some of the innovativeness is designed to improve the processes by which the work is performed. Employees who are assured in their efficacy to produce ideas and are proactively oriented generate and submit ideas that help to improve work processes (Frese, Tang, and Cees, 1996). With rapidly changing market environments operating globally, the modern workplace requires highly adaptable employees with multiple competencies who can perform many different functions rather than just a small piece of work repetitively (Lawler, 1994). Because of the self-construction aspect of jobs, successful occupational functioning is a dynamic process rather than a simple plugging of personal attributes into specified job requirements. Employees of high perceived efficacy are likely to perform occupational roles innovatively, whereas those of low perceived efficacy are prone to discharge occupational roles conventionally with little personal embellishment. The influence of perceived efficacy on the nature of role construction is evident even in the entry phase of career pursuits.

Newcomers to organizations have to adapt to the organizational environment and develop their occupational roles. Organizations differ in how they go about promoting occupational learning. They may do so through formal training or teach the roles informally on the job. They may prescribe how the roles should be performed or encourage newcomers to develop their own approach to the work role. Jones (1986) provides longitudinal evidence that newcomers' perceived efficacy at entry affects their responsiveness to different training orientations. Individuals low in perceived efficacy are most responsive to prescriptive training, which leads them to adopt the occupational roles as they are traditionally structured. Those high in perceived efficacy are more responsive to training that enables them to perform occupational roles innovatively. Self-efficacious newcomers incur some personal costs through their self-directedness, however. The perspective they bring to bear on their job may conflict with established practices and the preferences of existing workers. Therefore, incumbents usually have to negotiate the emergent elements of their role with their coworkers. With growing experience, individuals may add other emergent role elements to their job, requiring further renegotiations. Self-construction of roles can be more stressful because of the uncertainties and risks it involves, as opposed to simply adopting established role definitions and practices.

Changes in occupational activities are occurring rapidly nowadays, requiring a high sense of personal efficacy and versatility. These vocational changes are driven by a variety of influences. Many employees, of course, change their work roles through promotion to progressively higher job assignments. Work enrichment by job rotation that provides variety and new challenges is now widely used to sustain the interest and involvement of employees in their work when there is little prospect of upward mobility. The teamwork approach is often used for this purpose. Rather than segmenting a job into detached parts that become the sole work assignment for individuals day in and day out, the entire job is performed by self-managed team members. In team-based projects and production systems, each member learns every aspect of the job and rotates among the different subtasks. This type of organizational structure creates an enabling work environment that is well suited to producing a highly skilled, flexible workforce. The work life becomes more diversified and challenging and, through self-management, affords greater personal control.

Competitive economic forces are pruning the hierarchies of bureaucratic management. Increasingly, operational decisions and management functions are being assigned to the workers themselves in an effort to improve productivity and employee

satisfaction. Structuring work in ways that give operational control to those doing the projects removes bureaucratic impediments to initiative, creativity, and getting things done. The team members themselves decide how best to perform the job, structure the job assignments, make good use of complementary skills, and manage motivational and personnel problems. The team has full control over its own operation but must be accountable for its productivity. Otherwise, a group's self-interests may take precedence over productive performance. A sense of ownership of one's work enlists self-evaluative incentives, and personalized responsibility increases social incentives to do a good job.

Having workers manage themselves changes the model of supervisory managership. Managers must be willing to relinquish operational control and, instead, serve as facilitators who provide the resources, instructive guidance, and support that teams need to do their work effectively (Stewart & Manz, 1995). Managers serve as facilitators who provide the resources and support teams need to do the work effectively. Interestingly, enabling structures in the work environment build managers' sense of efficacy to operate as facilitators of productive teamwork (Laschinger & Shamian, 1994). Enabling experiences in the work life can affect perceived efficacy in other aspects of life. Workplace structures in which employees control their own work through a self-management system increase a sense of political efficacy and social participation in the political process (Elder, 1981).

Managers of low efficacy for enabling leadership are likely to create a disconcerting work life of illusory control in which work teams are held responsible for their performances but the managers continue to wield actual control by subtle means. The commitment to a self-managing work structure must be genuine and mutually supportive at all levels of the organization. Group self-management will not necessarily, in and of itself, make work more interesting or produce superior outcomes. Although self-managed teamwork generally improves productivity and quality of work life (Cohen, 1994), ineffectual self-managing groups are not uncommon. The variability in effectiveness needs explaining. Ineffectual self-managed groups abound. The benefits of group autonomy come with the cost of many managerial responsibilities. It is no easy task to maintain high productivity and manage the many psychosocial aspects of work life successfully. Effective teamwork, therefore, requires not only versatile technical efficacy but also self-regulatory and interpersonal efficacy to forge the group into a motivated and productive workforce. These vital self-management skills must be developed when lacking if group members are to work well together. Evidence suggests that perceived collective efficacy may be a key mechanism governing successful self-managed teamwork. Campion, Medsker, and Higgs (1993) examined a variety of processes and predictors of work group effectiveness. They report that perceived group efficacy, which they call potency, is positively associated with group self-management, flexibility and variety in job assignments, shared purposes and a sense of responsibility for the work, good communication among coworkers, managerial support, and mutual support and sharing of workloads. Perceived group efficacy was the strongest predictor of employee satisfaction and productivity. Potency treats collective efficacy as a general belief in a group's effectiveness assessed by a few global items (Guzzo, 1986). Perceived team efficacy tailored to the relevant domain is positively correlated with general team efficacy measured as potency (Lindsley, Mathieu, Heffner & Brass, 1994). The two determinants differ in predictiveness, however. Perceived team efficacy is a better predictor of subsequent group performance than potency. This is consistent with the common finding that globality sacrifices predictiveness.

During the course of their work life, some employees progress to positions of leadership. As is true of other aspects of occupational development, beliefs of personal efficacy affect aspirations to leadership. Singer (1991) studied professionals in middle management positions in different types of organizations. Leadership aspirations were predicted by the anticipated benefits of high rank for newcomers to the organization, but by perceived efficacy to fulfill the demands of leadership for those who had been with the organization longer. For female managers, even the

newcomers were basing their leadership aspirations on efficacy beliefs as well as on the desirability of the payoffs that come with being a leader.

Efficacious Adaptability

Job rotation, transfers, promotions, and geographic relocations require employees to develop whatever skills they lack to meet the new work demands (Dewhirst, 1991). Employees who have cultivated diverse talents can handle such occupational transitions better than those who are skilled in only a few things. Unfortunately, in the later years of their careers, employees whose work life is compartmentalized in hierarchically structured systems experience declining opportunities for challenging positions and enriching work assignments that foster career growth. Such organizational practices can gradually erode a sense of personal efficacy, which diminishes the level of work involvement and leads to occupational obsolescence. In addition to these common forms of occupational change, with increasing longevity, more and more people are seeking diversity and challenge in their lives by taking up second careers after retirement from their original careers.

The pace of technological change is so fast nowadays that knowledge and technical skills are quickly outmoded unless they are updated to fit the new technologies. Efficacious adaptability applies at the industry level as well as the workforce level. Organizations now have to be fast learners and rapid changers to remain successful in the future. Entire new industries spring up and established ones decline as a result of technological obsolescence. Established companies must be continuously innovative to survive and prosper in rapidly changing marketplaces. But such adaptability is not all that easy to accomplish. Not only does it require a good deal of forward thinking, but companies usually must do the developmental groundwork for change at the height of their success. They face the paradox of change under success. Prosperity breeds complacency, dampens interest in innovative renewal, and fuels the internal social dramas that impede change. The same inertial processes operate in sale strategies to increase market share as exist in product development. Prolonged success strengthens executives' beliefs in the efficacy of the old ways of doing business; fosters disinterest in, and dismissal of, unfavorable information; and promotes adherence to the old ways despite major changes in the marketplace that beget losses in operating profit (Audia, 1995). Those who are supremely self-assured have the tougher problem of forsaking what brought them success. Rapid cycles of change place increasing importance on adaptive forethought and skills for managing the inertia of success. Unwieldy decision-making systems make it difficult to capitalize on new trends early enough to secure the future leadership in the industry. Uncertainties about the likely payoff of unproved technologies and rivalries among organizational factions with vested interests create further sources of resistance to change.

Slow changers can become big losers. All too often, once-booming corporations with foreshortened perspectives fall victim to the constraints of success — they get locked into the technologies and products that produced their success and fail to change fast enough to the technologies of the future. Product cycles have become much shorter, requiring quicker changes. In the computer industry, for example, premier corporations that built their success on mainframe computer systems lost out to makers of minicomputers who, in turn, suffered sharp financial declines because they were slow to heed the technological change to microcomputers and workstations. As the next generation of computer technology passed them by, they suffered rapid decline and massive job cutbacks. Entrepreneurial companies can more quickly take advantages of the rapid pace of change. Thus, venturesome entrepreneurs, unhampered by unwieldy organizational systems and corporate inertia, often create new companies that take the lead in the new wave of technologies.

There are three types of changes, requiring different forms of efficacy, that determine organizational growth and effectiveness (Binks & Vale, 1990). The first involves the ability to recognize and respond quickly to the changes occurring in the marketplace that affect products or services. Reactive efficacy requires close monitoring of trends in the marketplace and test marketing of variants likely to win popular favor. The second type of change, which is more proactive, relies on efficacy to create incremental improvements in existing products or services. These improvements are achieved through continued experimentation and a good deal of improvisational modeling of competitors' successful products or practices. The third type of change involves creative innovations that produce new products, services, or production systems. At this level of change, organizations create market demands rather than merely adapting to them. Unlike the ecological view of organizational change, in social cognitive theory, organizations create niches as well as fill them. In innovative efficacy, knowledge is synthesized into new ways of thinking and doing things. A high sense of efficacy fosters innovativeness (Locke et al., 1984). In an effort to enhance innovativeness and responsiveness to trends in the marketplace, some of the larger organizations are giving their operating units greater autonomy to put their talents to best use. Others reorganize more radically by splitting into smaller entities that have full control over their operations. Organizational changes are extensively influenced by the actions of individuals who perform managerial roles. The influence of perceived managerial efficacy on organizational effectiveness will be examined shortly.

For the many reasons mentioned, people experience a high rate of change either within or across vocations over the full course of their working lives. Whatever the source of dislocation, they have to keep updating their knowledge and skills and learning new ones to keep up with technological developments. To do so, they must take charge of their own self-development. Any insecurities people have about their learning capabilities are reactivated when they have to learn new ways of thinking and doing things. A perceived sense of inefficacy is a contributor to occupational transition problems. Guided mastery programs provide effective ways of facilitating the transition to new occupational roles and levels of competency by enhancing efficacy beliefs and promoting skill development.

SELF-EFFICACY IN ORGANIZATIONAL DECISION MAKING

As in other aspects of life, those who preside over organizational activities are continuously faced with problems of choice. According to the rational model of human thinking, people thoroughly explore a wide range of possible options, calculate their advantages and disadvantages, and then select the course of action with the highest expected payoff. This rational model of good decision making presupposes extensive knowledge of alternatives and their likely consequences. It also assumes a stable ordering of preferences rooted in harmonious personal values. In making decisions in everyday life, however, people do not behave like wholly rational utility maximizers. At best, they exhibit only limited rationality. Cost-benefit considerations are only part of the bases of choice, and even the weighting of these factors is usually carried out inefficiently (Behling & Starke, 1973; Brandt, 1979; Simon, 1978). Moreover, in many of the decisions people make, they model the courses of action they see producing good results for others rather than going through elaborate calculations as if devoid of any social clues about the relative utility of various options (Bandura, 1986a). Given sufficient perceived efficacy and resources, they favor successful modeled options and shun inadequate ones.

The searches people conduct tend to be highly selective. They are rarely sufficiently informed to generate all the feasible options. Nor do they give detailed thought to all the possible consequences of the options they do consider. Indeed, it would take an inordinate amount of time to do so. To complicate matters, alternatives are not always well defined and outcomes are not easily foreseeable. Most actions have mixed effects, which requires a consideration of trade-offs. Typically, people pick, from a limited array of possibilities, the course of action that looks satisfactory rather than searching assiduously for the optimal one. Moreover, they are sometimes inconsistent in how they order alternatives,

have difficulty assigning relative weights to different types of outcomes, let the attractiveness of the outcomes color their judgments of how easy it might be to attain them, and opt for lesser outcomes because they can get them sooner. When faced with many alternatives and possible outcomes, they use simplifying decision strategies that may lead them to select alternatives that differ from those they would have selected had they weighed and ordered the various factors as presupposed by the benefit maximization model (Kahneman et al., 1982). All of this requires good weighting and computing capabilities.

Decision making is neither a dispassionate process nor one driven solely by the desire to maximize self-interest viewed mainly in hedonic terms. Emotional factors and group normative influences that favor or foreclose certain options affect the choices that are made (Etzioni, 1988). People do not seek mere utility in their choices. They adopt personal standards linked to self-evaluative outcomes that figure prominently in the calculus of decision making. Since they have to live with themselves, they tend to choose courses of action that bring them self-satisfaction and a sense of self-worth and reject those that are self-devaluating. When the self-evaluative effects of certain options conflict with material gain, people often settle for alternatives of marginal utility or even sacrifice substantial material payoff to preserve their positive self-regard (Bandura & Perloff, 1967; Simon, 1979b). They act in ways that hurt their material self-interest or, if they are moved by social compassion, they sacrifice their self-interest for the welfare of others. Evaluative self-regulation is a principal mechanism governing choice behavior (Bandura, 1986a). Within this broadened perspective, self-regard and social benefit become crucial aspects of one's self-interest.

In most of the important problems of choice that people face, they are not presented with a predetermined set of options. A comprehensive theory of decision making must specify where the options come from. We saw that, in the process of career decision making, efficacy beliefs determine the slate of options given consideration. People do not regard options in domains of perceived inefficacy as worth considering, whatever benefits they may hold. Such exclusions of large classes of options are made rapidly on self-efficacy grounds with little thought of costs and benefits. Perceived efficacy not only sets the slate of options for consideration but also influences other aspects of decision making. It affects what information is collected, how it is interpreted, and how it is converted into means for managing situational challenges. And finally, people have to be sufficiently secure in their efficacy to remain task-oriented in their decision making, especially when things go wrong.

If optimal decision making is hard to come by at the individual level, it is doubly difficult in organizations. Organizations pursue multiple goals that are not entirely compatible. For example, decisions that bring short-run successes may jeopardize long-term growth. Various factions in organizations often have differing views about the merits of alternative options and their likely consequences (March, 1981; Pfeffer, 1981). Conflicts of preference are common, and these are not easily resolvable. Organizational decisions, therefore, are products of compromises among factional interests seeking personal advantages as well as common benefits. Effective decision making in organizations requires a high sense of managerial efficacy not only in analytic thinking but also in social persuasion, management of power conflicts, and building coalitions.

Managerial Decision Making

In presiding over organizations, managers continuously make decisions and structure the efforts of others toward desired outcomes (Kotter, 1982; Mintzberg, 1973; Stewart, 1967). They must understand how their decisions affect the motivation and performance of others and how to make the best use of the personnel they are managing. Such managerial decisions must be made in the midst of a continual flow of activities on the basis of diverse sources of information that contain uncertainties and ambiguities. Much of the information may be tainted by the biases of those gathering and interpreting it (March, 1982). To complicate matters

further, feedback about the adequacy of decisions is often delayed and is rarely free of ambiguities or mixed outcomes. Moreover, decisions made at one point in time influence the options and effects of later decisions. Within this decisional context, managers must continually link short-run goals to more distal organizational objectives along equivocally structured means-ends pathways.

Many of the critical decisional rules governing the productivity of an organization must be discovered through exploratory means. The more novel and complex the environment, the greater the need to test different options and evaluate their effects to discover how one can best exercise influence over the system. Effective decision making in complex and dynamic environments requires a generative capability in which various cognitive skills are applied to ferret out information, interpret and integrate feedback, test and revise knowledge, and implement selected options. Managers have to live with the consequences of errors in judgment and faulty decisions.

Despite the evidence that much of what managers do involves decision making in complex and uncertain environments, little attention has been devoted to systematic analysis of managerial decision processes (Schweiger, Anderson, & Locke, 1985). Decision-making research conducted within the framework of cognitive psychology has contributed to our understanding of how perceptual and cognitive operations affect decision making. Much of the research on human decision making, however, involves single judgments in static environments under nontaxing conditions. In natural environments, multiple decisions must be made from a wide array of information generated by ongoing activities under time constraints and with social and self-evaluative consequences. Moreover, organizational decision making requires working through others and coordinating, monitoring, and managing collective efforts. Cognitive approaches to decision making are further limited by the fact that they usually ignore the impact of affective, motivational, and self-regulatory influences on how information is gathered, evaluated, integrated, and used. Managers do not simply react to decision-making systems that are demarcated for them. Rather, they create their own decision support systems and selectively process the information generated by these constructed environments (George, 1980; March, 1982). Managerial decision making requires working through others within organizational contexts characterized by hierarchy, division of labor, and specialization.

Because organizational outcomes must be achieved through the concerted efforts of others, some of the most important managerial decisions involve how to use human talent and how to guide and motivate human effort. This is not a dispassionate process. In executing this role, managers have to cope with numerous obstacles, failures, and setbacks that often carry perturbing self-evaluative implications as well as social consequences. These affective factors can undermine self-evaluations and motivation in ways that impair good use of decision-making skills. Effective decision making thus involves more than applying a set of cognitive operators to existing knowledge to generate desired solutions. Self-regulatory influences have considerable impact on how well cognitive-processing systems work.

It requires a strong sense of efficacy to deploy one's cognitive resources optimally and to remain task-oriented in the face of the many organizational complexities just described. Effective analytic thinking requires control over one's own thought processes and sufficient confidence in one's capabilities to continue systematic testing of options when selected courses of action produce inadequate results. People who judge themselves inefficacious in managing environmental demands tend to become more self-diagnostic than task-diagnostic (M. Bandura & Dweck, 1988). Self-referent intrusive thinking creates stress and undermines effective use of capabilities by diverting attention from how best to solve problems to concerns over personal deficiencies and possible adverse outcomes. As a result, managers get themselves thinking erratically and self-protectively rather than strategically. In contrast, people who believe strongly in their problem-solving capabilities remain highly efficient in their analytic thinking in

complex decision-making situations. Quality of analytic thinking, in turn, fosters performance accomplishments.

When research has addressed motivational mechanisms, it has often been conducted with relatively simple tasks for which people already possess the knowledge and means to manage the task demands and need only to intensify their effort to obtain higher levels of performance. In complex activities, increased effort will not be translated into productivity gains unless effective strategies are developed for deploying that effort productively (Wood & Locke, 1990). Simple tasks limit the applicability of findings to managerial decision making where performance accomplishments must be achieved through group effort. A good case in point is goal setting, which is the most widely researched and validated theory of work motivation (Locke & Latham, 1990). Until recently, in many of the studies of goal setting, people perform rudimentary tasks on their own (Wood et al., 1987). In contrast, achievement of organizational performance goals requires creating appropriate production functions, allocating people to those functions, and continually adapting the organizational practices to changes in available resources, situational circumstances, and the outcomes of the collective effort (Kotter, 1982; Mintzberg, 1973). Effective management of these ongoing activities calls for high levels of motivation and effective strategies for organizing the collective effort productively.

The multifaceted nature of managerial activities and their mazelike linkage to organizational functioning introduces complexities in the relationship between managers' goals and organizational attainment. The complexities of working through others create obstacles to transforming personal goals into group accomplishments. The more people one has to assign and guide with sensitivity to their personal attributes, the more difficult it is to raise collective performance through goal setting (Wood, Bandura, & Bailey, 1990). Sheer managerial effort alone does not ensure attainment of group goals. If strategies are poorly conceived, the guiding effort will not get a group to perform well. Moreover, efforts to enhance the level of organizational functioning often require constituent changes in particular aspects of the social system and the way in which social resources are allocated. Systematic pursuit of such operational subgoals contributes to eventual success but does not necessarily produce sizable gains in organizational performance in the short run. In fact, short-run gains often may have to be sacrificed for desired distal attainments.

In organizational environments requiring complex decision making, managers must figure out managerial rules that enable them to predict and exercise influence over the collective effort. Discernment of predictive organizational rules requires effective cognitive processing of multifaceted information that contains ambiguities and uncertainties. Decision rules are discovered through systematic application of analytic strategies. Initially, managers must draw on their existing state of knowledge in constructing provisional composite rules for how various motivational factors may affect group performance. The optimal value of the various predictive factors must be tested by varying them systematically and assessing how they affect group performance. Less skilled decision makers formulate vague composite rules; tend to alter many factors concurrently, which makes it difficult to figure out what produced the effects; and make less effective use of informative outcome feedback (Bourne, 1965; Bruner, Goodnow, & Austin, 1956).

The determinants and mechanisms governing managerial decision making do not lend themselves readily to experimental analysis in actual organizational settings. Such situations include a multiplicity of interacting influences that are difficult to identify, let alone control experimentally. An understanding of the mechanisms through which decision making operates can be advanced by experimental analysis of complex decision making in simulated organizational environments based on extensive observation of actual organizational functioning. A realistic simulated organization permits systematic variation of theoretically relevant factors and precise assessment of their impact on organizational performance and the psychological mechanisms through which they achieve their effects.

The simulated management system used in experiments to examine the role of self-regulatory mechanisms incorporated most of the complexities and dynamic features described in the previous sections (Wood & Bailey, 1985). In executing the managerial task, managers had to allocate employees from a roster to different production subfunctions so as to complete work assignments within optimal periods. By correctly matching employees to job requirements, the managers could attain a higher level of organizational performance than if employees were poorly matched to jobs. To assist them in this decision task, managers received descriptions of the skill and effort required for each of the production subfunctions and the characteristics of each employee. This information described each employee's particular skills, experience, expertise, motivational level, preference for routine or challenging work assignments, and standards of work quality. These aspects of the simulation addressed the requirements of socially mediated organizational functioning through division of labor and specialization.

In addition to allocating employees to jobs, the managers had to decide how to use goals, supervisory feedback and social incentives to guide and motivate their supervisees. To discover the rules about these motivational factors, managers had to test options, cognitively process the results of their decisions, and continue to apply analytic strategies in ways that would reveal the optimal managerial rules. To complicate matters further, the motivational factors involved both nonlinear and compound rules, which are especially difficult to learn. For example, goals that present a moderate challenge foster higher performance than easy goals or ones that are so difficult that they are essentially unattainable. Social commendations must be both appropriate to employees' attainments and equitable to the commendations given to others, thus requiring use of a compound rule. After discovering the set of rules, the managers had to figure out the best way to integrate them into a coherent and equitable managerial effort.

Knowing managerial rules does not ensure optimal implementation of them. Managers also had to gain proficiency in tailoring their supervisory actions to the particular characteristics of individual employees. Repeated mismanagement of the personnel increasingly impaired the quality of their functioning. Including multiple production tasks made it possible to examine the cumulative effects of good and faulty decision making. Periodic assessment of managers' perceived managerial efficacy, their aspirations for the organizations they were overseeing, and the quality of their analytic thinking provided insight into how these changing self-regulatory factors contribute to organizational functioning over time.

Recall that social cognitive theory explains human functioning in terms of triadic reciprocal causation. In this causal model, cognitive and other personal factors, behavior, and environmental events all influence one another bidirectionally. The dynamic simulated environment permits detailed analyses of how this interactional causal structure operates and changes over time. Each of the major interactants in the triadic causal structure — cognition, behavior, and environment — functions as an important constituent of the organizational process. The cognitive determinant is represented by beliefs of managerial efficacy, personal goal setting, and quality of analytic thinking. The managerial choices that are actually executed constitute the behavioral determinant. The portrayed and objective properties of the organizational environment, the level of challenge it prescribes, and the responsiveness of employees to managerial interventions represent the environmental determinant.

Chapter 4 presented detailed analyses of managerial decision making under conditions in which certain properties of the simulated organization were varied and belief systems were instilled that enhanced or undermined managers' beliefs in their managerial efficacy (Bandura & Jourden, 1991; Bandura & Wood, 1989; Jourden, 1991; Wood & Bandura, 1989b). Otherwise talented managers who were led to believe that complex decision making is an inherent aptitude, that organizations are not easily controllable, and that other managers perform better than they do, and who received feedback highlighting shortfalls in their managerial performance exhibited progressive deterioration of their managerial functioning. They were beset by increasing self-doubts about their managerial efficacy as they encountered problems. They became more and more erratic in their analytic thinking. They lowered their organizational aspirations. And they achieved progressively less with the organization they were managing. Failing organizational performances further undermined perceived managerial efficacy. In marked contrast, belief that complex decision making is an acquirable skill and that organizations are controllable, and feedback that highlighted the managers' comparative capabilities and the performance gains they were achieving fostered organizational productivity. Managers operating under these self-enhancing belief systems displayed a resilient sense of efficacy even when assigned productivity standards were exceedingly difficult to reach. They set themselves increasingly challenging organizational goals. And they used good analytic thinking for discovering managerial rules. Such a self-efficacious orientation paid off in high organizational productivity. Taken collectively, these studies clarify some of the dynamics of the rise, maintenance, and decline of organizational functioning as a result of the perceived self-efficaciousness of the managership.

In organizational milieus, a low sense of efficacy to produce desired results generally fosters the ascribing of blame to the deficiencies of others. For example, teachers who have a low sense of instructional efficacy tend to regard difficult students as lacking ability and unteachable, whereas those who have a strong belief in their instructional efficacy view student problems as surmountable through extra effort and variation of educational approach (Ashton & Webb, 1986). Similarly, many of the managers in the present studies who had suffered losses in perceived managerial efficacy were quite uncharitable in their views of their employees. They regarded some of them as unmotivatable and unworthy of supervisory effort and thought they should be summarily fired. Had this option existed, it is likely that managers with a low sense of efficacy would have worked their way through a large workforce by numerous dismissals of employees they had mismanaged.

The findings of field studies on the impact of managerial self-efficacy on career success are in accord with those of laboratory investigations of effective management. Onglatco and her colleagues measured managers' beliefs in their efficacy to perform technical, human relations, administrative, and conceptual managerial functions (Onglatco, Yuen, Leong, & Lee, 1993). The higher the managers' sense of efficacy, the greater their managerial success as measured by rate of upward mobility in the career path, level of salary, and perceived career success compared to their peers. Efficacy beliefs account for variation in managerial success even when controlling for the importance attached to performing the key managerial tasks well.

Appraising Opportunities and Risks and Managing Constraints

The development of new business ventures and the renewal of established ones depends heavily on innovativeness and entrepreneurship. With many resourceful competitors around, viability requires continual ingenuity. In corporate settings, managers constantly face decisions involving dilemmas and gambles. Some managers view such situations as presenting opportunities; others see them mainly as posing threats. Krueger and Dickson (1993, 1994) provide evidence that managers' beliefs in their decisional efficacy affect their appraisal orientations. Managers' whose perceived efficacy is raised focus on opportunities worth pursuing, whereas those whose sense of efficacy is lowered dwell on risks to be avoided. Perceived decisional efficacy affects risk taking through its impact on perceptions of opportunities and threats. These findings are in accord with those of Heath and Tversky (1991) showing that perceived competence increases willingness to take risks under uncertainty.

Entrepreneurship, which is driven by the envisioned opportunities of new ventures, rests heavily on a robust sense of efficacy to sustain one through the stresses and discouragements inherent in innovative pursuits. Strong belief that one can produce results lowers the perceived odds against success. Indeed, perceived entrepreneurial efficacy is higher in business majors who intend to start new ventures (Krueger, 1994). Moreover, they judge themselves better capable of beating the odds than other venturers. There is evidence to suggest that entrepreneurial efficacy has familial roots. Having an entrepreneurial parent, especially a successful one, raises offsprings' perceived efficacy to start and manage their own business (Scherer, Adams, Carley, & Wiebe, 1989). The stronger the perceived entrepreneurial efficacy, the higher the aspiration for preparatory education and training and the stronger the expectation of undertaking an entrepreneurial career.

Baum (1994) extended this line of research to actual venture growth in several hundred firms in the architectural woodwork industry. He studied entrepreneurs who were either the founders of the companies or transformers of those they bought. Entrepreneurial success was measured in terms of growth in sales, employment, and profits over a four-year period. General personality traits bore little relationship to successful entrepreneurial performance. The venturers who achieved high growth had a vision of what they wished to achieve, had firm belief in their efficacy to realize it, set challenging growth goals, had good technical skills, and came up with innovative production and marketing strategies.

An exaggerated sense of personal efficacy of course can blind one to substantial difficulties and risks. Having committed themselves to a pursuit that is not producing results, some individuals may attempt to recoup their losses by investing more resources and taking greater risks. Their decisions are swayed by bygone investments rather than by full consideration of future costs and benefits of given courses of action. Once decisions get framed as choices among losses, people are likely to end up, as the saying goes, throwing good money after bad. In laboratory tests, administrators of investment projects whose perceived decisional efficacy is raised are prone to escalate commitment to previous investments in an effort to salvage failing ventures. Those whose perceived efficacy is lowered are quick to abandon failing ventures that incur early costs (Whyte, Saks, & Hook, in press). A high sense of efficacy similarly predicts greater investment in unproductive ventures by technical experts, in this case by petroleum geologists exploring for oil in a site producing dry wells (Whyte & Saks, 1995).

Being mired in the past should be distinguished from belief that one can beat tough odds in the future. In the latter case, one learns from earlier failures how to improve the odds for success. Diagnosing "realism" and gauging its effects are no easy matters. Telling self-efficacious managers to remedy problems that are inherently unsolvable stacks the deck in favor of early quitting as the functional option. If continued investment eventually pays off, then early quitting is the losing option. But the costs of giving up too early receive little attention because unrealized futures are not easily researchable. The history of innovation vividly documents that premature abandonment of advantageous ventures because of early failures and discouraging setbacks would have deprived societies of the major advances they enjoy in virtually every aspect of life. It was Edison's unshakeable belief in his inventive efficacy that illuminated our environment and spawned the recording and movie industries, just to mention a few of his wondrous creations. As he so aptly put it, "The trouble with other inventors is that they try a few things and quit. I never quit until I get what I want" (Josephson, 1959). How lucky we are that he was unfazed by failure. In most human endeavors, it is not that problems are insoluble but that the intractable ones present unmercifully tough odds. Most people are not about to invest the inordinate amount of time and energy needed to succeed. There is much to be said for the efficacious "unrealists" who persevere in innovative endeavors despite considerable costs that eventually produce highly beneficial results.

The benefits of perceived managerial efficacy are especially evident when many external constraints are imposed on carrying out the managerial role (Jenkins, 1994a). Chief executives who have a high sense of efficacy manage to achieve good organizational functioning under both high and low perceived constraints, whereas organizations run by managers of low efficacy perform poorly under high perceived constraints but do somewhat better when there are fewer impediments to overcome. Managers of low perceived efficacy not only achieve less organizationally but fault external assessments of their organizations' performances as biased and unfair (Jenkins, 1994b).

A strong sense of personal efficacy has high functional value under organizational constraints for employees as well, as shown by Speier and Frese (in press) in a longitudinal study of East German workers during the historic transition from the communist system. They examined changes in personal initiative as reflected in employees' going beyond the formal duties of their jobs to improve the work process and taking proactive steps on their own in continuing education. Employees' efficacy beliefs both partially mediated and moderated the effect of organizational constraints on changes in their level of initiative in the workplace. Self-efficacious employees exhibited high initiative regardless of the amount of control they could exercise over their work activities, whereas those of lower efficacy showed little initiative under low controllability but were more enterprising when they had substantial leeway on how to perform their jobs.

Enhancing Resilience to Managerial Stressors

Managerial roles are often plagued with high pressure, perpetual evaluative threats, and potentially debilitating social comparisons that can easily drive one to the sauce. The evidence that belief systems can markedly affect, for better or for worse, the quality of managerial functioning through the efficacy mechanism prescribes ways of preserving a strong sense of efficacy that is resilient to organizational stressors. The first strategy involves the conception of ability. To construe managerial capability as an inherent aptitude heightens the threat value of missteps that are a natural part of any complex activity, shifts concern to self-protection of one's public image of smartness, and stifles risk-taking and creative ventures. In contrast, construal of managerial capability as acquirable skills removes the perceived threat of mistakes as diagnostic of inherent personal deficiencies, fosters development of potentialities, converts threats into challenges, and minimizes self-protective preoccupations that impair the quality of functioning. Thus, managers led to believe in these different conceptions of decision-making ability read the same level of managerial performance very differently (Wood & Bandura, 1989b). Their beliefs bias how they cognitively process their successes and failures. Managers who subscribe to the inherent-aptitude view regard substandard attainments as indicants of personal deficiencies and become beset with increasing doubts about their managerial efficacy as they encounter further difficulties. Managers who subscribe to the acquirable-skills view construe similar substandard attainments as instructive guides for improving their managerial competencies and sustain a self-efficacious outlook in the face of difficulties that leads to organizational attainments.

Conception of managerial ability in terms of acquirable skills reduces vulnerability not only to the adverse effects of mistakes but also to the debilitating effects of unfavorable social comparisons. Managers are continually confronted with comparative appraisals whether they seek them or not, especially in competitively structured systems. Since they are not about to forsake competitive pursuits, they must minimize the demoralizing effects of social comparison and instead use it constructively as an impetus and guide for self-development. If ability is regarded as reflecting inherent aptitude, being outperformed by others carries threatening diagnostic implications that one is lacking in basic intelligence. But if ability is construed as an acquirable skill, being surpassed by others is of little diagnostic import because it is changeable. One can always match, or even surpass, the attainments of others by gaining more knowledge and perfecting one's skills. Evidence of self-improvement that reduces the performance disparity from others boosts managers' perceived efficacy with concomitant benefits in organizational functioning (Bandura & Jourden, 1991).

The debilitating effects of social comparison can also be reduced by judging one's accomplishments against personal standards of self-improvement rather than against the attainments of others. By adopting a self-comparative focus, individuals gain the benefits of personal challenges for self-development without being haunted and debilitated by how others do. A self-comparative focus alone is not an unmitigated benefit, however. Self-improvement never follows a uniform, ever-rising course. Rather, it is characterized by spurts of improvement, setbacks, plateaus, and variations in the rate of progress. Hence, self-comparison can be self-demoralizing or self-enhancing depending on whether individuals mainly dwell on their shortfalls in the mixed constellation of changes or accent their gains. Framing performance feedback in ways that give salience to the gains being made enhances beliefs of managerial efficacy and resultant organizational attainments even when organizational standards are set at a level that is well nigh out of reach (Jourden, 1991). But even performance gains carry no guarantee of efficacy enhancement. Gains can be construed in ways that undermine efficacy beliefs or strengthen them. In most undertakings, people's rate of improvement is rapid at the outset as they acquire proficiencies but slows down over time as they refine their skills and approach the upper limits of possible accomplishments. To preserve a sense of efficacy amidst such mixed changes, people must view negative fluctuations in the context of a trajectory of improvement over time and recognize a declining rate of improvement as inherent in the mastery of any complex activity rather than a sign of personal deficiency.

Personal efficacy is always exercised within certain environmental opportunities and constraints. The issues of interest include unrealized opportunities as well as thwarted aspirations. Belief in the controllability of the environment partly determines the extent to which potential opportunities are realized and constraints are circumvented. Belief in controllability, therefore, is another means of creating resilient managerial self-efficacy. Viewing an organization as changeable increases one's perceived efficacy to manage it, whereas regarding it as relatively uninfluenceable undermines one's beliefs of managerial efficacy (Bandura & Wood, 1989). Indeed, approaching an organization with the view that there are severe limits on how much it can be changed instills a sense of personal inefficacy even when productivity standards are within easy reach and thus permit a high rate of organizational goal attainment. With that cognitive set, failures are taken as confirmatory evidence of organizational recalcitrance. While belief in one's powerlessness to effect change is self-handicapping, viewing an organizational environment as personally influenceable promotes resiliency of self-efficacy even when productivity standards are exceedingly difficult to fulfill. With belief that obstacles are surmountable, substandard attainments lead one to intensify one's efforts and search for more productive solutions. Thus, given the same simulated organization, managers led to believe that it was changeable created increasingly productive organizations, whereas managers led to believe that it was refractory to change created deteriorating organizations. These divergent organizational trajectories were largely driven by altered beliefs of managerial efficacy.

Self-Efficacy in Policy Making and Receptivity to Innovations

Many of the consequential decisions that managers have to make involve matters of policy and organizational mission as well as management of personnel. For these purposes, they must gather relevant information about the advantages and disadvantages of alternative courses of action, assess the reliability of the information, and decide how to interpret and weigh it in forming their policy decisions. Information is often collected for political and self-protective purposes rather than solely to illuminate costs and benefits. Moreover, the way in which decision makers gather and use information is partly influenced by their sense of personal efficacy.

Jatulis and Newman (1991) examined under simulated conditions the influence of potential risks, time pressure, and the perceived efficacy of program managers in the health field on their search for evaluative information about whether or not to institute a given health care program. When faced with time pressure and mixed support from their governing boards, program managers with a low sense of efficacy sought more information, spent more time talking to others about the matter, and procrastinated longer in making a decision than did managers who had a high sense of efficacy. Apparently, managers who distrust their ability to make good decisions and to defend and stick to those they have made spend a lot of time gathering information largely for self-protective purposes. It is not that self-inefficacious managers are simply slow decision makers. When governing boards are supportive and adequate time is available, managers do not embark on lengthy searches for evaluative program information.

Effective leadership requires receptivity to innovations that can improve the quality and productivity of organizations. Although benefits can be realized through innovations, many factors operate as barriers to their adoption. Innovations involve uncertainties about potential costs and benefits, commitment of limited financial resources that are being vied for by different factions, temporary disorganization of established structures and practices, and the hassles of retraining a workforce to use the new technologies (Bandura, 1986a). In organizations containing competing subgroups, as many do, an innovation that increases the power of one faction is resisted by rival factions that perceive change as detracting from their influence (Zaltman & Wallendorf, 1979). If an innovation should fail to live up to expectations, the promoter can incur heavy personal costs. Clearly, a high level of self-assurance is needed to override these many disincentives to adoption decisions.

The beliefs of school administrators in their efficacy to implement the use of microcomputers distinguished those who introduced them in their system from those who did not (Jorde-Bloom & Ford, 1988). The degree to which perceived efficacy affected adoption decisions, however, varied depending on whether microcomputers were adopted for managerial purposes or for instructional purposes.

In the more limited use as a tool for word-processing and information management, administrators' computer knowledge and experience, professional status, efficacy beliefs, and background in mathematics and science emerged as determinants of adoption decisions, in that order of importance. Using microcomputers as an instructional tool involves many staff members, who often have differing views on how students should be taught and who have insecurities about computers. Administrators' beliefs in their efficacy to implement the technology was the primary determinant of adoption, followed by professional status, maleness, and computer knowledge and experiences. Innovativeness is not a personality trait. Rapid adopters of computers, for example, are not necessarily speedy adopters of new clothing fashions. Not surprisingly, a trait measure of innovativeness did not contribute to prediction of which administrators introduced microcomputers in their organizations.

Efficacy beliefs affect not only administrators' receptivity to technological innovations but also the readiness with which employees adopt them (Hill, Smith, & Mann, 1987). That efficacy beliefs increase receptivity of technological innovations is corroborated experimentally. Business students whose sense of computer efficacy was arbitrarily lowered resisted computer aids in performing their work assignments (Ellen, 1988). In contrast, those whose perceived efficacy was raised abandoned manual methods for computer-aided ones. A supportive organizational milieu facilitates adoption of computing technology by managers in financial and consulting firms (Compeau & Higgins, 1995). Encouragement and modeling by coworkers of the use of computer systems raises managers' perceived efficacy to master the technology. High perceived efficacy, in turn, is accompanied by less anxiety and more enjoyment from working with computers, greater expected benefits in productivity and quality of job performance, and more extensive use of the computing technology. Technical assistance with hardware and software difficulties, however, had a negative impact on managers' perceived efficacy and outcome expectations. These findings underscore the importance of offering technical assistance in ways that are enabling rather than solving problems for workers in ways that leave them dependent and more doubtful of their capabilities.

New technologies are periodically introduced to the workplace to increase productivity by displacing labor-intensive operations. In these instances, employees must adopt the advanced technologies whether they like them or not. Such changes require employees to master new skills and to adapt to the mechanization of the work process. McDonald and Siegall (1992) examined how perceived efficacy for technical learning affected adaptation in a telecommunications company during a change-over period in which field technicians had to learn to manage their daily work activities through contact with a central computer rather than with a human operator. Employees who were self-assured in their learning efficacy were more satisfied with their job, were more committed to the organization, were less inclined to dwell on unrelated matters while doing their work, and performed their jobs better than employees who approached the changeover beset with self-doubts. When job opportunities are limited, a low sense of efficacy is expressed in avoidance behavior, such as tardiness and absenteeism, rather than in quitting the job. In redesigning work, trainers must focus not only on imparting knowledge and skills but also on enabling employees with the efficacy beliefs needed to profit from instruction and to execute the skills well once they are acquired.

Technological innovations are embedded in the network structures and power relations of organizations. Adoption of innovations, therefore, can have sociostructural reverberations. Early adopters of beneficial technologies not only increase their productivity but can gain influence in ways that change the structural patterns of organizations. Burkhardt and Brass (1990) report a longitudinal study showing that efficacy beliefs promote adoption of new technologies, which, in turn, alter the organizational network structure. They traced the diffusion within an agency of a computerized system that performed a variety of functions in data management and dissemination that were previously contracted out. Beliefs of personal efficacy to master computers were predictive of early adoption of the computerized system. Early adopters gained more influence and centrality within the organization over time than did later adopters. Structurally situated efficacy can clearly have widespread effects that extend beyond individual productivity.

Perceived self-efficacy influences the use of new technologies for household and leisure activities as it does in the workplace (Stern & Kipnis, 1993). The more people distrust their efficacy, the more they shy away from activities and products requiring higher cognitive skills. Those who feel sufficiently efficacious to purchase new products have to contend with the opaque prose of product operating manuals. As most readers would testify, the common manual formats actually weaken perceived efficacy to use the products appropriately (Celuch, Lust, & Showers, 1995). Efficacy beliefs about new technologies and products thus operate at both prepurchase and postpurchase phases. Marketers typically exalt the attributes and utility of their products but ignore the self-efficacy determinant in their promotional efforts. Knowledge that efficacy beliefs affect purchasing behavior will not be lost for long on enterprising advertisers.

SELF-EFFICACY IN ENACTMENT OF OCCUPATIONAL ROLES

After receiving training in their occupational roles, employees put into practice their knowledge and skills and continue to develop them over time. Perceived self-efficacy affects how well they manage the requirements and challenges of their occupational pursuits. The evidence for the contributing role of efficacy beliefs comes from a wide range of occupational domains.

Jobs vary in their degree of clarity about the roles employees are expected to play and how their role performances are evaluated. Much of the research on occupational role ambiguity has centered

on its stressful effects. McEnrue (1984) examined how perceived occupational role ambiguity affects the performance of managers of high and low perceived efficacy to manage the job demands of a large public utility. Conflicting views have been voiced on this subject. Some theorists contend that when job roles are unclear, the more competent employees will outperform the less competent ones. Others maintain that competent employees will put their capabilities to optimal use when they know what they need to do but not if their occupational role is ambiguous. The evidence shows that role ambiguity impedes use of personal capabilities. Thus, managers of high and low perceived efficacy do not differ in their performance when their roles are ambiguously structured. When role expectations and performance standards are clear, however, managers who have a high sense of efficacy exhibit marked gains in performance, whereas those of low perceived efficacy improve only slightly. These findings suggest different remedial measures for low organizational productivity. Self-efficacious managers need role clarification; inefficacious ones need both role clarification and guided mastery experiences that build their sense of managerial efficacy.

Self-Efficacy in Management by Goal Setting

Organizations often use goal setting as a way to increase their productivity. Goals improve level of functioning in several ways. The overreaching distal goals projected by leaders are typically cast as the vision being pursued. These goals provide a sense of purpose and direction for the organization's work. However, unless a vision is translated into concrete goals and strategies for their realization, it is but an idle fantasy. Interim goals help to move the organization ahead to the accomplishment of its mission. There is some evidence that the vision conveyed by leaders does not affect the performances of others directly. Rather, it enhances productivity to the extent that it inspires others to adopt the challenging goals embodied in the vision and strengthens their sense of efficacy to realize them (Kirkpatrick & Locke, 1996). Providing concrete strategies for how to implement the vision further aids group accomplishments. We have seen that goals have strong motivational effects. By providing challenges, goals raise and sustain the level of effort needed to be successful (Locke & Latham, 1990). When people are unclear about what they are trying to accomplish, their motivation is low and their efforts are poorly directed. Goals not only provide guides and motivators for performance, they also help to build and strengthen a sense of efficacy both individually and collectively. Success in attaining challenging goals increases people's beliefs in their capabilities (Bandura & Schunk, 1981). Accomplishing desired goals also creates self-satisfaction and increases interest in what one is doing (Bandura, 1986a; Locke, Cartledge, & Knerr, 1970; Morgan, 1984b).

Goals have these beneficial effects when they serve as challenges. Motivation through aspiration provides a continuing source of direction, personal efficacy, interest, and satisfaction. Without aspiration and active involvement in what they are doing, people are unmotivated, bored, and uncertain about their capabilities. If presented solely as general organizational objectives, such goals are usually too indefinite and remote to produce consistent results. General objectives that neither say much concretely about what is expected nor provide a clear timetable of advancement offer little basis for altering performance. To motivate and guide efforts, goal systems must be explicit, must be segmented into attainable progressive subgoals leading to long-range objectives, and must provide good feedback of performance on a regular basis. Under such conditions, people know what they are aiming for, know how they are doing, and can identify the corrective changes needed to achieve success.

Locke and Latham (1984) provide detailed guidelines for how to design and implement goal systems to enhance organizational performance. Pritchard and his colleagues specify concrete guidelines for how to devise good feedback systems for this purpose (Pritchard, Roth, Jones, Galgay, & Watson, 1988). A quality feedback system requires good measures of performance for different aspects of the work. It should include only aspects of the work over which the workers have control. It should provide an overall index of organizational productivity but also separate how the different parts of the organization are achieving their respective goals. Separable assessments identify where the system is working well and where improvements are needed. The unit workers thus become accountable for the work that is under their control. The feedback should be provided on a regular basis, along with information on how the level of performance is changing over time.

Goal systems have proved effective in increasing the organizational performance of all levels of personnel in virtually every type of activity (Locke & Latham, 1990). Goal systems, of course, will not enhance organizational productivity if they are imposed as onerous dictates. Such systems are resisted or subverted if they merely increase workloads without improving the work life or livelihood of employees. To gain high acceptance of, and commitment to, goal systems, employees should have a say in their development and implementation. Goals should be structured as challenges to aim for rather than as minimal levels of acceptable performance. Goal systems should promote the development of competencies that enable employees to perform better and derive pride from their work. Employees will regard a goal system favorably if it betters their work life or if they can share in some of the benefits of their improved productivity. In the growing competition of the global market, their very livelihood may rest upon such improved productivity.

Experimental analyses reviewed earlier reveal that perceived efficacy is a major mechanism through which goals affect motivation and performance. People's beliefs in their efficacy determine the goals they adopt and the strength of their commitment to them. Substandard performances diminish effort in individuals who doubt their capabilities but lead self-assured individuals to redouble their efforts to succeed. Organizational applications of goal setting corroborate the contributory role of efficacy beliefs to level of productivity.

Earley (1986) compared the effects on tire production in manufacturing facilities in the United

States and England of goal setting, strategy training, and whether the trainers were supervisors or union representatives. The employees' acceptance of the assigned goals, their commitment to them, the goals they set for themselves, and their perceived efficacy were also measured. Employees who were taught improved production strategies raised their perceived efficacy, set higher goals for themselves, were more committed to them, and increased their productivity. Training by union representatives produced higher goal acceptance and performance than did training by supervisors, especially in England where there is more labor-management antagonism. Both goal acceptance and efficacy beliefs enhanced productivity. Perceived self-efficacy raised productivity both directly and indirectly by fostering goal acceptance.

Participative Goal Setting

Organizations differ in the extent to which employees exercise control over the work process and allocation of resources. These variations in managerial practices partly reflect the cultural systems within which organizations are embedded (Erez & Earley, 1993; Tannenbaum, Kavcic, Rosner, Vianello, & Wieser, 1974). In collectivistic cultures, organizational decision making is generally more widely shared with workers than in cultures that are highly individualistic. The effects of participatory management have been evaluated most systematically in terms of organizational goal setting. This line of research has been extended to analyses of mediating psychological mechanisms, which is essential to a full understanding of participatory systems. Participation in goal setting can affect group performance by fostering acceptance of group goals and strengthening commitment to their attainment. When people have a say in the goals that are selected, they hold themselves responsible for fulfilling them and thereby engage self-evaluative motivators in the process. When goals are imposed by others, individuals do not necessarily accept them or feel obligated to meet them. Self-evaluative inducements for goal attainment, therefore, may be weaker when

performance standards are prescribed by others. The effects of assigned versus collaborative goal setting have been examined extensively in relation to job performance (Locke & Latham, 1990; Wagner & Gooding, 1987). People perform better with goals. Although participative goal setting increases satisfaction, it has no consistent effect on performance. Several factors may explain why allowing people to participate in determining their goals fails to improve their performance.

People are rarely of one mind on any subject, and group deliberation rarely forges unanimity. For members whose preferences differ from those of the prevailing view, participative decision-making will not bring them an increased sense of personal determination. As Locke and Schweiger (1979) point out, groups can be quite autocratic and their dictates highly constraining. Moreover, opportunities for participative decision-making by a group does not necessarily mean that most members exercise their influence in the formulation of group goals. A few influential members usually determine, in large part, what gets decided. Subordinate members may assent to decisions without feeling any personal commitment to them. So unless there is a high level of genuine involvement by all concerned in the formulation of collective goals, the differences between participative and prescriptive decision-making are more illusory than real.

When supervisors set goals and provide evaluative feedback, they create strong organizational pressure for improvements in performance. Concern over evaluation of one's work by others and the modeled productivity of coworkers can override the influence of how goals are set (White, Mitchell, & Bell, 1977). Once people get immersed in an activity, it appears that the goal itself becomes more salient than how it was set. The fewer the environmental sanctions and constraints, the more likely are self-evaluative motivators arising from personal commitment to exert their effects.

Collaborative decision making involves much more than goal setting, which serves mainly as a motivational device. In group transactions, members share knowledge about how best to perform their work. Improved plans and strategies can enhance the quality and productivity of group efforts. The cognitive benefits of participation will depend, in large part, on who can provide the best ideas. When members have better ideas than their managers, as is often the case because of their greater familiarity with the tasks, the collaborative decision making has a good payoff. Indeed, Latham, Winters & Locke (1994) found that the benefits of participation in decision making stem from the exchange of ideas rather than from how goals are set. Collaboration generated good strategies, raised members' sense of efficacy, and enhanced performance. Tests of mediating processes revealed that participant decision making improved performance entirely through its effects on development of task strategies and perceived personal efficacy. These are the processes that probably account for the effectiveness of self-managed teams. Perceived self-efficacy also helps to explain the variability in the effects of participant goal setting on performance (Latham, Erez, & Locke, 1988). Goals set through participation prove superior to assigned ones when encouragement of collaboration is accompanied by persuasory comments that boost members' sense of personal efficacy. Differences between how goals are set disappear or are markedly reduced when variations in efficacy beliefs are removed.

When personal contributions to group performance are not individually identified, people usually perform at a lower level when working together than when working alone. Some of the decline in productivity may stem from reduced incentive motivation. If people can gain the benefits of group accomplishments irrespective of how hard they work, some will slacken their efforts. When coworkers see other group members profit from the group's labors without contributing their fair share, they feel exploited. The productive ones slacken their own efforts, even though it reduces rewards to themselves and to the group, rather than suffer the exploitation (Kerr, 1983). Some discontent may arise, though to a lesser extent, even without big disparities in relative contributions. Ross (1981) has shown that people observe and recall more of their own contribution to a collective effort than that of their coparticipants. Consequently, they take more

credit for a group accomplishment than their coparticipants rightfully grant them. Because the self-focused bias in evaluating personal contribution is pervasive, group ventures can easily arouse feelings of exploitation or insufficient recognition.

Incentive factors may be part of the story, but they leave unexplained why everyone does not lapse into progressive idleness or why individuals continue to contribute insufficiently even though coworkers do not take kindly to loafers. Collective endeavors create social dynamics involving differential power, status, and comparative evaluation of personal capabilities. The mere presence of highly confident individuals, or being cast in a subordinate role, reduces effective use of even routine skills (Langer, 1979). For people who are easily socially intimidated, these types of social factors can impair performance by undermining perceived efficacy in group endeavors.

Individualism is not uniformly enhancing nor is collectivism uniformly dampening. Whether working together produces better or worse performances than working independently depends on members' perceived efficacy, the identifiability of their contribution to the group performance, and how they expect their work to be evaluated socially. Members with a high sense of efficacy expect positive outcomes for their efforts and consequently perform better when their work is individually identified than when it is merged into a group attainment. On the other hand, members with low perceived efficacy, who expect their deficient work to meet with disfavor, perform more poorly when they are singled out individually than when their contribution is an unidentifiable part of a team effort. As these findings and those reported next reveal, self-efficacy theory helps to explain the diverse effects on productivity of working alone or working together.

Contribution of Self-Efficacy to Creative Productivity

Success in academia rests heavily on research productivity. The process of scientific discovery is usually a tortuous one with uncertain outcomes.

Clearly, research is not a pursuit in which it is easy to ordain one's destiny. It requires considerable creativity, staying power, and fortuitous elements to achieve new knowledge that can have consequential social impact. Researchers must proceed on a strong sense of personal efficacy that their efforts will eventually prove successful. Indeed, high assurance in one's investigatory efficacy accounts for research productivity after controlling for the effects of years of experience, academic rank, and disciplinary affiliation (Vasil, 1992). Taylor and her colleagues examined the way in which perceived self-efficacy operates in concert with other factors in determining faculty research productivity (Taylor et al., 1984). They found that perceived efficacy contributes to productivity both directly and indirectly by influencing the goals of scholarship the faculty set for themselves and by enabling them to work flexibly on multiple research and writing projects at the same time. High productivity harvests citations in professional journals and commands good salaries and promotions.

Complaints are often registered over institutional pressures to publish or perish and to the heavy weighting of research publications in decisions about academic advancement and salary levels. One might view the dispute over research scholarship not as a matter of publish or perish but with puzzlement that the quest for new knowledge in academia would require social coercion. Schoen and Winocur (1988) provide a partial explanation for why this might be so. Faculty members hold weaker beliefs in their efficacy for research than for teaching or administration. Teaching lends itself more readily to personal control than do research activities, for which needed funding is difficult to secure, the outcomes of investigative efforts are uncertain, manuscripts are often rejected, and the pages of periodicals are littered with critiques of works that have managed to survive the grueling publication process. Skillful teaching, on the other hand, brings immediate personal satisfactions. In short, research is not the easiest pursuit in the academic arena. People generally shun what they feel inefficacious to perform, despite institutional mandates. Simply mandating creativity will not necessarily promote it.

Occupational Stress and Dysfunction

The findings reviewed in the previous sections were primarily concerned with the development of occupational efficacy and its impact on productivity and job satisfaction. Perceived self-efficacy to fulfill occupational demands also affects level of stress and the physical health of employees (McAteer-Early, 1992). Those who have a low sense of efficacy suffer anxiety, health problems, and health-impairing habits such as heavy drinking and sleep disturbances. Occupational stress is not just an employee problem. Certain organizational conditions can undermine employees' beliefs in their occupational capabilities and exacerbate the adverse effects of a low sense of coping efficacy. These include heavy workloads with accelerating technical demands, limited opportunities for continuing personal development to prevent technical obsolescence, poor prospects for occupational advancement, and an unsatisfying imbalance between one's work life and one's personal life. Some occupational pursuits are conducted at a demanding, frenetic pace that allows little time for much of a personal life outside of work.

Occupational stress is a pervasive problem that has both personal and organizational sources. Workplaces are often structured in ways that breed conflicts and create impediments to fulfilling role demands within available resources. Job overload and tedium exact an emotional toll. Much of the work is now driven by computerized technologies. Computerized workplaces provide continuous tracking of employee performance. Such information can be used to structure work processes, adjust workloads, and manage resources. Computer monitoring can adversely affect the quality of work life, however, when it is used as a coercive means of managerial control. In automated forms of surveillance, computers replace supervisors, creating increased depersonalization of supervisory functions and social isolation from coworkers. Electronic pacing and monitoring systems that enforce heavy workloads with little control over the work process convert workplaces into electronic sweatshops in routinized jobs and fishbowl environments in close scrutiny of higher level ones. Eliminating two of the major stress reducers, perceived control and social support, from the workplace creates a stressful work environment that saps job satisfaction. Heightened international competitiveness in the global market demands shorter developmental cycles for products and further tightening of control over work productivity. Job insecurities arising from corporate reorganizations, retrenchments, takeovers, mergers, and internationalizations present major stressors at all organizational levels.

Within the interactional model, efficacy beliefs affect appraisal and impact of organizational stressors on the physical health and emotional life of employees. Human stress has been viewed mainly in terms of task demands that tax or exceed individuals' perceived capability to manage them. This is, indeed, the most common source of emotional strain. Occupational stress also arises, however, when people find themselves trapped in jobs below their capabilities (Osipow & Davis, 1988) or are plateaued in their careers with little opportunity to make full use of their skills or to enhance them. Under these circumstances, stress is produced by self-devaluation for not making better use of one's talents and by social stigmatization upon being passed over for promotion rather than by the anticipated negative consequences of failure to manage burdensome workloads. What is experienced as an occupational stressor depends partly on level of perceived self-efficacy (Matsui & Onglatco, 1992). Employees who have a low sense of efficacy are stressed by heavy work demands and role responsibilities. Those with a high sense of efficacy are frustrated and stressed by limited opportunities to make full use of their talents. This process operates similarly at the level of collective efficacy. Employees who believe their departments are capable of performing well are more frustrated by organizational constraints and restrictive rules and procedures than are employees who have a low opinion of their departments' collective efficacy (Jex & Gudanowski, 1992).

There is some evidence to suggest that beliefs in individual and collective efficacy may contribute to different forms of occupational stress arising from organizational constraints, role ambiguity, and workloads (Jex & Gudanowski, 1992). A low sense of personal efficacy to fulfill job demands arouses anxiety, whereas a low opinion of the collective efficacy of one's department to do its job well contributes to job dissatisfaction and intention to quit the present job. Organizational constraints affect satisfaction and the intent to quit the firm mainly through their effects on perceived collective efficacy. The preceding studies were concerned solely with the impact on occupational stress of perceived efficacy to exercise control behaviorally. We saw earlier that efficacy beliefs affect stress reactions not only through perceived behavioral control but also through perceived capability to manage perturbing thoughts and affective states. Therefore, a comprehensive test of a self-efficacy theory of stress should include all three facets of controlling efficacy.

People in service occupations have to deal with recurrent human demands and problems day in and day out. It is all too easy to routinize and depersonalize services to the point where people are treated like faceless objects. Boredom and apathy set in when perceived efficacy to render significant benefits declines. The chronic stressors in emotionally taxing occupations can give rise to the syndrome of reactions described as "burnout" (Maslach, 1982). The depersonalization aspect of the syndrome is unique to human services, but the other two aspects — emotional exhaustion and lack of any sense of personal accomplishment — can occur in any occupation where people face an unceasing workload and view what they are doing as neither much valued nor doing much good. For occupations that do not involve provision of human services, the occupational disengagement takes the form of cynicism about one's work rather than depersonalization of clients (Leiter & Schaufeli, 1996). The net effect of this wear-out is decline in performance, low morale, absenteeism, and job turnover (Jackson et al., 1986; Maslach & Jackson, 1982). Moreover, these occupational difficulties tend to carry over into the personal life in substance abuse, health problems, and marital discord.

People resort to behavioral or cognitive efforts to manage or cope with stressors. Coping with aversive organizational demands takes different forms.

Employees can try to restructure their work situations, increase their knowledge and skills, and figure out ways to manage their job demands better. Or they can perform their work perfunctorily and turn inward to lessen their distress. Perceived self-efficacy is one factor that predicts the form the adaptation to emotionally taxing work takes. Chwalisz, Altmaier, and Russell (1992) examined the extent to which teachers' causal attributions for their job stress and their perceived efficacy to manage stressors affected their style of coping and the different types of burnout reactions. Figure 10.3 summarizes the pattern of relationships. Although belief in personal causation is related to perceived efficacy, neither belief about the causes of job stress, their persistence, nor their changeability were related to coping strategies or burnout reactions. Perceived occupational inefficacy, however, is a central mediator of burnout. Those who have a high sense of efficacy resort to problem-solving coping designed to improve their work situation. In contrast, those who believe there is little they can do to change the stressful aspects of their job resort to dysfunctional ways of coping to relieve their stress.

Some strategies for relieving stress rely on cognitive reappraisals of situations to make them less aversive (Lazarus & Folkman, 1984). These include viewing problems as challenges and incentives to improve one's skills, focusing on positive aspects in otherwise negative situations, considering how things could be much worse, placing petty problems in larger perspective, reexamining one's priorities, and seeking solace from others. Other stress-reducing strategies are more escapist, such as use of diversions to put the problems out of mind, resorting to drinking, drug use, or overeating to reduce tension, and withdrawal of involvement in the work life. A low sense of efficacy fosters escapist coping, which is apt to make the work life even worse. This type of coping is associated with high levels of emotional exhaustion and feelings of futility concerning personal accomplishments (Chwalisz et al., 1992; Leiter, 1991). Problem-solving coping helps employees to manage their work environment better and thus prevents the types of adverse effects that have come to be characterized as burnout (Leiter, 1991). The relationship between coping style and burnout is undoubtedly bidirectional. Escapist reactions to chronic job stressors contribute to burnout, and the aversive burnout experiences, in turn, prompt escape reactions. Some people, of course, leave their line of work in search of an occupational pursuit that might bring them some measure of success and satisfaction.

Prevention and reduction of occupational stress requires both personal and organizational correctives. At the personal level, employees need to develop the skills and self-efficacy needed to manage their work life in ways that provide them with a sense

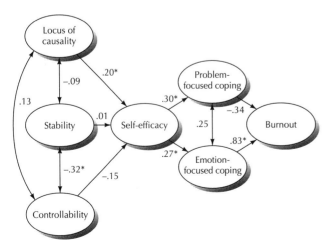

FIGURE 10.3. Analysis of the causal relationships among causal attributions, perceived coping efficacy, and coping strategies with regard to teacher burnout, as measured by physical and emotional exhaustion, depersonalization, and a low sense of personal accomplishment. The path coefficients with asterisks are significant beyond the *p* < .05 level. (Chwalisz et al., 1992)

of accomplishment and pride in their work. The perceived inability to turn off perturbing ruminations about negative work experiences is often more self-debilitating than are workloads themselves. Employees, therefore, need to learn how to achieve recuperative breaks from emotionally taxing work by not bringing work-related problems home either in the form of homework or as ruminative thinking. This is achieved both by development of efficacy to control aversive ruminations about the job during off-hours and by engagement in relaxing and revitalizing activities in everyday life. Such changes are not produced by social prescription alone. Harried individuals usually have a low sense of diversionary efficacy, so they quickly convince themselves that they can neither afford the time nor have the energy at the end of an exhausting day to pursue enjoyable leisure interests (Rosenthal & Rosenthal, 1985). They need a guided mastery program for how to restore enjoyable leisure activities to their lives. They might be apprised of Tsongos' basic maxim that no one on his deathbed has ever expressed regret for not having spent more time in the office.

The organizational sources of burnout involve the nature and structure of the work life and the quality of the social milieu in which the work is carried out (Maslach & Jackson, 1982). Among the organizational factors identified as contributory to burnout are prolonged and intensive contact with people presenting intractable problems, few breaks with nonpersonal work to reduce the emotional strain, unvaried work routines that make insufficient use of one's skills, lack of personal control over the policies and practices of one's work environment, little feedback about how one is doing on the job, and lack of social support from colleagues to ease the burden of some aspects of work life. Exposure to inefficacious and cynical views of colleagues accelerates this process through contagious modeling.

Efforts to reduce vulnerability to occupational stress and burnout at the organizational level must address the various ways in which employees' efficacy is undermined by the institutional practices. Employees need some control over matters that affect their work life and give them a sense of ownership for what they produce. Their work should be evaluated on the basis of what they can control. To have little control over the way in which the work life is structured but to be held accountable for the results is exasperating and stress-provoking. Employees need the benefit of programs for developing and upgrading their skills and helpful feedback systems that enable them to achieve a greater sense of efficacy and success in their work (Leiter, 1992). Restructuring of work into meaningful activities with variety, challenge, and opportunities to exercise initiative counteracts stressful stagnation. And finally, people need to be provided with a system of social support from co-workers along with efficacious leadership that creates a sense of mission and purpose.

Employee absenteeism is a chronic problem incurring costs that run into the billions of dollars annually by disrupting work schedules and lowering productivity. Absenteeism is not simply a matter of job dissatisfaction. Employees disclose a variety of factors that keep them from getting to work. They include family problems, conflicts with supervisors and coworkers, transportation difficulties, job stressors, personal problems with alcohol and drugs, boredom with their jobs, medical appointments and illnesses, and viewing some time off from work as an employee privilege (Latham & Frayne, 1989). Frequent absences from work only exacerbate the difficulties, resulting in escalating organizational sanctions from official warnings to placement on probation to termination.

Frayne and Latham (1987) devised an effective program to reduce absenteeism through development of self-regulatory efficacy. Neither organizational threats and penalties for absenteeism nor positive incentives for job attendance had made much of a dent in the absentee problem. Employees who often missed work were taught in groups how to manage their own motivation and behavior more effectively. They monitored their job attendance. They analyzed the personal and social problems that interfered with them getting to work and were taught strategies for overcoming these obstacles. They set themselves subgoals for increasing their job attendance and rewarded themselves for meeting their goals. To build resiliency, they analyzed the conditions that might produce a reversion to absenteeism and developed coping strategies for dealing with these conditions should they arise. A control group of employees did not receive the program in self-regulation.

Training in self-regulation increased employees' beliefs in their efficacy to overcome the obstacles that led them to miss work, and their sense of self-regulatory efficacy continued to gain strength over time (Fig. 10.4). They not only improved their job attendance but maintained these changes as assessed over a nine-month period (Latham & Frayne, 1989). The more the program raised employees' beliefs in their self-regulatory efficacy, the better their job attendance. Perceived self-regulatory efficacy at the end of training predicted job attendance nine months later. In confidential self-reports, employees acknowledged that before the training in self-management, they often used sickness as the reason for absences from work due to personal and social problems. After they gained efficacy to manage their life problems, they took leave from work almost solely because of illness or for medical appointments, and sick leave absenteeism declined over the follow-up period. The employees expressed a strongly positive attitude toward the training program. By increasing their job

attendance, they were spared aversive organizational sanctions and gained personal and occupational benefits for themselves.

COLLECTIVE ORGANIZATIONAL EFFICACY

Most occupational activities are directed at group goals achieved in organizational structures through collective effort. The effective exercise of collective action involves more complex, socially mediated paths of influence than does individual self-direction. People have to depend upon one another in performing tasks and in carrying out their complementary roles. Group success requires effective interdependent linkage of tasks, skills, and roles. Group members not only have to coordinate what they are doing individually with the work of others, but they are affected by the beliefs, motivation, and quality of performance of their coworkers. These interactive effects make collective efficacy an emergent group attribute. Although perceived collective efficacy is widely recognized to be highly important to a full understanding of organizational functioning, it has been the subject of little research. Perceived collective efficacy is concerned with the

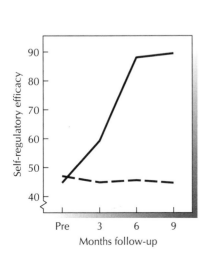
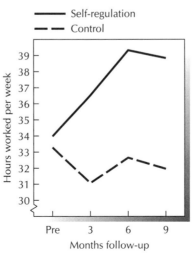

FIGURE 10.4. Reduction in absenteeism of employees who had the benefit of the self-regulatory program and those who did not. (After Frayne & Latham, 1987).

performance capability of a social system as a whole. Belief of collective efficacy affects the sense of mission and purpose of a system, the strength of common commitment to what it seeks to achieve, how well its members work together to produce results, and the group's resiliency in the face of difficulties.

In some organizations, the subsystems and activities must be tightly integrated, whereas in others they are only loosely coupled. In activities requiring low system interdependence, members of the group need to coordinate their efforts and support one another, but the group's level of attainment is the sum total of the outcomes produced independently. In endeavors requiring high system interdependence, members must work in concert to achieve group outcomes. Aggregating members' beliefs in their own efficacy is most relevant when the group outcome largely represents the summed contributions of members working independently within an organized structure. Aggregating members' beliefs in their group's efficacy is the more relevant measure when the group outcome is produced through highly interdependent effort.

Although perceived personal and group efficacy are clearly separable conceptually, in reality they usually go together because people have to rely, at least to some extent, on others in accomplishing their tasks. People working independently within a group structure do not function as social isolates totally immune to the influence of those around them. Their sense of efficacy is likely to be lower amidst a group of chronic losers than amidst habitual winners. Moreover, the resources, impediments, and opportunities provided by a given system partly determine how efficacious individuals can be, even though their work may be only loosely coupled. Conversely, when people work interdependently, their sense of group efficacy rests heavily on the personal efficacies of its members. Consequently, perceived personal and group efficacy are likely to be related to some extent across varied levels of organizational interdependence.

The determinants and mechanisms of organizational performance must be evaluated, for the most part, as they operate in the real world rather than through systematic variation of influential factors. Analysis of collective efficacy must distinguish between dynamic and stable phases of social system functioning. The impact of perceived collective efficacy on group performance is easiest to verify when the attainments of social systems are analyzed at the point at which they are undergoing major changes. It takes time for increases in a group's sense of collective efficacy to get fully translated into notable organizational accomplishments. When systems are in a dynamic phase of change, time-lagged effects remove some of the ambiguity about the source and direction of causation. Assessment of causal contribution is more complicated when organizations are in a relatively stable state. Consider, for example, a vitalizing coach who builds former losers into perennial winners and a demoralizing coach who manages to convert former winners into perennial losers. The teams now perform regularly at markedly different levels. If differences in the teams' performance attainments are removed statistically, quality of coaching will emerge as contributing little to the differential success of the teams when, in fact, those team performances are largely the products of the collective beliefs instilled in the players by the coaches when the teams were in flux. The problem of overcorrection is reduced if the contribution of perceived efficacy is removed from the index of prior performance.

The analysis of perceived collective efficacy is limited here because it receives detailed treatment in the next chapter. The research cited earlier on the productivity of schools as social systems provides one example of the contribution of perceived collective efficacy to organizational performance (Bandura, 1993). Teachers' beliefs in their collective efficacy contribute significantly to how well their schools perform academically after controlling for the socioeconomic and racial composition of the student bodies, teachers' experience level, and prior school-level achievement. Schools in which the staff members have a strong sense of collective efficacy flourish academically. Schools in which the staff members have serious doubts about their collective efficacy achieve little progress or decline academically.

Most organizational activities require a high degree of coordination to produce good results. This is especially so for self-managing teams whose success depends heavily on adept teamwork. Team members not only must perform their tasks interdependently but also must manage the instructional, motivational, interpersonal, and operational aspects of their work. Work teams vary in how effectively they manage these multiple functions. Little and Madigan (1994) provide some evidence that perceived collective efficacy operates as a group-level influence on how well self-managing teams perform their work. There are differences between work teams but consensus within teams about their perceived capabilities to perform their production activities well. The higher the sense of collective efficacy, the better the team performance. As is true at the individual level, perceived team efficacy is not a static group attribute. It rises and falls with fluctuations in the interlinking relationships among the members and changing external realities and pressures.

Individualistic versus Collectivistic Efficacy

Societies differ in the extent to which their social practices are rooted in individualism or in collectivism. Individualistic systems provide extensive opportunities for personal development, encourage self-initiative, and generously reward pursuit of personal success. In contrast, societies favoring a collectivistic ethic subordinate self-interest to group welfare and promote a strong sense of shared responsibility. Individual benefits and satisfactions are tied to group accomplishments. These different socialization experiences would tend to foster high perceived efficacy in individualists working independently and in collectivists working as a group. Studies of managerial performance suggest that this is the case. The effects of a collectivistic orientation on efficacy beliefs and productivity, however, are more complex than the unqualified view that collectivists routinely work better in groups than independently.

Earley (1993) compared the perceived efficacy and productivity of individualist and collectivist managers when they worked independently or as part of a group. The in-basket simulation tasks they performed included such activities as writing memos, completing requisition forms, rating job applicants, and evaluating product plans. American managers represented an individualistic culture, Israeli and Chinese managers collectivistic cultures. To evaluate the contribution of a collective orientation per se, the members of the groups were either ethnically homogeneous or ethnically diverse.

American managers expressed their highest level of perceived efficacy and performed best under an individual managerial system, whereas they perceived themselves as least efficacious and were least productive under a group management system. Managers from the collectivistic cultures exhibited the opposite pattern of functioning. They judged themselves most efficacious and worked most productively as members of an ethnically homogeneous managerial team and were least self-efficacious and productive as independent managers or in a managerial team with members from other cultural backgrounds. Interestingly, collectivists do not view themselves as uniformly efficacious in all group systems, but only with members from similar cultural backgrounds. Collectivists display a lowered sense of personal and group efficacy and diminished productivity in a group of culturally dissimilar members.

Individualists expected better self-evaluative and other outcomes for performing well independently than for performing well in a group; collectivists expected better outcomes for contributing to accomplishments of an in-group team than for performing well on their own or in a team of out-group members. The variation in productivity under individual and group managerial systems mainly reflects the different patterns of perceived efficacy cultivated by the different cultural practices. Personal and group efficacy beliefs account for most of the variation in managerial performance. When the effects of efficacy beliefs and anticipated outcomes are controlled, national origin explains only about 5 percent of the variation in performance.

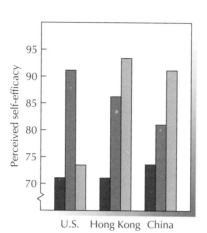
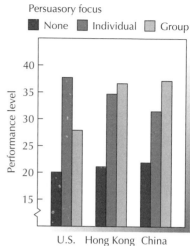

FIGURE 10.5. The differential effect of efficacy-boosting influences on the perceived efficacy and productivity of managers in individualistic and collectivistic cultures depending on whether the social influence was individually oriented or group oriented. (After Earley, 1994).

Experimental analyses further advance understanding of how efficacy beliefs are altered and function in divergent cultures. Earley (1994) examined the way in which persuasory efficacy influences that are individually or group oriented affect the efficacy beliefs, motivation, and productivity of managers in individualistic and collectivistic cultures. The managers were given preset diagnostic information that either they personally or their group possessed the attributes needed to perform a given managerial activity well. Figure 10.5 shows that managers from an individualistic culture exhibited higher efficacy beliefs and productivity gains when the efficacy-boosting influence was individually oriented, whereas those from collectivistic cultures achieved higher gains in perceived efficacy and productivity when the same efficacy-boosting influence was group oriented. Cultural context similarly moderates the impact of training on the perceived efficacy and performance of service representatives instructed either individually or collectively as a work unit in telecommunication companies in China and the United States.

Because there is variability within cultures, understanding how cultural background affects efficacy beliefs and functioning requires analysis of individual orientations as well as the prevailing cultural orientation. Regardless of cultural background, employees achieve the greatest sense of personal efficacy and productivity gains when training is congruent with their personal orientations than when it is discordant. Both at the cultural and individual levels of analysis, a strong sense of efficacy fosters high effort and productivity. The effects of individualistic or collectivistic orientation and of training focus on performance attainments are heavily mediated through efficacy beliefs and their motivational effects. These findings underscore the general principle that efforts to improve human well-being and accomplishments must be tailored to the values and attributes of individuals, whether shaped by the prevailing cultural influences or by divergent influences within a given culture.

In occupational roles that do not involve high interdependence in the execution of the work, interest centers more on individual than on group performance. Sales work requires a good deal of effort, resourcefulness, and perseverance. Barling and Beattie (1983) examined, among other factors, the relative contribution of efficacy beliefs and outcome expectations to insurance sales. Interpersonal and communication skills conducive to successful performance constituted the perceived self-efficacy. Outcome expectations were assessed in terms of a wide range of possible social, monetary, and career advancement benefits that good performance would produce. Sales personnel with a high sense of efficacy made more sales contacts and sold more policies and for a higher total value over a one-year period than did those of low perceived efficacy. Neither outcome expectations nor sales experience influenced any of these aspects of sales performance.

Organizational Learning

Under conditions of low interdependence, organizations serve mainly as contextual influences on individual performances. The relationship between individual and organizational effectiveness assumes special significance when individuals have to work interdependently to produce results. The issues of theoretical interest are how organizations learn and change and the relationship between individual and organizational learning. Organizations are changed by the behavior of individuals. Hence, the impact of sociostructural factors on organizational performance is mediated through motivational and learning mechanisms operating at the individual level. Learning occurs through several interrelated subfunctions. The first phase in the process requires monitoring and interpreting the environmental opportunities, constraints, preferences, and demands. Developing a conception of the relevant environment suggests the courses of action that may be needed to adapt to it or change it. The next phase involves strategic selection or construction of alternative solutions. In the third phase, the alternatives that look promising are tested and revised. The alternatives are initially tested by symbolic exploration of the capabilities required to produce them and the outcomes they are likely to yield. The solution emerging as the best from this cognitive simulation, considering perceived efficacy, outcome expectations, and reality constraints, is then implemented. The chosen course of action is adopted, modified, or discarded depending on the results it produces. Careful deliberation, of course, does not always precede action, nor is deliberation always optimal. But people are more successful in achieving their goals if they think before they leap into uncertain situations.

Although the generic process of learning is the same, there are fundamental differences between individual and organizational learning arising from differences in the locus of the subfunctions and the interplay between them. At the individual level, the same person performs each of the key subfunctions. At the organizational level, these different subfunctions have to be separated to a large extent and assigned to different subgroups to perform because of the magnitude and complexities of organizational activities. This is not to say that the subfunctions of organizational learning and innovation are rigidly departmentalized. Rather, each subfunction requires a great deal of specialized knowledge and no subset of individuals has the time and expertise to do everything well. Although there is, by necessity, some specialization of function, learning is an organization-wide activity to which any member can contribute creative ideas. The interrelatedness of the subfunctions requires exchange of ideas among the various constituencies. To complicate matters further, the segmentation of subfunctions activates social dynamics that can facilitate, retard, or block organizational learning and change. Viewed from the perspective of social cognitive theory, organizational learning occurs through interactive psychosocial processes rather than through reified organizational attributes operating independently of the behavior of individuals. Hidden agendas, biases, and inadequate understanding detract from the rationality of organizational efforts at innovative renewal (Shoemaker & Marias, in press).

Consider how the basic subfunctions are performed organizationally. With regard to the environmental monitoring or diagnostic function, a subsystem of an organization is assigned major responsibility for assessing the preferences, needs, and trends in the marketplace. Those who specialize in environmental monitoring conduct surveys, scan periodicals and electronic networks for information about emerging technologies, attend industry trade shows and meetings of professional societies to keep abreast of innovations, and analyze market trends and new product opportunities (Daft & Huber, 1987). In addition, monitors examine closely what successful competitors are doing and seek the views of knowledgeable advisors outside the organization The monitoring subfunction requires development of systems for gathering information, interpreting it, and disseminating it to promote shared understanding of the consumer environment. The broader social, political, and economic context within which organizations operate must also be closely monitored because the values and regulatory structures of the broader society play an influential role in shaping organizational life (Powell, 1990). With rapid changes in products and global markets, the environment has become more complex, less stable, and less predictable. Information seekers who doubt their ability to diagnose and predict the market environment reduce their monitoring efforts (Boyd & Fulk, 1996). The successful ones are not dissuaded by complexity. High-performing firms have better monitoring practices for charting their course than their low-performing counterparts. Judgment of the organization's capability to achieve success with envisaged options is an influential factor in the simulations that guide the decision making. The psychological mechanisms governing the selection and cognitive processing of environmental information are similar regardless of whether people are doing it individually or organizationally, but the segmentation of this subfunction with multiple players introduces social aspects that partly determine how well this activity is performed. Moreover, learning at the organizational level is a collaborative endeavor in which members generate new ideas by sharing their knowledge and interacting with each other. This adds another social process to collective learning. Computer technology using groupware enables individuals to work collaboratively on problems through on-line discussion freed from constraints of time and place (Wang, 1996).

After diagnosing the situation and deciding suitable directions for change, the aim must be translated into organizational activities designed to realize it. Radical innovations encounter more problems in product development and therefore require greater organizational support than do incremental improvements in existing products or processes. Organizations must continue to innovate

to survive and prosper. The innovating subfunction of developing new products or services is delegated to another subsystem. Missteps are part and parcel of experimentation with new ideas. Therefore, learning from failure is a critical part of organizational learning that requires allowance in creative work life (Frese & van Dyck, in press; Sitken, 1992). The customary incentives create a tension between sticking with what works now and developing what might work better in the future. Sufficing success can be an impediment to creating even better solutions. Innovating organizations set up special operating structures and incentive systems that are highly conducive to generating new ideas and translating them into promising innovations (Galbraith, 1982). Such arrangements not only promote innovativeness but shield innovators from the usual organizational resistance to ideas that do not fit the existing mold. Innovations can be created through three major processes. Some innovations are the products of exploratory experimentation. The prolific inventor, Thomas Edison, probably holds a record for discovery through dogged experimentation. For example, he tested 1600 different filaments before finding one that was suitable for light bulbs and then continued to search for the best filament by testing more than 6000 novel materials.

Few innovations are entirely new. The second type of creativity largely involves synthesizing existing knowledge into new ways of thinking and doing things. Many innovations, in fact, are achieved through modeling. Organizations engage in a great deal of selective modeling of competitors' successful practices and products. Modeling is more than simply a process of copying one another, however. Rather, useful elements are selected from various sources and synthesized into new versions (Bandura, 1986a). Modeling by breaking down a competitor's product and improving upon it is a widespread organizational practice that goes under the euphemism of "reverse engineering" (Eells & Nehemkis, 1984). Bolton (1993) builds a strong case that selective modeling is a competitive necessity because of the high discovery costs and the technical and market uncertainties associated with entirely new products. Organizations do not have the time and money to keep reinventing the core characteristics of good products, services, and systems.

The third process of creativity is serendipity. It gives birth, from time to time, to innovations (Austin, 1978). In the pithy words of Kettering, "Keep on going and the chances are that you will stumble on something." New products and sometimes even major industries spring from happenstance. For example, the Kellogg brothers managed a health sanitarium designed to rid the body of what they saw to be the evils of meat and liquor (Sinclair, 1981). One day, while boiling wheat dough to prepare a nutriment that might add some needed variety to the sanitarium menu, they were called away. Upon their return hours later, they decided to run the dough through steel rollers anyway. Much to their surprise, they got flakes for their patrons, rather than the sheets of wheat biscuits they set out to make. The fortuitous delay gave birth to the breakfast cereal industry. Fortuitous happenings similarly play an important role in many scientific discoveries. Alexander Fleming, the Nobel laureate, discovered the bactericidal effect of penicillin because his tardiness in discarding old culture dishes gave the penicillin mold sufficient time to develop. Organizational creativity is the product of these three modes of innovation.

The final subfunction that is critical to organizational learning involves test marketing the products that are produced and devising strategies for their distribution and promotion. Feedback from consumer markets provides guidance for further product development. If organizations lose touch with consumer markets, they are headed for serious trouble. It requires efficacious management to coordinate the expertise of the different subfunctions.

Organizational learning not only divides the subfunctions across subsystems but also activates influential group processes that operate as impeders or facilitators of organizational learning and change. The social drama of organizational functioning facilitates organizational learning and performance if members make good use of their complementary knowledge and expertise but hinders it if they view proposed changes as threatening their

vested interests and act in oppositional ways that undermine organizational efforts at change. Deficiencies or breakdowns in any of the major subfunctions of learning or in their social coordination will impair an organization's capability to innovate and to capitalize on emerging market opportunities. The basic subfunctions of organizational learning may be orchestrated differently in different settings, but they are essential for success regardless of whether organizations operate with a centralized hierarchical structure or a decentralized participatory one.

Assessment of perceived efficacy for organizational learning should measure members' beliefs about how well their organizational subsystems can perform their various functions and how well they can work together. The efficacy subfunctions include organizational capabilities to discern market opportunities and future trends, generate innovative ideas, translate them into superior products or services, and devise effective strategies for national or global marketing. Managers serve a vital coordinative function. We have already seen the influential role played by managers' beliefs in their decision-making efficacy in the quality of organizational functioning. In addition to measuring perceived subsystem and coordinative efficacy, the participants' beliefs in their organization's efficacy for innovation as a whole and for achieving different levels of financial gain should be assessed.

Organizational Culture

Perceived collective efficacy is also relevant to issues of organizational culture. This line of inquiry is concerned with the shared values and belief systems in an organization that shape its formal and informal practices (Martin, 1992; Schein, 1985). Organizational values are reflected in the rituals, norms, and priorities of an organization; the styles of behavior it rewards and penalizes; and the types of attitudes and behaviors that are modeled. Organizational cultures perpetuate themselves not only by their socialization practices but also through selective recruitment of people who readily fit into the prevailing system. The notion of an organization-wide culture is intuitively appealing but fraught with difficulties. To begin with, it is not clear exactly what an organizational culture is. A vaguely defined phenomenon embracing many different things is not easy to specify. To complicate matters further, organizations do not have a unitary character. They may espouse a uniform set of values and perspective but in practice be ruled by subcultures, each with its own view about how things should be done (Martin & Siehl, 1983). The various factions within an organization, whether complementary or partially conflicting, have their own social ties, normative standards, identities, and statuses (Young, 1989). The particular pattern of affinities, however, can shift depending on the issues of concern. Periodic changes in leadership create conflicts between members allied to the old and new organizational practices. A lack of explicit theories on how different aspects of a culture affect organizational functioning and a dearth of methods for measuring group cultures further retard research in this field. The difficulties in characterizing the current culture of an organization are amplified in efforts to reconstruct its history. There is a lot of invention in such retrospections.

Much of the evidence offered in support of organizational cultures is in the form of anecdotal reports about financially successful companies. More systematic empirical efforts to link organizational culture to financial performance have been ambiguous and inconsistent in their findings (Siehl & Martin, 1990). Many of the proponents of organizational culture dismiss quantitative methodologies. They question the appropriateness of standardized measures of core factors on which organizations can be compared and prefer phenomenological analyses of the social climates unique to given organizations. This argument is not without its problems. Successful organizations must have some features in common that can be measured reliably. If the factors that make organizations successful are peculiar to each organization, research on the cultures of successful organizations would have little generalizable value. Why waste time studying successes, other than for aesthetic reasons, if there

is nothing generalizable about them? Qualitative methods that rely on interviews and on-site observations provide essential insights for inductive theorizing and for constructing measures for analytic empirical studies. They yield quantitative data for sets of factors that characterize the cultures of organizations. Without quantitative assessment, it is difficult to evaluate the relative contribution of different factors and their interaction to organizational success.

In the study of workplace cultures, some postmodernists carry to a nihilistic extreme the view that there is no accurate representation of events but just differing points of view. Certainly no representations of the external world are entirely independent of interpretation, but neither are interpretations completely independent of the actual state of affairs in the external world. Life is full of reality checks that, in consequential matters, can bear down unmercifully on foolish actions spawned by faulty judgment. To cite a simple example, leaping off heights based on an erroneous interpretation of gravitational reality will promptly land one in a hospital intensive care unit. Existing social contingencies between actions and outcomes can similarly be quite unforgiving if misread. Some interpretations of reality have greater explanatory, predictive, and operative power than do others. To the radical postmodernist, however, no one version of reality is better than another. This type of argument has a self-negating quality because it renders the proponent's own view just another idiosyncratic version without any particular truth value. The radical brand of postmodernism begets ensnarlment in the egocentric predicament. Indeed, it is amusing to see radical postmodernists arguing authoritatively for the correctness of their view that there is no single correct view!

The linkage of organizational factors to effectiveness is not simply a matter of epistemological taste. Improvement and survival of organizations under the stiff competition in the global marketplace can be well served by knowledge of what makes organizations successful and adaptable to rapidly changing demands of the marketplace. After all, a major purpose for studying organizations is to gain knowledge that can inform beneficial organizational practices rather than just to tell engaging stories with egocentric analyses of the storytellers. Progress in understanding organizational functioning is better achieved by treating functionalist and phenomenological perspectives as complementary rather than as rival approaches (Denison & Mishra, 1995). The vagueness of the term *culture*, however, can retard quantitative analyses of organizational functioning. Efforts to verify the structures and processes conducive to successful organizational performance get diverted into disputes about whether a particular constellation of core factors selected for study really represents the culture. Progress in understanding organizational life may benefit from reframing the issue, not in amorphous cultural terms but in sociostructural terms that provide more fruitful directions for research.

Resistance to a functionalist perspective is often cloaked in critiques of the scope and adequacy of outcome measures. The choice of outcomes is more a value issue than an epistemological one, however. The outcomes of organizational practices can be measured in financial, humanistic, ecological, and social terms. Reliance on financial performance to the neglect of other aspects of work life, such as employees' morale, well-being, and turnover, provides a narrow view of organizational functioning. Moreover, the general public holds corporations to a broader social obligation than only serving shareholders' interests. Clearly, the measure of organizational success should be broadened. But financial performance must remain an important criterion. After all, if a firm cannot make a profit, it is soon put out of business. And finally, verification of theoretical propositions about organizational values and practices requires longitudinal evidence that culture affects subsequent organizational performance rather than simply cross-sectional evidence that culture and organizational performance are related when measured at the same time.

Organizational practices obviously affect the quality of work life and level of organizational performance. Advances in this field require specification of the multiple facets of organizational practices and the mechanisms through which they create organizational outcomes. Analysis of the culture of organizations should be concerned not only with traditions of how things are done but also with shared beliefs about the organization's capabilities to innovate and perform productively. Because of their diverse impact, an organization's beliefs about its efficacy to produce results is undoubtedly an important feature of its operative culture. Beliefs of organizational efficacy are created and transmitted through a variety of means. These include social modeling, incentive systems, personnel selection practices, staff development activities, the way in which jobs are structured, and relative success in the marketplace. Analyses of the determinants of perceived organizational efficacy can make a valuable contribution to the understanding of organizational performance.

11

Collective Efficacy

THE ANALYSES IN THE EARLIER chapters have focused mainly on the exercise of perceived personal efficacy in individual pursuits. But people do not live in social isolation, nor can they exercise control over major aspects of their lives entirely on their own. Many of the challenges of life center on common problems that require people to work together with a collective voice to change their lives for the better. The strength of families, communities, organizations, social institutions, and even nations lies partly in people's sense of collective efficacy that they can solve the problems they face and improve their lives through unified effort. To further their common interests, their actions have to be taken through groups and organizations. Increasingly, people's lives are being shaped by powerful influences operating outside their traditional institutions and across lines of nation states. Widespread technological changes and globalization of economic forces are creating transnational interdependencies that place an increasing premium on the exercise of collective agency to retain some measure of personal control over one's life course.

There is much talk of "empowerment" as the vehicle for bettering personal lives. This is a badly misused construct that has become heavily infused with promotional hype, naive grandiosity, and virtually every brand of political rhetoric. "Empowerment" is not something bestowed through edict. It is gained through development of personal efficacy that enables people to take advantage of opportunities and to remove environmental constraints guarded by those whose interests are served by them. Those who exercise authority and control do not go around voluntarily granting to others power over resources and entitlements in acts of beneficence. A share of benefits and control must be negotiated through concerted effort and, oftentimes, through prolonged struggle. Sociocognitive theory approaches the enhancement of human agency, whether in individual or collective form, in terms of enablement. Equipping people with a firm belief that they can produce valued effects by their collective action and providing them with the means to do so are the key ingredients in an enablement process.

Perceived collective efficacy is defined as *a group's shared belief in its conjoint capabilities to organize and execute the courses of action required to produce given levels of attainments*. The collective belief centers on the group's operative capabilities. Group functioning is the product of the interactive and coordinative dynamics of its members. Interactive dynamics create an emergent property that is more than the sum of the individual attributes. A host of factors contribute to the interactive effects. Some of these factors are the mix of knowledge and competencies in the group, how the group is structured and its activities coordinated, how well it is led, the strategies it adopts, and whether members interact with one another in mutually facilitory or undermining ways. The same participants can achieve different results depending on how well their particular skills and efforts are coordinated and guided. A group's capability to perform as a whole can vary widely under different blends of interactive dynamics. Therefore, perceived collective efficacy is an emergent group-level attribute rather than simply the sum of the members' perceived personal efficacies.

Perceived personal and collective efficacy differ in the unit of agency, but in both forms efficacy beliefs have similar sources, serve similar functions, and operate through similar processes. Although members behave collectively, their actions are regulated by the psychosocial processes analyzed in some detail in Chapter 10. Thus, people's beliefs in their collective efficacy influence the type of future they seek to achieve, how they manage their resources, the plans and strategies they construct, how much effort they put into their group endeavor, their staying power when collective efforts fail to produce quick results or encounter forcible opposition, and their vulnerability to discouragement. These processes, which shared efficacy beliefs activate, affect how well group members work together and how much they accomplish collectively. This chapter examines the role of shared beliefs of efficacy in different pursuits and sizes of collectivity.

GAUGING COLLECTIVE EFFICACY

Advancement of knowledge about the determinants, mechanisms, and outcomes of collective efficacy calls for a broad and comprehensive research effort. Progress in this field of study requires the development of suitable tools for measuring groups' shared beliefs of efficacy to achieve varying levels of results. Lack of sound measures places a methodological damper on research. The greatest progress can be made in explaining the development, decline, and restoration of collective efficacy, and how it affects group functioning, if multifaceted measures of perceived collective efficacy are tied to valid indices of group performance.

One can distinguish between two approaches to the measurement and evaluation of perceived collective efficacy in group functioning. The first involves aggregating members' appraisals of their personal capabilities for the particular functions they perform in the group. The second involves aggregating members' appraisals of their group's capability as a whole. The latter holistic judgment encompasses the coordinative and interactive influences operating within the group. Although these two indices of perceived collective efficacy differ in the relative weight given to individual factors and social interactive factors, they are not as distinct as they might appear at first sight. Beliefs of personal efficacy are not detached from the larger social system in which members function. In appraising their personal efficacies, individuals inevitably consider group processes that enhance or hinder their efforts. For example, in judging personal efficacy, a football quarterback obviously considers the quality of his offensive line, the fleetness of his running backs, the adroitness of his receivers, and how well they all work together. Conversely, in judging the efficacy of the team as a whole, members certainly consider how well key teammates can execute their roles. They would judge their team's efficacy quite differently depending on whether their star quarterback or an inexperienced understudy is at the helm. Thus, when participants are judging perceived efficacy in a group endeavor, they are not plumbing an abstract group mind in which the members are detached from one another. For the reasons given, linking efficacy assessed at the individual level to performance at the group level does not necessarily represent a cross-level relation. An assessment focus at the individual level is steeped in processes operating within the group. Nor does a focus at the group level remove all thought about the individuals who contribute to the collective effort. Not surprisingly, the two indices of collective efficacy are at least moderately correlated.

The interdependence of judgments of personal and group efficacy create analytic challenges for verifying emergent properties. It is commonly assumed that an emergent property is operative if groups continue to differ after controlling statistically for individual differences within the groups. The emergent attribute arising from the social dynamics of the group is presumably responsible for the group effects. Conversely, if differences between groups disappear when controlling for variations in individual characteristics within groups, then the individuals added together, rather than some unique or emergent characteristics of the groups, account for the group effects. The analytic logic is fine, but the findings of such statistical analyses can be misleading. As just explained, judgments of personal efficacy are heavily infused with the unique dynamics of the group. Therefore, individual-level controls can inadvertently remove most of the emergent social properties.

One could also measure perceived collective efficacy by having group members make the judgment together. This approach has serious limitations, however. Group members are rarely of one mind in their appraisals. A group belief, therefore, is best characterized by a representative value for the beliefs of its members and the degree of variability or consensus around that central belief. Forming a consensual judgment of a group's efficacy by group discussion is subject to the vagaries of social persuasion and pressures for conformity. A few influential individuals, especially the ones with more prestige or those in positions of authority, can sway the group to a judgment that does not accurately represent the views of many of its members. A single judgment forged by group discussion masks the variability in members' beliefs about their group's' capabilities. A forced consensus, therefore, can be highly misleading. Moreover, assessment of collective efficacy by group deliberation can raise or lower the very belief being measured, depending on the direction the discussion

takes to achieve the consensual judgment. If the reactive effects are short-lived, as is likely, this method may yield a nonrepresentative index of a group's sense of its efficacy. Where people vary in their responsiveness to conformity pressures, as they do cross-culturally (Bond & Smith, 1996), a deliberative method of assessment can introduce serious confoundments in comparative studies of collective efficacy. Even if a group judgment provided a sound index of collective efficacy, this assessment procedure would be unmanageable with large groups.

Commonality of efficacy belief does not mean that every member is of exactly the same view on every aspect of group functioning. In any mix of individuals — who inevitably differ in competencies, interests, roles, and statuses — complete uniformity would be rare. Indeed, group life is rarely tranquil. There are contentions from time to time across interdependent subunits, within subunits, and between hierarchical levels of group structure. Some of the clashes are dysfunctional. These tend to capture the major share of attention in analyses of group functioning. But other disagreements serve a useful purpose in setting challenging group goals, devising appropriate strategies to realize them, and building the social consensus to sustain the level of effort needed to succeed.

Perceived collective efficacy is not a monolithic group attribute. Within a school system, for example, teachers at different grade levels face different challenges that vary in amenability to personal control. Students' academic problems are more easily surmountable in the early grades than in later grades, where many may come with glaring academic deficiencies and a sense of futility, if not antagonism, toward academic activities. Hence, individuals occupying different positions or serving different functions within the same social system may differ somewhat in how they view their group's collective efficacy (Bandura, 1993). To complicate matters further, the level of collective efficacy for any given group may vary across different domains of activities. Although unanimity of efficacy belief within a group is rare, the differences in efficacy beliefs between groups should be greater than the variation within groups. Where individuals differ as widely in efficacy beliefs within groups as between groups, there is no distinguishable shared efficacy attribute for the group as a whole. Note that the major criterion of a shared belief is agreement within groups rather than differences across groups. For example, the members of various groups may have an equally high consensual belief in their groups' efficacy. Lack of differences across groups does not mean that the groups have no shared belief. They do, but it happens to be equally high.

The relative predictiveness of indices of perceived collective efficacy based on aggregated individual and holistic belief will depend, in large part, on the degree of interdependent effort required to produce group results. In activities involving low system interdependence, members of the group do not have to rely on one another to perform their job, even though they have shared goals and provide mutual social support. The group's level of attainment is the sum of the outcomes produced individually. Under low interdependence, an aggregate of individual efficacies would have predictive value. In endeavors involving high system interdependence, members must work well together to achieve group results. Such endeavors require close coordination of roles and strategies, effective communication, cooperative goals, and mutual adjustments to one another's performances (Saavedra, Earley, & Van Dyne, 1993). An aggregate of holistic judgments of the group's efficacy would have the better predictive value for group performances achieved through interdependent action. Variation in level of group interdependence is well illustrated in athletic teams. The accomplishment of a gymnastics team is the sum of the outcomes achieved independently by each gymnast. In contrast, the accomplishment of a soccer or football team is the product of players working closely together. They have to rely on one another for effective performance. Any breakdown in a subsystem can have disastrous effects on group performance. Gibson (1995) provides some evidence about the predictive benefits of congruence between type of collective efficacy belief and level of system interdependence. Perceived holistic efficacy is a better predictor of

group performance in activities requiring members to coordinate their efforts to do well than in activities that can be done well without members having to rely much on one another.

Collective efficacy is, of course, rooted in self-efficacy. A collection of inveterate self-doubters is not easily forged into a collectively efficacious force. Moreover, as previously noted, judgment of personal efficacy in a group context is not detached from coordinative and interactive group processes that affect the individual member's operative capabilities. There are certain conditions, however, under which aggregated personal and holistic judgments of collective efficacy are likely to diverge. A weak link in an activity that has to be performed interdependently can spell group failure even though the remaining members are highly efficacious. Similarly, a collection of supremely efficacious individuals may perform poorly as a unit if they do not work well together. In both of these instances, the aggregate of personal efficacies would overpredict the level of group performance. When a key function for group success is performed by a highly efficacious individual, members will have a higher opinion of their group's capability than of their own individual capabilities. A phenomenal soccer goalie who elevates an otherwise mediocre team's competitive capability is a good case in point. Where success rests heavily on the shoulders of a few extraordinarily efficacious members in crucial positions, aggregated personal efficacies would underpredict group attainments.

Studies of perceived collective efficacy demonstrate that it exists as a group attribute. Moreover, beliefs of collective efficacy predict level of group performance (Bandura, 1993; Hodges & Carron, 1992; Little & Madigan, 1995). The stronger the beliefs people hold about their collective capabilities, the more they achieve. This is true regardless of whether the group's sense of efficacy develops naturally or is created experimentally. The contribution of perceived collective efficacy to group performance is replicated across diverse social systems, including schools, organizations, and athletic teams.

The academic domain is especially well suited for studying the impact of perceived collective efficacy on organizational accomplishments: Each educational district includes multiple schools administered centrally, they pursue the same mission, and their productivity is assessed with standardized instruments regularly at the same time. In addition, school systems provide uniform measures of a variety of characteristics of the staff members and student bodies for evaluating the relative contribution of such factors to school-level performance. In a project analyzing perceived collective efficacy, a total of 79 elementary schools within the same large school district were studied using the school as the unit of analysis (Bandura, 1993).

The findings of this research shed light on a long-standing debate over the magnitude of school effects. Some researchers have argued that variations in socioeconomic status and racial composition of schools' student bodies account for the major share of differences among schools in achievement and that the characteristics of the school systems themselves have a relatively small effect. Figure 11.1 shows that although student body characteristics have some direct effect on school achievement, they influence school achievement largely by altering the staff members' beliefs about their collective efficacy to motivate and educate their students. The stronger the staff members' shared beliefs in their instructional efficacy, the

better their schools performed academically. When variations in staff members' beliefs in their collective efficacy are controlled, the relationship between students' characteristics and school attainment is considerably reduced. School systems involve an intermediate level of interdependence in that group attainments are the product of staff members' working both independently and collectively. The totality of teachers' beliefs in their own efficacy is just as predictive of school performance as the totality of teachers' beliefs in their schools' efficacy as a whole.

Prussia and Kinicki (1996) provide further support for the extension of social cognitive theory to the collective level. They examined experimentally how perceived collective efficacy operates in concert with other sociocognitive determinants — namely, group goals and affective evaluative reactions — in determining group effectiveness. Eighty-one groups engaged in brainstorming activities to generate feasible solutions for different types of problems. They received videotaped instruction in brainstorming strategies either in a lecture format or by observing a group modeling the same strategies behaviorally and cognitively. The groups received accurate feedback about their performance attainments but prearranged comparative

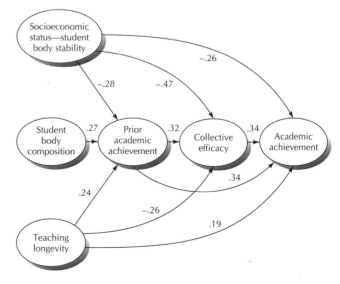

FIGURE 11.1. Path analysis showing the mediational role of perceived collective efficacy on school staff in the causal structure of school-level achievement in reading and mathematics. The sociodemographic characteristics of the student body and the staff's experiential level and perceived collective efficacy were measured at the beginning of the academic year. Prior academic achievement was the school-level achievement at the end of the prior year, and the predicted school-level academic achievement was assessed at the end of the succeeding year. (Bandura, 1993).

feedback leading them to believe that their group performed either above or below the normative productivity standard. The sociocognitive factors were then measured and related to the groups' subsequent success in adopting the strategic processes and generating novel solutions. Figure 11.2 presents the pattern of influences.

The impact of performance feedback on group performance operated entirely through its effects on affective reactions and perceived collective efficacy. Dissatisfaction with substandard performance combined with a strong sense of collective efficacy spurred group productivity. Perceived collective efficacy also completely mediated the effects of feedback on the goals the groups set for themselves and partially mediated the benefits of instructive modeling on group effectiveness. Modeling enhanced group effectiveness both directly and by raising members' beliefs in their collective capabilities. The strong impact of perceived collective efficacy on groups' aspirations rendered group goals a redundant predictor that did not yield further gains in predictive power. The overall findings corroborate that sociocognitive determinants operate in much the same way at the collective level as they do at the individual level.

POLITICAL EFFICACY

The quality of life in a society rests partly on its political culture and governmental practices. Because of increasing complexity in the economic, technological, and social realities of life, governmental agencies perform many functions that were formerly carried out by other social systems. Therefore, if people are to have some command of their lives, they must exercise influence over the political process. Those who doubt they can have any effect see little point in attempting to shape legislative activities. The politically uninvolved relinquish influence to politically efficacious constituencies who are more than happy to use the governmental system as an agency to advance their parochial interests. A low level of political participation has not only personal consequences but systemic consequences as well. It breeds growing public discontent and cynicism with the political system. A cynical populace lacking civic trust and engagement is not easy to govern. If political trust in the fairness of the system is seriously eroded, public officials cannot gain support for unpopular reforms that require some sacrifices in the short run for long-term

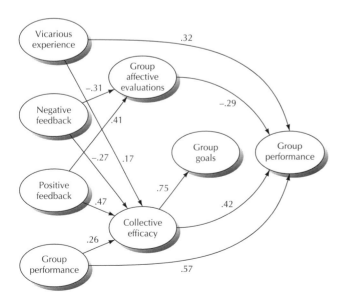

FIGURE 11.2. Path analysis showing that the impact of modeling and feedback influences on group problem solving are largely mediated through affective evaluative reactions and perceived collective efficacy. (Prussia & Kinicki, 1996)

benefits. Under these unfavorable incentive conditions, many political officials not only evade intractable social problems but often act in ways that exacerbate them.

Perceived political efficacy involves people's beliefs that they can influence the political system. There are two aspects to the exercise of control that are especially relevant to social change through political effort (Bandura, 1986a; Gurin & Brim, 1984). The first is the level of personal efficacy needed to produce results by enlistment of effort and proficient use of capabilities and resources. This constitutes the personal side of the transactional control process. The second aspect is how amenable social systems are to change by individual and collective influence. This facet represents the opportunity structures provided by the social system to exercise personal efficacy and enterprise, the ease of access to those opportunity structures, and the level of constraints and types of countermeasures imposed by the system to the exercise of personal efficacy. These properties of social systems determine how responsive they are to social action and how difficult they are to change.

The responsiveness or changeableness of the governmental system is neither a fixed characteristic nor independent of personal efficacy. Influential constituents shape the form of governmental functioning and to whom the officeholders are most responsive. Human behavior is governed largely by beliefs about personal efficacy and the controllability of social systems rather than simply by their objective properties. Thus, individuals who believe themselves to be inefficacious effect little change even in social systems that provide many potential opportunities (Bandura & Wood, 1989). Conversely, those who have a firm belief in their efficacy, through ingenuity and perseverance, figure out ways to exercise some measure of control over social systems containing limited opportunities and many constraints. Given a social environment with surmountable barriers, people who have a high sense of efficacy will be able to exercise more control over it, and will view it as more changeable, than will self-doubters who give up quickly in the face of difficulties.

People's beliefs about how much they can influence a given social system by personal means affect how they perceive their personal efficacy and the extent to which they change the social environment over time. This is strikingly revealed by the research cited earlier in which individuals managed a simulated organization under an instilled belief either that the organizational system was not easily controllable or that it was (Bandura & Wood, 1989). Viewing a social system as intractable weakens a sense of personal efficacy, which, in turn, impairs group functioning even when the desired social outcomes are within reach. Whereas beliefs of uncontrollability are personally and socially handicapping, viewing a social system as personally influenceable fosters productive thought and action that can improve the social environment. Moreover, belief that a social system is modifiable fosters resiliency of self-efficacy in the face of repeated disappointments and setbacks.

Research that measures beliefs of political efficacy speaks directly to the issue of how these beliefs affect participation in political activities. Unfortunately, some of the measures of perceived political efficacy used in this field of study do not actually assess political efficacy beliefs. Perceived political efficacy should be measured in terms of belief that one can produce effects through political action. Some of the measures instead assess such behavioral effects of political efficacy as level of participation in voting and community affairs, rather than belief in one's capability to influence the political process (Zurcher & Monts, 1972). Others assess political knowledge rather than belief that one can influence political affairs (Paige, 1971). Many investigators use a four-item scale designed to tap two factors of perceived political efficacy that might affect electoral participation (Campbell, Gurin, & Miller, 1954). The first is personal efficacy, as indicated by people's beliefs that they have a say in what government does, that they can influence how government works only by voting, and that they are capable of understanding how the system operates. The second factor is people's beliefs about the responsiveness of the social system. This factor is measured in terms of judgments that the political system is unresponsive to people's needs and that public officials are uncaring. Other investigators use variants of one or both of these themes.

These survey items purporting to measure perceived personal efficacy either do not really do so or assess it only partially. A perception that one does not have a say about what governments do pertains largely to beliefs about the unresponsiveness of the system. Perceived personal efficacy involves the power to produce effects, not just to understand political processes. One can comprehend fully the machinations of governmental systems but lack a sense of efficacy to influence them. There are many ways other than voting to influence governmental practices. Political efficacy is also exercised by campaigning for parties and candidates, fundraising, registering and mobilizing voters, petitioning, lobbying, and protesting rather than just by voting. Because of the limitations of these measures of perceived political efficacy, the findings of studies relying on them must be interpreted with considerable caution. Despite acknowledgment of the limitations (Balch, 1974; McPherson, Welch, & Clark, 1977), surprisingly, many researchers continue to use these measures rather than replace them with ones of greater explanatory and predictive value. Preserving the continuity and cumulativeness of research by sticking with a deficient measure is not the way to achieve reliable knowledge.

Other researchers emphasize vicarious sources of political efficacy in which the successes and failures of others instill beliefs in the utility or disutility of collective action (Muller, 1972). In the rational choice model, people presumably weigh the costs and benefits of given courses of political action and behave accordingly. The determinants in such rationalistic models of political action, therefore, are confined to the outcomes expected for different types of political tactics. The assumed utility of a given political means assesses the perceived efficacy of that means. As in the expectancy-value model discussed earlier, action is the product of expected outcomes and the probability that a given means will produce them. The failure to distinguish between means efficacy and personal efficacy is a major limitation of such models. A certain means

may be judged to be effective in producing desired results. But whether or not one can wield that means effectively is a separate issue. Thus, for example, people may be fully convinced that forceful coercive tactics could eventually bring change but feel inefficacious to mount and sustain the coercive effort needed in confrontations with intimidating authorities. People do not take upon themselves what they firmly believe is not within their power to do. They weigh heavily their perceived collective efficacy to overcome opposing forces in judging the benefits they are likely to gain and the costs they may incur by their actions. Hence, perceived efficacy should not only be included but should be given causal priority in reasoned choice models of action. It has been amply documented that reasoned choice models that focus on outcome expectations but ignore perceived efficacy to execute the means needed to produce those outcomes sacrifice predictive power.

There are other important determinants that expectancy-value models of political action neglect. Political participation cannot be fully understood without considering goal aspirations. Most political participation is channeled through membership in various groups that unite shared interests into common goals. The affiliations may involve political parties, special interest associations, formal or informal community pressure groups, or particular advocacy organizations that fight for causes of deep concern to their members. Groups target certain changes and then strive to accomplish them by mobilizing the combined resources and efforts of their members. The politically inactive lack such group ties, whereas the politically engaged are linked to participatory channels for political action (Wolfsfeld, 1986). The crucial factor, however, is not organizational membership per se but collective mobilization for the solution of problems. An aimless group will accomplish little. The goals on which people set their sights energize and channel their political activities and provide the basis for judging the success of their efforts. A given level of progress may be discouraging or a source of considerable satisfaction that strengthens political participation, depending on the goals against which it is measured.

Conceptual models must capture the full richness of determinants of political action. As in other domains of functioning, a comprehensive theory of political action from a sociocognitive perspective would encompass agentic efficacy beliefs, not just means efficacy; anticipated costs and benefits of alternative course of action as reflected in the three major classes of outcome expectations; short-run and long-range goals; and perceived sociostructural impediments. The theory would require sound measures of the determinants rather than substitute indices based on disputable assumptions.

Most of the research on political activism relies on global indices of perceived personal efficacy assessed by a few general items. Global indices are limited in what they can reveal about the contribution of efficacy beliefs to political and social change. As we have seen, efficacy beliefs are multifacetedly dispositional, not globally dispositional. Beliefs of personal efficacy vary across domains of activities, situational circumstances, and functional roles. Hence, informative empirical tests of theory require particularized, multifaceted measures of people's beliefs in their capabilities to fashion good strategies and to execute them with the tenacity needed to change social conditions. The interpretive problem is further complicated when beliefs about personal efficacy are combined with other factors into a single index of perceived control (Balch, 1974). Conglomerate indices obscure which of the constituent factors contribute to the observed effects, how heavily they do so, and whether they exert their effect independently or interactively.

The field of perceived political efficacy raises important conceptual issues as well as methodological ones. Personal efficacy and system responsiveness are not monolithic, self-contained entities as commonly portrayed in a static dualism. Both elements operate in dynamic interplay. System responsiveness is not independent of the types of social influences brought to bear upon it. Some institutional policies and practices are more influenceable than others. Officeholders may be more responsive to some types of social pressures than to others. Measures of perceived personal efficacy stripped of any context have limited predictive value. People vary in their beliefs of political efficacy to affect different governmental policies, to carry out different types of political tactics, and to sway different officeholders. Informative measures of political efficacy must reflect this diversity. Perceived political efficacy is best measured in terms of the impediments to change people believe they can surmount. Those of weak political efficacy view moderate obstacles as insurmountable, whereas reformers with a resolute sense of efficacy, such as the Ghandhis and Mandelas, regard even the most intransigent political systems as changeable through the power of collective action. The sections that follow present empirical evidence bearing on some of these issues.

Structure of Political Efficacy Beliefs

Political life has diverse aspects that differ widely in their changeability. Social cognitive theory posits that political activity is better explained and predicted by particularized efficacy beliefs that bear on the legislative activities and institutional practices of interest than by global measures of general life efficacy or nondescript political influence. The predictive benefits of specifying the domain over which influence is exercised are well documented. Perceived political efficacy is more predictive of political activity than is general life efficacy, which yields few significant relationships (Gootnick, 1974). In tests of relative predictiveness involving different types of political activities, locus of control is nonpredictive of political action; the widely used general measure of perceived political efficacy varies from weakly predictive to nonpredictive; and particularized beliefs of political efficacy are most predictive (Fox & Schofield, 1989; Wollman & Stouder, 1991). Not only do global measures not predict political activism, they are insensitive to the effects of disappointing political defeats (Huebner & Lipsey, 1981). These findings suggest that global efficacy measures may underestimate, or even misrepresent, the contribution of efficacy beliefs to political behavior.

The predictive value of particularized measures of perceived efficacy for different political strategies is further illustrated in research by Wiegman, Taal, Van den Bogaard, and Gutteling (1992). They measured people's willingness to protest the placement in their community of a chemical plant that would pose environmental hazards. The more strongly they believed that they could get themselves to use various protest strategies — such as petitioning, pressuring their local government, taking legal action, and participating in public demonstrations — the firmer was their intention to take coercive action. Perceived protest efficacy combined with outcome expectations of severe hazard contributed heavily to protest intention. These factors operate analogously as motivators in nuclear threats (Wolf, Gregory, & Stephan, 1986). Visualizing potentially catastrophic outcomes with belief that one can do something to prevent them heightens willingness to engage in political activities to promote nuclear disarmament.

Failed political efforts do not shake the perceived efficacy of resolute activists, as shown in a study of reactions to the defeat of a ballot referendum to increase safety standards for nuclear power plants (Huebner & Lipsey, 1981). A disappointing defeat of the political initiative for which the participants campaigned actively did not lower their belief in their ability to influence ecological policies, but they came to view their opposition as more formidable than originally assumed. Such an outlook would encourage greater effort and a search for better strategies, rather than demoralization. Those who are not active politically have little reason to engage in political activity not only because they feel personally inefficacious but also because they view the opposing forces as wielding considerable political power. Even successful political action does not necessarily raise faith in the responsiveness of governmental systems. Successful encounters with public officials raise perceived personal efficacy but not the view of governmental responsiveness, whereas failed encounters leave perceived efficacy intact but instill an even lower opinion of the responsiveness of the system (Madsen, 1987). The maintenance of some measure of personal efficacy in the face of system intransigence helps to sustain engagement in political affairs. Otherwise, belief

that political action is inconsequential would produce massive political alienation.

A number of researchers have examined the role of perceived efficacy in the realm of nuclear threat. This is an issue of special interest because of the striking discordance between the destructive horridness of the threat and the lack of public political action to prevent the international production and proliferation of nuclear weapons. Most people acknowledge the enormity of the nuclear threat, believe that a nuclear conflagration is likely to happen in their lifetime, and believe that they would not survive it (Fox & Schofield, 1989). But only a relatively small number get involved in activities designed to promote global nuclear disarmament. The rest remain concerned but inactive.

The nuclear age has ushered in a ghastly risk that creates major paradoxes and moral imperatives. Threats of nuclear retaliation are used to deter a nuclear attack. Retaliatory threats have no deterrent effect, however, unless there is every intention to react to an attack with nuclear force. A counterstrike launched if deterrence failed would be a ghastly act of vengeance that would wreak vast human and ecological devastation on foes, friends, and retaliators alike. In the aftermath of nuclear exchanges, survivors would find themselves in a largely uninhabitable environment. Drifting radioactive fallout would spread the human and ecological devastation indiscriminately worldwide. Because of the self-destructive consequences of a counterstrike, a nuclear deterrence doctrine, paradoxically, seeks to achieve a deterrent effect with a retaliatory threat that no one in their right mind could conceive of ever using.

No technical system is ever foolproof. As long as nuclear weapons exist, there is continual risk that someday they may be fired accidentally through malfunction of missile-monitoring systems or human error, or launched intentionally in an extreme crisis by an enraged, panic-stricken, or suicidal leadership. On four occasions, the United States has gone into a state of nuclear war alert, and only last-minute efforts revealed malfunctions or errors in the computer warning system (Falk, 1983). Nuclear proliferation and swifter missile systems that cut short the time for decisions raise the level of risk. To seek security in a fallible system that can produce massive nuclear annihilation is to invite human calamity of appalling proportions. Because of the vast scope and magnitude of indiscriminate nuclear devastation, the traditional just-war tenets that sanction self-defense to avert grave harm are inapplicable to nuclear weapons (Bandura, 1991d; Kavka, 1988; Lackey, 1985).

Human survival in the nuclear age requires the inhabitants of nations to challenge the military doctrines and justifications for nuclear weapons and to promote multilateral de-escalative steps to eliminate nuclear arsenals. Despite the catastrophic risks, many people are lulled by political rhetoric and by thinking in terms of conventional weaponry into a false sense of safety. Most feel powerless to do anything about the stockpiling and proliferation of nuclear weapons. But not all regard attempts to influence policies in the nuclear domain as futile.

The people who choose to become involved in activities directed at nuclear disarmament have a higher sense of efficacy than those who remain inactive (Edwards & Oskamp, 1992; Fox & Schofield, 1989; Tyler & McGraw, 1983). A resilient belief provides the needed protection against discouragement. Other predictors of political activism include a deep concern about the likelihood of a nuclear holocaust, personalization of the destructive threat to oneself and one's family, and a sense of personal moral responsibility to avert nuclear destruction. When combined with an efficacy belief that one can have an impact, these various outcome expectations provide the incentive and staying power for political action. Success in global disarmament is a tortuous long-range struggle. Even the signs of progress along the way are few and far between. To sustain their efforts, activists must rely on mutual social support and moral self-sanctions. It is the social support from fellow peace workers rather than from other sources that help to sustain political efforts.

Political efficacy is exercised in communal contexts. Localities vary in their level of community and civic commitment. Moreover, residents differ in their social status and the strength of their ties to the localities in which they reside. It is easier to mobilize and exert collective influence in close-knit communities where people support one another than in communities where they feel disconnected or alienated from one another and their social system. Research on citizens' perceived efficacy to influence their local governments provides interesting insights into the role of social status and communality in political efficacy (Steinberger, 1981). In accord with expectation, residents of high social status, as measured by education and wealth, believe that they can affect governmental policies and practices, whereas those of low status feel powerless to do so. Communality is more complexly related to perceived political efficacy, however. The strength of communal ties was assessed by the extent of residents' positive relationships to others living in their locality, how long they and their parents resided there, and whether they were economically dependent upon their community or commuted to work elsewhere. Residents of low status felt politically inefficacious regardless of level of communality. Social ties alone are not enough. It takes efficacious individuals to organize and activate a public constituency for change. Therefore, it is high-status individuals who raise their sense of political efficacy if they have strong communal ties.

Political processes are altered by people acting together rather than by individual feats. In the political arena, perceived efficacy is reflected in participants' beliefs in their collective capabilities to accomplish social changes through political action. To make change, they must be able to convert diverse self-interests into a common purpose. They have to enlist supporters and needed resources and form coalitions, if necessary, to strengthen their influence. They have to devise and carry out appropriate strategies of action. Because efforts at significant social change usually elicit forceful resistance, reformers must be able to withstand failures, setbacks, and reprisals. Perceived efficacy to cope with oppositional reactions of vested interests is thus a vital contributor to persevering reform efforts. A comprehensive assessment of collective political efficacy would address each of these major facets of collective effort. Such measures would advance our understanding of the process of efficacious political action as well as the attainment of legislative successes.

Participatory Dilemmas in Collective Action

Mobilization of collective effort to further common interests poses participatory dilemmas. This is especially true in large-scale endeavors where people can easily persuade themselves that what they have to contribute will not really matter in a huge collective effort. The larger the collectivity, the more insignificant the individual effort may appear (Kerr, 1996). Nor do the incentives of social change involving nonexclusive distribution of benefits for the group of beneficiaries naturally favor participatory involvement. As long as enough people work collectively to accomplish desired changes, the inactive ones cannot be excluded from enjoying the benefits as well. For example, a law enacted through collective pressure that bans discrimination based on gender or race benefits activists and nonactivists alike. One might argue from a rationalistic model that there is little reason to participate in collective endeavors, particularly under intimidating conditions, if one can reap the benefits and avoid the costs through the labor of others. Why pay if one can get a free ride? Feelings of exploitation by those bearing the burden can add further disincentive for personal involvement in collective endeavors. Felt inequities may arise even among the activists. Depending on the functions they perform, some members bear a disproportionate share of burdens but receive no greater benefits. What motivates and sustains engagement in collective action under conditions of free riding is an issue of considerable interest.

Given that significant social changes are typically spearheaded by a minority bearing the full burden, it is not freeloading but cost-bearing that poses the explanatory challenge. The incentives for engagement in collective endeavors not only are varied but can change over the course of social events. Moreover, social activism is a dynamic affair, not a static one. The initial challengers, who share the belief and commitment that they can

produce results by group pressure, are usually small in number. They act on the shared belief that their numbers will grow as officials reject justifiable demands under pressure or overreact with countermeasures of excessive force. Sympathizers will be moved by the grievances of the challengers and incensed by their harsh mistreatment. Indeed, some of the confrontational strategies serve the very purpose of provoking officials to react excessively, which enlists supporters to the challengers' cause (Bandura, 1973; King, 1958; Searle, 1968).

Group success, of course, brings benefits to the participants. Individuals who desire the benefits of collective triumphs and have a strong sense of efficacy that their contribution raises the chances of group success have a self-interested reason to join the ranks of reformers. They may not like shouldering the extra load and personal costs for inactive beneficiaries, but they have some incentive to do so if they believe that their actions will make a difference and they will be better off by helping to bring about valued outcomes than by doing nothing. Participants are not only pulled by expected shared benefits but pushed by the continuing costs of inaction. There are those who assume that if they do not help improve life conditions, the conditions won't get changed or will worsen. As a consequence, they and their families will continue to suffer inequities, indignities, or hardships. It would be collectively irrational for efficacious individuals to sink into a state of docility that continues to make life miserable for them just because some group members do not do their fair share in the collective effort.

Belief that one can help to ameliorate adverse conditions provides additional self-interested reasons to participate in collective action. One would be better off doing so than not. The stronger the belief in the group's efficacy to mobilize the level of participation needed to succeed, and the greater the expected shared benefits, the higher the participation rate (Kerr, 1996). In some approaches to social change through collective action, linking diverse self-interests to a common goal serves as a key motivational device (Alinsky, 1971). The more people who participate, the stronger the sense of collective efficacy to overcome oppositional forces. The perceived power and safety in numbers increases belief of likely benefits and lowers appraisal of likely costs.

People are not driven solely by consideration of material benefits. Self-evaluative sanctions, rooted in personal standards of fairness and justice, also serve as powerful motivators. People derive self-respect from challenging social practices that violate their ethical standards, and they react with outrage to harmful practices and with self-reproach for acquiescing to inhumanities. Submission carries self-devaluative costs. Those with a strong civic ethic are willing to endure a great deal of hardship and punitive treatment for the self-respect they gain from upholding their moral convictions and contesting injustices and inhumanities. Such leaders of reform efforts as Gandhi, King, and Mandela bore grave costs for their political dissent based on their personal integrity and moral convictions. Some sacrifice their lives for their convictions. A strong sense of collective self-worth can help support tough struggles for social betterment. Groups devoted to ecological causes invest their time, effort, and money in activities designed to save endangered species or habitats in foreign locales that do not touch their lives. Such collective efforts are supported by the internal payoff of self-respect rather than by material benefits.

Participants in collective endeavors are usually united in a cohesive community that touches many aspects of their lives. They develop close personal relationships, educate themselves on the rightness of their cause and effective strategies, and offer mutual aid and support in the struggle to accomplish their goals. A strong sense of camaraderie provides sustaining interpersonal rewards at a time when the tangible benefits of social change may be long in coming. Groups not only reward contributors to worthy causes but reprove shirkers who profit from others' labors. The ingrained norm of doing one's fair share creates social pressure to assist in collective struggles to effect desired changes (Goldstone, 1994). The more an individual's well-being and sense of identity are tied to a group, the stronger the felt social obligation for mutual assistance. Social and self-evaluative incentives have to carry the major share of support for reform efforts during the long haul toward uncertain outcomes.

The vast majority of those who benefit from social reforms are not active participants in bringing about the changes. A number of factors keep people politically inactive. As already noted, the conditions of distributed benefits, in which inactive members can enjoy the fruits of reformers' labors, are not especially conducive to widespread participation. Many people shy away from collective action, however, not because they can gain the benefits without the costs of participation but because they seriously doubt the group's efficacy to secure any benefits at all. They see little purpose in taking ineffectual action that will only inflict troublesome costs with little prospect of benefits. Perceived inefficacy to alter entrenched institutional practices breeds especially pessimistic outcome expectations. Retaliatory threats that are viewed as collectively unmanageable put a further damper on reform efforts. The weariness and stress of prolonged effort with little success to show for it additionally undermine a sense of collective efficacy and discourage continuing participation.

Belief in collective efficacy rests on the expectation that social reforms are achievable by a critical mass of activists rather than requiring universal participation. If social change depended on everyone participating, it would rarely be attempted because few would believe that a huge populace can be mobilized. In fact, social reforms are typically the product of an efficacious and highly committed minority of people who invest themselves in shaping a better future. They are the driving force for social change. Their belief that they can bring about change and mutual support insulate them against discouragement.

Political activists override the free-rider dilemma by belief that acting on one's personal efficacy in concert with enough others will raise perceived collective efficacy for collective action to a level that is likely to succeed in producing valued material, social, and self-evaluative outcomes. Finkel, Muller, and Opp (1989) report findings that are congruent with this view. The more strongly people believe that their actions will contribute to group success, that unified effort is necessary, and that they have a moral obligation to do their part, the more they will engage in collective political action to change governmental policies that adversely affect the quality of life.

Joint Impact of Efficacy and System Trust on Political Activism

According to Gamson (1968), people are moved to social action when they feel politically efficacious but mistrustful of their leaders and government. Studies testing this proposition, in its sparse form, have produced mixed findings. People who believe they can help to achieve desired futures will act on that belief regardless of whether they hold the political system in high or low regard. Indeed, politically efficacious individuals are more apt to take action if they trust their governmental system than if they are cynical about it (Hawkins, Marando, & Taylor, 1971; Fraser, 1970). There are different avenues and incentives for social change. People engage in political activity proactively to accomplish desired changes as well as reactively to blocked opportunities to effect changes by conventional means. The conflicting findings underscore the need to consider the form the political activism takes and the level of governmental operations targeted for change. Moreover, the anticipated countermeasures taken by the regime in response to reform efforts will shape the form of the political activism. Coercive or severely punitive counterresponses can keep militant activism under restraint.

People who are assured of their political efficacy and perceive their governmental system to be responsive to citizens' demands show high involvement in conventional modes of political action (Craig, 1979; Finkel, 1985; Pollock, 1983; Zimmerman & Rappaport, 1988). They work on behalf of political parties or candidates, contribute money to them, participate in campaign activities, try to influence the votes of others, voice their views to politicians and other public officials to sway them to their position on issues of concern, and wield their voting influence. Because they believe that

legislative changes are achievable by legitimate means, they do not condone unorthodox political activities. In contrast, individuals who believe they can bring about social change but who take a cynical view of authorities and the system over which they preside do not lapse into political passivity. Rather, they favor more confrontive, coercive tactics outside the traditional political channels. A politically efficacious outlook can thus support a good deal of activism, albeit of different forms, at both high and low levels of political trust. Because action is predicated on the belief that one can execute it competently, political activism is better predicted by efficacy belief than by trustfulness alone.

Research that measures only conventional forms of political behavior — such as electioneering, petitioning, contacting legislators, community work, and voting — is well suited for verifying the link between efficacy belief and activism for the politically efficacious, trustful citizenry. But measuring only lawful forms of political activism will yield misleading findings for efficacious citizens who repudiate major governmental practices, view politicians as self-serving obstructionists to needed social reforms, and consider conventional means for achieving social change to be ineffective. Their activism is more likely to take the form of protests, demonstrations, boycotts, civil disobedience, and even political violence (Seligson, 1980). For this group, a weak link between political efficacy and activism would be an artifact of failure to measure the more confrontational forms of activism. Finkel and his colleagues show that people resort to the form of political influence for which they feel most self-efficacious (Finkel et al., 1989). Conventional political activism is better predicted by perceived efficacy to exert influence through lawful means, whereas unlawful forms of protest are better predicted by perceived efficacy to effect change by confrontational tactics.

The research of Wolfsfeld (1986) further underscores the need to distinguish between different facets of political efficacy beliefs and their selective linkage to different modes of activism. The politically inactive have a low sense of political efficacy and view all modes of political activity as ineffective.

Those who are active within the political system believe they can influence it. They express high efficacy and approval for conventional forms of political action but low efficacy and disapproval for protest modes of activism. Dissidents also express strong belief in their efficacy to exert political influence, but they regard conventional tactics as ineffective and view protest tactics as the efficacious modes of influence. Pragmatists, who favor both conventional and confrontational tactics, express high approval and efficacy for all forms of political action.

A full understanding of the role that efficacy beliefs play in the political process also requires assessment of political participation at different levels of governmental systems. Many people have become skeptical about whether central governments gridlocked by competing special interest groups can solve intractable social problems. Citizens who have a low sense of political efficacy feel powerless to change governmental practices at any level. Those who believe they can accomplish some social change intensify their efforts to alter institutional policies and practices at regional and local levels over which they can command greater control. Research on political efficacy, therefore, must assess not only a multifaceted efficacy belief system but also different forms of political activism at different levels of governmental systems. The studies that are especially problematic rely on skimpy general measures or substitute indices dressed up in the correct terminology but of questionable equivalence to the determinants of interest. These analytic problems are endemic to secondary analyses of data collected for other purposes. All too often, the factors that were measured are poor substitutes for the ones in the theories being tested. Deficient substitutes can yield misleading findings.

Development of Political Efficacy and System Trust

The development of beliefs that one can influence the political system and that governmental institutions and officeholders are trustworthy starts early in life. Children neither have much political

knowledge nor participate in political activities. Therefore, their appraisals of their political efficacy and the political system must be shaped by other sources of influence. Children's beliefs about the political system develop in much the same way as do their beliefs in other areas of life. They develop beliefs about adult roles and institutional practices long before they become adults. Some of the beliefs about the realities of political life can be acquired through modeling rather than direct experience. Children have ample opportunities to observe the animated comments of adults around them and in the mass media about the influenceability of the political system and the trustworthiness of elected officials. Children's beliefs about their capabilities to influence governmental functioning may also be partially generalized from their experiences in trying to influence adults in educational and other institutional settings with which they must deal. Institutional experiences that imbue children with a sense of efficacy are more likely to instill a belief that political systems are also responsive and influenceable than are experiences that breed a sense of futility that one can do much to affect authorities.

Much of the research on developmental changes in perceived political efficacy has centered on racial differences in youth rather than on longitudinal analyses of how these belief systems are acquired and change over the course of development. From elementary to high school, children's beliefs in their efficacy for political action increases, but their cynicism about government and those who run it also increases. The findings generally show that African-American youths have a lower sense of political efficacy and higher political cynicism than do white youths (Lyons, 1970; Rodgers, 1974). Controls for socioeconomic status, however, qualify these differences. Youths of low socioeconomic status feel politically inefficacious and disaffected from the political system regardless of race. The racial differences emerge at the high socioeconomic level where African-American youths express lower political efficacy and greater cynicism than do their white counterparts. This is especially true for perceived efficacy to affect the political process.

Group averages must be interpreted with caution, however, because they mask substantial diversity within ethnic and racial groupings. For example, academically achieving African-American students, regardless of whether they live in advantaged or disadvantaged milieus, come to feel more politically efficacious but no less cynical about the political system as they advance in their schooling. Thus, for high achievers, racial differences disappear in perceived efficacy for political action but remain in political cynicism. The more minority youths learn about the political system academically, the more cynical they become about it. Knowing how the system is supposed to work in the interests of the public only reinforces dissatisfaction with how it actually functions. Nor do the machinations of political life aired daily on the broadcast news media inspire adults' faith in the integrity of governmental operations. Although heavy use of the news media raises personal political efficacy, it breeds disaffection with the political system (Newhagen, 1994b).

Analyses of alternative causal explanations indicate that the racial differences arise primarily from more limited opportunity structures to affect the political system and less responsiveness of the system to minority concerns. By reducing involvement in the political process, political inefficacy and cynicism create a cycle of growing alienation. Political apathy further reduces the power to affect legislation that can improve the conditions of life and leads to even lower institutional responsiveness through loss of electoral leverage on political officials.

Social impediments and socialization practices may also be important contributors to sex differences in perceived political efficacy. No such differences are observed in childhood, but adult females feel less politically efficacious than males (Campbell et al., 1954; Easton & Dennis, 1967). Studies of currently held efficacy beliefs are needed to determine whether the increased participation of women in political and legislative activities is reducing the gender gap in perceived efficacy to influence the political system. The gender variability in political efficaciousness is, in many respects, more informative than faceless group averages. The suffragists were unshakable in their efficacy and unfazed by public ridicule and vigorous attacks on their efforts to secure voting rights for women. The members of the League of Women Voters, of which there are large numbers nationwide, are exceedingly well informed, highly self-efficacious, and politically active. Increasing numbers of women are becoming legislators, political leaders, and policymakers. In the words of the popular ballad, clearly, the times they are a'changing.

Electronic Campaigning and the Political Process

The way the mass media are used in the political arena is undergoing major changes that are transforming political and governing processes. The political call-in system, in which political candidates field questions from callers on radio or television, has become a new interactive vehicle of political influence. In addition, political officials enlist talk-show hosts of similar ideological persuasion to mobilize public support for their legislative initiatives and opposition to those they dislike. We are entering an era of governance by television and of advertising wars over public policies. Public support for reform legislation is weakened by 30-second ads depicting common folks in conversations that misinform and scare the public about proposed changes. The special interests doing the influencing with the televised advocacy advertising masquerade under front groups with public caring names. In short, political parties and commercial interests with a lot of financial clout are increasingly orchestrating legislative activities in the media airways. These political battles for public support of policy initiatives are waged more deftly by well-crafted ads on the airways than in legislative chambers.

Talk radio provides easy access to a broad audience. In this interactive system, callers lobby for their political agenda with candidates and other listeners. Those who have a high sense of political efficacy use call-in political television more than those of low perceived efficacy (Newhagen, 1994a). Efficacy beliefs continue to predict listeners' use of the media to influence others after taking into account socioeconomic status, race, and amount of news viewing and newspaper reading. Neither trust in the political system nor trust in its leaders affects political use of the media. This finding further underscores the fact that people act politically more on beliefs of their ability to influence the system than on the stock they place in the system. Perceived political efficacy and participation in broadcast politicking have bidirectional effects. The self-efficacious use the broadcast media, and hearing people of similar political persuasion berating their foes and extolling the superiority of the policies and officeholders they favor boosts participants' beliefs in their own efficacy for political action (Newhagen, 1994b). Broadcast politicking raises perceived political efficacy more than does newspaper reading or news viewing.

The evolving telecommunication technologies may alter the mode of political influence used by people of different socioeconomic status. The call-in media are readily accessible to those of limited means because they require no special resources. By contrast, the more advantaged electorate is cruising the Internet. Interactive communication through computer networks brings perceived efficacy even more heavily into the political influence process. There are fewer social constraints to overcome because of the anonymity of the interactors. Users with strong political efficacy and convictions can now transcend time, place, and national boundaries in debating political issues. The views they express on the Internet quickly spread worldwide. To take one example, when a prestigious university press, fearing reprisals, rejected a manuscript on a volatile nationalist conflict, outraged academics promptly issued an Internet protest worldwide. They urged colleagues to boycott the press, resign editorial advisorships, and refuse to review manuscripts for this publishing house. Mobilization of collective influence via the Internet is swift, wide reaching, and free of institutional constraints. Given its ready accessibility, the Internet will be used increasingly as a vehicle for enlisting social forces and shaping the strategies and tactics for desired changes.

Limited public access to the media has been a major obstacle to participatory politics. During political campaigns, moneyed interests flood the airways with slick imagery ads that effectively evade serious discussion of issues that bear importantly on the social and economic life of the nation. Some critics have argued that, with media ownership concentrated in the hands of a few and with the costliness of access to it, free speech is turning into profitable speech. The public is getting increasingly exasperated with seeing the electoral process degraded to contrived images, sound bites, and incessant personal attacks. The media coverage of electoral campaigns has shifted the emphasis from substantive policy issues to the dynamics and tactics of electoral races (Patterson, 1993). Instant polls identify winners, losers, and changes in momentum as though elections were athletic contests. Newscasts exploit the main features of captivating drama. These elements highlight conflict between factions, emotive words that magnify the drama, and negativity that fuels animosities (Abel, 1981). The demand for quick fixes to complex problems fosters a foreshortened perspective toward the persistent troubles of society.

This negative state of affairs is driving a frustrated electorate to spurn the manipulative imagery of televised politics and instead share information, exchange ideas, debate the political issues among themselves, and build coalitions through the Internet. Politicians, of course, are not about to surrender their hold on political communications in this wide-reaching medium. Legislators and political parties have now adopted Internet politicking. They are presenting their views and spin on issues through speeches, press releases, position papers, and video clips on their own Internet sites. Politicians will have to monitor and battle their opponents on the Internet as well as in other locales.

Unfiltered, ready access by anyone to the system inevitably produces some perturbing speech. Freelancers are parodying, unmasking, and discrediting political figures they hold in low regard on unofficial cybersites. People defend and promote the speech they like, but they try to curb or silence the speech they do not like. One can expect efforts to regulate computer communication on the grounds of protecting the public from dangerous, malicious, and raunchy material. Established legal principles will be extended to incendiary forms of speech likely to incite injurious actions and to harassing or other pernicious actions directed by cyberspace users toward others. The major legal battles will be fought over controversial speech where what is highly objectionable to some people is not objectionable to others. The ready access and anarchic vastness of computer networks unconstrained by national boundaries, however, defies workable regulation of what appears on the worldwide Internet. The only viable solution is to put the control in the hands of the users. Software filters enable users to screen out the parts of the Internet that do not suit their sensibilities.

Computerized politicking provides vast opportunities for participatory discourse but does not dictate its quality. People behave quite differently in computer-mediated networks than they do in face-to-face interchanges. This is because the social influences that regulate how people behave toward one another in direct social relationships are much weaker and lack immediacy in computerized communications. Kiesler, Siegel, and McGuire (1984) document the many ways in which depersonalization of communication alters what people say to one another. The force of status and prestige is diminished so that individuals participate more equally in the computer-mediated system. When interchanges are conducted anonymously, participants behave more uninhibitedly and express views and feelings they would never voice in face-to-face communication. Thus, the superhighway can easily get flooded with misinformation, deceitful accusations, scurrilous commentaries, and a lot of unintelligible babble. How people sift through and evaluate the avalanche of information of varying credibility remains to be seen. Although a political communications system accessible to all vastly expands participation in the political process, it can bring out the worst in political campaigning but on an enlarged scale — because anyone who wishes can be a freelancing trickster, not only the advertising agencies that do the bidding of well-heeled interests. Computerized politicking shifts the locus of the battles but does not provide salvation from political foulness.

Voter turnout in America has been continuously declining to the point where only about 40 percent of the eligible electorate bothers to vote. Those who choose to vote tend to be older, wealthier, and of nonminority status. The combined effect of eroding party loyalties and growing public cynicism about the responsiveness of the political system accounts for most of the decline in electoral participation (Abramson & Aldrich, 1982). Much of the disaffection stems from political polarization over whether social problems reflect personal failings or failings of the social systems (Miller, 1974). Partisan solutions to the social problems please neither faction. They dislike the remedies offered by the opposing party but are also not contented with those of their own party because they do not go far enough in the direction they desire. Independents, who are growing in number and in political estrangement, perceive little difference between the political parties. Erosion of party ties and televised politicking have transformed the electoral process.

In this era of electronic campaigning, image politics orchestrated by pollsters, computer programmers, and adept image makers has become the major vehicle for influencing the electorate. It is easier to shape images of candidates by portraying favorable personal characteristics than to try to sway the electorate by addressing important issues nonevasively. As a seasoned legislator put it succinctly: "It's easier to buy an image than to earn it through deeds." Most candidates avoid like the plague proposing needed but unpopular remedies for growing social problems. Image management is more effectively achieved by contrived media portrayals than by public appearances. Professional image makers draw heavily on the mass media to heighten the attractiveness of their candidates to voters (Nimmo, 1976). Pollsters probe the public's likes, dislikes, fears, concerns, and hopes. With this information and that obtained from focus groups, political handlers cast their candidate in a marketable positive image and their opponents in a negative image through mass-marketing techniques using television advertisements, radio spots, and personalized mailers targeted to specific categories of voters identified by computers. Issues of substance get converted to exercises in political spin. The political handlers become media celebrities who, allied with reporters seeking something of interest in tightly scripted campaigns, channel much of the press coverage to the strategic and tactical features of political contests. Many of the prominent newscasters and political commentators enrich thenselves on the speaker circuit with lavish fees paid by influential lobbying groups. The more voters rely on television for their information, the more their voting decisions are influenced by candidates' imaged qualities rather than by their position on issues (McLeod, Glynn & McDonald, 1983).

Electronic campaigning significantly alters how candidates do their politicking, as well as the content of media messages. Candidates must spend much of their time preparing television advertisements and radio spots, staging media events likely to be reported in newscasts, and raising vast sums of money to buy the expensive media time. These polling operations and new tools of politics continue to be used during the time the victors are in office to ensure future electoral success.

Politicians do the bidding of those who bankroll their campaigns. The regulation of tobacco products illustrates both the political power of moneyed interests and the shifting dynamics of control as the public reasserts its influence by bypassing the barriers erected by political officeholders. Despite the fact that tobacco products are the most toxic legalized substances and kill hundreds of thousands of people annually, lawmakers have exempted nicotine from bills controlling drugs. Moreover, they have federalized control with preemptive laws that ban states and local governments from regulating tobacco products and advertising (Lynch & Bonnie, 1994). Figure 11.3 shows the power of tobacco money over the behavior of federal lawmakers. The more tobacco campaign money they receive, the more likely they are to fend off legislation to regulate tobacco products. Most of the proposed legislation is killed privately in committee. This legislative behavior protects the reelection of lawmakers at the heavy cost of national health.

Gardner (1972), a masterful and forceful advocate for the public interest, created Common Cause, a national citizens' force to curb the inordinate power of entrenched moneyed interests and to revitalize the governmental system to serve as an instrument of the public will. The entrenched controls weaken the ability of government to reform itself from within. Some of the efforts of this citizens' organization are directed toward shaping congressional reforms to correct structural flaws in the system of governance that make it all too easy to slight the public interest. These reforms include ending secrecy in the conduct of legislative business by making committee votes public, preventing conflicts of interest by public officials voting on legislation in which they have a financial stake, reducing the excessive power of committee chairpersons that

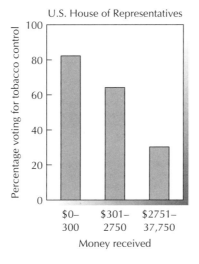
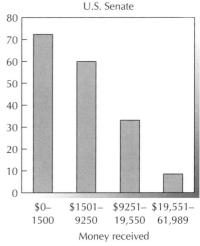

FIGURE 11.3. Relationship between the amount of campaign money legislators receive from the tobacco industry and their likelihood of voting against legislation to regulate tobacco products. (Public Citizen Health Research Group, 1993)

enables them to divert the governmental apparatus from its civic function, and abolishing the seniority system that confers power over congressional activities by longevity rather than by competence. To cite but one example, Common Cause worked successfully for a law requiring disclosure of political expenditures so that the public can know the financial interests backing various political candidates and how much money is spent for what purposes.

It is not enough to increase access to governmental systems. Effective public advocacy is needed to shape policies and to prevent or correct faulty legislation that looks good but subverts the intended public purpose. Regulatory agencies must be monitored to ensure that they implement the laws adequately — because if special interests fail to block policy initiatives at the legislative stage, they can negate them at the implementation stage by getting enacted laws translated into ineffectual regulations or weakening the enforcement practices. Therefore, in addition to working for structural reforms that make the governmental system more responsive to the public will, this citizens' organization exerts its influence on legislative actions in support of new solutions to a broad range of intractable social problems. Among the familiar candidates on the social agenda are education, health, employment, affordable housing, consumer and environmental protection, and law enforcement. In some of these areas, inequitable practices that adversely affect the less advantaged are sufficiently beneficial to large segments of the population to gain popular support. Common Cause provides a convenient vehicle for organized citizens' efforts to improve and invigorate the public process to accomplish shared purposes.

As people become cynical about their central government, they strive to regain control through local and regional ordinances over which they have greater influence. They got smoke-free workplaces, smoke-free restaurants, and smoke-free airliners by their own collective action, not through the governmental agencies entrusted with the responsibility to protect national health. When local efforts succeed, moneyed interests move in to preempt local control. A misleading ballot measure, heavily financed by the tobacco industry, was introduced in California to repeal all local tobacco ordinances and substitute a less restrictive statewide law under the guise of tougher tobacco control. This effort at preemption of local control was defeated by a resounding public counteraction. The same political scenarios are replayed in other legislative domains. Legislators fight to remove federalized control when it encroaches on their interests but push for preemptive federalized control that protects their interests. When a leader of a state legislature was once asked about his legendary broker politics with power blocks, he replied that "sometimes you have to rise above principle." With political stalemates pervading the central systems, the social battles over legislative remedies shift increasingly to local levels. Much of the innovation and experimentation with programs designed to address common social problems are being conducted at state and local levels.

The weakening of party ties enables legislators to operate as a collection of political freelancers. This makes it difficult to transcend individual interests in the service of national vision and purpose and to enlist the collective support needed to realize national goals. There are strong personal incentives, getting reelected being foremost among them, for legislators to promote their constituents' local interests even though many of the programs may not be in the best national interest. Legislators who routinely face weak opposition gain seniority in the governance system with power to deliver generous patronage benefits to their constituents. With power to bring home generous benefits from government coffers, incumbency becomes self-perpetuating. Special interests pour money into campaign coffers of legislators who gain political clout through senority. It should come as no surprise that local constituents generally like their incumbent legislators and routinely reelect them but regard the governmental system and its body of legislators as unresponsive to the interests of the people and out of touch with them. One of the more amusing expressions of this self-contradiction occurred in a California election where the voters reelected virtually all of their incumbent legislators while simultaneously voting overwhelmingly to limit the terms of legislators! By seeking to get a goodly share of the spoils of the system for their own localities, the public also promotes broker politics that worsen national fiscal and regulatory problems. In their conflicting demands on the governmental system, constituents want their representatives to spend money that serves their local interests but, at the same time, to vote for tax and spending limitations and decry pork-barrel politics. They want less government but the same or increased level of services, entitlements, subsidies, and patronage benefits. How well government works is thus a product of the dynamic interplay among the local interests of constituents, competing power blocks, and the ambitions and commitments of political leaders.

All too often, what is good public policy is self-jeopardizing politics for lawmakers. As a result, heavily lobbied lawmakers promote policy initiatives that favor the special interests on whom they depend for their campaign financing. In trying to get reelected, many candidates resort to policy by sound bites. In 30-second advertisements, they reduce intractable social problems to simple solutions that are popular in the abstract but would be disliked by many people if spelled out in specifics. Artful wordsmiths couch the legislative solutions in generalities that effectively evade coming to grips with the problems that concern the public. Some inspirational homilies and skillful flaunting of the wisdom of hindsight further help to brighten the image.

Political candidates can boost their chances of victory not only by mobilizing their supporters to vote but also by dissuading their opponents from voting. With expressions of political cynicism gaining vogue, efficacious political partisans are beginning to use cynicism as an electoral strategy. Political strategists usually try to promote cynicism among the sectors of the electorate whose vote the dissuaders are unlikely to gain. Lobbyists and those in the upper echelons of society are rarely, if ever, seen on television proclaiming voting as an act of futility, whereas those of lower status readily give vent to their cynicism about the government and their intention not to vote. Those who do not vote have little voice in legislative matters. By not exercising their political influence, the disaffected thus become accomplices to their own disempowerment. With low voter turnouts, well-organized political partisans can carry the day with relatively small numbers. The politically apathetic thus relinquish their influence to the active partisans and then complain about the kind of government they end up with.

Clearly, electronic politicking is changing the form and content of the political process. It also shapes the political system by its impact on candidates' self-selection. The realities of political life give high priority to interminable fund raising. Candidates inevitably get drawn into the seamy side of politics through negative advertising battles on the airwaves. Over the years, the political air wars have been getting nastier (West, 1993). Politics is not a vocation for those who bruise easily. It is difficult to retain one's integrity and preserve a sense of dignity in this process. Of those who judge they have the efficacy to withstand the grueling electoral demands and demeaning aspects of the political process, most are dissuaded from seeking office by the intense media scrutiny of the personal lives of candidates. The research on political efficacy has given us a better understanding of how the complex interplay of constituents, officeholders, and governmental systems determines governmental performance and level of satisfaction with it. The way in which the changing realities of political life affect people's willingness to become political actors in this drama remains an unexplored issue of considerable importance.

Collective Efficacy and Militant Social Action

The task of social change has never been an easy one, even in representative political systems. Those who seek to alter inequitable institutional practices encounter stiff opposition from powerholders and vested interests, who benefit from the system and use their power to keep it in place. The beneficiaries build their privileges and entitlements into protective laws, processes, and institutional structures (Gardner, 1972). When large sectors of society also benefit from inequitable social arrangements, these sectors lend widespread support to perpetuation of the status quo. They excuse high levels of physical force for social control but disapprove of protest for social change (Blumenthal, Kahn, Andrews, & Head, 1972). Institutional barriers and coercive threats deter attempts to alter social conditions that adversely affect human lives.

Authoritarian regimes wield control by brute force. They go to great lengths to curb the mobilization of collective action by challengers. Autocratic rulers keep a tight hold on the mass media and other vehicles of expression. They ban public associations, infiltrate covert ones, and operate elaborate surveillance systems to block people from organizing themselves into a forceful opposition. These suppressive practices create suspicion and distance among people. Repressive regimes stifle opportunities to build a sense of collective efficacy through group attainments. Challengers, therefore, have to create belief in their collective capability to rout their oppressors largely through the modeled successes of others who, under similar circumstances, toppled autocratic regimes by massive collective action.

Warranted social reforms can be blocked for some time by the rule of force, but at high costs to the society and the enlargement of oppositional activities. Powerholders find it progressively more difficult to exercise social control as harsh conditions and maltreatment heighten the level of resistance. They are eventually forced to make small concessions in an effort to placate the public demand. In doing so, they expose their vulnerability. Concessions raise challengers' sense of collective efficacy to force major reforms. Others who had believed that collective action would be futile are emboldened by the modeled successes to join the ranks of the challengers. Boosts in perceived collective efficacy are accompanied by rising expectations of gaining benefits and lowered perceived risk of incurring costs.

It is often said that hopelessness breeds militant social action, but the evidence disputes this view. Of the people living under inequitable and degrading conditions, comparatively few take active measures to force desired social change (Bowen, Bowen, Gawser, & Masotti, 1968; Sears & McConahay, 1969). In fact, severe privation is more likely to produce feelings of hopelessness and fatalistic resignation than militant action. The challenging question is not why some people who are subjected to maltreatment protest, but why most of them acquiesce to dismal living conditions amidst affluence. Threat of punitive sanctions can stifle protest and forceful action, but that is only part of the story. Explanations of political activism under conditions of impoverishment and degradation have been recast in terms of relative privation rather than in terms of objective levels of aversive conditions. For example, Davies (1969) reports that revolutions are most likely to occur when a period of social and economic betterment that instills rising expectations is followed by a sharp reversal in living conditions. Level of privation alone, whether measured in absolute or relative terms, is a weak predictor of militant action (McPhail, 1971).

Since most people who feel relatively deprived do not resort to forceful means, aversive privation is not in itself a sufficient cause of collective action. Additional factors determine whether discontent will take confrontational forms or some other behavioral expression. We saw earlier that confrontational activism is governed by a sense of purpose, a sense of efficacy to carry out protest activities in the face of risks, and expectations that such a course of actions will eventually bring about meaningful change. Applying a multideterminant approach to militant activism, Gurr (1970) examined the magnitude of civil disorder in Western nations as a function of three sets of factors. The first is the level of social discontent arising from economic decline, oppressive restrictions, and social inequities. The second factor is the traditional acceptance of force to achieve social change. Some societies disavow militant tactics, while others regard mass protests and coups d'état as legitimate means of change. The third factor is the balance of coercive power between the system and the challengers as measured by the amount of military, police, industrial, labor, and foreign support the protagonists can marshal on their side. Having coercive power raises people's beliefs that they have the means to compel change. The analysis reveals that when the tactics used are considered acceptable and challengers possess coercive power, they will use less extreme forms of collective protest to produce desired changes within the social system, and not much discontent is required. Revolutionary violence, however, requires widespread discontent and strong coercive power by challengers, whereas tactical traditions are of less importance.

People are not empty vessels shuffled about mechanically by external forces. Structural social conditions operate through the psychosocial processes of the individuals executing the actions. Goldstone (1994) casts the structural conditions conducive to collective militant action into the rationalistic process model. Groups resort to protest when they believe the payoffs exceed the penalties for such actions. The social dynamics shift expectations in favor of protest action as the strength of the regime weakens, the elite sectors of the society withdraw their support, and the protestors grow in number and solidarity. These are the types of social conditions that would instill in challengers a strong belief that it is within their power to force social changes. Otherwise, they would have little reason to expect that group protest would be effective. Any rationalistic model of political activism should include efficacy beliefs that have been shown in other applications of such models to increase explanatory and predictive power.

Consistent with efficacy theory, studies of militant activism indicate that detrimental conditions instigate collective protest not in those who have lost hope but in the more efficacious members whose efforts at social and economic betterment have met with at least some success (Bandura, 1973). Consequently, they have reason to believe that changes in social systems or their practices can be brought about through forceful group action. Among the members of dissident groups, those who protest social inequities and maltreatment, compared to inactive members, are generally better educated; have greater self-pride; have a stronger belief in their ability to influence events in their lives; and favor coercive measures, if necessary, to improve their living conditions (Caplan, 1970; Crawford & Naditch, 1970). In most nations, university students, rather than the severely underprivileged segments of the society, are the

spearhead of political activism (Lipset, 1966). They are the ones most likely to initiate protest movements that eventually force social reforms and topple oppressive regimes. Results of comparative studies indicate that people who are most disposed to social activism generally come from family backgrounds in which the exercise of social influence has been modeled and rewarded (Keniston, 1968; Rosenhan, 1970). Successful modeling, however, which serves as a major vehicle of social diffusion, can substantially alter the personal and social correlates of social activism over time. Those who initiate collective action are likely to believe more strongly in their efficacy to accomplish social changes than do later adopters. Later adopters need greater assurance that they can successfully execute forceful tactics and have something to gain by it. Modeled capability and utility can, over time, enable and embolden the initially less confident.

The media system is now a major vehicle for political and social change. The rate of change is greatly accelerated by instantaneous televised modeling of efficacious collective action. This is strikingly illustrated in the unprecedented speed with which the Communist regimes were toppled in Eastern Europe. People living under oppressive rule watched, on television, the East Germans bring down the Berlin Wall and topple their autocratic rulers by massive collective action. The tactic of successful mass action was immediately adopted by those in despotic regimes. The challengers in Germany carried placards in English, French, and Spanish, as well as in German, to gain worldwide support. They selected leaders who spoke English and could talk in sound bites. They transformed the sociopolitical order with an astounding rapidity that stunned the world, including political specialists.

Dispersed occurrences of similar practices do not necessarily reflect modeling processes. Common circumstances can produce similar behavior in different places without there having been any communication between them. A modeling enablement process is indicated by several criteria (Bandura, 1986a). First, there is close resemblance of the key features between the modeled activities and the occurrences elsewhere. When the modeled practices include a novel combination of elements, there is no mistaking the source, because there is little chance that unique resemblances could appear in so many places by sheer coincidence. Second, the modeled practices and the ones that occur elsewhere appear close together in time, with the originating ones appearing first. Third, the diffusion follows a differential spatial pattern — similar practices appear in locales where the novel behavior has been saliently modeled, but not in the places where it received little notice or was not displayed. Fourth, modeling influences spark an accelerating rise in similar practices as widespread adoptions create increasing modeling supports for further occurrences of the new behavior. And finally, the rate of adoption varies as a function of factors that are known to facilitate or deter modeling.

The rapid toppling of various Communist regimes by the similar strategy of massive collective action indicates a modeling enablement process rather than independent concurrent origination. The social discontent was widespread but, as Braithwaite (1994) documents, the same collective strategy was adopted in countries with quite different structural conditions. They differed in oppressiveness, economic viability, ethnic diversity, size, strength of the ruling clique, and degree of evolution from a centrally planned economy toward a market economy. Structural conditions are clearly only part of the story. Braithwaite argues that the modeling theory of political enablement provides a better explanation than does structural theory for the timing and form of collective action that swept the regimes. The collective strategy rapidly diffused because it was shown to be achieving successful results. Televised influence in contests of power can serve to fortify social control as well as promote social change. The Chinese dissidents were similarly emboldened by the modeled emancipatory success of forceful collective action against oppressive regimes. But the publicized counterreactions were different. The Chinese populace watched on CNN the militia breaking down doors and arresting student activists as it was happening. Live portrayal of brutal countermeasures promptly curbed the spread of the uprising.

Building Community-Wide Efficacy for Social Change

Shaping the social future through genuine institutional change is a long, tortuous process. There are many steps that people can take in the interim, however, to change their lives for the better by exercising control over local living conditions over which they can command influence. The formidable challenge is to build and mobilize a community-wide sense of efficacy in people who have come to regard many of the aversive aspects of their lives as beyond their control. Among community organizers, Alinsky devised some of the most insightful principles and strategies for converting social apathy to community-wide efficacy (Alinsky, 1969, 1971; Reitzes & Reitzes, 1984).

Alinsky was a masterful community organizer and strategist, but his acerbic and flamboyant style did not endear him to academicians, political radicals, or political operatives. He regarded militant activists as "rhetorical radicals" delivering fiery polemics without producing any tangible results. He viewed large-scale federalized programs for the disadvantaged as patronizing self-maintaining bureaucracies rather than as vehicles for enabling the disadvantaged with the means and self-beliefs to exert better control over their lives. His approach to collective enablement was founded on the cardinal principle of self-reliance: "Never do anything for someone that they can do for themselves."

Disillusionment with large bureaucratized programs is no grounds for pessimism about people's capability to shape a better future for themselves if they are helped in the right way. The history of social interventions amply documents that the programs that work best are those that promote self-help. Disenchantment with many of the large-scale government programs has shifted emphasis from doing things for people to finding ways of enabling them by developing their talents and providing support structures to do things for themselves.

In Alinsky's enablement model, social changes are accomplished through the exercise of power. Equitable services and treatment, he argued, are not acts of charity by powerholders but must be extracted from them by concerted effort. Social power comes in three forms: political power, the power of money, and the power of numbers. The disadvantaged lack political leverage and economic clout. But they have the power of numbers if their efforts are well organized and channeled. Collective community action provides the vehicle for effecting desired changes.

The role of a community organizer is not to solve people's problems for them but to help develop their capabilities to operate as a continuing potent force for bettering their lives and upholding their sense of self-worth and dignity. The organizer serves as the community enabler rather than as the implementer of action plans. The initial task is to ferret out and develop local leaders who can unite the community for common cause. The community must set up an organization to shape its collective efforts if it is to achieve its common interests. People have to develop organizational mechanisms for identifying key issues, selecting common goals, and devising and applying strategies for collective action. The disconsolate and fragmented character of disadvantaged communities impedes effective unified action. Therefore, the major task is to construct a self-directing community that unifies, enables, and motivates its residents. They are made aware that many of their individual problems are shared social problems that can be alleviated only by working together. Once mobilized, they have the means to improve their social and economic life.

The divergent factions in the community are forged into a unified force by appeal to their self-interests. None of the factions are likely to achieve what they want on their own, but by supporting one another's aspirations they can realize those of special personal concern. This is by no means an easy task. The more diverse the self-interests, the harder it is to unite people in collective action. To maintain a coalition of diverse self-interest requires the pursuit of solutions to the various problems plaguing the community. Residents are also unified around shared concerns. These include deficient municipal and health services, failing schools, exploitive landlords and merchants, and lack of job opportunities. A council representing the different social factions serves as the bargaining agent for the community. Successes in working together help to establish a norm of mutual assistance.

This enablement model enlists motivational goals in their most effective forms. Goals should be explicit ones that bear on people's daily lives rather than abstract ones. They should be realizable through concerted effort. They should be structured proximally to provide tangible evidence of progress. The careful structuring of goals is especially crucial for the initial life problems selected for improvement when community leaders are unpracticed in dealing with the establishment and most participants harbor doubts about their collective capability to extract major concessions from ruling officials. Early successes build trust in the leaders and affirm the community's power to effect changes. Once the credibility of a community to take unified action is established by deed, the mere threat of group action can be effective without having to carry it out. Perceived power is sufficient to goad negotiations.

Enablement of communities for social change produced many tangible victories in the face of daunting obstacles (Horwitt, 1989). A sense of community efficacy is not an everlasting property, however. Communities change in their social makeup over time. Moreover, changing social realities present new problems calling for new types of solutions that must be negotiated in different power relations. Collective community efficacy, therefore, may require periodic renewal with fresh leadership and revitalized communal commitments organized and channeled by supportive guidance. The staying power of community organizations depends heavily, of course, on continued success in producing tangible results. Problems of perceived powerlessness are no longer confined to the urban poor. Members of the shrinking middle class similarly express a growing sense of powerlessness to exercise control over their economic livelihood and the deteriorating quality of urban life. Many see the future as holding even more insecurity and social malaise for them and their children. More and more of them are losing faith in the integrity and ability of their governmental systems to act in their interests. The net result is a growing social fragmentation and civic and political disengagement. The mobilization of the middle class for efficacious citizen action was an emerging interest in Alinsky's model of collective enablement for social change (Nordon, 1972).

The vehicle for developing talented community organizers is a major legacy of Alinsky to the field of community enablement (Horwitt, 1989; Reitzes & Reitzes, 1984). The inherent strength of an operative model is best shown if it continues to function successfully after undergoing a change in leadership. Clearly, community enablement is very much alive and thriving. It is not only dispersing nationally but is expanding in scope and social influence. New protégés are building constituencies for efficacious collective action in more and more communities throughout the nation at a time of growing estrangement from governmental systems. Many of the elements of the Alinsky model are rooted in sound principles of social change and, hence, are essential ingredients in any effective approach to collective enablement. The new adaptations of the model, however, have shed the blazoned confrontational tactics and the strident language of power politics. The confrontational mode has been supplanted by a negotiatory mode. There has also been a shift in the focus of efforts from galvanizing a community around contentious issues to developing people's competencies, raising faith in their capabilities, and building strong communal ties for accomplishing shared purposes. By acting on their belief of collective efficacy, people are improving many aspects of their lives through collective self-help.

This is not to say that the exercise of group coercive power is now passé in community efforts to alter social systems or their practices. Quite the contrary. Even the nonviolent tactical approaches used by Gandhi (1942) and King (1958) were socially and morally coercive weapons wielded in a principled way through the force of numbers to change power relations and oppressive institutional practices that violated the most basic of human values. Many of the changes people seek cannot be achieved without fighting for them, because those of entrenched power are intent on preserving arrangements that protect their vested interests. The modern version of the community enablement model alters the style of how group pressure is wielded. Once the fight for recognition is won, community agents can transact their negotiations in a more courtly manner in accordance with the altered power relations. In addition, the modern model devotes greater effort to building people's efficaciousness and communal bonds as the source of collective power for effecting social change.

Many of the social and economic problems communities face are of regional and national origin. Therefore, efforts to improve the quality of life must extend beyond the confines of the community to regional and national legislative activities. Local power bases are being merged into regional alliances for this purpose (Greider, 1992). For example, Cortes, a brilliant Alinsky protégé who oversees a growing Texas network of organized constituencies, convened 150 community organizers and their delegates from across the state to address solutions to seemingly intractable educational problems. They gave progress reports on local projects designed to increase parents' involvement in the educational process, enhance students' scholastic attainments, raise scholarship funds from the business community, reduce violence in the schools, and promote school-based management. By sharing information about successful programs, people are spared the failures of trial and error and can effect desired changes faster. They also drafted an action agenda for school reform. Political candidates did attend this gathering, but they were invited to listen to the participants rather than to deliver their customized self-serving speeches. The coalition convenes huge statewide conventions. Electoral power commands political attention and strengthens social influence.

Other alliances of constituencies modeled on collective enablement are being formed elsewhere (Horwitt, 1989). Some of these efforts are shaping public policies. For example, one such project transformed, with interdenominational political and financial support, a devastated area of Brooklyn into several thousand new houses for families with low incomes. Federal regulations were altered to encourage similar housing projects supported by a combination of public and private financing. These wide-reaching efforts at building efficacious communities illustrates how participatory politics at the local level can be forged into a strong national force for social change. There are different paths to social change (Goldstone, 1994). In the centralized approach, reform efforts are directed at the national level. In the decentralized approach, national changes are achieved by expanding local power bases to the point at which they can exercise considerable influence over central political systems. These are complementary, rather than incompatible, strategies of social change.

Changing social realities call for additional adaptations of models of collective enablement for bettering the quality and course of people's lives. The internationalization of monetary and market forces is exerting a strong influence on the economic and social life of societies. Controlling influences that act remotely through mazelike global networks are not easily modifiable. Because they operate outside national borders, people have to rely heavily on national leaders to act on their behalf as negotiating agents with transnational systems. In short, in seeking to exercise some measure of control over their lives, people have to direct their efforts at the practices not only of local, regional, and national systems but of international ones as well. We will revisit this issue later.

The preceding model of collective enablement strives for a broad scope and reach of social influence. Some people collectively seek better access to, and control over, services and resources that are specific to their life circumstances. Their efforts tend to be more limited in scope but no less important to their lives. Many are members of disadvantaged or marginalized sectors of society who lack resources and see few opportunities to improve their plight. Much of their effort is consumed by the daily struggle for survival. Such deleterious social conditions incur heavy personal and social costs. The need to focus on prevention of human problems rather than on costly remediation or social control has been widely acknowledged but not practiced much. Some advocates of the preventive approach set it within a broader social-systems perspective that promotes not only personal change to deal more effectively with the environment but also collective community enablement to change environmental conditions that stunt human development and breed dysfunction (Rappaport, 1987; Rappaport & Seidman, in press).

In these group enablement programs, which are usually couched in the language of empowerment, people are taught how to exert influence over community practices that affect their well being. In this efficacy-building process, they need early experiences in producing tangible results to convince themselves that they have the capability to change the environment in which they live. Having gained some success, they come to believe that they can overcome tougher problems. Much is written about collective empowerment, with anecdotal reports of success. But there is a paucity of empirical evidence on how well such interventions work, and even less on how they produce their effects when they do succeed. The vagueness of the omnibus term *empowerment*— which is often presented as a mix of action strategies, psychological states, likely outcomes, and contexts of application — impedes advances in the field. The few efforts at empirical verification of effectiveness typically rely on time-series designs that assess the changes accompanying the introduction of a group enablement intervention (Fawcett, Seekins, Whang, Muiu, & Balcazar, 1984). When the essential ingredients of collective enablement models are poorly specified, there is uncertainty about how to put them into practice and disseminate those that happen to work.

The collective enablement programs take different forms, but the shared assumption is that they work in part by enhancing people's sense of efficacy to bring about changes in their lives. Studies in which this mediating process is assessed provide some evidence that training in group advocacy skills raises both personal and collective efficacy and increases actions designed to bring about desired changes (Yeich & Levine, 1994). Indeed, groups with good leadership can become quite re-sourceful in altering community policies and practices through collective initiatives that improve everyday life (Balcazar, Mathews, Francisco, Fawcett, & Seekins, 1994). A group acting alone, however, is less successful in producing legislative changes despite repeated efforts. Influencing legislators requires greater leverage through alliances with groups of diverse constituencies working in partnership.

In most of the forgoing applications, groups are taught how to negotiate collectively with agencies to increase access to public resources and improve social services. There are self-help groups in which people organize to help themselves to overcome intractable problems by creating their own subcommunity and resources. In this more generative form of collective efficacy, people create a self-governing community where they educate themselves, manage their own affairs, and create their own businesses that provide opportunities and resources for their self-development. The adaptation problems may involve, among other things, severe narcotic addiction, alcoholism, or debilitating psychosocial dysfunctions. These self-governing communities approach tenacious problems of living from a different perspective than do professional service systems (Riessman & Carroll, 1995). The latter tend to view such difficulties as symptoms of underlying pathologies or inherent defects. The remediations, which are heavily centered on the individual, focus on symptom management, medications, and fortifying personal vulnerabilities with coping skills to withstand environmental demands. The collective enablement approach is more socially oriented, builds on strengths rather than dwelling on deficits, and encompasses sociostructural factors among the sources and remedies for human problems (Azrin, 1976; Fairweather, Sanders, Cressler, & Maynard, 1969; Silbert, 1984). Through mutual help, members develop their competencies, strengthen beliefs in their capabilities, and garner needed resources to improve their lives. They achieve this not only by changing themselves but by creating living environments that remove impediments and expand opportunities. The communal ties, social supports, and guidance about how to exercise better control over their lives instill a sense of purpose and hope.

Self-help groups usually make no pretense of being service systems. Consequently, they do not systematically measure attrition rates, outcomes, and follow-up success rates. There is no question, however, that they often succeed in restructuring the lives of people who lack resources and who have histories of having gained little from professional services. Moreover, the few comparative studies that are available affirm the efficacy of approaches that operate on a collective enablement model (Azrin, 1976; Fairweather et al., 1969). Self-governing communities are more successful in changing people's lives for the better than are professional services.

ENABLEMENT BY MEDIA MODES OF INFLUENCE

An uninformed public is apt to be an ineffective, if not an apathetic, one. The mass media provide a major forum for bringing public attention to issues of social concern. Moreover, the media shape how people think about the issues by the way in which they structure them. The social debate takes different forms depending on whether the common problems people face are framed in terms of public policy solutions or individual remedies. Human problems need to be personalized to generate public interest and support, but then the concern should be shifted to policy considerations. The general public must be informed, motivated, and its collective efforts channeled to promote enactment of desired policies and to ensure their implementation in accordance with policy objectives. Effective use of the media, therefore, is an integral part of collective efforts to influence policymakers, legislators, and those who run regulatory and service agencies. The broadcast media enable advocates to reach millions of people simultaneously. Moreover, the discourse the media generate amplifies their efforts.

Media Use for Policy Initiatives

The general public has neither the economic resources nor the political clout to gain easy access to the broadcast media. Given these impediments, it requires a great deal of ingenuity to gain entry to the communications media and dramatize issues of concern in ways that can move the public to action. Wallack and his colleagues have codified many of the principles and effective strategies for using the media to influence public policies that can improve people's lives (Wallack et al., 1993). The authors remind us that media advocacy involves much more than just strategies for how to gain access to media outlets and frame issues for high social impact.

The responsiveness of the media to the public interest will depend partly on the strength of the public voice. Therefore, a good part of media advocacy is devoted to building coalitions and teaching community groups how to promote their policy initiatives through a variety of media outlets. Advocates must cultivate relationships with newscasters and journalists as trustworthy resources for ideas and background information on contentious issues. In the interest of objectivity and a lively story, the media usually air both sides of an issue, which provides advocates with a lot of free coverage. Indeed, presenting one's messages on newscasts, either in reaction to news events or by creating newsworthy ones that capture public attention, is considered to be the core of media advocacy.

Science plays an influential role in shaping public policy. Public advocacy needs to draw on credible data to add force to policy efforts and inform the policy recommendations. For example, evidence that second-hand smoke is a health hazard made it in most people's self-interest to support a ban on smoking in the workplace and various public places. Advocates must know how to translate scientific evidence into language that the public can understand and to counter efforts to discredit the integrity of the data. The targeted industries typically mount public relations campaigns and heavy lobbying efforts to thwart the public initiatives. It takes sustained effort, usually by a coalition of advocacy groups with common purpose working together, to prevail. Forging working alliances with diverse interest groups that have their own agendas and internal politics calls for a high level of perceived coordinative efficacy. The coordinators must focus the groups' efforts on a common purpose, negotiate consensus on the best way to pursue it, and garner the necessary resources and technical assistance. Electronic networking makes it easier to build relationships, exchange plans and strategies, and monitor advocacy activities both locally and nationally. Alliances will not stick together for long, especially in the face of intimidating counterreactions, unless they are strongly committed to a common guiding purpose and firmly believe that they can fulfill it collaboratively.

Entertainment Media in Social Change

Fictional dramatic presentations in the broadcast media provide another means of enabling people to achieve changes that have widespread social impact. Curbing global population growth is one example. Burgeoning population growth is the foremost and by far the most urgent global problem. The environmental degradation that it produces increasingly threatens the very habitability of the planet. Environmental degradation is affected by population size, the level of consumption, and the damage to the ecosystem caused by the technologies used to supply the consumable products (Ehrlich, Ehrlich, & Daily, 1995). The global ecosystem cannot sustain burgeoning populations and high consumption of finite resources.

There are finite limits to the earth's carrying capacity. The combination of high fertility rates, increased longevity, and consumptive appetites whetted by aggressive marketing and pressures for continuous economic growth thwart progress toward ecologically sustainable development in which economic betterment is achieved without destroying the environment. In the absence of disastrous ecological effects, economic forces typically override environmental concerns. Sustainability concerns not only ecological and economic conditions but also the quality of social life. Arresting population growth has become an imperative for survival. The challenge is to reduce the number of offspring to or below replacement levels. Widespread poverty in developing nations contributes to this mounting crisis. A burdensome population growth, in turn, degrades the standard of living by depleting resources produced through economic development. Altering consumptive styles of behavior in keeping with sustainable development presents the other formidable challenge to forestall mounting degradation of the global condition. Moreover, people need to be provided with guidance, incentives, and social supports for livelihoods that ensure the sustainability of the environment.

There are many factors that give rise to large families. Children serve as a source of labor and support parents in their older years. Male resistance to contraception and viewing offspring as symbols of male virility adds to the family count. Relegating women to a subservient role in which they have little say about family matters and restricting their educational opportunities commits them to a life of early and frequent childbearing. Stemming the tide of the soaring population, therefore, requires not only economic remedies but also changes in social norms and in people's belief systems and behavioral practices. People must understand how frequent childbearing compromises the kind of life that they and their offspring will be able to lead. Unless they see family planning as improving their welfare, they have little incentive to adopt it. Simply providing contraceptive services is not enough. The creative use of the communications media for motivating people to regulate their child bearing provides one illustration of human enablement to limit family size. Unlike ethnically objectionable approaches that impose coercive sanctions, violate human rights, or disregard the welfare of women, this approach favors personal choice in childbearing.

The format, which has now been adopted worldwide, was originally developed by Sabido (1981) to promote society-wide changes through televised modeling in dramatic serials. The episodes depict in captivating drama the daily lives of people, some of whom are on ruinous life-course trajectories, while others strive resiliently to improve their quality of life. The format was creatively founded on the basic sociocognitive principles in which efficacious modeling serves as the principal means to inform, motivate, and enable people to make a better life for themselves (Bandura, 1986a). The dramatic serials serve as an excellent vehicle for modeling family planning, women's equality, good health practices, and a variety of effective life skills in family, occupational, and community relations. The first feature capitalizes on the power of social modeling to alter attitudes, values, and lifestyle patterns. Positive models depict beneficial lifestyles, negative models portray detrimental ones, and transitional models are shown transforming their lives by discarding deleterious styles of behavior and adopting beneficial ones. In the literacy dramatic series, the most popular soap opera performer was cast in the role of instructor to take advantage of the attractable and aspirational value of prestigeful modeling.

The initial project addressed the problem of illiteracy in Mexico. In an effort to reduce widespread illiteracy, the government had launched a national self-instruction program. People who were skilled at reading were urged to organize small self-study groups in which they would teach others how to read with instructional material that had been specifically developed for this purpose. The national appeal produced a disappointing social response, however. Sabido selected the soap opera serial, which has a vast loyal following, as the best format for reaching, enabling, and motivating people with problems of illiteracy. The main story line in the dramatic series centered on the engaging and informative experiences of a self-instruction group.

The second feature relied on model similarity to persuade viewers that they too possessed the capabilities to master the skills that were being modeled. Actors in the learner roles were cast to represent the different segments of the population that presented problems of illiteracy. The self-study group included adolescents, young adults, and middle-aged and elderly individuals. Another feature was designed to gain and hold attentional engagement in the broadcast series. Melodramatic embellishments and emotive music gave dramatic intensity to the episodes to ensure high attentional involvement of the viewers.

Still another feature provided vicarious motivators to pursue the self-education program. The dramatic series depicted the substantial benefits of literacy both for personal development and for national efficacy and pride. The power of vicarious influence can be enhanced by contrasting modeling. The benefits of the functional lifestyle are contrasted with the miseries of the dysfunctional one by different characters in the drama. Other characters personify models accomplishing desired changes in their lives by adopting the functional values and lifestyles. Viewers are especially prone to draw inspiration from, and identify with, such transforming models through perceived similarity in life circumstances. Seeing models similar to themselves change their lives for the better not only conveys strategies for how to do it but raises viewers' sense of efficacy that they too can succeed.

Another feature was designed to increase the memorability of the modeled events. Epilogues summarizing the modeled messages were added to aid the symbolic coding of information for memory representation. It is of little value to motivate people to change if they are not provided with appropriate guides, resources, and environmental supports to realize those changes. Enlisting and creating environmental supports is an additional and especially helpful feature for expanding and sustaining social changes encouraged by the communications media. To facilitate media-promoted changes, all the instructional material was provided in an easily accessible way by the educational agency. In addition, the series often used real-life settings showing the actors obtaining the instructional material from an actual distribution center and eventually graduating in an actual graduation ceremony. The epilogues informed the viewers of this national self-education program and encouraged them to take advantage of it. Epilogues serve as a convenient vehicle for providing referrals to agencies and self-help groups where viewers can gain useful information and the services they need.

A prior interview study had revealed a pervasive self-inefficacy barrier that dissuaded people from enrolling in the national program. Some believed that reading skills could be acquired only when one is young. Since they had passed the critical period, they could no longer learn to read. Many others believed that they personally lacked the capabilities to master such a complex skill. Still others felt that they were unworthy of having an educated person devote their time to them. These self-handicapping misbeliefs were modeled by the actors and corrected by the instructor as she persuaded them that they possessed the capabilities to succeed. The dramatic series included humor, conflict, and engrossing discussions of the subjects being read. The episodes showed the models struggling in the initial phases of learning and then gaining progressive mastery and self-pride in their accomplishments.

Millions of viewers watched this series faithfully. Indeed, the viewership exceeded that of the standard soap operas. In the assessment of effects, compared to nonviewers, viewers of the dramatic series were much more informed about the national literacy program and expressed more positive attitudes about helping one another to learn. The rate of enrollment in the national self-instruction program was 99,000 in the year before the televised series and 840,000 during the year of the series. As people develop self-conceptions and skills that enable them to exercise better control over their lives, they serve as models, inspirations, and even tutors for others. This concomitant social influence can vastly extend the direct impact of televised modeling. In the year following the series, another 400,000 people enrolled in the self-instruction program.

A similar televised modeling series was developed to promote society-wide family planning in an effort to reduce the nation's burgeoning population growth. Before broadcasting the series, the producers enlisted the endorsement of Catholic Church leaders by focusing on family planning rather than promoting particular contraceptive devices. A creative format of contrasting modeling portrayed the process and benefits of family planning. The positive family life of a small family, whose wife worked in a family planning clinic, was contrasted with that of a married sister burdened by a huge family and the accompanying impoverishment and distress. Much of the drama focused on the married daughter from the huge family, who was beginning to experience severe marital conflicts and distress over a rapidly expanding family. Consultation with the aunt served as the vehicle for modeling a great deal of information about how to manage marital discord and machismo behavior, how to deal with male resistance to contraception and family planning, how to communicate openly in the family, and how to escape the many problems caused by a family overburdened with children. The young couple, who served as the transitional model, were shown gaining control over their family life and enjoying the accruing benefits with the help of a family planning center. A priest, who emphasized the need for responsible family planning, occasionally appeared in the dramas. At the end of some of the programs, viewers were informed about existing family planning services to facilitate media-promoted changes.

Records of the family planning centers revealed a 32 percent increase in the number of new contraceptive users over the number for the previous year of operation, before the series was televised. People reported that the television portrayal served as the impetus for consulting the centers. National sales of contraceptives rose between 4 and 7 percent in the preceding two years, whereas they increased by 23 percent in the year the program was aired. A set of serial dramas broadcast over several years was accompanied by a 34 percent drop in the birthrates.

Efforts to bring down the rate of population growth must address not only the strategies and benefits of family planning but also the role and status of women in societies in which they are treated subserviently. This was the dual message of a soap opera series televised in India. Sociocognitive principles are generalizable, but they must be tailored to the cultural context and social practices that spawn large families. In some societies, the status problems stem from machismo dominance; in others, from marriage and pregnancy at the onset of puberty with

no say in the choice of husband or the number and spacing of children; and in still others, from dispossession by polygamous marriages. In some societies, women are subjugated to the point where they are repeatedly beaten and are not even allowed to turn on a family radio. The modeling series in India was designed to raise the status of women as well as promote smaller family size. The drama centered on three generations of a lower middle class family who lived together in the same household (Singhal & Rogers, 1989). The episodes addressed a variety of themes about family life in the context of broader social norms and practices. The subthemes devoted particular attention to family harmony amidst differences among family members, elevation of the status of women in family life and their welfare socially, equal educational opportunities, gender bias in child rearing, choice in spouse selection, teenage marriage and parenthood, social integration, and family planning to limit family size. Some of the actors personified positive role models for gender equality; others were proponents of the traditional subservient role for women. Still others were transitional models. A famous Indian film actor reinforced the modeled messages in epilogues.

The melodramatic series was immensely popular, enjoying the top viewership on television and eliciting hundreds of thousands of letters from viewers offering advice and support to the characters. A study of a random sample of viewers revealed that the televised modeling promoted attitudes supportive of gender equality and limiting family size. Specifically, viewers reported that they had learned from the program that women should have equal opportunities and a say in decisions that affect their lives, that programs advancing the welfare of women should be encouraged, that cultural diversity should be respected, and that family size should be limited. The more aware viewers were of the messages being modeled, the greater was their support of women's freedom of choice in matters that affect them and of planning for small families (Brown & Cody, 1991).

Effective models of change often have limited social impact because they lack an adequate mechanism for social diffusion. Lack of expertise and resources creates a low sense of efficacy that operates as a barrier to adoptive behavior. Population Communications International removes this impediment by serving as the mechanism for diffusing globally the use of televised dramas to enhance the quality of family life and the status of women and to promote the use of family planning (Ryerson, 1994). This center acts as a liaison between governmental and nongovernmental agencies and private sectors in getting funding for the productions. In addition, it provides technical assistance in training television producers and writers, who sensitively tailor the dramas to their own cultural circumstances and values. Through this global effort, the serial dramas are now being used worldwide. The center also promotes cooperation and collaboration among nongovernmental organizations concerned with population, environmental, and health problems. Alliances increase the chances of success by mobilizing and focusing people's efforts to improve the quality of life for themselves and their children. In addition, the center also works with media personnel to heighten their sensitivity to issues of population growth and environmental degradation in their broadcasts and in the story lines they create for fictional dramas. The success of these efforts is measured mainly in terms of lowered family size and increased contraceptive usage.

The diverse applications have yielded uniform findings. The dramatic serials are an extraordinarily effective vehicle for reaching vast numbers of people over a prolonged period. Viewers get deeply involved in the lives of the televised characters. These serials are among the most popular on television, each engaging millions of fans. Radio versions of the televised series can reach vast rural populations. Airing of the televised serials is consistently followed by an appreciable drop in birthrates in country after country. For example, the decline in births per woman was 34 percent in Mexico and 23 percent in Brazil, and Kenya achieved a 58 percent increase in contraceptive usage and a 24 percent drop in birthrate. These types of changes call into question the widespread belief that economic development is a prerequisite for reducing fertility rates. One need not wait until the populace gets rich to bring birthrates down.

Changes following the introduction of dramatic serials must be interpreted with caution, of course, because some of the changes may be due to other social influences operating concurrently. Consistent evidence that, in each country, birthrates decline upon introduction of the dramatic serials increases confidence that they had something to do with the changes. This is especially true if births were rising over the preceding years. A decline following a rising baseline is more persuasive than a decline following a stable baseline, but it is suspect in the context of a declining baseline unless the introduction of the dramatic serial accelerates the rate of decline. Given that the countries are adopting the serial dramas because of a burgeoning population, it is reasonable to assume that birth trajectories are rising rather than declining. Over time, large families typically sprout offspring exponentially.

Interpretation of the relationship between the serial dramas and birthrates presupposes knowledge about time lags as to when the changes in reproductive behavior and birthrates should begin to appear. The serial dramas run for at least a year. Some are rerun or broadcast as new sequels. The decision to use contraceptives and to have fewer children can affect birthrates during the serials or shortly thereafter. So the time lags can be short. The time lag for additive secondary effects — where the lifestyle changes of viewers, in turn, alter the lifestyles of their associates — can occur over a variable period. Changes in birthrates over time reflect both the first-order and second-order influences. The presence of secondary effects in the time-lag results is of little pragmatic concern because the more positive influences televised modeling sets in motion, the better. But these effects do complicate evaluation of how much the observed changes are due directly to the serial dramas alone. Interviews with viewers about their decisions about contraceptive usage and the desired number and spacing of children could tell us what time lag to expect. Interviews could also identify whether the decision to limit family size was due to the influence of the serial dramas, to the lifestyle changes of viewers affected by the drama, or to some other sources.

Thus, assessment of the impact of serial dramas requires time-series analyses in which the direction and rate of change following the introduction of the dramas in a society is evaluated against the birthrate trajectory over the preceding years. Moreover, multiple statistical controls are needed for changes in governmental policies, incentives, and resources that could affect birthrates. Televised modeling can have substantial impact if it serves as a means for bringing people to community settings and support groups, which then provide the extensive guidance and continuing incentives needed to realize personal changes. For example, the Sabido project designed to promote literacy through self-education explicitly linked media modeling to community educational services. The synergistic effect of modeling combined with the national effort enlisted numerous participants, whereas the national effort alone gained relatively few recruits.

The findings of other applications of the dramatic format on family planning speak more directly to the issue of causation. In Kenya, the higher the exposure to the series, the stronger the effects on birthrate and on reproductive behavior (Westoff & Rodriguez, 1995). Specifically, the broadcasts increased women's desire to limit family size and to achieve longer spacing between births. Higher media exposure also increased adoption and consistent use of new methods of contraception. These effects remained after controlling for life-cycle status and a host of socioeconomic factors such as ethnicity, religion, education, and urban-rural residence. Internal analyses of evaluation surveys revealed that the media influence was a major factor in raising motivation to limit birthrate and adopt contraception practices.

Countries containing regions with separate transmitters provide a natural control group. Under these conditions, the serial dramas can be aired in one region with another serving as a control. Following the formal evaluation, the serial can be aired in the control region and its effects measured. Comparative tests of this type are most informative if the regions do not differ initially in population characteristics, in governmental initiatives that can affect birthrates, or in their preceding birthrate trajectories. With only two regions available, random assignment of the intervention cannot ensure that the regions are similar to begin with. Should they differ at the outset, statistical adjustments can be made for the variation.

A controlled study was conducted in Tanzania to compare changes in contraception use in broadcast areas that received a radio dramatic series with a large area that did not (Vaughan, Rogers, & Swalehe, 1995). The program targeted both family planning and sexual and drug injection practices that increase vulnerability to infection with the AIDS virus. This study sheds light on a number of issues. Although, at the outset, the populace was reasonably well informed about contraception and AIDS prevention and favorably disposed toward such practices, they did not translate these attitudes into action. The problem was neither informational nor attitudinal but motivational. The dramatic series provided the impetus for action. Compared to the control region, exposure to the radio series significantly increased adoption of contraceptive methods, family planning services, and AIDS prevention practices. As in the Kenya study, the higher the exposure across national regions, the stronger were the effects. Perceived self-efficacy emerged as an important factor in regulating reproductive and risky behavior. The radio series increased listeners' beliefs that they could exercise control over their family size. Frequent listeners expressed a higher sense of efficacy than nonlisteners. Frequent listenership similarly increased both perceived efficacy and adoption of practices that prevent infection with the AIDS virus. This study also provides evidence of second-order influences. The more people listened to the broadcasts, the more they talked about family planning with friends and spouses.

Further refinement of the dramatic format requires assessment of mediating processes as well as outcomes. Such analyses examine how modeling episodes are structured and socially perceived and the types of efficacy and outcome beliefs they instill. Such knowledge provides guidelines for how to maximize intended positive effects and minimize unintended negative effects. Negative modeling must be structured with care. For example, in the

Indian serial drama, some of the viewers who subscribed to the culturally stereotypic role ended up siding with the negative stereotype being modeled as the desired exemplar (Singhal & Rogers, 1989). There are two ways in which this unintended effect can be weakened. One strategy is to accent the adverse consequences of the dysfunctional lifestyle. The second strategy is to have the contrasting negative models begin to express some self-doubt about their life view and acknowledge, albeit grudgingly, the legitimacy of granting women a greater say in their lives.

Showing models breaking subservient roles and cultural norms requires some negative reactions to reflect the social reality. But these discordant episodes should model effective strategies for managing such events successfully so that viewers come to believe that they can improve the quality of their lives by similar means used perseveringly. This requires incorporating many efficacy-enhancing elements in the transactional episodes. Occasional references to women leaders worldwide working to raise the status of women can serve as an additional source of inspiration and support. In cultures where women are massively subjugated, changing entrenched cultural norms is a slow, gradual process. They have a long way to go. When large power differentials exist in gender relations, the modeled strategies must be judicious rather than blatantly confrontational — which, in real life, can be risky.

As is true of any intervention, the use of television to foster social development raises ethical issues. How such efforts are evaluated will depend on the types of changes being promoted, the agents of change, the means used, and the choice and voluntariness of exposure to the influence. Dramatic serials for social change do not introduce influences where none existed before. Rather, they usually supplant daytime serials that focus heavily on the seamy side of human affairs in a social world full of discord, deception, and indignities. In contrast, the prosocial messages of the development serials encouraging literacy, family planning, gender equality, and social harmony and dignity operate in the service of personal and social betterment. In addition to upholding basic human values, safe-guards must be built into broadcasting operations to ensure that they are not perverted from their prosocial function. There is less chance of misuse when people have choices about what to watch rather than having messages imposed upon them by a monolithic system. Enlisting the broadcast media for social change thus calls for sensitivity to the social structures into which prosocial serials are introduced to ensure that the changes they promote will better people's lives.

ENABLEMENT FOR SOCIOCULTURAL CHANGE

Societies are continuously faced with pressures to change some of their traditional institutions and social practices in efforts to improve the quality of life. These benefits cannot be gained without displacing some entrenched customs and adopting new social organizations and technologies. The benefits of change thus carry some social costs. The basic principles governing the diffusion of innovations within a society operate similarly in the intercultural dissemination of new ideas and practices. Yet there are notable differences in how the principles are converted to functional systems and implemented. Foreign practices are rarely adoptable unaltered and in their entirety. Rather, imported elements are usually reshaped and synthesized with indigenous patterns into new forms befitting the host culture. In most instances, it is functional equivalents rather than exact replicas of foreign ways that are adopted. In addition, unless the borrowed elements are valued highly, advocates of new practices are likely to encounter stronger resistance in diffusing behavior from one culture to another than in diffusing behavior within the same culture.

Obstacles to Social Change

Adopting new institutional arrangements and practices initially has some negative effects that serve as impediments to change. Some of these are inherent in the acquisition process itself, especially during early transitional phases. New practices usually threaten existing status and power relations. In addition, adopters have to abandon secure routines and learn new ways of doing things. Many are reluctant to go through the intimidating and tedious process of mastering new competencies. Those with an insecure sense of efficacy are intimidated by the new demands and the prospect of failure. Adoption of innovations involving complex skills that are not easily acquirable is slow (Rogers & Shoemaker, 1971).

In addition to the demands for new competencies, uncertainties about the effects of the unfamiliar ways arouse apprehensions. If new practices were instantly beneficial, change would be welcomed. But social and physical technologies cannot be transplanted from one milieu to another without some adaptation and experimentation. Preliminary applications are usually plagued with problems and temporary setbacks. It is only after corrective adjustments have been made that success may be achieved in the new contexts. Even after the new ways have been adapted to local conditions and needs, the advantages that may accrue from the innovations usually do not become evident until they have been tried for a while. Promissory outcomes of unaccustomed practices are not the kinds of events that impel an uncertain public to action. The more delayed and the less obvious the outcomes, the weaker are the incentives for the adoptive behavior. It takes some doing to convert abstract futures into concrete, current motivators.

Judging the costs and benefits of innovations is further complicated by the fact that social functions are interdependent. A favorable change in one area of functioning can produce unforeseen adverse effects in other areas of life. Some sectors of society may profit from the innovations; others may suffer losses. Because innovations have mixed effects and promoters generally overstate their value, people are understandably wary of forsaking practices of established utility for new ones of possibly better but uncertain benefit. Those with limited means or insecure status can ill-afford to risk mistakes. As a result, most adhere to traditional ways until they see innovations produce benefits for the bolder adopters.

Innovations vary in how discordant they are with the prevailing values and social practices. Innovations that clash with existing customs create additional impediments to their adoption and diffusion. Some customs are fortified by beliefs and moral codes that portend hazardous consequences for the new ways. The influence exerted by belief over adoptive behavior derives partly from the social and moral sanctions applied to conduct that violates strongly held belief systems.

Even greater obstacles to sociocultural change can be erected by privileged groups that benefit from the existing social arrangements and, thus, have a strong vested interest in preserving them. They support changes that enhance their well-being but oppose those that jeopardize their social and economic status. They mount counterinfluence by bringing coercive pressure to bear on those who have the most to gain from reforms and are, therefore, more receptive to them. Under these conditions, little change will result unless adopters are protected from unauthorized coercion and the new practices are structured in ways that provide some benefits for all concerned. This requires creating interdependent arrangements that tie people's benefits to progress toward common goals. Through interdependence, people become vested in one another's gains.

If a privileged minority continues to undermine or block beneficial reforms, then institutional sanctions must be applied if any changes are to be achieved. But privilege is not so easily contravened. Enforcement of change presupposes that the implementing agencies have rewarding resources to offer to communities and their leaders, that the agencies possess the power to impose negative sanctions, and that they have sufficient public support to withstand the political repercussions of challenging privileged groups. All too often, those social agencies are run by officials who are beholden to the very vested interests opposing changes that do not suit them. With sufficient controlling influence, vested local interests can easily exploit programs for change to their own advantage. Those seeking to accomplish significant social changes must have a resilient sense of collective efficacy that the tough odds can be surmounted.

Properties of Efficacious Models of Diffusion

Much time and effort is spent developing effective models of social change, but there is little research on how best to promote their widespread adoption. Creating effective models alone does not guarantee their acceptance and social diffusion. Quite the contrary: New programs often arouse resistance to adoption for the many reasons already given. If efforts to diffuse effective programs are to succeed, people must be equipped with the skills, beliefs of personal efficacy, and incentives needed to overcome the initially unfavorable conditions associated with adopting new ways. A successful model of social diffusion has four major phases: (1) selecting an optimal site for introducing the innovation; (2) creating the necessary preconditions for change; (3) implementing a demonstrably effective program for the adoption of the innovations; and (4) using the power of successful example to disperse the innovation to other settings. The essential features of each of these phases of a diffusion model are presented in the paragraphs that follow.

With regard to site selection, some sectors of society are more receptive to new ways than others. Foisting new practices on those who oppose them does more harm than good. If new practices are forced upon unwilling sectors, they will implement them in deficient ways that ensure their failure. The failed trial removes further pressures for change. Such campaigns not only waste effort and resources and have discouraging results, but they also impede later applications, when conditions may be more favorable for change. Innovations are best introduced initially in settings where people are willing to try them, at least on a provisional basis. Successes can then serve as demonstration models for those who resist adopting the innovations because they are unsure about their feasibility and likely outcomes. The evident benefits gained by

successful adopters carry substantially more force than exhortations in overcoming resistance to innovation.

The preconditions for change are created by increasing people's awareness of the nature and potential benefits of the innovations. They need to be provided with information about the purpose of new practices, their relative advantages, and the ways in which adopting them are likely to improve their lives. Both direct and media presentations serve to inform and arouse interest in new practices. Failure to tailor information about the innovation to the particular interests and capabilities of would-be adopters hampers a diffusion program at the outset (Rogers & Adhikarya, 1979).

Programs of social change often fail because they do not proceed beyond the precondition stage aimed at informing people and altering their attitudes toward the innovations. Focus on attitude change as the principal means of promoting innovations assumes that attitudes determine behavior. This approach has not met with notable success. There is much debate as to whether attitudes influence behavior or behavior alters attitudes. Evidence suggests that both attitudinal and behavioral changes are best achieved by creating conditions that foster the desired behavior. After people behave in new ways, their attitudes accommodate to their actions (Abelson et al., 1968). It might be argued, however, that it is exceedingly difficult to get people to behave in ways that contradict entrenched attitudes. Such a view assumes that there is a tight linkage between attitudes and behavior. In fact, different types of behavior can be construed as consistent with the same attitude. If the new practices are highly beneficial, adopters either alter their attitudes to coincide with their new behavior or construe it in a manner consistent with their traditional beliefs.

Social cognitive theory addresses the motivation for change not as a problem of attitudes but in terms of explicit cognitive factors known to regulate human motivation and action (Bandura, 1986a). These factors include efficacy beliefs, various forms of outcome expectations, aspirations, and perceived impediments. These are the factors that must be addressed in efforts to motivate people to adopt new social practices that can improve their well-being.

A variety of supportive aids must be enlisted in the adoption phase. Social persuasion alone is not enough to promote adoptive behavior. To increase receptivity one must also create optimal conditions for learning the new ways, provide the resources and positive incentives for adopting them, and build supports into the social system to sustain them. Social persuasion and positive incentives are widely used as motivators when the changes being implemented depend on the consent of those whose lives are being affected. In authoritarian societies, coercive methods are heavily used as inducements for the changes sought by those who wield power. Change through coercion is achieved at the price of regimentation. There are other social costs as well. By arousing opposition, enforced change is difficult to maintain without continued social surveillance and punitive sanctions for noncompliance. All too often, the coterie of advisors to power-holders are too similar in their views, and pressures for consensus are too strong, to ensure that their collective judgments remain in close touch with social realities. When a centralized system does not allow for critical evaluation of its decisions by outsiders, there is high risk of misjudgment that can have ruinous social consequences (Barnett, 1967; Janis, 1972).

Implementing a program of social change requires transmitting knowledge and new sets of competencies to potential adopters. This is an especially crucial aspect of the process when the changes require mastering new technologies and ways of thinking and doing things, rather than merely tinkering with existing practices. Extra motivational aids and social supports are called for when the new practices clash with entrenched traditional ones, as is often the case. If new patterns of behavior are to be acquired, potential adopters must be provided with emulatable models to impart the necessary knowledge, values, and skills. These models must affirm adopters' capabilities to master the new ways. There are many ways of implementing modeling principles, some of which are more effective than others. The three-facet approach — modeling of the desired competencies, guided enactments that build proficiencies, and generalized applications of the new ways that verify their functional value — yields the most impressive results (Goldstein, 1973; Latham & Saari, 1979; Rosenthal & Bandura, 1978).

New practices must produce benefits if they are to gain wide acceptance. Unfortunately, the benefits of many innovations do not become evident until they have been applied for some time. Such temporal lags pose special motivational problems. Advocates often find themselves faced with the task of getting skeptical people to adopt and continue new practices for a long time before they can obtain any convincing evidence that the programs really bring desired results. As Erasmus (1961) has noted, innovations are most readily accepted when they produce prompt observable benefits and the causal relationship between new practices and favorable results can be easily verified.

When the advantages to be gained from innovations are considerably delayed, it is necessary to provide current incentives to sustain adoptive behavior until its inherent value becomes apparent. The temporary, substitute incentives may include monetary benefits, special privileges, social recognition, and other status-conferring rewards. Aspirations translated into attainable interim goals that convey a sense of progress also serve as motivators that help sustain efforts to realize hoped for changes (Bandura, 1991b; Locke & Latham, 1990). Many diffusion failures that are attributed to resistance arising from incompatible beliefs probably result from insufficient guidance and incentives to adopt unaccustomed practices.

Initiating the dissemination phase of sociocultural change can benefit greatly from the aid of vicarious motivators. There is nothing more persuasive than seeing effective practices in use. Successes achieved through innovation by initial adopters can be used to encourage others to try the new ways themselves. The greater the demonstrable benefits, the greater the dispersive power of example (Ostlund, 1974; Rogers & Shoemaker, 1971). This applies to social as well as technical innovations. New policies that provide improved solutions to social problems spread nationwide (Gray, 1973; Poel, 1976). Widespread modeling of beneficial innovations helps to weaken the various social impediments to adoption of new ways (Mansfield, 1968).

In early phases of dissemination, communications media can play an important role in fostering change by stimulating interest in new practices, teaching the needed skills, and publicizing the results. Positive incentives accelerate the diffusion of innovations. For example, in efforts to supplant burdensome agricultural practices with more productive ones in China, model villages and members who excelled in the new knowledge and skills were singled out and publicly honored to spread the practices to other regions (Munro, 1975). When the vicarious incentives of seeing benefits gained by adopters are insufficient to overcome resistance, direct incentives can aid the diffusion process. Oshima (1967) illustrates how the adoption of advanced agricultural and production technologies was hastened in Japan by offering subsidies to villages willing to serve as demonstration models. The model villages were then used to publicize the benefits of the new methods. In the United States, federal grants are given to states and localities as incentives to adopt new policies and programs. Policies with monetary incentives for adopting them diffuse to states faster than those without such incentives (Welch & Thompson, 1980).

Not only is verbal advice not enough to get adoption of innovations, neither is it sufficient to disperse them, even if they can change people's lives for the better. Promoting widespread social diffusion of programs of demonstrated value requires an effective mechanism for doing so. It must provide prospective adopters with instructive guidance, essential resources, and positive incentives for successful change. This point is illustrated in the research by Fairweather and his coworkers (1969). They compared three diffusion strategies for promoting a model of residential treatment for psychiatric populations that was more humane, less expensive, and considerably more effective in restoring positive functioning than the existing institutional approaches. Several hundred psychiatric hospitals were encouraged in one of three ways to adopt the model. In the informational strategy, the hospitals received an informative report describing the model with evidence of its multiple benefits. In the social persuasion strategy, the diffusers offered on-site workshops on how to implement the model with documentation of its benefits. In the enablement strategy, the diffusers offered to teach the staff how to implement the model and to provide them supportive supervision. The adoption rates were 1 percent for the informational strategy, 16 percent for the persuasory strategy, and 29 percent for the enablement strategy. Clearly, service bureaucracies are not easily influenceable, but a supportive enablement approach works best. This project underscores the need to examine the efficacy of alternative modes of diffusion with the same care and rigor as is devoted to the development of the models being diffused.

It is difficult to alter the practices of social systems, even those that are only marginally effective, from within. Those who run such systems have a vested interest in preserving the existing arrangements and are wary of trying new approaches. There is little incentive to do so, especially when the benefits of reform receive little public notice, but the failure of efforts to make changes are widely publicized, often with social repercussions that can jeopardize statuses or careers. Changes from within usually replace existing procedures and organizational arrangements with new versions that manage to leave the system functioning in essentially the same old way.

Social programs are often established by the government on a national scale before they have been tested adequately, if at all, for their effectiveness and unintended adverse consequences. Untested programs do not enjoy a high rate of functional effectiveness. Once such programs are instituted, those whose jobs depend on their continuance and special interest beneficiaries have a strong vested interest in preserving them (Gardner, 1972). Dysfunctional systems persist even when better ones are available if there is no adequate performance evaluation and no system of accountability, and significant changes carry some risk. Under such circumstances, agencies can be changed or replaced faster by devising successful programs on a limited scale outside the traditional structure. Concerned officials may be willing to risk a demonstration trial, but they understandably resist large-scale changes with uncertain costs and benefits of the innovation. With demonstrated success, the power of a superior alternative can then serve as the instrument of influence for social diffusion. If officials are held answerable for the results of their programs, ineffective practices cannot be long defended after new ones have been tried and proved better. In an enabling diffusion model, the diffusers provide the guidance and support for adapting and implementing the new system in different social settings.

Progress in improving social systems would be greatly facilitated if, as a standard policy, some resources were regularly allocated for developing and testing innovations. Development funding is a vital feature of production industries, which must improve what they produce if they are to survive. Competition provides a strong incentive to innovate. In public agencies that enjoy monopolies over given services, many of the practices that evolve are more likely to serve the interests and convenience of the staff than to maximize benefits for those the agencies are designed to serve. This is because better service to others often means more work for the staff without increased recompense. Improvements in service organizations are achieved more rapidly by rewarding good performances by alternative systems than by criticizing poor performances by a single system. Providing alternatives creates incentives for organizations to improve the quality of their services; otherwise, they lose their patronage.

Social Impact of Innovations

Major innovations can have profound impact on the society at large. They create new industries, alter institutional practices, and restructure how people live their lives. The benefits are usually bought at the price of some undesirable social consequences, not all of which are foreseeable. The mixed effects of innovations and the thorny value issues they raise have been analyzed extensively

elsewhere and will be discussed only briefly here (Bandura, 1986a). The social effects of innovations have received their greatest attention from programs designed to "develop" and "modernize" so-called underdeveloped societies with Western technologies. All too often, modernization gets defined largely as urbanization and industrialization, to the neglect of community self-development tailored to fit the indigenous conditions (McPhail, 1981; Rogers & Adhikarya, 1979).

When new technologies are introduced without addressing the social conditions that control access to them, development programs intended for the public good may, in fact, exacerbate social problems. One must distinguish between adverse effects that are part and parcel of an innovation and those that flow mainly from the social structure into which they have been injected. Gotsch (1972) illustrates how the same innovation creates a markedly different distribution of benefits in societies under different social structures. The innovation of tube wells enabled farmers to grow a second crop using irrigation during the arid summer season. In the social system of Pakistan, factional dissension among farmers of small landholdings impeded the cooperative pooling of resources needed to purchase the innovation. The development agencies gave the subsidized financial credit to the larger landholders who installed the irrigation system with profitable results. Virtually none of those with small landholdings did so. In the more cooperatively structured system of Bangladesh, the owners of minifarms formed cooperatives to install, in partnership, the technology they could not afford individually and nearly doubled their profits. Thus, the same technology widened the disparity between social and economic classes in one society but produced shared benefits in another one.

Goss (1979) argues that diffusion programs should be evaluated in terms of social distribution of benefits as well as their aggregate utility. This raises issues of equity. Verdicts about the worth of innovations ultimately rest on value systems. The same distribution of benefits can be viewed favorably or unfavorably, depending on whether it is judged from a utilitarian perspective or an equity perspective. In the utilitarian calculus, bringing the greatest sum benefit to the greatest number may require undermining the livelihood of some members in the system. For example, agriculture technologies that drive small farmers off their land into cities in search of work as laborers (Havens & Flinn, 1975) would be justified by utilitarians on the grounds that large-scale mechanized farming with fertilizers and insecticides produces crops more abundantly and more cheaply for the greatest number of consumers. When diffusion of innovations is viewed from an equity standpoint, the challenge is to create social arrangements that enable all to share in the benefits of innovation. The example just cited of cross-cultural diffusion of an irrigation system that distributes benefits evenly is a good case in point.

Self-efficacy theory approaches the issue of inequitable distribution of benefits in terms of creating equitable opportunity to make use of innovations. Opportunities to share in the proceeds of technical innovations are expanded for the less advantaged members of society by cultivating their talents, strengthening their belief in their capabilities to master the technologies, and assisting them with needed resources that enable them to succeed. The work of Roling and his colleagues typifies this approach (Roling, Ascroft, & Chege, 1976). Development agencies are usually created to encourage technical innovations in the society. Their location and operating procedures determine the ease of access to innovations and where the innovations will spread (Brown, 1981). Such agencies usually offer most assistance to those who are better off, because they tend to be more knowledgeable, have some capital or are good loan risks, and command the social power to get preferential treatment. In an effort to produce more equitable benefits, Roling instructed development agencies to identify less advantaged farmers who had consistently passed up agricultural innovations. The agencies tried to dissuade the researchers from their seemingly frivolous pursuit of seeking to convert chronic resisters of new technologies to eager adopters. Persistence produced the list of reputed resisters. After the farmers were taught the innovation and given loans, virtually all of them not only adopted the innovation but passed it on to others. Their previous "intransigence" reflected access barriers, not personal resistance to innovation.

The structuring of social agencies to ensure access to opportunities should be considered as much a part of an innovation as the physical technology itself. Otherwise, developers become technocrats for hire, changing communities without much regard to the social consequences of their activities. The internationalization of financial capital seeking high profits increases the likelihood that many of the innovations being injected into societies serve the interests of the outsiders better than they do the inhabitants of the host country. The social component of a diffusion model is often addressed in sweeping terms calling for the need to transform the entire social system. A society may well need major changes. But since developers view direct social change as outside their purview, wholesale prescriptions provide ready excuses for evading otherwise achievable changes in agencies that influence who enjoys the benefits and who pays the costs of technical innovations.

Communications Innovations and Social Diffusion of Ideas and Social Practices

The scope of social diffusion is greatly expanded and its rate accelerated by coupling complementary communications technologies. Video systems can portray and edify almost every aspect of life. Fiber optics deliver thousands of communications simultaneously. Computer systems with huge storage capacities provide ready interactive access to all kinds of information and services. Satellite communication systems distribute information instantaneously nationwide or transnationally. These technologies provide interactive communication systems with tremendous capabilities to inform, teach, and transact. They have transformed the social diffusion process.

Social cognitive theory analyzes social diffusion of ideas, values, and social practices in terms of three constituent processes and the psychosocial factors that govern them (Bandura, 1986a). They include the acquisition of knowledge about the new ways and their functional value, adoption of these behavioral practices, and their diffusion through various social networks.

Symbolic modeling usually functions as the principal conveyer of innovations to widely dispersed areas. It plays an especially influential role in the early phases of diffusion. The print media, radio, and television inform people about new practices and their likely risks and benefits. Early adopters, therefore, come from among those who have had ready access to media sources of information about innovations (Robertson, 1971). The psychosocial determinants and mechanisms of modeling, which were reviewed earlier, govern the rate at which innovations are acquired. Theories of mass communication have commonly assumed that modeling influences operate through a two-step diffusion process. Opinion leaders pick up new ideas from the media and pass them on to their followers through personal influence. The view that diffusion is exclusively a filter-down process is disputed by a large body of evidence on modeling influences. The media can instill ideas for change either directly or through adopters. Human judgment, values, and conduct are often altered by television modeling without having to wait for an influential intermediary to adopt and model the new ways.

Differences in the knowledge, skills, and resources required by particular innovations produce variations in rate of acquisition. Innovations that are difficult to understand and use are given less consideration than simpler ones (Rogers, 1983; Tornatzky & Klein, 1982). Perceived personal efficacy largely determines how complex things look. Activities that exceed perceived capabilities appear complex, whereas those that fall within the bounds of perceived capabilities are viewed as doable. Analyses of how mass media effect changes reveal that both the preexisting and the induced level of perceived self-efficacy play an influential role in the adoption and social diffusion of behavioral practices (Maibach et al., 1991; Slater, 1989). The stronger the people's preexisting perceived efficacy,

and the more the media messages enhance beliefs in their capabilities, the more likely they are to adopt beneficial practices.

When television models new practices on the screens in virtually every household, people in widely dispersed locales can learn them. Not all innovations, however, are promoted through symbolic modeling in the mass media. Some innovations are disseminated through informal personal channels. In such instances, the circles in which people travel determine which innovations will be repeatedly observed and thoroughly learned. The personal model of diffusion has a considerably narrower reach, but it can be more efficacious because of the interpersonal influences that come into play.

The acquisition of knowledge and skills about innovations is necessary but not sufficient for their regular adoption. A number of factors determine whether people will put into practice what they have learned. Environmental inducements serve as one set of regulators. Adoptive behavior is also highly susceptible to incentive influences. Some of the motivating incentives derive from the inherent utility of the adoptive behavior. The greater the tangible benefits provided by an innovation, the higher is the incentive to adopt it (Downs & Mohr, 1979; Ostlund, 1974; Rogers & Shoemaker, 1971). But benefits cannot be experienced until the new practices are tried. Promoters, therefore, strive to get people to adopt new practices by altering their preferences and beliefs about likely outcomes, mainly by enlisting vicarious incentives. Advocates of new ideas and technologies create outcome expectations that the innovations offer better solutions than the established ways. Modeled benefits increase adoptive decisions. Modeling influences can of course impede as well as promote the diffusion process (Midgley, 1976). Modeling disappointing reactions to a particular innovation dissuades others from trying it. Even modeled indifference to an innovation, in the absence of any personal experience with it, will dampen the interests of others. Many innovations serve as a means of gaining social recognition and status. Adoptive behavior is also partly governed by self-evaluative reactions to one's own behavior. People adopt what they value, but they resist innovations that violate their social and moral standards or that conflict with their self-conception. The more compatible an innovation is with prevailing social norms and personal values, the greater its adoptability (Rogers & Shoemaker, 1971).

The amenability of an innovation to brief trial is another relevant characteristic that can affect the ease of adoption. Innovations that can be tried on a limited basis are more readily adoptable than those that have to be tried on a large scale with substantial effort and costs. And finally, people will not adopt innovations even though they are favorably disposed toward them if they lack the accessory resources that may be needed. The more resources innovations require, the lower is their adoptability.

Not all innovations are useful, nor is resistance to them necessarily dysfunctional (Zaltman & Wallendorf, 1979). The number of deficient innovations that are introduced exceeds the number of those with truly beneficial possibilities. Both personal and social well-being are well served by initial wariness to new practices promoted by unsubstantiated or exaggerated claims. The designations "venturesome" for early adopters and "laggards" for later adopters may befit innovations that hold promise. When people are mesmerized by alluring appeals into trying deficient innovations, however, the more suitable designation is "gullibility" for early adopters and "astuteness" for resisters. Rogers (1983) has criticized the prevalent tendency to conceptualize social diffusion from the perspective of the promoters. This limits the search for explanations of nonadoptive behavior to negative attributes of nonadopters.

The third major factor that affects social diffusion involves the structure of social networks. People are enmeshed in networks of relationships that include kinship, friendships, occupational colleagues, and organizational members, just to mention a few. They are linked not only directly by personal relationships. Because acquaintanceships overlap different network clusters, many people become linked to one another indirectly by interconnected ties. Thus, information about new ideas and practices is often conveyed through connections in a variety of social clusters (Rogers & Kincaid, 1981). One is more likely to learn about new ideas and practices from brief contacts with different casual acquaintances than from intensive contact in the same circle of close associates. This path of influence creates the seemingly paradoxical effect that innovations are extensively spread to cohesive groups through weak social ties (Granovetter, 1983).

People with many social ties are more apt to adopt innovations than are those who have few ties to others (Rogers & Kincaid, 1981). Moreover, adoption rates increase as more and more people in one's personal network adopt an innovation. Social connectedness can raise adoptive behavior through several processes. Multilinked relationships may convey more information through multiple modeling (Bandura, 1986a), they may mobilize stronger social influences, or it may be that people with close ties are more receptive to new ideas than those who are socially estranged. Seeing associates adopt innovations with beneficial results boosts personal efficacy and instills positive outcome expectations, both of which promote innovativeness.

There is no single social network in a community that serves all purposes. Different innovations engage different networks. For example, birth control practices and agricultural innovations diffuse through quite different networks within the same community (Marshall, 1971). To complicate matters further, the social networks that help launch an innovation may differ from those that spread it in subsequent phases (Coleman, Katz, & Menzel, 1966). Adoption rates are better predicted from the network that subserves a particular innovation than from a more general communication network.

Interactive computer networking is creating new social structures that link people together in widely dispersed locales in ways that transcend the barriers of time and space (Hiltz & Turoff, 1978). Through this interactive electronic format, people exchange information, share new ideas, and take part in any number of pursuits. Computerized networking provides a ready vehicle for creating diffusion structures, expanding their membership, extending them geographically, and disbanding them when they have outlived their usefulness.

Although social interconnectedness provides potential diffusion paths, psychosocial factors largely determine the fate of what spreads through those paths. In other words, it is the transactions that occur within social relationships rather than the ties themselves that explain adoptive behavior. The course of social diffusion is best understood by the interactions among psychosocial determinants of adoptive behavior, the properties of innovations that facilitate or impede their adoption, and the network structures that provide the social pathways of influence. Structural and psychological determinants of adoptive behavior, therefore, should be included as complementary factors in a comprehensive theory of social diffusion, rather than being cast as rival theories of the diffusion of innovations.

UNDERMINERS OF COLLECTIVE EFFICACY

Today's societies are going through drastic technological and social changes that present unique opportunities, challenges, and constraints. Wrenching social changes that dislocate lives are not new in history. What is new is the accelerated pace of informational and technological change and the extensive globalization of human interdependence. Computerized technologies and global market forces are restructuring and relocating work activities on which people's livelihood depends. These transformations are creating social, economic, and political upheavals. Nation states no longer operate as a collection of self-governing entities but as intertwined realms in a global system of influences. These new transnational realities place increasing demands on the exercise of collective efficacy to gain some measure of control over the courses lives take. Many human activities are impairing the quality of life and degrading on a global scale the intertwined ecosystems needed to sustain a habitable earth environment. The new dimensions of change, which have far-reaching consequences,

call for strong commitment to shared purposes and wide-ranging solutions to social problems. The needed changes can be achieved only through the united effort of people who have the skills, the sense of collective efficacy, and the incentives to shape their future life circumstances. As the need for efficacious group action grows, so does the sense of collective powerlessness.

Many factors undermine the development of collective efficacy. Life in the societies of today is increasingly shaped by transnational interdependencies and the power of international capital (Keohane & Nye, 1977). What happens economically and politically in one part of the world can affect the welfare of vast populations elsewhere. The growing transnational interconnectedness of human life poses new challenges to social adaptation and change. The power of transnational forces in the world economy — which affect the security of work life in nations, employment levels, wages, and even the value of national currencies — are more remote and harder to disentangle, let alone control. The increasing internationalization of financial capital challenges the efficacy of governmental systems to exert a determining influence over nations' economic and national life. There are no handy social mechanisms or global agencies through which people can shape and moderate transnational practices that affect their daily lives. As nations wrestle with the weakening of controlling influence, they experience a crisis in confidence in whether their leaders and institutions can work for them to improve their lives. National surveys have been conducted periodically of people's general sense of political efficacy, their confidence in their social institutions, and how they view the competence of those chosen to lead them. Although such omnibus measures leave much to be desired, they do provide evidence of a growing erosion of the perceived efficacy of social institutions to solve human problems (Guest, 1974; Lipset, 1985). People view inefficacy in leadership and governance as specific to their own social institutions, but the problem is worldwide.

To the general public, governmental systems seem incapable of playing a major role in the economic life of the nation. Political opportunists do a brisk business in panaceas. Since panaceas fail to provide remedies, many people express increasing disillusionment and cynicism over their leaders and centralized institutions. Under such conditions, people strive to regain control over their lives by seeking to improve their local circumstances, over which they have some command. Some of this effort is directed at restoring the past to the future rather than shaping a more promising social future attuned to the changing times. Local influence affirms personal efficacy. Not surprisingly, people have a higher sense of personal efficacy than institutional efficacy. The major challenge to leadership is to forge a national sense of efficacy to take advantage of the opportunities of globalization while minimizing the price that the changes extract from local cultures. All too often, short-run material benefits for influential players in the global financial markets create long-run social costs for local cultures. These new realities create major impediments and challenges to people's ability to exercise some control over the direction and quality of their lives.

The retreat to localism fueled by the public's disillusionment with its national systems ironically comes at a time that requires strong national leadership to manage powerful influences from abroad and to exercise some measure of control over the nation's own destiny. To increase their domestic effectiveness, nations must enlarge their influence over the actions of other nations and international institutions. Barring large power imbalances, nations have to strike mutually advantageous agreements through compromise rather than authoritative imposition. Paradoxically, to gain international control, nations have to negotiate reciprocal pacts that place some constraints on how they can conduct their national affairs (Keohane, 1993). For example, trade agreements usually impose certain limits on the practices of nation states. Thus, the gain in international control comes at the expense of some loss of national autonomy.

Under the new realities of growing transnational control, nation states seek to increase their controlling leverage by merging into larger functional units. For example, the nations of Western Europe formed the European Union to exercise greater control over their economic life. Other nation states will similarly be forced to merge into larger blocks; otherwise, they will have little bargaining power in transnational relations. As in the case of individual nations, however, the regional marriages do not come without a price. They too require some relinquishment of national sovereignty and changes in some traditional ways of life. For example, to reduce agricultural subsidies in member nations to a common level, the European Union lowered the subsidies the French government could provide their farmers. The reduced supplemental income will change the lifestyle of rural France by driving family farmers off the land. While regional control extracts costs from some sectors of society, it benefits other sectors through increased competitiveness in the global marketplace. Imposed constraints generate fragmenting internal disputes between those who are adversely affected by the accords and those who benefit from them. Whether the economic advantage of regional alignments is turned into improved quality of life is another matter. Some of the economic practices that are good for the market operators may not be all that good for the national community. If the financial powerholders have little allegiance to the national community, exploitive pursuit of self-interest can sow a lot of social discord and discontent.

Modern life is increasingly regulated by complex physical technologies that most people neither understand nor believe they can do much to influence. Pervasive dependence on the technologies that govern major aspects of life imposes dependence on specialized technicians. The very technologies that people create to control their life environment can become a constraining force that, in turn, controls their thinking and actions. As an example of such paradoxical consequences, the citizens of nations that are heavily dependent on deteriorating atomic plants for their energy feel powerless to remove the potentially catastrophic hazard from their lives, even though they acknowledge the systems to be unsafe. The devastating consequences of mishaps do not respect national borders. International consequences create imperatives for international solutions.

The social machinery of society is no less challenging. The functions of most social systems are heavily bureaucratized. In getting anything of significance done, one must wade through labyrinthine rules and regulations presided over by a hierarchy of authority. Some of these rules are designed to preserve the fairness of the systems. Others diffuse and depersonalize responsibility for unpopular decisions. Still others serve as coercive means of guarding the status quo. And many of the rules are designed more to benefit the people who run the social systems than to serve the public. Layers of bureaucratic structures thwart effective social action. Collective efforts at social change are sustained, in large part, by the modeled successes of other reformers and by evidence of progress toward desired goals. It is difficult to sustain expectations of success when the struggle is wearisome and bureaucratic practices continually thwart change. Even the more efficacious individuals, who are not easily deterred, find their efforts blunted by mazelike organizational mechanisms that diffuse and obscure responsibility. Pitting oneself repeatedly against bureaucratic gauntlets eventually exacts its toll. Rather than developing the means for shaping their own future, most people grudgingly relinquish control to technical specialists and public officials.

Effective action for social change requires merging diverse self-interests in support of common core values and goals. Disagreements among different constituencies who have a personal stake in the matters of concern create additional obstacles to successful collective action. Leadership increasingly faces the challenge of governing over diversity in ways that permit both autonomy for constituent communities to manage their own affairs and unity through shared values and purposes (Esteve, 1992). The voices for parochial interests are typically much stronger than those for collective responsibility. Electronic activism makes it easier to develop strong partisanships around special interests. It requires efficacious and inspiring leadership to forge mutually beneficial unity within diversity.

Recent years have witnessed growing social fragmentation of societies into special-interest groups, each exercising its own factional power.

Those seeking greater local rule argue that the national governance system is too centralized, too bureaucratized and gridlocked, and too wastefully inefficient. Nationalists, in turn, argue that local interests must be balanced by accomplishment of shared purposes. If carried too far, localism breeds fragmentation and social disconnectedness. Both dysfunctions in governmental systems and pursuit of individual advantage with little regard to the common good lead people to challenge the legitimacy of central governments to intrude in their lives (Hobsbawm, 1996). Estrangement from governmental systems undermines their efficacy to fulfill their civic functions. Computer mass mailing systems provide an easy vehicle for creating narrow-interest pressure groups of people who neither know nor see each other. Mail solicitations provide the funds to promote causes they hold dear and to contest those of which they disapprove. All too often, political alignments are formed by divisive appeals to racial and ethnic prejudices. Pluralism is taking the form of antagonistic factionalism. As a result, it is easier to get people to block courses of action than to merge them into a unified force for social change. Consensus gets forged around collective antipathies. Unbridled factionalism erodes connectedness to the larger society and undermines the collective efficacy needed to find solutions to common life problems.

In the more extreme forms of social fragmentation, countries are being dismantled with a vengeance along racial, religious, and ethnic lines. In many regions, removal of autocratic control begets resurgence of militant nationalism rather than unifying democratic nationhood. Social changes resulting from the influx of people from impoverished regions with diverse cultural and ethnic identities place further strains on governmental systems to shape the course of national life. These social realities pose increasing challenges of how to preserve collective identity and local control within the context of the growing interdependence of human life.

While some forces are creating social fragmentation, others are breaking down national identities. Advanced telecommunications technologies are spreading ideas, values, and styles of behavior transnationally at an unprecedented rate. The symbolic environment feeding off communication satellites is supplanting national cultures and homogenizing collective consciousness. People around the world are also gaining information and interacting on issues of interest through the global web of computer networks. In this global electronic communication, people look beyond their national boundaries for ideas and try to influence others worldwide. With further development of telecommunications technologies, people will become increasingly embedded in global symbolic environments. In addition, mass migrations of people, driven largely by privation and huge economic imbalances between countries, are changing cultural landscapes. As migration changes the ethnic composition of populations, cultures are becoming less distinctive. Global market forces are restructuring national economies and shaping the social life of societies. These various influences transcend national boundaries. People are increasingly forming collective identities around functional ties rather than national ties. This change in the locus of allegiance and control favoring regionalism is summed up well in the words of a spokesman for the Lombard League in northern Italy: "We care about being Lombards first and Europeans second. Italy means nothing to us."

In addition to the difficulties of enlisting shared purposes and collective effort in their service, the institutions that are the objects of change mount their own forceful countermeasures. Because of the many conflicting forces that come into play, attempts to produce socially significant changes do not bring quick successes. Even if desired reforms are officially adopted, their implementation is forestalled by defeated factions using legal challenges in an effort to restore some of the power and privileges they have lost. Long delays between action and noticeable results discourage many of the advocates along the way, even though changes of long-term significance may eventually occur. A sense of collective efficacy is difficult to develop and to sustain when there is heavy institutional opposition and the outcomes of group effort are so long delayed that their origins become obscured.

Those who seek to bring about major changes in their society need a resilient sense of efficacy to withstand the wearisome obstacles to their reform efforts. They must rely on their own support systems to see them through tough times. These supports take a variety of forms. Social reformers must have a tenacious belief in the worth of what they are doing. Given a resolute commitment to valued principles, reformers derive satisfaction and self-respect from the rightness of the effort alone. Others engaged in the collective endeavor provide mutual support as well. A firm sense of community is a strong sustaining force. In addition, reformers find inspiration and encouragement in the successes of others who shaped the social future through steadfast effort. Protection against discouragement requires not only a strong sense of collective efficacy to bring about change but also a long time perspective. Resilient reformers judge their successes in terms of progressive gains rather than heroic victories. Although diverse supports can be enlisted for collective action, unless groups are fully convinced they can effect social change, however daunting the obstacles, they will not have much staying power in pursuit of their vision.

The scope and magnitude of human problems also undermine the perceived efficacy to find effective solutions for them. Profound global changes in the form of burgeoning populations, shrinking resources, ozone depletion, and mounting environmental devastation are destroying the interdependent ecosystems that sustain life. These changes are creating new problems that require transnational remedies. Worldwide problems of growing magnitude and complexity instill a sense of paralysis, a feeling that there is little people can do that would have a significant impact on such massive problems. The larger the collectivity, the weaker the sense of efficacy that people can mobilize themselves to accomplish needed changes (Kerr, 1996). National self-interests and the fear of infringement of sovereignty create further obstacles to developing transnational mechanisms for change. Effective remedial and preventive measures call for concerted action at the local, national, and transnational levels. Global effects are the products of local practices. Each person, therefore, has a part to play in the solution. The strategy of "Think globally, act locally" is an effort to restore people's sense of efficacy that there are many things they can do to make a difference. The annual Goldman awards honor dedicated individuals who, with little more than an unshakable efficacy belief and a motivating vision, mobilized people to preserve the ecological resources in their region, often in the face of daunting opposition and grave personal threats.

Factional Efficacy and Gridlocking of Social Initiatives

The "social system" is not a monolith. Rather, it comprises numerous constituencies each vying for power and lobbying for its own interests in shifting coalitions. In this continual interplay, the same faction may be transmuted from a challenger of the system to an influential confederate in the system opposing rival factions, depending on the issues at stake. Thus, for example, agribusinesses fight the "system" in federal efforts to regulate their operations and processing of food products, but they become the "system" fighting the efforts of challengers to curtail federal subsidies to them. Whether people want government in or out of their lives depends on the particular interests being serviced. They actively lobby for government in their lives when it subsidizes and protects their self-interests, but they tend to view government as an intrusive agent that they want "off their backs" when its civic function is not to their advantage.

The rise of narrow-interest groups flexing their factional efficacy does not jibe with the diagnoses of growing public apathy and feelings of helplessness. Clearly there exists a paradox to be explained. Viewed from the efficacy perspective, in the absence of shared imperatives, growing factional efficacy undermines the exercise of collective efficacy through mutual immobilization. Efficacious factional initiatives, often fragmented and rivalrous, create an overload of programs and regulations,

force divisive issues on officeholders, weaken their capabilities to deal with intractable problems satisfactorily, and obfuscate a sense of national purpose (Atkin, 1980; Barton, 1980; Fiorina, 1980). Thus, people are exercising greater factional influence but achieving less collectively and becoming more discontented. Changing the officeholders beholden to factional interests does not eliminate the social problems people face. As a result, they become disillusioned about the prospect of effecting significant change in their social and economic way of life by the institutional means available to them.

Bidirectionality of Social Influence

In analyzing the impediments to human endeavors, it is all too easy to lose sight of the fact that human influence, whether individual or collective, is a two-way process rather than flowing unidirectionally. The degree of reciprocity may vary from one domain of activity to another, but social transactions are rarely unilateral. The degree of imbalance of social power depends partly on the extent to which people exercise the influence that is theirs to command. The less they bring their influence to bear on the conditions that affect their lives, the more control they relinquish to others.

The psychological barriers created by beliefs of collective powerlessness are especially pernicious because they are more demoralizing and debilitating than external impediments. People who have a sense of collective efficacy refuse to have their lives dictated by detrimental institutional practices. They mobilize their efforts and resources to surmount the external impediments erected to the changes they seek. In the metaphoric words of social analysts, social progress must be measured in inches, not miles. Even though accomplishments may fall short of aspirations, there is victory in the incremental changes people do achieve. Evidence of progress sustains their efforts and helps others to believe themselves capable of changing their lives for the better. People who are convinced of their collective powerlessness will cease trying even though changes are attainable through perseverant collective effort. They see no point in trying to change their life circumstances.

Achievement of collective efficacy requires cogent means of relating factional interests to shared purposes. The unifying purposes must be explicit and attainable through concerted effort. There is no single grand design for changing entrenched social practices. Because success calls for sustained effort over a long time, proximal subgoals are needed to provide incentives and evidence of progress along the way. As a society, we enjoy the benefits left by those before us who collectively fought inhumanities and worked for social reforms that permit a better life. Our own collective efficacy, in turn, will shape how future generations live their lives. Considering the pressing worldwide problems that loom ahead, people can ill-afford to trade efficacious endeavor for public apathy or mutual immobilization. The times call for social initiatives that build people's sense of collective efficacy to influence the conditions that shape their lives and those of future generations.

References

Aas, H., Klepp, K., Laberg, J. C., & Aaro, L. E. (1995). Predicting adolescents' intentions to drink alcohol: Outcome expectancies and self-efficacy. *Journal of Studies on Alcohol, 56,* 293–299.

Abdalla, I. A. (1995). Sex, sex-role self-concepts and career decision-making self-efficacy among Arab students. *Social Behavior and Personality, 23,* 389–402.

Abel, E. (Ed.). (1981). *What's news: The media in American society.* San Francisco: Institute for Contemporary Studies.

Abelson, R. P., Aronson, E., McGuire, W. J., Newcomb, T. M., Rosenberg, M. J., & Tannenbaum, P. H. (1968). *Theories of cognitive consistency: A sourcebook.* Chicago: Rand McNally.

Abramson, P. R., & Aldrich, J. H. (1982). The decline of electoral participation in America. *The American Political Science Review, 76,* 502–521.

Ader, R., & Cohen, N. (1993). Psychoneuroimmuniology: Conditioning and stress. In L. W. Porter & M. R. Rosenzweig (Eds.), *Annual Review of Psychology, 44,* 53–85.

Adler, A. (1956). (H. C. Ansbacher & R. R. Ansbacher, Eds.). *The individual psychology of Alfred Adler.* New York: Harper & Row.

Adler, N. E., Boyce, T., Chesney, M. A., Cohen, S., Folkman, S., Kahn, R. L., & Syme, S. L. (1994). Socioeconomic status and health: The challenge of the gradient. *American Psychologist, 49,* 15–24.

Affleck, G., Tennen, H., Pfeiffer, C., & Fifield, J. (1987). Appraisals of control and predictability in adapting to a chronic disease. *Journal of Personality and Social Psychology, 53,* 273–279.

Agnew, R., & Jones, D. H. (1988). Adapting to deprivation: An examination of inflated educational expectations. *The Sociological Quarterly, 29,* 315–337.

Agras, W. S. (1987). *Eating disorders: Management of obesity, bulimia and anorexia nervosa.* Elmsford, N.Y.: Pergamon.

Ahles, T. A., Blanchard, E. B., & Leventhal, H. (1983). Cognitive control of pain: Attention to the sensory aspects of the cold pressor stimulus. *Cognitive Therapy and Research, 7,* 159–178.

Ainsworth, M. D. S., & Bell, S. M. (1974). Mother-infant interaction and the development of competence. In K. Connolly & J. Bruner (Eds.), *The growth of competence* (pp. 97–118). London: Academic.

Ajzen, I. (1985). From intentions to actions: A theory of planned behavior. In J. Kuhl & J. Beckman (Eds.), *Action-control: From cognition to behavior* (pp. 11–39). Heidelberg: Springer.

Ajzen, I., & Fishbein, M. (1980). *Understanding attitudes and predicting social behavior.* Englewood Cliffs, NJ: Prentice-Hall.

Ajzen, I., & Madden, T. J. (1986). Prediction of goal-directed behavior: Attitudes, intentions, and perceived behavioral control. *Journal of Experimental Social Psychology, 22,* 453–474.

Alagna, S. W., & Reddy, D. M. (1984). Predictors of proficient technique and successful lesion detection in breast self-examination. *Health Psychology, 3,* 113–127.

Albert, M. S., Savage, C. R., Blazer, D., Jones, K., Berkman, L., Seeman, T., & Rowe, J. W. (1995). Predictors of cognitive change in older persons: MacArthur studies of successful aging. *Psychology and Aging, 10,* 578–589.

Alden, L. (1986). Self-efficacy and causal attributions for social feedback. *Journal of Research in Personality, 20,* 460–473.

Alden, L. (1987). Attributional responses of anxious individuals to different patterns of social feedback: Nothing succeeds like improvement. *Journal of Personality and Social Psychology, 52,* 100–106.

Alden, L. E., Bieling, P. J., & Wallace, S. T. (1994). Perfectionism in an interpersonal context: A self-regulation analysis of dysphoria and social anxiety. *Cognitive Therapy and Research, 18,* 297–316.

Alinsky, S. D. (1969). *Reveille for radicals.* New York: Vintage Books.

Alinsky, S. D. (1971). *Rules for radicals.* New York: Random House.

Allen, J. K., Becker, D. M., Swank, R. T. (1990). Factors related to functional status after coronary artery bypass surgery. *Heart Lung, 19,* 337–343.

Allen, J. P., Leadbeater, B. J., & Aber, J. L. (1990). The relationship of adolescent's expectations and values to delinquency, hard drug use and unprotected sexual intercourse. *Development and Psychopathology, 2,* 85–98.

Alloy, L. B., & Abramson, L. Y. (1988). Depressive realism: Four theoretical perspectives. In L. B. Alloy (Ed.), *Cognitive processes in depression* (pp. 223–265). New York: Guilford.

Alloy, L. B., & Clements, C. M. (1992). Illusion of control: Invulnerability to negative affect and depressive symptoms after laboratory and natural stressors. *Journal of Abnormal Psychology, 101,* 234–245.

Alloy, L. B., Abramson, L. Y., & Viscusi, D. (1981). Induced mood and the illusion of control. *Journal of Personality and Social Psychology, 41,* 1129–1140.

Alloy, L. B., Clements, C. M., & Koenig, L. J. (1993). Perceptions of control: Determinants and mechanisms. In G. Weary, F. Gleicher, & K. L. Marsh (Eds.), *Control motivation and social cognition* (pp. 33–73). New York: Springer-Verlag.

Altmaier, E. M., Russell, D. W., Kao, C. F., Lehmann, T. R., & Weinstein, J. N. (1993). Role of self-efficacy in rehabilitation outcome among chronic low back pain patients. *Journal of Counseling Psychology, 40,* 1–5.

Ames, C. (1984). Competitive, cooperative, and individualistic goal structures: A cognitive-motivational analysis. In R. E. Ames & C. Ames (Eds.), *Research on motivation in education: Student motivation* (Vol. 1, pp. 177–207). New York: Academic.

Anderson, C. A., & Jennings, D. L. (1980). When experiences of failure promote expectations of success: The impact of attributing failure to ineffective strategies. *Journal of Personality, 48,* 393–407.

Anderson, D. C., Crowell, C. R., Doman, M., & Howard, G. S. (1988). Performance posting, goal setting, and activity-contingent praise as applied to a university hockey team. *Journal of Applied Psychology, 73,* 87–95.

Anderson, J. R. (1980). *Cognitive psychology and its implications.* San Francisco: W. H. Freeman.

Anderson, N. H. (1981). *Foundations of information integration theory.* New York: Academic.

Anderson, R. B., & McMillion, P. Y. (1995). Effects of similar and diversified modeling on African American women's efficacy expectations and intentions to perform breast self-examination. *Health Communication, 7,* 327–343.

Anderson, R. N., Greene, M. L., & Loewen, P. S. (1988). Relationships among teachers' and students' thinking skills, sense of efficacy, and student achievement. *The Alberta Journal of Educational Research, 34,* 148–165.

Annis, H. M. (1982). Situational confidence

questionnaire ((C) A.R.F.). Toronto: Addiction Research Foundation.

Annis, H. M., & Davis, C. S. (1989). Relapse prevention. In R. K. Hester & W. R. Miller (Eds.), *Handbook of alcoholism treatment approaches: Effective alternatives* (pp. 170–182). New York: Pergamon.

Anson, A. R., Cook, T. D., Habib, F., Grady, M. K., Haynes, N., & Comer, J. P. (1991). The Comer school development program: A theoretical analysis. *Urban Education,* 26, 56–82.

Antoni, M. H., Schneiderman, N., Fletcher, M. A., Goldstein, D. A., Ironson, G., & Laperriere, A. (1990). Psychoneuroimmunology and HIV-1. *Journal of Consulting and Clinical Psychology,* 58, 38–49.

Antonuccio, D., Danton, W. G., & DeNelsky, G. Y. (1995). Psychotherapy vs. medication for depression: Challenging the conventional wisdom. *Professional Psychology,* 26, 574.

Appley, M. H. (1991). Motivation, equilibration, and stress. In R. A. Dienstbier (Ed.), *Perspectives on motivation: Nebraska symposium on motivation* (Vol. 38, pp. 1–67). Lincoln: University of Nebraska Press.

Arbona, C. (1990). Career counseling research and Hispanics: A review of the literature. *The Counseling Psychologist,* 18, 300–323.

Arch, E. C. (1992a). Affective control efficacy as a factor in willingness to participate in a public performance situation. *Psychological Reports,* 71, 1247–1250.

Arch, E. C. (1992b). Sex differences in the effect of self-efficacy on willingness to participate in a performance situation. *Psychological Reports,* 70, 3–9.

Arisohn, B., Bruch, M. A., & Heimberg, R. G. (1988). Influence of assessment methods on self-efficacy and outcome expectancy ratings of assertive behavior. *Journal of Counseling Psychology,* 35, 336–341.

Armstrong, C. A., Sallis, J. F., Hovell, M. F., & Hofstetter, C. R. (1993). Stages of change, self-efficacy, and the adoption of vigorous exercise: A prospective analysis. *Journal of Sport and Exercise Psychology,* 15, 390–402.

Arnold, H. J. (1976). Effects of performance feedback and extrinsic reward upon high intrinsic motivation. *Organizational Behavior and Human Performance,* 17, 275–288.

Ashby, M. S., & Wittmaier, B. C. (1978). Attitude changes in children after exposure to stories about women in traditional or nontraditional occupations. *Journal of Educational Psychology,* 70, 945–949.

Ashton, P. T., & Webb, R. B. (1986). *Making a difference: Teachers' sense of efficacy and student achievement.* White Plains, N.Y.: Longman, Inc.

Astin, H. S. (1984). The meaning of work in women's lives: A sociopsychological model of career choice and work behavior. *The Counseling Psychologist,* 12, 117–126.

Atkin, C. K. (1993). Effects of media alcohol messages on adolescent audiences. *Adolescent Medicine,* 4, 527–542.

Atkin, J. M. (1980). The government in the classroom. *Daedalus,* 109, 85–89.

Atkinson, J. W. (1964). *An introduction to motivation.* Princeton, N.J.: Van Nostrand.

Audia, G. (1995). The effect of organizations' and individuals' past success on strategic persistence in changing environments. Ph.D. diss., University of Maryland.

Austin, J. H. (1978). *Chase, chance, and creativity: The lucky art of novelty.* New York: Columbia University Press.

Averill, J. R. (1973). Personal control over aversive stimuli and its relationship to stress. *Psychological Bulletin,* 80, 286–303.

Azrin, N. H. (1976). Improvements in the community-reinforcement approach to alcoholism. *Behaviour Research and Therapy,* 14, 339–348.

Azrin, N. H., Acierno, R., Kogan, E. S., Donohue, B., Besalel, V. A., & McMahon, P. T. (1996). Follow-up results of supportive versus behavioral therapy for illicit drug use. *Behaviour Research and Therapy,* 34, 41–46.

Baer, J. S., Holt, C. S., & Lichtenstein, E. (1986). Self-efficacy and smoking reexamined: Construct validity and clinical utility. *Journal of Consulting and Clinical Psychology,* 54, 846–852.

Balcazar, F. E., Mathews, R. M., Francisco, V. T., Fawcett, S. B., & Seekins, T. (1994). The empowerment process in four advocacy organizations of people with disabilities. *Rehabilitation Psychology,* 39, 189–203.

Balch, G. I. (1974). Multiple indicators in survey research: The concept "sense of political efficacy." *Political Methodology,* 1, 1–43.

Baltes, M. M. (1988). The etiology and maintenance of dependency in the elderly: Three phases of operant research. *Behavior Therapy,* 19, 301–319.

Baltes, M. M. (1996). *The many faces of dependency in old age.* New York: Cambridge University Press.

Baltes, M. M., & Baltes, P. B. (Eds.). (1986). *The psychology of control and aging.* Hillsdale, N.J.: Erlbaum.

Baltes, M. M., & Wahl, H. (1991). The be-

havioral and social world of the institutionalized elderly: Implications for health and optimal development. In M. G. Ory & R. P. Abeles (Eds.), *Aging, health, and behavior* (pp. 83–108). Newbury Park, Calif.: Sage.

Baltes, P. B. (1983). Life-span developmental psychology: Observations on history and theory revisited. In R. M. Lerner (Ed.), *Developmental psychology: Historical and philosophical perspectives* (pp. 79–111). Hillsdale, N.J.: Erlbaum.

Baltes, P. B. (in press). *Wisdom.* Boston: Blackwell .

Baltes, P. B., & Baltes, M. M. (Eds.). (1990). *Successful aging: Perspectives from the behavioral sciences.* Cambridge: Cambridge University Press.

Baltes, P. B., & Labouvie, G. V. (1973). Adult development of intellectual performance: Description, explanation, and modification. In C. Eisdorfer & M. P. Lawton (Eds.), *The psychology of adult development and aging* (pp. 157–219). Washington, D.C.: American Psychological Association.

Baltes, P. B., & Lindenberger, U. (1988). On the range of cognitive plasticity in old age as a function of experience: 15 years of intervention research. *Behavior Therapy,* 19, 283–300.

Baltes, P. B., Lindenberger, U., Staudinger, U. M. (in press). Life-span theory in development psychology. In R. M. Lerner (Ed.), *Handbook of child psychology* (Vol. 1, 5th ed., Theoretical models of human development.). New York: Wiley.

Baltes, P. B., & Smith, J. (1990). Toward a psychology of wisdom and its ontogenesis. In R. J. Sternberg (Ed.), *Wisdom: Its nature, origins, and development* (pp. 87–120). New York: Cambridge University Press.

Bandura, A. (1964). The stormy decade: Fact or fiction? *Psychology in the Schools,* 1, 224–231.

Bandura, A. (1969a). *Principles of behavior modification.* New York: Holt, Rinehart & Winston.

Bandura, A. (1969b). Social-learning theory of identificatory processes. In D. A. Goslin (Ed.), *Handbook of socialization theory and research* (pp. 213–262). Chicago: Rand McNally.

Bandura, A. (1973). *Aggression: A social learning analysis.* Englewood Cliffs, N.J.: Prentice-Hall.

Bandura, A. (1977). Self-efficacy: Toward a unifying theory of behavioral change. *Psychological Review,* 84, 191–215.

Bandura, A. (1978). Reflections on self-efficacy. In S. Rachman (Ed.), *Advances in behaviour research and therapy* (Vol. 1., pp. 237–269). Oxford: Pergamon.

Bandura, A. (1982a). Self-efficacy mechanism in human agency. *American Psychologist, 37*, 122–147.

Bandura, A. (1982b). The psychology of chance encounters and life paths. *American Psychologist, 37*, 747–755.

Bandura, A. (1983). Self-efficacy determinants of anticipated fears and calamities. *Journal of Personality and Social Psychology, 45*, 464–469.

Bandura, A. (1984). Recycling misconceptions of perceived self-efficacy. *Cognitive Therapy and Research, 8*, 231–255.

Bandura, A. (1986a). *Social foundations of thought and action: A social cognitive theory.* Englewood Cliffs, N.J.: Prentice-Hall.

Bandura, A. (1986b). The explanatory and predictive scope of self-efficacy theory. *Journal of Clinical and Social Psychology, 4*, 359–373.

Bandura, A. (1988a). Self-regulation of motivation and action through goal systems. In V. Hamilton, G. H. Bower, & N. H. Frijda (Eds.), *Cognitive perspectives on emotion and motivation* (pp. 37–61). Dordrecht, the Netherlands: Kluwer Academic Publishers.

Bandura, A. (1988b). Perceived self-efficacy: Exercise of control through self-belief. In J. P. Dauwalder, M. Perez, & V. Hobi (Eds.), *Annual series of European research in behavior therapy* (Vol. 2, pp. 27–59). Amsterdam/Lisse, Netherlands: Swets & Zeitlinger.

Bandura, A. (1988c). Self-efficacy conception of anxiety. *Anxiety Research, 1*, 77–98.

Bandura, A. (1989a). Regulation of cognitive processes through perceived self-efficacy. *Developmental Psychology, 25*, 729–735.

Bandura, A. (1989b). A social cognitive theory of action. In J. P. Forgas & M. J. Innes (Eds.), *Recent advances in social psychology: An international perspective* (pp. 127–138). North Holland: Elsevier.

Bandura, A. (1990a). Reflections on nonability determinants of competence. In R. J. Sternberg & J. Kolligian, Jr. (Eds.), *Competence considered* (pp. 315–362). New Haven, Conn.: Yale University Press, 1990.

Bandura, A. (1990b). *Multidimensional scales of perceived academic efficacy.* Stanford University, Stanford, Calif.

Bandura, A. (1991a). Self-efficacy mechanism in physiological activation and health-promoting behavior. In J. Madden, IV (Ed.), *Neurobiology of learning, emo-*

tion and affect (pp. 229–270). New York: Raven, 1991.

Bandura, A. (1991b). Self-regulation of motivation through anticipatory and self-regulatory mechanisms. In R. A. Dienstbier (Ed.), *Perspectives on motivation: Nebraska symposium on motivation* (Vol. 38, pp. 69–164). Lincoln: University of Nebraska Press.

Bandura, A. (1991c). Social cognitive theory of self-regulation. *Organizational Behavior and Human Decision Processes, 50*, 248–287.

Bandura, A. (1991d). Social cognitive theory of moral thought and action. In W. M. Kurtines & J. L. Gewirtz (Eds.), *Handbook of moral behavior and development: Theory, research and applications* (Vol. 1, pp. 71–129). Hillsdale, N.J.: Erlbaum.

Bandura, A. (1991e). Human agency: The rhetoric and the reality. *American Psychologist, 46*, 157–162.

Bandura, A. (1992a). Exercise of personal agency through the self-efficacy mechanism. In R. Schwarzer (Ed.), *Self-efficacy: Thought control of action* (pp. 3–38). Washington, D.C.: Hemisphere.

Bandura, A. (1992b). Self-efficacy mechanism in psychobiologic functioning. In R. Schwarzer (Ed.), *Self-efficacy: Thought control of action* (pp. 355–394). Washington, D.C.: Hemisphere.

Bandura, A. (1992c). Psychological aspects of prognostic judgments. In R. W. Evans, D. S. Baskin, & F. M. Yatsu (Eds.), *Prognosis of neurological disorders* (pp. 13–28). New York: Oxford University Press.

Bandura, A. (1993). Perceived self-efficacy in cognitive development and functioning. *Educational Psychologist, 28*, 117–148.

Bandura, A. (1994). Social cognitive theory and exercise of control over HIV infection. In R. DiClemente and J. Peterson (Eds.), *Preventing AIDS: Theories and methods of behavioral interventions* (pp. 25–59). New York: Plenum.

Bandura, A. (1995a). On rectifying conceptual ecumenism. In J. E. Maddux (Ed.), *Self-efficacy, adaptation, and adjustment: Theory, research and application* (pp. 347–375). New York: Plenum.

Bandura, A. (1995b). Comments on the crusade against the causal efficacy of human thought. *Journal of Behavior Therapy and Experimental Psychiatry, 26*, 179–190.

Bandura, A. (1995c). Manual for the construction of self-efficacy scales. Available from Albert Bandura, Department of Psychology, Stanford University, Stanford, CA 94305-2130.

Bandura, A. (1996). Ontological and episte-

mological terrains revisited. *Journal of Behavior Therapy and Experimental Psychiatry, 27*, 323–345.

Bandura, A., & Abrams, K. (1986). Self-regulatory mechanisms in motivating, apathetic, and despondent reactions to unfulfilled standards. Manuscript, Stanford University, Stanford, Calif.

Bandura, A., & Adams, N. E. (1977). Analysis of self-efficacy theory of behavioral change. *Cognitive Therapy and Research, 1*, 287–308.

Bandura, A., Adams, N. E., & Beyer, J. (1977). Cognitive processes mediating behavioral change. *Journal of Personality and Social Psychology, 35*, 125–139.

Bandura, A., Adams, N. E., Hardy, A. B., & Howells, G. N. (1980). Tests of the generality of self-efficacy theory. *Cognitive Therapy and Research, 4*, 39–66.

Bandura, A., Barbaranelli, C., Caprara, G. V., & Pastorelli, C. (1996a). Multifaceted impact of self-efficacy beliefs on academic functioning. *Child Development, 67*, 1206–1222.

Bandura, A., Barbaranelli, C., Caprara, G. V., & Pastorelli, C. (1996b). Mechanisms of moral disengagement in the exercise of moral agency. *Journal of Personality and Social Psychology, 71*, 364–374.

Bandura, A., Barbaranelli, C., Caprara, G. V., & Pastorelli, C. (1997). Efficacy beliefs as shapers of aspirations and occupational trajectories. In preparation.

Bandura, A., Blanchard, E. B., & Ritter, B. (1969). Relative efficacy of desensitization and modeling approaches for inducing behavioral, affective, and attitudinal changes. *Journal of Personality and Social Psychology, 13*, 173–199.

Bandura, A., & Cervone, D. (1983). Self-evaluative and self-efficacy mechanisms governing the motivational effects of goal systems. *Journal of Personality and Social Psychology, 45*, 1017–1028.

Bandura, A., & Cervone, D. (1986). Differential engagement of self-reactive influences in cognitive motivation. *Organizational Behavior and Human Decision Processes, 38*, 92–113.

Bandura, A., Cioffi, D., Taylor, C. B., & Brouillard, M. E. (1988). Perceived self-efficacy in coping with cognitive stressors and opioid activation. *Journal of Personality and Social Psychology, 55*, 479–488.

Bandura, A., Jeffery, R. W., & Gajdos, E. (1975). Generalizing change through participant modeling with self-directed mastery. *Behaviour Research and Therapy, 13*, 141–152.

Bandura, A., Jeffery, R. W., & Wright, C. L.

(1974). Efficacy of participant modeling as a function of response induction aids. *Journal of Abnormal Psychology*, 83, 56–64.

Bandura, A., & Jourden, F. J. (1991). Self-regulatory mechanisms governing the impact of social comparison on complex decision making. *Journal of Personality and Social Psychology*, 60, 941–951.

Bandura, A., & Menlove, F. L. (1968). Factors determining vicarious extinction of avoidance behavior through symbolic modeling. *Journal of Personality and Social Psychology*, 8, 99–108.

Bandura, A., O'Leary, A., Taylor, C. B., Gauthier, J., & Gossard, D. (1987). Perceived self-efficacy and pain control: Opioid and nonopioid mechanisms. *Journal of Personality and Social Psychology*, 53, 563–571.

Bandura, A., & Perloff, B. (1967). Relative efficacy of self-monitored and externally imposed reinforcement systems. *Journal of Personality and Social Psychology*, 7, 111–116.

Bandura, A., Reese, L., & Adams, N. E. (1982). Microanalysis of action and fear arousal as a function of differential levels of perceived self-efficacy. *Journal of Personality and Social Psychology*, 43, 5–21.

Bandura, A., & Schunk, D. H. (1981). Cultivating competence, self-efficacy and intrinsic interest through proximal self-motivation. *Journal of Personality and Social Psychology*, 41, 586–598.

Bandura, A., & Simon, K. M. (1977). The role of proximal intentions in self-regulation of refractory behavior. *Cognitive Therapy and Research*, 1, 177–193.

Bandura, A., Taylor, C. B., Williams, S. L. Mefford, I. N., & Barchas, J. D. (1985). Catecholamine secretion as a function of perceived coping self-efficacy. *Journal of Consulting and Clinical Psychology*, 53, 406–414.

Bandura, A., & Walters, R. H. (1959). *Adolescent aggression*. New York: Ronald Press.

Bandura, A., & Wood, R. E. (1989). Effect of perceived controllability and performance standards on self-regulation of complex decision-making. *Journal of Personality and Social Psychology*, 56, 805–814.

Bandura, M. M., & Dweck, C. S. (1988). The relationship of conceptions of intelligence and achievement goals to achievement-related cognition, affect and behavior. Manuscript, Harvard University.

Barling, J., & Abel, M. (1983). Self-efficacy beliefs and tennis performance. *Cognitive Therapy and Research*, 7, 265–272.

Barling, J., & Beattie, R. (1983). Self-efficacy beliefs and sales performance. *Journal of*

Organizational Behavior Management, 5, 41–51.

Barlow, D. H. (1986). A psychological model of panic. In Shaw, B. F., Segal, Z. V., Vallis, T. M., & Cashman, F. E. (Eds.), *Anxiety disorders. Psychological and biological perspectives* (pp. 93–114). New York: Plenum.

Barlow, D. H., Leitenberg, H., Agras, W. S., & Wincze, J. P. (1969). The transfer gap in systematic desensitization: An analogue study. *Behaviour Research and Therapy*, 7, 191–196.

Barnett, A. D. (1967). A note on communication and development in communist China. In D. Lerner & W. Schramm (Eds.), *Communication and change in the developing countries* (pp. 231–234). Honolulu: East-West Center Press.

Baron, M., Dutil, E., Berkson, L., Lander, P., & Becker, R. (1987). Hand function in the elderly: Relation to osteoarthritis. *Journal of Rheumatology*, 14, 815–819.

Baron, R. A. (1988). Negative effects of destructive criticism: Impact on conflict, self-efficacy, and task performance. *Journal of Applied Psychology*, 73, 199–207.

Barrios, F. X. (1985). A comparison of global and specific estimates of self-control. *Cognitive Therapy and Research*, 9, 455–469.

Barrios, F. X., & Niehaus, J. C. (1985). The influence of smoker status, smoking history, sex, and situational variables on smokers' self-efficacy. *Addictive Behaviors*, 10, 425–430.

Barton, A. H. (1980). Fault lines in American elite consensus. *Daedalus*, 109, 1–24.

Barzon, J. (1964). Calamaphobia, or hints towards a writer's discipline. In H. Hull (Ed.), *The writer's book* (pp. 84–96). New York: Barnes & Noble.

Basen-Engquist, K., & Parcel, G. S. (1992). Attitudes, norms and self-efficacy: A model of adolescents' HIV-related sexual risk behavior. *Health Education Quarterly*, 19, 263–277.

Bastone, E. C., & Kerns, R. D. (1995). Effects of self-efficacy and perceived social support on recovery-related behaviors after coronary artery bypass graft surgery. *Annals of Behavioral Medicine*, 17, 324–330.

Bates, J. A. (1979). Extrinsic reward and intrinsic motivation: A review with implications for the classroom. *Review of Educational Research*, 49, 557.

Bauer, R. H. (1987). Control processes as a way of understanding, diagnosing, and remediating learning disabilities. In H. L. Swanson (Ed.), *Memory and learning disabilities. Advances in learning and behavioral disabilities* (Suppl. 2, 41–81). Greenwich, Conn.: JAI.

Baum, A., Cohen, L., & Hall, M. (1993). Control and intrusive memories as possible determinants of chronic stress. *Psychosomatic Medicine*, 55, 274–286.

Baum, J. R. (1994). The relation of traits, competencies, vision, motivation, and strategy to venture growth. Ph.D. diss., University of Maryland.

Beach, L. R., Barnes, V. E., & Christensen-Szalanski, J. J. J. (1986). Beyond heuristics and biases: A contingency model of judgmental forecasting. *Journal of Forecasting*, 5, 143–157.

Beck, A. T. (1973). *The diagnosis and management of depression*. Philadelphia: University of Pennsylvania Press.

Beck, A. T. (1976). *Cognitive therapy and the emotional disorders*. New York: International Universities Press.

Beck, A. T. (1984). Cognitive therapy of depression: New perspectives. In P. Clayton & J. E. Barnett (Eds.), *Treatment of depression: Old controversies and new approaches* (pp. 265–284). New York: Raven.

Beck, A. T., & Emery, G. (1985). *Anxiety disorders and phobias*. New York: Basic Books.

Beck, A. T., Laude, R., & Bohnert, M. (1974). Ideational components of anxiety neurosis. *Archives of General Psychiatry*, 31, 319–325.

Beck, K. H., & Frankel, A. (1981). A conceptualization of threat communications and protective health behavior. *Social Psychology Quarterly*, 44, 204–217.

Beck, K. H., & Lund, A. K. (1981). The effects of health threat seriousness and personal efficacy upon intentions and behavior. *Journal of Applied Social Psychology*, 11, 401–415.

Becker, L. J. (1978). Joint effect of feedback and goal setting on performance: A field study of residential energy conservation. *Journal of Applied Psychology*, 63, 428–433.

Becker, M. H. (1990). Theoretical models of adherence and strategies for improving adherence. In S. A. Shumaker, E. B. Schron, & J. K. Ockene (Eds.), *The handbook of health behavior change* (pp. 5–43). New York: Springer.

Becker, M. H. (Ed.). (1974). The health belief model and personal health behavior. *Health Education Monographs*, 2, 324–473.

Beckham, J. C., Rice, J. R., Talton, S. L., Helms, M. J., & Young, L. D. (1994). Relationship of cognitive constructs to adjustment in rheumatoid arthritis patients. *Cognitive Therapy and Research*, 18, 479–496.

Becoña, E., Frojan, M. J., & Lista, M. J. (1988). Comparison between two self-efficacy scales in maintenance of smoking cessation. *Psychological Reports*, 62, 359–362.

Behling, O., & Starke, F. A. (1973). The postulates of expectancy theory. *Academy of Management Journal*, 16, 373–388.

Bekkers, M. J. T. M., van Knippenberg, F. C. E., van den Borne, H. W., & vanBerge-Henegouwen, G. P. (1996). Prospective evaluation of psychosocial adaptation to stoma surgery: The role of self-efficacy. *Psychosomatic Medicine*, 58, 183–191.

Bélisle, M., Roskies, E., & Lévesque, J. (1987). Improving adherence to physical activity. *Health Psychology*, 6, 159–162.

Benight, C. C., Antoni, M. H., Kilbourn, K., Ironson, G., Kumar, M. A., Schneiderman-Redwine, L., Baum, A., & Schneiderman, N. (1996). Coping self-efficacy predicts less psychological and physiological disturbances following a natural disaster. Manuscript, University of Colorado at Colorado Springs.

Bereiter, C., & Scardamelia, M. (1987). *The psychology of written composition*. Hillsdale, N.J.: Erlbaum.

Bergeron, L. M., & Romano, J. L. (1994). The relationships among career decision-making self-efficacy, educational indecision, vocational indecision, and gender. *Journal of College Student Development*, 35, 19–24.

Bergin, D. A. (1987). Intrinsic motivation for learning, out-of-school activities, and achievement. Ph.D. diss., Stanford University, Stanford, Calif.

Berlin, J. A., & Colditz, G. A. (1990). A meta-analysis of physical activity in the prevention of coronary heart disease. *American Journal of Epidemiology*, 132, 253–287.

Berlyne, D. E. (1960). *Conflict, arousal, and curiosity*. New York: McGraw-Hill.

Berman, P., & McLaughlin, M. W. (1977). *Federal programs supporting educational change*. Vol. 7, *Factors affecting implementation and continuation* (R-1589/7-HEW). Santa Monica, Calif.: Rand Corporation.

Berman, P., McLaughlin, M., Bass, G., Pauly, E., & Zellman, G. (1977). *Federal programs supporting educational change*. Vol. 7, *Factors affecting implementation and continuation*. Santa Monica, Calif.: Rand Corporation.

Bernier, M., & Avard, J. (1986). Self-efficacy, outcome and attrition in a weight reduction program. *Cognitive Therapy and Research*, 10, 319–338.

Berry, J. M. (1996). A self-efficacy model of memory function in adulthood. Submitted for publication.

Berry, J. M. (Ed.). (1989). Cognitive efficacy:

A life span development perspective (Special issue). *Developmental Psychology*, 35, 683–735.

Berry, J. M., West, R. L., & Dennehey, D. (1989). Reliability and validity of the memory self-efficacy questionnaire. *Developmental Psychology*, 25, 701–713.

Betz, N. E., & Fitzgerald, L. F. (1987). *The career psychology of women*. Orlando, Fla.: Academic.

Betz, N. E., & Hackett, G. (1981). The relationship of career-related self-efficacy expectations to perceived career options in college women and men. *Journal of Counseling Psychology*, 28, 399–410.

Betz, N. E., & Hackett, G. (1983). The relationship of mathematics self-efficacy expectations to the selection of science-based college majors. *Journal of Vocational Behavior*, 23, 329–345.

Betz, N. E., & Hackett, G. (1986). Applications of self-efficacy theory to understanding career choice behavior. *Journal of Social and Clinical Psychology*, 4, 279–289.

Betz, N. E., & Hackett, G. (1987). Concept of agency in educational and career development. *Journal of Counseling Psychology*, 34, 299–308.

Betz, N. E., Klein, K. L., & Taylor, K. M. (1996). Evaluation of a short form of the career decision making self-efficacy scale. *Journal of Career Assessment*, 4, 47–58.

Bien, T. H., Miller, W. R., & Tonigan, J. S. (1993). Brief interventions for alcohol problems: A review. *Addiction*, 88, 315–336.

Bieschke, K. J., Bishop, R. M., & Garcia, V. L. (1996). The utility of the research self-efficacy scale. *Journal of Career Assessment*, 4, 59–75.

Binks, M., & Vale, P. (1990). *Entrepreneurship and economic change*. London: McGraw-Hill.

Binswanger, L. (1958). The case of Ellen West. In R. May, E. Angel, & H. F. Ellenberger (Eds.), *Existence: A new dimension in psychiatry and psychology* (pp. 237–264). New York: Basic Books.

Biran, M., & Wilson, G. T. (1981). Treatment of phobic disorders using cognitive and exposure methods: A self-efficacy analysis. *Journal of Counseling and Clinical Psychology*, 49, 886–899.

Birren, J. E. (1969). Age and decision strategies. *Interdisciplinary Topics in Gerontology*, 4, 23–36.

Bishop, J. H. (1989). Why the apathy in American high schools? *Educational Researcher*, 18, 6–10.

Black, A. H. (1965). Cardiac conditioning in curarized dogs: The relationship between

heart rate and skeletal behaviour. In W. F. Prokasy (Ed.), *Classical conditioning: A symposium* (pp. 20–47). New York: Appleton-Century-Crofts.

Blackburn, I. M., Eunson, K. M., & Bishop, S. (1986). A two-year naturalistic follow-up of depressed patients treated with cognitive therapy, pharmacotherapy, and a combination of both. *Journal of Affective Disorders*, 10, 67–75.

Blair, S. N., Kohl, H. W., III, Barlow, C. E., Paffenbarger, R. S., Gibbons, L. W., & Macera, C. A. (1995). Changes in physical fitness and all-cause mortality: A prospective study of health and unhealthy men. *Journal of the American Medical Association*, 273, 1093–1098.

Blane, H. T., & Leonard, K. E. (Eds.). (1987). *Psychological theories of drinking and alcoholism* (pp. 1–11). New York: Guilford.

Blittner, M., Goldberg, J., & Merbaum, M. (1978). Cognitive self-control factors in the reduction of smoking behavior. *Behavior Therapy*, 9, 553–561.

Block, J. H., Efthim, H. E., & Burns, R. B. (1989). *Building effective mastery learning schools*. White Plains, N.Y.: Longman.

Bloom, B. S., Madaus, G. F., & Hastings, J. T. (1981). *Evaluation to improve learning*. New York: McGraw-Hill.

Bloom, C. P., Yates, B. T., & Brosvic, G. M. (1984). Self-efficacy reporting, sex-role stereotyping, and sex differences in susceptibility to depression. Manuscript, The American University, Washington, D.C.

Blumenthal, M., Kahn, R. L., Andrews, F. M., & Head, K. B. (1972). *Justifying violence: The attitudes of American men*. Ann Arbor, Mich.: Institute for Social Research.

Blustein, D. L. (1989). The role of goal instability and career self-efficacy in the career exploration process. *Journal of Vocational Behavior*, 35, 194–203.

Boggiano, A. K., & Ruble, D. N. (1979). Competence and the overjustification effect: A developmental study. *Journal of Personality and Social Psychology*, 37, 1462–1468.

Bok, S. (1980). The self deceived. *Social Science Information*, 19, 923–936.

Bolles, R. C. (1975a). *Theory of motivation* (2nd ed.). New York: Harper & Row.

Bolles, R. C. (1975b). *Learning theory*. New York: Holt, Rinehart, & Winston.

Bolton, M. K. (1993). Imitation versus innovation: Lessons to be learned from the Japanese. *Organizational Dynamics*, 30–45.

Bond, R., & Smith, P. B. (1996). Culture and conformity: A meta-analysis of studies using

Asch's (1952b, 1956) line judgment task. *Psychological Bulletin,* 119, 111–137.

Bootzin, R. R., Herman, C. P., & Nicassio, P. (1976). The power of suggestion: Another examination of misattribution and insomnia. *Journal of Personality and Social Psychology,* 34, 673–679.

Bores-Rangel, E., Church, A. T., Szendre, D., & Reeves, C. (1990). Self-efficacy in relation to occupational consideration and academic performance in high school equivalency students. *Journal of Counseling Psychology,* 37, 407–418.

Boring, E. G. (1957). When is human behavior predetermined? *The Scientific Monthly,* 84, 189–196.

Borkovec, T. D., Wilkinson, L., Follensbee, R., & Lerman, C. (1983). Stimulus control applications to the treatment of worry. *Behaviour Research and Therapy,* 21, 247–251.

Bortz, W. M. (in press). Human aging, normal and abnormal. In R. Schrier & D. Jahnigen (Eds.), Geriatric medicine. Cambridge: Blackwell Scientific.

Bortz, W. M., II (1982). Disuse and aging. *Journal of the American Medical Association,* 248, 1203–1208.

Botvin, G. (1990). Substance abuse prevention: Theory, practice and effectiveness. In M. Tonry & J. Q. Wilson (Eds.), *Drugs and crime* (pp. 461–519). Chicago, Ill.: University of Chicago Press.

Botvin, G. J., & Dusenbury, L. (1992). Substance abuse prevention: Implications for reducing risk of HIV infection. *Psychology of Addictive Behaviors,* 6, 70–80.

Bouchard, S., Gauthier, J., LaBerge, B., French, D., Pelletier, M., & Godbout, C. (1996). Exposure versus cognitive restructuring in the treatment of panic disorder with agoraphobia. *Behaviour Research and Therapy,* 34, 213–224.

Bouffard-Bouchard, T. (1990). Influence of self-efficacy on performance in a cognitive task. *Journal of Social Psychology,* 130, 353–363.

Bouffard-Bouchard, T., Parent, S., & Larivée, S. (1991). Influence of self-efficacy on self-regulation and performance among junior and senior high-school age students. *International Journal of Behavioral Development,* 14, 153–164.

Bourne, L. E., Jr. (1965). Hypotheses and hypothesis shifts in classification learning. *The Journal of General Psychology,* 72, 251–262.

Bovbjerg, D. H., Redd, W. H., Maier, L. A., et al. (1990). Anticipatory immune suppression and nausea in women receiving cyclic chemotherapy for ovarian cancer.

Journal of Consulting and Clinical Psychology, 58, 153–157.

Bowen, D. R., Bowen, E. R., Gawser, S. R., & Masotti, L. H. (1968). Deprivation, mobility, and orientation toward protest of the urban poor. *American Behavioral Scientist,* 11, 20–24.

Bower, G. H. (1981). Mood and memory. *American Psychologist,* 36, 129–148.

Bower, G. H. (1983). Affect and cognition. *Philosophical Transactions of the Royal Society of London* (Series B), 302, 387–402.

Boyd, B. K., & Fulk, J. (1996). Executive scanning and perceived uncertainty: A multidimensional model. *Journal of Management,* 22, 1–21.

Bradley, R. D. (1993). The use of goal-setting and positive self-modeling to enhance self-efficacy and performance for the basketball free-throw shot. Ph.D. diss., University of Maryland.

Bradley, R. H., Caldwell, B. M., & Elardo, R. (1979). Home environment and cognitive development in the first two years: A cross-lagged panel analysis. *Developmental Psychology,* 15, 246–250.

Bradley, R. H., Caldwell, B. M., & Rock, S. L. (1988). Home environment and school performance: A ten-year follow-up and examination of three models of environmental action. *Child Development,* 59, 852–867.

Bradley, R. H., Caldwell, B. M., Rock, S. L., Barnard, K. E., Gray, C., Hammond, M. A., Mitchell, S., Siegel, L., Ramey, C. T., Gottfried, A. W., & Johnson, D. L. (1989). Home environment and cognitive development in the first 3 years of life: A collaborative study involving six sites and three ethnic groups in North America. *Developmental Psychology,* 25, 217–235.

Brafford, L. J., & Beck, K. H. (1991). Development and validation of a condom self-efficacy scale for college students. *Journal of American College Health,* 39, 219–225.

Braithwaite, J. (1994). A sociology of modelling and the politics of empowerment. *British Journal of Sociology,* 45, 445–479.

Brandt, R. (1989). On parents and schools: A conversation with Joyce Epstein. *Educational Leadership,* October, 24–27.

Brandt, R. B. (1979). *A theory of the good and the right.* Oxford: Clarendon.

Brandtstädter, J. (1989). Personal self-regulation of development: Cross-sequential analyses of development-related control beliefs and emotions. *Developmental Psychology,* 25, 96–108.

Brandtstädter, J. (1992). Personal control over development: Implications of self-effi-

cacy. In R. Schwarzer (Ed.), *Self-efficacy: Thought control of action* (pp. 127–145). Washington, D.C.: Hemisphere.

Brandtstädter, J., & Baltes-Götz, B. (1990). Personal control over development and quality of life perspectives in adulthood. In P. B. Baltes & M. M. Baltes (Eds.), *Successful aging: Perspectives from the behavioral sciences* (pp. 197–224). Cambridge: Cambridge University Press.

Brehmer, B. (1980). In one word: Not from experience. *Acta Psychologica,* 45, 223–241.

Brehmer, B., Hagafors, R., & Johansson, R. (1980). Cognitive skills in judgment: Subject's ability to use information about weights, function forms, and organizing principles. *Organization and Human Performance,* 26, 373–385.

Brehmer, B., & Joyce, C. R. B. (Eds.) (1988). *Human judgment: The SJT view.* Amsterdam: North-Holland.

Brewer, W. F. (1974). There is no convincing evidence for operant or classical conditioning in adult humans. In W. B. Weimer & D. S. Palermo (Eds.), *Cognition and the symbolic processes* (pp. 1–42). Hillsdale, N.J.: Erlbaum.

Brim, B. (1992). *Ambition: How we manage success and failure throughout our lives.* New York: Basic Books.

Brim, O. G., Jr., & Ryff, C. D. (1980). On the properties of life events. In P. B. Baltes & O. G. Brim, Jr. (Eds.), *Life-span development and behavior* (Vol. 3, pp. 367–388). New York: Academic.

Brod, M. I., & Hall, S. M. (1984). Joiners and nonjoiners in smoking treatment: A comparison of psychosocial variables. *Addictive Behaviors,* 9, 217–221.

Brody, E. B., Hatfield, B. D., & Spalding, T. W. (1988). Generalization of self-efficacy to a continuum of stressors upon mastery of a high-risk sport skill. *Journal of Sport and Exercise Psychology,* 10, 32–44.

Bronfenbrenner, U. (1958). The study of identification through interpersonal perception. In R. Tagiuri & L. Petrullo (Eds.), *Person, perception and interpersonal behavior* (pp. 110–130). Stanford, Calif.: Stanford University Press.

Brookover, W. B., Beady, C., Flood, P., Schweitzer, J., & Wisenbaker, J. (1979). *School social systems and student achievement: Schools make a difference.* New York: Praeger.

Brooks-Gunn, J. (1991). Consequences of maturational timing variations in adolescent girls. In R. M. Lerner, A. C. Petersen, & J. Brooks-Gunn (Eds.), *Encyclopedia of adolescence* (Vol. 2, pp. 614–618). New York: Garland.

Brooks-Gunn, J., & Furstenberg, F. F., Jr. (1989). Adolescent sexual behavior. *American Psychologist, 44,* 249–257.

Brown, A. L. (1984). Metacognition, executive control, self-regulation, and other even more mysterious mechanisms. In F. E. Weinert & R. H. Kluwe (Eds.), *Metacognition, motivation, and learning* (pp. 60–108). Stuttgart, West Germany: Kuhlhammer.

Brown, I., Jr., & Inouye, D. K. (1978). Learned helplessness through modeling: The role of perceived similarity in competence. *Journal of Personality and Social Psychology, 36,* 900–908.

Brown, J. D., Childers, K. W., & Waszak, C. S. (1990). Television and adolescent sexuality. *Journal of Adolescent Health Care, 11,* 62–70.

Brown, J. S. (1953). Comments on Professor Harlow's paper. In *Current theory and research on motivation: A symposium* (pp. 49–55). Lincoln: University of Nebraska Press.

Brown, L. A. (1981). *Innovation diffusion: A new perspective.* New York: Methuen.

Brown, S. D. (1980). Videotape feedback: Effects on assertive performance and subjects' perceived competence and satisfaction. *Psychological Reports, 47,* 455–461.

Brown, S. D., Lent, R. W., Ryan, N. E., & McPartland, E. B. (1996). Self-efficacy as an intervening mechanism between research training environments and scholarly productivity: A theoretical and methodological extension. *The Counseling Psychologist, 24,* 535–544.

Brown, S. J., Lieberman, D. A., Gemeny, B. A., Fan, Y. C., Wilson, D. M., & Pasta, D. J. (in press). Educational video game for juvenile diabetes care: Results of a controlled trial. *Medical Informatics.*

Brown, W. J., & Cody, M. J. (1991). Effects of a prosocial television soap opera in promoting women's status. *Human Communication Research, 18,* 114–142.

Brownell, K. D., & Jeffery, R. W. (1987). Improving long-term weight loss: Pushing the limits of treatment. *Behavior Therapy, 18,* 353–374.

Brownell, K. D., Marlatt, G. A., Lichtenstein, E., & Wilson, G. T. (1986). Understanding and preventing relapse. *American Psychologist, 41,* 765–782.

Brownell, K. D., & Rodin, J. (1994). The dieting maelstrom: Is it possible and advisable to lose weight? *American Psychologist, 49,* 781–791.

Brownell, K. D., & Stunkard, A. J. (1980).

Physical activity in the development and control of obesity. In A. J. Stunkard (Ed.), *Obesity* (pp. 300–324). Philadelphia: W. B. Saunders Co.

Brownell, K. D., & Wadden, T. A. (1992). Etiology and treatment of obesity: Understanding a serious, prevalent, and refractory disorder. *Journal of Consulting and Clinical Psychology, 60,* 505–517.

Bruner, J. S., Goodnow, J., & Austin, G. A. (1956). *A study of thinking.* New York: Wiley.

Brunswik, E. (1952). *The conceptual framework of psychology.* Chicago: University of Chicago Press.

Bruvold, W. H. (1993). A meta-analysis of adolescent smoking prevention programs. *American Journal of Public Health, 83,* 872–880.

Bryan, J. F., & Locke, E. A. (1967). Goal-setting as a means of increasing motivation. *Journal of Applied Psychology, 51,* 274–277.

Buckelew, S. P., Parker, J. C., Keefe, F. J., Deuser, W. E., Crews, T. M., Conway, R., Kay, D. R., & Hewett, J. E. (1994). Self-efficacy and pain behavior among subjects with fibromyalgia. *Pain, 59,* 377–384.

Buescher, K. L., Johnston, J. A., Parker, J. C., Smarr, K. L., Buckelew, S. P., Anderson, S. K., & Walker, S. E. (1991). Relationship of self-efficacy to pain behavior. *Journal of Rheumatology, 18,* 968–972.

Bull, S. J. (1991). Personal and situational influences on adherence to mental skills training. *Journal of Sport and Exercise Psychology, 13,* 121–132.

Bullock, D., & Merrill, L. (1980). The impact of personal preference on consistency through time: The case of childhood aggression. *Child Development, 51,* 808–814.

Bunge, M. (1977). Emergence and the mind. *Neuroscience, 2,* 501–509.

Bunge, M. (1980). *The mind-body problem: A psychological approach.* Oxford: Pergamon.

Burke, M. J., & Day, R. R. (1986). A cumulative study of the effectiveness of management training. *Journal of Applied Psychology, 71,* 232–245.

Burkhardt, M. E., & Brass, D. J. (1990). Changing patterns or patterns of change: The effects of a change in technology on social network structure and power. *Administrative Science Quarterly, 35,* 104–127.

Burnett, K. F., Nagel, P. E., Harrington, S., & Taylor, C. B. (1989). Computer-assisted behavioral health counseling for high school students. *Journal of Counseling Psychology, 36,* 63–67.

Burns, T. R., & Dietz, T. (in press). Human agency and evolutionary processes: Institutional dynamics and social revolution. In B. Wittrock (Ed.), *Agency in social theory.* Thousand Oaks, Calif.: Sage.

Buske-Kirschbaum, A., Kirschbaum, C., Stierle, H., Lehnert, H., & Hellhammer, K. (1992). Conditioned increase of natural killer cell activity (NKCA) in humans. *Psychosomatic Medicine, 54,* 123–132.

Butler, R. N., & Brody, J. A. (1995). *Delaying the onset of late-life dysfunction.* New York: Springer.

Butterfoss, F. D., Goodman, R. M., & Wandersman, A. (1993). Community coalitions for prevention and health promotion. *Health Education Research, 8,* 315–330.

Calder, B. J., & Staw, B. M. (1975). Self-perception of intrinsic and extrinsic motivation. *Journal of Personality and Social Psychology, 31,* 599–605.

Call, K. T., Mortimer, J. T., Lee, C., & Dennehy, K. (1993). High risk youth and the attainment process. Manuscript, University of Minnesota.

Campbell, A., Gurin, G., & Miller, W. E. (1954). *The voter decides.* Evanston, Ill.: Row, Peterson.

Campbell, M. K., DeVellis, B. M., Strecher, V. J., Ammerman, A. S., DeVellis, R. F., & Sandler, R. S. (1994). Improving dietary behavior: The effectiveness of tailored messages in primary care settings. *American Journal of Public Health, 84,* 783–787.

Campbell, N. K., & Hackett, G. (1986). The effects of mathematics task performance on math self-efficacy and task interest. *Journal of Vocational Behavior, 28,* 149–162.

Campion, M. A., & Lord, R. G. (1982). A control systems conceptualization of the goal-setting and changing process. *Organizational Behavior and Human Performance, 30,* 265–287.

Campion, M. A., Medsker, G. J., & Higgs, C. (1993). Relations between work group characteristics and effectiveness: Implications for designing effective work groups. *Personnel Psychology, 46,* 823–850.

Cannon, A. (1988, February 13). Getting minorities into college. *San Francisco Chronicle,* p. A2.

Cantor, N., & Harlow, R. E. (1994). Personality, strategic behavior and daily life problem-solving. *Current Directions in Psychological Science, 3,* 169–172.

Caplan, N. (1970). The new ghetto man: A review of recent empirical studies. *Journal of Social Issues, 26,* 59–73.

Cappell, H., & Greeley, J. (1987). Alcohol

and tension reduction: An update on research and theory. In H. T. Blance & K. E. Leonard (Eds.), *Psychological theories of drinking and alcoholism* (pp. 15–54). New York: Guilford.

Carey, K. B., & Carey, M. P. (1993). Changes in self-efficacy resulting from unaided attempts to quit smoking. *Psychology of Addictive Behaviors, 7,* 219–224.

Carey, M. P., Kalra, D. L., Carey, K. B., Halperin, S., & Richards, C. S. (1993). Stress and unaided smoking cessation: A Prospective investigation. *Journal of Consulting and Clinical Psychology, 61,* 831–838.

Carroll, D. L. (1995). The importance of self-efficacy expectations in elderly patients recovering from coronary artery bypass surgery. *Heart and Lung, 24,* 50–59.

Carroll, K. M., Rounsaville, B. J., & Keller, D. S. (1991). Relapse prevention strategies for the treatment of cocaine abuse. *American Journal of Drug and Alcohol Abuse, 17,* 249–265.

Carroll, W. R., & Bandura, A. (1982). The role of visual monitoring in observational learning of action patterns: Making the unobservable observable. *Journal of Motor Behavior, 14,* 153–167.

Carroll, W. R., & Bandura, A. (1985). Role of timing of visual monitoring and motor rehearsal in observational learning of action patterns. *Journal of Motor Behavior, 17,* 269–281.

Carroll, W. R., & Bandura, A. (1987). Translating cognition into action: The role of visual guidance in observational learning. *Journal of Motor Behavior, 19,* 385–398.

Carroll, W. R., & Bandura, A. (1990). Representational guidance of action production in observational learning: A causal analysis. *Journal of Motor Behavior, 22,* 85–97.

Carron, A. V. (1984). Cohesion in sport teams. In J. M. Silva, III & R. S. Weinberg (Eds.), *Psychological foundations of sport* (pp. 340–351). Champaign, Ill.: Human Kinetics Publ.

Carstensen, L. L. (1992). Selectivity theory: Social activity in life-span context. In K. W. Schaie (Ed.), *Annual review of gerontology and geriatrics* (Vol. 11, pp. 195–217). New York: Springer.

Carver, C. S., & Scheier, M. F. (1981). *Attention and self-regulation: A control-theory approach to human behavior.* New York: Springer-Verlag.

Celuch, K. G., Lust, J. A., & Showers, L. S. (1995). An investigation of the relationship between self-efficacy and the communication effectiveness of product manual

formats. *Journal of Business and Psychology, 9,* 241–252.

Cervone, D. (1985). Randomization test to determine significance levels for microanalytic congruences between self-efficacy and behavior. *Cognitive Therapy and Research, 9,* 357–365.

Cervone, D. (1989). Effects of envisioning future activities on self-efficacy judgments and motivation: An availability heuristic interpretation. *Cognitive Therapy and Research, 13,* 247–261.

Cervone, D., & Palmer, B. W. (1990). Anchoring biases and the perseverance of self-efficacy beliefs. *Cognitive Therapy and Research, 14,* 401–416.

Cervone, D., & Peake, P. K. (1986). Anchoring, efficacy, and action: The influence of judgmental heuristics on self-efficacy judgments and behavior. *Journal of Personality and Social Psychology, 50,* 492–501.

Cervone, D., Jiwani, N., & Wood, R. (1991). Goal-setting and the differential influence of self-regulatory processes on complex decision-making performance. *Journal of Personality and Social Psychology, 61,* 257–266.

Chamberlain, C. J., Coelho, A. J. (1993). The perceptual side of action: Decision-making in sport. In J. L. Starkes & F. Allard (Eds.), *Cognitive issues in motor expertise* (pp. 135–157). North-Holland: Elsevier Science Publishers B. V.

Chambliss, C. A., & Murray, E. J. (1979a). Cognitive procedures for smoking reduction: Symptom attribution versus efficacy attribution. *Cognitive Therapy and Research, 3,* 91–96.

Chambliss, C. A., & Murray, E. J. (1979b). Efficacy attribution, locus of control, and weight loss. *Cognitive Therapy and Research, 3,* 349–354.

Champlin, T. S. (1977). Self-deception: A reflexive dilemma. *Philosophy, 52,* 281–299.

Chaney, E. F., O'Leary, M. R., & Marlatt, G. A. (1978). Skill training with alcoholics. *Journal of Consulting and Clinical Psychology, 46,* 1092–1104.

Chapman, M., Skinner, E. A., & Baltes, P. B. (1990). Interpreting correlations between children's perceived control and cognitive performance: Control, agency, or means-ends beliefs? *Developmental Psychology, 26,* 246–253.

Church, A. T., Teresa, J. S., Rosebrook, R., & Szendre, D. (1992). Self-efficacy for careers and occupational consideration in minority high school equivalency students. *Journal of Counseling Psychology, 39,* 498–508.

Churchill, A. C. (1991). Metacognitive self-efficacy and intrusive thought. Ph.D. diss., University of Melbourne.

Churchill, A. C., & McMurray, N. E. (1989). Self-efficacy and unpleasant intrusive thought. Manuscript, University of Melbourne.

Chwalisz, K. D., Altmaier, E. M., & Russell, D. W. (1992). Causal attributions, self-efficacy cognitions, and coping with stress. *Journal of Social and Clinical Psychology, 11,* 377–400.

Cialdini, R. B., Borden, R. J., Thorne, A., Walker, M. R., Freeman, S., & Sloan, L. R. (1976). Basking in reflected glory: Three (football) field studies. *Journal of Personality and Social Psychology, 34,* 366–375.

Ciminero, A. R., & Steingarten, K. A. (1978). The effects of performance standards on self-evaluation and self-reinforcement in depressed and nondepressed individuals. *Cognitive Therapy and Research, 2,* 179–182.

Cioffi, D. (1991a). Beyond attentional strategies: A cognitive-perceptual model of somatic interpretation. *Psychological Bulletin, 109,* 25–41.

Cioffi, D. (1991b). Sensory awareness versus sensory impression: Affect and attention interact to produce somatic meaning. *Cognition and Emotion, 5,* 275–294.

Cioffi, D. (1993). Sensate body, directive mind: Physical sensations and mental control. In D. M. Wegner & J. W. Pennebaker (Eds.), *The handbook of mental control* (pp. 410–442). Englewood Cliffs, N.J.: Prentice-Hall.

Clance, P. R. (1985). *The impostor phenomenon.* Atlanta, Ga.: Peachtree.

Clark, D. M. (1988). A cognitive model of panic attacks. In S. Rachman & J. D. Maser (Eds.), *Panic: Psychological perspectives* (pp. 71–90). Hillsdale, N.J.: Erlbaum.

Clark, L. V. (1960). Effect of mental practice on the development of a certain motor skill. *Research Quarterly, 31,* 560–569.

Clark, M., Ghandour, G., Miller, N. H., Taylor, C. B., Bandura, A., & DeBusk, R. F. (in press). Development and evaluation of a computer-based system for dietary management of hyperlipidemia. *Journal of the American Dietetic Association.*

Clark, M. M., Abrams, D. B., Niaura, R. S., Eaton, C. A., & Rossi, J. S. (1991). Self-efficacy in weight management. *Journal of Consulting and Clinical Psychology, 59,* 739–744.

Clifford, S. A. (1988). Cause of termination and self-efficacy expectations as related to reemployment status. Ph.D. diss., University of Toledo, Ohio.

Coelho, R. J. (1984). Self-efficacy and cessation of smoking. *Psychological Reports*, 54, 309–310.

Cohen, E. G. (1990). Teaching in multiculturally heterogeneous classrooms: Findings from a model program. *McGill Journal of Education*, 26, 7–22.

Cohen, E. G. (1993). From theory to practice: The development of an applied research program. In J. Berger & M. Zelditch (Eds.), *Theoretical research programs: Studies in the growth of theory* (pp. 385–415). Stanford, Calif.: Stanford University Press.

Cohen, J. (1986). Theoretical considerations of peer tutoring. *Psychology in the Schools*, 23, 175–185.

Cohen, S., & Herbert, T. B. (1996). Health psychology: Psychological factors and physical disease from the perspective of human psychoneuroimmunology. In J. T. Spence, J. M. Darley, & D. J. Foss (Eds.), *Annual Review of Psychology*, 47, 113–142.

Cohen, S., & Lichtenstein, E. (1990). Partner behaviors that support quitting smoking. *Journal of Consulting and Clinical Psychology*, 58, 304–309.

Cohen, S., Tyrrell, D. A. J., & Smith, A. P. (1991). Psychological stress and susceptibility to the common cold. *New England Journal of Medicine*, 325, 606–612.

Cohen, S. G. (1994). Designing effective self-managing work teams. In M. M. Beyerlein & D. A. Johnson (Eds), *Advances in interdisciplinary studies of work teams* (Vol. 1, pp. 67–102). Greenwich, Conn.: JAI.

Cohn, E., & Rossmiller, R. (1987). Research on effective schools: Implications for less developed countries. *Comparative Education Review*, 31, 377–399.

Coladarci, T. (1992). Teachers' sense of efficacy and commitment to teaching. *Journal of Experimental Education*, 60, 323–337.

Coleman, J. S., Katz, E., & Menzel, H. (1966). *Medical innovation: A diffusion study*. New York: Bobbs-Merrill.

Coletti, G., Supnick, J. A., & Payne, T. J. (1985). The smoking self-efficacy questionnaire (SSEQ): Preliminary scale development and validation. *Behavioral Assessment*, 7, 249–260.

Collins, J. L. (1982, March). Self-efficacy and ability in achievement behavior. Paper presented at the annual meeting of the American Educational Research Association, New York.

Collins, R. L., & Lapp, W. M. (1991). Restraint and attributions: Evidence of the abstinence violation effect in alcohol consumption. *Cognitive Therapy and Research*, 15, 69–84.

Collins, R. L., & Marlatt, G. A. (1981). Social modeling as a determinant of drinking behavior: Implications for prevention and treatment. *Addictive Behaviors*, 6, 233–239.

Collis, B. (1985). Psychosocial implications of sex differences in attitudes toward computers: Results of a survey. *International Journal of Women's Studies*, 8, 207–213.

Comer, J. P. (1980). *School power*. New York: Free Press.

Comer, J. P. (1985). The Yale-New Haven primary prevention project: A follow-up study. *Journal of the American Academy of Child Psychiatry*, 24, 154–160.

Comer, J. P. (1988). Educating poor minority children. *Scientific American*, 259, 42–48.

Compeau, D. R., & Higgins, C. A. (1995). Computer self-efficacy: Development of a measure and initial test. *MIS Quarterly*, 19, 189–212.

Condiotte, M. M., & Lichtenstein, E. (1981). Self-efficacy and relapse in smoking cessation programs. *Journal of Consulting and Clinical Psychology*, 49, 648–658.

Connell, D. B., Turner, R. R., & Mason, E. F. (1985). Summary of findings of the school health education evaluation: Health promotion effectiveness, implementation, and costs. *Journal of School Health*, 55, 316–321.

Connolly, J. (1989). Social self-efficacy in adolescence: Relations with self-concept, social adjustment, and mental health. *Canadian Journal of Behavioural Science*, 21, 258–269.

Cooley, E. J., & Klinger, C. R. (1990). Academic attributions and coping with tests. *Journal of Social and Clinical Psychology*, 8, 359–367.

Cooney, N. L., Gillespie, R. A., Baker, L. H., & Kaplan, R. F. (1987). Cognitive changes after alcohol cue exposure. *Journal of Consulting and Clinical Psychology*, 55, 150–155.

Cooney, N. L., Kopel, S. A., & McKeon, P. (1982). Controlled relapse training and self-efficacy in ex-smokers. Paper presented at the annual meeting of the American Psychological Association, Washington, D.C.

Coopersmith, S. (1967). *The antecedents of self-esteem*. San Francisco: W. H. Freeman.

Corbin, C. (1972). Mental practice. In W. Morgan (Ed.), *Ergogenic aids and muscular performance* (pp. 93–118). New York: Academic.

Corbin, C. B., Laurie, D. R., Gruger, C., & Smiley, B. (1984). Vicarious success experience as a factor influencing self-confidence, attitudes, and physical activity of adult women. *Journal of Teaching in Physical Education*, 4, 17–23.

Cordua, G. D., McGraw, K. O., & Drabman, R. S. (1979). Doctor or nurse: Children's perceptions of sex-typed occupations. *Child Development*, 50, 590–593.

Council, J. R., Ahern, D. K., Follick, M. J., & Kline, C. L. (1988). Expectancies and functional impairment in chronic low back pain. *Pain*, 33, 323–331.

Courneya, K. S., & McAuley, E. (1993). Efficacy, attributional, affective responses of older adults following an acute bout of exercise. *Journal of Social Behavior and Personality*, 8, 729–742.

Courtney, A. E., & Whipple, T. W. (1974). Women in TV commercials. *The Journal of Communication*, 24, 110–118.

Covington, M. V., & Omelich, C. L. (1979). Are causal attributions causal? A path analysis of the cognitive model of achievement motivation. *Journal of Personality and Social Psychology*, 37, 1487–1504.

Coyne, J. C. (1976b). Toward an interactional description of depression. *Psychiatry*, 39, 28–40.

Coyne, J. C. (1988). Strategic therapy with couples having a depressed spouse. In G. Haas, I. Glick, & J. Clarkin (Eds.), *Family intervention in affective illness* (pp. 89–114). New York: Guilford.

Coyne, J. C. (1990). Interpersonal processes in depression. In G. I. Keitner (Ed.), *Depression and families: Impact and treatment* (pp. 33–53). Washington, D.C.: American Psychiatric Press.

Coyne, J. C. (Ed.). (1985). *Essential papers on depression*. New York: New York University Press.

Cozzarelli, C. (1993). Personality and self-efficacy as predictors of coping with abortion. *Journal of Personality and Social Psychology*, 65, 1224–1236.

Crabtree, M. K. (1986). Self-efficacy beliefs and social support as predictors of diabetic self-care. Ph.D. diss., University of California, San Francisco.

Craig, K. D. (1978). Social modeling influences on pain. In R. A. Sternbach (Ed.), *The psychology of pain* (pp. 73–109). New York: Raven.

Craig, K. D. (1983). A social learning perspective on pain experience. In M. Rosenbaum, C. M. Franks, & Y. Jaffe (Eds.), *Perspectives on behavior therapy in the eighties* (pp. 311–327). New York: Springer.

Craig, K. D. (1986). Social modeling influences. In R. A. Sternbach (Ed.), *The Psy-*

chology of pain (2nd ed., pp. 73–109). New York: Raven.

Craig, K. D., & Neidermayer, H. (1974). Autonomic correlates of pain thresholds influenced by social modeling. *Journal of Personality and Social Psychology, 29,* 246–252.

Craig, S. C. (1979). Efficacy, trust, and political behavior: An attempt to resolve a lingering conceptual dilemma. *American Politics Quarterly, 7,* 225–239.

Craighead, L. W., Stunkard, A. J., & O'Brien, R. M. (1981). Behavior therapy and pharmacotherapy for obesity. *Archives of General Psychiatry, 38,* 763–768.

Crandall, V. C. (1978, August). Expecting sex differences and sex differences in expectancies: A developmental analysis. In *Role of belief systems in the production of sex differences.* Symposium presented at the meeting of the American Psychological Association, Toronto.

Crawford, T., & Naditch, M. (1970). Relative deprivation, powerlessness, and militancy: The psychology of social protest. *Psychiatry, 33,* 208–223.

Creer, T. L., & Miklich, D. R. (1970). The application of a self-modeling procedure to modify an inappropriate behavior. *Behavior Research and Therapy, 8,* 91–92.

Crick, N. R., & Dodge, K. A. (1994). A review and reformulation of social information-processing mechanisms in children's social adjustment. *Psychological Bulletin,* 115, 74–101.

Crites, J. O. (1974). Career development processes: A model of vocational maturity. In E. L. Herr (Ed.), *Vocational guidance and human development* (pp. 296–320). Boston: Houghton Mifflin.

Crundall, I., & Foddy, M. (1981). Vicarious exposure to a task as a basis of evaluative competence. *Social Psychology Quarterly,* 44, 331–338.

Csikszentmihalyi, M. (1975). *Beyond boredom and anxiety.* San Francisco: Josey-Bass.

Csikszentmihalyi, M. (1979). Intrinsic rewards and emergent motivation. In M. R. Lepper & D. Greene (Eds.), *The hidden costs of reward.* (pp. 205–216). Morristown, N.J.: Erlbaum.

Cummings, C., Gordon, J. R., & Marlatt, G. A. (1980). Relapse: Strategies of prevention and prediction. In W. R. Miller (Ed.), *The addictive behaviors: Treatment of alcoholism, drug abuse, smoking and obesity* (pp. 291–321). Oxford: Pergamon.

Cunningham, A. J., Lockwood, G. A., & Cunningham, J. A. (1991). A relationship between perceived self-efficacy and quality of life in cancer patients. *Patient Education and Counseling,* 17, 71–78.

Curry, S. J., & McBride, C. M. (1994). Relapse prevention for smoking cessation: Review and evaluation of concepts and interventions. *Annual Review of Public Health,* 15, 345–366.

Cutler, J. C., & Arnold, R. C. (1988). Venereal disease control by health departments in the past: Lessons for the present. *American Journal of Public Health,* 78, 372–376.

Cutrona, C. E., & Troutman, B. R. (1986). Social support, infant temperament, and parenting self-efficacy: A mediational model of postpartum depression. *Child Development,* 57, 1507–1518.

Daft, R. L., & Huber, G. P. (1987). How organizations learn: A communication framework. In S. B. Bacharach (Ed.) & N. DiTomaso (Guest Ed.), *Research in the sociology of organizations* (Vol. 5, pp. 1–36). Greenwich, Conn.: JAI.

Dale, J., & Weinberg, R. (1990). Burnout in sport: A review and critique. *Applied Sport Psychology,* 2, 67–83.

Danehower, C. (1988). An empirical examination of the relationship between self-efficacy and expectancy. In D. F. Ray (Ed.), *Southern Management Association Proceedings* (pp. 128–130). Mississippi State: Southern Management Association.

Davey, G. C. L., Jubb, M., & Cameron, C. (1996). Catastrophic worrying as a function of changes in problem-solving confidence. *Cognitive Therapy and Research,* 20, 333–344.

Davidson, D. (1971). Agency. In R. Binkley, R. Bronaugh, & A. Marras (Eds.), *Agent, action, and reason* (pp. 3–37). University of Toronto Press.

Davidson, P., & Bucher, B. (1978). Intrinsic interest and extrinsic reward: The effects of a continuing token program on continuing nonconstrained preference. *Behavior Therapy,* 9, 222–234.

Davies, D. (1991). Schools reaching out: Family, school, and community partnerships for student success. *Phi Delta Kappan,* January, 376–382.

Davies, J. C. (1969). The J-curve of rising and declining satisfactions as a cause of some great revolutions and a contained rebellion. In H. D. Graham & T. R. Gurr (Eds.), *Violence in America: Historical and comparative perspectives* (Vol. 2, pp. 547–576). Washington, D.C.: U.S. Government Printing Office.

Davis, F. W., & Yates, B. T. (1982). Self-efficacy expectancies versus outcome expectancies as determinants of performance deficits and depressive affect. *Cognitive Therapy and Research,* 6, 23–35.

Davis-Berman, J. (1989). Physical self-efficacy, perceived physical status, and depressive symptomatology in older adults. *The Journal of Psychology,* 124, 207–215.

Dawes, R. M., Faust, D., & Meehl, P. E. (1989). Clinical versus actuarial judgment. *Science,* 31, 1668–1674.

DeBusk, R. F., Kraemer, H. C., & Nash, E. (1983). Stepwise risk stratification soon after acute myocardial infarction. *The American Journal of Cardiology,* 12, 1161–1166.

DeBusk, R. F., Miller, N. H., Superko, H. R., Dennis, C. A., Thomas, R. J., Lew, H. T., Berger III, W. E., Heller, R. S., Rompf, J., Gee, D., Kraemer, H. C., Bandura, A., Ghandour, G., Clark, M., Shah, R. V., Fisher, L., & Taylor, C. B. (1994). A case-management system for coronary risk factor modification after acute myocardial infarction. *Annals of Internal Medicine,* 120, 721–729.

Decety, J., & Ingvar, D. H. (1990). Brain structures participating in mental simulation of motor behavior: A neuropsychological interpretation. *Acta Psychologica,* 73, 13–34.

Decety, J., Jeannerod, M., Durozard, D., & Baverel, G. (1993). Central activation of autonomic effectors during mental simulation of motor actions in man. *Journal of Physiology,* 461, 549–563.

DeCharms, R. (1968). *Personal causation: The internal affective determinants of behavior.* New York: Academic.

Deci, E. L., & Ryan, R. M. (1985). *Intrinsic motivation and self-determination in human behavior.* New York: Plenum.

Decker, P. J., & Nathan, B. R. (1985). *Behavior modeling training: Principles and applications.* New York: Praeger.

DeGeest, S., Borgermans, L., Gemoets, H., Abraham, I., Vlaminck, H., Evers, G., & Vanrenterghem, Y. (1995). Incidence, determinants, and consequences of subclinical noncompliance with immunosuppressive therapy in renal transplant recipients. *Transplantation,* 59, 340–346.

Del Rey, P. (1971). The effects of videotaped feedback on form, accuracy, and latency in an open and closed environment. *Journal of Motor Behavior,* 3, 281–287.

DeMonbreun, B. G., & Craighead, W. E. (1977). Distortion of perception and recall of positive and neutral feedback in depression. *Cognitive Therapy and Research,* 4, 311–329.

Denison, D. R., & Mishra, A. K. (1995). Toward a theory of organizational culture and effectiveness. *Organization Science,* 6, 204–223.

DeRubeis, R. J., Evans, M. D., Hollon, S. D., Garvey, M. J., Grove, W. M., & Tuason, V. B. (1990). How does cognitive therapy work? Cognitive change and symptom change in cognitive therapy and pharmacotherapy for depression. *Journal of Consulting and Clinical Psychology*, 58, 862–869.

Desharnais, R., Bouillon, J., & Godin, G. (1986). Self-efficacy and outcome expectations as determinants of exercise adherence. *Psychological Reports*, 59, 1155–1159.

Deshler, D. D., Warner, M. M., Schumaker, J. B., & Alley, G. R. (1983). Learning strategies intervention model: Key components and current status. In J. D. McKinney & L. Feagans (Eds.), *Current topics in learning disabilities* (Vol. 1, pp. 245–279). Norwood, N.J.: Ablex.

Des Jarlais, D. C., & Friedman, S. R. (1988a). The psychology of preventing AIDS among intravenous drug users: A social learning conceptualization. *American Psychologist*, 43, 865–870.

Desmond, S. M., & Price, J. H. (1988). Self-efficacy and weight control. *Health Education*, 19, 12–18.

Devins, G. M., Binik, Y. M., Gorman, P., Dattel, M., McCloskey, B., Oscar, G., & Briggs, J. (1982). Perceived self-efficacy, outcome expectations, and negative mood states in end-stage renal disease. *Journal of Abnormal Psychology*, 91, 241–244.

Devins, G. M., & Edwards, P. J. (1988). Self-efficacy and smoking reduction in chronic obstructive pulmonary disease. *Behaviour Research Therapy*, 26, 127–135.

deVries, H., & Backbier, M. P. H. (1994). Self-efficacy as an important determinant of quitting among pregnant women who smoke: The Ø-pattern. *Preventive Medicine*, 23, 167–174.

deVries, H., Dijkstra, M., Grol, M., Seelen, S., & Kok, G. (April, 1990). Predictors of smoking onset and cessation in adolescents. Paper presented at the 7th World Conference on Tobacco and Health, Perth, Australia.

deVries, H., Dijkstra, M., & Kuhlman, P. (1988). Self-efficacy: The third factor besides attitude and subjective norm as a predictor of behavioural intentions. *Health Education Research*, 3, 273–282.

deVries, H., Kok, G., & Dijkstra, M. (1990). Self-efficacy as a determinant of the onset of smoking and interventions to prevent smoking in adolescents. In R. J. Takens, et al. (Eds.), *European perspectives in psychology* (Vol. 2, pp. 209–224). London: Wiley.

Dewhirst, H. D. (1991). Career patterns: Mobility, specialization, and related career issues. In R. F. Morrison & J. Adams (Eds.), *Contemporary career development issues* (pp. 73–107). Hillsdale, N.J.: Erlbaum.

DiClemente, C. C. (1981). Self-efficacy and smoking cessation maintenance: A preliminary report. *Cognitive Therapy and Research*, 5, 175–187.

DiClemente, C. C. (1986). Self-efficacy and the addictive behaviors. *Journal of Social and Clinical Psychology*, 4, 302–315.

DiClemente, C. C., Carbonari, J. P., Montgomery, R. P. G., & Huges, S. O. (1994). The alcohol abstinence self-efficacy scale. *Journal of Studies on Alcohol*, 55, 141–148.

DiClemente, C. C., Fairhurst, S. K., & Piotrowski, N. A. (1995). Self-efficacy and addictive behaviors. In J. E. Maddux (Ed.), *Self-efficacy, adaptation, and adjustment: Theory, research and application* (pp. 109–141). New York: Plenum.

DiClemente, C. C., & Hughes, S. O. (1990). Stages of change profiles in outpatient alcoholism treatment. *Journal of Substance Abuse*, 2, 217–235.

DiClemente, C. C., Prochaska, J. O., Fairhurst, S. K., Velicer, W. F., Velasquez, M. M., & Rossi, J. S. (1991). The process of smoking cessation: An analysis of precontemplation, contemplation, and preparation stages of change. *Journal of Consulting and Clinical Psychology*, 59, 295–304.

DiClemente, C. C., Prochaska, J. O., & Gilbertini, M. (1985). Self-efficacy and the stages of self-change of smoking. *Cognitive Therapy and Research*, 9, 181–200.

Dienstbier, R. A. (1989). Arousal and physiological toughness: Implications for mental and physical health. *Psychological Review*, 96, 84–100.

Dishman, R. K. (1982). Compliance/adherence in health-related exercise. *Health Psychology*, 1, 237–267.

Dittmann-Kohli, F., Lachman, M. E., Kliegl, R., & Baltes, P. B. (1991). Effects of cognitive training and testing on intellectual efficacy beliefs in elderly adults. *Journal of Gerontology: Psychological Sciences*, 46, 162–164.

Dobson, K. S., & Pusch, D. (1995). A test of the depressive realism hypothesis in clinically depressed subjects. *Cognitive Therapy and Research*, 19, 179–194.

Dolce, J. J. (1987). Self-efficacy and disability beliefs in behavioral treatment of pain. *Behaviour Research and Therapy*, 25, 289–300.

Dollard, J., & Miller, N. E. (1950). *Personality and psychotherapy*. New York: McGraw-Hill.

Donovan, J. E., & Jessor, R. (1985). Structure of problem behavior in adolescence and young adulthood. *Journal of Consulting and Clinical Psychology*, 53, 890–904.

Dornbusch, S. M. (February, 1994). Off the track. Presidential Address to the Society for Research on Adolescence, San Diego, Calif.

Downs, G. W., Jr., & Mohr, L. B. (1979). Toward a theory of innovation. *Administration and Society*, 10, 379–408.

Dowrick, P. W. (1983). Self modelling. In P. W. Dowrick & S. J. Biggs (Eds.), *Using video: Psychological and social applications* (pp. 105–124). London: Wiley.

Dowrick, P. W. (1986). *Social survival for children: A trainer's resource book*. New York: Brunner/Mazel.

Dowrick, P. W. (1991). *Practical guide to using video in the behavioral sciences*. New York: Wiley.

Dowrick, P. W., Holman, L., & Kleinke, C. L. (1993). *Video feedforward: Promoting self-efficacy in swimming*. Submitted for publication.

Dowrick, P. W., & Jesdale, D. C. (1990). Effects on emotion of structured video replay: Implications for therapy. *Bulletin de Psychologie*, 43, 512–517.

Drummond, D. C., & Glautier, S. (1994). A controlled trial of cue exposure treatment in alcohol dependence. *Journal of Consulting and Clinical Psychology*, 62, 809–817.

Duda (1988). The relationship between goal perspectives, persistence and behavioral intensity among male and female recreational sport participants. *Leisure Sciences*, 10, 95–106.

Duncan, T. E., & McAuley, E. (1993). Social support and efficacy cognitions in exercise adherence: A latent growth curve analysis. *Journal of Behavioral Medicine*, 16, 199–218.

Dunham, P., Dunham, F., Hurshman, A., & Alexander, T. (1989). Social contingency effects on subsequent perceptual-cognitive tasks in young infants. *Child Development*, 60, 1486–1496.

Dunning, D. (1995). Trait importance and modifiability as factors influencing self-assessment and self-enhancement motives. *Personality and Social Psychology Bulletin*, 21, 1297–1306.

Duval, S., & Wicklund, R. (1972). *A theory of self-awareness*. New York: Academic.

Dweck, C. S. (1991). Self-theories and goals: Their role in motivation, personality, and development. In R. A. Dienstbier (Ed.), *Nebraska symposium on motivation, 1990: Perspectives on motivation* (Vol. 38, pp.

199–235). Lincoln: University of Nebraska Press.

Dweck, C. S., Davidson, W., Nelson, S., & Enna, B. (1978). Sex differences in learned helplessness: II. The contingencies of evaluative feedback in the classroom; III. An experimental analysis. *Developmental Psychology, 14*, 268–276.

Dweck, C. S., & Elliott, E. S. (1983). Achievement motivation. In P. H. Mussen (General Ed.) & E. M. Heatherington (Vol. Eds.), *Handbook of child psychology: Socialization, personality & social development* (4th ed., Vol. 4, pp. 644–691). New York: Wiley.

Dweck, C. S., & Leggett, E. L. (1988). A social-cognitive approach to motivation and personality. *Psychological Review, 95*, 256–273.

Dzewaltowski, D. A. (1989). Towards a model of exercise motivation. *Journal of Sport and Exercise Psychology, 11*, 251–269.

Dzewaltowski, D. A., Noble, J. M., & Shaw, J. M. (1990). Physical activity participation: Social cognitive theory versus the theories of reasoned action and planned behavior. *Journal of Sport and Exercise Psychology, 12*, 388–405.

Earley, P. C. (1986). Supervisors and shop stewards as sources of contextual information in goal setting: A comparison of the United States with England. *Journal of Applied Psychology, 71*, 111–117.

Earley, P. C. (1993). East meets West meets Mideast: Further explorations of collectivistic and individualistic work groups. *Academy of Management Journal, 36*, 319–348.

Earley, P. C. (1994). Self or group? Cultural effects of training on self-efficacy and performance. *Administrative Science Quarterly, 39*, 89–117.

Earley, P. C., Connolly, T., & Ekegren, C. (1989). Goals, strategy development and task performance: Some limits on the efficacy of goal-setting. *Journal of Applied Psychology, 74*, 24–33.

Earley, P. C., Connolly, T., & Lee, C. (1989). Task strategy interventions in goal setting: The importance of search in strategy development. *Journal of Management, 15*, 589–602.

Earley, P. C., & Lituchy, T. R. (1991). Delineating goal and efficacy effects: A test of three models. *Journal of Applied Psychology, 76*, 81–98.

Eastman, C., & Marzillier, J. S. (1984). Theoretical and methodological difficulties in Bandura's self-efficacy theory. *Cognitive Therapy and Research, 8*, 213–230.

Easton, D., & Dennis, J. (1967). The child's acquisition of regime norms: Political efficacy. *The American Political Science Review, 35*, 25–38.

Eaton, C. A., & Rossi, J. S. (1991). Self-efficacy in weight management. *Journal of Consulting and Clinical Psychology, 59*, 739–744.

Ebbesen, E. B., & Konecni, V. J. (1975). Decision making and information integration in the courts: The setting of bail. *Journal of Personality and Social Psychology, 32*, 805–821.

Eccles, J. S. (1989). Bringing young women to math and science. In M. Crawford & M. Gentry (Eds.), *Gender and thought* (pp. 36–58). New York: Springer-Verlag.

Eccles, J. S., & Midgley, C. (1989). State-environment fit: Developmentally appropriate classrooms for young adolescents. In R. Ames & C. Ames (Eds.), *Research on motivation in education.* Vol. 3, *Goals and cognitions* (pp. 139–186). New York: Academic.

Edelman, R. E., & Chambless, D. L. (1995). Adherence during sessions and homework in cognitive-behavioral group treatment of social phobia. *Behaviour Research and Therapy, 33*, 573–577.

Eden, D. (1988). Pygmalion, goal setting, and expectancy: Compatible ways to boost productivity. *Academy of Management Review, 13*, 639–652.

Eden, D., & Aviram, A. (1993). Self-efficacy training to speed reemployment: Helping people to help themselves. *Journal of Applied Psychology, 78*, 352–360.

Eden, D., & Zuk, Y. (1995). Seasickness as a self-fulfilling prophecy: Raising self-efficacy to boost performance at sea. *Journal of Applied Psychology, 80*, 628–635.

Edmonds, R. (1979). Effective schools for the urban poor. *Educational Leadership, 37*, 15–24.

Edwards, S., & Dickerson, M. (1987). On the similarity of positive and negative intrusions. *Behaviour, Research and Therapy, 25*, 207–211.

Edwards, T. C., & Oskamp. S. (1992). Components of antinuclear war activism. *Basic and Applied Social Psychology, 13*, 217–230.

Eells, R., & Nehemkis, P. (1984). Corporate intelligence and espionage: A blueprint for executive decision making. New York: MacMillan.

Egeland, B., Carlson, E., & Sroufe, L. A. (1993). Resilience as process. *Development and Psychopathology, 5*, 517–528.

Ehlers, A., Margraf, J., Roth, W. T., Taylor, C. B., & Birbaumer, N. (1988). Anxiety induced by false heart rate feedback in patients with panic disorder. *Behaviour Research and Therapy, 26*, 1–11.

Ehrlich, P. R., Ehrlich, A. H., & Daily, G. C. (1995). *The stork and the plow: The equity answer to the human dilemma.* New York: Putnam.

Eich, E. (1995). Searching for mood dependent memory. *Psychological Science, 6*, 67–75.

Elden, J. M. (1981). Political efficacy at work: The connection between more autonomous forms of workplace organization and a more participatory politics. *The American Political Science Review, 75*, 43–58.

Elder, G. H., Jr. (1981). History and the life course. In D. Bertaux (Ed.), *Biography and society: The life history approach in the social sciences* (pp. 77–115). Beverly Hills, Calif.: Sage.

Elder, G. H., Jr. (1994). Time, human agency, and social change: Perspectives on the life course. *Social Psychology Quarterly, 57*, 4–15.

Elder, G. H., Jr. (1995). Life trajectories in changing societies. In A. Bandura (Ed.), *Self-efficacy in changing societies* (pp. 46–68). New York: Cambridge University Press.

Elder, G. H., Jr. & Ardelt, M. (March 18–20, 1992). Families adapting to economic pressure: Some consequences for parents and adolescents. Paper presented at the Society for Research on Adolescence, Washington, D.C.

Elder, G. H., Jr., Eccles, J. S., Ardelt, M., & Lord, S. (1995). Inner city parents under economic pressure: Perspectives on the strategies of parenting. *The Journal of Marriage and the Family, 57*, 771–784.

Elder, G. H., Jr., & Liker, J. K. (1982). Hard times in women's lives: Historical influences across forty years. *American Journal of Sociology, 88*, 241–269.

Elkin, F., & Westley, W. A. (1955). The myth of adolescent culture. *American Sociological Review, 20*, 680–684.

Elkin, I., Shea, M. T., Watkins, J. T., Imber, S. D., Sotsky, S. M., Collins, J. F., Glass, D. R., Pilkonis, P. A., et al. (1989). National Institute of Mental Health treatment of depression collaborative research program: General effectiveness of treatments. *Archives of General Psychiatry, 46*, 971–983.

Ellen, P. S. (1988). The impact of self-efficacy and performance satisfaction on resistance to change. *Dissertation Abstracts International, 48*, 2106–2107A. University of South Carolina.

Ellickson, P. L., & Hays, R. D. (1990–1991). Beliefs about resistance self-efficacy and drug prevalence: Do they really affect drug use? *The International Journal of the Addictions*, 25, 1353–1378.

Elliott, D. S. (1993). Health-enhancing and health compromising lifestyles. In S. G. Millstein, A. C. Petersen, & E. O. Nightingale (Eds.), *Promoting the health of adolescents: New directions for the twenty-first century* (pp. 119–145). New York: Oxford University Press.

Ellis, A., & Dryden, W. (1987). *The practice of rational-emotive therapy* (RET). New York: Springer.

Ellis, R. A., & Lane, W. C. (1963). Structural supports for upward mobility. *American Sociological Review*, 28, 743–756.

Emmelkamp, P. M. G., Kuippers, A. C. M., & Eggaraat, J. B. (1978). Cognitive modification versus prolonged exposure in vivo: Comparison with agoraphobics as subjects. *Behavior Research and Therapy*, 16, 33–42.

Emmelkamp, P. M. G., & Mersch, P. P. (1982). Cognition and exposure in vivo in the treatment of agoraphobia: Short-term and delayed effects. *Cognitive Therapy and Research*, 6, 77–90.

Emmelkamp, P. M. G., van der Helm, M., van Zangen, B. L., & Plochg, I. (1980). Treatment of obsessive compulsive patients: The contribution of self-instructional training to the effectiveness of exposure. *Behaviour Research and Therapy*, 18, 61–66.

Emrick, C. D., Tonigan, J. S., Montgomery, H., & Little, L. (1993). Alcoholics anonymous: What is currently known? In B. S. McCrady & W. R. Miller (Eds.), *Research on Alcoholics Anonymous: Opportunities and alternatives* (pp. 41–76). New Brunswick, N.J.: Rutgers Center of Alcohol Studies.

Endler, N. S., & Magnusson, D. (Eds.). (1976). *Interactional psychology and personality*. Washington, D.C.: Hemisphere.

Engel, G. L. (1977). The need for a new medical model: A challenge for biomedicine. *Science*, 196, 129–136.

England, S. L., & Dickerson, M. (1988). Intrusive thoughts: Unpleasantness not the major cause of uncontrollability. *Behaviour Research and Therapy*, 26, 279–282.

Enochs, L. G., & Riggs, I. M. (1990). Further development of an elementary science teaching efficacy belief instrument: A preservice elementary scale. *School Science and Mathematics*, 90, 694–706.

Enzle, M. E., & Ross, J. M. (1978). Increasing and decreasing intrinsic interest with contingent rewards: A test of cognitive evaluation theory. *Journal of Experimental Social Psychology*, 14, 588–597.

Epley, S. W. (1974). Reduction of the behavioral effects of aversive stimulation by the presence of companions. *Psychological Bulletin*, 81, 271–283.

Epstein, J. L. (1990). School and family connections: Theory, research, and implications for integrating sociologies of education and family. In D. G. Unger & M. B. Sussman, *Families in community settings: Interdisciplinary perspectives* (pp. 99–126). New York: Haworth.

Epstein, J. L., & Scott-Jones, D. (1988, November). School, family, community connections for accelerating student progress in elementary and middle grades. Paper presented at the Conference on Accelerated Schools, Stanford University, Stanford, Calif.

Epstein, L. H., Wing, R. R., Koeske, R., Ossip, D., & Beck, S. (1982). A comparison of lifestyle change and programmed aerobic exercise on weight and fitness changes in obese children. *Behaviour Therapy*, 13, 651–665.

Erasmus, C. J. (1961). *Man takes control*. Minneapolis: University of Minnesota Press.

Erdley, C. A., & Asher, S. R. (1996). Children's social goals and self-efficacy perceptions as influences on their responses to ambiguous provocation. *Child Development*, 67, 1329–1344.

Erez, M., & P. C. Earley (1993). *Culture, self-identity, and work*. Oxford: Oxford University Press.

Erez, M., & Zidon, I. (1984). Effect of goal acceptance on the relationship of goal difficulty to performance. *Journal of Applied Psychology*, 69, 69–78.

Eriksen, C. W. (1958). Unconscious processes. In M. R. Jones (Ed.), *Nebraska symposium on motivation* (pp. 169–227). Lincoln: University of Nebraska Press.

Eriksen, C. W. (1960). Discrimination and learning without awareness: A methodological survey and evaluation. *Psychological Review*, 67, 279–300.

Erwin, E. (1996). *A final accounting: Philosophical and empirical issues in Freudian psychology*. Cambridge, Mass.: MIT Press.

Esteve, J. M. (1992). Multicultural education in Spain: The autonomous communities face the challenge of European unity. *Educational Review*, 44, 255–272.

Etzioni, A. (1988). Normative-affective factors: Toward a new decision-making model. *Journal of Economic Psychology*, 9, 125–150.

Evans, D. M., & Dunn, N. J. (1995). Alcohol expectancies, coping responses and self-efficacy judgments: A replication and extension of Cooper et al.'s 1988 study in a college sample. *Journal of Studies on Alcohol*, 56, 186–193.

Evans, E. D., & Tribble, M. (1986). Perceived teaching problems, self-efficacy, and commitment to teaching among preservice teachers. *Journal of Educational Research*, 80, 81–85.

Evans, K., & Heinz, W. (1993). Studying forms of transition: Methodological innovation in a cross-national study of youth transition and labour market entry in England and Germany. *Comparative Education*, 29, 145–158.

Evans, K., & Heinz, W. R. (1991). Career trajectories in Britain and Germany. In J. Bynner & K. Roberts (Eds.), *Youth and work: Transition to employment in England and Germany* (pp. 205–228). London: Anglo-German Foundation.

Evans, M. D., Hollon, S. D., DeRubeis, R. J., Piasecki, J. M., Grove, W. M., Garvey, M. J., & Tuason, V. B. (1992). Differential relapse following cognitive therapy and pharmacotherapy for depression. *Archives of General Psychiatry*, 49, 802–808.

Evans, R. I., Rozelle, R. M., Maxwell, S. E., Raines, B. E., Dill, C. A., Guthrie, T. J., Henderson, A. H., & Hill, P. C. (1981). Social modeling films to deter smoking in adolescents: Results of a three-year field investigation. *Journal of Applied Psychology*, 66, 399–414.

Everett, S. A., Price, J. H., Tellijohann, S. K., & Durgin, J. (1996). The elementary health teaching self-efficacy scale. *American Journal of Health Behavior*, 20, 90–97.

Ewart, C. K. (1992). Role of physical self-efficacy in recovery from heart attack. In R. Schwarzer (Ed.), *Self-efficacy: Thought control of action* (pp. 287–304). Washington, D.C.: Hemisphere.

Ewart, C. K., Stewart, K. J., Gillilan, R. E., & Kelemen, M. H. (1986). Self-efficacy mediates strength gains during circuit weight training in men with coronary artery disease. *Medicine and Science in Sports and Exercise*, 18, 531–540.

Ewart, C. K., Taylor, C. B., Reese, L. B., & DeBusk, R. F. (1983). Effects of early post-myocardial infarction exercise testing on self-perception and subsequent physical activity. *American Journal of Cardiology*, 51, 1076–1080.

Eysenck, H. J., & Wilson, G. D. (1973). *The experimental study of Freudian theories*. London: Methuen.

Fairburn, C. G. (1984). Cognitive-behavioral treatment for bulimia. In D. M. Garner and P. E. Garfinkel (Eds.), *Handbook of psychotherapy for anorexia nervosa and bulimia* (pp. 160–192). New York: Guilford.

Fairweather, G. W., Sanders, D. H., Cressler, D. L., & Maynard, H. (1969). *Community life for the mentally ill: An alternative to institutional care.* Chicago: Aldine.

Falk, J. (1983). *Taking Australia off the map.* New York: Penguin Books.

Fanselow, M. S. (1986). Conditioned fear-induced opiate analgesia: A competing motivational state theory of stress analgesia. In D. D. Kelly (Ed.), Stress-induced analgesia. *Annals of the New York Academy of Sciences* (Vol. 467, pp. 40–54). New York: New York Academy of Sciences.

Farquhar, J. W., Fortmann, S. P., Flora, J. A., Taylor, C. B., Haskell, W. L., Williams, P. T., Maccoby, N., & Wood, P. D. (1990). Effects of communitywide education on cardiovascular disease risk factors: The Stanford five-city project. *Journal of the American Medical Association,* 264, 359–365.

Farquhar, J. W., Maccoby, N., & Solomon, D. S. (1984). Community applications of behavioral medicine. In W. D. Gentry (Ed.), *Handbook of behavioral medicine.* (pp. 437–78). New York: Guilford.

Farquhar, J. W., Maccoby, N., Wood, P. D., et al. (1977, June). Community education for cardiovascular health. *Lancet,* 1192–1195.

Farquhar, J. W., Maccoby, N., & Wood, P. D. (1985). Education and communication studies. In W. W. Holland, R. Detels, & G. Knox (Eds.), *Oxford textbook of public health* (Vol. 3, pp. 207–221). Oxford, London: Oxford University Press.

Fawcett, S. B., Seekins, T., Whang, P. L., Muiu, C., & Balcazar, Y. S. (1984). Creating and using social technologies for community empowerment. *Prevention in the Human Services,* 3, 145–171.

Feather, N. T. (Ed.) (1982). *Expectations and actions: Expectancy-value models in psychology.* Hillsdale, N.J.: Erlbaum.

Featherman, D. L., Smith, J., & Peterson, J. G. (1990). Successful aging in a postretired society. In P. B. Baltes & M. M. Baltes (Eds.), *Successful aging: Perspectives from the behavioral sciences* (pp. 50–93). Cambridge: Cambridge University Press.

Fecteau, G. W., & Stoppard, M. M. (1983, December). The generalization of self-efficacy to a cognitive-behavioural treatment for speech anxiety and the verbal persuasion source of efficacy information. Paper

presented at the annual meeting of the American Association of Behavior Therapy, Washington, D.C.

Feist, J. R., & Rosenthal, T. L. (1973). Serpent versus surrogate and other determinants of runway fear differences. *Behaviour Research and Therapy,* 11, 483–489.

Felson, R. B., & Reed, M. (1986). The effect of parents on the self-appraisals of children. *Social Psychology Quarterly,* 49, 302–308.

Feltz, D. L. (1982). Path analysis of the causal elements in Bandura's theory of self-efficacy and an anxiety-based model of avoidance behavior. *Journal of Personality and Social Psychology,* 42, 764–781.

Feltz, D. L. (1988a). Self-confidence and sports performance. In K. B. Pandolf (Ed.), *Exercise and sport sciences reviews* (pp. 423–457). New York: Macmillan.

Feltz, D. L. (1988b). Gender differences in the causal elements of self-efficacy on a high avoidance motor task. *Journal of Sport and Exercise Psychology,* 10, 151–166.

Feltz, D. L., & Albrecht, R. R. (1986). The influence of self-efficacy on the approach/avoidance of a high-avoidance motor task. In J. H. Humphrey & L. Vander Velden (Eds.), *Psychology and sociology of sport* (pp. 3–25). New York: AMS Press.

Feltz, D. L., & Landers, D. M. (1983). Effects of mental practice on motor skill learning and performance: A meta-analysis. *Journal of Sport Psychology,* 5, 25–57.

Feltz, D. L., Landers, D. M., & Raeder, U. (1979). Enhancing self-efficacy in high avoidance motor tasks: A comparison of modeling techniques. *Journal of Sport Psychology,* 1, 112–122.

Feltz, D. L., & Mugno, D. A. (1983). A replication of the path analysis of the causal elements in Bandura's theory of self-efficacy and the influence of autonomic perception. *Journal of Sport Psychology,* 5, 263–277.

Feltz, D. L., & Riessinger, C. A. (1990). Effects of in vivo emotive imagery and performance feedback on self-efficacy and muscular endurance. *Journal of Sport and Exercise Psychology,* 12, 132–143.

Feltz, D. L., & Weiss, M. R. (1982). Developing self-efficacy through sport. *Journal of Physical Education, Recreation and Dance,* 53, 24–26.

Fenichel, O. (1945). *The psychoanalytic theory of neurosis.* New York: Norton.

Ferrari, M., & Bouffard-Bouchard, T. (1992, June). Self-efficacy and expertise in motor learning and performance. Paper presented at the annual meeting of the Canadian Psychological Association, Quebec City.

Feske, U., & Chambless, D. L. (1995). Cog-

nitive behavioral versus exposure only treatment for social phobia: A meta-analysis. *Behavior Therapy,* 26, 695–720.

Festinger, L. (1942). A theoretical interpretation of shifts in level of aspiration. *Psychological Review,* 49, 235–250.

Festinger, L. (1954). A theory of social comparison processes. *Human Relations,* 7, 117–140.

Festinger, L. (1957). *A theory of cognitive dissonance.* Evanston, Ill.: Row, Peterson.

Fimrite, R. (1977). A melding of men all suited to a T. *Sports Illustrated,* September, 91–100.

Finkel, S. E. (1985). Reciprocal effects of participation and political efficacy: A panel analysis. *American Journal of Political Science,* 29, 891–913.

Finkel, S. E., Muller, E. N., & Opp, K. (1989). Personal influence, collective rationality, and mass political action. *American Political Science Review,* 83, 885–903.

Finkelstein, N. W., & Ramey, C. T. (1977). Learning to control the environment in infancy. *Child Development,* 48, 806–819.

Fiorina, M. P. (1980). The decline of collective responsibility in American politics. *Daedalus,* 109, 25–45.

Fisher, J. D. (1988). Possible effects of reference group-based social influence on AIDS-risk behavior and AIDS prevention. *American Psychologist,* 43, 914–920.

Fitzgerald, L. F., & Crites, J. O. (1980). Toward a career psychology of women: What do we know? What do we need to know? *Journal of Counseling Psychology,* 27, 44–62.

Fitzgerald, S. T., Becker, D. M., Celantaro, D. D., Swank, R., & Brinker, J. (1989). Return to work after percutaneous translumina coronary angioplasty. *American Journal of Cardiology,* 64, 1108–1112.

Flammer, A. (1995). Developmental analysis of control beliefs. In A. Bandura (Ed.), *Self-efficacy in changing societies* (pp. 69–113). New York: Cambridge University Press.

Flavell, J. H. (1970). Developmental studies of mediated memory. In H. W. Reese & L. P. Lipsitt (Eds.), *Advances in child development and behavior* (Vol. 5, pp. 181–211). New York: Academic.

Flavell, J. H. (1978a). Metacognitive development. In J. M. Scandura & C. J. Brainerd (Eds.), *Structural-process theories of complex human behavior* (pp. 213–245). Alphen a.d. Rijn, Netherlands: Sijithoff and Noordhoff.

Flavell, J. H. (1978b). Developmental stage: Explanans or explanadum? *The Behavioral and Brain Sciences,* 2, 187–188.

Flavell, J. H. (1979). Metacognition and cognitive monitoring: A new area of cognitive-developmental inquiry. *American Psychologist, 34,* 906–911.

Flerx, V. C., Fidler, D. S., & Rogers, R. W. (1976). Sex role stereotypes: Developmental aspects and early intervention. *Child Development, 47,* 998–1007.

Forgas, J. P., Bower, G. H., & Moylan, S. J. (1990). Praise or blame? Affective influences on attributions for achievement. *Journal of Personality and Social Psychology, 59,* 809–819.

Forste, R., & Tienda, M. (1992). Race and ethnic variation in the schooling consequences of female adolescent sexual activity. *Social Science Quarterly, 73,* 12–30.

Forward, J. R., & Williams, J. R. (1970). Internal-external control and black militancy. *Journal of Social Issues, 26,* 75–92.

Fowler, H. (1971). Implications of sensory reinforcement. In R. Glaser (Ed.), *The nature of reinforcement* (pp. 151–195). New York: Academic.

Fox, D. L., & Schofield, J. W. (1989). Issue salience, perceived efficacy and perceived risk: A study of the origins of anti-nuclear war activity. *Journal of Applied Social Psychology, 19,* 805–827.

Frankenhaeuser, M. (1975). Experimental approaches to the study of catecholamines and emotion. In L. Levi (Ed.), *Emotions: Their parameters and measurement* (pp. 209–234). New York: Raven.

Franks, I. M., & Maile, L. J. (1991). The use of video in sport skill acquisition. In P. W. Dowrick (Ed.), *Practical guide to using video in the behavioral sciences* (pp. 231–243). New York: Wiley.

Fraser, J. (1970). The mistrustful-efficacious hypothesis and political participation. *Journal of Politics, 32,* 444–449.

Frayne, C. A., & Latham, G. P. (1987). Application of social learning theory to employee self-management of attendance. *Journal of Applied Psychology, 72,* 387–392.

Free, M. L., & Oei, T. P. S. (1989). Biological and psychological processes in the treatment and maintenance of depression. *Clinical Psychology Review, 9,* 653–688.

Frese, M., Teng, E., & Cees, J. D. (1996). Helping to improve suggestion systems: Psychological predictors of giving suggestions in a Dutch company. Manuscript, University of Amsterdam.

Frese, M., & van Dyck, C. (1995). Error management: Learning from errors and organizational design. Manuscript, Department of Psychology, University of Amsterdam.

Fretz, B. R., Kluge, N. A., Ossana, S. M., Jones, S. M., & Merikangas, M. W. (1989). Intervention targets for reducing preretirement anxiety and depression. *Journal of Counseling Psychology, 36,* 301–307.

Freuh, B. C., Turner, S. M., Beidel, D. C., Mirabella, R. F., & Jones, W. J. (1996). Trauma management therapy: A preliminary evaluation of a multicomponent behavioral treatment for chronic combat-related PTSD. *Behaviour Research and Therapy, 34,* 533–543.

Frey, K. S., & Ruble, D. N. (1990). Strategies for comparative evaluation: Maintaining a sense of competence across the lifespan. In R. J. Sternberg & J. Kolligian, Jr. (Eds.), *Competence considered* (pp. 167–189). New Haven, Conn.: Yale University Press.

Friedman, S. R., de Jong, W. M., & Des Jarlais, D. C. (1988). Problems and dynamics of organizing intravenous drug users for AIDS prevention. *Health Education Research, 3,* 49–57.

Fries, J. F. (1989). *Aging well.* Menlo Park, Calif.: Addison-Wesley.

Fries, J. F., & Crapo, L. M. (1981). *Vitality and aging: Implications of the rectangular curve.* San Francisco: W. H. Freeman.

Fries, J. F., Koop, C. E., Beadle, C. E., Cooper, P. P., England, M. J., Greaves, R. F., Sokolov, J. J., Wright, D., & the Health Project Consortium (1993). Reducing health care costs by reducing the need and demand for medical services. *New England Journal of Medicine, 329,* 321–325.

Fries, J. F., Singh, G., Morfeld, D., Hubert, H., Lane, N. E., & Brown, B. W., Jr. (1994). Running and the development of disability with age. *American College of Physicians, 121,* 502–509.

Frieze, I. H. (1980). Beliefs about success and failure in the classroom. In J. H. McMillan (Ed.), *The social psychology of school learning* (pp. 39–78). New York: Academic.

Fry, L., Mason, A. A., & Pearson, R. S. B. (1964). Effect of hypnosis on allergic skin responses in asthma and hay fever. *British Medical Journal, 5391,* 1145–1148.

Fuchs, V. (1974). *Who shall live? Health, economics, and social choice.* New York: Basic Books.

Fuchs, V. R. (1990). The health sector's share of the gross national product. *Science, 247,* 534–538.

Fukuyama, M. A., Probert, B. S., Neimeyer, G. J., Nevill, D. D., & Metzler, A. E. (1988). Effects of DISCOVER on career self-efficacy and decision making of undergraduates. *The Career Development Quarterly, 37,* 56–62.

Furstenberg, F. F., Jr. (1976). *Unplanned parenthood: The social consequences of teenage childbearing.* New York: Free Press.

Furstenberg, F. F., Jr., Brooks-Gunn, J., & Morgan, S. P. (1987). Adolescent mothers in later life. New York: Cambridge University Press.

Furstenberg, F. F., Eccles, J., Elder, G. H., Jr., Cook, T., & Sameroff, A. (in press). *Urban families and adolescent success.* Chicago: University of Chicago Press.

Futoran, G. C., Schofield, J. W., & Eurich-Fulcer, R. (1995). The Internet as a K-12 educational resource: Emerging issues of information access and freedom. *Computers Education, 24,* 229–236.

Gadow, K. D. (1985). Relative efficacy of pharmacological, behavioral, and combination treatments for enhancing academic performance. *Clinical Psychology Review, 5,* 513–533.

Gagnon, J., & Simon, W. (1973). *Sexual conduct, the social sources of human sexuality.* Chicago: Aldine.

Galbraith, J. R. (1982). Designing the innovating organization. *Organizational Dynamics,* Winter, 5–25.

Gallie, D. (1991). Patterns of skill change: Upskilling, deskilling or the polarization of skills? *Work, Employment and Society, 5,* 319–351.

Gamson, W. A. (1968). *Power and discontent.* Homewood, Ill.: Dorsey.

Gandhi, M. K. (1942). *Nonviolence in peace and war.* Ahmedabad, India: Navajivan.

Gans, J. S., & Shepherd, G. B. (1994). How are the mighty fallen: Rejected classic articles by leading economists. *Journal of Economic Perspectives, 8,* 165–179.

Garber, J., Hollon, S. D., & Silverman, V. (1979, December). Evaluation and reward of self vs. others in depression. Paper presented at the meeting of the Association for the Advancement of Behavior Therapy, San Francisco.

Garber, J., & Seligman, M. E. P. (Eds.). (1980). *Human helplessness: Theory and applications.* New York: Academic.

Garcia, A. W., & King, A. C. (1991). Predicting long-term adherence to aerobic exercise: A comparison of two models. *Journal of Sport and Exercise Psychology, 13,* 394–410.

Garcia, M. E., Schmitz, J. M., & Doerfler, L. A. (1990). A fine-grained analysis of the role of self-efficacy in self-initiated attempts to quit smoking. *Journal of Consulting and Clinical Psychology, 58,* 317–322.

Gardner, J. W. (1972). *In common cause.* New York: W. W. Norton.

Garland, H. (1983). Influence of ability, assigned goals, and normative information on personal goals and performance: A challenge to the goal attainability assumption. *Journal of Applied Psychology, 68,* 20–30.

Garland, H. (1985). A cognitive mediation theory of task goals and human performance. *Motivation and Emotion, 9,* 345–367.

Garlington, W. K., & Dericco, D. A. (1977). The effect of modeling on drinking rate. *Journal of Applied Behavior Analysis, 10,* 207–212.

Gattuso, S. M., Litt, M. D., & Fitzgerald, T. E. (1992). Coping with gastrointestinal endoscopy: Self-efficacy enhancement and coping style. *Journal of Consulting and Clinical Psychology, 60,* 133–139.

Gaupp, L. A., Stern, R. M., & Galbraith, G. G. (1972). False heart-rate feedback and reciprocal inhibition by aversion relief in the treatment of snake avoidance behavior. *Behavior Therapy, 3,* 7–20.

Gauthier, J., Laberge, B., Fréve, A., & Dufour, L. (1986, June). The behavioural treatment of dental phobia: Interaction between therapeutic expectancies and exposure. Paper presented at the 47th Annual Meeting of the Canadian Psychological Association, Toronto.

Gauthier, J., & Ladouceur, R. (1981). The influence of self-efficacy reports on performance. *Behavior Therapy, 12,* 436–439.

Gecas, V. (1989). The social psychology of self-efficacy. *Annual Review of Sociology, 15,* 291–316.

Geer, J. H., Davison, G. C., & Gatchel, R. I. (1970). Reduction of stress in humans through nonveridical perceived control of aversive stimulation. *Journal of Personality and Social Psychology, 16,* 731–738.

Gelfand, D. M., & Teti, D. M. (1990). The effects of maternal depression on children. *Clinical Psychology Review, 10,* 329–353.

Gellatly, I. R., & Meyer, J. P. (1992). The effects of goal difficulty on physiological arousal, cognition, and task performance. *Journal of Applied Psychology, 77,* 694–704.

George, A. L. (1980). *Presidential decision-making in foreign policy.* Boulder, Colo.: Westview Press.

George, T. R. (1994). Self-confidence and baseball performance: A causal examination of self-efficacy theory. *Journal of Sport and Exercise Psychology, 16,* 381–399.

George, T. R., Feltz, D. L., & Chase, M. A. (1992). Effects of model similarity on self-efficacy and muscular endurance: A second look. *Journal of Sport and Exercise Psychology, 14,* 237–248.

Gerin, W., Litt, M. D., Deich, J., & Pickering, T. G. (1995). Self-efficacy as a moderator of perceived control effects on cardiovascular reactivity: Is enhanced control always beneficial? *Psychosomatic Medicine, 57,* 390–397.

Gerin, W., Litt, M. D., Deich, J., & Pickering, T. G. (1996). Self-efficacy as a component of active coping effects on cardiovascular reactivity. *Journal of Psychosomatic Research, 40,* 485–494.

Gerst, M. S. (1971). Symbolic coding processes in observational learning. *Journal of Personality and Social Psychology, 19,* 7–17.

Gettys, L. D., & Cann, A. (1981). Children's perceptions of occupational sex stereotypes. *Sex Roles, 7,* 301–308.

Gibson, C. B. (1995). Determinants and consequences of group-efficacy beliefs in work organizations in U.S., Hong Kong, and Indonesia. Ph.D. diss., University of California, Irvine.

Gibson, S., & Dembo, M. H. (1984). Teacher efficacy: A construct validation. *Journal of Educational Psychology, 76,* 569–582.

Giddens, A. (1984). *The constitution of society: Outline of the theory of structuration.* Cambridge: Polity Press; Berkeley: University of California Press.

Gilchrist, L. D., & Schinke, S. P. (1983). Coping with contraception: Cognitive and behavioral methods with adolescents. *Cognitive Therapy and Research, 7,* 379–388.

Gilchrist, L. D., & Schinke, S. P. (Eds.). (1985). *Preventing social and health problems through life skills training.* Seattle: University of Washington Press.

Gilchrist, L. D., Schinke, S. P., Trimble, J. E., & Cvetkovich, G. T. (1987). Skills enhancement to prevent substance abuse among American Indian adolescents. *International Journal of the Addictions, 22,* 869–879.

Gill, D. L. (1984). Individual and group performance in sport. In J. M. Silva & R. S. Weinberg (Eds.), *Psychological foundations of sport* (pp. 315–328). Champaign, IL: Human Kinetics.

Gilovich, T. (1984). Judgmental biases in the world of sports. In W. F. Straub & J. M. Williams (Eds.), *Cognitive sport psychology* (pp. 31–41). Lansing, N.Y.: Sport Science Associates.

Gilovich, T., Kerr, M., & Medvec, V. H. (1993). Effect of temporal perspective on subjective confidence. *Journal of Personal-ity and Social Psychology, 64,* 552–560.

Gilovich, T., Vallone, R., & Tversky, A. (1985). The hot hand in basketball: On the misperception of random sequences. *Cognitive Psychology, 17,* 295–314.

Gist, M. E. (1989). The influence of training method on self-efficacy and idea generation among managers. *Personnel Psychology, 42,* 787–805.

Gist, M. E., Bavetta, A. G., & Stevens, C. K. (1990). Transfer training method: Its influence on skill generalization, skill repetition, and performance level. *Personnel Psychology, 43,* 501–523.

Gist, M. E., Schwoerer, C., & Rosen, B. (1989). Effects of alternative training methods on self-efficacy and performance in computer software training. *Journal of Applied Psychology, 74,* 884–891.

Gist, M., Rosen, B., & Schwoerer, C. (1988). The influence of training method and trainee age on the acquisition of computer skills. *Personnel Psychology, 41,* 255–265.

Glasgow, R. E., & Arkowitz, H. (1975). The behavioral assessment of male and female social competence in dyadic heterosexual interactions. *Behavior Therapy, 6,* 488–498.

Glass, D. C., & Carver, C. S. (1980). Helplessness and the coronary-prone personality. In J. Garber & M. E. P. Seligman (Eds.), *Human helplessness: Theory and applications* (pp. 223–243). New York: Academic.

Glass, D. C., Reim, B., & Singer, J. (1971). Behavioral consequences of adaptation to controllable and uncontrollable noise. *Journal of Experimental Social Psychology, 7,* 244–257.

Glass, D. C., Singer, J. E., Leonard, H. S., Krantz, D., & Cummings, H. (1973). Perceived control of aversive stimulation and the reduction of stress responses. *Journal of Personality, 41,* 577–595.

Glickman, C. D., & Tamashiro, R. T. (1982). A comparison of first-year, fifth-year, and former teachers on efficacy, ego development, and problem solving. *Psychology in the Schools, 19,* 558–562.

Glynn, S. M., & Ruderman, A. J. (1986). The development and validation of an eating self-efficacy scale. *Cognitive Therapy and Research, 10,* 403–420.

Godding, P. R., & Glasgow, R. E. (1985). Self-efficacy and outcome expectations as predictors of controlled smoking status. *Cognitive Therapy and Research, 9,* 583–590.

Goethals, G. R., & Darley, J. M. (1977). Social comparison theory: Attributional approach. In J. M. Suls & R. L. Miller (Eds.), *Social comparison processes: Theoretical and empirical perspectives* (pp. 259–278). Washington, D.C.: Hemisphere.

Goldfried, M. R., & Robins, C. (1982). On the facilitation of self-efficacy. *Cognitive Therapy and Research*, 6, 361–379.

Goldstein, A. P. (1973). *Structured learning therapy*. New York: Academic.

Goldstein, A. P., & Sorcher, M. (1974). *Changing supervisor behavior*. New York: Pergamon.

Goldstone, J. A. (1994). Is revolution individually rational? *Rationality and Society*, 6, 139–166.

Golin, S., & Terrill, F. (1977). Motivational and associative aspects of mild depression in skill and chance tasks. *Journal of Abnormal Psychology*, 86, 389–401.

Gonzales, F. P., & Dowrick, P. W. (1982, November). The mechanism of self-modeling: Skills acquisition versus raised self-efficacy. Paper presented at 16th annual convention of the Association for Advancement of Behavior Therapy, Los Angeles.

Good, T. L., & Brophy, J. E. (1986). School effects. In M. C. Wittrock (Ed.), *Handbook of research on teaching* (3rd ed., pp. 570–602). New York: MacMillan.

Goodwin, D. W. (1985). Genetic determinants of alcoholism. In J. H. Mendelson & N. K. Mello (Eds.), *The diagnosis and treatment of alcoholism* (pp. 65–88). New York: McGraw-Hill.

Gootnick, A. T. (1974). Locus of control and political participation of college students: A comparison of unidimensional and multidimensional approaches. *Journal of Consulting and Clinical Psychology*, 42, 54–58.

Gordon, A. J., & Zrull, M. (1991). Social networks and recovery: One year after inpatient treatment. *Journal of Substance Abuse Treatment*, 8, 143–152.

Gorrell, J., & Capron, E. (1990). Cognitive modeling and self-efficacy: Effects on preservice teachers' learning of teaching strategies. *Journal of Teacher Education*, 41, 15–22.

Gortner, S. R., & Jenkins, L. S. (1990). Self-efficacy and activity level following cardiac surgery. *Journal of Advanced Nursing*, 15, 1132–1138.

Goss, K. F. (1979). Consequences of diffusion of innovations. *Rural Sociology*, 44, 754–772.

Gossop, M., Green, L., Phillips, G., & Bradley, B. (1990). Factors predicting outcome among opiate addicts after treatment. *British Journal of Clinical Psychology*, 29, 209–216.

Gotlib, I. H. (1981). Self-reinforcement and recall: Differential deficits in depressed and nondepressed psychiatric inpatients. *Journal of Abnormal Psychology*, 90, 521–530.

Gotlib, I. H., & Colby, C. A. (1987). *Treatment of depression: An interpersonal systems approach*. Elmsford, N.Y.: Pergamon.

Gotsch, C. H. (1972). Technical change and the distribution of income in rural areas. *American Journal of Agricultural Economics*, 54, 326–341.

Gould, D., & Krane, V. (1992). The arousal-athletic performance relationship: Current status and future directions. In T. S. Horn (Ed.), *Advances in sport psychology* (pp. 119–141). Champaign, Ill.: Human Kinetics Publ.

Gould, D., Hodge, K., Peterson, K., & Giannini, J. (1989). An exploratory examination of strategies used by elite coaches to enhance self-efficacy in athletes. *Journal of Sport and Exercise Psychology*, 11, 128–140.

Gould, D., Jackson, S. A., & Finch, L. M. (1993). Life at the top: The experiences of U.S. national champion figure skaters. *The Sport Psychologist*, 7, 354–374.

Gould, D., & Weiss, M. (1981). Effect of model similarity and model self-talk on self-efficacy in muscular endurance. *Journal of Sport Psychology*, 3, 17–29.

Gould, J. D. (1980). Experiments on composing letters: Some facts, some myths, and some observations. In L. Gregg & E. Steinberg (Eds.), *Cognitive processes in writing* (pp. 97–127). Hillsdale, N.J.: Erlbaum.

Gracely, R. H., Dubner, R., Wolskee, P. J., & Deeter, W. R. (1983). Placebo and naloxone can alter postsurgical pain by separate mechanisms. *Nature*, 306, 264–265.

Graham, S., & Harris, K. R. (1989a). Components analysis of cognitive strategy instruction: Effects on learning disabled students' compositions and self-efficacy. *Journal of Educational Psychology*, 81, 353–361.

Graham, S., & Harris, K. R. (1989b). Improving learning disabled students' skills at composing essays: Self-instructional strategy training. *Exceptional Children*, 56, 210–214.

Granovetter, M. (1983). The strength of weak ties: A network theory revisited. In R. Collins (Ed.), *Sociological theory 1983* (pp. 201–233). San Francisco: Jossey-Bass.

Gray, V. (1973). Innovation in the States: A diffusion study. *The American Political Science Review*, 4, 1174–1185.

Grayson, G. (1980, November 20). "Coding" athletes to win. *St. Louis Post-Dispatch*, pp. 1, 4.

Green, B. L., & Saenz, D. S. (1995). Tests of a mediational model of restrained eating: The role of dieting self-efficacy and social

comparisons. *Journal of Social and Clinical Psychology*, 14, 1–22.

Greene, D., Sternberg, B., & Lepper, M. R. (1976). Overjustification in a token economy. *Journal of Personality and Social Psychology*, 34, 1219–1234.

Greider, W. (1992). *Who will tell the people: The betrayal of American democracy*. New York: Simon & Schuster.

Grembowski, D., Patrick, D., Diehr, P., Durham, M., Beresford, S., Kay, E., & Hecht, J. (1993). Self-efficacy and health behavior among older adults. *Journal of Health and Social Behavior*, 34, 89–104.

Gresham, F. M., Evans, S., & Eliott, S. N. (1988). Academic and social self-efficacy scale: Development and initial validation. *Journal of Psychoeducational Assessment*, 6, 125–138.

Gross, D., Conrad, B., Fogg, L., & Wothke, W. (1994). A longitudinal model of maternal self-efficacy, depression, and difficult temperament during toddlerhood. *Research in Nursing and Health*, 17, 207–215.

Gross, D., Fogg, L., & Tucker, S. (1995). The efficacy of parent training for promoting positive parent-toddler relationships. *Research in Nursing and Health*, 18, 489–499.

Grossman, H. Y., Brink, S., & Hauser, S. T. (1987). Self-efficacy in adolescent girls and boys with insulin-dependent diabetes mellitus. *Diabetes Care*, 10, 324–329.

Grove, J. R. (1993). Attributional correlates of cessation self-efficacy among smokers. *Addictive Behaviors*, 18, 311–320.

Grow, G. O. (1991). Teaching learners to be self-directed. *Adult Education Quarterly*, 41, 125–149.

Gruber, B., Hall, N. R., Hersh, S. P., & Dubois, P. (1988). Immune system and psychologic changes in metastatic cancer patients using relaxation and guided imagery: A pilot study. *Scandinavian Journal of Behaviour Therapy*, 17, 25–46.

Grünbaum, A. (1984). *The foundations of psychoanalysis: A philosophical critique*. Berkeley: University of California Press.

Guest, A. M. (1974). Subjective powerlessness in the United States: Some longitudinal trends. *Social Science Quarterly*, 54, 827–842.

Gulliver, S. B., Hughes, J. R., Solomon, L. J., & Dey, A. N. (1995). An investigation of self-efficacy, partner support and daily stresses as predictors of relapse to smoking in self-quitters. *Addiction*, 90, 767–772.

Gunnar, M. R. (1980a). Contingent stimulation: A review of its role in early development. In S. Levine & H. Ursin (Eds.),

Coping and health (pp. 101–119). New York: Plenum.

Gunnar, M. R. (1980b). Control, warning signals, and distress in infancy. *Developmental Psychology,* 16, 281–289.

Gunnar-von Gnechten, M. R. (1978). Changing a frightening toy into a pleasant toy by allowing the infant to control its actions. *Developmental Psychology,* 14, 147–152.

Gurin, P., & Brim, O. G., Jr. (1984). Change in self in adulthood: The example of sense of control. In P. B. Baltes & O. G. Brim, Jr. (Eds.), *Life-span development and behavior* (Vol. 6, pp. 281–334). New York: Academic.

Gurin, P., Gurin, G., & Morrison, B. M. (1978). Personal and ideological aspects of internal and external control. *Social Psychology,* 41, 275–296.

Gurr, R. T. (1970). Sources of rebellion in Western societies: Some quantitative evidence. *Annals of the American Academy of Political and Social Science,* 391, 128–144.

Gustkey, E. (1979, December 21). The computerized athlete is here. *San Francisco Chronicle,* pp. 67, 70.

Guzzo, R. A. (1986). Group decision making and group effectiveness in organizations. In P. S. Goodman (Ed.), *Designing effective work groups* (pp. 34–71). San Francisco: Jossey-Bass.

Haaga, D. A. F. (1989). Articulated thoughts and endorsement procedures for cognitive assessment in the prediction of smoking relapse. *Psychological Assessment,* 1, 112–117.

Haaga, D. A. F., Davison, G. C., McDermut, W., Hillis, S. L., & Twomey, H. B. (1993). "States-of-mind" analysis of the articulated thoughts of exsmokers. *Cognitive Therapy and Research,* 17, 427–439.

Haaga, D. A. F., & Stewart, B. L. (1992). Self-efficacy for recovery from a lapse after smoking cessation. *Journal of Consulting and Clinical Psychology,* 60, 24–28.

Hackett, G. (1985). The role of mathematics self-efficacy in the choice of math-related majors of college women and men: A path analysis. *Journal of Counseling Psychology,* 32, 47–56.

Hackett, G., & Betz, N. E. (1981). A self-efficacy approach to the career development of women. *Journal of Vocational Behavior,* 18, 326–339.

Hackett, G., & Betz, N. E. (1989). An exploration of the mathematics self-efficacy/mathematics performance correspondence. *Journal of Research in Mathematics Education,* 20, 261–273.

Hackett, G., Betz, N. E., Casas, J. M., & Rocha-Singh, I. A. (1992). Gender, eth-

nicity, and social cognitive factors predicting the academic achievement of students in engineering. *Journal of Counseling Psychology,* 39, 527–538.

Hackett, G., Betz, N. E., & Doty, M. S. (1985). The development of a taxonomy of career competencies for professional women. *Sex Roles,* 12, 393–409.

Hackman, J. R., & Lawler, E. E., III. (1971). Employee reactions to job characteristics. *Journal of Applied Psychology* (Monograph), 55, 259–286.

Hafner, R. J., & Marks, I. M. (1976). Exposure in vivo of agoraphobics: Contributions of diazepam, group exposure, and anxiety evocation. *Psychological Medicine,* 6, 71–88.

Hagberg, J. M. (1994). Physical activity, fitness, health, and aging. In C. Bouchard, R. J. Shephard, & T. Stephens (Eds.), *Physical activity, fitness, and health: International proceedings and consensus statement* (pp. 993–1005). Champaign, Ill.: Human Kinetics Publ.

Haight, M. R. (1980). *A study of self deception.* Atlantic Highlands, N.J.: Humanities Press.

Hall, H. K., & Byrne, A. T. J. (1988). Goal setting in sport: Clarifying recent anomalies. *Journal of Sport and Exercise Psychology,* 10, 184–198.

Hallie, P. P. (1971). Justification and rebellion. In N. Sanford & C. Comstock (Eds.), *Sanctions for evil* (pp. 247–263). San Francisco: Jossey-Bass.

Halter, L. L., & Walker, H. (1983). The use of self-modeling and feedback procedures to improve the basketball performance of an NBA athlete. Manuscript, Sport Science Associates, Portland, Oregon.

Hamburg, B. A. (1974). Early adolescence: A specific and stressful stage of the life cycle. In G. V. Coelho, D. A. Hamburg, & J. E. Adams (Eds.), *Coping and adaptation* (pp. 101–124). New York: Basic Books.

Hamburg, D. A. (1992). *Today's children: Creating a future for a generation in crisis.* New York: Times Books.

Hamilton, S. F. (1987). Apprenticeship as a transition to adulthood in West Germany. *American Journal of Education,* 95, 314–345.

Hamilton, S. F. (1994). Social roles for youth: Interventions in unemployment. In A. C. Peterson & J. T. Mortimer (Eds.), *Youth unemployment and society* (pp. 248–269). London: Cambridge University Press.

Hammond, K. R., McClelland, G. H., & Mumpower, J. (1980). *Human judgment and decision making.* New York: Praeger.

Hampden-Turner, C. (1976). *Sane asylum.* San Francisco: San Francisco Book Co.

Hancock, T., & Garrett, M. (1995). Beyond medicine: Health challenges and strategies in the 21st century. *Futures,* 27, 935–951.

Hannah, J. S., & Kahn, S. E. (1989). The relationship of socioeconomic status and gender to the occupational choices of grade 12 students. *Journal of Vocational Behavior,* 34, 161–178.

Hannaway, J. (1992). Breaking the cycle: Instructional efficacy and teachers of "at risk" students. Manuscript, Stanford University, Stanford, Calif.

Harackiewicz, J. M., Sansone, C., & Manderlink, G. (1985). Competence, achievement orientation, and intrinsic motivation: A process analysis. *Journal of Personality and Social Psychology,* 48, 493–508.

Harlow, H. F. (1953). Motivation as a factor in the acquisition of new responses. In *Current theory and research in motivation: A symposium* (pp. 24–49). Lincoln: University of Nebraska Press.

Harré, R., & Gillet, G. (1994). *The discursive mind.* Thousand Oaks, Calif.: Sage.

Harris, P. L. (1989). *Children and emotion: The development of psychological understanding.* Oxford: Basil Blackwell.

Harris, S. S., Caspersen, C. J., DeFriese, G. H., & Estes, E. H. (1989). Physical activity counseling for healthy adults as a primary preventive intervention in the clinical setting. *Journal of the American Medical Association,* 261, 3590–3598.

Harter, S. (1981). A model of mastery motivation in children: Individual differences and developmental change. In W. A. Collins (Ed.), *Aspects of the development of competence: Minnesota Symposia on child psychology* (Vol. 14, pp. 215–255). Hillsdale, N.J.: Erlbaum.

Harter, S. (1990). Causes, correlates, and the functional role of global self-worth: A life-span perspective. In R. J. Sternberg & J. Kolligian, Jr. (Eds.), *Competence considered* (pp. 67–97). New Haven, Conn.: Yale University Press.

Harvey, V., & McMurray, N. (1994). Self-Efficacy: A means of identifying problems in nursing education and career progress. *International Journal of Nursing Studies,* 31, 471–485.

Haskell, W. L., Alderman, E. L., Fair, J. M., Maron, D. J., Mackey, S. F., Superko, H. R., Williams, P. T., Johnstone, I. M., Champagne, M. A., Krauss, R. M., & Farquhar, J. W. (1994). Effects of intensive multiple risk factor reduction on coronary atherosclerosis and clinical cardiac events in men and women with coronary artery disease. *Circulation*, 89, 975–990.

Haskell, W. L., Montoye, H. J., & Orenstein, D. (1985). Physical activity and exercise to achieve health-related physical fitness components. *Public Health Reports*, 100, 202–212.

Hattiangadi, N., Medvec, V. H., & Gilovich, T. (1995). Failing to act: Regrets of Terman's geniuses. *International Journal of Aging and Human Development*, 40, 175–185.

Havens, A. E., & Flinn, W. (1975). Green revolution technology and community development: The limits of action programs. *Economic Development and Cultural Change*, 23, 469–481.

Hawkins, B. W., Marando, V. L., & Taylor, G. A. (1971). Efficacy, mistrust, and political participation: Findings from additional data and indicators. *Journal of Politics*, 33, 1130–1136.

Hayes, C. D. (Ed.) (1987). *Risking the future: Adolescent sexuality, pregnancy and childbearing.* (Vol. 1). Washington, D.C.: National Academy Press.

Hays, R. D., & Ellickson, P. L. (1990). How generalizable are adolescents' beliefs about pro-drug pressures and resistance self-efficacy? *Journal of Applied Social Psychology*, 20, 321–340.

Heath, C., & Tversky, A. (1991). Performance and belief: Ambiguity and competence in choice under uncertainty. *Journal of Risk and Uncertainty*, 4, 5–28.

Heather, N., & Robertson, I. (1981). *Controlled drinking.* London: Methuen.

Heather, N., Rollnick, S., & Winton, M. (1983). A comparison of objective and subjective measures of alcohol dependence as predictors of relapse following treatment. *British Journal of Clinical Psychology*, 22, 11–17.

Heather, N., & Stallard, A. (1989). Does the Marlatt model underestimate the importance of conditioned craving in the relapse process? In M. Gossop (Ed.), *Relapse and addictive behaviour* (pp. 180–208). London: Tavistock/Routledge.

Heckhausen, J. (1987). Balancing for weaknesses and challenging developmental potential: A longitudinal study of mother-infant dyads in apprenticeship interactions. *Developmental Psychology*, 23, 762–770.

Heckhausen, J. (1992). Adults expectancies about development and its controllability: Enhancing self-efficacy by social comparison. In R. Schwarzer (Ed.), *Self-efficacy: Thought control of action* (pp. 107–126). Washington, D.C.: Hemisphere.

Heffernan, T., & Richards, S. (1981). Self-control of study behavior: Identification and evaluation of natural methods. *Journal of Counseling Psychology*, 28, 361–364.

Heiby, E. M. (1983a). Depression as a function of the interaction of self- and environmentally controlled reinforcement. *Behavior Therapy*, 14, 430–433.

Heiby, E. M. (1983b). Toward the prediction of mood change. *Behavior Therapy*, 14, 110–115.

Heiby, E. M. (1986). Social versus self-control skills deficits in four cases of depression. *Behavior Therapy*, 17, 158–169.

Heinrich, L. B. (1993). Contraceptive self-efficacy in college women. *Journal of Adolescent Health*, 14, 269–276.

Heller, M. C., & Krauss, H. H. (1991). Perceived self-efficacy as a predictor of aftercare treatment entry by the detoxification patient. *Psychological Reports*, 68, 1047–1052.

Herbert, T. B., & Cohen, S. (1993a). Depression and immunity: A meta-analytic review. *Psychological Bulletin*, 113, 472–486.

Herbert, T. B., & Cohen, S. (1993b). Stress and immunity in humans: A meta-analytic review. *Psychosomatic Medicine*, 55, 364–379.

Herman, C. P., & Polivy, J. (1983). A boundary model for the regulation of eating. In A. B. Stunkard & E. Stellar (Eds.), *Eating and its disorders* (pp. 141–156). New York: Raven.

Herrnstein, R. J. (1969). Method and theory in the study of avoidance. *Psychological Review*, 76, 49–69.

Hess, R. D., & Miura, I. T. (1985). Gender differences in enrollment in computer camps and classes. *Sex Roles*, 13, 193–203.

Hester, R. K., & Miller, W. R. (Eds.). (1995). *Handbook of alcoholism treatment approaches: Effective alternatives* (2nd ed.). Boston: Allyn & Bacon.

Highlen, P. S., & Bennett, B. B. (1983). Elite divers and wrestlers: A comparison between open- and closed-skill athletes. *Journal of Sport Psychology*, 5, 390–409.

Hill, G. J. (1989). An unwillingness to act: Behavioral appropriateness, situational constraint, and self-efficacy in shyness. *Journal of Personality*, 57, 871–890.

Hill, L. A., & Elias, J. (1990). Retraining midcareer managers: Career history and self-efficacy beliefs. *Human Resources Management*, 29, 197–217.

Hill, R. D. (1986). Prescribing relapse as a relapse prevention aid to enhance the maintenance of nonsmoking treatment gains. Ph.D. diss., Stanford University, Stanford, Calif.

Hill, T., Smith, N. D., & Mann, M. F. (1987). Role of efficacy expectations in predicting the decision to use advanced technologies: The case of computers. *Journal of Applied Psychology*, 72, 307–313.

Hiltz, S. R., & Turoff, M. (1978). *The network nation: Human communication via computer.* Reading, Mass.: Addison-Wesley.

Hineline, P. N. (1977). Negative reinforcement and avoidance. In W. K. Honing & J. E. R. Staddon (Eds.) *Handbook of operant behavior* (pp. 364–414). Englewood Cliffs, NJ: Prentice Hall, Inc.

Hinshaw, S. P. (1992). Externalizing behavior problems and academic underachievement in childhood and adolescence: Causal relationships and underlying mechanisms. *Psychological Bulletin*, 111, 127–155.

Hirt, E. R., Zillmann, D., Erickson, G. A., & Kennedy, C. (1992). Costs and benefits of allegiance: Changes in fans' self-ascribed competencies after team victory versus defeat. *Journal of Personality and Social Psychology*, 63, 724–738.

Hobsbawm, E. J. (1996). The future of the state. *Development and Change*, 27, 267–278.

Hodges, L., & Carron, A. V. (1992). Collective efficacy and group performance. *International Journal of Sport Psychology*, 23, 48–59.

Hoelscher, T. J., Lichstein, K. L., & Rosenthal, T. L. (1986). Home relaxation practice in hypertension treatment: Objective assessment and compliance induction. *Journal of Consulting and Clinical Psychology*, 54, 217–221.

Hofferth, S. L., & Hayes, C. D. (Eds.). (1987). *Risking the future* (Vol. 2). Washington, D.C.: National Academy Press.

Hoffman, H. S. (1969). Stimulus factors in conditioned suppression. In B. A. Campbell & R. M. Church (Eds.) *Punishment and aversive behavior* (pp. 185–234). New York: Appleton-Century-Crofts.

Hofstetter, C. R., Hovell, M. F., & Sallis, J. F. (1990). Social learning correlates of exercise self-efficacy: Early experiences with physical activity. *Social Science Medicine*, 31, 1169–1176.

Hofstetter, C. R., Sallis, J. F., & Hovell, M. F. (1990). Some health dimensions of self-efficacy: Analysis of theoretical specificity. *Social Science Medicine*, 31, 1051–1056.

Hogarth, R. (1981). Beyond discrete biases: Functional and dysfunctional aspects of judgmental heuristics. *Psychological Bulletin*, 90, 197–217.

Holahan, C. K., & Holahan, C. J. (1987a). Self-efficacy, social support, and depression in aging: A longitudinal analysis. *Journal of Gerontology*, 42, 65–68.

Holahan, C. K., & Holahan, C. J. (1987b). Life stress, hassles, and self-efficacy in aging: A replication and extension. *Journal of Applied Social Psychology*, 17, 574–592.

Holden, G. (1991). The relationship of self-efficacy appraisals to subsequent health related outcomes: A meta-analysis. *Social Work in Health Care*, 16, 53–93.

Holden, G., Moncher, M. S., Schinke, S. P., & Barker, K. M. (1990). Self-efficacy of children and adolescents: A meta-analysis. *Psychological Reports*, 66, 1044–1046.

Holland, J. L. (1985). *Making vocational choices: A theory of vocational personalities and work environments* (2nd ed.). Englewood Cliffs, N.J.: Prentice-Hall.

Hollandsworth, J. G., Jr., Glazeski, R. C., Kirkland, K., Jones, G. E., & van Norman, L. R. (1979). An analysis of the nature and effects of test anxiety: Cognitive, behavioral, and physiological components. *Cognitive Therapy and Research*, 3, 165–180.

Hollon, S. D., & Beck, A. T. (1994). Cognitive and cognitive-behavioral therapies. In A. E. Bergin & S. L. Garfield (Eds.), *Handbook of psychotherapy and behavior change* (3rd. ed., pp. 443–482). New York: Wiley.

Holloway, J. B., Beuter, A., & Duda, J. L. (1988). Self-efficacy and training for strength in adolescent girls. *Journal of Applied Social Psychology*, 18, 699–719.

Holman, H., & Lorig, K. (1992). Perceived self-efficacy in self-management of chronic disease. In R. Schwarzer (Ed.), *Self-efficacy: Thought control of action* (pp. 305–323). Washington, D.C.: Hemisphere.

Holmes, D. S. (1993). Aerobic fitness and the response to psychological stress. In P. Seraganian (Ed.), *Exercise psychology: The influence of physical exercise on psychological processes*. New York: Wiley.

Holroyd, K. A., Penzien, D. B., Hursey, K. G., Tobin, D. L., Rogers, L., Holm, J. E., Marcille, P. J., Hall, J. R., & Chila, A. G. (1984). Change mechanisms in EMG biofeedback training: Cognitive changes underlying improvements in tension headache. *Journal of Consulting and Clinical Psychology*, 52, 1039–1053.

Hoover-Dempsey, K. V., Bassler, O. C., & Brissie, J. S. (1987). Parent involvement: Contributions of teacher efficacy, school socioeconomic status, and other school characteristics. *American Educational Research Journal*, 24, 417–435.

Hoover-Dempsey, K. V., Bassler, O. C., & Brissie, J. S. (1992). Parent efficacy, teacher efficacy, and parent involvement: Explorations in parent-school relations.

Journal of Educational Research, 85, 287–294.

Horwitt, S. D. (1989). *Let them call me rebel: Saul Alinsky: His life and legacy*. New York: Knopf.

Hotz, V. J., & Tienda, M. (in press). Education and employment in a diverse society: Generating inequality through the school-to-work transition. In N. Denton and S. Tolnay (Eds.), *American diversity: A demographic challenge for the twenty-first century*. Albany, N.Y.: SUNY Press.

Hoy, W. K., & Woolfolk, A. E. (1993). Teacher's sense of efficacy and the organizational health of schools. *The Elementary School Journal*, 93, 355–372.

Huebner, R. B., & Lipsey, M. W. (1981). The relationship of three measures of locus of control to environmental activism. *Basic and Applied Social Psychology*, 2, 45–58.

Hull, C. L. (1943). *Principles of behavior*. New York: Appleton-Century-Crofts.

Hultsch, D. F., & Plemons, J. K. (1979). Life events and life-span development. In P. B. Baltes & O. G. Brim, Jr. (Eds.), *Life-span development and behavior* (Vol. 2, pp. 1–36). New York: Academic.

Hung, J. H., & Rosenthal, T. L. (1981). Therapeutic videotaped playback. In J. L. Fryrear & R. Fleshman (Eds.), *Videotherapy in mental health* (pp. 5–46). Springfield, Ill.: Thomas.

Hunt, G. M., & Azrin, N. H. (1973). A community-reinforcement approach to alcoholism. *Behaviour Research and Therapy*, 11, 91–104.

Hunt, J. McV., Cole, M. W., & Reis, E. E. S. (1958). Situational cues distinguishing anger, fear, and sorrow. *American Journal of Psychology*, 71, 136–151.

Hurley, C. C., & Shea, C. A. (1992). Self-efficacy: Strategy for enhancing diabetes self-care. *The Diabetes Educator*, 18, 146–150.

Hurrelmann, K., & Roberts, K. (1991). Problems and solutions. In J. Bynner & K. Roberts (Eds.), *Youth and work: Transition to employment in England and Germany* (pp. 229–250). London: Anglo-German Foundation.

Hyman, D. J., Maibach, E. W., Flora, J. A., & Fortmann, S. P. (1992). Cholesterol treatment practices of primary care physicians. *Public Health Reports*, 107, 441–448.

Ilgen, D. R. (1994). Jobs and roles: Accepting and coping with the changing structure of organizations. In M. G. Rumsey, C. B. Walker, & J. H. Harris (Eds.), *Personnel selection and classification* (pp. 13–32). Hillsdale, N.J.: Erlbaum.

Irwin, F. W. (1971). *Intentional behavior and motivation: A cognitive view*. Philadelphia: Lippincott.

Isen, A. M. (1987). Positive affect, cognitive processes, and social behavior. In L. Berkowitz (Ed.), *Advances in experimental social psychology* (Vol. 20). New York: Academic.

Jacklin, C. N., & Mischel, H. N. (1973). As the twig is bent: Sex role stereotyping in early readers. *The School Psychology Digest*, 2, 30–38.

Jackson, B. (1972). Treatment of depression by self-reinforcement. *Behavior Therapy*, 3, 298–307.

Jackson, C., Fortmann, S. P., Flora, J. A., Melton, R. J., Snider, J. P., & Littlefield, D. (1994). The capacity-building approach to intervention maintenance implemented by the Stanford five-city project. *Health Education Research*, 9, 385–396.

Jackson, S. E., Schwab, R. L., & Schuler, R. S. (1986). Toward an understanding of the burnout phenomenon. *Journal of Applied Psychology*, 71, 630–640.

Jacobs, B., Prentice-Dunn, S., & Rogers, R. W. (1984). Understanding persistence: An interface of control theory and self-efficacy theory. *Basic and Applied Social Psychology*, 5, 333–347.

Jacobs, J. A. (1989). *Revolving doors: Sex segregation and women's careers*. Stanford, Calif.: Stanford University Press.

Jacobson, N. S., Holtzworth-Munroe, A. (1986). Marital therapy: A social learning-cognitive perspective. In N. S. Jacobson & A. S. Gurman (Eds.), *Clinical handbook of marital therapy* (pp. 29–70). New York: Guilford.

Janal, M. N., Colt, E. W. D., Clark, W. C., & Glusman, M. (1984). Pain sensitivity, mood and plasma endocrine levels in man following long-distance running: Effects of naloxone. *Pain*, 19, 13–25.

Janis, I. L. (1972). *Victims of groupthink: A psychological study of foreign-policy decisions and fiascoes*. Boston: Houghton Mifflin.

Janis, I. L., & Mann, L. (1977). *Decision making*. New York: Free Press.

Jansen, A., Broekmate, J., & Heymans, M. (1992). Cue-exposure vs. self-control in the treatment of binge eating: A pilot study. *Behavior Research Therapy*, 30, 235–241.

Janz, N. K., & Becker, M. H. (1984). The health belief model: A decade later. *Health Education Quarterly*, 11, 1–47.

Jaremko, M. E. (1979). A component analysis of stress inoculation: Review and prospectus. *Cognitive Therapy and Research*, 3, 35–48.

Jatulis, L. L., & Newman, D. L. (1991). The role of contextual variables in evaluation decision making: Perceptions of potential loss, time, and self-efficacy on nurse managers' need for information. *Evaluation Review*, 15, 364–377.

Jeffrey, R. W., Bjornson-Benson, W. M., Rosenthal, B. S., Lindquist, R. A., Kurth, C. L., & Johnson, S. L. (1984). Correlates of weight loss and its maintenance over two years of follow-up among middle-aged men, *Preventive Medicine*, 13, 155–168.

Jellinek, E. M. (1960). *The disease concept of alcoholism.* Highland Park, N.J.: Hillhouse Press.

Jemmott, J. B., III, Jemmott, L. S., & Fong, G. T. (1992). Reductions in HIV risk-associated sexual behaviors among black male adolescents: Effects of an AIDS prevention intervention. *American Journal of Public Health*, 82, 372–377.

Jemmott, J. B., III, Jemmott, L. S., Spears, H., Hewitt, N., & Cruz-Collins, M. (1992). Self-efficacy, hedonistic expectancies, and condom-use intentions among inner-city black adolescent women: A social cognitive approach to AIDS risk behavior. *Journal of Adolescent Health*, 13, 512–519.

Jenkins, A. L. (1994a). The role of managerial self-efficacy in corporate compliance with the law. *Law and Human Behavior*, 18, 71–88.

Jenkins, A. L. (April, 1994b). Self-efficacy and the assessment environment: Bandura's social cognitive theory on work performance and appraisal. Paper presented at the 23rd Meeting of Australian Social Psychologists, Cairns, Queensland.

Jensen, K., Banwart, L., Venhaus, R., Popkess-Vawter, S., & Perkins, S. B. (1993). Advanced rehabilitation nursing care of coronary angioplasty patients using self-efficacy theory. *Journal of Advanced Nursing*, 18, 926–931.

Jensen, M. P., & Karoly, P. (1991). Control beliefs, coping efforts, and adjustment to chronic pain. *Journal of Consulting and Clinical Psychology*, 59, 431–438.

Jensen, M. P., Turner, J. A., & Romano, J. M. (1991). Self-efficacy and outcome expectancies: Relationship to chronic pain coping strategies and adjustment. *Pain*, 44, 263–269.

Jerusalem, M., & Mittag, W. (1995). Self-efficacy in stressful life transitions. In A. Bandura (Ed.), *Self-efficacy in changing societies* (pp. 177–201). New York: Cambridge University Press.

Jessor, R. (1986). Adolescent problem drinking: Psychosocial aspects and developmental outcomes. In R. K. Silbereisen et al. (Eds.), *Development as action in context* (pp. 241–264). Berlin: Springer-Verlag.

Jessor, R., Donovan, J. E., & Costa, F. M. (1991). *Beyond adolescence: Problem behavior and young adult development.* Cambridge: Cambridge University Press.

Jex, S. M., & Gudanowski, D. M. (1992). Efficacy beliefs and work stress: An exploratory study. *Journal of Organizational Behavior*, 13, 509–517.

Jobe, L. D. (1984). Effects of proximity and specificity of goals on performance. Ph.D. diss., Murdoch University, Western Australia.

Johansson, G. (1973). Visual perception of biological motion and a model for its analysis. *Perception and Psychophysics*, 14, 201–211.

Johnson, D. W., & Johnson, R. T. (1985). Motivational processes in cooperative, competitive, and individualistic learning situations. In C. Ames & R. Ames (Eds.), *Research on motivation in education.* Vol. 2, *The classroom milieu* (pp. 249–277). New York: Academic.

Johnson, D. W., Maruyama, G., Johnson, R., Nelson, D., & Skon, L. (1981). Effects of cooperative, competitive, and individualistic goal structures on achievement: A meta-analysis. *Psychological Bulletin*, 89, 47–62.

Joiner, T. E., Jr. (1994). Contagious depression: Existence, specificity to depressed symptoms, and the role of reassurance seeking. *Journal of Personality and Social Psychology*, 67, 287–296.

Jones, G. R. (1986). Socialization tactics, self-efficacy, and newcomers' adjustments to organizations. *Academy of Management Journal,* 29, 262–279.

Jones, R. A. (1977). *Self-fulfilling prophesies: Social, psychological, and physiological effects of experiences.* Hillsdale, N.J.: Erlbaum.

Jones, R. J., & Azrin, N. H. (1973). An experimental application of a social reinforcement approach to the problem of job-finding. *Journal of Applied Behavior Analysis*, 6, 345–353.

Jorde-Bloom, P., & Ford, M. (1988). Factors influencing early childhood administrators' decisions regarding the adoption of computer technology. *Journal of Educational Computing Research*, 4, 31–47.

Josephson, M. (1959). *Edison.* New York: McGraw-Hill.

Joss, J. E., Spira, J. L., & Speigel, D. S. (1994). The Stanford cancer self-efficacy

scale: Development and validation of a self-efficacy scale for patients living with cancer. Manuscript, Stanford University, Stanford, California.

Jourden, F. (1991). The influence of feedback framing on the self-regulatory mechanisms governing complex decision making. Ph.D. diss., Stanford University, Stanford, Calif.

Jourden, F. J., Bandura, A., & Banfield, J. T. (1991). The impact of conceptions of ability on self-regulatory factors and motor skill acquisition. *Journal of Sport and Exercise Psychology*, 8, 213–226.

Judd, C. M., & Kenny, D. A. (1981). Process analysis: Estimating mediation in treatment evaluations. *Evaluation Reviews*, 5, 602–619.

Juneau, M., Rogers, F., Bandura, A., Taylor, C. B., & DeBusk, R. (1986). Cognitive processing of treadmill experiences and self-appraisal of cardiac capabilities. Manuscript, Stanford University, Stanford, Calif.

Junge, M. E., & Dretzke, B. J. (1995). Mathematical self-efficacy gender differences in gifted/talented adolescents. *Gifted Child Quarterly*, 39, 22–26.

Jussim, L. (1986). Self-fulfilling prophecies: A theoretical and integrative review. *Psychological Review*, 93, 429–445.

Kagan, J. (1981). *The second year: The emergence of self-awareness.* Cambridge, Mass.: Harvard University Press.

Kahn, J. S., Kehle, T. J., Jenson, W. R., & Clark, E. (1990). Comparison of cognitive-behavioral, relaxation, and self-modeling interventions for depression among middle-school students. *School Psychology Review*, 19, 196–211.

Kahn, R. L., Wolfe, D. M., Quinn, R. P., & Snoek, J. D. (1964). *Organizational stress: Studies in role conflict and ambiguity.* New York: Wiley.

Kahneman, E. (1973). *Attention and effort.* Englewood Cliffs, N.J.: Prentice-Hall.

Kahneman, E., Slovic, P., & Tversky, A. (Eds.). (1982). *Judgment under uncertainty: Heuristics and biases.* New York: Cambridge University Press.

Kaivanto, K. K., Estlander, A.-M., Moneta, G. B., & Vanharanta, H. (1995). Isokinetic performance in low back pain patients: The predictive power of the self-efficacy scale. *Journal of Occupational Rehabilitation*, 5, 87–99.

Kane, T. D., Marks, M. A., Zaccaro, S. J., & Blair, V. (1996). Self-efficacy, personal goals, and wrestlers' self-regulation. *Journal of Sport and Exercise Psychology*, 18, 36–48.

Kanfer, F. H., & Gaelick, L. (1986). Self-management methods. In F. H. Kanfer & A. P. Goldstein (Eds.), *Helping people change* (pp. 283–345). New York: Pergamon.

Kanfer, F. H., & Hagerman, S. (1981). The role of self-regulation. In L. P. Rehm (Ed.), *Behavior therapy for depression: Present status and future directions* (pp. 143–180). New York: Academic.

Kanfer, R., & Hulin, C. L. (1985). Individual differences in successful job searches following lay-off. *Journal of Vocational Behavior, 38, 835–847.*

Kanfer, R., & Zeiss, A. M. (1983). Depression, interpersonal standard-setting, and judgments of self-efficacy. *Journal of Abnormal Psychology, 92, 319–329.*

Kaplan, R. M., Atkins, C. J., & Reinsch, S. (1984). Specific efficacy expectations mediate exercise compliance in patients with COPD. *Health Psychology, 3, 223–242.*

Kaplan, R. M., & Simon, H. J. (1990). Compliance in medical care: Reconsideration of self-predictions. *Annals of Behavioral Medicine, 12, 66–71.*

Karasek, R., & Theorell, T. (1990). *Healthy work: Stress, productivity, and the reconstruction of working life.* New York: Basic Books.

Karniol, R. (1989). The role of manual manipulative stages in the infant's acquisition of perceived control over objects. *Developmental Review, 9, 205–233.*

Karniol, R., & Ross, M. (1976). The development of causal attributions in social perception. *Journal of Personality and Social Psychology, 34, 455–464.*

Kasen, S., Vaughan, R. D., & Walter, H. J. (1992). Self-efficacy for AIDS preventive behaviors among tenth grade students. *Health Education Quarterly, 19, 187–202.*

Katch, F. I., & McArdle, W. D. (1977). *Nutrition, weight control, and exercise.* Boston: Houghton Mifflin.

Kato, M., & Fukushima, O. (1977). The effects of covert modeling in reducing avoidance behavior. *Japanese Psychological Research, 19, 199–203.*

Katz, R. C., Stout, A., Taylor, C. B., Horne, M., & Agras, W. S. (1983). The contribution of arousal and performance in reducing spider avoidance. *Behavioural Psychotherapy, 11, 127–138.*

Kavanagh, D. J. (1983). Mood and self-efficacy. Ph.D. diss., Stanford University, Stanford, Calif.

Kavanagh, D. J., & Bower, G. H. (1985). Mood and self-efficacy: Impact of joy and sadness on perceived capabilities. *Cognitive Therapy and Research, 9, 507–525.*

Kavanagh, D. J., Gooley, S., & Wilson, P. H. (1993). Prediction of adherence and control in diabetes. *Journal of Behavioral Medicine, 16, 509–522.*

Kavanagh, D. J., Pierce, J., Lo, S. K., & Shelley, J. (1993). Self-efficacy and social support as predictors of smoking after a quit attempt. *Psychology and Health, 8, 231–242.*

Kavanagh, D. J., & Wilson, P. H. (1989). Prediction of outcome with a group version of cognitive therapy for depression. *Behaviour Research and Therapy, 27, 333–347.*

Kavka, G. S. (1988). *Moral paradoxes of nuclear deterrence.* New York: Cambridge.

Kaye, K. (1982). *The mental and social life of babies: How parents create persons.* Chicago: University of Chicago Press.

Kazdin, A. E. (1973). Covert modeling and the reduction of avoidance behavior. *Journal of Abnormal Psychology, 81, 87–95.*

Kazdin, A. E. (1974a). Comparative effects of some variations of covert modeling. *Journal of Behavior Therapy and Experimental Psychiatry, 5, 225–232.*

Kazdin, A. E. (1974b). Self-monitoring and behavior change. In M. J. Mahoney & C. E. Thoresen (Eds.), *Self-control: Power to the person* (pp. 218–246). Monterey, Calif.: Brooks-Cole.

Kazdin, A. E. (1974c). Covert modeling, model similarity, and reduction of avoidance behavior. *Behavior Therapy, 5, 325–340.*

Kazdin, A. E. (1974d). The effect of model identity and fear-relevant similarity on covert modeling. *Behavior Therapy, 5, 624–635.*

Kazdin, A. E. (1975). Covert modeling, imagery assessment, and assertive behavior. *Journal of Consulting and Clinical Psychology, 43, 716–724.*

Kazdin, A. E. (1976). Effects of covert modeling, multiple models, and model reinforcement on assertive behavior. *Behavior Therapy, 7, 211–222.*

Kazdin, A. E. (1978). Covert modeling: The therapeutic application of imagined rehearsal. In J. L. Singer & K. S. Pope (Eds.) *The power of human imagination: New methods in psychotherapy. Emotions, personality, and psychotherapy* (pp. 255–278). New York: Plenum.

Kazdin, A. E. (1979). Imagery elaboration and self-efficacy in the covert modeling treatment of unassertive behavior. *Journal of Consulting and Clinical Psychology, 47, 725–733.*

Kazdin, A. E., & Wilcoxon, L. A. (1976). Systematic desensitization and nonspecific treatment effects: A methodological evaluation. *Psychological Bulletin, 83, 729–758.*

Kegeles, S. S., & Lund, A. K. (1982). Adolescents' health beliefs and acceptance of a novel preventive dental activity: Replication and extension. *Health Education Quarterly, 9, 192–208.*

Kelley, D. D. (Ed.). (1986). Stress-induced analgesia. *Annals of the New York Academy of Sciences* (Vol. 467). New York: New York Academy of Sciences.

Kellogg, R., & Baron, R. S. (1975). Attribution theory, insomnia, and the reverse placebo effect: A reversal of Storms and Nisbett's findings. *Journal of Personality and Social Psychology, 32, 231–236.*

Kelly, J. A. (1995). *Changing HIV risk behavior: Practical strategies.* New York: Guilford.

Kelly, J. A., St. Lawrence, J. S., Stevenson, L. Y., Houth, A. C., Kuliehman, S. C., Diaz, Y. E., Brasfield, T. L., Koob, J. J., & Morgan, M. G. (1992). Community AIDS/HIV risk reduction: The effects of endorsements by popular people in three cities. *American Journal of Public Health, 82, 1483–1489.*

Kempner, K., Castro, C. D., & Bas, D. (1993). Apprenticeship: The perilous journey from Germany to Togo. *International Review of Education, 39, 373–390.*

Keniston, K. (1968). *Young radicals.* New York: Harcourt, Brace, & World.

Kent, G. (1987). Self-efficacious control over reported physiological, cognitive and behavioural symptoms of dental anxiety. *Behaviour Research and Therapy, 25, 341–347.*

Kent, G., & Gibbons, R. (1987). Self-efficacy and the control of anxious cognitions. *Journal of Behavior Therapy and Experimental Psychiatry, 18, 33–40.*

Kent, G., & Jambunathan, P. (1989). A longitudinal study of the intrusiveness of cognitions in test anxiety. *Behaviour Research and Therapy, 27, 43–50.*

Kent, R. N., Wilson, G. T., & Nelson, R. (1972). Effects of false heart-rate feedback on avoidance behavior: An investigation of "cognitive desensitization." *Behavior Therapy, 3, 1–6.*

Keohane, R. O. (1993). Sovereignty, interdependence and international institutions. In L. Miller & M. Smith (Eds.), *Ideas and ideals: Essays on politics in honor of Stanley Hoffman* (91–107). Boulder, Colo.: Westview Press.

Keohane, R. O., & Nye, J. S. (1977). *Power and interdependence: World politics in transition.* Boston: Little, Brown.

Kerr, N. L. (1983). Motivation losses in small groups: A social dilemma analysis. *Journal of Personality and Social Psychology, 45,* 819–828.

Kerr, N. L. (1996). Does my contribution really matter?: Efficacy in social dilemmas. In W. Stroebe & M. Hewstone (Eds.), *European Review of Social Psychology* (Vol. 7) (209–240). Chichester, England: Wiley.

Kessler, K. A. (1978). Tricyclic anti-depressants: Mode of action and clinical use. In M. A. Lipton, A. DiMascio, & K. F. Killam (Eds.), *Psychopharmacology: A generation of progress* (pp. 1289–1302). New York: Raven.

Kiecolt-Glaser, J. K., & Glaser, R. (1988). Behavioral influence on immune function: Evidence for the interplay between stress and health. In T. Field, P. McCabe, & N. Schneiderman (Eds.), *Stress and coping* (Vol. 2, pp. 189–206). Hillsdale, N.J.: Erlbaum.

Kiecolt-Glaser, J. K., Glaser, R., Strain, E. C., Stout, J. C., Tarr, K. L., Holliday, J. E., & Speicher, C. E. (1986). Modulation of cellular immunity in medical students. *Journal of Behavioral Medicine, 9,* 5–21.

Kiecolt-Glaser, J. K., Glaser, R., Williger, D., Stout, J., Messick, G., Sheppard, S., Ricker, D., Romisher, S. C., Briner, W., Bonnell, G., & Donnerberg, R. (1985). Psychosocial enhancement of immunocompetence in a geriatric population. *Health Psychology, 4,* 25–41.

Kiesler, S., Siegel, J., & McGuire, T. W. (1984). Social psychological aspects of computer-mediated communication. *American Psychologist, 39,* 1123–1134.

Killen, J. D., Hayward, C., Wilson, D. M., Haydel, K. F., Robinson, T. N., Taylor, C. B., Hammer, L. D., & Varady, A. (1996). Predicting onset of drinking in a community sample of adolescents: The role of expectancy and temperament. *Addictive Behaviors, 21,* 473–480.

Killen, J. D., Maccoby, N., & Taylor, C. B. (1984). Nicotine gum and self-regulation training in smoking relapse prevention. *Behavior Therapy, 15,* 234–248.

Killen, J. D., Robinson, T. N., et al. (1989). The Stanford adolescent heart health program. *Health Education Quarterly, 16,* 263–283.

Kim, U., Triandis, H. D., Kâğitçibasi, C., Choi, S., & Yoon, G. (1994). *Individualism and collectivism: Theory, method, and applications.* Thousand Oaks, Calif.: Sage.

King, A. C., & Frederiksen, L. W. (1984). Low-cost strategies for increasing exercise behavior: Relapse preparation training and social support. *Behavior Modification, 8,* 3–21.

King, A. C., Kiernan, M., Oman, R. F., Kraemer, H. C., Hull, M., & Ahn, D. (in press). Towards a biobehavioral approach for predicting physical activity adherence across time: Applications of signal detection methodology. *Health Psychology.*

King, A. C., Taylor, C. B., Haskell, W. L., & DeBusk, R. F. (1988). Strategies for increasing early adherence to and long-term maintenance of home-based exercise training in healthy middle-aged men and women. *American Journal of Cardiology, 61,* 628–632.

King, M. L. (1958). *Stride toward freedom.* New York: Ballantine Books.

King, V., & Elder, G. H., Jr. (1996). *Self-efficacy and grandparenthood.* Submitted for publication.

Kipnis, D. (1974). The powerholders. In J. T. Tedeschi (Ed.), *Perspectives on social power* (pp. 82–122). Chicago: Aldine.

Kirkpatrick, S. A., & Locke, E. A. (1996). Direct and indirect effects of three core charismatic leadership components on performance and attitudes. *Journal of Applied Psychology, 81,* 36–51.

Kirsch, I. (1982). Efficacy expectations as response predictors: The meaning of efficacy ratings as a function of task characteristics. *Journal of Personality and Social Psychology, 42,* 132–136.

Kirsch, I. (1990). *Expectancy modification: A key to effective therapy.* Belmont, Calif.: Brooks-Cole.

Kirsch, I. (1995). Self-efficacy and outcome expectancy. In J. E. Maddux (Ed.), *Self-efficacy, adaptation, and adjustment: Theory, research and application* (pp. 331–345). New York: Plenum.

Kitchener, K. S. (1983). Cognition, metacognition, and epistemic cognition: A three-level model of cognitive processing. *Human Development, 26,* 222–232.

Klepac, R. K., Dowling, J., & Hauge, G. (1982). Characteristics of clients seeking therapy for the reduction of dental avoidance: Reactions to pain. *Journal of Behaviour Therapy and Experimental Psychiatry, 13,* 293–300.

Klerman, G. L., & Weissman, M. M. (1982). Interpersonal psychotherapy: Theory and research. In A. J. Rush (Ed.), *Short-term psychotherapies for depression* (pp.. 88–106). New York: Guilford Press.

Klorman, R., Hilpert, P. L., Michael, R., La-Gana, C., & Sveen, O. B. (1980). Effects of coping and mastery modeling on experienced and inexperienced pedodontic patients' disruptiveness. *Behavior Therapy, 11,* 156–168.

Koch, P. B. (1991). Sex education. In R. M.

Lerner, A. C. Petersen, & J. Brooks-Gunn (Eds.), *Encyclopedia of adolescence* (Vol. 2, pp. 1004–1006). New York: Garland.

Kok, G., deVries, H., Mudde, A. N., & Strecher, V. J. (1991). Planned health education and the role of self-efficacy: Dutch research. *Health Education Research, 6,* 231–238.

Kopel, S., & Arkowitz, H. (1975). The role of attribution and self-perception in behavior change: Implications for behavior therapy. *Genetic Psychology Monographs, 92,* 175–212.

Kortenhaus, C. M., & Demarest, J. (1993). Gender role stereotyping in children's literature: An update. *Sex Roles, 28,* 219–232.

Kotler-Cope, S., & Camp, C. J. (1990). Memory interventions in aging populations. In E. A. Lovelace (Ed.), *Aging and cognition: Mental processes, self awareness and interventions* (pp. 263–280). North-Holland: Elsevier Science Publishers B. V.

Kotter, J. P. (1982). What effective general managers really do. *Harvard Business Review, 60,* 156–167.

Krampen, G. (1988). Competence and control orientations as predictors of test anxiety in students: Longitudinal results. *Anxiety Research, 1,* 185–197.

Krantz, D. S., Grunberg, N. E., & Baum, A. (1985). Health psychology. *Annual Reviews in Psychology, 36,* 349–383.

Krantz, S. E. (1985). When depressive cognitions reflect negative realities. *Cognitive Therapy and Research, 9,* 595–610.

Krauss, I. (1964). Sources of educational aspirations among working-class youth. *American Sociological Review, 29,* 867–879.

Kroll, W. (1982). Competitive athletic stress factors in athletes and coaches. In L. D. Zaichkowsky & W. E. Sime (Eds.), *Stress management for sport* (pp. 1–10). Reston, Va.: AAHPERD.

Krueger, N. F. (1994). Strategic optimism: Antecedents of perceived success probabilities of new ventures. Paper presented at the meeting of the Academy of Management, Dallas, Texas.

Krueger, N. F., Jr., & Dickson, P. R. (1993). Self-efficacy and perceptions of opportunities and threats. *Psychological Reports, 72,* 1235–1240.

Krueger, N., Jr., & Dickson, P. R. (1994). How believing in ourselves increases risk taking: Perceived self-efficacy and opportunity recognition. *Decision Sciences, 25,* 385–400.

Kruglanski, A. W. (1975). The endogenous-exogenous partition in attribution theory. *Psychological Review, 82,* 387–406.

Kuiper, N., & Higgins, E. T. (Eds.). (1985).

Social cognition and depression [Special Issue]. *Social Cognition*, 3, 1–15.

Kuiper, N. A., & Olinger, L. J. (1986). Dysfunctional attitudes and a self-worth contingency model of depression. In P. C. Kendall (Ed.), *Advances in cognitive-behavioral research and therapy* (Vol. 5, pp. 115–142). New York: Academic.

Kuiper, N. A., Olinger, L. J., & MacDonald, M. R. (1988). Depressive schemata and the processing of personal and social information. In L. B. Alloy (Ed.), *Cognitive processes in depression* (pp. 289–309). New York: Guilford.

Kun, A. (1977). Development of the magnitude-covariation and compensation schemata in ability and effort attributions of performance. *Child Development*, 48, 862–873.

Kun, A. (1978, August). Perceived additivity of intrinsic and extrinsic motivation in young children. Paper presented at the meeting of the American Psychological Association, Toronto.

Kupfersmid, J. H. & Wonderly, D. M. (1982). Disequilibrium as a hypothetical construct in Kholbergian moral development. *Child Study Journal*, 12, 171–185.

Kyllo, L. B., & Landers, D. M. (1995). Goal setting in sport and exercise: A research synthesis to resolve the controversy. *Journal of Sport and Exercise Psychology*, 17, 117–137.

Kyriacou, C. (1987). Teacher stress and burnout: an international review. *Educational Research*, 29, 146–152.

Laberge, B., & Gauthier, J. (1986). The interaction between deadlines, therapeutic expectancies, perceived self-efficacy and phobic behaviour. Manuscript, Laval University, Ste-Foy, Quebec.

Lacey, H. M. (1979a). Control, perceived control and the methodological role of cognitive constructs. In L. C. Perlmuter & R. A. Monty (Eds.), *Choice and perceived control* (pp. 5–16). Hillsdale, N.J.: Erlbaum.

Lacey, J. I. (1967). Somatic response patterning and stress: Some revisions of activation theory. In M. H. Appley & R. Trumbull (Eds.), *Psychological stress: Issues in research* (pp. 14–42). New York: Appleton-Century-Crofts.

Lachman, M. E. (1986). Personal control in later life: Stability, change, and cognitive correlates. In M. M. Baltes & P. B. Baltes (Eds.), *The psychology of control and aging* (pp. 207–236). Hillsdale, N.J.: Erlbaum.

Lachman, M., Bandura, M., Weaver, S. L., & Elliott, E. (1995). Assessing memory control beliefs: The memory controllability inventory. *Aging and Cognition*, 2, 67–84.

Lachman, M. E., & Leff, R. (1989). Perceived control and intellectual functioning in the elderly: A 5-year longitudinal study. *Developmental Psychology*, 25, 722–728.

Lachman, M. E., Steinberg, E. S., & Trotter, S. D. (1987). Effects of control beliefs and attributions on memory self-assessments and performance. *Psychology and Aging*, 2, 266–271.

Lachman, M. E., Weaver, S. L., Bandura, M. M., Elliott, E., & Lewkowicz, C. J. (1992). Improving memory and control beliefs through cognitive restructuring and self-generated strategies. *Journal of Gerontology: Psychological Sciences*, 47, 293–299.

Lackey, D. P. (1985). Immoral risks: A deontological critique of nuclear deterrence. *Social Philosophy and Policy*, 3, 154–175.

Lackner, J. M., Carosella, A. M., & Feuerstein, M. (1996). Pain expectancies, pain, and functional self-efficacy expectancies as determinants of disability in patients with chronic low back disorders. *Journal of Consulting and Counseling Psychology*, 64, 212–220.

Ladouceur, R. (1983). Participant modeling with or without cognitive treatment of phobias. *Journal of Consulting and Clinical Psychology*, 51, 942–944.

LaGuardia, R., & Labbé, E. E. (1993). Self-efficacy and anxiety and their relationship to training and race performance. *Perceptual and Motor Skills*, 77, 27–34.

Lamson, R. J., & Meisner, M. (June 8–10, 1994). The effects of virtual reality immersion in the treatment of anxiety, panic, & phobia of heights. Paper presented at the Second Annual International Conference on Virtual Reality and Persons with Disabilities, California State University, Northridge.

Lang, P. J. (1977). Physiological assessment of anxiety and fear. In J. D. Cone & R. P. Hawkins (Eds.), *Behavioral assessment: New directions in clinical psychology* (pp. 178–195). New York: Brunner/Mazel.

Lang, P. J. (1985). The cognitive psychophysiology of emotion: Fear and anxiety. In A.H. Tuma & J. D. Maser (Eds.), *Anxiety and the anxiety disorders* (pp. 131–170). Hillsdale, N.J.: Erlbaum.

Langer, E. J. (1975). The illusion of control. *Journal of Personality and Social Psychology*, 32, 311–328.

Langer, E. J. (1979). The illusion of incompetence. In L. C. Perlmuter & R. A. Monty (Eds.), *Choice and perceived control* (pp. 301–313). Hillsdale, N.J.: Erlbaum.

Langer, E. J. (1983). The psychology of control. Beverly Hills, Calif.: Sage.

Langer, E. J., & Park, K. (1990). Incompetence: A conceptual reconsideration. In R. J. Sternberg & J. Kolligian, Jr. (Eds.), *Competence considered* (pp. 149–166). New Haven, Conn.: Yale University Press.

Langer, E. J., & Rodin, J. (1976). The effects of choice and enhanced personal responsibility for the aged: A field experiment in an institutional setting. *Journal of Personality and Social Psychology*, 34, 191–198.

Lapan, R. T., Boggs, K. R., & Morrill, W. H. (1989). Self-efficacy as a mediator of investigative and realistic general occupational themes on the Strong-Campbell interest inventory. *Journal of Counseling Psychology*, 36, 176–182.

Lareau, A. (1987). Social class differences in family-school relationships: The importance of cultural capital. *Sociology of Education*, 60, 73–85.

Laschinger, H. K. S., & Shamian, J. (1994). Staff nurses' and nurse managers' perceptions of job-related empowerment and managerial self-efficacy. *Journal of Nursing Administration*, 24, 38–47.

Latham, G. P., Erez, M., & Locke, E. A. (1988). Resolving scientific disputes by the joint design of crucial experiments by the antagonists: Application to the Erez-Latham dispute regarding participation in goal setting. *Journal of Applied Psychology* (Monograph), 73, 753–772.

Latham, G. P., & Frayne, C. A. (1989). Self-management training for increasing job attendance: A follow-up and a replication. *Journal of Applied Psychology*, 74, 411–416.

Latham, G. P., & Saari, L. M. (1979). Application of social learning theory to training supervisors through behavioral modeling. *Journal of Applied Psychology*, 64, 239–246.

Latham, G. P., & Seijts, G. H. (1995). The effects of proximal and distal goals on performance on a moderately complex task. Manuscript, University of Toronto.

Latham, G. P., Winters, D. C., & Locke, E. A. (1994). Cognitive and motivational effects of participation: A mediator study. *Journal of Organizational Behavior*, 15, 49–63.

Lauver, P. J., & Jones, R. M. (1991). Factors associated with perceived career options in American Indian, White, & Hispanic rural high school students. *Journal of Counseling Psychology*, 38, 159–166.

Lawler, E. E., III (1994). From job-based to competency-based organizations. *Journal of Organizational Behavior*, 15, 3–15.

Lawrance, L., & Rubinson, L. (1986). Self-efficacy as a predictor of smoking behavior in young adolescents. *Addictive Behaviors,* 11, 367–382.

Lawrence, C. P. (1988). The perseverance of discredited judgments of self-efficacy: Possible cognitive mediators. Ph.D. diss., Stanford University, Stanford, Calif.

Lazarus, R. S., & Folkman, S. (1984). *Stress, appraisal, and coping.* New York: Springer.

Leary, M. R., & Atherton, S. C. (1986). Self-efficacy, social anxiety, and inhibition in interpersonal encounters. *Journal of Social and Clinical Psychology,* 4, 256–267.

Lechner, L., & deVries, H. (1995). Starting participation in an employee fitness program: Attitudes, social influence, and self-efficacy. *Preventive Medicine,* 24, 627–633.

Ledwidge, B. (1978). Cognitive behavior modification: A step in the wrong direction? *Psychological Bulletin,* 85, 353–375.

Lee, C. (1984a). Accuracy of efficacy and outcome expectations in predicting performance in a simulated assertiveness task. *Cognitive Therapy and Research,* 8, 37–48.

Lee, C. (1984b). Efficacy expectations and outcome expectations as predictors of performance in a snake-handling task. *Cognitive Therapy and Research,* 8, 509–516.

Lee, C. (1986). Efficacy expectations, training performance, and competitive performance in women's artistic gymnastics. *Behaviour Change,* 3, 100–104.

Lee, C. (1988). The relationship between goal setting, self-efficacy, and female field hockey team performance. *International Journal of Sport Psychology,* 20, 147–161.

Lee, C., & Bobko, P. (1994). Self-efficacy beliefs: Comparison of five measures. *Journal of Applied Psychology,* 79, 364–369.

Lee, T. W., Locke, E. A., & Phan, S. H. (in press). Explaining the assigned goal-incentive interaction: The role of self-efficacy and personal goals. *Journal of Management.*

Lefcourt, H. M. (1976). *Locus of control: Current trends in theory and research.* Hillsdale, N.J.: Erlbaum.

Leibel, R. L., Rosenbaum, M., & Hirsch, J. (1995). Changes in energy expenditure resulting from altered body weight. *The New England Journal of Medicine,* 332, 621–628.

Leitenberg, H. (1995). Cognitive-behavioural treatment of bulimia nervosa. *Behaviour Change,* 12, 81–97.

Leitenberg, H., Gross, J., Peterson, J., & Rosen, J. C. (1984). Analysis of an anxiety model and the process of change during exposure plus response prevention treatment of bulimia nervosa. *Behavior Therapy,* 15, 3–20.

Leiter, M. P. (1991). Coping patterns as predictors of burnout: The function of control and escapist coping patterns. *Journal of Organizational Behaviour,* 12 123–144.

Leiter, M. P. (1992). Burnout as a crisis in self-efficacy: Conceptual and practical implications. *Work and Stress,* 6, 107–115.

Leiter, M. P., & Schaufeli, W. B. (1996). Consistency of the burnout construct across occupations. *Anxiety, Stress, and Coping,* 9, 229–243.

Leland, E. I. (1983). Self-efficacy and other variables as they relate to precompetitive anxiety among male interscholastic basketball players. Ph.D. diss. Stanford University, 1983. *Dissertation Abstracts International,* 44, 1376A.

Lent, R. W., Brown, S. D., & Hackett, G. (1994). Toward a unifying social cognitive theory of career and academic interest, choice, and performance. *Journal of Vocational Behavior,* 45, 79–122.

Lent, R. W., Brown, S. D., & Larkin, K. C. (1984). Relation of self-efficacy expectations to academic achievement and persistence. *Journal of Counseling Psychology,* 31, 356–362.

Lent, R. W., Brown, S. D., & Larkin, K. C. (1986). Self-efficacy in the prediction of academic performance and perceived career options. *Journal of Counseling Psychology,* 33, 265–269.

Lent, R. W., Brown, S. D., & Larkin, K. C. (1987). Comparison of three theoretically derived variables in predicting career and academic behavior: Self-efficacy, interest congruence, and consequence thinking. *Journal of Counseling Psychology,* 34, 293–298.

Lent, R. W., & Hackett, G. (1987). Career self-efficacy: Empirical status and future directions. *Journal of Vocational Behavior,* 30, 347–382.

Lent, R. W., Larkin, K. C., & Brown, S. D. (1989). Relation of self-efficacy to inventoried vocational interests. *Journal of Vocational Behavior,* 34, 279–288.

Lent, R. W., Lopez, F. G., & Bieschke, K. J. (1991). Mathematics self-efficacy: Sources and relation to science-based career choice. *Journal of Counseling Psychology,* 38, 424–430.

Lent, R. W., Lopez, F. G., & Bieschke, K. J. (1993). Predicting mathematics-related choice and success behaviors: Test of an expanded social cognitive model. *Journal of Vocational Behavior,* 42, 223–236.

Lent, R. W., Lopez, F. G., Bieschke, K. J., & Socall, D. W. (1991). Mathematics self-efficacy: Sources of relations to science-

based career choice. *Journal of Counseling Psychology,* 38, 424–431.

Lent, R. W., Lopez, F. G., Mikolaitis, N. L., Jones, L., & Bieschke, K. J. (1992). Social cognitive mechanisms in the client recovery process: Revisiting hygiology. *Journal of Mental Health Counseling,* 14, 196–207.

Leon, G. R., Sternberg, B., & Rosenthal, B. S. (1984). Prognostic indicators of success or relapse in weight reduction. *International Journal of Eating Disorders,* 3, 15–24.

Lepper, M. R. (1981). Intrinsic and extrinsic motivation in children: Detrimental effects of superfluous social controls. In W. A. Collins (Ed.), *Minnesota symposium on child psychology* (Vol. 14, pp. 155–214). Hillsdale, N.J.: Erlbaum.

Lepper, M. R., & Greene, D. (1978). Overjustification research and beyond: Toward a means-end analysis of intrinsic and extrinsic motivation. In M. R. Lepper & D. Greene (Eds.), *The hidden costs of reward: New perspectives on the psychology of human motivation* (pp. 109–148). Hillsdale, N.J.: Erlbaum.

Lerner, B. S., & Locke, E. A. (1995). The effects of goal setting, self-efficacy, competition and personal traits on the performance of an endurance task. *Journal of Sport and Exercise Psychology,* 17, 138–152.

Leslie, A. M. (1982). The perception of causality in infants. *Perception,* 11, 173–186.

Leventhal, H. (1970). Findings and theory in the study of fear communications. In L. Berkowitz (Ed.), *Advances in experimental social psychology* (Vol. 5, pp. 119–186). New York: Academic.

Leventhal, H., & Mosbach, P. A. (1983). The perceptual-motor theory of emotion. In J. T. Cacioppo & R. E. Petty (Eds.), *Social psychophysiology* (pp. 353–388). New York: Guilford.

Levi, L. (Ed.) (1972). Stress and distress in response to psychosocial stimuli. *Acta Medica Scandinavica,* 191, Supplement No. 528.

Levin, H. M. (1987). New schools for the disadvantaged. *Teacher Education Quarterly,* 14, 60–83.

Levin, H. M. (1991). *Learning from accelerated schools. Policy perspectives.* Philadelphia: The Pew Higher Education Research Program.

Levin, H. M. (1993). Accelerated schools in the United States: Do they have relevance for developing countries? In H. M. Levin & M. E. Lockheed, *Effective schools in developing countries* (pp. 158–172). London and Washington, D.C.: Falmer.

Levin, H. M. (1996). Accelerated schools after eight years. In R. Glaser and L. Schauble (Eds.), *Innovations in learning: New environments in education* (pp. 329–352). Mahway, N.J.: Lawrence Erlbaum.

Levin, H. M., & Lockheed, M. E. (1993). Creating effective schools. In H. M. Levin & M. E. Lockheed (Eds.), *Effective schools in developing countries* (pp. 1–20). London and Washington, D.C.: Falmer.

Levine, D. U. (1991). Creating effective schools: Findings and implications from research and practice. *Phi Delta Kappan*, January, 389–393.

Levine, J. D., & Gordon, N. C. (1984). Influence of the method of drug administration on analgesic response. *Nature*, 312, 755–756.

Levine, J. D., Gordon, N. C., & Fields, H. L. (1978, September 23). The mechanism of placebo analgesia. *Lancet*, 654–657.

Levine, J. D., Gordon, N. C., Jones, R. T., & Fields, H. L. (1978). The narcotic antagonist naloxone enhances clinical pain. *Nature*, 272, 826–827.

Levine, S., & Ursin, H. (Eds.) (1980). *Coping and health.* New York: Plenum.

Levinson, R. A. (1986). Contraceptive self-efficacy: A perspective on teenage girls' contraceptive behavior. *Journal of Sex Research*, 22, 347–369.

Levy, D. M. (1943). *Maternal overprotection.* New York: Columbia University Press.

Lewinsohn, P. M., Antonuccio, D. O., Steinmetz, J. L., & Teri, L. (1984). *The coping with depression course.* Eugene, Oregon: Castalia.

Lewinsohn, P. M., Hoberman, H. M., & Clarke, G. N. (1989). The coping with depression course: Review and future directions. *Canadian Journal of Behavioural Science*, 21, 470–493.

Lewinsohn, P. M., Hoberman, H. M., Teri, L., & Hautzinger, M. (1985). An integrative theory of depression. In S. Reiss & R. Bootzin (Eds.), *Theoretical issues in behaviour therapy* (pp. 331–359). New York: Academic.

Lewinsohn, P. M., Mischel, W., Chaplin, W., & Barton, R. (1980). Social competence and depression: The role of illusory self-perceptions. *Journal of Abnormal Psychology*, 89, 203–212.

Lewis, M., & Brooks-Gunn, J. (1979). *Social cognition and the acquisition of self.* New York: Plenum.

Lewit, E. M. (1989). U.S. tobacco taxes: Behavioral effects and policy implications. *British Journal of Addiction*, 84, 1217–1235.

Lieberman, D. A. (in press). Interactive video games for health promotion: Effects on knowledge, self-efficacy, social support, and health. In R. L. Street, W. R. Gold, & T. Manning (Eds.), *Health promotion and interactive technology: Theoretical applications and future directions.* Hillsdale, N.J.: Lawrence Erlbaum.

Lieberman, D. A., & Brown, S. J. (1995). Designing interactive video games for children's health education. In K. Morgan, R. M. Satava, H. B. Sieburg, R. Mattheus, & J. P. Christensen (Eds.), *Interactive technology and the new paradigm for healthcare.* (pp. 201–210). Amsterdam: IOS Press and Ohmsha.

Lin, C., & Ward, S. E. (1996). Perceived self-efficacy and outcome expectancies in coping with chronic low back pain. *Research in Nursing & Health*, 19, 299–310.

Lindsay, C. M. (Ed.) (1980). *New directions in public health care* (3rd ed.). San Francisco: Institute for Contemporary Studies.

Lindsley, D. H., Brass, D. J., & Thomas, J. B. (1995). Efficacy-performance spirals: A multilevel perspective. *Academy of Management Review*, 20, 645–678.

Lindsley, D. H., Mathieu, J. E., Heffner, T. S., & Brass, D. J. (1994, April). Team efficacy, potency, and performance: A longitudinal examination of reciprocal processes. Paper presented at the Society of Industrial-Organizational Psychology, Nashville, Tenn.

Lipset, S. M. (1966). University students and politics in underdeveloped countries. *Comparative Education Review*, 10, 132–162.

Lipset, S. M. (1985). Feeling better: Measuring the nation's confidence. *Public Opinion*, 2, 6–9, 56–58.

Lipset, S. M., & Schneider, W. (1983). *The confidence gap: Business, labor and government in the public mind.* New York: Free Press.

Lirgg, C. D., & Feltz, D. L. (1991). Teacher versus peer models revisited: Effects on motor performance and self-efficacy. *Research Quarterly for Exercise and Sport*, 62, 217–224.

Lissner, L., Odell, P. M., D'Agostino, R. B., Stokes, J., III, Kreger, B. E., Belanger, A. J., & Brownell, K. D. (1991). Variability of body weight and health outcomes in the Framingham population. *New England Journal of Medicine*, 324, 1839–1844.

Litt, M. D. (1988). Self-efficacy and perceived control: Cognitive mediators of pain tolerance. *Journal of Personality and Social Psychology*, 54, 149–160.

Litt, M. D., Nye, C., & Shafer, D. (1993). Coping with oral surgery by self-efficacy enhancement and perceptions of control. *Journal of Dental Research*, 72, 1237–1243.

Litt, M. D., Nye, C., & Shafer, D. (1995). Preparation for oral surgery: Evaluating elements of coping. *Journal of Behavioral Medicine*, 18, 435–459.

Little, B. L., & Madigan, R. M. (1994, August). Motivation in work teams: A test of the construct of collective efficacy. Paper presented at the annual meeting of the Academy of Management, Houston, Texas.

Little, T. D., Lopez, D. F., Oettingen, G., & Baltes, P. B. (1995). A comparative-longitudinal study of action-control beliefs and school performance: Their reciprocal nature and the role of context. Submitted for publication.

Little, T. D., Oettingen, G., Stetsenko, A. & Baltes, P. B. (1995). Children's action-control beliefs about school performance: How do American children compare with German and Russian children? *Journal of Personality and Social Psychology*, 69, 686–700.

Lloyd, C. (1980). Life events and depressive disorder reviewed: II. Events as precipitating factors. *Archives of General Psychiatry*, 37, 541–548.

Lobitz, W. C., & Post, R. D. (1979). Parameters of self-reinforcement and depression. *Journal of Abnormal Psychology*, 81, 33–41.

Locke, E. A. (1991a). Goal theory vs. control theory: Contrasting approaches to understanding work motivation. *Motivation and Emotion*, 15, 9–28.

Locke, E. A. (1991b). Problems with goal-setting research in sports — and their solution. *Journal of Sport and Exercise Psychology*, 8, 311–316.

Locke, E. A. (1994). The emperor is naked. *Applied Psychology: An International Review*, 43, 367–370.

Locke, E. A., Cartledge, N., & Knerr, C. S. (1970). Studies of the relationship between satisfaction, goal setting, and performance. *Organizational Behavior and Human Performance*, 5, 135–158.

Locke, E. A., Frederick, E., Lee, C., & Bobko, P. (1984). Effect of self-efficacy, goals, and task strategies on task performance. *Journal of Applied Psychology*, 69, 241–251.

Locke, E. A., & Latham, G. P. (1984). *Goal-setting: A motivational technique that works.* Englewood Cliffs, N.J.: Prentice-Hall.

Locke, E. A., & Latham, G. P. (1985). The application of goal setting to sports. *Journal of Sport Psychology*, 7, 205–222.

Locke, E. A., & Latham, G. P. (1990). *A theory of goal setting and task performance.* Englewood Cliffs, N.J.: Prentice-Hall.

Locke, E. A., & Schweiger, D. M. (1979). Participation in decision-making: One more look. In B. M. Staw (Ed.), *Research in organizational behavior* (Vol. 1, pp. 265–339). Greenwich, Conn.: JAI.

Locke, E. A., Zubritzky, E., Cousins, E., & Bobko, P. (1984). Effect of previously assigned goals on self-set goals and performance. *Journal of Applied Psychology, 69,* 694–699.

Lockheed, M. E. (1985). Women, girls, and computers: A first look at the evidence. *Sex Roles, 13,* 115–122.

Loeb, A., Beck, A. T., Diggory, J. C., & Tuthill, R. (1967). Expectancy, level of aspiration, performance, and self-evaluation in depression. *Proceedings of the 75th Annual Convention of the American Psychological Association, 2,* 193–194.

Longo, D. A., Lent, R. W., & Brown, S. D. (1992). Social cognitive variables in the prediction of client motivation and attrition. *Journal of Counseling Psychology, 39,* 447–452.

Lord, C. G., Umezaki, K., & Darley, J. M. (1990). Developmental differences in decoding the meanings of the appraisal actions of teachers. *Child Development, 61,* 191–200.

Lord, R. G., & Hanges, P. J. (1987). A control system model of organizational motivation: Theoretical development and applied implications. *Behavioral Science, 32,* 161–178.

Lord, R. G., & Levy, P. E. (1994). Moving from cognition to action: A control theory perspective. *Applied Psychology: An International Review, 43,* 335–398.

Lorig, K., (1990, April). Self-efficacy: Its contributions to the four year beneficial outcome of the arthritis self-management course. Paper presented at the meeting of the Society for Behavioral Medicine, Chicago.

Lorig, K., Chastain, R. L., Ung, E., Shoor, S., & Holman, H. (1989). Development and evaluation of a scale to measure perceived self-efficacy in people with arthritis. *Arthritis and Rheumatism, 32,* 37–44.

Lorig, K., Seleznick, M., Lubeck, D., Ung, E., Chastain, R. L., & Holman, H. R. (1989). The beneficial outcomes of the arthritis self-management course are not adequately explained by behavior change. *Arthritis and Rheumatism, 32,* 91–95.

Lorig, K., Sobel, D., Bandura, A., Holman, H. (1993). Chronic disease self-management: Preliminary behavioral, health status, and health care utilization outcomes. Manuscript, Stanford University, Stanford, Calif.

Love, S. Q., Ollendick, T. H., Johnson, C., & Schlezinger, S. E. (1985). A preliminary report of the prediction of bulimic behavior: A social learning analysis. *Bulletin of the Society of Psychologists in Addictive Behavior, 4,* 93–101.

Loveland, K. K., & Olley, J. G. (1979). The effect of external reward on interest and quality of task performance in children of high and low intrinsic motivation. *Child Development, 50,* 1207–1210.

Luepker, R. V., et al. (1994). Community education for cardiovascular disease prevention: Risk factor changes in the Minnesota Hearth Health Program. *American Journal of Public Health, 84,* 1383–1393.

Luepker, R. V. et al. (1996). Outcomes of a field trial to improve children's dietary patterns and physical activitiy: The child and adolescent trial for cardiovascular health (CATCH). *Journal of the American Medical Association, 275,* 768–776.

Luria, A. (1961). *The role of speech in the regulation of normal and abnormal behavior.* New York: Liveright.

Lyman, R. D., Prentice-Dunn, S., Wilson, D. R., & Bonfilio, S. A. (1984). The effect of success or failure on self-efficacy and task persistence of conduct-disordered children. *Psychology in the Schools, 21,* 516–519.

Lynch, B. S., & Bonnie, R. J. (Eds.) (1994). *Growing up tobacco free: Preventing nicotine addiction in children and youths.* Washington, D.C.: National Academy Press.

Lyons, B., Harrell, E., & Blair, S. (1990). Predicting exercise adherence: A test of the self-efficacy model. Manuscript, North Texas State University.

Lyons, S. R. (1970). The political socialization of ghetto children: Efficacy and cynicism. *Journal of Politics, 32,* 288–304.

Lyubomirsky, S., & Nolen-Hoeksema, S. (1994). Self-perpetuating properties of dysphoric rumination. *Journal of Personality and Social Psychology, 65,* 339–349.

Maccoby, N., & Farquhar, J. W. (1975). Communication for health: Unselling heart disease. *Journal of Communication, 25,* 114–126.

Maddux, J. E., & Rogers, R. W. (1983). Protection motivation and self-efficacy: A revised theory of fear appeals and attitude change. *Journal of Experimental Social Psychology, 19,* 469–479.

Madsen, D. (1987). Political self-efficacy tested. *American Political Science Review, 81,* 571–581.

Magnusson, D., Stattin, H., & Allen, V. L. (1985). Biological maturation and social development: A longitudinal study of some adjustment processes from mid-adolescence to adulthood. *Journal of Youth and Adolescence, 14,* 267–283.

Mahoney, M. J. (1979). Cognitive skills and athletic performance. In P.C. Kendall & S. D. Hollen (Eds.), *Cognitive-behavioral interventions: Theory, research, and procedures* (pp.423–443). New York: Academic.

Maibach, E. W., & Flora, J. A. (1993). Symbolic modeling and cognitive rehearsal: Using video to promote AIDS prevention self-efficacy. *Communication Research, 20,* 517–545.

Maibach, E., Flora, J., & Nass, C. (1991). Changes in self-efficacy and health behavior in response to a minimal contact community health campaign. *Health Communication, 3,* 1–15.

Maier, S. F. (1986). Stressor controllability and stress-induced analgesia. In D. D. Kelly (Ed.), *Stress-induced analgesia. Annals of the New York Academy of Sciences* (Vol. 467, pp. 55–72). New York: New York Academy of Sciences.

Maier, S. F., Laudenslager, M. L., & Ryan, S. M. (1985). Stressor controllability, immune function, and endogenous opiates. In F. R. Brush & J. B. Overmier (Eds.), *Affect, conditioning, and cognition: Essays on the determinants of behavior* (pp. 183–201). Hillsdale, N.J.: Erlbaum.

Maisto, S. A., Sobell, L. C., & Sobell, M. B. (1979). Comparison of alcoholics' self-reports of drinking behavior with reports of collateral informants. *Journal of Consulting and Clinical Psychology, 47,* 106–112.

Major, B., Cozzarelli, C., Sciacchitano, A. M., Cooper, M. L., Testa, M., & Mueller, P. M. (1990). Perceived social support, self-efficacy, and adjustment to abortion. *Journal of Personality and Social Psychology, 59,* 452–463.

Major, B., Mueller, P., & Hildebrandt, K. (1985). Attributions, expectations, and coping with abortion. *Journal of Personality and Social Psychology, 48,* 585–599.

Mallams, J. H., Godley, M. D., Hall, G. M., & Meyers, R. J. (1982). A social-systems approach to resocializing alcoholics in the community. *Journal of Studies on Alcohol, 43,* 1115–1123.

Malone, T. W. (1981). Toward a theory of intrinsically motivating instruction. *Cognitive Science, 5,* 333–370.

Malone, T. W., & Lepper, M. R. (1987). Making learning fun: A taxonomy of intrinsic motivations for learning. In R. E.

Snow & M. J. Farr (Eds.), *Aptitude, learning, and instruction: III. Cognitive and affective process analysis* (pp. 223–253). Hillsdale, N.J.: Erlbaum.

Mandel, B. (1993, July 25). Barbeque: The link to success. *San Francisco Examiner*, pp. B1–B2.

Manderlink, G., & Harackiewicz, J. M. (1984). Proximal versus distal goal setting and intrinsic motivation. *Journal of Personality and Social Psychology*, 47, 918–928.

Mandler, G. (1975). *Mind and emotion.* New York: Wiley.

Mandler, J. M. (1992). How to build a baby: II. Conceptual primitives. *Psychological Review*, 99, 587–604.

Manning, M. M., & Wright, T. L. (1983). Self-efficacy expectancies, outcome expectancies, and the persistence of pain control in childbirth. *Journal of Personality and Social Psychology*, 45, 421–431.

Mansfield, E. (1968). *Industrial research and technological innovation: An econometric analysis.* New York: Norton.

March, J. G. (1981). Decisions in organizations and theories of choice. In A. Van de Ven & W. Joyce (Eds.), *Perspectives on organization design and behavior* (pp. 205–244). New York: Wiley.

March, J. G. (1982). Theories of choice and making decisions. *Transaction: Social Science and Modern Society*, 20, 29–39.

Marcus, B. H., & Owen, N. (1992). Motivational readiness, self-efficacy and decision-making for exercise. *Journal of Applied Social Psychology*, 22, 3–16.

Marcus, B. H., Selby, V. C., Niaura, R. S., & Rossi, J. S. (1992). Self-efficacy and the stages of exercise behavior change. *Research Quarterly for Exercise and Sport*, 63, 60–66.

Marcus, B. H., & Stanton, A. L. (1993). Evaluation of relapse prevention and reinforcement interventions to promote exercise adherence in sedentary females. *Research Quarterly for Exercise and Sport*, 64, 447–452.

Marcus, D. K., & Nardone, M. E. (1992). Depression and interpersonal rejection. *Clinical Psychology Review*, 12, 433–449.

Marks, I. (1987). Benefits of behavioural psychotherapy. In J. P. Dauwalder, M. Perrez & V. Hobi (Eds.), *Annual series of European research in behavior therapy*, Vol. 2, *Controversial issues in behavior modification* (pp. 77–85). Amsterdam: Swets & Zeitlinger.

Markus, H., Cross, S., & Wurf, E. (1990). The role of the self-system in competence. In R. J. Sternberg & J. Kolligian, Jr. (Eds.), *Competence considered* (pp. 205–225). New Haven, Conn.: Yale University Press.

Markus, H., & Nurius, P. (1986). Possible selves. *American Psychologist*, 41, 954–969.

Marlatt, G. A., & Gordon, J. R. (1980). Determinants of relapse: Implications for the maintenance of behavior change. In P. O. Davidson & S. M. Davidson (Eds.), *Behavioral medicine: Changing health lifestyles* (pp. 410–452). New York: Brunner/Mazel.

Marlatt, G. A., & Gordon, J. R. (1985). *Relapse prevention: Maintenance strategies in the treatment of addictive behaviors.* New York: Guilford.

Marlatt, G. A., Larimer, M. E., Baer, J. S., & Quigley, L. A. (1993). Harm reduction for alcohol problems: Moving beyond the controlled drinking controversy. *Behavior Therapy*, 24, 461–504.

Marsh, A. (1977). *Protest and political consciousness.* Beverly Hills, Calif.: Sage.

Marshall, G. D., & Zimbardo, P. G. (1979). Affective consequences of inadequately explained physiological arousal. *Journal of Personality and Social Psychology*, 37, 970–988.

Marshall, G. N., & Lang, E. L. (1990). Optimism, self-mastery, and symptoms of depression in women professionals. *Journal of Personality and Social Psychology*, 59, 132–139.

Marshall, H. H., & Wienstein, R. S. (1984). Classroom factors affecting students' self-evaluations: An interactional model. *Review of Educational Research*, 54, 301–325.

Marshall, J. F. (1971). Topics and networks in intravillage communication. In S. Polgar (Ed.), *Culture and population: A collection of current studies* (pp. 160–166). Chapel Hill: Carolina Population Center.

Marshall, W. L. (1985). The effects of variable exposure in flooding therapy. *Behavior Therapy*, 16, 117–135.

Martin, D. J., Abramson, L. Y., & Alloy, L. B. (1984). Illusion of control for self and others in depressed and nondepressed college students. *Journal of Personality and Social Psychology*, 46, 125–136.

Martin, J. (1992). *Cultures in organizations: Three perspectives.* New York: Oxford University Press.

Martin, J., & Siehl, C. (1983). Organizational culture and counterculture: An uneasy symbiosis. *Organizational Dynamics*, Autumn, 52–64.

Martin, J. J., & Gill, D. L. (1991). The relationships among competitive orientation, sport-confidence, self-efficacy, anxiety, and performance. *Journal of Sport and Exercise Psychology*, 13, 149–159.

Martin, N. J., Holroyd, K. A., & Rokicki, L. A. (1993). The headache self-efficacy scale: Adaptation to recurrent headaches. *Headache Journal*, 33, 244–248.

Martinez-Pons, M. (1996). Test of a model of parental inducement of academic self-regulation. *Journal of Experimental Education*, 64, 213–227.

Maslach, C. (1979). Negative emotional biasing of unexplained arousal. *Journal of Personality and Social Psychology*, 37, 953–969.

Maslach, C. (1982). *Burnout: The cost of caring.* Englewood Cliffs, N.J.: Prentice-Hall.

Maslach, C., & Jackson, S. E. (1982). Burnout in health professions: A social psychological analysis. In G. S. Sanders & J. Suls (Eds.). *Social psychology of health and illness* (pp. 227–251). Hillsdale, N.J.: Erlbaum.

Masten, A. S., Best, K. M., & Garmezy, N. (1990). Resilience and development: Contributions from the study of children who overcome adversity. *Development and Psychopathology*, 2, 425–444.

Mathews, A., & Milroy, R. (1994). Effects of priming and suppression of worry. *Behaviour Research and Therapy*, 32, 843–850.

Mathews, A., Teasdale, J., Munby, M., Johnson, D., & Shaw, P. (1977). A home-based treatment program for agoraphobia. *Behavior Therapy*, 8, 915–924.

Mathews, A. M., Gelder, M., & Johnston, D. (1981). *Agoraphobia: Nature and treatment.* New York: Guilford.

Matsui, T., Ikeda, H., & Ohnishi, R. (1989). Relations of sex-typed socializations to career self-efficacy expectations of college students. *Journal of Vocational Behavior*, 35, 1–16.

Matsui, T., Konishi, H., Onglatco, M. L. U., Matsuda, Y., & Ohnishi, R. (1988). Self-efficacy and perceived exerted effort as potential cues for success-failure attributions. *Surugadai University Studies*, 1, 89–98.

Matsui, T., & Onglatco, M. L. (1991). Instrumentality, expressiveness, and self-efficacy in career activities among Japanese working women. *Journal of Vocational Behavior*, 39, 241–250.

Matsui, T., & Onglatco, M. L. (1992). Career self-efficacy as a moderator of the relation between occupational stress and strain. *Journal of Vocational Behavior*, 41, 79–88.

Matsui, T., & Tsukamoto, S. (1991). Relation between career self-efficacy measures based on occupational titles and Holland codes and model environments: A methodological contribution. *Journal of Vocational Behavior*, 38, 78–91.

McAlister, A., Perry, C., Killen, J., Slinkard, L. A., & Maccoby, N. (1980). Pilot study of smoking, alcohol and drug abuse prevention. *American Journal of Public Health*, 70, 719–721.

McAlister, A., Puska, P., Orlandi, M., Bye, L. L., & Zbylot, P. (1991). Behaviour modification: Principles and illustrations. In W. W. Holland, R. Detels, & F. G. Knox (Eds.), *Oxford textbook of public health* (2nd ed.). Vol. 3, *Applications in Public Health* (pp. 3–16). Oxford: Oxford University Press.

McArthur, L. Z., & Eisen, S. V. (1976). Achievements of male and female storybook characters as determinants of achievement behavior by boys and girls. *Journal of Personality and Social Psychology*, 33, 467–473.

McAteer-Early, T. (1992, August). The impact of career self-efficacy on the relationship between career development and health-related complaints. Paper presented at the Academy of Management Meeting, Las Vegas, Nev.

McAuley, E. (1985). Modeling and self-efficacy: A test of Bandura's model. *Journal of Sport Psychology*, 7, 283–295.

McAuley, E. (June, 1990). Attributions, affect, and self-efficacy: Predicting exercise behavior in aging individuals. Paper presented at the American Psychological Society Meeting, Dallas.

McAuley, E. (1991). Efficacy, attributional, and affective responses to exercise participation. *Journal of Sport and Exercise Psychology*, 13, 382–393.

McAuley, E. (1992). Understanding exercise behavior: A self-efficacy perspective. In G. C. Roberts (Ed.), *Motivation in sport and exercise*. (pp. 107–127). Champaign, Ill.: Human Kinetics.

McAuley, E. (1993). Self-efficacy, physical activity, and aging. In J. R. Kelly (Ed.), *Activity and aging: Staying involved in later life*. (187–206). Newbury Park, Calif.: Sage.

McAuley, E., & Courneya, K. S. (1992). Self-efficacy relationships with affective and exertion responses to exercise. *Journal of Applied Social Psychology*, 22, 312–326.

McAuley, E., Courneya, K. S., & Lettunich, J. (1991). Effects of acute and long-term exercise on self-efficacy responses in sedentary, middle-aged males and females. *The Gerontologist*, 31, 534–542.

McAuley, E., Courneya, K. S., Rudolph, D. L., & Lox, C. L. (1994). Enhancing exercise adherence in middle-aged males and females. *Preventive Medicine*, 23, 498–506.

McAuley, E., Duncan, T. E., & McElroy, M.

(1989). Self-efficacy cognitions and causal attributions for children's motor performance: An exploratory investigation. *The Journal of Genetic Psychology*, 150, 65–73.

McAuley, E., & Gill, D. (1983). Reliability and validity of the physical self-efficacy scale in a competitive sport setting. *Journal of Sport Psychology*, 5, 410–418.

McAuley, E., & Jacobson, L. (1991). Self-efficacy and exercise participation in sedentary adult females. *American Journal of Health Promotion*, 5, 185–207.

McAuley, E., Lox, C., & Duncan, T. E. (1993). Long-term maintenance of exercise, self-efficacy, and physiological change in older adults. *Journal of Gerontology: Psychological Sciences*, 48, 218–224.

McAuley, E., & Rowney, T. (1990). Exercise behavior and intentions: The mediating role of self-efficacy cognitions. In L. V. Velden and J. H. Humphrey (Eds.), *Psychology and sociology of sport* (Vol. 2, pp. 3–15). New York: AMS Press.

McAuley, E., Shaffer, S. M., & Rudolph, D. (1995). Affective responses to acute exercise in elderly impaired males: The moderating effects of self-efficacy and age. *International Journal of Aging and Human Development*, 41, 13–35.

McAuley, E., Wraith, S., & Duncan, T. E. (1991). Self-efficacy, perceptions of success, and intrinsic motivation for exercise. *Journal of Applied Social Psychology*, 21, 139–155.

McAuliffe, W. E., Albert, J., Cordill-London, G., & McGarraghy, T. K., (1991). Contributors to a social conditioning model of cocaine recovery. *International Journal of the Addictions*, 25, 1141–1177.

McCann, B. S., Bovbjerg, V. E., Brief, D. J., Turner, C., Follette, W. C., Fitzpatrick, V., Dowdy, A., Retzlaff, B., Walden, C. E., & Knopp, R. H. (1995). Relationship of self-efficacy to cholesterol lowering and dietary change in hyperlipidemia. *Annals of Behavioral Medicine*, 17, 221–226.

McCarthy, P., Meier, S., & Rinderer, R. (1985). Self-efficacy and writing: A different view of self-evaluation. *College Composition and Communication*, 36, 465–471.

McCaul, K. D., Glasgow, R. E., & Schafer, L. C. (1987). Diabetes regimen behaviors: Predicting adherence. *Medical Care*, 25, 868–881.

McCaul, K. D., O'Neill, K., & Glasgow, R. E. (1988). Predicting the performance of dental hygiene behaviors: An examination of the Fishbein and Ajzen model and self-efficacy expectations. *Journal of Applied Social Psychology*, 18, 114–128.

McCaul, K. D., Sandgren, A. K., O'Neill,

H. K., & Hinsz, V. B. (1993). The value of the theory of planned behavior, perceived control, and self-efficacy expectations for predicting health-protective behaviors. *Basic and Applied Social Psychology*, 14, 231–252.

McCullagh, P. (1993). Modeling: Learning, developmental, and social psychological considerations. In R. N. Singer, M. Murphey, & L. K. Tennant, (Eds.), *Handbook of research on sport psychology* (pp. 106–126). New York: MacMillan.

McCullagh, P., Noble, J. M., & Deakin, J. (1996). An examination of a commercial video as an observational learning tool. Submitted for publication.

McDonald, T., & Siegall, M. (1992). The effects of technological self-efficacy and job focus on job performance, attitudes, and withdrawal behaviors. *The Journal of Psychology*, 126, 465–475.

McDougall, G. J. (1994). Predictors of metamemory in older adults. *Nursing Research*, 43, 212–218.

McEnrue, M. P. (1984). Perceived competence as a moderator of the relationship between role clarity and job performance: A test of two hypotheses. *Organizational Behavior and Human Performance*, 34, 379–386.

McFarlane, A. H., Bellissimo, A., & Norman, G. R. (1995). The role of family and peers in social self-efficacy: Links to depression in adolescence. *American Journal of Orthopsychiatry*, 65, 402–410.

McGhee, P. E., & Frueh, T. (1980). Television viewing and the learning of sex-role stereotypes. *Sex Roles*, 6, 179–188.

McGinnis, J. M., & Foege, W. H. (1993). Actual causes of death in the United States. *Journal of the American Medical Association*, 270, 2207–2212.

McGue, M., & Slutske, M. (1996). The inheritance of alcoholism in women. In J. M. Howard, S. E. Martin, P .D. Mail, M.E. Hilton, & E. D. Taylor (Eds.). Women and alcohol: Issues for prevention research (65–91). National Institute on Alcohol Abuse and Alcoholism Research Monograph #32, NIH Publication #96–3817, Washington, D.C.: NIAAA.

McGuire, W. J. (1984). Public communication as a strategy for inducing health-promoting behavioral change. *Preventive Medicine*, 13, 299–319.

McIntyre, K. O., Lichtenstein, E., & Mermelstein, R. J. (1983). Self-efficacy and relapse in smoking cessation: A replication and extension. *Journal of Consulting and Clinical Psychology*, 51, 632–633.

McKinlay, J. B., & McKinlay, S. M. (1986).

Medical measures and the decline of mortality. In P. Conrad & R. Kern (Eds.), *The sociology of health and illness: Critical perspectives* (2nd ed., pp. 10–23). New York: St. Martin's.

McKusick, L., Coates, T. J., Morin, S. F., Pollack, L., & Hoff, C. (1990). Longitudinal predictors of reductions in unprotected anal intercourse among gay men in San Francisco: The AIDS behavioral research project. *American Journal of Public Health*, 80, 978–983.

McLeod, J. M., Glynn, C. J., & McDonald, D. G. (1983). Issues and images: The influence of media reliance in voting decisions. *Communication Research*, 10, 37–58.

McLoyd, V. C. (1979). The effects of extrinsic rewards of differential value on high and low intrinsic interest. *Child Development*, 50, 1010–1019.

McMullin, D. J., & Steffen, J. J. (1982). Intrinsic motivation and performance standards. *Social Behavior and Personality*, 10, 47–56.

McNab, T. (1980). *The complete book of track & field*. New York: Exeter Books.

McPhail, C. (1971). Civil disorder participation: A critical examination of recent research. *American Sociological Review*, 36, 1058–1072.

McPhail, T. L. (1981). *Electronic colonialism: The future of international broadcasting and communication*. Beverly Hills, Calif.: Sage.

McPherson, B. D. (1980). Retirement from professional sport: The process and problems of occupational and psychological adjustment. *Sociological Symposium*, 30, 126–143.

McPherson, J. M., Welch, S., & Clark, C. (1977). The stability and reliability of political efficacy: Using path analysis to test alternative models. *The American Political Science Review*, 71, 509–521.

Medvec, V. H., Madey, S. F., & Gilovich, T. (1995). When less is more: Counterfactual thinking and satisfaction among Olympic medalists. *Journal of Personality and Social Psychology*, 69, 603–610.

Meece, J. L., Wigfield, A., & Eccles, J. S. (1990). Predictors of math anxiety and its influence on young adolescents' course enrollment intentions and performance in mathematics. *Journal of Educational Psychology*, 82, 60–70.

Mefford, I. N., Ward, M. M., Miles, L., Taylor, B., Chesney, M. A., Keegan, D. L., & Barchas, J. D. (1981). Determination of plasma catecholamines and free 3,4–dihydroxyphenylacetic acid in continuously collected human plasma by high performance liquid chromatography with electrochemical detection. *Life Sciences*, 28, 447–483.

Meharg, S. S., & Woltersdorf, M. A. (1990). Therapeutic use of videotape self-modeling: A review. *Advances in Behaviour Research and Therapy*, 12, 85–99.

Meichenbaum, D. (1984). Teaching thinking: A cognitive-behavioral perspective. In R. Glaser, S. Chipman, & J. Segal (Eds.), *Thinking and learning skills*. Vol. 2, *Research and open questions* (pp. 407–426). Hillsdale, N.J.: Erlbaum.

Meichenbaum, D. (1985). *Stress inoculation training*. Oxford: Pergamon.

Meichenbaum, D. H. (1971). Examination of model characteristics in reducing avoidance behavior. *Journal of Personality and Social Psychology*, 17, 298–307.

Meichenbaum, D. H. (1977). *Cognitive-behavior modification: An integrative approach*. New York: Plenum.

Meichenbaum, D., & Asarnow, J. (1979). Cognitive-behavioral modification and metacognitive development: Implications for the classroom. In P. C. Kendall & S. D. Hollon (Eds.), *Cognitive-behavioral interventions: Theory, research, and procedures* (pp. 11–35). New York: Academic.

Meichenbaum, D., & Cameron, R. (1983). Stress inoculation training: Toward a general paradigm for training coping skills. In D. Meichenbaum & M. E. Jaremko (Eds.), *Stress reduction and prevention* (pp. 115–154). New York: Plenum.

Meichenbaum, D., & Gilmore, J. B. (1982). Resistance from a cognitive-behavioral perspective. In P. L. Wachtel (Ed.), *Resistance: Psychodynamic and behavioral approaches* (pp. 133–156). New York: Plenum.

Meichenbaum, D., & Jaremko, M. E. (Eds.). (1983). *Stress reduction and prevention*. New York: Plenum.

Meichenbaum, D. H., & Turk, D. (1976). The cognitive-behavioral management of anxiety, anger and pain. In P. Davidson (Ed.) *Behavioral management of anxiety, depression and pain* (pp. 1–34). New York: Brunner/Mazel.

Meichenbaum, D., & Turk, D. C. (1987). *Facilitating treatment adherence: A practitioner's guidebook*. New York: Plenum.

Melby, L. C. (1995). Teacher efficacy and classroom management: A study of teacher cognition, emotion, and strategy usage associated with externalizing student behavior. Ph.D. diss., University of California, Los Angeles.

Meltzoff, A. N. (1988a). Imitation of televised models by infants. *Child Development*, 59, 1221–1229.

Meltzoff, A. N. (1988b). Infant imitation after a 1-week delay: Long-term memory for novel acts and multiple stimuli. *Developmental Psychology*, 24, 470–476.

Meltzoff, A. N., & Moore, M. K. (1983). The origins of imitation in infancy: Paradigm, phenomena, and theories. In L. P. Lipsitt & C. K. Rovee-Collier (Eds.), *Advances in infancy research* (Vol. 2, pp. 266–301). Norwood, N.J.: Ablex Publishing.

Mento, A. J., Steel, R. P., & Karren, R. J. (1987). A meta-analytic study of the effects of goal setting on task performance: 1966–1984. *Organizational Behavior and Human Decision Processes*, 39, 52–83.

Meyer, A. J., Maccoby, N., & Farquhar, J. W. (1977). The role of opinion leadership in a cardiovascular health education campaign. In B. D. Ruben (Ed.), *Communication yearbook I* (pp. 579–591). New Brunswick, N.J.: Transaction Books.

Meyer, A. J., Nash, J. D., McAlister, A. L., Maccoby, N., & Farquhar, J. W. (1980). Skills training in a cardiovascular health education campaign. *Journal of Consulting and Clinical Psychology*, 48, 129–142.

Meyer, H. H., & Raich, M. S. (1983). An objective evaluation of a behavior modeling training program. *Personnel Psychology*, 36, 755–761.

Meyer, V. (1966). Modification of expectations in cases with obsessional rituals. *Behaviour Research and Therapy*, 4, 273–280.

Meyer, W. (1982). Indirect communications about perceived ability estimates. *Journal of Educational Psychology*, 74, 259–268.

Meyer, W. (1992). Paradoxical effects of praise and blame on perceived ability. In W. Stroebe & M. Hewstone (Eds.), *European review of social psychology*. (Vol. 3, pp. 259–283). Chichester, England: Wiley.

Meyer, W. U. (1987). Perceived ability and achievement-related behavior. In F. Halisch & J. Kuhl (Eds.), *Motivation, intention and volition* (pp. 73–86). Berlin, Germany: Springer-Verlag.

Meyerowitz, B. E., & Chaiken, S. (1987). The effect of message framing on breast self-examination attitudes, intentions, and behavior. *Journal of Personality and Social Psychology*, 52, 500–510.

Michaels, G. Y., & Goldberg, W. A. (Eds.). (1988). *The transition to parenthood: Current theory and research*. New York: Cambridge University Press.

Midgley, C., Feldlaufer, H., & Eccles, J. S. (1989). Change in teacher efficacy and student self- and task-related beliefs in mathematics during the transition to junior high school. *Journal of Educational Psychology*, 81, 247–258.

Midgley, D. F. (1976). A simple mathematical theory of innovative behavior. *Journal of Consumer Research*, 3, 31–41.

Millar, W. S. (1972). A study of operant conditioning under delayed reinforcement in early infancy. Monographs of the Society for Research in *Child Development,* 37(2, Serial No. 147).

Millar, W. S. (1974). The role of visual-holding cues and the simultanizing strategy in infant operant learning. *British Journal of Psychology,* 65, 505–518.

Millar, W. S., & Schaffer, H. R. (1972). The influence of spatially displaced feedback on infant operant conditioning. *Journal of Experimental Child Psychology,* 14, 442–453.

Miller, A. H. (1974). Political issues and trust in government: 1964–1970. *American Political Science Review,* 68, 951–972.

Miller, G. A., Galanter, E., & Pribram, K. H. (1960). *Plans and the structure of behavior.* New York: Holt.

Miller, P. J., Ross, S. M., Emmerson, R. Y., & Todt, E. H. (1989). Self-efficacy in alcoholics: Clinical validation of the situational confidence questionnaire. *Addictive Behaviors,* 14, 217–224.

Miller, S. M. (1979). Controllability and human stress: Method, evidence and theory. *Behaviour Research and Therapy,* 17, 287–304.

Miller, S. M. (1980). Why having control reduces stress: If I can stop the rollercoaster I don't want to get off. In J. Garber & M. E. P. Seligman (Eds.), *Human helplessness: Theory and applications* (pp. 71–95). New York: Academic.

Miller, S. M. (1981). Predictability and human stress: Towards a clarification of evidence and theory. In. L. Berkowitz (Ed.), *Advances in experimental social psychology* (Vol. 14, pp. 204–256). New York: Academic.

Miller, S. M., Lack, E. R., & Asroff, S. (1985). Preference for control and the coronary-prone behavior pattern: "I'd rather do it myself." *Journal of Personality and Social Psychology,* 49, 492–499.

Miller, S., & Weinberg, R. (1991). Perceptions of psychological momentum and their relationship to performance. *The Sport Psychologist,* 5, 211–222.

Miller, W. R., Brown, J. M., Simpson, T. L., Handmaker, N. S., Bien, T. H., Luckie, L. F., Montgomery, H. A., Hester, R. K., & Tonigan, J. S. (1995). What works? A methodological analysis of the alcohol treatment outcome literature. In R. K. Hester, & W. R. Miller, (Eds.), *Handbook of alcoholism treatment approaches: Effective alternatives* (2nd ed., pp. 12–44). Boston: Allyn & Bacon.

Miller, W. R., Leckman, A. L., Delaney, H. D., & Tinkcom, M. (1992). Long-term follow-up of behavioral self-control training. *Journal of Studies on Alcohol,* 53, 249–261.

Miller, W. R., & Muñoz, R. F. (1982). *How to control your drinking* (2nd ed.). Albuquerque: University of New Mexico.

Miller, W. R., & Rollnick, S. (1991). *Motivational interviewing: Preparing people to change addictive behavior.* New York: Guilford.

Millstein, S. G., Petersen, A. C., & Nightingale, E. O. (Eds.). (1993). *Promoting the health of adolescents: New directions for the twenty-first century.* New York: Oxford University Press.

Mineka, S., Gunnar, M., & Champoux, M. (1986). Control and early socioemotional development: Infant rhesus monkeys reared in controllable versus uncontrollable environments. *Child Development,* 57, 1241–1256.

Mintzberg, H. (1973). *The nature of managerial work.* Englewood Cliffs, N.J.: Prentice-Hall.

Mischel, W. (1968). *Personality and assessment.* New York: Wiley.

Mitchell, C., & Stuart, R. B. (1984). Effect of self-efficacy on dropout from obesity treatment. *Journal of Consulting and Clinical Psychology,* 52, 1100–1101.

Mitchell, L. K., & Krumboltz, J. D. (1984). Research on human decision making: Implications for career decision making and counseling. In S. D. Brown & R. W. Lent (Eds.), *Handbook of counseling psychology* (238–280). New York: Wiley.

Mitchell, T. R. (1974). Expectancy models of job satisfaction, methodological, and empirical appraisal. *Psychological Bulletin,* 81, 1053–1077.

Mittag, W., & Schwarzer, R. (1993). Interaction of employment status and self-efficacy on alcohol consumption: A two-wave study on stressful life transitions. *Psychology and Health,* 8, 77–87.

Miura, I. T. (1987a). A multivariate study of school-aged children's computer interest and use. In M. E. Ford & D. H. Ford (Eds.), *Humans as self-constructing living systems: Putting the framework to work* (pp. 177–197). Hillsdale, N.J.: Erlbaum.

Miura, I. T. (1987b). The relationship of computer self-efficacy expectations to computer interest and course enrollment in college. *Sex Roles,* 16, 303–311.

Mizes, J. S. (1985). Bulimia: A review of its symptomatology and treatment. *Advances in Behaviour Research and Therapy,* 7, 91–142.

Mone, M. A. (1994). Comparative validity of two measures of self-efficacy in predicting academic goals and performance. *Educational and Psychological Measurement,* 54, 516–529.

Mone, M. A., Baker, D. D., & Jeffries, F. (1995). Predictive validity and time dependency of self-efficacy, self-esteem, personal goals, and academic performance. *Educational and Psychological Measurement,* 55, 716–727.

Monti, P. M., Rohsenow, D. J., Rubonis, A. V., Niaura, R. S., Sirota, A. D., Colby, S. M., Goddard, P., & Abrams, D. B. (1993). Cue exposure with coping skills treatment for male alcoholics: A preliminary investigation. *Journal of Consulting and Clinical Psychology,* 61, 1011–1019.

Morelli, E. A., & Martin, J. (1982). Self-efficacy and athletic performance of 800 meter runners. Manuscript, Simon Fraser University, Vancouver, B.C.

Morgan, M. (1981). The overjustification effect: A developmental test of self-perception interpretations. *Journal of Personality and Social Psychology,* 40, 809–821.

Morgan, M. (1984). Reward-induced decrements and increments in intrinsic motivation. *Review of Educational Research,* 54, 5–30.

Morgan, M. (1985). Self-monitoring of attained subgoals in private study. *Journal of Educational Psychology,* 77, 623–630.

Morgan, W., & Pollock, M. (1977). Psychologic characterization of the elite distance runner. *Annals of the New York Academy of Sciences,* 301, 382–403.

Morris, J. N., Everitt, M. G., Pollard, R., Chave, S. P. W., & Semmence, A. M. (1980). Vigorous exercise in leisure-time: Protection against coronary heart disease. *Lancet,* 2, 1207–1210.

Morris, W. N., & Nemcek, D., Jr. (1982). The development of social comparison motivation among preschoolers: Evidence of a stepwise progression. *Merrill-Palmer Quarterly of Behavior and Development,* 28, 413–425.

Mortimore, P. (1995). The positive effects of schooling. In M. Rutter (Ed.), *Psychosocial disturbances in young people* (pp. 333–363). New York: Cambridge University.

Moss, M. K., & Arend, R. A. (1977). Self-directed contact desensitization. *Journal of Consulting and Clinical Psychology,* 45, 730–738.

Mossholder, K. W. (1980). Effects of externally mediated goal setting on intrinsic motivation: A laboratory experiment. *Journal of Applied Psychology,* 65, 202–210.

Mowrer, O. H. (1950). *Learning theory and*

personality dynamics. New York: Ronald Press.

Mowrer, O. H. (1960). *Learning theory and behavior.* New York: Wiley.

Mueller, P., & Major, B. (1989). Self-blame, self-efficacy, and adjustment to abortion. *Journal of Personality and Social Psychology,* 57, 1059–1068.

Mullen, B., & Copper, C. (1994). The relation between group cohesiveness and performance: An integration. *Psychological Bulletin,* 115, 210–227.

Muller, E. N. (1972). A test of a partial theory of potential for political violence. *The American Political Science Review,* 66, 928–959.

Muller, E. N. (1979). *Aggressive political participation.* Princeton, N.J.: Princeton University Press.

Multon, K. D., Brown, S. D., & Lent, R. W. (1991). Relation of self-efficacy beliefs to academic outcomes: A meta-analytic investigation. *Journal of Counseling Psychology,* 38, 30–38.

Muñoz, R. F., & Ying, Y. (1993). *The prevention of depression: Research and practice.* Baltimore: The Johns Hopkins University Press.

Munro, D. J. (1975). The Chinese view of modeling. *Human Development,* 18, 333–352.

Murphy, C. A., Coover, D., & Owen, S. V. (1989). Development and validation of the computer self-efficacy scale. *Educational and Psychological Measurement,* 49, 893–899.

Murphy, S. A. (1987). Self-efficacy and social support mediators of stress on mental health following a natural disaster. *Western Journal of Nursing Research,* 9, 58–86.

Murphy, S. M., & Jowdy, D. P. (1992). Imagery and mental practice. In T. S. Horn (Ed.), *Advances in sport psychology* (pp. 221–250). Champaign, Ill.: Human Kinetics Publ.

Murray, D. M., Pirie, P., Luepker, R. V., & Pallonen, U. (1989). Five- and six-year follow-up results from four seventh-grade smoking prevention strategies. *Journal of Behavioral Medicine,* 12, 207–218.

Myers, D. G. (1990). *Social psychology* (3rd ed.). New York: McGraw-Hill.

Nahinsky, I. D. (1991). Bouncing back in the World Series. *Bulletin of the Psychonomic Society,* 29, 131–132.

Neimeyer, R. A., & Feixas, G. (1990). The role of homework and skill acquisition in the outcome of group cognitive therapy for depression. *Behavior Therapy,* 21, 281–292.

Nelson, R. E., & Craighead, W. E. (1977). Selective recall of positive and negative

feedback, self-control behaviors, and depression. *Journal of Abnormal Psychology,* 86, 379–388.

Nevill, D. D., & Schlecker, D. I. (1988). The relation of self-efficacy and assertiveness to willingness to engage in traditional/nontraditional career activities. *Psychology of Women Quarterly,* 12, 91–98.

Newell, K. M. (1976). Motor learning without knowledge of results through the development of a response recognition mechanism. *Journal of Motor Behavior,* 8, 209–217.

Newhagen, J. E. (1994a). Self-efficacy and call-in political television show use. *Communication Research,* 21, 366–379.

Newhagen, J. E. (1994b). Media use and political efficacy: The suburbanization of race and class. *Journal of the American Society for Information Science,* 45, 386–394.

Newman, C., & Goldfried, M. R. (1987). Disabusing negative self-efficacy expectations via experience, feedback, and discrediting. *Cognitive Therapy and Research,* 11, 401–417.

Newman, R. S. (1991). Goals and self-regulated learning: What motivates children to seek academic help? In M. L. Maehr & P. R. Pintrich (Eds.), *Advances in motivation and achievement: A research annual* (Vol. 7, pp. 151–183). Greenwich, Conn.: JAI.

Nicholls, J. G. (1984). Achievement motivation: Conceptions of ability, subjective experience, task choice, and performance. *Psychological Review,* 91, 328–346.

Nicholls, J. G. (1990). What is ability and why are we mindful of it? A developmental perspective. In R. J. Sternberg & J. Kolligian, Jr. (Eds.), *Competence considered* (pp. 11–40). New Haven, Conn.: Yale University Press.

Nicholls, J. G., & Miller, A. T. (1984). Development and its discontents: The differentiation of the concept of ability. In J. G. Nicholls (Ed.), *Advances in motivation and achievement.* Vol. 3, *The development of achievement motivation* (pp. 185–218). Greenwich, Conn.: JAI.

Nicki, R. M., Remington, R. E., & MacDonald, G. A. (1984). Self-efficacy, nicotine-fading/self-monitoring and cigarette-smoking behaviour. *Behavior Research Therapy,* 22, 477–485.

Nimmo, D. (1976). Political image makers and the mass media. *The Annals of the American Academy of Political and Social Science,* 427, 33–44.

Nisbett, R., & Ross, L. (1980). *Human inference: Strategies and shortcomings of social*

judgment. Englewood Cliffs, N.J.: Prentice-Hall.

Nisbett, R. E. (Ed.). (1993). *Rules for reasoning.* Hillsdale, N.J.: Erlbaum.

Nisbett, R. E., & Wilson, T. D. (1977). Telling more than we can know: Verbal reports on mental processes. *Psychological Review,* 84, 231–259.

Nolen-Hoeksema, S. (1990). *Sex differences in depression.* Stanford, Calif.: Stanford University Press.

Nolen-Hoeksema, S. (1991). Responses to depression and their effects on the duration of depressive episodes. *Journal of Abnormal Psychology,* 100, 569–582.

Nolen-Hoeksema, S., Girgus, J. S., & Seligman, M. E. P. (1986). Learned helplessness in children: A longitudinal study of depression, achievement, and explanatory style. *Journal of Personality and Social Psychology,* 51, 435–442.

Nordon, E. (1972). Saul Alinsky: A candid conversation with the feisty radical organizer. *Playboy,* March, 59.

Norem, J. K., & Cantor, N. (1990). Cognitive strategies, coping, and perceptions of competence. In R. J. Sternberg & J. Kolligian, Jr. (Eds.), *Competence considered* (pp. 190–204). New Haven, Conn.: Yale University Press.

Nottelmann, E. D. (1987). Competence and self-esteem during transition from childhood to adolescence. *Developmental Psychology,* 23, 441–450.

Notterman, J. M., Schoenfeld, W. N., & Bersh, P. J. (1952). A comparison of three extinction procedures following heart rate conditioning. *Journal of Abnormal and Social Psychology,* 47, 674–677.

Novaco, R. W. (1979). The cognitive regulation of anger and stress. In P. Kendall & S. Hollon (Eds.), *Cognitive-behavioral interventions: Theory, research and procedures* (pp. 241–285). New York: Academic.

Oatley, K., & Bolton, W. (1985). A social-cognitive theory of depression in reaction to life events. *Psychological Review,* 92, 372–388.

O'Brien, G. T., & Borkovec, T. D. (1977). The role of relaxation in systematic desensitization: Revisiting an unresolved issue. *Journal of Behavior Therapy and Experimental Psychiatry,* 8, 359–364.

O'Brien, T. P., & Kelley, J. E. (1980). A comparison of self-directed and therapist-directed practice for fear reduction. *Behaviour Research and Therapy,* 18, 573–579.

O'Bryant, S. L., & Corder-Bolz, C. R. (1978). The effects of television on children's stereotyping of women's work roles. *Journal of Vocational Behavior*, 12, 233–244.

Oettingen, G. (1995). Cross-cultural perspectives on self-efficacy. In A. Bandura (Ed.), *Self-efficacy in changing societies* (pp. 149–176). New York: Cambridge University Press.

Ogbu, J. U. (1990). Cultural model, identity, and literacy. In J. W. Stigler, R. A. Shweder, & G. H. Herdt (Eds.), *Cultural psychology: Essays on comparative human development* (pp. 520–541). New York: Cambridge University Press.

Oka, R. K., Gortner, S. R., Stotts, N. A., & Haskell, W. L. (1996). Predictors of physical activity in patients with chronic heart failure secondary to either ischemic or idiopathic dilated cardiomyopathy. *American Journal of Cardiology*, 77, 159–163.

O'Leary, A. (1990). Stress, emotion, and human immune function. *Psychological Bulletin*, 108, 363–382.

O'Leary, A., Goodhart, F., Jemmott, L. S., & Boccher-Lattimore, D. (1992). Predictors of safer sexual behavior on the college campus: A social cognitive theory analysis. *Journal of American College Health*, 40, 254–263.

O'Leary, A., Shoor, S., Lorig, K., & Holman, H. R. (1988). A cognitive-behavioral treatment for rheumatoid arthritis. *Health Psychology*, 7, 527–544.

O'Leary, K. D., & Wilson, G. T. (1987). *Behavior therapy: Application and outcome* (2nd ed.). Englewood Cliffs, N.J.: Prentice-Hall.

Olioff, M., & Aboud, F. E. (1991). Predicting postpartum dysphoria in primiparous mothers: Roles of perceived parenting self-efficacy and self-esteem. *Journal of Cognitive Psychotherapy*, 5, 3–14.

Olioff, M., Bryson, S. E., & Wadden, N. P. (1989). Predictive relation of automatic thoughts and student efficacy to depressive symptoms in undergraduates. *Canadian Journal of Behavioural Science*, 21, 353–363.

Olivier, T. E. (1985). The relationship of selected teacher variables with self-efficacy for utilizing the computer for programming and instruction. Ph.D. diss., University of Houston. *Dissertation Abstracts International*, 46, 1501-A.

Onglatco, M., Yuen, E. C., Leong, C. C., & Lee, G. (1993). Managerial self-efficacy and managerial success in Singapore. *International Journal of Management*, 10, 14–21.

Orenstein, H., & Carr, J. (1975). Implosion therapy by tape-recording. *Behaviour Research and Therapy*, 13, 177–182.

Osberg, T. M., & Shrauger, J. S. (1990). The role of self-prediction in psychological assessment. In J. N. Butcher & C. D. Spielberger (Eds.), *Advances in personality assessment* (Vol. 8, pp. 97–120). Hillsdale, N.J.: Erlbaum.

Oshima, H. T. (1967). The strategy of selective growth and the role of communications. In D. Lerner & W. Schramm (Eds.), *Communication and change in the developing countries* (pp. 76–91). Honolulu: East-West Center.

Osipow, S. H., & Davis, A. S. (1988). The relationship of coping resources to occupational stress and strain. *Journal of Vocational Behavior*, 32, 1–15.

Ossip-Klein, D. J., Emont, S. L., Giovino, G. A., Shulman, E., LaVigne, M. B., Black, P. M., Stiggins, J., Shapiro, R., & Krusch, D. A. (in press). Predictors of smoking abstinence following a relapse crisis.

Ossip-Klein, D. J., Giovino, G. A., Megahed, N., Black, P. M., Emont, S. L., Stiggins, J., Shulman, E., & Moore, L. (1991). Effects of a smokers' hotline: Results of a 10-county self-help trial. *Journal of Consulting and Clinical Psychology*, 59, 325–332.

Osterman, P. (1980). *Getting started: The youth labor market.* Cambridge, Mass.: MIT Press.

Ostlund, L. E. (1974). Perceived innovation attributes as predictors of innovativeness. *Journal of Consumer Research*, 1, 23–29.

O'Sullivan, F., & Harvey, C. B. (1993). The effect of feedback given to groups of normal fifth-grade students. Manuscript, University of Victoria.

Ozer, E. M. (1995). The impact of childcare responsibility and self-efficacy on the psychological health of working mothers. *Psychology of Women Quarterly*, 19, 315–336.

Ozer, E. M., & Bandura, A. (1990). Mechanisms governing empowerment effects: A self-efficacy analysis. *Journal of Personality and Social Psychology*, 58, 472–486.

Ozer, M. N. (1988). *The management of persons with spinal cord injury.* New York: Demos.

Padgett, D. K. (1991). Correlates of self-efficacy beliefs among patients with non-insulin dependent diabetes mellitus in Zagreb, Yugoslavia. *Patient Education and Counseling*, 18, 139–147.

Paffenbarger, R. S., Hyde, R. T., Wing, A. L., Lee, I., Jung, D. L., & Kampert, J. B. (1993). The association of changes in physical-activity level and other lifestyle characteristics with mortality among men. *The New England Journal of Medicine*, 328, 538–545.

Paige, J. M. (1971). Political orientation and riot participation. *American Sociological Review*, 36, 810–820.

Pajares, F. (1996). Self-efficacy beliefs and mathematical problem-solving of gifted students. *Contemporary Educational Psychology*, 21, 325–344.

Pajares, F., & Johnson, M. J. (1994). Confidence and competence in writing: The role of self-efficacy, outcome expectancy, and apprehension. *Research in the Teaching of English*, 28, 316–331.

Pajares, F., & Johnson, M. J. (1996). Self-efficacy beliefs and the writing performance of entering high school students. *Psychology in the Schools* 33, 163–175.

Pajares, F., & Kranzler, J. (1995). Self-efficacy beliefs and general mental ability in mathematical problem-solving. *Contemporary Educational Psychology*, 20, 426–443.

Pajares, F., & Miller, M. D. (1994a). Role of self-efficacy and self-concept beliefs in mathematical problem solving: A path analysis. *Journal of Educational Psychology*, 86, 193–203.

Pajares, F., & Miller, M. D. (1994b). Mathematics self-efficacy and mathematical problem-solving: Implications for using varying forms of assessment. *Florida Educational Research Council*, 26, 33–56.

Pajares, F., Urdan, T. C., & Dixon, D. (1995). Mathematics self-efficacy and performance attainments of mainstreamed regular, special education, and gifted students. Submitted for publication.

Pajares, F., & Valiante, G. (in press). The predictive and mediational roles of the writing self-efficacy beliefs of elementary students. *Journal of Educational Research*.

Palincsar, A. S., & Brown, A. L. (1989). Instruction for self-regulated reading. In L. B. Resnick, & L. E. Klopfer (Eds.), *Toward the thinking curriculum: Current cognitive research* (pp. 19–39). Alexandria, Va.: ASCD.

Papousek, H., & Papousek, M. (1979). Early ontogeny of human social interaction: Its biological roots and social dimensions. In M. von Cranach, K. Foppa, W. LePenies, & D. Ploog (Eds.), *Human ethology: Claims and limits of a new discipline* (pp. 456–478). Cambridge, England: Cambridge University Press.

Paris, S. G., Cross, D. R., & Lipson, M. Y. (1984). Informed strategies for learning: A program to improve children's reading awareness and comprehension. *Journal of Educational Psychology*, 76, 1239–1252.

Paris, S. G., & Newman, R. S. (1990). Developmental aspects of self-regulated learning. *Educational Psychologist*, 25, 87–102.

Parker, L. (1989). Perceived control at the

workplace: Relationship with health and attitudes towards work. Ph.D. diss., Stanford University, Stanford, Calif.

Parker, L. (1993). When to fix it and when to leave: Relationships among perceived control, self-efficacy, dissent, and exit. *Journal of Applied Psychology*, 78, 949–959.

Parks, P. L., & Bradley, R. H. (1991). The interaction of home environment features and their relation to infant competence. *Infant Mental Health Journal*, 12, 3–16.

Parsons, J. E., Moses, L., & Yulish-Muszynski, S. (1977). The development of attributions, expectancies, and persistence. Symposium presented at the meeting of the American Psychological Association, San Francisco.

Parsons, J. E., & Ruble, D. N. (1977). The development of achievement-related expectancies. *Child Development*, 48, 1075–1079.

Pastorelli, C., Barbaranelli, C., Bandura, A., & Caprara, G. V. (1996). Impact of multifaceted self-efficacy beliefs on childhood depression. Submitted for publication.

Patkai, P. (1971). Catecholamine excretion in pleasant and unpleasant situations. *Acta Psychologica*, 35, 352–363.

Patterson, G. R., DeBaryshe, B. D., & Ramsey, E. (1989). A developmental perspective on antisocial behavior. *American Psychologist*, 44, 329–335.

Patterson, G. R., Dishion, T. J., & Bank, L. (1984). Family interaction: A process model of deviancy training. *Aggressive Behavior*, 10, 253–267.

Patterson, T. E. (1993). *Out of order: How the decline of the political parties and the growing power of the news media undermine the American way of electing presidents.* New York: Knopf.

Paul, G. L. (1986). Can pregnancy be a placebo effect?: Terminology, designs, and conclusions in the study of psychosocial and pharmacological treatments of behavior disorders. *Journal of Behavior Therapy and Experimental Psychiatry*, 17, 61–81.

Payne, C. (1991). The Comer intervention model and school reform in Chicago: Implications of two models of change. *Urban Education*, 26, 8–24.

Peake, P. K., & Cervone, D. (1989). Sequence anchoring and self-efficacy: Primacy effects in the consideration of possibilities. *Social Cognition*, 7, 31–50.

Pearlin, L. I., & Schooler, C. (1978). The structure of coping. *Journal of Health and Social Behavior*, 19, 2–21.

Peele, S. (1992). Alcoholism, politics, and bureaucracy: The consensus against con-

trolled-drinking therapy in America. *Addictive Behaviors*, 17, 49–62.

Pennebaker, J. W., Gonder-Frederick, L., Cox, D. J., & Hoover, C. W. (1985). The perception of general vs. specific visceral activity and the regulation of health-related behavior. In E. S. Katkin & S. B. Manuck (Eds.), *Advances in behavioral medicine: A research annual* (Vol. 1, pp. 165–198). Greenwich, Conn.: JAI.

Pennebaker, J. W., & Lightner, M. (1980). Competition of internal and external information in an exercise setting. *Journal of Personality and Social Psychology*, 39, 165–174.

Pentz, M. A. (1985). Social competence and self-efficacy as determinants of substance abuse in adolescence. In T. A. Wills & S. Shiffman (Eds.), *Coping and substance use* (pp. 117–142). New York: Academic.

Perri, M. G. (1985). Self-change strategies for the control of smoking, obesity, and problem drinking. In T. A. Wills & S. Shiffman (Eds.), *Coping and substance use* (pp. 295–317). New York: Academic.

Perri, M. G., McAllister, D. A., Gange, J. J., Jordan, R. C., McAdoo, W. G., & Nezu, A. M. (1988). Effects of four maintenance programs on the long-term management of obesity. *Journal of Consulting and Clinical Psychology*, 56, 529–534.

Perri, M. G., Nezu, A. M., & Wiegener, B. J. (1992). *Improving the long-term management of obesity: Theory, research, and clinical guidelines.* New York: Wiley.

Perri, M. G., Richards, C. S., & Schultheis, K. R. (1977). Behavioral self-control and smoking reduction: A study of self-initiated attempts to reduce smoking. *Behavior Therapy*, 8, 360–365.

Perry, C. L., Kelder, S. H., Murray, D. M., & Klepp, K. (1992). Communitywide smoking prevention: Long-term outcomes of the Minnesota heart health program and the class of 1989 study. *American Journal of Public Health*, 82, 1210–1216.

Perry, D. G., & Bussey, K. (1979). The social learning theory of sex differences: Imitation is alive and well. *Journal of Personality and Social Psychology*, 37, 1699–1712.

Perry, D. G., & Bussey, K. (1984). *Social development.* Englewood Cliffs, N.J.: Prentice-Hall.

Perry, D. G., Perry, L. C., & Rasmussen, P. (1986). Cognitive social learning mediators of aggression. *Child Development*, 57, 700–711.

Perry, H. M. (1939). The relative efficiency of actual and "imaginary" practice in five selected tasks. *Archives of Psychology*, 34 (No. 243).

Pervin, L. A., & Lewis, M. (Eds.). (1978). *Perspectives in interactional psychology.* New York: Plenum.

Petersen, A. C. (1987). The nature of biological-psychosocial interactions: The sample case of early adolescence. In R. M. Lerner & T. T. Foch (Eds.), *Biological-psychological interactions in early adolescence* (pp. 35–61). Hillsdale, N.J.: Erlbaum.

Petersen, A. C. (1988). Adolescent development. In M. R. Rosenzweig & L. W. Porter (Eds.), *Annual review of psychology* (pp. 583–607). Palo Alto, Calif.: Annual Reviews.

Peterson, C., & Seligman, M. E. P. (1984). Casual explanations as a risk factor for depression: Theory and evidence. *Psychological Review*, 91, 347–374.

Peterson, C., & Stunkard, A. J. (1989). Personal control and health promotion. *Social Science Medicine*, 28, 819–828.

Peterson, J. M. (1989). Remediation is no remedy. *Educational Leadership*, March, 24–25.

Peterson, S. L. (1993). Career decision-making self-efficacy and institutional integration of underprepared college students. *Research in Higher Education*, 34, 659–685.

Pfeffer, J. (1981). *Power in organizations.* Cambridge, Mass.: Ballinger.

Phares, E. J. (1976). *Locus of control in personality.* Morristown, N.J.: General Learning Press.

Phillips, D. A., & Zimmerman, M. (1990). The developmental course of perceived competence and incompetence among competent children. In R. J. Sternberg & J. Kolligian, Jr. (Eds.), *Competence considered* (pp. 41–66). New Haven, Conn.: Yale University Press.

Piaget, J. (1952). *The origins of intelligence in children.* New York: International Universities Press. (Originally published in French, 1936.)

Piaget, J. (1960). Equilibrium and the development of logical structures. In J. M. Tanner & B. Inhelder (Eds.), *Discussions on child development* (Vol. 4, pp. 98–115). New York: International Universities Press.

Piaget, J. (1970). Piaget's theory. In P. H. Mussen (General Ed.), W. Kessen (Vol. Ed.), *Handbook of child psychology* (4th ed., Vol. 1, pp. 103–128). New York: Wiley.

Pintrich, P. R., & DeGroot, E. V. (1990, April). Quantitative and qualitative perspectives on student motivational beliefs and self-regulated learning. Paper presented at the annual American Educational Research Association convention, Boston.

Pintrich, P. R., & Schrauben, B. (1992). Students' motivational beliefs and their cognitive engagement in classroom academic tasks. In D. Schunk & J. Meece (Eds.), *Student perceptions in the classroom: Causes and consequences* (pp. 149–183). Hillsdale, N.J.: Erlbaum.

Pittman, D. J., & White, H. R. (Eds.). (1991). *Society, culture, and drinking patterns reexamined.* New Brunswick, N.J.: Rutgers Center of Alcohol Studies.

Plimpton, G. (1965). Ernest Hemingway. In G. Plimpton (Ed.), *Writers at work: The Paris Review interviews* (2nd series). New York: Viking.

Plotnikoff, N. P., Faith, R. E., Murgo, A. J., & Good, R. A. (Eds.). (1986). *Enkephalins and endorphins: Stress and the immune system.* New York: Plenum.

Poag-DuCharme, K. A., & Brawley, L. R. (1993). Self-efficacy theory: Use in the prediction of exercise behavior in the community setting. *Journal of Applied Sport Psychology,* 5, 178–194.

Poel, D. H. (1976). The diffusion of legislation among the Canadian provinces: A statistical analysis. *Canadian Journal of Political Science,* 9, 605–626.

Polivy, J., & Herman, C. P. (1985). Dieting and binging: A causal analysis. *American Psychologist,* 40, 193–201.

Polivy, J., & Herman, C. P. (1992). Undieting: A program to help people stop dieting. *International Journal of Eating Disorders,* 11, 261–268.

Pollock, P. H. (1983). The participatory consequences of internal and external political efficacy. *Western Political Quarterly,* 36, 400–409.

Pond, S. B., III, & Hay, M. S. (1989). The impact of task preview information as a function of recipient self-efficacy. *Journal of Vocational Behavior,* 35, 17–29.

Porras, J. I., & Anderson, B. (1981). Improving managerial effectiveness through modeling-based training. *Organizational Dynamics,* Spring, 60–77.

Porras, J. I., Hargis, K., Patterson, K. J., Maxfield, D. G., Roberts, N., & Bies, R. J. (1982). Modeling-based organizational development: A longitudinal assessment. *Journal of Applied Behavioral Science,* 18, 433–446.

Post-Kammer, P., & Smith, P. (1985). Sex differences in career self-efficacy, consideration, and interests of eighth and ninth graders. *Journal of Counseling Psychology,* 32, 551–559.

Powell, G. E. (1973). Negative and positive mental practice in motor skill acquisition. *Perceptual and Motor Skills,* 37, 312.

Powell, W. W. (1990). The transformation of

organizational forms: How useful is organization theory in accounting for social change? In R. Friedland & A. F. Robertson (Eds.), *Beyond the marketplace: Rethinking economy and society* (pp. 310–329). New York: Aldine.

Powers, W. T. (1973). *Behavior: The control of perception.* Chicago: Aldine.

Pretty, G. H., & Seligman, C. (1984). Affect and the overjustification effect. *Journal of Personality and Social Psychology,* 46, 1241–1253.

Pretzer, J., Epstein, N., & Fleming, B. (1991). Marital attitude survey: A measure of dysfunctional attributions and expectancies. *Journal of Cognitive Psychotherapy,* 5, 131–148.

Primakoff, L., Epstein, N., & Covi, L. (1986). Homework compliance: An uncontrolled variable in cognitive therapy outcome research. *Behavior Therapy,* 17, 433–446.

Prince, J. S. (1984). The effects of the manipulation of perceived self-efficacy on fear-avoidant behavior. Ph.D. diss., Northern Illinois University, De Kalb.

Pritchard, R. D., Roth, P. L., Jones, S. D., Galgay, P. J., & Watson, M. D. (1988). Designing a goal-setting system to enhance performance: A practical guide. *Organizational Dynamics,* Summer, 69–78.

Prochaska, J. O., & DiClemente, C. C. (1992). Stages of change in the modification of problem behaviors. In M. Hersen, R. M. Eisler, & P. M. Miller (Eds.), *Progress in behavior modification* (Vol. 28, pp.184–218). Terre Haute, Ind.: Sycamore.

Prussia, G. E., & Kinicki, A. J. (1996). A motivational investigation of group effectiveness using social cognitive theory. *Journal of Applied Psychology,* 81, 187–198.

Public Citizen Health Research Group (1993). The influence of tobacco money on the U.S. Congress. *Health Letter,* 9, (No. 11), 1–7.

Puska, P., Nissinen, A., Salonen, J. T., & Toumilehto, J. (1983). Ten years of the North Karelia project: Results with community-based prevention of coronary heart disease. *Scandinavian Journal of Social Medicine,* 11, 65–68.

Rachman, S., Craske, M., Tallman, K., & Solyom, C. (1986). Does escape behavior strengthen agoraphobic avoidance? *Behavior Therapy,* 17, 366–384.

Rachman, S., & Hodgson, R. J. (1980). *Obsessions and compulsions.* Englewood Cliffs, N.J.: Prentice-Hall.

Rachman, S. J., & Wilson, G. T. (1980). *The effects of psychological therapy* (2nd ed.). Oxford: Pergamon.

Ramey, C. T., & Finkelstein, N. W. (1978). Contingent stimulation and infant competence. *Journal of Pediatric Psychology,* 3, 89–96.

Ramey, C. T., McGinness, G. D., Cross, L., Collier, A. M., & Barrie-Blackley, S. (1982). The Abecedarian approach to social competence: Cognitive and linguistic intervention for disadvantaged preschoolers. In K. Borman (Ed.), *The social life of children in a changing society* (pp. 145–174). Hillsdale, N.J.: Erlbaum.

Ramey, C. T., & Ramey, S. L. (1992). At risk does not mean doomed. National Health/Education Consortium Occasional Paper No. 4. National Commission to Prevent Infant Mortality, Institute for Educational Leadership, Washington D.C.

Randhawa, B. S., Beamer, J. E., & Lundberg, I. (1993). Role of mathematics self-efficacy in the structural model of mathematics achievement. *Journal of Educational Psychology,* 85, 41–48.

Rappaport, J. (1987). Terms of empowerment/exemplars of prevention: Toward a theory for community psychology. *American Journal of Community Psychology,* 15, 121–148.

Rappaport, J., & Seidman, E. (Eds.). (in press). *The handbook of community psychology.* New York: Plenum.

Raudenbush, S. W., Rowan, B., Cheong, Y. F. (1992). Contextual effects on the self-perceived efficacy of high school teachers. *Sociology of Education,* 65, 150–167.

Rebok, G. W., & Balcerak, L. J. (1989). Memory self-efficacy and performance differences in young and old adults: The effect of mnemonic training. *Developmental Psychology,* 25, 714–721.

Rebok, G. W., Offermann, L. R., Wirtz, P. W., & Montaglione, C. J. (1986). Work and intellectual aging: The psychological concomitants of social-organizational conditions. *Educational Gerontology,* 12, 359–374.

Reese, L. (1983). Coping with pain: The role of perceived self-efficacy. Ph.D. diss., Stanford University, Stanford, Calif.

Rehm, L. P. (1981). A self-control therapy program for treatment of depression. In J. F. Clarkin & H. Glazer (Eds.), *Depression: Behavioral and directive treatment strategies* (pp. 68–110). New York: Garland Press.

Rehm, L. P. (1982). Self-management in depression. In P. Karoly & F. H. Kanfer (Eds.), *Self-management and behavior change: From theory to practice* (pp. 522–567). New York: Pergamon.

Rehm, L. P. (1988). Self-management and

cognitive processes in depression. In L. B. Alloy (Ed.), *Cognitive processes in depression* (pp. 143–176). New York: Guilford.

Rehm, L. P. (1995). Psychotherapies for depression. In K. S. Dobson & K. D. Craig (Eds.), *Anxiety and depression in adults and children* (pp. 183–208). Thousand Oaks, Calif.: Sage.

Rehm, L. P., Fuchs, C. Z., Roth, D. M., Kornblith, S. J., & Ramono, J. M. (1979). A comparison of self-control and assertion skills treatments of depression. *Behavior Therapy*, 10, 429–442.

Reid, C. M., Murphy, B., Murphy, M., Maher, T., Ruth, D., & Jennings, G. (1994). Prescribing medication versus promoting behavioural change: A trial of the use of lifestyle management to replace drug treatment of hypertension in general practice. *Behaviour Change*, 11, 77–185.

Reilly, P. M., Sees, K. L., Shopshire, M. S., Hall, S. M., Delucchi, K. L., Tusel, D. J., Banys, P., Clark, H. W., & Piotrowski, N. A. (1995). Self-efficacy and illicit opioid use in a 180-day methadone detoxification treatment. *Journal of Consulting and Clinical Psychology*, 63, 158–162.

Reitzes, D. C., & Reitzes, D. C. (1984). Alinsky's legacy: Current applications and extensions of his principles and strategies. In R. E. Ratcliff (Ed.), *Research in social movements, conflicts and change* (Vol. 6, pp. 31–56). Greenwich, Conn.: JAI.

Relich, J. D., Debus, R. L., & Walker, R. (1986). The mediating role of attribution and self-efficacy variables for treatment effects on achievement outcomes. *Contemporary Educational Psychology*, 11, 195–216.

Rescorla, R. A., & Solomon, R. L. (1967). Two-process learning theory: Relationships between Pavlovian conditioning and instrumental learning. *Psychological Review*, 74, 141–182.

Reynolds, R., Creer, T. L., Holroyd, K. A., & Tobin, D. L. (1982, November). Assessment in the treatment of cigarette smoking: The development of the smokers' self-efficacy scale. Paper presented at the meeting of the Association of Behavior Therapy, Los Angeles.

Richardson, A. (1967). Mental practice: A review and discussion. Part I. *Research Quarterly*, 38, 95–107.

Riessman, F., & Carroll, D. (1995). *Redefining self-help: Policy and practice*. San Francisco: Jossey-Bass.

Riley, M. W., Kahn, R. L., & Foner, A. (Eds.). (1994). *Age and structural lag*. New York: Wiley.

Rimer, B. K., Orleans, C. T., Fleisher, L.,

Cristinzio, S., Resch, N., Telepchak, J., & Keintz, M. K. (1994). Does tailoring matter? The impact of a tailored guide on ratings and short-term smoking-related outcomes for older smokers. *Health Education Research*, 9, 69–84.

Rippetoe, P. A., & Rogers, R. W. (1987). Effects of components of protection-motivation theory on adaptive and maladaptive coping with a health threat. *Journal of Personality and Social Psychology*, 52, 596–604.

Rist, F., & Watzl, H. (1983). Self assessment of relapse risk and assertiveness in relation to treatment outcome of female alcoholics. *Addictive Behaviors*, 8, 121–127.

Rizley, R. (1978). Depression and distortion in the attribution of causality. *Journal of Abnormal Psychology*, 87, 32–48.

Robertson, D., & Keller, C. (1992). Relationships among health beliefs, self-efficacy, and exercise adherence in patients with coronary artery disease. *Heart & Lung*, 21, 56–63.

Robertson, T. S. (1971). *Innovative behavior and communication*. New York: Holt, Rinehart, & Winston.

Rodgers, H. R. (1974). Toward explanation of the political efficacy and political cynicism of black adolescents: An exploratory study. *American Journal of Political Science*, 18, 257–282.

Rodin, J. (1986). Health, control, and aging. In M. M. Baltes & P. B. Baltes (Eds.), *The psychology of control and aging* (pp. 139–165). Hillsdale, N.J.: Erlbaum.

Rodin, J., & Langer, E. J. (1977). Long-term effects of a control-relevant intervention with the institutionalized aged. *Journal of Personality and Social Psychology*, 35, 897–902.

Rodin, J., Rennert, K., & Solomon, S. K. (1980). Intrinsic motivation for control: Fact or fiction. In A. Baum & J. E. Singer (Eds.), *Advances in environmental psychology* (Vol. 2, pp. 131–148). Hillsdale, N.J.: Erlbaum.

Roemer, L., & Borkovec, T. D. (1994). Effects of suppressing thoughts about emotional material. *Journal of Abnormal Psychology*, 103, 467–474.

Rogers, C. R. (1959). A theory of therapy, personality, and interpersonal relationships, as developed in the client-centered framework. In S. Koch (Ed.), *Psychology: A study of a science. Vol. 3, Formulations of the person and the social context* (pp. 184–256). New York: McGraw-Hill.

Rogers, E. M., & Adhikarya, R. (1979). Dif-

fusion of innovations: Up-to-date review and commentary. In D. Nimmo (Ed), *Communication Yearbook 3* (pp. 67–81). New Brunswick, N.J.: Transaction Books.

Rogers, E. M., & Kincaid, D. L. (1981). *Communication networks: Toward a new paradigm for research*. New York: Free Press.

Rogers, E. M., & Larsen, J. K. (1984). *Silicon valley fever: Growth of high-technology culture*. New York: Basic Books.

Rogers, E. M., & Shoemaker, F. (1971). *Communication of innovations: A cross-cultural approach* (2nd ed.). New York: Free Press.

Rogers, R. W. (1983). Cognitive and physiological processes in fear appeals and attitude change: A revised theory of protection motivation. In J. T. Cacioppo & R. E. Petty (Eds.), *Social psychophysiology* (pp. 153–176). New York: Guilford.

Rohsenow, D. J., Niaura, R. S., Childress, A. R., Abrams, D. B., & Monti, P. M. (1990–1991). Cue reactivity in addictive behaviors: Theoretical and treatment implications. *The International Journal of the Addictions*, 25, 957–993.

Roling, N. G., Ascroft, J., & Chege, F. W. (1976). The diffusion of innovations and the issue of equity in rural development. In E. M. Rogers (Ed), *Communication and development* (pp. 63–79). Beverly Hills, Calif.: Sage.

Rollnick, S., & Heather, N. (1982). The application of Bandura's self-efficacy theory to abstinence-oriented alcoholism treatment. *Addictive Behaviors*, 7, 243–250.

Rooney, R. A., & Osipow, S. H. (1992). Task-specific occupational self-efficacy scale: The development and validation of a prototype. *Journal of Vocational Behavior*, 40, 14–32.

Rosen, G. J., Rosen, E., & Reid, J. B. (1972). Cognitive desensitization and avoidance behavior: A reevaluation. *Journal of Abnormal Psychology*, 80, 176–182.

Rosenbaum, J. E. (1978). The structure of opportunity in school. *Social Forces*, 57, 236–256.

Rosenbaum, J. E., & Kariya, T. (1989). From high school to work: Market and institutional mechanisms in Japan. *American Journal of Sociology*, 94, 1334–1365.

Rosenbaum, J. E., Kariya, T., Settersten, R., & Maier, T. (1990). Market and network theories of the transition from high school to work: Their application to industrialized societies. *Annual Review of Sociology*, 16, 263–99.

Rosenbaum, M., & Hadari, D. (1985). Personal efficacy, external locus of control, and perceived contingency of parental reinforcement among depressed, paranoid, and normal subjects. *Journal of Personality and Social Psychology, 49,* 539–547.

Rosenberg, H. (1993). Prediction of controlled drinking by alcoholics and problem drinkers. *Psychological Bulletin, 113,* 129–139.

Rosenfield, D., Folger, R., & Adelman, H. F. (1980). When rewards reflect competence: A qualification of the overjustification effect. *Journal of Personality and Social Psychology, 39,* 368–378.

Rosenhan, D. L. (1970). The natural socialization of altruistic autonomy. In J. Macaulay & L. Berkowitz (Eds.), *Altruism and helping behavior: Social psychological studies of some antecedents and consequences* (pp. 251–268). New York: Academic.

Rosenholtz, S. J., & Rosenholtz, S. H. (1981). Classroom organization and the perception of ability. *Sociology of Education, 54,* 132–140.

Rosenholtz, S. J., & Simpson, C. (1984). The formation of ability conceptions: Developmental trend or social construction? *Review of Educational Research, 54,* 31–63.

Rosenholtz, S. J., & Wilson, B. (1980). The effect of classroom structure on shared perceptions of ability. *American Educational Research Journal, 17,* 75–82.

Rosenstock, I. M. (1974). Historical origins of the health belief model. *Health Education Monographs, 2,* 328–335.

Rosenstock, I. M., Strecher, V. J., & Becker, M. H. (1988). Social learning theory and the health belief model. *Health Education Quarterly, 15,* 175–183.

Rosenthal, D., Moore, S., & Flynn, I. (1991). Adolescent self-efficacy, self-esteem, and sexual risk-taking. *Journal of Community and Applied Social Psychology, 1,* 77–88.

Rosenthal, R. (1978). Interpersonal expectancy effects: The first 345 studies. *Behavioral and Brain Sciences, 1,* 377–415.

Rosenthal, T. L. (1980). Modeling approaches to test anxiety and related performance problems. In I. G. Sarason (Ed.), *Test anxiety* (pp. 245–270). Hillsdale, N.J.: Erlbaum.

Rosenthal, T. L. (1993). To soothe the savage breast. *Behaviour Research and Therapy, 31,* 439–462.

Rosenthal, T. L., & Bandura, A. (1978). Psychological modeling: Theory and practice. In S. L. Garfield & A. E. Bergin (Eds.), *Handbook of psychotherapy and behavior change: An empirical analysis* (2nd ed., pp. 621–658). New York: Wiley.

Rosenthal, T. L., Edwards, N. B., & Ackerman, B. J. (1987). Students' self-ratings of subjective stress across 30 months of medical school. *Behaviour Research Therapy, 25,* 155–158.

Rosenthal, T. L., & Rosenthal, R. H. (1985). Clinical stress management. In D. Barlow (Ed.), *Clinical handbook of psychological disorders* (pp. 145–205). New York: Guilford.

Rosenthal, T. L., & Steffek, B. D. (1991). Modeling applications. In F. H. Kanfer & A. P. Goldstein (Eds.), *Helping people change* (4th ed., pp. 70–121). New York: Pergamon.

Rosenthal, T. L., & Zimmerman, B. J. (1978). *Social learning and cognition.* New York: Academic.

Ross, D. M., & Ross, S. A. (1984). Childhood pain: The school-aged child's view. *Pain, 20,* 179–191.

Ross, L., Lepper, M. R., & Hubbard, M. (1975). Perseverance in self-perception and social perception: Biased attributional processes in the debriefing paradigm. *Journal of Personality and Social Psychology, 32,* 880–892.

Ross, M. (1976). The self-perception of intrinsic motivation. In J. H. Harvey, W. J. Ickes, & R. F. Kidd (Eds.), *New directions in attribution research* (Vol. 1, pp. 121–141). Hillsdale, N.J.: Erlbaum.

Ross, M. (1981). Self-centered biases in attributions of responsibility: Antecedents and consequences. In E. T. Higgins, C. P. Herman, & M. P. Zanna (Eds.), *Social cognition: The Ontario symposium* (Vol. 1, pp. 305–321). Hillsdale, N.J.: Erlbaum.

Ross, S. M., & Brown, J. (1988). A scale to measure anticipatory self-efficacy in treatment of depression. Paper presented at the Annual Meeting of the American Psychological Association, Atlanta.

Rothbaum, B. O., Hodges, L. F., Kooper, R., Opdyke, D., Williford, J. S., & North, M. (1995). Effectiveness of computer-generated (virtual reality) graded exposure in the treatment of acrophobia. *American Journal of Psychiatry, 152,* 626–628.

Rothbaum, F., Weisz, J. R., & Snyder, S. S. (1982). Changing the world and changing the self: A two-process model of perceived control. *Journal of Personality and Social Psychology, 42,* 5–37.

Rothman, A. J., Salovey, P., Antone, C., Keough, K., & Martin, C. (1993). The influence of message framing on health behavior. *Journal of Experimental Social Psychology, 29,* 408–433.

Rothstein, A. L., & Arnold, R. K. (1976). Bridging the gap: Application of research

on videotape feedback and bowling. *Motor Skills: Theory into Practice, 1,* 35–62.

Rotter, J. B. (1966). Generalized expectancies for internal versus external control of reinforcement. *Psychological Monographs, 80* (1, Whole No. 609)).

Rotter, J. B. (1982). Social learning theory. In N. T. Feather (Ed.), *Expectations and actions: Expectancy-value models in psychology* (pp. 241–260). Hillsdale, N.J.: Erlbaum.

Rotter, J. B., Chance, J. E., & Phares, E. J. (1972). *Applications of a social learning theory of personality.* New York: Holt, Rinehart & Winston.

Rottschaefer, W. A. (1985). Evading conceptual self-annihilation: Some implications of Albert Bandura's theory of the self-system for the status of psychology. *New Ideas Psychology, 2,* 223–230.

Ruble, D. N. (1983). The development of social-comparison processes and their role in achievement-related self-socialization. In E. T. Higgins, D. N. Ruble, & W. W. Hartup (Eds.), *Social cognition and social development* (pp. 134–157). New York: Cambridge University Press.

Ruble, D. N., & Frey, K. S. (1991). Changing patterns of comparative behavior as skills are acquired: A functional model of self-evaluation. In J. Suls & T. A. Wills (Eds.), *Social comparison: Contemporary theory and research* (pp. 79–113). Hillsdale, N.J.: Erlbaum.

Ruddy, M. G., & Bornstein, M. H. (1982). Cognitive correlates of infant attention and maternal stimulation over the first year of life. *Child Development, 53,* 183–188.

Ruderman, A. J. (1986). Dietary restraint: A theoretical and empirical review. *Psychological Bulletin, 99,* 247–262.

Rudkin, L., Hagell, A., Elder, G. H., & Conger, R. (1992). Perceptions of community well-being and the desire to move elsewhere. Manuscript, University of North Carolina at Chapel Hill.

Rudolph, D. L., & McAuley, E. (1995). Self-efficacy and salivary cortisol responses to acute exercise in physically active and less active adults. *Journal of Sport and Exercise Psychology, 17,* 206–214.

Rudolph, D. L., & McAuley, E. (1996). Self-efficacy and perceptions of effort: A reciprocal relationship. *Journal of Sport and Exercise Psychology, 18,* 216–223.

Ruiz, B. A. A. (1992). Hip fracture recovery in older women: The influence of self-efficacy, depressive symptoms and state anxiety. Ph.D. diss., University of California, San Francisco. *Dissertation Abstracts International, 54*–03B, 1337.

Ruiz, B. A., Dibble, S. L., Gilliss, C. L., & Gortner, S. R. (1992). Predictors of general activity 8 weeks after cardiac surgery. *Applied Nursing Research, 5,* 59–65.

Rutter, M. (1979). Protective factors in children's responses to stress and disadvantage. In M. W. Kent & E. J. Rolf (Eds.), *Primary prevention of psychopathology.* Vol. 3, *Social competence in children* (pp. 49–74). Hanover, N.H.: University of New England Press.

Rutter, M. (1990). Psychosocial resilience and protective mechanisms. In J. Rolf, A. S. Masten, D. Cicchetti, K. H. Nuechterlein, & S. Weintraub (Eds.), *Risk and protective factors in the development of psychopathology* (pp. 181–214). New York: Cambridge University Press.

Rutter, M., Graham, P., Chadwick, O. F. D., & Yule, W. (1976). Adolescent turmoil: Fact or fiction? *Journal of Child Psychology and Psychiatry, 17,* 35–56.

Ryan, T. A. (1970). *Intentional behavior.* New York: Ronald Press.

Rychtarik, R. G., Fairbank, J. A., Allen, C. M., Roy, D. W., & Drabman, R. S. (1983). Alcohol use in television programming: Effects on children's behavior. *Addictive Behaviors, 8,* 19–22.

Rychtarik, R. G., Prue, D. M., Rapp, S. R., & King, A. C. (1992). Self-efficacy, aftercare and relapse in a treatment program for alcoholics. *Journal of Studies on Alcohol, 53,* 435–440.

Ryckman, R. M., Robbins, M. A., Thornton, B., & Cantrell, P. (1982). Development and validation of a physical self-efficacy scale. *Journal of Personality and Social Psychology, 42,* 891–900.

Ryerson, W. N. (1994). Population Communications International: Its role in family planning soap operas. *Population and Environment: A Journal of Interdisciplinary Studies, 15,* 255–264.

Saavedra, R., Earley, P. C., & Van Dyne, L. (1993). Complex interdependence in task-performing groups. *Journal of Applied Psychology, 78,* 61–72.

Sabido, M. (1981). *Towards the social use of soap operas.* Mexico City, Mexico: Institute for Communication Research.

Sadri, G., & Robertson, I. T. (1993). Self-efficacy and work-related behaviour: A review and meta-analysis. *Applied Psychology: An International Review, 42,* 139–152.

Sagotsky, G., & Lewis, A. (1978, August). Extrinsic reward, positive verbalizations, and subsequent intrinsic interest. Paper presented at the meeting of the American Psychological Association, Toronto.

Saklofske, D. H., Michayluk, J. O., & Randhawa, B. S. (1988). Teachers' efficacy and teaching behaviors. *Psychological Reports, 63,* 407–414.

Saks, A. M. (1994). Moderating effects of self-efficacy for the relationship between training method and anxiety and stress reactions of newcomers. *Journal of Organizational Behavior, 15,* 639–654.

Saks, A. M. (1995). Longitudinal field investigation of the moderating and mediating effects of self-efficacy on the relationship between training and newcomer adjustment. *Journal of Applied Psychology, 80,* 211–225.

Saks, A. M., Wiesner, W. H., & Summers, R. J. (1994). Effects of job previews on self-selection and job choice. *Journal of Vocational Behavior, 44,* 297–316.

Salkovskis, P. M., & Clark, D. M. (1990). Affective responses to hyperventilation: A test of the cognitive model of panic. *Behavior Research Therapy, 28,* 51–61.

Salkovskis, P. M., & Harrison, J. (1984). Abnormal and normal obsessions: A replication. *Behaviour Research and Therapy, 22,* 549–552.

Sallis, J. F., Haskell, W. L., Fortmann, S. P., Vranizan, M. S., Taylor, C. B., & Solomon, D. S. (1986). Predictors of adoption and maintenance of physical activity in a community sample. *Preventive Medicine, 15,* 331–341.

Sallis, J. F., & Hovell, M. F. (1990). Determinants of exercise behavior. In J. O. Holloszy & K. B. Pandolf (Eds.), *Exercise and sport sciences reviews* (Vol. 18, pp. 307–330). Baltimore: Williams & Wilkins.

Sallis, J. F., Hovell, M. F., Hofstetter, C. R., & Barrington, E. (1992). Explanation of vigorous physical activity during two years using social learning variables. *Social Science Medicine, 34,* 25–32.

Sallis, J. F., Pinski, R. B., Grossman, R. M., Patterson, T. L., & Nader, P. R. (1988). The development of self-efficacy scales for health-related diet and exercise behaviors. *Health Education Research, 3,* 283–292.

Salomon, G. (1984). Television is "easy" and print is "tough": The differential investment of mental effort in learning as a function of perceptions and attributions. *Journal of Educational Psychology, 76,* 647–658.

Salovey, P., & Birnbaum, D. (1989). Influence of mood on health-relevant cognitions. *Journal of Personality and Social Psychology, 57,* 539–551.

Salthouse, T. A. (1987). Age, experience, and compensation. In C. Schooler & K. W. Schaie (Eds.), *Cognitive functioning and social structure over the life course* (pp. 142–157). Norwood, N.J.: Ablex.

Sandahl, C., Lindberg, S., & Rönnberg, S. (1990). Efficacy expectations among alcohol-dependent patients: A Swedish version of the situational confidence questionnaire. *Alcohol and Alcoholism, 25,* 67–73.

Sanderson, W. C., Rapee, R. M., & Barlow, D. H. (1989). The influence of an illusion of control on panic attacks induced via inhalation of 5.5% carbon dioxide-enriched air. *Archives of General Psychiatry, 46,* 157–162.

Sanna, L. J. (1992). Self-efficacy theory: Implications for social facilitation and social loafing. *Journal of Personality and Social Psychology, 62,* 774–786.

Sarason, I. G. (1975a). Anxiety and self-preoccupation. In I. G. Sarason & D. C. Spielberger (Eds.), *Stress and anxiety* (Vol. 2, pp. 27–44). Washington, D.C.: Hemisphere.

Sarason, I. G., (1975b). Test anxiety and the self-disclosing coping model. *Journal of Consulting and Clinical Psychology, 43,* 148–153.

Saunders, B., & Allsop, S. (1989). Relapse: A critique. In M. Gossop (Ed.), *Relapse and addictive behaviour* (pp. 249–277). London: Tavistock/Routledge.

Savard, C. J., & Rogers, R. W. (1992). A self-efficacy and subjective expected utility theory analysis of the selection and use of influence strategies. *Journal of Social Behavior and Personality, 7,* 273–292.

Scarr-Salapatek, S., & Williams, M. L. (1973). The effects of early stimulation on low-birth-weight infants. *Child Development, 44,* 94–101.

Schachter, S. (1964). The interaction of cognitive and physiological determinants of emotional state. In L. Berkowitz (Ed.), *Advances in experimental social psychology* (Vol. 1, pp. 49–80). New York: Academic.

Schachter, S., & Singer, J. E. (1962). Cognitive, social, and physiological determinants of emotional state. *Psychological Review, 69,* 379–399.

Schachter, S., & Singer, J. E. (1979). Comments on the Maslach and Marshall-Zimbardo experiments. *Journal of Personality and Social Psychology, 37,* 989–995.

Schaie, K. W. (1995). *Intellectual development in adulthood: The Seattle longitudinal study.* New York: Cambridge University Press.

Scheier, M. F., Carver, C. S., & Matthews, K. A. (1983). Attentional factors in the perception of bodily states. In J. T. Cacioppo & R. E. Petty (Eds.), *Social psychophysiology* (pp. 510–542). New York: Guilford.

Schein, E. (1985). *Organizational culture and leadership.* San Francisco: Jossey-Bass.

Scherer, R. F., Adams, J. S., Carley, S. S., &

Wiebe, F. A. (1989). Role model performance effects on development of entrepreneurial career preference. *Entrepreneurship Theory and Practice*, Spring, 53–71.

Scheye, P. A., & Gilroy, F. D. (1994). College women's career self-efficacy and educational environments. *The Career Development Quarterly*, 42, 244–251.

Schiaffino, K. M., & Revenson, T. A. (1992). The role of perceived self-efficacy, perceived control, and causal attributions in adaptation to rheumatoid arthritis: Distinguishing mediator from moderator effects. *Personality and Social Psychology Bulletin*, 18, 709–718.

Schiaffino, K. M., Revenson, T. A., & Gibofsky, A. (1991). Assessing the impact of self-efficacy beliefs on adaptation to rheumatoid arthritis. *Arthritis Care and Research*, 4, 150–157.

Schifter, D. E., & Ajzen, I. (1985). Intention, perceived control, and weight loss: An application of the theory of planned behavior. *Journal of Personality and Social Psychology*, 49, 843–851.

Schimmel, G. T. (1986). Prediction of premature termination from inpatient alcoholism treatment: An application of multidimensional measurement concepts and self-efficacy ratings. Ph.D. diss., University of Delaware, 1985. *Dissertation Abstracts International*, 46, 4028B.

Schneider, J. A., O'Leary, A., & Agras, W. S. (1987). The role of perceived self-efficacy in recovery from bulimia: A preliminary examination. *Behaviour Research and Therapy*, 25, 429–432.

Schneiderman, N., McCabe, P. M., & Baum, A. (Eds.). (1992). *Stress and disease processes: Perspectives in behavioral medicine*. Hillsdale, N.J.: Erlbaum.

Schoemaker, P. J. H., & Marais, M. L. (in press). Technological innovation and large firm inertia. In G. Dosi & F. Malerba (Eds.), *Organization and strategy in the evolution of the enterprise*. London: McMillan.

Schoen, L. G., & Winocur, S. (1988). An investigation of the self-efficacy of male and female academics. *Journal of Vocational Behavior*, 32, 307–320.

Schoenberger, N. E., Kirsch, I., & Rosengard, C. (1991). Cognitive theories of human fear: An empirically derived integration. *Anxiety Research*, 4, 1–13.

Schooler, C. (1987). Psychological effects of complex environments during the life span: A review and theory. In C. Schooler & K. W. Schaie (Eds.), *Cognitive functioning and social structure over the life course* (pp. 24–49). Norwood, N.J.: Ablex.

Schooler, C. (1990). Individualism and the historical and social-structural determinants of people's concerns over self-directedness and efficacy. In J. Rodin, C. Schooler, & K. W. Schaie (Eds.), *Self-directedness: Cause and effects throughout the life course* (pp.19–58). Hillsdale, N.J.: Erlbaum.

Schooler, C. (1992). Enhancing cognitive and behavioral responses to televised health messages: The role of positive appeals. Ph.D. diss., Stanford University, Stanford, Calif.

Schroeder, H. E., & Rich, A. R. (1976). The process of fear reduction through systematic desensitization. *Journal of Consulting and Clinical Psychology*, 44, 191–199.

Schunk, D. H. (1981). Modeling and attributional effects on children's achievement: A self-efficacy analysis. *Journal of Educational Psychology*, 73, 93–105.

Schunk, D. H. (1982a). Effects of effort attributional feedback on children's perceived self-efficacy and achievement. *Journal of Educational Psychology*, 74, 548–556.

Schunk, D. H. (1982b). Verbal self-regulation as a facilitator of children's achievement and self-efficacy. *Human Learning*, 1, 265–277.

Schunk, D. H. (1983a). Reward contingencies and the development of children's skills and self-efficacy. *Journal of Educational Psychology*, 75, 511–518.

Schunk, D. H. (1983b). Ability versus effort attributional feedback: Differential effects on self-efficacy and achievement. *Journal of Educational Psychology*, 75, 848–856.

Schunk, D. H. (1984a). Self-efficacy perspective on achievement behavior. *Educational Psychologist*, 19, 48–58.

Schunk, D. H. (1984b). Sequential attributional feedback and children's achievement behaviors. *Journal of Educational Psychology*, 76, 1159–1169.

Schunk, D. H. (1984c). Enhancing self-efficacy and achievement through rewards and goals: Motivational and informational effects. *Journal of Educational Research*, 78, 29–34.

Schunk, D. H. (1985). Participation in goal setting: Effects on self-efficacy and skills of learning-disabled children. *Journal of Special Education*, 19, 307–317.

Schunk, D. H. (1987). Peer models and children's behavioral change. *Review of Educational Research*, 57, 149–174.

Schunk, D. H. (1989). Self-efficacy and cognitive skill learning. In C. Ames and R. Ames (Eds.), *Research on motivation in education*. Vol. 3, *Goals and cognitions* (pp. 13–44). San Diego: Academic.

Schunk, D. H. (1991). Goal setting and self-evaluation: A social cognitive perspective on self-regulation. In M. L. Maehr & P. R. Pintrich (Eds.), *Advances in motivation and achievement* (Vol. 7, pp. 85–113). Greenwich, Conn.: JAI.

Schunk, D. H. (1995). Self-efficacy and education and instruction. In J. E. Maddux (Ed.), *Self-efficacy, adaptation, and adjustment: Theory, research, and application* (pp. 281–303). New York: Plenum.

Schunk, D. H. (1996). Goal and self-evaluative influences during children's cognitive skill learning. *American Educational Research Journal*, 33, 359–382.

Schunk, D. H., & Cox, P. D. (1986). Strategy training and attributional feedback with learning disabled students. *Journal of Educational Psychology*, 78, 201–209.

Schunk, D. H., & Gunn, T. P. (1985). Modeled importance of task strategies and achievement beliefs: Effect on self-efficacy and skill development. *Journal of Early Adolescence*, 5, 247–258.

Schunk, D. H., & Gunn, T. P. (1986). Self-efficacy and skill development: Influence of task strategies and attributions. *Journal of Educational Research*, 79, 238–244.

Schunk, D. H., & Hanson, A. R. (1985). Peer models: Influence on children's self-efficacy and achievement. *Journal of Educational Psychology*, 77, 313–322.

Schunk, D. H., & Hanson, A. R. (1989a). Self-modeling and children's cognitive skill learning. *Journal of Educational Psychology*, 81, 155–163.

Schunk, D. H., & Hanson, A. R. (1989b). Influence of peer-model attributes on children's beliefs and learning. *Journal of Educational Psychology*, 81, 431–434.

Schunk, D. H., Hanson, A. R., & Cox, P. D. (1987). Peer-model attributes and children's achievement behaviors. *Journal of Educational Psychology*, 79, 54–61.

Schunk, D. H., & Lilly, M. W. (1984). Sex differences in self-efficacy and attributions: Influence of performance feedback. *Journal of Early Adolescence*, 4, 203–213.

Schunk, D. H., & Rice, J. M. (1984). Strategy self-verbalization during remedial listening comprehension instruction. *Journal of Experimental Education*, 53, 49–54.

Schunk, D. H., & Rice, J. M. (1985). Verbalization of comprehension strategies: Effects on children's achievement outcomes. *Human Learning*, 4, 1–10.

Schunk, D. H., & Rice, J. M. (1986). Extended attributional feedback: Sequence effects during remedial reading instruction. *Journal of Early Adolescence*, 6, 55–66.

Schunk, D. H., & Rice, J. M. (1987). Enhancing comprehension skill and self-efficacy with strategy value information. *Journal of Reading Behavior*, 19, 285–302.

Schunk, D. H., & Rice, J. M. (1989). Learning goals and children's reading comprehension. *Journal of Reading Behavior*, 21, 279–293.

Schunk, D. H., & Rice, J. M. (1991). Learning goals and progress feedback during reading comprehension instruction. *Journal of Reading Behavior*, 23, 351–364.

Schunk, D. H., & Rice, J. M. (1992). Influence of reading-comprehension strategy information on children's achievement outcomes. *Learning Disability Quarterly*, 15, 51–64.

Schunk, D. H., & Rice, J. M. (1993). Strategy fading and progress feedback: Effects on self-efficacy and comprehension among students receiving remedial reading services. *Journal of Special Education*, 27, 257–276.

Schunk, D. H., & Swartz, C. W. (1993). Writing strategy instruction with gifted students: Effects of goals and feedback on self-efficacy and skills. *Roeper Review*, 15, 225–230.

Schwab, D. P., Olian-Gottlieb, J. D., & Heneman, H. G., III (1979). Between-subjects expectancy theory research: A statistical review of studies predicting effort and performance. *Psychological Bulletin*, 86, 139–147.

Schwartz, B. (1978). *Psychology of learning and behavior*. New York: Norton.

Schwartz, B. (1982). Reinforcement-induced behavioral stereotype: How not to teach people to discover rules. *Journal of Experimental Psychology*, 111, 23–59.

Schwartz, G. E. (1971). Cardiac responses to self-induced thoughts. *Psychophysiology*, 8, 462–467.

Schwartz, G. E., Weinberger, D. A., & Singer, J. A. (1981). Cardiovascular differentiation of happiness, sadness, anger, and fear following imagery and exercise. *Psychosomatic Medicine*, 43, 343–364.

Schwartz, J. L. (1974). Relationship between goal discrepancy and depression. *Journal of Consulting and Clinical Psychology*, 42, 309.

Schwartz, N., & Clore, G. L. (1988). How do I feel about it? The informative function of affective states. In K. Fiedler & J. Forgas (Eds.), *Affect, cognition and social behavior: New evidence and integrative attempts* (pp. 44–62). Toronto: C. J. Hogrefe.

Schwartz, R. M., & Gottman, J. M. (1976). Toward a task analysis of assertive behavior. *Journal of Consulting and Clinical Psychology*, 44, 910–920.

Schwarzer, R. (1992). Self-efficacy in the adoption and maintenance of health behaviors: Theoretical approaches and a new model. In R. Schwarzer (Ed.), *Self-efficacy: Thought control of action* (pp. 217–243). Washington, D.C.: Hemisphere.

Schweiger, D., Anderson, C., & Locke, E. (1985). Complex decision-making: A longitudinal study of process and performance. *Organizational Behavior and Human Decision Processes*, 36, 245–272.

Sclafani, A., & Springer, D. (1976). Dietary obesity in rats: Body weight and fat accretion in seven strains of rats. *Physiology and Behavior*, 17, 461–471.

Scraba, P. J. (1990). Self-modeling for teaching swimming to persons with physical disabilities. Ph.D. diss., University of Connecticut, 1989. *Dissertation Abstracts International*, 50, 2830A.

Scully, D. M., & Newell, K. M. (1985). Observational learning and the acquisition of motor skills: Toward a visual perception perspective. *Journal of Human Movement Studies*, 11, 169–186.

Searle, J. R. (1968, December 29). A foolproof scenario for student revolts. *The New York Times Magazine*, p. 4.

Sears, D. O., & McConahay, J. B. (1969). Participation in the Los Angeles riot. *Social Problems*, 17, 3–20.

Sears, R. R., Maccoby, E. E., & Levin, H. (1957). *Patterns of child rearing*. Evanston, Ill.: Row, Peterson.

Seeman, T., McAvay, G., Merrill, S., Albert, M., & Rodin, J. (1996). Self-efficacy beliefs and change in cognitive performance: MacArthur studies of successful aging. *Psychology and Aging*, 11, 538–551.

Seligman, M. E. P. (1975). *Helplessness: On depression, development, and death*. San Francisco: W. H. Freeman.

Seligman, M. E. P. (1990). Why is there so much depression today? The waxing of the individual and the waning of the commons. In R. E. Ingram (Ed.), *Contemporary psychological approaches to depression: Theory, research, and treatment* (pp. 1–9). New York: Plenum.

Seligson, M. A. (1980). Trust, efficacy and modes of political participation: A study of Costa Rican peasants. *British Journal of Political Science*, 10, 75–98.

Seltenreich, J. J., III. (1990). The multivariate analyses of self-efficacy factors in a drunken driving population. Ph.D. diss., University of Oregon, 1989. *Dissertation Abstracts International*, 50, 4786B.

Seydel, E., Taal, E., & Wiegman, O. (1990). Risk-appraisal, outcome and self-efficacy expectancies: Cognitive factors in preventive behaviour related to cancer. *Psychology and Health*, 4, 99–109.

Shadel, W. G., & Mermelstein, R. J. (1993). Cigarette smoking under stress: The role of coping expectancies among smokers in a clinic-based smoking cessation program. *Health Psychology*, 12, 443–450.

Shannon, B., Bagby, R., Wang, M. Q., & Trenkner, L. (1990). Self-efficacy: A contributor to the explanation of eating behavior. *Health Education Research*, 5, 395–407.

Shavit, Y., & Martin, F. C. (1987). Opiates, stress, and immunity: Animal studies. *Annals of Behavioral Medicine*, 9, 11–20.

Shell, D. F., Murphy, C. C., & Bruning, R. H. (1989). Self-efficacy and outcome expectancy mechanisms in reading and writing achievement. *Journal of Educational Psychology*, 81, 91–100.

Shepherd, G. (Ed.). (1995). *Rejected: Leading economists ponder the publication process*. Sun Lakes, Ariz.: Thomas Horton.

Sherer, M., Maddux, J. E., Mercandante, B., Prentice-Dunn, S., Jacobs, B., & Rogers, R. W. (1982). The self-efficacy scale: Construction and validation. *Psychological Reports*, 51, 663–671.

Shiffman, S., Hickcox, M., Paty, J. A., Gnys, M., Kassel, J. D., & Richard, T. J. (1996). *The abstinence violation effect following smoking lapses and temptations*. Submitted for publication.

Shoor, S. M., & Holman, H. R. (1984). Development of an instrument to explore psychological mediators of outcome in chronic arthritis. *Transactions of the Association of American Physicians*, 97, 325–331.

Short, J. F., & Wolfgang, M. E. (1972). *Collective violence*. Chicago: Aldine-Atherton.

Shrauger, J. S., & Osberg, T. M. (1982). Self-awareness: The ability to predict one's future behavior. In G. Underwood & R. Stevens (Eds.), *Aspects of consciousness*. Vol. 3, *Awareness and self-awareness* (pp. 267–330). New York: Academic.

Siegel, K., Mesagno, F. P., Chen, J., & Christ, G. (1989). Factors distinguishing homosexual males practicing risky and safer sex. *Social Science Medicine*, 28, 561–569.

Siegel, R. G., Galassi, J. P., & Ware, W. B. (1985). A comparison of two models for predicting mathematics performance: Social learning versus math aptitude-anxiety. *Journal of Counseling Psychology*, 32, 531–538.

Siegel, S. (1983). Classical conditioning, drug tolerance, and drug dependence. In R. G. Smart, F. B. Glaser, Y. Israel, H. Kalant, R. E. Popham, & W. Schmidt (Eds.), *Research advances in alcohol and drug problems* (Vol. 7, pp. 207–246). New York: Plenum.

Siehl, C., & Martin, J. (1990). Organizational culture: A key to financial performance? In B. Schneider (Ed.), *Organizational climate and culture* (pp. 241–281). San Francisco: Jossey-Bass.

Signorella, M. L., & Liben, L. S. (1984). Recall and reconstruction of gender-related pictures: Effects of attitude, task difficulty, and age. *Child Development*, 55, 393–405.

Signorielli, N. (1985). *Role portrayal on television: An annotated bibliography of studies relating to women, minorities, aging, sexual behavior, health, and handicaps.* Westport, Conn.: Greenwood Press.

Signorielli, N. (1990). Children, television, and gender roles: Messages and impact. *Journal of Adolescent Health Care*, 11, 50–58.

Signorielli, N., & Morgan, M. (Eds.).(1989). *Cultivation analysis: New directions in media effects research.* Newbury Park, Calif.: Sage.

Silbert, M. H. (1984). Delancy Street Foundation: Process of mutual restitution. In F. Riessman (Ed.), *Community psychology series* (Vol. 10, pp. 41–52). New York: Human Sciences Press.

Silver, E. J., Bauman, L. J., & Ireys, H. T. (1995). Relationships of self-esteem and efficacy to psychological distress in mothers of children with chronic physical illnesses. *Health Psychology*, 14, 333–340.

Silver, W. S., Mitchell, T. R., & Gist, M. E. (1995). Responses to successful and unsuccessful performance: The moderating effect of self-efficacy on the relationship between performance and attributions. *Organizational Behavior and Human Decision Processes*, 62, 286–299.

Simon, H. A. (1976). *Administrative behavior: A study of decision-making processes in administrative organization* (3rd ed.). New York: Free Press.

Simon, H. A. (1978). Rational decision making in business organizations. *American Economics Review*, 69, 493–514.

Simon, K. M. (1979a). Effects of self comparison, social comparison, and depression on goal setting and self-evaluative reactions. Manuscript, Stanford University, Stanford, Calif.

Simon, K. M. (1979b). Relative influence of personal standards and external incentives

on complex performance. Ph.D. diss., Stanford University, Stanford, Calif.

Simon, K. M. (1979c). Self-evaluative reactions: The role of personal valuation of the activity. *Cognitive Therapy and Research*, 3, 111–116.

Simons, A. D., Murphy, G. E., Levine, J. L., & Wetzel, R. D. (1986). Cognitive therapy and pharmacotherapy for depression: Sustained improvement over one year. *Archives of General Psychiatry*, 43, 43–48.

Sinclair, W. (1981, July 26). The empire built on corn flakes. *San Francisco Chronicle*, p. 5.

Singer, M. (1991). The relationship between employee sex, length of service and leadership aspirations: A study from valence, self-efficacy and attribution perspectives. *Applied Psychology: An International Review*, 40, 417–436.

Singer, M. S. (1993). Starting a career: An intercultural choice among overseas Asian students. *International Journal of Intercultural Relations*, 17, 73–88.

Singerman, K. S., Borkovec, T. D., & Baron, R. S. (1976). Failure of a "misattribution therapy" with a clinically relevant target behavior. *Behavior Therapy*, 7, 306–313.

Singhal, A., & Rogers, E. M. (1989). Pro-social television for development in India. In R. E. Rice & C. K. Atkin (Eds.), *Public communication campaigns* (2nd ed., pp. 331–350). Newbury Park, Calif.: Sage.

Sitharthan, T. (1989). The role of efficacy expectations in the treatment of drug and alcohol problems. *National Drug and Alcohol Research Center*, Monograph 7, 37–45.

Sitharthan, T., & Kavanagh, D. J. (1990). Role of self-efficacy in predicting outcomes from a programme for controlled drinking. *Drug and Alcohol Dependence*, 27, 87–94.

Sitharthan, T., McGrath, D., Cairns, D., & Saunders, J. B. (1993). Heroin use precipitant inventory (HUPI): Development of a scale assessing the situations leading to opiate use. Manuscript, Royal Prince Alfred Hospital, N.S.W., Australia.

Sitkin, S. (1992). Learning through failure: The strategy of small losses. *Research in Organizational Behavior*, 14, 231–266.

Skelton, J. A., & Pennebaker, J. W. (1982). The psychology of physical symptoms and sensations. In G. Sanders & J. Suls (Eds.), *Social psychology of health and illness* (pp. 99–128). Hillsdale, N.J.: Erlbaum.

Skinner, B. F. (1971). *Beyond freedom and dignity.* New York: Knopf.

Skinner, B. F. (1974). *About behaviorism.* New York: Alfred A. Knopf.

Skinner, C. S., Strecher, V. J., & Hospers, H. (1994). Physicians' recommendations for mammography: Do tailored messages make a difference? *American Journal of Public Health*, 84, 43–49.

Skinner, E. A. (1991). Development and perceived control: A dynamic model of action in context. In M. Gunnar & L. A. Sroufe (Eds.), *Minnesota symposium on child psychology* (Vol. 23, pp. 167–216). Minneapolis: University of Minnesota Press.

Skinner, E. A. (1995). *Perceived control, motivation, & coping.* Thousand Oaks, Calif.: Sage.

Skinner, E. A., Chapman, M., & Baltes, P. B. (1988). Control, means-ends, and agency beliefs: A new conceptualization and its measurement during childhood. *Journal of Personality and Social Psychology*, 54, 117–133.

Slanger, E., & Rudestam, K. E. (1996). Factors of motivation and disinhibition in participation in high risk sports. Manuscript, The Fielding Institute, Santa Barbara, Calif..

Slater, M. D. (1989). Social influences and cognitive control as predictors of self-efficacy and eating behavior. *Cognitive Therapy and Research*, 13, 231–245.

Slovic, P., Fischhoff, B., & Lichtenstein, S. (1977). Behavioral decision theory. In M. R. Rosenzweig & L. W. Porter (Eds.), *Annual review of psychology* (Vol. 28, pp. 1–39). Palo Alto, Calif.: Annual Reviews.

Smith, G. R., & McDaniel, S. M. (1983). Psychologically mediated effect on the delayed hypersensitivity reaction to tuberculin in humans. *Psychosomatic Medicine*, 45, 65–70.

Smith, R. E. (1980). Development of an integrated coping response through cognitive-affective stress management training. In I. G. Sarason & C. D. Spielberger (Eds.), *Stress and anxiety* (Vol. 7, pp. 265–280). Washington, D.C.: Hemisphere.

Smith, R. E. (1989). Effects of coping skills training on generalized self-efficacy and locus of control. *Journal of Personality and Social Psychology*, 56, 228–233.

Smith, R. J., Arnkoff, D. B., & Wright, T. L. (1990). Test anxiety and academic competence: A comparison of alternative models. *Journal of Counseling Psychology*, 37, 313–321.

Snyder, M. (1987). *Public appearances/private realities: The psychology of self-monitoring.* New York: W. H. Freeman.

Solberg, V. S., O'Brien, K., Villareal, P., Kennel, R., & Davis, B. (1993). Self-efficacy and Hispanic college students: Validation of the college self-efficacy instrument. *Hispanic Journal of Behavioral Sciences*, 15, 80–95.

Solomon, D. S., & Maccoby, N. (1984). Communication as a model for health enhancement. In J. D. Matarazzo, N. E. Miller, S. M. Weiss, J. A. Herd, & S. M. Weiss (Eds.), *Behavioral Health: A handbook of health enhancement and disease prevention* (pp. 209–221). Silver Spring, Md.: Wiley.

Solomon, K. E., & Annis, H. M. (1989). Development of a scale to measure outcome expectancy in alcoholics. *Cognitive Therapy and Research*, 13, 409–421.

Solomon, K. E., & Annis, H. M. (1990). Outcome and efficacy expectancy in the prediction of posttreatment drinking behaviour. *British Journal of Addiction*, 85, 659–666.

Solomon, R. P. (1992). *Black resistance in high school*. Albany, N.Y.: State University of New York Press.

Solomon, Z. (1993). *Combat stress reaction: The enduring toll of war*. New York: Plenum.

Solomon, Z., Benbenishty, R., & Mikulincer, M. (1991). The contribution of wartime, prewar and postwar factors to self-efficacy: A longitudinal study of combat stress reaction. *Journal of Traumatic Stress*, 4, 345–361.

Solomon, Z., Weisenberg, M., Schwarzwald, J., & Mikulincer, M. (1988). Combat stress reaction and posttraumatic stress disorder as determinants of perceived self-efficacy in battle. *Journal of Social and Clinical Psychology*, 6, 356–370.

Soman, V. R., Koivisto, V. A., Deibert, D., Felig, P., & DeFronzo, R. A. (1979). *New England Journal of Medicine*, 301, 1200–1204.

South, S. J., & Tolnay, S. E. (Eds.). (1992). *The changing American family: Sociological and demographic perspectives*. Boulder, Colo.: Westview Press.

Speier, C., & Frese, M. (in press). Self-efficacy as a mediator and moderator between resources at work and personal initiative: A longitudinal field study in East Germany. *Human Performance*.

Spence, K. W. (1956). *Behavior theory and conditioning*. New Haven, Conn.: Yale University Press.

Sperry, R. W. (1993). The impact and promise of the cognitive revolution. *American Psychologist*, 48, 878–885.

Spink, K. S. (1990). Group cohesion and collective efficacy of volleyball teams. *Journal of Sport Exercise Psychology*, 12, 301–311.

Spink, K. S. (1992). Group cohesion and starting status in successful and less successful elite volleyball teams. *Journal of Sports Sciences*, 10, 379–388.

Stall, R., & Biernacki, P. (1986). Spontaneous remission from the problematic use of substances: An inductive model derived from a comparative analysis of the alcohol, opiate, tobacco, and food/obesity literatures. *International Journal of the Addictions*, 21, 1–23.

Stanley, M. A., & Maddux, J. E. (1986). Cognitive processes in health enhancement: Investigation of a combined protection motivation and self-efficacy model. *Basic and Applied Social Psychology*, 7, 101–113.

Stanley, M. A., & Maddux, J. E. (1986a). Self-efficacy expectancy and depressed mood: An investigation of causal relationships. *Journal of Social Behavior and Personality*, 1, 575–586.

Steele, C. M. (in press). A threat in the air: How stereotypes shape the intellectual identities and performance of women and African-Americans. *American Psychologist*.

Steinberger, P. J. (1981). Social context and political efficacy. *Sociology and Social Research*, 65, 129–141.

Stephens, R. S., Wertz, J. S., & Roffman, R. A. (1995). Self-efficacy and marijuana cessation: A construct validity analysis. *Journal of Consulting and Clinical Psychology*, 63, 1022–1031.

Steptoe, A., & Appels, A. (Eds.). (1989). *Stress, personal control and health*. New York: Wiley.

Steptoe, A., & Vögele, C. (1992). Individual differences in the perception of bodily sensations: The role of trait anxiety and coping style. *Behaviour Research Therapy*, 30, 597–607.

Stern, S. E., & Kipnis, D. (1993). Technology in everyday life and perceptions of competence. *Journal of Applied Social Psychology*, 23, 1892–1902.

Sternberg, R. J., & Kolligian, J., Jr. (Eds.). (1990). *Competence considered*. New Haven, Conn.: Yale University Press.

Stevens, C. K., Bavetta, A. G., Gist, M. E. (1993). Gender differences in the acquisition of salary negotiation skills: The role of goals, self-efficacy, and perceived control. *Journal of Applied Psychology*, 78, 723–735.

Stevens, V. J., & Hollis, J. F. (1989). Preventing smoking relapse, using an individually tailored skills-training technique. *Journal of Consulting and Clinical Psychology*, 57, 420–424.

Stewart, G. L., & Manz, C. C. (1995). Leadership for self-managing work teams: A typology and integrative model. *Human Relations*, 48, 747–770.

Stewart, R. (1967). *Managers and their jobs*. London: Macmillan.

Stickel, S. A., & Bonett, R. M. (1991). Gender differences in career self-efficacy: Combining a career with home and family. *Journal of College Student Development*, 32, 297–301.

Stock, J., & Cervone, D. (1990). Proximal goal-setting and self-regulatory processes. *Cognitive Therapy and Research*, 14, 483–498.

Stoffelmayr, A. S. (1994). Physician self-efficacy in the treatment of obesity. Ph.D. diss., Michigan State University, 1994. *Dissertation Abstracts International*, 55–12A, 3751.

Stone, A. A., Neale, J. M., Cox, D. S., Napoli, A., Valdimarsdottir, H., & Kennedy-Moore, E. (1994). Daily events are associated with a secretory immune response to an oral antigen in men. *Health Psychology*, 13, 440–446.

Stotland, S., & Zuroff, D. C. (1991). Relations between multiple measures of dieting self-efficacy and weight change in a behavioral weight control program. *Behavior Therapy*, 22, 47–59.

Stotland, S., Zuroff, D. C., & Roy, M. (1991). Situational dieting self-efficacy and short-term regulation of eating. *Appetite*, 17, 81–90.

Strang, H. R., Lawrence, E. C., & Fowler, P. C. (1978). Effects of assigned goal level and knowledge of results on arithmetic computation: Laboratory study. *Journal of Applied Psychology*, 63, 446–450.

Strecher, V. J., Bauman, K. E., Boat, B., Fowler, M. G., Greenberg, R., & Stedman, H. (1993). The role of outcome and efficacy expectations in an intervention designed to reduce infants' exposure to environmental tobacco smoke. *Health Education Research*, 8, 137–143.

Strecher, V. J., Becker, M. H., Kirscht, J. P., Eraker, S. A., & Graham-Tomasi, R. P. (1985). Psychosocial aspects of changes in cigarette-smoking behavior. *Patient Education and Counseling*, 7, 249–262.

Strecher, V. J., Kreuter, M., Den Boer, D.-J., Kobrin, S., Hospers, H. J., & Skinner, C. S. (1994). The effects of computer-tailored smoking cessation messages in family practice settings. *Journal of Family Practice*, 39, 262–268.

Streiner, D. L., & Norman, G. R. (1989). *Health measurement scales: A practical guide to their development and use*. Oxford: Oxford University Press.

Striegel-Moore, R. H., Silberstein, L. R., & Rodin, J. (1986). Toward an understanding of risk factors in bulimia. *American Psychologist*, 41, 246–263.

Stunkard, A. J. (1975). From explanation to action in psychosomatic medicine: The case of obesity. *Psychosomatic Medicine,* 37, 195–236.

Stunkard, A. J. (1988, Nov.). Some perspectives on human obesity: Its causes. *Bulletin of the New York Academy of Medicine,* 64, 902–923.

Suinn, R. M. (1983). Imagery and sports. In A. A. Sheikh (Ed.), *Imagery: Current theory, research, and applications* (pp. 507–534). New York: Wiley.

Suls, J. M., & Miller, R. L. (1977). *Social comparison processes: Theoretical and empirical perspectives.* Washington, D.C.: Hemisphere.

Suls, J., & Mullen, B. (1982). From the cradle to the grave: Comparison and self-evaluation across the life-span. In J. Suls (Ed.), *Psychological perspectives on the self* (Vol. 1, pp. 97–125). Hillsdale, N.J.: Erlbaum.

Surber, C. F. (1984). The development of achievement-related judgment processes. In J. Nicholls (Ed.), *Advances in motivation and achievement: The development of achievement motivation* (Vol 3., pp. 137–184). Greenwich, Conn.: JAI.

Surber, C. F. (1985). Applications of information integration to children's social cognitions. In J. B. Pryor & J. D. Day (Eds.), *The development of social cognition* (pp. 59–94). New York: Springer-Verlag.

Sushinsky, L. W., & Bootzin, R. R. (1970). Cognitive desensitization as a model of systematic desensitization. *Behaviour Research and Therapy,* 8, 29–33.

Sutton, S. (1996). Can "stages of change" provide guidance in the treatment of addictions?: A critical examination of Prochaska and DiClemente's model. In G. Edwards & C. Dare (Eds.), *Psychotherapy, psychological treatments and the addictions* (pp. 189–205). Cambridge: Cambridge University Press.

Swallow, S. R., & Kuiper, N. A. (1993). Social comparison in dysphoria and nondysphoria: Differences in target similarity and specificity. *Cognitive Therapy and Research,* 17, 103–122.

Taal, E., Rasker, J. J., Seydel, E. R., & Wiegman, O. (1993). Health status, adherence with health recommendations, self-efficacy and social support in patients with rheumatoid arthritis. *Patient Education and Counseling,* 20, 63–76.

Taal, E., Seydel, E., & Wiegman, O. (1990). Self-efficacy, protection motivation and health behaviour. In L. R. Schmidt, P. Schwenkmezger, J. Weinman, & S. Maes (Eds.), *Theoretical and applied aspects of health psychology* (pp. 113–120). Chur: Harwood Academic Publishers.

Takata, C., & Takata, T. (1976). The influ-

ence of models in the evaluation of ability: Two functions of social comparison processes. *Japanese Journal of Psychology,* 47, 74–84.

Tannenbaum, P. H., Kavcic, B., Rosner, M., Vianello, M., & Wieser, G. (1974). *Hierarchy in organizations.* San Francisco: Jossey-Bass.

Taylor, C. B., Bandura, A., Ewart, C. K., Miller, N. H., & DeBusk, R. F. (1985). Exercise testing to enhance wives' confidence in their husbands' cardiac capabilities soon after clinically uncomplicated acute myocardial infarction. *American Journal of Cardiology,* 55, 635–638.

Taylor, J. (1988). Slumpbusting: A systematic analysis of slumps in sports. *The Sport Psychologist,* 2, 39–48.

Taylor, K. M., & Betz, N. E. (1983). Applications of self-efficacy theory to the understanding and treatment of career indecision. *Journal of Vocational Behavior,* 22, 63–81.

Taylor, K. M., & Popma, J. (1990). An examination of the relationships among career decision-making self-efficacy, career salience, locus of control, and vocational indecision. *Journal of Vocational Behavior,* 37, 17–31.

Taylor, M. S., Locke, E. A., Lee, C., & Gist, M. E. (1984). Type A behavior and faculty research productivity: What are the mechanisms? *Organizational Behavior and Human Performance,* 34, 402–418.

Taylor, S. E. (1989). *Positive illusions: Creative self-deception and the healthy mind.* New York: Basic Books.

Taylor, S. E., & Brown, J. D. (1988). Illusion and well-being: A social psychological perspective on mental health. *Psychological Bulletin,* 103, 193–210.

Teasdale, J. D. (1983). Negative thinking in depression: Cause, effect, or reciprocal relationship? *Advances in Behaviour Research and Therapy,* 5, 3–25.

Teasdale, J. D. (1988). Cognitive vulnerability to persistent depression. *Cognition and Emotion,* 2, 247–274.

Telch, M. J., Bandura, A., Vinciguerra, P., Agras, A., & Stout, A. L. (1982). Social demand for consistency and congruence between self-efficacy and performance. *Behavior Therapy,* 13, 694–701.

Telch, M. J., Killen, J. D., McAlister, A. L., Perry, C. L., & Maccoby, N. (1982). Long-term follow-up of a pilot project on smoking prevention with adolescents. *Journal of Behavioral Medicine,* 5, 1–8.

Tenenbaum, G., Pinchas, S., Elbaz, G., Bar-Eli, M., & Weinberg, R. (1991). Effect of goal proximity and goal specificity on muscular endurance performance: A replica-

tion and extension. *Journal of Sport and Exercise Psychology,* 13, 174–187.

Terry, D. J., & O'Leary, J. E. (1995). The theory of planned behaviour: The effects of perceived behavioural control and self-efficacy. *British Journal of Social Psychology,* 34, 199–220.

Testa, M., & Major, B. (1990). The impact of social comparisons after failure: The moderating effects of perceived control. *Basic and Applied Social Psychology,* 11, 205–218.

Teti, D. M., & Gelfand, D. M. (1991). Behavioral competence among mothers of infants in the first year: The mediational role of maternal self-efficacy. *Child Development,* 62, 918–929.

Thalberg, I. (1972). *Enigmas of agency: Studies in the philosophy of human action.* New York: Humanities Press.

Tharp, R. G., & Gallimore, R. (1985). The logical status of metacognitive training. *Journal of Abnormal Child Psychology,* 13, 455–466.

Tharp, R. G., Gallimore, R. (1976). What a coach can teach a teacher. *Psychology Today,* 9, 74–78.

Thase, M. E., & Moss, M. K. (1976). The relative efficacy of covert modeling procedures and guided participant modeling on the reduction of avoidance behavior. *Journal of Behavior Therapy and Experimental Psychiatry,* 7, 7–12.

Thomas, J. P. (1993). Cardiac inpatient education: The impact of educational technology on self-efficacy. *Journal of Cardiopulmonary Rehabilitation,* 13, 398-405.

Thompson, J. K., Jarvie, G. J., Lahey, B. B., & Cureton, K. J. (1982). Exercise and obesity: Etiology, physiology, and intervention. *Psychological Bulletin,* 91, 55–79.

Timko, C., Moos, R. H., Finney, J. W., & Moos, B. S. (1994). Outcome of treatment for alcohol abuse and involvement in Alcoholics Anonymous among previously untreated problem drinkers. *Journal of Mental Health Administration,* 21, 145–160.

Tinetti, M. E., Mendes de Leon, C. F., Doucette, J. T., & Baker, D. I. (1994). Fear of falling and fall-related efficacy in relationship to functioning among community-living elders. *Journal of Gerontology: Medical Sciences,* 49, M140–M147.

Tobler, N. S. (1986). Meta-analysis of 143 adolescent drug prevention programs: Quantitative outcome results of program participants compared to a control or comparison group. *Journal of Drug Issues,* 16, 537–567.

Tolman, E. C. (1932). *Purposive behavior in animals and men.* New York: Century.

Tolman, E. C. (1951). *Collected papers in*

psychology. Reprinted as *Behavior and psychological man.* Berkeley: University of California Press.

Tornatzky, L. G., & Klein, K. J. (1982). Innovation characteristics and innovation adoption-implementation: A meta-analysis of findings. *IEEE Transactions of Engineering and Management,* EM-29, 28–45.

Tough, A. M. (1981). *Learning without a teacher* (Research Series No. 3). Toronto: The Ontario Institute for Studies in Education.

Toumilehto, J., Geboers, J., Salonen, J. T., Nissinen, A., Kuulasmaa, K., & Puska, P. (1986). Decline in cardiovascular mortality in North Karelia and other parts of Finland. *British Medical Journal,* 293, 1068–1071.

Tracy, D. C., & Adams, P. H. (1984, February). Self-efficacy: A crucial factor in the job-search process. *Dickinson Magazine,* 8–9.

Treasure, D. C., Monson, J., & Cox, C. L. (1996). Relationship between self-efficacy, wrestling performance, and affect prior to competition. *The Sport Psychologist,* 10, 73–83.

Triandis, H. C. (1995). *Individualism and collectivism.* Boulder, Colo.: Westview Press.

Trichopoulos, D., & Willett, W. C. (1996). Harvard report on cancer prevention. *Cancer Causes and Control,* 7, S3–S17, S55–S58.

Trope, Y. (1983). Self-assessment in achievement behavior. In. J. Suls & A. G. Greenwald (Eds.), *Psychological perspectives on the self* (Vol. 2, pp. 93–121). Hillsdale, N.J.: Erlbaum.

Tuckman, B. W. (1990). Group versus goal-setting effects on the self-regulated performance of students differing in self-efficacy. *Journal of Experimental Education,* 58, 291–298.

Tuckman, B. W., & Sexton, T. L. (1990). The relation between self-beliefs and self-regulated performance. *Journal of Social Behavior and Personality,* 5, 465–472.

Tuckman, B. W., & Sexton, T. L. (1991). The effect of teacher encouragement on student self-efficacy and motivation for self-regulated performance. *Journal of Social Behavior and Personality,* 6, 137–146.

Turk, D., Meichenbaum, D., & Genest, M. (1983). *Cognitive therapy of pain.* New York: Guilford.

Turkat, I. D. (1982). An investigation of parental modeling in the etiology of diabetic illness behavior. *Behavior Research and Therapy,* 20, 547–552.

Turkat, I. D., & Guise, B. J. (1983). The effects of vicarious experience and stimulus intensity of pain termination and work avoidance. *Behavior Research and Therapy,* 21, 241–245.

Turkat, I. D., Guise, B. J., & Carter, K. M. (1983). The effects of vicarious experience on pain termination and work avoidance: A replication. *Behaviour Research and Therapy,* 21, 491–493.

Tuscon, K. M., & Sinyor, D. (1993). On the affective benefits of acute aerobic exercise: Taking stock after twenty years of research. In P. Seraganian (Ed.), *Exercise psychology: The influence of physical exercise on psychological processes.* New York: Wiley.

Tversky, A., & Kahneman, D. (1974). Judgment under uncertainty: Heuristics and biases. *Science,* 185, 1124–1131.

Tversky, A., & Kahneman, D. (1981). The framing of decisions and the psychology of choice. *Science,* 211, 453–458.

Tyler, T. R., & McGraw, K. M. (1983). The threat of nuclear war: Risk interpretation and behavioral response. *Journal of Social Issues,* 39, 25–40.

Ulrich, E. (1967). Some experiments on the function of mental training in the acquisition of motor skills. *Ergonomics,* 10, 411–419.

Ungerleider, S., & Golding, J. M. (1991). Mental practice among Olympic athletes. *Perceptual and Motor Skills,* 72, 1007–1017.

Urakami, M. (1996). Career exploration processes in women's junior college students: An examination of the relationships among career decision-making self-efficacy, vocational exploration activity and self-concept crystallization. *Japanese Journal of Educational Psychology,* 44, 195–203.

Vaillant, G. E. (1995). *The natural history of alcoholism revisited.* Cambridge, Mass.: Harvard University Press.

van den Hout, M., Arntz, A., & Hoekstra, R. (1994). Exposure reduced agoraphobia but not panic, and cognitive therapy reduced panic but not agoraphobia. *Behaviour Research Therapy,* 32, 447–451.

van Ryn, M., & Vinokur, A. D. (1992). How did it work? An examination of the mechanisms through which an intervention for the unemployed promoted job-search behavior. *American Journal of Community Psychology,* 20, 577–597.

Vasil, L. (1992). Self-efficacy expectations and causal attributions for achievement among male and female university faculty. *Journal of Vocational Behavior,* 41, 259–269.

Vasta, R. (1976). Feedback and fidelity: Effects of contingent consequences on accuracy of imitation. *Journal of Experimental Child Psychology,* 21, 98–108.

Vaughan, P. W., Rogers, E. M., & Swalehe, R. M. A. (1995). The effects of "Twende Na Wakati," an entertainment-education radio soap opera for family planning and HIV/AIDS prevention in Tanzania. Manuscript, University of New Mexico, Albuquerque.

Velicer, W. F., DiClemente, C. C., Rossi, J. S., & Prochaska, J. O. (1990). Relapse situations and self-efficacy: An integrative model. *Addictive Behaviors,* 15, 271–283.

Vinokur, A. D., van Ryn, M., Gramlich, E. M., & Price, R. H. (1991). Long-term follow-up and benefit-cost analysis of the jobs program: A preventive intervention for the unemployed. *Journal of Applied Psychology,* 76, 213–219.

Voudouris, N. J., Peck, C. L., & Coleman, G. (1985). Conditioned placebo responses. *Journal of Personality and Social Psychology,* 48, 47–53.

Vroom, V. H. (1964). *Work and motivation.* New York: Wiley.

Vygotsky, L. (1962). *Thought and language.* Cambridge, Mass.: MIT Press.

Wachtel, P. L. (1977). *Psychoanalysis and behavior therapy.* New York: Basic Books.

Wadden, T. A., & VanItallie, T. B. (1992). *Treatment of the seriously obese patient.* New York: Guilford.

Wagner, J. (1987). *The search for signs of intelligent life in the universe.* New York: Harper & Row.

Wagner, J. A., & Gooding, R. Z. (1987). Shared influence and organizational behavior: A meta-analysis of situational variables expected to moderate participation-outcome relationships. *Academy of Management Journal,* 30, 524–541.

Wahler, R. G., Berland, R. M., & Coe, T. D. (1979). Generalization processes in child behavior change. In B. B. Lahey & A. E. Kazdin (Eds.), Advances in clinical child psychology (Vol. 2, pp. 35–69). New York: Plenum.

Walker, W. B., & Franzini, L. R. (1983, April). Self-efficacy and low-risk aversive group treatments for smoking cessation. Paper presented at the annual convention of the Western Psychological Association, San Francisco.

Wallace, I., & Pear, J. J. (1977). Self-control techniques of famous novelists. *Journal of Applied Behavior Analysis,* 10, 515–525.

Wallace, S. T., & Alden, L. E. (1991). A comparison of social standards and perceived ability in anxious and nonanxious men. *Cognitive Therapy and Research,* 15, 237–254.

Wallace, S. T., & Alden, L. E. (1995). Social anxiety and standard setting following social success or failure. *Cognitive Therapy and Research,* 19, 613–631.

Wallack, L., Dorfman, L., Jernigan, D., & Themba, M. (1993). *Media advocacy and public health: Power for prevention.* Newbury Park, Calif.: Sage.

Wallston, K. A., Wallston, B. S., & DeVellis, M. R. (1978). Development of a multidimensional health locus of control (MHLC) scale. *Health Education Monographs,* 6, 160–170.

Walsh, B., & Dickey, G. (1990). *Building a champion: On football and the making of the 49ers.* New York: St. Martin's Press.

Walter, H. J., Vaughn, R. D., Gladis, M. M., Ragin, D. F., Kasen, S., and Cohall, A. T. (1992). Factors associated with AIDS risk behaviors among high school students in an AIDS epicenter. *American Journal of Public Health,* 82, 528–532.

Walter, H. J., Vaughn, R. D., Gladis, M. M., Ragin, D. F., Kasen, S., and Cohall, A. T. (1993). Factors associated with AIDS-related behavioral intentions among high school students in an AIDS epicenter. *Health Education Quarterly,* 20, 409–420.

Wang, F. (1996) *Constructing a learning organization using groupware through cognitive apprenticeship and case-based learning.* Unpublished manuscript, University of Indiana, Bloomington, IN.

Ware, M. C., & Stuck, M. F. (1985). Sex-role messages vis-à-vis microcomputer use: A look at pictures. *Sex Roles,* 13, 205–214.

Wason, P.C. (1980). Specific thoughts on the writing process. In L. W. Gregg & E. R. Steinberg (Eds.), *Cognitive processes in writing* (pp. 1229–1237). Hillsdale, N.J.: Erlbaum.

Watkins, L. R., & Mayer, D. J. (1982). Organization of endogenous opiate and nonopiate pain control systems. *Science,* 216, 1185–1192.

Watson, J. S. (1977). Depression and the perception of control in early childhood. In J. G. Schulterbrandt & A. Raskin (Eds.), *Depression in childhood: Diagnosis, treatment, and conceptual models* (129–139). New York: Raven.

Watson, J. S. (1979). Perception of contingency as a determinant of social responsiveness. In E. B. Thoman (Ed.), *Origins of the infant's social responsiveness* (Vol. 1, pp. 33–64). New York: Halsted.

Webb, J. A., & Baer, P. E. (1995). Influence of family disharmony and parental alcohol use on adolescent social skills, self-efficacy, and alcohol use. *Addictive Behaviors,* 20, 127–135.

Webster, M., Jr., & Sobieszek, B. (1974). *Sources of self-evaluation: A formal theory of significant others and social influence.* New York: Wiley.

Wegner, D. M. (1994). Ironic processes of mental control. *Psychological Review,* 101, 34–52.

Wegner, L. D. M. (1989). *White bears and other unwanted thoughts.* New York: Viking Press.

Weinberg, R. (1986). Relationship between self-efficacy and cognitive strategies in enhancing endurance performance. *International Journal of Sport Psychology,* 17, 280–293.

Weinberg, R., Bruya, L., Longino, J., & Jackson, A. (1988). Effect of goal proximity and specificity on endurance performance of primary-grade children. *Journal of Sport and Exercise Psychology,* 10, 81–91.

Weinberg, R., & Jackson, A. (1990). Building self-efficacy in tennis players: A coach's perspective. *Applied Sport Psychology,* 2, 164–174.

Weinberg, R. S., Gould, D., & Jackson, A. (1979). Expectations and performance: An empirical test of Bandura's self-efficacy theory. *Journal of Sport Psychology,* 1, 320–331.

Weinberg, R. S., Gould, D., Yukelson, D., & Jackson, A. (1981). The effect of preexisting and manipulated self-efficacy on a competitive muscular endurance task. *Journal of Sport Psychology,* 4, 345–354.

Weinberg, R. S., Hughes, H. H., Critelli, J. W., England, R., & Jackson, A. (1984). Effects of preexisting and manipulated self-efficacy on weight loss in a self-control program. *Journal of Research in Personality,* 18, 352–358.

Weinberg, R. S., Yukelson, D., & Jackson, A. (1980). Effect of public and private efficacy expectations on competitive performance. *Journal of Sport Psychology,* 2, 340–349.

Weiner, B. (1985). An attributional theory of achievement motivation and emotion. *Psychological Review,* 92, 548–573.

Weiner, B. (1986). *An attributional theory of motivation and emotion.* New York: Springer-Verlag.

Weinstein, C. E., & Mayer, R. E. (1986). The teaching of learning strategies. In M. C. Wittrock (Ed.), *Handbook of research on teaching* (3rd ed., pp. 315–327). New York: Macmillan.

Weiss, J. M. (1991). Stress-induced depression: Critical neurochemical and electrophysiological changes. In J. Madden, IV (Ed.), *Neurobiology of learning, emotion and affect* (pp. 123–154). New York: Raven.

Weisz, J. R., & Cameron, A. M. (1985). Individual differences in the student's sense of control. In R. Ames & C. Ames (Eds.), *Research on motivation in education.* Vol. 2,

The classroom milieu (pp. 93–140). Orlando, Fla.: Academic.

Welch, S., & Thompson, K. (1980). The impact of federal incentives on state policy innovation. *American Journal of Political Science,* 24, 715–729.

Wener, A. E., & Rehm, L. P. (1975). Depressive affect: A test of behavioral hypotheses. *Journal of Abnormal Psychology,* 84, 221–227.

Wenzlaff, R. M., Wegner, D. M., & Roper, D. W. (1988). Depression and mental control: The resurgence of unwanted negative thoughts. *Journal of Personality and Social Psychology,* 55, 882–892.

Werner, E. E. (1992). The children of Kauai: Resiliency and recovery in adolescence and adulthood. *Journal of Adolescent Health,* 13, 262–268.

Werner, E. E., & Smith, R. S. (1992). *Overcoming the odds: High risk children from birth to adulthood.* Ithaca, N.Y.: Cornell University Press.

Werthner, P., & Orlick, T. (1986). Retirement experiences of successful Olympic athletes. *International Journal of Sport Psychology,* 17, 337–363.

West, D. M. (1993). *Air wars.* Washington, D.C.: Congressional Quarterly.

West, R. L., Berry, J. M., & Powlishta, K. K. (1983). Self-efficacy and prediction of memory task performance. Manuscript, Washington University, St. Louis, Mo.

Westling, B. E., & Ost, L. (1995). Cognitive bias in panic disorder patients and changes after cognitive-behavioral treatments. *Behaviour Research and Therapy,* 33, 585–588.

Westoff, C. F., & Rodriguez, G. (1995). The mass media and family planning in Kenya. *International Family Planning Perspectives,* 21, 26–31,36.

Whalen, C. K. (1989). Attention deficit and hyperactivity disorders. In T. H. Ollendick & M. Hersen (Eds.), *Handbook of child psychopathology* (2nd ed., 131–169). New York: Plenum.

Wheeler, K. G. (1983). Comparisons of self-efficacy and expectancy models of occupational preferences for college males and females. *Journal of Occupational Psychology,* 56, 73–78.

Wheeler, V. A., & Ladd, G. W. (1982). Assessment of children's self-efficacy for social interactions with peers. *Developmental Psychology,* 18, 795–805.

White, J. (1982). *Rejection.* Reading, Mass.: Addison-Wesley.

White, M., & Smith, D. J. (1994). The causes of persistently high unemployment. In A. C. Peterson & J. T. Mortimer (Eds.), *Youth unemployment and society* (pp.

95–144). London: Cambridge University Press.

White, R. W. (1959). Motivation reconsidered: The concept of competence. *Psychological Review*, 66, 297–333.

White, R. W. (1960). Competence and the psychosexual stages of development. In M. R. Jones (Ed.), *Nebraska symposium on motivation* (Vol. 8, pp. 97–141). Lincoln: University of Nebraska Press.

White, S. E., Mitchell, T. R., & Bell, C. H. (1977). Goal setting, evaluation apprehension, and social cues as determinants of job performance and job satisfaction in a simulated organization. *Journal of Applied Psychology*, 62, 665–673.

Whiting, S. (1991, June 20). Return of a master vintner. *San Francisco Chronicle*, pp. B3–B4.

Whyte, G., & Saks, A. (1995). Expert decision making in escalation situations: The role of self-efficacy. Submitted for publication.

Whyte, G., Saks, A., & Hook, S. (in press). When success breeds failure: The role of perceived self-efficacy in escalating commitment to a losing course of action. *Journal of Organizational Behavior*.

Wiedenfeld, S. A., O'Leary, A., Bandura, A., Brown, S., Levine, S., & Raska, K. (1990). Impact of perceived self-efficacy in coping with stressors on components of the immune system. *Journal of Personality and Social Psychology*, 59, 1082–1094.

Wiegman, O., Taal, E., Van den Bogaard, J., & Gutteling, J. M. (1992). Protection motivation theory variables as predictors of behavioural intentions in three domains of risk management. In J. A. M. Winnubst & S. Maes (Eds.), *Lifestyles, stress and health: New developments in health psychology* (pp. 55–70). Leiden: DSWO Press, Leiden University.

Wigal, J. K., Creer, T. L., & Kotses, H. (1991). The COPD self-efficacy scale. *Chest*, 99, 1193–1196.

Wiggins, J. S. (1973). *Personality and prediction: Principles of personality assessment.* Reading, Mass.: Addison-Wesley.

Wilkins, W. (1971). Desensitization: Social and cognitive factors underlying the effectiveness of Wolpe's procedure. *Psychological Bulletin*, 76, 311–317.

Will, G. F. (1990). *Men at work.* New York: Macmillan.

Willemsen, M. A., & DeVries, H. (1996). Saying "no" to environmental tobacco smoke: Determinants of assertiveness among nonsmoking employees. *Preventive Medicine*, 25, 575–582.

Williams, S. L. (1987). On anxiety and phobia. *Journal of Anxiety Disorders*, 1, 161–180.

Williams, S. L. (1990). Guided mastery treatment of agoraphobia: Beyond stimulus exposure. In M. Hersen, R. M. Eisler, & P. M. Miller (Eds.), *Progress in behavior modification* (Vol. 26, pp. 89–121). Newbury Park, Calif.: Sage.

Williams, S. L. (1992). Perceived self-efficacy and phobic disability. In R. Schwarzer (Ed.), *Self-efficacy: Thought control of action* (pp. 149–176). Washington, D.C.: Hemisphere.

Williams, S. L. (1996). Overcoming phobia: Unconscious bioinformational deconditioning or conscious cognitive reappraisal? In R. M. Rapee (Ed.), *Current controversies in the anxiety disorders* (pp. 373–376). New York: Guilford.

Williams, S. L., Dooseman, G., & Kleifield, E. (1984). Comparative power of guided mastery and exposure treatments for intractable phobias. *Journal of Consulting and Clinical Psychology*, 52, 505–518.

Williams, S. L., & Falbo, J. (1996). Cognitive and performance-based treatments for panic attacks in people with varying degrees of agoraphobic disability. *Behaviour Research and Therapy*, 34, 253–264.

Williams, S. L., & Kinney, P. J. (1991). Performance and nonperformance strategies for coping with acute pain: The role of perceived self-efficacy, expected outcomes, and attention. *Cognitive Therapy and Research*, 15, 1–19.

Williams, S. L., Kinney, P. J., & Falbo, J. (1989). Generalization of therapeutic changes in agoraphobia: The role of perceived self-efficacy. *Journal of Consulting and Clinical Psychology*, 57, 436–442.

Williams, S. L., & Rappoport, A. (1983). Cognitive treatment in the natural environment for agoraphobics. *Behavior Therapy*, 14, 299–313.

Williams, S. L., Turner, S. M., & Peer, D. F. (1985). Guided mastery and performance desensitization treatments for severe acrophobia. *Journal of Consulting and Clinical Psychology*, 53, 237–247.

Williams, S. L., & Watson, N. (1985). Perceived danger and perceived self-efficacy as cognitive mediators of acrophobic behavior. *Behavior Therapy*, 16, 136–146.

Williams, S. L., & Zane, G. (1989). Guided mastery and stimulus exposure treatments for severe performance anxiety in agoraphobics. *Behaviour Research Therapy*, 27, 238–245.

Williams, T. M., Joy, L. A., Travis, L., Gotowiec, A., Blum-Steele, M., Aiken, L. S., Painter, S. L., & Davidson, S. M. (1987). Transition to motherhood: A longitudinal study. *Infant Mental Health Journal*, 8, 251–265.

Willis, S. L. (1990). Current issues in cognitive training research. In E. A. Lovelace (Ed.), *Aging and cognition: Mental processes, self awareness and interventions* (pp. 263–280). North-Holland: Elsevier Science Publishers B. V.

Willis, S. L., & Schaie, K. W. (1986). Training the elderly on the ability factors of spatial orientation and inductive reasoning. *Psychology and Aging*, 1, 239–247.

Wilson, D. K., Wallston, K. A., & King, J. E. (1990). Effects of contract framing, motivation to quit, and self-efficacy on smoking reduction. *Journal of Applied Social Psychology*, 20, 531–547.

Wilson, G. T. (1982). Alcohol and anxiety: Recent evidence on the tension reduction theory of alcohol use and abuse. In J. Polivy & K. Blankstein (Eds.), *Self control of emotional behavior* (pp. 742–775). New York: Plenum.

Wilson, G. T. (1986). Cognitive-behavioral and pharmacological therapies for bulimia. In K. D. Brownell & J. Foreyt (Eds.), *Physiology, psychology, and treatment of eating disorders* (pp. 450–475). New York: Basic Books.

Wilson, G. T. (1988). Alcohol use and abuse: A social learning analysis. In A. Wilkinson & D. Chandron (Eds.), *Theories of alcoholism* (pp. 239–287). Toronto: Addiction Research Foundation.

Wilson, G. T. (1989). The treatment of bulimia nervosa: A cognitive-social learning analysis. In A. J. Stunkard & A. Baum (Eds.), *Eating, sleep and sexual disorders* (pp. 73–98). New York: Erlbaum.

Wilson, G. T., & Brownell, K. D. (1980). Behavior therapy for obesity: An evaluation of treatment outcome. *Advances in Behavior Research and Therapy*, 3, 49–86.

Wilson, G. T., Rossiter, E., Kleifield, E. I., & Lindholm, L. (1986). Cognitive-behavioral treatment of bulimia nervosa: A controlled evaluation. *Behavior Research and Therapy*, 24, 277–288.

Wilson, J. W. (1987). *The truly disadvantaged: The inner city, the underclass, and public policy.* Chicago: University of Chicago Press.

Wine, J. D. (1982). Evaluation anxiety: A cognitive-attentional construct. In H. W. Krohne & L. Laux (Eds.), *Achievement, stress, and anxiety* (pp. 207–219). Washington, D.C.: Hemisphere.

Winett, R. A. (1996). Activity and exercise guidelines: Questions concerning their scientific basis and health outcome efficacy. Submitted for publication.

Winett, R. A., King, A. C., & Altman, D. G. (1989). *Health psychology and public health: An integrative approach.* Elmsford, New York: Pergamon.

Winkleby, M. A. (1994). The future of community-based cardiovascular disease intervention studies. *American Journal of Public Health,* 84, 1369–1373.

Witte, K. (1992). The role of threat and efficacy in AIDS prevention. *International Quarterly of Community Health Education,* 12, 225–249.

Wolf, S., Gregory, W. L., & Stephan, W. G. (1986). Protection motivation theory: Prediction of intentions to engage in anti-nuclear war behaviors. *Journal of Applied Social Psychology,* 16, 310–321.

Wolfsfeld, G. (1986). Evaluational origins of political action: The case of Israel. *Political Psychology,* 7, 767–788.

Wollman, N., & Stouder, R. (1991). Believed efficacy and political activity: A test of the specificity hypothesis. *Journal of Social Psychology,* 131, 557–566.

Wolpe, J. (1974). *The practice of behavior therapy.* New York: Pergamon.

Wood, J. V. (1989). Theory and research concerning social comparisons of personal attributes. *Psychological Bulletin,* 106, 231–248.

Wood, R. E., & Bailey, T. (1985). Some unanswered questions about goal effects: A recommended change in research methods. *Australian Journal of Management,* 10, 61–73.

Wood, R. E., & Bandura, A. (1989a). Social cognitive theory of organizational management. *Academy of Management Review,* 14, 361–384.

Wood, R. E., & Bandura, A. (1989b). Impact of conceptions of ability on self-regulatory mechanisms and complex decision making. *Journal of Personality and Social Psychology,* 56, 407–415.

Wood, R. E., Bandura, A., & Bailey, T. (1990). Mechanisms governing organizational performance in complex decision-making environments. *Organizational Behavior and Human Decision Processes,* 46, 181–201.

Wood, R. E., & Locke, E. A. (1987). The relation of self-efficacy and grade goals to academic performance. *Educational and Psychological Measurement,* 47, 1013–1024.

Wood, R. E., & Locke, E. A. (1990). Goal-setting and strategy effects on complex tasks. In B. M. Staw & L. L. Cummings (Eds.), *Research in organizational behavior* (Vol. 12, pp. 73–109). Greenwich, Conn.: JAI.

Wood, R. E., Mento, A. J., & Locke, E. A. (1987). Task complexity as a moderator of goal effects: A meta-analysis. *Journal of Applied Psychology,* 72, 416–425.

Woodruff, T. J., Rosbrook, B., Pierce, J., & Glantz, S. A. (1993). Lower levels of cigarette consumption found in smoke-free workplaces in California. *Archives of Internal Medicine,* 153, 1485–1493.

Woodward, N. J., & Wallston, B. S. (1987). Age and health care beliefs: Self-efficacy as a mediator of low desire for control. *Psychology and Aging,* 2, 3–8.

Woolfolk, A. E., & Hoy, W. K. (1990). Prospective teachers' sense of efficacy and belief about control. *Journal of Educational Psychology,* 82, 81–91.

Woolfolk, A. E., Rosoff, B., & Hoy, W. K. (1990). Teachers' sense of efficacy and their beliefs about managing students. *Teaching and Teacher Education,* 6, 137–148.

Wortman, C. B., Panciera, L., Shusterman, L., & Hibscher, J. (1976). Attributions of causality and reactions to uncontrollable outcomes. *Journal of Experimental Social Psychology,* 12, 301–316.

Wright, J., & Mischel, W. (1982). Influence of affect on cognitive social learning person variables. *Journal of Personality and Social Psychology,* 43, 901–914.

Wright, P. M. (1989). Test of the mediating role of goals in the incentive-performance relationship. *Journal of Applied Psychology,* 74, 699–705.

Wulfert, E., & Wan, C. K. (1993). Condom use: A self-efficacy model. *Health Psychology,* 12, 346–389.

Wulfert, E., & Wan, C. K. (1995). Safe sex intentions and condom use viewed from a health belief, reasoned action, and social cognitive perspective. *Journal of Sex Research,* 32, 299–311.

Wurtele, S. K., & Maddux, J. E. (1987). Relative contributions of protection motivation theory components in predicting exercise intentions and behavior. *Health Psychology,* 6, 453–466.

Wylie, R. C. (1974). *The self-concept: A review of methodological considerations and measuring instruments* (rev. ed.). Lincoln: University of Nebraska Press.

Wynne, L. C., & Solomon, R. L. (1955). Traumatic avoidance learning: Acquisition and extinction in dogs deprived of normal peripheral autonomic function. *Genetic Psychology Monographs,* 52, 241–284.

Yalom, I. D., & Yalom, M. (1971). Ernest Hemingway: A psychiatric view. *Archives of General Psychiatry,* 24, 485–494.

Yamagishi, T. (1988). The provision of a sanctioning system in the United States and Japan. *Social Psychology Quarterly,* 51, 265–271.

Yarrow, L. J., McQuiston, S., MacTurk, R. H., McCarthy, M. E., Klein, R. P., & Vietze, P. M. (1983). Assessment of mastery motivation during the first year of life: Contemporaneous and cross-age relationships. *Developmental Psychology,* 19, 159–171.

Yarrow, L. J., Rubenstein, J. L., & Pedersen, F. A. (1975). *Infant and environment: Early cognitive and motivational development.* New York: Halsted.

Yates, A. J., & Thain, J. (1985). Self-efficacy as a predictor of relapse following voluntary cessation of smoking. *Addictive Behaviors,* 10, 291–298.

Yeich, S., & Levine, R. (1994). Political efficacy: enhancing the construct and its relationship to mobilization of people. *Journal of Community Psychology,* 22, 259–271.

Yin, Z., Simons, J., & Callaghan, J. (1989). The application of goal-setting in physical activity: A field study. Paper presented at the meeting of the Association for the Advancement of Applied Sport Psychology, Seattle.

Yordy, G. A., & Lent, R. W. (1993). Predicting aerobic exercise participation: Social cognitive, reasoned action, and planned behavior models. *Journal of Sport and Exercise Psychology,* 15, 363–374.

Young, E. (1989). On the naming of the rose: Interests and multiple meanings as elements of organizational culture. *Organization Studies,* 10, 187–206.

Young, J. D. (1996). The effect of self-regulated learning strategies on performance in learner controlled computer-based instruction. *Educational Technology Research and Development,* 44, 17–27.

Young, R. M., Oei, T. P. S., & Crook, G. M. (1991). Development of a drinking self-efficacy questionnaire. *Journal of Psychopathology and Behavioral Assessment,* 13, 1–15.

Zailian, M. (1978, April 30). Interview with Victor Borge: "If I were not a humorist, I'd be a pianist." *San Francisco Chronicle,* p. 22.

Zajonc, R. B., & Markus, G. B. (1975). Birth order and intellectual development. *Psychological Review,* 82, 74–88.

Zaltman, G., & Wallendorf, M. (1979). *Consumer behavior: Basic findings and management implications.* New York: Wiley.

Zane, G., & Williams, S. L. (1993). Performance-related anxiety in agoraphobia: Treatment procedures and cognitive mechanisms of change. *Behavior Therapy,* 24, 625–643.

Zautra, A. J., Reich, J. W., & Newsom, J. T. (1995). Autonomy and sense of control among older adults: An examination of their effects on mental health. In L. Bond, S. Culter, & A. Grams (Eds.), *Promoting successful and productive aging*. Newbury Park, Calif.: Sage Publications.

Zeiss, A. M., Lewinsohn, P. M., & Muñoz, R. F. (1979). Nonspecific improvement effects in depression using interpersonal skills training, pleasant activity schedules, or cognitive training. *Journal of Consulting and Clinical Psychology*, 47, 427–439.

Zigler, E., & Butterfield, E. C. (1968). Motivational aspects of changes in IQ test performance of culturally deprived nursery school children. *Child Development*, 39, 1–14.

Zillmann, D. (1983). Transfer of excitation in emotional behavior. In J. T. Cacioppo & R. E. Petty (Eds.), *Social psychophysiology* (pp. 215–240). New York: Guilford.

Zimbardo, P. G. (1977). *Shyness: What it is, what to do about it*. Reading, Mass.: Addison-Wesley.

Zimmerman, B. J. (1989). A social cognitive view of self-regulated academic learning. *Journal of Educational Psychology*, 81, 329–339.

Zimmerman, B. J. (1990). Self-regulating academic learning and achievement: The emergence of a social cognitive perspective. *Educational Psychology Review*, 2, 173–201.

Zimmerman, B. J., & Bandura, A. (1994). Impact of self-regulatory influences on writing course attainment. *American Educational Research Journal*, 31, 845–862.

Zimmerman, B. J., Bandura, A., & Martinez-Pons, M. (1992). Self-motivation for academic attainment: The role of self-efficacy beliefs and personal goal-setting. *American Educational Research Journal*, 29, 663–676.

Zimmerman, B. J., & Martinez-Pons, M. (1986). Development of a structured interview for assessing student use of self-regulated learning strategies. *American Educational Research Journal*, 23, 614–628.

Zimmerman, B. J., & Martinez-Pons, M. (1988). Construct validation of a strategy model of student self-regulated learning. *Journal of Educational Psychology*, 80, 284–290.

Zimmerman, B. J., & Martinez-Pons, M. (1990). Student differences in self-regulated learning: Relating grade, sex, and giftedness to self-efficacy and strategy use. *Journal of Educational Psychology*, 82, 51–59.

Zimmerman, B. J., & Ringle, J. (1981). Effects of model persistence and statements of confidence on children's self-efficacy and problem solving. *Journal of Educational Psychology*, 73, 485–493.

Zimmerman, M. A., & Rappaport, J. (1988). Citizen participation, perceived control, and psychological empowerment. *American Journal of Community Psychology*, 16, 725–750.

Zubin, J., Eron, L. D., & Schumer, F. (1965). *An experimental approach to projective techniques*. New York: Wiley.

Zurcher, L. A., & Monts, J. K. (1972). Political efficacy, political trust, and anti-pornography crusading: A research note. *Sociology and Social Research*, 56, 211–220.

Name Index

Subject Index

Albert Bandura is David Starr Jordan Professor of Social Science in Psychology at Stanford University and past president of the American Psychological Association. Among the awards he has received are the Distinguished Scientific Contributions Award of the American Psychological Association and the William James Award. He has been elected to the American Academy of Arts and Sciences and the Institute of Medicine of the National Academy of Sciences, and has received honorary degrees from eleven universities. He is the author of nine books, including, most recently, *Social Foundations of Thought and Action: A Social Cognitive Theory.*

W. H. Freeman and Company
41 Madison Avenue
New York, NY 10010
Houndmills, Basingstoke RG21 6XS, England

ISBN 0-7167-2850-8

90000

9 780716 728504